Phil Edmonston

LEMON-AID

1990-2016

NEW AND USED CARS AND TRUCKS

DUNDURN
TORONTO

Editor: Catherine Leek of Green Onion Publishing
Design: Kim Monteforte of WeMakeBooks.com
Printer: Webcom

ISBN: 978-1-45973-257-5 (pb)
ISBN: 978-1-45973-258-2 (pdf)
ISBN: 978-1-45973-259-9 (epub)

1   2   3   4   5   19   18   17   16   15

We acknowledge the support of the **Canada Council for the Arts** and the **Ontario Arts Council** for our publishing program. We also acknowledge the financial support of the **Government of Canada** through the **Canada Book Fund** and **Livres Canada Books**, and the **Government of Ontario** through the **Ontario Book Publishing Tax Credit** and the **Ontario Media Development Corporation**.

Visit us at

Dundurn.com | @dundurnpress | Facebook.com/dundurnpress
Pinterest.com/dundurnpress

Dundurn
3 Church Street, Suite 500
Toronto, Ontario, Canada
M5E 1M2

CONTENTS

CONTENTS

CONTENTS

KEY DOCUMENTS

Part Four

1990-2016 RATINGS "WHEN GOOD CARS GO BAD"

KEY DOCUMENTS

A YEAR OF LIVING DANGEROUSLY

Washington, May 14, 2014: "General Motors will pay $35 million to settle a federal probe into its 10-year delay of recalls related to an ignition switch flaw (*time.com/102906/gm-fine-ignition-recalls/*).

Ottawa, December 31, 2014: "To date, Transport Canada has no evidence to suggest GM Canada failed to comply with its legal obligations in Canada," ministry spokeswoman Lauren Armstrong said in an email. "Should evidence show that GM or any other company did not issue a notice once becoming aware of a defect, Transport Canada will not hesitate to prosecute." (*business.financialpost.com/2014/12/30/in-2014-recall-crisis-no-punishment-for-canadian-automakers/*).

Pathetic. Transport Canada has NO recall powers, Environment Canada sleeps while Volkswagen cheats on emissions tests with diesels that poison our lungs with excess NOx fumes (See Part 4, European Vehicles, Volkswagen) and our government adopts the "Mike Duffy-Sgt. Schultz defense:" "I see nothing, I know nothing."

Road Kill

Go ahead, choose your poison: 30.4 million GM cars using poorly-designed, "deadly" ignition switches (50% recalled, leaving 15.2 million to maim and kill); Toyota and Honda with detonators that spew out shrapnel making sashimi of your face and throat; or 2007-15 Chrysler/Jeeps that stall out, lose steering and brakes, and disable their airbags. These are all real dangers making 2014 a record year for safety-related recalls, not due so much to assembly line mistakes, but as a direct consequence of factory cost-cutting run wild, bad engineering, and poor design. Worst of all, 30% of the affected vehicles will never get fixed.

The biggest recall last year was GM's ignition failures that have cost the company over a $4.6 billion U.S. and allegedly led to 23 deaths (two deaths in Canada) and hundreds of injuries. A Canadian class action has been filed in Ontario (*www.gmclassactionsuit.ca*). The fix rate for this safety defect is only 56% despite massive publicity given to the hazard.

This recall would not have happened if GM had replaced the ignitions ten years ago when first alerted to the defect. The payout would have been $37.7 million, according to confidential General Motors documents released by the U.S. Congress. The cheaper $14.2 million repair that GM authorized saved the company $23.5 million—a savings that has ballooned into a loss of almost $5 billion.

GM's dangerous ignition switches and the company's coverup are the latest confirmation that automakers will deliberately manufacture a vehicle that will kill or maim simply because, in the long run, it costs less to stonewall complaints and pay off victims than to make a safer vehicle.

I first learned this lesson after reading the court transcripts of *Grimshaw v. Ford* (fire-prone Pintos) from 1981. Reporter Anthony Prince wrote the following assessment of Ford's indifference in an article titled "Lessons of the Ford/Firestone scandal: Profit motive turns consumers into road kill," *People's Tribune* (Online Edition), Vol. 26, No. 11, November 2000:

> Rejecting safety designs costing between only $1.80 and $15.30 per Pinto, Ford had calculated the damages it would likely pay in wrongful death and injury cases and pocketed the difference. In a cold and calculating "costs/benefits" analysis, Ford projected that the Pinto would probably cause 180 burn deaths, 180 serious burn injuries, [and] 2,100 burned vehicles each year. Also, Ford estimated civil suits of $200,000 per death, $67,000 per injury, [and] $700 per vehicle for a grand total of $49.5 million. The costs for installing safety features would cost approximately $137 million per year. As a result, the Pinto became a moving target, its unguarded fuel tank subject to rupture by exposed differential bolts shoved into it by rear-end collisions at speeds of as little as 21 miles per hour [34 km/h]. Spewing gasoline into the passenger compartment, the car and its passengers became engulfed in a raging inferno.

And here are more recent examples of corporate greed triumphing over public safety: 35 million vehicles worldwide equipped with "grenading" Takata-made air-bag inflaters used by 10 automakers since 2008; 16 million defective Ford cruise-control deactivation switches that catch fire while the vehicle is parked; millions of Jeeps with unprotected fuel tanks that burst into flames in a rear-ender (Jeep will install a free trailer hitch.); and Toyota, Honda, Chrysler, Ford, and GM minivan sliding doors that suddenly open while underway, or injure passengers when closing unexpectedly.

Putting profits first, carmakers don't give a damn for auto safety, building quality products, or protecting the environment. Instead, they lobby for "zombie" consumer protection laws (neither dead nor alive), set up "secret" warranties, hide behind bankruptcy filings, and slap gag orders on settlements. Where there has been progress in each of these areas, it has been due to successful lawsuits and government intervention, with Washington and California leading the way, while Transport Canada (unsafe vehicles), Canada's Competition Tribunal (price-fixing and misleading advertising), and Environment Canada (rigged fuel economy claims) exhibit a determined indifference to consumer complaints. Apparently, when it comes to auto safety, Ottawa is more comfortable singing "Kumbaya" with the Detroit Big Two than being a cop on the beat. (Chrysler, the traditional third Detroit-based company, is now London-based Fiat Chrysler Automobiles and uses Amsterdam as a tax-haven.)

HENRY FORD: AUTO CONSUMER ADVOCATE?

In 1916, the Ford Motor Company had a capital surplus of $60 million accumulated through cutting the price of its cars each succeeding year, increasing employee salaries, and sticking to a simple design and colour scheme (which shade of black do you prefer?). As the company's president and majority shareholder, Ford also wanted to end special dividends for shareholders and invest that money in building new factories that would dramatically increase production, improve quality, lower costs to car buyers, and employ more people with higher salaries at his plant. Ford declared:

What a shame that the automobile industry ignored Henry Ford's philosophy that reasonable prices and consistent quality attracts more buyers and produces better machines.

> My ambition is to employ still more men, to spread the benefits of this industrial system to the greatest possible number to help them build up their lives and their homes. To do this we are putting the greatest share of our profits back in the business.

Ford never expected that this philosophy would get him sued by John Francis and Horace Elgin Dodge who owned 10% of Ford shares. In *Dodge v. Ford Motor Company* (170 NW 668 (Mich. 1919)), the brothers asked Michigan's Supreme Court to order Ford to drop his pro-worker, quality-first policy and funnel the company's profits to shareholders, instead.

The court complied and held that Henry Ford's first duty was to shareholders rather than the community as a whole or employees. The trial court judgment was upheld, directors were forced to declare an extra dividend of $19.3 million, and Henry Ford was publicly rebuked by the court:

> A business corporation is organized and carried on primarily for the profit of the stockholders. The powers of the directors are to be employed for that end. The discretion of directors is to be exercised in the choice of means to attain that end, and does not extend to a change in the end itself, to the reduction of profits, or to the non-distribution of profits among stockholders in order to devote them to other purposes.

Henry Ford got the message, the Dodges got seed money to build their Dodge car plant, and American car buyers got a target painted on their backs.

WHAT YOU DON'T KNOW *CAN* HURT YOU

Lemon-Aid published this confidential 2005 GM service bulletin in its 2009 edition. It warns American and Canadian dealers (not car owners) that if a driver is short or uses a large ignition keyring, the car may stall, brakes and steering will fail, and the airbag won't deploy. An improved ignition switch is offered at no charge under this "secret" warranty extension. Incredibly, neither Transport Canada nor General Motors Canada sent out a warning to owners until February 2014 when 2.6 million cars were recalled. Worse, Transport Canada says GM will face charges only when there is proof GM Canada knew of the danger before 2014.

Service Bulletin

File In Section: 02 - Steering
Bulletin No.: 05-02-35-007
Date: December, 2005

INFORMATION

Subject: Information on Inadvertent Turning of Key Cylinder, Loss of Electrical System and No DTCs

Models:
2005-2006 Chevrolet Cobalt
2006 Chevrolet HHR
2005-2006 Pontiac Pursuit (Canada Only)
2006 Pontiac Solstice
2003-2006 Saturn ION

There is potential for the driver to inadvertently turn off the ignition due to low ignition key cylinder torque/effort.

The concern is more likely to occur if the driver is short and has a large and/or heavy key chain. In these cases, this condition was documented and the driver's knee would contact the key chain while the vehicle was turning and the steering column was adjusted all the way down. This is more likely to happen to a person who is short, as they will have the seat positioned closer to the steering column.

In cases that fit this profile, question the customer thoroughly to determine if this may be the cause. The customer should be advised of this potential and should take steps to prevent it – such as removing unessential items from their key chain.

Engineering has come up with an insert for the key ring so that it goes from a "slot" design to a hole design. As a result, the key ring cannot move up and down in the slot any longer – it can only rotate on the hole. In addition, the previous key ring has been replaced with a smaller, 13 mm design. This will result in the keys not hanging as low as in the past.

Parts Information

Part Number	Description
15842334	Cover, Dr Lk & Ign Lk Key

GM bulletins are intended for use by professional technicians, NOT a "do-it-yourselfer". They are written to inform these technicians of conditions that may occur on some vehicles, or to provide information that could assist in the proper service of a vehicle. Properly trained technicians have the equipment, tools, safety instructions, and know how to do a job properly and safely. If a condition is described, DO NOT assume that the bulletin applies to your vehicle, or that your vehicle will have that condition. See your GM dealer for information on whether your vehicle may benefit from the information.

WE SUPPORT VOLUNTARY TECHNICIAN CERTIFICATION

Copyright 2005 General Motors Corporation. All Rights Reserved.

The service bulletin above is that proof.

While Ottawa dithers as to whether GM Canada will be fined for delaying this recall, the U.S. Department of Transportation (NHTSA) has set up a website that not only tells car owners if their car has been recalled, but also if the recall correction has been done. All owners have to do is send their Vehicle Identification Number to *vinrcl.safercar.gov/vin/*. The VIN can be found on the driver-side dash or door jamb.

Secret Car Warranties

Automobile manufacturers use secret warranties to compensate car owners for safety-related and performance-related defects long after the original warranty has expired, sometimes up to ten years. These extended warranties are found in confidential Technical Service Bulletins (TSB) sent to the dealer, but seldom seen by car owners themselves, despite the fact that safety may be affected.

Part Four has an updated list of hundreds of car models covered by secret warranties that will pay for the repair or replacement of defective parts, including engines, transmissions, catalytic converters, brakes, and computer modules, even if you bought your vehicle used. Look at the following little-known warranty extensions that will pay huge repair bills up to 13 years out.

General Motors

SPECIAL COVERAGE ADJUSTMENT – CATALYTIC CONVERTER WARRANTY EXTENSION

BULLETIN NO.: 10134   DATE: NOVEMBER 17, 2010

2006–07 Chevrolet Malibu equipped with 2.2L Engine (L61)
2006–07 Pontiac G6 equipped with 2.4L Engine (LE5)

CONDITION: Some customers of 2006–07 model year Chevrolet Malibu vehicles with a 2.2L engine (L61) and Pontiac G6 vehicles equipped with a 2.4L engine (LE5) may comment about the illumination of the indicator lamp. This may be due to erosion of the mat within the catalytic converter.

SPECIAL COVERAGE ADJUSTMENT: This special coverage covers the condition described for a period of 10 years or 120,000 miles (193,000 km), whichever occurs first, from the date the vehicle was originally placed in service, regardless of ownership. The repairs will be made at no charge to the customer.

Catalytic converters attach to the exhaust system, usually last 5 years, and can cost $500 each to replace. GM's 10-year extended warranty may mean $1,000 savings for two converters. Remember, secret "goodwill" warranties apply whether the vehicle was bought new or used.

2005-07 SUVs with defective fuel level sensors will have the part replaced for free up to 10 years or 120,000 miles. Previous repair costs will be refunded. Affected models are 2005-06 Chevrolet SSR, Trailblazer EXT, GMC Envoy XL; and the 2005-07 Buick Rainier, Chevrolet Trailblazer, and GMC Envoy. Cite GM Campaign #10054E.

Honda

2006-09 Civic engines may have a cracked engine block. This warranty extension will pay for a new engine block. If the engine is "cooked" from overheating, the entire engine will be replaced, *gratis*.

ENGINE BLOCK WARRANTY EXTENSION

CAMPAIGN NO.: 10-048   DATE: DECEMBER 18, 2013

APPLIES TO: 2006-08 Civic - VINs beginning with 1HG or 2HG: 2009 Civic - VINs beginning with 1HG, 19X and 2HG

BACKGROUND: On some 2006-08 and early production 2009 Civics, the engine (cylinder) block may leak engine coolant, resulting in engine overheating. To increase customer confidence, American Honda is extending the warranty of the engine block to 10 years from the original date of purchase, with no mileage limit. The warranty extension does not apply to any vehicle that has ever been declared a total loss or sold for salvage by a financial institution or insurer, or has a branded, or similar title under any states law. To check for vehicle eligibility, you must do a VIN status inquiry.

CUSTOMER NOTIFICATION: Customers were originally sent a notification of this warranty extension that indicated the warranty on the engine block was being extended to eight years. They will receive another notification that the warranty on the block is being extended to 10 years.

CORRECTIVE ACTION: If confirmed by your diagnosis, install a new engine block.

Imagine, how many thousands of Honda owners may have paid for repairs that are covered up to 10 years. To save "he said, she said" disputes with the dealer service manager, present a copy of the above service bulletin. If that doesn't work, take the bulletin to small claims court.

2006-11 Civics with cracked or chalking paint on the hood, roof, trunk, or front fenders will be repainted at no charge up to seven years. Cite Honda Campaign #12-049.

Nissan

2002-05 Altima and Maxima models benefit from a 13-year extended warranty that pays for new bushings and seals, plus the complete replacement of the lower suspension assembly, all affected by premature corrosion. There is no mileage limit under Campaign #P5216.

Toyota, Lexus

Toyota and Lexus have 10-year secret warranties that cover repairs related to oil seepage from an engine oil cooler pipe, a clogged brake fluid reservoir assembly filter, and defective telescoping steering wheel clips.

- **2007-11 Siennas, 2008-11 Highlanders and 2009-11 Venzas. Lexus 2007-11 RX 350 and 2010-11 RX 450h:** In TSB #SC-ZE2 issued on Aug. 1, 2014, Toyota confirmed that oil seepage could occur in these models. They are also eligible for the same free repair according to TSB #SC-ZLC issued the same day. The part will have an unlimited mileage warranty through Jan. 31, 2016, and then be covered by a 10-year, 150,000-mile coverage. (Since these bulletins are American-inspired; no kilometer conversion is given.)

- **Camry Hybrids:** Clogged brake fluid reservoirs in these models are covered for 10 years, according to TSB #SC-E0U issued on July 10, 2014. Toyota is inspecting all Hybrids that may develop the problem until June 30, 2017. If needed, a new brake fluid reservoir will be installed.

- **2005-12 Avalons:** An extended warranty on the steering wheel telescoping clip is available, says TSB #CSP-ZTY issued on April 14, 2014. Toyota has found that the clips may not let the telescoping steering wheel stay in its set position. The part will be covered with no mileage limit until May 31, 2015, on all vehicles, followed by coverage of 10 years from the date of service with no mileage limit.

- **2004-09 Prius:** A faulty dash instrument cluster that suddenly goes dark will have the component replaced for free up to 9 years, with no mileage limit.

- **2004-10 Siennas:** Faulty sliding power doors will be fixed for free up to 9 years, or 120,000 miles. This is clearly a safety-related defect (see Toyota dealer bulletin, below).

TOYOTA

Toyota Motor Sales, U.S.A., Inc.
19001 South Western Avenue
Torrance, CA 90501
(310) 468-4000

2. **CSP Coverage Details**

> Toyota is offering a Warranty Coverage Extension (CSP) for the Rear Sliding Door Latch Assemblies and Power Sliding Door Cable Assembly* for a period of 9 years from the vehicle's date of first use or 120,000 miles, whichever comes first. If the condition is verified, the dealer will replace the Rear Sliding Door Latch Assemblies and/or the Power Sliding Door Cable Assembly* under the terms of this CSP.
>
> *Note: Warranty Extension Coverage for the _Power Sliding Door Cable Assembly_ only applies to Certain 2004 to Certain 2007 Model Year Sienna Vehicles equipped with a _power sliding door_.
>
> Please note that damage incurred from abuse, a crash, vandalism or other non-warrantable causes are not covered by the New Vehicle Limited Warranty or this Warranty Extension.

Lemon-Aid's "Last Ride"

Lemon-Aid has had a successful, though bumpy, ride since its debut in Montreal 45 years ago.

Running through territory that establishment auto critics feared to enter, even on tippy-toes, in 1971 this small 100-page bilingual book dared to oppose Allstate's insurance claims practices and exposed crooked Esso Diagnostic Clinics, gasoline price-fixing, car dealer scams, and automaker safety-related defects. The book sold well in 1971, coincidentally, that same year Ottawa passed the *Canadian Motor Vehicle Safety Act* and Esso began closing its controversial auto Diagnostic Clinics.

After publishing more than 160 annual *Lemon-Aid* guides in French and English and selling almost 2 million copies, I have arrived at where I want to be. Thanks in part to consumer advocacy in the courts, in the legislatures, and in street protests, vehicles are more crashworthy, car bodies are better built, and the avenues for consumer redress are less costly and impressively effective. We now have a $25,000-limit in small claims courts, a legacy of stunning class-action victories, and 50 years of pro-consumer jurisprudence from the Supreme Court down to administrative tribunals.

I am particularly proud of having founded the non-profit, national Automobile Protection Association over four decades ago. Under the capable leadership of its President, George Iny, the APA has worked closely with Quebec's Consumer Protection Bureau and carried out annual undercover exposés of car dealerships throughout Canada.

Best of all, the Association has won precedent-setting consumer protection lawsuits three of the four times it has appeared before Canada's Supreme Court during the past four decades. The one loss, where class-action status was refused to GM Firenza owners, created momentum for Canada's provinces to enact their own class-action laws.

In October 2014, the APA won its latest victory before the Supreme Court when the Court ruled that consumers pursuing a class action for price-fixing against gas station operators could get access to wiretaps made of the alleged conspirators during the government's criminal probe of the plot.

In its six-to-one ruling, the Court declared that parties in civil cases could seek access to those kinds of recordings made in criminal probes and rejected appeals from Imperial Oil Ltd. and other defendants arguing that the lower courts erred in allowing the consumers and the Automobile Protection Association to pursue a class action with damning wiretap information.

In a nutshell, this means that evidence from a criminal investigation can be leveraged by consumers to get compensation in civil court or through an out-of-court settlement. Not only did the government get to levy a huge fine, but motorists who paid too much for gas can now use the same proof to get their money back, as well (*scc-csc.lexum.com/scc-csc/scc-csc/en/item/14399/index.do*).

A precedent, for sure.

Inasmuch as consumer rights are essentially human rights transposed into the marketplace, Canadians have won the war for safe and reliable products, honest prices, and truthful representation of goods and services. And, when we are ripped off, there are myriad government agencies, media organizations, and independent consumer groups who will take up the cudgels to ensure that plaintiffs get an equitable, relatively inexpensive, and quick hearing.

In less than 50 years, *Lemon-Aid* has helped transform Canada's namby-pamby automobile consumer protection philosophy of "buyer beware" or "blame the victim," to one of "seller beware" – the gist of Henry Ford's philosophy and plain common sense.

Phil Edmonston

September 2015

Part One
CHEAP GAS AND COSTLIER CARS

What a difference a year makes, Fuel prices are hitting new lows, creating a seller's market for fully-loaded, Internet-connected large cars, trucks, SUVs, and vans, and a buyer's market for fuel-sipping compact cars, diesel-engine-equipped cars and trucks, hybrids, and electric vehicles.

GAS PUMP BUMP

The present oil glut and OPEC's inability to hike prices means cheap gasoline will be available for a few years before they return to their 2014 peak. In last year's blowout sellers' market, cheap gasoline and pent-up buyer demand, not quality or safety improvements, enabled Chrysler, Ford, and General Motors to make wind-fall profits selling fewer cars at higher prices. They pulled this rabbit out of the hat by pushing fully-loaded, high-tech equipped, large cars and trucks, offering generous leasing incentives, and extending financing to eight years.

In less than a year, oil prices have fallen precipitously, from over $110 U.S. per barrel to $45 for some grades of crude. Although motorists welcome the savings at the pump, lower gas prices aren't entirely good for the auto industry or the environment. Car-shoppers, are already turning away from "greener" mini-compacts, hybrid, and electric vehicles.

Governments are rightfully worried that cheaper fuel will be a game-changer that could spell the end of market forces driving shoppers to purchase smaller vehicles, keep their cars longer (about 11 years is the norm in North America), and drive less.

This concern is responsible for the passage of more restrictive government regulations to protect the environment and conserve oil. French Prime Minister Manuel Vallis, for example, says he wants to phase out the 10,000 euro bonus government gives to buyers of diesel-powered passenger cars. "In France, we have long favored the diesel engine," he said, according to *Reuters*. "This was a mistake, and we will progressively undo that, intelligently and pragmatically." Keep in mind this was said a year before Volkswagen admitted it had cheated on emissions tests and confirmed its diesels were spewing 40 times the nitrogen oxide permitted. from 2009-15.

This is a nightmarish scenario for automobile manufacturers who have bet big on diesels and don't believe there could be an orderly phaseout of diesel-equipped vehicles. In fact, one can predict the impact this policy will have on car sales in a nation where nearly 80 percent of light vehicles are diesel-powered. But that's just the beginning. Vallis also promises to rate cars according to how much they pollute, and let cities limit access for the most-polluting vehicles.

Presently, there's a global trend toward restricted vehicle use in large cities, and as driving costs go down these restrictions will surely tighten along with increased fuel taxes to maintain infrastructure and promote more efficient vehicles and mass transit. For example, a report by the U.S. Environmental Protection Agency (EPA) notes that:

> Several foreign cities, such as Athens, Mexico City, Santiago and Singapore, have established mandatory no-drive days, or severe restriction on driving into certain congested areas during specific time periods [e.g., during the morning peak period].
>
> In Singapore, special licenses are required for driving into the central business district during the morning peak period for all vehicles except busses, emergency vehicles, motorcycles, and vehicles with four or more occupants.

Closer to Canada, the EPA reports that Boston's "no car zone" "resulted in a 40 to 45 percent reduction in carbon monoxide levels within the restricted area with no corresponding or off-setting increase outside the area."

More Choice, Better Deals

2015 is shaping up as a banner year for new and used car sales in Canada, thanks to the resurgence of leasing, more sales incentives, lower fuel prices and interest rates, and increased competition from Asian automakers using devalued currency. This has resulted in a glut of 2015 models that has depressed prices and improved the availability of some of last year's more popular models. To "move the iron" dealers are sweetening rebates, adding standard equipment and several years of free maintenance, including plus zero percent financing, and offering new car loans for up to 96 months. Of course the longer the loan, the more the vehicle costs, but this isn't of much consequence, if you beat the depreciation demons by keeping the vehicle at least eight years and fuel stays cheap.

On the other hand, Canada's swooning loonie is wiping out any real savings from lower gas prices and opening the window for massive price gouging by auto manufacturers in Canada. The loonie has dropped to its lowest level since 2004, worth just $0.77 U.S. Put another way, a U.S. dollar is now worth $1.31 Canadian and falling.

Something Old, Something New

This year it will take a sharp eye to spot which of the new and upgraded models are worth more money than last year's offering.

2015-16 models that are new, upgraded or dropped.

NEW	UPGRADED	
*Acura TLX	BMW X6	Lincoln MKS
Alfa Romeo 4C	Buick LaCrosse	Mercedes-Benz
Audi Q3	*Cadillac Escalade	C-Class
Audi Q5	*Chevrolet City	Nissan Murano
Audi A5	Express	Smart ForTwo
BMW X4	Chevrolet Colorado	*Subaru Legacy
Chevroltet Trax	*Chevrolet Suburban	*Subaru Outback
*Honda CR-V	*Chevrolet Tahoe	*Toyota Camry
*Ifiniti Q30	Chevrolet Trax	*VW GTI
Jeep Renegade	Dodge Challenger	*VW Golf/
*Lexus NX	Dodge Charger	Sportswagen
*Lexus RC Coupe	Ford Edge	*VW Jetta
*Mercedes-Benz GLA	Ford F-150	Volvo XC90
Mini Cooper	Ford Econoline	
Nissan Versa Note	*Ford Mustang	**DROPPED**
Ram ProMaster City	*GMC Yukon	*Acura TL
*Tesla Model X	*GMC Yukon XL	*Acura TSX
VW eGolf	*Honda CR-V	BMW 1 Series
VW Phaeton	*Honda Fit	Cadillac CTS-V
	Hyundai Sonata	Chrysler 200
	Kia Sedona	Convertible
	Land Rover Discovery	Dodge Avenger
		Jeep Liberty

NOTE: Vehicles preceded by an * are "good buys" – new or used.

15 Buying Tips

Now's a particularly good time to be a patient shopper.

Time works to your advantage as better products make their debut and lower oil prices continue to drive down prices of fuel-sipping economy cars, compacts, hybrids, and electrics. Also, dealer inventories have to be cleaned out by year's end to make room for the 2016 model arrivals. Prices cut by 10-15 percent are commonplace with these smaller cars and will probably be more during the winter months. Conversely, with the money saved from cheaper fuel and home heating savings, Canadians are rushing to dealers to pick up over-priced, inefficient, bloated, all-dressed, large trucks, SUVs, vans, and European luxury cars. To hell with the fuel penalty. After being nagged for years about oil shortages and gas that would reach $7 a gallon, we have suddenly found ourselves awash in cheap oil and greater competition in the oil patch and among retailers. Our collective consciousness says, "It's time for a treat. I want mine. Bigger is better."

In addition to the oil glut savings, there are a number of other ways whereby car buyers can save from $10,000 to $15,000 on a car purchase:

1. Buy a vehicle that is relatively uncomplicated, is easy to service, and has been sold in large numbers over many years. This will ensure that cheaper, independent garages can provide service and parts.

2. Look for a vehicle that's finishing its model run, but steer clear of models that were axed because of poor reliability or mediocre performance, like GM's front-drive minivans, Jeeps, pre-2014 Chevrolet Impalas, Nissan's Quest, and American hybrids.

3. Don't buy European offerings, unless you *know* local servicing is competent and reasonably priced. Dealership networks are notoriously weak for these cars, parts are inordinately expensive and hard to find, and few independent garages will invest in the expensive equipment needed to service complicated emissions and fuel-delivery systems. Earlier this year CBC aired a story of an Ontario woman who bought a used 2010 BMW Mini and after seven months was given an estimate for a $10,000 engine rebuild. The old axiom that there is a right way, a wrong way, and an expensive European way to fix a car still holds true.

4. Don't buy a hybrid or electric model. Most give a poor return on investment, are complicated to service, dealer-dependent, and they don't always provide the fuel economy or savings they hype. A VW diesel is far more reliable and gives you a greater return on investment (see chart below). However, wait for the dust to settle before buying a new or used VW diesel. Performance and fuel economy will likely suffer on 2009-2015 models that don't meet emissions regulations.

The Dodge Ram is a good buy, when equipped with the Cummins diesel engine. It beats all the competition for power and reliability.

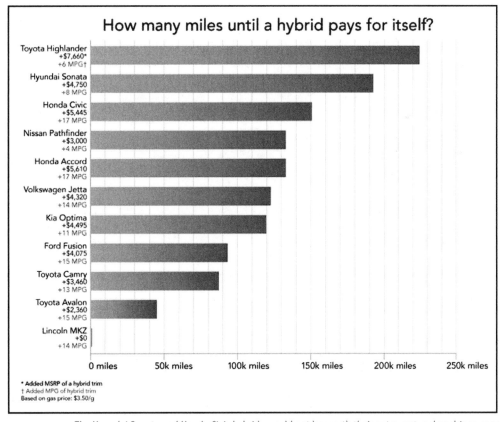

How many miles until a hybrid pays for itself?

Toyota Highlander +$7,660* +6 MPG†	
Hyundai Sonata +$4,750 +8 MPG	
Honda Civic +$5,445 +17 MPG	
Nissan Pathfinder +$3,000 +4 MPG	
Honda Accord +$5,610 +17 MPG	
Volkswagen Jetta +$4,320 +14 MPG	
Kia Optima +$4,495 +11 MPG	
Ford Fusion +$4,075 +15 MPG	
Toyota Camry +$3,460 +13 MPG	
Toyota Avalon +$2,360 +15 MPG	
Lincoln MKZ +$0 +14 MPG	

0 miles   50k miles   100k miles   150k miles   200k miles   250k miles

* **Added MSRP of a hybrid trim**
† Added MPG of hybrid trim
Based on gas price: $3.50/g

The Hyundai Sonata and Honda Civic hybrids would not be worth their extra cost, unless driven over 241,401.5 km (150,000 mi). BMW's Active 3 Hybrid? No problem. Simply drive it almost 3.25 million km (2 *million* mi) to balance out its higher purchase price — $6,400 more than a 335i.

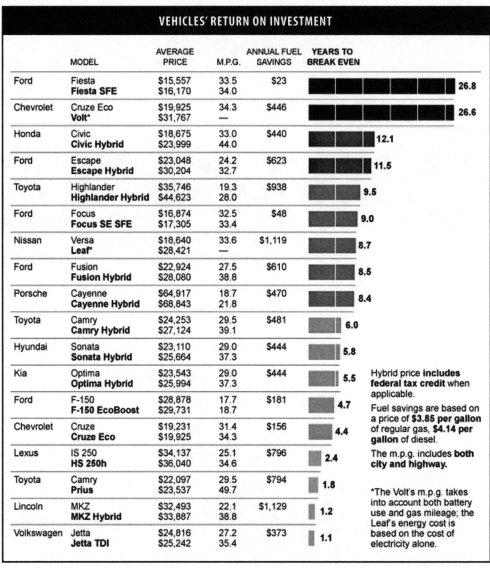

	MODEL	AVERAGE PRICE	M.P.G.	ANNUAL FUEL SAVINGS	YEARS TO BREAK EVEN
Ford	Fiesta **Fiesta SFE**	$15,557 $16,170	33.5 34.0	$23	26.8
Chevrolet	Cruze Eco **Volt***	$19,925 $31,767	34.3 —	$446	26.6
Honda	Civic **Civic Hybrid**	$18,675 $23,999	33.0 44.0	$440	12.1
Ford	Escape **Escape Hybrid**	$23,048 $30,204	24.2 32.7	$623	11.5
Toyota	Highlander **Highlander Hybrid**	$35,746 $44,623	19.3 28.0	$938	9.5
Ford	Focus **Focus SE SFE**	$16,874 $17,305	32.5 33.4	$48	9.0
Nissan	Versa **Leaf***	$18,640 $28,421	33.6 —	$1,119	8.7
Ford	Fusion **Fusion Hybrid**	$22,924 $28,080	27.5 38.8	$610	8.5
Porsche	Cayenne **Cayenne Hybrid**	$64,917 $68,843	18.7 21.8	$470	8.4
Toyota	Camry **Camry Hybrid**	$24,253 $27,124	29.5 39.1	$481	6.0
Hyundai	Sonata **Sonata Hybrid**	$23,110 $25,664	29.0 37.3	$444	5.8
Kia	Optima **Optima Hybrid**	$23,543 $25,994	29.0 37.3	$444	5.5
Ford	F-150 **F-150 EcoBoost**	$28,878 $29,731	17.7 18.7	$181	4.7
Chevrolet	Cruze **Cruze Eco**	$19,231 $19,925	31.4 34.3	$156	4.4
Lexus	IS 250 **HS 250h**	$34,137 $36,040	25.1 34.6	$796	2.4
Toyota	Camry **Prius**	$22,097 $23,537	29.5 49.7	$794	1.8
Lincoln	MKZ **MKZ Hybrid**	$32,493 $33,887	22.1 38.8	$1,129	1.2
Volkswagen	Jetta **Jetta TDI**	$24,816 $25,242	27.2 35.4	$373	1.1

VEHICLES' RETURN ON INVESTMENT

Hybrid price **includes federal tax credit** when applicable.

Fuel savings are based on a price of **$3.85 per gallon** of regular gas, **$4.14 per gallon** of diesel.

The m.p.g. includes **both city and highway.**

*The Volt's m.p.g. takes into account both battery use and gas mileage; the Leaf's energy cost is based on the cost of electricity alone.

Note: After these figures were published in the *New York Times* April 4, 2012, GM dropped the Volt price by $10,000 U.S. and Nissan cut the Leaf's MSRP by $15,000. The 2016 Volt has been revamped.

Source: *www.truecar.com*

OppositeLock.com updated and confirmed TrueCar's earlier study with 2014 model cars (*oppositelock.jalopnik.com/is-the-hybrid-trim-really-worth-it-1618280072/1625147629/+whitsongordon*). They found the purported savings on gas consumption doesn't justify the higher cost of most hybrids – unless you buy a Lincoln MKZ where there isn't much of a price difference.

Electrics: An analysis done by *MojoMotors.com* shows the $79,900 U.S. Tesla S is the best-performing electric car studied. The Chevy Spark EV came in second place. The worst vehicles? BMW's i3 BEV and the Toyota RAV4 EV. Ford's $36,199 Focus EV has also received underwhelming support.

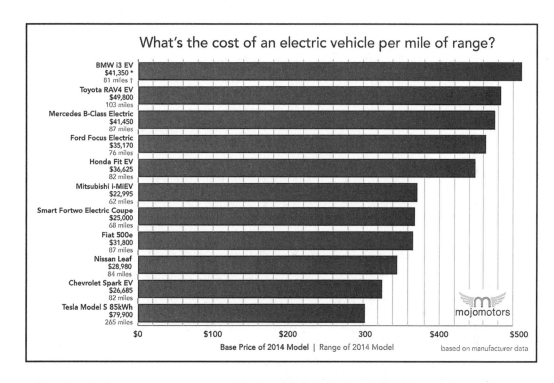

What's the cost of an electric vehicle per mile of range?

BMW i3 EV
$41,350 *
81 miles †

Toyota RAV4 EV
$49,800
103 miles

Mercedes B-Class Electric
$41,450
87 miles

Ford Focus Electric
$35,170
76 miles

Honda Fit EV
$36,625
82 miles

Mitsubishi i-MiEV
$22,995
62 miles

Smart Fortwo Electric Coupe
$25,000
68 miles

Fiat 500e
$31,800
87 miles

Nissan Leaf
$28,980
84 miles

Chevrolet Spark EV
$26,685
82 miles

Tesla Model S 85kWh
$79,900
265 miles

mojomotors

$0 $100 $200   300 $400 $500

Base Price of 2014 Model | Range of 2014 Model   based on manufacturer data

Who buys a $79,9000 U.S. Tesla to save money on fuel? Electrics will always have inherent limitations on range, especially in the North American context. It will never provide the travel distance that you require, especially based on what we know today about the limited storage capabilities of batteries and the small network of charging stations.

5. Be wary of Chrysler, Dodge, or Jeep models. Chrysler is the weakest of the Detroit Three and its lineup has a sad history of serious safety- and performance-related defects, with the TIMP module being a case in point. Automatic transmissions, brakes, the electrical system, and air conditioners are particularly troublesome. On the other hand, 2014-16 diesel and gasoline-powered Ram trucks break the mold and are recommended buys. Also, the Chrysler group will launch a plug-in hybrid version of the next-generation 2016 Chrysler Town & Country minivan this year. The minivan will be powered by a gasoline engine and a battery pack. Buyers are keeping their fingers crossed.

   Other hybrids will follow, including a Chrysler-badged full-size crossover. But CEO Sergio Marchionne warned that electrification is not a panacea to increase the fuel economy of his company's fleet. He believes that a plug-in minivan hybrid could achieve fuel economy that would rival the much smaller Toyota Prius, rated at 50 mpg for combined highway and city driving. The 2014 plug-in Prius is rated at 95 mpg-e, a rating for combined use of electricity and gasoline. After the battery is depleted, the vehicle is rated at 50 mpg combined highway and city.

6. Don't buy American Big Three front-drives. After three decades of trying, Chrysler, GM, and Ford still can't get it right. With the lone exception of the 2012-15 Chevrolet Impala and perhaps the 2016 Malibu, American front-drives have been plagued by serious powertrain, suspension, brake, and electronic glitches. Models that are co-productions like the GM-Toyota Vibe-Matrix built on Asian front-drive technology are recommended buys.

7. Don't be blinded by luxury, high-performance, or turbochargers; higher-priced cars don't ensure you will get a higher-level of quality or reliability. Think Cadillac ATS, XLR, and XTS, Lincoln MKS, MKT (with EcoBoost), MKX, and the VW Touareg.

   As for turbocharged small engines, they are often slower and less fuel efficient than larger four- and six-cylinder engines. For instance, *Consumer Reports* found that the 2013 Ford Fusion's EcoBoost four-cylinder (an $800 option), burned more gas (25 mpg) than similar models with conventional engines. Turbo-equipped vehicles that are less fuel efficient than V6 models in the same class are the Hyundai Sonata, Kia Sportage, and Ford Escape. Moreover, a turbocharged 1.6L Chevrolet Cruze got the same gas mileage as the same car powered by a larger 1.8L engine. On the other hand, BMW and VW turbocharged models did perform as advertised giving better mileage and faster acceleration times.

8. Steer clear of cars, parts, or tires made in China. Except for a five-star rating for the 2014 Qoros small sedan, European and Australian crash test scores for most Chinese-made vehicles are listed as "Poor," and their assembly quality is several notches below Tonka, at best.

Jacob George, vice-president of China operations for J. D. Power Asia Pacific says Chinese-built vehicles won't match U.S. average initial quality before 2016. *Lemon-Aid* believes that assessment is overly optimistic. For example, *Consumer Reports* tire testers reported last September that among 20 tires tested, three all-season brands exported from China (Geostar, Sunny, and Pegasus) finished last in the rankings for snow traction and tread life. The 2015 Volvo S60L stretched S60 sedan could be the first vehicle made in

China's Brilliant (no kidding!) large sedan was found to offer no occupant crash protection.

China to be exported to North America. Since Volvo was purchased by China's Zhejiang Geely Holdings in 2010, local buyers have created unprecedented sales for the once-Swedish automaker and this popularity may delay the car's arrival.

9. Don't buy a 2013-14 Ford vehicle equipped with an EcoBoost turbocharged engine. These powerplants are noted for their chronic loss of power, stalling, on-road bucking, and surging.

10. Choose a conventional hydraulic automatic transmission. Be wary of CVT and DCG automatics. Nissan CVT-equipped vehicles have been so failure prone that the company has extended its warranty up to ten years on most of the 2007-10 lineup.

NISSAN CVT – CUSTOMER SATISFACTION PROGRAM

The following is a list of vehicles included in the Nissan CVT Warranty Extension program:

2007	2008	2009	2010
Murano	–	Murano	Murano
–	Rogue	Rogue cube®	Rogue cube®
Sentra	Sentra	Sentra	Sentra
Versa 1.8SL	Versa 1.8SL	Versa 1.8SL	Versa 1.8SL
Maxima	Maxima	Maxima	Maxima
Altima	Altima	Altima	Altima
Altima Coupe	Altima Coupe	Altima Coupe	Altima Coupe
Altima Hybrid	Altima Hybrid	Altima Hybrid	Altima Hybrid

Nissan's ten-year "goodwill" warranty covers almost any … eventuality.

11. Make sure the vehicle comes with a full-sized spare tire and jack, not a spray can of sealant. Include this stipulation in the contract. If you wait until the vehicle is delivered, the dealer will likely charge you $200+ for a so-so original equipment tire.

12. Start shopping during the winter of 2016, when the auto show hoopla has died down and GM-sweetened rebates drive prices downward.

13. Don't buy from dual dealerships. Parts inventories at many dealerships may have been depleted due to slow sales, and qualified mechanic may be in short supply. The represented auto companies see the dealerships as less than loyal and will cut them little slack in vehicle deliveries and warranty assistance.

14. Don't buy any vehicle that requires an extended warranty due to a reputation for past failures. Choose a better car, instead.

15. Use your credit card for the down payment, and put down as little money as possible. Use credit instead of cash to pay for repairs and maintenance charges. If you want to cancel a sales contract or work order, it's easier to do with a credit card than with cash.

WHICH NEW CAR, TRUCK, SUV, OR VAN

I remember in the '70s, American Motors gave away free TVs with each new car purchase, just before shutting its doors. In the past decade, General Motors gave away free Dell computers and VW hawked free guitars with its cars. The Detroit Three automakers continue to build poor-quality cars and trucks, although there appears to be some improvement over the past three years. The gap between Asian and American automobile quality has narrowed; however, this may reflect only a lowered benchmark following recent Honda, Nissan, and Toyota powertrain, electrical system, and body fit glitches and a substantial increase in recalls. Nevertheless, Asian makes continue to dominate J.D. Power and Associates' dependability surveys, while other American and European models are mostly ranked below the industry average, but are trending upward.

Incidentally, Ford, long the darling for improved quality scores during the past five years, has crashed in the latest ratings charts due to chronic infotainment electronic failures, faulty EcoBoost (turbocharged) powertrains, and false fuel-economy ratings with its C-Max hybrid and Fusion compact. Ford was sued by owners of the 2013 Fusion Hybrid and C-Max Hybrid, who complained the company's official fuel economy figures were lies. The company settled out of court.

In their class-action petition filed in Philadelphia in April 2013, the owners claimed:

> Plaintiffs are some of the tens of thousands of consumers who purchased a Fusion Hybrid or C-Max Hybrid, only to be stuck with under-performing, less-valuable vehicles that inflict

higher fuel costs on their owners. Both cars are rated at 47 mpg in all three EPA categories (city, highway, combined), but in *Consumer Reports'* full test, the Fusion Hybrid returned 39 mpg, while the C-Max Hybrid returned 37 mpg.

Step 1: Be Patient and Practical

First, keep in mind that you are going to spend much more money than you may have anticipated – almost $28,000 for the average car and $40,000 for most minivans, according to Dennis DesRosiers, a Toronto-based auto consultant. The many hidden fees, like freight charges and so-called administrative costs, are added to the bottom line. But, with cut-throat discounts and armed with tips from this guide, you can bring that amount down by at least a couple thousand dollars.

According to the Canadian Automobile Association (CAA), the average household owns two vehicles, which are each driven about 20,000 km annually and cost an average of $800 a year for maintenance; DesRosiers estimates $1,100.

Keep in mind that it's practically impossible to buy a bare-bones car or truck because automakers know this is a seller's market until this winter, so they tend to cram new cars with costly, non-essential performance and convenience features in order to maximize their profits. Nevertheless, money-wasting features like factory-installed electronic navigation, self-parking, digital screens, and voice-command capability can easily be passed up with little impact on safety or convenience. In fact, voice command and in-dash computer screens can be very distracting while driving – producing a negative safety effect. Rear-view cameras, full-torso side curtain airbags and electronic stability control (ESC), however, are important safety options that are well worth the extra expense.

Our driving needs are influenced by where we live, our lifestyles, and our ages (see Cars for Seniors, below, for a discussion of vehicles best suited to mature drivers). The ideal car should be cheap (a three-year-old can easily save you $10,000), crashworthy and easy to drive, have minimal high-tech features to distract and annoy, and not cost much to maintain.

In the city, a small wagon or hatchback is more practical and less expensive than a mid-sized car like the Honda Accord or Toyota Camry. Furthermore, have you seen the newer Civic and Elantra? What once were small cars are now quite large, relatively fuel-efficient, and equipped with more horsepower than you'll ever likely need. Nevertheless, if you're going to be doing a lot of highway driving, transporting small groups of people, or loading up on accessories, a medium-sized sedan, wagon, or small sport-utility could be the best choice for price, comfort, and reliability.

Don't let low fuel prices stampede you into buying a vehicle unsuitable to your driving needs. If you travel less than 20,000 km per year, mostly in the city, choose a small car or SUV equipped with a 4-cylinder engine that produces about 140 hp to get the best fuel economy without sacrificing performance. Anything more powerful is just a waste. Extensive highway driving, however, demands the cruising performance, extra power for additional accessories, and durability of a larger, 6-cylinder engine. Believe me, fuel savings will be the last thing on your mind if you buy an underpowered vehicle.

Carrmakers give false figures in five areas: Fuel economy, emissions, rear legroom, payload, and towing capacity. Confirm these claims with a test drive, and get the recommendation of a dealer for the trailer or boat you intend to haul.

Be especially wary of the towing capabilities bandied about by automakers. They routinely exaggerate towing capability by removing the bumpers, spare tire, radio, consoles, thinning each passenger down to 150 pounds, and substituting lighter aluminum alloy wheels. Ford's deception spans its 2011-15 models; GM has been lying from 2014-15. Another towing caveat: Dealers seldom mention the need for expensive optional equipment, or that the top safe towing speed may be only 72 km/h (45 mph).

Generally, 3-3.8L V6 engines will safely accommodate most towing needs. The 4-cylinder engines may handle light loads, but will likely offer a white-knuckle experience when merging with highway traffic or travelling over hilly terrain.

Remember, you may have to change your driving habits to accommodate the type of vehicle you purchase. Front-drive braking is quite different from braking with a rear-drive, and braking efficiency on ABS-equipped vehicles is compromised if you pump the brakes. Also, rear-drive vans handle like trucks, and you may scrub the right-rear tire during sharp right-hand turns until you get the hang of making wider turns. Limited rear visibility is another problem with larger vans, forcing drivers to carefully survey side and rear traffic before changing lanes or merging.

Step 2: Explore Alternatives

Don't confuse styling with needs (do you have a bucket bottom to conform to those bucket seats?) or trendy with essential (will a cheaper down-sized SUV like a Hyundai Tucson or Subaru Forester suit you as well as, or better than, a mid-sized car?). Visiting the showroom with your spouse, a level-headed relative, or a sensible friend will help you steer a truer course through all the non-essential options you'll be offered.

Getting a female perspective can be really helpful. Women don't generally receive the same welcome at auto showrooms as men do, but that's because they make the salesmen (yes, usually less than 10 percent of the sales staff are women) work too hard to make a sale. Most sales agents admit that female shoppers are far more knowledgeable about what they want and more patient in negotiating contract details than men, who tend to be mesmerized by many of the techno-toys available.

In increasing numbers, women have discovered that minivans, SUVs, and small pickups are more versatile than passenger cars and station wagons. And, having spotted a profitable trend, automakers are offering increased versatility combined with unconventional styling in so-called "crossover" vehicles. These blended cars are part sedan and part station wagon, with a touch of sport-utility added for function and fun. For example, the Ford Flex is a smaller, sporty crossover vehicle that looks like a miniature SUV. First launched as a 2009 model, the Flex comes in an entry-level SE trim line that brings down the starting price a bit.

Small South Korean SUVs like this Hyundai Tucson ($21,999 plus, $1,760 freight) are ideal for small families and light commuting. Remember, Hyundai owns Kia and their vehicles are quite similar. So, if a Hyundai dealer doesn't have the model or offer the price you want, go to a Kia outlet.

2013 Ford Flex Technical Service Bulletins

TSB Number	TSB Date	TSB Title
14-0105	05/21/2014	Rough Idle
14-0083	04/30/2014	Door Ajar Lamp ON With Doors Closed
14-0057	03/19/2014	Leak From Differential Vent Cap
14-0051	03/13/2014	Poor AM/AM-HD Band Reception/Whistling Noise
14-0037	02/28/2014	Navigation System – Display Offset or Incorrect Position
13-10-17	10/25/2013	Power Liftgate Inop.
13-10-6	10/04/2013	MyFord/MyLincoln Touch Issues
13-9-22	09/27/2013	SYNC(R) – Various Concerns
13S04S4	08/19/2013	Fuel Leaks
12A04S4	08/09/2013	Campaign – MyFord/MyLincoln Touch(R) Performance Upgrade
13-5-14	05/21/2013	Pop/Click Noise On Acceleration
13-4-16	04/25/2013	Intermittent No Upshift
13-4-19	04/25/2013	Exhaust Sulfur Odor
13-3-11	03/21/2013	Unable To Locate Vehicle Or GPS Concerns
13-3-9	03/15/2013	Water Leak From Roof Opening Panel
13-2-6	02/14/2013	Rattle Or Scratching Noise From The Headliner Area
13-1-1	01/10/2013	Memory Sys – Incorrect Easy Entry/Exit Steering Column Position
12-12-11	12/31/2012	Seat Heaters Not Warm Enough
12-11-8	11/15/2012	Audio System – Display Stays On 20-30 Seconds After Key Off
12-11-1	11/05/2012	My Ford/Lincoln Touch(R) – Various Issues

Ford's $28,674 Flex is somewhat pricey, but it does offer car-like performance, SUV versatility, and excellent crashworthiness. A perusal of Ford service bulletins and owner complaints shows long-term reliability is worse than average.

Step 3: Stick to Your Budget

Determine how much money you can spend, and then decide which vehicles in that price range interest you. Have several models in mind so that the overpriced one won't tempt you as much. As your benchmarks, use the ratings, alternative models, estimated purchase costs, and residual value figures shown in Part Four of this guide. Remember, logic and prudence are the first casualties of showroom hype, so carefully consider what you actually need and how these things will fit into your budget before comparing models and prices at a dealership.

Write down your first, second, and third choices relative to each model and the equipment offered. Browse the automaker websites both in Canada and in the States, and consult *www.unhaggle.com* for the Canadian manufacturer's suggested retail price (MSRP), promotions, and package discounts. Look for special low prices that may apply only to Internet-generated referrals. Once you get a good idea of the price variations, get out the fax machine or PC at home or work (a company letterhead is always impressive) and then make the dealers bid against each other (see Cutting the Price, below). Call the lowest-bidding dealership, ask for an appointment to be assured of getting a sales agent's complete attention, and take along the downloaded price info from the Canadian and American automaker websites to avoid arguments.

Sometimes a cheaper "twin" will fit the bill. Twins are nameplates made by different auto manufacturers, or by different divisions of the same company, that are virtually identical in body design and mechanical components, like the Chevrolet Silverado and GMC Sierra pickups.

Let's look at the savings possible with "twinned" Chrysler minivans. A 2009 Grand Caravan SXT that was originally listed for $31,395 is now worth about $5,500. An upscale 2009 Town & Country Limited that performs similarly to the Grand Caravan, with just a few additional gizmos, first sold for $42,995 and is now worth about $10,500. Where once almost $11,500 separated the two minivans, the price difference is now only $5,000 – and you can expect the gap to close to almost nil over the next few years. Did the little extras really justify the Town & Country's higher price, or make it a better buy than the Grand Caravan? Obviously, the marketplace thinks not.

And don't get taken in by the "Buy Canadian!" chanting from Chrysler, Ford, General Motors, and the Canadian Auto Workers. It's pure hokum. While Detroit-based automakers are beating their chests over the need to buy American, they buy Asian automakers and suppliers and then market the foreign imports as their own. This practice has resulted in bastardized nameplates whose parentage isn't always easy to nail down. For example, is the Aveo a Chevy or a Daewoo? (For the record, it's a Daewoo, and not that reliable, to boot.) Beyond car makes, imported Chinese auto parts have had a poor reliability record over the past decade running the gamut of leaking tire valve stems affecting all automakers who bought "bargain-basement" imported stems to "grenading" 2011-13 5.0L Mustang GT high performance manual transmission, that also fail to go into Second gear.

This brings up the question as to whether Chinese automakers can be trusted to make safe, reliable parts and vehicles that aren't mis-represented. *Lemon-Aid* thinks not. We believe the corporate DNA of Chinese automakers is to maximize profits at all cost.

Chinese manufacturers sold millions of failure-prone tire stem valves to American car companies, have flooded the North American market with low-quality, counterfeit brand tires, and continue to fake the competition. They copied GM's Daewoo subcompact and renamed it the "Chery." GM sued when the Chinese manufacturer used a disguised GM Daewoo in a crash test in place of the Chery (China Motor Vehicle Documentation Centre. Retrieved 2011-03-12). And now they are ripping off Land Rover by selling a copy of the Evoque SUV and marketing it as the 2016 "Landwind X7."

According to *Autocar*, the Landwind X7 is expected to sell for the equivalent of $22,000 in China, or about $30,000 cheaper than the Evoque.

Vehicles that are produced through co-ventures between Detroit automakers and Asian manufacturers have better quality control than vehicles manufactured by companies that were bought outright, and this looks like one of the factors that may save the American auto industry. For example, Toyota and Pontiac churned out identical Matrix and Vibe compacts in Ontario and the U.S.; however, the cheaper, Ontario-built Matrix has the better reputation for quality. On the other hand, Jaguar and Volvo quality declined when Ford bought the companies and Volvo is just getting on its feet under Chinese ownership. GM-owned Saab has gone bankrupt, although General Motors still pledges to honour all warranties on Saabs it sold. As for Daimler's shotgun wedding with Chrysler, apart from dissension, what did they really build together – certainly no innovative, high-quality products.

Sometimes choosing a higher trim line that packages many options as standard features will cost you less when you take all the features into account separately. It's hard to compare these bundled prices with the manufacturer's base price and added options in Canada, though, U.S. automaker websites often provide more details. All of the separate prices are inflated and must be negotiated downward individually, while fully equipped vehicles don't allow for options to be deleted or priced separately. Furthermore, many of the bundled options are superfluous, and you probably wouldn't have chosen them to begin with.

In North America, auto buyers are moving upscale. There is a major shift from small to large cars, and large sedans to crossovers and full-sized SUVs. *TrueCar.com*, an American auto analyst, says transaction costs reflects this trend: Mid-size SUVs average $6,465 more than mid-size sedans and compact utilities sell for $5,379 more than compact cars. Since an SUV costs automakers only about $1,500 more to make than a sedan on the same platform, manufacturers are making record profits selling fewer vehicles. Also, not only are women joining the upscale crowd, seniors as well have embraced "bigger is better." *Edmunds*, a publisher of car reviews, says nearly half of compact SUV and crossover buyers are older than 55.

Minivans, SUVs and pickups, for example, often come in two versions: A base commercial (or cargo) version and a more luxurious model for private use. The commercial version doesn't have as many bells and whistles, but it's more likely to be in stock and will probably cost much less. And if you're planning to convert it, there's a wide choice of independent customizers that will likely do a better – and less expensive – job than the dealer. Of course, you will want a written guarantee from the dealer or customizer, or sometimes both, that no changes will invalidate the manufacturer's warranty. Also, look on the lot for a low-mileage (less than 10,000 km) demonstrator that has been carried over unchanged. You will get an end-of-model-year rebate, a lower price for the extra mileage, and sundry other sales incentives that apply. Remember, if the vehicle has been registered to another company or individual, it is no longer a demo and should be considered used and be discounted accordingly (by at least 25 percent). You will also want to carry out a CarProof (*www.carproof.com*) VIN search and get a complete printout of the vehicle's service history.

When and Where to Buy

When to Buy

Start doing your research now, but wait until the first of the year to get a more reasonable price. And shoppers who wait until next summer or early fall can double-dip from additional automakers' dealer incentive and buyer rebate programs. Remember, too, that vehicles made between March and August offer the most factory upgrades and fewer factory-related glitches.

Visit the showroom at the end of the month, just before closing, when the salesperson will want to make that one last sale to meet the month's quota. If sales have been terrible, the sales manager may be willing to do some extra negotiating in order to boost sales staff's morale.

Where to Buy

Large cities have more selection, and dealers offer a variety of payment plans that will likely suit your budget. Prices are also very competitive as dealers use sales volume to make most of their profit.

But, price isn't everything and good dealers aren't always the ones with the lowest prices. Buying from someone you know gives honest and reliable service is just as important as getting a low price. Check a dealer's honesty and reliability by talking with motorists in your community who drive vehicles purchased from the local dealer (identified by the nameplate on the vehicle's trunk). If these customers have been treated fairly, they'll be glad to recommend their dealer. You can also check the dealer's thoroughness in new-vehicle preparation and servicing by renting a vehicle for a weekend, or by getting your trade-in serviced.

How can you tell which dealers are the most honest and competent? Well, judging from the thousands of reports I receive each year, dealerships in small suburban and rural communities are often fairer than big-city dealers because they're more vulnerable to negative word-of-mouth testimonials and to poor sales – when their vehicles aren't selling, good service picks up the slack. Their prices may also be more competitive, but don't count on it. Unfortunately, as part of their bankruptcy restructuring, Chrysler and General Motors closed down many dealerships in suburban and rural areas because the dealers couldn't generate sufficient sales volume to meet the automakers' profit targets.

Dealers that sell more than one manufacturer's product line present special problems. Their overhead can be quite high, and the cancellation of a dual dealership by an automaker in favour of setting up an exclusive franchise elsewhere is an ever-present threat. Parts availability may also be a problem because dealers with two separate vehicle lines must split their inventory and may, therefore, have an inadequate supply on hand (read: Smart/Mercedes and former Mitsubishi/Chrysler partnerships).

The quality of new-vehicle service is directly linked to the number and competence of dealerships within the network. If the network is weak, parts are likely to be unavailable, repair costs can go through the roof, and the skill level of the mechanics may be subpar, since better mechanics command higher salaries. Among foreign manufacturers, Asian and South Korean have a much improved overall dealer representation across Canada, primarily due to record-breaking sales during the last few years.

European automaker profits aren't expected to grow much throughout 2015 as Europe's economic troubles continue to cut auto sales by about 10 percent. Nevertheless, the popularity of upscale European cars in China and North America should improve the bottom line of most European automakers this year.

Servicing has always been problematic with European makes. Prices tend to be costly and particularly dealer-dependent. You can always get better treatment by going to dealerships that are accredited by auto clubs such as the CAA or consumer groups like the Automobile Protection Association (APA) or Car Help Canada. Auto club accreditation is no ironclad guarantee that a dealership will be honest or competent; however, if you're insulted, cheated, or given bad service by one of their recommended garages (look for the accreditation symbol in a dealer's phone book ads, on the Internet, or on their shop windows), the accrediting agency is one more place to take your complaint to apply additional mediation pressure. And, as you'll see in Part Three, plaintiffs have won substantial refunds by pleading that an auto club is legally responsible for the actions of a garage it recommends.

Automobile Brokers and Vehicle-Buying Services

Brokers are independent agents who act as intermediaries to find the new or used vehicle you want at a price below what you'd normally pay. They have their smartphone contact lists, speak the sales lingo, know all of the angles and scams, and can generally cut through the bull to find a fair price – usually within days. Their services may cost a few hundred dollars, but you may save a few thousand. Additionally, you save the stress and hassle associated with the dealership experience, which for many people is like a trip to the dentist.

Brokers get new vehicles through dealers, while used vehicles may come from dealers, auctions, private sellers, and leasing companies. The broker's job is to find a vehicle that meets a client's expressed needs and then to negotiate its purchase (or lease) on behalf of that client. The majority of brokers tend to deal exclusively in new vehicles, with a small percentage dealing in both new and used vehicles. Ancillary services vary among brokers and may include such things as comparative vehicle analysis and price research.

The cost of hiring a broker can be charged either as a flat fee of a few hundred dollars or as a percentage of the value of the vehicle (usually 1-2 percent). The flat fee is usually best because it encourages the broker to keep the selling price low. Reputable brokers are not beholden to any particular dealership or make, and they'll disclose their flat fee up front or tell you the percentage amount they'll charge on a specific vehicle. Brokers employed to purchase cars in the States may charge a few thousand dollars, seriously cutting into the savings you may get from a lower purchase price. Seriously consider doing the transaction without a broker. It's that easy.

Finding the right broker

Good brokers are hard to find, particularly in western Canada. Buyers who are looking for a broker should first ask friends and acquaintances if they can recommend one. Word-of-mouth referrals are often the best because people won't refer others to a service with which they were dissatisfied. Your local credit union or the regional CAA office is also a good place to get a broker referral. For instance, Alterna Savings recommends a car-buying service called Dealfinder.

Dealfinder

For most buyers, going into a dealer showroom to negotiate a fair price is intimidating and confusing. Numbers are thrown at you, promises are made and broken, and after getting the "lowest price possible," you realize your neighbour paid a couple thousand dollars less for the same vehicle.

No wonder smart consumers are turning away from the "showroom shake-down" and letting professional buyers, like Ottawa-based Dealfinder Inc. (*www.dealfinder.ca*), separate the steak from the sizzle and real prices from "come-ons." In fact, simply by dealing with the dealership directly, Dealfinder can automatically save you the $200+ sales agent's commission before negotiations even begin.

For a $159 (plus tax) flat fee, Dealfinder acts as a price consultant after you have chosen the vehicle you want. The agency then shops dealers for the new car or truck of your choice in any geographic area you indicate. It gets no kickbacks from retailers or manufacturers, and if you can negotiate and document a lower price than Dealfinder gets, the fee will be refunded. What's more, you're under no obligation to buy the vehicle they recommend, since there is absolutely no collusion between Dealfinder and any manufacturer or dealership.

Dealfinder is a small operation that has been run by Bob Prest for over 19 years. He knows the ins and outs of automobile price negotiation and has an impressive list of clients, including some of Canada's better-known credit unions. His reputation is spread by word-of-mouth recommendations and the occasional media report. He can be reached by phone at 1-800-331-2044, or by e-mail at *dealfinder@magma.ca.*

Freight Scams

Lemon-Aid has always cautioned new-car buyers against paying transportation and PDI (pre-delivery inspection) fees or suggested they be whittled down by about half. This advice worked well until a couple of years ago when charges ballooned to $1,400-$2,000 and automakers made them part of the MSRP instead of listing the item separately or not at all. When rolled into the MSRP, the freight charge/PDI can be more easily negotiated downward with the car's price since they are no longer touted as a sacrosanct "must pay" item.

"FLEECING" BY LEASING

Why Leasing Costs More

From a low of 7 percent in 2009, now about 20 percent of cars are leased – still, well below the 45 percent spike in 2005. Because leases are so profitable for dealers and automakers, alike, the industry is throwing around a basketful of incentives to sell leasing contracts. All this effort is paying off with a proliferation of leasing deals mostly on high-end sports and luxury cars and fully-loaded trucks and SUVs. Insiders say that almost all vehicles costing $60,000 or more are leased vehicles.

Yet, there are many reasons why leasing is a bad idea. It's often touted as an alternative used to make high-cost vehicles more affordable, but for most people, it's really more expensive than buying outright. Lessees usually pay the full MSRP on a vehicle loaded with costly options, plus hidden fees and interest charges that wouldn't be included if the vehicle was purchased instead of leased. Researchers have found that some fully loaded entry-level cars leased with high interest rates and deceptive "special fees" could cost more than what some luxury models would cost to buy. A useful website that takes the mystery out of leasing is *www.federal-reserve.gov/pubs/leasing* (see Leasing under the Consumer Information tab), run by the U.S. Federal Reserve Board. It goes into incredible detail comparing leasing versus buying, and has a handy dictionary of the terms you're most likely to encounter.

Decoding "Lease-Talk"

Take a close look at the small print found in most leasing ads. Pay particular attention to words relating to the model year, condition of the vehicle ("demonstration" or "used"), equipment, warranty, interest rate, buy-back amount, down payment, security payment, monthly payment, transportation and preparation charges, administration fees ("acquisition" and "disposal" fees), insurance premiums, number of free kilometres, and excess-kilometre charges.

Leasing Advantages

Experts agree: If you must lease, keep your costs to a minimum by leasing for the shortest time possible, by assuming the unexpired portion of an existing lease, and by making sure that the lease is close-ended (meaning that you walk away from the vehicle when the lease period ends) – an option used by 75 percent of lessees, according to the CAA.

Leasing does have a few advantages, though. First, it saves some of your capital, which you can invest to get a return greater than the leasing interest charges. Second, if you are taking a chance on a new model that hasn't been proven, you know that yours can be dumped at the dealer when the lease expires.

But taking a chance on an unproven model raises several questions. What are you doing choosing such a risky venture in the first place? And will you have the patience to wait in the service bay while your luxury lemon waits for parts or a mechanic who's ahead of the learning curve? Plus, suppose you want to keep the car after the lease expires. Your guaranteed buy-out price will likely cost 10-15 percent more than what the vehicle is worth on the open market.

Some Precautions and an Alternative

On both new and used purchases and leases, be wary of unjustified hidden costs, like a $495 "administrative" or "disposal" fee, an "acquisition" charge, or boosted transport and freight costs that can collectively add several thousand dollars to a vehicle's retail price. Also, look at the lease transfer fee charged by the leasing company, the dealer, or both. This fee can vary considerably.

Instead of leasing, consider purchasing used. Look for a three- to five-year-old off-lease vehicle with 60,000-100,000 km on the clock and some of the original warranty left. Such a vehicle will be just as reliable for less than half the cost of one bought new or leased. Parts will be easier to find, independent servicing should be a breeze, insurance premiums will come down from the stratosphere, and your financial risk will be lessened considerably if you end up with a lemon.

Breaking a Lease

Not an easy thing to do, and you may wind up paying $3,000-$8,000 in cancellation fees.

The last thing you want to do is stop your payments, especially if you've leased a lemon. The dealer can easily sue you for the remaining money owed, and you will have to pay the legal fees for both sides. You won't be able to prove the vehicle was defective or unreliable, because it will have been seized after the lease payments stopped. So there you are, without the vehicle to make your proof and on the receiving end of a costly lawsuit.

There are several ways a lease can be broken. First, you can ask for free Canadian Motor Vehicle Arbitration Plan (CAMVAP) arbitration (see page 176) if you believe you have leased a lemon. A second recourse, if there's a huge debt remaining, is to send a lawyer's letter cancelling the contract by putting the leasing agency and automaker on notice that the vehicle is unacceptable. This should lead to some negotiation. If this fails, inspect the vehicle, take pictures of any defects, have it legally tendered back to the dealer, and then sue for what you owe plus your inconvenience and assorted sundry expenses. You can use the small claims court on your own if the amount in litigation is less than the court's claim limit ($7,000 in Quebec; $25,000-$30,000 elsewhere).

The leasing agency or dealer may claim extra money when the lease expires, because the vehicle may miss some original equipment or show "unreasonable" wear and tear (dings, paint problems, and excessive tire wear are the most common reasons for extra charges). Prevent this from happening by having the vehicle inspected by an independent retailer and taking pictures of the vehicle prior to returning it.

BUYING THE RIGHT CAR OR TRUCK

Front-Drives

Front-drives direct engine power to the front wheels, which pull the vehicle forward while the rear wheels simply support the rear. The biggest benefit of front-drives is foul-weather traction. With the engine and transmission up front, there's lots of extra weight pressing down on the front-drive wheels, increasing tire grip in snow and on wet pavement. But when you drive up a steep hill, or tow a boat or trailer, the weight shifts and you lose the traction advantage.

Although I recommend a number of front-drive vehicles in this guide, I don't like them as much as rear-drives. Granted, front-drives provide a bit more interior room (no transmission hump), more car-like handling, and better fuel economy than do rear-drives, but damage from potholes and fender-benders is usually more extensive, and maintenance costs (especially premature suspension, tire, and brake wear) may be a bit higher than with rear-drives.

Rear-Drives

Rear-drives direct engine power to the rear wheels, which push the vehicle forward. The front wheels steer and also support the front of the vehicle. With the engine up front, the transmission in the middle, and the drive axle in the rear, there's plenty of room for larger and more durable drivetrain components. This makes for less crash damage, lower maintenance costs, and higher towing capacities than with front-drives.

On the downside, rear-drives don't have as much weight over the front wheels as do the front-drives and, therefore, they can't provide as much traction on wet or icy roads and tend to fishtail unless they're equipped with an expensive traction-control system.

Ford's rear-drive 2013 Mustang ($15,000) comes with a V6 that's almost as powerful as its earlier V8 and it's $10,000 cheaper. Except for the 2006 V6 and 2012 V8, which aren't recommended, Mustangs are Average to Above Average performers that hold their value and are easily repaired by independent garages that are usually one-third cheaper than dealer repairs.

Four-Wheel Drive (4x4)

Four-wheel drive (4x4) directs engine power through a transfer case to all four wheels, which pull and push the vehicle forward, giving you twice as much traction. On most models, the vehicle reverts to rear-drive when four-wheel drive isn't engaged. The large transfer-case housing makes the vehicle sit higher, giving you additional ground clearance.

Keep in mind that extended driving over dry pavement with 4x4 engaged may cause the driveline to bind and result in serious damage. Some buyers prefer rear-drive pickups equipped with winches and large, deep-lugged rear tires.

Many 4x4 customers driving SUVs set on truck platforms have been turned off by the typically rough and noisy driveline, a tendency for the vehicle to tip over when cornering at moderate speeds, vague or truck-like handling, high repair costs, and poor fuel economy.

All-Wheel Drive (AWD)

Subaru has used AWD since 1972, but it became a standard feature on all Subarus beginning with the 1996 lineup. AWD is four-wheel drive that's on all the time. The lone exception is the rear-drive BRZ introduced in 2012. It's a great handling performance car, that's hobbled by serious reliability problems. Used mostly in sedans and minivans, AWD never needs to be deactivated when running over dry pavement and doesn't require the heavy transfer case that raises ground clearance and cuts fuel economy. AWD-equipped vehicles aren't recommended for off-roading because of their lower ground clearance and fragile driveline parts, which aren't as rugged as 4x4 components. But, you shouldn't be off-roading in a car or minivan in the first place.

Trucks and SUVs

Pickups trucks and SUVs (including "crossover" utility vehicles, or CUVs) tend to give automakers a higher profit margin than most vehicles, but, at the expense of fuel-economy estimates. For this reason truck- and SUV-laden Chrysler, part of Fiat Chrysler Automobiles, usually brings up the rear in government reports, just behind General Motors and Ford. Mazda, Honda and Subaru rank as the top performers?

Nevertheless, Texans aren't impressed by fuel-economy stats or big money when it comes to judging the best trucks and SUVs. The Steel Market Development Institute, a lobbyist for eight United States-based steel producers, found this out the hard way. Despite its sponsorship of the Texas Auto Writers Association's 2014 Truck Rodeo, Ford's aluminum-paneled 2015 F-150 trounced the steel bodied competition and took home the Truck of Texas title and four other awards. Needless to say, the steel industry grumbles that aluminum is just a passing nerd-inspired fad and "only steel is real." However 2016 Ford F-150 sales are strong.

Which Safety Features Are Best?

Automakers have loaded 2015-16 models with features that wouldn't have been imagined several decades ago, because safety devices appeal to families and some, like airbags, can be marked up by 500 percent. Yet some safety innovations, such as anti-lock brake systems (ABS) and adaptive cruise control (ACC), don't deliver the safety payoffs promised by automakers and may create additional dangers. For example, ABS often fail and are expensive to maintain, while ACC may slow the vehicle down when passing another car on the highway. Some of the more-effective safety features are head-protecting side airbags, ESC, rearview cameras, adjustable brake and accelerator pedals, standard integrated child safety seats, seat belt pretensioners, adjustable head restraints, and sophisticated navigation and communication systems.

Seat belts provide the best means of reducing the severity of injury arising from both low- and high-speed frontal collisions. In order to be effective, though, seat belts must be adjusted properly and feel comfortably tight without undue slack. Owners often complain that seat belts don't retract enough for a snug fit, are too tight, chafe the neck, or don't fit children properly. Some automakers have corrected these problems with adjustable shoulder-belt anchors that allow both tall and short drivers to raise or lower the belt for a snug, more comfortable fit. Another important seat belt innovation is the pretensioner (not found on all seat belts), a device that automatically tightens the safety belt in the event of a crash.

Crashworthiness

A vehicle with a high crash protection rating is a lifesaver. In fact, crashworthiness is the one safety improvement over the past 40 years that everyone agrees has paid off handsomely without presenting any additional risks to drivers or passengers. By surrounding occupants with a protective cocoon and deflecting crash forces away from the interior, auto engineers have successfully created safer vehicles without increasing vehicle size or cost. And purchasing a vehicle with the idea that you'll be involved in an accident someday is not unreasonable. According to IIHS (see below), the average car will likely have two accidents before ending up as scrap, and it's twice as likely to be in a severe front-impact crash as a side-impact crash.

Since some vehicles are more crashworthy than others, and since size doesn't always guarantee crash safety, it's important to buy a vehicle that gives you the best protection from frontal, frontal offset, small overlap frontal, side, and rear collisions while keeping its rollover and roof-collapse potential to a minimum.

Two Washington-based agencies monitor how vehicle design affects crash safety: The National Highway Traffic Safety Administration (NHTSA) and the

Insurance Institute for Highway Safety (IIHS). Crash information from these two groups doesn't always correspond because tests and testing methods vary.

NHTSA crash-test results for vehicles and tires are available at *www.safercar. gov/Safety+Ratings*. Information relating to safety complaints, recalls, defect investigations, and service bulletins can be found at *www.safercar.gov /Vehicle+Owners*. IIHS results may be found at *www.iihs.org/ratings*.

NHTSA archives millions of owner complaints from the last four decades and lists them by model and year.

Don't get taken in by the five-star crash rating hoopla touted by automakers. Except for the Tesla electric car, few vehicles can claim a prize for being the safest. Vehicles that do well in NHTSA side and front crash tests may not do very well in IIHS offset crash tests, or may have poorly designed head restraints that can increase the severity of neck injuries. Or a vehicle may have a high number of airbag failures, such as the bags deploying when they shouldn't or not deploying when they should.

Before making a final decision on the vehicle you want, look up its crashworthiness and overall safety profile in Part Four.

Cars versus trucks

Occupants of large vehicles have fewer severe injury claims than do occupants of small vehicles. This was proven conclusively in a 1996 NHTSA study showing that collisions between light trucks or vans and small cars resulted in the car occupants having an 81 percent higher fatality rate than the occupants of the light trucks or vans.

Vehicle weight offers the most protection in two-vehicle crashes. In a head-on crash, for example, the heavier vehicle drives the lighter one backward, which decreases forces inside the heavy vehicle and increases forces in the lighter one. All heavy vehicles, even poorly designed ones, offer this advantage in two-vehicle collisions. However, they may not offer good protection in single-vehicle crashes.

Crash test figures show that SUVs, vans, and trucks also offer more protection to adult occupants than do passenger cars in most crashes because their higher set-up allows them to ride over other vehicles (Ford's 2002 4x4 Explorer lowered its bumper height to prevent this hazard). Conversely, because of their high centre of gravity, easily overloaded tires, and unforgiving suspensions, these vehicles have a disproportionate number of single-vehicle rollovers, which are far deadlier than frontal or side collisions. In the case of the early Ford Explorer, Bridgestone/Firestone CEO John Lampe testified in August 2001 that 42 of the 43 rollovers involving Ford Explorers in Venezuela were on competitors' tires – shifting the rollover blame to the Explorer's design and crashworthiness.

Interestingly, a vehicle's past crashworthiness rating doesn't always guarantee that subsequent model years will be just as safe or safer. Take Ford's Escort as an example. It earned five stars for front-passenger collision protection in 1991 and then earned fewer stars every year thereafter, until the model was discontinued in 2002. The Dodge Caravan is another example. It was given five stars for driver-side protection in 2000, but earned only four stars ever since, until taken off the market in 2007. The Grand Caravan, though, has consistently earned five stars in the same category.

Rollovers

Although rollovers represent only 3 percent of crashes (out of 10,000 annual U.S. road accidents), they cause one-third of all traffic deaths from what are usually single-vehicle accidents.

Rollovers occur less frequently with passenger cars and minivans than with SUVs, trucks, and full-sized vans (especially the 15-passenger variety). That's why electronic vehicle stability systems aren't as important a safety feature on passenger cars as on vans, pickups, and SUVs.

More Safety Considerations

Unfortunately, there will never be enough simple safety solutions to protect us from ourselves. NHTSA has discovered that kids wear their seat belt 87 percent of the time if their parents do, and that 60 percent of children killed on the roads in 2005 were not wearing a seat belt.

Although there has been a dramatic reduction in automobile accident fatalities and injuries over the past four decades, safety experts feel that additional safety features will henceforth pay small dividends. They say it's time to target the driver. NHTSA believes that we could cut automobile accident fatalities by half through 100 percent seat belt use and the elimination of drunk driving.

This means that safety programs that concentrate primarily on motor vehicle standards won't be as effective as measures that target both the driver and the vehicle – such as more sophisticated "black box" data recorders, more-stringent licensing requirements, including graduated licensing and de-licensing programs directed at teens and seniors, and stricter law enforcement.

Incidentally, police studies have shown that there's an important side benefit to arresting traffic-safety scofflaws. They often net dangerous career criminals or seriously impaired drivers before they have the chance to harm others. Apparently, sociopaths and substance abusers don't care which laws they break.

Active safety

Advocates of active safety stress that accidents are caused by the proverbial "nut behind the wheel" and believe that safe driving can be best taught through schools or private driving courses. Active safety components are generally those mechanical systems, such as ABS, high-performance tires, and traction control, that may help a driver to avoid accidents if they're skillful and mature.

I am not a fan of ABS. The systems are often ineffective, failure-prone, and expensive to service. Yet they are an essential part of most systems' ESC, which is a proven lifesaver. Essentially, ABS prevents a vehicle's wheels from locking when the brakes are applied in an emergency situation, thus reducing skidding and the loss of directional control. When braking on wet or dry roads, your stopping distance will be about the same as with conventional braking systems. But in gravel, slush, or snow, your stopping distance will be greater.

The theory of active safety has several drawbacks. A study of seriously injured drivers at the Shock Trauma Center in Maryland showed that 51 percent of the sample tested positive for illegal drugs while 34 percent tested positive for alcohol (*www.druggeddriving.org/ddp.html*). Drivers who are under the influence of alcohol or drugs cause about 40 percent of all fatal accidents. All the high-performance options and specialized driving courses in the world will not provide much protection from impaired drivers who draw a bead on your vehicle. And, because active safety components get a lot of use – you're likely to need ABS 99 times more often than you'll need an airbag – they have to be well designed and well maintained to remain effective. Finally, consider that independent studies show that safe driving taught to young drivers doesn't necessarily reduce the number of driving-related deaths and injuries (*Lancet*, July 2001; 1978 DeKalb County, Georgia, Study):

> The DeKalb Study compared the accident records of 9,000 teens that had taken driver education in the county's high schools with 9,000 teens that had no formal driver training. The final results showed no significant difference between the two groups. In other words, DeKalb County, Georgia, paid a large amount of money for absolutely no value.

Passive safety

Passive safety assumes that you will be involved in life-threatening situations and should be either warned in time to avoid a collision or automatically protected from rolling over, losing traction, or bearing the brunt of collision forces. Head-protecting side airbags, ESC, brake override systems, daytime running lights, and a centre-mounted third brake light are five passive safety features that have paid off handsomely in reduced injuries and lives saved.

Passive safety features also assume that some accidents aren't avoidable and that, when those accidents occur, vehicles should provide as much protection as possible to drivers, passengers, and other vehicles that may be struck – without depending on the driver's reactions. Passive safety components that have consistently been proven to reduce vehicular deaths and injuries are seat belts, laminated windshields, and vehicle structures that enhance crashworthiness by absorbing or deflecting crash forces away from the vehicle's occupants.

HIGH TECH TAKES THE WHEEL

Faster wireless systems, dash-mounted video cameras, LED front lights, radar, and lithium ion batteries are five technologies that should post the most growth within the next five years.

High-speed 4G wireless connections, seven times as fast as previous 3G cellular services, have come to the car and are expected to make driving safer and highway travel more predictable. Audi offers it in the 2015 A3 and General Motors has included 4G in the 2015 Chevrolet Malibu. Thirty other GM models will have it by 2016.

With 4G, drivers can download directions, turning their cars into roving Wi-Fi hot spots for up to seven devices. In effect, the car will have access to the same information that one could get from home or off a smart phone, including

The G1W (top) and G1W-C (bottom) are recommended by a number of independent testers. They cost between $75-$100 U.S. (*thewirecutter.com/reviews/best-dash-cam/*).

the hundred of car-friendly "apps" that can make driving safer, cheaper, and more pleasant.

Get ready for dash-mounted event data video recorders. Widely used in commercial vehicles such as delivery trucks and police patrol cars, they are gaining popularity among auto owners as a safety feature that can record accidents, breakdowns, and crimes. Although dash cams have not been offered as a dealer option yet, they are widely available on the Internet, such as Amazon and Garmin, for less than $200. Be wary of fakes from China.

Helpful Automobile Apps

Applications are little, self-contained programs that come with powerful web browsers to increase the functionality of modern "smart"phones. Apps allow users to do with the phone's browser in a few clicks whatever can be done with a desktop computer. The accessed information doesn't need a Bookmark or URL to be found and the image is enlarged to be easily read on the phone's screen.

In the "connect-me-now" world of communication, smart phones have replaced cell phones, MP3 players, global positioning systems (GPS), personal data assistants (PDA), and, in some cases, even computers. That's because these phones are much cheaper, multi-functional, and more mobile than most computers. Here are a selection of apps that you may find useful.

1. Safer Car: A free app downloaded from the NHTSA, the Safercar mobile app is available for iPhones (*itunes.apple.com/us/app/safercar/id593086230?ls= 1&mt=8*) and Androids (*play.google.com/store/apps/details?id=gov*). The Safer Car app allows you to receive immediate information on your phone when you register to receive safety updates. Other aspects of the Safer Car app include:

   - *Real time news:* The app forwards NHTSA safety headlines and information, including recalls on vehicles you own. You receive timely news that may bear on the safety of you and your family.

   - *Complaints:* With the Safer Car app, you can notify NHTSA of a complaint, concern, or safety issue you discovered with your car. Other owner complaints are also listed.

- *Safety ratings:* Using the app, you can review and compare safety data for cars you own or are considering for purchase.
- *Safety seats:* Information on safely installing child safety and booster seats is provided, along with help finding local support to have your seat checked or properly installed.
- Recall cam*paigns:* Find out if your car is under investigation, has been recalled, *and* if it has been fixed according to automaker data.

2. iWrecked Auto Accident Assistant: Available for free from *Apple.com's* iTunes, the iWrecked app helps you make sense out of a stressful situation all while protecting your rights by taking the "he said, she said" out of the experience. This app helps you document pertinent facts about the other parties involved, the vehicle description, witness names, addresses and comments, insurance contacts, and license plate and drivers license numbers. There is also a place to show photos of the damage and accident scene taken by your iPhone.

3. Waze (*www.complex.com/sports/2014/02/best-smartphone-apps-for-drivers/waze*): This powerful navigation app is not only free, but it works on both the iPhone and Android platform and is applicable to drivers on both sides of our border. Accident and construction delays are indicated in real time in both official languages. This is the full-fledged navigation application that threatens most automaker navigation devices that sell for thousands of dollars and cost up to a hundred dollars each time they are updated by the dealer. Waze allows drivers to report police or hazards, and see what other people have reported.

Breaking the EDR Code

Since 1996, cars sold in the U.S. have been required to provide a connection for mechanics and inspectors to measure what's going on electronically under the hood. The system, called On-Board Diagnostics generation two (OBD-II), uses a 16-pin connector mounted somewhere near the instrument panel to gather maintenance, component failure, and safety information and stores it in a vehicle's "black box," much like airplane electronic data recorders (EDRs). The problem is that until recently, only dealers could read the codes and drivers paid dearly to have the EDR info decoded.

Fortunately, over the past half decade, the aftermarket has developed gadgets that use the OBD-II connection to transmit uncoded stats in real time, such as fuel economy, engine speed, temperature, vehicle speed, and pertinent safety information relative to airbag deployment and braking application. When this information is combined with a smart phone's accelerometer and GPS locating ability, you get a comprehensive view of your car's performance, efficiency, safety-related defects, and emissions control malfunctions. Here are just a few of these gadgets and apps.

1. **GoPoint** (*gopointtech.com/products/*): The free GoPoint app works with iPhones and uses a GoPoint cable (which costs $100, but can be purchased online for less) to plug into your car's (OBD) port to give you real-time information from the vehicle's built-in computer diagnostic system. It remove the risks, and surprises, from driving as it measures the efficiency of your vehicle and tells you when fuel economy is running low relative to your driving habits. For safety's sake and peace of mind, the BT1 will speak with your vehicle to interrupt the dreaded Check Engine light. Is your vehicle safe to drive? Will it cost a small fortune to repair? Find out quickly and painlessly using your iPhone, iPod touch, or iPad. It's like having your own personal mechanic riding next to you! Bosch offers a similar app for free, called "fun2drive." It is downloaded from the Google Play Store or the Apple App Store (for iOS products).

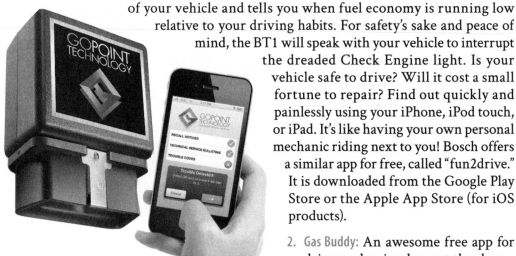

The Tata Nano is a primitive, no frills mini-compact. A radio and fire extinguisher are optional.

2. **Gas Buddy:** An awesome free app for drivers who simply want the cheapest gas available, thereby, avoiding the annoyance of fueling up and then spotting cheaper gas a mile down the road. Gas Buddy quickly locates stations in Canada or the States with the most competitive price. It searches by city, zip code, or your nearest GPS-mapped location. Plus, Gas Buddy will map the route to the cheapest station and show what other amenities the station provides – such as a car wash, compressed air, ATM, convenience store, etc.

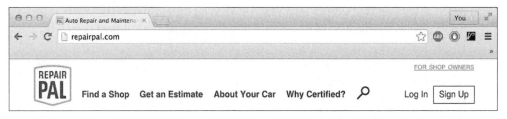

3. **Repair Pal:** This free iPhone application will quickly get you a repair estimate, and find a mechanic nearest your GPS location to do the work. Here's how it works. First, select the year, make, and model of your vehicle and add your zip code or iPhone's GPS location. Next, pick from a menu the repair that needs to be done. An estimated price range from both dealerships and independent shops will appear shortly on your phone screen. This will be followed by a list of other things that could go wrong and a local

mechanic's recommendation as to what should be tackled first. Repair Pal also provides a list of nearby shops, along with their star-based rating, and will map your route or call the garage automatically. And, if more assistance is required Repair Pal will connect you to roadside assistance or the manufacturer's customer assistance.

4. iLeaseMyCar Pro: This is an important $1.99 U.S. tool for iPhone users who aren't sure whether they want to buy or lease a new car. The application infuriates dealer sales people because it quickly determines the monthly payment for an auto loan or lease down to the penny by using the same information found in dealership programs. If you are new-car shopping, this app can save you calculations on different vehicles so you don't get confused by all the figures. There is also a useful reverse lease/loan calculator that shows the selling price that will meet your desired payment.

5. My Max Speed 2.0: Using the accelerometer in an Android phone, this $4.99 U.S. app logs speed and location every five seconds and can export the data to a spreadsheet. It's a great way to monitor a teen's driving habits, or beat a traffic ticket. The app also shows where the vehicle has travelled and sends a message if the phone carrying the app travels outside a preset boundary.

6. AccuFuel: A $0.99 U.S. iPhone app is primarily a fuel efficiency tracker, but also keeps a real time record of what you spend on fuel. Fuel use data is given in SAE, imperial, and metric units that can be stored for multiple vehicles.

7. How about a Car: A free appl similar to AccuFuel, but designed for the android platform. It also tells you when to get your oil changed, check tire pressure, etc.

Voice Controls – A Mixed Bag

Driving while distracted is a major cause of automobile accidents that can be prevented by driver's using common sense (active safety), which isn't very likely with the popularity of smart phones and the advent of cars that rove the Internet. For example, a driver talking with other passengers in the car is said to be the cause of 81 percent of auto crashes. Auto accident statistics show that other significant causes of car accidents are listening to or changing the radio stations (involved in 66 percent of all accidents) and talking on cell phones (25 percent).

Interestingly, a 2006 University of Utah study compared cell phone use to drunk driving (*www.distraction.gov/research/PDF-Files/Comparison-of-CellPhone-Driver-Drunk-Driver.pdf*). Researchers found impairments associated with using a cell phone while driving can be as profound as those associated with driving with a blood alcohol level at 0.08 percent, a "driving under the influence" level throughout Canada and the United States.

In another experiment, people using a driving simulator were more likely to hit a pedestrian when their cellphone rang, even if they had planned in advance not to answer it (*www.ncbi.nlm.nih.gov/pubmed/22871271*).

Phones don't have to be used to be a distraction; studies show that our antennas are always up. People's performance on basic laboratory tests of attention gets worse if a cellphone is merely visible nearby. (See: *psycnet.apa.org/index.cfm?fa=buy. optionToBuy&id=2014-52302-001.*)

What about stricter law enforcement? Don't get your hopes up. A 2010 study carried out by the Highway Loss Data Institute reviewed insurance claims in New York, Connecticut, and California and compared the data to other areas without cell phone bans. The conclusion? Laws banning the use of hand-held devices while driving did not reduce the rate of accidents in the three states and the District of Columbia (*www.cnn.com/2010/US/01/29/cellphone.study/index.html*).

Driven to Distraction

In order to make use of these above features less distracting, carmakers and infotainment suppliers have enthusiastically embraced "voice recognition." Even government agencies like NHTSA are backing voice controls since their own research has shown that the crash risk rises threefold when a driver takes their hands off the steering wheel and eyes off the road. They predict these new features will lead to fewer accidents as drivers keep their hands on the wheel and stay mentally "connected" to the road ahead.

Wrong.

Many of the new systems have simply changed one distraction for another. And, this is in addition to drivers balking at having to remember robotic phrases and practice Professor Higgins diction.

Actually features like Apple's Siri electronic assistant (first used in 2013 models) may be as mentally taxing as the buttons and knobs they replace, says the American Automobile Association's Foundation for Traffic Safety. Test subjects scored 4 points on a 5-point scale used to measure mental strain while using Siri – more of a distraction than talking on a cell phone or fooling with radio knobs. More worrisome? Siri was used when three simulated crashes were registered during the experiments. Researchers also tested Toyota Entune, Ford Sync, and Chevrolet MyLink.

Toyota's Entune did best with a 1.7 score on the 5-point cognitive workload scale (equivalent to listening to an audio book). The worst, Chevrolet MyLink, scored a 3.7 out of 5. GM was an early adopter of Siri, offering it into the Chevrolet Spark and Sonic starting in February 2013, and updated its MyLink system for 2015.

Research data now confirms that voice controlled systems don't make driving safer. Instead, they allow drivers to drift into a "zombie" state – the eyes look ahead, but don't see; hands are on the steering wheel, but don't react. Then, when the system doesn't work as expected, drivers will look at the screen to figure out what's wrong. And, we are back to square one.

Safety Features that Kill

In the late '60s, Washington forced automakers to include essential safety features like collapsing steering columns and safety windshields in their cars. Mandatory safety and crashworthiness standards were passed in 1966 U.S. legislation (Ottawa passed its own watered-down version in 1971's *Canadian Motor Vehicle Safety Act*). Since the American law came into force American highway fatalities dropped from 50,894 to 33,561 in 2012. As the years have passed, the number of mandatory safety features increased to include seat belts, airbags, and crashworthy construction. These improvements met with public approval until a decade ago, when reports of deaths and injuries caused by ABS and airbag failures showed that defective components and poor engineering negated the potential life-saving benefits associated with having these devices.

For example, one out of every five ongoing NHTSA defect investigations concerns inadvertent airbag deployment, deactivation of the front passenger airbag, failure of the airbag to deploy, or injuries suffered when the bag did go off. In fact, airbags are the agency's single largest cause of current investigations, exceeding even the full range of brake problems, which runs second.

Side Airbags – Good and Bad

Side and side curtain airbags are designed to protect drivers and passengers in rollovers and side-impact crashes, which are estimated to account for almost one-third of vehicular deaths. They have also been shown to help keep unbelted occupants from being ejected in rollovers. Head-protecting side airbags can reduce serious crash injuries by 45 percent. Side airbags without head protection reduce injuries by only 10 percent. Ideally, you want a side airbag system that protects both the torso and head.

There's a downside to increased side airbag protection. Sit properly in your seat, or face serious injury from the deploying side airbag. Preliminary safety studies show that side airbags may be deadly to children or to any occupant sitting too close to the airbag, resting his or her head on the side pillar, or holding onto the roof-mounted assist handle. Research carried out in 1998 by safety researchers (Anil Khadikar of Biodynamics Engineering Inc. and Lonney Pauls of Springwater Micro Data Systems, *Assessment of Injury Protection Performance of Side Impact Airbags*) shows there are four hazards that pertain to most airbag systems:

1. Inadvertent airbag firing (short circuits, faulty hardware or software);
2. Unnecessary airbag firing (sometimes the opposite-side airbag will fire; the airbag may deploy when a low-speed side-swipe wouldn't have endangered occupant safety);
3. A small child, say, a three-year-old, restrained in a booster seat could be seriously injured; and
4. Out-of-position restrained occupants could be seriously injured.

The researchers conclude with the following observation, "Even properly restrained vehicle occupants can have their upper or lower extremities in harm's way in the path of an exploding [side] airbag."

And don't forget NHTSA's side airbag warning issued on October 14, 1999:

Side impact airbags can provide significant supplemental safety benefits to adults in side impact crashes. However, children who are seated in close proximity to a side airbag may be at risk of serious or fatal injury, especially if the child's head, neck, or chest is in close proximity to the airbag at the time of deployment.

Protecting yourself

Because not all airbags function, or malfunction, the same way, *Lemon-Aid* has done an exhaustive analysis of American and Canadian recalls, crash data, and owner complaints to determine which vehicles and which model years use airbags that may seriously injure occupants or deploy inadvertently. That data can be found in Part Four's model ratings.

Additionally, you should take the steps below to reduce the danger from airbag deployment.

- Buy a vehicle with head-protecting side curtain airbags for front and rear passengers.
- Make sure that seat belts are buckled and all head restraints are properly adjusted (to about ear level).
- Choose vehicles with head restraints that are rated "Good" by IIHS (see Part Four).
- Insist that passengers who are frail or short or who have recently had surgery sit in the back and properly position themselves away from side airbags.
- Ensure that the driver's seat can be adjusted for height and has tracks with sufficient rearward travel to allow short drivers to remain at a safe distance (over 25 cm (10 in.)) away from the bag's deployment and still be able to reach the accelerator and brake.
- Consider buying pedal extensions to keep you at a safe distance away from a deploying airbag if you are short-statured.

Top 20 Safety Defects

The U.S. government's online safety complaints database contains well over 100,000 entries, going back to vehicles made in the late '70s. Although the database was originally intended to record only incidents of component failures that relate to safety, you will find every problem imaginable dutifully recorded by clerks working for NHTSA. This information is posted at NHTSA *safercar.gov* (see Helpful Automobile Apps, above).

A perusal of the listed complaints shows that some safety-related failures occur more frequently than others and often affect one manufacturer more than another. Here is a summary of the most commonly reported failures.

1. Sudden unintended acceleration
2. ABS total brake failure; wheel lock-up
3. Airbag malfunctions
4. Tire-tread separation
5. Electrical/fuel-system fires
6. Sudden stalling
7. Sudden electrical failures
8. Erratic transmission engagements
9. Unintended transmission shifts
10. Steering and suspension failures
11. Seat belt malfunctions
12. Collapsing seatbacks
13. Defective sliding doors and locks
14. Poor headlight illumination; glare
15. Dash reflecting onto windshield
16. Hood flying up
17. Wheel falling away
18. Steering wheel lifting off
19. Transmission lever pulling out
20. Exploding windshields

Note: Stalling while underway has been officially dismissed by NHTSA as a legitimate safety hazard. NHTSA Deputy Administrator, David Friedman, testified at a congressional hearing in September 2014, saying that stalling doesn't pose an unreasonable safety risk unless it can be linked to crashes or injuries. GM responded that stalling at any time is dangerous. The resulting bipartisan public outcry has forced NHTSA to review its policy.

Auto Recalls for Consumers (*www.arfc.org/complaints/*), a non-profit U.S. consumer group, has separated complaints and recalls since 1995, by automaker and the number of recalls and complaints posted by NHTSA.

	Top 10 cars with the most complaints filed			Top 10 cars with the most recalls filed	
1	2000 Ford Focus	5097 Complaints	1	2006 Ford E-350	30 Recalls
2	1995 Ford Windstar	4908 Complaints	2	2007 Ford E-350	26 Recalls
3	2002 Ford Explorer	3792 Complaints	3	2008 Ford E-350	23 Recalls
4	1997 Ford F-150	3249 Complaints	4	2006 Ford E-250	22 Recalls
5	2010 Ford Fusion	3215 Complaints	5	2007 Ford E-250	18 Recalls
6	1999 Dodge Durango	3089 Complaints	6	2009 Ford E-350	18 Recalls
7	1998 Ford Explorer	2334 Complaints	7	1994 Dodge Ram	18 Recalls
8	2006 Chevrolet Cobalt	2301 Complaints	8	2006 Chevrolet Express	16 Recalls
9	2007 Toyota Camry	2297 Complaints	9	2004 Ford E-250	16 Recalls
10	2001 Ford Focus	2261 Complaints	10	1997 Ford F-150	15 Recalls

Note: Ford has the dubious distinction of being the carmaker that appears the most frequently on the complaint and recall lists.

Do You Feel Comfortable in the Vehicle?

The advantages of many sports cars and minivans quickly pale in direct proportion to your tolerance for a harsh ride, noise, a claustrophobic interior, and limited visibility. Large minivans, SUVs and trucks often have awkwardly high step-ups, auto-regulated interior temperatures that range from Siberian to Death Valley, lots of buffeting from wind and passing trucks, and poor rear visibility. With these drawbacks, many buyers find that after falling in love with the showroom image, they end up hating their purchase – all the more reason to test drive your choice over a period of several days to get a real feel for its positive and negative characteristics.

Check to see if the vehicle's interior is user-friendly. For example, can you reach the sound system and AC controls without straining or taking your eyes off the road? Are the controls just as easy to operate by feel as by sight? What about dash glare onto the front windshield, and headlight aim and brightness? Can you drive with the window or sunroof open and not be subjected to an ear-splitting roar? Do rear-seat passengers have to be contortionists to enter or exit, as is the case with many two-door vehicles?

To answer these questions, you need to drive the vehicle over a period of time to test how well it responds to the diversity of your driving needs, without having some impatient sales agent yapping in your ear. If this isn't possible, you may find out too late that the handling is less responsive than you'd wanted and that the infotainment electronics create an Orwellian environment.

You can conduct a few showroom tests. Adjust the seat to a comfortable setting, buckle up, and settle in. Can you sit 25 cm (10 in.) away from the steering wheel and still reach the accelerator and brake pedals? Do the head restraints force your chin into your chest? When you look out the windshield and use the rear- and side-view mirrors, do you detect any serious blind spots? Will optional mirrors give you an unobstructed view? Does the seat feel comfortable enough for long trips? Can you reach important controls without moving your back from the seatback, or taking your eyes off the road? If not, shop for something that better suits your needs.

CARS FOR SENIORS

A group of pensioners were discussing their medical problems over coffee at Tim Hortons one morning.

"Can you believe it?" said one. "My arm is so weak I can hardly hold this coffee cup."

"Yes, I know." replied the second. "My cataracts are so bad I can't see the breakfast prices."

"I can't turn my head," rejoined the third, "because of the arthritis in my neck."

"My blood pressure pills make me dizzy," commented the fourth, adding, "I guess that's the price we pay for getting old."

"Well, it's not all bad," shouted out the first, "At least we can still drive Eh!"

– Anonymous

Seniors are the fastest growing segment of the driving population and driving is vital to their health and independence. Nevertheless, the Canadian Association of Occupational Therapists warns that older driver mortality and morbidity is on the rise for seniors:

> In fact, the leading cause of accidental deaths for persons 65 to 75 years old in Canada today is driving-related accidents. More specifically, individuals over 75 have a 3.5 times higher crash rate compared to 35 to 44 year olds (Canada Safety Council, 2005). With the senior population on the rise, it is projected that by 2040 there will be almost double the number of older drivers in Canada.

Those living in households that are car-dependent spend 25 percent of income on transportation. By living closer to work, shopping, restaurants, and other amenities, households can reduce transportation costs to 9 percent of their total income.

Husbands do the bulk of family driving, which usually involves short trips (11-17 km (6-10 mi) per day, on average) for medical appointments and visits to family, friends, and shopping malls. This puts older women, who tend to outlive their husbands, in a serious bind because of their lack of driving experience – particularly in rural areas, where driving is a necessity rather than a choice.

Nevertheless, seniors, like most other drivers, want cars that are reliable, relatively inexpensive, and fuel efficient. Additionally, older drivers need vehicles that compensate for some of the physical challenges associated with aging and provide protection for accidents more common with mature drivers (side impacts, for example). Furthermore, as drivers get older, they find that the very act of getting into a car (sitting down while moving sideways, without bumping their heads or twisting their necks) demands considerable acrobatic skill. And don't even ask about shoulder pain when reaching up and over for the shoulder belt!

Some head restraints are pure torture, especially for seniors. Some of the worst designs that push your head forward and into the chest to comply with new whiplash regulations appeared five years ago.

Driving Through the Ages

Accident death rates are much higher for older occupants than for younger age groups. This is because our fragility increases as we age, and our ability to withstand the forces involved in crashes become much lower. Of course, our driving skills also deteriorate as we age, although most of us are reluctant to admit it.

- **At age 40:** Thought processing starts slowing down, multi-tasking becomes more difficult, night and peripheral vision worsens, and glare blinds you for a longer period of time.
- **At age 50:** Nine in ten people use bifocals, reaction time slows, and distractions increase.
- **At age 60:** Muscle strength and range of motion decrease by as much as 25 percent. Hearing acuity is reduced.
- **At age 70:** Arthritic joints may make movement painful and restrict mobility, and conditions such as stroke, Parkinson's disease, hypertension, and diabetes may impair cognitive ability or affect behaviour.

Access and Comfort

Drivers with arthritic hands often have to insert a pencil into their key ring to twist the key in the ignition.

Since hand and grip strength can be a problem for seniors, make sure your ignition lock doesn't require that much effort. A thicker steering wheel also requires less hand and wrist strength to grip and handle to make turns. Power locks, trunk and tailgate closers, mirrors, and windows are a must, especially if the vehicle will be operated with hand controls. A remote keyless fob will allow entry without fumbling with the door lock. Cruise control can be helpful for those with lower-body mobility challenges. Also, consider vehicles with adjustable pedals, a tilt steering column, and a height-adjustable, power-assisted driver's seat with memory.

Ideally, you want to balance lumbar support with the ability to reach the pedals and see over the dashboard, without putting stress on muscles that are losing some flexibility.

Some vehicle types are more senior-friendly:

- **Four-door vehicles:** Doors are lighter and easier to open than two-door coupes.
- **Performance sports cars:** Usually have seats with more heavily padded side and thigh bolsters, which force occupants to "climb out" of their seats.
- **SUVs, trucks, and vans:** Easier to get in and out of than a sedan, since the higher seats require less bending. Minivans offer a higher seat, plus a more easily reached lower door.

 Look for vehicles that are easy to enter and exit, with door openings that are wide enough for easy access. Ensure that the door catches when opened on a slight incline so that it doesn't close as you are exiting. Vans, SUVs, and trucks should also have a low step-up and an easily reached inside-grip handle, as well as other handles located throughout the interior. Other vehicles need low thresholds beneath the doors because many older drivers have a great deal of difficulty lifting their legs to get out. The trunk or rear cargo area should also have a low liftover and room to stow a wheelchair or scooter.

Drivers with limited mobility need a seated position that is close to standard chair height: Not too low so that you fall into it, and not too tall that you have to climb up and then back down. Concave bucket seats may complicate exiting the vehicle, though heated seats with lumbar support are great for drivers with back pain.

Bench seats are preferable because they're roomier and easier to access. Incidentally, some General Motors' vans may be fitted with a removable Sit-N-Lift feature that provides a motorized, rotating lift-and-lower passenger seat accessed through the middle door.

Most people prefer the versatility of a van like the Toyota Sienna or the full-sized GM Express/Savana, but well-equipped smaller versions can accommodate the physically-challenged, just as well.

Safety Features for Older Drivers

Generally you want controls with larger buttons, more readable labeling, rear-backup cameras, blind-spot-detection systems, convex mirrors added to the side mirrors, and cross-traffic alerts that detect passing cars in the rear.

- A low beltline (the lower edge of the glass area) improves the driver's downward sightlines, making parking easier. As drivers age, reduced flexibility in the shoulders and neck can restrict head movement, so having more glass area is a huge help.

- Large, wide-angle side mirrors and rear-view mirrors help compensate for reduce vision caused by minor strokes and glaucoma, limited range of motion, or difficulties twisting to check for blind spots while merging or backing up. A rear-mounted camera helps when backing up; however, the rear image may be distorted, making it impossible to judge distance accurately.

- The driver's seat should be mounted high enough to give a commanding view of the road (with slower reaction times, seniors need earlier warnings). The driver's seat must offer enough rearward travel to attenuate the force of an exploding airbag, which can be particularly hazardous to older or small-statured occupants, and anyone recovering from surgery. Adjustable gas and brake pedals are a must for short-legged drivers.

- Head restraints shouldn't force your chin into your chest and should be easily adjustable.

- Cars that are brighter and lighter in colour are easier for other drivers to see at night and when it rains.

- Look for bright dashboard gauges that can be seen in sunlight, and instruments with large-sized controls. Drivers with diminished vision and sensitivity to glare will find extendable sun visors helpful.

- Remote-controlled mirrors are a must, along with adjustable, unobtrusive head restraints and a non-reflective front windshield (many drivers put a cloth on the dash-top to cut the distraction). Make sure that the brake and accelerator pedals aren't mounted too close together.

- A superior crashworthiness rating is essential, as well as dual-stage torso- and head-protecting side airbags, since many intersection collisions involving mature drivers occur when drivers are making a turn into oncoming traffic. The extra head protection can make a critical difference in side impacts. Dual-stage and dual-threshold airbags are recommended to attenuate the force of the airbags' deployment.

- The deployment force depends on crash severity, distance from the driver and passenger, and weight of the driver.

- Look for headlights that give you a comfortable view at night, as well as dash-mounted turn signal indicators that are easily seen and heard. Ensure that the vehicle's knobs and switches are large and easy to identify and that the gauges are sufficiently backlit that they don't wash out in daylight or produce too much glare at night.

- Features that are especially important to drivers wearing bifocals: A blue-green light colour that measures 505 nanometres is the ideal gauge colour in terms of being easiest to see. The belief that instruments illuminated or marked in red are easiest to see is a myth. Also, be sure to check that the dash doesn't cause windshield glare (a common problem with light-coloured dash panels).

- An antilock braking system, or ABS, prevents wheels from locking during emergency braking. Drivers using ABS can stop the car and retain control without "pumping" the brakes, which can be challenging for older drivers.

- Electronic traction and stability control (ESC) is a feature that helps prevent loss of control in turns, or during a sudden stop, especially on slippery roads. ESC allows drivers to compensate for slower reaction times and make quick corrections. Vehicles that come with ESC are listed on the National Highway Safety Administration website: *www.safercar.gov.*

- Having an easily accessed, full-sized spare tire and a user-friendly lug wrench and jack stand is also important.

A Feature of Limited Utility

Some safety, performance, and convenience features may not work as well as advertised and may issue false, distracting alerts, or be costly to service. A chief offender is Ford's MyTouch and SYNC options found on many of its cars since 2011. Owners find these features very buggy, slow, and not-at-all intuitive to use.

Says one Ford owner:

> Ford's MyTouch infotainment system integrates multiple controls and info readouts via what used to be the entertainment system in what is a way busier approach than reaching over towards the center stack to make adjustments via rotary knobs or push buttons. I don't need to be cursoring up and down through menu options – while I am driving in heavy traffic, period. It isn't as bad as texting while driving, but it is close.

Good "Senior" Car Choices

These new and used vehicles are recommended by *Lemon-Aid* for access, visibility, front-seat comfort, driving position, and controls. Most have a better-than-average reliability rating, for the Chevrolet Impala and Chrysler 300, and most have standard electronic stability control.

Audi A8 (all years)	Kia Soul (2014-16)
BMW 7 Series (all years)	Lexus LS 460 (all years)
Ford Five Hundred (all years)	Lexus RX (2004-16)
Honda Accord (2008-16)	Subaru Forester (2009-16)
Honda Odyssey (2011-16)	Toyota Avalon (2007-16)
Hyundai Tucson (2006-16)	Toyota Camry (2014-16)
Infiniti M35 (all years)	Toyota Highlander (2004-16)

Adaptive Aids

For most people, driving a motor vehicle has become essential to the tasks of everyday living – commuting to work, running errands, or taking children to school for example – and synonymous with freedom, independence, and self-sufficiency. Driving in vehicle-congested areas is challenging enough for drivers without disabilities; for a person with a physical disability driving to the local grocery store can be downright daunting. But it can be done. After rehabilitative assessment and evaluation, the driving needs of people with temporary or permanent disabilities can be accommodated through the use of adaptive vehicle equipment, safe driver training, or both.

Many persons with physical disabilities can safely drive using some of the considerable variety of adaptive devices available today. Some of these devices are found in almost all vehicles and are used by people with and without physical disabilities.

For example, some of the commonly found adaptive aids are:

- Left foot accelerator – eliminates left leg cross-over;
- Right hand turn signals – eliminate right hand cross-over;
- Foot pedal extensions – raise height of brake and accelerator pedals;
- Hand controls – operate horn, wipers, turn signals, dimmer switch; can also operate brake and accelerator;
- Steering devices – allow steering by spinner knobs, amputee ring, quad fork, or tri-pin;
- Custom seating – creates balance, positioning, and stability; and
- Lifts and ramps – permit access into and out of the vehicle.

Adaptive aids compensate for the disability or inability to perform the needed function. For example, if a driver is missing a right leg, a left foot gas pedal allows him to drive with his left foot.

Simple assistive devices are available to make driving safer and easier. Items such as seat belt adjusters, handibars, or expanded mirrors are available either in home catalogues or at medical supply or auto parts stores. Other items that do not require a specialist to install are easy-locking seat belts, visor extenders, steering wheel covers to improve grip, seat and back support cushions to relieve back pain or improve the ability to see over the steering wheel, keyless ignitions, and doors that automatically lock and open (see *www.colonial medical.com*).

To begin adaptive-on-the-road driving, a person should first become familiar with the current state-of-the-art adaptive vehicle equipment and rehabilitative driver training available in their province. A good place to start is by calling your local automobile dealer or e-mailing automobile manufacturers (with Google, put in the name of the car company followed by *@ca* or simply type GM Mobility, for example) or non-profit organization representing the physically handicapped. One Ottawa-based national group that works with many regional associations is: Independent Living Canada, 214 Montreal Road, Suite 402, Ottawa ON Canada K1L 8L8; Phone: 613/563.2581; TTY/TDD: 613/563.4215; E-mail: *info@ilc-vac*.

Where to Go for More Information

Simple assistive devices are available to make driving safer and easier. Items such as seatbelt adjusters, handibars, or expanded mirrors are available either in home catalogs or at medical supply or auto parts stores. Other items that do not require a specialist to install are easy-locking seatbelts, visor extenders, steering wheel covers to improve grip, seat and back support cushions to relieve back pain or improve the ability to see over the steering wheel, keyless ignitions, and doors that automatically lock and open. (See: *www.colonial medical.com*.) Here are some other websites that may be helpful.

- The National Mobility Equipment Dealers Association (NMEDA) supports the use of safe, reliable vehicles and modifications to enhance accessibility for people with special needs (see: *www.nmeda.org.*).

- The National Highway Traffic Safety Administration (NHTSA) addresses automotive safety issues for persons with disabilities (see: *www.nhtsa.dot.gov/ cars/rules/adaptive*).

- See AAA's "Safe Features for Mature Drivers" (*www.aaaexchange.com/Main/ Default.asp?CategoryID=18&SubCategoryID=86&ContentID=388*).

- AAA's list of vehicles and their options suitable for seniors can be accessed at: *www.aaapublicaffairs.com/Assets/Files/20083211031180.SFMD-VehicleListv6.2.pdf*.

OTHER BUYING CONSIDERATIONS

When "New" Isn't New

Nothing will cause you to lose money more quickly than buying a new car that's older than advertised, has previously been sold and then taken back, has accident damage, or has had the odometer disconnected or turned back.

Even if the vehicle hasn't been used, it may have been left outdoors for a considerable length of time, causing the deterioration of rubber components, premature body and chassis rusting, or severe rusting of internal mechanical parts, which leads to brake malfunction, fuel line contamination, hard starting, and stalling.

You can check a vehicle's age by looking at the date-of-manufacture plate usually found on the driver-side door pillar. If the date of manufacture is 7/13 or earlier, your vehicle was probably one of the last 2013 models made before the September changeover to the 2014s.

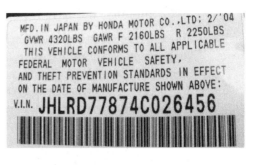

Redesigned vehicles or those new to the market are exceptions to this rule. They may arrive at dealerships in early spring or mid-summer and are considered to be next year's models. They also depreciate more quickly owing to their earlier launching, but this difference narrows over time.

Sometimes a vehicle can be too new and cost you more in maintenance because its redesign glitches haven't yet been worked out. As Honda's North American manufacturing chief, Koki Hirashima, so ably put it, carryover models generally have fewer problems than vehicles that have been significantly reworked or just introduced to the market. Newly redesigned vehicles get quality scores that are, on average, 2 percent worse than vehicles that have been around for a while, says J.D. Power. Some surprising poor performers have been the Honda Civic, Jaguar X-Type, Nissan Altima and Quest, and Toyota Corolla and Tundra.

Because they were the first off the assembly line for that model year, most vehicles assembled between September and February are called "first-series" cars. "Second-series" vehicles, made between March and August, incorporate more assembly-line fixes and are better built than the earlier models, which may depend on ineffective "field fixes" to mask problems until the warranty expires. Second-series vehicles will sell for the same price or less, but they will be a far better buy because of their assembly-line upgrades and more generous rebates. Service bulletins for Chrysler's Caliber and Charger; GM's Solstice, Torrent, and Sky roadsters; and the Ford Fusion, Zephyr, and Milan show these vehicles all had serious quality shortcomings during their first year on the market. It usually takes a couple of years for the factory to get most of the quality glitches corrected.

There's also the very real possibility that the new vehicle you've just purchased was damaged while being shipped to the dealer and was later fixed in the service bay during the PDI. It's estimated that this happens to about 10 percent of all new vehicles. Although there's no specific Canadian legislation allowing buyers of vehicles damaged in transit to cancel their contracts, B.C. legislation says that dealers must disclose damages of $2,000 or more. In a more general sense, Canadian common-law jurisprudence does allow for cancellation or compensation whenever the delivered product differs markedly from what the buyer expected to receive. Ontario's revised *Consumer Protection Act* is particularly hard-nosed in prohibiting this kind of misrepresentation.

Fuel Economy Fantasies

The mileage promised on car stickers is grossly inflated, sometimes by as much as 30 percent. *Consumer Reports* found some hybrids have fuel consumption discrepancies that average 12 L/100 km (19 mpg) worse than the city-driving rating given by the U.S. Environmental Protection Agency.

But Chrysler, Ford, GM, Honda, Lexus, Toyota, and VW don't tell the average buyer that their so-called fuel-frugal hybrids, ethanol-friendly, diesel-powered, and turbocharged models are simply high-tech, feel-good PR machines that often don't have as much power or fuel-efficiency as conventionally powered comparable models. Not only does it cost much more than advertised to run vehicles equipped with special engines and alternate fuels, but poor reliability and higher servicing costs also give these "green" vehicles a decidedly lemony flavour. And, there's Ford's EcoBoost turb noisemaker, as this owner discovered:

Ford doesn't seem to know how to combine EcoBoost virtues with a rewarding soundtrack. I own a car with a 3.5-liter EcoBoost, and it sounds like a whale with indigestion, all groans and clicks from the intake and injectors. Sometimes I don't know whether to take it to the dealer or a a gastroenterologist.

Yet most public environmental protection groups and government agencies, seconded by the major automobile clubs, genuflect whenever the hybrid, ethanol, or diesel alternative is proposed.

Once again, we have to be wary of the lies. Toyota, for example, seldom mentions the fact that its hybrid battery packs can cost about $4,000 U.S. to replace, or that *Automotive News*, *Car and Driver*, and *Edmunds* have also found that diesel and hybrid fuel consumption figures can be 30-40 percent more than advertised.

Why am I so hard on ethanol? After all, in its 2007 budget the federal Conservative government committed $2 billion in incentives for ethanol, made from wheat and corn, and for biodiesel. The Canadian Renewable Fuels Association says ethanol is "good for the environment," a position echoed by the Manitoba and Saskatchewan governments, which emphasize that ethanol "burns cleaner" than gasoline.

Hogwash! Environment Canada's own unpublished research says ethanol "burns no cleaner than gasoline."

Scientists at Environment Canada studied four vehicles of recent makes, testing their emissions in a range of driving conditions and temperatures. "Looking at tailpipe emissions, from a greenhouse gas perspective, there really isn't much difference between ethanol and gasoline," said Greg Rideout, head of Environment Canada's toxic emissions research. The study was broadcast by CBC on March 30, 2007, and can be found at *www.cbc.ca*.

Environment Canada found no statistical difference between the greenhouse gas emissions of regular unleaded fuel and 10 percent ethanol blended fuel. Although it did note a reduction in carbon monoxide, a pollutant that forms smog, emissions of some other gases, such as hydrocarbons, actually increased under certain conditions.

Other drawbacks of ethanol: It's hard to find, it eats fuel line and gas tank components, it performs poorly in cold climates, it gives you 25-30 percent less fuel economy than gasoline, and it adds to world hunger (the crop used to produce one SUV fill-up of ethanol could feed a person for a year).

Smart drivers should continue to ignore automaker gas-saving hype, hunker down, and keep their paid-for, reliable, gas-guzzling used vehicles, because the depreciation savings will more than offset the increased cost of fuel.

Hybrids

After reading the CAA's findings that a 2010 Toyota Prius hybrid will cost slightly more to run than a $15,496 2010 Chevrolet Cobalt, it's hard to comprehend how *Consumer Reports* can call the $26,100 hybrid a money-saver.

As practical as the promise of ethanol fuel for everybody seemed to be at first, hybrids use a pie-in-the-sky alternative fuel system that requires expensive and complex electronic and mechanical components to achieve the same fuel economy that a bare-bones Honda Civic can achieve for about two-thirds the cost of the Prius – and without polluting the environment with exotic toxic metals leached from battery packs and powertrain components.

Four years before the CAA findings, *Consumer Reports* tested six pairs of vehicles, with each pair including a conventional vehicle and the equivalent hybrid model, and published the astounding results in its April 2006 edition. *CR* found that in each category of car, truck, and SUV, the extra cost for the hybrid version was unacceptably *higher* than the cost of the same vehicle equipped with a conventional propulsion system.

Other disadvantages of hybrids are their mechanical and electronic complexities, dependence on specialized dealers for basic servicing, high depreciation rates and insurance costs, overblown fuel-efficiency numbers (owners report getting 40 percent less mileage than promised), and the $3,000 cost to replace their battery packs.

Finally, consider that Hybrid vehicles like the Toyota Prius use rare-earth minerals such as lanthanum, scandium, and yttrium mixed oxides and aluminas (which are used in almost all automotive emissions control systems). Neodymium is another rare element needed for the lightweight permanent magnets that power hybrid motors. It's a radioactive substance mined almost exclusively in China, which has threatened to restrict its sale for domestic use and slapped on heavy export duties. And there's a good reason why mining has been mostly restricted to China – the government there doesn't care if the mining and refining of these toxic minerals poisons the environment and sickens villagers – something North American "green" advocates overlook.

Western nations simply cannot afford to mine and refine neodymium within their borders due to the enormous environmental toxicity that mining it produces. In a sense, China is not cornering the neodymium market using their mineral reserves, but rather their willingness to sacrifice their environment and expose their populace to a higher cancer rate. In the end, North American motorists may trade a dependence on Middle Eastern oil for a troubling dependence on Chinese-sourced neodymium that's poisoning the Chinese people in the process.

Diesels

"Noisy, smokey, and slow," those are the three reasons why only one percent of car sales in North America are diesels, while 50 percent of Europeans choose a diesel powerplant (thanks, in part to France's €10,000 incentive). Yet, diesels run as clean as gasoline engines and are far more fuel-efficient than ever before. With the notable exception of VW "cheating" on tests, among the alternative fuels tested by independent researchers, diesel comes closest to the estimated fuel economy figures.

This increased fuel economy allows diesels to go up to 805 km (500 miles) between fill-ups. And you don't have to drive at a snail's pace. Modern diesels have gobs of low-end torque for fast acceleration from a standing position. The torque advantage also attracts SUV and truck owners who want good towing capability with quick pick up.

Dealerships and servicing are aren't hard to find and repairs require neither a steep learning curve in the service bay nor exotic replacement parts. Because of their higher compression, diesel engines are built with more rugged components like a strengthened crankshaft and more durable pistons. Additionally, unlike hybrids, diesels are reasonably priced (about $2,000 more than gasoline-powered vehicles) and hold their value quite well, which balances out the higher new purchase price.

Nevertheless, small diesels represent the future more than hybrids and electrics, however, as long as fuel prices remain low, diesel sales volume isn't likely to increase by much. Despite a limited market that's likely to remain small in the short term, a wide array of diesel-powered cars, sport utilities, and trucks are available from an increasing number of automakers, including BMW, Chrysler, Ford, General Motors, Jeep, Land Rover, Mercedes, Porsche, and Volkswagen. Mazda has promised a Mazda 6 diesel for 2016.

Diesel Reliability Varies

European imports offer the most reliable, durable diesel engines. Asians haven't done as well; Hyundai's Santa Fe SUV diesel sold in other countries has been a disaster. Except for Chrysler's Cummins diesel, most Detroit-made vehicles equipped with diesel engines are a big letdown. Owners report horrendously expensive maintenance costs, considerable repair downtime, and the worsening of the diesel's poor reliability trend, which was seen over the past decade with Ford's Powerstroke and GM's Duramax. Additionally, some of the diesel engines now require that owners regularly fill up with urea – an unexpected extra expense and annoyance.

Concentrated urea for diesels is sold at gas stations and
auto supply stores. Not for "do it yourselfers."

To pee or not to pee? Model diesel engines, like the Mercedes' Bluetec, inject a urea solution – known as AdBlue – into the exhaust to reduces nitrous oxide (NOx) emissions. Audi, BMW, VW, and the Detroit Three also use urea injection under different names.

A yearly urea refill can be expected since the urea tank contains roughly 8 gallons (U.S.), which is good for about 19,300 km (12,000 miles) of standard operation. Generally, automakers will add the urea solution at every scheduled maintenance visit.

Mercedes-Benz Blutec diesels will not run if the urea tank doesn't contain a certain amount. If the tank reaches one gallon, the car notifies the driver. It does so again with only 20 starts remaining. To reset the system, at least two gallons of AdBlue – or four half-gallon bottles at $7.75 each – must be added. Not a lot to clean the environment, you say? Read on.

Consumer Reports was charged an outrageous $317 to put 7.5 gallons of AdBlue in its Mercedes GL320 test car at $32/gallon for the fluid, even though 7.5 gallons would only cost $116.25 in half-gallon bottles elsewhere. So, what can you do if your car or truck is urea-immobilized, there is no dealership around, or you refuse to pay through the nose for a simple fill-up?

That brings us back to our original question: "To pee or not to pee?"

Don't pee, at least not into the urea tank. Yes, human urine contains 2-4 percent urea, but modern diesels won't use your pee because it's too diluted and full of other substances like salts, toxins, bile pigments, hormones, and up to 95 percent water. AdBlue, TDI, and other urea products have a concentration of 32.5 percent urea mixed with deionized water. If you put anything else in the urea tank, your car or truck won't start.

Fuel economy misrepresentation

So if you can't make a gas-saving product that pours into your fuel tank or attaches to the fuel or air lines, you have to use that old standby and, well, lie. Hell, if automakers and government fuel-efficiency advocates can do it, why not dealers?

Fuel economy misrepresentation is actionable, and there is Canadian jurisprudence that allows for a contract's cancellation if the gas-mileage figures are false (see Part Three). Most people, however, simply keep the car they bought and live with the fact that they were fooled.

There are a few choices you can make that will lower fuel consumption. First off, choose a smaller version of the vehicle style you are interested in buying. Second, choose a manual transmission or a hydraulic automatic with a fuel-saving fifth or sixth gear. Third, an engine with a cylinder-deactivation feature or variable valve timing will increase fuel economy by 8 and 3 percent, respectively.

Excessive Maintenance Fees

Maintenance inspections and replacement parts represent hidden costs that are usually exaggerated by dealers and automakers to increase their profits on vehicles that either rarely require fixing or are sold in insufficient numbers to support a service bay.

Alan Gelman, a well-known Toronto garage owner and co-host of Toronto AM740's "Dave's Corner Garage," warns drivers:

> There are actually two maintenance schedules handed out by car companies and dealers. The dealer inspection sheets often call for far more extensive and expensive routine maintenance checks than what's listed in the owner's manual. Most of those checks are padding; smart owners will stick with the essential checks listed in the manual and have them done by cheaper, independent garages.

Getting routine work done at independent facilities will cost about one-third to one-half the price usually charged by dealers. Just be sure to follow the automaker's suggested schedule so no warranty claim can be tied to botched servicing. Additionally, an inexpensive ALLDATA service bulletin subscription (see Appendix II) will keep you current as to your vehicle's factory defects, required check-ups, and recalls; tell you what's covered by little-known "goodwill" warranties; and save you valuable time and money when troubleshooting common problems.

Choosing a Reliable, Cheap Vehicle

Overall vehicle safety and body fit and finish on both domestic and imported vehicles are better today than they were four decades ago. Premature rusting is less of a problem, and reliability is improving. Repairs to electronic systems and powertrains, however, are outrageously expensive and complicated. Owners of cars and trucks made by General Motors, Ford, and Chrysler still report serious engine and automatic transmission deficiencies, often during the vehicle's first year in service. Other common defects include electrical system failures caused by faulty computer modules; malfunctioning ABS systems; brake rotor warpage; early pad wearout; failure-prone air conditioning and automatic transmissions; and faulty engine head gaskets, intake manifolds, fuel systems, suspensions, and steering assemblies.

Nothing shows the poor quality control of the Detroit Three automakers as much as the poor fit and finish of body panels. Next time you're stuck in traffic, look at the trunk lid or rear hatch alignment of the vehicle in front of you. Chances are, if it's a Detroit-bred model, the trunk or hatch will be so misaligned that there will be a large gap on one side. Then look at most Asian products. Usually, you will see perfectly aligned trunks and hatches without any large gaps on either side.

Detroit's "Good" Products

Don't get the impression that Detroit automakers can't make reasonably good vehicles, though. Ford's Mustang still gives you a big bang for your buck (some owners say that bang could be the Chinese-built manual transmission "grenading");

GM's full-sized rear-drive vans are good buys; and its Acadia, Enclave, Equinox, Terrain, and Traverse SUVs also perform well. Best of all, GM has dramatically improved the quality and reliability of its 2012-16 Chevrolet Impala and 2013-16 Silverado and Sierra small pickups.

General Motors' products are quite a mixed bag. Its full-sized vans, SUVs, small cars, and joint ventures with Toyota and Suzuki have all done well, but its front-drive minivans, small and mid-sized family cars (think early Malibu and Impala) are mediocre, at best.

Most studies done by consumer groups and private firms show that, in spite of improvements attempted over the past two decades, vehicles made by Chrysler, General Motors, and (to a greater extent) Ford still don't measure up to Japanese and some South Korean products, such as Hyundai, in terms of drivetrain quality and technology. This is particularly evident in SUVs and minivans, where Honda and Toyota have long retained the highest reliability and dependability ratings, despite some powertrain, brake, and fit and finish glitches (mostly sliding side door failures).

Chrysler

Chrysler doesn't have any cars that are popular or reliable; its minivan sales are struggling; and Fiat's money woes and lousy sales are a growing cancer that will drain the profits generated by Chrysler's Jeep and truck divisions.

Don't buy a Chrysler unless it's a well-inspected Ram pickup with a manual transmission and a diesel engine. Rams so equipped can be excellent buys from a reliability and durability standpoint. As far as Jeeps are concerned, they are excellent off-roaders – when they aren't off-road at the repair bay.

Ford

Ford sold off most of its assets and borrowed billions of dollars just before the 2008 recession hit. The fact that it didn't go bankrupt helped Ford keep its own loyal customers and put the company in a good position to poach Chrysler, GM, Honda, Nissan, and Toyota sales.

But, Ford dropped the ball.

Quality control went downhill. The Lincoln division became an embarrassment with no new models and a stinging failure in last year's IIHS small overlap crash test (driver-side front quarter panel), which gave the 2009-15 Lincoln MKZ large sedan a rating of "Poor."

Ford continues its downward spiral by equipping its cars with expensive and unreliable electronic infotainment devices that became a money-losing disaster. In a desperate move to fix its electronic woes, the company has announced that Microsoft will oversee the system in the future (OMG). Take a look at *Consumer Reports'* reliability ratings of Ford's lineup. Count CR's reliability black dots. And then ask yourself, "How could a company that was so far ahead screw things up so badly?"

Call it a bad case of hubris. Ford figured it was too big to fail and that North American customers would buy poorly-built products because there wasn't much competition. Moreover, there was always car-starved China, a country used to buying poor-quality automobiles – even if they are over-priced. Furthermore, Mother Nature was on Ford's side. In addition to Chrysler and GM's bankruptcy, Asian automakers were hobbled by both a tsunami and Fukushima's nuclear reactor near-meltdown.

It's hard to believe that a $48,000 Lincoln MKS large luxury sedan cannot pass with ease the same test that the $25,500 Mini Cooper Countryman small compact passed with flying colours.

General Motors

GM is back to making bundles of money, thanks to what's become a seller's market, outstanding sales in China (second only to VW), and a larger investment in new products.

Nevertheless, GM's past poor quality control is seriously affecting its reputation and bottom line. Quality deficiencies still affect most of GM's lineup, notably its Cadillac division, American-built front-drives, and imported pickups. Owners cite unreliable powertrains, poor braking performance, electrical problems, and subpar fit and finish as the main offenders.

The company's increased reliance on factories in China to build economy cars for North America is pretty scary. Imagine, not only are North Americans' bailout funds being used to create jobs in China, but we also will have the dubious pleasure of driving some of the worst-made automobiles in the world, imported from the country that sold us lead-laced-paint-coated kids' toys and poisoned pet food ingredients. Move over, Fiat! Here come the China-sourced Chery econobox and Brilliance luxury sedan – two cars that are cheap and not so crashworthy. (Don't just take my word that these are bad cars – watch the crash videos.)

An interesting conclusion relative to Chinese manufacturing, according to several independent studies – like those done by Christensen Associates, Inc. (*www.camcinc.com/library/SoYou'reBuyingFromChina.pdf*) and by Paul Midler in *Poorly Made in China: An Insider's Account of the Tactics Behind China's Production Game* (John Wiley & Sons, 2009) – is that safety and quality are trumped by price. Your car has no brakes? No problem. We'll give you a 10 percent discount and shoot the factory foreman.

Asian Automakers

Almost all of the Asian automakers make exceptionally good cars.

Kia has done extremely well this past year, selling its full lineup amid accolades for improved quality coming from *Consumer Reports* and independent auto reviewers. As for Hyundai, its parent company, sales are just as good and quality is a notch better. The Accent and Elantra are a big hit and good stand-ins for Honda, Mazda, Nissan, and Toyota small and family-sized cars.

Don't buy into the myth that parts for imports are overpriced or hard to find. It's actually easier to find parts for Japanese and South Korean vehicles than for domestic ones because of the large number of units produced, the ease with which relatively simple parts can be interchanged among different models, and the large reservoir of used parts available.

Sadly, customer relations have been the Japanese automakers' Achilles' heel. Dealers are spoiled rotten by decades of easy sales and have developed a "take it or leave it" showroom attitude, which is often accompanied by a woeful ignorance of their own model lineups.

But, there's no problem with discourteous or ill-informed South Korean automakers who have to try harder and haggle with customers to make their sales. True, poor quality has been a South Korean bugaboo, but this was also a problem with Japanese cars when they first arrived in the early '70s. Yet, like Honda's and Toyota's recoveries following start-up quality glitches, Hyundai (South Korea's biggest automaker) has made considerable progress in bringing quality up to Toyota's and Honda's level during the past decade.

Up to the mid-'90s, South Korean vehicles were merely cheap, poor-quality knock-offs of their Japanese counterparts. They would start to fall apart after their third year because of subpar body construction, unreliable automatic transmission and electrical components, and parts suppliers who put low prices ahead of reliability and durability. This was particularly evident with Hyundai's Pony,

Hyundai's 2015 $14,000 Accent and the 2015 $17,000 Kia Soul are inexpensive, reliable, and good overall entry-level performers.

Stellar, Excel, and early Sonata models. During the past decade, though, Hyundai's product lineup has been extended and refined, and quality is no longer a worry. In fact, Hyundai's 2015 upscale Genesis is a top-performing $39,999 (watch out for the $1,800 freight fee) luxury sedan that beats most European competitors and leaves both Cadillac and Lincoln in the dust. Also, Hyundai's comprehensive base warranty protects owners from most of the more expensive breakdowns that may occur.

Hyundais are easily repaired by independent garages, and their rapid depreciation doesn't mean much; they cost so little initially, and entry-level buyers are known to keep their cars longer than most, thereby easily amortizing the higher depreciation rate.

Kia, a struggling, low-quality, small South Korean compact automaker bought by Hyundai in October 1998, has come a long way. At first, it languished under Hyundai's "benign neglect," as Hyundai spent most of its resources on its own cars and SUVs. But, during the past five years, Hyundai has worked hard to improve Kia reliability and fit and finish by using more Hyundai parts in each Kia redesign and by improving quality control on the assembly line.

European Models

Lemon-Aid doesn't recommend many European cars; there are way too many with serious and expensive quality and servicing problems. Plus, a small dealer network doesn't give owners much choice if they find prices too high or servicing inadequate.

And there's more. In 2005, Britain's Warranty Direct, a third-party warranty provider, checked the cost of repairs and reliability of 250 of the most popular models sold in the British Isles. It found the Honda Accord to be the most reliable and the Fiat Punto to be the least reliable in its survey. (Are you listening, Chrysler?) Overall, Asian cars fared best in reliability and cost of repair ratings.

Honda was the brand least likely to require repairs, with Mazda, Toyota, Subaru, Nissan, Mitsubishi, and Lexus all top-ranking. Smart, Mini, and Porsche were the only European nameplates in the top ten.

Another poor performer was Land Rover. It recorded a horrendous warranty claim rate of 47 percent in an average year. This was followed up by Renault and Saab, both with a 38 percent chance of requiring a repair in an average year, while Jeep scored similarly low on the reliability index. Other reliability "bottom feeders" were Audi, Volvo, Chrysler, and Mercedes-Benz.

But not all the news is bad. VW's small cars and diesel-equipped models will continue to be strong sellers. Resale values are strong, and prices will be even more competitive. Plus, the automaker is offering substantial cash rebates in North America to compensate for poor sales in Europe.

Nevertheless, with European models, your service options are limited and customer-relations staffers can be particularly insensitive and arrogant. You can count on lots of aggravation and expense because of the unacceptably slow distribution of parts and their high markups. Because these companies have a quasi-monopoly on replacement parts, there are few independent suppliers you can turn to for help. And auto wreckers, the last-chance repository for inexpensive car parts, are unlikely to carry European parts for vehicles that are either more than three years old or manufactured in small numbers.

These vehicles also age badly after the five-year mark. The weakest areas remain the drivetrains, electronic control modules, electrical and fuel systems, brakes, accessories (including the sound system and AC), and body components.

Cutting Costs

Watch the Warranty

There's a big difference between warranty promise and warranty performance. Most automakers offer bumper-to-bumper warranties that are good for at least the first 3 years/60,000 km, and most models get powertrain coverage up to 5 years/100,000 km, although Mitsubishi offers a 5-year/100,000 km base warranty and a 10-year/160,000 km powertrain warranty. It's also becoming an industry standard for car companies to pay for roadside assistance, a loaner car, or hotel accommodations if your vehicle breaks down while you're away from home and it's still under warranty. This assistance may be for as long as five years, without any kilometre restriction. *Lemon-Aid* readers report few problems with these ancillary warranty benefits.

Don't buy a car that's warranty-dependent

If you pick a vehicle rated Recommended by *Lemon-Aid*, the manufacturer's warranty won't be that important and you won't need to spend money on additional warranty protection. On those vehicles that have a history of engine and transmission breakdowns, but the selling price is too good to turn down, budget about $1,500 for an extended powertrain warranty backed by an insurance policy. If the vehicle has a sorry overall repair history, you will likely need a $2,000 comprehensive warranty. But first ask yourself this question, "Why am I buying a vehicle that's so poorly made that I need to spend several thousand dollars to protect myself until the warranty company grows tired of seeing my face?"

Just like the weight-loss product ads you see on TV, what you see isn't always what you get. For example, bumper-to-bumper coverage usually excludes stereo components, brake pads, clutch plates, and many other expensive parts. And automakers will pull every trick in the book to make you pay for their factory screw-ups. These tricks include blaming your driving or your vehicle's poor maintenance, penalizing you for using an independent garage or the wrong fuel, or simply stating that the problem is "normal" and it's really you who is out of whack.

Part Three has all the answers to the above lame excuses. There, you will find plenty of court decisions and sample claim letters that will make automakers and their dealers think twice about rejecting your claim.

Don't pay for repairs covered by "secret" warranties

Automobile manufacturers are reluctant to publicize their secret warranty programs because they feel that such publicity would weaken consumer confidence in their products and increase their legal liability. The closest they come to an admission is to send out a "goodwill policy," "special policy," or "product update" service bulletin intended for dealers' eyes only. These bulletins admit liability and propose free repairs for defects that include faulty paint, air conditioning malfunctions, and engine and transmission failures.

If you're refused compensation, keep in mind that secret warranty extensions are, first and foremost, an admission of manufacturing negligence. You can usually find them in technical service bulletins (TSBs) that are sent daily to dealers by automakers. Your bottom-line position should be to accept a pro-rata adjustment from the manufacturer, whereby you, the dealer, and the automaker each accept a third of the repair costs. If polite negotiations fail, challenge the refusal in court on the grounds that you should not be penalized for failing to make a reimbursement claim under a secret warranty that you never knew existed!

Service bulletins are written by automakers in "mechanic speak" because service managers relate better to them that way. They're great guides for warranty inspections (especially the final one), and they're useful in helping you decide when it's best to trade in your car. Manufacturers can't weasel out of their obligations by claiming that they never wrote such a bulletin.

If your vehicle is passed warranty, show these bulletins to less-expensive, independent garage mechanics so they can quickly find the trouble and order the most recent upgraded part, ensuring that you don't replace one defective component with another. This is what a typical *Alldata.com* service bulletin summary looks like for the 2012 Chevrolet Malibu:

2012 Chevrolet Malibu L4-2.4L (Technical Service Bulletins)

Sort by Number	Sort by Date	Sort by Title
01-08-42-001J	04/22/2014	Exterior Lamp Condensation
02-08-42-001G	04/22/2014	Head/Tail/License/Fog/Driving Lamp Damage
PIC5491F	04/18/2014	OnStar Will Not Power Up
*14064	04/09/2014	Campaign – Engine Drive Belt Tensioner Noise
PIT5964	03/05/2014	OnStar(R) – Canadian Customers Unable to Make Calls in USA
PIC5959A	03/05/2014	No Audio on Certain Channels

Sort by Number	Sort by Date	Sort by Title
PIC4801F	03/04/2014	OnStar(R) – Turn-By-Turn Feature Inoperative
PIC3011H	02/26/2014	OnStar(R) – Voice Recognition Issues
12-03-10-002A	02/21/2014	Wheels/Tires – Vibration Felt Between 58-72 MPH
PI0388D	02/18/2014	Restraints – Seat Belt Webbing Latch Plate Twisted
08-03-10-006E	02/18/2014	Tire Goes Flat on Aluminum Rim
99-01-39-004E	02/10/2014	Eliminating A/C Odors
PIP5093A	01/30/2014	Oil Leaks From Rear of Engine
PIC5953	01/22/2014	Phone Voice Recognition Issues
PIP4112N	01/17/2014	Normal Sag or Hesitation on Acceleration
PI0281D	01/16/2014	Under Body Corrosion
PIP3140F	01/16/2014	Abnormal Noise/Vibration Due to Aftermarket Items
*01-07-30-042H	01/14/2014	A/T – 2-3 or 3-2 Shift Clunk Noise
PI1152	01/10/2014	A/C Stuck in Defrost Mode
00-06-01-026E	11/11/2013	Inspection After Severe Internal Engine Damage
PI0018B	11/08/2013	Front/Rear Side Door Windows Bind/Noisy/Move Slowly
06-08-51-005C	10/30/2013	Hem Flange Sealer for Corrosion Protection
07-02-32-002N	09/18/2013	Power Steering Fluid Leaks
10-08-44-006B	09/10/2013	Reporting Inaccurate Map Data
99-09-40-005G	08/15/2013	Seat Belt Extender Availability
*99-04-20-002H	04/11/2013	Information on Driveline Clunk
13-08-116-001A	03/22/2013	Electrical – Aftermarket Interface Devices Causing Issues
12-03-08-001	08/06/2012	Clunk or Thump Noise From Front Suspension
05-03-08-002E	05/31/2012	Shock Absorber/Strut Fluid Leak
08-05-23-006H	05/15/2012	Brake Rotor Noise/Pulsation
08-08-44-028A	04/11/2012	Audio – Inadvertent Steering Wheel Button Activation
11-08-44-005A	02/15/2012	Audio – Poor Radio Reception/Noise
09-09-40-001B	01/13/2012	Seat Belt Latching/Warning Lights
06-08-64-001C	12/23/2011	Side Window Chipping Info

Sort by Number	Sort by Date	Sort by Title
08-09-41-002G	12/16/2011	Air Bag Lamp ON/Multiple DTCs
*10-08-50-003B	11/10/2011	Driver/Passenger Seat Head Rest Info
09-01-37-002E	11/01/2011	Front/Rear Passenger Carpet Wet
08-08-49-004B	06/27/2011	Warped Instrument Panel Top Cover

Read this Alldata bulletin summary carefully paying close attention to bulletins marked with an *. For example, the *-marked Engine Drive Belt Tensioner Noise listing provides for the free replacement of that component under a secret warranty. The second marked bulletin addresses a "clunk" noise heard when shifting. Nothing too worrisome about that, until you download the actual bulletin from Alldata (see below). The last bulletin highlighted is GM's admission that its head restraints can force your head forward and downward. GM says a slight adjustment will correct their faulty design.

2014 CHEVROLET MALIBU L4-2.0L TURBO
A/T – 2-3 OR 3-2 SHIFT CLUNK NOISE INFORMATION

TSB: # 01-07-30-042H   DATE: JAN. 14, 2014

2014 and Prior GM Passenger Cars and Light Duty Trucks Equipped with 4L60-E, 4L65-E or 4L70-E Automatic Transmission (RPOs M30, M32, M70)

SUBJECT: Information on 2-3 Upshift or 3-2 Downshift Clunk Noise

IMPORTANT: For 2005 model year full size utilities and pickups, refer to Corporate Bulletin Number 05-07-30-012. Some vehicles may exhibit a clunk noise that can be heard on a 2-3 upshift or a 3-2 downshift. During a 2-3 upshift, the 2-4 band is released and the 3-4 clutch is applied. The timing of this shift can cause a momentary torque reversal of the output shaft that results in a clunk noise. This same torque reversal can also occur on a 3-2 downshift when the 3-4 clutch is released and the 2-4 band applied. This condition may be more pronounced on a 4-wheel drive vehicle due to the additional tolerances in the transfer case. This is a normal condition. No repairs should be attempted.

This bulletin makes a surprising admission: GM's "clunk" is a **decade-old** defect; **it affects all of GM's vehicles;** and **GM will do absolutely nothing for you** because clunking is considered "normal." Incidentally, no other automaker has the gall to admit their entire lineup is clunk-afflicted.

Canadian service managers and automakers may deny at first that these bulletins even exist, or they may shrug their shoulders and say that they apply only in the States. However, when they're shown a copy, they usually find the appropriate Canadian part number or bulletin in their files. The problems and solutions don't change from one side of the border to another. Imagine American and Canadian tourists' cars being towed across the border because each country's technical service bulletins were different? Mechanical fixes do differ in cases where, for example, a bulletin is for California only, or it relates to a safety or emissions component used only in the U.S. But these instances are rare, indeed. What is quite gratifying is to see some automakers, like Honda, candidly admit in their bulletins that "goodwill" repair refunds are available. What a shame other automakers aren't as forthcoming!

The best way to get bulletin-related repairs carried out is to visit the dealer's service bay and to attach the specific ALLDATA-supplied service bulletin covering your vehicle's problems to a work order.

Getting your vehicle's service bulletins

Free summaries of automotive recalls and technical service bulletins listed by year, make, model, and engine can be found at the ALLDATA (*www.alldata.com/TSB*) and NHTSA (*www.safercar.gov*) websites. But, like the NHTSA summaries, ALLDATA's summaries are so short and cryptic that they're of limited use. You can download the complete contents of all the bulletins applicable to your vehicle from ALLDATA at *www.orders.alldatadiy.com* if you pay the $26.95 U.S. annual subscription fee, which covers vehicles since 1982. Readers of this year's *Lemon-Aid* will find key 1982-2014 model bulletins listed by vehicle make and year in Part Four.

Trim Insurance Costs

Insurance premiums can average between $900 and $2,000 per year, depending on the type of vehicle you own, your personal statistics and driving habits, and whether you can obtain coverage under your family policy.

There are some general rules to follow when looking for insurance savings. For example, vehicles older than five years do not necessarily need collision coverage, and you may not need loss-of-use coverage or a rental car. Other factors that should be considered are noted below.

- When you phone for quotes, make sure you have your serial number in hand. Many factors, such as the make of the car, the number of doors, if there's a sports package, and the insurer's experience with the car, can affect the quote. And be honest, or you'll find your claim denied, the policy cancelled, or your premium cost boosted.

- Where you live and work also determine how much you pay. In the past, auto insurance rates have been 25-40 percent lower in London, Ontario, than in downtown Toronto because there are fewer cars in London and fewer kilometres to drive to work. Similar disparities are found in British Columbia and Alberta.

- Taking a driver-training course can save you hundreds of premium dollars.

- You may be able to include your home or apartment insurance as part of a premium package that's eligible for additional discounts.

InsuranceHotline.com, based in Ontario but with quotes for other provinces, says that it pays to shop around for cheap auto insurance rates. The group has found that the same insurance policy could vary in cost by a whopping 400 percent.

Depreciation

Depreciation is the biggest – and most often ignored – expense that you encounter when you trade in your vehicle or when an accident forces you to buy another vehicle before the depreciated loss can be amortized. Most new cars depreciate a whopping 30-45 percent during the first two years of ownership.

The best way to use depreciation rates to your advantage is to choose a vehicle listed as being both reliable and economical to own and then keep it for ten years or more. Generally, by choosing a lower-depreciating vehicle – such as one that keeps at least half its value over four years – you are storing up equity that will give you a bigger down payment and fewer loan costs with your next purchase.

Remember: Japanese cars are the slowest to depreciate, while American models lose their value the quickest. European models are in the middle range, and South Korean automakers' vehicles depreciate almost as slowly as the Japanese and offer additional savings due to their lower original purchase price.

If buying new, you want a vehicle that depreciates slowly, like a Subaru Forester, Mazda3, or Honda Civic, Accord, or CR-V. However, used car buyers should be on the lookout for fast-depreciating vehicles that are also reliable and overall good performers, like a recent Chevrolet Impala, Kia Soul, or a Hyundai Accent, Elantra, or Santa Fe. Anything from Ford, or Chrysler? Yes, a recently-minted Mustang or a diesel-equipped Ram pickup.

Gas Pains

With gas prices moderating at the 95 cents a litre mark, motorists are scratching their heads trying to find easy ways to cut gas consumption. Here are three simple suggestions.

1. Buy a used compact car for half its original price. Savings on taxes, freight fees, and depreciation is about $15,000.
2. Find low-cost fuel referrals on the Internet (*www.gasbuddy.com*). You can save about 15 cents a litre.
3. Keep your vehicle properly tuned for a 10 percent savings from improved fuel economy.

More dirt on diesels

The only reasons to buy a diesel-equipped vehicle are for their potential to deliver better-than average fuel economy and for their much lower maintenance and repair costs when compared with similar-sized vehicles powered by gasoline engines.

Let's examine the fuel-savings issue first. In theory, when compared with gasoline powerplants, diesel engines are up to 30 percent more efficient in a light vehicle and up to 70 percent cheaper to run in a heavy-duty towing and hauling truck or SUV. They become more efficient as the engine load increases, whereas gasoline engines become less so. This is the main reason diesels are best used where the driving cycle includes a lot of city driving – slow speeds, heavy loads, frequent stops, and long idling times. At full throttle, both engines are essentially equal from a fuel-efficiency standpoint. The gasoline engine, however, leaves the diesel in the dust when it comes to high-speed performance.

On the downside, fleet administrators and owners report that diesel fuel economy in real driving situations is much less than what's advertised – a complaint also voiced by owners of hybrids. Many owners say that their diesel-run rigs get about 30 percent less mileage than what the manufacturer promised.

Nevertheless, diesel fuel should cost about $0.05 a litre less than regular gasoline. However, in some regions, the increased cost of diesel fuel – because of high taxes and oil company greed, some say – can drive up the price by a dime over regular fuel.

The diesel engine's reputation for superior reliability may have been true in the past, but no longer. This fact is easily confirmed if you cross-reference owner complaints with confidential automaker service bulletins and independent industry polling results put out by J.D. Power and others, a task done for you in Part Four's ratings section. In a nutshell, Chrysler sells the best truck diesel while GM and Ford come in second and third among Detroit pickups. Some owners of diesel-equipped trucks have been frustrated by chronic breakdowns, excessive repair costs, and poor road performance. It's practically axiomatic that bad injectors have plagued Ford Power Stroke, GM Duramax engines, and (to a lesser extent) Dodge Cummins diesels.

In the past, defective injectors were often replaced at the owner's expense and at a cost of thousands of dollars. Now, General Motors and Ford use "secret warranty" programs to cover replacement costs long after the base warranty has expired (11-13 years). Chrysler has been more recalcitrant in making payouts, apparently because fewer vehicles may be involved and costs can be quite high (expensive lift pumps and injectors may be faulty).

As for diesel-equipped cars – VW and Mercedes have cornered that market.

Hybrid cars

Automakers have sold a number of different hybrids like the Prius, Honda Civic and Accord Hybrids, the Ford C-Max, and some Hyundai/Kia variants. They mostly use an engine/electric motor for maximum fuel economy and low emissions while providing the driving range of a comparable small car. Yet this latest iteration of the electric car still has serious drawbacks, which may drive away even the most green-minded buyers.

- Real-world fuel consumption may be 20 percent higher than advertised. This has resulted in several out-of-court settlements by Honda, Kia, and Ford for misleading advertising. These settlements compensate owners with a pre-paid fuel charge card that is renewed annually.

The Toyota Prius is the best of the Hybrid lineup from a reliability and performance standpoint. Its return on investment is still hotly debated. However, in a polling of a dozen Prius taxi drivers across Canada, the Prius is considered a definite money-saver when used as a high-mileage urban transporter.

- Cold weather and hilly terrain can cut fuel economy by almost 10-30 percent.
- AC and other options can increase fuel consumption even more.
- Interior cabin heat may be insufficient.
- Electrical systems can deliver a life-threatening 275-500 volts if tampered with through incompetent servicing or during an emergency rescue.
- Battery packs can cost up to $4,000 U.S., and fuel savings take time before they equal the hybrid's extra costs.
- Hybrids cost more to insure, and they depreciate just as quickly as non-hybrid vehicles that don't have expensive battery packs to replace.
- Hybrids make you a captive customer where travel is dependent on available service facilities.

If you find the limitations of an electric hybrid too daunting, why not simply buy a more fuel-efficient small car? Or, get a comfortable higher line of used car? Here are some environmentally friendly cars recommended by Toronto-based Environmental Defence Canada (*www.environmentaldefence.ca*) and by *Lemon-Aid*:

- Honda Civic and Fit
- Hyundai Accent and Tucson
- Mazda3 and Mazda5
- Nissan Sentra and Versa (although the Versa received a two-star crash rating)
- Toyota Corolla and Yaris
- VW Golf/Jetta TDI (2008 or earlier)

Test for "Real" Performance

Take the phrase "car-like handling" with a large grain of salt. A van isn't supposed to handle like a car. Since many rear-drive models are built on a modified truck chassis and use steering and suspension components from their truck divisions, they tend to handle more like trucks than cars, in spite of automakers' claims to the contrary. Also, what you see isn't necessarily what you get when you buy or lease a new sport-utility, van, or pickup, because these vehicles seldom come with enough standard features to fully exploit their versatility. Additional expensive options are usually a prerequisite to make them safe and comfortable to drive or capable of towing heavy loads. Consequently, the term "multipurpose" is a misnomer unless you are prepared to spend extra dollars to outfit your car or minivan. Even fully equipped, these vehicles don't always provide the performance touted by automakers.

Rust Protection

Most vehicles built today are much less rust-prone than they were several decades ago, thanks to more-durable body panels and better designs. When rusting occurs now, it's usually caused by excessive environmental stress (road salt, etc.), a poor paint job, or the use of new metal panels that create galvanic corrosion or promote early paint peeling – the latter two causes being ones that are excluded from most rustproofing warranties.

Invest in undercoating, and remember that the best rustproofing protection is to park the vehicle in a dry, unheated garage or under an outside carport and then wash it every few weeks. Never bring it in and out of a heated garage during the winter months, since it is most prone to rust when temperatures are just a bit above freezing; keep it especially clean and dry during that time. If you live in an area where roads are heavily salted in winter, or in a coastal region, have your vehicle's undercoating sprayed annually.

Annual undercoating, which costs around $150, will usually do as good a job as rustproofing. It will protect vital suspension and chassis components, make the vehicle ride more quietly, and allow you to ask a higher price at trade-in time. The only downside, which can be checked by asking for references, is that the undercoating may give off an unpleasant odour for months, and it may drip, soiling your driveway.

Whether you are rustproofing the entire vehicle or just undercoating key areas, make sure to include the rocker panels (make a small mark inside the door panels on the plastic hole plugs to make sure that they were removed and that the inside was actually sprayed), the rear hatch's bottom edge, the tailgate, and the wheelwells. It's also a smart idea to stay at the garage while some of the work is being done to see that the overspray is cleaned up and all areas have been covered.

Surviving the Options Jungle

The best options for your buck are a 5- or 6-speed hydraulic automatic transmission, an anti-theft immobilizer, a rearview camera, air conditioning, a premium sound system, and higher-quality tires – features that may bring back one-third to half their value come trade-in time. Rustproofing can also make cars easier to sell in some provinces where there's lots of salt on the roads in the winter, but paint protection and seat sealants are a waste of money. Most option packages can be cut by 20 percent, while extended warranties are overpriced by about 75 percent.

Dealers make at least twice as much profit as much profit selling options as they do selling most cars. No wonder their eyes light up when you start perusing their options list. If you must have some options, compare prices with independent retailers and buy where the price is lowest and the warranty is the most comprehensive. Buy as few options as possible from the dealer, since you'll get faster service, more comprehensive guarantees, and lower prices from independent suppliers. Remember, extravagantly equipped vehicles hurt your pocketbook in three ways: They cost more to begin with but return only a fraction of what they cost when the car is resold; they drive up maintenance costs; and they often consume extra fuel.

A heavy-duty battery and suspension, and perhaps an upgraded sound system, will generally suffice for American-made vehicles; most imports already come well equipped. An engine block heater with a timer isn't a bad idea, either. It's an inexpensive investment that ensures winter starting and reduces fuel consumption by allowing you to start out with a semi-warm engine.

When ordering parts, remember that purchases from American outlets can be slapped with a small customs duty if the part isn't made in the U.S. And then you'll pay the inevitable GST or HST levied on the part's cost and customs duty. Finally, your freight carrier may charge a $15-$20 brokerage fee for representing you at the border.

Must-Have Options

The problem with options is that you often can't refuse them. Dealers sell very few bare-bones cars and minivans, and they option-pack each vehicle with features that can't be removed. You'll be forced to dicker over the total cost of what you are offered, whether you need the extras or not. So it isn't a case of "yes" or "no," but more a decision of "at what cost?"

Adjustable Pedals and Extensions

This device moves the brake and accelerator pedals forward or backward about 10 cm (4 in.) to accommodate short-statured drivers and protect them from airbag-induced injuries.

If the manufacturer of your vehicle doesn't offer optional power-adjustable pedals, there are several companies selling inexpensive pedal extensions through the Internet; for example, go to HDS Specialty Vehicles' website at *hdsmn.stores.yahoo.net*. If you live in Toronto or London, Ontario, check out Kino Mobility (*www.kinomobility.com*).

Adjustable Steering Wheel

This option allows easier access to the driver's seat and permits a more-comfortable driving position. It's particularly useful if more than one person will drive the vehicle.

Air Conditioning

AC systems are far more reliable than they were a decade ago, and they have a lifespan of five to seven years. Sure, replacement and repair costs can hit $1,000, but that's very little when amortized over an eight- to ten-year period. AC also makes your car easier to resell.

Does AC waste or conserve fuel when a vehicle is driven at highway speeds? Edmunds, a popular automotive information website, conducted fuel-efficiency tests and concluded that there wasn't that much difference between open or closed windows, a finding confirmed by *Consumer Reports*. See *www.edmunds.com/advice/fueleconomy/articles/106842/article.html*:

> While the A/C compressor does pull power from the engine wasting some gas, the effect appears to be fairly minimal in modern cars. And putting the windows down tends to increase drag on most cars, canceling out any measurable gain from turning the A/C off. But this depends on the model you're driving. When we opened the sunroof in our SUV, the mileage did decrease even with the A/C off. Still, in our experience, it's not worth the argument because you won't save a lot of gas either way. So just do what's comfortable.

AC provides extra comfort, reduces wind noise (from not having to roll down the windows), and improves window defogging. Factory-installed units are best, however, because you'll get a longer warranty and improve your chances that everything was installed properly.

Anti-Theft Systems

You'd be a fool not to buy an anti-theft system, including a lockable fuel cap, for your much-coveted-by-thieves Japanese compact or sports car. Insurance Bureau of Canada (IBC) statistics for 2013 show that automobile theft costs Canadians close to $1 billion a year, including $542 million for insurers to fix or replace stolen cars, $250 million in police, health-care, and court-system costs and millions more for correctional services.

The IBC collects auto theft reports from its member insurance companies and government agencies throughout Canada and publishes its "most stolen vehicles" list each year. The insurance group says that despite declines in recent years, auto theft is still big business in Canada.

Rick Dubin, Vice-President of Investigative Services, reports that thieves have changed their strategy to avoid getting caught, "Organized criminals are now dismantling higher-end vehicles and exporting them in pieces instead of as whole vehicles because they are less likely to be detected." These vehicles get reassembled as far away as West Africa and then resold, he says.

"Thieves consistently target the Honda Civic to chop for parts. Those parts are easy to resell because there are so many Civics on the road," says Dubin.

Pickups and SUVs: A Hot Target

IBC research shows that high-end, four-wheel drive or all-wheel drive vehicles, including Ford F350 and 250 Series trucks along with Cadillac Escalades, remain targets for thieves. "This should come as no surprise," says Dubin. "Many of these higher-end vehicles are stolen in Atlantic Canada and Quebec and they end up being 'title-washed' and sold in other parts of the country. It's a lucrative market for big, rugged vehicles."

The Top 10 Most Frequently Stolen Vehicles Across Canada

Rank	Model	Rank	Model
#1	2007 Ford F350 Sd 4Wd Pu	#6	1999 Honda Civic 2Dr Coupe
#2	2006 Ford F350 Sd 4Wd Pu	#7	2004 Ford F350 Sd 4Wd Pu
#3	2007 Ford F250 Sd 4Wd Pu	#8	2006 Ford F250 Sd 4Wd Pu
#4	2003 Cadillac Escalade 4Dr 4Wd Suv	#9	2000 Honda Civic Sir 2Dr
#5	2005 Ford F350 Sd 4Wd Pu	#10	2003 Ford F350 Sd 4Wd Pu

Note: Everytime this list comes out, I yearn for a list of those cars that are so unwanted that no self-respecting thief would steal them. Until an official alert is sent out by the IBC, here's my own list of "Cars Thieves Hate:" The Chrysler Sebring/Avenger, Chevrolet Cavalier/Sunfire, Cobalt/Pontiac Pursuit, Dodge Caliber, GM minivans, Hyundai Pony, Nissan Quest, Saturn Ion, and VW New Beetle. All of the above cars can be safely parked on the street, unlocked, with the key in the ignition – except on trash pickup day.

There's a 1 in 130 chance that your vehicle will be stolen but only a 60 percent chance that you'll ever get it back.

Since amateurs are responsible for stealing most vehicles, the best theft deterrent is a visible device that complicates the job while immobilizing the vehicle and sounding an alarm. For less than $150, you can install both a steering-wheel lock and an engine ignition disabler. GPS tracking systems by independent retailers are cost-efficient and effective, as well.

Battery (Heavy-Duty)

The best battery for northern climates is the optional heavy-duty type offered by many manufacturers for about $100. It's a worthwhile purchase, especially for vehicles equipped with lots of electric options. Most standard batteries last only two winters; heavy-duty batteries give you an extra year or two for about 20 percent more than the price of a standard battery.

Make sure your new vehicle comes with a fresh battery – one manufactured less than six months earlier. Batteries are stamped with a date code, either on the battery's case or on an attached label. The vital information is usually in the first two characters – a letter and a numeral. Most codes start with a letter indicating the month: A for January, B for February, and so forth. The numeral denotes the year, say, 0 for 2000. For example, "B3" stands for February 2003.

Don't order an optional battery with cold cranking amps (CCA) below the one specified for your vehicle, or one rated 200 amps or more above the specified rating. It's a waste of money to go too high. Also, buy a battery with the longest reserve capacity you can find; a longer capacity can make the difference between driving to safety and paying for an expensive tow.

Central Locking Control

Costing around $200, this option is most useful for families with small children, car-poolers, or drivers of minivans who can't easily slide across the seat to lock the other doors.

Child Safety Seat (Integrated)

Integrated safety seats are designed to accommodate any child more than one year old or weighing over 9 kg (20 lb.). Since the safety seat is permanently integrated into the seatback, the fuss of installing and removing the safety seat and finding someplace to store it vanishes. When not in use, it quickly folds out of sight, becoming part of the seatback. Two other safety benefits: You know that the seat has been properly installed, and your child gets used to having his or her "special" seat in back, where it's usually safest to sit.

Electronic Stability Control (ESC)

IIHS studies conclude that as many as 10,000 fatal crashes could have been prevented if all vehicles were equipped with ESC. The insurance safety organization found that stability control is second only to seat belts in saving lives because it reduces the risk of fatal single-vehicle rollovers by 80 percent and the chance of having other kinds of fatal collisions by 43 percent.

ESC was first used by Mercedes-Benz and BMW on the S-Class and 7 Series models in 1995 and then was featured on GM's 1997 Cadillacs and Corvettes. It helps prevent the loss of control in turns, on slippery roads, or when you must make a sudden steering correction. The system applies the brakes to individual wheels or cuts back the engine power when sensors find the vehicle is beginning to spin or skid. It's particularly useful in maintaining stability with SUVs, but it's less useful with passenger coupes and sedans.

Keep in mind that not all ESC systems work as they should. In tests carried out by *Consumer Reports* on 2003 models, the stability control system used in the Mitsubishi Montero was rated "unacceptable," BMW's X5 3.0i system provided poor emergency handling, and Acura's MDX and Subaru's Outback VDC stability systems left much to be desired. NHTSA safety complaint postings are also full of incidents where the electronic stability control either kicked in at the wrong time, worked partially, or didn't work at all. As with airbags and ABS, the feature is a mixed blessing.

Engines (Cylinder Deactivation)

Choose the most powerful 6- or 8-cylinder engine available if you're going to be doing a lot of highway driving, if you plan to carry a full passenger load and luggage on a regular basis, or if you intend to load up the vehicle with convenience features like air conditioning. Keep in mind that minivans, SUVs, and trucks with 6-cylinder or larger engines are easier to resell and retain their value the longest. For example, Honda's '96 Odyssey minivan was a sales dud in spite of its bulletproof reliability, mainly because buyers didn't want a minivan with an underpowered 4-cylinder powerplant. Some people buy underpowered vehicles in the mistaken belief that tubocharging will give added power and increased fuel economy. It doesn't. That's why there's so much interest in peppy 4-cylinders hooked to 6-speed transmissions and in larger engines with a "cylinder deactivation," or start-stop feature.

Honda employs cylinder deactivation to cut fuel consumption by 20 percent on the Odyssey. It runs on all six cylinders when accelerating, and on three cylinders when cruising. So far, there have been neither reliability nor performance complaints related to the feature. On the other hand there have been many owner complaints relative to stop-start systems that work poorly.

Engine and Transmission Cooling System (Heavy-Duty)

This relatively inexpensive option provides extra cooling for the transmission and engine. It can extend the life of these components by preventing overheating when heavy towing is required. It's a recommended feature for large cars and trucks, especially those Ford and Chrysler models with a history of unreliable transmissions.

Extended Warranties

An acceptable buy if you limit the coverage to the powertrain; the warranty is backed by the vehicle manufacturer; and the dealer will cut the price by 50 percent. However, you are throwing away $1,500-$2,000 if you buy an extended warranty for vehicles rated Recommended in *Lemon-Aid* or for vehicles sold by automakers that have "goodwill" warranties covering engine and transmission failures (look in Part Four). If you can get a great price for a vehicle rated just Average or Above Average but want protection from costly repair bills, shop independent garages that offer lifetime warranties on parts listed in this guide as being failure-prone, such as powertrains, exhaust systems, and brakes.

Buy an extended warranty only as a last resort, and make sure you know what it covers and for how long. Budget $1,000 after dealer discounting for the powertrain warranty. Incidentally, auto industry insiders say the average markup on these warranties varies from 50-65 percent, which seems almost reasonable when you consider that some appliance warranties are marked up from 40-80 percent.

Keyless Entry (Remote)

This safety and convenience option saves you from fiddling with your key in a dark parking lot, or taking off a glove in cold weather to unlock or lock the vehicle. Try to get a keyless entry system combined with anti-theft measures, such as an ignition kill switch or some other disabler. Incidentally, some automakers no longer make vehicles with an outside key lock on the passenger's side and key fobs frequently fail. *Lemon-Aid* has found the locking systems also malfunction trapping occupants inside or barring them from entering. Make sure the vehicle has a manual over-ride.

Paint Colour

Choosing a popular colour can make your vehicle easier to sell at a good price. DesRosiers Automotive Consultants say that blue is the preferred colour overall, but green and silver are also popular with Canadians. Manheim auctioneers say that green-coloured vehicles brought in 97.9 of the average auction price, while silver ones sold at a premium 105.5 percent. Remember that certain colours require particular care.

- **Black (and other dark colours):** These paints are most susceptible to sun damage because of their heavy absorption of ultraviolet rays.
- **Pearl-toned colours:** These paints are the most difficult to work with. If the paint needs to be retouched, it must be matched to look right from both the front- and side-angle views.

- **Red:** This colour also shows sun damage, so keep your car in a garage or shady spot whenever possible.
- **White:** Although grime looks terrible on a white car, white is the easiest colour to care for. But the colour is also very popular with car thieves, because white vehicles can be easily repainted another colour.

Power-Assisted Sliding Doors, Mirrors, Windows, and Seats

Once merely a convenience feature, power-assisted windows and doors are a necessity as we age – crawling across the front seat a few times to roll up the passenger-side window or to lock the doors will quickly convince you of their value. Power mirrors are convenient on vehicles that have a number of drivers, or on minivans, vans, and SUVs. Power seats with memory are particularly useful, too, if more than one person drives a vehicle. Automatic window and seat controls currently have few reliability problems, and they're fairly inexpensive to install, troubleshoot, and repair. As a safety precaution, make sure the window control has to be lifted. This will ensure no child is strangled from pressing against the switch on older vehicles. Power-sliding doors on minivans are more dangerous. They continue to be failure-prone on all makes and shouldn't be purchased by families with children.

Suspension (Heavy-Duty)

Always a good idea, this inexpensive option pays for itself by providing better handling, allowing additional ride comfort (though a bit on the firm side), and extending shock life by an extra year or two.

Tires

There are three rules to remember when purchasing tires. First, neither brand nor price is a reliable gauge of performance, quality, or durability. Second, the cheapest prices are offered by tire discounters like Tire Rack (*www.tirerack.com*), *and Discount Tire Direct (www.discounttiredirect.com)*, and their Canadian equivalents like Canadian Tire and TireTrends (*www.tiretrends.com/index.php3*). Third, choosing a tire recommended by the automaker may not be in your best interest, since traction and long tread life are often sacrificed for a softer ride and maximum EPA (Environmental Protection Agency) mileage ratings.

Which tires are best?

There is no independent Canadian agency that evaluates tire performance and durability. However, the U.S.-based NHTSA rates tread wear, traction, and resistance to sustained high temperatures; etches the ratings onto the side walls of all tires sold in the States and Canada; and regularly posts its findings on the Internet (*www.safercar.gov*). NHTSA also logs owner complaints relative to different brands.

Lemon-Aid summarizes these complaints in the ratings of specific models in Part Four.

You can get more-recent complaint postings, service bulletins, and tire recall notices at the same government website, and check out independent owner performance ratings as compiled by Tire Rack, a large tire retailer, at *www.tirerack. com/tires/surveyresults/index.jsp.*

Two types of tires are generally available: All-season and performance. "Touring" is just a fancier name for all-season tires. Expect to pay $100 to $150 per tire. Basic all-season tires are the cheapest and last longer than performance tires. The best performers in this category are the Michelin Defender and energy saver, followed by the Continental Pro-Contact, and Goodyear Assurance. The Michelin Primacy and Continental PureContact are the best-handling all-seasons with H, V, and T speed ratings. High-performance all-season tires worth buying are those made by Continental, Goodyear, Hankook, Michelin, and Pirelli, while the most recommended summer high-performance tires are made by Continental, Goodyear, Michelin, Nokian, Pirelli, and Yokohama.

All-season tires are a compromise since, according to Transport Canada, they won't get you through winter with the same margin of safety as snow tires will and they don't provide the same durability on dry surfaces as do regular summer tires. In areas with low to moderate snowfall, however, all-season tires made by Continental, Goodyear, Michelin, Pirelli, and Cooper generally get high marks.

Mud or snow tires provide the best traction on snowy surfaces, but traction on wet roads is actually decreased. Treadwear is also accelerated by the use of softer rubber compounds. Beware of using wide tires for winter driving; 70-series or wider give poor traction and tend to float over snow. The better all-terrain tires are made by Cooper, Falken, Goodyear, Hankook, and Michelin; winter tires worth considering are those made by Continental, Michelin, and Nokia.

Remember, too, that buying slightly larger wheels and tires may improve handling, but there's a limit. For example, many cars come with 16-inch original equipment (OE) tires supplied by the carmaker. Moving up to a slightly larger size, say a 17-inch wheel, could improve your dry and wet grip handling. Getting any larger wheels can have serious downsides, though, like making the vehicle harder to control, providing less steering feedback, making the car more subject to hydroplaning ("floating" over wet surfaces), and causing SUVs and pickups to roll over more easily.

Don't over-inflate tires to lower their rolling resistance for better fuel economy. The trade-off is a harsher ride and increased risk of a blowout when passing over uneven terrain. Excessive tire pressure may also distort the tread, reducing contact with the road and increasing wear in the centre of the tread. Under-inflation is a far more common occurrence. Experts agree that tire life decreases by 10 percent for every 10 percent the tire is under-inflated, sometimes through lack of maintenance or due to the perception that an under-inflated tire improves traction. Actually, an under-inflated tire makes for worse traction. It breaks traction more easily than a tire that is properly inflated, causing skidding, pulling to the side when braking, excessive wheelspin when accelerating, and tire failure due to overheating.

Truck and SUV tires

All-season truck and SUV tires cost between $100 to $200 per tire. Tires imported from China are the cheapest but they are no bargain. They provide average handling and braking performance, but don't give sufficient traction in snow and have a short tread life.

Spare tires

Be wary of space-saver spare tires. They often can't match the promised mileage, and they seriously degrade steering control. Furthermore, they are usually stored in spaces inside the trunk that won't hold a normal-sized tire. The location of the stored spare can also have safety implications. Watch out for spares stowed under the chassis or mounted on the rear hatch. Frequently, the attaching cables and bolts rust out or freeze, so the spare falls off or becomes next to impossible to use when you need it.

Self-sealing and run-flat tires

Today, there are two technologies available to help maintain vehicle mobility when a tire is punctured: Self-sealing and self-supporting/run-flat tires.

- **Self-sealing:** Ideal if you drive long distances. Punctures from nails, bolts, or screws up to 3/16 of an inch (0.48 cm) in diameter are fixed instantly and permanently with a sealant. A low air-pressure warning system isn't required. Expert testers say a punctured self-sealing tire can maintain air pressure for up to 200 km (124.5 mi) – even in freezing conditions.

- **Self-supporting/run-flat:** Priced from $175-$350 per tire, 25-50 percent more than the price of comparable premium tires, Goodyear's Extended Mobility Tire (EMT) run-flat tires were first offered as an option on the 1994 Chevrolet Corvette and then became standard on the 1997 model. These tires reinforce the side wall so it can carry the weight of the car for 90 km (55 mi), or about an hour's driving time, even after all air pressure has been lost. You won't feel the tire go flat; you must depend on a $250-$300 optional tire-pressure monitor to warn you before the side wall collapses and you begin riding on your rim. Also, not all vehicles can adapt to run-flat tires; you may need to upgrade your rims. Experts say run-flats will give your car a harder ride, and you'll likely notice more interior tire and road noise. The car might also track differently. The Sienna's standard Dunlop run-flat tires have a terrible reputation for premature wear. At 25,000 km (15,534 mi), one owner complained that her Sienna needed a new set at $200 each. You can expect a backlog of over a month to get a replacement. Goodyear and Pirelli run-flat tires have been on the market for some time now, and they seem to perform adequately.

The NHTSA has seen reduced aging of tires filled with nitrogen. Claims have also been made that nitrogen maintains inflation pressure better than air. Though the data technically does support that passenger car tires could benefit from being filled with nitrogen, tire manufacturers say that they already design tires to perform well with air inflation. And while nitrogen will do no harm, manufacturers say that they don't see the need to use nitrogen, which generally adds $5 or more per tire charge. Drivers might appreciate the slight improvement in air retention provided, but you can do just as well without paying an extra penny by performing regular inflation checks.

Trailer-Towing Equipment

Just because you need a vehicle with towing capability doesn't mean that you have to spend big bucks. But you should first determine what kind of vehicle you want to do the job and whether your tires will handle the extra burden. For most towing needs (up to 900 kg/2,000 lb.), a passenger car, small pickup, or minivan equipped with a 6-cylinder engine will work just as well as a full-sized pickup or van (and will cost much less). If you're pulling a trailer that weighs more than 900 kg, most passenger cars won't handle the load unless they've been specially outfitted according to the automaker's specifications. Pulling a heavier trailer (up to 1,800 kg/ 4,000 lb.) will likely require a large vehicle equipped with a V8 powerplant.

Automakers reserve the right to change limits whenever they feel like it, so make any sales promise about towing an integral part of your contract. A good rule of thumb is to reduce the promised tow rating by 20 percent. In assessing towing weight, factor in the cargo, passengers, and equipment of both the trailer and the towing vehicle. Keep in mind that five people and luggage add 450 kg (almost 1,000 lb.) to the load, and that a full 227L (60 gal.) water tank adds another 225 kg (almost 500 lb.). The manufacturer's gross vehicle weight rating (GVWR) takes into account the anticipated average cargo and supplies that your vehicle is likely to carry.

Automatic transmissions are fine for trailering, although there's a slight fuel penalty. Manual transmissions tend to have greater clutch wear caused by towing than do automatic transmissions. Both transmission choices are equally acceptable. Remember, the best compromise is to shift the automatic manually for maximum performance going uphill and to maintain control, while not overheating the brakes, when descending mountains.

Unibody vehicles (those without a separate frame) can handle most towing chores as long as their limits aren't exceeded. Front-drives aren't the best choice for pulling heavy loads in excess of 900 kg (2,000 lb.), since they lose some steering control and traction with all the weight concentrated in the rear.

Whatever vehicle you choose, keep in mind that the trailer hitch is crucial. It must have a tongue capacity of at least 10 percent of the trailer's weight; otherwise, it may be unsafe to use. Hitches are chosen according to the type of tow vehicle and, to a lesser extent, the weight of the load.

Most hitches are factory-installed, even though independents can install them more cheaply. Expect to pay about $200 for a simple boat hitch and a minimum of $600 for a fifth-wheel version.

Equalizer bars and extra cooling systems for the radiator, transmission, engine oil, and steering are prerequisites for towing anything heavier than 900 kg (2,000 lb.). Heavy-duty springs and brakes are a big help, too. Separate brakes for the trailer may be necessary to increase your vehicle's maximum towing capacity.

Transmissions

Despite its many advantages, the manual transmission is an endangered species in North America. In fact, manuals have gone from 20 percent of sales to 5 percent in the last 20 years where they are mostly seen in high-performance sports cars, budget trucks, and small, inexpensive econocars. (The most recent casualties: The 2015 Subaru Legacy sedan and Outback crossover.) The brake pads on stick-shift vehicles tend to wear out less rapidly than those on automatics; a transmission with five or more forward speeds is usually more fuel-efficient than one with three forward speeds (hardly seen anymore); and manual transmissions usually add a mile or two per gallon over automatics, although this isn't always the case.

Of the three types of automatic gearboxes available, generally the most reliable and cheapest to repair are the conventional hydraulic automatics, with five to nine dedicated gears (speeds). However, the ZF 9HP automatic gearbox used in 2014-15 Acura, Chrysler, and Jeep models may be the quintiessential "lemon." It has generated over 145 safety-related complaints posted by NHTSA (in one rollaway, the Cherokee dragged its owner into 10 feet of water at a local lake). *Car and Driver* reports Jeep dealers are replacing 12-15 Cherokee transmissions a week (*blog.car anddriver.com/holy-shift-zf-9-speed-automatic-problems-mount-chrysler-releases-third-software-update-for-jeep-cherokee/*):

> [T]hese allegations are far worse than the sluggish and delayed gear changes we've experienced testing the Cherokee and Evoque (and yet absent in the 200 and TLX). Cherokee, 200, and TLX owners have each reported conditions such as sudden lunges from unexpected downshifts, a lack of kickdown upon entering highways, front-axle vibration in low gears, and complete failures in which the transmission shifts into neutral while driving and lights up the dash with warning lights. Other owners have reported rollaways in which the vehicle indicated it had engaged park when it was actually in neutral.

Incidentally, this problem may continue to grow in size. The 2015 Land Rover Discovery Sport, 2015 Jeep Renegade, and 2016 Fiat 500X will also carry the 9HP automatic.

A "Macho Machine" that will make you cry as it shifts from 9 to 0 gears while you're yelling "I'm gonna die."

From NHTSA postings:

Two times the Cherokee's transmission warning came on to "service transmission" with no response from depressing the accelerator. At these two times the vehicle was at a full stop and the dash was full of warning lights for different things. When the transmission was shifted from drive to park, there was a loud and violent jerking by the transmission. This transmission has had it's software updated many times, which has not helped. Dealer tech was able to observe this condition and replaced the transmission valve body. After replacing the valve body and after driving about 50 miles on an interstate highway, the service transmission warning came on, again. The car would lunge and jerk violently trying to go. Shut the engine off and let the car reset itself. I will not drive the vehicle again and will ask Chrysler to supply a rental vehicle at their expense until they have replaced my vehicle. This makes three times the vehicle has been in the shop for transmission problems. This transmission issue as far I am concerned is a major safety issue.

Fiat Chrysler CEO Sergio Marcionne had these words of sympathy for owners of Cherokees equipped with the failure-prone 9HP tranny. "We have had to do an inordinate amount of intervention on that transmission, surely beyond what any of us had forecast."

The two other choices are the ultra-expensive and failure-prone dual-clutch gearbox (DCG), a favourite with European automakers like Audi, BMW, and VW and the continuously variable automatic transmission (CVT), a variation used widely by American and Asian automakers. Most CVT transmissions don't have gears; they use less durable belts, instead. When the belts break, the whole transmission is overhauled at great expense. CVT gearboxes that use chains are a bit more durable, but they still break.

Both automatics claim improved performance and fuel efficiency, but what they actually deliver, judging by service bulletins and owner feedback, is early breakdowns near the five-year mark, rough shifting, excessive noise, less performance response or "feel," and expensive dealer-dependent repairs.

One theory regarding why the manual numbers keep falling? North American drivers are too busy with cell phones, text messaging, and cappuccinos to shift gears. Interestingly, European buyers opt for a manual transmission almost 90 percent of the time. (And they also drink cappuccinos, but usually not in 20 oz. paper takeout cups.)

Unnecessary Options

All-Wheel Drive (AWD)

Mark Bilek, editorial director of *Consumer Guide*'s automotive website (*consumerguideauto.howstuffworks.com*), is a critic of AWD. He says AWD systems generally encourage drivers to go faster than they should in adverse conditions, which creates trouble stopping in emergencies. Automakers like AWD as "a marketing ploy to make more money," Bilek contends. My personal mechanic adds, "Four-wheel drive will only get you stuck deeper, farther from home."

Anti-Lock Brakes (ABS)

Like ACC and backup warning devices, ABS is another safety feature that's fine in theory but often impractical under actual driving conditions. The system maintains directional stability by preventing the wheels from locking up. This will not reduce the stopping distance, however. In practice, ABS is said to make drivers overconfident. Many still pump the brakes and render them ineffective; total brake failure is common; and repairs are frequent, complicated, and expensive to perform.

Cruise Control

Automakers provide this $250-$300 option, which is mainly a convenience feature, to motorists who use their vehicles for long periods of high-speed driving. The constant rate of speed saves some fuel and lessens driver fatigue during long trips. Still, the system is particularly failure-prone and expensive to repair, can lead to driver inattention, and can make the vehicle hard to control on icy roadways. Malfunctioning cruise-control units are also one of the major causes of sudden acceleration incidents. At other times, cruise control can be very distracting, especially to inexperienced drivers who are unaccustomed to sudden speed fluctuations.

Adaptive cruise control is the latest evolution of this feature. It senses a vehicle ahead of you and then automatically downshifts, brakes, or cuts your vehicle's speed. This commonly occurs when passing another car or when a car passes you, and it can make for a harrowing experience, especially when you are in the passing lane.

Electronic Instrument Readout

If you've ever had trouble reading a digital watch face or resetting your VCR, you'll feel right at home with this electronic gizmo. Gauges are presented in a series of moving digital patterns that are confusing, distracting, and unreadable in direct sunlight. This system is often accompanied by a trip computer and vehicle monitor that indicate average speed, signal component failures, and determine fuel use and how many kilometres you can drive until the tank is empty. Figures are frequently in error or slow to catch up.

Fog Lights

A pain in the eyes for some, a pain in the wallet for others who have to pay the high bulb replacement costs. Fog lights aren't necessary for most drivers who have well-aimed original-equipment headlights on their vehicles.

Gas-Saving Gadgets and Fuel Additives

Ah, the search for the Holy Grail. Magic software and miracle hardware that will turn your gas-hungry Hummer into a fuel-frugal Prius when the right additive is poured into your fuel tank.

The accessory market has been flooded with hundreds of atomizers, magnets, and additives that purport to make vehicles less fuel-thirsty. However, tests on over 100 gadgets and fuel or crankcase additives carried out by the EPA have found that only a handful produce an increase in fuel economy, and the increase is tiny. These gadgets include warning devices that tell the driver to ease up on the throttle or shift to a more fuel-frugal gear, hardware that reduces the engine power needed for belt-driven accessories, cylinder deactivation systems, and spoilers that channel airflow under the car. The use of any of these products is a quick way to lose warranty coverage and fail provincial emissions tests.

GPS Navigation Systems

This navigation aid links a Global Positioning System (GPS) satellite unit to the vehicle's cellular phone and electronics. Good GPS devices cost $125-$1,500 U.S. when bought from an independent retailer. As a dealer option, you will pay $1,000-$2,000 U.S. For a monthly fee, the unit connects drivers to live operators who will help them with driving directions, give repair or emergency assistance, or relay messages. If the airbag deploys or the car is stolen, satellite-transmitted signals are automatically sent from the vehicle to operators who will notify the proper authorities of the vehicle's location.

Many of the systems' functions can be performed by a smart phone, and the navigation screens may be obtrusive, distracting, washed out in sunlight, and hard to calibrate. A portable Garmin GPS unit is more user-friendly and much cheaper.

High-Intensity Headlights

These headlights are much brighter than standard headlights, and they cast a blue hue. Granted, they provide additional illumination of the roadway, but they are also annoying to other drivers, who will flash their lights – or give you the middle finger – thinking that your high beams are on. These lights are easily stolen and expensive to replace. Interestingly, European versions have a device to maintain the light's spread closer to the road so that other drivers aren't blinded.

ID Etching

This $150-$200 option is a scam. The government doesn't require it, and thieves and joyriders aren't deterred by the etchings. If you want to etch your windows for your own peace of mind, several private companies will sell you a $15-$30 kit that does an excellent job (try *www.autoetch.net*), or you can wait for your municipality or local police agency to conduct one of their periodic free VIN ID etching sessions in your area.

Paint and Fabric Protectors

Selling for $200-$300, these "sealants" add nothing to a vehicle's resale value. Although paint lustre may be temporarily heightened, this treatment is less effective and more costly than regular waxing, and it may also invalidate the manufacturer's guarantee at a time when the automaker will look for any pretext to deny your paint claim.

Auto fabric protection products are nothing more than variations of Scotchgard, which can be bought in aerosol cans for a few dollars – a much better deal than the $50-$75 charged by dealers.

Power-Assisted Minivan Sliding Doors

Not a good idea if you have children. These doors have a high failure rate, opening or closing for no apparent reason and injuring children caught between the door and post.

Remote Starters (After-Market)

Remote starters are risky options. If they aren't original equipment there's a greater chance of having been installed improperly. Apart from being unreliable, after-market remote starters may cause a fire or damage electronic circuits and computers.

Reverse-Warning System

Selling for about $500 as part of an option package, this safety feature warns the driver of any objects in the rear when backing up. Although a sound idea in theory, in practice the device often fails to go off or sounds an alarm for no reason. Drivers eventually either disconnect or ignore it. Choose a rearview backup camera, instead.

Rollover-Detection System

This feature makes use of sensors to determine if the vehicle has leaned beyond a safe angle. If so, the side airbags are automatically deployed and remain inflated to make sure occupants aren't injured or ejected in a rollover accident. This is a totally new system that has not yet been proven. It could have disastrous consequences if the sensor malfunctions, as has been the case with front and side airbag sensors over the past decade.

Rooftop Carrier

Although this inexpensive option provides additional baggage space and may allow you to meet all your driving needs with a smaller vehicle, a loaded roof rack can increase fuel consumption by as much as 18 percent. An empty rack can increase your gas bill by about 10 percent.

Rustproofing

Rustproofing is no longer necessary, since automakers have extended their own rust warranties. In fact, you have a greater chance of seeing your rustproofer go belly up than having your untreated vehicle ravaged by premature rusting. Even if the rustproofer stays in business, you're likely to get a song and dance about why the warranty won't cover so-called internal rusting, or why repairs will be delayed until the sheet metal is actually rusted through.

Be wary of electronic rustproofing. Selling for $425-$700, these electrical devices claim to inhibit vehicle corrosion by sending out a pulse current to the grounded body panels, protecting areas that conventional rust-inhibiting products can't reach. There is much debate as to whether these devices are worth the cost, or if they work at all.

Seat Warmers

Over the years, the NHTSA has logged over 1,260 complaints on seat heaters, mostly concerning overheating, resulting in 287 injuries and over 500 fires.

Sunroof

Unless you live in a temperate region, the advantages of having a sunroof are far outweighed by the disadvantages. NHTSA's *safercar.gov* website is replete with owner complaints of the sunroof suddenly exploding when the car door is shut; the ambient temperature drops; or for no discernable reason when the vehicle is underway. Moreover, you aren't going to get better ventilation than a good AC system would provide, and a sunroof may grace the interior with painful booming wind noises, rattles, water leaks, and road dust accumulation. A sunroof also increases fuel consumption, reduces night vision because overhead highway lights shine through the roof opening, and can reduce headroom by several centimetres.

Tinted Glass

On the one hand, tinting jeopardizes safety by reducing your night vision. On the other hand, it does keep the interior cool in hot weather, reduces glare, and hides the car's contents from prying eyes. Factory applications are worth the extra cost, since cheaper aftermarket products (costing about $150) distort visibility and peel away after a few years. Some tinting done in the States can run afoul of provincial highway codes that require more transparency.

CUTTING THE PRICE

Bidding by Fax or E-mail

The process is quite easy: Simply fax or e-mail an invitation for bids to area dealerships, asking them to give their bottom-line price for a specific make and model. Be clear that all final bids must be sent within a week. When all the bids are received, the lowest bid is sent to the other dealers to give them a chance to beat that price. After a week of bidding, the lowest price gets your business. Incidentally, with the Canadian loonie headed to parity with the American dollar, try doing an Internet search for American prices and then using that lower figure to haggle with Canadian dealers.

Dozens of *Lemon-Aid* readers have told me how this bidding approach has cut thousands of dollars from the advertised price and saved them from the degrading song-and-dance routine between the buyer, sales agent, and sales manager ("he said, she said, the sales manager refused").

A *Lemon-Aid* reader sent in the following suggestions for buying by fax or e-mail.

First, I'd like to thank you for writing the *Lemon-Aid* series of books, which I have used extensively in the fax-tendering purchase of my '99 Accord and '02 Elantra. I have written evidence from dealers that I saved a bare minimum of $700 on the Accord (but probably more) and a whopping $900 on the Elantra through the use of fax-tendering, over and above any deals possible through Internet-tendering and/or showroom bargaining.

Based on my experience, I would suggest that in reference to the fax-tendering [or e-mail-tendering] process, future *Lemon-Aid* editions emphasize the issues below.

Casting a wide geographical net, as long as you're willing to pick the car up there. I faxed up to 50 dealerships, which helped tremendously in increasing the number of serious bidders. One car was bought locally in Ottawa, the other in Mississauga.

Unless you don't care much about what car you end up with, be very specific about what you want. If you are looking at just one or two cars, which I recommend, specify trim level and all extended warranties and dealer-installed options in the fax letter. Otherwise, you'll end up with quotes comparing apples and oranges, and you won't get the best deal on options negotiated later. Also, specify that quotes should be signed. This helps out with errors in quoting.

Dealerships are sloppy. There is a 25-30 percent error rate in quotes. Search for errors and get corrections, and confirm any of the quotes in serious contention over the phone.

Phone to personally thank anyone who submits a quote for their time. Salespeople can't help themselves, they'll ask how they ranked, and often want to then beat the best quote you've got. This is much more productive than faxing back the most competitive quote (I know, I've tried that too).

Another reader, in British Columbia, was successful with this approach.

Thanks for all the information that helped me decide to purchase a new Honda Odyssey EX-L for a super price from a good dealer.

After completing my research (and vacillating for a few weeks) I ended up issuing a faxed "request for quotation" (RFQ) from several dealerships. I can tell you that some of them were not happy and tried to tell me that Honda Canada was clamping down on this activity. In the end, one dealership did not respond and one "closer" salesperson called to attempt to get me in their dealership so he could "assess my needs." I told him that my needs were spelled out very specifically in my request but he refused to give me a price.

In the end, I received five quotations by phone, fax, and e-mail. I purchased my van in Chilliwack for about $2,200 off list. It turned out that the salesperson just started selling cars two months ago and was very appreciative of my business. The whole deal was completed in half an hour. I was in full control but treated every respondent fairly. I did not play dealers off one another and went with the lowest first offer.

GETTING A FAIR PRICE

"We Sell Below Cost"

This is no longer a bait-and-switch scam. Many dealers who are going out of business are desperate to sell their inventory, sometimes for 40 percent below the MSRP. Assuming the vehicle's cost price was 20 percent under the MSRP, astute buyers are getting up to a 20 percent discount. The chart lists the profit margins for various vehicle categories, excluding freight, PDI, and administrative fees, which you should bargain down or not pay at all. In addition to the dealer's markup, some vehicles may also have a 3 percent carryover allowance paid out in a dealer incentive program. Finance contracts may also tack on a 2 percent dealer commission.

Holdback

Ever wonder how dealers who advertise vehicles for "a hundred dollars over invoice" can make a profit? They are counting mostly on the manufacturer's holdback.

In addition to the MSRP, the invoice price, dealer incentives, and customer rebates (available to Canadians at *www.apa.ca*), another key element in every dealer's profit margin is the manufacturer's holdback – the quarterly payouts dealers depend on when calculating gross profit.

The holdback was set up almost 50 years ago by General Motors as a guaranteed profit for dealers tempted to bargain away their entire profit to make a sale. It usually represents 1-3 percent of the sticker price (MSRP) and is seldom given out by Asian or European automakers, which use dealer incentive programs instead. There are several free Internet sources for holdback information. The most recent and comprehensive are *www.edmunds.com* and *www.kbb.com*, two websites geared toward American buyers. Although there may be a difference in the holdback percentage between American automakers and their Canadian subsidiaries, it's usually not significant.

Some GM dealers maintain that they no longer get a holdback allowance. They are being disingenuous – the holdback may have been added to special sales "incentive" programs, which won't show up on the dealer's invoice. Options are the icing on the cake, with their average 35-65 percent markup.

Can You Get a Fair Price?

Yes, but you'll have to keep your wits about you and time your purchase well into the model year – usually in late winter or spring.

New-car negotiations aren't wrestling matches where you have to pin the sales agent's shoulders to the mat to win. If you feel that the overall price is fair, don't jeopardize the deal by refusing to budge. For example, if you've brought the contract price 10 percent or more below the MSRP and the dealer sticks you with a $200 "administrative fee" at the last moment, let it pass. You've saved money and the sales agent has saved face.

Of course, someone will always be around to tell you how he or she could have bought the vehicle for much less. Let that pass, too.

To calculate a fair price, subtract two-thirds of the dealer's markup from the MSRP and then trade the carryover and holdback allowance for a reduced delivery and transportation fee. Compute the options separately, and sell your trade-in privately. Buyers can more easily knock $3,000 off a $20,000 base price if they wait until the annual New Year "fire" sale in early 2016 that lasts until the

2017s arrive. This is best done by choosing a vehicle that's in stock, and avoiding unnecessary options.

Beware of Financing and Insurance Traps

Once you and the dealer have settled on the vehicle's price, you aren't out of the woods yet. You'll be handed over to an F&I (financing and insurance) specialist, whose main goal is to convince you to buy additional financing, loan insurance, paint and seat cover protection, rustproofing, and extended warranties. These items will be presented on a computer screen as costing only "a little bit more each month."

Compare the dealer's insurance and financing charges with those from an independent agency that may offer better rates and better service. Often, the dealer gets a kickback for selling insurance and financing. And guess who pays for it? Additionally, remember that if the financing rate looks too good to be true, you're probably paying too much for the vehicle. The F&I closer's hard-sell approach will take all your willpower and patience to resist, but when he or she gives up, your trials are over.

Add-on charges are the dealer's last chance to stick it to you before the contract is signed. Dealer PDI and transportation charges, "documentation" fees, and extra handling costs are ways that the dealer gets extra profits for nothing. Dealer preparation is often a once-over-lightly affair, with a car seldom getting more than a wash job and five dollars' worth of gas in the tank. PDI should cost no more than 2 percent of the car's selling price.

Some loan companies operating in Canada require borrowers to allow the installation of a starter-interrupter device that prevents the vehicle from starting if money is owing on the loan. Triggered by a remote signal from the loaner, the car can't be started until the device has been reset. Though it has yet to receive a formal complaint, the Office of the Privacy Commissioner of Canada is "actively following the issue, specifically the data collection made possible by the growing deployment of automotive sensors." In public hearings, some witnesses have complained the starter-interrupter shut off their cars while they were driving.

The borrower's vehicle is continuously tracked through these devices and drivers have to give up any right of privacy until their loan is paid.

after the time for me to cure this nonpayment has run out. I agree that I have no right to privacy regarding the use of the GPS device to track the location of the vehicle, but in the event that a court, arbitrator, dispute resolution organization or state or federal authority should determine that such a right exists, I hereby waive such right to the fullest extent possible. I understand the GPS unit is not being used to make monies beyond those due and owing under this Agreement and my Contract, but is being used to secure collection of monies I hereby acknowledge I owe and, where allowed, to repossess the Vehicle as allowed.

Buyer:		Co-Buyer:	

A contract template posted on the Passtime USA website. The driver gives up "the right to privacy."

Except for Quebec, neither Transport Canada nor the other provinces have legislation governing these devices. In Quebec, the government requires lenders to provide consumers with 30 days' notice before they repossess a car through a bailiff. Starter-interrupters aren't allowed for repossessions.

"No Haggle" Pricing Is "Price Fixing"

All dealers bargain. They hang out the "No dickering; one price only" sign simply as a means to discourage customers from asking for a better deal. Like parking lots and restaurants that claim they won't be responsible for lost or stolen property, they're bluffing. Still, you'd be surprised by how many people believe that if it's posted, it's non-negotiable.

Price Guidelines

When negotiating the price of a new vehicle, remember that there are several price guidelines and dealers use the one that will make them the most profit on each transaction. Two of the more common prices quoted are the MSRP (what the automaker advertises as a fair price) and the dealer's invoice cost (which is supposed to indicate how much the dealer paid for the vehicle). Both price indicators leave considerable room for the dealer's profit margin, along with some extra padding in the form of inflated transportation and preparation charges. If you are presented with both figures, go with the MSRP, since it can be verified by calling the manufacturer. Any dealer can print up an invoice and swear to its veracity. If you want an invoice price from an independent source, contact *www.apa.ca* or *www.carhelpcanada.com*.

Buyers who live in rural areas or in western Canada are often faced with grossly inflated auto prices compared to those charged in major metropolitan areas. A good way to get a more competitive price without buying out of province is to check online to see what prices are being charged in different urban areas. Show the dealer printouts that list selling prices, preparation charges, and transportation fees, and then ask for his or her price to come closer to the advertised prices.

Another tactic is to take a copy of a local competitor's car ad to a competing dealer selling the same brand and ask for a better price. Chances are they've already lost a few sales due to the ad and will work a little harder to match the deal; if not, they're almost certain to reveal the tricks in the competitor's promotion to make the sale.

Dealer Incentives and Customer Rebates

Sales incentives haven't changed much in the past 30 years. When vehicles are first introduced in the fall, they're generally overpriced; early in the new year, they'll sell for about 20-30 percent less. After a year, they may sell for less through a combination of dealer sales incentives (manufacturer-to-dealer), cash rebates (manufacturer-to-customer), zero percent interest financing (manufacturer's-finance-company-to-customer), and discounted prices (dealer-to-customer).

In most cases, the manufacturer's rebate is straightforward and mailed directly to the buyer from the automaker. There are other rebate programs that require a financial investment on the dealer's part, however, and these shared programs tempt dealers to offset losses by inflating the selling price or pocketing the manufacturer's rebate. Therefore, when the dealer participates in the rebate program, demand that the rebate be deducted from the MSRP, not from some inflated invoice price concocted by the dealer.

Some rebate ads will include the phrase "from dealer inventory only." So if your dealer doesn't have the vehicle in stock, you won't get the rebate.

Sometimes automakers will suddenly decide that a rebate no longer applies to a specific model, even though their ads continue to include it. When this happens, take all brochures and advertisements showing your eligibility for the rebate plan to provincial consumer protection officials. They can use false advertising statutes to force automakers to give rebates to every purchaser who was unjustly denied one.

If you are buying a heavily discounted vehicle, be wary of "option packaging" by dealers who push unwanted protection packages (rustproofing, paint sealants, and upholstery finishes) or who levy excessive charges for preparation, filing fees, loan guarantee insurance, and credit life insurance.

Price Swings

This year, the best prices will come early in the first quarter of 2016 and will continue through the fall, when most 2017s arrive. On the other hand, if your choice has an unusually low sticker price, find out why it's so unpopular and then decide if the savings are worth it. Vehicles that don't sell because of their weird styling are no problem, but poor quality control (think Chrysler minivans and Ford compacts) can cost you big bucks.

Leftovers

The 2015 leftovers are being picked clean as the 2016s arrive this fall. The older models can be good buys, if you can amortize the first year's depreciation by keeping the vehicle for eight years or more. But if you're the kind of driver who trades every two or three years, you're likely to come out a loser by buying an end-of-the-season vehicle. The simple reason is that, as far as trade-ins are concerned, a leftover is a "used" vehicle that has depreciated at least 20 percent in its first year. The savings the dealer gives you probably won't equal that first year's depreciation (a cost you'll incur without getting any of the first year's driving benefits). If the dealer's discounted price matches or exceeds the 30 percent depreciation, you're getting a pretty good deal.

Ask the dealer for all work orders relating to the vehicle, including the PDI checklist, and make sure that the odometer readings follow in sequential order. Remember as well that most demonstrators should have less than 5,000 km (3,100 mi) on the ticker and that the original warranty has been reduced from the day the vehicle was first put on the road. Also, make sure the vehicle is relatively "fresh" (about three months old) and check for warranty damage. With demos, have the dealer extend the warranty or lower the price about $100 for each month of warranty that has expired. If the vehicle's file shows that it was registered to a leasing agency or any other third party, you're definitely buying a used vehicle disguised as a demo. You should walk away from the sale – you're dealing with a crook.

CASH VERSUS FINANCING

Up until this year, car dealers preferred financing car sales instead of getting cash, because of the 1-2 percent kickbacks lenders gave them. This is less the case now, because fewer companies are lending money, and those that do are giving back very little to dealers and don't want to give loans for more than two-thirds of the purchase price. Dealers are scrambling for equity and will sell their vehicles for less than what they cost if the buyer pays cash. Cash is, once again, king.

If you aren't offered much of a discount for cash, financial planners say it can be smarter to finance the purchase of a new vehicle if a portion of the interest is tax deductible. The cash that you free up can then be used to repay debts that aren't tax deductible (mortgages or credit card debts, for example).

Rebates Versus Low or Zero Percent Financing

Low-financing programs have a number of disadvantages.
- Buyers must have exceptionally good credit.
- Shorter financing periods mean higher payments.
- Cash rebates are excluded.
- Only fully equipped or slow-selling models are eligible.
- Buyers pay full retail price.

The above stipulations can add thousands of dollars to your costs. Remember, to get the best price, first negotiate the price of the vehicle without disclosing whether you are paying cash or financing the purchase (say you haven't yet decided). Once you have a fair price, you can then take advantage of the financing.

Getting a Loan

Borrowers must be at least 18 years old (the age of majority), have a steady income, prove that they have discretionary income sufficient to make the loan payments, and be willing to guarantee the loan with additional collateral or with a parent or spouse as a co-signer.

Before applying for a loan, you should have established a good credit rating via a paid-off credit card and have a small savings account with your local bank, credit union, or trust company. Prepare a budget listing your assets and obligations. This will quickly show whether or not you can afford a car. Next, prearrange your loan with a phone call. This will protect you from much of the smoke-and-mirrors showroom shenanigans.

Incidentally, if you do get in over your head and require credit counselling, contact Credit Counselling Service (CCS), a not-for-profit organization located in many of Canada's major cities (*www.creditcanada.com*).

Hidden Loan Costs

The APA's undercover shoppers have found that most deceptive deals involve major banking institutions rather than automaker-owned companies.

In your quest for an auto loan, remember that the Internet offers help for people who need an auto loan and want quick approval, but don't want to face a banker. The BMO (Bank of Montreal: *www.bmo.com*), RBC (Royal Bank of Canada: *www.rbc.com*), and other banks allow vehicle buyers to post loan applications on their websites. Loans are available to any web surfer, including those who aren't current BMO or RBC customers.

Be sure to call various financial institutions to find out the following:

- The annual percentage rate on the amount you want to borrow, and the duration of your repayment period;
- The minimum down payment that the institution requires;
- Whether taxes and licence fees are considered part of the overall cost and, thus, are covered by part of the loan;
- Whether lower rates are available for different loan periods, or for a larger down payment; and
- Whether discounts are available to depositors, and, if so, how long you must be a depositor before qualifying.

When comparing loans, consider the annual rate and then calculate the total cost of the loan offer – that is, how much you'll pay above and beyond the total price of the vehicle.

Dealers may be able to finance your purchase at interest rates that are competitive with the banks' because of the rebates they get from the manufacturers and some lending institutions. Don't believe dealers who say they can borrow money at as much as 5 percentage points below the prime rate. Actually, they're jacking up the retail price to more than make up for the lower interest charges. Sometimes, instead of boosting the price, dealers reduce the amount they pay for the trade-in. In either case, the savings are illusory.

When dealing with banks, keep in mind that the traditional 36-month loan has now been stretched from 60-96 months. Longer payment terms make each month's payment more affordable, but over the long run, they increase the cost of the loan considerably. Therefore, take as short a term as possible or make sure you keep the car far longer than the term of the loan.

Be wary of lending institutions that charge a "processing" or "document" fee ranging from $25-$100. Sometimes consumers will be charged an extra 1-2 percent of the loan up front in order to cover servicing. This is similar to lending institutions adding "points" to mortgages, except that with auto loans, it's totally unjustified. In fact, dealers in the States are the object of several state lawsuits and class actions for inflating loan charges.

Some banks will cut the interest rate if you're a member of an automobile owners' association or if loan payments are automatically deducted from your chequing account. This latter proposal may be costly, however, if the chequing account charges exceed the interest-rate savings.

Loan Protection

Credit insurance guarantees that the vehicle loan will be paid if the borrower becomes disabled or dies. There are three basic types of insurance that can be written into an installment contract: Credit life, accident and health, and comprehensive. Some car companies, like Hyundai, will make some of your loan payments if you become unemployed. Most bank and credit union loans are already covered by some kind of loan insurance, but dealers sell the protection separately at an extra cost to the borrower. For this service, the dealer gets a hefty 20 percent commission. The additional cost to the purchaser can be significant.

Collecting on these types of policies isn't easy. There's no payment if your unemployment was due to your own conduct or if an illness is caused by some condition that existed prior to your taking out the insurance. Generally, credit insurance is unnecessary if you're in good health, you have no dependants, and your job is secure. Nevertheless, if you need to cancel your financial obligations, the same company that started LeaseBusters now offers FinanceBusters (*www. financebusters.com*). They provide a similar service to a lease takeover, but for customers who have vehicle loans.

Personal loans from financial institutions (particularly credit unions) now offer lots of flexibility, like fixed or variable interest rates, a choice of loan terms, and no penalties for prepayment. Precise conditions depend on your personal credit rating.

Leasing contracts are less flexible. There's a penalty for any prepayment, and rates aren't necessarily competitive.

Financing Scam: "Your Financing Was Turned Down"

This may be true, now that credit has become more difficult to get. But watch out for the scam that begins after you have purchased a vehicle and left your trade-in with the dealer. A few days later, you are told that your loan was rejected and that you now must put down a larger down payment and accept a higher monthly payment. Of course, your trade-in has already been sold.

Protect yourself from this rip-off by getting a signed agreement that stipulates that financing has been approved and that monthly payments can't be readjusted. Tell the dealer that your trade-in cannot be sold until the deal has closed.

THE CONTRACT

How likely are you to be cheated when buying a new car or truck? APA staffers posing as buyers visited 42 dealerships in four Canadian cities in early 2002. Almost half the dealers they visited (45 percent) flunked their test, and (hold onto your cowboy hats) auto buyers in western Canada were especially vulnerable to dishonest dealers. Either dealer ads left out important information or vehicles in the ads weren't available or were selling at higher prices. Fees for paperwork and vehicle preparation were frequently excessive.

Now, 13 years later, we know dealers are much more honest. Ahem … maybe.

The Devil's in the Details

Watch what you sign, since any document that requires your signature is a contract. Don't sign anything unless all the details are clear to you and all the blanks have been filled in. Don't accept any verbal promises that you're merely putting the vehicle on hold. And when you are presented with a contract, remember it doesn't have to include all the clauses found in the dealer's pre-printed form. You and the sales representative can agree to strike some clauses and add others.

When the sales agent asks for a deposit, make sure that it's listed on the contract as a deposit, try to keep it as small as possible (a couple hundred dollars at most), and pay for it by credit card – in case the dealer goes belly up. If you decide to back out of the deal on a vehicle taken from stock, let the seller have the deposit as an incentive to cancel the contract (believe me, it's cheaper than hiring a lawyer and probably equal to the dealer's commission).

Scrutinize all references to the exact model (there's a heck of an upgrade from base to LX or Limited), prices, and delivery dates. Make sure you specify a delivery date in the contract that protects the price.

Contract Clauses You Need

You can put things on a more equal footing by negotiating the inclusion of as many clauses as possible from the sample of additional contract clauses found on page

101. To do this, write in a "Remarks" section on your contract and then add, "See attached clauses, which form part of this agreement." Then attach a photocopy of the "Additional Contract Clauses" and persuade the sales agent to initial as many of the clauses as possible. Although some clauses may be rejected, the inclusion of just a couple of them can have important legal ramifications later if you want a full or partial refund.

ADDITIONAL CONTRACT CLAUSES

1. **Original contract:** This is the ONLY contract; i.e., it cannot be changed, retyped, or rewritten, without the specific agreement of both parties.
2. **Financing:** This agreement is subject to the purchaser obtaining financing at _____% or less within _____ days of the date below.
3. **"In-service" date and mileage:** To be based on the closing day, not the day the contract was executed, and will be submitted to the automaker for warranty and all other purposes. The dealership will have this date corrected by the automaker if it should become necessary.
4. **Delivery:** The vehicle is to be delivered by _____, failing which the contract is cancelled and the deposit will be refunded.
5. **Cancellation:**
    (a) The purchaser retains the right to cancel this agreement without penalty at any time before delivery of the vehicle by sending a notice in writing to the vendor.
    (b) Following delivery of the vehicle, the purchaser shall have two days to return the vehicle and cancel the agreement in writing, without penalty. After two days and before thirty-one days, the purchaser shall pay the dealer $25 a day as compensation for depreciation on the returned vehicle.
    (c) Cancellation of contract can be refused where the vehicle has been subjected to abuse, negligence or unauthorized modifications after delivery.
    (d) The purchaser is responsible for accident damage and traffic violations while in possession of the said vehicle.
6. **Protected price:** The vendor agrees not to alter the price of the new vehicle, the cost of preparation, or the cost of shipping.
7. **Trade-in:** The vendor agrees that the value attributed to the vehicle offered in trade shall not be reduced, unless it has been significantly modified or has suffered from unreasonable and accelerated deterioration since the signing of the agreement.
8. **Courtesy car:**
    (a) In the event the new vehicle is not delivered on the agreed-upon date, the vendor agrees to supply the purchaser with a courtesy car at no cost. If no courtesy vehicle is available, the vendor agrees to reimburse the purchaser the cost of renting a vehicle.
    (b) If the vehicle is off the road for more than two days for warranty repairs, the purchaser is entitled to a free courtesy vehicle for the duration of the repair period. If no courtesy vehicle is available, the vendor agrees to reimburse the purchaser the cost of renting a vehicle of equivalent or lesser value.
9. **Work orders:** The purchaser will receive duly completed copies of all work orders pertaining to the vehicle, including warranty repairs and the pre-delivery inspection (PDI).
10. **Dealer stickers:** The vendor will not affix any dealer advertising, in any form, on the vehicle.
11. **Fuel:** Vehicle will be delivered with a free full tank of gas.
12. **Excess mileage:** New vehicle will not be acceptable and the contract will be void if the odometer has more than 200 km at delivery/closing.
13. **Tires:** Original equipment Firestone or Bridgestone tires are not acceptable.

_____ _____ _____
  Date   Vendor's Signature   Buyer's Signature

"We Can't Do That"

Dealers and automakers facing bankruptcy can do almost anything to get your business. Don't take the dealer's word that "We're not allowed to do that" – heard most often in reference to reducing the PDI or transportation fee. Some dealers have been telling *Lemon-Aid* readers that they are "obligated" by the automaker to charge a set fee and could lose their franchise if they charge less. This is pure hogwash. No dealer has ever had their franchise licence revoked for cutting prices. Furthermore, the automakers clearly state that they don't set a bottom price, since doing so would violate Canada's *Competition Act* – that's why you always see them putting disclaimers in their ads saying the dealer can charge less.

The Pre-delivery Inspection

The best way to ensure that the PDI (written as "PDE" in some regions) will be completed is to write in the sales contract that you'll be given a copy of the completed PDI sheet when the vehicle is delivered to you. Then, with the PDI sheet in hand, verify some of the items that were to be checked. If any items appear to have been missed, refuse delivery of the vehicle. Once you get home, check the vehicle more thoroughly, and send a registered letter to the dealer if you discover any incomplete items from the PDI.

SELLING YOUR TRADE-IN

When to Sell

It doesn't take a genius to figure out that the longer one keeps a vehicle, the less it costs to own. If you're happy with your vehicle's styling and convenience features and it's safe and dependable, there's no reason to get rid of it. But when the cost of repairs becomes equal to or greater than the cost of payment for a new car, you need to consider trading it in. Shortly after your vehicle's fifth birthday (or whenever you start to think about trading it in), ask a mechanic to look at it to give you some idea of what repairs, replacement parts, or maintenance work it will need in the coming year. Find out if dealer service bulletins show that it will need extensive repairs in the near future (see Appendix II for how to order bulletins from ALLDATA). If it's going to require expensive repairs, you should trade the vehicle right away; if expensive work isn't predicted, you may want to keep it. Auto owners' associations provide a good yardstick. They figure that the annual cost of repairs and preventive maintenance for the average vehicle is about $800. If your vehicle is five years old and you haven't spent anywhere near $5,000 in maintenance, it would pay to invest in your old vehicle and continue using it while patiently searching for a new car. Document recent repairs and show warranty work as a selling tool to get a better price when you do sell and to help the buyer get a better price on a repair that had been fixed under warranty.

Consider whether your vehicle can still be serviced easily. If it's no longer on the market, the parts supply is likely to dry up and independent mechanics will be reluctant to repair it.

Don't trade for fuel economy alone. Most fuel-efficient vehicles, such as front-drives, offset the savings through higher repair costs. Also, the more fuel-efficient vehicles may not be as comfortable to drive because of their excessive engine noise, lightweight construction, stiff suspension, and torque steer.

Reassess your needs. Has your family grown to the point that you need a new vehicle? Are you driving less? Are you taking fewer long trips? Let your car or minivan show its age, and pocket the savings if its deteriorating condition doesn't pose a safety hazard and isn't too embarrassing. If you're in sales and are constantly on the road, it makes sense to trade every few years – in that case, the vehicle's appearance and reliability become a prime consideration, particularly since the increased depreciation costs are mostly tax deductible.

Getting the Most for Your Trade-In

Customers who are on guard against paying too much for a new vehicle often sell their trade-ins for too little. Before agreeing to any trade-in amount, read Part Four of this guide to compare the dealer price and what the vehicle is worth in a private sale.

Now that you've nailed down your trade-in's approximate value, here are some tips on selling it with a minimum of stress.

- Never sign a new vehicle sales contract unless your trade-in has been sold – you could end up with two vehicles.

- Negotiate the price from retail (dealer price) down to wholesale (private sales).

If you haven't sold your trade-in after two weekends, you might be trying to sell it at the wrong time of year or have it priced too high.

Make Money – Sell Privately

If you must sell your vehicle and want to make the most out of the deal, consider selling it yourself and putting the profits toward your next purchase. You'll likely come out hundreds of dollars ahead – buyers will pay more for your vehicle because they know cars sold by owners cost less. The most important thing to remember is that there's a large market for used vehicles in good condition in the $5,000-$7,000 range. Although most people prefer buying from individuals rather than from used-car lots, they may still be afraid that the vehicle is a lemon. By using the suggestions below, you should be able to sell your vehicle quite easily.

1. Know its value. Study dealers' newspaper ads and compare them with the prices listed in *Lemon-Aid*. Undercut the dealer's price by $300-$800, and be ready to bargain down another 10 percent for a serious buyer. Remember,

prices can fluctuate wildly depending on which models are trendy, so watch the want ads carefully.

2. Enlist the aid of the salesperson who's selling you your new car. Offer him or her a few hundred dollars to find you a buyer. The fact that one sale hinges on the other, along with the prospect of making two commissions, may work wonders.

3. Post notices on bulletin boards at your office or local supermarkets, and place a "For Sale" sign in the window of the vehicle itself. Place a newspaper ad only as a last resort.

4. Don't give your address right away to a potential buyer responding to your ad. Instead, ask for the telephone number where you may call that person back.

5. Be wary of selling to friends or family members. Anything short of perfection, and you'll be eating Christmas dinner alone.

6. Don't touch the odometer. If you do, you may get a few hundred dollars more – and a criminal record.

7. Paint the vehicle. Some specialty shops charge only $300 and give a guarantee that's transferable to subsequent owners.

8. Make minor repairs. This includes a minor tune-up and patching up the exhaust. Again, if any repair warranty is transferable, use it as a selling point.

9. Clean the vehicle. Go to a reconditioning firm, or spend the weekend scrubbing the interior and exterior. First impressions are important. Clean the chrome, polish the body, and peel off old bumper stickers. Remove butts from the ashtrays and clean out the glove compartment. Make sure all tools and spare parts have been taken out of the trunk. Don't remove the radio or speakers – the gaping holes will lower the vehicle's worth much more than the cost of the sound equipment. Replace missing or broken dash knobs and window cranks.

10. Change the tires. Recaps are good buys.

11. Let the buyer examine the vehicle. Insist that it be inspected at an independent garage, and then accompany the prospective buyer to the garage. This gives you protection if the buyer claims you misrepresented the vehicle.

12. Don't mislead the buyer. If the vehicle was in an accident or some financing is still to be paid, admit it. Any misleading statements may be used later against you in court. It's also advisable to have someone witness the actual transaction in case of a future dispute.

13. Keep important documents handy. Show prospective buyers the sales contract, repair orders, owner's manual, and all other documents that show how the vehicle has been maintained. Authenticate your claims about fuel consumption.

14. Write an effective ad, if you need to use one.

Selling to Dealers

Selling to a dealer means that you're likely to get 20 percent less than if you sold your vehicle privately, unless the dealer agrees to participate in an accommodation sale based on your buying a new vehicle from them. Most owners will gladly pay some penalty to the dealer, however, for the peace of mind that comes with knowing that their eventual buyer won't lay a claim against them. This assumes that the dealer hasn't been cheated by the owner. If the vehicle is stolen, isn't paid for, has had its odometer spun back (or forward to a lower setting), or is seriously defective, the buyer or dealer can sue the original owner for fraud. Sell to a dealer who sells the same make. He or she will give you more because it's easier to sell your trade-in to customers who are interested in only that make of vehicle.

Drawing Up the Contract

The province of Alberta has prepared a useful bill of sale applicable throughout Canada that can be accessed at *www.servicealberta.gov.ab.ca/pdf/mv/BillOfSaleReg3126.pdf*. Your bill of sale should identify the vehicle (including the serial number) and include its price, whether a warranty applies, and the nature of the examination made by the buyer.

The buyer may ask you to put in a lower price than what was actually paid in order to reduce the sales tax. If you agree to this, don't be surprised when a Revenue Canada agent comes to your door. Although the purchaser is ultimately the responsible party, you're an accomplice in defrauding the government. Furthermore, if you turn to the courts for redress, your own conduct may be put on trial.

SUMMARY

Now that we know how to get the cheapest, safest, and most reliable new car, lets take a look at the many used car buys that can save you up to $15,000 over a new car, and provide a decade's worth of cheap reliable transportation.

Part Two

OLD WHEELS: WHAT'S HOT, WHAT'S NOT

Old is the New Young

"The volume of 6–11-year-old vehicles is declining, while the group of vehicles older than 12 years is on the rise. This trend supports the increase in average age and creates a potential strategic shift in the aftermarket ... independent and chain repair shops should be paying close attention to their business plans and making concerted efforts to retain business among the do-it-for-me (DIFM) audience, while retailers have a unique and growing opportunity with potential consumers wrenching on their own vehicles."

R. L. Polk

(www.polk.com/company/news/polk_finds_average_age_of_light_vehicles_continues_to_rise)

Women ask the important questions and listen. Men get "gadget-giddy." Take your mother, wife, or sister along.

2015 Used Cars – A "Bumper" Crop

Canadians are buying new and used cars in record numbers. As used car loan rates stabilize, sales incentives multiply, and more vehicles end their five-year leases, shoppers are paying off their credit card debt and shopping for another car. Moreover, almost two-thirds of the cars sold in Canada are used, up from about 56 percent just over a decade ago.

Blame it on increased longevity – of the driver – and of the car (or more so, the truck). We discussed the phenomenon of senior drivers populating our highways in the previous chapter, but we also should mention that many older drivers are perfectly happy owning "senior" cars, as well. More than six million of the 31.7 million cars on the road (2013) are 11.4 years old or older and R. L. Polk Data says, half of all the cars manufactured in the last 25 years are still on the road today.

Trucks last almost three times longer than cars. By brand segment, over 20 percent of all the Chevrolet pickups sold 25 years ago are still chugging along our highways and Chrysler and Ford pickups aren't far behind.

Buy Used for Half Price – Sell for 20% More

Buying a used vehicle is easier than buying new one and with a little bit of homework and patience you can find reliable wheels for less than half what the car originally cost. Plus, there is less of a showroom shakedown – confusing figures, payment plans, and costly "extras" – awaiting you. You get a car that has already been scratched, dented, and corroded, but this saves you from that sickening feeling when that new car starts letting you down, or someone dents your car door while parked at the supermarket. The transformation from new to used occurs as soon as the sales title passes from dealer to a second owner, thus theoretically making every car sold a used vehicle that immediately loses about 20 percent of its original value. This instant morphing from new to used creates a huge pool of inexpensive used vehicles sold by dealers and private sellers who compete aggressively for every dollar and expect you to haggle.

Price haggling is encouraged because depreciation gives buyers a large margin to bring prices down. In fact, most private owners discover they can get about 20 percent more by selling their trade-in privately than what most dealers would offer. Dealers also make more money selling used vehicles than they make selling new cars and trucks, and they aren't burdened by such things as the manufacturer's suggested retail price, freight charges, options loading, high floor plan interest rates, reduced commissions, and warranty charge-backs. The savings generated by these simpler transactions often go straight into the dealer's and buyer's pockets.

Used Is the Smart Choice

It simply costs too much to own a new car or SUV. In fact, many of my readers tell me that the cost of their new car exceeded the downpayment on their first mortgage. No wonder that of the 4.4 million automobiles that were sold in Canada in 2010, most were second-hand (2.9 million).

Read on for more reasons why Canadians increasingly prefer to buy used vehicles rather than new ones.

Less Initial Cash Outlay, Slower Vehicle Depreciation, "Secret" Warranty Repair Refunds, and Better and Cheaper Parts Availability

New-vehicle prices average around $31,000 and insurance can cost almost $2,200 a year for young drivers. The Canadian Automobile Association (CAA) calculates that once you add financing costs, maintenance, taxes, and a host of other expenses over an average of 18,000 kilometers, the yearly outlay for a Honda Civix LX would be about $9,100 (or 51 cents per km). A Camry LE would cost over $1,400 more at $10,500 (58 cents per km) and the Chevrolet Equinox LT would require $11,900 (66 cents per km).

Inasmuch as these figures were estimated in 2014, the subsequent 50-percent cut in fuel costs (pegged to a $50 U.S. price for a barrel of oil) represents an annual savings of almost $2,000.

The above annual new-car disbursements can be reduced by almost 50 percent if a vehicle is purchased used, figuring in a substantially lower purchase price, taxes, financing charges, insurance premiums, and no freight or admininstrative fees. Also, moderating fuel prices could cut the CAA forecasted expenses by another 5 percent (*www.caa.ca/wp-content/uploads/2012/06/CAA_Driving_Cost_English_2013_web.pdf*).

For a comprehensive comparative analysis of all the costs involved in owning a vehicle over one- to 10-year periods, access Alberta's consumer information website at *www.agric.gov.ab.ca/app24/costcalculators/vehicle/getvechimpls.jsp*.

Depreciation works for you

If someone were to ask you to invest in stocks or bonds guaranteed to be worth less than half their initial purchase value after three to four years, you'd probably head for the door. But this is exactly the trap you're falling into when you buy a new vehicle that will likely lose up to 60 percent of its value after three years of use.

When you buy used, the situation is altogether different. That same vehicle can be purchased three years later, in good condition, and with much of the manufacturer's warranty remaining for less than half its original cost.

Secret warranty refunds

Almost all automakers use secret "goodwill" warranties to cover factory-related defects long after a vehicle's original warranty has expired. This creates a huge fleet of used vehicles that are eligible for free repairs.

We're not talking about merely a few months' extension on small items. In fact, some free repairs – like those related to Audi, Nissan, and VW transmissions – are authorized up to ten years under a variety of "goodwill" programs (see Introduction). Still, most secret warranty extensions hover around the five- to seven-year mark and seldom cover vehicles exceeding 160,000 km (almost 100,000 mi). Yet there are exceptions, like the secret catalytic converter warranty that will pay for the converter's replacement up to ten years, or 193,000 km (120,000 mi), on many Chevrolet models.

Incidentally, automakers and dealers claim that there are no "secret" warranties, since they are all published in service bulletins. Although this is technically correct, have you ever tried to get a copy of a service bulletin? Or, if you did manage to get a copy, did the dealer or automaker say the benefits are applicable only in the States? Pure weasel speak!

Secret warranty roundup

As a public service – and particularly because I enjoy getting the carmakers all riled up and giving auto owners more tools to get free repairs – here is a summary of the more important 2015-16 secret warranties currently in effect that may save you thousands of dollars.

ALL YEARS, ALL MODELS

Problem: Premature wearout of brake pads, calipers, and rotors. Produces excessive vibration, noise, and pulling to one side when braking. **Warranty coverage:** *Calipers and pads:* "Goodwill" settlements confirm that brake calipers and pads that fail to last 2 years/40,000 km will be replaced for half the repair cost; components not lasting 1 year/20,000 km will be replaced for free. *Rotors:* If they last less than

3 years/60,000 km, they will be replaced at half price; replacement is free up to 2 years/40,000 km.

Problem: Faulty automatic transmissions that self-destruct, shift erratically, gear down to "limp mode," are slow to shift in or out of Reverse, or are noisy. Warranty coverage: If you have the assistance of your dealer's service manager, or some internal service bulletin that confirms the automatic transmission may be defective, expect an offer of 50-75 percent (about $2,500) if you threaten to sue in small claims court. Acura, Honda, Hyundai, Lexus, and Toyota coverage varies between seven and eight years.

ACURA

2007-09 MDX; 2009-10 RL; and 2009-11 TL

Problem: Fix for a transmission judder. Warranty coverage: 8 years/169,000 km (105,000 mi) radiator assembly and automatic transmission warranty extension, which covers "damage, repairs, replacement, and related towing resulting from this issue." Original and subsequent owner coverage and retroactive reimbursement.

BMW

2004-06 models

Problem: Premature failure of the seat airbag occupant detection mat. Warranty coverage: BMW has extended the warranty to 10 years/unlimited mileage.

2007-10 models equipped with a high-pressure fuel pump

Problem: Premature failure. Warranty coverage: BMW has extended the emissions warranty to 10 years/193,000 km (120,000 mi.), according to bulletin #SI B13 03 09, announced in BMW's November 2010 dealer letter.

CHRYSLER

2007-12 Jeeps, Durangos, minivans, and trucks

Problem: Stalling, no starts, and various electrical malfunctions. A defective Totally Integrated Power Module (TIPM) will cause the car to play out a scene from *The Exorcist*: no starts, self-starts, stallouts, and headlights suddenly shutting off. Parked vehicles may produce other bizarre happenings, like the anti-theft alarm

going off for no apparent reason, the radio and blower motor coming on or electric windows that roll down by themselves. All this can happen while the vehicle is on the road or parked, without a key in the ignition or a key fob nearby. Warranty coverage: Dealers may charge up to $1,300 for out-of-warranty

TIPM repairs. However, owners who complain to Chrysler can get "goodwill" compensation on a case-by-case basis. This is a known "hidden" defect that affects a vehicle's "merchantability" as expressed in provincial consumer protection laws and business practices legislation.

Check out what some drivers reported in a California class-action lawsuit filed May 5, 2014, in California: *www.autosafety.org/sites/default/files/imce_staff_uploads/ Chrysler%20TIPM%20-%20Gibbs%202nd%20Amended%20Complaint%205-14.pdf*:

2008 Dodge Grand Caravan: While stopped at a red light, the van suddenly entered into an electrical chaos. The horn started blaring, the wipers started going full blast, and wiper fluid starting spraying. This kind of electrical problem has happened before but this time was the worst. The vehicle continued to drive while everything electrical flickered and continued to malfunction. Finally had to stop and remove fuses for horn and wiper fluid in order to get the malfunctions to stop. Van transmission also stopped shifting during this episode. Even after vehicle was stopped, there were multiple electrical popping noises throughout the engine as if it was trying to power up things that were no longer operational. I took vehicle into dealership and they identified problem as a failure of the TIPM. Looking online there are multiple complaints of similar problems and failures. The TIPM is actually backordered because of the demand.

. . .

2011 Dodge Durango: It began when the car would crank and not start several times before actually starting. I took it in (figuring at some point it would just not start at all and leave me stranded) and they said they couldn't duplicate it and sent me home. It started doing it again, so I took it back in and they reflashed something or other and sent me on my way. The reflash did not fix the problem, but I did not take it back in, figuring I would leave with same result. Finally, the car died on me while I was driving it, with my small children in the car. No power brakes, no power steering. I was able to pull over to the side of the road safely. Thankfully I was not going terribly fast and there were no other cars around. I took it back in again, and they told me it needed a new TIPM.

JEEP

2007 Dodge Calibers and Jeep Compasses and Patriots

Problem: Jeeps have serious corrosion issues that are addressed by a little-known extended warranty. We all know that the first Canadian Fiats were rustbuckets, but ironically, it now seems that Jeeps and Chrysler Calibers have contracted the same contagion. **Warranty coverage:** The premature corrosion of the front and rear suspension cross-members is now covered for 10 years with no mileage limitation. Cite TSB #23-012-14 issued on May 19, 2014 to get the free repairs. The first sign of this problem will be a vibration in the steering wheel.

FORD

2009-2011 Escape, Mariner; 2010-2011 Fusion and Milan vehicles equipped with a 2.5L or 3.0L engine built on or before 03/04/2011

Problem: A leaking/stuck canister purge valve. This condition may cause various intermittent driveability symptoms. Warranty coverage: 8 years under the Emissions Warranty.

Ford/Lincoln; 2009-11 Edge, Flex; 2011 Explorer; 2010–11 MXS; 2009-2011 MKX; 2010-11 MKT

Problem: Sluggish transmission. Warranty coverage: Change the valve body calibration under the 8-year Emissions Warranty.

2011-14 models equipped with the MyFord Touch touch screen entertainment and navigation system

Problem: Poor cell phone and Bluetooth compatibility; doesn't recognize voice commands; slow to respond; and not user-friendly. Warranty coverage: Ford is extending the warranty on the system to five years with unlimited miles, up from three years and 58,000 km (36,000 mi). Lincolns will be covered for six years with unlimited miles, up from four years and 80,000 km (50,000 mi).

GENERAL MOTORS

2000-03 GM S10 and Sonoma models

Problem: Corroded, fractured tailgate cables. Warranty coverage: GM warranty extension to 12 years/no mileage limitation.

2005-06 G6, Malibu, and Malibu Maxx; 2008 G6, Malibu, Malibu Maxx, and Aura

Problem: Loss of power-steering assist. Warranty coverage: Under Special Coverage Adjustment #10183, dated July 20, 2010, GM will replace the failed components free of charge up to 10 years/160,000 km (100,000 mi.).

2006-07 Cobalt, G4/G5, and Ion

Problem: A faulty fuel pump module may produce a fuel odour or spotting on the ground. Warranty coverage: GM has extended the fuel pump warranty to 10 years/ 193,000 km (120,000 mi.), says TSB #09275A, issued March 3, 2010.

2006-07 Malibu and G6

Problem: Catalytic Converter failure. Warranty coverage: Under Special Coverage Adjustment #10134, dated November 17, 2010, GM will replace the converter free of charge up to 10 years/193,000 km (120,000 mi.).

2006-07 Buick Terraza; 2010 Buick Lucerne; 2006-07 Chevrolet Monte Carlo; 2006-08 Chevrolet Uplander; 2006-10 Chevrolet Impala; 2008-09 Chevrolet Malibu; 2006-08 Pontiac Montana SV6; 2006-09 Pontiac G6; 2006-08 Saturn Relay; 2007-09 Saturn AURA; all equipped with a 3.5L or 3.9L Engine

Problem: Some customers may comment on a coolant leak. The comments may range from spots on the driveway to having to add more coolant. If the coolant leak is coming from the front (accessory drive end) of the engine, the coolant crossover gaskets should be replaced. If the leak is found to be coming from a cylinder head gasket, the gasket must be replaced. Warranty coverage: GM's 8-year Emissions Warranty.

2006-09 Cadillac STS-V, XLR, XLR-V; 2007-08 Cadillac Escalade, Escalade ESV, Escalade EXT, XLR; 2006-09 Chevrolet Corvette; 2007-08 Chevrolet Silverado; 2008 Chevrolet Suburban; 2007-08 GMC Sierra, Sierra Denali, Yukon Denali, Yukon XL Denali; 2008 GMC Yukon XL; 2008-09 HUMMER H2; and 2008-09 Pontiac G8

Problem: Slips in Reverse or Third, Delayed Reverse or Drive Engagement, DTC P0776, P2715, P2723, Harsh 2-3 Shifts (Inspect 1-2-3-4/3-5-R housing and pump seal rings). Warranty coverage: GM's base warranty. Eligible for "goodwill" consideration since the housing and pump seal rings weren't reasonably durable.

2006-11 models

Problem: Engine Oil Consumption on Aluminum Block/Iron Block Engines with Active Fuel Management. Install AFM Oil Deflector and Clean Carbon from Cylinder and/or Install Updated Valve Cover. Warranty coverage: The 8-year Emissions Warranty.

2007-12 Chevrolet Silverado and GMC Sierra

Problem: Excessive rear interior wind noise, which GM attributes to "a void in the body filler within the C-pillar" or "a result of the design of the body rear panel acoustic insulator that is mounted behind the rear seat. The insulator could be one of several early designs which demonstrated a lesser success of minimizing wind noise (Bulletin No.: 10-08-58-001F). Warranty coverage: GM will add padding in the cab area on a case-by-case basis at no charge under a "goodwill" policy. *GM P/N 12378195 is not available in Canada. However several equivalents such as Evercoat (Q-Pads) P/N 100116 and Dominion Sure Seal (Sound Deadener Pads) BSDE Part 110900 are available through NAPA Auto Parts retailers. Information for finding your local retail location can be obtained online at *www.napacanada.com*. Dominion Sure Seal (sound deadener pads) BSDE Part 110900 can be obtained by contacting Dominion Sure Seal at 1-800-265-0790.

HONDA

2006-09 Civic

Problem: The sun visor may come apart or split with use. Warranty coverage: Honda has extended the warranty to 10 years/161,000 km (100,000 mi).

2006-09 Civic

Problem: Engine overheats or leaks coolant because the engine block is cracking at the coolant passages. Warranty coverage: Honda will install a new engine block assembly free of charge under a "goodwill policy," as stated in its TSB #10-048, issued August 17, 2010.

2007-09 Civics

Problem: An engine oil leak from the front of the timing chain case cover on the oil pump assembly. Warranty coverage: Post-warranty free repairs may be eligible for goodwill consideration by the District Parts and Service Manager or your Zone Office.

2007-11 CR-Vs

Problem: AC failure. Warranty coverage: A warranty extension pays for a replacement up to seven years/100,000 miles (miles because these secret warranties are approved in the States only).

2008-09 Accord

Problem: The leather seat covers may crack or paint rub off, delaminate, or peel. Honda attributes the problem to "an insufficient buffing process and material problem." Warranty coverage: Honda will replace the seat-back or seat cushion cover.

LEXUS

2007-13 Lexus ES; 2006-12 Lexus IS; and 2013 Lexus GS models

Problem: Emergency trunk release can break, trapping an occupant inside. Warranty coverage: Trunk release will be replaced; no time or ownership limitation.

MAZDA

2007-11 CX7 and CX-9

Problem: These Mazdas may leak oil from the rear differential seal. In TSB 0300411, Mazda says the differential breather was placed too low and could easily become clogged by snow or water. Warranty coverage: A new differential with a raised breather covered by the breather boot will be installed for free on a case-by-case basis.

MERCEDES

Model Year 2005-06 ML (164), SLK (171), C (203), CLK (209), E (211), CLS (219), R (251), and Model Year 2005-08 G (463)

Problem: Faulty airbag wiring may cause the airbag warning light to remain lit. **Warranty coverage:** Mercedes has extended the warranty to 10 years/161,000 km (100,000 mi).

NISSAN

2005-08 models

Problem: Inaccurate fuel sending unit. **Warranty coverage:** Nissan extended the warranty to 7 years/116,000 km (72,000 mi).

2005-10 Frontier, Pathfinder, and Xterra models

Problem: Coolant may leak into the five-speed transmission. **Warranty coverage:** 8 years/129,000 km (80,000 mi) torque converter coverage for the original owner and any subsequent owners. Owners who already had the radiator or transmission repaired would be eligible for reimbursement.

2007-12 Altimas and Sentras and 2008-12 Rogues with 4-cylinder engines

Problem: A leak from the oil cooler may be a problem on some Nissans. In TSB NTB11015A, Nissan says the leak is from the upper end of the oil cooler. **Warranty coverage:** Removing the cooler and replacing the gaskets are covered under an undefined extended warranty.

TOYOTA

1995-2000 Tacoma and Tundra

Toyota's extended warranty provides a valuable 15-year durability benchmark of what manufacturers should do with rust-cankered vehicles. This example should be used in negotiations with any automaker where body defects are involved.

TOYOTA CUSTOMER SERVICES

Volume: __XV__
Number: __TC08-004__
Date: __03/07/2008__
X Action
X Retain
___ Information

TO: ALL REGION/PRIVATE DISTRIBUTOR GENERAL MANAGERS/ VICE PRESIDENTS

FROM: DAVID CAMDEN
VICE PRESIDENT, DEALER OPERATIONS

DAVE ZELLERS
VICE PRESIDENT, PRODUCT QUALITY AND SERVICE SUPPORT

BOB WALTZ
VICE PRESIDENT, CUSTOMER SATISFACTION, TOYOTA DIVISION

SUBJECT: CUSTOMER SUPPORT PROGRAM – WARRANTY COVERAGE EXTENSION FOR FRAME RUST CORROSION PERFORATION ON CERTAIN 1995 - 2000 MY TACOMA

Problem: Rust-damaged structural frames. The excessive rusting is caused by inadequate anti-corrosion undercoating applied at the factory. **Warranty coverage:** According to the April 14, 2008, edition of *Automotive News*, Toyota will repair or buy back the affected pickups. Dealers will inspect all affected Tacomas and Tundras free of charge and apply an extended 15-year frame-rust warranty. Trucks with minor frame pitting will be repaired for free; trucks with more serious damage will be bought back at 150 percent of the "excellent" value listed in the U.S.-published *Kelley Blue Book* guide, regardless of the truck's condition.

2006-08 RAV4, 2007-08 Solara, 200-709 Camry, 2007-2011 Camry Hybrid, 2009 Corolla, and 2009 Matrix

Problem: The 2.4L 4-cylinder engine may be an "oil-burner." In TSBs #SB002411 and #SB009411, the company said the problem was traced to the piston assembly. **Warranty coverage:** Toyota will replace the pistons and rings on a "goodwill," case-by-case basis.

VOLKSWAGEN

2009-11 Jettas and 2010-11 Golfs, all with the 2.0L TDI engine

Problem: The company says it may have a remedy for diesels that won't start in cold weather. In TSB #2111-06 Volkswagen confirms that some vehicles might not start if left in temperatures below freezing. Moisture from the air intake may condense in the intercooler. **Warranty coverage:** VW recommends adding a cold weather intercooler kit that will be provided free of charge on a case-by-case basis.

Parts

Used parts can have a surprisingly long lifespan. Generally, a new gasoline-powered car or minivan can be expected to run with few problems for at least 200,000-300,000 km (125,000-200,000 mi) in its lifetime and a diesel-powered vehicle can easily double those figures. Some repairs will crop up at regular intervals along with preventive maintenance, and your yearly running costs should average about $1,000. Buttressing the argument that vehicles get cheaper to operate the longer you keep them, the U.S. Department of Transportation points out that the average vehicle requires one or more major repairs after every five years of use. Once these repairs are done, however, the vehicle can then be run relatively trouble-free for another five years or more, as long as the environment isn't too hostile. In fact, residents in outlying regions keep their vehicles the longest – an average of 11 years, or longer in some provinces.

Time is on your side in other ways, too. Three years after a model's launch, the replacement parts market usually catches up to consumer demand, although low-volume European makes may take longer.

Parts are unquestionably easier to come by after this three-year point through bargaining with local garages, carefully searching of auto wreckers' yards, or looking on the Internet. And a reconditioned or used part usually costs one-third to half the price of a new part. There's generally no difference in the quality of reconditioned mechanical components, and they're often guaranteed for as long as, or longer than, new ones. In fact, some savvy shoppers use the ratings in Part Four of this guide to see which parts have a short life and then buy those parts from retailers who give lifetime warranties on their brakes, exhaust systems, tires, batteries, and so on.

Buying from discount outlets or independent garages, or ordering through the Internet, can save you big bucks (30-35 percent) on the cost of new parts and another 15 percent on labour when compared with dealer charges. Mass merchandisers like Costco are another good source of savings; they cut prices and add free services and lifetime warranties on some parts.

Body parts are a different story. Although car company repair parts can cost 50 percent more than certified generic aftermarket parts, buyers would be wise to buy only original equipment manufacturer (OEM) parts supplied by automakers in order to get body panels that fit well, protect better in collisions, and have maximum rust resistance. Insurance appraisers often substitute cheaper, lower-quality aftermarket body parts in collision repairs, however, policyholders who insist upon original equipment (OEM) parts usually get them with little or no hassle.

With some European models, you can count on a lot of aggravation and expense caused by the unacceptably slow distribution of parts and by the high markup. Because these companies have a quasi-monopoly on replacement parts, there are few independent suppliers you can turn to for help. And junkyards, the last-chance repository for inexpensive car parts, are unlikely to carry foreign parts for vehicles that are manufactured in small numbers.

It's a myth that Japanese and South Korean car parts are hard to find, or aren't very durable. Although this was true in the early 70s when Asian automakers just arrived in North America, there is now an abundance of foreign-made parts available. This is due in large part to the popularity of Japanese and Korean vehicles, an influx of independent suppliers, platform sharing where the same parts are used among many different models, and the large reservoir of used foreign parts stocked by junkyards.

Parts imported from China are a different story. The aftermarket parts arena has been flooded by cheap Chinese components that don't have the same durability as replacement parts made by auto manufacturers or well-known parts makers. Exhaust systems, brakes, tires, tire valve stems, and a host of other maintenance items are commonly brought in from China. Ironically, these parts of dubious value are snapped up by carmakers who are only interested in getting more for less and end up with poor-quality, failure-prone parts that cost far more to replace when they are recalled.

This is one of the reasons that cars made in China have done so poorly in crash tests. An American auto engineer asked his Chinese colleagues during one of these crashworthiness trials, "Where is the crash space where crash fores are deflected away from the occupants?" Answer: "There is no crash space."

This Chinese-built car obviously tested out as uncrashworthy.

Insurance Costs Less

The price you pay for insurance can vary significantly, not only between insurance companies but also within the same company over time. But one thing does remain constant – the insurance for used vehicles is a lot cheaper than new-car coverage, and through careful comparison shopping, insurance premium payouts can be substantially reduced.

Beware of "captive" brokers

Although the cost of insurance premiums for used cars is often one-third to half the cost of the premiums you would pay for a new vehicle, using the Internet to find the lowest auto insurance quote and accepting a large deductible are critical to keeping premiums low.

Use InsuranceHotline.com

InsuranceHotline.com is the largest online quoting service for car insurance in Canada. The agency will run applicants' profiles through its extensive database of insurance companies to find the insurer with the lowest rate.

Here are some *InsuranceHotline.com* findings.

- A family car under $35,000 can cost more to insure than one over $35,000.
- SUVs under $35,000 don't always cost more to insure than a family car or a small luxury model.
- Luxury cars mean luxury premiums, costing on average about $500 more annually to insure than family cars, SUVs, muscle cars, or hybrids.
- Hybrids' fuel savings can be wiped out by higher-cost insurance premiums that rival what you would pay to insure a muscle car.
- It does pay to shop around – sometimes, more than $900:

Comparing Insurance Company Rates

2013 Ford Focus SE (4 door) in Peace River, Alberta	
Intact Insurance Company (West)	$1902
SGI Canada	$2653
Peace Hills	$2705
Economical Mutual	$2879

In Ontario, the more expensive cities for auto insurance can be found in the Greater Toronto Area:

GTA Insurance Rates vs. Ontario Average

Rank	City	Avg. Annual Insurance Cost	Difference from ON Avg.
#1	Brampton	$2,393	+ 44%
#2	Woodbridge	$2,342	+ 41%
#3	Vaughan	$2,342	+ 41%
#4	Toronto	$2,017	+ 27%
#5	Mississauga	$1,998	+ 26%
#6	Hamilton	$1,987	+ 26%
#7	Thornhill	$1,884	+ 20%
#8	Markham	$1,829	+ 17%
#9	Richmond Hill	$1,755	+ 13%
#10	Ajax	$1,718	+ 11%

Ontario cities with the cheapest car insurance policies were: Belleville, Kingston, Cobourg, and Napanee. (The annual auto insurance premium average for Ontario of $1,538, was calculated by *Insurancehotline.com* based on a single, 35-year-old driver with a clean driving record).

ARC Insurance (*arcinsurance.ca/blog/average-car-insurance-rates-across-canadian-provinces/*) compared the cost of car insurance throughout Canada and found the following rates among the provinces:

10.	Quebec	$642	5.	Alberta	$1,004
9.	Prince Edward Island	$695	4.	Manitoba	$1,027
8.	New Brunswick	$728	3.	Saskatchewan	$1,049
7.	Nova Scotia	$735	2.	British Columbia	$1,112
6.	Newfoundland & Labrador	$749	1.	Ontario	$1,281

Of couse the type of vehicle that's insured affects the cost of insurance as well, sometimes in surprising ways. *Insurancehotline.com* compared insurance premium quotes on 2015 cars, SUVs, trucks, and minivans in six Ontario cities – Ajax, Cambridge, London, Ottawa, Peterborough, and Toronto, and ranked them based on which ones cost less to insure than the rest:

1. Chevrolet Corvette Stingray
2. Volkswagen Golf
3. Porsche Boxster
4. Tesla Model S*
5. Mazda6
6. Honda Accord
7. Mazda3
8. Volkswagen GTI
9. Cadillac CTS
10. Ford Mustang GT
11. BMW M235i
12. Porsche Cayman

Incredible that a Corvette would cost less to insure than a Mazda3, but that's the figure hotline agents came up with based on their fictional 40-year-old driver with a clean driving and insurance history. From the number one position to the twelvth, the difference in quoted premiums was $408.

There were similar surprises with insurance costs for trucks, SUVs, and minivans.

Trucks

1. Nissan Frontier
2. Honda Ridgeline
3. Nissan Titan
4. Toyota Tacoma
5. GMC Canyon
6. Dodge Ram
7. GMC Sierra
8. Chevrolet Silverado
9. Ford F-Series
10. Toyota Tundra

SUVs

1. Hyundai Santa Fe Sport
2. Dodge Journey
3. Jeep Wrangler
4. Ford Escape
5. Mazda CX-5
6. Jeep Cherokee
7. Nissan Rogue
8. Chevrolet Equinox
9. Honda CR-V
10. Toyota RAV4

Minivans

1. Kia Sedona
2. Chevrolet Orlando
3. Kia Rondo
4. Dodge Grand Caravan
5. Chrysler Town & Country
6. Honda Odyssey
7. Toyota Sienna
8. Mazda Mazda5

From the number one position to the tenth, the difference in quoted truck premiums was $165; SUV premium prices varied by $342; and the difference among minivans was $300.

Insured collision repairs

The Automobile Repair Regulatory Council says the owner of a motor vehicle damaged in an accident has the right to choose the shop that will do the repairs. Do not waste your time or that of several shops getting several estimates. Select a repair facility you feel comfortable with, then notify your agent or insurance company, or ask the shop to call on your behalf. Your insurance adjuster may require that the damage to the vehicle be inspected. This can be done at an insurance drive-in claim centre or at the shop you have chosen.

Here are some things to inspect yourself, before driving away with your repaired car.

- Check the appearance of the repaired area close up and at a distance.
- Examine the paint for colour match, texture, and overspray.
- Take a test drive to check mechanical repairs.
- Check that the vehicle is clean.

If you are not satisfied, mention your concerns immediately and follow up with a written claim (copy your insurer) and a time period for the work to be completed.

Notify your insurance company

Before you sign any work orders, notify your insurance company or agent, and tell them where the damaged vehicle can be inspected. Most collision and repair centres guarantee their work to some degree, which may not include the paint job. Ask to see a copy of the shop's guarantee and have any information you do not understand clarified. As for the paint warranty, try to get at least a one-year guarantee.

Choosing a qualified repair shop

Look for signs that indicate repair technician certification and training. Membership in professional trade associations indicates that the shop is keeping up with the latest repair procedures. Also, affiliation with automobile associations like the CAA, Alberta Motor Association (AMA), British Columbia Automobile Association (BCAA) or Automobile Protection Association (APA) is a plus, because you can use the association to exert pressure when the repair takes too long, or the work isn't done properly. In Part Three you will find jurisprudence where an Alberta auto association was found liable for the negligence of one of its member garages (see Cases to Consider, Repairs: Faulty Diagnosis).

Defects Can't Hide

You can easily avoid any nasty surprises by having your chosen used vehicle checked out by an independent mechanic (for $85-$100) before you purchase. This examination protects you against any of the vehicle's hidden defects; bolsters your claim against the seller in small claims court should you wind up with a lemon; makes the inspecting garage partially responsible for damages; and gives you a powerful negotiating tool, where the cost of any estimated repairs can be used to bargain down the purchase price.

It's easier to get permission to have the vehicle inspected if you promise to give the seller a copy of the inspection report should you decide not to buy it. If you still can't get permission to have the vehicle inspected elsewhere, walk away from the deal, no matter how tempting the selling price. The seller is obviously trying to put one over on you. Ignore the standard excuses that the vehicle isn't insured, that the registration plates have expired, or that the vehicle has a dead battery.

No Surprises

Smart customers shopping for a reliable used car can easily run an Internet history check on a vehicle and its previous owners through CarProof at *www.carproof. com/order*. A comprehensive search costs $51.45, or $71.45 if you want Insurance Corporation of British Columbia (ICBC) vehicle claims history info, as well. Try to get answers to the following questions from the seller or dealer before signing a contract: What did the vehicle first sell for, and what is its present insured value? Who serviced it? Has it had accident repairs? Are parts easily available? How much of the original warranty or repair warranties are left? Does the vehicle have a history of costly performance-related defects? What free repairs are available through "goodwill" warranty extensions? (See "Secret Warranties/Internal Bulletins" in Part Four.)

Quick and Cheap Justice

Lawyers win, regardless of whether you win or lose. And you're likely to lose more than you'll ever get back using the traditional court system in a used-car dispute.

But if you're just a bit creative, you'll discover there are many federal and provincial consumer-protection laws that go far beyond whatever protection may be offered by the standard new-vehicle warranty. While Nova Scotia has introduced a "lemon law," Manitoba is the only province with regulations in effect. Furthermore, buyers of used vehicles don't usually have to conform to any arbitrary rules or service guidelines to get this protection.

Let's say you do get stuck with a vehicle that's unreliable, has undisclosed accident damage, or doesn't perform as promised. Fortunately, small claims courts have a jurisdiction limit of $10,000-$30,000 – more than enough to cover the cost of repairs, or compensate you if the vehicle is taken back. That way, any dispute between buyer and seller can be settled within a few months, and without lawyers or excessive court costs. Furthermore, you're not likely to face a battery of lawyers standing in for the automaker and dealer in front of a stern-faced judge. You may not even have to face a judge at all, since many cases are settled through court-imposed mediators at a pretrial meeting that's usually scheduled a month or two after filing.

Car dealers get their vehicles from fleets, lessees, wholesalers, trade-ins, and private sales. Some of the less reputable dealers will buy at auction vehicles that other dealers unloaded because they weren't good enough to sell to their own customers. Other dealers will set up "curb-sider" scams where they sell used vehicles from private homes, using their employees as shills.

Presently dealers have an abundance of "young" three-year-old off-lease vehicles at unusually low prices because the buy-back prices at lease end were set low as the recession loomed. On the other hand, dealers now selling import brands are chronically short of product because owners keep these vehicles three to four years longer and use the buy-back option for themselves. The majority of private sales are comprised of vehicles six years or older, while independent used-car dealers get most of their profit from selling anything that can be driven away.

Asian Prices

Although used models may cost more this year, they won't cost that much more. We are heading into a buyer's new car market that will free up more used cars as shoppers exchange their trade-ins for new cars. Japanese new car prices will only be about 3 percent higher this year due to increased Detroit and South Korean competition. Detroit auto manufacturers, awash in profits from record sales, are stoking the incentive fires with rebate and other sales incentives that include free maintenance programs and 96-month financing.

Buying strategies

As new cars remain affordable, used cars, like the Honda Civic – Canada's most popular small car – become even more attractive. Civics are more in demand than ever now that the redesigned 2012 has been trashed by both independent consumer rating groups and a coterie of car columnists. Toyota is back on top, too, after being mauled by incessant safety recalls. Meanwhile, South Korean auto-makers like Hyundai and Kia have been riding a surge of record sales over the past few years thanks to *Consumer Reports* recommending most of Hyundai's cars and SUVs and a few (Omigod!) Kias.

Used Hondas are least likely to have servicing problems since over 90 percent of Honda's Canadian sales came from domestically manufactured cars like the Civic, Acura, and Ridgeline pickup. Mazda Canada is also well situated to service its products. Its two best-selling models in Canada, the Mazda3 and Mazda5, have been on the market long enough to build up a large supply of replacement parts and used models aren't hard to find at reasonable prices. Subarus (especially, the Forester) on the other hand, are over-priced due to a combination of their standard AWD, strong reliability ratings, and exceptional road performance. Since Suzuki left the North American market several years ago, used prices have tumbled. Inasmuch as Suzukis have always been reliable buys, smart consumers may wish to take advantage of the cars' depressed prices and uncomplicated servicing by independent garages. Parts availability and replacement costs are no problem, either.

Luxury Lemons

Buying used won't turn a luxury lemon into a cherry, but it will ensure that you lose far less money through depreciation and costly repairs. If you have been a steady reader of *Lemon-Aid* for the past several decades, you've been made wary of Mercedes' poor quality for over two decades and probably saved money buying a Lincoln Town Car or Toyota Avalon instead. Furthermore, BMW owners have proven to be some of the most satisfied with their cars' overall dependability when compared with most other European makes, especially, Audi, Jaguar, Porsche, Saab, and Volkswagen.

Lincoln's front-drive Continental (a failure-prone Taurus in disguise) and Mercedes' unreliable luxury cars and SUVs are proof positive that there's absolutely no correlation between safe, dependable transportation and the amount of money a vehicle costs, especially with most front-drive Lincoln and Cadillac luxury cars. Rear-drive Lincolns and Cadillacs, however, have always performed well after many years of use.

Chrysler "luxury" means beautiful styling and lousy quality control. Its luxury rear-drives, like the 300 and Magnum that once sold at a 10 percent premium, are now piling up on dealers' lots due to their reputation as gas-guzzlers with serious automatic transmission, fuel, and suspension system problems, as well as body deficiencies. It's hard to believe, but a 2009 Chrysler 300 Touring that originally sold for $32,095 is now worth barely $7,000. Depreciation also takes a pretty big bite out of Asian luxury car values, with a 2008 Lexus IS 250 that once cost $31,900 now selling for $13,500.

FIVE DECADES OF HITS AND MISSES

Hits

Acura – CL Series, Integra, and Legend; Audi – A3, A4, A6, R8, S4, S6, TT, TTs, TTRS; BMW – 135i, 3 Series, and 5 Series; Chrysler – Colt, 2000, Stealth, and Tradesman vans (invest in an extended warranty for the automatic transmission); Ford – Crown Victoria, Econoline vans, Freestyle/Taurus X, Grand Marquis, Mustang V6, and Ranger; GM – Acadia, Cruze, 2014 Impala, Enclave, Equinox, Express, Firebird, Rainier, Savana, Tahoe, Terrain, Traverse Vandura, and Yukon; Honda – Accord, Civic, CR-V, Element, Fit, Odyssey, Prelude, Pilot, and Ridgeline; Hyundai – Accent, Elantra, Genesis, Santa Fe, Tiburon, Tucson, Velostar and Veracruz; Kia – Forte, Rio, Rondo, and Soul; Lexus – All models; Lincoln – Mark series and Town Car; Mazda – 323, 626, CX-5, CX-7, Mazda3, Mazda5, Mazda6, Miata, Protegé, and Tribute; Mitsubishi – Outlander and Spyder; Nissan – Frontier, GT-R, Leaf, Rogue, Sentra, Versa, Xterra, and X-Trail; Subaru – Impreza, Legacy, Outback, and Forester; Suzuki – Aerio, Esteem, Kizashi, Swift, and SX4; Toyota – Avalon, Camry, Corolla, Cressida, Echo, Highlander, Matrix, Sienna, Sequoia, Tercel, and Venza; VW – Jetta TDI (without DSG trannies).

Misses

Audi – Early A3, A4, A6, A8, and Q7; BMW – 7 Series, Mini Cooper, and X5; Chrysler – 200, 300, Avenger, Caravan, Charger, Dakota, Durango, Grand Caravan, Intrepid, LHS, Magnum, Neon, New Yorker, Pacifica, PT Cruiser, Sebring, Sprinter, and

Owning a GM front-drive minivan is akin to owning beachfront property in Louisiana.

Town & Country; Daewoo – All models; Fiat – All early models and the 500; Ford – Aerostar, C-Max Contour, Edge, Explorer, F-150, Focus, Mystique, Sable, Taurus, Tempo, Topaz, and Windstar/ Freestar; GM – Avalanche, Aveo, Canyon, Catera, Cimarron, Cobalt, Colorado, CTS, Envoy, Fiero, G6, Grand Prix, HHR, Impala (through 2013), the Lumina/Montana/ Relay/Silhouette/Terraza/ Trans Sport/Venture/Uplander group of minivans, Malibu, SRX, STS, TrailBlazer, and Volt; Hyundai – Excel, Pony, pre-2006 4-cylinder Sonatas, and Stellar; Infiniti – G20; Jaguar – All models; Jeep – Cherokee, Commander, Compass, Grand Cherokee, Journey, and Patriot; Kia – Sedona, Sephia, Sorento, Spectra, and 2006 and earlier Sportages; Lada – All models; Land Rover – All models; Lincoln – Continental front-drive; Mercedes-Benz – 190, B-Class, C-Class, CLK, GL-Class (V8), M series, R-Class, S-Class, and SLK; Merkur – All models; Nissan – 240Z, 250Z, 260Z, Altimas, Armada, Cube, Juke, Quest, Titan; Porsche – All models; Saab – All models; Saturn – L-Series, ION, Relay, S-Series, and VUE; Suzuki – Forenza, Samurai, Verona, and X-90; Toyota – Previa; VW – EuroVan, Passat, Golf, Rabbit, Tiguan, and Touareg (with DSG transmissions).

Note in the list above how many so-called premium luxury brands have fallen out of favour and have been orphaned by shoppers and then abandoned by the automakers themselves. Their hapless owners are left with practically worthless, unreliable cars that can't be serviced properly.

Also, keep in mind that some Japanese makes from Honda, Lexus, Mazda, Nissan, and Toyota have had a resurgence of engine and transmission problems, in addition to an apparent overall decline in reliability and safety.

For example, Nissan engineers have worked overtime during the past seven years to correct Quest glitches, and Toyota's Tacoma and Tundra pickups have such serious corrosion problems (covered by a 15-year secret warranty that includes buying back the pickups at 150 percent of their resale value), and sudden acceleration, drivetrain, and suspension defects that the automaker has continually recalled the vehicles or extended their warranties to compensate owners.

Rank	Top 10 Cars with the Most Complaints Filed Since 1995 (www.arfc.org/complaints/)	Complaints	Rank	Top 10 Cars with the Most Recalls Filed Since 1995	Recalls
#1	2000 Ford Focus	5097	#1	2006 Ford E-350	30
#2	1995 Ford Windstar	4908	#2	22007 Ford E-350	26
#3	2002 Ford Explorer	3792	#3	2008 Ford E-350	23
#4	1997 Ford F-150	3249	#4	2006 Ford E-250	22
#5	2010 Ford Fusion	3215	#5	2007 Ford E-250	18
#6	1999 Dodge Durango	3089	#6	2009 Ford E-350	18
#7	1998 Ford Explorer	2334	#7	1994 Dodge Ram	18
#8	2006 Chevrolet Cobalt	2301	#8	2006 Chevrolet Express	16
#9	2007 Toyota Camry	2297	#9	2004 Ford E-250	16
#10	2001 Ford Focus	2261	#10	1997 Ford F-150	15

Chrysler Automatic Transmissions

Since the early '90s, practically all models in Chrysler's front-drive lineup have had failure-prone automatic transmissions. What adds insult to injury, though, is that Chrysler regularly stiffs its customers with transmission repair bills that average more than $3,000 – about half the average vehicle's worth after five years – when the warranty expires. Since this is far less than what a new car or minivan would cost, most owners pay the bill and then hop onto the transmission merry-go-round, replacing the same transmission at regular intervals. Go ahead, ask any transmission shop.

Keep in mind that during the past few years Chrysler has changed over to a new powertrain hookup with a re-engineered transmission that includes 8-speed gearing and a new Pentastar V6 engine. Early reports show the powertrain is still as unreliable as ever and dangerously defective.

The following owner review in *www.Edmunds.com* clearly shows its shortcomings:

We bought our 2011 Grand Cherokee Laredo 4X4 in December 2010 and it has been in the shop on and off for weeks since we bought it, with major engine-related problems. It only has 13000 km on it, but it blows black smoke out of the exhaust when it is started and sounds like an old diesel engine when it runs. The front crankshaft pulley came apart grinding the remaining pulley against the engine block (Chrysler called it "engine crankshaft damper problems" and "harmonizer balancer issues") and most recently the engine was "pulling in too much fuel" and Chrysler informed us the oil separator and PVC valve would need to be replaced. The gear shifter has broken, and was further damaged by the dealer 4 months ago and still has not been repaired due to "a lack of replacement parts."The engine has had declining performance since about 5000 km.

We didn't just get a lemon because we found out that in fact other 3.6-liter Pentastar V6 engines have come in with the same problems and there have been technical service bulletins released by Chrysler on these issues and on other Grand Cherokees.

This engine is scheduled to go into many more models in 2012 and I would strongly recommend avoiding this engine at all costs.

And from *www.dodgeforum.com:*

According to *Consumers Reports*, the transmission is "clunky" in their tests. Well, it is, especially when cold. It wants to get into 2nd and 3rd so quickly, that the shift is a bit jerky ... I bought my 2011 Dodge Grand Caravan in May and as soon as it hit 5000 miles, I noticed a bang between 1st and 2nd gear. It took 4 days to get an appointment at the local dealer. I told them I shouldn't be driving the car with this shifting problem, they didn't seem to be worried. I brought the van in and they had to wait 5 days for a part to come in for it. I got the van back to find out I had no reverse and the check engine light came on. Brought the van back the next morning and they told me they had done a complete rebuild on the transmission and that a pump had gone. Got the van back a week later and noticed the same banging from 1st to 2nd gear and a shudder when in reverse. Brought it back again, and just picked the van up today to find out it was low on transmission fluid. There is no dipstick, and the service manager said the only way to know the fluid is low is by going on the computer. The van still has the hesitation from 1st to 2nd but I have only driven it about 10 miles today.

Well, after driving the van for a week, out of the economy mode, it happened again. I was backing down a steep driveway and when I put it into drive it hopped and had about a 3-second delay, while on-coming traffic was approaching me at 50mph! Pretty scary. So I put it back into economy mode to have the same jerky shifting. Later that afternoon, I pulled out of my parking lot and it banged in between 1st and 2nd gear again. This is unacceptable. Calling the dealer today for the 4th fix on this tranny.

The 2014 Jeep Cherokee was the first light vehicle in the world with a 9-speed transmission – beating Land Rover, which promised to have a 9-speed on the market earlier. Chrysler says increasing the number of gears from six to nine helps to reduce emissions, improve fuel efficiency by 45 percent and adds to the vehicle's off-road capability. These claims are deisputed by owner postings to *safercar.gov* where the 2014 Cherokee has racked up 141 safety-related complaints (50 would be normal):

My transmission shifts hard from 1st to 2nd, and from 2nd to 3rd. It also has a pronounced "wobble" after it shifts from 1st into 2nd gear, and continues until it shifts hard into 3rd gear at about 20 mph. After a stop will not go into 1st gear for a second or two, then abruptly surges forward with more speed than the amount of accelerator you are giving it. When decelerating, the transmission will actually go into 4th gear and add fuel causing the tachometer to go up between 500 and 1000 rpm. The transmission although touted as a "9-speed", is useless, as it will not go in either automatically or manually at any speed below

75 or 76 mph even though it easily could at 67 or 68 mph with sufficient rpm to still maintain speed. This Jeep is equipped with the towing package from the factory. Towing a 17′ boat traveling over 300 miles, the car ran normally on the way to the destination shifting when it needed to and even going into 8th gear a good deal of the trip. On the return trip, the transmission refused to shift out of 5th gear even though the tach was registering 3k to 4k rpm even when going downhill. It also seemed to be losing power and having difficulty going up slight grades on the interstate. A few times I got it into 7th gear by completely letting up on the gas going downhill but as soon as we started up a slight grade it would again go into 5th and not shift into a higher gear. When I reported these problems to the dealer, I was told that this is normal operation for this transmission.

. . .

When driving at highway speeds (68 mph) and slowing down, the gears on the 2014 Jeep Cherokee downshifted, resulting in an increase in speed, despite pressure being applied to the breaks. This occurs with the automatic transmission when breaking and changing gears from 4th to 5th gear. The shift into 4th gear is followed immediately by a 500+ rpm increase in the engine. If heavy, consistent pressure is not applied to the break, the car will accelerate 1-2 mph. If heavy, consistent pressure is applied to the break, the car shifts violently and the car "lurches" forward due to the increase in rpm.

. . .

Transmission failure 3 times in the first 3000 miles. First failure was while stationary. Second was at approx 30 mph and 3rd at approx 65 mph. Failure is unpredictable and causes immediate drop in speed which could result in an accident. Car was "fixed" by Jeep dealer each time; car failed in same manner all 3 times.

Diesel Defects

Chrysler

Although Chrysler's Cummins engine has been the most reliable diesel sold by American automakers, it also has had some serious manufacturing flaws, involving lift-pump failures that compromise injector-pump performance. Here's how independent mechanic Chuck Arnold (*chuck@thepowershop.com*) describes the problem.

Low fuel pressure is very dangerous because it is possible for the engine to run very well right up to the moment of failure. There may be no symptom of a problem at all before you are walking. If you notice extended cranking before startup of your Cummins 24-Valve engine you should get your lift pump checked out fast. Addition of fuel lubricant enhancing additives to every tank of fuel may minimize pump damage and extend pump life. Finally, Cummins and Bosch should re-engineer their injector pump to make it less sensitive to low-fuel-pressure-induced failure. Existing safety systems designed to limit performance or signal engine trouble need to be redesigned to work when fuel pressure is inadequate so that very expensive injector pumps are not destroyed without warning.

Ford

F-Series equipped with the 6.0L Power Stroke diesel engine were so badly flawed that they couldn't be fixed, forcing Ford to buy back over 500 units. In late October 2013, the company settled a class-action lawsuit related to the 6.0L engine found in 2003-2007 SuperDuty trucks, vans, Excursions, and ambulances. Owners complained of a myriad of problems with the Navistar design. Components affected ranged from injectors, the fuel injection control module, EGR system, and turbocharger. Power Strokes have a history of fuel injectors that leak into the crankcase, and, on the 7.3L diesel, water can leak into the fuel tank, causing the engine to seize. Other glitches affect the turbocharger, the fuel injection control pressure sensor, and the engine control software.

Also, both Ford and General Motors have had problems with snow accumulation in the air filter element, restricting air passage to the engine and possibly causing severe engine damage. Both companies are liable for the free repair of any damage caused by this poor design. Or did they imagine Canada was a snow-free zone?

General Motors

GM's diesel engine failures primarily affect the 6.5L and 6.6L Duramax engine. The 6.5L powerplants are noted for cracked blocks, broken cranks, cracks in the main webbing, cracked cylinder heads, coolant in the oil, loss of power, hard starting, low oil pressure, and oil contamination. Duramax 6.6L engines have been plagued by persistent oil leaks and excessive oil burning, and by defective turbochargers, fuel-injection pumps, and injectors, causing seized engines, chronic stalling, loss of power, hard starts, and excessive gas consumption.

SAFETY FIRST

Looking through Part Four can help you make a list of safe and reliable used car buys to consider before you even leave the house.

Frontal-offset crash test of a Hyundai Tucson by the Insurance Institute for Highway Safety (IIHS).

The best indicator of a car's overall safety is National Highway Traffic Safety Administration (NHTSA) and Insurance Institute for Highway Safey (IIHS) crashworthiness ratings, applicable to most vehicles made and sold over the past several decades in North America. IIHS uses more severe standards and rates head restraint effectiveness, roof crush resistance, and front-quarter protection as well. Results from these two agencies are posted for each model rated in Part Four. For readers who wish to go directly to the respective website of either safety group, see *safercar.gov* or *www.iihs.org/ratings*.

However, there are many other national and international testing agencies that you may consult, and they can be found at *www.crashtest.com/netindex.htm*. This site shows the results of early crash tests of cars that were sold in Australia, Europe, and Japan and that are just now coming to the North American market.

Of course, no one expects to be in a collision, but NHTSA estimates that every vehicle will be in two accidents of varying severity during its lifetime. So why not put the averages on your side?

The Tata Nano is a primitive, no frills mini-compact. A radio and fire extinguisher are optional.

WHEN AND WHERE TO BUY

When to Buy

Unlike new cars that are best bought in the late fall or early winter months, used vehicles are best bought in the summer or fall when trade-ins swell dealer inventories and private sellers don't mind showing their vehicles outdoors. Prices are higher at this time of the year, but you'll have a greater choice of vehicles. In winter, prices decline substantially, and dealers and private sellers are generally easier to bargain with because buyers are scarce and weather conditions don't allow sellers to present their wares in the best light. In spring and summer, prices go up a bit as private sellers become more active and increased new-car rebates bring more trade-ins.

Private Sellers

Private sellers are your best source for a cheap and reliable used vehicle because you're on an equal bargaining level with a vendor who isn't trying to profit from your inexperience. A good private sale price would be about 5 percent *more* than the rock-bottom wholesale price, or approximately 20 percent *less* than the retail price advertised by local dealers. You can find estimated wholesale and retail prices in Part Four.

Remember, no seller, be it a dealer or a private party, expects to get his or her asking price. As with price reductions on home listings, a 10-20 percent reduction on the advertised price is common with private sellers. Dealers usually won't cut more than 10 percent off their advertised price.

It is also a good idea to draw up a bill of sale that gives all the pertinent details of your used-car transaction. (See the following pages for one that you may use as your guide.)

Buying with Confidence

No matter whom you're buying a used vehicle from, there are a few rules you should follow to get the best deal.

First, have a good idea of what you want and the price you're willing to pay. If you have a preapproved line of credit, that will keep the number crunching and extra fees to a minimum. Finally, be resolute and polite, but make it clear that you are a serious buyer and want to keep the transaction as simple as possible.

Here's a successful real-world technique used by Kurt Binnie, a frequent *Lemon-Aid* tipster.

> Imagine the surprise of the used-car salesman when I pulled out my BlackBerry and did a VIN search right in front of him using Carfax [*Lemon-Aid* recommends the Canadian firm CarProof]. Threw him right off balance. Carfax results for Ontario vehicles give a good indication, but not the complete MTO [Ministry of Transportation, Ontario] history. I bought the UVIP [Used Vehicle Information Package] ... before closing the deal. For the car I ended up buying, I didn't even tell the sales staff that I was running the VIN while I was there. I was able to see it wasn't an auction vehicle or a write-off. This technique should work with pretty much any WAP [Wireless Application Protocol] enabled phone.

Kurt's letter goes on to describe how he avoids negotiations with sales staff and managers. He figures out the price he's willing to pay beforehand, using a combination of book values and the prices listed at *www.autotrader.ca*. He then test drives the vehicle, runs the VIN through his BlackBerry, and then makes a point-blank, one-time offer to the dealer. He has also found that used-car staff often have no knowledge about the vehicles on their lots beyond their asking price, and they make no distinction between cars manufactured early or late in the model year.

Primary Precautions

Get a printed sales agreement, even if it's just handwritten, that includes a clause stating that there are no outstanding traffic violations or liens against the vehicle. It doesn't make a great deal of difference whether the car will be purchased "as is" or certified under provincial regulation. A vehicle sold as safety certified can still turn into a lemon or be dangerous to drive. The certification process can be sabotaged if a minimal number of components are checked, the mechanic is incompetent, or the instruments are poorly calibrated. "Certified" is not the same as having a warranty to protect you from engine seizure or transmission failure. It means only that the vehicle met the minimum safety standards on the day it was tested.

PLEASE PRINT CLEARLY

Bill of Sale

- **Sections 1 and 2 must be completed** in order to make this Bill of Sale acceptable for vehicle registration. Completion of section 3, on the back of this form, is optional.
- Two copies of this Bill of Sale should be completed. The buyer keeps the original and the seller keeps the copy.
- Alterations or corrections made while completing the vehicle information section should be initialled by the buyer and seller.

SECTION 1

SELLER(S) INFORMATION

Name(s) *(Last, First, Second)*				Telephone Number

Address	Street	City / Town	Province / State	Postal Code / Zip Code

Personal Identification:

VEHICLE INFORMATION

Year	Make	Model or Series	Style

Vehicle Identification Number (VIN) / Serial Number	Body Color	Roof Color	Odometer Reading

BUYER(S) INFORMATION

Name(s) *(Last, First, Second)*				Telephone Number

Address	Street	City / Town	Province / State	Postal Code / Zip Code

Personal Identification:

This vehicle was sold for the sum of:

_____ Dollars $ _____

(Sum written in full)

(Subject to the terms and special conditions which appear in Section 3 on the back of this form)

SECTION 2

GENERAL INFORMATION

Dated at: _____

               City / Town   Province / State   Country

on _____ .

I certify that all information shown above is true to the best of my knowledge.

_____	_____
Signature of Buyer	Signature of Seller

_____	_____
Signature of Buyer	Signature of Seller

_____	_____
Signature of Witness	Signature of Witness

REG3126 (2011/01)

SECTION 3 (OPTIONAL)

SPECIAL CONDITIONS OF SALE

1. The vehicle described on the front of this form is:
   Check the appropriate box(es)

   a) Free of all liens and encumbrances: ☐ Yes ☐ No   If No, please give names of lien holders:

   _____

   b) Being paid for in full: ☐ Yes ☐ No

   Being paid by: ☐ Cash ☐ Cheque ☐ Money Order ☐ Other *(please specify)*: _____

2. Payment Terms: _____

3. Vehicle was last registered in: _____

   Province / State   Country

4. Special conditions of sale *(if any)*: _____

   _____

   _____

   _____

General Information:

- The law in the Province of Alberta requires a vehicle to be insured prior to registration. Documentary proof of vehicle insurance is required. Legislation allows a person to whom a valid licence plate is issued to transfer the licence plate to a newly purchased vehicle to be registered within 14 days of the date on their Bill of Sale.

  The above does not apply to commercial vehicles used for the transportation of goods or passengers for compensation.

- A vehicle entering Alberta from another jurisdiction requires a safety inspection. Information can be obtained from a Registry Agent. A listing of local Registry Agents can be found in the telephone directory under Licence and Registry Services; or visit Service Alberta's website at www.servicealberta.gov.ab.ca for comprehensive registries and consumer information and services.

- In addition to the Bill of Sale, other identification is required to obtain Alberta registration. Where possible, obtain Section 2 of the previous Alberta vehicle registration certificate.

- The prospective purchaser can determine whether a vehicle is free of liens and encumbrances in Alberta by contacting a Registry Agent.

  In order to perform a search, a Registry Agent will require the vehicle identification number (VIN) / serial number of the vehicle. A request for a search can be made in person or in writing. There is a fee for this service.

- Vehicle Information Reports are available from a Registry Agent. There is a fee for each service.

- The buyer must produce a copy of a properly completed Bill of Sale, that includes the same information as shown on this standardized form, in order to register and licence a vehicle in Alberta.

This form is provided as a courtesy by Service Alberta to ensure that sufficient information is contained within the Bill of Sale to permit licensing and registration of the described vehicle by the new owner.

No liability attaches to the Crown through the use of this document in respect of the sale of this vehicle. Any dispute arising from the sale becomes a civil matter among the parties named in this document.

REG3126 (2011/01)

Source: Alberta government site: *www.registryedmonton.com/uploads/BillOfSaleReg3126.pdf.*

Make sure the vehicle is lien-free and has not been damaged in a flood or written off after an accident. Flood damage can be hard to see, but it impairs ABS, power steering, and airbag functioning (making deployment ten times slower).

Canada has become a haven for rebuilt American wrecks. Write-offs are also shipped from provinces where there are stringent disclosure regulations to provinces where there are lax rules or no rules at all.

If you suspect your vehicle is flood-damaged, is a rebuilt wreck from the States, or was once a taxi, there's a useful Canadian search agency called CarProof that can give you a complete history of any vehicle within a day (see No Surprises, above).

CarProof (www.carproof.com)

If a lien does exist, you should contact the creditor(s) listed to find out whether any debts have been paid. If a debt is outstanding, you should arrange with the vendor to pay the creditor the outstanding balance, or agree that you can put the purchase price in a trust account to pay the lender. If the debt is larger than the purchase price of the car, it's up to you to decide whether you wish to complete the deal. If the seller agrees to clear the title personally, make sure that you receive a written relinquishment of title from the creditor before transferring any money to the other party. Make sure the title doesn't show an "R" for "restored," since this indicates that the vehicle was written off as a total loss and may not have been properly repaired.

Even if all documents are in order, ask the seller to show you the vehicle's original sales contract and a few repair bills in order to ascertain how well it was maintained and if it has any unexpired repair warranties. The bills will show you if the odometer was turned back and will also indicate which repairs are still guaranteed. If none of these can be produced, leave. If the contract shows that the car was financed, verify that the loan was paid. If you're still not sure that the vehicle is free of liens, ask your bank or credit union manager to check for you. If no clear answer is forthcoming, look for something else.

Don't Pay Too Much

Prices for large- and mid-sized cars, trucks, and SUVs are soaring as fuel costs tumble. But this price increase hasn't been as severe with small cars and trucks, mini-minivans, downsized SUVs, or entry-level wagon crossovers. Their prices, both new and used, will remain relatively stable and are expected to stay that way through the summer.

If you'd like to save even more when buying used, consider the tips below.

- Choose a vehicle that's three to five years old and has a good reliability and durability record. Don't buy an extended warranty that may become worthless. The money you save from the extra years' depreciation and lower insurance premiums will make up for some additional maintenance costs.

- Look for discounted off-lease vehicles with low mileage and a good reputation.

- Buy a vehicle that's depreciated more than average simply because of its bland styling, unpopular colour (dark blue, white, and champagne are out; silver is in), lack of high-performance features, or discontinuation.

- Buy a cheaper twin or rebadged model like a fully loaded Camry instead of a Lexus ES, a Toyota Matrix in lieu of a Pontiac Vibe, or a Chevrolet Silverado instead of a GMC Sierra.

- Buy a fully equipped gas hog. Your $30,000 savings on a large SUV or pickup will pay the gas bill many times over, and the vehicle can be easily resold a few years down the road, with only moderate depreciation.

Price Guides

The best way to determine the price range for a particular model is to read the *Lemon-Aid* values found in Part Four. From there, you may wish to get a free second opinion by accessing Vehicle Market Research International's Canadian used-car prices at *www.vmrcanada.com*. It is one of the few free sources that list wholesale and retail values for used cars in Canada. The site even includes a handy calculator that adjusts a vehicle's value according to model, mileage, and a variety of options.

Black Book and *Red Book* price guides, found in most libraries, banks, and credit unions, are essential to anyone buying or selling a used vehicle. Both guides are easily accessible on the Internet. To read the *Canadian Black Book* values, simply copy the following URL into your web browser: *www.canadianblackbook.com/used-cars.html*. This site lists the vehicle's trade-in and future value, as well as the asking price based upon your Canadian postal code. No other identification is required.

Now, if you want to use the *Canadian Red Book Vehicle Valuation Guide*, which seems more attuned to Quebec and Ontario sales, you can order single copies of their used car and light truck wholesale and retail price guide for $19.95 at *www.canadianredbook.com* (an annual subscription costs $105). There are no restrictions as to who may subscribe.

You may also go to *Auto Trader* magazine's website at *www.autotrader.ca* to see at what prices other Canadians are trying to sell your chosen vehicle.

Don't be surprised to find that many national price guides have an Eastern Ontario and Quebec price bias, especially the *Red Book*. They often list unrealistically low prices compared with what you'll see in the eastern and western provinces and in rural areas, where good used cars are often sold for outrageously high prices or are simply passed down through the family for an average of eight to ten years. Other price guides may list prices that are much higher than those found in your region. Consequently, use whichever price guide lists the highest value when selling your trade-in or negotiating a write-off value with an insurer. When buying, use the guide with the lowest values as your bargaining tool.

Cross-Border Sales

Now that the Canadian dollar is worth about $0.77 U.S., there's not much to gain buying a car in the States. However, shopping in the States for upscale exotic sports cars, luxury vehicles, fully-loaded SUVs, trucks, and vans can save astute buyers some money. But for many, the small savings may not be worth the risk and hassle.

Here's what to do.

1. Check with Ottawa to see if the used vehicle you covet can be imported into Canada (call the Registrar of Imported Vehicles at 1-888-848-8240, or visit their website at *www.riv.ca*).

2. Take a trip across the border to scout out what is available from all dealers. Compare your findings with what's offered by Canadian cross-border brokers.

3. Verify if the price is fair once taxes and transport charges are considered.

Hire a broker or deal directly with the dealer. Be wary of private sellers, because your legal rights may be more limited in cross-border transactions.

Rental and Leased Vehicles

Next to buying privately, the second-best choice for getting a good used vehicle is a rental company or leasing agency. Due to our slumping economy, Budget, Hertz, Avis, and National are selling, at cut-rate prices, vehicles that have one to two years of service and approximately 80,000-100,000 km (approximately 50,000-60,000 mi) on the odometer. These rental companies will gladly provide a vehicle's complete history and allow an independent inspection by a qualified mechanic of the buyer's choice, as well as arrange for competitive financing.

Rental vehicles are generally well maintained, sell for a few thousand dollars more than privately sold vehicles, and come with strong guarantees, like Budget's 30-day money-back guarantee at some of its retail outlets (including three in B.C.). Rental-car companies also usually settle customer complaints without much hassle so as to not tarnish their images with rental customers.

Rental agencies tend to keep their stock of cars on the outskirts of town near the airport (particularly in Alberta and B.C.) and advertise in the local papers. Sales are held year-round as inventory is replenished. Late summer and early fall are usually the best times to see a wide selection because the new rentals arrive during this time period.

Vehicles that have just come off a three- or five-year lease are much more competitively priced than rentals, generally have less mileage, and are usually as well maintained. You're also likely to get a better price if you buy directly from the lessee, rather than going through the dealership or an independent agency. But remember that you won't have the dealer's leverage to extract post-warranty "goodwill" repairs from the automaker.

Repossessed Vehicles

Repossessed vehicles frequently come from bankrupt small businesses or subprime borrowers who failed to make their finance payments. They are usually found at auctions, but finance companies and banks sometimes sell them as well. Canadian courts have held that financial institutions are legally responsible for defects found in what they sell, so don't be at all surprised by the disclosure paperwork that will be shoved under your nose. Also, as with rental car company transactions, the combination of these companies' deep pockets and their abhorrence of bad publicity means you'll likely get your money back if you make a bad buy. The biggest problem with repossessed sport-utilities and pickups is that they may have been damaged by off-roading or neglected by their financially troubled owners. Although you rarely get to test drive or closely examine these vehicles, a local dealer may be able to produce a vehicle maintenance history by running the VIN through their manufacturer's database.

New-Car Dealers

New-car dealerships aren't bad places to pick up good used cars or trucks. Sure, prices are about 20 percent higher than those for vehicles sold privately, but rebates and zero percent financing plans can trim used-car prices dramatically. Plus, dealers are insured against selling stolen vehicles or vehicles with finance or other liens owing. They also usually allow prospective buyers to have the vehicle inspected by an independent garage, offer a much wider choice of models, and have their own repair facilities to do warranty work. In addition, if there's a possibility of getting post-warranty "goodwill" compensation from the manufacturer, your dealer can provide additional leverage, particularly if the dealership is a franchisee for the model you have purchased. Finally, if things do go terribly wrong, dealers have deeper pockets than private sellers, so there's a better chance of winning a court judgment.

Provinces are also cracking down on dealers who sell defective used cars. In addition to Manitoba's recently enacted "lemon law," Alberta now requires a thorough mechanical inspection of every used car sold by dealers. Under the revised regulations, a mechanical assessment will be completed by a licensed journeyman technician with a trade certificate as an Automotive Service Technician or Heavy Equipment Technician under the *Apprenticeship and Industry Training Act.*

A mechanical fitness assessment will be valid for 120 days from the time of completion. This is a change from 14 days for the previous certificate. The extended time period recognizes the broader nature of the assessment. More information about the amendments to the vehicle inspection regulation is available on the Alberta Transportation website at *www.transportation.alberta.ca* (under the "Drivers and Vehicles" tab).

"Certified" vehicles

The word "certified" doesn't mean much. Ideally, it tells us the vehicle has been inspected and reconditioned under the manufacturer's supervision. Of course, some dealers simply slap a "certified" sticker on the car. Remember, an automaker, auto association, dealer, or mechanic that certifies a vehicle becomes co-liable for your later troubles (See the jurisprudence in Part Three).

Used-car leasing

It isn't a good idea to lease either new or used vehicles. Leasing has been touted as a method of making the high cost of vehicle ownership more affordable, but don't you believe it. Leasing is generally costlier than an outright purchase, and, for most people, the pitfalls far outweigh any advantages. If you must lease, do so for the shortest time possible and make sure the lease is close-ended (meaning that you walk away from the vehicle when the lease period ends). Also, make sure there's a maximum mileage allowance of at least 25,000 km (about 15,500 mi) per year and that the charge per excess kilometre is no higher than 8-10 cents. (For information on leasing see "Fleecing" by Leasing in Part One.)

Used-Car Dealers

Used-car dealers usually sell their vehicles for a bit less than what new-car dealers charge. However, their vehicles may be worth a lot less because they don't get the first pick of top-quality trade-ins. Many independent urban dealerships are marginal operations that can't invest much money in reconditioning their vehicles, which are often collected from auctions and new-car dealers reluctant to sell the vehicles to their own customers. And used-car dealers don't always have repair facilities to honour the warranties they do provide. Often, their credit terms are easier (but more expensive) than those offered by franchised new-car dealers.

That said, used-car dealers operating in small towns are an entirely different breed. These small, often family-run businesses recondition and resell cars and trucks that usually come from within their communities. Routine servicing is usually done in-house, and more complicated repairs are subcontracted out to specialized garages nearby. On one hand, these small outlets survive by word-of-mouth advertising and wouldn't last long if they didn't deal fairly with local townsfolk. On the other hand, their prices will likely be higher than elsewhere due to the better quality of their used vehicles and the cost of reconditioning and repairing what they sell under warranty.

Auctions

First of all, make sure it's a legitimate auction. Many are fronts for used-car lots where sleazy dealers put fake ads in complicit newspapers, pretending to hold auctions that are no more than weekend selling sprees.

Furthermore, you'll need lots of patience, smarts, and luck to pick up anything worthwhile. Government auctions – places where the mythical $50 Jeeps are sold – are fun to attend but highly overrated as places to find bargains. The odds against you: It's impossible to determine the condition of the vehicles put up for bid, prices can go way out of control, and auction employees, professional sellers, their relatives, and their friends usually pick over the good stuff long before you ever see it.

To attend commercial auctions is to swim with the piranhas. They are frequented by "ringers" who bid up the prices, and by professional dealers who pick up cheap, worn-out vehicles unloaded by new-car dealers and independents. There are no guarantees, cash is required, and quality is likely to be as low as the price. Remember, too, that auction purchases are subject to provincial and federal sales taxes, the auction's sales commission (3-5 percent), and, in some cases, an administrative fee of $75-$100.

If you are interested in shopping at an auto auction, remember that certain days are reserved for dealers only, so call ahead. You'll find the vehicles locked in a compound, but you should have ample opportunity to inspect them and, in some cases, take a short drive around the property before the auction begins.

Used car predators troll the Internet. Here, Ziggy and Tigger, look for unwary prey.

The Internet

The Internet is a risky place to buy a used car. You don't know the seller, and you know even less about the car. It's easy for an individual to sell a car they don't own, and it's even easier to create a virtual dealership, with photos of a huge inventory and a modern showroom, when the operation is likely made up of one guy working out of his basement.

Rating systems are unreliable too. Ratings from "happy customers" may be nothing but ploys – fictitious postings created by the seller to give out five-star ratings and the appearance that the company is honest and reliable.

If you must use the Internet to buy a car, use it to protect your wallet, as well. Don't accept any of the seller's information as truthful. Instead, order an ovrernite comprehensive on-line title and accident report from CarProof or some other credible agency. Do this before wasting $100 or more inspecting the car by an independent mechanic. Be especially suspicious of vehicles brought in from the States or other provinces.

Although you take an even bigger risk buying out-of-province or in the States, there are a few precautions you can take to protect yourself. First off, compare shipping fees with a Canadian automobile transporter like Hansen's (*www.lhf.com*), and put your money into an escrow account until the vehicle is delivered in satisfactory condition.

If the car is located in the States, print out the tips found on eBay's website at *pages.ebay.ca/ebaymotors/explained/checklist/howtobuyUS.html*. The website takes you through each step in detail and will tell you if the vehicle is permitted in Canada and the likely modification requirements. If the vehicle needs alteration, you should check with a mechanic for an estimate. You will also need to get a recall clearance letter from the dealer or automaker in order to pass federal inspection. Additional information can be obtained from the Registrar of Imported Vehicles (1-888-848-8240 or *www.riv.ca*).

Beware of phony eBay solicitations that are sent via doctored e-mails selling out-of-province vehicles. In the e-mail the "owner" will even promise to deliver the car to you at no extra cost. Rather than paying through the relatively secure PayPal used in most legitimate transactions, you will be instructed to send payment through a Western Union or MoneyGram money transfer.

How prevalent is this scam? About a third of the ads in *Canadian Auto Trader* checked out several years ago by the non-profit Automobile Protection Association turned out to be phony. The most obvious indications these ads were placed by scam artists is that the same e-mail address kept reappearing, or the listed phone number was a dummy. Local newspapers are frequently complicit in this fraud. Always look for ads with recurring phone numbers.

Most of the fraudulent advertisements were placed outside Canada, apparently without the knowledge of the online sites that published them. Nevertheless, it's hard not to suspect some complicity because the ads are quite easy to verify by the hosting site. For example, *Wheels.ca* staffers say they refuse advertisers with an IP address outside of Canada and that ad claims and contact information are constantly checked by the business office.

Dishonest sellers aren't your only Internet trap. There are also plenty of crooks who will steal your car by pretending to be honest buyers. These phonies will take the delivery of the car, pay for it with a worthless cashier's cheque, and then disappear. Again, use PayPal or an independent third-party who can confirm payment has been received before releasing the vehicle.

There is some government help available to catch Internet used-car swindlers. PhoneBusters, the federal-provincial agency set up to deal with telephone and Internet scams (1-888-495-8501) has ties to the RCMP and OPP, and will investigate and arrest these high-tech crooks.

Here are some more tips for selling or purchasing vehicles online.

- Check out the listed phone number and ask for an address and independent reference.

- Insist that the car be inspected by a third party before closing the deal.
- Search the VIN or ad description using Google or *www.carproof.com*. Often the same wording or VIN will appear on different sites.
- Never use a money transfer service.
- Call the online escrow agency and speak with a representative before divulging any personal financial information.
- Be skeptical of eBay "second chance" offers.
- Always use the eBay "contact seller" process.
- Report all shady deals to the local RCMP detachment. Then, file a complaint with your local police service and at the same time voice your concerns with the Internet service provider (ISP) hosting the offensive material. The Canadian Association of Internet Providers (*www.caip.ca*) would also welcome your comments or concerns in regards to Canadian ISPs.

Canadian car sales websites

- *AMVOQ.ca* – Quebec used-car classifieds (in French)
- *AutoHunter.ca* – Alberta used-car classifieds
- *Autonet.ca* – New and used cars and trucks, new-car dealers, new-car prices, and reviews
- *AutoTrader.ca* – Used-car classifieds from all across Canada
- *BuySell.com* – Classifieds from all across Canada
- eBay Motors Canada (*cars.eBay.ca*) – The premiere site for used cars located in Canada or anywhere in the world
- North American Automobile Trade Association (*www.naata.org*) – This trade association lists dealers and brokers who will help you find a new or used cross-border bargain
- *RedFlagDeals.com* – A compendium of shopping tips, as well as advice on dealing with the federal and provincial governments
- Used Cars Ontario (*www.usedcarsontario.com*) – Used-car classifieds for major cities in Ontario, with links and articles

U.S. car sales websites

- *AutoTrader.com* – New- and used-car classifieds
- *Cars.com* – Ditto, except there's an "Advanced Search" option
- *CarsDirect.com* – One of the largest car-buying sites
- eBay Motors U.S. (*www.motors.ebay.com*) – Similar to the Canadian site
- *Edmunds.com* – Lots of price quotes and articles
- The Big Lot! (*www.thebiglot.com*) – Another large car-buying site

Financing Choices

Financing a car purchase is *never* a good idea. Instead, pay as much cash as possible by purchasing an older car, or by downsizing and simplifying your choice.

If financing is unavoidable, do this exercise to figure out how much financing you can afford. First deduct your recurring monthly expenses – living expenses such as groceries, rent, subscriptions, club memberships, etc. – from your monthly income after taxes. What's left over is your disposable income. Then calculate how much of that you can pay each month for a new or used car. Most financial planners recommend spending no more than 10 percent of take-home income for monthly car payments. Make sure you have enough left for emergencies and entertainment.

There are a lot of car-related "hidden" expenses that will eat into your disposable income, like depreciation (the largest expense of all), insurance, fuel, and maintenance. CAA's Driving Costs Annual Report puts the average total expenditure between $8,000 to $15,000 a year. A good rule of thumb is to plan on spending 10-15 percent of your total monthly budget on all automotive expenses. Remember to take into account such items as insurance costs, which can run as high as 12 percent, but more typically 5-8 percent of the purchase price.

Now don't panic. Depreciation can be reduced by half if the car is bought used; insurance premiums will be less if coverage is part of a total package and the car has a good claims history (find out before the purchase); fuel expenses can be lowered by 20 percent with an economy car and using *gasbuddy.com* to find the cheapest gas stations around; and maintenance can cost 30 percent less and carry longer warranties, if performed by independent garages.

By keeping the purchase price low, there is less money to lose, and the cash downpayment can be more substantial.

Credit Unions

A credit union is the best place to borrow money for a used car at competitive interest rates and with easy repayment terms. In fact, credit unions jumped into car financing in a big way when the major automakers pulled back, five years ago. Keep in mind, you'll have to join the credit union or have an account with it before the loan is approved. You'll also probably have to come up with a larger down payment.

Banks

Financing a car through a bank can mean either applying for a car loan or a line of credit. A loan will require a lien on your car and fixed monthly payments until the end of the term. Interest rates on car loans often vary considerably.

You can get a good idea of the different car-loan interest rates through an online comparison of bank rates. For purchases in the States, go to *www.bankrate.com*;

Canadian loan interest rates are updated by the individual banks and credit unions who mostly ask you to call toll-free to get a current quote.

Let's assume that your monthly budget is $400. The following table shows you the cost of the vehicle you can afford based on different repayment periods.

Monthly Payment	Loan Term	Interest Rate and APR[3]	Loan Amount
$400	4 years	7.59%[4]	$16,514.65
	5 years	7.49%[5]	$19,966.86
	6 years	7.49%[6]	$23,141.09
	7 years	7.49%[7]	$26,086.94
	8 years[2]	7.49%[8]	$28,820.85

As you can see, with an eight-year car loan (used mostly for new cars)[2], you can buy a more expensive vehicle while sticking to your monthly budget.

[2] Subject to credit approval by National Bank. Certain conditions apply.
[3] APR means "Annual Percentage Rate" and represents the total interest and fees charged by the Bank, expressed as an annual percentage. It corresponds to the annual interest rate if the cost of borrowing is comprised exclusively of interest.
[4] Example based on financing of $16,514.65, with a four-year term and a hypothetical rate of 7.59%.
[5] Example based on financing of $19,966.86, with a five-year term and a hypothetical rate of 7.49%.
[6] Example based on financing of $23,141.09, with a six-year term and a hypothetical rate of 7.49%.
[7] Example based on financing of $26,086.94, with a seven-year term and a hypothetical rate of 7.49%.
[8] Example based on financing of $28,820.85, with an eight-year term and a hypothetical rate of 7.49%.

Source: National Bank of Canada: *www.nbc.ca.*

Since you are already online, e-mail the lowest-interest lenders and get a loan commitment first, before you start shopping and the dealer's sales agent starts throwing different figures at you. Simply Google the bank's name and add "car loan interest rates."

Lines of credit, on the other hand, require no lien and offer the ability to pay a minimum each month, or as much as you can afford. The rates are often lower than traditional bank loans and there are no penalties for paying it off early, making it the preferred route for many car buyers.

Banks are always leery of financing used cars, but they generally charge rates that are competitive with what dealers offer.

In your quest for a bank loan, keep in mind that the loan officer will be impressed by a prepared budget and sound references, particularly if you seek out a loan before choosing a vehicle. If you don't have a preapproved loan, it wouldn't hurt to buy from a local dealer, since banks like to encourage businesses in their area.

The Internet offers help for people who need an auto loan and want quick approval but don't want to face a banker. For example, the Royal Bank website has a selected list of dealers who are empowered to process Royal Bank loans at their dealerships (see *www.rbcroyalbank.com/products/personalloans/installment_loan.html*). Attractive financing rates, including zero financing charges (watch out for an inflated purchase price or hidden fees), are available from automakers through their dealers, as well. Here are the interest rates Toyota advertises:

Toyota Certified Used Vehicle Rates

Vehicles	Finance (%) Terms in Months				
	24	36	48	60	72
Yaris, Yaris Hatchback, Corolla, Matrix, Camry	1.9%	2.9%	3.9%	3.9%	4.9%
SCION — IQ,XB,XD,TC,FRS	1.9%	2.9%	3.9%	3.9%	4.9%
Prius c, Prius, Prius v, Camry Hybrid, Highlander Hybrid	2.9%	2.9%	2.9%	3.9%	4.5%
Sienna, RAV4, Celica, Solara, Avalon, Highlander, FJ Cruiser, 4Runner, Sequoia, Venza, Tacoma 4x2, Tacoma 4x4, Tundra 4x2, Tundra 4x4	3.9%	3.9%	3.9%	4.9%	5.5%

*Limited time purchase financing offer provided through Toyota Financial Services on approved credit. Representative finance example based upon $10,000 financed at 1.9% APR equals $424.96 per month for 24 months, $0 down payment. Cost of borrowing is $199.04, for a total obligation of $10,199.04. Taxes, license, insurance, registration and applicable fees are extra. Dealer may sell for less. Offer subject to change without notice. See your participating Toyota dealer for full program details.

Dealers

Cash may be king with some Canadian retailers, but not at your local car dealership. It's a myth that dealers will treat you better if you pay cash. Dealers want you to buy a fully loaded vehicle and finance the whole deal. And, now that auto loans are easier to get than they were several years ago, dealers are financing everything in sight – especially used cars.

Dealer financing isn't the rip-off it once was, but there are some notable exceptions, as a CBC British Columbia television investigation concluded in January 2014. Reporters interviewed a couple who paid TD bank 25.44 percent in interest charges on a five-year-old Dodge Avenger that was financed for a 7-year term – costing more than double the price of their car.

"We're paying $21,000 for the loan – then $23,000 in interest," said Angie Hauser of Kelowna. "They're making money off of people who have no money...We've been robbed by a bank with the help of a car dealer. I mean, that's the only way I see it," said her husband Enzo Gamarra.

"Why would I want to pay $44,000 for a car that's now only worth $15,000?"

High-interest subprime loans are offered to buyers with poor credit by some of Canada's better-known financial institutions. *Canadian Auto World* magazine says subprime loans make up approximately 25 percent of all auto loans arranged by dealerships. Surprisingly, defaults on these high-cost loans are relatively low.

Dealers want to wring as much profit as possible from each loan contract, so be careful not to let the seller pencil in additional charges for sickness or unemployment protection insurance. Nevertheless, some dealers can finance your purchase at rates that compete with those of banks and finance companies, thanks to carmaker sales incentives. Make sure, though, financing at rates far below the prime rate isn't due to a jacked-up base price that compensates for the "bargain" loan rate.

Dealer Scams

One of the more common selling tricks is to not identify the previous owner because the vehicle was used commercially, was problem-prone, or had been written off as a total loss after an accident. It's also not uncommon to discover that the mileage has been turned back, particularly if the vehicle was part of a company's fleet. Your best defence? Demand the name of the vehicle's previous owner and then run a VIN check through CarProof as a prerequisite for purchasing.

It would be impossible to list all the dishonest tricks employed in used-vehicle sales. As soon as the public is alerted to one scheme, crooked sellers use other, more elaborate frauds. Nevertheless, under industry-financed provincial compensation funds, buyers can get substantial refunds if defrauded by a dealer.

Here are some of the more common fraudulent practices you're likely to encounter.

Declaring a False Price

Here's where your own greed will do you in. In a tactic used almost exclusively by small, independent dealers and some private sellers, the buyer is told that he or she can pay less sales tax by listing a lower selling price on the contract. But what if the vehicle turns out to be a lemon, or the sales agent has falsified the model year or mileage? The hapless buyer is offered a refund only on the fictitious purchase price indicated on the contract. If the buyer wanted to take the dealer to court, it's quite unlikely that he or she would get any more than the contract price. Moreover, both the buyer and dealer could be prosecuted for making a false declaration to avoid paying sales tax. Keep to the legal principle: "Come to the court with clean hands."

Dealers Disguised as Private Sellers

Individual transactions account for about three times as many used-vehicle sales as dealer sales, and crooked dealers get in on the action by posing as private sellers. Called "curbsiders," these scammers lure unsuspecting buyers through lower prices, cheat the federal government out of tax money, and routinely violate provincial registration and consumer protection regulations. Bob Beattie, executive director of the Used Car Dealers Association of Ontario (*www.ucda.org*), once estimated that about 20 percent of so-called private sellers in Ontario are actually curbsiders. Dealers in large cities like Toronto, Calgary, and Vancouver believe curbsiders sell half of the cars advertised in the local papers. This scam is easy to detect if the seller can't produce the original sales contract or show repair bills made out over a long period of time in his or her own name. You can usually identify a car dealer in the want ads section of the newspaper – just check to see if the same telephone number is repeated in many different ads. Sometimes you can trip up a curbsider by requesting information on the phone, without identifying the specific vehicle. If the seller asks you which car you are considering, you know you're dealing with a curbsider.

Legitimate car dealers claim to deplore the dishonesty of curbsider crooks, yet they are their chief suppliers. Dealership sales managers, auto auction employees, and newspaper classified ad sellers all know the names, addresses, and phone numbers of these thieves but don't act on the information. Newspapers want the ad dollars, auctions want the action, and dealers want someplace they can unload their wrecked, rust-cankered, and odometer-tricked junkers with impunity. Talk about hypocrisy, eh?

Curbsiders are particularly active in Western Canada, importing vehicles from other provinces where they were sold by dealers, wreckers, insurance companies, and junkyards (after having been written off as total losses). They then place private classified ads in B.C. and Alberta papers, sell their stock, and then import more.

Buyers taken in by these scam artists should sue in small claims court both the seller and the newspaper that carried the original classified ad. When just a few cases are won in court and the paper's competitors play up the story, the practice will cease.

"Free-Exchange" ("You Got a Lemon? Here's a Greener One")

How nice. The dealer offers to exchange any defective vehicle for any other vehicle in stock. What really happens, though, is that the dealer won't have anything else selling for the same price and so will demand a cash bonus for the exchange – or you may get the dubious privilege of exchanging one lemon for another.

"Money-Back" Guarantee

Once again, the purchaser feels safe in buying a used car with this kind of guarantee. After all, what could be more honest than a money-back guarantee? Dealers using this technique often charge exorbitant handling charges, rental fees, or mechanical repair costs to the customer who bought one of these vehicles and then returned it.

"50/50" Guarantee

The devil is definitely in the details with this trick. Essentially, the dealer will pay half of the repair costs over a limited period of time. It's a fair offer if an independent garage does the repairs. If not, the dealer can always inflate the repair costs to double their actual worth and then write up a bill for that amount (a scam sometimes used in "goodwill" settlements). The buyer winds up paying the full price of repairs that would probably have been much cheaper at an independent garage. The best kind of used-vehicle warranty is 100 percent with full coverage for a fixed term, even if that term is relatively short.

"As Is" and "No Warranty"

You will see from the jurisprudence in Part Three that these phrases are pure bluff, whether used in a dealer or private sale. Sellers insert these clauses much like parking lot owners or coat checkers at restaurants when they post warnings that they have no responsibility to indemnify your losses. In fact, when you pay for a custodial service or a used vehicle, the commission the seller of that service or product receives requires that you be protected.

Remember, every vehicle carries a provincial legal warranty protecting you from misrepresentation and the premature failure of key mechanical or body components. Nevertheless, sellers often write "as is" or "no warranty" in the contract in the hope of dissuading buyers from pressing legitimate claims.

Generally, when "as is" has been written into the contract or bill of sale, it usually means that you're aware of mechanical defects, you're prepared to accept the responsibility for any damage or injuries caused by the vehicle, and you're agreeing to pay all repair costs. However, the courts have held that the "as is" clause is not a blank cheque to cheat buyers, and must be interpreted in light of the seller's true intent. Was there an attempt to deceive the buyer by including this clause? Did the buyer really know what the "as is" clause could do to his or her future legal rights? It's also been held that the courts may consider oral representations ("parole evidence") as an expressed warranty, even though they were never written into the formal contract. So, if a seller makes claims as to the fine quality of the used vehicle, these claims can be used as evidence. Courts generally ignore "as is" clauses when the vehicle has been intentionally misrepresented, when the dealer is the seller, or when the defects are so serious that the seller is presumed to have known of their existence. Private sellers are usually given more latitude than dealers or their agents.

Odometer Fraud

Who says crime doesn't pay? It most certainly does if you turn back odometers for a living in Canada.

Estimates are that each year close to 90,000 vehicles with tampered odometers reach the Canadian marketplace – at a cost to Canadians of more than $3.56 million. This is about double the incidents one would expect based on a 2002 U.S. NHTSA study that pegs odometer fraud at 450,000 vehicles annually. NHTSA estimates that half of the cars with reset odometers are relatively new, high-mileage rental cars or fleet vehicles.

Odometer fraud is a pernicious crime that robs thousands of dollars from each victim it touches. See, for example, *United States v. Whitlow*, 979 F.2d 1008 (5th Cir. 1992), at 1012 (under sentencing guidelines, the court affirmed the estimate that consumers lost $4,000 per vehicle). The television news magazine *60 Minutes* once characterized odometer scams as the largest consumer fraud in America. Victims of this fraud are commonly the least able to afford it, since buyers of used cars include large numbers of low-income people. In addition, consumers generally are unaware of being victimized.

Odometer tampering involves several interrelated activities. Late-model, high-mileage vehicles are purchased at a low price. The vehicles are "reconditioned" or "detailed" to remove many outward appearances of long use. Finally, odometers are reset, typically removing more than 64,000 km (40,000 mi).

In addition to the cosmetic "reconditioning" of the car, the odometer tamperer "reconditions" the car's paperwork. Automobile titles include a declaration of mileage statement to be completed when ownership is transferred. To hide the actual mileage that is declared on the title when the car is sold to an odometer tamperer, the tamperer must take steps to conceal this information. These steps vary from simple alteration of mileage figures to creating transfers to fictitious "straw" dealerships to make it unclear who was responsible for the odometer roll-back and title alteration. Alternatively, the odometer tamperers frequently destroy original title documents indicating high mileage and obtain duplicate certificates of title from provincial or state motor vehicle departments, upon which the false, lower mileage figures are entered.

Odometer fraud is practiced by a variety of people, including:

- Organizations that roll back or forward ("clock") the odometers on thousands of cars, wholesaling them to dealers who resell them to the public;
- Groups of individuals who buy cars, clock them, and sell them through the classifieds, passing them off as cars of a friend or relative ("I'm selling Aunt Sally's Buick for her"); and
- Individuals who only clock their own car to defeat a lease provision or cheat on a warranty.

Gangs of odometer scammers ply their trade in Canada because it seems as if no one cares what they do, and they stand to gain thousands of dollars, or 10 cents profit for each mile erased from the odometer on the resale value of a doctored car. Moreover, electronic digital odometers make tampering child's play for anyone with a laptop computer, or anyone who has sufficient skill to simply replace the dashboard's instrument panel.

Think: When was the last time you heard of a Canadian dealership being charged with odometer fraud? Probably a long time ago, if at all. And what is the punishment for those dealers convicted of defrauding buyers? Not jail time or loss of their franchise. More than likely, it'll be just a small fine.

Not so in the States. Many victims can get compensation from dealers who sold cars with altered odometers, regardless of who was responsible for the alteration. For business and legal reasons, dealers frequently compensate consumers who purchased vehicles with altered odometers. U.S. federal law permits consumers to obtain treble damages or $1,500, whichever is greater, when they are victims of odometer fraud (49 U.S.C. section 32710). The courts have been hard-nosed in protecting consumers in these kinds of lawsuits against dealers.

How to spot a car that's been to a "spin doctor?"

- When calling a supposedly private seller, ask to see the car in the ad, without specifying which one.
- Ask the seller for a copy of the contract showing the name of the selling dealer and previous owner.
- Check the history of the car through CarProof.
- Look for uneven paint or body panels that don't line up. Do the doors, hood, and trunk open and close easily? Do the bumpers and fenders sit squarely?
- Examine brake and gas pedal wear as well as the driver's door sill. Does their wear match the kilometres? An average tire lasts 80,000 kilometres; any premature wear signals an odometer turnback or chassis misalignment.
- On older vehicles that don't use a digital odometer, check to see if the numbers on the odometer are lined up and snug. If they jiggle when you bang your hand on the dash, have an expert check for fraud.

- Have the car inspected by a franchised dealer for that make of vehicle, and ask for a copy of the service records, noting the mileage each time the vehicle was serviced.

Misrepresentation

Used vehicles can be misrepresented in a variety of ways. A used airport commuter minivan may be represented as having been used by a Sunday school class. A mechanically defective sports car that's been rebuilt after several major accidents may have plastic filler in the body panels to muffle the rattles or hide the rust damage, heavy oil in the motor to stifle the clanks, and cheap retread tires to eliminate the thumps. Your best protection against these dirty tricks is to have the vehicle's quality completely verified by an independent mechanic before completing the sale. Of course, you can still cancel the sale if you learn of the misrepresentation only after taking the vehicle home, but your chances of successfully doing so dwindle as time passes.

Both the federal and provincial governments have scored impressive victories resulting in fines of up to $10 million and personal damage awards of $15,000 against General Motors, *Time Magazine,* and Bell Telephone for misrepresenting their products. I'm not sure that these court decisions will create a cottage industry of misleading advertising plaintiffs, but Canadian businesses are terrified that it will (see Part Three, Supreme Court Tackles "Fine Print").

PRIVATE SCAMS

A lot of space in this guide is dedicated to describing how used-car dealers and scam artists cheat uninformed buyers. Of course, private individuals can be dishonest, too. In either case, protect yourself at the outset by keeping your deposit small and by getting as much information as possible about the vehicle you're considering. Then, after a test drive, you may sign a written agreement to purchase the vehicle and give a deposit of sufficient value to cover the seller's advertising costs, subject to cancellation if the automobile fails its inspection. After you've taken these precautions, watch out for the following private sellers' tricks.

Vehicles that Are Stolen or Have Finance Owing

Many used vehicles are sold privately without free title because the original auto loan was never repaid. You can avoid being cheated by asking for proof of purchase and payment from a private seller. Be especially wary of any individual who offers to sell a used vehicle for an incredibly low price. Check the sales contract to determine who granted the original loan, and call the lender to see if it's been repaid. Place a call to the provincial Ministry of Transportation to ascertain whether the car is registered in the seller's name. Find out if a finance company is named as beneficiary on the auto insurance policy. Finally, contact the original dealer to determine whether there are any outstanding claims.

In Ontario, all private sellers must purchase a Used Vehicle Information Package at one of 300 provincial Driver and Vehicle Licence Issuing Offices, or online at *www.mto.gov.on.ca/english/dandv/vehicle/used.htm*. This package, which costs $20, contains the vehicle's registration history in Ontario; the vehicle's lien information (i.e., if there are any liens registered on the vehicle); the fair market value on which the minimum tax payable will apply; and other information such as consumer tips, vehicle safety standards inspection guidelines, retail sales tax information, and forms for bills of sale.

In other provinces, buyers don't have easy access to this information. Generally, you have to contact the provincial office that registers property and then pay a small fee for a computer printout that may or may not be accurate. You'll be asked for the current owner's name and the car's VIN, which is usually found on the driver's side of the dashboard.

There are two high-tech ways to get the goods on a dishonest seller. First, have a dealer of that particular model run a vehicle history check through the automaker's online network. This will tell you who the previous owners and dealers were, what warranty and recall repairs were carried out, and what other free repair programs may still apply. Second, you can use CarProof (*www.carproof.com*) to carry out a background check.

Summary: Be Tough and Fair

Don't treat your used-car negotiation like a World Wrestling Federation title bout. You are no Vince McMahon and most private sellers are simple, honest folk. Dealers, on the other hand, will use every trick in the book to maximize their profit, but you will likely still get a good deal if the price and inspection results are acceptable. You will end up with a reliable used car, truck, or minivan at a reasonable price – through patience and homework.

Nevertheless, prevent potential headaches and hassles by becoming thoroughly familiar with your legal rights, as outlined in Part Three, and by buying a vehicle recommended in Part Four.

Here are the steps to take to keep your level of risk to a minimum.

1. Keep your present vehicle for at least 10 years. Don't get panicked over high fuel costs – depreciation is a greater threat to your pocketbook.
2. Sell to a dealer if the reduction in applicable taxes on your next purchase with that dealer is greater than the potential profit of selling privately.
3. Sell privately if you can get at least 15 percent more than what the dealer offered.
4. Buy from a private party, rental car outlet, or dealer – in that order.

5. Use an auto broker to save time and money, but pay a set fee, not a commission.

6. Buy only a *Lemon-Aid*-recommended three- to five-year-old vehicle with some original warranty left that can be transferred.

7. Carefully inspect front-drive vehicles that have reached their fifth year. Pay particular attention to the engine intake manifold and head gasket, CV joints, steering box, and brakes. Make sure the spare tire and tire jack haven't been removed.

8. Buy a full-sized, rear-drive delivery van and then add the convenience features that you would like (seats, sound system, etc.) instead of opting for a more-expensive, smaller, less-powerful minivan.

9. Buy a vehicle recommended by *Lemon-Aid*, thereby foregoing the need to purchase a $1,500–$2,000 extended warranty; many of these warranty providers may be headed for bankruptcy.

10. Have maintenance repairs done by independent garages that offer lifetime warranties on brakes, exhaust systems, and automatic transmissions.

11. Install used or reconditioned mechanical parts, demand that original parts be used for body repairs, and insist upon choosing your own repairer.

12. Keep all the previous owner's repair bills to facilitate warranty claims and to let mechanics know what's already been replaced or repaired.

13. Upon delivery, adjust mirrors to reduce blind spots and adjust head restraints to prevent your head from snapping back in the event of a collision. On airbag-equipped vehicles, move the seat backward more than half its travel distance and sit at least 30 cm away from the airbag housing.

14. Ensure that the side airbags include head protection.

15. Make sure that both the dealer and automaker have your name in their computers as the new owner of record. Ask for a copy of your vehicle's history, which is stored in the same computer.

16. Go to *www.safercar.gov* and look up all the free confidential service bulletins applicable to your vehicle and compare that to the free ALLDATA index of bulletins at *www.alldatadiy.com/recalls/index.html*. Get true copies of all the recalls and service bulletins that are particularly significant to your needs from ALLDATA's site (*www.alldatadiy.com/buy*). The cost is $26.95 (U.S.) for a one-year subscription, or $44.95 for five years. A one-year subscription for additional vehicles costs $16.95 per vehicle. Overnight, you will be sent an Internet download or data disc of all your vehicle's service bulletins going back to 1982. This will keep you current as to the latest secret warranties, recalls, and troubleshooting tips for correcting factory screw-ups. *Safercar.gov* can also give you details on all recalled vehicles and which ones have been fixed by the dealer.

Part Three

RECOURSES AND REFUNDS

Fifty Shades of Gray: If you bought a new or used 2006-2013 Honda Civic, 2007-2013 CR-V, 2009-2013 Pilot, or 2011-2013 Odyssey with cracked, chalking, or clouding paint, you may qualify for a free fix at your local Honda dealer, according to a series of technical service bulletins issued by Honda between January 2013 and June 2014.

CAMPAIGN – PAINT CHALKING, CRACKING, OR CLOUDING

SERVICE BULLETIN NO.: 14-034   DATE: JUNE 12, 2014

WARRANTY EXTENSION: 2006-13 Civic Paint Cracking, Chalking, or Clouding.

BACKGROUND: SB 14-034: Warranty Extension: 2006-13 Civic Paint Cracking, Chalking, or Clouding. Vehicles covered under this bulletin will have the warranty on their paint extended to 7 years from the original date of purchase with no mileage limit. The exterior paint on the hood and the leading edge of the front fenders may crack or look chalky or cloudy. Also the roof, trunk, upper portions of the quarter panel, and the upper portions of the doors may look chalky or cloudy.

CORRECTIVE ACTION: If necessary, repaint the entire affected panel(s) with an isocyanate two-part color and clearcoat paint after obtaining DPSM approval.

PARTS INFORMATION: If you need to replace any moldings or windshield clips, reference the parts catalog for the applicable part numbers, and submit them in your warranty claim.

Canadians complain just as much as Americans – but not as well. Americans fight back hard – with small claims and class action lawsuits, with mass demonstrations, and with media manipulation. In Canada, we are, well, *Canadian*. Our grievances are politely aired and, if they are not acted upon, we vow to take our business elsewhere. Granted, sometimes we will collectively forge institutional solutions to problems (such as making healthcare available to everyone, selling our products, and protecting our culture). But individually, we tend to be pushovers.

This section of *Lemon-Aid* seeks to change all that. *In the pages that follow, you will learn to see complaining in a new light and:*

- Discover the many benefits of complaining, be inspired by the success stories of other complainers, and learn when complaints are justified.

- Learn what are your legal rights with accurate and up-to-date summaries of consumer-rights legislation and related judicial decisions.

- Be encouraged to follow step-by-step instructions for effective consumer complaining, enabling you to act individually to get a refund for a new or used car "lemon," or service that was incompetent, over-priced, not needed, or covered by a "secret" warranty.

- Understand the benefits of collective complaining and the process through which effective outcomes can be achieved.

- Find tips for using the court system as a means to satisfy customer complaints, get practical information about choosing an appropriate venue, anticipating costs, and handling the actual litigation.

- Access detailed information pertaining to safety- and performance-related defects.

How Do You Know When to Complain?

First, let me be clear: There are times when *you should not complain*. Contrary to the popular adage, the customer is not *always right. Sure, we have all been spoiled by retailers who will take back a shirt or dress, no questions asked. But that is just good public relations. We don't have the right to a refund or exchange credit if we change our mind, paid too much* (unless there was misrepresentation), or can't find financing for the purchase. Actually, if the sale is cancelled because it can't be financed, the seller is entitled to charge a penalty to cover reasonable expenses caused by the lost sale – this is why contracts should spell out the costs that will result if they are broken.

Nonetheless, there are many times – particularly if you are faced with a defective product or an unsatisfactory service – when *you should complain. I recommend that you claim a full or partial refund (damages) if any of the following allegations can be substantiated.*

- **The product is unsafe or defective; service is inadequate, or incomplete:** This principle holds true even if the product was sold "as is" or "without warranty" if the buyer can prove the seller's bad faith.
- **The product or service does not meet the client's needs as expressed in the contract or promised in the sales representation:** For example, gas mileage isn't as represented; the voice-activated infotainment system doesn't respond in a way you can understand, navigation aids lead you into a lake; and dash gauges won't wash out in sunlight.

Cars that don't "listen:" In-car voice recognition systems work so poorly that automakers should give up trying to add new features and go back to the basics, says J.D. Power's 2014 Initial Quality Study of vehicle models sold in the United States. Twenty-three percent of the failures noted were related to audio, communication, entertainment, or navigation. Apparently, in-car systems often don't work as well as voice recognition features in smart phones because cars are exposed to road noise, engine noise, and passenger conversations.

- **The warranty has been breached:** This comes into play when the guarantee wasn't honoured or differs in its application from what was promised. Since the warranty is considered to be an integral part of the contract, when it is breached (not honoured), a full or partial refund and punitive damages can be claimed from the seller, warranty company, or manufacturer. Prudent plaintiffs usually hold all parties equally responsible and let the presiding judge decide how to apportion blame.

- **A consumer-protection law is violated:** Even if the seller is contravening only a technical requirement of the law, like not giving the buyer a copy of the contract, the contract can be cancelled. In some used car cases, buyers who had paid too much were able to get their money refunded because the mileage written on the contract was incorrect or the warranty wasn't clearly stated. Judges take a dim view of standard-form contracts that aren't in conformity with the law. In fact, many consumer-protection laws require that the judge give the consumer the edge when deciding responsibility.

- **The product or service doesn't last for a reasonable period of time:** A judge has the final say as to what is a reasonable period of time; the court's decision prevails over the contract's guarantee. This rule applies to all products and services, including a vehicle's durability and car repairs.

- **Delivery is delayed or the price is boosted:** The seller must respect the delivery date and price given verbally or written on the contract. If there is no promised delivery date, the court will decide what is a reasonable wait based upon the industry norm.

- **Parts availability or after-sales servicing is inadequate:** There is no legal requirement that manufacturers provide parts and service beyond the warranty period. However, judges can refund part of the purchase price and award damages, even if the warranty has expired and if a product's reliability or durability is reduced due to poor servicing or an inadequate supply of replacement parts.

- **A "fix" doesn't fix the problem:** When the seller's corrective warranty repairs don't fix the problem indicated on the work order after repeated customer visits, the seller and/or manufacturer should either replace the product or pay for repairs elsewhere. If the warranty period runs out during repeated repairs, coverage for the uncorrected problem must continue until it is fixed.

- **A secret "goodwill" warranty extension isn't honoured:** Carmakers often extend their warranties long after the original warranty has expired. A problem occurs when the company applies the longer warranty in the United States only, or restricts its extension to specific regions. For example, Firestone/Bridgestone tried to limit its tire warranty extension to cars registered only in hot-weather states, until the courts showed this was impractical because cars registered elsewhere could have a catastrophic tire failure when driving through a warmer region, or after having moved to a warmer state. Incidentally, carmakers still routinely restrict their post-warranty free repairs. Fortunately, in Canada, showing a service bulletin (like the one shown for Honda, above) will usually get the free repair. (See a comprehensive listing of current secret warranty extensions in Part Two and in Part Four's model reviews).

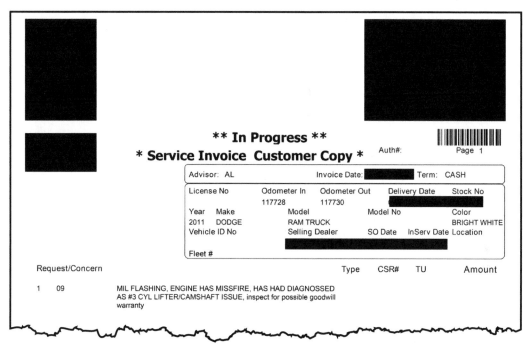

** In Progress **
* Service Invoice Customer Copy *   Auth#:   Page 1

| Advisor: AL | | Invoice Date: | | Term: CASH |

License No	Odometer In	Odometer Out	Delivery Date	Stock No
	117728	117730		

Year	Make	Model	Model No	Color
2011	DODGE	RAM TRUCK		BRIGHT WHITE

Vehicle ID No	Selling Dealer	SO Date	InServ Date	Location

Fleet #

Request/Concern		Type	CSR#	TU	Amount
1	09	MIL FLASHING, ENGINE HAS MISSFIRE, HAS HAD DIAGNOSSED AS #3 CYL LIFTER/CAMSHAFT ISSUE, inspect for possible goodwill warranty			

"Secret warranties" are often referred to as "product improvement" or, "Customer Satisfaction" programs – or GM's favourite: a "Special Policy." Bottom-line, both dealer and automaker split the cost.

- **There has been false representation or misinformation:** This applies when an important characteristic of the product or service was not as represented (cost, size, warranty, performance, fuel economy, towing specs, is the wrong model year, etc.), or important facts were not disclosed (vehicle had transport or accident damage repairs, etc.). (See pages 198 and 200.)

Times have changed as our governments and courts become more responsive to consumer issues and less tolerant of corporate crime. Small-claims "people's courts" allow claims for as much as $25,000. We have multi-million dollar class actions, government-run auto insurance, and more aggressive government regulators that ensure our rights are respected. Yes, there's a new sheriff in town.

Two Warranties

Like new cars, used-vehicle defects are covered by two warranties. The *expressed* or *written* warranty, which has a fixed time limit and lots of seller escape clauses, and the *implied* or *legal* warranty, are entirely up to a judge's discretion to apply based upon the vehicle's cost, how it was maintained, manufacturer and dealer assertions, the severity of the failure, the extent of that failure's consequences, and, I add only half-jokingly, the judge's own experience with car dealers.

Expressed

The expressed warranty given by the seller is often full of empty promises, and it allows the dealer and manufacturer to act as judge and jury when deciding whether a vehicle was misrepresented or is afflicted by defects they'll pay to correct. Rarely does it provide a money-back guarantee or last beyond five years. As of October 1, 2015, though, Volvo Canada is offering a Lifetime Replacement Parts & Labour Warranty on all parts purchased and installed at an authorized Volvo retailer. Simply put, Volvo customers now pay only once and never pay again for Volvo Car replacement parts and labour, for as long as they own their vehicle.

But, there are still a lot of loopholes carmakers can use. Some of the more familiar lame excuses used in denying expressed warranty claims are "You abused the car," "It was poorly maintained," "It's normal wear and tear," "It's rusting from the outside, not the inside," and "It passed the safety inspection." Ironically, the expressed warranty sometimes says there is no warranty at all, or that the vehicle is sold "as is." Fortunately, courts usually throw out these exclusions by upholding two legal concepts.

1. The vehicle must be fit for the purpose for which it was purchased.
2. The vehicle must be of merchantable quality when sold.

Not surprisingly, sellers use the expressed warranty to reject claims, while smart plaintiffs mention the expressed warranty, and they argue for a refund under the implied warranty, instead.

Implied

The implied warranty ("of fitness") is your ace in the hole. As clearly stated in the under-reported Saskatchewan decision *Maureen Frank v. General Motors of Canada Limited*, in which the judge declared that paint discoloration and peeling shouldn't occur within 11 years of the purchase of the vehicle, the implied warranty is an important legal principle. It is solidly supported by a large body of federal and provincial laws, regulations, and jurisprudence, and it protects you primarily from hidden defects that may be either dealer- or factory-related. But the concept also includes misrepresentation and a host of other scams.

This warranty also holds dealers to a higher standard of conduct than private sellers because, unlike private sellers, dealers and auto manufacturers are presumed to be aware of the defects present in the vehicles they sell. That way, they can't just pass the ball to the previous owner and then walk away from the dispute.

Dealers are also expected to disclose defects that have been repaired. For instance, in British Columbia, provincial law (the *Motor Dealer Act*) says that a dealer must disclose damages that cost more than $2,000 to fix. This is a good law to cite in other jurisdictions.

In spite of all your precautions, there's still a 10 percent chance you'll buy a lemon, says mobility services company Runzheimer International (a figure also cited by former GM VP Bob Lutz, who confirms that one out of every 10 vehicles produced by the Detroit automakers is likely to be a lemon).

Why the implied warranty is so effective

1. It establishes the concept of reasonable durability, meaning that parts are expected to last for a reasonable period of time, as stated in jurisprudence, judged by independent mechanics, or expressed in extended "goodwill" warranties given by automakers in the past (examples: 10 years/193,000 km for catalytic converters; 7 years/200,000 miles for diesel injectors as expressed in one U.S. service bulletin; and 7 years/160,000 km for engines and transmissions).

2. It covers the entire vehicle and can be applied for whatever period of time the judge decides.

3. It can order that the vehicle be taken back, or a major repair cost be refunded. One *Lemon-Aid* reader writes:

    > I wanted to let you and your readers know that the information you publish about Ford's paint failure problem is invaluable. Having read through your "how-to guide" on addressing this issue, I filed suit against Ford for the "latent" paint defect. The day prior to our court date, I received a settlement offer by phone for 75 percent of what I was initially asking for.

4. It can order that plaintiffs be given compensation for supplementary transportation, inconvenience, mental distress, missed work, screwed-up vacations, insurance paid while the vehicle was in the repair shop, repairs done by other repairers, and exemplary, or punitive, damages in cases where the seller was a real weasel. (Hello! VW diesel owners.)

5. It is often used by small claims court judges to give refunds to plaintiffs "in equity" (out of fairness), rather than through a strict interpretation of contract law.

MOTOR VEHICLE DIVISION
VEHICLE DOCUMENT/ALERT NOTICE
PERSONAL & CONFIDENTIAL

Notice Date: 3/19/2014

IMMEDIATE RESPONSE TO THIS NOTICE REQUIRED

TO
THE
ORDER
OF:

Vehicle Code:

Customer Service: 1-855-739-3773

Make: TOYOTA * HONDA * NISSAN

Program Term Deadline

3/29/2014

Call to verify the above information

Call to verify the above information

IMMEDIATE RESPONSE TO THIS NOTICE REQUIRED

Notice Date: 3/19/2014

Make: TOYOTA * HONDA * NISSAN

Code:	
Coverage:	AVAILABLE
Program Term Deadline:	3/29/2014

Attention:

Our records indicate that you have not contacted us to have your vehicle contract updated.

Please call 1-855-739-3773 today.

You are receiving the notice because your factory warranty will expire or may have already expired based on the mileage and age of your vehicle.

By neglecting to replace your coverage you will be at risk of being financially liable for any and all repairs after your factory warranty expires. However, you still have time left to activate your service contract on your vehicle before it's too late. No vehicle inspection will be required.

No other notices will be sent for this offer. This will be our only attempt to contact you about your expiring factory warranty.

Your file on this vehicle will be deleted and you may no longer be eligible for this offer regarding service coverage after 3/29/2014.

A recent Better Business Bureau (BBB) study says supplementary auto warranties may cost much more than they're worth. Sellers can reap huge profits because they are usually free to mark up the price to whatever the consumer will pay. A contract that cost the seller $1,000, for example, may be sold to a car owner for $2,000 or more. The average price paid by survey respondents who bought contracts was a whopping $2,146. (*stlouis.bbb.org/storage/142/documents/vehicleservicecontractstudy2011.pdf*).

Other tactics used by sellers included:

- Selling what are called "product warranties" or "additive contracts," which require buyers to use oil or another additive in their vehicle to make the service contract valid.

- Telling consumers their original warranties had expired or were about to expire.

- Creating a sense of urgency by saying the offer was only good that day.

- Using the "take-away" scheme in which the consumer doesn't qualify for the offer but an exception will be made in his or her case.

- Selling contracts of "limited value" because they contained numerous exclusions and conditions.

- Promising non-existent "bumper-to-bumper" coverage.

How "Protected" Are You?

In the BBB survey, vehicle protection was a roll of the dice. For example, vehicle claims were routinely denied because a covered part was damaged by an allegedly defective non-covered part. Some contracts required the owner to have maintenance done as recommended by the vehicle's manufacturer and to provide receipts of work done, including oil changes. Of the survey respondents, 93 percent said the company refused to pay for repair claims they covered by their contracts. Other reasons given for not covering the repair: 60 percent said the company told them the repair was not covered by the contract, 17 percent said they were told that they lacked proper maintenance documents, and 16 percent said the warranty company classified the defect as a pre-existing condition.

Reasons for denying claims in many instances were "questionable and even frivolous," according to the Missouri Attorney General, which noted the following examples in its suits:

- A consumer's claim was denied by one provider because the certified mechanic's maintenance records were handwritten and not printed by computer.

- Another consumer's claim was denied when the claims department stated they could not pay the claim because they did not have the original paperwork, only copies.

- An inspector for a provider denied a claim because he said damage was due to off-roading even though the consumer was 67 years old and never went off-roading.

- One consumer's claim to repair the water pump for $958.91 was denied because the customer changes his own oil and the contract requires that work be done by a state licensed mechanic.

The average amount spent for those repairs in spite of the extra warrany was $1,480, and totalled $2.7 million when applied to all complainants in the BBB database who incurred the same problem. One researcher noted, a casino would give you better odds of collecting.

Vehicle Service Contract Claims

Companies paid $27,250

Companies denied $388,544

Source: Survey of 660 complainants

Supreme Court Tackles "Fine Print"

Canada's courts have made a full-court press against misleading advertising. The Supreme Court has ruled that the omnipresent misleading advertising that has bombarded us in print, over the airwaves, and on the Internet for what seems forever must stop. In two powerful decisions, originating from Ontario and Quebec, Bell Canada and *Time* magazine were exposed as flim-flam hypocrites and hit with a record-breaking fine and precedent-setting damages.

On June 28, 2011, Bell Canada consented to pay a $10-million settlement (the first time that the maximum penalty for misleading advertising has ever been imposed) and change its advertising after the Canadian Competition Bureau said its ads were contrary to the *Competition Act's* civil prohibition against making representations that are false or misleading (*www.ct-tc.gc.ca*).

Bell lied continuously in its ads for over five years about the prices at which certain of its services were available (including home phones, Internet, satellite television, and wireless services). Bell's representations gave the "general impression" that the advertised monthly price for the services was sufficient, when in fact Bell used a variety of "fine-print disclaimers" to "hide" additional mandatory fees that made the actual price paid by consumers higher than the advertised price (in one instance 15% higher than advertised). According to the *Competition Act's* misleading advertising provisions, the "general impression" conveyed by the advertisement to the average consumer, as well as its literal meaning, were considered in determining that the representations made were false or misleading.

As with most businesses caught scamming the public, Bell maintained it did no wrong. Nevertheless, the company paid the $10-million fine and agreed to drop all non-compliant advertising within 60 days. In particular, Bell agreed not to use small print or other ancillary disclosures that contradict the general impression of its price representations. Bell also agreed to pay the Competition Bureau $100,000 to cover the costs of the Bureau's investigation.

Time Magazine

On February 12, 2012, Canada's Supreme Court threw the book at *Time* magazine for lying to readers in order to sell subscriptions. Yes, the same *Time* that pillories politicians for being untruthful has used its subscription sales department for years to give consumers false expectations that they have won a sweepstakes prize.

The ruling endorses Quebec's "seller beware" mindset in its precedent-setting judgment relating to false and misleading representations under the province's *Consumer Protection Act*. In *Richard v. Time Inc. (scc.lexum.org/decisia-scc-csc/scc-csc/scc-csc/en/7994/1/document.do)*, the Court held that a representation should be judged simply by what a credulous and inexperienced consumer would believe to be true – a position long held by the courts in matters relating to misleading advertising charges filed under the federal *Competition Act*.

The Court also stated that if a prohibited business practice exists, there is no need to prove actual damages; an irrefutable presumption of prejudice exists. This opens the door to punitive damages, even where the circumstances do not justify a compensatory award.

Although punitive, or exemplary damages, can go as high as $1 million (Cdn.) (see pages 173-174 and Appendix II: *Whiten v. Pilot – Complaint Letter). Time* magazine was ordered to pay (to the plaintiff, yippee!) only $15,000. Yet, the impact of this award has been far greater than the amount, as it serves as a reminder to business and government that lies won't be tolerated in Ottawa – except during Question Period ... smile.

YOU HAVE JUST WON $1 MILLION DOLLARS, IF YOU SUBSCRIBE TO TIME...HOLD YOUR BREATH FOR FIVE MINUTES, SING ALL STANZAS OF "O'CANADA" IN BOTH LANGUAGES, AND TELL US WHERE SENATOR MIKE DUFFY LIVES.

Angry consumer reading *Time* letter. "GRRRRRR!"

Auto Industry Fine Print

If qualifying information is necessary to prevent a representation from being false or misleading when read on its own, then that information should be presented clearly and conspicuously. "Fine print," which is the bread and butter of auto advertising, won't do.

The U.S. Federal Trade Commission defines misleading auto advertising this way in *United States of America v. Billion* (*www.ftc.gov/system/files/documents/cases/141211billioncmpt.pdf*):

This Consent Order defines "clearly and conspicuously" as

A. In a print advertisement, the disclosure shall be in a type size, location, and in print that contrasts with the background against which it appears, sufficient for an ordinary consumer to notice, read, and comprehend it.

B. In an electronic medium, an audio disclosure shall be delivered in a volume and cadence sufficient for an ordinary consumer to hear and comprehend it. A video disclosure shall be of a size and shade and appear on the screen for a duration and in a location sufficient for an ordinary consumer to read and comprehend it.

C. In a television or video advertisement, an audio disclosure shall be delivered in a volume and cadence sufficient for an ordinary consumer to hear and comprehend it. A video disclosure shall be of a size and shade, and appear on the screen for a duration, and in a location, sufficient for an ordinary consumer to read and comprehend it.

D. In a radio advertisement, the disclosure shall be delivered in a volume and cadence sufficient for an ordinary consumer to hear and comprehend it.

E. In all advertisements, the disclosure shall be in understandable language and syntax. Nothing contrary to, inconsistent with, or in mitigation of the disclosure shall be used in any advertisement or promotion.

Look at the above Federal Trade Commission standards and read the car ads in any Canadian newspaper. Can you see, let alone understand, the cryptic abbreviations at the bottom of each dealer/automaker ad? Or, what about the blue lettering on a darker blue or other colour background? How many brave Canadian journalists would submit their own newspaper ads to the FTC, let alone the provincial order of opthamologists and lawyers to confirm readability and clarity? Not the *Globe and Mail*. Not *La Presse*, and, most certainly, not the "Wheels" section of the *Toronto Star*.

'98 SEDAN – IMPORT 160K, 1 Acdnt, flpd 14x ovr clff into rvr, elctrcl sys fried. Nvr fxd. Box #43587
Research before you buy.
www.VehicleSalesAuthority.com

Motor
Vehicle Sales Authority
of British Columbia

Television commercials are slicker. You get twenty seconds of praise for the vehicle and then ten seconds of small type scrolled down the screen at break-neck speed telling you all of the exceptions to the foregoing. In effect, fine-print flashes "we were just kidding."

Carmakers have gotten more brazen in the lies they tell on TV. For example, Nissan ran a 30-second ad in 2011 extolling the prowess of its 2012 mid-size Frontier pickup. In the spot, the Frontier scoots up a steep dune to rescue a buggy stuck in the sand. Competitors cried foul, saying what was depicted couldn't be done. The U.S. Federal Trade Commission investigated and confirmed the actual truck couldn't pull off such a feat, cables were used to pull both vehicles, and the dune was "photo shopped" to look much steeper than it really was.

Nissan admitted its commercial was deceptive, and in an out-of-court settlement with the FTC the carmaker promised to henceforth tell the truth or face a $16,000 U.S. fine for each day a misleading commercial is run during the next 20 years.

The last time the FTC and an automaker settled such a case was with Volvo in 1992. That case involved an ad showing a monster truck crushing a lineup of cars but unable to damage a Volvo station wagon.

Broken Promises

New or used vehicles can turn out to be bad buys for various reasons. They were misrepresented by the seller, who sold for the wrong model year ("redated"), covered up damage, turned back the odometer, inflated their fuel economy, lied about its previous use (not really driven only on Sundays by a little old lady, etc.), or they are afflicted with factory-induced defects like sudden acceleration or brake failures. In some cases, abusive driving or poor maintenance by the previous owner can make a vehicle unreliable or dangerous to drive. Misrepresentation is relatively easy to prove. You simply have to show the vehicle doesn't conform to the oral or written sales representations made before or during the time of purchase. These representations include sales brochures and newspaper, radio, television, and Internet ads. Omission of key information can also fall under misrepresentation.

Private sales can easily be cancelled if the vehicle's mileage has been turned back, if accident damage hasn't been disclosed, or if the seller is really a dealer pretending to be a private seller ("curbsiding" (see Part Two)). Even descriptive phrases like "well-maintained," "driven by a woman" (whatever *that's* supposed to imply), or "excellent condition" can get the seller into trouble if misrepresentation was intended.

To get compensation or to have the car taken back, defects need to be confirmed by an independent garage examination that shows either that the deficiencies are premature, factory-related, or not maintenance-related or that they were hidden at the time of purchase. You can also make your proof by showing repetitive repairs for the same problem over a short period of time. It doesn't matter if the vehicle was sold new or used. In fact, many of the small claims court victories against automakers relating to defective paint, engines, and transmissions were won by owners who bought their vehicles used and then sued both the seller and the automaker.

Sure, automakers will sometimes plead they are not part of the chain of responsibility because they didn't sell the product to the plaintiff. Fortunately, as you will learn reading this section, Canadian judges do not buy that argument. Particularly if the defect was obviously factory-related and caused an injury or death.

Cases involving these kinds of failures are not that difficult to win in Canada under the doctrine of *res ipsa loquitur*, meaning "the thing speaks for itself," or in negligence cases, the liability is shown by the failure itself. Planes shouldn't fall and cars shouldn't suddenly accelerate or fail to stop. Under *res ipsa loquitur*, you don't have to pinpoint the exact cause of the failure, and judges are free to award damages by weighing the "balance of probabilities" as to fault.

This advantage found in Canadian law was laid out succinctly in the July 1, 1998, issue of the *Journal of Small Business Management* in its comparison of product liability laws on both sides of the border (see "Effects of Product Liability Laws on Small Business" at *www.allbusiness.com*).

> Although in theory the Canadian consumer must prove all of the elements of negligence (*Farro v. Nutone Electrical Ltd. 1990*; Ontario Law Reform Commission 1979; Thomas 1989), most Canadian courts allow injured consumers to use a procedural aid known as *res ipsa loquitur* to prove their cases (*Nicholson v. John Deere Ltd. 1986; McMorran v. Dom. Stores Ltd. 1977*). Under *res ipsa loquitur*, plaintiffs must only prove that they were injured in a way that would not ordinarily occur without the defendant's negligence. It is then the responsibility of the defendant to prove that he was not negligent. As proving the negative is extremely difficult, this Canadian reversal of the burden of proof usually results in an outcome functionally equivalent to strict product liability (*Phillips v. Ford Motor Co. of Canada Ltd. 1971*; Murray 1988). This concept is reinforced by the principal that a Canadian manufacturer does not have the right to manufacture an inherently dangerous product when a method exists to manufacture that product without risk of harm. To do so subjects the manufacturer to liability even if the safer method is more expensive (*Nicholson v. John Deere Ltd. 1986*).

Let's put the legalese aside and use the simple definition outlined by U.S. Supreme Court Justice Sotomayor. In *Jarvis v. Ford* (United States Second Circuit Court of Appeal, February 7, 2002), she rendered a judgment in favour of a driver who was injured when her six-day-old Ford Aerostar minivan suddenly accelerated as it was started and put into gear. What makes this decision unique is that the jury had no specific proof of a defect. The Court of Appeal agreed with the jury award, and Justice Sotomayor gave these reasons for the court's verdict:

> A product may be found to be defective without proof of the specific malfunction:
>   It may be inferred that the harm sustained by the plaintiff was caused by a product defect existing at the time of sale or distribution, without proof of a specific defect, when the incident that harmed the plaintiff:
>
>   (a) was of a kind that ordinarily occurs as a result of product defect; and
>   (b) was not, in the particular case, solely the result of causes other than product defect existing at the time of sale or distribution.
>
> Restatement (Third) of Torts: Product Liability §3 (1998). In comment c to this section, the Restatement notes:

The jury awarded Ms. Jarvis $24,568 in past medical insurance premiums, $340,338 in lost earnings, and $200,000 in pain and suffering. For future damages, the jury awarded $22,955 in medical insurance premiums, $648,944 in lost earnings, and $300,000 for pain and suffering.

You can definitely get a refund if a repair or part lasts beyond its guarantee but not as long as is generally expected. You'll have to show what the auto industry considers to be "reasonable durability," however.

This isn't all that difficult if you use the conservative benchmarks that automakers, mechanics, and the courts have recognized over the years (see the Reasonable Part Durability chart below).

REASONABLE DURABILITY			
Accessories		**Brake System (cont.)**	
Air conditioner	7 years/no mileage	Brake drum	120,000 km
Cruise control	7 years/140,000 km	Brake drum linings	35,000 km
Headlights (HID)	5 years/100,000 km	Brake rotor	60,000 km
Hybrid battery	10 years/no mileage	Brake calipers/pads	30,000 km
Power doors, windows	5 years/no mileage	Master cylinder	100,000 km
Power locks	8 years/no mileage	Wheel cylinder	80,000 km
Power seats	5 years/no mileage	**Engine and Drivetrain**	
Radiator	5 years/100,000 km		
Radio	7 years/no mileage	CV joint	6 years/120,000 km
Tire sensor	5 years/no mileage	Differential	7 years/140,000 km
Body		Engine (diesel)	15 years/300,000 km
		Engine (diesel) fuel pump	11 years/193,000 km
Door handles	10 years/160,000 km	Engine (diesel) NOx sensor	10 years/193,000 km
Liftgate struts	7 years/no mileage	Engine (gas)	7 years/140,000 km
Paint (peeling)	7–11 years/no mileage	Engine accessory power module	10 years/240,000 km
Rust (perforations)	15 years/no mileage		
Rust (surface)	5 years/no mileage	Engine block	10 years/no mileage
Water/wind/air leaks	5 years/no mileage	Engine control module	15 years/300,000 km
Brake System		Engine drivebelt (tensioner)	4 years/no mileage
ABS	100,000 km	Engine EGR bypass valve	10 years/193,000 km
ABS computer	10 years/200,000 km	Engine fuel flex sensor	10 years/240,000 km

REASONABLE DURABILITY (cont.)			
Engine and Drivetrain (cont.)		**Ignition System (cont.)**	
Engine fuel pump, module	10 years/193,000 km	Electronic module	5 years/100,000 km
Engine oxygen sensor	10 years/193,000 km	Retiming	20,000 km
Engine misfire, piston	8 years/no mileage	Spark plugs	20,000 km
Engine oil burning	10 years/193,000 km	Tune-up	20,000 km
Engine supercharger	10 years/193,000 km	**Safety Components**	
Engine turbocharger	7 years/140,000 km		
Engine water pump	10 years/240,000 km	Airbags	8 years/no mileage
Rear axle	4 years/no mileage	Airbag passenger sensors	15 years/no mileage
Transfer case	10 years/200,000 km	Seat belts	life of vehicle
Transmission, ECM	10 years/200,000 km	Stability control	5 years/100,000 km
Transmission (man.)	12 years/240,000 km	Tail lamp water leak	2 years/no mileage
Transmission oil cooler	10 years/240,000 km	**Steering and Suspension**	
Thrust bearing (new)	4 years/no mileage		
Torque converter clutch	10 years/193,000 km	Alignment	1 year/20,000 km
Exhaust System		Ball joints	10 years/200,000 km
		Coil springs	10 years/200,000 km
Catalytic converter	10 years/193,000 km	Power steering	10 years/240,000 miles
Exhaust manifold	10 years/193,000 km	Power steering hose	10 years/no mileage
Muffler	3 years/60,000 km	Power steering (Saturn 2003-09)	life of vehicle
Tailpipe	5 years/100,000 km		
Ignition System		Shock absorber	3 years/60,000 km
		Struts	5 years/100,000 km
Ignition key	10 years/no mileage	Tires (radial)	5 years/100,000 km
Ignition key (sticking)	15 years/no mileage	Truck tie-rod ends	5 years/100,000 km
Cable set	60,000 km	Wheel bearings	3 years/60,000 km

NOTE: Many of the above guidelines were copied from automaker service bulletin "campaigns," "goodwill" policies, and "product improvement" programs that OK'd payouts to thousands of dissatisfied customers over the past several decades. Other durability benchmarks come from out-of-court settlements and judgments that cite expert witnesses as to the reasonable durability of various vehicle components.

Let's use Honda as an example. Honda has a secret warranty extension covering engine blocks up to 10 years with no mileage limit (TSB #10-048). Another little-known warranty extension applies to engine misfiring and defective piston rings for 8 years/unlimited mileage due to Honda's settlement in *Soto v. American Honda Motor Co. Inc.* (Case No.3: 12-cv-1377-SI (N. D. Cal.)). Honda also will pay for paint defects up to 7 years with no mileage limit and power steering failures up to 10 years or 150,000 miles on 2006-09 Civics and Fits (TSB #14-058). Finally, 2007-09 CRV will get free door locks, even if the present ones aren't faulty with no time or mileage limitations (TSB #14-083).

With the exception of anti-lock brake systems (ABS), safety features generally have a lifetime warranty, but airbags are a different matter. Those that are deployed in an accident – and the personal injury and interior damage their deployment will likely have caused – are covered by your accident insurance policy. However, if there is a sudden deployment for no apparent reason, the automaker and dealer should be held jointly responsible for all injuries and damages caused by the airbag. Front seat side airbag inadvertent deployments are covered on 2008 Honda Accords in another court settlement up to December 2016 (TSB #14-023, May 24, 2014). You can confirm this defect through witnesses, photos, or by downloading data from your vehicle's data recorder (see Helpful Automobile Apps in Part One). This proof will likely lead to a more generous settlement from the dealer and automaker and prevent your insurance premiums from being jacked up. Be sure to use both the *Kravitz and Donoghue* judgments in holding the dealer and carmaker responsible for costs.

The Art of Complaining

Most Canadian consumers don't like to complain or get involved with the legal system. And, they have reason to be wary. Blood pressure rises, heated words are exchanged, and you always think of a better argument after the discussion is over.

Yet there are some complaint strategies that aren't hard to employ and can be successful.

Cold-calling

Phone the seller or automaker, but don't expect to get much out of the call. Private sellers won't want to talk with you, and service managers will simply apply the dealership's policy, knowing that 90 percent of complainers will drop their claims after venting their anger.

Still, try to work things out by contacting someone higher up who can change the policy to satisfy your request. In your attempt to reach a settlement, ask only for what is fair and don't try to make anyone look bad.

Speak in a calm, polite manner, and try to avoid polarizing the issue. Talk about cooperating to solve the problem. Let a compromise emerge – don't come in with a rigid set of demands. Don't insist on getting the settlement offer in writing, but make sure that you're accompanied by a friend or relative who can confirm the offer in court if it isn't honoured. Be prepared to act upon the offer without delay so that your hesitancy won't be blamed if the seller or automaker withdraws it.

Service manager help

Service managers have more power than you may realize. They make the first determination of what work is covered under warranty or through post-warranty "goodwill" programs, and they are directly responsible to the dealer and manufacturer for that decision (dealers hate manufacturer audits that force them to pay back questionable warranty decisions). Service managers are paid both to save the dealer and automaker money and to mollify irate clients – almost an impossible balancing act.

Nevertheless, when a service manager agrees to extend warranty coverage, it's because you've raised solid issues that neither the dealer nor the automaker can ignore. All the more reason to present your argument in a confident, forthright manner with your vehicle's service history and *Lemon-Aid*'s "Reasonable Part Durability" table in hand (above). Also, bring as many technical service bulletins (TSBs) and owner complaint printouts as you can find from National Highway Traffic Safety Administration's (NHTSA) website and similar sources. It's not important that they apply directly to your problem; they establish parameters for giving out after-warranty assistance, or "goodwill."

Don't use your salesperson as a runner, since the sales staff are generally quite distant from the service staff and usually have less pull than you do. If the service manager can't or won't set things right, your next step is to convene a mini-summit with the service manager, the dealership principal, and the automaker's service rep, if he or she represents that make. Regional service representatives are technicians who are regularly sent out by the manufacturer to help dealers with technical problems. By getting the automaker involved, you can often get an agreement where the seller and the automaker pay two-thirds of the repair cost, even when the vehicle was bought used.

Get an independent estimate

Dealers who sell a brand of vehicle used that they don't sell new will give you less latitude. You have to make the case that the vehicle's defects were present at the time of purchase or should have been apparent to the seller, or that the vehicle doesn't conform to the representations made when it was purchased. Emphasize that you intend to use the courts if necessary to obtain a refund – most sellers would rather settle than risk a lawsuit with all the attendant publicity. An independent estimate of the vehicle's defects and repair costs is essential if you want to convince the seller that you're serious in your claim and that you stand a good chance of winning your case in court. Come prepared with an estimated cost of repairs to challenge the dealer who agrees to pay half the repair costs and then jacks up the price 100 percent so that you wind up paying the whole shot.

Send a written complaint you can use in court

If you haven't sent a written claim letter, fax, or e-mail, you really haven't complained – or at least, that's the auto industry's mindset, often upheld by the courts. If your vehicle was misrepresented, has major defects, or wasn't properly repaired under warranty, the first thing you should do is give the seller a written summary of the outstanding problems or alleged misrepresentation and stipulate a time period within which the seller can fix the vehicle or refund your money.

If there are subsequent negotiations because a part isn't available or for other valid reasons, confirm the offer in a follow-up letter and issue another deadline. Should the second deadline pass without a satisfactory settlement, take your "paper trail" of letters and file a small claims court lawsuit.

Use the format of the following sample complaint letters that mirror most things that may go wrong. Add additional court decisions that bolster your complaint (see Cases to Consider, below).

Remember, you can ask for compensation for repairs that have been done or need to be done, insurance costs while the vehicle is being repaired, towing charges, supplementary transportation costs such as taxis and rented cars, and damages for inconvenience. If no satisfactory offer is made, ask for mediation, arbitration, or a formal hearing in your provincial small claims court. Make the manufacturer a party to the lawsuit, especially if the emissions warranty, a secret warranty extension, a safety recall campaign, or extensive chassis rusting is involved.

Product Complaint Letter/Email/Fax

Without Prejudice

Date

Seller, Manufacturer, or Distributor Name and Address

Dear Sir or Madam,

Please be advised that I am dissatisfied with my _____ that I bought from you for the following reasons:

1. _____ .
2. _____ .
3. _____ .

In compliance with Canadian consumer protection laws and the 'implied warranty' upheld by the Supreme Court of Canada in *Donoghue v. Stevenson and Kravitz v. GM*, I hereby request that these defects be repaired in the near future without charge, or the _____ taken back and my money refunded.

This product has not been reasonably durable, is not of merchantable quality, and is, therefore, not as represented to me.

Should you fail to repair these defects in a satisfactory manner and within a reasonable period of time, I reserve the right to have the repairs done elsewhere and claim reimbursement in court without further delay.

I also reserve my rights to punitive damages up to $1 million, pursuant to the Canadian Supreme Court's ruling in *Whiten v. Pilot* (February 22, 2002).

I believe your company wants to deal with its clients in an honest, competent manner and trust that my claim is the exception and not the rule.

A positive response within the next five (5) days would be appreciated.

Sincerely,

(signed with telephone number, email address, or fax number)

Service Complaint Letter/Email/Fax

Without Prejudice

Date

Seller or Service Provider Name and Address

Dear Sir or Madam,

Please be advised that I am dissatisfied with the following service you provided, namely _____ , for these reasons:

1. _____ .
2. _____ .
3. _____ .

You have not fulfilled our contract for services as specified. This is a clear violation of Canadian consumer protection laws as upheld by both common and civil law statutes. I hereby request that you correct the deficiencies without delay and respect the terms of our contract. Failing which, I want my money refunded.

If my request is denied, I reserve the right under *Sharman v. Ford*, Ontario Superior Court of Justice, No. 17419/02SR, 2003/10/07, to have the contracted work done elsewhere. I shall then claim reimbursement in court for that cost, plus punitive damages for my stress and inconvenience, without further delay, pursuant to the Canadian Supreme Court's ruling in *Whiten v. Pilot*.

I am sure you want to deal with your clients in an honest, competent manner and trust that my claim is the exception and not the rule.

A positive response within the next five (5) days would be appreciated.

Sincerely,

(signed with telephone number, email address, or fax number)

Fuel-Economy Misrepresentation

Without Prejudice

Date

Seller, Manufacturer, or Distributor Name and Address

Dear Sir or Madam,

Please be advised that I am dissatisfied with my _____ poor fuel economy. I bought this vehicle from you based upon your advertising that it would be fuel-efficient. It isn't. You indicated I could expect 12.7/8.3 L/100 km city/highway mileage but I am burning 14.7/10.3 L/100 km in careful, flat-highway driving.

I, therefore, seek $500 in compensation in compliance with *Sidney v. 1011067 Ontario Inc. (c.o.b. Southside Motors)* and provincial and federal misleading advertising statutes, upheld by the Supreme Court of Canada's recent award of punitive damages ($15,000) in *R. v. Time Inc.,* and ($10 million) in *R. v. Bell Canada.*

I also base my claim on the "implied warranty" of merchantability, and joint responsibility of automaker and dealer, also confirmed by the Supreme Court of Canada in *Donoghue v. Stevenson and Kravitz v. GM.*

This product is not as represented to me. Honda, in *Lockabey v. American Honda Motors,* Hyundai, and Kia have recently set up $200 owner refund programs and warranty extensions that compensate their customers misled by misrepresented fuel economy figures and faced with higher fuel costs. In *Paduano v. American Honda Motor Co., Inc.,* Honda later settled for $50,000, plus another $50,000 in attorneys' fees.

I also reserve my rights to punitive damages up to $1 million, pursuant to the Canadian Supreme Court's ruling in *Whiten v. Pilot* where an insurance settlement was unduly delayed.

I believe your company wants to settle these fuel-economy claims and move on. A positive response within the next five (5) days would be appreciated.

Sincerely,

(signed with telephone number, email address, or fax number)

Tire Defects or Premature Wear

Without Prejudice

Date

Seller, Manufacturer, or Distributor Name and Address

Dear Sir or Madam,

Please be advised that I am dissatisfied with my _____ that I bought from you for the following reasons:

1. _____.
2. _____.
3. _____.

In compliance with Canadian consumer protection laws and the "implied warranty" upheld by the Supreme Court of Canada in *Donoghue v. Stevenson, Kravitz v. GM,* Winnipeg Condominium v. Bird Construction *[1995] 1S.C.R.85* (negligence), and *Blackwood v. Ford Motor Company of Canada Ltd., 2006* (Provincial Court of Alberta, Civil Division; Docket: PO690101722; Registry: Canmore; 2006/12/08, I hereby request that the defective tire be replaced at no cost to me.

This product has not been reasonably durable, is not of merchantable quality, and is, therefore, not as represented to me.

Should you fail to deal with this claim in a satisfactory manner and within a reasonable period of time, I reserve the right to purchase a replacement from an independent retailer and claim reimbursement in court without further delay.

I also reserve my rights to punitive damages, pursuant to the Canadian Supreme Court's ruling in *Whiten v. Pilot* (February 22, 2002).

A positive response within the next five (5) days would be appreciated.

Sincerely,

(signed with telephone number, email address, or fax number)

Infotainment Device Failure

Without Prejudice

Date

Seller, Manufacturer, or Distributor Name and Address

Dear Sir or Madam,

Please be advised that I am dissatisfied with my car's Infotainment system _____ that I bought from you. This is what is wrong:

1. _____.
2. _____.
3. _____.

I want these defects repaired or my vehicle replaced and my money refunded under the "implied warranty" doctrine upheld by the Supreme Court of Canada in *Donoghue v. Stevenson, Kravitz v. GM,* and Winnipeg Condominium v. Bird Construction *[1995] 1S.C.R.85* (negligence). I also cite two pending class-actions: *Richards v. Ford Motor Co., Case No. 2:12-cv-00543 and Steven Rouse, et al. v. Ford Motor Company,* Case No. 11-CH-20581, Circuit Court of Cook County, Illinois, County Department, Chancery Division.

This product has not been reasonably durable, is not of merchantable quality, and is, therefore, not as represented to me.

Should you fail to satisfy my claim in a satisfactory manner and within a reasonable period of time, I reserve the right to have the repairs done elsewhere by an independent garage and claim reimbursement in court without further delay.

I also reserve my rights to punitive damages up to $1 million, pursuant to the Canadian Supreme Court's ruling in *Whiten v. Pilot* (February 22, 2002).

I believe your company wants to deal with its clients in an honest, competent manner and trust that my claim is the exception and not the rule.

A positive response within the next five (5) days would be appreciated.

Sincerely,

(signed with telephone number, email address, or fax number)

Mediation and Arbitration

If the formality of a courtroom puts you off, or you're not sure that your claim is all that solid and you don't want to pay legal costs to find out, consider using mediation or arbitration. These services are sponsored by the Better Business Bureau, the Automobile Protection Association, the Canadian Automobile Association, the Canadian Automobile Manufacturers Arbitration Plan, and by many small claims courts where compulsory mediation is a prerequisite to going to trial.

Beware of mandatory arbitration clauses

The Supreme Court of Canada in *Seidel v. Telus Communications Inc.* (2011 SCC 15), struck down mandatory arbitration clauses in "contracts of adhesion" in a narrow 5-4 split decision. Seidel signed a cell phone contract with TELUS and she was being charged for connection time and ring time instead of just the actual talking time. Seidel claimed that TELUS engaged in deceptive and unconscionable practices contrary to the British Columbia *Business Practices and Consumer Protection Act*. She also sought certification to act as a representative of a class of allegedly overcharged customers under the *Class Proceedings Act*.

Contracts of adhesion are standard form contracts drafted by sellers and signed by customers without negotiation and usually without even being read. The arbitration clauses say that in the event of a dispute, the parties agree to submit their dispute to arbitration rather than to the courts. Some provincial legislatures, however, have enacted laws to invalidate these arbitration clauses thereby allowing consumers to pursue class actions. Also, lower courts in several provinces have made rulings that invalidate arbitration clauses where they would prevent consumers from pursuing class proceedings.

Dealers and automakers favour arbitration because it's relatively inexpensive, decisions are rendered more quickly than through regular litigation, there is a less formalistic approach to the rules of evidence, jurisprudence isn't created, and they can dodge bad publicity.

The disadvantages to binding arbitration are many and include the following: Loss of recourse to the courts, no appeals, no jurisprudence to guide plaintiffs as to the rules of law used in prior decisions (which often leads to quicker settlements or encourages litigants to stand by their principles), and the chumminess that often develops between arbiters and dealer/automaker defendants who may meet often over similar issues throughout the year – a familiarity that breeds contempt.

Automakers want binding arbitration clauses in sales contracts because they can use them to oppose class actions related to their products and can more easily cover up design or production defects that are carried over year after year, since plaintiff's must file their cases individually and cannot pool their resources, or drum up media support.

Another drawback is that the defendant can refuse to take back the car or pay the cost of repairs simply by arguing that the arbitration process was flawed because the arbitrator exceeded his or her mandate. This objection puts the arbitration in the regular court system where each side has lawyers' fees and a final decision may take two years. This is what Ford of Canada did in refusing to take back a 2010 Focus that had abraded paint. Ford's appeal against the Canadian Motor Vehicle Arbitration Plan (CAMVAP) was tossed out of court.

Don't get the impression that binding arbitration is a useless tool to get redress. CAMVAP has worked fairly well with some new car disputes. On the other hand it proved woefully ineffective in resolving the "death wobble" on Dennis Warren's 2007 Dodge Ram 2500 (see *www.cbc.ca/m/touch/news/story/2011/05/16/bc-dodge problem.html*).

Using Government Agencies

"Zombie" Consumer Protection

Illusory consumer protection is created by legislation that defines consumer rights and obligations, but then sets up an enforcement branch that is ineffective for the purpose it was created. It is neither alive nor dead. It doesn't regulate nor deregulates. It's simply "there" – used as a "feel good" symbol of government's inactive action. Here's how a government "zombie" is created:

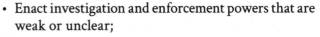

- Enact investigation and enforcement powers that are weak or unclear;
  - Ensure that investigation and enforcement are underfunded;
    - Keep civil penalties low and forego the use of criminal charges;
      - Choose staffers who were once employed by the industry to be regulated;
  - Don't lay charges if a sizeable charitable donation is made;
  - Channel settlement funds to lawyers and government, instead of to victims; and
- Set up an advisory board with limited powers and little knowledge of what's going on.

Seek Outside Help

Don't lose your case because of poor preparation or misleading advice. Ask government or trustworthy independent consumer protection agencies to evaluate how well you've prepared before going to your first hearing. Also, use the Internet to ferret out additional facts and gather support. (This guide's Appendix II listing of helpful website links is a good place to start.)

If there is no satisfactory response, *contact the media and register your complaint with the provincial government's consumer affairs ministry.* Ontario, for example, has a unique way of alerting businesses to your complaint by forwarding it with the government's own covering letter. In the government's letter the province's sly bureaucrats are careful to say they haven't initiated a *formal* investigation, yet – they are just passing on a consumer's complaint. Very subtle, eh?

What is most likely to stick in the letter recipient's mind is this paragraph:

> Where a Ministry investigation finds a violation of the Consumer Protection Act has occurred, charges may be laid. Successful prosecution under the CPA may result in fines of up to $50,000 for an individual or imprisonment for a term of not more than two years less a day or both and, if convicted, a corporation may be liable to a fine of not more than $250,000.

Ottawa will go one step further. Its online form solicits citizen reports of dishonest business practices. One such complaint lodged by *Lemon-Aid* and the Automobile Protection Association (APA) forced Toyota to settle a price-fixing investigation by giving $2 million to a Canadian charity, and a misleading advertising charge by the APA resulted in General Motors Canada paying a $20,000 fine after lying about its Firenza reliability.

Government investigators treat all information as confidential and look into allegations of price-fixing, misleading advertising, false weights and measures readings (such as car odometers), and a host of other prohibited activities – as described by the *Competition Act*, the *Consumer Packaging and Labelling Act*, the *Textile Labelling Act, and the Precious Metals Marking Act. Such complaints are administered by the Competition Bureau (see www.competitionbureau.gc.ca/eic/site/cbbc.nsf/frm-eng/GH%C3%89T-7TDNA5).*

But *what if you are ticked off about poor government service?* Well, the federal government has a bilingual free website for that, too. No kidding, it's called Service Canada (*www.servicecanada.gc.ca/eng/ocs*).

Pressure Tactics

It doesn't hurt to use independent, non-profit groups like the BBB, or other industry complaint agencies to get your claim resolved. Just don't expect rapid or consistent results. BBB offices throughout North America have come under fire over the years for being more a lap dog than a watch dog over business practices due to their close ties to business, as was the case in one television news expose that resulted in the closing of the Los Angeles (Southland) BBB office:

> The expulsion stems back to a pay-to-play scandal unearthed in 2010 by the ABC News show 20/20. The investigation showed extortion-type practices applied to local businesses: Those that paid annual dues to the BBB were handed accreditation and A ratings, while those that didn't play along were given subpar grades, even if they hadn't received complaints. Most

disturbingly, investigators were able to get accreditation and an A- grade for a fake, totally nonexistent business after paying a $425 fee to the local BBB. (The name of the dummy business was Hamas—yep, the same as the Middle Eastern terrorist organization.)

business.time.com/2013/03/19/why-the-better-business-bureau-should-give-itself-a-bad-grade/

You can put additional pressure on a seller or garage, and have fun at the same time, by putting a lemon sign on your car and parking it in front of the dealer or garage, by creating a "lemon" website, or by forming a self-help group. Angry Chrysler and Ford owners, for example, have received sizeable settlements in Canada by forming the Chrysler Lemon Owners Group (CLOG) and the Ford Lemon Owners Group (FLOG).

And get this: Apple Inc. co-founder Steve Wozniak repeatedly called Toyota over the course of several months to report brake failures with his Prius. Toyota officials ignored him. However, when he mentioned the problem in an aside during an Apple press conference, all hell broke loose. The company returned his call, apologized, fixed the car, and recalled thousands of others.

Use your website and social media (Twitter, Facebook, Yelp, etc.) to gather data from others who may have experienced a problem similar to your own. This can help you organize other auto owners for class action and small claims court lawsuits and it pressures the dealer or manufacturer to settle. Public demonstrations (picketing, decorating your car with lemons, etc.), websites and Twitter "buzz" often generate news stories that will take on a life of their own as others join the movement or add depth and breadth to the campaign.

Here's some more advice from this consumer advocate with hundreds of pickets and mass demonstrations under his belt. Keep a sense of humour, and never break off the negotiations. Flipping "the bird" to someone like Mercedes-Benz is counter-productive.

When you shell out $35,000 to $80,000 for a Lexus, you expect a quality-manufactured vehicle that's safe and lives up to the express warranty that it came with. If there is a flaw with your Lexus that reduces its value or that is a safety concern and the manufacturer has been unsuccessful in fixing it, you are likely entitled to damages under state and federal Lemon Laws.

Gaulitics (*www.gaulitics.com/2015/06/mercedes-benz-settlement-rips-off.html*) was set up to protest an MB engine settlement. Below is an "informational" protest site: *lemonlawexperts.com/lexus-repurchase-lemon-law/*. Courts generally rule that informational website are OK, while protest sites or signs that defame or interfere with customers' right to choose may be deemed illegal.

Finally, don't be scared off by threats that it's illegal to criticize a product or company. Unions, environmentalists, and consumer groups do it regularly (it's called informational picketing), and the Supreme Court of Canada in *R. v. Guinard* reaffirmed this right in February 2002 (see [2002] 1 S.C.R. 472). In that judgment, an insured posted a sign on his barn claiming the Commerce Insurance Company was unfairly refusing his claim. The municipality of Saint-Hyacinthe, Quebec, told him to take the sign down. He refused, maintaining that he had the right to state his opinion. The Supreme Court agreed.

This judgment means that consumer protests, signs, and websites that criticize the actions of corporations or government cannot be shut up or taken down simply because they say unpleasant things. However, what you say must be true, and your intent must be to inform, without malice.

Even if you do respectfully protest your treatment following a used car purchase from a dealer, on rare occasions that dealer may file suit against you for defamation or libel. Generally, Canadian courts take a dim view of consumers and non-government organizations, like unions and environmental groups, being sued for protesting, or even picketing. Nevertheless, some dealers will sue.

Fortunately, two other Supreme Court decisions buttress a citizen's right to engage in information protests or picketing. This assumes the protest is done without infringing upon the rights of others through actions such as assault, restricting access, defacing property, or harassing others.

The first decision overturned a lower court award of $1.5 million to a forestry executive who sued *The Toronto Star*. *The Star* alleged he had used political connections to get approval for a golf course expansion (*Grant v. Torstar Corp.*, [2009] 3 S.C.R. 640).

The Supreme Court struck down the judgment against the newspaper because that judgment had failed to give adequate weight to the value of freedom of expression. The court announced a new defense of "responsible communication on matters of public interest." In the court's opinion, anyone (journalists, bloggers, unions, picketers, etc.) can avoid liability if they can show that the information they communicated – whether true or false – was of public interest and they tried their best to verify it.

In another case, again involving a major Canadian newspaper, a former Ontario police officer sued *The Ottawa Citizen* after it reported he had misrepresented his search-and-rescue work at Ground Zero in New York City after the attacks of September 11, 2001. The Supreme Court reversed the $100,000 jury award because the judges felt the article was in the public interest (*Quan v. Cusson*, [2009] 3 S.C.R. 712).

Contact the Right People

Before we go any further, let's get one thing straight – a telephone call to a service manager or automaker may only be marginally effective. Auto manufacturers and their dealers want to make money, not give it back. Customer service advisors are paid to *apply* the warranty policy; don't expect them to *make* policy due to your claim's extenuating circumstances.

To get action, if you suspect a secret warranty applies or that your vehicle has an independently-confirmed factory-related defect, you have to kick your claim upstairs, where the company representatives have more power. This can usually be accomplished by sending your claim to the legal affairs department (typically found in Ontario). It should be a registered letter, fax, or e-mail – something that creates a paper trail and gets attention. What's more, that letter must contain the threat that you will use the implied warranty against the dealer and manufacturer and cite convincing jurisprudence to win your small claims court action in the same region where that business operates.

15 Legal "Tips" Lawyers Know

1. Don't Take NO for an Answer

There are a number of situations where a defect is clearly the auto manucturer's fault, yet, car owners's are capriciously denied assistance by customer affairs. Often, the owner is told to make an insurance claim.

Don't!

Here are five common failures where the automaker is at fault due to poor design, or poor-quality materials:

1. Airbag deploys when it shouldn't, or fails to deploy when it should.
2. Critters snack on engine compartment wiring and plastics.
3. AC compressor damaged by road debris.
4. Windshield or sunroof explodes without impact.
5. Paint cracks, peels, or delaminates.

As mentioned earlier, the manufacturer's or dealer's warranty is a written legal promise that a vehicle will be reasonably reliable, subject to certain conditions. Regardless of the number of subsequent owners, this promise remains in force as long as the warranty's original time/kilometre limits haven't expired. Tires aren't usually covered by car manufacturers' warranties; they're warranted instead by the tiremaker on a prorated basis. This isn't such a good deal, because the manufacturer is making a profit by charging you the full list price. If you were to buy the same replacement tire from a discount store, you'd likely pay less, without the prorated rebate.

But consumers have gained additional rights following Bridgestone/Firestone's massive recall in 2001 of its defective ATX II and Wilderness tires. Because of the confusion and chaos surrounding Firestone's handling of the recall, Ford's 575 Canadian dealers stepped into the breach and replaced the tires with any equivalent tires they had in stock, no questions asked. This is an important precedent that tears down the traditional wall separating tire manufacturers from automakers in product liability claims. In essence, whoever sells the product can now be held liable for damages. In the future, Canadian consumers will have an easier time holding the dealer, the automaker, and the tire manufacturer liable, not just for recalled products but also for any defect that affects the safety or reasonable durability of that product. This liability is one of the reasons why this year Honda replaced unsafe Takata airbags when the manufacturer dragged its feet – Honda had no choice.

This is particularly true now that the Supreme Court of Canada (*Winnipeg Condominium v. Bird Construction*, [1995] 1 S.C.R. 85) has ruled that defendants are liable in negligence for any designs that result in a risk to the public's safety or health. Sometimes automakers plead that their compliance with federal automobile safety laws immunizes them from product liability claims, but this argument has been shot down countless times by the courts. (Type "auto safety standards liability" into an Internet search engine.)

In the U.S., safety restraints such as airbags and safety belts have limited warranty coverage sometimes extended for the lifetime of the vehicle. In Canada, however, some automakers have tried to dodge this responsibility, alleging that they are separate entities, their vehicles are different, and no U.S. agreement or service bulletin can bind them. That distinction is both disingenuous and dishonest and wouldn't likely hold up in small claims court – probably the reason why most automakers relent when threatened with legal action.

Aftermarket products and services, such as gas-saving gadgets, rustproofing, and paint protectors, can render the manufacturer's warranty invalid, so make sure you're in the clear before purchasing any optional equipment or services from an independent supplier.

How fairly a warranty is applied is more important than how long it remains in effect. Once you know the normal wear rate for a mechanical component or body part, you can demand proportional compensation when you get less than normal durability – no matter what the original warranty says. Some dealers tell customers that they need to have original equipment parts installed in order to maintain their warranty. A variation on this theme requires that the selling dealer does routine servicing, including tune-ups and oil changes (with a certain brand of oil), or the warranty is invalidated. Nothing could be further from the truth. Canadian law stipulates that whoever issues a warranty cannot make that warranty conditional on the use of any specific brand of motor oil, oil filter, or any other component, unless it's provided to the customer free of charge.

Sometimes dealers will do all sorts of minor repairs that don't correct the problem, and then after the warranty runs out, they'll tell you that major repairs are needed. You can avoid this nasty surprise by repeatedly bringing your vehicle to the dealership before the warranty ends. During each visit, insist that a written work order include the specific nature of the problem, as you see it, and a statement that this is the second, third, or fourth time the same problem has been brought to the dealer's attention. Write this down yourself, if need be. This allows you to show a pattern of non-performance by the dealer during the warranty period and establishes that the problem is both serious and chronic. When the warranty expires, you have the legal right to demand that it be extended on those items consistently reappearing on your handful of work orders. *Lowe v. Fairview Chrysler* (see page 198) is an excellent judgment that reinforces this important principle. In another lawsuit, *François Chong v. Marine Drive Imported Cars Ltd. and Honda Canada Inc.* (see page 215), a Honda owner forced Honda to fix his engine six times – until they got it right.

A retired GM service manager suggests another effective tactic when you're not sure that a dealer's warranty "repairs" will actually correct the problem for a reasonable period of time after the warranty expires. Here's what he says you should do:

> When you pick up the vehicle after the warranty repair has been done, hand the service manager a note to be put in your file that says you appreciate the warranty repair, however, you intend to return and ask for further warranty coverage if the problem reappears before a reasonable amount of time has elapsed – even if the original warranty has expired. A copy of the same note should be sent to the automaker. ... Keep your copy of the note in the glove compartment as cheap insurance against paying for a repair that wasn't fixed correctly the first time.

2. Be Willing to Compromise

Winning litigants often end up losing their shirt after all the legal costs are included. This happens because once you are snared in the legal process, costs add up astronomically. Plus, the lawsuit can take on a life of its own and you may find yourself in too deep to drop the case. All the more reason to stay receptive to compromise motions from the other side. The old dictum that a fair compromise can be worth more than a winning judgment still holds true today.

3. Sue as a Last Resort

If the seller you've been negotiating with agrees to make things right, give him or her a deadline and then have an independent garage check the repairs. If no offer is made within ten working days, file suit in court. Make the manufacturer a party to the lawsuit only if the original, unexpired warranty was transferred to you; if your claim falls under the emissions warranty, a TSB, a secret warranty extension, or a safety recall campaign; or if there is extensive chassis rusting due to poor engineering and design, inferior paint, or improper paint application.

4. Choose the Right Court

You must decide what remedy to pursue: A partial refund (*quanti minoris*) or a cancellation of the sale. To determine the refund amount, add the estimated cost of repairing existing mechanical defects to the cost of prior repairs. Don't exaggerate your losses or claim for repairs that are considered routine maintenance listed in the owner's manual. If it's not listed, it's not *routine*. A suit for cancellation of sale should be thought out carefully since it involves a number of practical problems non-lawyers often ignore.

First, the court requires that the vehicle be "tendered," or taken back to the seller, at the time the lawsuit is filed. This means that you are without transportation for as long as the case continues, unless you purchase another vehicle in the interim. Secondly, after the five to seven years the case is appealed, if you lose, you must then take back the old vehicle, pay storage and expert witness fees, and pay back all of the monthly finance payemts. You could go from having no vehicle to having two, one of which is a clunker. Even if you win, you lose – about $5,000 to $10,000 for your own lawyer's fees. So, it's fair to ask – what did I really gain?

Generally, if the cost of repairs or the sales contract amount falls within the small claims court limit, file the case there to keep costs to a minimum and to get a speedy hearing. Small claims court judgments aren't easily appealed, lawyers aren't necessary, filing fees are minimal (about $125), and cases are usually heard within a few months.

Watch what you ask for. If you claim more than the small claims court limit, you'll have to go to a higher court, where court costs are Ebola-deadly and hearings are frequently delayed.

5. Can You Afford Justice?

The June 2009 issue of *The Canadian Lawyer* published a summary of average legal fees within Canada. From the following highlights of that article (*www. personal.umich.edu/~purzel/national_reports/Canada.pdf*), it is easy to see how difficult it would be for many Canadians to pay to have their "day in court" going through the regular court system.

- The average hourly fee for an Ontario lawyer with ten years experience was $382 – though some fees were as high as $900 per hour.

- The hourly fee for lawyers in the western provinces was $467.

- In Quebec, 2 percent of the profession was charging more than $500 per hour, with a further 1 percent at more than $400 (*Le Journal du Barreau du Québec*, May 2009).

- In Ontario, legal fees for a one-party, two-day trial would range from $18,738 to $90,404.
- The average cost (in Ontario) to each party in a two-day dispute would be $45,477.

Not surprisingly, litigants are fighting back by shunning lawyers and representing themselves, making contingency fee arrangements, asking for pay-as-you-go court costs, and searching out small claims courts where filing fees barely top $200 and lawyers are optional, if not barred entirely.

6. Find a Contingency-Fee Lawyer

Honest lawyers who see you are too poor to afford legal counsel but earn too much for legal aid will steer you toward a much cheaper contingency-fee lawyer to help you through the regular court system. In Canada contingency fees vary from 20-45 percent of the proceeds awarded, and the client pays nothing unless and until there is recovery in the lawsuit. This fee arrangement particularly suits plaintiffs with serious injury claims who likely have little income. All contingency fee agreements are subject to court review; however, the agreement you signed in the lawyer's office will carry a lot of weight as to your intentions. Note, however that *most contingency-fee agreements provide that although there is no legal fee payable if the case is lost, the client remains responsible for reimbursing the lawyer for disbursements paid out.*

There are many ways to structure a contingency-fee agreement that is fair to both client and lawyer. For example, one could provide for a percentage fee that decreases (or increases) depending on the level of financial recovery. In some Canadian personal injury and malpractice matters, a higher percentage is due on the first $100,000 awarded and a lower percentage on compensation recovered in excess of $100,000. *The contingency-fee percentage should apply to recovery less any costs awards.*

Another way to avoid excessive up-front legal costs is to ask the court to make provisional or interim costs orders as a means of financing the suit. This may be granted where the plaintiff cannot afford the litigation, appears to have a meritorious claim, and raises issues of public importance (*British Columbia [Minister of Forests] v. Okanagan Indian Band* [2003] 43 C.P.C. [5th] 1).

Watch out for unexpected legal expenses like "Court Costs" that come at the end of the trial. Although filing fees are quite low, a successful litigant's disbursements may be charged to the losing party. These can include costs of effecting service; expenses for travel, accommodation, and photocopying; witness expenses; and experts' reports. An unsuccessful party may also have to pay a self-represented successful party an amount as compensation for inconvenience and expense. If that plaintiff is represented by a lawyer, the court may award the winning side a reasonable representation fee at trial or at an assessment hearing.

7. Favour Small Claims Court

Crooked automakers scurry away from small claims courts like cockroaches from bug spray, not because the courts can issue million-dollar judgments or force litigants to spend millions in legal fees (they can't), but because they can award sizeable sums to plaintiffs ($25,000-$30,000) and make jurisprudence that other judges on the same bench are likely to follow.

Legal scholars look down their nose at small claims judgments, affirming that small claims decisions don't make "case" law or jurisprudence binding other magistrates. They are wrong. They are scholars, not judges, nor litigants.

It is *Lemon-Aid*'s experience, over 45-years, following thousands of lawsuits, that small claims judges discuss cases with their peers and develop a common perception relative to similar lawsuits. It happened with hundreds of prematures rusting and paint delamination complaints, as well as Ford and Nissan's "redating" of year-old vehicles as new, current models. In fact, both of these small claims collective actions (rust and redating) were upheld in two separate judgements by our Supreme Court. How's that for jurisprudence?

In Prebushewski v. Dodge City Auto (1985) Ltd. and Chrysler Canada Ltd., the Supreme Court ordered Chrysler to pay $25,000 in punitive damages for denying a Saskatoon Dodge Ram owner's refund request.

And small claims doesn't necessarily mean "small" judgments. For example, in *Dawe v. Courtesy Chrysler* (Dartmouth Nova Scotia Small Claims Court; SCCH #206825; July 30, 2004), Judge Patrick L Casey, Q.C., rendered an impressive 21-page decision citing key automobile product liability cases over the past 80 years. He awarded $5,037 to the owner of a new 2001 Cummins-equipped Ram pickup that suffered from myriad ailments. The truck shifted erratically, lost braking ability, wandered all over the road, lost power or jerked and bucked, bottomed out when passing over bumps, allowed water to leak into the cab, produced a burnt-wire and oil smell as the lights would dim, and produced a rear-end whine and wind noise around the doors and under the dash. Dawe had sold the vehicle and reduced his claim to meet the small claims threshold.

Small Claims Courts in Canada

There are small claims courts in most counties of every province, and you can make a claim either in the county where the problem happened or in the county where the defendant lives and conducts business. Simply go to the small claims court office and ask for a claim form. Instructions on how to fill it out accompany the form. Remember, you must identify the defendant correctly, and this may require some help from the court clerk or a law student because some automakers name local attorneys to handle suits (look for other recent lawsuits naming the same party). Crooks often change their company's name to escape liability; for example, it would be impossible to sue Joe's Garage (2008) if your contract is with Joe's Garage Inc. (2004).

Use the Maximum Limits for Small Claims Courts table to check your provincial or territorial court's website for specific rules and restrictions. Also, save time by downloading claim forms and other documents from the Internet (Google "small claims court Ontario," for example).

Claim Limits for Small Claims Courts

Province	Claim Maximum	Province	Claim Maximum
Alberta	$25,000	Nunavut	$20,000
British Columbia	$25,000	Ontario	$25,000
Manitoba	$10,000	Prince Edward Island	$8,000
New Brunswick	$12,500	Quebec	$15,000
Nova Scotia	$25,000	Saskatchewan	$20,000
Northwest Territories	$36,000	Yukon	$25,000

It is also important to note the following information:

- Plaintiffs with claims exceeding the maximum allowed may abandon the excess portion.

- Disputes involving title to land, slander, libel, bankruptcy, false imprisonment, or malicious prosecution must be handled in a superior court.
- In Quebec, people who appear before the Small Claims Division represent themselves, without a lawyer, and appeals are limited.

It wouldn't hurt to hire a lawyer or a paralegal for a brief walk-through of small claims court procedures to ensure that you've prepared your case properly and that you know what objections the other side will likely raise. If you'd like a lawyer to do all the work for you, there are a number of law firms around the country that specialize in small claims litigation. "Small claims" doesn't mean small legal fees, however. In Toronto, some law offices charge a flat fee of $1,500 for a basic small claims lawsuit and trial.

Remember that you're entitled to bring to court any evidence relevant to your case, including original copies of written documents such as contracts, letters, or bills of sale or receipts. If your car has developed severe rust problems, bring a photograph (signed and dated by the photographer) to court. You may also have witnesses testify in court. It's important to discuss a witness's testimony prior to the court date. If a witness can't attend the court date, he or she can write a report and sign it for representation in court. This situation usually applies to an expert witness, such as an independent mechanic who has evaluated your car's problems. Remember, however, that signed documents presented without a witness to guaranty their authenticity or to submit to cross-examination can be easily thrown out.

If you lose your case, some small claims court statutes allow a retrial, at a nominal cost, in exceptional circumstances. If a new witness has come forward, additional evidence has been discovered, or key documents that were previously not available have become accessible.

Finally in small claims court where informality and mediation rule, don't be a smart-aleck, and, above all, don't mouth off to the judge. Although an award of costs in small claims court, other than disbursements, should not exceed 15 percent of the amount claimed, a pissed-off presiding judge may increase the costs to penalize a party or a party's representative for unreasonable behaviour during the proceeding. Stay cool and let the facts carry the day.

Justice Marvin A. Zuker's *Ontario Small Claims Court Practice 2015* (Carswell, 2014) serves as an excellent reference full of tips on filing, pleading, and collecting a judgment. Judge Zuker's annual publication is easily understood by non-lawyers and uses court decisions from across Canada to help you plead your case successfully in any Canadian court.

Alan MacDonald, a *Lemon-Aid* reader won his small claims court case by presenting important facts and jurisprudence. Here's how he describes the experience (*MacDonald v. Highbury Ford Sales Limited*, Ontario Superior Court of Justice in the Small Claims Court London, June 6, 2000, Court File #0001/00, Judge J. D. Searle):

In 1999 after only 105,000 km the automatic transmission went. I took [my 1994 Ford Taurus wagon] to Highbury Ford to have it repaired. We paid $2,070 to have the transmission fixed, but protested and felt the transmission failed prematurely. We contacted Ford, but to no avail: their reply was we were out of warranty period. The transmission was so poorly repaired (and we went back to Highbury Ford several times) that we had to go to Mr. Transmission to have the transmission fixed again nine months later at a further $1,906.02. ....

My observations with going through small claims court involved the following: I filed in January of 2000, the trial took place on June 1 and the judgment was issued June 6.

At pretrial, a representative of Ford (Ann Sroda) and a representative from Highbury Ford were present. I came with one binder for each of the defendants, the court, and one for myself (each binder was about 3 inches thick – containing your reports on Ford Taurus automatic transmissions, ALLDATA Service Bulletins, [and extracts from the following websites:] Taurus Transmissions Victims (Bradley website), Center for Auto Safety ... Read This Before Buying a Taurus ... and the Ford Vent Page ....

The representative from Ford asked a lot of questions (I think she was trying to find out if I had read the contents of the information I was relying on). The Ford representative then offered a 50 percent settlement based on the initial transmission work done at Highbury Ford. The release allowed me to still sue Highbury Ford with regards to the necessity of going to Mr. Transmission because of the faulty repair done by the dealer. Highbury Ford displayed no interest in settling the case, and so I had to go to court.

For court, I prepared by issuing a summons to the manager at Mr. Transmission, who did the second transmission repair, as an expert witness. ... Next, I went to the law school library in London and received a great deal of assistance in researching cases pertinent to car repairs. I was told that judgments in your home province (in my case, Ontario) were binding on the court; that cases outside of the home province could be considered, but not binding, on the judge.

The cases I used for trial involved *Pelleray v. Heritage Ford Sales Ltd.*, Ontario Small Claims Court (Scarborough) SC7688/91 March 22, 1993; *Phillips et al. v. Ford Motor Co. of Canada Ltd. et al, Ontario* Reports 1970, 15th January 1970; *Gregorio v. Intrans-Corp.*, Ontario Court of Appeal, May 19, 1994; *Collier v. MacMaster's Auto Sales*, New Brunswick Court of Queen's Bench, April 26, 1991; *Sigurdson v. Hillcrest Service & Acklands (1977)*, Saskatchewan Queen's Bench; *White v. Sweetland*, Newfoundland District Court, Judicial Centre of Gander, November 8, 1978; *Raiches Steel Works v. J. Clark & Son*, New Brunswick Supreme Court, March 7, 1977; *Mudge v. Corner Brook Garage Ltd.*, Newfoundland Supreme Court, July 17, 1975; *Sylvain v. Carroseries d'Automobiles Guy Inc. (1981)*, C.P. 333, Judge Page; and *Gagnon v. Ford Motor Company of Canada, Limited et Marineau Automobile Co. Ltée. (1974)*, C.S. 422–423.

In court, I had prepared the case, as indicated above, and had my expert witness and two other witnesses who had driven the vehicle (my wife and my 18-year-old son). As you can see by the judgment, we won our case and I was awarded $1,756.52, including prejudgment interest and costs.

8. Reject Unfair Contract Clauses

Don't let anyone tell you that contracts and warranties are iron-clad and cannot be broken. In fact, a judge can cancel an unfair sales contract or extend your warranty at any time, even though corporate lawyers spend countless hours protecting their clients with one-sided standard-form contracts. Judges look upon these agreements, called "contracts of adhesion," with a great deal of skepticism. They know these loan documents, insurance contracts, automobile leases, and guarantees grant consumers little or no bargaining power. So when a dispute arises over terms or language, provincial consumer protection statutes require that judges interpret these contracts in the way most favourable to the consumer. Simply put, ignorance can sometimes be a good defence.

9. Avoid Hearsay and Annoying Courtroom Tactics

Judges have considerable latitude in allowing hearsay evidence if it's introduced properly. But it is essential that printed evidence and/or witnesses (relatives are not excluded) be available to confirm that a false representation actually occurred, that a part is failure-prone, or that its replacement is covered by a secret warranty or internal service bulletin alert. If you can't find an independent expert, introduce this evidence through the automaker reps and dealership service personnel who have to be at the trial anyhow. They know all about the service bulletins and extended warranty programs cited in *Lemon-Aid* and will probably contradict each other, particularly if they are excluded from the courtroom prior to testifying. Incidentally, you may wish to have the court clerk send a subpoena requiring the deposition of the documents you intend to cite, all warranty extensions relevant to your problem, and other lawsuits filed against the company for similar failures. This will make the fur fly in Oshawa, Oakville, and Windsor, and will likely lead to an out-of-court settlement. Sometimes, the service manager or company representative will make key admissions if questioned closely by you, a court mediator, or the trial judge. Here are three important questions to ask:

1. Is this a common problem?
2. Do you recognize this service bulletin?
3. Is there a case-by-case "goodwill" plan covering this repair?

Automakers often blame owners for having pushed their vehicle beyond its limits. Therefore, when you seek to cancel the contract or get repair work reimbursed, it's essential that you get an independent mechanic or your co-workers to prove the vehicle was well maintained and driven prudently.

10. Complain Early ("Reasonable Diligence")

When asking for a refund, keep in mind the "reasonable diligence" rule that requires that a suit be filed within a reasonable amount of time after the purchase, repair, accident, or personal knowledge that a secret warranty applies. Because many factory-related deficiencies take years to appear, the courts have ruled that the reasonable diligence clock starts clicking only after the defect is confirmed to be manufacturer- or dealer-related (powertrain, paint, etc.). For powertrain components like engines and transmissions, this allows you to make a claim seven to ten years after the vehicle was originally put into service, regardless of whether it was bought new or used. Body failures like paint delamination (see *Frank v. GM*) are reimbursable for up to 11 years; severe rusting for up to 15 years. If there have been negotiations with the dealer or the automaker, or if either the dealer or the automaker has been promising to correct the defects for some time or has carried out repeated unsuccessful repairs, the deadline for filing the lawsuit can be extended.

11. Ask for Exemplary, Punitive Damages

Yes, you can claim for hotel and travel costs or compensation for general inconvenience. Fortunately, when legal action is threatened, usually through small claims court, automakers quickly up their out-of-court offer to include most of the owner's expenses because they know the courts will be far more generous. For example, a British Columbia court's decision gave $2,257 for hotel and travel costs, and then capped it off with a $5,000 award for "inconvenience and loss of enjoyment of their luxury vehicle" to a motorist who was fed up with his lemon Cadillac (see *Wharton v. Tom Harris Chevrolet Oldsmobile Cadillac Ltd. and General Motors of Canada Limited*; B.C. Supreme Court, Vancouver; 1999/12/02; Docket C982104). In the *Sharman v. Ford* case (see page 211), the judge gave the plaintiff $7,500 for "mental distress" caused by the fear that his children would fall out of his 2000 Windstar equipped with a faulty sliding door.

As of March 19, 2005, the Supreme Court of Canada confirmed that car owners can ask for punitive, or exemplary, damages when they feel the seller's or the automaker's conduct has been so outrageously bad that the court should protect society by awarding a sum of money large enough to dissuade others from engaging in similar immoral, unethical conduct. In *Prebushewski v. Dodge City Auto (1984) Ltd. and Chrysler Canada Ltd.* (2001 SKQB 537; QB1215/99JCS), the plaintiff got $25,000 in a judgment handed down December 6, 2001, in Saskatoon. The award followed testimony from Chrysler's expert witness that the company was aware of many cases where daytime running lights shorted and caused 1996 Ram pickups to catch fire. The plaintiff's truck had burned to the ground, and Chrysler refused the owner's claim, saying it had fulfilled its expressed warranty obligations, in spite of its knowledge that fires were commonplace. The plaintiff sued on the grounds that there was an implied warranty that the vehicle would be safe. Justice Rothery gave this stinging rebuke in his judgment against Chrysler and its dealer:

> Not only did Chrysler know about the problems of the defective daytime running light modules, it did not advise the plaintiff of this. It simply chose to ignore the plaintiff's requests for compensation and told her to seek recovery from her insurance company. Chrysler had replaced thousands of these modules since 1988. But it had also made a business decision to neither advise its customers of the problem nor to recall the vehicles to replace the modules. While the cost would have been about $250 to replace each module, there were at least one million customers. Chrysler was not prepared to spend $250 million, even though it knew what the defective module might do.
>
> Counsel for the defendants argues that this matter had to be resolved by litigation because the plaintiff and the defendants simply had a difference of opinion on whether the plaintiff should be compensated by the defendants. Had the defendants some dispute as to the cause of the fire, that may have been sufficient to prove that they had not willfully violated this part of the *Act*. They did not. They knew about the defective daytime running light module. They did nothing to replace the burned truck for the plaintiff. They offered the plaintiff no compensation for her loss. Counsel's position that the definition of the return of the purchase price is an arguable point is not sufficient to negate the defendants' violation of this part of the *Act*. I find the violation of the defendants to be willful. Thus, I find that exemplary damages are appropriate on the facts of this case.
>
> In this case, the quantum ought to be sufficiently high as to correct the defendants' behaviour. In particular, Chrysler's corporate policy to place profits ahead of the potential danger to its customers' safety and personal property must be punished. And when such corporate policy includes a refusal to comply with the provisions of the *Act* and a refusal to provide any relief to the plaintiff, I find an award of $25,000 for exemplary damages to be appropriate. I therefore order Chrysler and Dodge City to pay: Damages in the sum of $41,969.83; Exemplary damages in the sum of $25,000; Party and party costs.

12. Make Dealers Honour Third-Party Warranties

When a company goes bankrupt, its extended warranties become worthless unless successfully litigated. At best, payouts will be parsimonious. Supplementary warranties providing extended coverage may be sold by the manufacturer, the dealer, or an independent third party and are automatically transferred when the vehicle is sold. They cost between $1,500 and $2,000 and are usually a waste of money. You can protect yourself better by steering clear of vehicles that have a reputation for being unreliable or expensive to service (see Part Four ratings), and using the threat of small claims courts when factory-related trouble arises. Don't let the dealer pressure you into deciding right away.

Generally, you can purchase an extended warranty any time during the period in which the manufacturer's warranty is in effect or, in some cases, shortly after buying the vehicle from a used-car dealer. An automaker's supplementary warranty will likely cost about a third more than warranties sold by independents. And in some parts of the country, notably B.C., dealers have a quasi-monopoly on selling warranties, with little competition from the independents.

Dealers love to sell extended warranties, whether you need them or not, because dealer markup represents up to 60 percent of the warranty's cost. Out of the remaining 40 percent comes the sponsor's administration costs and profit margin, calculated at another 15 percent. What's left to pay for repairs is a paltry 25 percent of the original amount. The only reason that automakers and independent warranty companies haven't been busted for this Ponzi scheme is that only half of the car buyers who purchase extended service contracts actually use them.

It's often difficult to collect on supplementary warranties because independent companies frequently go out of business or limit the warranty's coverage through subsequent mailings. Provincial laws cover both situations. If the bankrupt warranty company's insurance policy won't cover your claim, take the dealer to small claims court and ask for repair costs and the refund of the original warranty payment. Your argument for holding the dealer responsible is a simple one. By accepting a commission to act as an agent of the defunct company, the dealer took on the obligations of the company as well. As for limiting the coverage after you have bought the warranty policy, this is illegal, and it allows you to sue both the dealer and the warranty company for a refund of both the warranty and the repair costs.

13. Enforce "Secret" Warranties

Ford Focuses and Escapes with steering issues, GM's biodegrable catalytic converters, Honda's overheating engines and paint delamination, Nissan's glitch-prone CVT trannies, Toyotas needing new pistons and rings, and VWs that leak when it rains are only a few of the hundreds of car models covered by service bulletin "secret" warranties unearthed by *Lemon-Aid*.

Lawyers know manufacturers are reluctant to make free repair programs public because they feel that doing so would increase their legal liability. The closest they come to an admission is sending a "goodwill program," or "special customer service policy" TSB to dealers or first owners of record. Consequently, the only motorists who find out about these policies are the original owners who haven't changed their addresses or leased their vehicles. The other motorists who get compensated for repairs are the ones who read *Lemon-Aid* each year, staple TSBs to their work orders, and yell the loudest.

Remember, vehicles bought used and repairs done by independent garages are included in these secret warranty programs. Large, costly repairs, such as blown engines, burned transmissions, and peeling paint, are often covered. Even mundane little repairs, which can still cost you $100 or more, are frequently included in these programs. If you have a TSB but you're still refused compensation, keep in mind that secret warranties are an admission of manufacturing negligence. Owners who have been refused compensation should send an e-mail claim to the automaker and selling dealer and then file a small-claims court claim if no settlement is reached within a week.

14. Demand Recall Compensation

Following the government bailout of Chrysler and GM in 2009 most auto industry pundits predicted that automobile quality would improve and safety-related defects would decline. Wrong. Almost half of the 30 million recall notices sent out to General Motors customers in 2014 disproportionately involved vehicles made within the last few years rather than defects affecting GM's "old" pre-bankruptcy lineup.

As of October 2014, 51 of GM's 78 recalls covered 2014- or 2015-model year vehicles. Twelve of the recalls affected recently built Chevrolet Silverado and GMC Sierra pickups, making them the most frequently recalled pickups. They were also recalled three times in 2013, for a total of 15 callbacks since their introduction, which was hailed by then-CEO Dan Akerson, as "probably our best launch ever."

Vehicles are recalled for one of two reasons. Either they are potentially unsafe or they don't conform to federal pollution control regulations, like Volkswagen's recent diesel emissions confession. Whatever the reason, recalls are a great way to get free repairs and other compensation – if you know which ones apply to you and you have the patience of Job. NHTSA says about 25 percent of the recalled vehicles never made it back to the dealership for repairs, because owners were never informed, didn't consider the defect to be that hazardous, or gave up waiting for corrective parts.

Carmakers usually limit their safety or emissions recall to simply fixing the problem for free. But, lawyers know that the recall notice is an admission of negligence by the dealer and manufactuer. From that admission flows the obligation to reimburse the affected car owner for supplementary transportation, missed vacation, insurance premiums paid while car was in the shop, and an additional amount for the owner's time spent and inconvenience.

If you've moved or bought a used vehicle, it's smart to pay a visit to your local dealership, give them your address, and get a report card on which recalls, warranties, and free service campaigns apply to your vehicle. Simply give the service advisor the vehicle identification number – found on your insurance card, or on your dash just below the windshield on the driver's side – and have the number run through the automaker's computer system. Ask for a computer printout of the vehicle's history (have it e-mailed to you or a friend), and make sure you're listed in the automaker's computer as the new owner. This ensures that you'll receive notices of warranty extensions and emissions and safety recalls.

In order to cut recall costs, many automakers try to limit a recall to vehicles in a certain designated region. This practice doesn't make sense, since cars are mobile and an unsafe, rust-cankered steering unit can be found anywhere, not just in certain rust-belt provinces or American states. For instance, in 2001, Ford attempted to limit to five American states its recall of faulty Firestone tires. Public ridicule of the company's proposal led to an extension of the recall throughout North America.

Car companies hate to admit their mistakes because they know that lawsuits and bad publicity will inevitably ensue. Automobile manufacturers and dealers take a restrictive view of what constitutes a manufactured safety or emissions defect and frequently charge for repairs that should be free under federal safety or emissions legislation. To counter this tendency, look at the chart of Reasonable Part Durability (above). If you experience similar problems, insist that the automaker fix the problem at no expense to yourself, including paying for a car rental while corrective repairs are done.

Recall campaigns in the U.S. force automakers to pay the entire cost of fixing a vehicle's safety-related defect for any vehicle purchased up to eight years before the recall's announcement. A reasonable period beyond that time is usually a slam dunk in small claims court. In Canada, there is no specific time limit.

Voluntary recall campaigns are a real problem, though. The government doesn't monitor the notification of owners; dealers and automakers routinely deny there's a recall, thereby dissuading most claimants; and the company's so-called fix, not authorized by any governing body, may not correct the hazard at all. Also, the voluntary recall may leave out many of the affected models, or unreasonably exclude certain owners. Think of GM's voluntary ignition-switch fiasco this year that prompted a mandatory federal safety recall.

15. Use "Black Box" Snitches

If your car has an airbag, it's probably spying on you. And if you get into an accident caused by a mechanical malfunction, you will be glad that it is.

Event data recorders (EDRs) the size of a VCR tape have been hidden near the engine, under the seat, or in the centre consoles of airbag-equipped vehicles since the early '90s. To find out if your car or truck carries an EDR, read your owner's manual, contact the regional office of your car's manufacturer, or go to any dealer or independent garage.

Data recorders operate in a similar fashion to flight data recorders used in airplanes. They record data from the last five seconds before impact, including the force of the collision, the airbag's performance, when the brakes were applied, engine and vehicle speed, gas pedal position, and whether the driver was wearing a seat belt.

EDRs are an excellent tool to assess culpability in criminal and civil trials. Car owners who wish to dispute criminal charges, oppose their insurer's decision as to fault, or hold an automaker responsible for a safety device's failure (airbags, seat belts, or brakes) will find this data invaluable.

Getting EDR Data

Access your vehicle's EDR data using one of the smartphone Apps listed in Part 1 under "Helpful Automobile Apps". In the past, automakers have systematically hidden their collected data from government and insurance researchers, citing concerns for drivers' privacy. This argument, however, has been roundly rejected by law enforcement agencies, the courts, and car owners who need the independent information to prove negligence in court (see *www.harristechnical.com/downloads/cdrlist.pdf).*

Car owners, rental agencies, and fleet administrators are also using EDR data to pin legal liability on automakers for accidents caused by the failure of safety components, such as airbags that don't deploy when they should (or do deploy when they shouldn't) and anti-lock brakes that don't brake.

KEY COURT DECISIONS

The following Canadian and U.S. lawsuits and judgments cover typical problems that are likely to arise. Use them as leverage when negotiating a settlement or as a reference should your claim go to trial. Legal principles applying to Canadian and American law are similar; Quebec court decisions, however, may be based on legal principles that don't apply outside of that province. Nevertheless, you can find a comprehensive listing of Canadian decisions from small claims courts all the way to the Supreme Court of Canada at *www.legalresearch.org or www.canlii.org.*

You can find additional court judgments in the legal reference section of your city's main public library or at a nearby university law library. Ask the librarian for help in choosing the court decisions that best support your claim. LexisNexis (*www.lexisnexis.com*) and FindLaw (*www.findlaw.com*) are two useful Internet sites for legal research. Their main drawback, though, is that you may need to subscribe or use a friendly student's or lawyer's password to access jurisprudence on these sites. Check out your local library to see what online databases you can access with your library card. Lawsource, LexisNexis and other current resources will help you find Canadian legislation, case law, commentaries, and much more. Sometimes, just inserting the appropriate latin phrases in Google will bring up additional Canadian case law.

Legal Phrases You Should Know

When using our courts, it's a good idea to be trilingual, with a good knowledge of English, French, and *Legalese*. The following phrases are ones that you are mostly likely to encounter when filing or pleading a lawsuit:

- *Audi alteram partem* (Hear the other side). This is most often used to refer to the principle that no person should be judged without a fair hearing in which each party is given the opportunity to respond to the evidence against him or her.

- *Caveat emptor* (Let the buyer beware). Purchasers are responsible for checking whether goods suit their needs. This concept ruled the consumer protection movement until the publication of Ralph Nader's *Unsafe at Any Speed* in the '60s. That book, which exposed the design deficiencies of GM's Corvair, argued that more effective legislation was needed to forge a "seller beware" mindset. British Columbia, Saskatchewan, and Quebec were the first provinces to apply this doctrine in legislation relative to automobile warranties and the interpretation of what is reasonable durability.

- *Ex post facto* law (From after the action). A law that retroactively changes the legal consequences (or status) of actions committed or relationships that existed prior to the enactment of the law. This phrase is used to describe unfair laws that seek to punish retroactively.

- *Ignorantia juris non excusat* (Ignorance of the law excuses no one). A legal principle holding that a person who is unaware of a law may not escape responsibility for violating that law.

- *Pro bono publico* (For the public good). The term is generally used to describe professional work undertaken voluntarily, and without payment.

- *Mens rea* (A guilty mind). This goes to the defendant's intent, and is considered one of the necessary elements of a crime.

- *Quanti minoris* (A reduced amount, or diminished value). A partial refund may be claimed based upon the reduced value of a product caused by the manufacturer's or seller's negligence or misrepresentation.

  This principle was used successfully against Nissan and Ford of Canada by the Automobile Protection Association (APA) in hundreds of small claims court cases during the '70s. Refunds of up to $300 were awarded as compensation to buyers who were sold "redated" new vehicles that were the previous year's model. Nissan appealed the awards to the Supreme Court of Canada, claiming small claims courts were unconstitutional because lawyers were barred from pleading. A second argument was that the small claims courts lacked jurisdiction because the proper remedy was a cancellation of the sale. This would have taken the cases out of the courts' $300 maximum jurisdiction. The Supreme Court rejected both arguments (see *Nissan v. Pelletier and St.-Onge v. Nissan*).

- *Ratio decidendi* (The point in a case which determines the judgment, or the principle which the case establishes).

- *Res ipsa loquitur* (The thing speaks for itself). The elements of duty of care and breach can be sometimes inferred from the very nature of an accident or other outcome, even without direct evidence of how any defendant behaved.

- *Restitutio in integrum* (Restoration to the original condition). This is one of the primary guiding principles behind the awarding of damages in common law negligence claims. The general rule is that the amount of compensation awarded should put the successful plaintiff in the position he or she would have been in had the wrongful action not been committed. Thus, the plaintiff should clearly be awarded damages for direct expenses, such as medical bills, property repairs, and the loss of future earnings attributable to the injury (which often involves difficult speculation about future career and promotion prospects). This is also a term used to describe how far insurance companies must go in repairing accident damage.

Finally, I get asked this one all the time: What's the latin phrase for "sue the bastards?" There are two directions to go with this – literally: *"Endum adulteri"* or prosaic: *Illegitimi non carborundum*, or "Don't let the bastards grind you down."

CASES TO CONSIDER

Class Actions

A class action is a special form of lawsuit in which one plaintiff brings a claim against one or more defendants based on allegations that are common to a group, or class, of people. In order for the action to become a class action, it must proceed through a stage known as "certification."

Canadian automobile class actions often copy U.S. judgments or settlements and are usually settled out of court. However, 28 price-fixing class action lawsuits have been consolidated in a suit for $700 million. These suits have been filed by Canadian auto dealers against parts suppliers and are scheduled for "certification" November 16, 2015. Defendants, Yazaki, Denso, and Furukawa, paid US$748 million in criminal fines in the United States several years ago for their role in price-fixing and bid-rigging conspiracies related to the sale of wire harnesses, fuel senders, instrument panel clusters, electronic control units, and heater control panels. Two law firms are leading the charge: Toronto-based Sotos LLP (*info@sotosllp.com*) and Siskinds LLP in London, Ontario (*www.siskinds.com/*).

Some Canadian law firms who have been successful in automobile class actions:

Stevensons LLP
144 Front Street, Suite 400
Toronto, ON M5J 2L7
Phone: 416-599-7900
(647-847-3811)
E-mail: *cstevenson@stevensonlaw.net*
bkirkland@stevensonlaw.net

Koskie Minsky LLP
20 Queen Street West,
Suite 900, Box 52
Toronto, Ontario, M5H 3R3
Phone: (416) 977-8353
Class Actions Department
Kirk Baert: *kbaert@kmlaw.ca*

Automatic Transmission Failures (Chrysler)

Lowe v. Fairview Chrysler-Dodge Limited and Chrysler Canada Limited (No. 1224/95; Ontario Court, General Division; Burlington Small Claims Court; May 14, 1996): This judgment, in the plaintiff's favour, raises important legal principles relative to Chrysler.

- TSBs are admissible in court to prove that a problem exists and that certain parts should be checked out.
- If a problem is reported prior to a warranty's expiration, warranty coverage for the problematic component(s) is automatically carried over after the warranty ends.
- It's not up to the car owner to tell the dealer/automaker what the specific problem is.
- Repairs carried out by an independent garage can be refunded if the dealer/automaker unfairly refuses to apply the warranty.
- The dealer/automaker cannot dispute the cost of the independent repair if they fail to cross-examine the independent repairer.
- Auto owners can ask for and win compensation for their inconvenience, which in this judgment amounted to $150.

Court awards quickly add up. The plaintiff was given $1,985.94, with the addition of court costs and prejudgment interest, plus costs of inconvenience fixed at $150. The final award amounted to $2,266.04.

False Advertising

Misrepresentation

Goldie v. Golden Ears Motors (1980) Ltd. (Case No. CO8287; Port Coquitlam, British Columbia Small Claims Court; June 27, 2000; Justice Warren): In a well-written, eight-page judgment, the court awarded plaintiff, Goldie, $5,000 for engine repairs on a 1990 Ford F-150 pickup in addition to $236 court costs. The dealer was found to have misrepresented the mileage and sold a used vehicle that didn't meet Section

8.01 of the provincial Motor Vehicle Act Regulations due to its unsafe tires and defective exhaust and headlights.

In rejecting the seller's defence that he disclosed all information "to the best of his knowledge and belief" as stipulated in the sales contract, Justice Warren stated:

> The words "to the best of your knowledge and belief" do not allow someone to be willfully blind to defects or to provide incorrect information. I find as a fact that the business made no effort to fulfill its duty to comply with the requirements of this form. . . . The defendant has been reckless in its actions. More likely, it has actively deceived the claimant into entering into this contract. I find the conduct of the defendant has been reprehensible throughout the dealings with the claimant.

This judgment closes a loophole that sellers have used to justify their misrepresentation, and it allows for cancellation of the sale and damages if the vehicle doesn't meet highway safety regulations.

MacDonald v. Equilease Co. Ltd. (Ontario Supreme Court; January 18, 1979; Judge O'Driscoll): The plaintiff leased a truck that was misrepresented as having an axle stronger than it really was. The court awarded the plaintiff damages for repairs and set aside the lease.

Seich v. Festival Ford Sales Ltd. ((1978), 6 Alta. L.R. (2d) 262): The plaintiff bought a used truck from the defendant after being assured that it had a new motor and transmission. It didn't, and the court awarded the plaintiff $6,400.

"The 2015 Chevrolet Corvette ranks #2 out of 16 luxury sports cars. Drivers are blown away by its incredible acceleration, agile handling and ride comfort."
– U.S. News & World Report.

"In spite of the marketing claims, the paint on the newest cars, along with fit and finish of the body, along with a variety of mechanical and electrical problems plus an eye opening number of engine and transmission failures rendered the newest Corvette a certifiable piece of shit and overall failure."
– corvettec7.iasco.blogspot.com/.

Used car sold as new (demonstrator)

Bilodeau v. Sud Auto (No. 09-000751-73; Quebec Court of Appeal; 1973; Judge Tremblay): This appeals court cancelled the contract and held that a car can't be sold as new or as a demonstrator if it has ever been rented, leased, sold, or titled to anyone other than the dealer.

Rourke v. Gilmore (January 16, 1928; as found in *Ontario Weekly Notes*, vol. XXXIII, at p. 292): Before discovering that his new car was really used, the plaintiff drove it for over a year. For this reason, the contract couldn't be cancelled. However, the appeals court instead awarded damages for $500, which was quite a sum in 1928!

Vehicle not as ordered

Whether you're buying new or used, the seller can't misrepresent the vehicle. Anything that varies from what one would commonly expect, or from the seller's representation, must be disclosed prior to signing the contract. Typical misrepresentation scenarios include odometer turnbacks, undisclosed accident damage, used or leased cars being sold as new, new vehicles that are the wrong colour or the wrong model year, and vehicles that lack promised options or standard features.

Chenel v. Bel Automobile (1981) Inc. (Quebec Superior Court, Quebec City; August 27, 1976; Judge Desmeules): The plaintiff didn't receive his new Ford truck with the Jacob brakes essential for transporting sand in hilly regions. The court awarded the plaintiff $27,000, representing the purchase price of the vehicle less the money he earned while using the truck.

Lasky v. Royal City Chrysler Plymouth ((1987), 59 O.R. (2d) 323 (H.C.)): The plaintiff bought a 4-cylinder 1983 Dodge 600 that was represented by the salesman as being a 6-cylinder model. After putting 40,000 km on the vehicle over a 22-month period, the buyer was given her money back, without interest, under the provincial *Business Practices Act.*

Used car fuel-economy

Sidney v. 1011067 Ontario Inc. (c.o.b. Southside Motors) (Ontario Provincial Court): The court ruled that fuel economy misrepresentation can lead to a contract's cancellation if the dealer gives a higher-than-actual figure, even if it's claimed it was an innocent misrepresentation. In this case, the buyer was awarded $11,424.51 plus prejudgment interest because of a false representation made by the dealer regarding fuel efficiency. The plaintiff claimed that the defendant advised him that the vehicle could run 800-900 km per tank of fuel, when in fact the maximum distance was only 500 km per tank.

Car owners, panicked over soaring fuel prices, have been scammed by carmakers and dealers alike with bogus fuel economy claims.

Fortunately, the courts are cracking down on sellers who use false gas consumption figures to sell both new and used cars. For example, Ontario's revised *Consumer Protection Act*, 2002 (available through the province's searchable law database, *www.e-laws.gov.on.ca*), lets consumers cancel a contract within one year of entering into the agreement if a dealer makes a false, misleading, deceptive, or unconscionable representation. This includes false fuel economy claims.

Dealers cannot make the excuse that they were fooled or that they were simply providing data supplied by the manufacturer. The law clearly states that both parties are jointly liable, and therefore the dealer is presumed to know the history, quality, and true performance of what is sold.

Implied Warranty Rulings

Reasonable durability

This is that powerful "other" warranty that they never tell you about. It applies during and after the expiration of the manufacturer's or dealer's expressed or written warranty and requires that a part or repair will last a reasonable period of time. What is reasonable depends in a large part on benchmarks used in the industry, the price of the vehicle, and how it was driven and maintained. Look at the "Reasonable Part Durability" table, above, for some guidelines as to what you should expect. Judges usually apply the implied or legal warranty when the manufacturer's expressed warranty has expired and the vehicle's manufacturing defects remain uncorrected.

Chevrier v. General Motors du Canada (No. 730-32-004876-046; Quebec Small Claims Court, Joliette District (Repentigny); October 18, 2006; Justice Georges Massol) (you can find the full judgment (French) at *www.canlii.org*): The plaintiff leased and then bought a 2000 Montana minivan. At 71,000 km the automatic transmission failed and two GM dealers estimated the repairs to be between $2,200 and $2,500. They refused warranty coverage because the warranty had expired after the third year of ownership or 60,000 km of use. The owner repaired the transmission at an independent garage for $1,869 and kept the old parts, which GM refused to examine.

A small claims court lawsuit was filed, and Judge Massol gave the following reasons for ruling against GM's two arguments that (1) there was no warning that a claim would be filed, and (2) all warranties had expired:

1. GM filed a voluminous record of jurisprudence in its favour, relative to other lawsuits that were rejected because they were filed without prior notice. The judge reasoned that GM could not plead a "failure to notify," because the owner went to several dealers who were essentially agents of the manufacturer.

2. The judge also reasoned that the expiration of GM's written warranty does not nullify the legal warranty set out in articles 38 and 39 of the *Consumer Protection Act*. The legal warranty requires that all products be "reasonably durable," which did not appear to be the case with the plaintiff's vehicle, given its low mileage and number of years of use.

GM was ordered to pay the entire repair costs, plus interest, and the $90 filing fee.

Dufour v. Ford Canada Ltd. (No. 550-32-008335-009; Quebec Small Claims Court, Hull; April 10, 2001; Justice P. Chevalier): Ford was forced to reimburse the cost of engine head gasket repairs carried out on a 1996 Windstar 3.8L engine – a vehicle not covered by the automaker's Owner Notification Program, which cut off assistance after the '95 model year.

Schaffler v. Ford Motor Company Limited and Embrun Ford Sales Ltd. (Court File No. 59-2003; Ontario Superior Court of Justice; L'Orignal Small Claims Court; July 22, 2003; Justice Gerald Langlois): The plaintiff bought a used 1995 Windstar in 1998. Its engine head gasket was repaired for free three years later, under Ford's seven-year extended warranty. In 2002, at 109,600 km, the head gasket failed again, seriously damaging the engine. Ford refused a second repair. Justice Langlois ruled that Ford's warranty extension bulletin listed signs and symptoms of the covered defect that were identical to the problems written on the second work order ("persistent and/or chronic engine overheating; heavy white smoke evident from the exhaust tailpipe; flashing 'low coolant' instrument panel light even after coolant refill; and constant loss of engine coolant"). Judge Langlois concluded that "the problem was brought to the attention of the dealer well within the warranty period; the dealer was negligent." The plaintiff was awarded $4,941 plus 5 percent interest. This judgment included $1,070 for two months' car rental.

John R. Reid and Laurie M. McCall v. Ford Motor Company of Canada (Claim No: #02-SC-077344; Superior Court of Justice; Ottawa Small Claims Court; July 11, 2003; Justice Tiernay): A 1996 Windstar, bought used in 1997, experienced engine head gasket failure in October 2001 at 159,000 km. Judge Tiernay awarded the plaintiffs $4,145 for the following reason:

A Technical Service Bulletin dated June 28, 1999, was circulated to Ford dealers. It dealt specifically with "undetermined loss of coolant" and "engine oil contaminated with coolant" in the 1996-98 Windstar and five other models of Ford vehicles. I conclude that Ford owed a duty of care to the Plaintiff to equip this vehicle with a cylinder head gasket of sufficient sturdiness and durability that would function trouble-free for at least seven years, given normal driving and proper maintenance conditions. I find that Ford is answerable in damages for the consequences of its negligence.

Dawe v. Courtesy Chrysler (SCCH #206825; Dartmouth Nova Scotia Small Claims Court; July 30, 2004; Judge Patrick L Casey, Q.C.): "Small claims" doesn't necessarily mean small judgments. This 21-page, unreported Nova Scotia small claims court decision is impressive in its clarity and thoroughness. It applies *Donoghue, Kravitz, and Davis, et al.,* in awarding a 2001 Dodge Ram owner over $5,000 in damages. Anyone with engine, transmission, and suspension problems or water leaking into the interior will find this judgment particularly useful.

Fissel v. Ideal Auto Sales Ltd. ((1991), 91 Sask. R. 266): Shortly after the vehicle was purchased, its motor seized and the dealer refused to replace it, even though the car was returned on several occasions. The court ruled that the dealer had breached the statutory warranties in sections 11(4) and (7) of the *Consumer Products Warranties Act*. The purchasers were entitled to cancel the sale and recover the full purchase price.

Friskin v. Chevrolet Oldsmobile (72 D.L.R. (3d) 289): A Manitoba used-car buyer asked that his contract be cancelled because of his car's chronic stalling problem.

The garage owner did his best to correct it. Despite the seller's good intentions, the *Manitoba Consumer Protection Act* allowed for cancellation.

Graves v. C&R Motors Ltd. (British Columbia County Court; April 8, 1980; Judge Skipp): The plaintiff bought a used car on the condition that certain deficiencies be remedied. They never were, and he was promised a refund, but it never arrived. The plaintiff brought suit, claiming that the dealer's deceptive activities violated the provincial *Trade Practices Act*. The court agreed, concluding that a deceptive act that occurs before, during, or after the transaction can lead to the cancellation of the contract.

Hachey v. Galbraith Equipment Company ((1991), 33 M.V.R. (2d) 242): The plaintiff bought a used truck from the dealer to haul gravel. Shortly thereafter, the steering failed. The plaintiff's suit was successful because expert testimony showed that the truck wasn't roadworthy. The dealer was found liable for damages for being in breach of the implied condition of fitness for the purpose for which the truck was purchased, as set out in section 15(a) of the New Brunswick *Sale of Goods Act*.

Henzel v. Brussels Motors ((1973), 1 O.R. 339 (County Court)): The dealer sold a used car, brandishing a copy of the mechanical fitness certificate as proof that the car was in good shape. The plaintiff was awarded his money returned because the court held the certificate to be a warranty that was breached by the car's subsequent defects.

Johnston v. Bodasing Corporation Limited (No. 15/11/83; Ontario County Court, Bruce; February 23, 1983; Judge McKay): The plaintiff bought a used 1979 Buick Riviera that was represented as being "reliable" for $8,500. Two weeks after purchase, the motor self-destructed. Judge McKay awarded the plaintiff $2,318 as compensation to fix the Riviera's defects. One feature of this particular decision is that the trial judge found that the *Sale of Goods Act* applied, notwithstanding the fact that the vendor used a standard contract that said there were no warranties or representations. The judge also accepted the decision in *Kendall v. Lillico* (1969) (2 Appeal Cases 31), which indicates that the *Sale of Goods Act* covers not only defects that the seller ought to have detected but also latent defects that even his or her utmost skill and judgment could not have detected. This places a very heavy onus on the vendor, and it should prove useful in actions of this type in other common-law provinces with laws similar to Ontario's *Sale of Goods Act*.

General Motors Products of Canada Ltd. v. Kravitz ((1979), 1 S.C.R. 790): The court said the seller's warranty of quality was an accessory to the property and was transferred with it on successive sales. Accordingly, subsequent buyers could invoke the contractual warranty of quality against the manufacturer, even though they did not contract directly with it. This precedent was then codified in articles 1434, 1442, and 1730 of Quebec's *Civil Code*.

Morrison v. Hillside Motors (1973) Ltd. ((1981), 35 Nfld. & P.E.I.R. 361): A used car advertised to be in "A1" condition and carrying a 50/50 warranty developed a number of problems. The court decided that the purchaser should be partially compensated because of the ad's claim. In deciding how much compensation to award, the presiding judge considered the warranty's wording, the amount paid for the vehicle, the model year of the vehicle, the vehicle's average life, the type of defect that occurred, and the length of time the purchaser had use of the vehicle before its defects became evident. Although this judgment was rendered in Newfoundland, judges throughout Canada have used a similar approach for more than a decade.

Neilson v. Maclin Motors (71 D.L.R. (3d) 744): The plaintiff bought a used truck on the strength of the seller's allegations that the motor had been rebuilt and that it had 210 hp. The engine failed. The judge awarded damages and cancelled the contract because the transmission was defective and the motor had not been rebuilt and did not have 210 hp.

Parent v. Le Grand Trianon and Ford Credit (C.P., 194; Quebec Provincial Court; February 1982; Judge Bertrand Gagnon): Nineteen months after paying $3,300 for a used 1974 LTD, the plaintiff sued the Ford dealer for his money back because the car prematurely rusted out. The dealer replied that rust was normal, there was no warranty, and the claim was too late. The court held that the garage was still responsible. The plaintiff was awarded $1,500 for the cost of rust repairs.

Narbonne v. Glendale Recreational Véhicules (Reference: 2008 QCCQ 5325; Quebec Small Claims Court; June 2, 2008; Judge Richard Landry): Three years after the plaintiff purchased a travel trailer, the manufacturer sent a recall notice to the wrong address. Seven years after that, the vehicle broke down when the recalled part failed. The manufacturer said it had done its part in sending out the recall notice. The judge disagreed, and found the company responsible for the full cost of the repairs, lodging, and $500 for general inconvenience, for a total of $5,792.

"As is" clauses

Since 1907, Canadian courts have ruled that a seller can't exclude the implied warranty as to fitness by including such phrases as "there are no other warranties or guarantees, promises, or agreements than those contained herein." See *Sawyer-Massey Co. v. Thibault* ((1907), 5 W.L.R. 241).

Adams v. J&D's Used Cars Ltd. ((1983), 26 Sask. R. 40 (Q.B.)): Shortly after the plaintiff purchased a car, its engine and transmission failed. The court ruled that the inclusion of "as is" in the sales contract had no legal effect. The dealer breached the implied warranty set out in Saskatchewan's *Consumer Products Warranties Act*. The sale was cancelled, and all monies were refunded.

Inaccurate odometer (quanti minoris)

Everyone knows that dealers and private sellers take advantage of lax federal sanctions to turn back odometer readings to get a better selling price. But, few buyers know that inaccurate odometers are also a common factory-related defect resulting in the premature expiry of the warranty, more frequent vehicle servicing costs, and accelerated depreciation. Fortunately, in *St. Onge v. Nissan Canada,*

Quebec Small Claims Court, Quebec, case no. 200-32-059430-131, October 1, 2013, Justice Andre Brochet) Quebec's small claims court has ruled that carmakers have to pay owners for these losses.

Daniel St. Onge bought a used 2010 Infiniti EX35 from a Nissan dealer for $31,138 and shortly discovered the odometer was adding between 5 and 11.1 percent more kilometers than were actually travelled – a variance confirmed by his personal GPS navigator. Nissan Canada refused to fix the odometer and St. Onge sued the manufacturer for damages on the grounds that he would not have paid so much for the vehicle if he had known it had this problem (*quanti minoris*).

This kind of lawsuit was used successfully by the Automobile Protection Association in the '70s against Nissan when the company sold leftover cars as the latest model. Small claims courts throughout the province awarded owners $300 per car – an amount later upheld by the Supreme Court of Canada (see *Nissan Automobile Co. (Canada) Ltd. v. Pelletier*, [1981] 1 S.C.R. 67.)

Nissan raised five defenses:

1. **We didn't do it. Nissan Canada is just a distributor for vehicles it imports from an independent foreign subsidiary** (Canadian affiliates of multinational automakers try this excuse fairly regularly): Judge André Brochet rejected this argument and ruled that Nissan Canada was part of the Nissan Motor Company Ltd. family, who manufactured the Infiniti EX35.

2. **The federal Motor Vehicle Safety Act allows an odometer and speedometer to be off by up to ten percent:** The judge concluded that the federal safety act did not protect Nissan from selling a vehicle that records false mileage readings under the provincial *Consumer Protection Act.* The duration of a warranty in Quebec must be determined in a precise manner. If an odometer were to record the incorrect mileage, the manufacturer has a duty to disclose it before the consumer consents to the purchase. Failure to do so is an omission of an important fact that affects the car's price.

3. **Nissan had won an earlier class action involving its faulty odometers:** The earlier case was never judged on its merits due to flaws in the selection of the class representative. Judge Brochet concluded that the issue of Nissan's odometer errors had never been tried before a court in Quebec.

4. **St. Onge's GPS was not a certified testing device:** The Nissan dealer had used the consumer's own unit to run their tests, which confirmed St. Onge's findings. In the absence of any other evidence, the judge affirmed he could rely on the best evidence available, which were St. Onge's figures.

5. **Weather, road conditions, poor maintenance, or St. Onge's driving habits could have affected the odometer reading:** This defense is often made by automakers to shift the blame for a defect to other factors (like GM's testimony that its paint delamination is due to acid rain or bird droppings). The Court threw out this argument after considering Nissan's lack of proof that other causes could be involved.

Judge Brochet awarded the full $3,000 claimed by Mr. St. Onge as a reasonable reduction of the $31,000 purchase price, plus 5 percent interest assessed over 15 months. Nissan also had to pay $135 court costs.

This case is a very good template of how to win a settlement or lawsuit where a car's performance doesn't match its representation, or there is a failure to disclose an important fact by the seller. Furthermore, the judgment confirms that automakers continue to be liable, even if a vehicle is sold used. Misrepresented fuel-economy savings, towing payloads, and horsepower ratings are three areas where this judgment will likely have the most impact. The complete decision in *St. Onge vs. Nissan Canada appears in French at www.apa.ca/userfiles//St-Ongevs Nissanpetitescr%C3%A9ancesfactoryodoerror.pdf.* Auto owners who wish to join the APA can go to *www.apa.ca/join.asp.*

Leasing

Ford Motor Credit v. Bothwell (No. 9226-T; Ontario County Court, Middlesex; December 3, 1979; Judge Macnab): The defendant leased a 1977 Ford truck that had frequent engine problems, characterized by stalling and hard starting. After complaining for one year and driving 35,000 km, the defendant cancelled the lease. Ford Credit sued for the money owing on the lease. Judge Macnab cancelled the lease and ordered Ford Credit to repay 70 percent of the amount paid during the leasing period. Ford Credit was also ordered to refund repair costs, even though the corporation claimed that it should not be held responsible for Ford's failure to honour its warranty.

Salvador v. Setay Motors/Queenstown Chev-Olds (Case No.1621/95; Hamilton Small Claims Court): The plaintiff was awarded $2,000, plus costs, from Queenstown Leasing. The court found that the company should have tried harder to sell the leased vehicle, and at a higher price, when the "open lease" expired.

Schryvers v. Richport Ford Sales (No. C917060; B.C.S.C.; May 18, 1993; Justice Tysoe): The court awarded $17,578.47, plus costs, to a couple who paid thousands of dollars more in unfair and hidden leasing charges than if they had simply purchased their Ford Explorer and Escort. The court found that this price difference constituted a deceptive, unconscionable act or practice, in contravention of the *Trade Practices Act* (R.S.B.C. 1979, c. 406).

Judge Tysoe concluded that the total general damages awarded to the Schryvers for both vehicles would be $11,578.47. He then proceeded to give the following reasons for awarding an additional $6,000 in punitive damages:

Little wonder Richport Ford had a contest for the salesperson who could persuade the most customers to acquire their vehicles by way of a lease transaction. I consider the actions of Richport Ford to be sufficiently flagrant and high handed to warrant an award of punitive damages.

There must be a disincentive to suppliers in respect of intentionally deceptive trade practices. If no punitive damages are awarded for intentional violations of the legislation, suppliers will continue to conduct their businesses in a manner that involves deceptive trade practices because they will have nothing to lose. In this case I believe that the appropriate amount of punitive damages is the extra profit Richport Ford endeavoured to make as a result of its deceptive acts. I therefore award punitive damages against Richport Ford in the amount of $6,000.

See also:

- *Barber v. Inland Truck Sales* (11 D.L.R. (3d) 469)
- *Canadian-Dominion Leasing v. Suburban Super Drug Ltd.* ((1966), 56 D.L.R. (2d) 43)
- *Neilson v. Atlantic Rentals Ltd.* ((1974), 8 N.B.R. (2d) 594)
- *Volvo Canada v. Fox* (No. 1698/77/C; New Brunswick Court of Queen's Bench; December 13, 1979; Judge Stevenson)
- *Western Tractor v. Dyck* (7 D.L.R. (3d) 535)

Paint and Body Defects

The following tips on making a successful claim apply mainly to paint defects, water and air leaks, and subpar fit and finish, but you can use the same strategy for any other vehicle defect that you believe is the automaker's or dealer's responsibility. If you're not sure whether the problem is a factory-related deficiency or a maintenance item, have it checked out by an independent garage or get a TSB summary for your vehicle. The summary may include specific bulletins relating to the diagnosis, correction, and ordering of upgraded parts needed to fix your problem.

1. If you know that your vehicle's paint problem is factory-related, take your vehicle to the dealer and ask for a written, signed estimate. When you're handed the estimate, ask if the paint job can be covered by some "goodwill" assistance. (Ford's euphemism for this secret warranty is "Owner Notification Program" or "Owner Dialogue Program;" GM's term is "Special Policy;" and Chrysler simply calls it an "Owner Satisfaction Notice." Don't use the term "secret warranty" yet. You'll just make everyone angry and evasive.)

2. Your request will probably be met with a refusal, an offer to repaint the vehicle for half the cost, or (if you're lucky) an agreement to repaint the vehicle free of charge. If you accept the half-the-cost offer, make sure that it's based on the original estimate you have in hand, since some dealers jack up their estimates so that your 50 percent is really 100 percent of the true cost.

3. If the dealer or automaker has already refused your claim and the repair hasn't been done yet, get an additional estimate from an independent garage that shows the problem is factory-related.

4. If the repair has yet to be done, mail or fax a registered claim to the automaker (and send a copy to the dealer) claiming the average of both estimates. If the repair has been done at your expense, mail or fax a registered claim with a copy of your bill.

5. If you don't receive a satisfactory response within a week, deposit a copy of the estimate or paid bill and claim letter/fax before the small claims court and await a trial date. This means that the automaker/dealer will have to appear, no lawyer is required, and costs should be minimal (under $100). Usually, an informal pretrial mediation hearing with the two parties and a court clerk will be scheduled within a few months, followed by a trial a few weeks later (the time varies depending on region). Most cases are settled at the mediation stage. You can help your case by collecting photographs, maintenance work orders, previous work orders dealing with your problem, TSBs, and by speaking to an independent expert (the garage or body shop that did the estimate or repair is best, but you can also use a local teacher who instructs automotive repair). Remember, service bulletins can be helpful, but they aren't critical to a successful claim.

Other situations

- If the vehicle has just been repainted or repaired but the dealer says that "goodwill" coverage was denied by the automaker, pay for the repair with a certified cheque and write "under protest" on the cheque. Remember, though, if the dealer does the repair, you won't have an independent expert who can affirm that the problem was factory-related or that it was a result of premature wear. Plus, the dealer can say that you or the environment caused the paint problem. In these cases, TSBs can make or break your case.

- If the dealer or automaker offers a partial repair or refund, take it. Then sue for the rest. Remember, if a partial repair has been done under warranty, it counts as an admission of responsibility, no matter what "goodwill" euphemism is used. Also, the repaired component or body panel should be just as durable as if it were new. Hence the clock starts ticking from the time of the repair until you reach the original warranty parameter – no matter what the dealer's repair warranty limit says.

Very seldom do automakers contest these paint claims before small claims court, instead opting to settle once the court claim is bounced from their customer relations people to their legal affairs department. At that time, you'll probably be offered an out-of-court settlement for 50-75 percent of your claim.

Stand fast, and make reference to the service bulletins you intend to subpoena in order to publicly contest in court the unfair nature of this "secret warranty" program (automakers' lawyers cringe at the idea of trying to explain why consumers aren't made aware of these bulletins) – 100 percent restitution will probably follow.

Four pro-consumer paint judgments

In *Dunlop v. Ford of Canada* (No. 58475/04; Ontario Superior Court of Justice, Richmond Hill Small Claims Court; January 5, 2005; Deputy Judge M.J. Winer), the owner of a 1996 Lincoln Town Car, purchased used in 1999 for $27,000, was awarded $4,091.64. Judge Winer cited the *Shields* decision (following) and gave these reasons for finding Ford of Canada liable:

> Evidence was given by the Plaintiff's witness, Terry Bonar, an experienced paint auto technician. He gave evidence that the [paint] delamination may be both a manufacturing defect and can be caused or speeded up by atmospheric conditions. He also says that [the paint on] a car like this should last ten to 15 years, [or even for] the life of the vehicle....
>
> It is my view that the presence of ultraviolet light is an environmental condition to which the vehicle is subject. If it cannot withstand this environmental condition, it is defective in my view.

In *Shields v. General Motors of Canada* (No. 1398/96; Ontario Court, General Division; Oshawa Small Claims Court; July 24, 1997; Deputy Judge Robert Zochodne), the owner of a 1991 Pontiac Grand Prix purchased the vehicle used with over 100,000 km on its odometer. Beginning in 1995, the paint began to bubble and flake and eventually peeled off. Deputy Judge Robert Zochodne awarded the plaintiff $1,205.72 and struck down every one of GM's environmental/acid rain/UV rays arguments. Here are the other important aspects of this 12-page judgment that General Motors did not appeal.

1. The judge admitted many of the TSBs referred to in *Lemon-Aid* as proof of GM's negligence.

2. Although the vehicle already had 156,000 km on it when the case went to court, GM still offered to pay for 50 percent of the paint repairs if the plaintiff dropped his suit.

3. The judge ruled that the failure to protect the paint from the damaging effects of UV rays is akin to engineering a car that won't start in cold weather. In essence, vehicles must be built to withstand the rigours of the environment.

4. Here's an interesting twist: The original warranty covered defects that were present at the time it was in effect. The judge, taking statements found in the GM technical service bulletins, ruled that the UV problem was factory-related, existed during the warranty period, and represented a latent defect that appeared once the warranty expired.

5. The subsequent purchaser was not prevented from making the warranty claim, even though the warranty had long since expired from a time and mileage standpoint and he was the second owner.

Bentley v. Dave Wheaton Pontiac Buick GMC Ltd. and General Motors of Canada (Victoria Registry No. 24779; British Columbia Small Claims Court; December 1, 1998; Judge Higinbotham). This small claims judgment builds on the Ontario *Shields v. General Motors of Canada* decision and cites other jurisprudence as to how long paint should last on a car. If you're wondering why Ford and Chrysler haven't been hit by similar judgments, remember that they usually settle out of court. (See also *Maureen Frank v. General Motors of Canada Limited* (No. SC#12 (2001); Saskatchewan Provincial Court; October 17, 2001; Provincial Court Judge H.G. Dirauf), discussed on page 160.)

More paint and rust cases

In *Whittaker v. Ford Motor Company* ((1979), 24 O.R. (2d) 344). A new Ford developed serious corrosion problems in spite of having been rustproofed by the dealer. The court ruled that the dealer, not Ford, was liable for the damage for having sold the rustproofing product at the time of purchase. This is an important judgment to use when a rustproofer or paint protector goes out of business or refuses to pay a claim, since the decision holds the dealer jointly responsible.

Martin v. Honda Canada Inc. (Ontario Small Claims Court, Scarborough; March 17, 1986; Judge Sigurdson). The original owner of a 1981 Honda Civic sought compensation for the premature "bubbling, pitting, [and] cracking of the paint and rusting of the Civic after five years of ownership." Judge Sigurdson agreed with the owner and ordered Honda to pay $1,163.95.

Thauberger v. Simon Fraser Sales and Mazda Motors (3 B.C.L.R. 193). This Mazda owner sued for damages caused by the premature rusting of his 1977 Mazda GLC. The court awarded him $1,000. Thauberger had previously sued General Motors for a prematurely rusted Blazer truck and was also awarded $1,000 in the same court. Both judges ruled that the defects could not be excluded from the automaker's expressed warranty or from the implied warranty granted by British Columbia's *Sale of Goods Act*.

See also:

- *Danson v. Chateau Ford (1976) C.P.* (No. 32-00001898-757; Quebec Small Claims Court; 1976; Judge Lande)
- *Doyle v. Vital Automotive Systems* (Ontario Small Claims Court, Toronto; May 16, 1977; Judge Turner)
- *Lacroix v. Ford* (Ontario Small Claims Court, Toronto; April 1980; Judge Tierney)
- *Marinovich v. Riverside Chrysler* (No. 1030/85; District Court of Ontario; April 1, 1987; Judge Stortini)

Product Liability

Almost four decades ago, in *Kravitz v. GM* (the first case where I was called as a pro bono expert witness), the Supreme Court of Canada clearly affirmed that automakers and their dealers are jointly liable for the replacement or repair of a vehicle if independent testimony shows that it is afflicted with factory-related defects that compromise its safety or performance. The existence of a secret warranty extension or TSB also helps prove that the vehicle's problems are the automaker's responsibility. For example, in *Lowe v. Fairview Chrysler* (see page 198), TSBs were instrumental in showing an Ontario small claims court judge that Chrysler's history of automatic transmission failures went back to 1989.

In addition to replacing or repairing the vehicle, an automaker can also be held responsible for any damages arising from the defect. This means that loss of wages, supplementary transportation costs, and damages for personal inconvenience can be awarded. In the States, product liability damage awards often exceed millions of dollars. Canadian courts, however, are far less generous.

Punitive Damages

Punitive damages (also known as "exemplary damages") awards the plaintiff compensation that exceeds his or her losses in order to deter those who carry out dishonest or negligent practices. These kinds of judgments have been quite common in the U.S. for almost 50 years, and they sometimes reach hundreds of millions of dollars.

Punitive damages are rarely awarded in Canadian courts and are almost never used against automakers. When they are given out, it's usually for sums less than $100,000. During the past decade, though, our courts have cracked down on business abuses and awarded plaintiffs amounts varying from $5,000 to $1 million.

In February 2002, the Supreme Court of Canada let stand an unprecedented million-dollar award against what one of the justices called "the insurer from hell." In *Whiten v. Pilot Insurance Co.*, the couple's home burned down and the insurer refused to pay the claim. The jury was so outraged that it ordered the company to pay $345,000 for the loss, plus $320,000 for legal costs and $1 million in punitive damages, making it the largest punitive damage award in Canadian history. The Supreme Court refused to overturn the jury's decision. This judgment scares the dickens out of insurers, who fear that they face huge punitive damage awards if they don't pay promptly.

In May 2005, the Supreme Court of Canada once again reaffirmed the use of punitive damages in *Prebushewski v. Dodge City Auto (1984) Ltd. and Chrysler Canada Ltd.* (2001 SKQB 537; Q.B. No. 1215). The Court backed the Saskatchewan court's $25,000 punitive damage award against Chrysler, rendered in Saskatoon on December 6, 2001, which cited egregious violations of provincial consumer protection statutes (see part of the judgment on page 78). The Supreme Court of Canada's confirmation of the judgment can be found at *scc.lexum.umontreal.ca*.

Canadian courts have become more generous in awarding plaintiffs money for mental distress experienced when defects aren't repaired properly under warranty. In *Sharman v. Formula Ford Sales Limited, Ford Credit Limited, and Ford Motor Company of Canada Limited* (No.: 17419/02SR; Ontario Superior Court of Justice; October 7,

2003), Justice Shepard of the Ontario Superior Court in Oakville awarded Mr. Sharman (a Ford of Canada customer relations staffer in Oakville) $7,500 because Ford had breached the implied warranty of fitness and made him fearful his children would fall out of his 2000 Windstar due to a faulty sliding door. Another $7,207 was given for breach of contract and breach of warranty because the minivan's sliding door wasn't secure and still leaked air and water after many attempts to repair it. Interestingly, the judge cited the *Wharton* decision as support for his award for mental distress.

The plaintiff and his family have had three years of aggravation, inconvenience, worry, and concern about their safety and that of their children. Generally speaking, our contract law did not allow for compensation for what may be mental distress, but that may be changing. I am indebted to counsel for providing me with the decision of the British Columbia Court of Appeal in *Wharton v. Tom Harris Chevrolet Oldsmobile Cadillac Ltd.*, [2002] B.C.J. No. 233, 2002 BCCA 78. This decision was recently followed in *T'avra v. Victoria Ford Alliance Ltd.*, [2003] BCJ No. 1957.

In *Wharton*, the purchaser of a Cadillac Eldorado claimed damages against the dealer because the car's sound system emitted an annoying buzzing noise and the purchaser had to return the car to the dealer for repair numerous times over two and a half years. The trial court awarded damages of $2,257.17 for breach of warranty with respect to the sound system, and $5,000 in non-pecuniary damages for loss of enjoyment of their luxury vehicle and for inconvenience, for a total award of $7,257.17. The Court of Appeal upheld the decision of the trial judge and Levine J.A. spent considerable time reviewing the law, but in particular the law relating to damages for breach of implied warranty of fitness: "The principles applicable to an award of damages for mental distress resulting from a breach of contract were thoroughly and helpfully analyzed in the recent judgment of the House of Lords in *Farley v. Skinner*, [2001] 3 W.L.R. 899, [2001] H.L.J. No. 49, affirming and clarifying the decision of the English Court of Appeal in *Watts v. Morrow*, [1991] I W.L.R. 142 1. Both of those cases concerned a claim by a buyer of a house against a surveyor who failed to report matters concerning the house as required by the contract. In *Watts*, the surveyor was negligent in failing to report defects in the house, and non-pecuniary damages of $6,750 were awarded to each of the owners for the inconvenience and discomfort experienced by them during repairs. In *Farley*, the surveyor was negligent in failing to discover, as he specifically undertook to do, that the property was adversely affected by aircraft noise. The House of Lords upheld the trial judge's award of non-pecuniary damages of $610,000, reversing the Court of Appeal, principally on the grounds that the object of the contract was to provide 'pleasure, relaxation, peace of mind, or freedom from molestation' and also because the plaintiff had suffered physical discomfort and inconvenience from the aircraft noise."

· · ·

The reasons for judgment in *Farley* provide a summary and survey of the law as it has developed, in England, to date. They are helpful in analyzing and summarizing the principles derived from *Watts*, which are, in my view, applicable to the case at bar. In summary they are (borrowing the language from both *Watts* and *Farley*):

(a) A contract-breaker is not in general liable for any distress, frustration, anxiety, displeasure, vexation, tension, or aggravation which the breach of contract may cause to the innocent party.

(b) The rule is not absolute. Where a major or important part of the contract is to give pleasure, relaxation or peace of mind, damages will be awarded if the fruit of the contract is not provided or if the contrary result is instead procured.

(c) In cases not falling within the "peace of mind" category, damages are recoverable for inconvenience and discomfort caused by the breach and the mental suffering directly related to the inconvenience and discomfort. However, the cause of the inconvenience or discomfort must be a sensory experience as opposed to mere disappointment that the contract has been broken. If those effects are foreseeably suffered during a period when defects are repaired, they create damages even though the cost of repairs are not recoverable as such.

Application of Law to the Facts of this Case

In the *Wharton* case (see pages 190 and 212), the respondent contracted for a "luxury" vehicle for pleasure use. It included a sound system that the appellant's service manager described as "high end." The respondent's husband described the purchase of the car in this way:

> [W]e bought a luxury car that was supposed to give us a luxury ride and be a quiet vehicle, and we had nothing but difficulty with it from the very day it was delivered with this problem that nobody seemed to be able to fix.... So basically we had a luxury product that gave us no luxury for the whole time that we had it.

It is clear that an important object of the contract was to obtain a vehicle that was luxurious and a pleasure to operate. Furthermore, the buzzing noise was the cause of physical, in the sense of sensory, discomfort to the respondent and her husband. The trial judge found it inhibited listening to the sound system and was irritating in normal conversation. The respondent and her husband also bore the physical inconvenience of taking the vehicle to the appellant on numerous occasions for repairs. The inconvenience and discomfort was, in my view, reasonably foreseeable, if the defect in the sound system had been known at the date of the contract. The fact that it was not then known is, of course, irrelevant.

The award of damages for breach of the implied warranty of fitness satisfies both exceptions from the general rule that damages are not awarded for mental distress for breach of contract, set out in *Watts* as amplified in *Farley* (both cases discussed in the excerpt to this case, above).

The justice continued and said (at para. 63), "... awards for mental distress arising from a breach of contract should be restrained and modest."

The court upheld the trial judge's award of $5,000 in *Wharton* where the issue was a buzzing in the sound system.

In my view, a defect in manufacture which goes to the safety of the vehicle deserves a modest increase. I would assess the plaintiff's damage for mental distress resulting from the breach of the implied warranty of fitness at $7,500. Judgment to issue in favour of the plaintiff against the defendants, except Ford Credit, on a joint and several basis for $14,707, plus interest and costs.

Provincial business practices acts and consumer protection statutes prohibit false, misleading, or deceptive representations and allow for punitive damages should the unfair practice toward the consumer amount to an unconscionable representation (see *Canadian Encyclopedic Digest* (3d) s. 76, pp. 140-45). "Unconscionable" is defined as "where the consumer is not reasonably able to protect his or her interest because of physical infirmity, ignorance, illiteracy, or inability to understand the language of an agreement or similar factors." This concept has been successfully used in consumer, environmental, and labour law.

- Exemplary damages are justified where compensatory damages are insufficient to deter and punish. See *Walker v. CFTO Ltd.* ((1978), 59 O.R. (2d) 104 (C.A.)).

- Exemplary damages can be awarded in cases where the defendant's conduct was "cavalier." See *Ronald Elwyn Lister Ltd. v. Dayton Tire Canada Ltd.* ((1985), 52 O.R. (2d) 89 (C.A.)).

- The primary purpose of exemplary damages is to prevent the defendant and all others from doing similar wrongs. See *Fleming v. Spracklin* (1921).

- Disregard of the public's interest, lack of preventive measures, and a callous attitude all merit exemplary damages. See *Coughlin v. Kuntz* ((1989), 2 C.C.L.T. (2d) (B.C.C.A.)).

- Punitive damages can be awarded for mental distress. See *Ribeiro v. Canadian Imperial Bank of Commerce* ((1992), 13 O.R. (3d) 278 (C.A.), leave to appeal to Supreme Court of Canada refused [1993] 2 S.C.R. x)) and *Brown v. Waterloo Regional Board of Commissioners of Police* ((1983), 43 O.R. (2d) 113, affirming in part (1982), 37 O.R. (2d) 277).

In the States, punitive damage awards have been particularly generous. Whenever big business complains of an "unrestrained judiciary," it trots out a 20-year-old case where an Alabama BMW 500 series owner was awarded $4 million because his new car had been repainted before he bought it and the seller didn't tell him. Under appeal, the owner was offered $50,000.

The case was *BMW of North America, Inc. v. Gore* (517 U.S. 559, 116 S. Ct. 1589 (S.C. (1996))). In this case, the Supreme Court cut the damages award and established standards for jury awards of punitive damages. Nevertheless, million-dollar awards continue to be quite common. In the following example, an Oregon dealer learned that a $1-million punitive damages award was not excessive under *Gore* and under Oregon law.

The Oregon Supreme Court determined that the standard it set in *Oberg v. Honda Motor Company* (888 P.2d 8 (Or. Sup. Ct. (1996)), on remand from the Supreme Court, survived the Supreme Court's subsequent ruling in *Gore*. The court held that the jury's $1-million punitive damages award, 87 times larger than the plaintiff's compensatory damages in *Parrott v. Carr Chevrolet, Inc.* (2001 Ore. LEXIS), wasn't excessive. In that case, Mark Parrott sued Carr Chevrolet, Inc., over a used 1983 Chevrolet Suburban under Oregon's *Unlawful Trade Practices Act.* The jury awarded Parrott $11,496 in compensatory damages and $1 million in punitive damages because the dealer failed to disclose collision damage to a new-car buyer.

See also:

- *Vlchek v. Koshel* ((1988), 44 C.C.L.T. 314 (B.C.S.C.))
- *Granek v. Reiter* (No. 35/741; Ontario Court, General Division)
- *Morrison v. Sharp* (No. 43/548; Ontario Court, General Division)
- *Schryvers v. Richport Ford Sales* (B.C.S.C., No. C917060; May 18, 1993; Judge Tysoe)
- *Varleg v. Angeloni* (No. 41/301; B.C.S.C.)
- *Grabinski v. Blue Springs Ford Sales, Inc.* (U.S. App. LEXIS 2073 (8th Cir. W.D. MO (2000))

Repairs: Faulty Diagnosis

Davies v. Alberta Motor Association (No. P9090106097; Alberta Provincial Court; Civil Division; August 13, 1991; Judge Moore): The plaintiff had the AMA's Vehicle Inspection Service check out a used 1985 Nissan Pulsar NX prior to buying it. The car passed with flying colours. A month later, the clutch was replaced and numerous electrical problems ensued. At that time, another garage discovered that the car had been involved in a major accident, had a bent frame, a leaking radiator, and was unsafe to drive. The court awarded the plaintiff $1,578.40 plus three years' interest. The judge held that the AMA set itself out as an expert and should have spotted the car's defects. The AMA's defence – that it was not responsible for errors – was thrown out. The court held that a disclaimer clause could not protect the association from a fundamental breach of contract.

Secret Warranty Rulings

It's common practice for manufacturers to secretly extend their warranties to cover components with a high failure rate. Customers who complain vigorously get extended warranty compensation in the form of "goodwill" adjustments.

François Chong v. Marine Drive Imported Cars Ltd. and Honda Canada Inc. (No. 92-06760; British Columbia Provincial Small Claims Court; May 17, 1994; Judge C.L. Bagnall): The plaintiff was the first owner of a 1983 Honda Accord with 134,000 km on the odometer. He had six engine camshafts replaced – four under Honda "goodwill" programs, one where he paid part of the repairs, and one via this small claims court judgment.

In his ruling, Judge Bagnall agreed with Chong and ordered Honda and the dealer to each pay half of the $835.81 repair bill for the following reasons:

The defendants assert that the warranty, which was part of the contract for purchase of the car, encompassed the entirety of their obligation to the claimant, and that it expired in February 1985. The replacements of the camshaft after that date were paid for wholly or in part by Honda as a "goodwill gesture." The time has come for these gestures to cease, according to the witness for Honda. As well, he pointed out to me that the most recent replacement of the camshaft was paid for by Honda and that, therefore, the work would not be covered by Honda's usual warranty of 12 months from date of repair. Mr. Wall, who testified for Honda, told me there was no question that this situation with Mr. Chong's engine was an unusual state of affairs. He said that a camshaft properly maintained can last anywhere from 24,000 to 500,000 km. He could not offer any suggestion as to why the car keeps having this problem.

The claimant has convinced me that the problems he is having with rapid breakdown of camshafts in his car is due to a defect, which was present in the engine at the time that he purchased the car. The problem first arose during the warranty period and in my view has never been properly identified nor repaired.

Tire Failures: Premature Wear

Blackwood v. Ford Motor Company of Canada Ltd., 2006 (Docket: PO690101722; Provincial Court of Alberta, Civil Division; Registry: Canmore; December 8, 2006; Honourable J. Shriar): This four-page judgment gives important guidelines as to how a plaintiff can successfully claim a refund for a defective tire.

The plaintiff bought a new 2005 Ford Focus. After ten months and 22,000 km, his dealer said all four tires needed replacing at a cost of $560.68. Both the dealer and Ford refused to cover the expense under the 3-year/60,000 km manufacturer's tire warranty, alleging that the wear was "normal wear and tear." Judge Shriar disagreed and awarded the plaintiff the full cost of the replacement tires, plus the filing fee and costs related to the registered mail and corporate records address check. An additional $100 was awarded for court costs, plus interest on the total amount from the date of the filing.

Unsafe Vehicles

Incidents of airbags that deploy for no reason, or don't deploy when they should, sudden unintended acceleration, and brake failure are among the top most frequent complaints logged by Transport Canada and NHTSA. However, the cause of these failures can be very difficult to diagnose, and individual cases are treated very differently by federal safety agencies. Sudden acceleration is considered to be a safety-related problem – stalling isn't always given the same priority. Never mind that a vehicle's sudden loss of power on a busy highway (as happens with 2001-05 Toyota and Lexus models) puts everyone's lives at risk. The same problem exists with engine and transmission powertrain failures, which are only occasionally considered to be safety-related. Anti-lock Braking Systems (ABS) and airbag failures are universally considered to be life-threatening defects.

If a death or injury is caused by a safety-related defect:

1. Use the "balance of probabilities." For example, sudden acceleration or stalling out in traffic can be difficult to duplicate and is often blamed on driver error. This was GM's strategy when faced with hundreds of accident reports relating to defective ignition switches. The real reason the ignition switches shut off inadvertently was a defective "switch detent plunger." General Motors was aware of this potential problem, and held meetings about it, as early as 2005. By the end of September 2014 *Reuters* stated in an article that 153 deaths were linked to the faulty ignition switch. So how do you satisfy the burden of proof showing that the problem exists and is the automaker's responsibility? Use the legal doctrine called "the balance of probabilities" by eliminating all of the possible dodges the dealer or manufacturer may employ. Show that proper maintenance has been carried out, that you're a safe driver, and that the incident occurs frequently and without warning. Remember, U.S. Supreme Court Justice Sotomayor's ruling against Ford for its "runaway" Aerostar? You don't need an engineering analysis to prove product liability – common sense can be proof enough *(www.suddenacceleration.com/jarvis-v-ford-motor-company/)*.

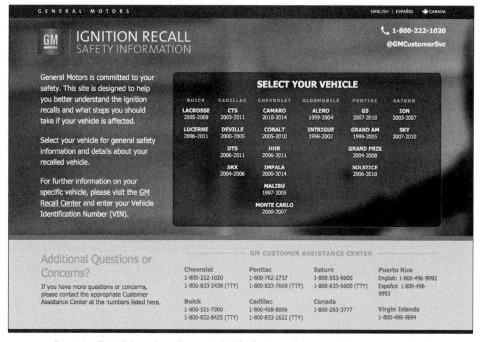

Over 16 million GM cars have been recalled for faulty ignition switches, including 2011-13 Chevrolet Caprice and 2008-09 Pontiac G8 sedans and 1.5 million 2008 Jeeps, Chrysler 300s, Dodge Chargers, and the Dodge Magnum station wagon (see *www.gmignitionupdate.com/*).

2. Get independent witnesses to confirm the problem exists. Confirmation includes verification by an independent mechanic, passenger testimony, downloaded data from your vehicle's data recorder, and lots of Internet browsing using *www.lemonaidcars.com* and a search engine like Google. Notify the dealer or manufacturer by fax, e-mail, or registered letter that you consider the problem to be a factory-induced, safety-related defect. Make sure you address your correspondence to the manufacturer's product liability or legal affairs department. At the dealership's service bay, make sure that every work order clearly states the problem as well as the number of previous attempts to fix it. (You should end up with a few complaint letters and a handful of work orders confirming that this is an ongoing deficiency.) If the dealer won't give you a copy of the work order because the work is a warranty claim, ask for a copy of the order number "in case your estate wishes to file a claim, pursuant to an accident." (This will get the service manager's attention.) Leaving a paper trail is crucial for any later claim, because it shows your concern and persistence and clearly indicates that the dealer and manufacturer had ample time to correct the defect.

3. Note on the work order that you expect the problem to be diagnosed and corrected under the emissions warranty or a "goodwill" program. It also wouldn't hurt to add the phrase on the work order or in your claim letters that "any deaths, injuries, or damage caused by the defect will be the dealer's and manufacturer's responsibility" since this work order (or letter, fax, or e-mail) constitutes you putting them on formal notice.

4. If the dealer does the necessary repairs at little or no cost to you, send a follow-up confirmation saying that you appreciate the assistance. Also, emphasize that you'll be back if the problem reappears, even if the warranty has expired, because the repair renews your warranty rights applicable to that defect. In other words, the warranty clock is set back to its original position. You won't likely get a copy of the repair bill, because dealers don't like to admit that there was a serious defect present. Keep in mind, however, that you can get your complete vehicle file from the dealer and manufacturer by issuing a subpoena, which costs about $75 (refundable), if the case goes to small claims or a higher court. This request has produced many out-of-court settlements when the internal documents show extensive work was carried out to correct the problem.

5. If the problem persists, send a letter, fax, or e-mail to the dealer and manufacturer saying so, look for ALLDATA service bulletins to confirm that your vehicle's defects are factory-related, and call Transport Canada or NHTSA, or log onto NHTSA's website, to report the failure. Also, contact the Center for Auto Safety in Washington, D.C. at 202-328-7700 or visit *www.autosafety.org* for a lawyer referral and an information sheet covering the problem. To find an expert Canadian lawyer familiar with auto defects

and sales scams, contact the non-profit Automobile Protection Association (contact info available at *www.APA.ca*).

6. Now come two crucial questions: Should you repair the defect now or later, and should you use the dealer or an independent? Generally, it's smart to use an independent garage if you know the dealer isn't pushing for free corrective repairs from the manufacturer, if weeks or months have passed without any resolution of your claim, if the dealer keeps claiming that it's a maintenance item, or if you know an independent mechanic who will give you a detailed work order showing the defect is factory-related and not a result of poor maintenance. Don't mention that a court case may ensue, since this will scare the dickens out of your only independent witness. The bonus of using an independent garage is that the repair charges will be about half what a dealer would demand. Incidentally, if the automaker later denies warranty "goodwill" because you used an independent repairer, use the argument that the defect's safety implications required emergency repairs to be carried out by whoever could see you first.

7. Take note of the manufacturer's own safety warnings. Dashboard-mounted warning lights usually come on prior to airbags suddenly deploying, ABS brakes failing, or engine glitches causing the vehicle to stall out. (Sudden acceleration, however, usually occurs without warning.) Automakers consider these lights to be critical safety warnings and generally advise drivers to immediately have the vehicle serviced to correct the problem (advice that can be found in the owner's manual) when any of the above lights come on. This bolsters the argument that your life was threatened, emergency repairs were required, and your request for another vehicle or a complete refund isn't out of line.

8. If any of the above defects causes an accident, the airbag fails to deploy, or you're injured by its deployment, ask your insurance company to have the vehicle towed to a neutral location and clearly state that neither the dealer nor the automaker should touch the vehicle until your insurance company and Transport Canada have completed their investigation. Also, get as many witnesses as possible and immediately go to the hospital for a check-up, even if you're feeling okay. You may be injured and not know it because the adrenalin coursing through your veins is masking your injuries. A hospital exam will easily confirm that your injuries are related to the accident, which is essential in court or for future settlement negotiations.

9. Peruse NHTSA's online accident database to find reports of other accidents caused by the same failure, or open or closed government investigations. Ironically, NHTSA had closed two GM ignition switch probes, before public pressure resulted in the government-forced recall of 2.6 million cars a decade later.

10. Don't let your insurance company settle the case if you're sure the accident was caused by a mechanical failure. Even if an engineering analysis fails to directly implicate the manufacturer or dealer, you can always plead the aforementioned balance of probabilities. If the insurance company settles, your insurance premiums will probably increase.

Part Four

1990-2016 RATINGS "WHEN GOOD CARS GO BAD"

Like a box of chocolates, when you drive a minivan you never know what you'll get.

While driving my 2014 Toyota Sienna on a sunny 65 degree morning, we hear a loud boom. Nothing was in front of us, no overpass. I slide the moonroof (all other cars call it a sunroof) cover back and glass falls in – it look as if it had exploded upward. Thank goodness I had the cover closed. Dealership determines it was caused by impact because of the glass break pattern. I asked him if he had ever seen the pattern of glass if it was defective, if there would show a weak point. He said he had not and then said he did not know for sure – it was just from his experience he determined this – everyone at dealership had never heard of a spontaneous blow out in the moonroof/sunroof. There is a lot documented on *edmunds.com* and at other places.

• • •

My daughter was in the back seat of my 2014 Grand Caravan when the seatbelt started to retract itself at the point that she was immobilized and it started choking her. We called the police and the fire department so they could release her. They cut the seatbelt.

Of course, buying a new or used car is always a scary experience. In either case you're buying someone's problems: The automaker's or the seller's. With this in mind, many people prefer to forgo the experience, skip car ownership altogether, and find other ways to get around.

GOING "CAR-LESS"

Before we go into what makes a good car buy and lead you through the jungle of new and used choices, I'll take one last stab at explaining why a car isn't a smart buy – at all.

Let's do the math. Figure $8,000 a year as your average new car expense, including a $200 monthly finance payment. Consider, too, that just the extra freight/administrative fee of $2,000 is almost as much as the cost of one year's financing.

Now, as mentioned in Part Two, you can buy a used car and cut $8,000 to $4,000 and ditch the freight charge and interest costs. So, that's by far a better buy.

But, here's the kicker. **Don't buy a car.**

Instead, budget $10 each weekday for public transportation to work or school, or for downtown entertainment or strolling. That's $50 weekly or $200 a month – equal to the cost of financing a new car, or paying just its freight cost. For special occasions, splurge with a $100 rental.

There are also lots of advantages to being "car-less."

There's no "showroom shakedown" where you are assailed by fast-talking sales people and end up buying what you don't need at an inflated price you can't afford. You leave with a feeling in the pit of your stomach that you've been "had". It's a common feeling that was first highlighted in 1977 when Gallup found that only 8% of respondents rated car salespeople "high" or "very high" for honesty and ethics. In the latest December 2014 survey that number was – 8%. Meanwhile, a full 45% in the latest poll rated salespeople low or very low – not much better than the 47% responding in 1977.

U.S. Views on Honesty and Ethical Standards in Professions

	% Very high or high	% Average	% Very low or low
Nurses	80	17	2
Medical doctors	65	29	7
Pharmacists	65	28	7
Police officers	48	31	20
Clergy	46	35	13
Bankers	23	49	26

	% Very high or high	% Average	% Very low or low
Lawyers	21	45	34
Business executives	17	50	32
Advertising practitioners	10	44	42
Car salespeople	8	46	45
Members of Congress	7	30	61

Dec. 8-11, 2014. Rated in order of % Very high or high. GALLUP

In addition to the above damning survey results, auto manufacturers themselves are warning customers of illegal activities practiced by their own dealerships. Last March, Fiat Chrysler Automobiles' senior vice president for communications warned that a "handful of dealers had accepted large numbers of orders for the 707-hp Dodge Charger and Challenger SRT Hellcat without regard to available supply and without advising their customers that orders may not be filled, if at all, for many months or longer. We believe such a practice is 'unscrupulous' and may constitute a breach of the Dealer's Sales and Service Agreement with FCA US LLC and a violation of other applicable laws."

- The savings accrued by going car-less can pay down college costs or a home mortgage – both good investments.
- Car pooling builds social skills and makes for lasting friendships.
- You're in tune with the environment; you see more, hear more, and know more about your surroundings.
- Environmentalist David Suzuki would be proud. Save money and cut pollution by using a rental, taxi, bus, subway, or ride-sharing service like Toronto-based Uber, accessible via a smartphone (*www.uber.com/cities/toronto*). With these alternatives, and no additional vehicle pollutants in the environment, how's that for going "green?"
- Going car-less leads to less worry in bad weather over starting, driving, parking, and windshield ice.
- And there's always the peace of mind of letting someone else take you to your destination. There's no fear of other drivers, traffic jam histrionics, and lots of time to read, write, think, or simply take a nap.

2015-16: A "PERFECT STORM" FOR BUYERS

Pent up demand, lower fuel prices, and easier low-interest credit have produced a "perfect storm" favourable to buyers of new and used cars and trucks. Following last year's record sales, carmakers are again imprudently flooding the market with more vehicles than they can sell. New cars have huge discounts, trade-ins are more plentiful, and used car prices are generally softer than usual because new cars are so plentiful and cheap. Furthermore, the market distortion caused by cheaper gas makes "gas guzzlers", "luxo-cars", and all-dressed SUVs and trucks more attractive, even at higher prices, than discounted econoboxes, diesels, hybrids, and electrics.

Five Ways to Get a "Good" Car

1. **Treat the purchase as an investment:** Buy a vehicle that is reasonably priced, requires a low down-payment, is financed at a competitive interest rate, has a high predicted resale value, provides reasonable fuel economy, and can be serviced at most independent garages.

2. **Look for above-average reliability and durability:** Factory-related auto defects can't hide from the Internet. Thanks to information put out by government safety agencies, independent consumer groups, and private auto safety associations, we can easily separate the cherries from the lemons and get a car that will last 15 years or more – 4 years longer than the time most Canadians keep their vehicles.

   For example, last June the Internet reported that Jeep and Fiat were at the bottom of J.D. Power and Associates' *Initial Quality Study*. Then in October, Chrysler's Dodge, Ram, Jeep and Fiat brands were shown to be the bottom-four finishers in *Consumer Reports* Annual Owner Survey. The Chrysler brand fell four places to rank 22nd out of 28 brands listed. On the other hand, the *Consumer Reports* reliability study awarded the highest marks to Toyota and Lexus, perennial front runners for several decades.

   Fiat responded to its low scores by stressing that its quality control manager had been "let go" to pursue other interests and that the company was countering the bad publicity through a television campaign making fun of Fiat's ("fix it again, Tony") reputation. It didn't work. Fiat still has a low-rank.

3. **Load up on safety features:** This means getting a vehicle that has at least three essential safety features: A high crash-protection test score, electronic stability control (all 2012 and later models), fail-safe accelerator over-rides, and a rear-view camera.

4. **Don't go overboard on performance and comfort:** More gadgets mean more glitches. Look for easy-to modulate acceleration, stopping, steering, and shifting, without undue noise or jostling. Exterior styling should focus on functionality and interior amenities must be practical, comfortable, and convenient to access. Beware of chin-to-chest head restraints.

5. Be wary of infotainment features: Opt for the latest electronic safety gear and infotainment features that have proven reliability and are not simply "bolt-on" hardware and software systems peddled by outside suppliers. Unfortunately, the stampede for optimum "connectivity" has resulted in failure-prone electronic systems like Ford's MyFord Touch (2011-14 models) and systems that are dangerously distracting.

Several years ago the Ford brand fell from 5th to 27th in J. D. Power & Associates' new-car quality survey, largely because of complaints with MyFord Touch. On the other hand, Chrysler's Uconnect touch-screen infotainment system is ranked as one of the *best* in the industry, followed by Chevrolet, Hyundai, Kia, and Toyota.

NARROWING DOWN THE CHOICES

Consider buying a *Lemon-Aid* approved new or used vehicle identified by an asterisk (*) in the sales charts below, which apply to 2015 and 2016 models. Be mindful that a car or truck should be kept at least 10 years or longer to compensate for depreciation and assorted acquisition fees. A new well-equipped compact car or small SUV will run between $18,000 and $25,000; a 3-year-old used version sells for only half as much. Add a couple more years and shave two-thirds off the original selling price.

Best-Selling 2015 Cars

Sales	Model	Sales	Model	Sales	Model
#1	*Honda Civic	#10	*Honda Accord	#19	Chrysler 200
#2	*Hyundai Elantra	#11	*Toyota Camry	#20	*Subaru Impreza
#3	*Toyota Corolla	#12	Nissan Sentra	#21	*BMW 3-Series
#4	*Mazda 3	#13	*Kia Rio	#22	*Kia Soul
#5	Chevrolet Cruze	#14	Hyundai Sonata	#23	Nissan Altima
#6	*Volkswagen Jetta	#15	Nissan Versa	#24	Ford Fiesta
#7	*Hyundai Accent	#16	*Volkswagen Golf	#25	*Subaru Outback
#8	Ford Focus	#17	*Kia Forte		
#9	Ford Fusion	#18	*Honda Fit		

Best-Selling 2015 SUV/Crossovers

Sales	Model	Sales	Model	Sales	Model
#1	Ford Escape	#10	*Chevrolet Equinox	#19	*Toyota Highlander
#2	*Honda CR-V	#11	Ford Edge	#20	Nissan Pathfinder
#3	*Toyota RAV4	#12	*Kia Sorento	#21	Chevrolet Trax
#4	*Nissan Rogue	#13	Jeep Grand Cherokee	#22	*Lexus RX
#5	*Hyundai Santa Fe Sport	#14	Ford Explorer	#23	Audi Q5
#6	Dodge Journey	#15	*Subaru Forester	#24	Mitsubishi RVR
#7	Jeep Wrangler	#16	*Hyundai Tucson	#25	*Acura RDX
#8	Jeep Cherokee	#17	*GMC Terrain		
#9	*Mazda CX-5	#18	Volkswagen Tiguan		

Sources: Automakers & Automotive News Data

Best-Selling 2015 Trucks

Sales	Model	Sales	Model	Sales	Model
#1	Ford F-Series	#6	*Toyota Tundra	#11	Chevrolet Colorado
#2	*Dodge Ram	#7	*Nissan Frontier	#12	*Chevrolet Avalanche
#3	*GMC Sierra	#8	Nissan Titan	#13	*Cadillac Escalade EXT
#4	*Chevrolet Silverado	#9	*Honda Ridgeline		
#5	*Toyota Tacoma	#10	GMC Canyon		

2015 Minivans

Sales	Model	Sales	Model	Sales	Model
#1	Chevrolet Orlando	#5	Kia Rondo	#9	*Toyota Sienna
#2	Chrysler Town & Country	#6	Kia Sedona	#10	Volkswagen Routan
#3	Dodge Grand Caravan	#7	*Mazda 5		
#4	*Honda Odyssey	#8	Nissan Quest		

2015 Commercial Vans

Sales	Model	Sales	Model	Sales	Model
#1	*Chevrolet Express	#5	*GMC Savana	#9	Ram Cargo Van
#2	Ford E-Series	#6	Mercedes-Benz Sprinter	#10	Ram ProMaster
#3	Ford Transit	#7	Nissan NV		
#4	Ford Transit Connect	#8	Nissan NV200		

New or used, the vehicle you buy must meet your everyday driving needs and have high crashworthiness and reliability scores. Annual maintenance should cost no more than the CAA-and-DesRosiers-estimated average of $800 to $1,100. The depreciation rate should have leveled off, so that subsequent years won't cut the car's price by more than a couple thousand dollars, leaving you with some resale equity. Parts and servicing costs shouldn't be excessive either, which means checking out maintenance costs from Internet owner forums before you buy.

SOUTH KOREA: SOARING; JAPAN: SNORING

The best vehicles come from South Korea, which has made an amazing quality/sales turnaround in just a decade, followed by Japan automakers who appear to be coasting on past glories. A few European makes (mostly Audi, BMW, and Volkswagen), and even fewer American models bring up the rear, led by General Motors. Chrysler/Fiat comes a distant second, and finally Ford, which continues to be trapped in its self-inflicted poor-quality funk.

This year small cars and family sedans give the most performance and reliability for the money. And, throughout 2016 their prices will continue to decline because the buying crowd has so much fuel-savings bling in its pockets to spend. Customers who once were ready to buy smaller, or consider getting a hybrid or electric vehicle, are now marching in tandem toward fully-loaded luxury cars, SUVs, trucks, and vans. This will create a bonanza of cheap small cars this winter and, likely lead to the demise of the Chevy Volt electric car, hybrid price-cutting, and fewer diesel-equipped cars. Still some bargain-priced fuel-efficient models will remain, like Honda's Fit, Civic, and Accord; Hyundai's Accent and Elantra; Subaru's Forester and Legacy; Toyota's Corolla; and Volkswagen's diesel-equipped TDI (with manual transmission).

Luxury models, American minivans, and small to large Chrysler and Ford passenger cars, SUVs, and trucks represent the worst value among new and used vehicles. If interior room is your paramount concern, consider a Mazda 5 microvan, a Subaru Outback or Forester, or a downsized Hyundai Tucson or Toyota RAV4.

The best values for your purchasing dollar among luxury cars are the BMW 3 Series, including the X3, Acura RDX, and MDX, Infiniti EX, and the Lexus lineup.

Luxury vehicles that don't provide much value as they age are those built by Cadillac, Jaguar, Land Rover, and Lincoln.

Researchers at the University of Michigan publish an annual record, listing which automakers make the most and least satisfying vehicles. Called the American Customer Satisfaction Index (ACSI), the group pulls no punches in naming which manufacturers build the best and worst vehicles in terms of owner satifaction. ACSI's most surprising conclusions, excerpted below, confirm that there is no correlation between the cost of an automobile and its inherent quality, although foreign makes generally have the most satisfied customers.

Car buyer satisfaction is down for a third straight year as prices rise and recalls continue. Customer satisfaction with automobiles fell 3.7 percent to 79 on ACSI's 100-point scale.

While it is true that all cars are now much better than they were 10 to 20 years ago, it is alarming that so many of them have quality problems. This should not happen with modern manufacturing technology and has negative consequences for driver safety, costs and customer satisfaction.

Car owners report a 40 percent increase in recalls compared to the second quarter of 2014, which – along with rising prices – is damaging driver satisfaction. While quality problems abound, rising prices also are contributing to the decline in buyer satisfaction.

- Among 27 nameplates tracked by the ACSI, 15 lose ground in customer satisfaction and only 2 improve from a year ago – both foreign-made. Foreign-made cars have a significant advantage in customer satisfaction and 77% of the above-average nameplates in the ACSI are imports.

- At the top of the industry overall, Toyota's Lexus plateaus at 84%, taking the lead from Mercedes-Benz, which falls 3% to 83%. After a sharp drop to the bottom of the industry a year ago, Honda's luxury brand Acura appears to have turned a corner. One of only two brands to improve this year, Acura rebounds 8% to 83%, tied with Mercedes and Lincoln for second place.

- BMW – the other gainer – rises 3% to 82%. Also at 82% are Subaru (-4%) and Toyota (-1%), the top-scoring mass market automakers. Volkswagen (-5%), Buick (-4%) and Honda (-4%) all slip into a tie at 80%. Cadillac and Mazda also score 80%, unchanged since last year. Meanwhile, the Ford nameplate (-2%) and Chevrolet (-4%) drop to 79% alongside Volvo, which returns to the ACSI near the bottom of the luxury category.

- The remaining automakers are below the industry average. GMC and Kia (each down 5%) match Audi (-1%) at 78%, just ahead of Nissan (-5%) and Nissan's luxury nameplate Infiniti, which debuts at 77%. Mitsubishi also posts its first ACSI score of 77%. BMW's MINI enters the Index at 76%, tying Fiat Chrysler's Dodge. At the bottom of the category are all four Fiat Chrysler brands: Dodge (-3% to 76%), Jeep (-5% to 75%), Chrysler (-9% to 74%) and Fiat (73%).

The charts that follow show 5-year customer satisfaction trends for domestic automakers in comparison with international manufacturers, as well as results for Detroit's Big Three.

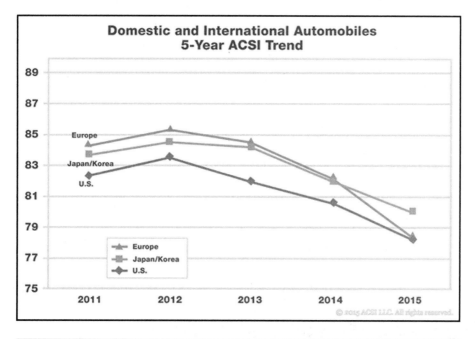

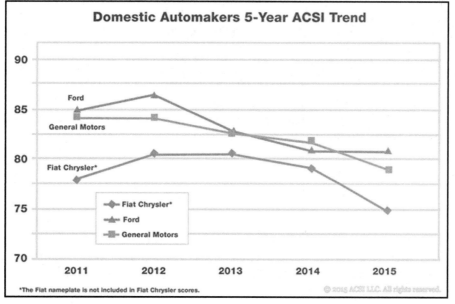

The Fiat nameplate is not included in Fiat Chrysler scores.

Lemon-Aid believes low quality scores are due to the following three factors: Cost cutting, increased electronic and mechanical complexity, and the use of outside suppliers making the cheapest parts.

Don't Believe in the "Fuel Fairy"

Fuel economy isn't all that important when you are buying used, since all of your other savings should easily compensate for the extra fuel costs.

We don't recommend most gas-electric engine hybrids; their retail prices are mostly at the high end and long-term reliability can be problematic. *Consumer Reports'* April 2013 issue targets the 2009 Honda Civic Hybrid as the worst of a bad lot:

> [It] has a big problem with the drive battery. The 2009 model was the worst: almost one in five owners needed a replacement hybrid battery in our 12-month survey period...more than ten percent of owners of the 2003, 2004, and 2010 models also needed one.

Honda provided a software update to owners of 2006-08 Civic Hybrids to help extend the life of the IMA battery and issued a technical service bulletin (TSB) for the States in late 2012 which extends the IMA battery warranty. Batteries that were once covered for 10 years/100,000 miles, are now warranteed for 11 years/137,000 miles; vehicles covered for 8 years/80,000 miles, are now covered for 9 years/96,000 miles; and replacement batteries that were bought are covered for 36,000 miles, or three years. Furthermore, imagine looking for a replacement battery while in another town or on vacation. As for guaranteeing the $3,000 replacement up to the equivalent of three years driving? Try telling that to the dealer when negotiating its trade-in price.

Honda Civic Hybrid (above). Sure, check the oil and water – oh! – and replace the battery.

Hybrid fuel sipping can save gas as advertised – 4.5L/100km (2013 Toyota Prius), or much less – with some owners claiming a 40% reduction in the fuel economy hyped by automakers. There have also been reports that hybrid motors have a high failure rate due to corrosion; battery replacement costs are estimated to run as high as $3,000 (U.S.) for the Toyota Prius and $10,000 for other makes; and their 8-year resale values are no better than similar vehicles equipped with conventional engines. Look again at a 2010 Toyota Prius that originally sold for $27,400. It is now valued at almost a third of its original price (and approaching the end of the battery-pack warranty).

Take our Part Four fuel economy estimates with a large grain of salt and blame it on the feds, since Ottawa is in cahoots with automakers in coming up with fanciful fuel economy ratings. It's not a criminal conspiracy; it's just lazy complacency that they are just now correcting. Nevertheless, up to 2014, the Canadian mileage figures were "cooked" by as much as 22%.

In November of 2011, CBC News and the Automobile Protection Association (APA) compared the Canadian and American fuel consumption ratings of various 2012 models. The survey showed that Canadian fuel-economy estimates were inflated by 16-22% compared to the U.S. estimates, for the same vehicles. Since this is L/100km, a lower number is better.

More accurate U.S. fuel economy figures for 2014 and earlier models can be found at: *www.fueleconomy.gov*, while the puffed-up Canadian figures reside at *oee. nrcan.gc.ca/transportation/tools/fuelratings/ratings-search.cfm.*

APA President George Iny says Canadian numbers were generated by the industry from standardized lab tests, not real-life road conditions. Back in 2008 the U.S. government got rid of the lab tests.

TAKE ADVANTAGE OF DEPRECIATION

Not all cars and trucks are born with equal attributes, and they age (depreciate) at different rates. When buying new, you want a reliable model that depreciates slowly; when buying used, consider a vehicle that has prematurely lost much of its value but is still dependable and inexpensive to maintain. Fortunately, there are plenty of the latter on the market due to the increased number of trade-ins as new car sales rebound in Canada.

During the past year, rebates, cut-rate financing, subsidized leasing, and fluctuating fuel costs, along with poor reputations for quality, have depressed the residual values of most American cars and trucks. According to the Automotive Lease Guide (*www.alg.com*), Detroit-made vehicles barely keep 33% of their sticker values after 4 years, while the average Japanese make is predicted to keep 46% of its value after 4 years. Residual values can be accessed free of charge at *www.cars. com/go/alg/index.jsp#*. Here are a few predicted residual values for some popular 2015 models.

2015 Dodge Grand Caravan

	24 months	36 months	48 months	60 months
MSRP	$22,060	$22,060	$22,060	$22,060
ALG Residual %	56	45	38	32
ALG Residual Value	$12,850	$10,400	$8,700	$7,250

2015 Chevrolet Silverado 1500 2WD

	24 months	36 months	48 months	60 months
MSRP	$28,172	$28,172	$28,172	$28,172
ALG Residual %	55	45	41	36
ALG Residual Value	$15,875	$13,025	$11,650	$10,275

2015 Mazda MX-5 Miata Convertible Sport MT

	24 months	36 months	48 months	60 months
MSRP	$25,088	$25,088	$25,088	$25,088
ALG Residual %	63	53	46	39
ALG Residual Value	$15,975	$13,475	$11,725	$9,775

2015 Audi TT Coupe 2.0T Quattro

	24 months	36 months	48 months	60 months
MSRP	$41,245	$41,245	$41,245	$41,245
ALG Residual %	68	59	51	44
ALG Residual Value	$28,925	$25,250	$21,675	$18,800

How Lemon-Aid Picks the "Best" and "Worst"

Lemon-Aid doesn't give a rating for every vehicle make sold in Canada. We focus primarily on new and used vehicles, sold in relatively large numbers, considered to be the best and worst buys. Often, we may suggest buying a high-ranking used car that is similar to the new version, but sold for much less (the Mazda Miata and Audi TT Coupe are good examples).

If you have a question about a vehicle not found in *Lemon-Aid*, send us an email at *lemonaid@earthlink.net*. We will be glad to send you a free update with the information we have available.

Lemon-Aid has been giving honest, independent, and dependable auto ratings for over 4 decades by following these simple rules.

- Ratings should be used primarily as a comparative database that combines a driving test with an owners' survey of past models (only *Consumer Reports* does this). Unfortunately, *Consumer Reports'* annual April edition has dropped its reliability ratings for specific components of the past 12 model years. Instead, there is just a black or red circle indicating which model year is more reliable than another. Nowhere is survey information provided on which mechanical components or body parts are failure-prone, essential data useful when arguing for extended warranty coverage or compensation. Used car buyers are further penalized in not knowing which problem areas an independent mechanic or body shop should check first before the vehicle is purchased.

- Failure trends should first be gathered from owner complaints posted on the National Highway Traffic Safety Administration (NHTSA) *safercar.gov* site. It's a treasure trove of auto-failure anecdotes that show which cars have repeated failures or outstanding recalls, or are part of an ongoing safety probe, and which particular component is faulty. It also helps owners to get secret warranty repairs through the use of confidential service bulletins found on the site.

- Survey responses must come from a large owner pool (over 1.1 million responses from *Consumer Reports* subscribers, for example). Anecdotal responses should then be cross-referenced, updated, and given depth and specificity through NHTSA's safety complaint prism. Responses must be cross-referenced again through automaker internal service bulletins to determine the extent of the defect over a specific model and model-year range and to alert owners to problems likely to occur and the recommended fix.

- Rankings should be predicated on important characteristics measured over a significant period of time, unlike Car of the Year contests, owner-perceived values, or J.D. Power – "first impression" owner surveys carried out after only 3 months of ownership. This is particularly important for first-year cars and models that have undergone a major redesign. As for awards given by auto clubs, car critics, and magazines like *Car and Driver* and *Motor Trend*, be on your guard. Any car can be Car of the Year – if the advertising payoff is big enough.

This includes the venerable 18 million member ADAC German Auto Club, founded in 1903 (*www.stuff.co.nz/motoring/news/9637705/Falsified-voting-tatters-award-reputation*):

Volkswagen said it was considering giving back the award.

ADAC communications director Michael Ramstetter resigned in disgrace after conceding he manipulated the results of the car club's coveted Yellow Angel award for Germany's favourite car, which was won last week by the Volkswagen Golf model.

ADAC conceded that Ramstetter, the editor of ADAC's popular *ADAC Motorwelt* magazine that called itself Europe's biggest monthly with 18 million readers, massively inflated the results of votes, saying 34,299 motorists had voted for the Golf as Germany's favourite car when it had only been 3409 votes.

The ADAC affair recalled another scandal about German car testing in 1997 when a Swedish motor magazine found Mercedes' A-Class tended to flip while undergoing its "elk test," or evasive manoeuvre test. German magazines did not detect the flaw. Mercedes first declined to comment but later recalled the cars to retrofit added safety features.

- A vehicle should not be rated during the first 6 months it has come on the market or undergone a complete redesign. Look at the much heralded Honda Fit for example. The Fit has always been a reliable, well-performing small car. But, the redesigned 2015 model was not as good, due to its new design and relocation to another manufacturing plant in Mexico. Below are three typical examples of safety-related complaints received by NHTSA (*safercar.gov*) for the 2015 Fit. Some other incidents are quite bizarre like flea infestation, Marquis de Sade head restraints, airbag failure to deploy, reversed rear seatbelt buckles, sudden acceleration, sudden brake failures, rainwater leaks, and the smell of rotten meat coming through the AC vents. Complaints are entered into *Lemon-Aid*'s complaint database and are used to determine if a safety-related defect trend exists and whether or not a vehicle's rating should be downgraded. (In the case of the Fit, the noted complaints apparently affected only a few cars.)

New or used, Honda's Fit offers bulletproof reliability, superior driving performance, and excellent fuel economy, all at a reasonable cost.

The contact owns a 2015 Honda Fit. While driving approximately 30 mph downhill, the vehicle accelerated independently and the brakes failed. The vehicle crashed into a building. The passenger sustained a cracked vertebrae in the neck that required medical attention. The failure mileage was 1,300.

. . .

Unpleasant smells started coming out of vents in early July 2014 (I purchased the vehicle new on June 13, 2014). They started as smelling like fresh mulch or dog poo, but became more like mold/mildew, sometimes smelling like wet dirty gym socks and getting as bad as smelling like rotting meat. Several attempts (one by me and three by the service department where I'd purchased the vehicle) have been made to correct the problem. Chemical cleaners, replacing the cabin air filter have been done. I have inspected the cowl intakes, cabin air filter and blower box myself and the smells do not emanate from them. I was informed there was a worker walkout at the new Mexico-based plant (the real reason for the launch delay in the US from mid-April to mid-June), where the 2015 Honda Fits for North America are made, and that many vehicles were left standing where they were when the walkout commenced, and the walkout lasted weeks. Someone should investigate this and see what else may have happened to these vehicles while they sat stagnant during the walkout.

. . .

The front seats are really uncomfortable. The head restraints on the front seats force our heads too far forwards, causing neck pains and sometimes neck aches or headaches. The front seats don't offer sufficient lumbar support. After 30-45 minutes of riding or driving, our lower backs start to hurt. This pain can last a while after exiting the vehicle. The front seat cushion cuts off circulation below the waist after 40-45 minutes of sitting in them. This numbs my legs, which can reduce reaction time in case I need to try to avoid an accident.

- Ratings must come from unimpeachable sources. There should be no conflicts of interest due to ties with advertisers or consultants, and no results gathered from self-serving tests done under ideal conditions, like previous years' Transport Canada fuel economy tests.

- Tested cars must be bought, not borrowed, and serviced, not pampered, as part of a journalists' fleet lent out for ranking purposes. Also, automakers must be judged equally and not penalized if they refuse to "pay to play" in annual car of the year rankings handed out by car critics. Of course, automobile manufacturers must not be members of the ranking body.

- Again, we are wary of self-administered fuel economy ratings used by automakers in complicity with the federal government and some car enthusiast magazines. *Automotive News* added its name to the list of skeptics when it found that some Honda and Toyota hybrids get 20-40% less real-world gas mileage than advertised. The car industry publication also discovered that hybrids need to be driven in a particular way in order to be fuel efficient, use more fuel than ordinary cars on short trips or when using air conditioning, and are affected by colder climates, resulting in increased fuel consumption way beyond what the ratings figures indicate.

DEFINITION OF TERMS

Ratings

We rate vehicles on a scale of one to five stars, with five stars being our top ranking. Models are designated as "Recommended," "Above Average," "Average," "Below Average," or "Not Recommended," with the most recent year's rating indicated by the number of stars beside the vehicle's name.

Recommended

We don't give this rating out very often, and we are quick to drop it if safety, servicing, or overall quality control decline. We don't believe for one moment that the more you spend, the better performing, more reliable, or safer the vehicle. For example, most Hondas are as good as Acuras, which cost thousands of dollars more for their luxury cachet. The same is true when you compare Toyota and Lexus. Even more surprising, some luxury makes, such as Jaguar, are "pseudo-luxe," because the older models may be merely dressed-up Fords sold at a luxury-car price. The extra money only buys you more features of dubious value and newer, failure-prone electronic gadgetry. Also, luxury models are just as likely to have factory-related defects as cheaper cars. For example, BMW's high-tech 2014 i8 plug-in hybrid was recently recalled because the gas tank might leak fuel due to an inadequate weld. The i8 sells for $150,000 Canadian.

In fact, the simplest choice is often the best buy. Ford's Mustang, Hyundai's Elantra and Tucson, and the Mazda3 get positive ratings because they are easy to find, fairly reliable, and reasonably priced – not the case with many over-priced Hondas and Toyotas. The above vehicles are good buys new, though used model recommendations may vary by year, just like Mustangs with made-in-China "grenading" manual transmissions or the 26.2 million 2000-11 models (worldwide) equipped with shrapnel-shooting Takata air bags (recalled by BMW, Chrysler/Jeep, Ford, General Motors, Honda, Mazda, Mitsubishi, Nissan, Subaru, and Toyota), or the 2015-16 Chevrolet Impala and Dodge Ram which slipped a couple of notches from their almost-perfect 2014 model scores.

Above Average/Average

Vehicles that are given an Above Average or Average rating are good second choices if a Recommended vehicle isn't your first choice, isn't available, or isn't within budget.

Below Average/Not Recommended

Many vehicles are given a Below Average rating by *Lemon-Aid* because we know they will likely be troublesome; however, we also believe their low price and reasonably priced independent servicing may make them acceptable buys to some do-it-yourselfers who have put aside sufficient money saved from the transaction to cover expected failures. Chrysler minivans, for example, are relatively cheaper than other minivans principally due to their reputation for poor reliability, failure-prone powertrains, and rapid depreciation.

Vehicles with a history of unforeseeable, recurring, and expensive defects are most likely to be given a Not Recommended rating. They are best avoided altogether, no matter how low the price, because they're so likely to suffer from many durability and performance problems that you may never stop paying for repairs. Sometimes, however, a Not Recommended model will improve over several model years and garner a better rating.

Incidentally, for those owners who wonder how I can stop recommending model years I once recommended, let me be clear. As vehicles age, their ratings change to reflect new information from owners and from service bulletins relating to durability and the automaker's warranty performance. For example, Honda's Civic, Nissan's Quest, Toyota's Sienna, and BMW's Mini have been downgraded for some years because new service bulletins and additional owner complaints show disturbing trends in crashworthiness, dependability, or overall performance.

For 45 years, I have been an active consumer advocate and auto journalist. When I uncover fraud, unsafe designs, or failure-prone components, I first expose the problem. Then I take a second step, one rarely taken by journalists who want to keep their jobs. I become part of the story by mobilizing owners, lawyers, and independent mechanics to force automaker recalls or set up reimbursement programs.

Some Lemon-Aid Victories

- Published the warning ("Your Key Ring may Kill You") about GM "killer" ignition switches (2003-07 models) in the 2009-10 edition of *Lemon-Aid* and supported that warning with GM's own internal service bulletins. In 2014, six years after *Lemon-Aid*'s warning, GM admitted liability for the deadly switches, recalling 6 million vehicles, earmarked over a $1 billion in compensation through the 2013 model-year production, and paid a $35 million fine to the U.S. government. GM Canada admitted no liability, saying it was unaware that the defect existed. Transport Canada bought this fabrication.

- Forged an out-of-court, class-action settlement in 2006 making GM Canada pay back millions of dollars to Canadian car owners stuck with "cooked" V6 engines afflicted by warped intake manifold gaskets in GM's 1995-2005 models. GM paid Canadians an estimated $40 million in repairs because the automaker used faulty engine gaskets made out of plastic to save a few pennies per car.

- Beat GM and Nissan in two separate Supreme Court actions in the early 70s and 80s. The Court ruled GM and its dealers were equally liable for auto defects and the Nissan decision nailed down the constitutionality of small claims court and forced Nissan, along with other automakers to quit selling year-old models as the latest model-year.

- Forced GM Canada to pay a $20,000 fine for criminal conduct after lying about its 1978 Firenza's poor reliability; getting the car taken off the market, negotiating cash refunds for Firenza owners; and successfully lobbied provincial legislatures for class-action laws to prevent future Firenza abuses.

Throughout the year, *Lemon-Aid* gets refunds for buyers cheated by dealers and automakers. We lobby automakers to compensate owners of out-of-warranty vehicles either through formal warranty extension programs or on a case-by-case basis. We also publish little-known lawsuits, judgments, and settlements to help car owners and their lawyers win their cases or get a fair settlement.

Reliability is defined as anything that causes one to return the car for non-maintenance repairs; it doesn't include recalls, because recalls are not a measure of initial quality. Rating data is compiled from a number of sources, including confidential technical service bulletins, owner complaints sent to me each year by *Lemon-Aid* readers, owners' comments posted on the Internet, and survey reports and tests done by auto associations, consumer groups, and government organizations. Some auto columnists feel this isn't a scientific sampling, and they're right. Nevertheless, the results shown above confirm we have been mostly on the mark over the past four decades.

Lemon-Aid reviews and reliability rankings have nothing to do with how popular cars are, nor do they impact future sales. Take a look at the 2015-16 Jeep line. The cars are quntiessential lemons, fire-prone, and service-challenged, yet sales are "red hot" (pun intended).

Not all cars and trucks are profiled; those that are new to the market or relatively rare may receive only an abbreviated mention in the Appendix until sufficient owner or service bulletin information becomes available. Some cars aren't profiled at all due to page limitations.

Strengths and Weaknesses

With the Detroit automakers, engine head gasket, automatic transmission, brake, steering, and electrical failures are omnipresent. Ford infotainment systems are chaotic and annoying. South Korean vehicles have weak transmissions, electrical systems, and electronic control modules. Japanese makes are noted mostly for their brake, minivan door, AC, window, sound system, electrical, and fuel delivery glitches, though engine and transmission failures have been appearing more frequently, especially with Toyota and Lexus models built during the past decade. Finally, the European automakers are in a high-tech bind. Like Ford, electronic demons constantly bedevil older Audi, BMW, Jaguar, Land Rover, Mercedes and VW high-end products, making them unreliable and costly to service after only a few years of ownership; plus, these vehicles are so complicated to diagnose and service that many mechanics simply throw up their hands in dismay.

Unlike other auto guides, *Lemon-Aid* knows where automotive skeletons are buried and pinpoints potential parts failures, explains why those parts fail, and advises you as to your chances of getting a repair refund under a "goodwill warranty" program. We also offer troubleshooting tips direct from the automakers' bulletins so that your mechanic won't replace parts unrelated to your troubles before coming upon the defective component that is actually responsible.

Parts supply can be a real problem. It's a myth that automakers have to keep a supply of parts sufficient to service what they sell, as any buyer of a Chevrolet/Daewoo Aveo, a front-drive Lincoln Continental, or a Ford Windstar/Freestar will quickly tell you. Additionally, apart from *Lemon-Aid*, there's no consumer database that warns prospective purchasers as to which models are "parts-challenged."

Major Redesign

This section outlines a vehicle's differences between model years, including overhauls in design and other modifications. If a model is unchanged from one model year to the next, why pay a premium for it simply because it is one year newer?

CURRENT LATCH RATINGS (2015 models unless otherwise noted)

Good

BMW 5 series	Mercedes-Benz GL-Class	Volkswagen Passat

Acceptable

Acura MDX	Dodge Durango	Honda Odyssey	Mazda 3
Buick Enclave	Dodge Grand Caravan	Honda Pilot	Mazda CX-5
Chevrolet Cruze	Ford Edge	Hyundai Santa Fe	Mercedes-Benz C-Class
Chevrolet Equinox	Ford Expedition	Jeep Cherokee	Mercedes-Benz E-Class
Chevrolet Impala	Ford Explorer	Jeep Compass	Mitsubishi Outlander Sport
Chevrolet Malibu	Ford Flex	Kia Forte	2014 Nissan Maxima
Chevrolet Tahoe	Ford Focus	Kia Optima	Nissan Murano
Chevrolet Traverse	Ford Taurus	Kia Sedona	Nissan Pathfinder
Chrysler 300	GMC Terrain	Kia Sorento	Nissan Versa
Chrysler Town & Country	GMC Yukon XL	Kia Soul	Toyota Camry
Dodge Dart	Honda Civic	Lexus GX	Volvo S60

Marginal

2016 Acura RDX	Ford Escape	Lexus CT 200h	Subaru Impreza
Audi Q7	Ford F-150	Lexus NX	Subaru Outback
BMW 3 series	Ford Fusion	Lexus RC	Subaru XV Crosstrek
2016 BMW X3	GMC Acadia	Lexus RX	Toyota 4Runner
BMW X5	Honda Accord	Mazda CX-9	Toyota Avalon
Buick LaCrosse	Honda CR-V	Mini Cooper	Toyota Corolla
Cadillac SRX	Hyundai Elantra	Nissan Frontier	Toyota Highlander
Chevrolet Sonic	Hyundai Sonata	Nissan Quest	Toyota Prius
Chrysler 200	Infiniti QX60	Nissan Rogue	Toyota RAV4
Dodge Charger	Jeep Grand Cherokee	Nissan Sentra	Volvo V60
Dodge Journey	Jeep Wrangler	Subaru Forester	Volvo XC60
Dodge Ram 1500			

Poor

Chevrolet Silverado 1500	Hyundai Accent	Nissan Altima	Toyota Tundra
Ford Fiesta	Lexus ES	Toyota Sienna	Volkswagen Jetta
GMC Sierra 1500	Mazda 6		

Source: *http://www.iihs.org/iihs/news/desktopnews/iihs-launches-ease-of-use-ratings*

Or, if a vehicle was redesigned a few years ago, don't you want that vehicle a year after the redesign, when most of the factory kinks have been ironed out?

Safety

Child Safety Seat Setup

New this year, we show whether the vehicle is user-friendly for the installation of a safety seat as judged by the Insurance Institute for Highway Safety (IIHS). As you can see in the Current Latch Ratings chart, the ease of installation doesn't relate to vehicle cost, size, or origin (a KiaRio or Soul is "Acceptable," whereas a GM Silverado/Sierra truck and VW luxury Passat are rated as "Poor."

Crashworthiness

How much crash protection can you expect per model year, going back at least a decade? *Lemon-Aid* cites many NHTSA (*safercar.gov*) owner consumer complaints by model year, even though they aren't all safety related. These independent confirmations by other owners are key to proving your failure is factory related and widespread. Readers often use this corroboration to get free "goodwill" repairs or to win lawsuits involving accident damage, injuries, or death. These complaints are also supportive in countering automaker/dealer dismissive responses like "We never saw that before," "No one else has complained," "It could be your driving or poor maintenance," "We couldn'duplicate the failure," and the most arrogant response of all, "That's normal, they all operate like that."

NHTSA records list many common safety-related failures that include vehicles rolling away with the transmission in Park, sliding minivan doors that don't open when they should or open when they shouldn't, or electronic computer modules that cause a vehicle to "lag and lurch." The vehicle won't accelerate from a stop for a few seconds, and then it will lurch out into traffic after the accelerator has been floored to get the vehicle out of harm's way.

Be wary and persistent in protecting your family. Heretofore, the auto industry, with Transport Canada complicity, buried (literally) its mistakes, like Takata refusing to call its shrapnel-shooting airbags "defective," or Honda hiding thousands of accident reports from government investigators and waiting a decade to recall Takata airbags it knew in 2004 could be killers.

If *Lemon-Aid* doesn't list a problem you have experienced (safety related, or not), go directly to the NHTSA website's database at *www.safercar.gov* for an update. Your vehicle may be currently under investigation, or may have been recalled since this year's guide was published. *Lemon-Aid* doesn't list most recalls because there are so many. In 2014, 600 recall notices were sent out in Canada covering 8 million vehicles, while the U.S. recalled almost 64 million vehicles with about 700 recall announcements over the same period.

Local dealers can also be helpful. They can easily run your car's Vehicle Identication Number (VIN) through their computers, since they hope to snag the extra recall repair dollars. Just make sure you ask the dealer to also check for a "customer satisfaction program," a "service policy," a "goodwill" warranty extension, or a free emissions warranty service.

Owner-reported Safety-related Failures

We list safety failures reported by owners, ensuing investigations, lawsuits, and court settlements.

Stonewall, then Recall

Don't be surprised if your vehicle is covered by a "phantom" recall where the defect is known but the remedy hasn't been approved, or the corrected parts aren't yet available. For example, in October 2014, Chrysler recalled nearly 500,000 2011 through 2014 cars and SUVs for faulty alternators that would make the 3.6L V6 engine stall unexpectedly. By early 2015 many owners were still waiting for a fix. Why the delay? There's a U.S.-imposed $35 million fine for taking more than five days to announce a recall once an automaker discovers a defect is safety related – there is no fine in the U.S., or in Canada, for late repairs, although legislation is in the works.

Alert

The ALERT! section clearly points out those vehicles that may be exceptional buys, or are seriously flawed, or require special maintenance.

Vehicle Profile Tables

Prices

Dealer profit margins on new and used cars vary considerably – giving lots of room to negotiate a fair price if you take the time to find out what the vehicle is really worth. The manufacturer's suggested retail price (MSRP) in the Prices and Specs box is a useful benchmark to spot inflated prices on 2015-16 models .

Used prices are based on sales recorded as of August 2015. Prices are for the lowest-priced standard model that is in good condition with a maximum of 20,000 km for each calendar year. Watch for price differences reflecting each model's equipment upgrades, designated by a numerical or alphabetical abbreviation. For example, L, LX, and LXT usually mean more standard features are included, progressively, in each model. Numerical progression usually relates to engine size.

Prices reflect the automarkets in Quebec and Ontario, where the majority of used-vehicle transactions take place. Residents of Eastern Canada should add 10%, and Western Canadians should add at least 15-20% to the listed price. Why the higher costs? Less competition, combined with inflated new-vehicle prices in these regions. Don't be too disheartened, though; you'll recoup some of what you overpaid down the road when you sell the vehicle.

Why are *Lemon-Aid*'s used car prices sometimes lower than the prices found in dealer guides such as *Red Book*? The answer is simple. Much like a homeowner selling a house, dealers inflate their prices so that you can bargain the price down and wind up convinced that you made a great deal.

We use newspaper classified ads from Quebec, Ontario, and British Columbia, as well as auction reports, to calculate my used-vehicle values. We then check these figures against *Red Book* and *Black Book* prices. We then project what the value will be by mid-model year, and that lowers prices further.

The average price is given to leave some margin for negotiation as well as to account for the regional differences in prices, and the sudden popularity of certain models or vehicle classes.

Since no evaluation method is foolproof, check dealer prices against newspaper- and Internet-sourced private classified ads and then add the option values listed on the next page to come up with a fairly representative offer. Don't forget to bargain the price down further if the odometer shows a cumulative reading of more than 20,000 km per calendar year. Interestingly, the value of anti-lock brakes in trade-ins plummeted during the last few years as they became a standard feature on many entry-level vehicles.

Value of Options by Model Year

OPTION	2005	2006	2007	2008	2009	2010	2011	2012	2013
Air conditioning	$200	$200	$250	$300	$300	$300	$325	$325	$350
Radio & CD player	100	100	100	100	100	100	100	100	100
Anti-lock brakes	50	50	50	50	50	75	75	100	100
Automatic transmission	150	150	150	150	150	175	175	175	200
Cruise control	50	50	50	50	50	50	50	50	75
Electric six-way seat	25	25	25	25	25	25	25	50	50
GPS	50	50	50	50	50	75	75	75	100
Leather upholstery	0	0	0	0	0	25	25	25	50
Paint protector	0	0	0	0	0	25	25	25	50
Power door locks	0	0	0	0	50	50	50	50	50
Power windows	0	0	0	0	0	50	50	50	50
Rustproofing	0	0	0	0	25	25	50	50	50
Stability control	50	50	50	50	50	50	50	0	0
Sunroof	50	50	50	75	125	125	150	150	200
T-top roof	150	150	150	150	150	150	150	200	200
Tilt steering	0	50	50	75	75	75	75	75	100
Tinted windows	0	0	0	0	0	0	0	0	0
Tires (Firestone)	−100	−100	−100	−100	−100	−150	−150	−150	−150

Note: Electronic stability control has been a mandatory feature since 2012.

It will be easier to match the lower used prices if you buy privately. Dealers rarely sell much below the maximum prices; they claim that they need the full price to cover the costs of reconditioning and paying future warranty claims. If you can come within 5-10% of this guide's price, you'll have done well.

In the Value of Options by Model table, take note that some options, such as a DVD/GPS infotainment system, paint protector, rustproofing, and tinted windows, have little worth on the resale market, though they may make your vehicle easier to sell. Other options, like a rear-view camera, high-performance tires with more than half their tread left, and a supplementary warranty all add value. Electronic stability control, on the other hand, may not. It has been a mandatory feature in Canada on 2012-13 light-duty vehicles built since September 1, 2011. The extra cost has been figured into the base price of subsequent models.

Ten Ways to Maximize Residual Value

1. Choose a vehicle that's popular but production doesn't exceed demand, which can drive down values. Remember, vehicles with high fleet or consumer rebates are cheapened, thus negating the upfront discount.

2. Choose options that have the most demand at resale, such as air conditioning, power windows, automatic transmissions, and a rear-view camera. Adding upgraded sound systems or interior trim is worthwhile only with higher-level models, not compact cars.

3. Factory-installed navigation systems are notorious for being over-priced and losing half their value when the car leaves the showroom.

4. Choose a colour that's popular with buyers, such as silver, white, or black. Don't experiment with unusual colours or excessive accessorizing.

5. Invest in smart reconditioning. Although it is said that every $1 spent on detailing a car will return $1.50 upon resale, this doesn't work with entry-level vehicles as much as it does with more expensive, fully-equipped cars and trucks.

6. Wash and vacuum is essential, especially, higher mileage units.

7. Avoid major collision repairs and replace tires with less than 50% tread life.

8. For vehicles in rough condition, consider using brokers. They have more contacts and can auction the car if necessary.

9. In general, cars put on the market in early spring and summer will sell more easily.

10. Market timing is also influenced by the type of vehicle and region of the country. That is, 4x4s will be more valuable in the cold climate provinces in the late fall and winter. Convertibles produce a better return on investment when marketed during the summer months.

Reliability

The older a vehicle gets (at five to seven years old), the greater the chance that major components, such as the engine and transmission, will fail as the result of high mileage and environmental wear and tear. Surprisingly, a host of other expensive-to-repair failures are just as likely to occur in new vehicles as in older ones. The air conditioning, electronic computer modules, electrical systems, and brakes are the most troublesome components, manifesting problems early in a vehicle's life. Other deficiencies that will appear early, due to sloppy manufacturing and harsh environments, include failure-prone body hardware (trim, finish, locks, doors, and windows), susceptibility to water leakage or wind noise, and peeling and/or discoloured paint.

Owners with cracked or exploding windows or windshields are often told by dealers to make an insurance claim, instead. Don't do it. If there is no proof that the window was impacted by a foreign object, the window should be replaced by the automaker. Breakage may occur for all sorts of reason: A change in temperature, shutting the car door, or passing over a bump in the road. VW is recalling its 2013-15 Beetles for just that reason: The sunroof glass panel may shatter when passing over a bump, particularly in cold weather. Smart owners should use the Beetle recall as the benchmark to get their window, windshield, or sunroof replaced *gratis* by the auto manufacturer, instead of incurring an insurance premium increase.

A "star score" in the Profile shows a model year's degree of overall reliability.

NOT RECOMMENDED   BELOW AVERAGE   AVERAGE   ABOVE AVERAGE   RECOMMENDED

Repairs

The cost and frequency of repairs are major factors considered in each vehicle's ranking. With this 1990-2016 edition we've listed five problem areas: The electrical system, base engine, fit and finish, infotainment features, and automatic transmission. The higher the number inside the money bag in this category, the more frequent or expensive the repairs.

REASONABLE   SOMEWHAT COSTLY   CALL THE BANK

Electronic stability control (ESC)

ESC is one of the most effective safety technologies to be mandated since vehicle safety standards were introduced in the States in 1967 and in Canada in 1971. Since 2012, all vehicles sold in Canada must have ESC; in the States ESC became mandatory 3 years earlier.

Secret Warranties/Internal Bulletins

The "Secret Warranties/Internal Bulletins" section provides details as to which specific model years pose the most risk and why. This helps you direct an independent mechanic to check out the likely trouble spots before you make your purchase.

It's not enough to know which parts on your vehicle are likely to fail. You should also know which repairs will be done for free by the dealer and automaker, even though you aren't the original owner and the manufacturer's warranty has long since expired.

Welcome to the hidden world of secret warranties, found in confidential technical service bulletins (TSBs) published in *Lemon-Aid* or gleaned from owners' feedback from Internet auto forums.

Almost all automakers have "secret warranty" or "warranty adjustment" programs. Under these programs, the manufacturer will do free repairs on vehicles with persistent problems, even after the warranty expires, in order to avoid a recall, bad press, or a small claims court lawsuit. According to the Center for Auto Safety (*www.autosafety.org/secret-warranties*), at any given time there are approximately 500 secret warranty programs available through automobile manufacturers.

For years, the NHTSA has declined to post on its Web site complete service bulletins from automakers about problems with their cars and about specialized warranty extensions that could save car owners thousands of dollars on repairs. Usually, what you will find on NHTSA's website (*www.safercar.gov*) is a cryptic reference to some service campaign or the bulletin itself. As for Transport Canada help, don't hold your breath.

How much money can be saved by knowing which secret warranties apply to your vehicle? Here are three recent examples where the savings could be enormous.

- **BMW** – Sensors that detect the presence of a passenger in the front seat are getting 15-year warranties. A defective sensor will cause the airbag warning light on the dashboard to illuminate. TSB #010914 issued on Aug. 2, 2014, confirms that a 15-year warranty now applies to 2006-7 5 Series sedans and station wagons with the comfort seat option and to 2006-7 Z4 Roadsters and 3 Series sedans and wagons with either manual or power seats.

- **GENERAL MOTORS** – Warranty coverage for intermittent loss of power steering in large crossover models has been extended. In TSB #14329 issued on Sept. 16, 2014, GM said that premature wear in the power steering pump might be to blame and has extended the pump warranty up to 10 years or 193,000 km. Affected model years: 2008-11 Buick Enclaves, 2009-11 Chevrolet Traverses, 2007-11 GMC Acadias and 2007-10 Saturn Outlooks.

- **LEXUS** – Repairs needed to stop engine oil cooler pipe leakage are covered by an extended warranty. Instead of the standard four-year/50,000-mile warranty, the part will have an unlimited mileage coverage through Jan. 31, 2016, and after that a 10-year/193,000 km warranty. In TSB #SC-ZLC issued on Aug. 1,

2014, Lexus said the leak might develop in 2007-11 RX 350 and 2010-11 RX 450h models.

In addition to using *Alldatadiy.com* and *safercar.gov* there are several other places where service bulletins can be found:

- **AUTOMD.COM** – This free site lists a summary of 1980-2015 model technical service bulletins in an easy-to-access format. Unfortunately, like the free *safercar.gov* bulletin summaries, the original bulletin isn't published. This makes it difficult to find out which other models are affected, what specific repairs are needed, and what is the automaker's admission of liability. ALLDATA's collection of original bulletins gives this information.

- **MITCHELL 1 DIY (*eautorepair.net*)** – Like ALLDATA, Mitchell subscribers pay an annual fee per car model researched ($49.99 U.S.). This allows a free download of all pertinent TSBs throughout the year.

AMERICAN MODELS

Merge Fiat with Chrysler: Voilà! A Jeep flambée.

While Jeep is putting out fires, GM has scored with better-built cars and trucks. *Consumer Reports* gave an unexpected rave review of the redesigned 2014 Chevrolet Impala, calling it the "best new sedan tested." The 2014 Silverado pickup got similar praise.

GM and Chrysler deserved to go bankrupt. Ford should have closed down as well, but it had a few pennies in the till after selling off its assets, including rights to its Blue Oval logo. The Detroit Three were flying high in 1965 with a 90% U.S. market share. Now, after emerging from bankruptcy 6 years ago, they have 42% of the auto market, counting GM's 17.8%, Ford's 14.7%, and Chrysler's 11.7%. Most auto writers believe American carmakers lost the public's confidence through sheer arrogance and poor quality products.

Let's be clear. American automakers took every last dime out of their cars for profit, pushed junk out the door, and made hapless owners unwilling victims of their unsafe designs and poor quality control. An entire generation of consumers ran to Asian and German products, while American automakers showed an abject disdain for auto safety, reliable vehicles, and honest transactions. All this became clearly apparent from Ford's Firestone Tire stonewalling, GM's faulty ignition switch coverup, and Chrysler's initial refusal and foot-dragging related to the recall of its fire-prone Jeeps.

American Car Quality

Going into the 2016 model year, shoppers are faced with a diminishing number of Detroit-made vehicles that are safe, dependable, and durable. This is made all the more incredible when we see the billion-dollar bailout Chrysler and GM were given by Ottawa and Washington to make better cars and trucks.

In fact, the post-bankrupt 2009-2015 Detroit-made models are less safe and more poorly-built than ever before. Counting the recalls for 2014 alone, we see a clustering of American-made cars that fall into the 2009-15 model years. For example, Canadian auto recalls hit an all-time high in 2014. With more than eight million vehicles affected, automakers issued nearly 600 recall notices on Canadian vehicles. Both the number of recalls and the number of vehicles affected are significantly higher than in any other year. So much for better quality vehicles after the bankruptcy bailout.

Fiat Chrysler/Jeep: Mama Mia!

In 2014 the Detroit Big Three became the Detroit Big Two-and-a Half, after Chrysler was taken over by Fiat and became part of Fiat Chrysler Automobiles NV (FCA), a Netherlands-based automotive holding company. As for the Chrysler name, it is now *non grata*, having been ditched by Fiat in favour of a new moniker: FCA US LLC (akin to the singer "formerly known as Prince"). The renamed group houses many other auto brands such as Abarth, Alfa Romeo, Ferrari (up for sale), Lancia, Fiat, and Maserati.

Dodging taxes by moving overseas is commonly called corporate "inversion" and ensures that the newly-minted Dutch company pays minimal taxes in North America and Italy where most of its customers and workers reside.

This tax dodge is all the more shameful when one considers the architect of FCA's flight from North American and Italian taxes is Fiat CEO Sergio Marchionne – a Canadian/Italian dual national. Take note that this is the second time Fiat has abandoned its North American customers. The company left Canadians with their rust-ravaged cars and worthless warranties in 1987, only to return 25 years later as Chrysler's self-styled financial savior feeding from Ottawa and Washington's bailout trough while marketing the mediocre Fiat 500 hatchback and convertible.

Ironic. Fiat was "rescued" by Chrysler, thanks to its strong Jeep and truck sales.

Fiat's accomplishment? Putting its crown jewel, Ferrari, on the auction block and being rebuffed by Ottawa in its request for a $700-million Canadian handout to retool its Windsor and Brampton, Ontario plants. When the government grants and loans didn't appear, Mr. Marchionne withdrew his request and ponied up the money from Chrysler's profits.

His parting shot? "Canada was acting like 'a guppy in shark-infested waters' (meaning American and Mexican man-eaters were swimming by with looser purse strings).

Fiat/Chrysler

Although all three American carmakers are flush with money, the strongest contender for biggest gains for 2016 is Chrysler thanks to the resurgence of car, minivan, SUV, and truck sales. Dodge has its Ram 1500 pickup, that's the best of a bad lot, but still not as well-made as the Asian competition.

In fact, after fawning over the 2014 truck as a Recommended Buy, *Consumer Reports* cut its rating a year later due to a storm of infotainment and other complaints from readers. The consumer group reasons that overly-complicated in-car electronics that have unresponsive touchscreens, dysfunctional controllers, and unreliable phone synchronicity will probably have other serious deficiencies down the road. Incidentally, other first-year models from Cadillac, Fiat, Ford, Honda, Jeep, and Infiniti were seen as the worst offenders according to *Consumer Reports'* latest study.

Chrysler's lineup won't change much until the second half of 2016, when a reworked Dart and Jeep Journey will appear. Until then, the low-volume Viper will get some simple upgrades along with the addition of high performance SRT (Street Racing Technology) versions of the Charger and Challenger. Dodge's Avenger mid-size sedan was dropped earlier last year.

Chrysler minivans and passenger cars may get hockey moms to a few games, but they'll likely miss the playoffs while pacing in their dealer's service bay's penalty box. The minivans are heavily-discounted jack-in-the-boxes that are all sizzle (snap, crackle, and pop electronics), but no steak (drivetrain reliability).

Jeep

The Jeep lineup is all about macho cachet, superior off-road performance, electrical short-circuits (TIMP module) that threaten your life and pocketbook, and Tonka-inspired, unreliable powertrains. Not a single new or used Jeep is recommended and most have been relegated to Appendix 1 due to their low-volume sales.

Jeep Renegade

Fiat's Chrysler alliance will be field-tested this year with the 2016 Jeep Renegade, a $20,000 compact entry in the Jeep lineup, replacing the Compass and the Patriot. Mostly a Fiat 500X crossover marketed as an American SUV with Fiat innards and a Jeep logo slapped on the body (go figure). Fiat press flacks say the 500X/Renegade is an amalgam of the best components of both companies; independent reviewers aren't so sure after looking at long-term owner reviews in Europe combined with safety-related complaints posted by NHTSA relative to the 2012 Fiat 500's performance in the States.

For those who may think we are too concerned that Fiat's poor quality will afflict the new Renegade, take a look at the 55 safety-related complaints posted by NHTSA against Fiat's imported 500 series econocar. Here are just a few: Engine compartment fires; fuel tank leaks caused by road debris; no airbag deployment during an accident; airbag, engine, and transmission warning lights that are continuously lit; persistent stallout in traffic and sudden unintended acceleration; automatic transmission-equipped cars that roll backwards when stopped on a hill;

clutches that self-destruct; flying hubcaps; keys that stick in the ignition and engines cannot be turned on or off; and persistent wiper fluid leaks. Owners also give a failing grade for fit and finish, warranty service, and parts availability.

This is some heavy baggage for the new Jeep Renegade to carry on-road or off-road.

Two wrongs don't make it right. Fiat is combining the low-rated Fiat 500 SUV with an equally low-rated Chrysler Jeep brand. Of course, neither car is recommended during its first year in Canada. When betting on vehicle quality, only in algebra do two negatives make a positive.

FORD

As deficient as we find Fiat Chrysler Automobiles' 2015-16 lineup, Ford's offerings are much worse. Ford took advantage of the 2009 Chrysler and GM bankruptcy bailout to successfully hype its "no bailout, better car quality" image and trounce the competition. Unfortunately, both parts of the statement were a lie. Ford, along with Chrysler and General Motors, got millions in "soft" grants from the Bush White House ostensibly to research the development of fuel-efficient vehicles and Ford's 2009-15 quality control shortly became even worse than Fiat Chrysler's.

Lemon-Aid has noted a steady erosion of quality in Ford products over the past five years where the company's "Quality is Job 1" has apparently been changed to "Quality is Job Gone." No where is this more evident than with one of the company's most popular small cars and a *Consumer Reports* 2015 Recommended Buy – the Ford Fusion.

Normally, *safercar.gov* registered about 50 safety-related complaints per model year for most cars. For instance, a 2010 model would likely have a cumulative total of a bit more than 250 registered complaints. Hold your breath. The 2010 Fusion has amassed over 2,050 owner complaints.

Back to the Future

Not since the bad old days in 1995-2001, when Ford's Taurus, Sable, Windstar, and front-drive Lincoln Continental generated thousands of complaints of self-destructing engines and automatic trannies, has Ford's product line been so bad. Fortunately, former Ford Canada President Bobbie Gaunt saw the problems, met with angry consumers, extended the powertrain warranty, paid off the outstanding customer claims, and set up a small group to swiftly act on incoming complaints – all in a period of a few months.

Bobbie Gaunt retired from Ford in December of 2000 and Ford's integrity and honest customer relations went with her. Ford's lousy customer relations – part *Mad Magazine* Alfred E. Neuman ("What? Me Worry?"), part Marquis de Sade – now quickly turns owner anger into pure rage.

I know of no other company whose customer relations staffer had to take the company to court to fix his Windstar minivan. He was fearful his kids would fall out when the side door opened on turns. (See: *Sharman v. Ford* in Part Three).

This year most of Ford's 2015-16 production is not recommended by *Lemon-Aid* due to major quality and performance deficiencies seen throughout the company's lineup. It appears that Ford puts all sorts of innovative infotainment features, gadgets, and drivetrains into their vehicles without phasing them in slowly as does Toyota and General Motors. This leaves us with infotainment systems that neither inform nor entertain, powertrains that are powerless, and faulty steering assemblies with replacement costs that may steer you into bankruptcy. Both *Consumer Reports* and J. D. Power & Associates have come to the same conclusion, though, their Ford ratings aren't as harsh as *Lemon-Aid*'s.

Ford's mid-size Fusion and F-series trucks are especially vulnerable to power-train breakdowns, EcoBoost turbos that gulp gas, stall out or suddenly lose power, plus steering, electronic, and infotainment failures.

Ford first responded to owners' infotainment complaints in 2007 with constant software updates that didn't work. In 2010 the system was replaced by complex touch-screen menus and glitch-prone voice software. Now the automaker is rediscovering knobs and buttons and dumping its Microsoft-based MyFord Touch in favour of the Blackberry OS Sync 3 system expected by 2016. Actually, the company had no choice. One senior analyst for *AutoTrader.com* says the five-year-old MyFord Touch feature was on a fast track to become "the modern-day equivalent of an Edsel."

Insiders also predict the 2015-16 aluminum panel-equipped pickups will likely have various fit and finish issues during their first year on the Canadian market. In the meantime, smart shoppers should steer clear of Ford's F-series trucks and Fusions, at least until its EcoBoost turbo engines provide a safer ride.

My F-150 EcoBoost almost killed us!

My wife and I were almost killed three times now when trying to pass a slower vehicle and/or merging on to an interstate. My 2011 Ford EcoBoost motor lost power and started shaking violently like it was about to fall apart and we had to pull over to avoid a collision! The last time it happened was yesterday March 26, 2013. I had to drive 2 miles on the side of the interstate at 20 mph just to get off and away from danger and then had to get a tow truck to come get me since it wouldn't drive over 20 mph.

Fusion Confusion

There are 517 NHTSA-recorded safety-related complaints on the 2012 Fusion – a model year where most of the base warranty will soon expire. (There are only 23 recorded complaints on the 2012 Fusion Hybrid, which makes one ask, "What is going on?") These reports show how dangerously defective Ford's products can be and how little the company cares.

> As I was driving down the road yesterday, I suddenly lost all power steering in my 2012 Ford Fusion ... I am a 23-year-old female and it takes every bit of strength I have to maneuver the vehicle at this time. Very disappointed that a vehicle 2 years old would need the entire power steering system replaced (according to Ford this will cost me around $2,400).

> • • •

> 2013 Ford Fusion SE 2.0LT EcoBoost. When coming to an idle my car always acts like it is going to stall. It idles really hard and the rpms always jump real low. There are never any warning lights/messages that appear. Extremely poor gas mileage – this is a 4 cylinder and an EcoBoost that should be getting a hell of a lot better gas mileage – city and highway! My 2012 Fusion V6 had wayyyy better mpg. I have read in forums about both of these issues and found related problems. Ford wanted $180.00 just to 'look' at my driveability. Just to plug my car computer into their scanner. There are no recalls on this for my specific car even though I am finding a lot of the same issues as some recalls on other model Fusions. I should not have to pay for this to be fixed

Gas Savings? Just Kidding

Ford's deception when it comes to fuel economy and towing payload figures is another indication that the automaker has a "customer be damned" mindset. Last June, Ford cut the mileage rating on six new models, most of them hybrids, and paid between $125 US and $1,050 US to owners of four versions of the 2014 Ford Fiesta, hybrid and plug-in hybrid versions of the 2013-14 C-Max and Ford Fusion, and the hybrid version of the 2013-14 Lincoln MKZ.

150-pound Truckers?

Since 2010, Ford has measured its Super Duty pickups' payload capacities only after throwing out the spare tire, jack, radio, and centre console and adding the weight of two 68-kilogram (150-pound) occupants. Deleting those items and slimming down the driver and passenger lowers a pickup's weight giving it a false maximum payload rating. In fact, the F-450 has a payload capacity number 3% higher than an honest measurement.

This fraud also affects a pickup's safety and warranty. For example, a base F-450 loaded to Ford's advertised maximum payload capacity would exceed its Class 3 gross vehicle weight rating by 27.7 kilograms (61 pounds). As for warranty eligibility, Ford advises dealers to warn customers that they could lose warranty coverage if the truck's weight rating is exceeded. Huh?

GENERAL MOTORS

The 2015-16 model-year finds GM with the strongest lineup of the Detroit Three. Five major car launches are planned by late 2015 or early 2016. The next generations of the Volt plug-in hybrid, Malibu and Cruze sedans, the Spark minicar, and the Camaro sports car are set to be revealed. The Chevrolet and GMC divisions have completed a top-to-bottom upgrade of their lucrative truck offerings, Cadillac and Buick dealers are selling more refined passenger cars, and buyers have a wider choice of new, or refreshed, crossovers and SUVs with Buick adding a mid-sized crossover slotted between the entry-level Encore and large Enclave. GM's percentage of sales from new or enhanced models has shot up to 34% versus 18% for the industry overall, mostly due to its redesigned pickups and SUVs. Moreover, industry watchers predict a 26% "replacement rate" over the next two years, five points higher than the industry's 21% average,

A faster replacement time has produced a number of other new and refreshed models this year, like the second-generation Chevy Cruze compact and an upgraded Volt plug-in hybrid – two reworked cars redesigned after only a five-year wait. Chevy's new 2016 Camaro has also beaten the clock, returning less than seven years after its re-launch while Ford's 2015 Mustang took almost ten years to go from the drawing board to dealers' showrooms.

CAMARO: A winner. The redesigned 2016 Camaro will see strong sales as long as fuel prices remain low and the economy doesn't tank.

VOLT: A loser. Buyers won't pay a $39,000 premium for a plug-in hybrid fuel-sipper when gasoline costs half as much as a year ago. It temporarily shut down the plant.

Cadillac

Like Ford's Lincoln division, Cadillac has a somber future. GM is playing catch-up to get decent luxury car sales as German automakers led by Audi, BMW, and Mercedes Benz run away with the market. Cadillac sales fell in North America last year at a time when sales of other luxury brands were booming. GM sold just over 170,000 Cadillacs in 2014, down 6.5% from 2013. That's about half what BMW and Mercedes reported. Their sales were up nearly 10%, while Mercedes grew 6.5%, according to Autodata Corp.

Hyundai is also making inroads with its $45,000 Genesis sedan, a cheaper, more reliable, and better-performing competitor that's much cheaper than the similarly-equipped $53,000 Cadillac CTS sedan.

Cadillac needs to build more Escalades and trim sticker prices on its CTS and other models. The brand's biggest blunder for 2015 was its outrageously over-priced $80,300 Cdn (plus a $2,050 freight fee) Cadillac ELR plug-in hybrid. GM officials say the high price was meant to give the car a cachet of exclusivity, but ended up driving customers away. Sales were predicted to be 2,100; actual ELRs sold through November were 1,192 coupes. Customers figured, "Why pay an extra $45,000 for a Cadillac with the heart and chassis of the Chevrolet Volt."

Secret Warranties and Crashworthiness

All car companies make "lemons" and unsafe cars – GM just builds more of them and got caught with a decade-old paper-trail of internal service bulletins outlining secret warranties that confirmed its engine ignition switch could be a killer. Although General Motors will likely spend several billion dollars in safety fines, court settlements, and underwriting corrective repairs, the company remains unrepentant, despite the 50 deaths linked to the switch and the company's promises in 2009 bailout hearings to make auto safety a priority.

In fact, GM has just kicked its hypocrisy up a notch with two other secret warranty programs that should have been recalls.

The first "goodwill" program will replace ignition keys on trucks so the shift lever doesn't bump the key and shut off the engine. General Motors maintains this is not a safety defect because it occurs only when the driver has a foot on the brake and is shifting gears.

GM issued a technical service bulletin to dealers on November 6, instructing them to replace keys for customers who complain of a problem. The bulletin covers 2014-15 Silverado/Sierra 1500 pickups, and 2015 Suburban/Tahoe/Yukon/Yukon XL SUVs. Trucks with keyless start buttons aren't covered by the bulletin.

Dealers are to give a redesigned key to customers who complain of the problem.

The second secret warranty that should be a recall is GM's warranty extension for the intermittent loss of power steering in large crossover models. In TSB #14329 issued on September 16, 2014, GM said that wear in the power steering pump might cause the problem in 2008-11 Buick Enclaves, 2009-11 Chevrolet Traverses, 2007-11 GMC Acadias, and 2007-10 Saturn Outlooks. The pumps are now covered for ten years or 150,000 miles – a warranty extension unknown to many affected owners.

If crashworthiness is your primary concern, forget most Detroit-bred cars and trucks. Out of 195 vehicles tested in 2014, only ten Detroit models were designated a Top Safety Pick by the Insurance Institute for Highway Safety (*www.iihs.org/iihs/ratings/TSP-List*).

To qualify for 2015 Top Safety Pick, a vehicle must earn good ratings in the moderate overlap front, side, roof strength, and head restraint tests, as well as a good or acceptable rating in the small overlap front test.

To qualify for 2015 Top Safety Pick+, a vehicle must meet the Top Safety Pick criteria, plus earn an advanced or superior rating for front crash prevention. Top Safety Pick+ winners with optional front crash prevention qualify for the higher award only when equipped with the technology. However when not equipped, they still meet the criteria for Top Safety Pick.

Models that earn Top Safety Pick+ or Top Safety Pick are the best vehicle choices for safety within size categories. Size and weight influence occupant protection in serious crashes. Larger, heavier vehicles generally afford more protection than smaller, lighter ones. Thus, a small car that's a Top Safety Pick+ or Top Safety Pick doesn't necessarily afford more protection than a bigger car that doesn't earn the award.

TSP+ indicates a Top Safety Pick+ winner

TSP indicates a Top Safety Pick winner

Minicars

- **TSP** 2015 Chevrolet Spark
- **TSP** 2015 Honda Fit
- **TSP+** 2016 Scion iA
- **TSP** 2015 Toyota Prius c
  Applies only to vehicles built after May 2015.

Small cars

- **TSP** 2015 Chevrolet Sonic
  Applies only to vehicles built after February 2015.
- **TSP** 2015 Chevrolet Volt
- **TSP** 2015 Dodge Dart
- **TSP** 2015 Ford C-Max Hybrid
- **TSP** 2015 Ford Focus
- **TSP** 2015 Honda Civic 2-door coupe
- **TSP** 2015 Honda Civic 4-door sedan
- **TSP** 2015 Hyundai Elantra
  Applies only to sedan models.
- **TSP** 2015 Kia Soul
- **TSP+** 2015 Lexus CT 200h
  with optional front crash prevention
  Applies only to vehicles built after September 2014.
- **TSP+** 2015 Mazda 3
  with optional front crash prevention
  4-door hatchback | 4-door sedan
- **TSP** 2015 Mini Cooper Countryman
- **TSP** 2015 Mitsubishi Lancer
  Does not apply to Ralliart and Evolution models.
- **TSP** 2015 Nissan Sentra
- **TSP** 2015 Scion FR-S
- **TSP** 2015 Scion tC

- **TSP** 2015 Subaru BRZ
- **TSP+** 2015 Subaru Impreza
  with optional front crash prevention
- **TSP+** 2016 Subaru WRX 4-door sedan
  with optional front crash prevention
- **TSP** 2015 Subaru WRX 4-door sedan
- **TSP+** 2015 Subaru XV Crosstrek
  with optional front crash prevention
- **TSP+** 2015 Toyota Prius
  with optional front crash prevention
- **TSP+** 2016 Volkswagen Golf 4-door hatchback
  with optional front crash prevention Applies only to 4-door and SportWagen models.
- **TSP** 2015 Volkswagen Golf 4-door hatchback
  Applies only to 4-door and SportWagen models.
- **TSP+** 2016 Volkswagen GTI 4-door hatchback
  with optional front crash prevention Applies only to 4-door models.
- **TSP** 2015 Volkswagen GTI 4-door hatchback
  Applies only to 4-door models.

Midsize moderately priced cars

- **TSP** 2015 Chevrolet Malibu
- **TSP+** 2015 Chrysler 200
  with optional front crash prevention
- **TSP** 2015 Ford Fusion
- **TSP** 2015 Honda Accord 2-door coupe

- **TSP** 2015 Honda Accord 4-door sedan
- **TSP** 2015 Hyundai Sonata
- **TSP** 2015 Kia Optima
- **TSP+** 2015-16 Mazda 6 4-door sedan
  with optional front crash prevention
  2016 | 2015
- **TSP** 2015 Nissan Altima
- **TSP+** 2015 Subaru Legacy
  with optional front crash prevention
- **TSP+** 2015 Subaru Outback
  with optional front crash prevention
- **TSP+** 2015 Toyota Camry
  with optional front crash prevention
- **TSP+** 2015 Toyota Prius v
  with optional front crash prevention
- **TSP+** 2016 Volkswagen Jetta 4-door sedan
  with optional front crash prevention
- **TSP** 2015 Volkswagen Jetta 4-door sedan
- **TSP** 2015 Volkswagen Passat

Midsize luxury/near luxury cars

- **TSP+** 2015 Acura TLX
  with optional front crash prevention
- **TSP+** 2015 Audi A3
  with optional front crash prevention
- **TSP+** 2015 BMW 2 series
  with optional front crash prevention

TSP+ 2015 Infiniti Q50
with optional front crash prevention

TSP+ 2016 Lexus ES 350
with optional front crash prevention

TSP 2015 Lincoln MKZ

TSP+ 2015 Volvo S60

TSP+ 2015 Volvo V60

Large family cars

TSP 2015 Toyota Avalon

Large luxury cars

TSP+ 2015-16 Acura RLX 4-door sedan
with optional front crash prevention (2015 models); standard on 2016 models
2016 | 2015

TSP+ 2016 Audi A6
with optional front crash prevention
Applies only to vehicles built after January 2015.

TSP+ 2015 Hyundai Genesis
with optional front crash prevention

TSP+ 2015 Infiniti Q70
with optional front crash prevention
Does not apply to V8 4-wheel-drive models.

TSP+ 2015 Lexus RC
with optional front crash prevention

TSP+ 2015 Mercedes E class

TSP+ 2015 Volvo S80

Small SUVs

TSP 2016 Audi Q3

TSP 2015 Buick Encore

TSP 2015 Chevrolet Trax

TSP+ 2015 Honda CR-V
with optional front crash prevention

TSP+ 2015-16 Mazda CX-5 4-door SUV
with optional front crash prevention
2016 | 2015

TSP+ 2015 Mitsubishi Outlander
with optional front crash prevention

TSP 2015 Mitsubishi Outlander Sport

TSP 2015 Nissan Rogue

TSP+ 2015 Subaru Forester
with optional front crash prevention

TSP 2015 Toyota RAV4
Applies only to vehicles built after November 2014.

Midsize SUVs

TSP 2015 Chevrolet Equinox

TSP 2015 Ford Flex

TSP 2015 GMC Terrain

TSP+ 2016 Honda Pilot
with optional front crash prevention

TSP 2016 Kia Sorento

TSP+ 2015 Nissan Murano
with optional front crash prevention

TSP 2015 Nissan Pathfinder

TSP+ 2015 Toyota Highlander
with optional front crash prevention

Midsize luxury SUVs

TSP+ 2015-16 Acura MDX 4-door SUV
with optional front crash prevention
2016 | 2015

TSP+ 2015 Audi Q5
with optional front crash prevention
Applies only to vehicles built after January 2015.

TSP 2015 Infiniti QX60

TSP+ 2015 Lexus NX
with optional front crash prevention

TSP+ 2015 Mercedes M class
with optional front crash prevention

TSP+ 2015 Volvo XC60

TSP+ 2016 Volvo XC90

Minivans

TSP 2015 Honda Odyssey

TSP 2015 Kia Sedona

TSP+ 2015 Toyota Sienna
with optional front crash prevention

Large pickups

TSP 2015 Ford F-150
Applies only to SuperCrew models.

Quality

Since emerging from bankruptcy in 2009, most of GM's trucks, SUVs, and full-sized vans are better built than equivalent models made by Chrysler and Ford. But, when it comes to passenger cars, except for recent Impalas and Malibus, the company's lineup consists of mediocre performers and overpriced Cadillacs.

Parts suppliers say GM, Ford, and Chrysler won't pay for quality parts and this is a major reason why their vehicles can't compete with Asian and some European makes. According to a December 2014 report by IHS Automotive, manufacturers are demanding annual price decreases as high as 10%, when historically the standard annual price reduction sought by automakers has been about 2-3%.

Suppliers said that the focus on cutting costs is what's compromising quality and safety and it's not limited to the Detroit Three (*insights.globalspec.com/article/ 165/global-study-on-automaker-supplier-relations*):

> For most volume carmakers, including VW, Fiat Chrysler, Ford, General Motors and Renault, cost pressures on the supply base are increasingly overriding the quality performance demanded of their suppliers.

GM had the worst supplier relations among major automakers from 2002 to 2005, according to an annual survey of more than 250 suppliers conducted by researcher Planning Perspectives Inc. of Birmingham, Michigan. In 2005, 85% of GM suppliers characterized their relationship with the automaker as "poor," and 53% would "prefer not to do business" with the company or were "ambivalent" about it, according to the survey.

What's particularly ironic about the "bean-counter" takeover of GM is that cheapening the product will likely be more costly in the long run due to recalls, lawsuits, and lost sales. The company's initial refusal to change its lethal ignition switches, for example, saved 90 cents (US) per vehicle, but will cost GM several billion dollars when recall expenses and victim compensation are included.

200/AVENGER/SEBRING ★

bad buy

The Chrysler 200.

RATING: *200:* Not Recommended (2011-16). Superior crashworthiness for what is to many owners, an unsafe car. *Avenger, Sebring:* Not Recommended (1995-2013). Used models are poor buys, despite their "bargain" price tag. 2010 was the Sebring's last model year; the 200 is a reworked Sebring in disguise up to its 2015 redesign. **Road performance:** Considerably improved in 2011 with stiffened body mounts, a smoother suspension, a raised roll centre, an upgraded rear sway bar and tires, improved noise reduction, and a softened ride. The base 4-cylinder engine coupled to the Jurassic 4-speed tranny is a puny performer and lacks reserve power for passing and merging. **Strong points:** 2015-16 models have a well-designed infotainment system, more stylish appearance; a gentler, more comfortable ride; and a classier, quieter interior. V6 engine gives plenty of power when it isn't stalling out. Brakes work well. Easy access to the interior. Standard side curtain airbags and electronic stability control. **Weak points:** Noisy 4-cylinder engine. The 6- and 9-speed transmissions shift harshly and too frequently. Clumsy handling. Only average fuel economy. Uncomfortable front seats have insufficient thigh room. Interior feels small, closed in. Cramped rear seating. Smallish trunk.

Prices and Specs

Prices (Soft): $19,495-$25,195 **Freight:** $1,700 **Powertrain (Front-drive/AWD):** Engines: 2.4L 4-cyl. (184 hp), 3.6L V6 (295 hp); Transmission: 9-speed manumatic **Dimensions/capacity (sedan):** Passengers: 2/3; Wheelbase: 108 in.; H: 59/L: 192/W: 74 in.; Headroom F/R: 3/3.5 in.; Legroom F/R: 42.4/36.2 in.; Cargo volume: 16 cu. ft.; Fuel tank: 60L/regular; Tow limit: 2,000 lb.; Load capacity: 900 lb.; Turning circle: 39.2 ft.; Ground clearance: 6.1 in.; Weight: 3,475 lb.

Other Opinions: "The 2015 Chrysler 200 ranks #10 among affordable mid-size cars. It has a nine-speed automatic transmission that shifts smoothly but is a little slow to downshift during hard acceleration and sometimes has trouble finding the right gear." – *U.S. News & World Report.* "There are a lot of 'mosts' in the mid-size sedan segment: most fun, most spacious, most stylish, most likely to be painted Champagne Mica and driven through parking lots at 4 mph. The new 200 is none of the mosts we care most about, but neither is it the least of anything. In a high-volume class that prioritizes practicality, somewhere in the middle is not a bad place to be." – *Car and Driver.* **Major redesign:** *Avenger:* 2008, 2011; *Sebring:* 2001, 2007; *200 Series:* 2015. **Highway/city fuel economy:** *2.4L 9-speed auto.: 6.4/10.2 L/100 km.* **Best alternatives:** The Mazda3, Honda Accord, and Hyundai Elantra.

SAFETY: Child safety seat setup: "Marginal." **Crashworthiness:** NHTSA: Awarded the 2001-13 Sebring and Avenger five stars for frontal crash safety and three and four stars for side and rollover protection. The 200 got four stars for overall crash protection. The 2015 model added a star for a five-star overall score, while IIHS rates the 200 sedan and convertible "Good" in all its crashworthiness tests. **Owner-reported safety-related failures:** Horrific 9-speed automatic transmission gives you nine ways to kill yourself by losing power on the highway.

> Without notice, my 2015 Chrysler 200 did not want to pick up speed going up hill. Almost got rear ended. Also when trying to stop the car – it jolts forward before slowing down. This is dangerous – I was told by an employee of the rental agency that 2 other people had the same incident happen to them and they returned the cars. I fear someone will get seriously injured or killed. Chrysler needs to recall these vehicles before precious lives are lost or permanently injured.

> • • •

> Limited three-quarter rear visibility. Owners report a suspension "death wobble" after passing over potholes, etc. and get used to making constant steering corrections as the vehicle wanders all over the road. Also, Chrysler's infamous Totally Integrated Power Module (TIPM) causes non-deployment of front airbags, hard starts and frequent stalling in traffic on cars equipped with the 3.6L V6. Chrysler recalled the 2011-13 Avenger, Sebring, 200, and Jeeps but owners say this didn't correct the stalling, starting problem, They want a recall that works and they want the 'fix' extended to 2007-2014 model years.

> *– carcomplaints.com*

> It didn't take long after the 2011 Chrysler 200 release date for owners to start complaining that their dream car was turning into a nightmare. That's because the car's engine was dangerously prone to shutting off when idling or coming to a stop without any warning signs of when it would happen. This issue was listed as the 5th worst problem on *CarComplaints. com's* "Top Vehicle Problem Trends of 2012" and it also affected the 2011 Dodge Avenger."

> *– carcomplaints.com/Chrysler/200/*

Replacing Chrysler's ubiquitous TIPM module may cost as much as $1,200 (US) A number of class actions are winding their way through the American courts. If no settlement or favourable decision is reached, use the small claims court to claim a refund for the TIPM replacement due to its "premature failure," or "lack of reasonable durability."

ALERT! Don't accept poor-performing Nexen original equipment tires:

The factory-installed tires for the 200 are unsafe for winter driving. Not only do they not grip from a complete stop but they are also ineffective in stopping and turning. The brand of tire installed is Nexen P235/40/19. I had contacted Chrysler customer service but they simply laid the blame upon me and stated that I should've chosen all-season tires. I explained that I didn't have a choice in the type of tire that was mounted, only the wheel size and that all-season tires were supposedly mounted at the factory. I then received a response refusing to address the issue directly and that I contact the tire manufacturer. I have since installed winter tires at my own cost.

200/Avenger/Sebring Profile

	2006	2007	2008	2009	2010	2011	2012	2013	2014
Used Values ($)									
200	—	—	—	—	—	11,500	13,000	12,500	14,500
Avenger SE	—	—	5,000	5,500	6,500	9,000	11,000	13,000	15,000
Sebring	3,500	4,000	4,500	5,000	7,500	—	—	—	—
Convertible	5,000	—	6,000	8,500	11,000	15,000	17,000	21,000	23,000
Reliability	②	②	②	②	②	②	②	③	③
Repairs ($$$)	❸	❸	❸	❸	❸	②	②	②	②
Electrical	①	①	①	①	①	①	①	①	②
Engine (base)	①	②	②	②	②	③	③	③	③
Fit/Finish	①	①	①	①	①	②	③	③	③
Infotainment	—	—	—	—	—	③	③	④	④
Transmission (auto.)	①	①	①	①	①	①	①	①	②

SECRET WARRANTIES, INTERNAL BULLETINS: 2007-08—Tips on silencing noisy seats and rear suspension rattles. Sunroof water leaks. Rear-door glass comes out of its track; won't roll up. Engine surge or gear hunting upon deceleration. Steering honk, moan, or grinding sound when making left turns (replace the power steering fluid reservoir). Broken transmission gearshift-lever interlock spring retainer hook "freezes" lever in Park position. Customer Satisfaction Notification Program

K16, dated August 2010, says steel reinforcement clip will be installed for free, if needed. 2007-09—Difficult to fill fuel; nozzle shut off. Horn honks or moans on hard left-hand turns. 2007-10—AC leaks water onto passenger floor. Lower door hinge popping, groaning noises. 2008—Hard starts; no-starts. 2010—Cold start is followed by rough idle. Automatic transmission transfer gear beating noise. Rear-door glass may make a "shuttering" noise when raised or lowered. Trunk release operates even though vehicle is locked. 2011—RPM fluctuations and hard starting are addressed in TSB# 18-028-11, issued May 27, 2011. Both problems are reimbursable under warranty. 2011-12—Hard shifting can be resolved by reflashing the PCM says TSB# 18-020-12. 2011-13—3.6L V6 engine cylinder leakage may require a new cylinder head covered by an extended warranty (Chrysler X56 Warranty Extension). This little-known program is confirmed by TSB #09-002-14 REV.8, published December 15, 2014. 2011-14—Headliner falls down. 2012-13—A poor upshifting automatic transmission is covered in TSB# 21-013-12, issued November 10, 2012. 2013—Fix for off-centre steering wheels. 2015—Silencing rear brake squeal in Reverse. 5 to 4 poor shift quality requires the replacement of the C-clutch snap ring. *Avenger* 2013-14—Silencing left front door wind noise. *200:* 2011—Silencing rear door wind noise. *Avenger and 200:* 2014—On vehicles carrying the 3.6L engine, extended crank time can be corrected by inspecting the Bank 1 position camshaft sensor and replacing it, if needed.

CHARGER/CHALLENGER

RATING: *Charger:* Average (2013-16); Below Average (2007-2012), because it costs more, depreciates faster, and elicits more safety-related complaints than its cheaper, high-performance brother. *Challenger:* Average (all years). In a nutshell, the Challenger remains the premiere muscle car with a retro look and a small horsepower edge over its Dodge rival, while the Charger continues as Dodge's slightly higher-priced muscle car, now sporting an 8-speed automatic transmission. Both cars offer a choice of the Hemi or the head gasket-challenged Pentastar V6. *Challenger Hellcat:* The most powerful, regular production muscle car ever made, combining 1970's styling and today's more refined driveline and suspension. It's powered by a supercharged 6.2L V8 engine that delivers a respectable 10.7 L/100 km highway fuel mileage. One novel feature: Owners get two key fobs to start the car. One – a black fob – limits power output to 500 horsepower. The other, a red fob, lets the driver add 207 horses. **Road performance:** In past model years, the Challenger's lack of agility made it more of a Clydesdale than a "pony car," but recent suspension and steering tweaks have made the car more responsive. The Charger's performance is also better than average, particularly with the 8-speed automatic transmission. **Strong points:** These are comfortable, spacious, and affordable sports cars with a healthy dose of muscle car flair (especially the 2012 Challenger). Challenger's bigger back seat and larger trunk give it an edge when compared with the Chevrolet Camaro and Ford Mustang. The infotainment system, unlike Ford/Lincoln's, is first class. It's undeniable that both cars have exceptional styling, horsepower to burn (as in, "What do you mean the fuel tank is on empty again?"), and attitude. **Weak points:** A stiff, jarring ride, handling that's not particularly agile, overly assisted steering that requires constant correction, and marginal rear headroom. The Challenger is in dire need of an interior face-lift similar to the Charger's. There are many quality issues that mostly concern the 305 hp 3.6L V6 and powertrain dependability has come under fire from owners of 2009-12 models. Drivetrain electronics, airbags, steering, brakes, suspension, and fit and finish all need to be checked carefully prior to buying any used model.

Prices and Specs

Prices (Firm): *Charger SE:* $33,195, *Charger SXT:* $36,295, *Charger SXT Plus:* $38,790, *R/T:* $37,995, *R/T AWD:* $39,996, *SRT8:* $47,995, *Challenger SXT:* $29,695, *Challenger SXT Plus:* $33,695, *Challenger R/T:* $37,695, *Challenger SRT 392:* $52,695, *Challenger Hellcat:* $69,840-$73,000 (Costa Nostra firm) **Freight:** $1,700 **Powertrain (Rear-drive/AWD):** Engines: 3.6L V6 (292 hp), 3.6L V6 (305 hp), 5.7L V8 (370 hp), 5.7L V8 (375 hp), 6.4L V8 (470 hp), 6.2L HEMI V8 (707 hp); Transmissions: 5-speed auto., 8-speed auto.; *Challenger:* 6-speed man., 6-speed auto. **Dimensions/capacity:** Passengers: 2/3; Wheelbase: 116/120 in.; *Charger:* H: 58/L: 200/W: 75 in.; *Challenger:* H: 57/L: 198/W: 76 in., Headroom F/R: *Charger:* 3/2.5 in.; *Challenger:* 3.5/2 in.; Legroom F/R: *Charger:* 41.5/28 in.; Cargo volume: 16 cu. ft.; Fuel tank: 68-72L/regular; Tow limit: *Challenger:* Not recommended, *Charger:* 1,000 lb.; Load capacity: 865 lb. est.; Turning circle: 41 ft.; Ground clearance: 4.5 in.; Weight: *Challenger:* 3,720-4,140 lb.; *Charger:* 3,728-4,268 lb.

Other Opinions: "The 2015 Dodge Challenger ranks #8 out of 11 affordable sports cars. Automotive writers are impressed with the Challenger's roomy, high-end cabin and potent V8 engines, but they say it isn't as agile as some competitors. The 2015 Dodge Charger ranks #9 out of 11 affordable large cars." – *U.S. News & World Report.* "With Chrysler working so hard to fill all of the orders for the 2015 model year Hellcat cars, Chrysler hasn't had a single word to say about the 2016 model year versions of the high performance Challenger and Charger, so anything that you read on the internet right now is purely rumor – but with the 2015 models being such a hit, I wouldn't expect any changes for the 2016 model year." – *www.torquenews.com.* **Major redesign:** *Charger/Intrepid:* 1998, 2006, 2011, 2015; *Challenger:* 2008 and 2015 (slightly restyled). A Hellcat-powered SRT arrived in the winter of 2014. No other major action is planned on the large coupe until a redesign in 2018. **Highway/city fuel economy:** *Charger 3.6L: 7.3/11.7 L/100 km. Charger 5.7L: 8/13.5 L/ 100 km. Charger 5.7L AWD: 8.5/14.4 L/100 km. Challenger 3.6L: 7.3/11.7 L/100 km. Challenger 5.7L, man.:* 8.2/13.8 L/100 km. *Challenger 6.4L, SRT8:* 8.8/15.1 L/100 km. *Challenger 6.4L, SRT8 auto.:* 9.2/15.6 L/100 km. *Challenger 6.2L, Hellcat:* 18/10L/100km **Best alternatives:** The Chevrolet Camaro and Hyundai Genesis. Why not the Mustang? Way too many safety-related defects and internal service bulletins decrying the 'Stang's poor highway performance and abysmal reliability.

SAFETY: Child safety seat setup: "Marginal." **Crashworthiness:** *Charger:* NHTSA: Four stars for frontal collision and rollover protection and three stars for side crashworthiness. 2005 and earlier models did almost as well, except that side passenger protection earned three stars. The IIHS rates recent model Chargers "Good" for frontal, side, and head-restraint protection and roof strength. *Challenger:* Since 2009 NHTSA has given five stars for front and side crashworthiness and four stars for rollover resistance. **Owner-reported safety-related failures:** Powertrains, electronics, electrical shorts, and suspension/steering defects in addition to failures of the front lower control arm and tension strut bearings. Post-2012 model problems are similar, but not as severe. But what makes a bad situation worse is Chrysler's poor servicing, frequently backordered parts, and refusal to provide a loaner vehicle:

> My 2014 Charger's transmission started to slip/skip and shift roughly. After a few visits to dealer and after they kept my car for a week, it was determined that the tranny valve body needed replacing, and Chrysler won't provide a loaner due to my vehicle still being drive-able (WTF?). The part is on backorder and Chrysler doesn't know when they will have it in. So, now I am stuck with a $40,000 paperweight in my driveway until Chrysler gets off their sorry butts to get this problem resolved. This is obviously a common problem.
>
> *– safercar.gov posting*

ALERT! Can you read the dash gauges during daytime driving?

Charger/Challenger Profile

	2006	2007	2008	2009	2010	2011	2012	2013	2014
Used Values ($)									
Charger SE	4,000	4,500	5,500	7,000	8,500	10,500	3,500	16,000	19,500
SXT AWD	—	6,500	8,000	9,000	12,000	—	15,500	17,000	23,000
SRT8	9,000	11,500	14,000	18,000	21,500	—	30,000	34,000	39,000
Challenger SXT	—	—	—	13,000	16,000	19,000	16,500	19,000	22,000
SRT8	—	—	—	18,000	22,000	29,500	32,000	37,000	42,000
Reliability	★2	★2	★2	★2	★2	★2	★2	★3	★3
Repairs ($$$)	3	3	3	3	3	2	2	2	2
Electrical	★1	★1	★1	★1	★1	★1	★1	★1	★2
Engine (base)	★1	★2	★2	★2	★2	★3	★3	★3	★3
Fit/Finish	★1	★1	★1	★1	★1	★2	★3	★3	★3
Infotainment	—	—	—	—	—	★3	★3	★4	★4
Transmission (auto.)	★1	★1	★1	★1	★1	★1	★1	★1	★2

SECRET WARRANTIES, INTERNAL BULLETINS: *All*—Long crank time and RPM fluctuations; rear door; wind noise; and light to moderate paint defects. 2009-12—In TSB #P01, Chrysler warns that some 300s, Chargers, and Challengers with Hemi engines and automatic transmissions may develop a fracture in the engine timing chain. If the chain breaks, severe engine damage can result. The timing chain, tensioner, and guide will be replaced free on affected models, regardless of warranty status. Owners of the company's large sedans may wonder what trouble could pop up next. 2011-13—Chrysler trunk lids may pop open on some 2011-13 Chrysler 300s and Dodge Chargers when the vehicle is in park and the keyless remote is nearby. Some of the passive entry switches on the trunk lids let water get into the switch and corrode. Replacing the switch (a free repair for this safety hazard) should keep the lid shut. *Charger:* 2005-10—Inoperative door locks remedy found in TSB #08-061-12, issued Nov. 29, 2012. 2011-12—A front-end clunk can be silenced by replacing both the left and right side front tension struts (under warranty), says TSB #02-005-12. Automatic transmission controls cause a shudder, shift concern; deck lid spoiler rattle, chatter; front door wind noise; battery drain; radio powers itself on with the ignition off; fix for the rear chime; false chime from the blind spot system; trunk won't open with passive switch; and coolant leaks. 2012—There's a free fix under warranty for front shocks that may be out of specification (TSB #02-006-12, issued Oct. 13, 2012). 2014—Rear shock absorbers with reduced performance or leakage should be replaced under warranty. *Challenger:* 2011-12—Intermittent no-start; automatic transmission malfunctions; booming noise at idle; door glass self-cycling/battery drain; passive door handles inoperative; and deck lid and trunk can be opened without the key fob nearby. Incorrect ride height can be fixed by replacing the right and left rear spring. 2015—Loss of power steering assist can be traced to a faulty steering gear pinion cover retaining washer. Wind noise from the doors can be fixed by repositioning the outer door mounted window seal flag. *Charger and Challenger:* 2011-13—3.6L V6 engine cylinder leakage may require a new cylinder head covered by an extended warranty (Chrysler X56 Warranty Extension). This little-known program is confirmed by TSB #09-002-14 REV.8, published Dec. 15, 2014. 2014—On vehicles carrying the 3.6L engine, extended crank time can be corrected by inspecting the Bank 1 position camshaft sensor and replacing it, if needed.

300, 300C/MAGNUM ★★★/★

RATING: Average (2011-16); *Magnum:* Not Recommended (all years). Introduced as a 2005 model, this large rear-wheel drive station wagon was dropped at the end of the 2008 model year. It was Dodge's first car to use the new Chrysler LX platform, shared with the Chrysler 300 and Dodge Charger. **Road performance:** Here's your dilemma: The relatively new Pentastar 3.6L V6 gives the car power and fuel economy it has always lacked, but skimps on reliability; the V8 has much more power, but it guzzles fuel; not much of a penalty with cheap gas. Early 300 models provide so-so handling that was improved with the 2011 models. The Touring model gives a smoother, more-comfortable ride than does the Magnum, 300M, or 300C. **Strong points:** You will enjoy a remarkably quiet, luxurious, and spacious (up front) interior, and a large trunk. Uconnect infotainment system works flawlessly and is easily mastered. The Garmin-based navigation system is one of the most intuitive systems available. **Weak points:** Subpar powertrain electronics and head gasket failures with the Pentastar powerplant. Mercedes-sourced electronics have had serious, head-scratching reliability glitches that defy correction. Airbag and engine warning lights are constant and not always meaningful. Limited backseat head- and legroom. Options can send the already-high base price soaring. Hemi-equipped models are overpriced, and the 300's resale value falls quickly. Standard towing capability is less than one would expect from a reardrive.

Prices and Specs

Prices (Soft): *Touring: $37,895, 300S: $40,595, C: $41,595, Platinum: $43,595,* **Freight:** $1,700 **Powertrain (Rear-drive /AWD):** Engines: 3.6L V6 (292 hp), 3.6L V6 (300 hp), 5.7L V8 (363 hp); 6.4L V8 (465 hp) Transmissions: 5-speed auto., 8-speed auto. **Dimensions/capacity (base):** Passengers: 2/3; Wheelbase: 120 in.; H: 58.4/L: 199/W: 75 in.; Headroom F/R: 3/2.5 in.; Legroom F/R: 41.8/40.1 in.; Cargo volume: 16.3 cu. ft.; Fuel tank: 68L/regular; Tow limit: 2,000 lb.; Load capacity: 865 lb.; Turning circle: 41 ft.; Ground clearance: 4.7-5 in.; Weight: *300:* 3,961-4,513 lb.

Other Opinions: "The Chrysler 300 ranks #7 out of 10 affordable large cars. [It] has one of the nicest interiors in the class, according to auto writers, and they also like its abundant power and smooth, quiet ride." – *U.S. News & World Report.* "Only slightly new but certainly improved, the Chrysler 300 remains a top contender in the full-size sedan segment." – *Left Lane News.* "Driving on a well cleared interstate in light snow conditions, the rear of the vehicle sways back and forth like there is no traction while the front end has traction and tries to maintain traction. Once stabilized and only driving 20-25mph when going over a bridge or under an overpass, the little bit of moisture in those areas makes the rear of the car slide side to side. Driving over expansion joints in the highway makes the rear of the vehicle jump to the right. Driving is stabilized on completely dry roads or in town on snowpacked but treated roads. The car cannot be driven over 25 mph without out the rear end swaying back and forth." – *NHTSA safercar.gov.* **Major redesign:** 1999, 2005, and 2011 (no more wagons). **Highway/city fuel economy:** *3.6L:* 7.3/11.7 L/100 km. *5.7L 300C (cylinder deactivation):* 8/13.5 L/100 km. *5.7L AWD:* 8.7/13.4 L/100 km. Owners report that real-world fuel consumption for both engines is far more than these estimates. **Best alternatives:** Honda Accord, Hyundai Azera, Subaru Forester or Legacy, Toyota Avalon, and Sienna.

SAFETY: Child safety seat setup: "Acceptable." Crashworthiness: NHTSA: Impressive crashworthiness, which gave the 2001-04 models four stars for frontal and side crash protection. The 2005-10 models earned five and four stars, while the 2011 through 2014 cars got five stars in all categories. 2010 through 2015 models tested by IIHS also garnered top scores in all categories. Earlier versions had mixed results. Owner-reported safety-related failures: Powertrain, electronic, electrical system, and steering/suspension failures are endemic to most of Chrysler's lineup. Brakes on heavier vehicles also need frequent replacement.

ALERT! Before purchasing any one of these models, have an independent garage check the brake calipers and rotors (pull the wheels), the steering assembly, and the condition of the transmission fluid. Also, ensure that the tilted head restraints aren't a pain in the neck (especially on the 2009 and later SRT8).

300/300C/Magnum Profile

	2006	2007	2008	2009	2010	2011	2012	2013	2014
Used Values ($)									
300 Touring	5,000	6,000	7,000	8,000	9,500	12,500	15,000	18,000	22,000
300C, Ltd. AWD	6,500	7,500	9,000	10,500	12,500	17,500	20,500	23,000	28,000
Magnum SE	4,500	5,500	6,500	—	—	—	—	—	—
SRT8	6,000	8,500	10,500	—	—	—	—	30,000	34,000
Reliability	★	★	★	★	★	★	★	★	★
Repairs ($$$)	💰3	💰3	💰3	💰3	💰3	💰2	💰2	💰2	💰2
Electrical	★	★	★	★	★	★	★	★	★
Engine (base)	★	★	★	★	★	★	★	★	★
Fit/Finish	★	★	★	★	★	★	★	★	★
Infotainment	—	—	—	—	—	★	★	★	★
Transmission (auto.)	★	★	★	★	★	★	★	★	★

SECRET WARRANTIES, INTERNAL BULLETINS: 2005-10—Inoperative door locks remedy found in TSB #08-061-12, issued Nov. 29, 2012. 2006-10—Lower door hinge popping, groaning. 2007-10—Harsh 4-3 shift; poor shift quality. 2008-09—How to reduce engine whistling. 2009—Poor steering wheel returnability. 2010—Inoperative side windows and MIL light warnings. MIL light may be signaling the need to install a shim onto the thermostat, or replace the thermostat housing. 2011-12—Radio malfunctions; a fix for water infiltrating into the mirror turn-signal housing; Forward-Collision warning system light comes on when no threat is imminent; airbag light also activates for no reason; hard starts and no-starts; car may not shift from Neutral to Drive; warning chime that there is another vehicle in close proximity may malfunction; poor headlight and side light illumination; rear-view and side-view mirrors give too dark an image; fuel spills out after refueling; computer malfunction causes excessive amounts of fuel to be dumped into the engine cylinders. 2011-13—3.6L V6 engine cylinder leakage may require a new cylinder head covered by an extended warranty (Chrysler X56 Warranty Extension). This little-known program is confirmed by TSB #09-002-14 REV.8, published Dec. 15, 2014. 2014—On vehicles carrying the 3.6L engine, extended crank time can be corrected by inspecting the Bank 1 position camshaft sensor and replacing it, if needed.

CARAVAN, GRAND CARAVAN/TOWN & COUNTRY ★★★/★

RATING: Average (2011-16); Not Recommended (1990-2010). Although the Caravan has been gone since 2007, the Grand Caravan has been a fixture in the Dodge lineup ever since Chrysler invented the minivan in 1983. Now, that Fiat is calling the shots, this twin to the Chrysler Town & Country will be dropped from the Dodge lineup after 2015, as Fiat trims its product lineup. The 2011 refinements corrected many of these minivans' past deficiencies and added a few new ones (as in Pentastar V6). As for long-term servicing, it seems repairs and parts aren't as much a problem as the minivan's overall poor reliability. Road performance: Post-2010 models' tight chassis and responsive steering provide a comfortable, no-surprise ride. Their stiffer springs have greatly improved handling and comfort. Manoeuvring around town is easy, though high-speed merging with a full load takes some skill. Too bad the 2011 Pentastar V6 is such a hound. The engine tends to run roughly and suddenly lose power, and the transmission shifts erratically, mostly due to faulty engine head gaskets and poorly calibrated electronics. Power steering is vague and over-assisted as speed increases. Downshifting from the electronic gearbox provides practically no braking effect. The brake pedal feels mushy, and the brakes tend to heat up after repeated applications, causing considerable loss of effectiveness (fade) and warping of the front discs. The ABS has proved to be unreliable on older vans and costly to repair. Strong points: Very reasonably priced and subject to deep discounting. Rapid depreciation lures bargain hunters who then faint at the first tranny or Pentastar V6 repair bill. Lots of innovative convenience features; user-friendly instruments, controls; and infotainment features. Weak points: A sad history of chronic powertrain and electronic module (TIPM) failures. The AC, ABS, suspension (Ram and Jeep "death wobble"), and body defects are exacerbated by Chrysler Canada's hard-nosed attitude in interpreting its warranty obligations.

Prices (Negotiable): *Grand Caravan Value Package:* $19,895, *SE Plus:* $21,690, *SXT:* $25,795, *SXT Plus:* $27,890, *SXT Premium Plus:* $27,295, *Blacktop:* $28,690, *Crew:* $28,995, *Crew Plus:* $31,995, *R/T:* $34,195, *Town & Country Touring:* $33,995, *S:* $35,790, *Touring-L:* $35,995, *Premium:* $37,495, *Limited:* $39,995 **Freight:** $1,700 **Powertrain (Front-drive):** Engine: 3.6L V6 (283 hp); Transmission: 6-speed auto. **Dimensions/capacity:** Passengers: 2/2/3; Wheelbase: 121 in.; H: 68/W: 79/L: 203 in.; Headroom F/R1/R2: *Grand Caravan:* 3/3/1.5 in., *Town & Country:* 3/3/1.5 in.; Legroom F/R1/R2: *Grand Caravan:* 41/32.5/27 in., *Town & Country:* 41/32.5/27 in.; Cargo volume: 61.5 cu. ft.; Fuel tank: 76L/regular; Tow limit: 3,600 lb.; Load capacity: 1,150 lb.; Turning circle: 41 ft.; Ground clearance: 5 in.; Weight: *Grand Caravan:* 4,685 lb., *Town & Country:* 4,685 lb.

Other Opinions: "The Grand Caravan ranks #6 out of 7 minivans (the Town and Country rates #3). [It] appeals to critics because of its low starting price and flexible Stow 'n Go seats, but its rivals are more comfortable and refined." – *U.S. News & World Report.* "The Grand Caravan is priced right and chock-full of handy features, but its lack of refinement keeps it a notch below the Japanese-brand competition." – *Edmunds.* **Major redesign:** 2001, 2008, and 2011. Grand Caravan will be dropped in 2016. **Highway/city fuel economy:** *Caravan 2.4 4-cylinder:* 11.8/8.2 L/100 km. *Caravan 3.0 V6:* 12.7/8.3 L/100 km. *Caravan 3.3 V6:* 12.2/8.2 L/100 km. *Grand Caravan 3.3 V6:* 12.9/8.5 L/100 km. *Grand Caravan 3.8 V6:* 13.2/8.7 L/100 km. *Town & Country 2.7:* 15.5/10 L/100 km. *Town & Country 4.0:* 12.2/7.9 L/100 km. *Town & Country AWD:* 13.6/9.1 L/100 km. *3.6L: 7.9/12.2 L/100 km.* **Best alternatives:** First, think small and consider the six-passenger Mazda5. Honda's Odyssey should be your next choice, with the Toyota Sienna placing third. Full-sized GM rear-drive vans are also worth looking at. They are more affordable and practical buys if you intend to haul a full passenger load or do regular heavy hauling, are physically challenged, use lots of accessories, or take frequent motoring excursions. Sure, they're less fuel-efficient, but they are often discounted over 30%. Don't splurge on a new luxury Chrysler minivan. Chrysler's upscale Town & Country may cost up to $10,000 more than a Grand Caravan yet be worth only a few thousand dollars more after six years on the market.

SAFETY: **Child safety seat setup:** "Acceptable." **Crashworthiness:** NHTSA: *Grand Caravan:* 2011-15s were given an overall four-star rating. Earlier 2005-10 models earned an impressive five stars. 1999-2004 versions again posted four stars or more. 1998 and earlier Caravans were average performers. IIHS ranks 2008-15 frontal offset, side impact, roof strength, and head-restraint protection as "Good," however, small overlap front protection was judged "Poor." 2002 through 2007 models were judged "Average" overall. *Town & Country:* Identical rankings as the Grand Caravan. **Owner-reported safety-related failures:** *All 2003-07 minivans:* Over 700 stalling complaints. Owners say the vehicles stall out immediately after filling up the fuel tank, or when turning.

ALERT! The chrome ring around the passenger-side heater deck may cause a distracting reflection in the side-view mirror in the Town & Country; the backup camera image is too dim in daytime to be useful; and the third-row seat belt is a hostage-taker.

Caravan/Grand Caravan/Town & Country Profile

	2006	2007	2008	2009	2010	2011	2012	2013	2014
Used Values ($)									
Caravan	3,500	4,000	—	—	—	—	—	—	—
Grand Caravan	4,500	5,000	5,500	6,500	7,500	12,000	14,500	16,000	18,000
Town & Country	6,000	7,500	8,500	11,000	13,000	16,000	20,000	23,000	26,500
Reliability	★	★	★	★	★	★	★	★	★
Repairs ($$$)	3	3	3	3	3	2	2	2	2
Electrical	★	★	★	★	★	★	★	★	★
Engine (base)	★	★	★	★	★	★	★	★	★
Fit/Finish	★	★	★	★	★	★	★	★	★
Infotainment	—	—	—	—	—	★	★	★	★
Transmission (auto.)	★	★	★	★	★	★	★	★	★

SECRET WARRANTIES, INTERNAL BULLETINS: 2008—Harsh shifting. Abnormal front brake pad wear. Outside sliding-door handle is inoperative in freezing temperatures. Roof rack howling sound. Howl, honk from the front windshield. Front door rattle or window won't roll down. Exhaust system rattle, clunk. Slow fuel tank fill; pump shuts off prematurely. **2008-09**—Roof rack crossbar adjuster corroded/seized. **2008-10**—Front wheel bearing growling, humming will be corrected by the free replacement of the front wheel bearings under a 5-year/145,000 km "goodwill" warranty extension, as outlined in TSB #02-003-11, published Sept. 29, 2011. Power steering fluid leaks. An inoperative power sliding door may only require a reflashing of the sliding-door computer module. **2008-14**—A sliding door rattle is caused by the door panel bowing and contacting the rear quarter panel when the door is opened. Battery may be drained due to a faulty Fold and Stow module that creates a continuous electrical draw. **2009**—Remedy for front brake squeal, pulsation. **2009-10**—Correction for sliding-door binding. **2009-11**—A front end vibration or short front brake pad life may require installing new brake linings and replacing both brake rotors under warranty (TSB# 05-005-12, issued Sept. 20, 2012). **2010**—Silencing transfer-gear bearing noise. Water leakage onto the front floort (create a drain hole in the foam at the lower cowl to allow water to drain). **2010-12**—Remedy for a water leak in the jack storage area. **2011-13**—3.6L V6 engine cylinder leakage may require a new cylinder head covered by an extended warranty (Chrysler X56 Warranty Extension). This little-known program is confirmed by TSB #09-002-14 REV.8, published Dec. 15, 2014. Erratic automatic transmission shifting may be corrected by flash reprogramming the Powertrain Control Module (PCM) with new software covered by the 8-year Emissions warranty. 2012-13—Sunroof opens but won't close; scratched glass. 2013-15—A fix for rear sliding door rattling. 2014—On vehicles carrying the 3.6L engine, extended crank time can be corrected by inspecting the Bank 1 position camshaft sensor and replacing it, if needed. Power liftgate won't close (passenger-side pinch sensor wire harness may be misrouted). 2014-15—Steering wheel or seat vibration when the brakes aren't applied may still require new front brake rotors.

DODGE DURANGO ★★

The Durango

RATING: Below Average (2012-16); Not Recommended (2011 and earlier). **Strong points:** This four-door large SUV is spacious, quiet, easy-handling, provides a comfortable ride, and offers a practical, easy-to-understand Uconnect infotainment system. Fuel economy has improved with the advent of the 8-speed automatic transmission. However, low-cost gasoline and problematic Pentastar powertrain performance chip away at the fuel savings. **Weak points:** In theory, this is the ideal large SUV capable of handling both on- and off-road duties with aplomb. The problem is that it's "possessed." Electronic module demons (TIPM) wreck havoc on the car's safety and reliability. Like *The Sorcerer's Apprentice,* Durango owners have incredible power ... that they can't control.

Other Opinions: "The Dodge Durango ranks #5 out of 13 affordable large SUVs." – *U.S. News & World Report.*

I put the vehicle in park at the end of my driveway so I could check the mail. While walking back to the vehicle form the mailbox, the vehicle starting backing up a hill on its own. I had to run next to the vehicle, hanging partially inside the cab, to attempt to shut off vehicle. Vehicle would not shut off. I had to push down emergency brake with my hand in order to get vehicle to stop.

The active braking alarm has sounded to inform me that I was too close to a vehicle, though there was no vehicle in sight (this has happened 3 times). Vehicle randomly starts on it own. Sometimes the vehicle states it is not in park when it clearly is in park.

Vehicle has gone from park to drive on one occasion, as well. The vehicle back hatch opened on its own while driving down the highway and my belongings fell out all over the road. Vehicle fails to accelerate correctly when I press the gas pedal intermittently, sometimes from a stop but usually from a slow speed. This causes other drivers to come close to rear-ending me because I am going slower than the speed of traffic (because my foot is depressing the gas pedal but the vehicle is not reacting).

– safercar.gov posting

Major redesign: A spin-off of the quality- and sales-challenged Dodge Dakota, Durango's first two generations were sold between 1998 and 2003. A 235-310 hp, 4.7L PowerTech V8 replaced the 5.2L 230 hp Magnum V8 engine for 2000; however, the 5.2L was still kicking around in some early 2000 models. In that same year a special AWD performance version called the R/T was released with a 5.9L, 250 hp Magnum V8, which became the engine of choice until it was replaced on the 2004 model by the 5.7L, 345 hp Hemi V8 and used throughout the Chrysler, Dodge, Ram lineup to this day. The Durango along with its Aspen luxury SUV twin were discontinued in 2008 along with their respective 385 hp hybrid versions that had an abbreviated 2008-09 model run A third-generation Durango returned as a 2011 model powered by a base 290 hp 3.6 V6 and an optional 5.7L, 360 hp Hemi V8. Refreshed for 2004, the car got sportier-looking styling, and an 8-speed automatic transmission. Industry insiders predict the Durango will stick around for a few more years before it's replaced by an upscale, resurrected 2018 Grand Wagoneer. This will put the Durango on a highway to nowhere and likely cause resale values to plummet. Highway/city fuel economy: *3.9L 4x2:* 15.9/11 L/100 km. *5.2L 4x4:* 18.9/13.1 L/100 km. *Hemi V8 with Multi-Displacement System:* 13.9/8.8 L/100 km. *V6:* 12.2/8.1 L/100 km. Best alternatives: Buick Enclave, Chevrolet Tahoe, and GMC Yukon. The Enclave has a better-appointed interior, third-row seating that actually comfortably accommodates adults, and you will find more cargo space than the Durango. Toyota's Highlander is more reliable than the other choices; it can seat one more person than the Durango; and owners laud its quiet, comfortable ride. Other pluses to consider are the top-drawer cabin materials and well thought out ergonomics; the many small storage spaces; and the Highlander's higher resale value.

 SAFETY: Child safety seat setup: "Acceptable." Crashworthiness: NHTSA: Gives 2012-15 models four star crash protection scores with three stars awarded for rollover resistance. 2001-09 Durangos also had above average (except for average, three-star rollover protection) scores. IIHS gave "Good" crash protection ratings to 2011-15 models in all test categories. Owner-reported safety-related failures: Many owner reports of mediocre braking. Limited rear visibility; also, if you are of shorter stature, you may not be able to see over the raised hood. Invest in a rear-view camera. The TIPM electronic control module often shorts out causing a variety of hazardous electrical malfunctions.

ALERT! Fit and finish have always been problematic with Durangos. Chrysler will offer "goodwill" body repairs, if pushed.

Durango Profile

	2011	2012	2013	2014
Used Values ($)				
SXT	16,000	21,000	25,000	29,000
Crew Plus/LTD	20,000	25,000	30,000	34,000
R/T	21,000	26,000	31,000	37,000
Citadel	23,000	28,000	32,000	39,000
Reliability	★1	★2	★2	★2
Repairs ($$$)	3	3	3	3
Electrical	★1	★2	★2	★2
Engine (base)	★2	★2	★3	★3
Fit/Finish	★1	★1	★1	★1
Infotainment	★3	★3	☆	☆
Transmission (auto.)	★1	★2	★2	★2

SECRET WARRANTIES, INTERNAL BULLETINS: 2006-08—Fuel spitback can be prevented by replacing the fuel filler tube under an extended warranty that has no time nor mileage limitation.

FUEL SPIT BACK	
SERVICE BULLETIN NO.: 14-001-12 REV. A	DATE: MARCH 01, 2012

CHRYSLER   **SUBJECT:** Fuel Spit Back During Refueling Due To Inlet Check Valve X39 (Unlimited Time And Mileage Warranty Extension).

2011-12—Excessive transfer case noise when shifting from Drive to Neutral can be remedied by installing a revised separator plate into the transmission valve body (reimbursable under warranty, says TSB# 21-010-12, issued July 16, 2012). Noise from the instrument panel may be caused by an improperly adjusted hood hinge. 2011-13—3.6L V6 engine cylinder leakage may require a new cylinder head covered by an extended warranty (Chrysler X56 Warranty Extension). This little-known program is confirmed by TSB #09-002-14 REV.8, published Dec. 15, 2014. A rattle or clunk noise from the rear of vehicles equipped with Load Leveling suspension may mean the rear shock absorbers need to be replaced. Front brake squealing when braking can be corrected by installing a front brake pad kit (68052370AC) under warranty. 2011-14—Remedy for a rear suspension rattle, chuckle. Front brake squealing when braking can be corrected by installing a front brake pad kit (68052370AC) under warranty. 2012—Troubleshooting engine misfiring and power loss. Engine power sag; hesitation may be fixed by replacing the power control module. A shudder felt when accelerating, decelerating, or when coasting may require only the reflashing or changing of the drivetrain control module. Power liftgate won't open or close. A rear shock absorber buzz, squeak, or rattle may signal the need to replace both rear upper shock mounts. Excessive exhaust noise can be corrected by replacing the exhaust pipe/catalytic converter assembly. Light to moderate paint imperfections. 2013—A second row head restraint squeak or creak may require the replacement of the head restraint mechanism. 2013-14—A click, creak, or groaning sound near the C-pillar, Dual Plane sunroof may require the replacement of the rear sunroof glass or adding structural adhesive at the rear right corner. Rear brake rattling can be silenced by replacing the caliper adapter mounting bolts. 2014—On vehicles carrying the 3.6L engine, extended crank time can be corrected by inspecting the Bank 1 position camshaft sensor and replacing it, if needed. If the truck won't shift out of Park, the electronic shifter may need to be replaced. Replace it under warranty. Remedy for a rear suspension rattle, chuckle: Replace both rear shock upper mounts.

Ram 1500

RATING: *1500 Series:* An Above Average buy (2014-16); Average (2012-13); Below Average (1994-2011). *2500 Series:* A Recommended buy (2013-16); Above Average (2009-12); Not Recommended (2008 or earlier). *3500 Series:* Recommended (2013-16); Below Average (2012); Above Average (2011 and earlier). Recent model Ram 1500s are dramatically improved after the truck lineup was lost in the wilderness following its 1994 redesign. Reliability has improved and powertrain failures are less frequent, but still nowhere near the quality of most Asian products. Nevertheless, Ram pickups are unique. They are the only models with a half-ton 1500 with a diesel engine, or a coil-sprung 2500 Heavy Duty pickup. When equipped with a manual tranny and a diesel engine, Rams are more than adequate for most chores, even with their "death wobble" suspension/steering assemblies for which most affected models have been recalled. **Road performance:** Compare the stability and ride with Asian trucks, and you will be impressed by the newest Ram's better handling and more comfortable ride. Mercifully, this may mean the end of the Chrysler/Ram "death wobble," where the truck loses steering control after passing over potholes or uneven terrain. **Strong points:** In a recent comparison test run by *Consumer Reports* magazine, Ram was ranked "Recommended" after beating out the Ford F-150 and Toyota Tundra. Only the Chevrolet Avalanche and Silverado/ Sierra out-pointed the Ram (by a few points). The test Ram was a four-wheel-drive 1500 Crew Cab, with an optional 5.7L Hemi V8 coupled with a more efficient 8-speed automatic transmission. This setup provided seamless power along with a 15 mpg fuel economy rating. The lockable "Ram box" storage compartment keeps items secure and out of the weather. **Weak points:** The Pentastar and 8-speed tranny have yet to prove they are dependable performers. So far, Pentastar hook-ups with 6-speeds aren't that impressive. The fuel-thirsty Hemi V8 isn't a wise choice, either. Its cylinder-deactivation feature is helpful, but not very. The Hemis are also complicated to service, and parts are often back ordered. The "Ram box" takes up some of the bed width. Two other minuses: A high step up and a heavier than usual tailgate.

Other Opinions: "The Ram 1500 ranks #1 out of 6 full size pickup trucks. It impresses reviewers with its best-in-class ride, excellent cabin materials, responsive transmission and class-exclusive diesel engine option." – *U. S. News & World Report.* "The Ram 1500 lineup is now even more unique and appealing with the addition of the EcoDiesel option. It isn't the motor for everyone – the cheaper, punchier and more characterful Hemi is still a stellar choice – but its combination of low-end torque and efficiency will undoubtedly win over many hearts and wallets." – *Left Lane News.* **Major redesign:** 1981, 1994, and 2013. The wimpy 2012 V6 had only a 4-speed automatic. Carried over this year is the 305 hp 3.6L V6, which, with 305 hp, is up 42% over the old 3.7L. Add the 8-speed automatic combined with the peppier V6, and you won't need a V8. In addition to the 2014 Ram's 1500 EcoDiesel and new engine and suspension options for the heavy-duties, there's also an all-new 6.4L Hemi V8 used with the 4500 and 5500 models. This will give buyers two different horsepower and torque ratings with the 6.7L Cummins engine and two gasoline engines with two different horsepower ratings (at less than 10,000 pounds GVW, it's 410; more than 10,000 pounds GVW it's 367). Chassis cabs use reinforced steel frames to allow for much bigger payloads and trailer towing. **Highway/city fuel economy:** *3.9 4x2:* 15.9/11 L/100 km. *5.2 4x4:* 18.9/13.1 L/100 km. *Hemi V8 with Multi-Displacement System:* 13.9/8.8 L/100 km. V6: 12.2/8.1 L/100 km. *3.0L V6 EcoDiesel:* 8.8/12.1/100 km. **Best alternatives:** Honda Ridgeline and the Nissan Frontier. Chevrolet's Silverado and the GMC Sierra are the best Detroit alternatives to the Ram.

SAFETY: **Child safety seat setup:** "Marginal." **Crashworthiness:** Few crash tests have been carried out. Nevertheless, NHTSA gives 2003-10 models five star crash protection scores with four stars awarded for rollover resistance. Earlier models also had above average scores through 2000. *All 2010 1500 models:* IIHS gave frontal crash protection and head restraints a "Good" rating. IIHS gave side crash protection a "Marginal" rating. **Owner-reported safety-related failures:** Many owner reports of mediocre braking. If you are of shorter stature driver, you may not be able to see over the raised hood. Some 2015 2500 model owners have gotten sick from exhaust fumes entering the cabin. Owners say factory suggested 80 psi tire pressure is too high; causes excessive skidding. *3500 Series:* Reports that the "Ram death wobble" (severe shaking when passing over a pothole) has been carried over to the 2014 3500 series. Acceleration lag is another safety-related problem affecting the 2014s.

> This truck has been to the dealership several times for the "dead pedal" issue. There is a 3-4 second delay from the moment you ask the truck to accelerate before there is any throttle response. And then once it does respond, the power delivery is extremely slow. I have had several near accidents when I was attempting to turn left in front of oncoming traffic, and the truck does not respond to full throttle.

> • • •

> While leaving the lot I go to accelerate and the truck slowly increases speed and then starts to move. This happens all the time and I took the truck into the dealership and they stated this is Chryslers torque management system. This system has almost caused me to get into a wreck twice. I know of one friend who has gotten into a wreck. I researched this issue and sure enough there are hundreds of members on Dodge and Cummins forums complaining of this issue and Chrysler will not do anything about it.
>
> Here are links to some threads: *www.cumminsforum.com/forum/2013-general-discussion/ 1193537-quick-rant.html* and *www.cumminsforum.com/forum/2013-general-discussion/ 1179305-dead-pedal.html*

ALERT! Check your truck's axle. Chrysler has been sued in a class action where a 2014 Ram 1500 wasn't equipped with the heavy-duty axle for which the owner had paid extra. Instead of the pickup's heavy-duty rear axle that had a ratio of 3.55-to-1, the truck had a standard 3.21-to-1 rear axle. (*Beasly vs. FCA US*). A higher axle ratio usually gives more torque to the rear wheels, improving towing performance, though you will burn more fuel. Chrysler wouldn't say how many other Rams were misrepresented. Be wary of "pain in the neck" front head restraints on some model years. They could be a dealbreaker. Look for paint flaws, particularly on the hood. Trucks equipped with the 3.0L Ecodiesel engine may not start in cold weather. Faulty TIMP computer modules affect all Ram model lines since 2007.

> I parked my 2004 3500 series Ram in a parking space in front of the office at about 7:30 and came out·at approx.4:45. Noticed the windshield wipers were on but the switch was off; then noticed the message center said air bag mat. required but then went away very quickly; then went to put on my seat belt then thought what I saw was smoke coming from the steering column; then saw a red seat belt lite come on in the instrument cluster; then the air bag blew out in my face causing bruising and abrasions to my face and upper body area and stinging to my face.

Ram 1500/2500/3500

	2006	2007	2008	2009	2010	2011	2012	2013	2014
Used Values ($)									
1500 ST 2X4	5,000	5,500	6,500	7,500	9,000	12,500	15,500	18,000	20,500
1500 ST 4x4	7,500	7,000	8,500	10,000	11,500	14,500	17,500	21,000	23,500
2500 ST 2X4	8,000	8,500	10,000	12,000	14,000	16,000	18,000	22,500	25,500
2500 ST 4x4	9,000	10,000	12,000	14,500	16,000	18,500	21,000	24,500	27,000
Reliability	★	★	★	★	★	★	★	★	★
Repairs ($$$)	3	3	3	3	3	2	2	1	1
Electrical	★	★	★	★	★	★	★	★	★
Engine (base)	★	★	★	★	★	★	★	★	★
Fit/Finish	★	★	★	★	★	★	★	★	★
Infotainment	—	—	—	—	—	4	4	★	★
Transmission (auto.)	★	★	★	★	★	★	★	★	★

SECRET WARRANTIES, INTERNAL BULLETINS: 2006-08—Horizontal paint etching. 2007—Automatic transmission torque converter shuddering. Transmission defaults to neutral. 2009—Steering wander may require installation of a steering shaft kit. Under a special warranty extension campaign, Dodge will replace free of charge torn seat cushion covers or seat cushions. Hood squeaking, creaking sound on turns or when passing over bumps. AC hissing noise. 2009-10—Quad rear doors won't lock or unlock. Water leaks diagnostic tips. Under Customer Satisfaction Notification K23, Dodge will replace a corroded front bumper for free. No mileage or time limitations have been imposed. Another Campaign will tackle poor AC performance by replacing defective air door actuators free of charge. 2009-11—Excessive steering wheel vibration on the 1500 model may require a new steering wheel assembly under warranty, says Chrysler. Fuel filler housing pops out of opening. A wind noise from the front door area can be silenced by adding more soundproofing material under warranty. 2010-14—Brake squealing can be silenced by installing a brake pad kit (#68034093AD). 2011-12—Excessive transfer case noise when shifting from Drive to Neutral can be remedied by installing a revised separator plate into the transmission valve body (reimbursable under warranty, says TSB# 21-010-12, issued July 16, 2012). 2011-13—3.6L V6 engine cylinder leakage may require a new cylinder head covered by an extended warranty (Chrysler X56 Warranty Extension). This little-known program is confirmed by TSB #09-002-14 REV.8, published December 15, 2014. 2012-13—A howl, and/or humming noise at speeds below 48 kph (30 mph) may be silenced by installing an insulating package onto the transmission cooling lines. 2013-14—If the truck wonj't shift out of Park, the electronic shifter may need to be replaced. 2014—A rear high-speed vibration can be corrected by replacing the rear propeller shaft (driveshaft assembly). *3500 Series:* On vehicles carrying the 3.6L engine, extended crank time can be corrected by inspecting the Bank 1 position camshaft sensor and replacing it, if needed. Metallic rattle from the roof headliner area. Excessive tire wear. 2015—Steering column noise and/or minor movement can be corrected by replacing the brake pedal bracket bolts. A lower instrument panel noise may be due to loose centre instrument panel fasteners. *2500, and 3500 Series:* 2015—Transmission slip and premature wear under hnigh engine load; replace the torque converter.

> Vehicle is designed and constructed with non adjustable camber for the front wheels. This is causing uneven wear to the front tires, outside edge now bald while rest of tire tread is intact. The only known repair is using aftermarket parts and a proper alignment along with new tires costing the consumer $1000 and $1500 per vehicle.

JEEP

Chrysler's ... er ... Fiat's Jeep division is proof positive that basement ratings published by *Lemon-Aid*, *Consumer Reports*, and J. D. Powers don't mean a darn to buyers who will pay lots of cash for a little *macho* cachet, even if that means taking home one of the lowest-rated brands.

Indeed, the Jurassic Wrangler is a perennial bestseller for off-roaders and the Mercedes-designed Grand Cherokee continues to be the preferred model in the higher performance ranges. Then, there is the recently-launched, Fiat-inspired, Dart-based Cherokee that manages to be both underpowered and a fuel hog, thanks to its 9-speed automatic transmission and wimpy 4-cylinder engine that are still not ready for prime time. Bringing up the undistinguished rear are the Compass, Patriot, and Renegade.

All Jeeps are rated Below Average or Not Recommended buys because they are mostly unsafe, unreliable, uncomfortable, gaz-guzzling, and exhibit a Salvadore Dali approach to fit and finish. Apart from fire-prone fuel tanks and biodegradable bodies, the entire Jeep lineup for the past several decades has been bedeviled by powertrain, fuel system, electrical system, brakes, suspension, and body deficiencies. Depreciation? A 2010 Grand Cherokee Laredo that cost $43,000 new, now sells for $21,000. OUCH!

The 2016 Renegade: A Fiat Jeeplet

RATING: Not Recommended (2015-16) during its first year on the market, especially with its dependence upon crude and untested Fiat technology and spotty servicing. Typically, Chrysler needs a couple of years to fix early-production defects; wait at least until the arrival of the second-series 2016 models before buying a Renegade. This said, the Renegade remains a true off-roader, while rivals are either crossovers or SUVs that offer only limited off-road capability in exchange for a smoother ride. **Road performance:** Weighing in at 3400+ pounds, the Renegade is heavier than the Buick Encore, Kia Soul, or Nissan Juke. It has a relatively quiet powertrain that's a bit on the rough side when pushed and the 9-speed tranny constantly "gear hunts" to save the most gas. So, the car lugs along, conserving fuel while fraying nerves. Renegade is the first small SUV to use a disconnecting rear axle and power take-off feature to improve 4WD fuel economy by about 1-2%. The system instantly engages when 4WD traction as needed. The Trailhawk model delivers best-in-class 4WD trail rated capability with features such as a 20:1 crawl ratio and 20mm (0.8 inches) increased ride height. Although the new 9-speed automatic is the the most commonly ordered gearbox, two manual and one dual-dry clutch transmissions are also available. **Strong points:** This is Jeep's first model developed from scratch by Fiat and Chrysler. It shares about 40% of its components with Fiat's 500X. Both are built at Fiat's plant in Melfi, central Italy. There's a nicely-appointed cabin, a spacious (up front) interior, a large trunk, and two removable "My Sky" roof panels. Chrysler's much-praised Uconnect infotainment system works flawlessly and is easily mastered. The Garmin-based navigation system is one of the most intuitive systems available. **Weak points:** Acceleration is only mid-pack. Lots of wind and road noise, Many buyers fear a "witches brew" of defects caused by the mix-match of Fiat and Chrysler componentry.

Other Opinions: "During 2015, that class is due to more than double in size, with newcomers to include the Chevrolet Trax, aforementioned Fiat 500X, Honda HR-V, Mazda CX-3, and the Jeep Renegade. Among these, however, the Renegade is the only one capable of anything close to severe off-road use, all the others primarily being all-weather on-road vehicles. That sets the Renegade apart, but also means it might not be the best choice if an 'all-weather runabout' better fits your needs." – *Consumer Guide.*" It offers off-road skills, towing and cargo hauling that trump most other subcompact crossovers." – *Edmunds.* "Jeep targeted the Nissan Juke, Buick Encore and Kia Soul as primary competition. The Renegade is quieter and sportier than the Soul (no mean feat), more comfortable and drivable than the Juke, and more aggressive and capable than the Encore." – *Left Lane News.* "Silly, engine is a 180-hp vibrator, you will never be taken seriously while driving it. If there were a Jeep emoji, it would look like this." – *Car and Driver.* Major redesign: Renegade will get some minor improvements in mid-2017 for the 2018 model year. Highway/city fuel economy: 7.6/9.8L/100 km. Best alternatives: All of the above models.

SAFETY: Child safety seat setup: Untested. Crashworthiness: Untested. The driver's view is blocked by pillars on either side of the small back window. Owner-reported safety-related failures: Too early to report.

ALERT! In your test-drive, put the automatic transmission through its paces. Some reviewers say it's not sufficiently responsive. Also, make sure that the large side pillars don't obstruct your forward or rearward visibility.

WRANGLER ★★

RATING: Below Average (all years). Jeeps are all about *cachet* and cash. The cash is needed to pay for the biodegradable 3.6L V6 repairs and to correct the many electronic and tranny failures. Yet, in spite of its dated design, the Wrangler is one of the most off-road-capable Jeeps ever made. That's it. The little SUV falls far short when driven on-road. Road performance: This entry-level Jeep's impressive "bush" performance is taken away by its overall poor reliability and dangerous on-road performance, highlighted by the powertrain suddenly jumping out of gear when the outside temperature drops, or the steering and suspension going into a "death wobble" after passing over potholes or speed bumps. Plus, its short wheelbase, loud and porous cabin, and mediocre highway performance makes the Wrangler annoying at best as a daily commuter and outright uncomfortable as a road trip vehicle. The V6 engine is powerful enough for most chores, but fuel economy suffers with the automatic 5-speed. Handling is compromised by vague steering and low cornering limits (standard stability control is a plus). A rigid frame makes for a stiff, jiggly ride and clumsy handling. Overall, the Rubicon is a better performer than the $600 cheaper Unlimited Sahara. **Strong points:** The Wrangler comes with a roomy, plush cabin with plenty of headroom. Unlimited models with four doors have 1.6 inches more legroom in the back and lots of cargo space. **Weak points:** All Wranglers sell at their full list price and are not likely to be discounted by much as the year progresses. Fortunately, slow depreciation takes the bite out of its hefty price tag. Getting in and out takes some acrobatics and patience; the two-door interior is comfortable; and there is only a small amount of cargo room in the back.

Prices and Specs

Prices (Firm): *Sport: $21,195, Sport S: $26,645, Unlimited Sport S: $29,695, Sahara: $32,870, Unlimited Sahara: $35,270, Rubicon: 35,870, Unlimited Rubicon: $38,270* **Freight:** $1,700 **Powertrain (Rear-drive / part-time/full-time AWD):** Engine: 3.6L V6 (285 hp); Transmissions: 6-speed man., 5-speed auto. **Dimensions/capacity (base):** Passengers: 2/3; Wheelbase: 116 in.; H: 71/W: 74/L: 173 in.; Headroom F/R: 5.5/5 in.; Legroom F/R: 41/28 in.; Cargo volume: 34.5 cu. ft.; Fuel tank: 70L/regular; Tow limit: 3,500 lb.; Load capacity: 850 lb.; Turning circle: 43 ft.; Ground clearance: 8 in.; Weight: *Sport:* 3,849 lb., *Rubicon:* 4,165 lb.

Other Opinions: "The 2015 Jeep Wrangler ranks #21 out of 25 affordable compact SUVs. Although test drivers agree that the 2015 Jeep Wrangler is an incredible off-road vehicle, its stiff ride and lack of standard features may make it less than ideal for some drivers." – *U.S. News & World Report.*" The *Edmunds* car guide takes a similar tack: "An SUV unlike any other, the 2015 Jeep Wrangler offers exceptional off-road capability, though its lack of refinement makes it an acquired taste." **Major redesign:** 1997, 2007, and 2011. The next redesign is scheduled for the 2018 version. It is expected to have an aluminum body and 8-speed automatic transmission. **Highway/city fuel economy:** Fuel economy? Much less than advertised (don't believe government-posted figures). *3.6L V6 man.:* 9.3/12.7 L/100 km. *3.6L V6 auto.:* 9.5/12.6 L/100 km. **Best alternatives:** Honda CR-V or Element, Hyundai Tucson, Nissan Xterra, Subaru Forester, and Toyota RAV4. Remember, none of these other models do as well as the Wrangler off-road.

SAFETY: Child safety seat setup: "Marginal." **Crashworthiness:** NHTSA: 2007-15 Wranglers not crash-tested, though rollover resistance predicted to be average from 1997 through 2014. 1997-2006 models earned four-star scores, but driver frontal crash safety was given only two stars on 1994-1996 models. **Owner-reported safety-related failures:** Many electrical failures caused by a faulty TIPM module: Stalling, sudden acceleration, loss of steering, inoperative locks, and malfuntioning lights and gauges. Loss of power while underway, especially when cresting a hill or driving on a level surface; a cracked oil cooler/filter housing results in an oil leak and burning oil at the top of engine; and water leaks throughout the interior.

> At around 3:45 am, while I was sleeping, the horn started intermittently blaring. I looked out the window and the reverse lights were on (at full brightness). For the next hour, it would start and stop randomly. I finally disconnected the battery in frustration. Earlier the previous evening, the headlights came on and stayed on. I had not used the Jeep for the previous two days. This issue is clearly related to the totally integrated power module (TIPM) which has already been replaced once in this vehicle (which had caused my 2014 Jeep to stall – and completely die – several times). I am extremely concerned for my safety with this vehicle and this issue.

ALERT! Owners report that the Wrangler's off-road prowess is compromised by poor original equipment tires and thin body panels. Although there's not much you can do about the body panels, *www.tirerack.com* can give you invaluable, unbiased tips on the best and cheapest tires for the kind of driving you intend to do. 2012 and newer Jeeps have the more powerful 3.6L engine, compared to the lazy 3.8L in the pre-2012 models. It makes a big difference with an automatic transmission, less so for a manual. If you're looking at pre-2012, at least drive a newer Jeep to see whether you can live with the difference. Be sure to lift up the carpet and check out the undercarriage for rust and off-road damage. Stay away from heavily modified vehicles. You can't tell the quality of the components that were used or how well the customizing was done. Older Jeeps tend to burn oil. This was especially true for the 2007 model year. More recent Pentastar 3.6L V6 models have had early engine head gasket failures covered by a little-known Chrysler extended warranty. Beware of windshield stress fractures. They are a common Wrangler defect and a replacement should be covered by the warranty – not you insurance policy.

> I took the jeep to the local dealer who said it was a stress fracture probably due to freezing conditions along with the heat from the defroster. The individual I spoke with conceded it was in all probability a manufacturing defect since he had heard of "a lot of other cases like mine" but would not be quoted on that. He contacted Chrysler who refused to cover the windshield damage because although I only had the vehicle for seven months, the mileage was over 12,000. I have continued to investigate incidences of stress fracture damage to front windshields in the Jeeps and have collected a significant amount of data through numerous complaint blogs that support the fact that either the Jeep windshields themselves are defective or some problem with the vehicle design itself makes it possible for considerable heat to be trapped between the windshield and dashboard to the point where stress causes the window to crack. Rather than address the issue, Chrysler is instead forcing owners to go through their private insurance for repairs.

Wrangler SUV Profile

	2006	2007	2008	2009	2010	2011	2012	2013	2014
Used Values ($)									
X/Sport	4,000	5,000	6,000	7,000	8,000	10,000	12,500	20,000	22,500
Sahara	5,500	6,500	8,000	9,500	11,500	15,000	18,500	22,000	25,000
Rubicon	7,500	8,500	10,000	11,500	13,500	16,500	20,000	25,000	27,500
Unltd. TJ, X, Sport	5,500	6,500	8,000	9,000	10,500	13,500	16,500	20,000	22,500
Reliability	★	★	★	★	★	★	★	★	★
Repairs ($$$)	3	3	3	3	3	3	2	2	2
Electrical	★	★	★	★	★	★	★	★	☆
Engine (base)	★	★	☆	☆	☆	☆	☆	☆	☆
Fit/Finish	★	★	★	★	★	☆	☆	☆	☆
Infotainment	—	—	—	—	—	☆	☆	☆	☆
Transmission (auto.)	★	★	★	★	★	★	★	★	☆

SECRET WARRANTIES, INTERNAL BULLETINS: 2007-09—Excessive steering vibration when passing over rough surfaces. Difficult fuel fill. Wind noise and water leaks from the windshield/soft top header. 2007-10—Manual transmission pops out of First gear when upshifting. Hard starts, no-start, or dead battery. Special Campaign #J34 for free replacement of the steering damper hardware. 2007-14—Remedy for cowl trim panel water leakage. 2008-10—Warranty is extended to 7 years/70,000 miles to cover the replacement of the automatic transmission cooler line on vehicles equipped with a 3.8L engine. 2009-10—Transmission fluid may overheat; a chime will be installed to alert the driver when this happens. This is a Customer Satisfaction Program, not a safety recall. 2009-12—Replace the wireless control module under warranty if your radio clock loses time. 2011-12—Countermeasures to eliminate engine misfiring. Manual transmission pops out of gear (TSB #21-002-12, issued Jan. 12, 2012). Light to moderate paint imperfections. Inoperative front heated seats. Front water leak onto front floor. 2011-13—3.6L V6 engine cylinder leakage may require a new cylinder head covered by an extended warranty (Chrysler X56 Warranty Extension). This little-known program is confirmed by TSB #09-002-14 REV.8, published Dec. 15, 2014. 2012-14—Tailgate retaining strap over extends and breaks. This is a warrantable repair due to the premature failure. 2013—A cracked upper swing gate hinge cover should be replaced under warranty. Windshield wiper vibration may be caused by a faulty wiper module linkage bolt. Replace the front windshield if it appears chipped along the bottom edge. 2014—On vehicles carrying the 3.6L engine, extended crank time can be corrected by inspecting the Bank 1 position camshaft sensor and replacing it, if needed. A rear high-speed vibration can be corrected by replacing the rear propeller shaft (drive-shaft assembly). Intermittent cooler operation may be fixed by replacing the cooling fan module under warranty. Fix for hard-to-adjust front passenger seat. 2015—Replace the hard top if it leaks at the rear seam.

GRAND CHEROKEE ★★★

RATING: Average (2015-16); Not Recommended (2011-14); Average (2009-10); Not Recommended (2008 and earlier). Jeep's 2011 redesign spawned an incredible proliferation of factory-related defects that have taken 4 years to correct. Although it's too early to tell for certain, apparently, the latest Grand Cherokees have more performance and reliability potential than earlier models. The car comes well-equipped with a user-friendly Uconnect infotainment system, Bluetooth, a USB port, rearview camera, a 19-speaker Harman Kardon audio system, navigation, adaptive cruise control, and a rear-seat entertainment feature. Here's the downside: During the past decade the Grand Cherokee has been beset with chronic automatic transmission, engine head gasket, brake, and electrical system defects in addition to abysmally bad fit and finish with an affinity for premature rusting in the wheel-wells, doors, and rocker panels. **Road performance:** The Grand Cherokee is built on a proven rear drive unibody platform that the Mercedes-Benz ML has used for years; when combined with front and rear independent suspension systems, the result is enhanced on-road handling and comfort. A small turning circle enhances maneuverability. On the other hand, the 3.6L V6 has to be pushed to move this heavy SUV and its lack of midrange torque makes for scary passing maneuvers. The previous 5-speed transmission often went AWOL while gear-hunting over hilly terrain. Choose a later model equipped with an 8-speed, although its electronic shifter takes some practice. Low-range gearing for off-road driving is lacking on most models. **Strong points:** The 290 hp Pentastar V6 boosts power with 80 horses more than the previous V6 engine. The cabin is quiet and well-appointed with high-quality materials, comfortable seats, and good ergonomics. Fit and finish has been much improved since 2014. **Weak points:** New, Grand Cherokees sell way above their real value and the recommended diesel option is way over-priced as an $8,000 option. Two good reasons to wait until mid-2016 for prices to settle down, or to invest in a leftover 2015 version. The engine, automatic transmission, and electrical system continue to be unreliable and expensive to diagnose and repair. Fit and finish on pre-2015 models is quite poor. Owners report engine surges when brakes are applied and that the soft brake pedal, doesn't provide much stopping power until halfway through its travel. The 6-speed manual transmission sometimes pops out of gear and the automatic transmission slips erratically in and out of Second gear, suddenly downshifts, or leaks fluid.

> The 2015 I had just purchased with the V-6 and 8-speed transmission, due to my 2014 Dodge Durango with the same engine and transmission being bought back by Chrysler, is exhibiting the same unsafe shifting and stalling conditions.

Other opinions: "The 2015 Jeep Grand Cherokee is ranked #7 out of 12 affordable mid-size SUVs." – *U.S. News & World Report.* "The Grand Cherokee's off-roading abilities are exceptional, while an inviting interior and a platform co-developed with Mercedes-Benz give it the daily-driving refinement of a more expensive luxury vehicle." – *Left Lane News.* **Major redesign:** 1999, 2005, and 2011. The next redesign is scheduled for the 2017 model year. **Highway/city fuel economy:** *3.6L:* 8.9/ 13L/100 km. *5.7L:* 10.6/15.7 L/100 km. *3.0L V6 diesel:* 8.4/11.2L/100 km. **Best alternatives:** A 2015 or later diesel would be your best used investment. If you don't have the patience to wait for new prices to go down, consider a Honda CR-V or Element, a Hyundai Santa Fe or Tucson, a Subaru Forester, or a Toyota RAV4. Remember, none of these other models can follow the Grand Cherokee off-road, but on the other hand, they won't be following it in for repairs, either.

SAFETY: Child safety seat setup: "Marginal." **Crashworthiness:** NHTSA: Gives the 2015 AWD model five stars for overall crashworthiness; 2WD gets four stars. 2011-14 models were awarded five stars for side-impact crash protection, four stars for side protection, and three stars for rollover resistance. The 4x4 model has a similar rating, except that rollover resistance was a bit better, at four stars. 2001-04s were given a "marginal" rating for frontal offset protection and three stars for full-frontal crashworthiness. IIHS gave the 2015 version a "Good" rating in all categories, except for "small overlap front," where it was rated "Marginal." Earlier models got a "Good" ranking for roof strength, frontal offset, side, and head restraint effectiveness. **Owner-reported safety-related failures:** Make sure the headlights provide sufficient illumination during a night road test; many dissatisfied drivers wish they had tested this before buying their Grand Cherokee.

ALERT! 1993-2004 Jeeps may have fire-prone fuel tanks similar to the Ford Pintos recalled in the 70s: Chrysler will install a free hitch, if needed. Safety advocates, however, say the hitch doesn't make the car less dangerous. Ralph Nader calls the Jeeps a "modern day Pinto for soccer moms." Last March, a Georgia jury agreed and awarded $150 million to the family of Remington Walden, 4, who died in 2012 when his family's 1999 Jeep Grand Cherokee was rear-ended and burst into flames, burning the child alive.

The jury in Decatur County, Georgia, found that Chrysler acted with "reckless and wanton disregard" for consumers' safety and ordered it to pay 99% of the damages in the case. This ruling followed Fiat Chrysler CEO Sergio Marchionne's videotaped testimony that he had "no way of knowing" whether newer Jeeps, with the gas tanks in front of the rear axle, are safer.

There have been 395 fatal fire crashes of the 1993-2004 Jeep Grand Cherokee, 1993-2001 Jeep Cherokee, and 2002-2007 Jeep Liberty.

A fatal fire involving a 1999 Jeep Grand Cherokee that was rear-ended by a pickup.

Grand Cherokee Profile

	2006	2007	2008	2009	2010	2011	2012	2013	2014
Used Values ($)									
North/Laredo	5,500	7,000	8,500	10,000	13,000	16,000	20,000	25,000	29,000
V8	—	—	—	—	21,000	24,000	28,000	31,500	33,000
SRT8	8,500	11,500	14,000	16,500	19,500	—	32,500	39,000	48,000
Limited V6	8,000	10,000	13,000	16,000	18,500	22,500	25,000	27,000	30,500
Overland V6	9,500	12,000	15,000	18,500	—	23,500	28,000	35,000	40,000
Reliability	1	1	1	1	1	1	1	3	3
Repairs ($$$)	3	3	3	3	3	2	2	2	2
Electrical	1	1	1	1	1	1	1	1	2
Engine (base)	1	1	1	1	1	2	2	2	3
Fit/Finish	1	1	1	1	1	1	1	2	2
Infotainment	—	—	—	—	—	3	3	4	5
Transmission (auto.)	1	1	1	1	1	1	2	2	2

SECRET WARRANTIES, INTERNAL BULLETINS: 2005-10—Lower door hinge popping or groaning noises can be silenced by spraying lithium grease between the roller and roller pin. 2011—A shudder or bump felt through the steering wheel under moderate braking and/or driving over rough roads may require a new intermediate steering column shaft covered by warranty. If the torque converter drive plate fasteners are loose, you will hear a knocking or rattling from the automatic transmission on vehicles equipped with the 3.6L engine. A rear shock buzz, squeak, or rattle may mean you need new rear upper shock mounts. A fuel tank sloshing noise remedy is to replace the fuel tank. 2011-12—Excessive transfer case noise when shifting from Drive to Neutral can be remedied by installing a revised separator plate into the transmission valve body (reimbursable under warranty, says TSB #21-010-12, issued July 16, 2012). 2011-13—3.6L V6 engine cylinder leakage may require a new cylinder head covered by an extended warranty (Chrysler X56 Warranty Extension). This little-known program is confirmed by TSB #09-002-14 REV.8, published Dec. 15, 2014. 2011-14—Remedy for a rear suspension rattle, chuckle. Front brake squealing when braking can be corrected by installing a front brake pad kit (68052370AC) under warranty. 2012—Troubleshooting engine misfiring and power loss. Engine power sag; hesitation may be fixed by replacing the power control module. A shudder felt when accelerating, decelerating, or when coasting may require only the reflashing or changing of the drivetrain control module. Power liftgate won't open or close. A rear shock absorber buzz, squeak, or rattle may signal the need to replace both rear upper shock mounts. Excessive exhaust noise can be corrected by replacing the exhaust pipe/catalytic converter assembly. Light to moderate paint imperfections. 2013—A second row head restraint squeak or creak may require the replacement of the head restraint mechanism. 2013-14—A click, creak, or groaning sound near the C-pillar, Dual Plane sunroof may require the replacement of the rear sunroof glass or adding structural adhesive at the rear right corner. Rear brake rattling can be silenced by replacing the caliper adapter mounting bolts. 2014—On vehicles carrying the 3.6L engine, extended crank time can be corrected by inspecting the Bank 1 position camshaft sensor and replacing it, if needed. Excessive steering wheel vibration may signal the need to replace the wheel bearings. A rattle from the driver side instrument panel or steering wheel may require the replacement of the steering column lock control module wiring harness bracket. An exhaust system rattle or squeak may be caused by a loose heat shield.

Automakers know judges can't be hood-winked.

PAINT DEGRADATION/ROAD ABRASION

BULLETIN NO.: 10-15-6

DATE: AUGUST 16, 2010

2008–11 Focus

ISSUE: Some 2008–11 Focus vehicles may experience paint damage or road abrasion on the rocker panel and on the side of the vehicle located slightly ahead of the rear tires on both 2 door and 4 door models. Rocker Panel, 1/4 panel, dog leg and/or rear door, dependent on model. This has been reported in geographical areas that commonly experience snow and ice conditions and use various forms of traction enhancers.

ACTION: Follow the Service Procedure steps to correct the condition.

NOTE: Per the warranty and policy manual paint damage caused by conditions such as chips, scratches, dents, dings, road salt, stone chips or other acts of nature are not covered under the warraty. However, paint abrasion at the dog leg area due to the above circumstances is a unique condition on the focus and, as a result, repairs are eligible for basic warranty coverage.

Focus Fizzles; F-150 Sizzles

Actually, all of Ford's small cars are incurring large losses, while the company's high performance cars, SUVs, trucks, and vans are seeing record-breaking sales. Mustangs, Edges, Escapes, and F-150s are chronically backordered, and sell for thousands of dollars more than MSRP (manufacturer's suggested retail price). Meanwhile, the Fiesta, Focus, and Fusion stagnate in dealer inventories. Lincoln is on life-support.

Bye-bye, Town Car (1981-2011). You were better than Lincoln. Dealers are crying for your return.

Ford Quality Not "Job 1"

J.D. Power and Associates' 2012 Initial Quality Study (IQS) blasted Ford over its poor quality and complicated MyFord Touch and MyLincoln Touch electronic systems and other controls. The company's dual clutch automatic transmission was also singled out as being balky and unpredictable. Owners reported that the Fiesta and Focus Power Shift automatic transmission was particularly troublesome and that Ford's C-Max and Fusion hybrid fuel savings claims were as believable as former Alberta Premier Jim Prentice's provincial Budget math skills.

FORD SYNC(R) – UNABLE TO LOCATE VEHICLE, GPS ISSUES

SERVICE BULLETIN NO.: 12-11-2   DATE: 11/15/12

GLOBAL POSITION SATELLITE MODULE – TRAFFIC DIRECTIONS AND INFORMATION/ NAVIGATION – UNABLE TO LOCATE VEHICLE – BUILT ON OR BEFORE 5/14/2012

FORD: 2010-211 Fiesta, Focus, Mustang; 2010-12 Fusion, Taurus; 2010 Explorer Sport Trac; 2010-11 Explorer; 2010-12 E-Series, Edge, Escape, Expedition, F-150, F-Super Duty, Flex; **LINCOLN:** 2010-12 MKS, MKZ; 2010-11 MKX; 2010-12 Navigator; **MERCURY (U.S.):** 2010 Milan, Mountaineer; and 2010-11 Mariner.

"Dammit, honey, will you PLEASE ask someone for directions."

Some of Ford's model offerings fall far short of the company's carefully orchestrated hype. Highway performance is much less than promised, head restraints are poorly designed, interior instruments and controls are far from user-friendly, high-tech communication and navigation gizmos are needlessly complicated, and quality control is woefully inadequate (see the reports on "lag and lurch" self-destructing manual transmissions in the Mustang section and failure-prone automatics in the Fusion ratings). Yet, Ford's products represent the best of what was formerly called the Detroit Big Three – shows how far the benchmark has been lowered.

In the past decade, powertrain defects, faulty suspensions and steering components, and premature brake wear and brake failures were the primary concerns of Ford owners. The company's engine and automatic transmission deficiencies affected most of its products, and these deficiencies have existed since the early '80s, judging by *Lemon-Aid* reader reports, NHTSA complaints, confidential Ford internal documents, and technical service bulletins. And we aren't talking about mechanical and electronic components only; Ford's fit and finish has traditionally also remained far below Japanese and South Korean standards.

EcoBoost or EcoBust?

EcoBoost Stalling

Ford Motor Co. is being sued by three vehicle owners in Ohio because of alleged defects in the automaker's six-cylinder EcoBoost engine. According to the lawsuit, the 3.5-liter V6 EcoBoost engine "contained serious latent design, manufacturing, or assembly defects" that cause vehicles to shake, misfire and rapidly lose power.

Ford knew of the problem, the suit says, because it published several technical service bulletins and suggested potential fixes to dealers covering the F-150.

The problematic V6 EcoBoost was introduced in the 2010 Ford Flex crossover, Taurus SHO, Lincoln MKT crossover and MKS sedan, the 2011 pickups, and the 2013 Ford Explorer Sport.

The National Highway Traffic Safety Administration has received nearly 100 complaints about the engine, the lawsuit states.

– Vince Bond Jr.
Automotive News, May 15, 2013

Although disgruntled Ford owners call the feature "EcoBust," Ford is hyping its "EcoBoost" family of new turbochargers as an innovative attempt to provide fuel savings and added power throughout the automaker's entire lineup. This is the opposite direction that GM and Chrysler are going in using traditional engines but, with added features like cylinder deactivation and engine shut-offs at idle, EcoBoost is used by Ford to describe a new family of turbocharged and direct-injected 4-cylinder and 6-cylinder gasoline engines that deliver power and torque consistent with larger displacement powerplants. Engines using this design are touted to be 20% more fuel-efficient than naturally aspirated engines. Ford says the EcoBoost's power output and fuel efficiency rival hybrid and diesel engine technology, and the company intends on using it extensively in future vehicle applications.

Independent testers, like *Consumer Reports*, say the EcoBoost engines don't live up to their fuel-saving, nor their performance hype:

> Its 25 mpg overall places it among the worst of the crop of recently redesigned family sedans. The Toyota Camry, Honda Accord, and Nissan Altima, all with conventional 2.4- or 2.5-liter four-cylinder engines, get an additional 2, 5, and 6 mpg, respectively. And all accelerate more quickly.

Owners claim in several lawsuits that Ford knew the Fusion and C-Max hybrids would never match the glowing mileage figures hyped by the automaker (*editorial. autos.msn.com/2013-ford-c-max-hybrid-review*):

> I thought my 2013 C-MAX would be a Prius Killer? NOT! As a returning Ford buyer I feel deceived. I want to support US companies and US jobs. What was Ford thinking when they published 47/47/47 estimates? Based on the advertised EPA estimates, I would have been ok with low 40's but 28-33 mpg is not even in the ballpark. This is not an issue about EPA testing standards, but rather an issue about setting false customer expectations in order to promote sales. Ford's "47mpg" marketing campaign tarnished what should have been the roll out of a truly remarkable vehicle, the C-MAX. Real world mpg estimates should have been promoted in the mid-30's.

Ford may yet improve overall quality by joining the competition and shifting its product mix to vehicles that use more reliable Asian-supplied turbo components. Like most major automakers, the company is copying more fuel-efficient European designs, importing some models directly from Europe, then transferring their production to North America. By selling and building worldwide models that are virtually identical, Ford can keep production costs down and quickly get to market better-performing, more fuel-efficient, and higher-quality vehicles.

Sure, Ford still makes some worthwhile vehicles like the Edge, Mustang, and F-150 series and its quality control is on a par with Chrysler's, but that benchmark is way too low.

FIESTA ★★★

Fuel economy at all costs. This includes a quirky transmission and engine malfunctions, a cramped interior, and poor overall reliability. Buy a Honda Fit or Hyundai Accent instead.

RATING: Average (2015-16); Below Average (2011-14). Available as a five-door hatchback or sedan, the Fiesta is borrowed from Ford of Europe. Interestingly, Ford has never imported a European-derived vehicle that went on to become a success in North America. (Remember the Cortina? The Merkur XR4TI?) Poor quality, performance, and servicing afflicted most of these imports and sent them packing back to Europe. Will the Fiesta repeat history? If low fuel prices continue, it's quite likely. **Road performance:** Good driving dynamics with responsive steering, easily-modulated brakes, and nimble, better-than-average handling. Base engine could use more power for passing and merging and there's a choppy ride on uneven roadways. The PowerShift automatic transmission shifts erratically and unexpectedly. The car accelerates best with the manual gearbox. **Strong points:** Stylish with plenty of high-tech interior features and great gas mileage with a manual gearbox. There is also just adequate space in the front of this five-seater for the driver and passenger. Little noise intrudes into the well-appointed cabin. A tilt and telescopic steering wheel, height-adjustable driver's seat, and capless fuel filler also come with the car. A relatively high ground clearance reduces "belly drag" in the snow (an inch higher than the Toyota Yaris and VW Jetta). **Weak points:** A policy of fuel economy at all costs, including engine and transmission failures, results in poor overall reliability and a cramped interior. Buy a Honda Fit or Hyundai Accent, instead. Owners report that the automatic transmission cuts gas mileage by almost 15%. Rear passenger space is cramped; even Honda's Fit has more storage area than the Fiesta five-door hatchback. Drivers find the head restraints force a chin-to-chest driving position that's so uncomfortable they're removing the head restraints altogether. Audio control takes getting used to. Seats could use a bit more lumbar and thigh bolstering. Armrest is too far forward on the Fiesta's door. Limited cargo and rear seat space. The dash houses angled keys that look good but lack functionality. Owners report the following failures: Oil pan, water pump, and front crank seal leaks; engine stalling and surging along with poor transmission performance; electrical shorts; excessive steering-wheel vibration; noisy brakes; and various fit and finish deficiencies (for example, door panels fall apart or the doors suddenly fly open).

Prices and Specs

Prices (Soft): *Base:* $15,349, *Sedan SE:* $16,000, *S:* $17,000, *Sedan ST:* $23,024, *Titanium:* $20,000 **Freight:** $1,700 **Powertrain (Front-drive):** Engine: 1.5 3-cyl. (123 hp), 1.6L DOHC 4 (120 hp); Transmissions: 5-speed man., 6-speed manumatic **Dimensions/capacity:** Passengers: 2/3; Wheelbase: 98 in.; H: 57.1-58.1/L: 159.7-160.1/W: 71.8-77.8 in.; Headroom F/R: 5/1.5 in.; Legroom F/R: 42.2/31.2 in.; Cargo volume: 12.8 cu. ft.; Fuel tank: 46.9L/regular; Tow limit: Not recommended; Turning circle: 34.4 ft.; Ground clearance: 6.7 in.; Weight: 2,537-2,742 lb.

Other opinions: "The 2015 Ford Fiesta ranks #12 out of 42 affordable small cars." – *U.S. News & World Report.* "While its quirky dual-clutch automatic transmission and limited rear seat/cargo space mean it won't be perfect for everyone, the Fiesta does impress with sporty driving dynamics and a boatload of available technology and comfort features." – *Left Lane News.* "The contact owns a 2014 Ford Fiesta. The hard edge on the trim of the steering wheel would constantly cut the contact's hand. Also, the contact mentioned that the steering wheel would vibrate and a buzzing noise emitted from the steering column. In addition, the vehicle failed to shift when in reverse, grind, and independently shift into neutral. The traction control and hill assist also intermittently illuminate while driving. The vehicle was taken to two different dealers, on 5 separate occasions. The technician diagnosed that the power steering module, sensors, NVH tape, steering wheel, steering module, reprogrammed main computer, and air bags were all replaced. All failures except the traction control and hill assist light were not rectified. The failure mileage was 2,420." – *safercar.gov.* **Major redesign:** The 2011-16 models aren't very different from each other; for sport car thrills, the ST is faster and smoother than the base version. **Highway/city fuel economy:** *Man.:* 6.5./8.5L/100km. *Auto:* 5.5./7.5L/100km. *16-valve:* 6.8./8.9L/100km. **Best alternatives:** Honda Civic or Fit, Hyundai Accent or Elantra, Kia Rio, Mazda2 or Mazda3, and Nissan's Versa. Don't be tempted by the Ford Focus as a second choice. Sure, its fuel economy is tempting, and you get a more comfortable ride with more room, but an unbelievably high number of mechanical and body defects wipe out any advantage.

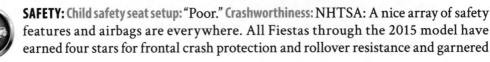

SAFETY: Child safety seat setup: "Poor." **Crashworthiness:** NHTSA: A nice array of safety features and airbags are everywhere. All Fiestas through the 2015 model have earned four stars for frontal crash protection and rollover resistance and garnered five stars for side crashworthiness. IIHS gave it top marks in frontal offset, side, and rear impact occupant protection, as well as protection from excessive roof intrusion into the cabin. On the other hand, the 2015 model scored "Marginal" in the front small overlap test. **Owner-reported safety-related failures:** A serious safety problem has surfaced with the 2011-14 Fiesta and 2013-14 Fusion/Lincoln MKZ: Their doors may suddenly fly open due to a faulty door latch. Ford has known about this defect for the past several years and has repaired over a thousand cars *gratis* on a case-by-case basis under a "goodwill" warranty extension. Owners tell the NHTSA these Mexican-made vehicles are unsafe and should be recalled to have all their latches replaced. One Fiesta owner wrote NHTSA's *safercar.gov:* "When I made a turn, one of the doors came flying open. I had to use a cargo strap to keep the door shut both times while taking it to the dealership for repair." Other owner complaints: Airbags failed to deploy; rear seatbacks may not lock into position, allowing any cargo to fly forward as a deadly projectile in a sudden stop; and fuel leaks under the car.

ALERT! Brake and accelerator pedals are placed too close together; be wary of the front head restraints:

> The headrest is causing me to have headaches due to the forward leaning position of the headrest. I have tried all the situations of the seat and it is the same for all of them. I am 5'2" and in my research have found most other short people have the same issue.

Fiesta Profile

	2011	2012	2013	2014
Used Values ($)				
S	6,500	7,500	9,500	11,000
SE	8,000	9,500	11,000	13,000
SEL	9,000	11,000	13,000	15,500
ST	—	—	—	19,000
Titanium	—	—	13,500	16,000
Reliability	★1	★1	★1	★2
Repairs ($$$)	💰3	💰3	💰3	💰2
Electrical	★1	★1	★1	★2
Engine (base)	★1	★1	★2	★2
Fit/Finish	★1	★1	★1	★1
Infotainment	★1	★1	★1	★2
Transmission (auto.)	★1	★1	★1	★1

SECRET WARRANTIES, INTERNAL BULLETINS: 2011—Customer Satisfaction Program 11B31 (secret warranty) calls for a free upgraded clutch replacement on the DPS6 automatic transmission. Engine stalling and surging along with poor transmission performance may be due to a malfunctioning transmission control module. Automatic transmission grind or rattle noise in Second, Fourth, or Reverse gear. Poor or no engine start, or transmission engagement. Engine block heater coolant leakage and spillover into the spark plug well. Some Fiestas may exhibit an oil leak at the cylinder head oil galley located behind the exhaust cam phaser. On Fiestas equipped with manual windows, the window glass may suddenly drop due to a defective window regulator (a warranty item, for sure). AC condensation may collect on the front passenger floor. 2011-12—Automatic transmission fluid leak from the clutch housing will require a major repair covered by the base warranty (TSB #12-4-6, issued April 20, 2012). Some Fiestas equipped with a manual transaxle may exhibit a transmission disengagement from reverse gear on high tip-in RPM (2500-3000 RPM). Steering column pop, clunk, knock during slow-speed turns. 2011-13—Some cars may produce a thump, rattle in the fuel filler neck area. Ford will correct the problem free of charge under its Emissions Warranty. 2011-14—AC lack of heat; blower motor frozen in cold weather. This may be caused by snow entering through the cowl top area. The snow melts and the water enters the blower motor and refreezes during a below freezing overnight soak. The blower motor fuse at location F4 in the Power Distribution Box may also be open (repair covered under the base warranty). Vehicles equipped with air conditioning and built on or before Sept. 10, 2013, may leak water onto the front passenger floor area in high temperature and high humidity conditions. Remedies for clutch shudder or automatic transmission fluid leaks may include installing a seal kit, replacing the clutch, and reprogramming the PCM/TCM module. This is an expensive repair that's covered up to 7 years, 100,000 miles under Ford's Customer Satisfaction Program #14M01, created July 21, 2014.

EXCESSIVE TRANSMISSION CLUTCH SHUDDER AND/OR AUTOMATIC TRANSMISSION FLUID LEAK

SERVICE BULLETIN NO.: 14-0131   DATE: 07/23/14

2011-14 Fiesta and Focus

ISSUE: Vehicles equipped with a DPS6 automatic transmission may exhibit an excessive transmission clutch shudder on light acceleration. Some vehicles may or may not exhibit transmission fluid leaking from the clutch housing.

2012-13—Various SYNC malfunctions are tackled (TSB# 13-9-22, published Sept, 27, 2013). 2012-14—Vehicles equipped with 1.6L Twin Independent Variable Cam Timing (Ti-VCT) may exhibit a whirring, buzz, or saw-type noise from the engine after a cold start between 950-1200 RPM from the timing belt cover. Ford suggests changing the engine timing chain under warranty.

FOCUS ★

RATING: Not Recommended (2000-03; 2012-16); Average (2004-11); *Electric*: Not Recommended (2013-16). **Road performance:** This small car is fun to drive and a fairly good highway performer when the transmission is working properly – which isn't often. Like the Fiesta's similar transmission, overall performance both on the highway and in town is hampered by a failure-prone, poorly designed, and often badly-calibrated PowerShift automatic that stumbles and surges. Its deficiencies compromise safety and fuel economy and lead to white-knuckle driving when merging or when slowing down. Nevertheless, the car usually gives a smooth, supple ride, shows excellent handling and road holding, and provides a commanding view of the highway. Titanium models come with a sport-tuned suspension, which provides a ride that may be too firm for some. Electric versions are basically a one-trick pony: A conclusion buttressed by *U.S. News & World Report*'s ranking the car #26 out of 42 affordable small cars. **Strong points:** Stylish, with a well-appointed interior and plenty of high-tech options. The 2015-16 Focus comes standard with a user-friendly rear-view camera and Ford's SYNC voice-control system, which includes Bluetooth and a USB port. Available features include dual-zone automatic climate control, navigation, blind-spot monitoring, and the MyFord Touch infotainment system with an 8-inch touch screen. Do the reworked infotainment features work better than previous versions? Early owner reports say *"nyet."* **Weak points:** Infotainment controls are distracting, uncooperative, and glitch-prone. Backseat legroom is minimal. What a difference a few years make; good thing *Lemon-Aid* is an annual guide, because the redesigned 2012-14 Focus has been transformed back into its lemony former state. The car's deficiencies are legion – mostly related to the powertrain (engine and transmission), brakes, electronics (infotainment) and electrical systems, steering, and fit and finish. *Electric:* This plug-in electric car has an upscale interior and agile handling for an EV, but there's a high learning curve to understanding the car's confusing and failure-prone infotainment system. Apparently, Ford Customer Assistance is of limited assistance as this owner points out to *consumeraffairs.com*:

Last July I leased a 2014 Ford Focus EV (electric vehicle). This has proven to be the worst overall experience I have ever had with any car. Dealing with Ford has been a disaster. I've never been treated so rudely by a company like that. One of the issues I have is with the window in the rear hatch. It has a pattern in it that looks like it was put through a waffle iron. It is extremely distracting when you are looking through the rear view mirror and it's worse in certain lighting conditions. When I bring this to the attention of the dealer and also to Ford customer disservice they only will say that other cars have it too so that means it's normal. With that philosophy how do recalls ever happen? If thousands of cars have the same defect doesn't that make it normal? I don't think so but apparently Ford does.

I'm also having problems with the SYNC system. As I'm driving along my phone just disconnects and I have to manually reconnect again. This can happen multiple times in one day and then it may not happen again for a week. It's totally random. When I brought it in for service they hooked up another phone to it overnight and in the morning it was still connected so in their minds there is nothing wrong. I am told the SYNC system as a whole is functioning fine with no problems yet a while back I received either a letter or an e-mail from Ford saying that the warranty on the SYNC system has been extended to five years due to the problems. In addition the letter said that Ford would no longer be using Microsoft and would be switching companies in the future. That doesn't sound like the system is just fine to me. In addition, another problem with that same system is it changes the input source at will. I can be listening to music from one source and it will just switch to radio.

Prices and Specs

Price (Very soft): *Sedan S:* $16,799, *ST:* $30,349, *Electric:* $35,449 **Freight:** $1,700 **Powertrain (Front-drive):** Engine: 2.0L DOHC 4 (160 hp), Electric motor (143 hp); Transmissions: 5-speed man., 6-speed auto. **Dimensions/capacity:** Passengers: 2/3; Wheelbase: 104.3 in.; H: 57.7-58.2/L: 171.6-178.5/ W: 71.8-80.5 in.; Headroom N/A; Legroom F/R: 43.7/33.2 in.; Cargo volume: 13.2 cu. ft.; Fuel tank: 47L/ regular; Tow limit: Not recommended; Turning circle: 36 ft.; Weight: 2,919-3,622 lb.

Other opinions: "The 2015 Ford Focus ranks #9 out of 42 affordable small cars. Test drivers note the automatic transmission is sluggish at low speeds. An optional turbocharged three-cylinder engine paired with a six-speed manual transmission generates plenty of power, but critics say for low-speed driving the manual transmission could be better geared." – *U.S. News & World Report.* "My 2013 Ford Focus almost got me killed. I was on the Bay Bridge in the middle lane, when I experienced extreme loss of power. I was moving with the speed of traffic, and all of a sudden no power. I had to cut across three lanes of traffic to get to the shoulder, just missed getting smashed by a Mac Truck. I had just gotten the car back from the dealer two weeks earlier for the same problem. They assured me that it was fixed and that what was going on was 'normal.' I am scared to drive it, I am scared to sell it to someone because they might hurt themselves or others. This is the worst lemon around. People are going to die because the car is not reliable, perhaps they already have. Ford has a responsibility to protect its customers." – *www. consumeraffairs.com/automotive/ford_focus.html.* Major redesign: 2000 and 2012 models. The car got an updated interior and exterior for 2015, but it really hasn't been fully redesigned since 2012. Highway/city fuel economy: *Auto.:* 6.7/9.2 L/100 km. *Electric:* 110/99 mpg-e (miles per gallon-equivalent) city/highway and can travel 76 miles on a fully charged battery. Best alternatives: Take a good look at the Honda Fit, Hyundai Accent or Elantra, Mazda3, or the VW Golf for exceptionable performance, cabin space to comfortably seat five, high fuel economy, and a reasonable price. A good alternatives to the Focus Electric is the Nissan Leaf. Industry insiders say, however, that Ford may drop the Focus Electric in 2016 due to poor sales in North America. Ford has sold its Focus Electric for more than three years, and has delivered just over 4,600 units. During that time, Nissan sold 66,500 Leafs.

SAFETY: Child safety seat setup: "Acceptable." **Crashworthiness:** NHTSA: Gives the 2012 models a four-star overall rating while 2013-15 models do even better with an overall five-star score. It's likely the 2016 will do as well. 2000-10 models got three to five stars for frontal/side crashworthiness and rollover resistance. The 2000 and 2001 two-door models only got one star for passenger side-impact protection. IIHS gave its top rating ("Good") for frontal offset, rear, and side crash protection and roof strength. However, head restraints receive criticism for being angled downward too sharply, forcing the head to bend forward. The 2015 got just an "Acceptable" front small overlap rating. Owner-reported safety-related failures: Mostly stalling, brake, and electrical failures.

ALERT! Watch out for the driver head restraints pushing your chin to your chest, especially with the Recaro seats on the ST. Once you get the creak out of your neck, contort your body to hold the door shut, because over a thousand owners have had the doors suddenly open while cruising on the highway.

Focus Profile

	2006	2007	2008	2009	2010	2011	2012	2013	2014
Used Values ($)									
S	3,000	3,500	4,000	5,000	6,000	7,500	10,000	1,500	13,000
SE	3,500	4,500	5,000	6,000	7,000	9,000	11,500	12,500	13,500
SEL	—	—	—	6,500	8,000	10,000	12,500	—	—
Titanium	—	—	—	—	—	—	13,500	17,500	20,500
*Electric	—	—	—	—	—	—	—	22,500	26,500
Reliability	⭐	⭐	⭐	⭐	⭐	⭐	⭐	⭐	⭐
Repairs ($$$)	2	2	2	2	2	2	3	3	3
Electrical	⭐	⭐	⭐	⭐	⭐	⭐	⭐	⭐	⭐
Engine (base)	⭐	⭐	⭐	⭐	⭐	⭐	⭐	⭐	⭐
Fit/Finish	⭐	⭐	⭐	⭐	⭐	⭐	⭐	⭐	⭐
Infotainment	—	—	—	⭐	⭐	⭐	⭐	⭐	⭐
Transmission (auto.)	⭐	⭐	⭐	⭐	⭐	⭐	⭐	⭐	⭐

Note: After two model years the 2013 Electric is worth barely half its original $42,000 selling price. Not much of a money-saver when all the costs are added up.

SECRET WARRANTIES, INTERNAL BULLETINS: 2000-11—Excessive engine vibration at idle may be caused by small stones, road debris, ice, or snow packed/lodged in the rear engine roll restrictor. 2008-10—Ignition key binds in the ignition cylinder. 2008-11—Some Focus models equipped with a 4F27E transmission may exhibit a 2-3 or 2-4 upshift flare, or lack of Third and/or Fourth gear along with burnt automatic transmission fluid and lit diagnostic trouble codes (DTCs) P0733, P0734, P0751, and/or P0972. A direct clutch repair kit is available under warranty to fix these powertrain malfunctions. Vehicles may exhibit a whine, howl, or groan type noise from the intermediate shaft bearing with the vehicle in motion. This maybe due to moisture getting past the bearing seals. An underbody squeak or creaking noise may be silenced by replacing the parking brake cables and routing eyelets (TSB #10-24-06, issued Dec 16, 2011). Paint damage? Here is Ford's "secret warranty" that will pay for a new paint job. 2009-10—A fix for inoperative door locks. 2010-11—If the idle speed intermittently drops lower than desired and/or fluctuates, the throttle body may be the culprit. 2011—Ford says excessive road wander, steering drift, or uneven rear tire wear may require the installation of a new right rear lower control arm (TSB #11-1-1, issued Jan. 25, 2011). 2011-14—A clutch shudder or automatic transmission fluid leaks require a new seal kit, clutch, and reprogramming of the PCM/TCM module. This is an expensive repair that's covered up to 7 years, 100,000 miles under Ford's Customer Satisfaction Program #14M01, created July 21, 2014. 2012—AC Engine controls/drivability issues. Automatic transmission controls have various drivability concerns. Free transmission clutch replacement. Steering wander. Front-end crunching, creaking when passing over bumps. MyFord Touch glitches. Loss of steering power assist. Erratic fuel gauge readings. Fixing a depression in the hood's surface. 2012-13—A crunching or creaking-type noise from the front suspension on low-speed turns and over bumps may be corrected by installing a new strut bearing on the affected side. Water leaking into the passenger side front footwell is likely due to leaking climate control condensate from the AC. If the instrument panel cluster won't light up on start-up, the body control module ISP may need rebooting after fuse #69 has been removed for a minute and reinserted. 2012-14—If there is early nozzle shut off, or a slow fuel fill, clean out the EVAP canister fresh air hose vent hose and the screen filter. Some vehicles may exhibit a clunk and/or rattle-type noise from the left and/or right front strut area at speeds between 8-32 km/h (5-20 mph) over minor road surface imperfections. First, lubricate both front strut shafts before investing more money in changing any components. Another problem that falls under both the regular and Emissions warranty: Some vehicles may have inaccurate fuel gauge indication and/or inaccurate distance to empty readings. The Check Engine may also be lit. More infotainment failures: Some vehicles equipped with MyFord Touch/MyLincoin Touch may screw up navigation data, voice recognition, call sound quality, phone pairing, clock, media indicators, WiFi pass code entry, rear-view camera guide lines, and other system performances. Ford says troubleshooting the above problems should take no more than 20 minutes of electronic module tinkering (under warranty). 2013—Tire "slapping" and vehicle vibration may be caused by faulty Continental tires. Ford assumes responsibility for their replacement.

FUSION/LINCOLN MKZ ★/★★★★

RATING: *Fusion:* Not Recommended (2013-16); Not Recommended (2010-12); Below Average (2006-09). *MKZ:* Above Average (all years). After seeing all the quality mistakes in Ford's Focus since year 2000, it's no surprise that the Fusion, launched in 2006 with many of the same mechanical components, is a risky buy. What is surprising is that its Lincoln counterpart is an all-around much better car. A fusion of Dr. Jekyll and Mr. Hyde. Lincoln's Dr. Jekyll delivers adequate acceleration and fair handling; steering that is tight, precise, and vibration-free; and 4-cylinder and V6 engines that are adequate, but not as thrifty or dependable as presented. The Fusion's Mr. Hyde gives you a 19th century brew that includes a demonic automatic transmission; a dysfunctional infotainment system; a car that runs off in all directions; 2013-14 models with doors that suddenly fly open on turns and braking that's far scarier than anything Robert Louis Stevenson or Stephen King could imagine. **Road performance:** *Fusion and MKZ:* Good acceleration and fair handling; steering is tight, precise, and vibration free; and the 4-cylinder and V6 engines borrowed from Mazda are competent. Added rigidity and additional chassis tweaking have resulted in a car that will seat five passengers (four in comfort) and corner reasonably well. On 2013s, AWD is again available, a fuel-saving engine stop-start system is standard on 1.6L models, and hybrid buyers get a new 2.0L. An Atkinson-cycle 4-cylinder replaced the outgoing 2.5L. The high-performance Fusion ST uses a refined version of the much-criticized EcoBoost 2.0L powerplant. More negatives: Both cars carry a dangerously flawed automatic transmission; brake performance is unreliable, brake calipers and rotors frequently need replacing; and the Fusion tends to wander all over the road, forcing drivers to constantly correct the steering. **Strong points:** Stylish and cheap (used). The Lincoln can run on one or both of its power sources and requires no plug-in charging. **Weak points:** Cramped rear seating and tilted-forward head restraints can be pure torture; owners say the front seats are painful to sit in due to a hard block within the seat. An accident survivor says Lincoln airbags failed to deploy, and both front seatbacks collapsed in a rear-ender. Fusion owners say the knee airbag restricts brake pedal access and the brakes are too weak. Chronic automatic transmission failures and erratic shifting with the Fusion; sudden stalling when the car is underway; Hybrid brake pedal is mounted too close to the accelerator pedal. Fuel economy estimates (Hybrid included) can't be trusted. Hybrid batteries don't hold their charge. One Edmonton owner wrote this to his local TV station:

> My 2013 Ford Fusion vehicle has been in the service department for a total of 3 months (8 times) for the same issue and no dealership can fix it (I have had it to 2 different dealerships) with no luck currently it is being towed to Metro Ford for the 4th time (9 times total including this time).
>
> The issue is the hybrid system. The dealers have replaced the battery 3 times and now it is dead again. Ford Canada has been notified on several occasions and has done nothing to resolve these issues.

This morning the car is dead again and Ford Canada has said that they can't do anything and it will be 2 days before a representative will get back to me.

This vehicle has only a little over 18,000 kms and is usually in the service dept. at least once a month (one time it was in for 33 days straight).

It has also been in for "no key detected" at least 3 times, as well. When this happens the car is dead and the only way to get into it is by using a dummy key which will open the doors but nothing else.

These vehicles are not very good for the environment as they have been replacing batteries left and right over the last 18 months and can't fix the issues.

Three weeks ago they replaced a main mother board in the dash and it solved the problem for less than three weeks and it is dead again this morning.

• • •

We finally get to pick the car up from the dealer today (9 more days with a rental). The funny thing is they gave us a new battery because the other one was weak (4th new one) but said that they can't find the problem with the help from Ford Canada Techs. The Service Manager pulled my girlfriend to the side and basically told her that they don't know what is wrong with it, that they can't find the problem. She said to him that the car was a "Lemon" and he said "I would have to agree".

Prices and Specs

Prices (Negotiable; Lincolns: Deeply discounted): *Fusion S:* $24,199, *SE:* $26,099, *Titanium:* $34,999, *SE Hybrid:* $30,399, *SE Energi:* $40,099, *MKZ Front-drive, 4-cyl.:* $38,860, *AWD V6:* $43,000, *Hybrid:* $38,860 **Freight:** $1,600; Note: 2016 Hybrid and Energi versions are discounted by $1,000 due to low fuel prices deflating the value of all fuel-sippers **Powertrain (Front-drive/AWD):** Engines: *Fusion:* 1.6L EcoBoost 4-cyl. (179 hp), 2.0L EcoBoost 4-cyl. (240 hp), 2.5L 4-cyl. (170 hp), 2.0L 4-cyl. hybrid (185 hp) and plug-in electric; *Fusion ST:* 2.0L EcoBoost 4-cyl. (252 hp); *Lincoln:* 3.7L V6 (300 hp), 2.0L 4-cyl. hybrid (188 hp); Transmissions: 6-speed man., 6-speed auto., CVT **Dimensions/capacity:** *Fusion:* Passengers: 2/3; Wheelbase: 107 in.; H: 56.9/L: 190.6/W: 72 in.; Headroom F/R: 2.5/2.5 in.; Legroom F/R: 40.5/28 in.; Cargo volume: 16 cu. ft.; Fuel tank: 45L/regular; Tow limit: No towing; Load capacity: 850 lb.; Turning circle: 39 ft.; Ground clearance: 5 in.; Weight: 3,285 lb.

Other opinions: "The 2015 Ford Fusion ranks #9 out of 18 affordable mid-size cars; the Lincoln MKZ scores last out of 17 upscale mid-size cars. Though critics say the Fusion has a clunky touch-screen infotainment system and an underpowered base engine, they like the car's enjoyable feel while driving and its spacious interior. MKZ's cheap cabin materials and the poorly-designed infotainment system leave critics disgruntled." – *U.S. News & World Report.* "I bought a brand new 2015 Ford Fusion. My knee has hit the key fob multiple times while driving and the car has turned off while in motion. This is a very dangerous situation because the car shuts off while in traffic. The key fob sticks way out and for a guy who is 6ft it is very hard to avoid hitting the key fob with my knee. This will kill someone." – *safercar.gov*. **Major redesign:** *Fusion:* 2006 and 2010 models; *MKZ:* 2006. NHTSA recorded 2167 safety-related complaints on the redesigned 2010 Fusion; 250 would be normal. Fusion will be slightly upgraded in 2016 as a 2017 model. **Highway/city fuel economy:** *2.5L:* 6.9/9.4 L/100 km. *Auto.:* 6.9/9.4 L/100 km. *3.0L:* 7.3/11.1 L/100 km. *3.0L AWD:* 7.8/11.8 L/100 km. *3.5L AWD:* 8.3/12.7 L/100 km. *Hybrid:* 5.4/4.6 L/100 km. Owners say facetiously that the only way these cars save fuel is by spending most of their time in the dealer's service bay. **Best alternatives:** *Fusion:* Honda Accord, Hyundai Elantra or Tucson, Mazda6, and Toyota Camry. *MKZ:* Toyota Avalon, BMW 5-Series, and Mercedes-Benz E-Class.

SAFETY: Child safety seat setup: "Marginal." **Crashworthiness:** NHTSA: Gives the 2006-16 Fusion/MKZ four to five stars for crashworthiness, although the 2011-12 MKZ earned only three stars for passenger side-impact protection. IIHS ranked the 2012 Fusion/MKZ "Good" for roof strength, frontal offset, side, and rear crash safety. **Owner-reported safety-related failures:** Owners note poor visibility through the rear windshield and intermittent loss of braking ability:

> The contact owns a 2014 Lincoln MKZ Hybrid. The contact stated during the winter, the transmission would shift gears to low independently. Also, the contact stated that without the vehicle being on, the transmission shifted out of Park and rolled away. As a result of the failure, the vehicle crashed into a barrier.

ALERT! Ford says bolts used in the assisted-steering system could rust and fracture, causing the 2013-15 Fusion or Lincoln MKZ to lose power steering. Affected cars will be repaired free of charge if the vehicle has been registered in a province that uses road salt in the winter, which may have accelerated the corrosion. Limiting liability to certain areas means some dangerous vehicles will not be fixed if they were driven in one area and sold in another. Logically, Ford must accept the warranty claim if the defect exists, no matter where the car was bought or registered. Automatic transmission may not hold the Lincoln on an incline. Sometimes the vehicle lurches forward in Park:

> I pulled into a parking space (space in front of a canal) and pushed buttoned into park and the car then lurched forward, going into the canal (front half only, the back half was stopped by the sea wall). We see there was a recall for the same problem for 2013 Lincoln MKZ Hybrids (ours is not a hybrid).

Fusion/Lincoln MKZ Profile

	2006	2007	2008	2009	2010	2011	2012	2013	2014
Used Values ($)									
S	—	—	—	—	—	9,500	11,500	16,000	18,500
SE	3,500	4,000	5,000	6,000	7,500	10,000	12,500	16,500	19,500
SEL	4,500	5,500	6,500	7,500	9,000	11,500	14,000	—	—
SEL V6	5,500	6,500	7,500	8,500	9,500	12,000	16,000	—	—
HYBRID	—	—	—	—	8,000	12,500	16,500	19,500	22,000
MKZ	7,500	9,000	10,500	13,500	16,000	17,000	22,500	28,000	32,000
HYBRID	—	—	—	—	—	17,500	23,000	28,500	1,000

Reliability

	2006	2007	2008	2009	2010	2011	2012	2013	2014
Fusion	★2	★2	★2	★2	★	★	★	★2	★2
MKZ	★4	★4	★4	★4	★4	★4	★4	★4	★5
Repairs ($$$)	💰3	💰3	💰3	💰3	💰3	💰3	💰2	💰2	💰2
Electrical	★	★	★	★	★	★	★	★	★2
Engine (base)	★1	★2	★2	★2	★1	★1	★2	★2	★2
Fit/Finish	★	★	★	★	★	★	★	★	★2
Infotainment	—	—	—	—	—	★	★	★	★2
Transmission (auto.)	★	★	★	★	★	★	★	★	★2

SECRET WARRANTIES, INTERNAL BULLETINS: *Fusion:* 2009-13—A throttle body replacement is covered by Customer Satisfaction Program #13N03 until January 31, 2015. After that date owners should petition the small claims court if Ford refuses their claim. 2012-13—SYNC malfunctions diagnosed. 2013—Fusion Hybrid and Fusion Energi models may make a noise that could be described as a ting, pop, or click from the front wheel area when accelerating from a stop or when shifting between Drive/Reverse and Reverse/Drive. *MKZ:* 2012—More SYNC malfunctions addressed. *Fusion, MKZ:* 2007-11—Vehicles equipped with AWD systems and built on or before Aug. 13, 2010, may exhibit a driveline vibration or a howl noise at highway speeds in cold temperatures. 2010—Vehicles equipped with AWD may exhibit a shudder/chatter/vibration driveline sensation during a tight turn, or a thump/clunk noise on light acceleration. These symptoms may also occur under 40 mph (64 km/h), on tip-in, driving uphill, or towing under heavy acceleration. 2010-11—Vehicles may experience a leaking/stuck canister purge valve. This condition may cause various intermittent driveability symptoms without any diagnostic trouble codes (DTC). The condition may also cause driveability symptoms with malfunction indicator light lit. 2010-12—Transmission fluid leak from the left-hand halfshaft seal. This may be due to seal and/or bushing wear caused by the halfshaft surface finish. 2011-12—Look out for an intermittent harsh 1-2 shift or harsh 5-6 shift regardless of temperature or soak time. Additionally, 4-5 shift flare may be experienced after an extended cold soak on the first few 4-5 shifts of the day. 2.5L-equipped vehicles with late 4-5 shift events and/or high RPMs may also benefit from a calibration of the PCM. SYNC infotainment functionality concerns. 2011-14—An extended warranty (Customer Satisfaction Program 14N02) applies to PCM reprogramming in the event of ABS brake communication failures. 2013—Vehicles that won't start may need to reprogram the radio transceiver module (RTM). 2013-14—Vehicles equipped with an HF35 transmission may exhibit a thumping, rubbing or grinding noise coming from the transmission. This noise may be present in all gear ranges, including Neutral when the vehicle is moving, but will not be present when the vehicle is stationary or in Park. Remedy is to replace the transfer shaft gear assembly, transmission assembly, and exhaust manifold gasket, per instructions in TSB #14-0176, dated Sept. 24, 2014. Inoperative ambient lighting can be turned on by reprogramming the body control module. Some vehicles equipped with MyFord Touch/MyLincoln Touch may have problems with navigation data, voice recognition, call sound quality, phone pairing, clock, media, Wi-Fi pass code entry, rear view camera guide lines and/or overall system performance. TSB #13-10-6, dated Oct. 4, 2013, troubleshoots all of the above failures.

MUSTANG ★★★★

Ford's 2011 rear-drive Mustang came with a better V6 engine and other improvements that took a couple of years to perfect.

RATING: Above Average (2013-16; 2008-10); Below Average (2011-12); Average (2000-07). The 2016 Mustang has been carried over without any significant changes, nevertheless, it has been downgraded this year due to a flood of owner complaints relating to earlier versions. Owners cite chronic manual and automatic transmission failures and "shift lag," "unfixable" electrical shorts, electronic module malfunctions, and rattling door panels. **Road performance:** Fast acceleration and impressive handling and braking, thanks to last year's independent rear suspension and better brakes. The V8 is a pocket rocket, but the automatic transmission robs the engine of some of its performance, particularly in cold weather. The manual tranny is more responsive with crisp short-throws, yet, it tends to grind when upshifting, especially when engaging Fifth gear. Sudden acceleration when downshifting. The engine also sometimes shuts off when the car slows down with the clutch applied. **Strong points:** Base models come equipped with a host of safety, luxury, and convenience features. There's easy access into the interior and comfortable, upright front seating gives an excellent view of the road. Resale value is better than average. **Weak points:** The automatic transmission "hunts" for the proper gear. Numerous complaints of failing rear ends and driveshafts on all cars equipped with manual transmissions. Chronic power steering failures. Limited rear seat room, heat vents overheat, and poor quality fit and finish, highlighted by doors that open when the car is underway.

Prices and Specs

Prices (Firm): *Fastback V6:* $27,099, *Fastback EcoBoost:* $30,099, *V6 Premium:* $26,999, *V6 Convertible:* $32,099, *EcoBoost Premium Fastback:* $35,599, *GT Fastback:* $39,099, *EcoBoost Premium Convertible:* $41,199, *GT Premium Fastback:* $44,599, *GT Premium Convertible:* $50,149, *Shelby GT500 Convertible:* $66,249
Freight: $1,700 **Powertrain (Rear-drive):** Engines: 3.7L V6 (300 hp), 5.0L 2.3L EcoBoost (310 hp), 5.0L V8 (435 hp); Transmissions: 6-speed man., 6-speed auto. **Dimensions/capacity:** Passengers: 2/2; Wheelbase: 107.1 in.; H: 54.4-54.9/L: 188.3/W: 8.2-81.9 in.; Headroom F/R: 5/1 in.; Legroom F/R: 39.5/23 in.; Cargo volume: 13 cu. ft.; Fuel tank: 60.1L/regular, EcoBoost 58L/regular; Tow limit: 1,000 lb.; Load capacity: 700 lb.; Turning circle: 33.4 ft.; Ground clearance: 5.7 in.; Weight: 3,585 lb.

Other opinions: "The 2015 Ford Mustang ranks #1 out of 11 affordable sports cars and convertibles (Chevrolet's Camaro ranks #6) … The Mustang's robust engine options, athletic handling and high-end interior render it a thoroughly modern muscle car." – *U.S. News & World Report.* "While turning our 2012 Mustang, my wife heard something loose and rattling in the steering wheel. She then pulled into a parking space. She shook the steering wheel side to side and a large broken black bolt fell out. After that she realized that the wheel was free and fell off into her hands." – *safercar.gov.* **Major redesign:** 1994, 2005, and 2011. The Shelby GT350 returns as a 2016 model and offers a new, 5.2L naturally-aspirated V8 with a racing-style crankshaft and a better cylinder-head and valvetrain setup. You will also find lightweight aluminum body panels from the A-pillar forward. Going back to the earlier Mustang redesigns, used car buyers should take note that a huge horsepower boost on the base 2011 Mustang turned its wimpish 210 hp V6 into a sizzling 305 hp racer that's one of the best bargains around. Incidentally, the

2011-12 GT500 ratcheted up its performance by a few notches, too, with an aluminum-block engine that produced 550 hp. Other goodies on the 2011-12 Mustangs: A new limited-clip differential, larger brakes (taken from the 2010 GT), electronic power steering, a retuned suspension, stiffer rear anti-roll bars, and convertibles that get less body flexing through the use of shock-tower braces. Another welcome change on these earlier models: Fold-down rear head restraints to improve visibility. **Highway/city fuel economy:** *2.3L 4-cyl. man.:* 7.5/10.6 L/100 km. *2.3L 4-cyl. auto.:* 7.4/11 L/100 km. *3.7L V6 man.:* 8.3/13.5 L/100 km. *3.7L V6 auto.:* 8.5/ 12.8 L/100 km. *3.7L V6 convertible auto:* 7.8/11.9 L/100 km. *5.0L V8 man.:* 9.3/15.2 L/ 100 km. *5.0L V8 auto.:* 9.5/14.9 L/100 km. **Best alternatives:** The resurrected Camaro is looking better and better as it boosts horsepower and offers more standard gear and less drivetrain failures than Ford. Forget about the Dodge Challenger. Its 250 hp engine and heavy body take it out of the running. In summary, four fun and reliable competitors are the Chevrolet Camaro, Hyundai Genesis, 2012 Infiniti G25 or G27, and Mazda Miata.

SAFETY: **Child safety seat setup:** Unrated. **Crashworthiness:** NHTSA: Gives the 2015 Mustang an overall five-star score. 2012-14 models earned four stars for overall crashworthiness and five stars for rollover resistance. 2001-10 models are rated five stars for frontal offset crash protection. 2001-04 models merited three stars for side-impact crashworthiness while the 2005-10 models earned four to five stars. The IIHS's crash protection rating for 2010-15 models was "Good" for moderate overlap front protection, frontal offset collision safety, and head restraint effectiveness. Side crashworthiness was ranked only "Acceptable," however. Ironically, the 2010-15 convertible version, a car style that usually doesn't do well in crash tests, outperformed the two-door hardtop with a "Good" rating in all categories. 2005-09 convertibles failed the rear crashworthiness test. Door flies open on the hghway. **Owner-reported safety-related failures:** Exhaust fumes enter into the cabin. Fuel tank may fall off due to the mounting bracket bolts failing. Engine throttle body frequently fails.

ALERT! Hold your horses! Make sure the car is delivered with all its advertised equipment:

> Ford has failed to make a spare wheel/tire available for the 2015 Mustang. It is not standard on all vehicles (a tire inflation kit is all it comes with) and the spare wheel/tire is on back order for all dealerships because supply is low and production is being prioritized over owner availability. Three different tire stores have told me they do not have a compatible spare available.

> . . .

> My 2015 convertible was delivered without protective tonneau covers/caps. When convertible is in down position, there are big holes in top of rear panel exposing the mechanical arms. Apparently the OEM [Original Equipment Manufacturer] of these parts could not make them properly and if an owner tries to put up top without removal, the whole convertible

top mechanism gets destroyed. Right now all sorts of dirt and debris gets into these big gapping holes.

Invest in an anti-theft system (one that includes an engine immobilizer) and good tires recommended by *www.tirerack.com.* Stay away from the notchy, erratic-shifting 6-speed Getrag manual transmission. It has performed poorly on 2011-13 models and the jury's still out on the 2014s (see *mustangsdaily.com/blog/2011/11/09/ford-responds-to-nhtsasinvestigation-of-the-mustangs-mt82-6-speed-transmission*).

My 2012 Mustang GT was most likely totaled tonight when the transmission did not allow a shift into 5th gear. It slid into 3rd [gear] and caused the wheels to spin resulting in the car fishtailing and hitting a tree in the median.

Mustang Profile

	2006	2007	2008	2009	2010	2011	2012	2013	2014
Used Values ($)									
Coupe	5,500	7,000	8,500	10,000	11,500	13,000	14,000	16,500	18,500
Coupe Premium	—	—	—	—	—	—	16,500	19,500	22,000
Convertible	8,000	9,000	11,000	13,000	14,500	18,500	21,500	24,000	27,000
Coupe GT	7,500	8,500	10,000	12,500	15,000	18,500	22,500	26,500	30,000
Convertible GT	10,500	12,500	14,000	16,000	19,000	22,500	26,000	29,500	31,500
Coupe Boss	—	—	—	—	—	—	30,500	35,000	—
Shelby Coupe	—	17,000	21,000	24,000	27,500	33,000	39,500	48,500	54,000
Coupe Cvt.	—	21,000	24,500	27,500	32,000	38,000	45,000	54,000	60,000
Reliability	3	3	☆	☆	☆	2	2	☆	☆
Repairs ($$$)	1	1	1	1	1	3	3	1	1
Electrical	3	3	4	4	4	2	2	4	4
Engine (base)	2	2	3	3	3	1	1	2	2
Fit/Finish	2	2	2	2	2	1	1	3	3
Infotainment	—	—	—	1	1	1	1	2	2
Transmission (auto.)	2	2	2	2	3	1	1	3	3

SECRET WARRANTIES, INTERNAL BULLETINS: 2005-15—Airbags fail to deploy. 2005-12—May have a major fluid leak from the rear axle vent. 2011—Some fuel gauge indicators may drop from approximately 1/2 to 1/4 full to E, and the Message Center may show 0 Miles to Empty. Owners may also notice that when refueling, the vehicle may only take half a tank. 2011-12—SYNC voice recognition system may ignore your voice … "Hello, Hal, do you hear me?" Manual transmission can be difficult to shift in cold weather. Front-end suspension may produce a grunt, creak, chirp, or squeak. Owners say the same noise affects 2013-14 suspensions. 2011-13—Mustangs that won't start, or are rough running, may simply have a blown #13 fuse in the battery junction box. 2011-14—Vehicles may have a delayed Park to Forward or Reverse transmission engagement on startup after parking several hours or overnight. The vehicle functions normally after the initial engagement has completed. Ford suggests replacing the transmission pump assembly – a six-hour repair. This repair should not be needed before 7-10 years. So, naturally, any refusal by Ford to pass this repair under warranty should prompt owners to file a claim in small claims court. Use TSB #14-0076 as proof of the company's responsibility. Mustangs equipped with a 3.7L, 5.0L 4V DOHC and 5.0L 4V DOHC SEFI with a rear axle vent located on the left axle tube may exhibit a fluid leak from the rear axle vent. Ford will install a vent kit under warranty (takes about a half-hour).

REAR AXLE VENT – OIL LEAK

SERVICE BULLETIN NO.: 14-0046   DATE: 03/06/14

ISSUE: Some 2011-2014 Mustang vehicles equipped with a 3.7L, 5.0L 4V DOHC and 5.0L 4V DOHC SEFI with a rear axle vent located on the left axle tube may exhibit a fluid leak from the rear axle vent.

ACTION: Install a new vent kit following the instructions included in the kit.

A Mustang that grunts, chirps, creaks, or squeaks when passing over bumps may need a new lower control arm (about a 2-hour job). Many complaints of exhaust funes entering into the cabin. Wheel stems valves may rupture and cause sudden tire deflation. 2012—Engine cold start-up ticking noises with 3.5L and 3.7L engines; the repairs require installing a camshaft kit that takes 2 hours of labour. Automatic transmission fluid leak from the bell housing. Squealing, squeaking rear brakes. 2012-13—Vehicles equipped with a 3.7L engine may produce a chirping or squealing noise from the accessory drive belt during idle and acceleration. You may need to replace the accessory drive belt and tensioner. 2013—Mustangs equipped with a MT-82 manual transmission, may experience a hard to shift or grind condition during a 1-2 upshift, or a pop-out of Second gear condition during acceleration. Ford says to check the clutch pedal reserve and replace the synchronizers, if needed (almost a 6-hour job). 2013-14—Vehicles may make a growl or buzz noise coming from the transmission that occurs when shifting from Park to Drive or Park to Reverse most often after the vehicle has been parked and then restarted. Ford says the main control valve body separator plate may need to be replaced under warranty. 2014—Water that enters the front driver's side of the vehicle will be corrected under warranty. Vehicle doesn't decelerate when foot is taken off the gas pedal.

RATING: *Edge, MKX:* Below Average (2014-16); Not Recommended (2011-13); Average (2007-10). A five-passenger wagon/SUV crossover based on the same platform as the Fusion sedan. *Lincoln MKX:* A near-mechanical twin of the Ford Edge, the MKX has a plusher interior, a quieter, smoother ride, and a more powerful engine. It offers the luxury doodads and high seating position that premium crossover buyers want, but shortchanges buyers with substandard mechanicals. Much like the smaller crossover Ford Escape's Lincoln MKC twin, the MKX is "all hat, but no cattle." This kind of skullduggery was last seen when Cadillac dressed up a rebadged variant of GM's compact, front-drive J-cars (the Chevrolet Cavalier, Buick Skyhawk, Oldsmobile Firenza, Pontiac 2000, and Sunbird from 1982 through 1988) and called it a Cimarron. Car shoppers called it a misrepresentation. **Road performance:** The Edge comes in either all-wheel drive or front-drive. Power-wise, the 2016 Ford Edge offers three different engines. The base engine is a 2.0L EcoBoost 4-cylinder turbo driving 245 horses and will easily tow as much as 3,500 pounds (AWD); the 3.5L 265 hp V6 returns with 20 fewer horses; and the 2.7L turbo-charged 300 hp V6 will make the high-performance crowd giddy. They'll get quicker turbo-assisted acceleration while risking premature powertrain failures. When accelerating the vehicle veers to the right and frequently loses all power before stalling out:

> On April 11, 2015, the throttle body assembly on the engine of my 2011 Ford Edge failed while in heavy traffic at highway speed on a 6-lane highway. I was traveling in the inside lane when the failure occurred. There was no power to the engine, and I coasted quickly across 2 lanes to a right turn lane. Fortunately, everyone reacted positively to my emergency flashers as I decelerated. On Monday, April 13, the local Ford dealership repaired the car. After returning home, I checked the internet for information on this failure mode and was surprised to read that Ford had a couple years earlier settled a NHTSA complaint for several Ford models that exhibited the problem my car experienced. The Ford Edge was not part of the settlement. Further research revealed other Ford Edges with the same problem as mine. Apparently, Ford won a partial settlement on the throttle body issue. The failure mode is as dangerous as the General Motors ignition switch failure.

Last year's standard 3.5L V6 engine is a better performer than the 2016 powerplant. The 6-speed automatic transmission lacks refinement, however, and shifts roughly. There's also lots of road noise and the ride is jiggly. *Lincoln MKX:* 2015 Lincolns don't offer an optional 4-cylinder, but both nameplates come with standard 6-cylinder engines. The MKX base engine is a 305 hp 3.7L, while the Edge carries a 285 hp 3.5L 6-cylinder. Edge Sport models are equipped with the 3.7L. **Strong points:** A well-appointed interior includes a rear-view camera, push-button start, a USB port, and an improved SYNC infotainment system that uses voice commands to control compatible mobile devices. Easy to park. **Weak points:** Sudden automatic transmission failures (Reverse gear, Fifth and Sixth gear, and clutch);

defective transmission power transfer unit (PTU); interior lights come on and shut off for no reason; radio can't be shut off; push-button starter takes several pushes to turn off the car.

Prices and Specs

Edge Prices (Firm): *SE:* $31,999, *SEL:* $35,099, *Titanium:* $39,199, *Sport:* $45,199 **MKX Price (Soft):** $45,000 **Freight:** $1,700-1,800 **Powertrains (Front-drive/AWD):** Engines: 2.0L turbo 4-cyl. (245 hp); 3.5L V6 (365 hp); 2.7L EcoBoost (335 hp) V6; 3.7L (330 hp) V6 Transmission: 6-speed manumatic **Dimensions/capacity:** Passengers: 2/3; Wheelbase: 112.2 in.; H: 68.6/L: 188; *MKX:* 190.5 in./W: 75.9 in.; Headroom F/R: 3.0/2.0 in.; Legroom F/R: 41.5/31 in.; Cargo volume: 39.2 cu. ft.; Fuel tank: 68.1L/regular; Tow limit: 3,500 lb.; Load capacity: 910 lb.; Turning circle: 38.8 ft.; Ground clearance: 7.9; *MKX:* 8.5 in.; Weight: 3,927-4,401 lb.

Other opinions: "The 2015 Ford Edge ranks #5 out of 12 affordable mid-size SUVs; it has poised handling and an upscale interior with plenty of available high-end features ... The 2015 Lincoln MKX ranks #17 out of 17 luxury mid-size SUVs. Underwhelming power, uninspired handling and a troublesome infotainment system leave the Lincoln MKX well behind its competition, critics say." – *U.S. News & World Report.* "There's no denying that this Lincoln is showing its age compared to newer rivals that have better fuel efficiency, easier-to-use technology and more advanced safety features." – *Kelley Blue Book.* "The Edge's 'door ajar' switch is faulty on most Ford Flex and Edge models. While the door is completely shut, the door ajar light stays on resulting in the doors not locking. Even if you press the automatic lock they simply unlock. Ford is not willing to address the issue or fix the issue. The way the faulty part is built into the lock mechanism requires the owner to replace the entire lock mechanism. This part cost $230.00 and due to the number of issues is not available on the market currently. As a result of the safety issue, we were required to force the switch to ground itself out, meaning we grounded out the wires linked to the door ajar light so the light is no longer on and the doors were locked." – *safercar.gov.* **Major redesign:** *Edge:* 2016 versions have restyled front and rear ends, better interior appointments, and an improved infotainment system. Keep your fingers crossed on the infotainment upgrade. *MKX:* The 2016 standard engine is a 3.7L 330 hp V6; a new 2.7L 335 hp EcoBoost V6 is optional. A lower, wider look sets the car apart from the Ford Edge. Also new this year is a camera that gives a 360-degree view around the vehicle, self-parking, self-braking, and an anti-collision feature. **Highway/city fuel economy:** *3.5 V6:* 9.5/13.3 L/100 km.; *MKX:* 3.7L: 10.3/13.7 L/100 km. Many drivers say actual gas mileage is much less than advertised. **Best alternatives:** *Edge:* GM Equinox and Terrain, Honda CR-V, Hyundai Tucson and Santa Fe, Kia Sorento and Sportage, Nissan Rogue, and the Toyota RAV4. *MKX:* Lexus RX 350 and RX 350 Hybrid.

SAFETY: Child safety seat setup: "Acceptable." **Crashworthiness:** NHTSA: 2011-15 models got four-star crash safety ratings. 2007-2010 versions did much better. They scored five stars in all categories, except for rollover protection which was four stars. IIHS rated the 2015 Edge "Good" for moderate overlap front and side collisions. 2011-15 versions scored "Good" in all crash tests carried out by IIHS, while the 2007-10 failed the roof strength test. Standard safety features that are part of the 2016 Edge trim lineup include 4-wheel antilock brakes, traction and stability control, front side-mounted airbags, front and rear head airbags, a post-collision safety system, and a programmable speed and audio volume limiting system (when junior borrows the car). **Owner-reported safety-related failures:** Fuel and exhaust fumes leak into the interior through the air vents *MKX:* Vehicle destroyed by fire while parked; car rolls away when parked on an incline; shuts down on the highway as dash control panel goes blank; sudden loss of brakes; faulty blind spot and cross traffic sensors; often electronic keys are way too sensitive:

> The keys can be in a purse or backpack and the buttons can be pressed down. They are also easily pressed down if you have them in your pocket with another item. On multiple occasions we have walked out to our car and had the windows all down, the sun roof open and or the tailgate up. We frequently will set off the alarm. One time it had started raining heavily and the windows had gotten rolled down. Consequently the interior of the car was soaked.

Windshield wiper motor burns out; just like the Edge, the "door ajar" light comes on for no reason, whether the car is underway or parked, and unlocks the doors. *Edge:* Models have had various electrical fires, (apparently from the fuse box); airbags that fail to deploy; sudden unintended acceleration; loss of power on the highway or when turning (throttle body sensor); collision warning alert sounded without any cars or objects nearby; car in Park rolled back and hit another parked car; brake failures (faulty brake booster); stop/brake/signal light frequently burns out; windows fog up in cold weather and sometimes suddenly shatter for no reason:

> The rear window of vehicle shattered simultaneous to turning the ignition switch. There was no impact to the window; it just shattered. Nothing dropped from the sky; the vehicle was parked in the driveway well away from traffic both vehicle and pedestrian. I repeat it just spontaneously shattered. There is only two thousand miles on this vehicle. This should not have happened.

ALERT! The MyFord Touch infotainment feature needs to be part of your test drive. Despite some improvements this year, critics say it is still complicated to use and often malfunctions. Warning lights indicating danger of crash activate when no other vehicle is nearby. Waits of up to six months for some MKX recall repairs.

Edge/Lincoln MKX Profile

	2007	2008	2009	2010	2011	2012	2013	2014
Used Values ($)								
SE	5,500	6,500	8,000	9,500	13,000	16,500	19,000	22,500
SEL V6	—	—	—	—	—	19,500	23,500	26,000
LTD AWD	—	—	—	15,000	18,500	21,500	24,500	27,500
Lincoln MKX	8,500	11,000	14,000	17,500	20,000	28,000	33,000	37,500
Reliability	☆	☆	☆	☆	★	★	★	☆
Reliability (MKX)	☆	☆	☆	☆	★	★	☆	☆
Repairs ($$$)	2	2	2	2	3	3	2	1
Electrical	☆	☆	★	☆	★	★	★	☆
Engine (base)	☆	☆	★	☆	★	★	☆	☆
Fit/Finish	☆	☆	☆	☆	★	★	★	☆
Infotainment	—	—	—	—	★	★	★	★
Transmission (auto.)	☆	☆	☆	☆	★	★	★	☆

SECRET WARRANTIES, INTERNAL BULLETINS: 2007-10—Some Edge and MKX vehicles may exhibit a growl or howl type-noise coming from the left or right rear wheel area. Consider changing the hub assembly. 2009-11—Transmission and camera malfunctions may have a simple solution covered by the Emissions Warranty (see service bulletin in Flex *Secret Warranties*). This bulletin also applies to the Lincoln MKS and MKX and the 2010-11 Lincoln MKT. 2010-13—Edge and Lincoln MKX brake booster warranty extension to 10 years/150,000 miles (Customer Satisfaction Program #13N02, Sept. 30, 2014). 2011—Some 2011 Edge Sport, Limited, and Lincoln MKX vehicles may exhibit a stress crack(s) in the front door window glass. Typical complaint is stress crack that originates from glass edge(s). Ford will replace the window under warranty per TSB #12-1-5, dated Jan. 2, 2012. 2011-13—Fluid leak from rear differential vent cap (2011-12 MKZ; 2011-13 MKT and MKX, and 2011-14 MKS). 2011-2013 Edge, MKX, 2013 Flex and MKT vehicles and 2013 Explorers may exhibit a door ajar warning light illuminated with all doors closed. Ford says new push pins will solve the problem. This is a major complaint of Ford owners who say the defect locks and unlocks the doors while the vehicle is in motion and costs $200+ dollars to fix. Ford should pay for this safety-related failure. Cite Ford TSB No. #14-0154, published Aug. 29, 2014. Intermittent power liftgate operation (Lincoln MKX). 2011-14—Edge and Lincoln MKX various infotainment upgrades. 2012-14—Edge and Lincoln MKX headliner sagging near roof opening panel. 2013—Exterior lights that flash on and off may need a new front lighting control module. 2014—Glass fogging, slow to clear with defroster.

2013 Ford Flex.

RATING: Above Average (2009-16). This boxy front-drive, or AWD four-door wagon seats either six or seven passengers in three rows of seats. Power comes from a 262 hp 3.5L V6 mated to a 6-speed automatic transmission and an optional turbocharged 3.5L that unleashes 355 horses while mated to the same gearbox. A crossover SUV, the Flex is built alongside Ford's Edge and the Lincoln MKX mid-size crossovers at the Oakville, Ontario, factory. **Road performance:** The standard V6 engine is adequate. High performance fans wanting quicker acceleration are risking premature powertrain failures. Ordinarily, the 6-speed automatic transmission shifts smoothly. The car handles well for an SUV, gives a smooth, quiet ride, provides good steering response, and is easy to maneuver in the city. **Strong points:** An astoundingly low number of owner complaints since its introduction as a 2009 spin-off of the Ford Freestyle and Taurus. Shortly after its introduction, the Flex was listed as the #3 affordable mid-sized SUVs in *U.S. News & World Report* behind the Buick Enclave and Chevrolet Traverse. It also was rated the most reliable large sized SUV and Ford's most reliable vehicle by *Consumer Reports*. This positive reception by Ford owners is reinforced by NHTSA's *safercar.gov* website that shows few owner complaints from 2009 through the 2015 model year. A large, well laid-out cabin with plenty of amenities. Nice standard features include heated side mirrors, rear parking sensors and Ford's voice-controlled SYNC system with Bluetooth and a USB port. **Weak points:** EcoBoost engines almost always undershoot their promised fuel savings and work poorly with automatic transmissions. Interior plastic garnishings look cheap. MyFord Touch returns with an 8-inch touch screen and other improvements. Is it now glitch free? No, not to many observers.

Prices and Specs

Prices (Firm): *S:* $30,899, *SEL:* $37,699, *Limited:* $44,799 **Freight:** $1,700-1,800 **Powertrain (Front-drive):** Engines: 3.5L V6. (287 hp); 3.5L V6 EcoBoost (365 hp) Transmission: 6-speed manumatic **Dimensions/capacity:** Passengers: 2/3/2; Wheelbase: 118 in.; H: 68/L: 202/W: 80 in.; Headroom F/R: 6.5/7.5 in.; Legroom F/R: 41.5/31.5 in 2F/R: 2.0/28 in.; Cargo volume: 47.5 cu. ft.; Fuel tank: 70L/regular; Tow limit: 4,500 lb.; Load capacity: 1,160 lb.; Turning circle: 40.7 ft.; Ground clearance: 5.9 in.; Weight: 4,820 lb.

Other opinions: "The 2015 Ford Flex ranks #8 out of 13 affordable large SUVs. Though it has minimal cargo area and a perplexing infotainment system, reviewers like the 2015 Ford Flex's nimble handling and roomy seating for seven." – *U.S. News & World Report.* "The 'door ajar' switch is faulty on most Ford Flex and Edge models. While the door is completely shut, the door ajar light stays on resulting in the doors not locking. Even if you press the automatic lock they simply unlock. Ford is not willing to address the issue or fix the issue. The way the faulty part is built into the lock mechanism requires the owner to replace the entire lock mechanism. This part cost $230.00 and due to the number of issues is not available on the market currently. As a result of the safety issue, we were required to force the switch to ground itself out, meaning we grounded out the wires linked to the door ajar light so the light is no longer on and the doors were locked." – *safercar.gov.* **Major redesign:** 2016s will have restyled front and rear ends, better interior appointments and an improved infotainment system. Keep your fingers crossed on the infotainment upgrade. A 355 hp EcoBoost V6 was added along with updated styling in 2010 and the 2013 model got a major body update (boxy... still boxy). **Highway/city fuel economy:** *3.5 V6:* 9.5/13.3 L/100 km. **Best alternatives:** GM Tahoe, Yukon, Escalade, and Enclave. Smaller choices: GM Equinox and Terrain, Honda CR-V, Hyundai Tucson, Kia Sportage, Nissan Rogue, and the Toyota RAV4.

SAFETY: **Child safety seat setup:** "Acceptable." **Crashworthiness:** NHTSA: 2011-15 models weren't fully-rated; only rollover protection was given as four stars. 2009-15 versions scored "Good" in all crash tests carried out by IIHS. **Owner-reported safety-related failures:** Airbags fail to deploy; sudden loss of power on the highway; vehicle goes forward when put into Reverse; liftgate glass shatters when it is closed; and frequent reports of brake failures when the car is parked on an incline:

My 2014 Flex was parked on side of road, on an incline facing uphill, with engine running. 2 adult passengers in vehicle. Without notice vehicle began rolling backwards. Passenger turned wheel in an attempt to stop vehicle on curb. Center console prevented passenger from being able to access vehicle brakes or parking brake. Vehicle ended up striking another vehicle before it came to rest. Luckily there were no injuries as hill ends in cul-de-sac with large drop off. I requested local Ford dealers inspect powertrain system as a car in park should not suddenly begin rolling. 2 local dealers have refused to look at vehicle citing they do not want to get involved.

ALERT! The MyFord Touch infotainment feature needs to be part of your test drive. Despite some improvements this year, critics say it is still complicated to use and often malfunctions.

Flex Profile

	2009	2010	2011	2012	2013	2014
Used Values ($)						
SE	9,500	10,500	14,000	17,000	19,000	21,500
SEL	10,500	11,500	14,500	17,500	19,500	27,000
LTD AWD	13,000	15,500	20,500	23,500	29,500	32,500
Reliability	☆	☆	☆	☆	☆	☆
Repairs ($$$)	2	2	2	2	1	1
Electrical	☆	☆	☆	☆	☆	☆
Engine (base)	★	★	★	★	★	★
Fit/Finish	☆	☆	☆	☆	☆	☆
Infotainment	—	—	★	★	★	★
Transmission (auto.)	★	★	★	★	★	★

SECRET WARRANTIES, INTERNAL BULLETINS: 2009—Water leaks from the rear of the roof opening panel. This may be more pronounced when parked with the front of the vehicle elevated. Likely cause is the headliner foam panels restricting the rear drain tubes for the roof opening panel. Some 2009 Taurus, Taurus X, Sable, Flex, and MKS vehicles equipped with an automatic tranny may have a moan or buzz type noise during upshifts. This may be due to the cooler lines grounding out on the vehicle body. **2009-10**—Owners of vehicles equipped with power folding second row seats may find the seat not fully lifting and folding forward (tumble) after the power release switch is depressed. The seat track riser assembly may need to be replaced. **2009-11**—Some 2009 Edge, MKX, and Flex vehicles built on or after May 4, 2009, 2010-2011 Edge, Flex, MKS, MKT, MKX, Taurus, and 2011 Explorer vehicles built on or before April 15, 2011, may have a sluggish acceleration or hesitation feel during a rolling stop 0-8 km/h (0-5 mph) followed by a harsh bump or feel like a slip on take-off from a stop followed by a harsh bump. Ford says you may need to change the valve body separater plate. Transmission and camera malfunctions may have a simple solution covered by the Emissions Warranty:

2009-13—A remedy for headliner scratching or rattling. 2010—Some Taurus, Edge, Flex, Fusion, Milan, MKS, MKT, MKX, and MKZ vehicles equipped with AWD may exhibit a shudder/chatter/vibration driveline sensation during a tight turn, or a thump/clunk noise on light acceleration. These symptoms may also occur under 40 mph (64 km/h), when driving uphill, or towing under heavy acceleration. A faulty power transfer unit (PTU) may be the culprit, says Ford. 2010-14—Some 2010-2014 Flex, MKS, MKT, Taurus, and 2013-2014 Explorers vehicles equipped with a 3.5L Turbocharged engine with an aluminum valve cover may burn oil and/or produce excessive engine oil smoking from the tail pipe at idle during normal engine operating temperatures. Ford TSB #14-0113, dated Oct. 3, 2014, says the the valve cover, crankcase vent oil separator, and upper manifold gasket may need replacing. 2011-13—Fluid may leak from the rear differential vent cap. Some 2011-2013 Edge, MKX, 2013 Flex, and MKT vehicles and 2013 Explorers may exhibit a door ajar warning light illuminated with all doors closed. Ford says new push pins will solve the problem. This is a major complaint of Ford owners who say the defect locks and unlocks the doors while the vehicle is in motion and costs $200+ dollars to fix. Ford should pay for this safety-related failure. Cite Ford TSB No. #14-0154, published Aug. 29, 2014. 2013-14—Vehicles equipped with a power liftgate that's inoperative, or pruduces a crunching noise, may have a faulty liftgate motor. A wind or whistle-type noise from the left and/or right A-pillar area at highway speeds in crosswind conditions may be due to the A-pillar window moulding not being fully seated.

Ford Escape

RATING: Average (2013-16); Below Average (2004-12). The Lincoln MKC is similar to the Escape and is reviewed in the Appendix. After its 2013 model overhaul, the Escape has been carried over relatively unchanged. Then, the decade-old Escape was in dire need of improvements to save fuel, provide a roomier interior, and improve overall ride and handling. The Hybrid version was dropped after the 2012 model year in favour of two direct-injected and turbocharged 1.6L and 2.0L EcoBoost 4-cylinder engines. The 2013 model also features improved interior space and technology, and accessibility that tops the previous model and much of the competition. For 2016, the 2.0L EcoBoost engine is replaced by a 2.3L variant that's more powerful and smoother running. **Road performance:** Improved considerably with its last redesign. The new Escape is much more agile and comfortable and has more power and quicker engine response. Steering and braking are just adequate and ride comfort is average. **Strong points:** A roomy, well-finished interior that provides lots of high-tech content and plenty of cargo space. *Hybrid:* Surprisingly for a vehicle that has such a complicated electrical system, there aren't many complaints concerning the hybrid components. One would normally expect to see, on average, 50 or so reports per model year. Owners do report some brake and steering failures. **Weak points:** Owners are complaining that EcoBoost engines don't always deliver the promised fuel savings and work poorly with automatic transmissions.

Other opinions: "The Ford Escape ranks #5 out of 25 affordable compact SUVs. Powerful turbocharged engine options, athletic handling and an upscale cabin help the Escape stand out among its rivals." – *U.S. News & World Report.* "Purchased vehicle 1/30/2015 and drove off lot with 3 miles on it. Less than a week later vehicle started stalling at traffic lights and hesitating upon acceleration. Vehicle was in Ford repair shop for 12 days with $1200 worth of parts replaced on transmission. Picked up vehicle with 810 miles on it and less than a week and 150 miles later the vehicle is again stalling at traffic lights upon acceleration. The vehicle is dangerous to drive!" – *safercar.gov.* **Major redesign:** 2001, 2008, and 2013 models. **Highway/city fuel economy:** *FWD, 2.5L:* 6.3/9.5 L/100 km. *FWD, 2.0L:* 6.7/9.5 L/100 km. *AWD, 2.0L:* 6.9/9.8 L/100 km. *2012 Hybrid:* 6.5/5.8 L/100 km. *Hybrid AWD:* 7.4/7 L/ 100 km. **Best alternatives:** Chevrolet Equinox, GMC Terrain, Honda CR-V, Hyundai Tucson, Kia Sportage, Toyota RAV4, and Nissan Rogue.

SAFETY: Child safety seat setup: "Marginal." **Crashworthiness:** NHTSA: Gave the 2013-15 Escape five stars for side crashworthiness and four stars for frontal and rollover protection. 2011 and 2012 models earned Average crashworthiness scores (three stars) in all categories. The IIHS gave its top rating ("Good") to the 2009-15s for frontal offset protection, however the 2015 scored a "Poor" rating for small overlap front collision protection. 2005-08 models were ranked "Acceptable," and the 2001-04s got a "Marginal" rating in all categories. 2013 models were rated "Poor" in small overlap front crashes. Side crash scores were "Good" for 2001-13 Escapes with airbags; "Poor" for 2001-07 without airbags. Roof strength was rated "Marginal" on the 2008-12s, while the 2013 models excelled in the same test. Rear crash protection for 2005-08 models was judged "Acceptable" and 2009-13 Escapes merited a "Good" designation. **Safety-related failures reported by owners:** Airbags fail to deploy, driver's seat collapses, or seat belt latch pops open; spontaneous windshield cracks and sunroof/side window shattering; distorted windshields; and liftgate glass exploded.

ALERT! The Escape's luxury near-twin is the entry-level Lincoln MKC, which sells for about $20,000 Cdn. more. Some notable differences are the Lincoln's nicely restyled body, distinctive grille, lower, longer, and wider platform, and standard features such as xenon headlights and heated seats. The base 240-hp 2.0L turbocharged 4-cylinder is shared with the Escape; a new, 275-hp 2.3L turbo four is optional. Both cars use a 6-speed automatic; AWD versions come with a more refined adaptive suspension.

Escape Profile

	2006	2007	2008	2009	2010	2011	2012	2013	2014
Used Values ($)									
Escape XLS/Base	4,000	4,500	5,500	6,500	7,500	10,500	13,500	14,500	21,500
4x4	5,500	6,500	8,000	9,500	11,500	13,500	15,500	18,000	22,500
XLT 4x2/S 2.5	5,000	6,000	7,000	8,000	9,500	12,000	14,500	15,000	17,000
4x4	6,000	6,500	7,500	8,500	9,000	11,000	15,000	19,500	21,500
Hybrid 4x2	6,000	7,000	8,000	10,000	12,500	16,500	20,500	—	—
4x4	7,500	8,500	10,00	12,000	14,500	18,500	22,000	—	—
Reliability	★	★	★	★	★	★	★	★	★
Repairs ($$$)	③	③	③	③	③	③	③	②	②
Electrical	★	★	★	★	★	★	★	★	★
Engine (base)	★	★	★	★	★	★	★	★	★
Fit/Finish	★	★	★	★	★	★	★	★	★
Infotainment	—	—	—	—	—	★	★	★	★
Transmission (auto.)	★	★	★	★	★	★	★	★	★

SECRET WARRANTIES, INTERNAL BULLETINS: 2008-09—Steering column pop, clunk when turning. All instrument cluster warning lights come on intermittently. Uncommanded liftgate opening or closing. Exterior heated mirror glass cracking. Front grille chrome peeling. 2008-10—Steering wheel vibration can be remedied by installing a special damper Ford has devised. Special Ford fix for steering column pop or clunk. Windows squeak, grind when operated. Ignition key binds in ignition cylinder. Washer nozzles leak fluid onto the hood. Poor radio reception. 2008-12—Escapes equipped with electronic manual temperature control (EMTC) may find the AC blows warm air or lacks sufficient blower motor power. This may be due to a blower motor resistor damaged by water entering the heater core and evaporator core housing through the cowl. 2009—Ford Customer Satisfaction Program #10B15100419-001 (secret warranty) was set up April 19, 2010, to cover the cost of reprogramming the Power Control Module to reposition the solenoid regulator valve and eliminate bore wear. Mechanics are also empowered to replace the valve body, overdrive, and forward clutch. Ford says these measures are needed to increase the transmission's durability. If Ford says no to a free repair, ask them to apply the Emissions Warranty and threaten to go to small claims court with their own service bulletin as proof. Automatic transmission fluid leaks from the dipstick tube. Exterior door handles may be hard to open and may not be flush. 2009-10—Automatic transmission sticks in Fifth gear (reprogram the power control module). A harsh-shifting automatic transmission requires the same remedy. Harsh engagements, shifts, or starts in Fifth gear from a start signal; there's an open signal in the output shaft speed sensor or the main control lead frame connector. Automatic transmission axle shaft seal fluid leak. AWD models may produce a vibration, rumble, and/or excessive exhaust noise in cold temperatures. 2009-11—The rear axle may produce a "hoot" noise on light acceleration just before the 1-2 shift. 2009-12—An intermittent water leak originating from the liftgate glass/seal can be easily plugged says TSB #12-2-2. 2009-13—Ford has extended the throttle body warranty up to 10 years/150,000 miles per Customer Satisfaction Program #13N03. 2012—Transmission fluid leakage. Engine drone or rattle. 2.0L and 2.5L engines may constantly cause the MIL light to come on. Harsh or delayed shifts. Broken liftgate window. Water leaks from the liftgate area. 2012-14—Before spending big bucks, try simply lubricating the front strut shafts to eliminate a clunk or rattle from the front strut area. 2013—Per TSB # 13-4-25 models with noisy front brakes may need to replace the front disc brake caliper anchor plates with new service parts. Because this is a premature failure, Ford should cover the upgraded parts under a "goodwill" warranty. The high pitch squeal occurs during low to moderate brake pedal application after the brakes have warmed up. Tire "slapping" and excessive vibration may be caused by faulty Continental tires. Ford assumes responsibility for their replacement. 2013-14—Vehicles equipped with 1.6L or 2.0L gasoline turbocharged direct injection (GTDI) engines may be hard to start, run rough, lack power, or lose RPMs. These conditions may be caused by a wiring short in the signal return splices. Other vehicles equipped with a 1.6L or 2.0L may lose power, in cold weather. It may be necessary to replace the charge air cooler (CAC) tube and screen assembly from the CAC to the throttle body. Some Escapes equipped with 1.6L or 2.0L gasoline turbocharged direct injection (GTDI) engines may exhibit a rattle/buzz noise or vibration from the right rear floorboard on acceleration between 1500-2500 RPM. The fuel pump may need to be replaced under warranty. Vehicles equipped with AWD may exhibit rear drive unit (RDU) whine at highway speeds of 64-88 km/h (40-55 mph). Ford says the RDU front bushings may need to be replaced under warranty. Excessive windnoise at highway speeds or whistle in crosswind conditions may be due to the windshield A-pillar moulding lip not staying retained tightly to the pillar. An extended warranty (Customer Satisfaction Program 14N02) applies to PCM reprogramming in the event of ABS brake communication failures. Use TSB #13-10-6, dated Oct. 4, 2013, to troubleshoot a number of MyFord Touch/MyLincoin Touch failures with navigation, voice recognition, call sound quality, phone pairing, clock and media malfunction, WiFi pass code entry, rear-view camera guidelines, and overall poor system performance. An intermittent lack of air conditioning and/or a loss of airflow from the vents may occur after extended driving in hot, humid conditions. This is likely due to the evaporator core icing. 2014—Escapes equipped with a 1.6L EcoBoost engine may exhibit an illuminated malfunction indicator lamp (MIL) with a transmission overheat condition. Reprogram the powertrain control module to the latest calibration.

EXPLORER ★★★

Ford's 2016 Explorer: A unibody crossover pretending to be a real SUV?

RATING: Surprisingly, reliability varies considerably from one year to the other. Average (2015-16; 2007-10; 2001); Below Average (2012-14); Not Recommended (2011; 2002-06; 2000). A middle of the pack, clumsy gas hog that was underpowered with its earlier wimpy 2.0L optional 4-cylinder EcoBoost engine. The 2016 model comes with a new, more powerful EcoBoost I-4 engine, a new Platinum model provides more luxury, and the restyled exterior, lighting, and wheels all add to a more refined look. Ford uses its much-criticized, often dysfunctional, MyFord Touch electronics interface through 2015. Road performance: The Explorer's unibody construction cuts weight and gives car-like road manners to the SUV. It offers front-drive, AWD, or FWD that can be left engaged on dry pavement, and has a low-range gear for off-roading. Four-wheel drive is available with all models, including the 2.3L EcoBoost (the older 2.0L EcoBoost was limited to FWD). Downshifts can be slow and abrupt, and braking may be hard to modulate on hills. Strong points: Average performance and reliability with the V6 and a new turbocharged 4-cylinder engine that supplies the power lacking in last year's model, however, the fuel penalty and engine durability have yet to be determined. An upscale cabin. Lots of high-tech updates for the 2016 model year that include new exterior camera systems, improved infotainment performance, automated parking, a no-hands liftgate, and front grille shutters that enhance aerodynamics and airflow. **Weak points:** 2016 transaction prices are too high; bundled options are especially pricey; the longer you delay your purchase, the better quality you'll likely find as Ford tackles quality and design deficiencies that usually hang around for a few years on its new designs. The most likely areas of concern for the next several years are costly powertrain failures in addition to faulty brake, electrical system, steering and suspension components, and subpar body construction. The last few model years have featured electronic devices that are distracting and failure prone; a dash offering a confusing array of small buttons, crowded displays, and redundant controls; and head restraints that are literally a pain in the neck. The cabin is an adequate size, but it's not quite as roomy as what is offered by the Dodge Durango, Ford Flex, or Chevy Traverse. Cargo space is the smallest of the group, and the third row is somewhat cramped.

Prices and Specs

Prices (Firm): *Base FWD:* $30,700, *XLT V6 FWD:* $33,400, *Limited V6 FWD:* $38,407, *Limited:* $41,300, *Sport:* $43,300, *Platinum:* $52,600 **Freight:** $1,700 **Powertrain (Front-drive/4x4/AWD):** Engines: 2.3L 4-cyl. EcoBoost (280 hp), 3.5L V6 (290 hp); 3.5L EcoBoost (365 hp); Transmission: 6-speed auto. **Dimensions/capacity:** Passengers: 2/3/2; Wheelbase: 112.8 in.; H: 71/L: 198.3/W: 82.5-90.2 in.; Headroom F/R1/R2: 5.5/3.5/3 in.; Legroom F/R1/R2: 42/27/27 in.; Cargo volume: 42 cu. ft.; Fuel tank: 70.4L/regular; Tow limit: 5,000 lb.; Load capacity: 1,570 lb.; Turning circle: 38.9 ft.; Ground clearance: 7.5 ft.; Weight: 4,443 lb.

Other opinions: "The 2015 Ford Explorer ranked #12 out of 13 affordable large SUVs. Bewildering tech features and confining rear seats disappoint reviewers, who otherwise like the Explorer's first-rate interior." – *U.S. News & World Report.* **Major redesign:** 1995, 2002, 2006, 2011, and 2016 models. Ford's much ballyhooed, redesigned 2011-2015 Explorer handles less like a truck and provides better fuel economy now that Ford has replaced its body-on-frame platform with a car-like unibody chassis. This fifth generation Explorer shares the same platform with Ford's Flex and Lincoln MKT. Unfortunately, the reworked Explorer continues to have the same serious performance and quality control deficiencies decried by both *Consumer Reports* and *Motor Trend.* Surprisingly, *Consumer Reports* gave the Explorer an easier time than *Motor Trend* did in this May 2011 article:

> We didn't like driving the Explorer very much. ... Massive, freaky, comical torque steer (the vehicle pulls to one side when accelerating). The big Ford also rode worse than much of the competition. ... We also had issues with the seating position ... the chassis needs some refinement. ... Car feels wobbly at speed – not confidence inspiring...The MyFord Touch system shut down for about 60 seconds, taking away all climate, stereo, phone, and navigation controls.

The 6-speed automatic transmission shifts slowly at times, the engine is noisy, handling is mediocre with excessive body roll when cornering, and the slow steering transmits little road feedback. Interior ergonomics and comfort apparently wasn't Ford's "Job 1" with the reworked Explorer, either. The driving position is described as "flawed," with limited footroom, a poorly placed footrest, and pedals that are mounted too close together. Front seat cushions felt narrow and too short; rear cushions too hard, too low, or too short. *CR* rated fit and finish as average, and the MyFord Touch system was judged to be overly complicated, with the Sync-voice-command system often misunderstanding simple commands. **Highway/city fuel economy:** *3.5L V6:* 8/11.9 L/100 km; *4x4:* 8.8/12.5 L/100 km. Ford's "government-approved" gas mileage figures are pure fiction and actual fuel economy may be as much as 25 % worse, says *autoblog.com.* **Best alternatives:** Ford Flex, GMC Denali, Honda CR-V or Ridgeline, Hyundai Tucson or Santa Fe, and Toyota RAV4.

SAFETY: Child safety seat setup: "Acceptable." **Crashworthiness:** NHTSA: Gave the 2013-15 Explorer its top five-star overall crashworthiness rating; 2012 Explorers earned four stars; and 2006-10 versions scored five stars for frontal and side protection and three stars for rollover resistance. 2001-03 models scored only two stars in rollover resistance. IIHS crash tests of the 2015 Explorer rated small overlap frontal crashworthiness as "Marginal" and all other categories were "Good." Frontal offset protection was also "Good" with 2002-14 models, while 1995-2001 Explorers earned just "Acceptable" scores. Side protection was "Good" for 2011-14 and "Acceptable" for the 2006-10 Explorers. Head-restraint effectiveness was "Acceptable" and roof strength was deemed "Good." Head restraints were "Good" on 2004-08 models; "Acceptable" on the 2009-10s, and "Good" on the 2011-14 Explorers. **Owner-reported safety-related failures:** Chronic stalling, brake failures, and electronic malfunctions.

ALERT! Drivers say the obstructed front and rear visibility is a deal breaker:

> I am going into the 5th month of leasing my 2015 Ford Explorer and I am not happy with this vehicle. Currently the odometer reads 2,100 miles and they were not enjoyable miles. I have to say that this 2015 Explorer has the worst design on the inside that I've ever seen. The outward visibility from the driver's seat for the front and rear of this vehicle is severely compromised by the huge C pillars which create blind spots within the vehicle.

Other things to check out at the dealership: Exhaust fumes may leak into the interior; the brake and accelerator pedals are mounted too close to each other; narrow, poorly cushioned seats lack sufficient thigh support; the small rear window cuts visibility; and the headlights don't light up enough of the road. Other criticisms: The head restraints are literally a pain in the neck and can be dangerous if the airbags deploy; mediocre automatic transmission performance, and fit and finish deficiencies; sunvisors are poorly designed; sudden power-steering failure; and worst of all, unintended acceleration accompanied by loss of brakes.

Explorer Profile

	2006	2007	2008	2009	2010	2011	2012	2013	2014
Used Values ($)									
Base 4x2	—	—	—	—	—	13,500	16,500	20,500	26,000
XLT	—	—	—	—	—	17,500	22,000	24,500	28,000
4x4	5,500	6,500	8,000	10,000	13,500	19,000	24,000	26,500	32,000
Reliability	★	☆	☆	☆	☆	★	☆	☆	☆
Repairs ($$$)	3					3	2	2	2
Electrical	★	☆	☆	☆	★	★	☆	☆	☆
Engine (base)	★	☆	☆	☆	☆	★	☆	☆	☆
Fit/Finish	★	☆	☆	☆	☆	★	☆	☆	☆
Infotainment	—	—	—	—	—	★	★	★	★
Transmission (auto.)	★	★	★	★	★	★	★	★	☆

SECRET WARRANTIES, INTERNAL BULLETINS: 2011-12—There are a number of bulletins that address intermittent front brake squeal; a hard-to-open forward centre console storage bin door; interior rattle or buzz; and front bumper creaking. Troubleshooting power liftgate malfunctions. Countermeasures to silence a buzzing, howling, or rattle at higher vehicle speeds and/or cross winds coming from the windshield appliques. 2011-13—Explorer vehicles may exhibit a door ajar warning light illuminated with all doors closed. Ford says new push pins will solve the problem. This is a major complaint of Ford owners who say the defect locks and unlocks the doors while the vehicle is in motion and costs $200+ dollars to fix. Ford should pay for this safety-related failure. Cite Ford TSB No. #14-0154, published Aug. 29, 2014. If the front window glass jumps or chatters during up/down travel, replace the front window regulator motor on the affected door(s). 2011-14—An inoperative AWD may be fixed simply by recalibrating the ABS module. A whistle or buzz-type noise from the front cowl panel grille cover at highway speeds may be caused by the seal for the front cowl panel grille cover not making full contact with the windshield. Fixes for a host of infotainment failures are addressed in TSB #13-10-6, dated Oct. 4, 2013 and TSB #12A04S4. 2011-15—Troubleshooting tips to get rid of an exhaust odour in the cabin with the auxiliary climate control system engaged (TSB #14-0130). Another TSB (#14-0118) shows an inexpensive way to free up the interior front console door when it sticks shut. 2012—Power liftgate malfunctions. 2013-14—Explorers powered by a 3.5L engine with an aluminum valve cover may burn oil and/or show engine oil smoking in the exhaust at idle during normal engine operating temperatures. TSB #14-0113, dated Oct. 3, 2014, suggests changing the right-hand valve cover, upper intake manifold gasket, crankcase vent oil separator, valve cover, and PCV valve. May exhibit power transfer unit (PTU) fluid leaking, likely due to a missing or disconnected PTU vent hose. No audio output on startup during cold ambient temperatures or when abnormally low battery voltage levels are present. Take 20 minutes to reprogram the audio control module (ACM) to correct this problem. **2014**—A raw fuel odour that is most noticeable near the intake manifold can be eliminated by replacing the high-pressure fuel tube.

F-150 PICKUP

RATING: Average (2015-16; 2007-09); Below Average (2010-14); Not Recommended (2006 and earlier). The F-150 has been coasting on its past reputation before Detroit cost-cutters cheapened the product. Hopefully, the redesigned 2015-16 trucks will be more reliable and fuel frugal with a new lighter aluminum-clad body and offering 2016s that will allow the 5.0L V8 engine to run on propane or compressed natural gas, two money-saving factory options fleet buyers have wanted for decades. Give Ford some credit: Canada's most popular pickup survived a brutal, worldwide 2008-09 recession, that forced GM and Chrysler into bankruptcy, and is still hugging first place in sales despite increasing competition from competitors who are now building better drivetrains and infotainment systems in trucks that are more price-competitive. For several decades, Ford quality control has been the pits, with the automaker placing far behind Chevrolet, Chrysler, and the Japanese automakers in truck reliability. The Internet is full of F-series owners pointing out serious powertrain, steering, electronic module, and infotainment deficiencies, all confirmed by confidential service bulletins, *safercar.gov*, NHTSA-posted owner complaints, and multi-million dollar out-of-court settlements. Lying has become second nature to the Blue Oval Boys. Time and again, Ford has settled class action lawsuits over false fuel economy claims and, more recently, false truck payload ratings. And while truck buyers cry out for more reliable pickups, Ford goes into 2016 betting the farm on aluminum-bodied trucks to save fuel, which has hit historic lows. Without question, the redesigned 2015 F-150 has been much improved in areas that needed improving: An infotainment system that's user-friendly and responsive, a better interior and assembly quality, plus, a simpler powertrain lineup. **Road performance:** Ford has cut the number of trim levels from eight to five, while offering four engines, two of them with EcoBoost technology. The standard 3.5L V6 is adequate for most duties; though the new, optional turbocharged 2.7L V6 engine will provide quicker acceleration. Nevertheless, the turbo engine isn't worth the extra cost and uncertain durability of the new V6 turbo powerplants. Towing will require either the turbocharged 3.5L V6 or a V8, depending upon the load. Handling is a breeze, although the ride is a bit stiff; braking is mediocre, though. **Strong points:** A nice array of powertrain combinations heated, cooled memory seats; moonroof, rear-view camera, a multimedia hub, SYNC with MyFord Touch, and a voice-activated navigation feature connected to Sirius Travel Link. **Weak points:** Four things to worry about: EcoBoost engine failures and poor fuel economy; the "gear hunting" automatic transmission; a user-hostile infotainment system; and the long-term durability and repair costs of the 2015-16 model aluminum body panels. The tasilgate staircase is useless. Windshield dash glare. An "Omigod" high sticker price; less comfortable than comparable models (Ram 1500, for example); and long-term reliability of the redesign still has to be determined. Shoppers would be wise to wait a year for the inevitable factory-related "bugs" to be worked out. This is especially important because these trucks have disappointed owners after each redesign since the mid-80s.

Prices and Specs

Prices (Very firm): *F-150 Base model:* $24,899, *F-150 XL:* $26,699, *F-150 XLT:* $31,099, *Lariat:* $45,890, *King Ranch:* $62,299, *Platinum:* $64,299 **Freight:** $1,700 **Powertrain (Rear-drive/Part-time 4x4/AWD):** Engines: *2015-16 F-150:* 3.5L V6 (282 hp), 2.7L EcoBoost V6 (325 hp), 3.5L turbocharged V6 (365 hp), and a 5.0L V8 (385 hp), *Other models/engines:* 3.6L V8 (248 hp), 4.6L V8 (292 hp), 5.4L V8 (310 hp), 6.2L V8 (411 hp), 6.4L V8 diesel (350 hp), 6.7L V8 diesel (385 hp), 6.8L V10 (362 hp), 3.5L V6 (365 hp); EcoBoost: 3.7L V6 (302 hp), 5.0L V8 (360 hp), 6.2L V8 (411 hp); Transmissions: 6-speed auto., 6-speed man. **Dimensions/capacity:** Passengers: 2/1 up to 3/3; Wheelbase: 122.4-163.7 in.; H: 75.1-76.9/L: 231.9-243.7/W: 79.9 in.; Headroom F/R: 70/5.5 in.; Cargo box volume: 52.8/62.3/77.4 cu.ft.; *F-250:* Headroom F/R: 6/6 in.; Legroom F/R: 40/30.5 in.; Fuel tank: 87.1L/regular; Tow limit: *F-150:* 12,200 lb.; *F-250:* 12,500 lb.; Load capacity: 1,480-3,300 lb.; Turning circle: 40.7-47.1 ft.; Ground clearance: 8.5-9.3 in.; Weight: 4,050-4,930 lb.

Other opinions: "The 2015 Ford F-150 ranks #2 out of 6 full size pickup trucks (Ram scored #1). Drivers praise its agile handling, roomy interior and muscular turbocharged V6 engine options." – *U.S. News & World Report.* "The interior of the F150 is still plagued by the same kind of nonsense that's afflicted the Mustang for a decade. Rock-hard door panels, tons of greasy-looking, cheap-feeling plastic, and bunch of buttons vomited on the panel. Compared to the MyFordTouch system, though, the HVAC buttons are a paragon of usability. With MFT, there's a touchscreen with icons that are too tiny, so skip it and be safer on the road. SYNC3 can't arrive soon enough." – *The Truth About Cars.* **Major redesign:** 1987, 1992, 1997, 2004, 2009, and 2015. Some of the 2015 engine and model changes: A 3.5L V6 replaces the 3.7L V6, a new turbocharged 2.7L V6 arrives, the optional 6.2L V8 is dropped, and no more Raptor. **Highway/city fuel economy:** *3.5L V6:* 9.2/12.2 L/100 km; *6.2L V8:* 11.4/16.9 L/100 km; *3.5L V6 4x4:* 9/12.9 L/100 km; *6.2L V8 4x4:* 12.7/18.3 L/100 km; *3.7L V6:* 8.9/12.9 L/100 km; *3.7L 4x4:* 9.8/13.4 L/100 km; *5.0L V8:* 9.7/13.9 L/100 km; *5.0L V8 4x4:* 10.5/15 L/100 km; *Raptor 6.2L V8 4x4:* 14.2/19.1 L/100 km. **Best alternatives:** Chrysler's Ram equipped with a Cummins diesel and a more-reliable manual transmission, GM's Silverado or Sierra base models or HD series, Honda's Ridgeline, and Nissan's Titan. Nissan's Frontier or King Cab are also worth considering.

Rams have richer interiors and one of the best infotainment systems around (Uconnect). GM's duo are quieter, more refined, offer a small-block V8, and have slightly better ergonomics. Japanese models are competitive, though the new Nissan Titan costs more. Toyota's Tundra is a few thousand bucks cheaper and a bit more reliable to boot.

SAFETY: Child safety seat setup: "Marginal." **Crashworthiness:** NHTSA: Gave the 2015 its top five star rating for overall crashworthiness, although rollover protection garnered only four stars. 2013-14s earned five stars for side crashworthiness and four stars for frontal collision protection and rollover resistance. Earlier models scored between three and five stars through 1992, except for 2001-03 4x4 models that earned only two stars for rollover resistance. IIHS awarded the 2010-12 models a "Good" rating for head restraints; 2007-08 versions were rated "Marginal." **Owner-reported safety-related failures:** Speaking of head restraints – owners say headrests on some model years are uncomfortable and dangerous:

> Headrest forces driver's chin into the chest. Dealer stated that this is the new safety design. Headrests are non-adjustable. Also, they are very wide and, in conjunction with the frame post at the rear of the doors, create a blind spot on both sides of the pickup.

Ford's new EcoBoost engines have been heralded as providing plenty of turbo power and using less fuel than previous powerplants. This is true, but these redesigned engines have a nasty habit of losing power when most needed and then lurching forward, thereby exposing passengers and pedestrians to serious injury or death. Hundreds of owners are wary of this engine:

> While taking off from T-intersection and turning left crossing oncoming traffic the truck started to take off then lost all power for approximately 3-5 seconds. This left my family and I sitting in the oncoming traffic lane on a blind corner. The truck did not die (I thought it did), I mashed the accelerator to the floor and the truck did not respond whatsoever. My wife was screaming frantically at me asking what I was doing while I attempted to get the truck to move out of the oncoming lane. After approximately 5 seconds the truck regained power and accelerated normally. This has occurred 3X now and I am afraid to drive the truck but do and my wife will not drive it at all. [*www.blueovalforums.com/forums/index.php?/topic/49606-f-150-ecoboost-shutter*]

The owner of a 2014 F-150 describes his experience this way:

> As I accelerate, the truck seems to go into neutral for about three seconds. Then it re-engages and jerks violently. I have taken the truck to the dealership twice. The first time, they reprogrammed it but didn't repair the issue. This last time, the technician told me to pick up my truck because they couldn't recreate the issue I was experiencing. Another technician stated it was the eco-boost but that Ford was side stepping the issue because they couldn't find how to fix it.

2014 F-150 EcoBoost V6 – engine shudders and stalls upon rapid acceleration; issue has been addressed with "deflector shield" but this shield is already in place in my vehicle but the vehicle continues to have this issue – I feel the vehicle is unsafe but Ford offers no assistance with resolution of the issue.

There's much more: Windshield/windows shattering without cause; sticking cruise control; unintended acceleration; the sudden loss of power steering; passenger airbag wire harness breaking when seatback is moved forward; the rear passenger seats don't lock into place when in the lowered position, although the Ford manual says they must be locked to be safe; when parked on a down slope vehicle won't start even though almost a quarter of a tank of gas remains.

ALERT! If you need a truck as a workhorse, rather than a showhorse, get a stripped-down XL, instead of the $50,000+ SuperCrew. Owners of the just-launched trucks say the F-150's front windshield may crack for no apparent reason. If there is no evidence of an object impacting the windshield, don't let Ford refuse your claim:

I was parked in my driveway when a section of the rear window exploded. The vehicle was warming up (auto start) for about 5 minutes before my daughter and I got in to leave when we heard a loud pop. I looked back and noticed the rear driver side window was shattered. There were little pieces of glass throughout the back of the vehicle and I'm sure landed on my daughter's hair and clothes. The vehicle is a 4x4 SuperCrew cab with the sliding 3 piece rear window. I am located in Barrie, Ontario, Canada, and the weather was 0 degrees celcius when it happened.

Headlights also may not be too your liking:

This 2014 is equipped with div headlights. When turned on they have a distinct vertical line that runs from your far left vision to your far right vision. Below this line it is very bright and above this line it is total darkness. The line runs directly across the center of your vision. This line is constantly bouncing up and down with bumps and imperfections in the road. Extremely difficult to see. When driving through mountains, hills and low lines your vision is 100% blocked above the line. When the vehicle is driving down a grade you lose all vision to the upcoming grade. Please, have someone drive one of these trucks at night in the hills.

	2006	2007	2008	2009	2010	2011	2012	2013	2014
Used Values ($)									
Base 4x2	6,000	6,500	7,500	8,500	10,500	13,000	16,500	20,000	22,000
F-250 XLT	7,000	7,500	9,000	10,500	13,000	15,500	18,500	22,000	24,500
Reliability	★	★	★	★	★	★	★	★	★
Repairs ($$$)	💰	💰	💰	💰	💰	💰	💰	💰	💰
Electrical	★	★	★	★	★	★	★	★	★
Engine (base)	★	★	★	★	★	★	★	★	★
Fit/Finish	★	★	★	★	★	★	★	★	★
Infotainment	—	—	—	—	—	★	★	★	★
Transmission (auto.)	★	★	★	★	★	★	★	★	★

Note: After each redesign, quality suffers. Will the 2015-16s be any different?

SECRET WARRANTIES, INTERNAL BULLETINS: 2009—Harsh shifting at low speeds. 2009-10—F-150, 250, 350, and F-Super Duty vehicles equipped with a 4.6L 3V or 5.4L 3V engine may emit a low frequency engine knocking noise at hot idle. 6R80 transmission bulkhead connector sleeve leaking fluid. Shudder, vibration on moderate acceleration. Before springing for costly repairs, simply ask mechanic to adjust the rear axle pinion angle under warranty. Water stains the rear portion of the headliner due to the high mounted stoplamp assembly leaking water. Water leak at satellite antenna. Remedies for Sync phone problems affecting most of Ford's lineup. The new SYNC service Microphone kit now includes a voltage filter incorporated into the jumper harness. The foam seal detaches between the instrument panel and the windshield glass (covered under a "goodwill" extended warranty on a case-by-case basis. Likely a sure-fire winner for small claims court). Headline droops, sags at rear of roof opening panel. 2009-10 *F-150*; and 2011 *F-250 and F-350:* Vehicles may exhibit an audible clicking noise in the engine compartment and/or a hard start after refueling. Some F-150, Expedition, Explorer Sport Trac, Explorer, Mountaineer, and Navigator vehicles equipped with a 6R80 transmission may show signs of transmission fluid leakage around the transmission bulkhead connector sleeve. Install a seal kit. 2009-12—Trucks equipped with a 9.75 traction-lok differential rear axle assembly may produce a shudder, chatter and/or vibration during slow, tight turns. This concern may be more noticeable after cold startup and less noticeable once the rear axle fluid warms up. Ford says a clutch pack replacement kit may be needed. Excessive vibration, a thump, or clunk noise from under the vehicle can be corrected by replacing the driveshaft assembly. Trucks equipped with a 2-piece driveshaft may exhibit a rear driveshaft slip/bump on light to moderate acceleration from a stop or when coming to a stop with light braking. Remedy: Replace the slip yoke. If the gear selector lever takes excessive effort to shift in cold weather, snow may have built up around the shift cable and lever. A new snow shield kit will alleviate this problem. Water staining the rear portion of the headliner in the area(s) above the back glass and at both cab corners is likely due to the high mounted stoplamp assembly leaking water. Simply replace the stoplamp assembly. 2010—A service kit has been released to assist in repairing of the 4R75E transmission in 2008 Mark LT, 2008-10 F-150, E-Series, 2008-211 Crown Victoria, Grand Marquis, and Town Car vehicles that exhibit a grinding, whine-type noise, vibration and/or gear slippage while driving or a loss of Reverse resulting from a planetary gear assembly failure. 2010-13— Repair tips for a water leak at the rear glass sliding center panel. 2011—Trucks equipped with a 6R80 automatic transmission may have transmission fluid leaking from the bell housing area. Install a pump kit. A harsh 1-2 shift at or below 24 km/h (15 mph), harsh downshifts, and/or a flare on upshifts can all be corrected by recalibrating the PCM module. 2011-12—Vehicles equipped with a 3.5L gasoline turbocharged direct injection (GTDI) EcoBoost engine may exhibit an intermittent engine surge during moderate to light loads at cruise, stumble and/ or misfire on hard acceleration after an extended drive at highway speeds during humid or damp conditions. This could result in a steady or flashing malfunction indicator lamp (MIL). 2011-13—Vehicles equipped with a 6R80 transmission may exhibit a transmission engagement in higher (Fifth) gear when starting. The wrench indictor and/or the seat belt minder may be illuminated, the speedometer reads zero and the odometer displays flashes while driving. Symptoms may clear after an ignition key cycle. Replace the molded leadframe on the main control assembly to fix the problem. Engine misfiring on trucks equipped with a 3.5L turbo engine may need new spark plugs and coil boots. F-150s equipped with a turbocharged 3.5L engine that buck/jerk at steady cruise with the transmission in Sixth gear and experience engine lugging up grades at 1500-2000 RPM, may siply need a PCM recalibration. 2011-14—Vehicles may have a delayed park to forward or reverse transmission engagement on startup after parking several hours or overnight. The vehicle functions normally after the initial engagement has completed. Ford suggests replacing the transmission pump assembly – a six-hour repair. This repair should not be needed before 7-10 years. So, naturally, any refusal by Ford to pass this repair under warranty should prompt owners to file a claim in small claims court. Use TSB #14-0076 as proof of the company's responsibility. 2011-14—Trucks equipped with a 3.5L turbo engine may exhibit a hard start or no start condition after using the block heater when temperatures are below -15°C (0°F). Ford suggests installing an immersion block heater kit under warranty. An intermittent click or snap from the rear axle on initial light acceleration from a stop while in drive or reverse may occur on light acceleration after changing direction from drive to reverse, or reverse to drive. Ford suggests changing the rear pinion seal. If there is a delayed engagement when shifting between Park and Reverse, the transmission pump assembly may be defective.

2011-2014 Expedition, F-150, Mustang; LINCOLN: 2011-2014 Navigator.

ISSUE: Some 2011-2014 Expedition, Mustang, F-150 and Navigator vehicles may exhibit a delayed park to forward or reverse transmission engagement only on initial vehicle start up after parking several hours or overnight. The vehicle functions normally after the initial engagement has completed.

ACTION: It may be necessary to replace the transmission pump assembly.

Fixes for a host of infotainment failures are addressed in TSB #13-10-6, dated Oct. 4, 2013, and TSB #12A04S4. 2012—Vehicles equipped with a 3.7L engine may produce a chirping or squealing noise from the accessory drive belt during idle and acceleration. You may need to replace the accessory drive belt and tensioner. Water leaking onto the front passenger side floor when the climate control system is in either air conditioning or defrost mode may be due to an incorrectly assembled heater core and evaporator core housing. 2012-13—Repair tips for headliner sagging along the windshield or rear window glass. 2013—Trucks equipped with electronic automatic temperature control or an electronic manual temperature control remote mount only, may lack sufficient heat. This may be caused by ice accumulation in the heater core And evaporator core housing affecting operation of the temperature blend door. 2013-14—Vehicles may make a growl or buzz noise coming from the transmission that occurs when shifting from Park to Drive or Park to Reverse most often after the vehicle has been parked and then restarted. Ford says the main control valve body separator plate may need to be replaced under warranty. No audio output on startup during cold ambient temperatures or when abnormally low battery voltage levels are present. Take 20 minutes to reprogram the audio control module (ACM) to correct this problem. 2014—Trucks equipped with a 3.7L engine may leak coolant at the rear of the engine at the heater hose. 2015—Inoperative or frozen door latches on the Super Cab may require the installation of a new rear door lower latch assembly or latch cable.

GENERAL MOTORS

GM out of Touch?

"We seem to forget that a cloistered executive, whose only social contacts are with similar executives who make $500,000 a year, and who has not really bought a car the way a customer has in years, has no basis to judge public taste."

— John DeLorean, 1979
On a Clear Day You Can See General Motors

John DeLorean was right. America's premier automaker has steadily lost touch with what car buyers want. DeLorean was the youngest division head in General Motors in the mid-60s, and designed a number of iconic, classic vehicles including the Pontiac GTO (*Gran Turismo Omologato*) muscle car, Grand Prix, and Firebird.

GM's 2016 model lineup doesn't have similar winners and DeLorean is long gone. The company faces an uphill battle as it brings back cars no one wants. Market share that hovered in the upper 40s during DeLorean's tenure will slide to 17.9% by the end of 2015, say auto analysts at *Edmunds*.

Although the company will launch a redesigned 2016 Volt

GM's Corvette brings new meaning to "topless."

electric car, many industry insiders say General Motors' electric car brand is dead and point to the Volt's delayed 2016 startup as proof. Except for the popular sub-compact Spark EV, the Volt and Cadillac ELR electric cars can't compete due to their poor design and price-gouging resulting in thousands of dollars in discounts that leave buyers with the feeling they paid too much. In fact, auto critics are calling the $80,000 (Cdn.) 2016 ELR a Chevy Volt in disguise, at twice the price.

Cadillac is a brand in shambles. Offering overpriced and under-performing cars, most of its product line has been met with buyer indifference. The only standout being the Escalade, which is really an SUV. European and Asian auto-makers have filled the void in supplying luxury cars that are stylish, fun to drive, and price competitive. GM should drop the Cadillac division and use the savings to beef up warranties, merge GMC into Chevrolet to save production costs, and expand its crossover models as a hedge against volatile fuel prices that see-saw customer preferences.

Quality: Promise vs. Performance

Generally, new and redesigned vehicles or those with the latest electronic gadgets, tend to have more problems than carry-over models that undergo fewer design, engineering, and equipment changes. This is not the case, however, with the Impala and Silverado/Sierra pickups – three vehicles reworked as 2014 models that have proven to be better perfomers and more reliable than previous iterations.

For example, the much maligned Chevrolet Impala, voted "best sedan tested" by *Consumer Reports* in 2014, is riding high, along with the afore-mentioned pickups with sustained popularity and dependability going into 2016. It will be joined by a redesigned Malibu, which GM promises will replicate the Impala's success.

GM quality has definitely improved with other models, as well – not across the board, but in key areas like fit and finish, fuel economy, and infotainment features. Nevertheless, General Motors still lags far behind Asian and European carmakers in making dependable and durable engines and transmissions, a 5-decade-old problem shared with Ford and Fiat Chrysler. Now, all three automakers say those bad old days are gone and that the 2016 models will have first-class engines, transmissions, and fuel delivery systems.

Don't believe it!

GM and Fiat Chrysler have just announced they are cutting back their 2016 powertrain warranty coverage in the States from 100,000 to 60,000 miles, an action that belies their promise of better quality engines and transmissions in the future.

GM still has some serious electrical and fuel system shortcomings, but despite the above glitches, the automaker now ranks near the top of J.D. Power's annual Initial Quality Index survey.

GM's limited powertrain warranty and existing free scheduled maintenance in Canada is unchanged so far. The base guarantee is for five years or 160,000 km, whichever comes first, while Chrysler, Ford, Honda, and Toyota currently offer a five-year/100,000-km. limited warranty. Furthermore, GM has softened a bit of its consumer-hostile attitude as of late (multi-million dollar fines help). Now, when it does make a major screw-up it is quicker than the other Detroit automakers to set things right by extending its warranty coverage or issuing a recall.

One recent example of this is its 2015 OnStar system that would drain the battery if the car sits unused for four days or longer. The company sent this letter to affected owners of almost its entire lineup of vehicles:

November 2014   Bulletin No.: 14395

Dear General Motors Customer:

We have learned that your 2015 model year Buick Encore, LaCrosse, Regal, or Verano; Cadillac ATS, CTS, ELR, Escalade, SRX or XTS; Chevrolet Colorado, Corvette, Cruze, Equinox, Impala, Malibu, Silverado, Sonic, Spark, SS, Suburban, Tahoe, Trax, or Volt; or GMC Canyon, Sierra, Terrain, or Yukon vehicle may have a performance issue with the OnStar® module that could impact your vehicle's battery life. **This condition can cause a dead battery if your vehicle is not started for approximately 4 days, and can occur even if you do not have an active OnStar® subscription.**

Your satisfaction with your GM vehicle is very important to us, so we are announcing a program to prevent this condition or, if it has occurred, to fix it.

What We Will Do:

Your GM dealer will replace the OnStar® module. If you do not have an active OnStar® subscription, your dealer will temporarily activate the OnStar® system and upon replacing the module, your dealer will deactivate the system. **This module replacement will be performed for you at no charge until November 30, 2017.**

Unlike GM, Ford continues to be dragged down by "stonewalling" owner complaints over its unreliable powertrain, power steering, and electronic features, in addition to its disappointing "real" world fuel-economy. Chrysler's momentum has been sustained by its improved quality control and popular truck offerings, although its cars remain poor choices.

SPARK/SPARK EV   ★★/★★★

RATING: *Spark:* Below Average (2013-16); Once you accept the fact that this is a slow four-passenger urban econocar you won't be too disappointed. A front-drive, four-door hatchback, Spark is smaller than Chevy's Aveo subcompact. Since it's built by GM Daewoo, think of it as the Aveo's smaller brother. The restyled 2016 Spark has 17% more horsepower, but adds a roof that's several inches lower. *Spark EV:* Average (2015-16). A 2016 Spark EV will be sold in Canada this year (earlier 2015 models were offered only to fleet buyers) in British Columbia, Ontario, and Quebec – three provinces that offer generous incentives for plug-in electric cars. Road performance: Handling is mediocre; the CVT transmission is slow to respond; and the ride is stiff and jittery. Loud and slow acceleration. How slow is Spark slow? Well, the British *Fifth Gear* TV show clocked the acceleration time for the 2015 model at 0-97 km/h (0-60 mph) with the 1.0L and 1.2L engines. The results? 15.5 and 12.1 seconds, respectively, so bring along a good book and an hourglass. Some other faults: The steering is a bit light for highway driving; gear shifts aren't always smooth; steering column doesn't telescope; and it's harsh riding when going over uneven terrain. *Spark EV:* In spite of the Spark EV's 81-mile (131-km) range rating, GM markets the car mainly to "city residents whose transportation needs can be met with an all-electric vehicle." Strong points: The 2016 car's low price is quite reasonable with the base model and EV version. Good acceleration time of 0-97 km/h (0-60 mph) in 7.2 seconds. OnStar 4G LTE with Wi-Fi is available. Other new features for 2016: The interior gets upgraded fabrics and better seat foam to make the ride a little more bearable; there's an upgraded LCD control screen and easy access to the media and climate controls; and a new MyLink radio controls most features like a smartphone. The Spark EV is one of the very few low-volume battery-electric vehicles to offer DC quick charging as well as conventional 240-Volt charging. In a practical sense, this means 80% of the battery can be charged in just 20 minutes. Weak points: Firm prices; cabin a bit narrow. *2015:* The hatchback's load floor is quite high – the Honda Fit is more useful and versatile. Mushy brakes and chronic rear brake squeal (corrosion).

Prices and Specs

Prices (Firm): *LS man.:* $12,145; *LS auto:* $15,095; *1LT auto.:* $17,245; *2LT auto:* $19,170; *Electric Vehicle:* $29,000, less government rebates **Freight:** $1,850-1,950 **Powertrain (Front-drive):** Engine: 1.4L Ecotec 4-cyl. (98 hp); Transmissions: 5-speed man., CVT **Dimensions/capacity:** Passengers: 2/3; Wheelbase: 94 in.; H: n/a/L: 144.1/W: 62.9 in.; Headroom F/R: 4.0/2.0 in.; Legroom F/R: 39/26 in.; Cargo volume: 11 cu. ft.; Fuel tank: 35L/regular; Tow limit: Not recommended; Load capacity: 660 lb.; Turning circle: 32.5 ft.; Ground clearance: 4.9 in.; Weight: 2,269-2,368 lb.

Other opinions: "The 2015 Chevrolet Spark ranks #29 out of 42 affordable small cars." – *U.S. News & World Report.* "Aside from the usual slew of advantages (efficiency, value and ease of parking) and disadvantages (glacial acceleration, chintzy interior trim) associated with a tiny city car, the Spark offers useful high-tech features and a surprisingly roomy interior with space for four adults." – *Left Lane News.* "It appears the [2016 Spark] will continue to live in rental car lots and in the driveways of those that are unaware of the much better choices available. Sub-100HP in the US market just seems like a death wish for this vehicle." – *Car and Driver.* Major redesign: 2016; the Spark EV is carried over unchanged until late 2016 when it will be replaced by the 2017 Chevrolet Bolt concept car shown at last January's Detroit Auto Show. That car will have a range rating of 200 miles, and a price before incentives of $37,500 U. S. Ouch! Highway/city fuel economy (2015): *1.8L man.:* 6.8/9.0 L/100 km. *Auto.:* 6.7/9.6 L/100 km. *1.4L Turbo man.:* 6.2/8.5 L/100 km. *Auto.:* 6.8/9.0 L/100 km. *RS:* 6.8/9.0 L/100 km. *2016 1.4 L Ecotec:* 5.9 L/100 km. (highway). Best alternatives: Honda Fit, Hyundai Accent, Mazda2, Nissan Versa, and Toyota Yaris. The Kia Rio has a stronger base engine, and provides a comfortable and quieter ride.

SAFETY: Child safety seat setup: Not rated. Crashworthiness: NHTSA: The 2013-15 models were given four stars for overall crash protection; EV not crash-tested. IIHS rated the 2013-15s "Acceptable" for small overlap front protection; "Good" in all other categories. Both a rear-view camera and rear parking-assist sensors are standard on every model, as are no fewer than ten airbags. **Owner-reported safety-related failures:** Owners say the front passenger-side airbag sensor doesn't recognize that the seat is occupied; engine lags and lurches when accelerating; car rolls backwards when stopped on a hill, even though Hill Holder is engaged; engine loses power when merging with highway traffic; the transmission sometimes hesitates before shifting; windshield wiper motor overheats and stops working; hood may fly open into the windshield; car doesn't come with a spare tire; and the front end of the vehicle is too low and drags on the ground when passing over uneven terrain. Spark EV:

> After fully charging up the electric vehicle, going down hill at approx 40mph, lost all power in brakes, steering control and the forward propulsion system. Due to loss of power veered out of control onto oncoming traffic and braking system was not responding to pumps. After pulling on steering wheel hard finally got vehicle under control and pulled to the side. Vehicle would not restart and had to be towed to dealer. Did not have vehicle and did not drive the vehicle more than 30 miles before incident happened. Returned 2014 chevy spark electric vehicle to dealership permanently.

ALERT! Vehicle shuts down if the driver's knee jostles the ignition keychain. This is the same defect mentioned for the Sonic and responsible for millions of recalled GM cars.

Spark Profile

	2013	2014
Used Values ($)		
LS	8,500	9,500
1LT (auto)	11,000	12,500
2LT (auto)	12,000	13,500
Reliability	★3	★
Repairs ($$$)	💰2	💰
Electrical	★	★
Engine (base)	★2	★2
Fit/Finish	★3	★
Infotainment	★3	★3
Transmission (auto.)	★2	★2

SECRET WARRANTIES, INTERNAL BULLETINS: 2013—GM will replace broken engine mounts free of charge. 2013-14—GM will repair the AC at no charge:

CAMPAIGN – A/C COOLING ISSUES	
SERVICE BULLETIN NO.: 13434C	DATE: JUNE 23, 2014

AIR CONDITIONING SYSTEM INOPERATIVE OR COOLS INTERMITTENTLY

2013-2014 Chevrolet Spark

*****THIS PROGRAM IS IN EFFECT UNTIL APRIL 30, 2016.*****

CONDITION: Certain 2013-2014 model year Chevrolet Spark vehicles may have a condition where the air conditioning (A/C) system does not work or cools intermittently due to inaccurate control of the evaporator temperature sensor.

CORRECTION: Dealers are to inspect and, if necessary, replace the A/C compressor. Dealers are to also, if necessary, replace the Evaporative Air Temperature (EAT) Sensor, install a low pressure switch adaptor kit, and reprogram the Body Control Module.

SONIC ★★★

RATING: Average (2012-16). Just a small step up in reliability from the Spark, This econocar proves that cheap small cars can be better performers than equivalent or slightly larger models costing thousands of dollars more ("Hello, Fiat, Fiesta, Focus, Cruze, and SMART"). The turbocharged hatchback offers the best combination for power and interior space. Basically a second-generation South Korean Aveo, the Sonic offers more refinement, enhanced crashworthiness, better performance, and an irresistibly low entry price. Sonic fits into GM's small car lineup between the Spark and Cruze and is evidence that cheap subcompact cars don't mean you have to endure an uncomfortable ride and white-knuckle highway performance. **Road performance:** Fast and smooth acceleration; the optional turbocharged 1.4L engine has more torque and a nicely refined power curve. Steering is precise and responsive, with no torque steer pulling the car to the side when accelerating, however, some reports of excessive steering shake and vehicle wander. **Strong points:** Reasonably priced, refined, and well appointed. The interior is comfortable and practical, with little noise intrusion into the cabin. Sedans are about a foot longer than hatchbacks. **Weak points:** The hatchback's load floor is quite high – the Honda Fit is more useful and versatile. Mushy brakes and chronic rear brake squeal (corrosion). Owners also report that the front passenger-side airbag sensor doesn't recognize that the seat is occupied; the transmission sometimes hesitates before shifting; and the front end of the vehicle is too low and drags on the ground when passing over uneven terrain.

Other opinions: "The 2015 Chevrolet Sonic ranks #15 out of 42 affordable small cars; With a large rear seat, numerous available features and agile handling, the Sonic earns reviewers' appreciation" – *U.S. News & World Report.* "I understand that NHTSA has mandated forward-leaning head restraints on all late-model vehicles. The head restraint in my 2014 Sonic is terrible; it shoves my head forward, forcing me to either stare at the instrument cluster or raise my eyes in a kubrick stare to see the road. It wasn't immediately apparent during the test drive, but after 200+ miles of driving in less than a week, my neck is stiff and shoulders feel like rocks." – *safercarcar.gov.* **Major redesign:** 2016 model year has only been slightly restyled. In mid-2016, an electric variant will debut. **Highway/city fuel economy:** *1.8L man.:* 6.8/9.0 L/100 km. *Auto.:* 6.7/9.6 L/100 km. *1.4L Turbo man.:* 6.2/8.5 L/100 km. *Auto.:* 6.8/9.0 L/100 km. *RS:* 6.8/9.0 L/100 km. Owners have complained to NHTSA that gas mileage is much less than advertised. Wrote one frustrated owner:

> I'm only getting about 14 to 16 mpg on my car. I went to the dealer and was told that it was normal. I said that its impossible to get such low mpg when the paperwork says that I should get 25/35 mpg. I spoke to the service manager and he said that it's normal to get 14 to 16 mpg. I told him, 'You're telling me my 2005 Nissan Altima 3.5 gets better gas milage and a Dodge Durango gets better gas milage??' Well the service department can't seem to find the problem. They recalibrated everything and its even worse. I spend $300 in gas a month which is unheard of.
>
> *– safercar.gov*

Best alternatives: Honda Fit, Hyundai Accent, Mazda2, Nissan Versa, and Toyota Yaris.

SAFETY: **Child safety seat setup:** "Marginal." **Crashworthiness:** NHTSA: The 2015-16 models are the first subcompacts to receive a five-star overall score for safety and the first cars in their class to offer ten standard airbags. 2012-14 models earned five stars from NHTSA for front, side, and rollover crash protection. IIHS also gave its "Good" top score for small and moderate front overlap, frontal offset, side, rear, and roof crashworthiness. **Owner-reported safety-related failures:** Several incidents where the ignition key, if bumped, can cause the vehicle to shut down in traffic. Car rolls backwards when stopped on a hill, even though Hill Holder is engaged.

ALERT! Owners note that the Sonic wanders at cruising speed with original equipment tires and wheels; if a road test confirms this wandering, change the tires and wheels. Also, make sure the front head restraints are comfortable.

Sonic Profile

	2012	2013	2014
Used Values ($)			
LS	8,500	9,500	11,500
LT	9,000	11,500	13,500
Reliability	★	★	★
Repairs ($$$)	2	1	1
Electrical	★	★	★
Engine (base)	★	★	★
Fit/Finish	★	★	★
Infotainment	★	★	★
Transmission (auto.)	★	★	★

SECRET WARRANTIES, INTERNAL BULLETINS: 2012—The driver airbag module retainers may not be fully engaged in the steering wheel. A rattle or clunk noise during turns or over bumps may require the free replacement of the stabilizer bars, which may have lower ball joint boots that are subject to water and dirt intrusion. There is a free service campaign to replace the fuel pipe and quick connect on certain 2012 Sonics equipped with a 1.4L turbo engine and 6-speed manual transmission. In high speed front crash tests, the nylon fuel feed pipe quick connect fractured and released a small amount of fuel after the crashed vehicle was rolled 90 to 180 degrees. A bump feeling, surge, or an engine vibration while stopped at idle with the transmission in Drive and the foot on the service brake may be caused by the transmission Neutral Idle feature. 2012-14—Inoperative heated seats is a seat module software issue. 2013-14—Oil leaks, high oil consumption, or blue exhaust smoke may be caused by an improperly seated exhaust manifold, or one with a missing non-return valve. Malfunction Indicator Lamp (MIL) on and/or hard cold starts, rough idle during cold ambient temperatures on vehicles equipped with a 1.8L engine. This may be caused by fuel being leaner for cleaner combustion, at lower ambient temperatures with low volatility fuel. Changing to top tier fuels may correct this condition. GM says it's normal for a cold Sonic engine to be slow in providing adequate cabin heat.

CRUZE ★

A "Cruze" to nowhere.

RATING: Not Recommended (2011-16). This car could have been a contender. Right size, right equipment, reasonably-priced, and available with a diesel option. But GM screwed it up. Launched two years after the company got out of bankruptcy with the promise to make quality products, the Cruze has distinguished itself as unsafe, unreliable, and anything but fuel-efficient. Even with "goodwill" warranty extensions to cover the car's many factory-related defects, the free repairs remain a secret to many Cruze owners (see Secret Warranties below). The 2016-17 redesign is a two-edged sword that adds some performance and convenience features, while risking more production snafus. So far, the only announced changes on the 2016 Cruze are interior and exterior improvements, making the car larger, lower, lighter, and sleeker, and offering Android Auto and Apple CarPlay smartphone interfaces. Although these changes may be tempting, smart shoppers should wait for the 2016 second series (April-May) to have early production glitches ironed out. **Road performance:** A peppy, smooth, and efficient turbocharged engine, plus good steering and handling. Automatic transmission sometimes is slow to down-shift. The firm suspension makes you feel every bump in the road. **Strong points:** The 2016 redesign is expected to offer a new platform carrying a more powerful 4-cylinder Ecotec turbo engine, and a 7-speed dual-clutch automatic in place of the existing 6-speed autoshifter. **Weak points:** Cramped rear seating with seat cushions set too low; limited storage area; and terrible long-term reliability. Early exhaust manifold replacement (see Secret Warranties, below); cracked engine head gasket; leaking engine, tranny, and axle seals; hesitation when accelerating; heater and AC often don't work; heater overheats, or can't be shut off; rear windshield water leaks (covered by a secret warranty; see Secret Warranties); all dash lights suddenly come on for no reason; leaking water pump; key sticks in the ignition when in Park; smart key locks owners in and out of their car (see Secret Warranties, below); rear engine mount failures; "clunky" steering covered by a "secret" warranty (see Secret Warranties, below).

Prices and Specs

Prices (Soft): *1LS:* $16,075, *2LS:* $18,775, *LT:* $20,040, *Eco:* $21,740, *2LT:* $22,140, *Diesel:* $25,540, *LTZ:* $27,195 **Freight:** $1,850-$1,950 **Powertrain (Front-drive):** Engines: 1.8L 4-cyl. (136 hp), 1.4L turbocharged 4-cyl. (138 hp); 2.0L turbocharged diesel 4-cyl. (151 hp); Transmissions: 6-speed man., 6-speed auto. **Dimensions/capacity:** Passengers: 2/3; Wheelbase: 105.7 in.; H: 58.1/L: 181/W: 70.7 in.; Headroom F/R: 6/30 in.; Legroom F/R:43/26 in.; Cargo volume: 15 cu. ft.; Fuel tank: 59L/regular; Tow limit: 1,000 lb.; Load capacity: 900 lb.; Turning circle: 35.7 ft.; Ground clearance: 6.5 in.; Weight: 3,056 lb.

Other opinions: "The 2015 Chevrolet Cruze ranks #6 out of 42 affordable small cars. Reviewers like the pleasant ride, even handling, powerful available diesel engine and spacious trunk" – *U.S. News & World Report.* "The 20-per-cent improvement in fuel economy provided by diesel is quickly reduced, if not eliminated, by its higher price. Using Natural Resources Canada ratings, the 2014 Chevrolet Cruze will use about 1,200 litres of diesel fuel per year on average, compared to 1,520 for the gasoline version of the same car. However, Canada's most popular car, the Honda Civic in comparable EX trim, will use 1,220 litres of fuel per year, as will the Mazda3. Using recent prices in downtown Toronto, the Cruze diesel would consume $1,618 worth of fuel, and the Civic/Mazda3 $1,511 over a year. Makes diesels a pretty tough sell, despite their longevity and lower maintenance costs." – Richard Russell, *Toronto Globe & Mail.* **Major redesign:** 2016 redesign includes a new coupe and SS model; an improved ride; restyled front and rear ends; interior trim improvements; and more rear passenger room. If fuel prices remain low, the diesel engine may be ditched in mid-2016. **Highway/city fuel economy:** *Eco 1.4L man.:* 4.6/7.2 L/100 km. *Eco 1.4L auto.:* 5.1/7.8 L/100 km. *1.8L man.:* 5.4/7.8L/100 km. *1.8L auto.:* 5.6/9.2 L/100 km., *2.0L diesel auto.:* 5.1/8.7 L/100 km. **Best alternatives:** Some good alternative models to save fuel and also stay out of the repair bay are the Honda Civic, Hyundai Elantra, Mazda3, and VW Jetta. One family complained to CBC Calgary TV that their 2011 Cruze LT's "real" gas mileage is half what's touted by General Motors:

I strongly feel cheated … we didn't save any money – quite the opposite. We know that in most cases the [fuel efficiency] tests are done under specific conditions, but this was really grossly different.

– *Farah Mocquais, vehicle owner*

The family expects to spend $3,500 more on gas than expected by the time the odometer reaches 100,000 kilometres.

SAFETY: Child safety seat setup: "Acceptable." Crashworthiness: NHTSA: 2011-15 models earned five stars in overall crashworthiness tests carried out; IIHS rated the same cars "Good" for frontal, side, head-restraint, and roof crash protection. However, they were given a "Marginal" score for small overlap front protection. Owner-reported safety-related failures: Safety-related Cruze complaints increased incrementally after the car's first year on the market. Up to 350 incidences per some Cruze model years is astoundingly high, whereas 50 complaints is the norm for most vehicles. The experiences described in this section have been taken from the first 90 complaints posted by 2014-15 model year owners. There are hundreds other equally harrowing postings covering the Cruze's 2011-15 model run. The worst of the worse follow: Sudden stallout followed by unintended acceleration ("lag and lurch"), when accelerating:

> My 2014 Cruze has a safety issue, so scary I am afraid of driving it now: the gas pedal has a delay in it and scared me to death several times, trying to come out of a stop light on a busy intersection as the car had a 2-3 second delay in responding to the gas pedal, and then whooshed out on top of incoming traffic!!! On the highway it happened several times that changing lanes becomes an issue as this delay in responding and sudden acceleration almost got me into an accident last week.

GM Says "lag and lurch" acceleration and "sag or hesitation" on acceleration is a normal characteristic.

"SAG OR HESITATION" ON ACCELERATION – NORMAL

SERVICE BULLETIN NO.: PIP4112P   DATE: JUN 26, 2014

MODELS:

2008-2012 Buick Enclave	2009-2012 Chevrolet Traverse
2010-2011 Buick LaCrosse MH7	2011 Chevrolet Cruze
2010-2013 Buick LaCrosse MH2, MH4	2012 Chevrolet Cruze MH9
2011 Buick Regal MH7	2010-2015 Chevrolet Camaro, Express
2006-2009 Cadillac XLR, XLR-V	2011-2015 Chevrolet Caprice
2006-2011 Cadillac STS, STS-V	2012 Chevrolet Captiva Sport MHJ, MHK
2007-2012 Cadillac SRX	2012 Orlando
2007-2015 Cadillac Escalade, Escalade EXT, Escalade ESV	2012 Chevrolet Sonic MH9
	2012-2013 Chevrolet Impala
2008-2015 Cadillac CTS	2014 Chevrolet SS
2013-2015 Cadillac ATS	2007-2015 GMC Sierra, Yukon, Yukon XL
2006-2015 Chevrolet Corvette	2008-2012 GMC Acadia
2007-2013 Chevrolet Avalanche	2010-2012 GMC Terrain MH2, MH7
2007-2015 Chevrolet Silverado, Suburban, Tahoe	2010-2011 GMC Terrain MHC, MH7
	2010-2015 GMC Savana
2008-2011 Chevrolet Malibu MH8	2008-2011 HUMMER H2
2008-2013 Chevrolet Malibu MH2	2007-2010 Pontiac G6 MH2
2008-2012 Chevrolet Equinox MH2, MH4	2009-2010 Pontiac G6 MH8
2009-2011 Chevrolet Equinox MHC, MH7	2008-2009 Pontiac G8

2008-2009 Pontiac Torrent MH2, MH4	2008-2010 Saturn Outlook, Vue MH2, MH4
2007-2009 Saturn Aura MH2	Equipped With a Gasoline Engine and
2009 Saturn Aura MH8	Automatic Transmission

CONDITION/CONCERN: Some customers may comment on a sag or hesitation when accelerating under the following conditions: When coasting at low speeds of less than 15 miles per hour with a closed throttle and then aggressively applying the throttle. Examples of this maneuver include a rolling stop or a lane change maneuver. In this type of maneuver, even though the accelerator is applied aggressively, the throttle blade is opened slowly for up to 0.7 seconds to help minimize drive-line lash and clunking. Also, in a vehicle equipped with a six speed automatic transmission when making a hard, complete stop with a closed throttle, immediately followed by an aggressive throttle opening the transmission down-shifts may not be completed by the time the throttle is opened. As a result approximately 0.5 seconds of "zero" torque may be commanded to allow the shift to first gear to occur.

RECOMMENDATION/INSTRUCTIONS: Both of the above conditions are a result of Torque Management and both of these conditions should be considered normal and no repairs should be attempted.

Additional safety related failures: Airbags fail to deploy when they're needed; frequent stallouts in traffic; ignition keyring may cause the ignition switch to shut off the car; brake/accelerator mounted too close together, they both can be applied at the same time, or the wrong pedal may be applied; accelerator pedal fractured; floor mats slide up under the pedals; loss of braking when backing up or underway (vacuum pump suspected).

> The driver owns a 2015 Chevrolet Cruze. While driving at an unknown speed, the brakes were engaged and failed to stop the vehicle. Driver had to stand on the brake pedal in order to stop the vehicle. He was able to turn off and restart the vehicle successfully. The failure recurred on 3 separate occasions.

Front axle shaft failure and wheel came off; chronic automatic transmission failures and malfunctions; rear-view mirror blocks the view through the front windshield, reflects excessive headlight glare, and vibrates constantly; sidewall "bubbling" with Firestone tires; "sticky" power steering binds or fails completely (see Secret Warranties below); exhaust, AC, and anti-freeze fumes leak into the cabin; extensive undercarriage rusting; dangerous doors suddenly slam shut:

> The doors should definitely be recalled. They are a safety concern. They slam back on you even if opened all the way, if on an uneven pavement or slight incline.

Headlights shut off; windows slow to defog and, don't clear completely; and in one incident, the steering wheel came off in the driver's hands.

ALERT! If you *must* buy a Cruze, consider the purchase of a more reliable and fuel-efficient 2015-16 diesel-equipped version. This will provide a good hedge against rising fuel prices and make the car easier to sell at a good price. On the other hand, don't count on lower fuel costs and better mileage to balance out the diesel's higher fuel cost. As for recall repairs, you will need the patience of Job. Owners say a three month's wait for repairs is not unusual.

> After 5 recalls and an accident caused by my brakes failing, I now have to replace the entire engine because of cracked pistons. This just doesn't make sense. How is this car still on the road? Someone is going to get killed driving one of these cars."
>
> — *www.consumeraffairs.com/automotive/chevy-cruze.html*

Cruze Profile

	2011	2012	2013	2014
Used Values ($)				
LS	7,000	8,500	10,500	12,000
LT	9,000	11,500	13,500	15,500
Eco	—	12,500	14,500	17,000
LTZ	9,500	12,500	14,500	20,500
Diesel	—	—	—	17,500
Reliability	★	★	★	★
Repairs ($$$)	③	③	③	③
Electrical	★	★	★	★2
Engine (base)	★	★	★	★
Fit/Finish	★2	★2	★2	★3
Infotainment	★	★	★	★2
Transmission	★	★	★	★

 SECRET WARRANTIES, INTERNAL BULLETINS: 2011—Power-steering fluid leaks. Shock absorber/strut fluid leaks; tire slowly goes flat. Automatic transmission clunk noise. Engine hesitation at start-up requires reprogramming the engine control module. 2011-12—Uneven brake pedal feel. This bulletin provides a service procedure to reprogram the electronic brake control module. 2011-14—Coolant loss free refill ("secret" warranty). Don't pay attention to the expiry date; consumer laws say: "If they broke it, they fix it."

2011-2014 Chevrolet Cruze With 1.4L Engine

****THIS PROGRAM IS IN EFFECT UNTIL AUGUST 12, 2016.****

CONDITION: Cruze vehicles equipped with the 1.4L engine may have a low engine coolant level even though there are no external leaks present. Some customers may have noticed that the coolant level was full when the vehicle was new but the coolant level decreased over time.

CORRECTION: Dealers are to inspect the cooling system level and fill it to the appropriate level if it is low.

2012—Engine hesitation at start-up under high accessory loads requires repro-gramming of the ECM under the Emissions Warranty. 2012-14—Engine oil leaks, burning oil, and turbo failures are covered in the following service bulletin:

EXCESSIVE OIL CONSUMPTION – OIL LEAKS – BLUE EXHAUST SMOKE – MIL – OR FUEL TRIM CODES
SERVICE BULLETIN NO.: PIP5197   DATED: MAY 6, 2014

2012-2014 Chevrolet Cruze; 2013-2014 Buick Encore; 2013; 2014 Chevrolet Sonic; 2013; 2014 Chevrolet Trax (Canada Only) equipped with 1.4L.

CONDITION/CONCERN: You may encounter a customer concern of oil consumption, oil leaks, and blue smoke from the exhaust, MIL or fuel trim codes.

CORRECTION: Check for a missing or improperly seated intake manifold Non Return Valve that may have damaged the PCV orifice diaphragm. If the intake manifold Non Return Valve is missing or not properly seated, then replace the intake manifold assembly. Check the PCV orifice for leaking oil or drawing vacuum at idle thru its external port.

2013—On certain Buick LaCrosse, Regal, Verano, Cadillac SRX, and Chevrolet Cruze and Malibu vehicles there may be an interference condition between the outside door handle and the door handle bracket assembly. This could cause the outside door handle to stick or bind in the open position when the door is opened from outside of the vehicle. To correct, Dealers are to inspect and modify the front and rear outside door handles, free of charge. GM dealers will also repair, for free, vehicles that produce a steering clunking noise when turning. Offer expires after May 31, 2015, but may be extended by the small claims court, inasmuch as steering gear boots should last longer than 2 years.

2013-14—A notchy or stick/slip feel in the steering wheel when turning near center wheel position can be easily corrected by reprogramming the power steering control module. Also applies to same-year GM Verano and Malibu. (TSB #P11239, dated July 24, 2014.) Again this GM admission makes the company and dealer jointly responsible for the free correction of this defect. 2014—Incorrect door lock power switches will be replaced, *gratis:* Certain 2014 model year Chevrolet Cruze vehicles may have had an incorrect power switch installed on the driver door. Dealers are to inspect and, if necessary, install the correct door switch. *This program is in effect until March 31, 2016.* GM will also replace all door strikers on certain 2014 Cruze vehicles. The door strikers may have been incorrectly plated, giving the appearance of "pitting." Water leak free repair ("secret" warranty). Expiry date can be extended in small claims court:

More water leaks covered under a "secret" warranty:

CUSTOMER SATISFACTION PROGRAM – WET CARPET ON DRIVER'S SIDE

SERVICE BULLETIN NO.: #14490   DATE: AUGUST 11, 2014

2014 Chevrolet Cruze

*****THIS PROGRAM IS IN EFFECT UNTIL AUGUST 31, 2016.*****

CONDITION: Certain 2014 model year Chevrolet Cruze vehicles may not have an adequate seal on the driver's side lower windshield panel-to-cowl interface. This could allow water to enter the vehicle and moisten the front and rear carpet on the driver's side.

CORRECTION: Dealers are to reseal the windshield panel-to-cowl interface seam.

MALIBU/HYBRID

RATING: An Average Buy (2016) if improved performance is matched by improved quality. Below Average Buy (1997-2015). The 2016 mid-size Malibu has gone up a notch in its rating because the car has been totally redesigned in a similar way as was the much-improved 2014 Impala. This year's Malibu is powered by a new turbocharged 1.5L 4-cylinder, 160 hp engine coupled to a front-drive, 6-speed automatic transmission. An optional 250 hp, 2.0L 4-cylinder engine comes with a new 8-speed automatic tranny. The gasoline-electric hybrid has a 1.8-L 182 hp 4-cylinder engine that works with a two-motor electric drive unit taken from the 2016 Volt plug-in hybrid. Electric power comes from a 1.5 kilowatt-hour lithium-ion battery pack. Prior versions elicited few owner complaints. The Malibu Hybrid also shares the 2016 Volt's blended regenerative braking system, which helps keep the battery charged. More of a five-seater this year, the longer and sleeker 2016 has 1.3 more inches of rear-seat legroom than the 2015. Standard features include Bluetooth phone connectivity, a six-speaker audio system and OnStar 4G LTE with a built-in Wi-Fi hot spot. Some must-have options: A rear-view camera, USB port, and MyLink infotainment system with a new 8-inch touch screen. Lane keep assist, forward collision alert, adaptive cruise control, front pedestrian detection with automatic braking, and automatic parking assist are newly available features that have drawn mixed reactions when used with some upper-level models. One sneaky addition is Chevrolet's new Teen Driver system, which mutes the audio system when front seat belts aren't buckled, alerts occupants when the vehicle is exceeding a preset speed, and allows parents to monitor their teen's driving habits. Yikes! Road performance: Earlier standard 4-cylinder engines hooked to an automatic transmission were barely adequate for highway driving with a full load. 2016 models also seem underpowered. Nevertheless, the car does give a comfortable though firm ride and offers better-than-average handling, thanks to its independent suspension. Strong points: Well-appointed, with many advanced high-tech features; an improved hybrid powerplant, adequate passenger and luggage space, a roomier, more comfortable interior; increased rear legroom; fewer squeaks and rattles; and higher-grade cabin materials. Weak points: Premature wheel bearing replacement; trunk opens on its own. As with earlier redesigns, expect premature brake wear, electrical shorts, a sticky, binding steering wheel, and powertrain failures, chief of which is a tendency to lag and then lurch forward when accelerating or decelerating:

> The sudden downshifts cause the vehicle to suddenly propel forward, especially when cruising to slow down or while brake is depressed, causing an unsafe change in vehicle speed that requires sudden need to brake or increase brake pressure to avoid striking vehicle in front. Transmission also at times has an "engine miss" type jolt while at cruising speed on flat pavement 30-45mph that has at one time repeated for 3 minutes straight. Majority of time transmission behaves normally and without incident and then suddenly goes nuts.

Prices and Specs

(2015) Prices (Firm): *LS:* $25,140, *LT:* $26,990, *Eco:* $28,500, *1LZ:* $33,250 **Freight:** $2,000 **Powertrain (Front-drive):** Engines: 1.5L turbocharged 4-cyl. (160 hp); 2.0L turbocharged 4-cyl. (250 hp); 1.8L Transmission: 6-speed auto.; 8-speed auto. **Dimensions/capacity:** Passengers: 2/3; Wheelbase: 107.8 in.; H: 57.6/L: 191.6/W: 73 in.; Headroom F/R: 3.5/3; Legroom F/R: 42.1/36.8; Cargo volume: 16.3 cu. ft.; Fuel tank: 70L/regular; Tow limit: NR; Load capacity: 905 lb.; Turning circle: 37.4 ft.; Ground clearance: 5 ft.; Weight: 3,393 lb.

Other opinions: The 2015 Chevrolet Malibu, ranked #12 out of 18 affordable mid-size cars in *U.S. News & World Report's* annual review of new cars. "I have been having numerous problems with a pause in the engine when I'm speeding up onto a highway or to pass on the highway. It's most dangerous when I enter the highway. The car instead of just speeding up has been known to pause, and then speed up. This is very dangerous because it's hard to determine when the car is going to 'pause'. I was almost in an accident because I had enough time to enter the highway and the car decided to 'pause' and then go but that slight pause effects the timing of entering traffic." Major redesign: 1997, 2004, 2008, 2013, 2016, and a 2014 "refresh." Four redesigns in 6 years and buyers remain unimpressed. 2014 models boast a restyled front end, an upgraded interior, and a more fuel-efficient powertrain. Did these changes improve Malibu's fortunes? Nope, sales continue to nosedive. Highway/city fuel economy: *2.4L:* 6.5/9.5 L/100 km. *2.4L 6-speed:* 5.9/9.4 L/100 km. *V6:* 7.8/12.2 L/100 km. 2014 fuel economy may increase 3-5%, thanks to start-stop feature and variable valve lift control. The Hybrid's real fuel economy isn't much more than what the 4-cyl.-powered Hyundai Sonata and Toyota Camry provide. Also, owners say that Malibu's mileage figures on all models are impossible to achieve: "This vehicle should have an average of 36 mpg for hwy. I drive 100 miles every day round trip and 98 miles of that is highway at posted speed of 60-65 mph. I am still getting only about 27.5 mpg almost a year later." Best alternatives: The Honda Accord has more usable interior space, is much more reliable, gives good gas mileage, and has quicker and more accurate steering; Hyundai's Elantra is cheaper and just as well put together; and Toyota's Camry is plusher, though not as driver oriented. Other cars worth considering are the Mazda3 and Mazda6. Another possibility is the afore-mentioned reworked 2014-16 Chevy Impala, a slightly larger and higher-priced in-house competitor.

SAFETY: Child safety seat setup: "Acceptable." Crashworthiness: NHTSA: Beginning with the 2004 models, the Malibu was awarded its five-star crashworthiness score for frontal and side protection and four stars for frontal rollover resistance. IIHS says frontal offset, side, rear, and roof crash protection is "Good." Owner-reported safety-related failures: 2015 Malibus are afflicted with a dangerous "lag and lurch" powertrain. Since GM calls the loss of power and sudden acceleration "normal" it's doubtful the reworked 2016 version will perform any better. 2004s noted for driver's seat toggling back and forth due to inadequate welds to the frame cross-bars (see Secret Warranties, below). Excessive dash glare into the front windshield;. steering wheel binds, doesn't track straight, or jerks to one side (see Secret Warranties, below); and the stop-go gas-saving feature can leave the car without power when stopped. Sudden engine failure; won't restart (see Secret Warranties, below).

ALERT! Next spring's models will be better built; keep your powder dry for at least six months until Malibu's 2016 model upgrades have been owner tested. Be wary of overpriced, bundled option packages.

Malibu Profile

	2006	2007	2008	2009	2010	2011	2012	2013	2014
Used Values ($)									
LS	4,000	5,000	6,000	7,000	8,000	10,500	12,000	15,000	18,500
LT	5,000	6,000	7,000	8,000	9,500	11,500	13,000	16,000	20,000
LTZ	6,000	7,000	8,000	9,500	11,000	13,000	15,500	18,000	—
MAXX LT	5,500	6,500	7,500	—	—	—	—	—	—
Hybrid	—	—	7,000	8,000	9,500	—	—	—	—
ECO	—	—	—	—	—	—	—	17,000	—
Reliability	★	★	☆	☆	☆	☆	☆	☆	☆
Repairs ($$$)	③	③	③	③	③	③	②	②	②
Electrical	★	★	★	★	★	★	☆	☆	☆
Engine (base)	★	★	★	★	★	☆	☆	★	★
Fit/Finish	★	★	★	★	★	☆	☆	☆	☆
Infotainment	—	—	—	—	—	☆	☆	☆	☆
Transmission (auto.)	★	★	★	★	★	★	★	★	★

SECRET WARRANTIES, INTERNAL BULLETINS: 2004-08—Front-end clunk or rattle when passing over small bumps at low speeds. 2005-08—2005-06 G6, Malibu, and Malibu Maxx; 2008 G6, Malibu, Malibu Maxx, and Aura may have a sudden loss of steering power-assist. Under Special Coverage Adjustment #10183, dated July 20, 2010, GM will replace the failed components free of charge up to 10 years/ 100,000 mi. (160,000 km). 2006-07—TSB #10134A, published Aug. 24, 2011, says that cars with the 2.2L 4-cylinder engine and those with the 2.4L 4-cylinder with 4-speed automatic transmission may have a deteriorating catalytic converter, causing the engine light to illuminate. The warranty is extended to 10 years/192,000 km. for 2006-07 Cobalt, G4/G5, and Ion. 2010-14—Here is a free fix for a sticking, binding steering wheel (covered by a secret warranty). This warranty extension applies to new and used car owners:

SPECIAL COVERAGE ADJUSTMENT – POWER STEERING STICK-SLIP

SERVICE BULLETIN NO.: 14232   DATE: NOVEMBER 21, 2014

2012-2014 Buick Verano; 2011-2014 Chevrolet Cruze, Volt; 2010-2014 Chevrolet Equinox; 2013-2014 Chevrolet Malibu; 2010-2014 GMC Terrain.

CONDITION: Some vehicles may have increased friction in the steering system. This could cause the steering wheel to stick in the straight-ahead position after driving long distances on a straight highway. The steering wheel can be turned but it may require increased effort.

SPECIAL COVERAGE ADJUSTMENT: This special coverage covers the condition described above for a period of 10 years or 150,000 miles (240,000 km), whichever occurs first, from the date the vehicle was originally placed in service, regardless of ownership. Dealers are to 1) replace the steering gear on 2010-2012 model year vehicles; or 2) reprogram the power steering control module on 2013-2014 model year vehicles. The repairs will be made at no charge to the customer.

2011—Power-steering fluid leaks. Airbag warning light comes on intermittently (likely caused by a loose, missing, or damaged connector position assurance retainer). Shock absorber fluid leaks. Wet front or rear passenger-side carpet (this condition may be caused by a plugged HVAC evaporator drain – in some cases, water from the HVAC system will drain back though the front of the dash). Clunking automatic transmission shifts are called "normal" by GM. 2012-15— Driver's front seat moves, makes noise when turning:

FRONT SEAT LATERAL MOVEMENT, CLUNK, SQUEAK, CLICK NOISE OR SHIFT WHILE CORNERING

SERVICE BULLETIN NO.: PI0686C   DATE: AUGUST 27, 2014

2012-2015 Buick Regal; 2012-2015 Buick Verano; 2011-2015 Chevrolet Cruze; 2013-2015 Chevrolet Malibu; 2014-2015 Chevrolet Impala; 2014 Chevrolet SS.

CONDITION/CONCERN/ACTION: Some customers may comment on a lateral movement in the seat while cornering. This condition has also been described as a clunk, squeak, click noise or shift in the seat. This condition occurs on the driver side 6-way manual or power adjusted seat. This condition may also be present on the passenger side seat if the vehicle is equipped with a 6-way adjustable passenger seat. This condition may be caused by movement between the seat pan and the seat cross tube. A clip has been made available to eliminate the lateral seat movement (TSB: PI0686C, Dated: August 27, 2014)

2013—Inoperative voice recognition feature. Some 2013 Malibu and Cadillac ATS models equipped with a 2.0L turbo engine may complain of a rough-running engine with a "check engine light" on/low compression, and misfiring. This condition may be caused by a cracked piston. 2013-14—Unwanted trunk opening. Water leaking from the AC can be remedied by repositioning the AC evaporator and blower module drain hose. 2013-14—Sudden loud engine noise or engine seizure:

BEARING DAMAGED OR ENGINE WILL NOT ROTATE

SERVICE BULLETIN NO.: PI1171   DATE: FEBRUARY 6, 2014

2013-2014 Buick Regal; 2013-2014 Cadillac ATS; 2014 Cadillac CTS Sedan; 2014 Chevrolet Impala; 2013-2014 Chevrolet Malibu; Equipped with 2.0L Engine or 2.5L Engine.

CONDITION/CONCERN: Some customers may comment on a loud engine noise or that the engine is seized. In some cases, the engine will stop running and will not restart.

RECOMMENDATION/INSTRUCTIONS: This may be caused by one or more of the rod or main bearings being damaged or spun. The bearing material will enter the oil and be distributed throughout the engine. The damaged bearing material cannot be completely removed from the engine and may cause future damage. The only way to assure a complete repair is to replace the engine assembly. Replacing the crankshaft and bearings should not be attempted. Replace the engine assembly.

IMPALA/ALLURE, LACROSSE/LUCERNE ★★★★★/★★★★★/★★

Consumer Reports' rave review of the 2014 Impala proves that
GM can build high-quality vehicles — when it wants to.

RATING: *Impala:* Recommended (2015-16); Above Average (2012-13) The 2016 Impala and LaCrosse are carried over relatively unchanged, except for Impala's redesigned SS and a jet black version called the Midnight Edition. The reworked 2014-16 versions offer plenty of space, lots of family-friendly features and impressive safety and reliability ratings; Average (2006-11); Not Recommended (2000-05). For most of the past decade, the Impala was one of GM's least competitive products and was almost culled from the herd years ago. GM knew that keeping the Impala without major upgrades soiled the Chevrolet brand and gave Ford's Fusion and Chrysler's 200 a big sales boost. That's why GM poured millions into the car's 2014 redesign. It has upgraded the car in almost every way to make it leap past its sorry history with fine handling and even better styling. *Allure/LaCrosse:* Above Average (2011-16); Average (2005-10). There is very little "new" in the 2016 LaCrosse; its redesign is scheduled for 2017. *Lucerne*: Below Average (2006); Average (2007-11). LaCrosse and Lucerne are similarly equipped large front-drive sedans that have been hobbled by mediocre road performance and poor quality control. The discontinued Lucerne was the larger of the two cars and its debut 2006 model accumulated the most performance- and safety-related complaints. As the car steadily improved, GM dropped it in 2011. **Road performance:** The V6 provides smooth acceleration and works well with the 6-speed automatic transmission, though it could use more high-speed torque. Handling and ride are better than average, owing to recent suspension and steering refinements. A few years ago, the mid-sized LaCrosse was completely restyled and its 4-wheel independent suspension was retuned to improve the ride and handling. The available AWD system employs a limited-slip differential to send torque to whichever wheel has more traction for better control on slippery roads. **Strong points:** *Impala:* With its 2014 transformation, the Impala won the top spot among all sedans recommended by *Consumer Reports;* only the $90,000 Tesla S luxury electric car and the BMWi did better in their categories. And for 2016 it continues to get high marks for peppy acceleration, agile handling, and a comfy ride, a spacious cabin, and big trunk. Both models come with an array of standard features, plenty of rear seat room, and a refined interior. They also provide a comfortable ride, and have an easily accessed interior and rear seatbacks that fold flat, opening up cargo storage space. *LaCrosse:* Adequate rear legroom, and a front bench seat. LaCrosse also has a much better reliability record than the Impala. **Weak points:** Other shortcomings: Engine rear main seal leak; loud engine knocking, ticking noise; horn is difficult to activate; and water leaks into the trunk area, promoting mold growth and foul odours coming from the AC: "The car was now smelling so bad with mildew and mold even the service technician could hardly stand to sit in it at all. They have tried to change the underlay, and it still smells bad."

Prices and Specs

Prices (Negotiable): *Base Impala LS:* $28,795, *LT:* $31,995, *1LZ:* $36,795; *Base LaCrosse:* $36,095, *Leather AWD:* $42,045; *Premium 1:* $40,945; *Premium II:* $42,945 **Freight:** $2,000 **Powertrain (Front-Drive/AWD):** Engines: *Impala:* 2.5L (195 hp), 3.6L V6 (305 hp), 3.9L V6 (230 hp), 5.3L V8 (303 hp); *Hybrid:* 2.4L (182 hp); *LaCrosse:* 2.4L 4-cyl. (182 hp), 3.0L V6 (255 hp), 3.6L V6 (280 hp); Transmissions: *Impala:* 4-speed auto.; *LaCrosse:* 6-speed auto. **Dimensions/capacity:** Passengers: 2/3; Wheelbase: *Impala:* 110.5 in.; *LaCrosse:* 111.7 in.; *Impala:* H: 58.7/L: 200.4/W: 72.9 in.; *LaCrosse:* H: 58.9/L: 197/W: 73.1 in.; Headroom: F/R: 3.5/3.5 in.; Legroom F/R: 44/31 in.; Cargo volume: 11 cu. ft.; Fuel tank: 64L/regular/premium; Tow limit: NR; Load capacity: *Impala:* 905 lb., *LaCrosse:* 905 lb.; Turning circle: 38.8 ft.; Ground clearance: 6 in.; Weight: *Impala LS, LT:* 3,555 lb., *LTZ:* 3,649 lb.; *LaCrosse CX:* 3,948 lb.

Other opinions: "The 2015 Chevrolet Impala ranks #1 out of 10 affordable large cars … The car has a powerful V6 engine and a high-end cabin that can stand toe-to-toe with some luxury cars." – *U.S. News & World Report.* "Impala is competitive with cars that cost $20,000 more, including the Audi A6 and Lexus LS 460L, as well as the recently reviewed Acura RLX and Jaguar XF." – *Consumer Reports.* **Major redesign:** *Impala:* 2014; *LaCrosse:* 2010. **Highway/city fuel economy:** *Impala 3.5L:* 6.7/10.8 L/100 km. *3.9L:* 7.4/12 L/100 km. *LaCrosse 2.4L:* 6.5/10.8 L/100 km. *3.6L:* 7.3/12.2 L/100 km. *AWD 3.6L:* 7.7/12.7 L/100 km. **Best alternatives:** There's always the tried and proven Honda Accord, Mazda6, Hyundai Elantra, and Toyota Camry or Avalon. Those wanting a bit more performance should consider the BMW 3 Series. More room and better performance can be had by purchasing a Hyundai Tucson or a Honda CR-V.

SAFETY: Child safety seat setup: "Acceptable." Crashworthiness: NHTSA: Gave the 2015 Impala and LaCrosse a five-star overall crashworthiness, except for four stars for rollover resistance. 2012-13 versions got four-star scores across the board. However, year 2000-11 models posted impressive four- and five-star rankings. IIHS judged overall crash protection for the 2010-15 versions as "Good" however, roof strength and rear crash protection (head restraints) were judged to be only "Acceptable." 2006-09 scores varied from "Acceptable" to "Good," while 2006-08 models were rated "Marginal" for rear crashworthiness. 2005-2001 Impalas were "Good" for front protection, but rated "Poor" in rear crash tests. The 2010-15 LaCrosse/Allure has similar scores as the Impala. During its six years on the market, the Lucerne earned a "Good" overall score in the IIHS front impact tests, and an "Acceptable" score side impact crash protection. Surprisingly, for such a large car, the IIHS found that 2006-08 model year Lucernes had the highest fatality rate in the large 4-door car class. **Owner-reported safety-related failures:** Chronic stalling; car can be left in Park, and roll away; wheel lug nut studs snap off; and large tires and wheels on the redesigned Impala (2014) may provoke blowouts:

I can deal with the poor visibility headlamps, the front camera that keeps flagging "service front camera" and camera false alarms but the huge 19 inch wheels and tires with hardly any sidewall to absorb rough roads are a recipe for disaster and dangerous. I live in the northeast and it is loaded with potholes. When I hit one yesterday the tire blew causing a very dangerous situation.

Other failures: Sudden unintended acceleration:

My 2011 Lucerne accelerated unintentionally without warning. As a result, the contact crashed the vehicle into a wall. The air bags failed to deploy. The contact sustained chest injuries that required medical attention. In addition, the driver sustained neck and back injuries that required medical attention.

Airbags frequently fail to deploy in a collision; loss of brakes; loss of steering; inadequate headlight illumination; and visibility is obstructed by the tall, wide rear-seat head restraints. Says one owner of a 2012 LaCrosse:

The "Blind Spots" on this vehicle are outrageous. The front seat head restraints are so big it is not possible to look out the driver's side rear window when backing up. I would remove the headrests to make the car safer for others (the ones you can't see), but they cannot be removed. The deck lid is so high that the rear-view mirror shows only one half of the outside – the rest of the mirror shows the interior of the car. The pillar between the rear side windows and the back window is so wide this also obscures the view when backing up.

Also, be wary of the car's collision warning device giving out false alerts, possibly causing an accident, as this driver told NHTSA:

About 1/2 dozen occasions the vehicle's early detection system has engaged without any vehicles in front. These occurrences seem to be on days when it is raining and there are reflections off the road, or very sunny days (again causing reflections). The flashing light, loud alarm, and interruption with regular audio is very jarring (scary). On one occasion I applied my brakes very hard because of the alarm (but there was no car in front) – this almost caused the car behind to hit me.

ALERT! Test drive both cars at night to see if the narrow headlight beams are acceptable. One driver's family reported he was run over by his 2014 LaCrosse parked in the driveway:

Car was parked on driveway, driver door was open, driver leaned into car and shut off car engine with push button ignition switch, vehicle immediately rolled back, open door knocked driver down, and he was run over and died at hospital. Bystander tried to assist and was knocked down by open door and dragged a short distance by the door.

Impala: Check out the steering, as well. Many owners complain of it binding as if it were stuck in a notch.

Impala/Allure, LaCrosse/Lucerne Profile

	2006	2007	2008	2009	2010	2011	2012	2013	2014
Used Values ($)									
Impala LS	5,000	6,000	7,000	8,000	9,000	11,500	13,500	16,500	21,00
LT	6,000	6,500	7,500	8,500	9,500	12,000	14,500	17,500	24,000
LTZ	6,500	7,500	8,500	10,500	13,500	14,000	17,500	21,0 00	29,000
SS	6,500	6,000	7,000	9,000	—	—	—	—	—
Allure/LaCrosse	6,000	7,000	8,000	10,000	11,500	15,500	19,500	23,500	27,500
AWD	—	—	—	—	13,500	17,000	23,000	28,500	31,500
Lucerne	6,000	7,000	8,500	10,500	12,000	15,500	—	—	—
Super	—	9,500	12,000	14,000	16,000	22,500	—	—	—
Reliability	★	★	★	★	★	★	☆	☆	☆
Repairs ($$$)	2	2	2	2	1	1	2	2	2
Electrical	1	1	1	1	1	2	2	2	2
Engine (base)	2	2	2	2	2	3	3	3	3
Fit/Finish	1	1	1	1	1	2	3	3	3
Infotainment	—	—	—	—	—	3	3	3	3
Transmission (auto.)	1	1	1	1	1	1	2	2	3

SECRET WARRANTIES, INTERNAL BULLETINS: All model years: General Motors says it's "normal" for your automatic transmission to "clunk" when changing gears. No wonder GM went bankrupt with this attitude:

INFORMATION ON 2-3 UPSHIFT OR 3-2 DOWNSHIFT CLUNK NOISE

SERVICE BULLETIN NO: 01-07-30-042H   DATE: JAN 14, 2014

2014 and Prior GM Passenger Cars and Light Duty Trucks Equipped with 4L60-E, 4L65-E or 4L70-E Automatic Transmission (RPOs M30, M32, M70)

IMPORTANT: Some vehicles may exhibit a clunk noise that can be heard on a 2-3 upshift or a 3-2 downshift. During a 2-3 upshift, the 2-4 band is released and the 3-4 clutch is applied. The timing of this shift can cause a momentary torque reversal of the output shaft that results in a clunk noise. This same torque reversal can also occur on a 3-2 downshift when the 3-4 clutch is released and the 2-4 band applied. This condition may be more pronounced on a 4-wheel drive vehicle due to the additional tolerances in the transfer case.

    This is a normal condition. No repairs should be attempted.

    This is NOT a normal condition. GM has been sending out this bulletin for decades, rather than fix these transmissions. Owners with this problem can ask small claims court to refund part of the price they paid for their vehicle under the *quanti minoris* doctrine. ("I would have paid this much less (your claim amount) if I knew I'd be getting less performance.").

2005-08—Countermeasures for harsh shifting and slipping. Repair for a steering column clunk heard when turning. 2005-09—Automatic transmission slips in gear; left-side axle seal leaks. Wind noise diagnostic tips. Airbag warning light comes on intermittently. 2005-11—Reduced power, as MIL alert lights up (see bulletin). 2006-09—Airbag warning light stays lit. 2007-09—Steering gear mount to frame may make a pop, creak, or click noise. 2008—Power steering leak may require the replacement of the steering gear cylinder line. 2008-09—Poor AC performance. Inaccurate fuel gauge readings. V8 engine oil leak from the rear cover assembly area. 2009—V8 engine valve tick noise remedy (replace the valve lifters). *Impala:* 2006-08—GM bulletin #08-06-04-039, published Aug. 7, 2008, says that if the car cranks but won't start, the likely culprit is a blown fuel pump fuse. Coolant leaks that can cause engine overheating usually require that the engine head gasket be replaced. Again, this is a warranty item that is often covered up to 7 years/160,000 km. under "goodwill" warranty extensions. 2006-09—Rear suspension creak, clunk, pop noise. Power-steering noise reduction measures. 2007—Troubleshooting wind/road noise. 2007-08—AC won't maintain desired temperature. Ignition key cannot be removed. No shift out of Park. Undercar noises. Rear speaker rattling. 2008—Inaccurate fuel gauge readings. 2011—Automatic transmission clunks when shifted. Power-steering leakage. Airbag warning light comes on intermittently. 2012-13—Some owners may comment on an engine oil leak under their vehicle. Upon inspection, the service technician may observe an engine oil leak between the engine and transmission mounting surfaces. This may be caused by the crankshaft #3 thrust bearing wing separating from the thrust bearing, resulting in excessive crankshaft end play and damaging the crankshaft rear oil seal and housing. Inasmuch as this is a manufacturing defect, GM and the dealer should pay the repair bill. Provincial consumer laws say vehicles should be "reasonably" durable. 2014—Some 2014 Impala or 2010-14 LaCrosse models with 3.0L and 3.6L V6 engines produce a rubber squeak type noise when the steering wheel is turned. This may be caused by the intermediate shaft seal rubbing on the rotating intermediate steering shaft. The EPS wire harness bracket may also be contacting the steering column seal. This repair may take two hours and is a warrantable item. Another free repair involves water leaking into the trunk, here's the "secret" warranty that will cover the repair cost:

CUSTOMER SATISFACTION PROGRAM – TAIL LAMP GASKET SEAL

SERVICE BULLETIN NO.: 14047　　　　　　　　　　　　　　　　　　DATE: MAY 8, 2014

TAIL LAMP GASKET SEAL

2014 Chevrolet Impala

**********THIS PROGRAM IS IN EFFECT UNTIL MAY 31, 2016.**********

CONDITION: With heat and age, the tail lamp gasket on certain 2014 model year Chevrolet Impala vehicles may lose the ability to seal. This could allow water to leak into the trunk area.

CORRECTION: Dealers are to replace the tail lamp gaskets and inspect the trunk for water damage or odor.

It goes without saying that the dealer and GM are also rersponsible for repairing the damage and getting rid of any noxious odours.

Lucerne: 2006-08—Inoperative Park Assist feature. Frayed headliner (front edge). 2006-09—Airbag warning light stays lit (replace the right front seat belt buckle). Vehicle pulls to the right when accelerating. Bump, clunk on slow speed turns. Front door won't open or unlock. Inoperative inside and outside rear door handles. Hard to view instrument panel cluster in sunlight. Hard starts, no-starts (repair and re-route transmission wiring harnesses). 2006-11—Reduced power as MIL alert lights up. 2007-10—Low-speed automatic transmission moan or whine noise. 2009—Parking Assist gives erratic visual and audio warnings. 2009-10—Engine coolant leaks (replace coolant crossover pipe gaskets). Campaign and TSB #10142, dated May 12, 2010, provides for the re-securing of the electronic brake control module at no charge to the vehicle owner. Courtesy transportation will also be provided. This is not a recall. Oil leak at the front of the engine (replace the front cover seal). 2009-11—Procedures outlined to reduce front brake rotor noise and pulsation.

CAMARO ★★★★

RATING: Above Average, bordering on Recommended, if first year production glitches are minor and quickly corrected (2016). This year's Camaro has been completely redesigned to provide a faster, more responsive driving experience. It offers an all-new vehicle platform borrowed from Cadillac's ATS and XTS, as well as a simpler and more efficient powertrain lineup. Curb weight has been trimmed by more than 300 pounds. Buyers have three engine choices: A 2.0L 275 hp turbocharged in-line 4-cylinder; an optional 3.6L 335 hp V6; and a high-performance 6.2L 455 hp V8. All three engines can be coupled to either a 6-speed manual or 8-speed automatic transmission. **Road performance:** 2016 model feels much lighter, more nimble and more secure than earlier versions; the harder you drive, the better it performs. It brakes more powerfully, dives into corners without losing control, and accelerates faster than ever before. **Strong points:** The revamped interior has more of an upscale, high-tech look and feel with two 8-inch screens for instrumentation readouts, controls, and infotainment. Audio and climate controls consist of user-friendly buttons and dials. Outward visibility – a weakness in the current Camaro – has improved slightly, thanks, to a lower dash and improved side mirrors. Ride comfort and handling are enhanced with the car's new, multi-link MacPherson strut front suspension and quick-ratio electric power steering. These two features produce a more precise feeling of control and additional road "feedback." The new 5-link independent rear suspension also makes for better control and reduces acceleration "squat." All model years have shown impressive V6 and V8 acceleration with reasonable fuel economy and competent steering/handling. Interior trim looks and feels to be of good quality, and the seats provide sufficient lateral support and are easy to adjust. Very few serious reliability complaints. **Weak points:** (2016) Expect long delivery delays and no-haggle prices. The interior feels tighter than last year's version. (2010-15) No headroom; if you are 6'2" or taller, your head will be constantly brushing up against the headliner; rear seating is a "knees-to-chin" affair; not much cargo room; small trunk and trunk opening. Owners report and *Consumer Reports* confirms that fit and finish glitches are everywhere; exterior styling seems to have been slapped together by a committee; the rear, especially, is ugly and obstructs rear visibility; plus, the car is set too high to look "sporty." Fuel sloshes in the fuel tank.

Prices and Specs (2015)

Prices (Firm): *1LS man.:* $29,095, *2LS auto.:* $30,295, *1LT man.:* $30,110, *2LT man.:* $35,495, *1SS:* $39,390, *2SS:* $44,655, *1LT Conv.:* $37,330, *2LT Conv.:* $41,475, *1SS man.:* $45,850, *2SS auto.:* $43,220, *1SS Conv.:* $44,820, *2SS Conv.:* $50,525, *ZL1:* $65,650 **Freight:** $2,000 **Powertrain (Rear-drive):** Engines: 3.6L V6 (323 hp), 6.2L V8 (400-426 hp), 6.2L supercharged V8 (580 hp); Transmissions: 6-speed man., 6-speed auto. **Dimensions/capacity:** Passengers: 2/2; Wheelbase: 112.3 in.; H: 54.2/L: 190.4/W: 75.5 in.; Headroom F/R: 3.5/0 in.; Legroom F/R: 40/22 in.; Cargo volume: 11. cu. ft.; Fuel tank: 71.9L/regular, 64L/ premium; Tow limit:1,000 lb.; Load capacity: 730 lb.; Turning circle: 37.7 ft.; Weight: 3,769-3,849 lb.

Other opinions: "The 2016 Camaro still makes you feel like you're sitting in a bunker, looking out of a gun slit." – *Aaron Bragman, cars.com.* Major redesign: 1993, 2010 and 2016. Highway/city fuel economy: *3.6L V6:* 7.1/12.4 L/100 km. *Auto.:* 6.8/11.4 L/100 km. *SS man. and 6.2L V8:* 8.2/13.2 L/100 km. *Auto.:* 8/13.3 L/100 km. Best alternatives: Camaros are "hot," and last year's sales beat the equally popular Ford Mustang by a small margin. Smart buyers will wait on the more reasonably priced, leftover models available in the spring of 2016. The Hyundai Genesis Coupe, Mustang, and Mazda Miata are good alternative models. When comparing the Mustang and Camaro for overall reliability, the Camaro has a slight edge due to the 'Stang's infotainment, powertrain, and fit and finish deficiencies. 2002 and earlier Camaros are cheap project cars that sell for $4,000 to $5,000, depending upon whether you pick up a base, no frills model or a V8-equipped convertible (prices can be confirmed on the Internet at VMR Canadian Used Car Prices). Another Camaro advantage over older Mustangs is the less likelihood of finding rust rot in the rocker (door) panels and trunk.

SAFETY: Child safety seat setup: Not tested. Crashworthiness: NHTSA: Awarded the 2012-15 models its top five-star rating for frontal, side, and rollover crashworthiness. Earlier models going back to 1991 are rated mostly four and five stars in overall crash protection. IIHS hasn't crash-tested the Camaro. Owner-reported safety-related failures: Passenger-side airbag doesn't recognize the seat is occupied; sudden unintended acceleration; and car shuts down on the highway; airbags failed to deploy. 2016 brakes feel less squishy and fade less than previous years' models.

ALERT! Convertible tops on 2011-15 Camaros are known for water leaks. Check for this during your test drive. A class action was authorized in March 2015 in Louisiana under *Cain v. General Motors LLC* (Civil Action #14-1077). The lawsuit alleges that the plaintiff purchased a 2011 Chevrolet Camaro Convertible on April 14, 2011, and had the vehicle in the repair shop on 12 separate occasions for a cumulative total of 125 days due to the water leaks in the Camaro because of a defective convertible top design. 2010 through 2015 models are also noted for suddenly stalling out on the highway:

> I was driving my 2014 camaro at approximately 70 mph. I slowed to get off the exit and as I did the engine died and the power steering and brakes were inoperative. Luckily I didn't hit anyone. The engine failed again later in the same evening and twice 2 days later.

Camaro Profile

	2010	2011	2012	2013	2014
Used Values ($)					
Camaro LS	12,000	14,500	18,000	21,500	23,000
LT	14,000	16,500	19,500	22,500	24,000
SS	17,500	22,000	25,000	30,000	34,000
Convertible LT	—	20,000	23,500	27,500	31,000
Convertible SS	18,500	25,000	28,000	30,500	40,500
Reliability	☆	☆	☆	☆	☆
Repairs ($$$)	💰	💰	💰	💰	💰
Electrical	★	★	★	★	★
Engine (base)	★	★	★	★	★
Fit/Finish	★	★	★	★	★
Infotainment	—	★	★	★	☆
Transmission (auto.)	★	★	★	★	☆

SECRET WARRANTIES, INTERNAL BULLETINS: 2008-14—Troubleshooting tips for front and rear windows that bind, fit poorly, are misaligned, rattle or squeak, move slowly or don't move at all. Tips on silencing a chatter noise from the rear of the vehicle that occurs when making low speed turns. 2009-14—Some vehicles may not crank or start, caused by excessive leakage from cylinder past exhaust or exhaust intake valve, low static compression, sensor is disconnected, or while cranking, valve train fails to move. 2011—Automatic transmission makes a clunk sound when shifted. Recalibration of the electronic brake control module to improve cold weather braking performance. Likely causes of power-steering fluid leaks; lower rear window seal loose or missing. Side window glass won't clear moulding. Door light bar inoperative or loses intensity. Noisy six-way power front seats. Rear bumper facia contacting body/paint peeling. Door and quarter panel paint appearance. Convertible top spots, indentation/damage. 2011-12—Convertible top headliner tears near the support brackets; excessive wind intrusion. 2012—The correction for an airbag warning light that stays on for no reason. Vehicle may not crank or start due to excessive leakage from cylinder past exhaust or intake valve, low static compression, or a disconnected sensor. 2012-14—When trying to shift into First or Second gear, the manual transmission may bind and a clunk/grind/rattle noise may be heard. 2013-15—GMC/Cadillac/Chevrolet: After shifting into Park, the vehicle rolls when brake pedal is released (TSB: #380746, dated: Nov. 1, 2014). 2014-15—When braking or accelerating, a clunking or a popping sound noise can be heard from the rear of the vehicle. The upper control arm/ball joint may be loose.

CORVETTE ★★★

Super-fast – DEPRECIATION. A 2010 Z06 that sold for $95,620 is now barely worth $40,000.

RATING: Average (2006-16); a brawny, bulky sport coupe that's slowly evolving into a more refined machine since its 2014 redesign targeting younger, high-performance enthusiasts. Known as an "old man's toy," studies cited by Wikipedia say that about 46% of Corvette buyers in 2012 were 55 or older, compared with 22% of Audi R8 and 30% of Porsche 911 customers. For 2016, the Corvette is carried over without any significant changes. Buyers get a new flat-bottomed steering wheel, new two-tone GT seats in either red or gray, and when the 3LT Jet Black interior is chosen, there's a choice of red or yellow stitching. Stingrays now offer the Magnetic Ride Control suspension setup without getting the entire Z51 handling package. The Corvette does deliver high-performance thrills – along with an automatic transmission that tends to overheat, suspension hop, and numb steering. Overall, get the quieter and less temperamental base Corvette; it delivers the same cachet for a lot less money. **Road performance:** A powerful and smooth powertrain that responds quickly to the throttle; the 8-speed gearbox performs well in all gear ranges and makes shifting smooth, with short throws and easy entry into all gears. Easy handling; enhanced side-slip angle control helps to prevent skidding and provides better traction control. No oversteer (in fact, steering is a little vague), wheel spinning, breakaway rear ends, or nasty surprises, thanks partly to standard electronic stability control. Better-than-average braking, though some drivers have reported excessive brake fade after successive stops; the ABS-vented disc brakes are easy to modulate, and they're fade-free. **Strong points:** The car has a relatively roomy interior, a user-friendly cabin, easily accessed instruments and controls, and lots of convenience features. Comfortable and supportive leather bucket seats are standard along with a nine-speaker Bose audio system, a rear-view camera, satellite radio, and GM's much-lauded MyLink infotainment system. Security is secured with a key-controlled lockout feature that discourages joy riding by cutting engine power in half. All Corvettes are also equipped with an impressively effective PassKey theft-deterrent system that uses a resistor pellet in the ignition to disable the starter and fuel system when the key code doesn't match the ignition lock. Cars equipped with manual transmissions get a Performance Traction Management system that modulates the engine's torque output for fast starts. This feature also manages engine power when the driver floors the accelerator when coming out of a corner. **Weak points:** Stunning depreciation. Quality control continues to be subpar, and safety-related powertrain, suspension, and body deficiencies are common. NHTSA recorded this 2015 Corvette owner's lament, "Water leaking into rear cargo hold area. Accumulating and not draining out. Don't know why." The car is so low that its front air dam scrapes over the smallest rise in the road. Expect lots of visits to the body shop. Sophisticated electronic suspension and powertrain components have a low tolerance for real-world conditions. Independent automobile journalists have been particularly critical of the C7's Active Fuel Management System and C6 Z06's valve guide failures:

> Due to the lack of effective vibration suppression measures that are typically used in four-cylinder engines, such as a balance shaft, the AFM literally wreaks havoc on the engine, under best scenario obliterating the under designed hydraulic serpentine belt tensioner and in more drastic situations, shuttering the thrust bearing and destroying the crankshaft and ultimately the entire engine.
>
> On top of it, the excessive oil consumption directly related to AFM and specifically, oil getting pushed by the rings on the deactivated cylinders is becoming the norm as well, forcing owners to check the oil frequently.
>
> Add to it the ill thought out direct injection system and flawed PCV system and the ownership of the Stingray can easily turn into a big nightmare, making old Lancias and Fiats look like a Honda Accord.
>
> *— corvettec7fiasco.blogspot.com/*

. . .

> The LS7 that powers the mighty, high-performance, super-cool C6 Z06 (see what I did there?) is subject to valve guide failure. GM claims that the problem affects a small percentage of LS7s built before Feb 2011, when a new inspection procedure "100% eliminated" the failure. The problem is that this might not be true, with some mechanics reporting heavy valve guide wear on all LS7 engines regardless of age. There's even a suggestion that the faulty head design continues into the Camaro Z/28, which would be a shame.
>
> *— www.thetruthaboutcars.com/2014/09/fixed-abode-holding-corvette-standard*

Owners also complain that the airbag warning light comes on randomly, the Active Handling and traction control systems malfunction, windows and doorlocks operate erratically, convertible top problems, and an overheating centre console:

> Lift up a suitcase or put arm on console storage area and you would burn your arm or hand. Heat inside storage area exceeded est. of 130 deg and burned spots in cell phone screen and computer in suitcase melted hard drive and ruined computer.

Other opinions: "The 2015 Chevrolet Corvette ranks #2 out of 16 luxury sports cars. Drivers are blown away by its incredible acceleration, agile handling and ride comfort." – *U.S. News & World Report.* "In spite of the marketing claims, the paint on the newest cars, along with fit and finish of the body, along with a variety of mechanical and electrical problems plus an eye opening number of engine and transmission failures rendered the newest Corvette a certifiable piece of shit and overall failure." – *corvettec7fiasco.blogspot.com/.* **Major redesign:** 1997, 2003, 2008, and 2014 (Stingray). The seventh generation Stingray is faster, fuel-efficient, more powerful, more refined, and offers a much better interior (smaller steering wheel and better seats) than previous model years. The 6.2L V8 coupled to a 7-speed manual transmission produces 455 hp (with cylinder deactivation). **Highway/city fuel economy:** *6.2L man.:* 7.7/12.9 L/100 km. *Auto.:* 8.1/14.3 L/100 km. *7.0L man.:* 8.2/14.2 L/100 km. *Auto.:* 8.2/14.2 L/100 km. *ZR1 man.:* 10.2/15.5 L/100 km. **Best alternatives:** Other sporty models worth considering are the Porsche 911 or Boxster. The Nissan 370Z looks good on paper, but its quality problems carried over year after year make it a risky buy.

SAFETY: **Child safety seat setup:** Untested. **Crashworthiness:** Untested. **Owner-reported safety-related failures:** Worried about low-flying drones? Low-flying Corvette roofs may be a greater safety hazard. According to the December 31, 2009, *New York Times,*

General Motors recalled 22,000 Corvettes [2005-07 Corvettes and 2006-07 Z06], because the roof might fly off. What do you think kicked the company into action? Complaints on the National Highway Traffic Safety Administration website from owners? Was it the safety agency itself, worried about the complaints? Concerns raised by the Federal Aviation Administration? Nope. it was the Japanese Ministry of Land Infrastructure and Transport, unhappy about the problem on imported Corvettes.

Vehicle rolls away when parked on an incline; Goodyear Eagle F1 tires hydroplane on wet roadways; leaking fuel pump; both headlights suddenly shut off and limited rearward visibility. Complaints posted at *safercar.gov* point out that the suspension is unstable when passing over uneven roads and the wheels hop when turning:

There are already a few reports on the skipping and hopping at low speeds when the wheels are locked all the way left or right while turning. I experienced this on delievery and have owned the car for 9 months. Since the cold weather has arrived the issue has gotten even more severe, like the front end is going to fall off. Chevrolet will not admit to this problem/issue but it is a generally know issue related to the "Ackerman" effect. *Motor Trend* identified it and resorted to saying the 2014 Corvette is no parking lot car.

. . .

Chevy is selling 2015 Z-51 Corvettes with summer only run-flat tires. Michelin indicates that these tires severely lose traction whenever temperatures fall below 40 degrees F. They are also not appropriate for use in wet or snowy conditions. Michelin or any other tire manufacturer does not make an all-season tire that is a run-flat.

– safercar.gov

ALERT! Some optional features aren't worth the extra money. For example, the Performance Data Recorder, which you can use to record driving videos and collect performance data isn't as useful as some smart phone apps and raises some serious privacy concerns. Also, the Competition Sport bucket seats are more about cachet than support and comfort. Beware of classic car dealers who tout the Corvette as an investment "vehicle." Think about this – a 2010 Corvette ZR1 that sold new for $128,515 is now worth barely $60,000. And, if you look at the entire Corvette lineup since 2010, you will see an even worse return on investment. In fact, almost all American, Asian, and European luxury sports cars lose more than half their value after five years. Remember, depreciation is a car's biggest expense. The more you pay up front, the more you lose down the road.

Corvette Profile

Used Values ($)	2006	2007	2008	2009	2010	2011	2012	2013	2014
Coupe	14,000	17,500	20,000	25,000	29,000	33,000	39,000	44,000	50,000
Convertible LT	18,000	22,000	26,000	30,000	35,000	41,000	46,000	53,000	60,000
Z06	23,000	27,000	31,000	36,000	41,000	48,000	56,000	70,000	—
ZR1	—	—	—	4,000	59,000	70,000	80,000	90,000	—
Reliability	★1	★1	★1	☆2	☆2	☆2	☆2	☆3	☆3
Repairs ($$$)	3	3	3	3	3	3	2	2	2
Electrical	☆2	☆2	☆2	☆2	☆2	☆2	☆3	☆3	☆3
Engine (base)	☆2	☆2	☆2	☆2	☆2	☆2	☆2	☆2	☆2
Fit/Finish	☆2	☆2	☆2	☆3	☆3	☆3	☆3	☆3	☆3
Infotainment	—	—	—	—	—	☆2	☆3	☆3	☆3
Transmission (auto.)	★1	★1	★1	★1	★1	★1	★1	★1	☆2

SECRET WARRANTIES, INTERNAL BULLETINS: 1997-2013—Front or rear composite springs may crack or break for no apparent reason. 2005-12—Be wary that top doesn't lift off while driving. Snap, pop, creak, or rattle noise from lift-off roof panel while driving (verify condition and perform appropriate repairs). 2005-13—Brake rotor may have surface cracks. Folding top contacts stowage compartment lid (tonneau) and/or tonneau contacts rear window during top operation (verify condition and perform appropriate adjustments). 2006-14—TSB #09-04-20-001D, dated Nov. 8, 2011 addresses a chatter noise during low speed tight turn conditions (i.e. parking lot, driveway, etc.) primarily during cooler ambient temperatures. The condition can be experienced in all directions: Right, left, forward, reverse. For the 2011-2013 model years, the Goodyear F1 tire, available on Corvette Grand Sports and Z06 models, has a significant tread design change. This new design is more susceptible to tire chatter or hop than the previous design. 2006-15—GM service bulletin #PIP4112P says "lag and lurch" acceleration is "normal." 2008-13—When the engine is warm, the underhood bussed electrical center (UBEC) housing will expand, causing the headlamp low-beam relay control circuit routed wire to bend slightly. After the wire is repeatedly bent, it can fracture and separate. When this occurs, the low-beam headlamps will not illuminate. Dealers are to install a jumper wire. 2008-13—Window malfunctions explained. 2009-14—Some vehicles may not crank or start, caused by excessive leakage from cylinder past exhaust or exhaust intake valve, low static compression, sensor is disconnected, or while cranking, valve train fails to move. 2011—Wheel hop and differential chatter, under-hood rattle, engine tapping noise, and automatic transmission clunks. Power-steering and shock absorber fluid leakage. Airbag warning light comes on intermittently. Cracks in transparent removable roof panel. Convertible headliner frayed at outer edges. Troubleshooting tips for eliminating various noises from lift-off roof while driving. 2012-13—Campaign allows for the free replacement of the air inlet grille panel. 2012-14—GM bulletin confirms poor shifting into First or Second gear; clutch pedal clunk, grind, or rattle.

CONVERTIBLE TOP COVER SEPARATION

BULLETIN NO.: 08312A   DATE: JULY 1, 2010

CUSTOMER SATISFACTION, CONVERTIBLE ROOF COVER SEPARATION – INSTALL NEW RETAINER BRACKET

2008-09 Chevrolet Corvette With Manual or Power Roof Convertible

CONDITION: Certain 2008 and 2009 model year Chevrolet Corvette manual or power roof convertible vehicles may have a condition in which the fabric roof cover may begin to separate from its retainer bracket near the top edge of the windshield. When the vehicle reaches speeds of approximately 100 mph (160 km/h) or greater, the roof cover could begin to pull away from the retainer bracket and, depending on the speed of the vehicle and duration at that speed, could tear to the rear glass. If this were to occur, the headliner would remain intact and the roof cover would not separate from the vehicle.

CORRECTION: Dealers are to install a new design retainer bracket.

2013—Low engine oil pressure, no oil pressure, and/or engine noise could be the result of a sticking oil pump pressure relief valve. 2013-15—When gear is in Park, it may fail to hold the vehicle when the brake is released. 2014—An engine that ticks or runs hot, may have a faulty head gasket. Vehicle may have a cooler outlet connector pipe on the auxiliary transmission cooler that may not be properly sealed to its mating connection. The improper seal may cause transmission oil to leak or, under certain conditions, the connector pipe to disconnect from the mating connection. The disconnection of the connector pipe may result in a stall out, and leaking transmission oil could cause smoldering if it contacts the heated intake exhaust pipes or mufflers. GM bulletin says manual transmission may not shift from Sixth to Seventh gear. Another TSB says Performance Traction Management feature may fail. 2014-15—If car cranks, but won't start, GM says the camshaft position actuator solenoid valve may need to be replaced (TSB #PIP5130E). Sierras, Silverados, Suburbans, and Yukons are also affected (see Silverado section).

CADILLAC CTS ★★★

RATING: Average (2008-16); Below Average (2004-2007). The Cadillac CTS is one rung up from today's entry-level Cadillac ATS. It's the successor of GM's Catera, a poor-quality, mid-size, entry-level luxury sedan imported from Germany and noted for serious powertrain and reliability problems and mediocre highway performance. CTS continues that tradition with a wimpy and problematic base powertrain. Unfortunately, as Cadillac reinvents itself in a futile attempt to lure well-to-do younger buyers, its cars are ridiculously over-priced, more complex, and less distinctive. Road performance: Competent and secure handling; a pleasant ride; manually tuned suspension settings for all tastes; and available AWD. The 3.6L V6 is smooth and adequate, if not pushed. The 2016 CTS has a new 3.6L V6 LGX with Active Fuel Management and automatic start/stop – a feature shared with the turbocharged 2.0L I4 LTG engine. There's also an 8-speed automatic transmission that replaces the 6-speed and an external engine oil cooler. *CTS-V:* The 2016 CTS-V presents a more powerful supercharged V8, making it essentially a Corvette Z06 clone driving 640 horses. It launches to a top speed of 200 mph and reaches 60 mph in 3.7 seconds. The compact four-lobe supercharger works with GM's much-criticized Active Fuel Management system (see the Corvette critique) to deliver both high-performance thrills and promised low fuel and repair bills. Strong points: Roomier cabin than with other cars in this class (the Sport Wagon's generous cargo space is especially noteworthy); and offers a tasteful, well-appointed interior loaded with high-tech gadgetry, like OnStar with 4G LTE data connectivity. CUE infotainment has been upgraded on 2016 models. Weak points: Excessive oil burning, prematurely-worn timing chains and/or camshafts on earlier models. Shoppers should be especially wary of 2008 and 2009 models. The brake system and rear differential are also prone to early wearout. Be wary of rough shifting or transmission slippage. Power seats and the navigation and stereo are also problematic. Interior squeaks and rattles, especially from the rear parcel shelf, and weather stripping that creates wind noise on coupe models. This Cadillac is not as agile as its rivals. Owners complain of fit and finish defects and frequent electronic module malfunctions. Rear-seat access requires some acrobatics due to the low rear roofline, and the rear seatback could use additional bolstering. Also, the small trunk's narrow opening adds to the difficulty of loading bulky items. *CTS-V:* The revamped 2016 CTS-V is only available as a coupe; the sedan and wagon are gone. Optional Recaro seats may be too stiff for some; and the interior is outdated. Privacy advocates are sure to rise up against GM's Performance Data Recorder gadget that offers up to 30 channels of performance data and real-time audio and video. Cadillac boasts that the front-view camera will capture each curve and straightaway and, when parked, will let you watch and analyze your driving performance on the Cadillac CUE screen. The footage can be saved on an SD card to share later at your DUI trial.

Prices and Specs

Prices (Very Negotiable): *CTS 2.0L:* $48,730, *CTS 2.0L AWD:* $51,355, *CTS 3.6L LuxuryL:* $56,255, *AWD:* $58,275, *3.6L Performance AWD:* $56,255 *3.6L Performance AWD:* $62,490 **Freight:** $2,150 **Powertrain (Rear-drive/AWD):** Engines: 2.0L Turbo (272 hp), 3.6L V6 (220 hp), 3.6L V6 (304 hp), 6.2L Supercharged V8 (640 hp); Transmissions: 6-speed man., 8-speed auto. **Dimensions/capacity:** *Base CTS:* Passengers: 2/3; Wheelbase: 115 in.; H: 57/L: 196/W: 72 in.; Headroom F/R: 3/1.5 in.; Legroom F/R: 44/28.5 in.; Cargo volume: 14 cu. ft.; Fuel tank: 70L/premium; Tow limit: 1,000 lb.; Load capacity: 890 lb.; Turning circle: 38 ft.; Ground clearance: 5 in.; Weight: 3,915, *CTS-V:* 4,145 lb.

Other opinions: "The 2015 Cadillac CTS ranks #1 out of 18 upscale mid-size cars. Automotive journalists write that CUE's touch screen and center console buttons react slowly to user inputs, which can make the system frustrating to use, especially while driving." – *U.S. News & World Report.* "[GM] compared the V's horsepower, torque, and power-to-weight ratio to those of the BMW M5 and Mercedes-Benz E63 AMG. Needless to say, the Cadillac cleans house." – *Car and Driver.* **Major redesign:** 1997, 2003, 2008, 2014, and 2016. **Highway/city fuel economy (2015):** *3.0L:* 7.2/11.23 L/100 km. *3.6L:* 6.9/11.4 L/100 km. *3.6L AWD:* 7.9/13 L/100 km. *CTS-V man.:* 10.5/14.9 L/100 km. *CTS-V auto.:* 11/17.5 L/100 km. **Best alternative:** Acura TL SH-AWD, BMW 3 Series, Hyundai Genesis, and Infiniti G37.

SAFETY: Child safety seat setup: Untested. **Crashworthiness:** NHTSA: Gives the CTS four and five stars in crash tests going back to 2003. IIHS awarded its top rating of "Good" for frontal offset, side, roof, and rear (head-restraint) crashworthiness. **Owner-reported safety-related failures:** Sudden stalling when the car is underway.

ALERT! You may want to take a pass on the panoramic sunroof in view of reports that sunroofs often crack or implode for no apparent reason. Also, think carefully about whether you want AWD. That option will cost you about $4,500 more.

Cadillac CTS Profile

	2006	2007	2008	2009	2010	2011	2012	2013	2014
Used Values ($)									
Coupe	—	—	—	—	—	21,000	27,000	30,500	36,500
Sedan	6,500	8,000	9,500	11,000	14,000	18,000	23,500	32,500	42,500
Wagon	—	—	—	—	15,500	20,500	25,000	29,500	36,000
CTS-V	10,500	14,500	—	21,500	27,000	35,500	44,500	53,000	61,500
Reliability	✪	✪	✪	✪	✪	✪	✪	✪	✪
Repairs ($$$)	💰3	💰3	💰2	💰2	💰2	💰2	💰2	💰2	💰2
Electrical	★	★	✪	✪	✪	✪	✪	✪	✪
Engine (base)	★	★	★	★	★	★	★	✪	✪
Fit/Finish	★	★	★	★	★	✪	✪	✪	✪
Infotainment	—	—	—	—	—	✪	✪	✪	✪
Transmission (auto.)	★	★	★	★	★	★	★	★	✪

SECRET WARRANTIES, INTERNAL BULLETINS: All models/years: Reverse servo cover seal leak. Paint delamination, peeling, or fading. *CTS:* 2003-15—Drivetrain chatter or rear axle clunk (TSB #10-04-20-001F); Replace the rear differential fluid. 2005-11—Loss of engine power may be caused by water intrusion into the instrument panel (TSB #07-06-04-019D). 2008-09—Clunk noise while turning, or automatic transmission extension housing leaks. Front brakes squeal when braking. GM suggests owners replace the brake pads with Kit #PN 25958115). Front door window drops incrementally. Rear door windows may go down by themselves. Front door latch freezing; seal the latch housing on both front doors to prevent water intrusion. 2008-10—Front door window is slow or noisy when activated. 2008-11—Noise heard when shifting between Reverse and Drive. Inoperative low-beam headlights. 2008-12—Front seat lateral movement/clunking noise. 2008-13—Clunk noise heard when shifting out of Drive to Reverse or Reverse into Drive:

This 90-minute job should be covered up to 7 years/160,000 km.,
the benchmark for what qualifies as "reasonable durability."

2011—Slow, noisy operation of the front door glass. Power steering/shock absorber
leaks. The airbag warning light comes on intermittently. An easy, inexpensive way
to eliminate a chatter-type noise or rear axle clunk. 2012-13—Crankshaft rear oil
seal leaks:

This is a warrantable item inasmuch as this oil leak has more to do with
mechanical failure than owner maintenance. Stand your ground.

2012-14—Remedy for a water leak or wind noise from passenger front door glass
according to TSB #PI0748A, dated Jan. 31, 2014. Remember, body defects like this
are the responsibility of both the dealer and manufacturer. 2014—GM bulletin

#13429 provides a service procedure to replace the hazard warning switch. Software in the hazard warning switch may cause the activation of the hazard warning lamps when the vehicle has been turned off. If the hazard warning lamp activation goes unnoticed, it could drain the battery.

EQUINOX/TERRAIN ★★★★★/★★★★★★

The Chevrolet Equinox

RATING: Recommended (2010-16); Below Average (2005-09). 2016 models are carried over relatively unchanged except for a slight restyling of the front and rear ends. The interior has been dressed up, as well. **Road performance:** These tall wagons handle very well, provide a comfortable ride, and are easily controlled with precise steering. Thrilling acceleration with the V6 and manual transmission; the 4-cylinder engine and automatic gearbox are acceptable and fairly quiet, but the V6 is the better performer with little fuel penalty. The most important change among model years is the choice of a potent 301 hp 3.6L V6, which has 14% more horsepower and 22% more torque than the 3.0L V6. Interestingly, fuel-economy figures for the 3.6L are the same as with the 3.0L. *Terrain:* Acceptable handling and braking combined with a comfortable ride. **Strong points:** The Terrain shares its basic design and powertrain with the Chevrolet Equinox. Besides a plethora of airbags, the Terrain also comes with ABS, traction control, and an antiskid system. A rear-view camera is standard on all Terrain models. Plenty of passenger room; a quiet interior; most controls are well laid out; and very comfortable seating. **Weak points:** The 4-cylinder engine comes up short when passing other vehicles or merging into traffic; handling is better with the Honda competition; tall head restraints cut rear visibility; the dash buttons all look the same; cheap-looking, easily scratched, and hard-to-keep-clean door panels and dash materials.

Overall reliability has been only average. The transmission, suspension, electrical, and fuel systems have been problematic, and fit and finish continues to get low marks. Not quite as much cargo space as seen in some rival makes; and some dash controls are difficult to reach.

Prices and Specs

Prices (Firm): *LS:* $26,405, *AWD:* $28,605, *1LT:* $29,670, *AWD:* $31,870, *2LT:* $30,560, *AWD:* $32,760, *Terrain: SLE-1:* $28,295, *AWD:* $30,495, *SLE-2:* $30,745, *AWD:* $32,945, *SLT-1:* $32,445, *AWD:* $34,645, *SLT-2:* $37,145, *AWD:* $39,345, *Denali AWD:* $42,245 **Freight:** $2,000 **Powertrain (Front-drive/AWD):** Engines: 2.4L 4-cyl. (182 hp), 3.6L V6 (301 hp); Transmission: 6-speed auto. **Dimensions/capacity:** Passengers: 2/3; Wheelbase: 112.5 in.; H: 66.3/L: 187.8/W: 72.5 in.; Headroom F/R: 5/4 in.; Legroom F/R: 43/31 in.; Cargo volume: 33.5 cu ft.; Load capacity: 1,070 lb.; Fuel tank: 59L/regular; Tow limit: 3,500 lb.; Turning circle: 40 ft.; Ground clearance: 7.8 in.; Weight: 3,786 lb.

Other opinions: "The 2015 Chevrolet Equinox ranks #8 out of 25 affordable compact SUVs. The 2015 Chevrolet Equinox has spacious seating and a quiet, comfortable ride, but it isn't very engaging to drive and the base engine could use more power." – *U.S. News & World Report.* "Alongside its GMC counterpart, the Terrain, the Equinox is well rounded with equal strengths in quality, functionality and drivability ... With the Equinox, you get a jack-of-all-trades vehicle but, as the rest of the saying goes, a master of none. For a family-centric people mover, that can be a good thing." – *AutoTrader.* **Major redesign:** 2005 and 2010. **Highway/city fuel economy:** *2.4L auto.:* 6.1/9.2 L/100 km. *AWD:* 6.9/10.1 L/100 km. *3.0L auto.:* 8.1/12.4 L/100 km. *AWD:* 8.6/12.9 L/100 km. **Best alternatives:** Honda CR-V, Hyundai Tucson, Mazda CX5, Nissan Rogue, Subaru Forester, and Toyota RAV4.

SAFETY: Child safety seat setup: "Acceptable." **Crashworthiness:** NHTSA: Both cars have earned a good reputation for safety, with four- and five-star federal ratings plus top "Good" ratings from IIHS, including the tough small overlap frontal test. Of particular note is the 2016's inclusion of a rear-view camera system as a standard feature. **Owner-reported safety-related failures:** Outward visibility is obstructed by thick rear pillars.

ALERT! These cars are hobbled by the turbocharged 4-cylinder engine; go for a V6-equipped version.

Equinox/Terrain Profile

	2006	2007	2008	2009	2010	2011	2012	2013	2014
Used Values ($)									
4x2 LS	5,500	6,500	7,500	8,500	9,500	12,000	14,500	17,500	20,500
LT V6	—	—	—	—	11,500	15,000	17,500	21,000	23,000
LS 4x4	—	7,500	8,500	10,000	11,500	13,500	15,500	19,000	21,500
LT	—	8,500	9,500	10,500	12,000	15,000	17,500	21,000	23,500
Reliability	★	★	★	★	☆	☆	☆	☆	☆
Repairs ($$$)	3	3	3	3	2	1	1	1	1
Electrical	★	★	★	★	★	☆	☆	☆	☆
Engine (base)	★	★	★	★	★	★	☆	☆	☆
Fit/Finish	★	★	★	★	★	☆	☆	☆	☆
Infotainment	—	—	—	—	—	★	☆	☆	☆
Transmission (auto.)	★	★	★	★	★	★	★	★	☆

SECRET WARRANTIES, INTERNAL BULLETINS: *Acadia, Enclave, Equinox, OUTLOOK, Terrain, Torrent, Traverse, and VUE:* 2007-12—Transfer case fluid leak. *Avalanche, Escalade, Sierra, Silverado, Suburban, Tahoe, and Yukon:* 2007-13—Tapping/clicking/ticking noise at windshield area. *Avalanche, Equinox, Escalade, Sierra, Silverado, Suburban, Tahoe, Terrain, Yukon, and Yukon Denali:* 2010-12—Roof panel flutters/rattle noise when doors close. 2010-14—*Troubleshooting various front end noises on bumps. Terrain:* Power steering sticks or slips ("secret" warranty):

SPECIAL COVERAGE ADJUSTMENT – POWER STEERING STICK-SLIP

SERVICE BULLETIN NO.:14232 — DATE: NOV 21, 2014

2012-2014 Buick Verano; 2011-2014 Chevrolet Cruze, Volt; 2010-2014 Chevrolet Equinox; 2013-2014 Chevrolet Malibu; 2010-2014 GMC Terrain.

CONDITION: Some 2012-2014 model year Buick Verano, 2011-2014 Chevrolet Cruze and Volt, 2010-2014 Chevrolet Equinox and GMC Terrain, and 2013-2014 Chevrolet Malibu vehicles may have increased friction in the steering system. This could cause the steering wheel to stick in the straight-ahead position after driving long distances on a straight highway. The steering wheel can be turned but it may require increased effort.

SPECIAL COVERAGE ADJUSTMENT: This special coverage covers the condition described above for a period of 10 years or 150,000 miles (240,000 km), whichever occurs first, from the date the vehicle was originally placed in service, regardless of ownership. Dealers are to 1) replace the steering gear on 2010-2012 model year vehicles; or 2) reprogram the power steering control module on 2013-2014 model year vehicles. The repairs will be made at no charge to the customer.

2010-15—Power steering noise or hose leaks are addressed in TSB #13-02-32-001C, dated Aug. 6, 2014. Steering shudder during slow speed maneuvers:

STEERING SHUDDER (VIBRATION) DURING SLOW SPEED MANEUVERS

SERVICE BULLETIN NO.:#PI0814D   DATE: APRIL 15. 2014

2010-2015 Chevrolet Equinox; 2010-2015 GMC Terrain.

CONCERN: Some customers may comment they are experiencing a steering vibration, felt through the steering wheel and vehicle structure, combined with a moan type noise. This condition is most noticed during low speed parking lot maneuvers or when the vehicle is stationary and the steering wheel is turned.

IMPORTANT: The following repair will make noticeable improvements to the shudder (vibration) condition. However, in most cases it will not completely eliminate a common hydraulic power steering system noise. This condition can be corrected by replacing the following components: power steering gear inlet hose assembly, generator (alternator) assembly and the emission evaporative hose. The revised power steering hose assembly is longer and provides a dampening quality. The revised generator has an isolation pulley and the revised evaporative hose is designed to clear the revised power steering hose.

2011—Automatic transmission clunks when shifting. Trouble-shooting tips to plug transfer case fluid leaks. Power steering, shock absorber leaks. Tire-pressure monitor system update for Canadians only. *Equinox, LaCrosse, Malibu ECO, Regal, Terrain, Verano:* 2012-13—Voice recognition feature inoperative. *Equinox:* 2013—The flexible fuel sensor may fail prematurely; a "secret" warranty covers the replacement cost (see Silverado section). GM will replace a defective starter motor for free under its base warranty. *Equinox:* 2013-14—Power steering "secret" warranty (see TSB, above). 2014—Water leaks on front carpet. Creak or pop from right front of body.

ACADIA/ENCLAVE/TRAVERSE

RATING: Recommended (2013-16); Above Average (2011-12); Average (2010); Below Average (2005-09). These are practically identical seven- and eight-passenger crossover SUVs, with the Traverse being the most recent addition in 2009 with the other models launched in 2008 (Enclave) and 2007 (Acadian), respectively. **Road performance:** The smooth-running 3.6L V6 has plenty of power for most chores and isn't as fuel-thirsty as other SUVs in the same class; a taut and comfortable ride; and standard stability control. On the negative side: The automatic transmission sometimes hesitates when shifting. **Strong points:** Strong acceleration; many powertrain configurations; a quiet interior; good towing capability; parts aren't hard to find and are reasonably priced; mechanical/body failures aren't excessive; and repairs can be done by independent garages. **Weak points:** Transmission oil leaks

The Buick Enclave (left), Chevrolet Traverse (right), and GMC Acadia (bottom) are all quite similar mid-size SUVs that are reasonably reliable and perform well. The downside: Poor fuel economy, and an over-priced sticker price for the Enclave. Consider the cheaper Chevrolet Traverse, or GMC Acadia, or beat the high prices by getting a used version of one of the above (Pssst… you'll also save the infamous $2,000 "freight fee").

and malfunctions; fuel-pump flow module fails, making the engine run rough or stall; inaccurate fuel gauges; a noisy, failure-prone suspension; and headlight failures. Middle-row passenger windows vibrate and make a loud noise when partially rolled down; excessive seat creaking and squeaking and overall fit and finish is subpar.

Prices and Specs

Prices (Firm): *Enclave 2x4:* $48,060, *AWD:* $51,060, *Premium AWD:* $55,560, *Traverse 1LS 2x4:* $33,655, *AWD:* $36,655, *LT:* $37,110, *AWD:* $40,110, *2LT:* $40,760, *AWD:* $43,760, *LTZ AWD:* $50,295, *Acadia: SLE-1:* $36,345, *AWD:* $39,345, *SLE-2:* $40,045, *SLT-1:* $44,960, *AWD:* $47,960, *Denali:* $56,760 **Freight:** $2,000 **Powertrain (Front-drive/AWD):** Engine: 3.6L V6 (288 hp); Transmission: 6-speed auto. **Dimensions/ capacity:** *Enclave:* Passengers: 7/8; Wheelbase: 119 in.; H: 70/L: 201.5/W: 78 in.; Headroom F/RR: 3.5/4/0 in.; Legroom F/RR: 41.5/30/24 in.; Cargo volume: 44 in. (behind first row).; Fuel tank: 83L/regular; Tow limit: 4,500 lb.; Load capacity: 1,335 lb.; Turning circle: 40.4 ft.; Ground clearance: 8.4 in.; Weight: 5,100 lb.

Other opinions: "The 2015 Buick Enclave ranks #3 out of 13 affordable large SUVs. Critics appreciate the 2015 Enclave's generous cargo space, upscale interior and refined ride." – *U.S. News & World Report.* "As with its mainstream siblings the Chevrolet Traverse and GMC Acadia, the Enclave is larger than its rivals, making it ideal for those requiring extra space for passengers and cargo. Despite its bigger footprint, the Enclave's sub-$40,000 ($50,000 Cdn.) starting price undercuts rivals by thousands. Buick's 3-row SUV may not have the brand cachet or sleek design of some rivals, but what it lacks in those areas it makes up for in value." – *Kelley Blue Book.* **Major redesign:** *Acadia:* 2007; *Enclave:* 2008; and *Traverse:* 2009. **Highway/city fuel economy:** *Front-drive:* 8.4/12.7 L/100 km. *AWD:* 9/13.4 L/100 km.

Best alternatives: The 2010-14 models are your best buys for the lowest price/highest quality advantage now that GM has corrected some of the first-year production quirks. Higher fuel prices and new products are also pushing leftover SUV and truck base prices way down; $15,000 discounts are commonplace. The Ford Flex, Honda Pilot, Hyundai Veracruz, and Mazda CX-9. If you don't mind downsizing a notch, consider the Ford Edge, Hyundai Santa Fe, and Nissan Xterra. Be wary of the Saturn Outlook. It has many identical features and components, but not the equivalent quality nor reliability.

SAFETY: Child safety seat setup: "Acceptable." Crashworthiness: NHTSA: Since 2007 these vehicles have received five stars for overall crashworthiness. IIHS awarded the trio identical "Good" ratings for overall crash protection, including the more stringent moderate overlap front collision crash test. Owner-reported safety-related failures: Side airbags sometimes fail to deploy, side panels create a huge blind spot, and there's limited rear visibility. Check this out with a test drive.

ALERT! Again, those pesky head restraints can make your driving a living hell if you are not the ideal size. Stay away from Firestone and Bridgestone original-equipment tires; www.tirerack.com is your best contact for dependable and well-performing tires.

Acadia/Enclave/Traverse Profile

	2006	2007	2008	2009	2010	2011	2012	2013	2014
Used Values ($)									
Acadia SLE	—	7,500	9,000	10,500	12,500	16,500	21,000	25,000	29,500
AWD	—	8,500	10,500	12,000	13,500	18,500	23,000	27,500	32,000
SLT	—	10,000	12,000	14,000	16,500	21,000	26,000	31,500	36,000
AWD	—	12,000	14,000	16,500	18,500	23,500	29,000	34,000	38,500
Denali	—	—	—	—	—	25,000	34,000	40,500	46,000
Enclave	—	—	12,500	13,000	15,000	20,500	24,000	29,000	34,500
AWD	—	—	13,000	14,500	16,500	21,500	26,500	32,000	37,000
Traverse LS	—	—	—	10,500	12,500	16,000	19,500	23,500	26,500
AWD	—	—	—	12,000	14,000	17,500	21,000	25,500	29,000
Reliability	★	★	★	★	◐	☆	☆	☆	☆
Repairs ($$$)	②	②	②	②	②	①	①	①	①
Electrical	★	★	★	★	★	☆	☆	☆	☆
Engine (base)	★	★	★	★	☆	☆	☆	☆	☆
Fit/Finish	★	★	★	★	★	★	★	☆	☆
Infotainment	—	—	—	—	—	★	★	☆	☆
Transmission (auto.)	★	★	★	★	★	☆	☆	☆	☆

SECRET WARRANTIES, INTERNAL BULLETINS: 2007-10—"Secret" warranty coverage on the water pump shaft seals up to ten years or 120,000 miles. In TSB #13091 issued on May 20, 2013, GM said the seal might fail and cause coolant leaks. Affected models: 2007-10 GMC Acadias and Saturn Outlooks; 2008-10 Buick Enclaves; and 2009-10 Chevrolet Traverses. Should the leak develop, a new water pump will be installed. 2011—Electrical/water issues. Troubleshooting tips to plug transfer case fluid leaks. Power-steering, automatic transmission clunks. Second-row "Easy Entry" seats may not work. Engine won't shut off or start (see bulletin, below).

ELECTRICAL – ENGINE WON'T SHUT OFF/ELECTRICAL ISSUES

BULLETIN NO.: 08-08-57-003C   DATE: JULY 15, 2011

FLOOR WET UNDER CARPET/ENGINE CONTINUES TO RUN WITH KEY OFF/POSSIBLE NO CRANK/NO START/COMMUNICATION LOSS/VARIOUS ELECTRICAL CONCERNS (SEAL SEAM)

2008-12 Buick Enclave; 2007-12 GMC Acadia; and the 2007-10 Saturn Outlook.

CONDITION: Some customers may comment on any, or a combination of, the following conditions:
- Evidence of a water leak at the right side A-pillar and/or the right front floor is wet under the carpet.
- Various electrical concerns such as: Engine Continues to Run with Key Off/Possible No Crank/ No Start/Communication Loss/Various Electrical Concerns, which may be a result of a water leak on the IP BEC.
- Other electrical related conditions that may be communication issues between certain electrical modules due to water dripping on the IP BEC.

CAUSE: Water from the right front sunroof drain hose exits the vehicle through the plenum (upper arrow) and may re-enter through the un-sealed seam at the front of the dash. In more current models and years, sunroof drain hose and windshield related issues have sometimes been found to be a source of a water leak in the A-pillar area. This water can also sometimes leak on the IP BEC and/or onto the floor area.

ESCALADE/SUBURBAN/TAHOE/YUKON/HYBRID ★★★★/★

RATING: Above Average buy (2011-16); Average buy (2004-10). *Hybrid*: Not recommended (2007-13). The Hybrid was dropped in 2013 because it was "the right airplane at the wrong airport" according to *Los Angeles Times* car critic, Dan Neil. After last year's redesign, these models are carried over into 2016 with modest improvements – and not so modest price increases. Most of the changes involve upgrades to the CUE infotainment system to improve system speed and performance. Additional standard features: Lane Keep Assist; a front camera view of the Surround Vision feature that's selectable via the Cadillac CUE screen; and "Intellibeam" headlights. These large SUVs are for those who need rugged, truck-like capabilities, a nine-passenger capacity, and lots of cargo space. All four vehicles are practically identical, though the Escalade comes with a plusher interior and is more gadget laden. Road performance: Surprisingly good handling for an SUV this large. Comfortable for highway cruising, and very agile around town as well. **Strong points:** Robust acceleration; many powertrain configurations; standard stability control since 2006; a quiet interior and comfortable ride; good towing capability; parts aren't hard to find and are reasonably priced; and repairs can be done by independent garages. Less reliability problems since the last redesign in 2007. A used hybrid version is available, though, it's a risky investment. **Weak points:** Mediocre fuel economy; surprisingly rapid depreciation (can you say "used car bargain?"); on earlier models, small third-row seat sits too low and doesn't fold into the floor; long braking distances; and spotty fit and finish. Specific problem areas include loss of brakes; faulty powertrain, suspension, and climate controls; chronic electrical shorts; and various body glitches.

Prices and Specs

Prices (Firm): *Escalade Base:* $82,195, *Escalade Luxury:* $87,795, *Premium:* $92,795, *Platinum:* $101,735, *ESV:* $85,595, *Suburban 2x4 LS 1500:* $54,150, *AWD LS 1500:* $57,450; *Tahoe LS 2x4:* $51,200, *AWD:* $54,500, *LT:* $59,000, *AWD:* $62,300, *Yukon SLE 2x4:* $52,900, *4x4:* $56,200, *Denali AWD:* $75,650 **Freight:** $2,150 **Powertrain (Front-drive/AWD):** Engines: 5.3L V8 (320 hp), 6.2L V8 (403 hp), 6.0L V8 (332 hp); Transmissions: 6-speed auto., 8-speed auto. (Denali),CVT **Dimensions/capacity:** Passengers: *Escalade:* 3/3/2; *Tahoe:* 3/3/3; Wheelbase: *Escalade:* 116 in.; *Hybrid:* 202.5 in.; H: 74.3/L: 202.5/W: 79 in.; Headroom F/RR: 3/3.5/0 in.; Legroom F/RR: 40/27/28.5 in.; Cargo volume: 46.5 cu. ft.; Fuel tank: 98L/regular; Tow limit: *Escalade:* 8,100 lb.; *Hybrid:* 5,600lb.; Maximum load: *Escalade:* 1,330 lb.; *Hybrid:* 1,484 lb.; Turning circle: 40.4 ft.; Ground clearance: 9 in.; Weight: *Escalade:* 5,691-5,943 lb., *Hybrid:* 6,116 lb.

Other opinions: "The 2015 Chevrolet Tahoe ranks #1 out of 13 affordable large SUVs. Reviewers call the all-new Tahoe one of the best large SUVs on the market, pointing to its gentle ride, strong acceleration, refined cabin and favorable fuel economy." – *U.S. News & World Report.* "The forward collision alert system just doesn't work. I cannot make it produce a collision alert no matter what I do. For example it is advertised to provide a heads up visual warning as well as an audio warning if I approach the car in front of me to rapidly. It does not. The system also has a green automobile icon when you are following closer than about 200 feet to the vehicle in front of you. The green icon is advertised to turn yellow if you follow too close. It does not. The only time that I have ever seen the red heads-up display is when it is a false alert. All in all, this system which was touted to be a great safety feature is totally worthless." – *safercar.gov.* **Major redesign:** *Escalade:* 1999, 2002, 2007, and 2015; *Suburban, Tahoe, and Yukon:* 2000, 2007, and 2015. All these SUVs had a shortened 2014 model year starting in June 2013, and were replaced with a new version, based on the successful 2014 Silverado platform, in February 2014 as 2015 models. Upgrades include: Inlaid doors that tuck into the door sills, improved fuel economy, less interior noise, aluminum hoods and liftgate panels, and a more-efficient, direct-injected EcoTec3 powertrain. Also new are the addition of fold-flat second and third-row seats, and an additional two inches of leg room for second-row passengers. **Highway/city fuel economy:** *Escalade AWD:* 10 /15.3 L/100 km. *Escalade AWD auto.:* 13.8 /21.2 L/100 km. *Escalade Hybrid AWD:* 8.5/10.4 L/100 km. The other model spin-offs are within the same range. **Best alternatives:** Many SUV buyers can't resist the options and end up buying much more car than they need. Question the need for 4x4. If the weather is that bad, maybe you should stay at home. Did you know sunroofs are usually much more trouble than they're worth (shattering when a door is closed, or when the temperature drops, leaking, whistling)? Or, that most extras aren't worth much come trade-in time? Plus, the extra money for a "loaded" SUV or truck could be put to paying off the loan, fuel economy will suffer from the extra weight and 4x4 option, and a smaller car is easier to unload. If there's a need to trade up look at cheaper alternatives. For example, you can get eight-passenger seating and better fuel economy and manoeuvrability in the cheaper Chevy Traverse. Other good choices are the Buick Enclave, Chevrolet Avalanche, Equinox or Terrain, Ford Flex, GMC Acadia or Traverse, Honda Pilot, Hyundai Santa Fe, Mazda CX-5 or CX-9, and Toyota Highlander. The Ford Flex and the Mazda CX-9 get good fuel economy and are easier to drive, and their third-row seating outclasses what GM offers. Plus, crossover SUVs are available with AWD, which can provide a good amount of all-weather capability. In the new year, prices will fall and many of these large SUVs will sell with almost a third off their original price.

 SAFETY: **Child safety seat setup:** "Acceptable." **Crashworthiness:** NHTSA: 2000-15 models have earned top marks of four and five stars, except for three-star rollover resistance performance. IIHS hasn't yet tested these SUVs. **Owner-reported safety-related failures:** The headlights don't sufficiently illuminate the roadway:

> The contact owns a 2015 Chevrolet Tahoe. While driving various speeds at night, the exterior lighting was too dim because of an invisible line above the dashboard. The dealer adjusted the headlights, but the failure recurred.

Also, keep a wary eye on the rear hatch when loading or unloading cargo warns this Escalade owner in his *safercar.gov* posting:

> 2011 Cadillac Escalade power rear cargo door is a serious safety hazard. Son was seriously hurt at airport luggage claims when a power rear cargo door was closing, came down on his head and face without warning of any kind that this door was closing. The door is so large and heavy as it comes down, it's fast and does not retract back up when it hits something. The driver had no warning that a person was behind him as he closed the door.

ALERT! These SUVs are flying out of dealer showrooms as low fuel prices and pent-up demand create a seller's market. Some dealers report units being sold within 17 days after they arrive, with customers favouring fully-loaded LTZ and Suburban models. Interestingly, used trade-ins are marked down considerably making those SUVs the best buys.

Escalade/Suburban/Tahoe/Yukon/Hybrid Profile

	2006	2007	2008	2009	2010	2011	2012	2013	2014
Used Values ($)									
Escalade	14,000	18,000	21,000	27,000	31,500	39,500	48,000	55,000	63,000
ESV	—	20,000	23,500	28,000	33,500	41,500	51,500	58,000	66,000
EXT	—	24,500	27,000	31,000	29,000	37,500	44,000	53,000	—
Hybrid AWD	—	—	—	—	30,000	40,000	50,000	58,000	—
Suburban	10,500	12,000	13,500	17,500	20,000	24,500	31,000	37,000	43,000
Suburban AWD	—	—	—	—	—	—	—	—	46,000
Tahoe	8,000	9,000	10,500	14,500	17,000	20,500	26,500	34,000	37,000
Tahoe AWD	—	10,500	13,500	16,500	18,000	22,500	28,500	34,500	40,000
Hybrid	—	12,000	14,000	17,500	24,000	24,000	32,000	40,000	—
Hybrid AWD	—	—	13,000	16,000	18500	26,000	36,000	44,000	—
Yukon	8,000	9,000	10,500	12,000	15,500	21,000	26,500	32,000	37,000
Yukon AWD	—	10,000	12,500	15,500	18,000	22,500	28,500	34,500	40,000
Hybrid	—	12,000	14,500	16,000	19,000	25,000	34,000	41,000	—
Hybrid AWD	—	14,000	16,000	18,500	22,000	28,000	36,500	44,000	—
Reliability	★3	★3	★3	★3	★3	☆	☆	☆	☆
Repairs ($$$)	💰2	💰2	💰2	💰2	💰2	💰2	💰2	💰2	💰2
Electrical	☆	☆	☆	☆	☆	☆	☆	☆	☆
Engine (base)	★2	★2	★2	★2	★2	★2	★2	★2	★2
Fit/Finish	★1	★1	★1	★1	★1	★2	★2	★2	★2
Infotainment	—	—	—	—	—	★2	★2	☆	☆
Transmission (auto.)	★1	★1	★1	★1	★1	★1	★1	★2	★2

SECRET WARRANTIES, INTERNAL BULLETINS: 2007-13—Inoperative cruise control; inoperative or unwanted activation of radio controls; backlighting flashes, flickers, or inoperative due to possible short to ground on steering wheel coil connector. 2007-14—Excessive oil consumption, fouled, cracked spark plugs, and a rough running engine may need 10 hours of work and the replacement of key engine parts says TSB: #10-06-01-008M, dated Nov. 26, 2014. This repair is premature and should be covered up to 7 years 160,000 km.

ENGINE OIL CONSUMPTION ON ALUMINUM BLOCK/IRON BLOCK ENGINES WITH ACTIVE FUEL MANAGEMENT (AFM) (INSTALL AFM OIL DEFLECTOR AND CLEAN CARBON FROM CYLINDER AND/OR INSTALL UPDATED VALVE COVER)

SERVICE BULLETIN NO.: 10-06-01-008M   DATE: NOVEMBER 26, 2014

2007-2014 Cadillac Escalade; 2007-2013 Chevrolet Avalanche, Silverado; 2007-2014 Chevrolet Suburban, Tahoe; 2010-2012 Chevrolet Colorado; 2010-2015 Chevrolet Camaro; 2007-2013 GMC Sierra, Sierra Denali; 2007-2014 GMC Yukon; 2010-2012 GMC Canyon; 2008-2009 Pontiac G8 GT; Vehicles Built Prior to February 1, 2011 Require Updated Valve Cover and October 2010 Require AFM Shield; Equipped with Any of the Following Engines: Aluminum Block V8 Engine with Active Fuel Management (RPOs LH9, L94, LZ1, L99, LC9, LH6, L76, L92, LFA (Hybrid); Iron Block V8 Engine with Active Fuel Management (AFM) (RPOs LMG, LY5).

CONDITION: Some customers may comment about engine oil consumption of vehicles with higher mileage (approximately 48,000 to 64,000 km. (30,000 to 40,000 mi) and a service engine soon light being on and/or rough running engine. Verify that the PCV system is functioning properly. If the customer understands that some oil consumption is normal and still feels the consumption level is excessive, more than 1 quart per 2000 to 3000 miles of driving, perform the service indicated in this bulletin. It is no longer necessary to have the customer return multiple times to have the usage verified.

CAUSE: This condition may be caused by two conditions. Oil pulled through the PCV system or oil spray that is discharged from the AFM pressure relief valve within the crankcase. Under most driving conditions and drive cycles, the discharged oil does not cause a problem. Under certain drive cycles (extended high engine speed operation), in combination with parts at the high end of their tolerance specification, the oil spray quantity may be more than usual, resulting in excessive deposit formation in the piston ring grooves, causing increased oil consumption and cracked or fouled spark plugs (# 1 and/or # 7). Refer to the latest version of Corporate Bulletin Number 12-06-01-001.

NOTE: When installing the updated valve cover or reinstalling a used valve cover, verify that the baffles can hold water and do not leak. If any leaks are found, seal with RTV if possible or replace the valve cover. Thoroughly clean and dry the valve cover before installation.

Suburban, Tahoe, Yukon: 2009-14—Some vehicles may not crank or start, caused by excessive leakage from cylinder past exhaust or exhaust intake valve, low static compression, sensor is disconnected, or while cranking, valve train fails to move. 2011—Engine knocking on a cold start (GM says, "Don't worry, be happy"). Power-steering, shock absorber leaks. Airbag warning light comes on intermittently. Airbag isn't flush with the dash. Exhaust leak, rattle, and rumble noise. Tapping, clicking, and ticking noise at windshield area. Sun visor fails to stay in the up position. Sticking, binding door mounted seat switches. Front-door window regulator squeaks. Third-row seat hard to remove and install. Front seat cushion cover becomes detached and warped. Wavy front or rear fender liners. 2012-13—4WD fails to engage as Service alert lights up. What to do if the blower motor is noisy or doesn't work properly. 2014-15—Shift lever hits ignition key: Truck shuts down (see Silverado section). An engine that ticks or runs hot, may have a faulty head gasket. If the vehicle cranks, but won't start, GM says the camshaft position actuator solenoid valve may need to be replaced (TSB: # PIP5130E). **2015**—TSB #PIT5288A gives tips for troubleshooting electrical malfunctions: Dead battery, no entry/start, no audio, and an inoperative touch screen, rear wiper, rear power windows, and tire pressure warning device. Hood fluttering.

SILVERADO/SIERRA ★★★★★

Silverado/Sierra and Chrysler Ram have the edge over Ford's F-150, until we see how Ford's aluminum body and redesign hold up long-term.

RATING: Recommended (2014-16); Above Average (2011-13); Average (2010); Below Average (2004-09). General Motors introduced its first pickup truck in 1930 and these pickups have been essentially the same for their entire history, except for the redesigned 2008 and 2014 models. The Silverado is seen as the "standard" version aimed for use in agriculture, while the Sierra targets industrial workers and truck aficionados who want a bit more luxury. GM's pickup quality and performance have improved dramatically since its upgrades and the company no longer needs a "twin-brand" gimmick to sell trucks and SUVs. All the more reason why GM should merge GMC with Chevrolet. **Road performance:** Since its 2014 model redesign, the Silverado handles much better, offers more usable power, and gives a more-controllable ride (no more "Shakerado"). Nevertheless, some annoying and dangerous powertrain glitches remain. For example, many owner complaints target the engine's "Reduced Power Mode" feature and assorted engine/transmission malfunctions:

I have had a recurring problem with my new 2012 Chevrolet Silverado 1500 LT (5.3 liter engine) going into "Reduced Engine Power Mode" which also results in the disabling of stability control and traction control. This is a dangerous condition in that it results in a loss of power while operating the vehicle upon the roadway. An authorized repair facility has replaced the number one and two throttle sensors, the accelerator pedal assembly, the throttle body, the alternator, the computer, and a large ground wire behind the dash. A GM engineer has flown in and now the repair center is replacing the engine wiring harness. The vehicle (which was purchased less than three months ago) has been out of service for approximately 30 days. In researching this matter I have found that Chevy has had an ongoing problem with this in various vehicles in its product line since 2003. Although several service bulletins have been produced there does not seem to be a consensus regarding the cause of this problem. All of the parts associated with trouble codes C0242, P2127, and P2138 have been replaced without result. This condition could result in the affected vehicles being rear-ended, or, because of the loss of stability and traction control, result in a rollover. This needs to be addressed immediately.

• • •

Transmission shifts hard from a complete stop as 1st gear was being engaged. Drove it until break-in period was over and took it back to the dealer where the transmission body and valves were replaced. Now getting more problems with the transmission shifting between gears at a speed of 35-45 mph [56-72 km/h]. Transmission disengages and I have no power going to the wheels, like it shifts to Neutral for 5-10 seconds. This will cause an accident if transmission does not reengage while driving in traffic you will get rear ended.

Ford's F-Series and the Dodge Ram 1500 have had many recent refinements, sport better interiors, and more capable powertrains give a comfortable ride. But, from a quality and dependability standpoint, 2011-16 GM trucks have excelled. The Silverado 1500 Hybrid has a 6.0L V8 that pairs with an electric motor, producing 332 hp. It can run on one or both of its power sources depending on driving demands, and doesn't need to be plugged in. The Hybrid has a continuously variable automatic transmission and a maximum towing capacity of 6,100 lb. **Strong points:** *1500:* Comfortable seating; a quiet interior; lots of storage capability; generally good crashworthiness scores; and acceptable fuel economy with the 6-speed automatic transmission coupled to the 5.3L V8. *2500:* These heavy-duty work trucks are built primarily to be load carrying vehicles, capable of working off-road; the independent front end improves handling and smooths out the ride. The standard engine is a powerful 360 hp 6.0L V8 backed up by a 397 hp 6.6L turbodiesel. On the other hand, the GM Allison transmission dates to the late '40s, yet it hasn't performed as well as Ford's TorqShift 6-speed found in the Super Duty models. **Weak points:** *1500:* Powertrain smoothness and reliability doesn't measure up to what the Honda Ridgeline and Nissan Titan can provide, especially when comparing the performance of the V8 4x4 model. GM Duramax-equipped pickups need diesel exhaust fluid (urea) refills every 8,000 km. (5,000 mi.). This is more frequent than the oil change one usually does every 12,000 km. (7,500 mi.). Furthermore, the urea-filling process can be costly when done by the dealer, versus buying the product off the shelf and pouring it yourself.

Other opinions: "The 2015 Chevrolet Silverado 1500 ranks #3 out of 6 Full Size Pickup Trucks. Its smooth ride and low-noise interior make the 2015 Chevrolet Silverado 1500 an attractive truck, reviewers say, though it trails competitors in the use of cutting-edge technology." – *U.S. News & World Report.* "The rear headrest of the crew cabs are too small and do not raise up high enough to protect the head of anyone in the rear seat. There is also no center head rest for the rear seat. This is very dangerous and I wish I had seen it before I purchased the truck. This is a major safety concern that needs to be addressed asap. At least offer us the option to purchase larger headrests for the rear seat." – *safercar.gov.* **Major redesign:** *Silverado/Sierra 1500:* 1999, 2007, and 2014-15. The 2014 re-engineered 1500 model carries a new 355 hp V8 that gets better gas mileage, has a larger cargo bed, more payload capacity, and can tow up to 11,200 lb. The tailgate is easier to use, it has a lower step-in height than its rivals and there are steps to make it easy to climb into. **Highway/city fuel economy:** *4.3L 2WD:* 10/14.1 L/100 km. *4.3L 4WD:* 11.3/14.9 L/100 km. *4.8L 2WD:* 10.6/14.7 L/100 km. *4.8L 4WD:* 11.1/15.4 L/100 km. *5.3L 2WD:* 10.1/14.5 L/100 km. *5.3L 4WD:* 10.3/14.7 L/100 km. *6.2L AWD:* 10.8/17.7 L/100 km. *Hybrid 2WD:* 9.2/9.8 L/100 km. *Hybrid 4WD:* 9.8/10.5 L/100 km. **Best alternatives:** Any 2011 or later GM pickup will do, if cost is your primary concern. The Honda Ridgeline and Nissan Titan are good first choices, while the Nissan Rogue remains a competent crossover SUV with power and storage space to spare. Chrysler's Ram pickups have also raised the quality benchmark since 2014 and their new suspension offers one of the smoothest rides of any full-size pickup. On the other hand, Ford trucks still have some problems to work out, notably boosting its EcoBoost fuel economy and reliability and proving that its quality demons have been exorcized through the revamped 2015 F-series. Nevertheless, Ford's low quality and dependability ratings make its best-selling trucks also-rans in this year's *Lemon-Aid* ratings, where GM and Chrysler take the number one and two spot for most value for your buck.

SAFETY: Child safety seat setup: "Poor." **Crashworthiness:** NHTSA: Gave the redesigned 2014-16 Silverado/Sierra its top five-star overall crash protection scores; earlier models also did well, with four-star ratings from 2011 through 2013. The 2009 models tested surprisingly well, scoring five stars for overall crash safety. Earlier pickups and other models weren't tested. IIHS has given the 2014-16 Silverado 1500 a "Good" rating for overall crash protection. An "Acceptable" score was earned for side-impact crashworthiness and head-restraint effectiveness for 2010-13 models. IIHS says the 1500's roof crashworthiness merits a "Marginal" rating for 2011-13 versions. 1997 to 2009 trucks have safety ratings that aren't as good; their crash scores vary from "Good" to "Poor." **Owner-reported safety-related failures:** 2013 models may surge suddenly and the accelerator sometimes sticks when "floored."

ALERT! Owners of 2013 and earlier models say the climate control system doesn't defog the windshield adequately. Be sure to check this out in your test drive.

> I brought my '13 Silverado in for service because the a/c would not come on and defog the windshield in the recent snow storm. The service rep (correctly) informed me that the a/c compressor will not turn on if the temperature is below 40°F. So no fix by the dealer was done. This is a safety issue in cold/freezing weather conditions where the windshield fogs up severely when you get in the truck. The fogging continues even after the heater is warmed up and blowing hot air out the defroster ducts especially if the passengers are wet or snowy when they get in.
>
> *– safercar.gov*

Silverado/Sierra Profile

	2006	2007	2008	2009	2010	2011	2012	2013	2014
Used Values ($)									
Silverado 1500 4x2	6,000	7,000	8,000	9,500	11,000	14,500	17,500	20,000	22,500
Hybrid	—	8,000	—	13,000	17,000	22,000	26,000	—	—
Sierra	—	7,000	8,000	9,500	11,500	14,000	17,500	19,000	22,000
Hybrid AWD	—	—	—	13,000	17,500	22,500	26,500	30,000	—
Reliability	★	★	★	★	☆	☆	☆	☆	☆
Repairs ($$$)	3	3	3	3	2	2	2	2	1
Electrical	★	☆	☆	☆	☆	☆	☆	☆	☆
Engine (base)	★	★	★	☆	☆	☆	☆	☆	☆
Fit/Finish	☆	☆	☆	☆	☆	☆	☆	☆	☆
Infotainment	—	—	—	—	—	★	★	☆	☆
Transmission (auto.)	★	★	★	★	☆	☆	☆	☆	☆

SECRET WARRANTIES, INTERNAL BULLETINS: 2002-15—Leakage of EGR engine coolant into the combustion chamber 2002-15 Silverado, Sierra; 2004-09 Kodiak, C4500-C5500, Topkick C4500-C5500, 2006-15 Express, and Savana. By admitting this defect, GM admits liability. These engines should last at least 7 years/ 160,000 km. and GM should pay the estimated $3,000 repair when the engines fail prematurely. 2007-13—Inoperative cruise control; inoperative or unwanted activation of radio controls; backlighting flashes, flickers, or inoperative due to possible short to ground on steering wheel coil connector. Excessive oil consumption, fouled, cracked spark plugs, and rough running engines may need 10 hours of work and the replacement of key engine parts says TSB: #10-06-01-008M, dated Nov. 26, 2014. This repair is premature and should be covered up to 7 years 160,000 km. (see Tahoe, Yukon rating). 2009-13—Brake-induced pulsation/vibration felt in steering wheel, rumble noise from underbody during downhill descent (verify condition and replace front brake pads). GM admits this is a factory goof-up, so ask for a free pad replacement within 2 years, or a refund of 50% thereafter *Silverado, Sierra, Savana, Express:* 2009-14—Some vehicles many not crank or start, caused by excessive leakage from cylinder past exhaust or exhaust intake valve, low static compression, sensor is disconnected, or while cranking valve train fails to move. 2010-15—A fuel odour in the cabin may be caused by a leak at the bottom of the flywheel housing. 2011—Airbag light comes on intermittently. Side roof-rail airbags may not deploy as designed, says GM Customer Satisfaction Campaign bulletin #11288 (shh...it's a "secret warranty" – the fix is free). Automatic transmission clunks when shifted. Rear suspension clunk and squeaks. Rattle noise from wheel or hubcap. Underbody pop, clunk when turning. Rear leaf-spring slap or clunk noise. Exhaust leak, rattle, or rumble. Front-door regulator squeak. Tapping, clicking, or ticking at the windshield area. Shock absorber and power-steering leaks. Sun visor won't stay up. Water leaks through the headliner near the sunroof. Tires may slowly go flat. Warped or wavy fender liners. Rear-view mirror shake. Front brake vibration. *Express, Savana, Sierra, Silverado, Suburban, and Yukon XL:* 2011-12—Free fix to correct a rear axle grinding noise/vibration. Program was in effect until April 30, 2014; an extension can be requested through small claims court. Right side roof-rail airbags may be improperly mounted; GM will remount the airbags free of charge. 2012-13—4WD fails to engage as Service alert lights up. What to do if the blower motor is noisy doesn't work properly. 2013—Starter motor may short out after wearing through insulation. 2014—Some 2013 model year Buick LaCrosse and Regal; Cadillac ATS and SRX; Chevrolet Caprice, Captiva, Equinox, and Impala; and GMC Terrain vehicles, and 2014 Chevrolet Silverado 1500 and GMC Sierra 1500 vehicles, equipped with E85 flex fuel capability. The flexible fuel sensor may become inoperative during normal operation due to an electrical failure caused by road salt and other environmental contaminants. With a faulty flex fuel sensor, the Service Engine Soon light will illuminate and remote start will be inoperative. Special Coverage Adjustment: Dealers are to replace the fuel flex sensor, free of charge. This special coverage

(GM-speak for "secret" warranty) covers the condition described above for a period of 10 years or 150,000 miles (240,000 km.), whichever occurs first, from the date the vehicle was originally placed in service, regardless of ownership. The power sliding rear glass regulator may need to be replaced if the power window doesn't work. Want a laugh? Another TSB (#14002A) outlines a free "service procedure to inspect and, if necessary, repair the appearance of underbody components on our pickups that may not meet GM appearance requirements for new vehicles. These vehicles may exhibit signs of premature surface degradation on certain underbody components." Surface degradation is GM-speak for rust. 2014-15—Hood fluttering (TSB #PIT5288A). gives tips for troubleshooting electrical malfunctions: Dead battery, no entry/start, no audio, and inoperative touch screen, rear wiper, rear power windows, and tire pressure warning feature. An engine that ticks or runs hot, may have a faulty head gasket. If the truck cranks, but won't start, GM says the camshaft position actuator solenoid valve may need to be replaced (TSB # PIP5130E). In some trucks, various diagnostic trouble codes are displayed and panel cluster warning lamps and/or malfunction indicator lamp (MIL) illuminating diesel exhaust fluid (DEF) and engine may crank, not start, and runs rough or misfires. Shift lever hits ignition key: Truck shuts down.

SHIFT LEVER CONTACTS IGNITION KEY

SERVICE BULLETIN NO.: 14-00-89-005   DATE: NOV 6, 2014

2014 Chevrolet Silverado 1500; 2015 Chevrolet Silverado, Suburban, Tahoe; 2014 GMC Sierra 1500; 2015 GMC Sierra, Yukon, Yukon XL – Without Keyless Engine Start Switch (Push Button).

CONDITION: Some customers may comment that if the tilt steering column is in the full-up position and the shift lever is moved between gears, the shift lever contacts the head of the ignition key. Some contact force may rotate the ignition key and shut the engine off.

CORRECTION: A new design ignition key has been released. Technicians should replace the ignition key with the latest design. Refer to the pictures below for identification of the old key (1) versus new key (2).

2015—In response to owner complaints of dead batteries, GM will replace the OnStar feature, *gratis* because it could be draining the battery. You don't have to be an OnStar subscriber to get the replacement (see page 336).

ASIANS AND AUTO SAFETY

Takata Corp. is recalling over 35 million cars, built from 2000 to 2014 to replace deadly front-passenger airbags that "grenade" when they go off. Honda has sold almost 10% of the affected vehicles and has reassured owners it has their best interests at heart. Can we trust Honda?

"I did not have an airbag incident. I bought a 2015 honda odyssey two weeks ago. I read the newspaper article today, and called honda to find out whether the airbags installed in my car are takata. Honda declined to tell me, stating that they don't give that information to consumers unless their specific vehicle is subject to recall. My complaint is that the issues leading to the recalls seem shrouded in non-disclosure, and that consumers should be able to find out information about their vehicles."

– safercar.gov

Shameful. Canadian car owners will get more recall info from NHTSA's *safercar.gov* than from Transport Canada or automakers. Owners armed with the U.S. info should see a dealer for that make and ask for an appointment to repair the defect. At the same time, a letter should be sent to the Legal Affairs branch of the Canadian automaker (usually located in Toronto), warning that it will be liable for any injuries or deaths incurred while waiting for repairs.

ACURA

Acura, Honda's luxury division, has sold a variety of models in Canada, mostly as upscale Hondas with a luxury nameplate. Among its entry-level models is the ILX compact introduced in 2013 and the discontinued CSX and TSX. Larger, more expensive models include the TL performance luxury sedan, replaced by the 2015 TLX (a ZDX four-door sport coupe), the RL luxury performance sedan – replaced by the RLX – (a turbocharged RDX luxury crossover SUV), and the MDX luxury SUV. Some of these models are rated in Appendix I.

Acuras are good buys, but let's not kid ourselves – most Acura products are basically fully loaded Hondas with a few additional features and unjustifiably higher prices that drift downward to reasonable levels as the vehicles age.

This is no surprise, Acura buyers are willing to over-spend because they covet the Acura brand for its luxury cachet, even if they are simply all-dressed Hondas with luxury pretensions. *Automobile* magazine calls Acura "a lost brand" – a harsh judgment of the first Japanese nameplate (four years before Lexus) to take on the U.S. luxury market with its popular 1986 Legend and Integra. The brand is now less distinctive than it once was when Acura was a showcase for advanced technology. It has lost its leadership edge and now offers what everybody else provides, at a discount.

Acura has moved away from affordable, nimble, sporty cars to be a builder of high-end SUVs like the MDX – its bestseller that accounts for one-third of all Acura sales. Despite the fact that Acura and Honda dealers have abhorred real price competition for years, declining sales during the past few years have forced them to give sizeable rebates and other sales incentives to customers to keep market share. In their own right, maintenance costs are low, depreciation is generally slower than average, though there are some exceptions, and reliability and quality are much better than average. Still the driving experience is not all that extraordinary, interior amenities are fairly basic, and controls and touchscreens are counter-intuitive. MDX and RDX SUVs are the better performers, while the cheaper ILX and RLX models haven't lived up to owner expectations. Nevertheless, what few defects Acuras have mirror Honda's problems and are usually related to squeaks, rattles, minor trim glitches, infotainment malfunctions, and accessories such as the navigation, climate control, and sound systems.

Here's a tip for penny-pinchers. Despite being the best-selling vehicle in Acura Canada's lineup, Honda axed the Acura CSX after the 2011 model year and replaced it with the Civic-based ILX. Smart shoppers should consider buying a fully loaded 2011 CSX Sedan Tech, with some remaining warranty, for $13,500, a "steal" for a car that originally sold for almost double the price ($25,790).

And, speaking of the warranty, Acura has extended the warranty on some of its 2007-2011 models to cover an automatic transmission judder (shake) that may also damage the transmission's torque converter (below). Owners of 2009-11 TSX models also benefit from a "secret" warranty, covering sticking engine rings and high oil consumption. That warranty extension (TSB #13-006, dated April 3, 2015) extends coverage up to 8 years/125,000 miles for pistons and piston rings, no matter if the vehicle was bought new or used.

WARRANTY EXTENSION: TORQUE CONVERTER
PRODUCT UPDATE: PCM UPDATE FOR LOCK-UP CLUTCH FUNCTION

CSC-10049199-8317   SEPTEMBER 2012

ACURA

MDX 2007-09, RL 2009-10, and TL 2009-11

This letter is to notify you of a warranty extension and product update on your Acura.

WHAT IS THE REASON FOR THIS PRODUCT UPDATE?

A transmission judder (vibration) may sometimes be felt while driving between 20-45 mph. To minimize the opportunity for judder to occur, a software update for the transmission is available. If you do not feel the transmission judder, the software may prevent it from occurring. If the transmission software is not updated, the transmission may become damaged.

WHAT IS THE REASON FOR THIS WARRANTY EXTENSION?

If the judder goes away or never appears, no action is required on your part. If the judder appears or comes back after the product update is applied, the torque converter may need to be replaced. To ensure your confidence in your vehicle, American Honda is extending the warranty on the torque converter to 8 years from the original date of purchase or 105,000 miles, whichever comes first. This warranty extension provides coverage for the original owner and any subsequent owners.

MDX

RATING: Recommended (2015-16). Above Average (2007-14); Average (2001-06). **Road performance:** Good highway performance with commendable acceleration, nice handling, and good fuel economy. Although braking was improved in 2014, "feel" and braking distance still need improving. Steering is reasonably responsive, but the 6-speed automatic transmission isn't as efficient as the 7- or 8-speeds offered by German competitors. Furthermore, shifting Is a bit tardy when accelerating around curves. Recent models with a larger wheelbase and improved suspension help improve the ride quality and extra inches in length provide greater cargo capacity. **Strong points:** Loaded with goodies: The standard rear-view camera is a proven lifesaver; above-average reliability; and a roomy interior offers plenty of interior comfort and top-quality body and mechanical components. Excessive engine and road noise intrusion into the cabin has been muted by the 2014 redesign. Rear and middle seats fold flat and give easier rear seat access. **Weak points:** Overpriced and overweight; the rear third seat remains for kids only; the dash console isn't user-friendly; audio and navigation systems are needlessly complicated; and fuel consumption is on the high side. Owners report noisy brakes and premature brake wear; erratic cruise control; severe brake shimmy; windshield cracks for no reason; and malfunctioning power accessories and entertainment systems. Infotainment settings can be hard to find in the system's menus.

Other opinions: "The 2015 Acura MDX ranks #5 out of 18 luxury midsize SUVs ... [it has] outstanding fuel economy for the class, powerful performance and a roomy, high-end cabin." – *U.S. News & World Report.* "Dual-screen infotainment system's mediocre graphics and distracting interface; modest cargo space behind the third row." – (*Edmunds.com*). **Major redesign:** 2001, 2007, and 2014. The 2016 version offers a new standard 9-speed automatic transmission with push-button gear selection, an improved AWD system, and an easy-entry driver seat. Expect a mid-cycle change in mid-2016 and a revamped version in 2019. **Highway/city fuel economy:** 9.1/12.7 L/100 km. **Best alternatives:** The BMW X5, Buick Enclave, Chevrolet Traverse or Terrain, Infiniti FX35, and Lexus RX series. Would you like comparable Asian performance and reliability for $15,000 less? Try a Honda Pilot (the MDX's cheaper cousin), a Nissan Xterra, or a Toyota Highlander. The Volvo XC90 and Mercedes ML320, ML350, or ML550 have adequate cargo room with all the rows down, but they have neither comparable cargo room behind the second row nor quality control and dealer servicing.

SAFETY: **Child safety seat setup:** "Acceptable." **Crashworthiness:** NHTSA: 2014-16 models given the top five-star rating for all crash tests. 2001-13 models earned four and five stars for occupant crash protection. IIHS: Rear, offset, side, and roof protection are "Good." IIHS qualifies 2001-15 models' frontal offset, side protection, and head restraints as "Good." One discordant note: 2003-06 model head restraints were judged to be "Poor." **Owner-reported safety-related failures:** Sudden unintended acceleration; engine cuts out when turning; steering also locks up while turning; brake warning light comes on for no reason; steering doesn't respond, grinds or makes a rubbing sound when turned to maximum; 2015 model axle fractured after only 80 miles of use.

ALERT! This mid-size SUV's sporty suspension may not sit well with passengers who expect a smoother ride; although the redesigned 2014 model rides better, a Lexus RX is much smoother, even over the roughest roads. Another advantage of the RX is its lower starting price and reasonable fuel economy for an AWD.

MDX Profile

	2006	2007	2008	2009	2010	2011	2012	2013	2014
Used Values ($)									
MDX	11,000	13,000	15,500	19,500	23,000	27,500	32,500	38,000	42,500
Touring/Tech	13,500	16,000	18,500	22,000	24,500	29,000	35,500	44,000	52,000
Elite	—	19,500	22,000	25,000	28,000	33,000	38,500	47,500	57,000
Reliability	★	☆	☆	☆	☆	☆	☆	☆	☆
Repairs ($$$)	2	◉	◉	◉	◉	◉	◉	◉	◉
Electrical	★	☆	☆	☆	☆	☆	☆	☆	☆
Engine (base)	★	★	☆	☆	☆	☆	☆	☆	☆
Fit/Finish	2	★	★	★	★	★	★	☆	☆
Infotainment	—	—	—	—	—	2	2	2	★
Transmission (auto.)	2	★	★	★	★	★	★	★	☆

SECRET WARRANTIES, INTERNAL BULLETINS: 2007-09—Acura will cover the cost of replacing the transmission torque converter up to 8 years/105,000 miles. 2007-10—Warranty extension for a steering wheel that's hard to turn. Acura is extending the warranty on the power steering pump to 7 years from the original date of purchase or 100,000 miles, whichever comes first. A water leak at the rear of the moonroof signals the need for a moonroof drain channel seal. 2007-11—With a normal engine oil level, a "check engine oil level" message appears on the MID or the navigation screen. The low oil pressure indicator on the instrument panel may also be on. Acura will replace the engine oil pressure switch. 2007-13—Silence a squeaking, screeching window by removing the lower seal from the glass outer weatherstrips on each of the four doors. 2010-11—If the front or rear seat stays hot after the seat heater is turned off, the heater switch has to be replaced. 2010-13—A steering vibration/moan while turning at low speeds may be caused by a faulty alternator pulley. 2012—Running board step plate pad doesn't lay flat and the master key won't lock in the extended position. 2013—The front brakes may squeal when applied. In TSB #13-020 issued on April 13, 2013, Acura says the noise is caused by glazed brake pads. 2014—A second-row passenger seat rattle may be caused by the cable link contacting the seat frame. If the engine "chirps" when warmed up, chances are the timing belt is contacting the back edge of the crankshaft pulley. On the other hand, a grinding, rattling, vibrating, fluttering, or buzzing noise coming from the front of the vehicle under light acceleration may signal that the bulkhead cover fasteners (latches and strikers) are loose.

HONDA

Honda's 2016 lineup has a car, truck, SUV, or minivan for every need and, this year, the company will introduce its new HR-V compact crossover ranked #3 out of 27 affordable compact SUVs rated by *U.S. News & World Report*.

For over three decades Honda and its Acura spin-offs have taken top scores for reliable, well-performing, and fuel-efficient vehicles. However, during the past decade, the company has hid a dark secret – its life-saving airbags could be life-taking grenades and the company's much vaunted quality control was achieved by a system of "secret" warranties that swept production goofs under the rug and deliberately hid defect reports from U.S. officials.

Let's take the Takata issue first. Honda is Takata's biggest customer, and has been for well over a decade. The automaker received complaints of Takata airbag failures resulting in deaths and injuries. In late 2014, Honda acknowledged failing to tell NHTSA about 60% of accident reports, or 1,729 incidents involving injuries or deaths in its automobiles since 2003.

Regulators believe that some of Honda's unreported cases likely involve defective Takata airbags that are linked to six deaths – all in Hondas – and hundreds of injuries. In February and June 2007, Honda told Takata about additional airbag ruptures that year. But again, the automaker did not initiate a recall or provide information about the ruptures to federal regulators. U.S. federal safety regulators subsequently fined Honda $70 million – the maximum allowed – for failing to report deaths and injuries involving its vehicles in a timely manner. Honda claimed it missed the safety implications due to inaccurate data entry and computer coding errors, as well as a "narrow interpretation" of what incidents required a report to regulators.

This explanation didn't wash with U.S. federal investigators. In addition to levying a precedent-setting $70 million U.S. fine, Washington forced Honda to sign a consent order giving the government increased oversight over what Honda reports, and mandates third-party audits to ensure that all required reporting is completed honestly.

Auto shoppers are still casting a wary eye at Honda's recent lowered quality ratings from different independent consumer groups that concluded the automaker had been "coasting" on its previous high ranking by putting less into its more recent cars to boost profits. The *Nikkei Asian Review*, in its December 1, 2014, issue says the company has pursued expansion at the expense of product quality since 2012, after getting its marching orders from Honda President Takanobu Ito:

> Some observers trace the company's current crisis back to President Takanobu Ito. In September 2012, he said he would pursue a global sales target of over 6 million vehicles in fiscal 2016. Ito's declaration was a major departure from the company's management tradition. None of his predecessors announced medium- or long-term sales targets. The president's statement reflected a major shift in the company's focus from development of technologically sophisticated vehicles to price and sales volume. A mid-ranking manager at Honda said one indirect cause of the recalls is the absence of "product quality" from the company's future vision.

Ito missed his six-million-car target and now has forsworn making any more predictions, but the damage has been done.

New Products

Honda is investing heavily into turbocharging its small-displacement engines, dual-clutch transmissions with seven to nine gears, fuel-sipping Earth Dreams engines, and continuously variable transmissions (CVT). Keep in mind that each of these innovations has as many detractors as boosters due to their first-year troubles and inability to meet both fuel-economy and performance objectives.

And speaking of innovations that may be more trouble than they are worth – Welcome to Honda head-restraint hell!

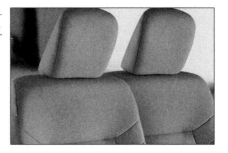

Marquis de Sade head restraints used by some penny-pinching automakers are a "pain in the – neck".

Some cars in Honda's lineup use front head restraints that have generated hundreds of NHTSA complaints, headline many Honda forums, and are literally an excruciating "pain in the neck" – and the shoulders, and lower spine. U.S. Government regulations require better whiplash protection for passengers and most automakers complied years ago with thoughtful, comfortable designs. Not Honda. Be wary. This *is* a deal-breaker.

FIT ★★★★

RATING: Above Average (2008-16); Average (2007). Within each one of these above ratings, the first year of each redesign had more factory-related problems than the ensuing model years. Slotted below the Civic, the Fit is a good choice among small compacts, however, the poor front seat design for some can be a deal-breaker. **Road performance:** Plenty of smooth, quiet power with either the manual or automatic transmission; handles and brakes like a sports car. The accelerator may be too sensitive and cause the car to over-accelerate. Handling is easy, but side winds require constant steering corrections. The ride is also somewhat choppy due to the car's small size. Unintentional drifting at highway speeds. **Strong points:** Small on the outside but big on the inside this mini-car sips fuel and still performs well in both city and highway driving. Its 1.5L engine isn't in the big leagues, but you will seldom realize you're driving a mini-compact. Innovative seats allow you to lift the rear seat's base up against the backrest to make room for bulky items, or the seat can be folded flat, which doubles the cargo space. You can even configure the seats to make a small bed. Honda offers lots of standard features; good interior ergonomics (front seats, excepted); ample and flexible interior space; quality craftsmanship; and good resale value. **Weak points:** Engine struggles going uphill with a full load; a busy ride; front seats aren't height-adjustable; and more legroom is needed for taller passengers. Headlights may not project far enough into the distance. Road debris easily destroys the AC condenser – an expensive repair not covered under warranty, says one angry Honda owner in this NHSTA-logged complaint:

There are "vents" which lie below the license plate holder near the road, wide enough to fit a fist and the length of the front bumper. This allows all kinds of road debris to enter and hit the A/C condenser only inches behind the opening. This damage has been reported on a number of websites since model year 2008. A similar issue has also been reported in a number of other Honda car models, including the CR-V and the Odyssey, which resulted in a successful class action lawsuit.

Owner-reported safety-related failures: Barely a handful of complaints were logged by NHTSA for the 2011-13 models when 50 per model year would be the norm. Owners report sudden acceleration and airbag failures; some transmission seal leaks; a weak AC; windshield stress fractures; paint chipping/delamination and premature cosmetic rusting; a small gas tank; and a fuel sloshing noise heard under the front seats.

Prices and Specs

Prices (Firm): *DX: $14,580, LX: $17,375, EX: $19,275, EX-L NAVI: $21,375* **Freight:** $1,610 **Powertrain (Front-drive):** Engine: 1.5L 4-cyl. (130 hp); Transmissions: 6-speed man., CVT auto. **Dimensions/ capacity:** Passengers: 2/3; Wheelbase: 99.6 in.; H: 60/L: 160/W: 67 in.; Headroom F/R: 5.5/4 in.; Legroom F/R: 45/27 in.; Cargo volume: 16.6 cu. ft.; Fuel tank: 40L/regular; Tow limit: No towing; Load capacity: 850 lb.; Turning circle: 34.1 ft.; Weight: 2,513 lb.

Other opinions: "The 2015 Honda Fit ranks #1 out of 42 affordable small cars; #1 in affordable subcompacts; and #1 in hatchbacks. It has exceptional fuel economy and impresses critics with generous cargo room, a spacious back seat and pleasant ride." – *U.S. News & World Report.* "I was so impressed with the 2015 Honda Fit after reading all the glowing ratings. Took two 20-minute test drives ... after a whole afternoon of riding around, my back was hurting. OK ... I was tired I told myself. Nope, every time I drive this car my lower back hurts. I took some others' advice and reversed the head rest. That was a bit better but did nothing for my lower back. Once or twice a year I do a 500 mile trip. I could drive 6-7 hours in the Vibe without issue. That trip is coming up again, and I am truly worried about doing it in the Fit. I am retired, and on a fixed income .... These old bones can't live in misery." – *www.carcomplaints.com/Honda/Fit/2015/.* **Major redesign:** 2007 and 2015. Car buyers seeking an excellent value should strongly consider the redesigned 2015 Fit, which is improved in nearly every way over the old model. **Highway/city fuel economy:** *Man.:* 6.4/8.1 L/100 km. *Auto.:* 5.7/7.0 L/100 km. Interestingly, tests prove the automatic gearbox is more fuel-efficient than the manual transmission. Whichever transmission you choose, owners say fuel economy claims are overstated by Honda. **Best alternatives:** Other good econocars are the Honda Civic, Hyundai Accent or Elantra, Mazda2 or Mazda3, and VW Golf. Mercedes' Smart Car and Toyota's Yaris aren't as refined or reliable as the Fit.

SAFETY: Child safety seat setup: Untested. **Crashworthiness:** NHTSA: 2015-16 models were awarded five stars for overall crash protection. Crashworthiness was cut to four stars on the 2011-14 models. Earlier 2007-10 models provide five-star frontal and side protection and score four stars for rollover resistance. IIHS: 2012-15 ratings are "Good" for offset frontal, side, rear, and roof crashworthiness; small front overlap protection varied from "Poor" to "Average." 2007-11 Fits continued to do poorly in the small front overlap test, while getting a "Good" rating in other crash tests. **Owner-reported safety-related failures:** Airbags that fail to deploy, "touchy" brakes, the dashboard's elevated design obstructs forward visibility; and drivers have a narrow view out the rear window. Other safety concerns include sudden unintended acceleration; insufficient legroom that leads drivers to apply the brakes and accelerator at the same time; extreme side wind sensitivity when cruising on windswept roadways; periodic brake failures; broken seat belts; rear seat belts that ratchet tighter around children; and tire jacks that sometimes bend sideways when lifting the car.

ALERT!:

The head rest pushes my head forward and strains my neck to the point that I either have to sit upright away from the seat or stretch my neck far out in pain. Either way it is not safe, whether in case of accident or generally for my health. With no cool-off period on new cars in California, I cannot return the car, which at this point has 12 miles [19 km] on it, so I am forced to drive unsafely. I ran Google search for Honda head rest complaints and found out that customers have been complaining about Honda's new head rests for the same very reason since 2007 through 2015 for most of their models – from Accord and Odyssey to Fit.

What makes the matter worse is that you cannot reverse the headrest as there are grooves only on one of the two support poles. By making head restraints painful to use, Honda is forcing its customers to drive unsafely, specifically without head restraints.

– safercar.gov

Fit Profile

	2007	2008	2009	2010	2011	2012	2013	2014
Used Values ($)								
DX	4,000	5,000	6,000	7,500	7,000	8,500	9,500	11,000
LX	5,000	6,000	7,000	8,000	8,500	9,500	11,500	13,500
Sport	6,000	7,000	8,500	9,500	10,500	12,500	14,000	15,500
Reliability	3	4	4	4	4	3	3	
Repairs ($$$)	2	1	1	1	1	2	2	
Electrical	2	3			3			
Engine (base)	3	3						
Fit/Finish	2	3						
Infotainment	—	—	—	—	3	3	3	
Transmission (auto.)	1	1	1	1	2	2	3	3

SECRET WARRANTIES, INTERNAL BULLETINS: 2007-08—A "secret" warranty extends the electric power steering warranty to 10 years/150,000 miles and covers all repairs, including the replacement of the EPS control unit. The steering will feel heavier than normal, or is hard to turn. 2009-12—The front windshield may have a vertical crack starting at the bottom, above the cowl, near the middle. Honda will replace the windshield as a "goodwill" gesture. Cite TSB #12-006, published Jan. 21, 2012. This defect is not an insurance claim. Honda is responsible 100% and must pay supplementary transport while car is out of service. Fix for a fuel filler door that won't open. If the A/C blower motor works on high speed only, Honda suggest changing the blower motor and resistor. 2009-13—The rear cargo and/or spare tire well areas may be wet or damp; replace the AM/FM antenna base and apply Konishi Bond to the seal prior to installation. Floor carpet tears or wears out prematurely. The legal principle of "reasonable durability" comes into play here. Try a 50% cost-sharing deal. 2014-15—Measures to correct rear-view camera malfunctions. 2015—The 2015 front bumper beam was changed to improve narrow offset (also known as small overlap) front crash test protection. Honda will provide owners of early-2015s those vehicles with the updated front bumper beam.

CIVIC ★★★★

RATING: Above Average (2015-16); Average (2001-14). **Road performance:** These cars are noted for good acceleration, a smooth-shifting automatic transmission, and reasonable fuel economy. Be careful, though, since a lot depends upon the model year chosen as Honda works through the mistakes it made in its 2012 redesign. It would be wise to get a second-series 2016 (built after April 2016). The restyled 2016 version will be a bit larger, harness a few more horses and offer a revised infotainment system. For the high-performance crowd, Honda will launch the Civic Type R, which it calls "the most extreme and high-performing Type R ever built." This sporty five-door comes with a new direct-injected turbocharged 2.0L

VTEC 310 hp engine hooked to a 5-speed manual transmission. Contrary to most vehicles, older Hondas are more reliable, than the post-2011 versions. A big fly in Honda's ointment, thougth, is its extensive use of Takata airbags in over 700,000 vehicles sold in Canada from 2001 through 2011. These shrapnel-spewing balls of hot air were recalled in December 2014, however, that recall has been re-opened because the replacements may contain the same over-aggressive ammonium nitrate propellant that was used in the recalled 2001-05 Civics. **Strong points:** Competent engines that will handle most duties; instruments and controls are easily accessed; a tilt/telescoping steering wheel is standard; and interior space is more than adequate for most adults. Civics also have a strong resale value. **Weak points:** Honda's redesigned 2012 model lost the quality and performance edge that made the Civic Canada's most popular small car for decades. Although they are slightly better built, the 2013-14 Civics continue to have serious safety and performance problems that are a repeat of the earlier model's deficiencies. So far, the 2015's haven't elicited many complaints, which bodes well for the reworked 2016 version. Brakes are a major sore point that includes premature brake caliper and rotor resurfacing. Rear brake rotors can also quickly rust and need resurfacing if the car isn't driven for several weeks. Tire pressure warning alert lights for no reason; fuel sloshes in the fuel tank when braking or going over bumps; paint delaminates and is easily scratched (see "Secret Warranties," below); and there's limited trunk space. Body fit and finish and accessories are also problematic: A-pillar, dash, or sunroof rattles; windows bind or come out of run channels; doors and trunk lids are hard to close; fuel-door handles don't work; driver's seat is poorly mounted; door locks and power windows malfunction, (see "Secret Warranties," below); the trunk cannot be opened from the cabin area; the driver-side window won't roll back up (see "Secret Warranties," below); sun visors fall apart; fuel gauge, speedometer, and tachometer can't be believed; lousy radio speakers; water leaks through the door bottoms, from the tail light into the trunk, and onto the driver-side footwell carpet; windows often come off their tracks; trunk springs fail; exterior and interior lights dim to an unsafe level; heated side mirrors gradually lose their reflective ability; and the AC condenser is easily destroyed by road debris.

Prices and Specs

Prices (negotiable): *DX:* $15,440, *LX Coupe:* $18,590, *EX-L, Sedan:* $25,240, *Si Sedan:* $26,191 **Freight:** $1,810 **Powertrain (front-drive):** Engines (2012 Hybrid): 1.5L 4-cyl. (110 hp) plus electric motor (23 hp), 1.8L 4-cyl. (140 hp), 2.4L 4-cyl. (201 hp); Transmissions: 5-speed man., 5-speed auto., 6-speed man., CVT auto. **Dimensions/capacity:** *Sedan:* Passengers: 2/3; Wheelbase: 105.1 in.; H: 56.5/L: 177.3/W: 69 in.; Headroom F/R: 5/2.5 in.; Legroom F/R: 41/27 in.; Cargo volume: 13 cu. ft.; Fuel tank: 50L/regular; Tow limit: 1,000 lb.; Load capacity: 850 lb.; Turning circle: 35.4 ft.; Weight: 2,725 lb. *2012 Hybrid:* Passengers: 2/3; Wheelbase: 105.1 in.; H: 56.5/L: 177.3/W: 69 in.; Headroom F/R: 5/2.5 in.; Legroom F/R: 41/27 in.; Cargo volume: 11 cu. ft.; Fuel tank: 47L/regular; Tow limit: N/A; Load capacity: 850 lb.; Turning circle: 35.4 ft.; Weight: 2,853 lb.

Other opinions: "The 2015 Honda Civic ranks #4 out of 42 affordable small cars. An upscale and roomy interior, silky transmission and solid fuel economy win over critics and help the 2015 Honda Civic shine in a crowded segment." – *U.S. News & World Report.* "I own a 2007 Honda Civic LX. Went to dealership regarding terrible paint fading, broken visor (which had been replaced once already for being defective). They said they will repaint car at no cost to me and they replaced visor again. I was also told the car's heavy vibration is due to a broken engine mount and given a quote of $477 to repair. They stated engine mount breakage is normal wear and tear issue … now I read numerous reports of this problem from 1992-2010." – *repairpal.com/bad-engine-mounts-may-cause-vibration-roughness-and-rattle-964.* **Major redesign:** 2001, 2006, 2012, and 2016. The latest Earth Dreams engine upgrade will be part of the Civic's spring 2016 redesign when lots of new content will go into the 2017 model. **Highway/city fuel economy:** *1.8L (140 hp) man.:* 5.4/7.4 L/100 km. *Auto.:* 5.7/8.2 L/100 km. *2012 Hybrid:* 5.3 L/100 km (combined highway/city). **Best alternatives:** Chevrolet Impala, Hyundai Elantra, Mazda3, Kia Forte, or the Volkswagen Golf.

SAFETY: Child safety seat setup: "Acceptable." **Crashworthiness:** NHTSA: 2012-15 Civics given four and five stars for overall crashworthiness. The 2011s didn't do as well: Four stars for front protection and rollover resistance, and only two stars for side crashworthiness. IIHS: Crash tests rate the 2006-15 models "Good" in all categories. 2001-05s also earned a "Good" score in frontal offset crash tests, but 2003-05 models got a "Poor" score for rear crash protection. **Owner-reported safety-related failures:** Seat belts tighten progressively when connected:

> Autistic child removed seat belt to exit my 2013 Civic, child somehow became tangled in seat belt. Belt started retracting. Could not remove child from belt after several attempts. Seat belt would not release and continued to dig itself farther into child's torso. Local fire department had to be called to cut child out of the seat belt.

The airbag warning light stays lit even though an adult passenger occupies the seat; and many instances of inadvertent side airbag deployment, or airbags failing to deploy in collisions:

> I was trying to back into a parking space with my 8-month-old 2012 Honda Civic. As I took my foot off the gas pedal to put the car into reverse and before I could step on the brake, the car surged forward at a tremendous rate of speed, jumped a curb and went straight into a brick building. The car bounced backwards onto the parking lot and I was able to step on the brake and regain control. This happened in a matter of a split second with no time to jam the brake on as the car lurched forward. Even though the car jolted tremendously, the airbag did not go off, but a service light came on the dash board indicating "Check Airbag System."

Sometimes, the driver's door cannot be unlocked from inside:

Upon viewing an accident in front of me, I parked on side of road, applied emergency flashers, called 911 (hand held – not attached to car) and was removing keys from ignition & trying to open driver side door & exit car to render aid. Car door would not open. I unlocked door manually at handle. Still would not open. I re-inserted key, turned engine on, pushed door open button. Door not open. (I was dialing & talking with 911 operator during this time). I was getting excited about need to get to victim(s) of accident, but couldn't get out of my car. I eventually climbed over middle console to exit car from passenger's door.

Windshield wipers freeze in their housing; sudden loss of power steering; fractured front tie rods, causing complete steering loss; sudden acceleration or surging when the AC or heater is engaged, or when the steering wheel is turned sharply; car veers sharply to the right when braking; the brake and accelerator pedal are mounted too close together; and the premature replacement of brake pads and discs. The Start/Stop button, located near the flasher button, can be easily pressed by accident; the gas pedal sticks to the floor; several seconds hesitation when accelerating from a stop, especially when in ECON mode, or engine surges when exiting an off-ramp or when the brakes are applied:

Car suddenly stops dead while accelerating to make left-hand turn. It will resume acceleration only after a 4-second pause. Turning into oncoming traffic with a dead vehicle is going to cause an accident involving injuries or death. This is the third time that this incident has occurred to my vehicle. The Honda dealer cannot find the cause.

ALERT! Hundreds of complaints that the head restraint pushes the driver's head downward and too far forward:

I have tilted the seat back as far as I safely can and still be able to drive. I am [a] 53-year-old female, 5'3" tall, and wear bifocals. I am having difficulty focusing from tachometer to speedometer to road because I cannot [move] my head to use the right part of my glasses to see. I cannot tilt my head back at all because of the headrest. I also experienced a headache that evening as well due to eye strain. The NHSTA changed their headrest regulations in 2008. Test dummies for large males were used and then standards were put in place. After spending thousands of dollars on a new car, I am unable to safely drive it. I have to either remove, turn around, or jerry-rig a remedy for the headrest in order to drive and not suffer neck, back, shoulder, and visual pain. The cost is my safety in an accident. Or, I can leave the headrest and drive with my posture in a horrid position. I cannot sit up straight, my head is forced downward so I cannot use my bifocals properly, and I cannot tilt the seat back any further and still see over the dashboard.

Other problems to look for during your test drive: Horn may not be loud enough; dim headlights; windshield fogs up faster than AC can cope with; and original equipment tires may be bottom-rung imports.

Civic Profile

	2006	2007	2008	2009	2010	2011	2012	2013	2014
Used Values ($)									
Sedan DX	4,000	4,500	5,000	6,000	6,500	7,500	8,500	10,000	12,000
Sedan DX-G	—	5,000	6,000	7,000	7,500	9,500	—	—	—
Sedan LX	5,000	6,000	7,500	—	—	—	10,500	13,000	15,000
Si	—	—	8,500	10,000	11,500	13,000	16,500	—	—
Hybrid	4,500	5,000	6,000	7,000	—	—	15,000	—	—
Coupe LX	4,500	5,500	6,500	7,500	8,500	—	11,000	13,000	15,000
Si	6,000	7,000	8,500	9,500	11,000	13,000	16,500	19,500	—
Reliability	★	★	★	★	★	★	★	★	★
Repairs ($$$)	2	2	2	2	2	2	3	1	1
Electrical	★	★	★	★	★	★	★	★	★
Engine (base)	★	★	★	★	★	★	★	★	★
Fit/Finish	★	★	★	★	★	★	★	★	★
Infotainment	—	—	—	—	—	★	★	★	★
Transmission (auto.)	★	★	★	★	★	★	★	★	★

SECRET WARRANTIES, INTERNAL BULLETINS: All models/years: Most Honda TSBs allow for special warranty consideration on a "goodwill" basis, even after the warranty has expired or the car has changed hands. Referring to the "goodwill" euphemism will increase your chances of getting some kind of refund for repairs that are obviously related to a factory defect. Paint defect claims sometimes require an accompanying digitized photo before they can be considered. Tips for submitting a successful paint claim can be found in TSB #10-002, published Jan. 20, 2010. *Hybrid:* 2006-07—Hybrids that lose power when accelerating need three different software updates. This will be done under a "goodwill" warranty at no charge to the customer, says Honda Service Bulletin #09-058, published July 30, 2009. Honda's 2006 Civic software update caused a dramatic drop in fuel economy. Accord Hybrid owners say they are also getting poor gas mileage, since the same revised engine/IMA battery software was installed in their Hybrids to extend IMA battery life. *CNG:* 2001-15—Inoperative fuel gauge. *Civic:* 2006-08—In TSB #13-047 Honda says uneven tire wear on 2006-07 Civics and 2006-08 Civic Hybrids might be caused by incorrect rear suspension geometry. Repairs include new upper control arms. 2006-09—Engine overheats or leaks coolant because the engine block is cracking at the coolant passages. Honda will install a new engine block assembly free of charge up to 10 years, with no mileage limit as stated in

TSB #10-048, issued Dec. 9, 2014. The sun visor may come apart or split with use. American Honda has extended that warranty, as well, to 7 years from the original date of purchase or 100,000 miles, whichever comes first. 2006-13—Roof and trunk paint cracking, chalking, or clouding. Cite Honda TSB #14-034, issued Sept. 23, 2014. This TSB is critical as a benchmark by Honda for any paint claims targeting other models, colours, model years, or automakers. Again, the legal principle of "reasonable durability" and negligence applies. Torn engine mounts cause a rattle or a knock coming from the right front of the vehicle when driving over bumps at 15-20 mph (24-32 km/h). It is likely the passenger's side hydraulic side engine mount is cavitating and making a rattling sound, or it is torn and making a knocking sound. It needs to be replaced under an extended warranty. Cite Honda TSB #06-060, issued Dec. 24, 2010. 2006-09—A "secret" warranty extends the electric power steering warranty to 10 years/150,000 miles and covers all repairs, including the replacement of the EPS control unit. The steering will feel heavier than normal, or is hard to turn. 2006-11—There may be a pop or clunk from the front suspension area when driving over bumps. This usually occurs after completing a tight (full lock) turn and the front bump stops become dislodged and then pops back into place. Cite TSB #078, issued March 2, 2012. 2006-11—Trunk lid repaint warranty extension. Dissimilar metals in the chrome trim and the trunk lid, along with road salt, may create a very low electrochemical reaction that forms corrosion, rust spots, or stains on the trunk lid. Honda is extending the warranty on the trunk lid to 7 years from the original date of purchase says TSB #13-004, issued Jan. 3, 2013. 2006-12—Honda admits it is looking into a clicking or clacking noise emitted when turning. 2012-13—More free paint jobs: Honda will repaint any Civic up to 7 years if the roof or trunk paint has a chalky appearance or the paint is cracked on the hood and the leading edge of the front fenders. This free repair is available to all owners, whether their vehicle was bought new or used. (A copy of Honda's authorization letter is kept by the NHTSA at *safercar.gov* under "2013 Honda service bulletins"). Incorrect fuel gauges fixed for free under the emissions warranty. Front windows may not go up due to lack of clearance between the window motor pinion and plate hole. Roof molding may be loose or missing. 2013—Rocker arm may need to be replaced. Remedy for front brake squeaking, squealing, or grinding. Honda confirms inner door handles or latches may pop or stick. 2014—Tire pressure alert may come on for no reason. 2014-15—Troubleshooting tips for rear-view camera, or audio malfunctions.

HR-V ★

RATING: The HR-V is Not Recommended during its first year on the Canadian market. Generally, the first year a vehicle earns a low rating due to factory-related defects, parts and servicing glitches, hyped introductory prices, and delivery delays. This is especially true of new Hondas or models that Honda redesigns.

Slotted between the Fit and CR-V, with the heart of a Civic, a second-series HR-V (built after March 2016) should be a good choice among small compacts. Surprisingly, the HR-V's wheelbase is only 0.3 inch shorter than the CR-V's, which explains why a 6-foot-plus passenger can comfortably sit behind a just as tall driver. On the other hand, the HR-V is 10 inches shorter in overall length, 1.5 inches lower in height and nearly 2 inches narrower, so enjoy the back seat, while you can. Rear cargo space is also impressive and the flat folded rear seat area is a dog owner's delight. **Road performance:** Plenty of pickup over most terrain, a quiet engine and little road or wind noise in the cabin. Brakes are efficient with minimal front-end plow, and little fading after successive stops. Annoying CVT transmission drone. **Strong points:** The HR-V has all the essentials: Perky engine around town and perfect for non-challenging terrain; a commodious, flexible, and well-appointed interior, a "Goldilocks" suspension that's not too firm, nor too soft; reliable and available components from the Fit, and good fuel consumption. **Weak points:** Engine struggles going uphill with a full load, however, short commutes and city chores are a breeze.

Prices and Specs

Price (Firm): $21,500 est. **Freight:** $1,800 **Powertrain (Front-drive/AWD):** Engine: 1.8L 4-cyl. (141 hp); Transmission: 6-speed man (only available on front-wheel drive models), CVT **Dimensions/capacity:** Passengers: 2/3; Wheelbase: 102.8 in.; H: 63.2/L: 169.1/W: 69.8 in.; Headroom N/A; Legroom N/A; Cargo volume: 24.3 cu. ft.; Fuel tank: 55L/regular; Tow limit: No towing; Ground clearance: 6.7 in.; Load capacity: 850 lb.; Turning circle: 37.4 ft.; Weight: N/A

Other opinions: "The all-new 2016 Honda HR-V's flexible interior and composed ride make it one of the most practical subcompact SUVs available ... [It] ranks #1 in affordable subcompact SUVs and #3 out of 27 affordable compact SUVs." – *U.S. News & World Report.* "Early subcompact SUVs like the Mitsubishi Outlander Sport and Nissan Juke required buyers to sacrifice interior roominess, but more recent additions like the Chevrolet Trax and Jeep Renegade are more accommodating. The HR-V's innovative layout takes it a step further with a roomy, versatile cabin and large cargo area. Combined with a high-grade interior and good estimated gas mileage." – *cars.com.* **Major redesign:** 2016. **Highway/city fuel economy:** N/A. Be wary of Honda's overly-optimistic gas consumption figures; instead, wait a few months for Ottawa NRC ratings at: *oee.nrcan.gc.ca/fcr-rcf/public/index-e.cfm.* **Best alternatives:** Other good econocars are the Chevrolet Trax (see chart below), Kia Soul, which doesn't come with four-wheel drive, Mazda2 or Mazda3, and the VW Golf. Upscale AWD models are fairly reliable and good performers are the Buick Encore, Chevrolet Equinox, GMC Terrain; Honda CR-V, Mazda CX-3, and Nissan Rogue.

	2016 Chevy Trax	2016 Honda HR-V
Wheelbase	100.6 in.	102.8 in.
Length	168.5 in.	169.1 in.
Width	69.9 in.	69.8 in.
Height	65.9 in.	63.2 in.
Curb weight	3,048 lbs.	2,888 lbs.
Base engine	Turbo 1.4-liter 4-cylinder	1.8-liter 4-cylinder
Horsepower	138 @ 4,900 rpm	141 @ 6,500 rpm
Torque, lbs.-ft.	148 @ 1,850 rpm	127 @ 4,300 rpm
NRC L/100 km	Hwy/City 6.9/9.1L	N/A
Base price*	$19,130	$21,500

*Shipping fee not included

SAFETY: Child safety seat setup: Untested. **Crashworthiness:** NHTSA: Five stars awarded for overall crash safety. Nevertheless, the HR-V has the same interior packaging as the Fit it is based on. This means the fuel tank is located under the front seats allowing the rear seats to fold lower and flatter than competitors', but also possibly increasing the risk of fire in rear and frontal collisions as the tank is "sandwiched" by crash forces. Still, the 2015-16 Fit crashworthiness scores have been outstanding. Standard safety features on the HR-V include four-channel anti-lock brakes (ABS) with Brake Assist and Hill Start Assist; Vehicle Stability AssistTM (VSA®) with Traction Control; an expanded view driver's mirror; a much-recommended multi-angle rear-view camera; dual-stage, multiple-threshold front airbags, driver and front passenger SmartVent side airbags and side-curtain airbags for all outboard seating positions; and the infamous federally-mandated Tire Pressure Monitoring System (TPMS) that gives wrong readings as often as right and have to be reset at $50 a pop. **Owner-reported safety-related failures:** Nothing reported.

ALERT! Be patient to get a better price. Dealers aren't expected to budge from the manufacturer's suggested retail price before mid-2016, when manufacturer rebates and discounts kick in.

RATING: Recommended (2007-16); Above Average (2001-06). Carried over with minor changes since last year's redesign, the 2016 CR-V continues to be a driver-communicative SUV that is as reliable as it is cheap to service. **Road performance:** A smooth-running 4-banger handles most chores adequately, but owners say they'd like a bit more grunt for merging and tackling steep grades with a full load. There are also complaints of a persistent hesitation before acceleration that crops up from time to time. On the other hand, the car got a new CVT automatic transmission last year that is more responsive and smoother, though a bit noisier. The updated suspension and steering systems for 2015 have also improved both handling and steering. The ride is firm but comfortable, though the steering is a bit stiff and vague. High-speed cornering is not recommended, due to excessive body lean. Also, annoying highway noises are omnipresent when at cruising speeds. **Strong points:** Equipped with more standard features than most competitors, the 2016 CR-V has a nicely outfitted cabin that includes comfortable front seating and roomy rear seats that recline and slide independently and fold down to create a flat cargo floor. The lift-up tailgate is much more convenient than the swing-out version used in previous years. Overall fuel economy is better than many SUVs in its class. **Weak points:** The infotainment system is seriously compromised by buttons that are hard to see and access while driving. The ignition key frequently gets stuck in the ignition; electrical system shorts; premature brake wear; AC condenser is destroyed by road debris (a chronic failure on most of Honda's lineup); engine oil pan leaks; windshield washer nozzles freeze up in cold weather; pervasive vibrations, rattles, and clunking, knocking sounds.

Prices and Specs

Prices (Firm): *LX:* $25,990, *LX 4WD:* $28,140, *EX:* $28,940, *EX 4WD:* $31,040, *EX-L 4WD:* $33,240, Touring: $35,140 **Freight:** $1,810 **Powertrain (Front-drive/AWD):** Engine: 2.4L 4-cyl. (185 hp); Transmission: CVT **Dimensions/capacity:** Passengers: 2/3; Wheelbase: 103.1 in.; H: 66.1/L: 177.8/W: 71.6 in.; Headroom F/R: 4/4 in.; Legroom F/R: 40.5/29 in.; Cargo volume: 36 cu. ft.; Fuel tank: 50L/regular; Tow limit: 1,500 lb.; Load capacity: 850 lb.; Turning circle: 39 ft.; Ground clearance: 7.2 in.; Weight: 3,404 lb.

Other opinions: "The 2015 CR-V is ranked #1 in affordable compact SUVs. Reviewers praise the 2015 Honda CR-V for its abundance of standard features and spacious cabin, and it gets excellent fuel economy." – *U.S. News & World Report.* "Just bought a Honda CR-V 2015 EX-L. After driving it for one day experienced serious vibrations in driver and passenger seat while driving and even more intense when idling. Extremely distracting almost causing an accident. I cannot drive in this car. Dealer and Honda have acknowledged this problem with the new CR-Vs (not all – its random) but do not have a solution. Some dealers have actually refunded customers and exchanged cars to customer satisfaction. Its the right thing to do. They should be applauded. Not mine. They won't exchange or refund. I will be miserable every day in this car. Saw there is a potential class action suit since so many customers from 2015 have been affected and Honda has acknowledged the defect." – *www.carcomplaints.com/Honda/CR-V/2015/.* **Major redesign:** 1997, 2002, 2007, and 2012. **Highway/city fuel economy:** *Front-drive:* 6.9/8.6 L/100 km. *AWD:* 7.5/10.1 L/100 km. **Best alternatives:** The CR-V's biggest competitor is the Toyota RAV4. If you don't mind going downscale a bit, consider a Hyundai Tucson. Mazda's CX-5 handles better on challenging roads than the afore-mentioned alternatives, but its problematic powertrain drives it to the end of the line. An often-overlooked alternative is the GMC Terrain. Drivers get plenty of back-seat room, cabin materials are first class, and there's power to spare with the available V6 engine. Chevrolet's Equinox and the Buick Encore are also worthy contenders.

SAFETY: **Child safety seat setup:** "Marginal." **Crashworthiness:** NHTSA: 2003-15 CR-Vs get an overall safety rating of four to five stars. IIHS: 2015 model gets the top rating of "Good" in all categories; 2012-14 models have similar marks, except for a "Marginal" score in the front overlap test. 2007-11 CR-Vs scored "Good" in all categories, except for a "Marginal" ranking relative to roof strength. **Owner-reported safety-related failures:** When the accelerator is pressed hard, there is a loss of power and downshifting is delayed, just when extra power is needed. Traction control has also been a problem with earlier models. Other safety-related failures: Airbags fail to deploy; bent wheel studs can easily snap; and sun visors fall out of their mounting

ALERT! Again, painful front seat head restraints:

> The head restraint pushes my head forward. There is no position in which an anatomical posture can be achieved. In order to be comfortable I either sit away from the back of the seat with essentially no back support, sit sideways on the seat so my head can clear to the side of the neck restraint, or turn the head rest around. This however is also unsafe.

A 2015 Honda CR-V vibration lawsuit has been filed that alleges the cars rattle and vibrate to the extent they can make an occupant nauseous. The lawsuit alleges Honda knows about the problem but has no idea how to fix it. The plaintiff says the 2015 Honda CR-V was modified to include a direct-injection engine called "Earth Dreams" that causes excessive vibration that doesn't exist in previous model years. The lawsuit was filed May 26, 2015, in the U.S. District Court for the Central District of California under *Vivian Romaya v. American Honda Motor Co. Inc.*

CR-V Profile

	2006	2007	2008	2009	2010	2011	2012	2013	2014
Used Values ($)									
EX/LX	5,000	6,000	7,000	8,000	10,000	13,000	15,500	18,000	21,000
4x4	—	7,000	8,000	9,000	11,000	14,500	17,500	20,500	22,500
EX	6,500	—	—	10,500	12,500	16,500	19,500	22,500	24,500
4x4	—	8,500	9,500	11,500	13,500	17,500	20,500	23,500	26,500
EX-L	—	9,500	10,500	13,000	14,500	18,500	22,000	24,000	27,500
Touring LX	—	—	—	—	—	—	23,500	26,500	29,500
Reliability	☆	☆	☆	☆	☆	☆	☆	☆	☆
Repairs ($$$)	🛍	🛍	🛍	🛍	🛍	🛍	🛍	🛍	🛍
Electrical	☆	☆	☆	☆	☆	☆	☆	☆	☆
Engine (base)	☆	☆	☆	☆	☆	☆	☆	☆	☆
Fit/Finish	☆	☆	☆	☆	☆	☆	☆	☆	☆
Infotainment	—	—	—	—	—	☆	☆	☆	☆
Transmission (auto.)	☆	☆	☆	☆	☆	☆	☆	☆	☆

SECRET WARRANTIES, INTERNAL BULLETINS: All years: Keep in mind that Honda service bulletins almost always mention that "goodwill" extended warranties may be applied to any malfunction. **2007-08**—Poor AC performance on acceleration; AC hoots or whistles. Headliner rattles or buzzes when driving. Tailgate rusting near license plate trim. False low tire pressure alert. **2007-09**—In *Kevin Davitt v. America Honda Motor Co., Inc.,* Honda settled claims over defective doorlocks. The settlement reimburses owners for repairs and extends the warranty (visit *www.doorlocksettlement.com*). **2008**—Cold engine whine may be corrected by replacing the engine oil pump. **2008-09**—Headliner sagging near the liftgate. **2010-11**—Fluid leaks from rear of vehicle. Low power on acceleration requires only a software update, says Honda. High oil consumption due to sticking rings will be remedied by a warranty extension on the pistons and piston rings up to 8 years/125,000 miles, says TSB #12-089. **2011-12**—An engine oil leak at the rear of the cylinder head cover may be caused by a defective No. 5 rocker shaft holder. The left rear wheel well doesn't have enough seam sealer, which may allow water to leak into the interior under the rear seat. A loss of power when accelerating may be caused by faulty PGM-FI software. **2012-14**—A front brake judder may be caused by a misaligned brake pad, disc, or caliper. Install new brake pads. **2015**—Until Honda corrects a serious vibration problem, owners suggest this stop-gap measure to reduce the vibration:

The vibration is felt through the cabin and the driver seat. This is totally unacceptable. The engine vibration is noticed around 550-600 rpms. If the AC is turned on the rpm increase and the vibration goes away. Switching the AC off the rpm drop to around 550-600 rpms and the vibration returns.

ACCORD/CROSSTOUR/HYBRID ★★★★ / ★★★★ / ★

RATING: Above Average (2014-16); Average (2010-13); Below Average (2008-09); Above Average (2001-07). The 2016 redesigned models will have a beefier, 285 hp V6, borrowed from the Pilot, a shorter wheelbase (coupe), a restyled front and rear end (looks like a large Civic), and possibly the addition of a 9-speed automatic transmission. Interestingly, some of the older models have generated fewer quality and performance complaints than recent Accords. But, be careful. The 2008 Accord has almost 992 safety-related failures posted to the NHTSA website. With 50 complaints per year the norm, that's three times the complaint average. *Crosstour:* Average (2010-2015). This hatchback/wagon SUV shares the Accord platform, advantages, and defects. Power is supplied by a 2.4L 189 hp 4-cylinder and a 3.5L 278 hp V6 engine coupled to either a front-wheel or AWD powertrain, It's essentially a smaller Pilot, with two rows of seating compared to the Pilot's three. *Hybrid:* Not Recommended (2005-07). The 2005 through 2007 model year Hybrid was Honda's third hybrid model, following the discontinued Insight and Civic Hybrid. It was priced US$3,000 higher than the similar gasoline-powered "EX V6," minus a power moonroof. The Hybrid uses the 2005 Odyssey engine for a combined 240 to 255 horsepower rating and can shut off three of its six cylinders under certain conditions for better fuel economy. This technology that Honda calls VCM, or Variable Cylinder Management, has come under fire by owners who say the feature works erratically and can be dangerous when stopping or accelerating from a stop. Most frugal buyers opted for the conventional powered V6 and the Hybrid got the axe after the 2007 model year. Although fuel economy was touted as 7.8L/100 km (city) and 6.4L/100 km (highway), many drivers said the cars never got near those figures and several class actions were initiated. Today, a 2005-07 Hybrid is worth between $3,000 and $4,000. It's a risky buy, though, as far as reliability and servicing are concerned. Early Accords are decent performers through 2007, but Honda's 2008 redesign, while adding more content, significantly lowered the car's overall quality and performance for several years. Honda is still working on serious factory-related glitches carried over from the earlier redesign – one of which is a deadly "lag and lurch" powertrain malfunction, posted at *safercar.gov* by this owner of a 2013 Accord:

This was instance #3 and worst occurrence. Stopped at traffic light, made a left turn when break in traffic, half way into turn engine lagged with no response like it shutdown, then took off. Almost T-boned by oncoming traffic. Lag between start of turn and then engine response was at least 2-3 seconds. Same issue has happened 2 times before. Both of those instances were right turns on red, with no oncoming traffic. I have searched the Internet forums and found similar occurrences with other Honda owners, not only of the Accord but also the Crosstour.

Road performance: Excellent acceleration with all engines. The Accord also handles and rides well, thanks to large tires, a sturdy chassis, and standard stability control. Like most Hondas, this is a driver's car, while its primary competitor, the Toyota Camry, is more of a mobile cocoon. *Crosstour:* More responsive handling, comfort, and a car-like driving position. A competent performer that suffers from a large turning radius, a confusing dash, and not as much cargo space expected of a wagon. **Strong points:** A well-designed family car, the Accord was last redesigned for the 2013 model year and jumped leagues ahead of the competition by giving owners superior road performance and a roomy interior with loads of safety and convenience features thrown in. If you want good fuel economy and performance with a conventional powertrain, choose one of the two 4-cylinder engines. The V6 is a bit of a gas hog and is necessary only for highway travel with a full load. Ride comfort and responsive handling are assured by a suspension and steering set-up that enhances driver control. And what about space? Recent model Accord sedans are roomier than ever before, with interior dimensions and capacity that provide more interior space than you'll likely need. Fast and nimble without a V6, this is the mid-sized sedan of choice for drivers who want maximum fuel economy and comfort along with lots of space for grocery hauling and occasional highway cruising. With the optional V6, the Accord is one of the most versatile mid-sized cars you can find. It offers something for everyone, and its reasonable resale value after 5 years means there's no way you can lose money buying one. **Weak points:** An astoundingly high number of performance and reliability defects on the 2008-09 models, with apparently biodegradable brakes topping the list. The thief-friendly trunk sometimes opens on its own when parked – a problem known for over 7 years that affects Acuras, as well. Trunk lid struts won't hold the lid up when parked on a hill; chronic stalling. Mediocre fuel economy with the V6. Excessive wind noise. Sunroof and moonroof open up on their own:

> Last night, my 2014 Honda Accord's windows and sunroof automatically opened; there have been other random electrical problems. The opening of the windows occurred during a rain storm and my brand new Honda is filled with water.

The driver's door collects and leaks water. Faulty tire pressure monitoring device; annoying windshield dash reflection; distorted windshields; and omnipresent creaks and rattles. "Hey, wanna $500 deal on a new AC condenser?"

> Air conditioner condenser damaged due to road debris. Vehicle design is poor leaving the condenser unprotected from road debris. Grill opening is large with no screen or mesh in front of the condenser. Repair cost is $786.

Crosstour: The 4-year-old Crosstour is billed as a "crossover utility vehicle," which is Honda-speak for a high-riding hatchback family station wagon equipped with four-wheel drive capability. This five-seater Accord spin-off offers a disappointing 22 cubic feet of cargo space and 51.3 cubic feet with the rear seatbacks folded. Strut towers intrude into storage space, and the sloping rear-end styling compromises the Crosstour's utility.

Prices and Specs

Prices (Negotiable): *Accord Coupe EX:* $24,630, *EX-L Navi:* $28,330, *EX-L V6 Navi:* $33,730, *Accord Sedan LX:* $24,050, *Sport:* $24,250, *EX-L:* $27,650, *V6:* $31,130, *Touring:* $29,050, *Touring V6:* $33,630 **Freight:** $1,810 **Powertrain:** *Accord front-drive: Engines:* 2.4L 4-cyl. (185 hp), 2.4L 4-cyl. (189 hp), 3.5L V6 (278 hp); Transmissions: 6-speed man., 6-speed auto., CVT; *Crosstour Front-drive/4WD: Engines:* 2.4L 4-cyl. (192 hp), 3.5L V6 (271 hp); Transmission: 6-speed auto. **Dimensions/capacity:** *Accord Sedan:* Passengers: 2/3; Wheelbase: 110.2 in.; H: 58.1/L: 191/W: 72.6 in.; Headroom F/R: 5/2 in.; Legroom F/R: 41 /30 in.; Cargo volume: 16 cu. ft.; Fuel tank: 65L/regular; Tow limit: 1,000 lb.; Load capacity: 850 lb.; Turning circle: 37.7 ft.; Weight: 3,236-3,298 lb. *Crosstour Sedan:* Passengers: 2/3; Wheelbase: 110.1 in.; H: 58.1/L: 196.8/W: 74.7 in.; Headroom F/R: 6.5/3.5 in.; Legroom F/R: 41.5/30 in.; Cargo volume: 25.7 cu. ft.; Fuel tank: 65L/regular; Tow limit: 1,500 lb.; Load capacity: 850 lb.; Turning circle: 40.2 ft.; Ground clearance: 8.1 in.; Weight: 3,852-4,070 lb.

Other opinions: "The 2015 Honda Accord ranks #3 out of 18 affordable midsize cars. It has crisp handling, a spacious back seat and good fuel economy, according to reviewers." – *U.S. News & World Report.* "American Honda Motor Co. has agreed to settle a class-action lawsuit over claims that it manufactured 1,593,755 defective vehicles that excessively burn oil and require frequent spark plug replacements. The settlement concerns the 2008-12 Accord, 2008-13 Odyssey, 2009-13 Pilot, 2010-11 Accord Crosstour and 2012 Crosstour equipped with 6-cylinder engines. The plaintiffs claimed Honda hid the problem from consumers. Honda denied the allegation, despite receiving hundreds of online complaints on the National Highway Traffic Safety Administration Web site, and about 130 on carcomplaints.com concerning the 2008 Accord alone." – *www.autonews.com/.* **Major redesign:** 2008, 2013, and 2016. **Highway/city fuel economy:** *2.4L 4-cylinder auto.:* 5.8/8.8 L/100 km. *3.5L V6 6-speed man.:* 7.8/12.6 L/100 km. *Auto.:* 6.7/11 L/100 km. *Crosstour auto. 2WD:* 7.2/11.5 L/100 km. *Auto. 4WD:* 8/12.3 L/100 km. **Best alternatives:** BMW 3 Series, Hyundai Elantra or Sonata, Mazda6, and Toyota Camry. *Crosstour:* Nissan Murano, Subaru Outback, and Toyota Venza (discontinued).

SAFETY: Child safety seat setup: "Marginal." **Crashworthiness:** NHTSA: Accord has earned five-star crash protection scores for front, side, and rollover protection from 2002 through 2015. Earlier models, through 1998 merited three- and four-star crashworthiness scores. Side protection for 1997 and earlier Accords scored three stars. IIHS: The car has garnered a "Good" rating since 2012 for head-restraint effectiveness, frontal offset, side, rear, and roof crashworthiness. 2008 to 2011 versions got similar marks, except for an "Acceptable" rating for roof strength. *Crosstour:* NHTSA: Four stars to 2012-15 models only for rollover resistance, while the 2010 Crosstour scored five stars in all test categories, except for rollover protection, which rated one star less. IIHS: 2012-15 Crosstours "Good" for frontal offset, side, and rear crashworthiness; 2008-11 models' roof strength protection was only "Acceptable." **Owner-reported safety-related failures:** Airbags may explode for no reason or fail to deploy; brake and steering failures:

> All of a sudden steering cut out on me in the middle of my turn. I narrowly missed oncoming traffic and stopped right before I hit the curb and a parked car. When I did stop and got my composure back I looked down and there was a steering wheel light on and a buzzing noise. All this while going no more then 6 miles an hour. At this current moment my car is less then 2 years old and has less then 400 miles on it.

Chronic stalling, and sudden, unintended acceleration. Horn honks on its own and drains battery, limited rear visibility, sunroof shatters for no discernable reason, poorly-designed, ineffective side mirrors, and soya-coated wiring and fuel line is "Kibbles" for rodents:

> The 2015 Honda vehicles have a "green" product that consists of fuel lines and various wiring that has a soy-based composition. Rodents are eating the fuel lines and wiring because of the soy-based ingredient. I know of numerous vehicles that have leaked gasoline due to the damage caused by rodents. I believe the problem includes numerous vehicle makes. I feel that our new Honda is a time bomb in terms of potential fires.

ALERT! God help you if your original-equipment sound system self-destructs just after 3 years of use. Dealer-quoted replacement price of $1,500 U.S. – No warranty and no "goodwill." Lesson learned: Independent retailers will install a comparable system for $300. Four things that must be verified during the Accord's test drive: Lag and lurch acceleration; low-beam headlights that may give insufficient illumination; blinding glare from the chrome lining around the cup holders and instrument panel; and poor seat and head restraint design that causes severe neck, back, and leg pain (a complaint over the past several years):

> My 2014 Accord's driver seat is defective. After driving a short distance I have experienced sciatic nerve pain down my leg, severe lower back pain and pelvic numbness. The design of the bottom and upright portion of the seat are not designed to support a driver correctly. After driving the car less than a thousand miles I am considering selling the vehicle and taking a loss. I love the Honda product but they should make captured terrorists drive this car instead of waterboarding.
>
> • • •
>
> I bought a 2013 Honda Accord knowing that there have been complaints online about the headrest issue, but brief test drives prior to purchase don't fully reveal the extent to which this is a safety defect. An Acura (also made by Honda) dealer even told me that Acura had

had these same complaints for several years, but modified the headrest design in the 2013 models to correct the flaw. Honda has not done this yet, though. I test drove many other manufacturers' cars and they comply with federal regulations without such an obvious design problem. I'm 5'4" and sit up straight when driving, which means the head restraint continually bumps or pokes the back of my head while providing no back support at all — which is itself a safety defect in a crash. So is the fact that it pushes my head so far forward that it impedes good visibility when I turn my head to look back over my right shoulder. Slumping causes back, shoulder and neck pain, untenable on a road trip and also impedes visibility. Earlier model head-restraints that don't have this issue won't fit due to different center-to-center post measurements, so there are no available parts to replace the existing restraint (I tried – even with one in my older Acura). I have read online forums in which desperate Honda drivers describe bending the posts or making other modifications to relieve their pain while driving. They shouldn't have to and this could jeopardize their safety.

Be careful where you put your knee when driving:

My car stopped when the start button was pressed while driving. The start button is near my knee and an accidental press caused my moving car to shut down – fortunately I was just starting and only going 5 mph. Can you imagine what would happen if my knee hit the start button while going 65 in traffic? The dealer said that is normal!!

Accord/Crosstour Profile

	2006	2007	2008	2009	2010	2011	2012	2013	2014
Used Values ($)									
Coupe SE/EX	5,000	6,000	7,000	9,000	11,000	13,500	17,000	19,000	21,500
EX V6/EX-L V6 Nav.	—	7,000	9,000	11,500	14,500	18,000	22,500	25,500	28,500
Sedan LX/SE	4,000	5,000	8,000	8,000	10,000	11,500	15,000	17,000	19,500
EX	6,000	—	—	9,000	11,000	13,500	17,500	21,500	24,000
EX-L V6 Nav.	—	—	9,500	11,500	14,000	18,000	21,000	23,500	26,500
Crosstour EX-L	—	—	—	—	15,000	18,500	21,000	23,500	30,000
EX-L Nav.	—	—	—	—	16,000	19,000	21,500	27,500	32,000
Hybrid	—	—	—	—	8,000	8,500	9,500	—	—
Reliability	☆	☆	★1	★1	★	★	☆	☆	☆
Repairs ($$$)	🛍	🛍	🛍3	🛍3	🛍	🛍	🛍	🛍	🛍
Electrical	☆	☆	★	★	★	★	★	★	☆
Engine (base)	☆	☆	★1	★2	★	★	★	☆	☆
Fit/Finish	★3	★3	★2	★2	★	★	★	★	☆
Infotainment	—	—	—	—	—	★	★	★	★
Transmission (auto.)	☆	☆	★1	★1	★2	★	★	★	★

SECRET WARRANTIES, INTERNAL BULLETINS: 2003-08—The 6-speed manual transmission grinds when shifted into Third gear, pops out of Third gear, or is hard to shift into Third gear. 2003-15—V6-equipped models may leak oil from the rear cylinder head cover gasket. 2005-10—Silencing a chirp coming from the engine timing belt area. 2008—Court settlement relative to side airbag deployment. Excessive oil consumption. Road debris continues to damage expensive AC compressors. Blower motor noisy or inoperative. Carpet on the passenger's side pulls out from under the door sill trim. 2008-09—Trouble-shooting an engine whining noise and a steering clicking. Fix for an engine that ticks or knocks at idle. 2008-12—High oil consumption due to sticking rings will be remedied by a warranty extension on the pistons and piston rings up to 8 years/125,000 miles, says TSB #13-078 (later extended to 2013s):

HIGH OIL CONSUMPTION—FAULTY ENGINE RINGS	
SERVICE BULLETIN NO.: 13-078	DATE: JULY 24, 2014

2008-12 Accord V6 A/T

BACKGROUND: American Honda is announcing a powertrain warranty extension as a result of a settlement of a class captioned, Soto et al. v. American Honda Motor Co., Inc., Case No. 3:12-cv-1377-SI (N.D. Cal.).The piston rings on certain cylinders may rotate and align which can lead to spark plug fouling. This can set DTCs P0301 through P0304 and cause the MIL to come on. **American Honda is extending the powertrain warranty to cover repairs related to engine misfire (that triggers DTCs P0301 through P0304) to 8 years with unlimited mileage from the original date of purchase and has settled a class action based on this remedial measure.**

2008-12 *(2010-13 Crosstour)*—A clunk is heard in the front suspension while driving over irregular surfaces and in hot weather. You may need to replace both of the front lower ball joints with updated service parts made to address this specific symptom. If the ball joints were previously replaced, then replace both front knuckle assemblies. 2011-12—Bulletin confirms leakage from the driveshaft seals. Windshield wind noise may be caused by deformed hood seal. Engine rattles on cold start-up. 2013—Engine oil leaks. Troubleshooting front and rear wheel bearing noise and rear head cover gasket oil leaks. Honda bulletin confirms some cars surge, hesitate, or judder. Driver airbag rattles and not centered; horn goes off by itself, measures to silence front door wind noise. 2013-14—Some vehicles produce a pop or clicking sound when turning the steering wheel. 2014-15—A front suspension clunk or rattle (see Hybrid, below). Front suspension clunks or rattles heard when driving over bumps or when turning may mean at least one self-locking nut at the top of the front damper spring assembly is loose. Repair tips to silence wind noise from the driver's or front passenger's side window. *Hybrid:* 2006-07—Hybrids that lose power when accelerating need three different software updates. Honda's

2006 Civic software update caused a dramatic drop in fuel economy and Accord Hybrid owners say they also get poor gas mileage, since the same revised engine/IMA battery software was installed in their Hybrids to extend IMA battery life.

ODYSSEY ★★★

RATING: Average (2009-16); Above Average (1997-08). This is not the "perfect minivan" that many car critics applaud. In fact, its many pluses are seriously undermined by innumerable design and factory defects. Yes, the Odyssey out-classes Toyota's Sienna in driving pleasure, but it's not as reliable. In a Sienna, the driver is "driven;" in an Odyssey, the driver is more actively involved in the over-all performance of the vehicle, which is both good and bad, as you will see. There have been frequent reports of safety- and performance-related failures, notably the airbags, seat belts, powertrain, suspension, and electrical system. Of particular concern are airbag malfunctions, brake defects leading to sudden brake loss, and the frequent replacement of the brake calipers and rotors. **Road performance:** Plenty of power for high-speed merging and lots of mid-range torque means less shifting when the engine is under load. Although owners speak highly of the car-like ride and handling, others say the transmission clunks or jerks so much when shifting that the car is unsafe:

> I was driving in traffic for an hour or so, in first or second gear. After a while, anytime we would accelerate to about 20 mph, we experienced a violent jerking as if we just ran over something. This happened consistently every time we accelerated to or decelerated to 2 0mph. Took it into Honda the next day and they couldn't find a problem. The jerking was very strong and consistent for about an hour of driving.
>
> *— safercar.gov*

Strong points: The Odyssey has a lean look, but the interior is wide and long enough to accommodate most large objects. Sliding doors are standard equipment, and if you buy the EX version, they will both be power-assisted. Sufficient power is supplied by a competent V6, which includes variable cylinder deactivation to increase fuel economy. The engine's ability to automatically switch between 6-cylinder and 3-cylinder activation, depending on engine load, may cut gas consumption by up to 10%. The Odyssey has remained relatively unchanged since the 2011s got a restyled interior and wider/lower exterior; a reworked front end; and user-friendly instruments and controls. The wider interior houses a versatile second-row bench seat that spreads the seats out and uses a total of five latch positions for child seats, as well as more ample third-row seats. If you need extra cargo space, you can easily fold the third-row seats, add the cargo, and bring the kids up into the second row. Honda also boasts that its 4-cylinder engine fuel economy has improved. **Weak points:** Fuel consumption isn't as low as Honda touts; noisy suspension caused by premature front strut wearout; fuel sloshes inside the fuel tank, and, when the ECO button is turned on, the transmission makes a rattling noise, as the car starts shaking. Second-row head restraints block visibility; dash instrument cluster is washed out in daylight; excessive wind noise at 50-100 km/h; major electronic problems on recent models include malfunctioning rear-view camera, electric doorlocks and sliding doors that are slow to respond, and the security alarm that goes off randomly due to a defective hood switch.

My 2014 Odyssey's blinker randomly refuses to turn off even after manually turning it off. The collision detection system malfunctions at times. It randomly beeps with no vehicle in sight and at other times, when it should beep, it doesn't. The navigation/radio screens completely black out, only showing yellow lines that you normally see when backing up. During this time, the collision detection system, backup camera, radio and heating controls all do not work. The screens stay blacked out even during driving/backing up, then once the vehicle is off and restarted, things go back to normal

Front passenger legroom is marginal, owing to the restricted seat travel on some models; it's difficult to calibrate the radio without taking your eyes off the road; and the storage well may not take any tire larger than a "space saver," meaning you'll carry your flat in the back. Watch out for AC problems. Owners say it comes on and won't shut off, the AC/heat blower randomly increases in power, and road debris frequently destroys the AC condenser. Sunroof may shatter for no apparent reason. Rain water leaks through windows and out of the electrical conduit entering into where the sliding door mechanism is located.

Prices and Specs

Prices (Firm): *LX:* $29,990, *EX:* $33,990, *EX RES:* $35,490, *EX-L RES:* $40,990, *Touring:* $46,990 **Freight:** $1,495 **Powertrain (Front-drive):** Engine: 3.5L V6 (248 hp); Transmission: 5-speed auto. **Dimensions/capacity:** Passengers: 2/3/3; Wheelbase: 118.1 in.; H: 68.8/L: 202.1/W: 77.1 in.; Headroom F/R1/R2: 2.5/5/3.5 in.; Legroom F/R1/R2: 41/32/29 in.; Cargo volume: 61.5 cu. ft.; Fuel tank: 80L/regular; Tow limit: 3,500 lb.; Load capacity: 1,340 lb.; Turning circle: 36.7 ft.; Ground clearance: 5 in.; Weight: 4,387 lb.

Other opinions: "The 2015 Honda Odyssey ranks #1 out of 7 minivans. Critics like the 2015 Honda Odyssey's comfortable ride, outstanding agility and feature-rich interior." – *U.S. News & World Report.*" Says *www.autobody-review.com:* "If you have a Honda Civic, chances are you have paint problems. And actually it is not limited to just Honda Civics. Certain CR-V's, Odyssey vans, and Pilots are also prone to paint issues. In fact the paint problems with Honda are so bad, that there are now Facebook pages dedicated to the subject. There is even a class action lawsuit that was filed against Honda. Here are the 4 top suggestions that Honda owners have been given by their Honda dealers. Keep the car out of the sun. Don't wash the car as often. Don't use harsh waxes. And avoid bird droppings." **Major redesign:** 1999, 2005, and 2011. A redesigned version is scheduled for 2017. **Highway/city fuel**

economy: 8.5/13.3 L/100 km. *EX-L and Touring:* 7.8/2.3 L/100 km. **Best alternatives:** For better handling and reliability, the closest competitor to the Odyssey is Toyota's Sienna minivan. One major difference between the two models is the seating. Toyota's are like La-Z-Boy armchairs and are a chore to remove. Honda seats are more basic and are easier to install or remove. The Toyota Sienna also has a more powerful engine than the Odyssey, and it's available with AWD. Its cargo area is best in class and seating is comfortable everywhere. The Mazda5 and Chrysler's Caravan are worth considering for different reasons. The Mazda5 has less room but burns less fuel (without a high-tech engine add-on), and Chrysler's many minivan defects can be an annoyance and a budget-buster as well, but they are dirt-cheap, offer lots of room for people and things, and have plenty of convenience and safety features. The Kia Sedona minivan is also a decent choice. If you're looking for lots of towing "grunt" and plenty of usable space, rear-drive GM full-sized vans are fairly reliable vehicles that often carry sizeable discounts in the summer of the following year. Try to resist the gimmicky video entertainment, DVD navigation system, and expensive leather seats. Try to trade the original-equipment Firestone or Bridgestone tires for something better (check with *www.tirerack.com*).

 SAFETY: **Child safety seat setup:** "Acceptable." **Crashworthiness:** NHTSA: Impressive. Top five-star score in all crash categories, except rollovers (four stars) for 1998 through 2015 models. IIHS: "Good" for frontal, side, rear, and roof crash protection. **Owner-reported safety-related failures:** Odysseys are very reliable and safe. Nevertheless, the few safety-related failures reported to *Lemon-Aid* and the government are scary. For example, look at this report found in the NHTSA's 2013-14 Odyssey database:

> My son almost choked to death on the middle row seat belt. I have three young kids of 7,6 and 4. The 7 and 6 year olds were playing and suddenly the seat belt wrapped around my sons neck. My wife quickly attempted to unattached and untangle and she could not. The seat belt just got tighter and tighter and there was no emergency release button either from the top or bottom of the seat belt. I quickly held him up in the air sideways to give him a little air while my wife ran to a stranger's house to borrow scissors. The only way for us to release him free was to cut the seat belt. We are fortunate that nothing serious happened to my son, only bruises around his neck.

Brakes are another major problem area highlighted by vehicles rolling away when parked on an incline; premature front brake wear, excessive noise; a history of mushy braking; sudden brake loss after the VSA light comes on (some dealers suggest unplugging the VSA); brake loss when backing out of a parking lot; brake pedal sometimes sinks to the floor; engine races when braking; and severe shimmying when the brakes are applied. On other model years we see warped airbag covers; early engine failure; severe drivetrain judder and bucking felt when accelerating uphill; electrical malfunction-caused stalling in traffic; third row cupholder area panel gets so hot passengers could be burned; driver-side mirrors give a blurred, distorted image; wipers leave streaks on the windshield that can't be polished out; and the van's headlights often blind oncoming drivers' eyes. Older models have even more to be wary of: Automatic transmission breakdowns; transmission slams into gear or suddenly locks in low gear while the vehicle is underway; erratic downshifts; steering pulls continually to the right; premature replacement of the front strut assemblies; poor handling in snow, despite traction control; windshield shattered on its own; third-row folding seat collapsed and broke a child's fingers; the side sliding door frequently malfunctions by closing unexpectedly, opening when the vehicle is underway, and failing to retract when closing on an object; the EXL's running board can be dangerously slippery when wet; and reports of some near-falls and many bruised shins.

ALERT! During your test drive see if the van has a tendency to lag, lurch, clunk or jerk when shifting gears (feels like the vehicle is running over a speed bump). Some owners say the headlights don't project far enough, the windshield is blurry, and the shiny dashboard reflects too much in the side mirrors – check that out, too.

Odyssey Profile

	2006	2007	2008	2009	2010	2011	2012	2013	2014
Used Values ($)									
DX/LX	5,500	7,000	8,500	10,500	13,000	16,000	19,000	22,000	23,500
SE/EX	6,500	8,000	10,000	12,500	14,500	18,000	21,500	24,000	26,000
EX-L Res	8,500	10,500	12,500	15,000	19,500	23,000	27,500	31,000	34,000
Touring	—	13,500	16,500	20,000	24,000	27,000	32,500	37,000	39,000
Reliability	4	4	3	3	3	3	3	3	3
Repairs ($$$)	1	1	1	2	2	2	2	2	2
Electrical	4	4	4	3	3	3	3	3	3
Engine (base)	3	3	3	2	2	2	2	2	2
Fit/Finish	2	2	2	2	2	2	2	2	2
Infotainment	—	—	—	—	—	3	3	3	3
Transmission (auto.)	3	3	3	2	2	2	2	2	2

SECRET WARRANTIES, INTERNAL BULLETINS: All years—Honda TSBs allow for special warranty consideration on a "goodwill" basis by the company's District Service Manager or Zone Office. There's an incredibly large number of sliding-door problems covered by a recall, and a plethora of service bulletins too numerous to print here. Ask Honda politely for the bulletins or "goodwill" assistance. If refused, subpoena the documents through small claims court, using NHTSA's complaint and service bulletin summaries as your shopping list. 1999-2003—Deformed windshield moulding. 1999-2006—Troubleshooting vehicle pull or drift to one side. 2003-07—Honda has a secret warranty extension that covers paint defects up to 7 years (no mileage or prior ownership limitation), says TSB #08-031, issued Jan. 8, 2010. Although this service bulletin is specifically for blue metallic paint defects, the coverage can be easily extrapolated to cover any other Honda colours, as indicated in TSB #10-002 "Paint Defect Claim Information," issued Jan. 20, 2010. 2005—Correction for middle-row seat that won't unlatch. 2005-06—Noise remedy for the power steering, front brakes, front wheel bearings, windshield, sliding door, and exhaust system. 2005-07—Drivetrain ping, squeal, or rattle. Power steering pump whine or buzz. Power seat won't move forward or backward. 2005-09—Engine timing belt chirp. Sliding door doesn't open all the way. Power door locks continually lock while driving. 2005-10—If the steering wheel is hard to turn at low speeds, Honda will replace the steering pump for free up to 7 years/100,000 miles (TSB #11-039). 2007—Delayed First gear engagement. Insufficient AC cooling at idle. 2007-08—If the brake pedal feels low and spongy, the dealer should replace the ABS/TCS or VSA modulator control unit under warranty, says Honda TSB #07-045 issued March 5, 2009. 2008—Engine knocking or ticking at idle. 2008-09—Water accumulates in the inner tail lights in the tailgate. 2008-10—A "secret" warranty extends powertrain coverage to 8 years/unlimited mileage as part of an out-of-court settlement in *Soto v. American Honda Motor Co.* Apparently, engine misfires due to spark plug fouling can damage the engine. Dealer may have to clean the pistons, and replace the piston rings in the affected cylinders. If the service manager looks at you quizzedly, cite TSB #13-080. A gap between the front passenger's airbag lid and the dashboard is Honda's problem. Front door glass opens/closes slowly or sticks. 2008-12—Remedy for engine ticking at idle (see TSB, below). 2010-12—Engine oil leaks in the B-cap side bolt area. 2011-12—Honda extends the warranty on stained or corroded tailgates and chrome trim. Troubleshooting complaints that when shifting into higher gears vehicle would hesitate. 2011-14—A rear suspension clunk or squeak may indicate lower spring seat deterioration. Replace the lower arm and the lower spring seat. 2011-15—Remedy for roof rack and tailgate rattling. 2014—Troubleshooting tips for a power sliding door that sticks in the unlocked position. 2013—Remedy for power sliding doors that detach from their rollers. 2014-15—Brakes may grind, rub, or screech due to the front brake caliper bracket contacting the brake rotor. Dealer must replace the brake caliper brackets and refinish or replace the affected disc. A hard downshift or clunk when slowing down to a rolling stop may simply require updated PCM A/T software. Honda service bulletin confirms the power sliding doors may detach from their rollers.

PILOT ★★★★

2016 Pilot: A metrosexual minivan?

RATING: Above Average (2014-16). Average (2011-13); Above Average (2007-10). **Road performance:** The third-generation 2016 Pilot has grown into a large-sized people carrier that offers adequate power for highway cruising, superb handling, and a fairly comfortable ride. Although the revised styling screams "Odyssey!" overall dimensions are larger, while weight is down approximately 300 pounds with noise, vibration, and harshness reduced. A new one-touch system slides the split-rear seat forward to ease third-row access, and the exterior is more sleek and modern in appearance compared to its boxy predecessor. Some minuses: Mediocre acceleration when fully loaded and so-so braking. **Strong points:** Pilot's a mouse that sometimes roars and at other times squeaks (rattles and clunks). Truck-like on the outside, but a much tamer vehicle when you look closely and get it on the road. It combines car-like comfort and handling in a crossover package where ride comfort, utility, and passenger accommodations are foremost. A versatile interior that could be more refined; plenty of passenger space; seating for up to eight; the third-row seat folds flat into sections to free up storage space; and there's a small storage area in the floor. Chock full of safety and convenience features and the GPS and voice operation feature are easy to use – with a little practice. Overall reliability has been better than average, except for the 2011-13 models. Weak points: Unimpressive fuel economy – the much-heralded cylinder deactivation system doesn't save as much fuel as Honda fantasizes. The new 9-speed transmission is said to be similar to Chrysler's. If so, trouble may be on the horizon. The premature replacement of brake calipers and discs is a major factor driving up repair costs (service managers say brakes wear out quickly because Pilot is so heavy). Excessive engine vibration, especially, when Variable Cylinder Management is engaged. Lots of shuddering and vibration when shifting gears; automatic transmission fluid leaks; whining and clicking noise from the power steering; rear AC system will not shut off from the front control panel; interior plastic materials and overall fit and finish aren't up to Honda's reputation for quality; water leaks into the passenger compartment; driver's door doesn't open or close smoothly because the front fender panel and door edge don't mesh; persistent rear rattling and grinding noise that gets louder with the AC on rear engine motor mounts; and some road noise is omnipresent. The centre console and the many buttons for other controls can be confusing to operate until you've mastered the layout.

Prices and Specs

Prices (Firm): *LX:* $30,400, *LX 4WD:* $33,400, *SE:* $37,800, *EX-L RES:* $39,800, *Touring:* $44,150 **Freight:** $1,810 **Powertrain (Front-drive/AWD):** Engine: 3.5L V6 (280 hp); Transmission: 6-speed auto., 9-speed **Dimensions/capacity (2015):** Passengers: 2/3/3; Wheelbase: 109.2 in.; H: 71.0/L: 190.9/W: 78.5 in.; Headroom: F/R1/R2: 40/39.8/38.2 in.; Legroom: F/R1/R2: 41.4/38.5/32.1 in.; Cargo volume: 1.5 cu. ft.; Fuel tank: 79.5L/regular; Tow limit: 3,500-4,500 lb.; Load capacity: 1,320 lb.; Turning circle: 39.4 ft.; Ground clearance: 8 in.; Weight: 4,319 lb.

Other opinions: "Drives and rides better – though not all models do so equally. We think the midlevel EX with AWD is the best overall, while the high-dollar Elite has a bit much "head toss," unpleasant diagonal pitching over some bumps. the kind of body motion that we'd worry could generate car-sickness." – *USA Today.* "The overwhelming feeling from behind the wheel is that you're driving a minivan – a plush, comfortable minivan, but a minivan all the same." – *www.thecarconnection. com.* Major redesign: 2003, 2009, and 2016; Highway/city fuel economy: *Front-drive:* 8.7/12.7 L/100 km. *AWD:* 9.1/13.1 L/100 km. Best alternatives: A Hyundai Sante Fe and Toyota Highlander top the list of alternate choices; GM's Terrain or Traverse would also be worth considering.

SAFETY: Child safety seat setup: "Acceptable." Crashworthiness: NHTSA: 2011-15 Pilots awarded four stars for frontal and rollover protection, and five stars for side protection. 2003-10 models have even better scores; five stars for both frontal and side impacts and four stars for rollover protection. IIHS: The 2015 Pilot given the top "Good" rating in all crash categories, except for tough overlap front protection, which was rated "Poor." There were similar scores, except for roof strength, on the 2009-11 models, which were judged "Marginal" and 2003-05 Pilot head restraints were rated both "Poor" and "Marginal." **Owner-reported safety-related failures:** Although owners reported barely 100 complaints to NHTSA during the past 3 years (most vehicles average 50 reports a year), some of the reported incidents are quite serious threats. For example, imagine getting seriously burned while sitting in the front passenger seat of a 2013 Pilot:

> We heard a grinding noise coming from beneath the front passenger side of the car. Seconds later, my wife grabs her foot and screams in excruciating pain. I pulled over and saw a .25 inch- thick by 5 inch long abrasion that ran across the arc of her right foot that tore the top layers of her skin. I checked my wife into urgent care at St. Jude's hospital. A physician diagnosed the abrasion as a second degree electrical burn (*tinyurl.com/pilot-injury-photos*).

Other complaints include airbags failed to deploy; inadvertent curtain airbag deployment; fuel leak under the vehicle; loss of power while underway, affects 2012-13 models (*www.piloteers.org*); sudden, unintended acceleration, long hesitation when accelerating; vehicle pulls to the right; when shifting from Park to Drive vehicle lurches forward; transmission also lurches back and forth between Fourth and Fifth gear; transmission doesn't hold when the Pilot is parked on an incline:

> I had put my car in park, it was still running, I reached in and turned the key off and the car immediately started to roll. I attempted to get in the car to brake, but was unable to do this and then was thrown away from the vehicle, hitting my head on my rock driveway. There was a slight incline where I parked but when it started to roll it reached a steeper incline and rolled down my driveway and hit a tree.

Sudden loss of braking; long braking distance; mushy brakes that lose pressure; electrical failures leading to stalling and hard starting:

> I was told not to bother to bring it in for service each time it stalled because they were waiting for a recall/fix from corporate. After six weeks, multiple stalls, which were all reported to my dealer as requested, dealer agreed to trade my vehicle in for a different Pilot. Within less than 24 hours of owning this second 2012 Honda Pilot, my new car stalled. I have recently been on YouTube and discovered that this is a common problem with the 2012 Honda Pilots, and has also been reported with some 2011 Honda Pilots.

Front wheel fell off; and several owners warn that unprotected wiring in the undercarriage area could be life-threatening if damaged:

> Wheel sensor wires on 2011 Honda Pilots are exposed and unprotected under the vehicle which when damaged, disable anti-lock braking system (ABS), vehicle stability assist (VSA), and the variable torque management (VTM-4) systems. Exposed wires are prone to be cut or damaged by road debris and hazards. Due to the wire being exposed, it was damaged and caused an out-of-pocket expense of approx. $266.00 to repair.

Other owner complaints include secondary hood latch failed when passing over rough roads; rear tailgate window exploded while vehicle was parked in a garage and the moonroof exploded while underway; original-equipment Goodyear tire sidewall failures; the key won't turn the ignition; and the driver's seat height adjustment lowers on its own while the Pilot is underway. Pilot dealer servicing has also been found wanting:

> Spontaneous star crack in lower center windshield, spontaneous rear hatch and passenger door opening while driving with my young child in the rear passenger seat (with "locked" doors), transmission rattle upon slow acceleration or coast at Second and Third gears … Honda dealer said call insurance about windshield, something must have "hit" windshield without me knowing it, said "found no abnormal noises" and "cannot duplicate" rattle noise because different people have different driving patterns, said "cannot duplicate" doors opening while driving, dealer did not "fix" any of these safety issues, just told us to pick up the car. … After research on Internet, I believe these to be manufacturer defects.

ALERT! During the test drive, watch how the engine and tranny perform; powertrain defects and excessive vibration are the primary source of owner complaints. Pilot sales have rebounded this year, as low gas prices give trucks and SUVs a second wind. Since dealers won't dicker over prices, delay your new car purchase until the first quarter of 2016 when the car will be cheaper and better made.

Pilot Profile

	2006	2007	2008	2009	2010	2011	2012	2013	2014
Used Values ($)									
EX/LX	8,500	10,500	12,000	13,500	15,500	19,500	24,000	26,500	29,500
4x4	—	11,500	13,000	14,500	17,500	21,500	26,000	28,500	32,500
EX-L Res	11,500	14,000	—	17,500	20,000	25,500	30,500	34,000	36,500
Touring	—	—	—	19,500	21,500	28,000	33,000	37,500	41,000
Reliability	☆	☆	☆	☆	☆	★2	★2	★2	☆
Repairs ($$$)	1	1	1	1	1	2	2	2	1
Electrical	☆	☆	☆	☆	☆	☆	☆	☆	☆
Engine (base)	☆	☆	★3	★3	★3	★2	★2	★2	☆
Fit/Finish	☆	☆	☆	★3	★3	★2	★2	★2	★3
Infotainment	—	—	—	—	—	★3	★3	★3	☆
Transmission (auto.)	☆4	☆4	☆4	★3	★3	★2	★2	★2	☆

SECRET WARRANTIES, INTERNAL BULLETINS: 2008-13—A "secret" warranty extends powertrain coverage to 8 years/unlimited mileage as part of an out-of-court settlement in *Soto v. American Honda Motor Co.* Apparently, engine misfires due to spark plug fouling can damage the engine. Dealer may have to clean the pistons, and replace the piston rings in the affected cylinders. If the service manager looks at you like you are the Antichrist, cite TSB #13-080. 2009-11—Honda will repair and repaint the tailgate for free, up to 7 years, if it is damaged or stained by rust (June 2014 Honda memo to owners). Another Honda service bulletin confirms the vehicle pulls to the right on a straight road, but offers no fix. 2009-14—Persistent wheel bearing noise confirmed by Honda; no specific fix. 2010—Honda bulletin admits the company is investigating inexplicable sunroof shattering (exploding). 2010-12—Engine oil leaks from the B-cap side bolts. 2011-12—Engine ticking or knocking at idle (see Odyssey). 2012-15—Excessive engine vibration between 60 and 100 kph: Update the PCM module and replace the propeller shaft (4WDs). 2014-15—Honda bulletin confirms there is excessive brake travel when applied and that brakes feel spongy.

RIDGELINE

RATING: Recommended (2006-16); not only a top-performer, but well-appointed, and very reliable, too. Biggest disappointment? There won't be any Ridgeline's available until early next year when the long-awaited 2016s arrive – maybe equipped with a small diesel. **Road performance:** Sustained and quiet acceleration; a smooth-shifting automatic transmission; and secure handling and good cornering control, thanks to communicative, direct steering and well-tuned shocks that also give a comfortable, supple ride. **Strong points:** The Ridgeline mixes performance with convenience. It's an ideal truck for most jobs, as long as you keep it on the highway. Off-road, this unibody pickup offers only medium performance relative to its nearest body-on-frame competitors, the Toyota Tacoma and the Nissan Frontier. Its long wheelbase and independent rear suspension give the Ridgeline an impressive in-bed trunk and excellent road manners, but make it difficult for the truck to traverse anything that's rougher than a stone road or has a breakover angle greater than 21 degrees. A friendly cabin environment where everything is easily accessed and storage spaces abound; a lockable trunk beneath the cargo bed; the tailgate opens either vertically or horizontally; and there's no intrusive wheel arch in the 5-foot-long bed. Reliability and overall dependability are legendary, and crashworthiness is exemplary. **Weak points:** A high sales price that will probably stay inflated until this summer when the new model hype subsides; first-year production glitches; and an untried powertrain configuration.

Other opinions: "Test drivers like the Ridgeline's innovative lockable in-bed trunk and car-like handling, but note that its cabin looks and feels outdated compared to more recently-redesigned pickup trucks' interiors. The Ridgeline is powered by a V6 engine that auto critics say makes adequate power for everyday driving, but may be strained if pulling a trailer as heavy as the Honda Ridgeline's 5,000 pound maximum tow rating. A 5-speed automatic transmission is standard, and reviewers say it occasionally has rough shifts and can make the Ridgeline feel sluggish at highway speeds." – *U.S. News & World Report.* "Upon accelerating from a stop and turning to either the left or right the throttle control would hesitate and not be responsive to the gas pedal. It was like a dead zone as the vehicle was moving." – *safercar.gov.* **Major redesign:** 2006 and 2016. Honda skipped the 2015 model year while it works on the redesigned 2016 version scheduled to arrive in early 2016. It is expected to continue using a closed-box unibody frame, for a smooth, car-like ride and will likely borrow the next-generation Pilot's 3.5L 280 hp V6 engine, hooked to a 9-speed automatic transmission. **Highway/city fuel economy:** 9.8/14.1 L 100 km. **Best alternatives:** GM's Silverado and Sierra duo, the Toyota Tacoma, or Nissan's Frontier. This year's Chevy Colorado, and GMC Canyon aren't in the running during their first year on the market.

SAFETY: **Child safety seat setup:** Untested. **Crashworthiness:** NHTSA: Exceptionally high marks given for passenger crash protection. 2011-14 models earned four stars for rollover resistance, however, 2006-10 Ridgelines did much better, with five stars for frontal and side protection in addition to four stars for rollover crashworthiness. IIHS: "Good" in offset frontal, side, rear, and roof crash protection going back to the 2006 model year. **Owner-reported safety-related failures:** Few safety-related incidents have been reported to NHTSA federal investigators or by *Consumer Reports* members. Internal manufacturer service bulletins show no major failure trends.

ALERT! Remember, small- and mid-sized pickups retain a higher resale value than most cars; it's the big rigs that depreciate the fastest, but also apparently last the longest, as well. So, even if you pay more than expected, you will recoup the difference by extending the trade-in time. If buying used, look for hesitation when accelerating – a common complaint heard over the years.

Ridgeline Profile

Used Values ($)	2006	2007	2008	2009	2010	2011	2012	2013	2014
LX/DX	8,000	9,500	11,000	13,000	16,000	20,000	25,000	28,000	30,500
VP	—	—	—	14,500	17,500	21,500	26,500	29,500	—
EX-L/Sport	12,000	14,000	16,000	18,000	21,000	24,500	27,500	30,500	32,000
EX-L Navi/Touring	—	15,500	17,500	19,500	22,500	25,000	29,000	33,500	40,000
Reliability	★	★	☆	☆	☆	☆	☆	☆	☆
Repairs ($$$)	◉	◉	◉	◉	◉	◉	◉	◉	◉
Electrical	☆	☆	☆	☆	☆	☆	☆	☆	☆
Engine (base)	☆	☆	☆	☆	☆	☆	☆	☆	☆
Fit/Finish	☆	☆	☆	☆	☆	☆	☆	☆	☆
Infotainment	—	—	—	—	—	★	★	☆	☆
Transmission (auto.)	☆	☆	☆	☆	☆	☆	☆	☆	☆

SECRET WARRANTIES, INTERNAL BULLETINS: 2006-07—Automatic transmission is hard to shift into Fourth gear. Vehicle pulls, drifts to one side. Drivetrain ping, squeal, or rattle upon light acceleration. Rear differential noise, judder on turns. 2006-09—Parking brake won't release in cold weather because of water infiltration. Noise and judder when turning. 2006-10—Steering column clicking when turning. 2006-11—Rear seat leg doesn't fold flat. 2009-10—Headliner vibrates or rattles. Whistling from the front door windows. Gap between the front bumper and the fender/headlamp. 2009-11—Tailgate won't open in swing mode; handle is stiff. Front seats squeak and creak. 2010-12—Engine oil leaks in the B-cap side bolt area.

HYUNDAI

Hyundai and its Kia subsidiary brand have racked up impressive sales across Canada during the past decade for three reasons: Cheaper prices, added content, and above average quality control backed by comprehensive warranties. Entry-level vehicles are relatively cheaper and loaded with more standard features when compared with the competition. Compare Accent, Genesis, and Tucson with other brands and laugh all the way to the bank. Hyundai quality and highway performance that was once a cruel joke played on Pony, Stellar, and Excel owners, now is recognized as equal to the best that comes from Japan (except for the Sonata's "wanderer" ways). Warranty performance is fair and issues are usually settled quickly, without lawsuits. The only exception has been Hyundai and its Kia brother's failure to "fess up" when they were caught lying about fuel economy and horsepower ratings a few years back. Both companies subsequently set up compensation programs to satisfy owners who claimed they were mislead.

Pilfered Quality?

Hyundai car quality over the past several decades has gone from risible to reliable, thanks to the use of better-made components and corporate espionage.

Over two decades ago, Hyundai hired away a handful of Toyota's top quality-control engineers – and got a satchel full of Toyota's secret quality-control documents in the bargain. Following a cease-and-desist letter from Toyota's lawyers in 2006, Hyundai returned the pilfered papers and swore to Toyota's lawyers that they never looked at the secret reports stolen from the company (wink, wink; nudge, nudge).

Funny thing, though, Hyundai quality immediately improved; and Kia followed. Industry insiders say the privileged information was a major factor in Hyundai's leapfrogging the competition with better quality-control systems and more reliable components. How ironic, too, that Hyundai and Kia have copied the marketing strategy employed by Japanese automakers since the early '70s: Secure a solid beachhead in one car segment, like the Accent econocar, and then branch out from there with new models, like the Elantra compact and the Genesis sports coupe and sedan.

Hyundai redesigns its lineup every 3 years. Models that flop, like the Entourage minivan, Tiburon, and Azera, get dumped. The company also shares components with its Kia subsidiary to keep production costs down while raising Kia quality (yes, *Consumer Reports* recommends the Kia Forte, Soul, and Sorento).

Hyundai Pony

Hyundai Genesis

"The $4,750 entry-level 1984 Pony was undoubtedly cheap and generally 'craptastic,' but it was a beginning. I knew a guy who drove one – and to say it was less than reliable would be an understatement." (See "Hyundai Pony, 1984-87" at *www.autos.ca/forum/index.php?topic=73546.0*.)

Has the Quality Bubble Burst?

Unfortunately, all is not rosy for Hyundai from a quality perspective. Its redesigned 2011 Sonata (the Kia Optima is the same car with different badging) is a mess – a potentially lethal mess – with over 500 safety-related complaints reported to NHTSA (100 complaints would be the norm after 2 years on the market).

Owners of 2011-13s decry sudden, unintended acceleration, malfunctioning powertrains, headlights that give inadequate lighting, and steering malfunctions that drive the Sonata to one side of the road or the other:

> 2012 Sonata will not drive straight, it pulls to the left mostly but also to the right. Basically the car swerves all over the road, especially at higher speeds. I took it back to the dealership and they told me all foreign cars drive like this. They adjusted the tire pressure but that did not solve the problem. I do not feel safe driving the car. Hyundai issued a service campaign to fix the 2011 Sonatas for this exact problem, why can't they just do the same for the 2012s?

To a lesser degree, similar safety problems (notably, steering malfunctions) have affected the Elantra. Apparently, Hyundai has followed Toyota and Honda quality cutbacks and is giving owners less content for more money.

Rocks on Your Roof

Both Hyundai and Kia take top prize for shattered sunroofs, a problem also shared with many other domestic and imported, entry-level and top luxury models, like Audi (A8 and S8), BMW (3-Series), Honda, and Toyota/Lexus. Here's what happens, while underway, or when parked: The sunroof explodes like a shotgun blast; pieces of glass fly throughout the cabin if the protective interior lining isn't closed; and afterwards the dealer/manufacturer will refuse the apprimately $1,500 warranty claim for a replacement under the pretext that the glass shattered after "being struck by an object."

This is a bogus excuse and automakers know it. They use a similar excuse when owners report a split sidewall on a brand new original equipment tire. But with exploding sunroofs, the theory of "rocks on the roof" just doesn't fly. Read the following scenario of what happened when a local TV station took up this story:

UC PROFESSOR SOLVES SHATTERED SUNROOF PROBLEM

MARCH 21, 2011

Michael Finney of "7 On Your Side," ABC News

FINNEY: A San Jose woman had a frightening experience when her sunroof suddenly shattered above her head while she was driving. Michelle Park asked BMW to cover her sunroof under warranty but the carmaker refused. That's when 7 On Your Side got involved.

PARK: It was like a little mini-explosion going right above your head and then you think, 'Oh my God, what just happened.

FINNEY: The explosion left a huge hole in her sunroof. Only the jagged edges remain.

Park brought her new 2010 328i into Stevens Creek BMW in Santa Clara for inspection. The service manager wrote in an email to BMW corporate saying, "The shop foreman found no signs of impact damage. The client is requesting this to be repaired under warranty."

An hour later, BMW replied saying, "I have picked up more rocks in the last three months and this is not a product issue. She will need to contact her insurance company."

PARK: He should have requested for pictures, he should have said, he'll send somebody out to inspect it, that was it, in 3 minutes he said it was a rock issue, how would he know.

FINNEY: Park searched the internet and found that car owners of various makes reported their sunroofs also suddenly shattered.

7 On Your Side then discussed this incident with Tarek Zohdi, a professor of mechanical engineering at UC Berkeley. He calculated a rock lofted into the air by a vehicle tire would reach a height of 10-15 feet and would have to come down at 70-80 miles an hour to break the sunroof.

ZOHDI: There is not a chance in the world that an unintentional rock that is lofted by a vehicle would ever break a sunroof panel.

FINNEY: Zohdi says the maximum velocity of a rock coming down would be 25 miles an hour, well short of the needed 70 miles an hour. He said it is more likely the sunroof broke due to the stress caused by changes in temperatures or from fatigue.

ZOHDI: In both cases I would say in my opinion the car manufacturer has the problem; basically it's a manufacturers defect.

FINNEY: 7 On Your Side called BMW corporate. It agreed to replace the sunroof free of charge even before we informed it of the professor's finding.

Tarek says it is possible a rock could break a windshield with a direct hit, but the same scenario is not true for a sunroof since the rock would have to be first lofted into the air.

During 2012, the South Koreans doubled-down their investments in North America as they snagged dealers dumped by the bankrupt Chrysler and General Motors. They have brought out an extensive lineup of fuel-efficient new cars, minivans, and SUVs, and are targeting increasingly upscale customers without forgetting their entry-level base. For example, Hyundai enhanced its luxury lineup with the Genesis luxury sedan and the Genesis Coupe, a Camaro/Mustang stalker. The 2012 Equus is a $64,499 (now worth $31,000, used), V8-powered, rear-drive luxury sedan aimed squarely at the BMW 5 Series and the Mercedes-Benz E-Class. Equus was developed on the rear-drive Genesis sedan platform, but the wheelbase was stretched by 10.9 cm (4.3 in.). It's 29 cm (11.4 in.) longer than the 2010 Mercedes E-Class. At the other end of the fuel economy spectrum, both Hyundai and Kia are focusing on fuel-frugal small cars and plan to offer drivers fuel-saving options that include smaller engines, direct-injection gasoline engines, plug-in hybrids, and fuel cell technology. Hyundai calls the fuel economy initiative "Blue Drive" – a fancy name for cheaper models with less content, less weight, and more miles per gallon. Blue Edition models have a lower gear ratio and tires with less rolling resistance. Power windows and door locks, as well as other formerly standard amenities, are optional, thereby trading convenience for cash savings. Hyundai is also giving each Sonata a Blue Link communications system that provides a direct connection to emergency services in the event of an accident. The feature also gives traffic and weather updates and allows owners easy access to roadside assistance. Smart phones can be connected with Blue Link to help owners locate their vehicle in large shopping malls or to follow "Junior" when he takes the car out on the weekend. The system can keep track of where the vehicle is being driven and how fast it's going.

"Hey son, I know you'll love this feature ... son, son?"

ACCENT ★★★★★

RATING: Recommended (2014-16); Above Average (2006-13); Below Average (2001-05). **Road performance:** Good engine and automatic transmission performance in most situations; but passing and merging requires some caution and patience. Easy handling; a reasonably comfortable and quiet ride; a relaxed driving position with good visibility. Some drivers feel the engine could use a bit more high-end torque and noise-vibration dampening and that the ride is a bit on the firm, jittery side. The Mazda2 is a better choice for winding roads. **Strong points:** Hyundai has transformed its entry-level Accent into a larger, upscale compact the same way the Civic was incrementally improved and enlarged to join the Accord in the family car class. All of these improvements have added to the Accent's base price over the years, however, it is still one of the cheapest and most reliable small cars sold in North America. Although the Accent does almost everything right at an affordable price, it has flown under the radar of most independent rating agencies, keeping a low suggested retail and resale price. Carrying a homegrown direct-injection

1.6L 4-cylinder engine coupled to a standard 6-speed manual transmission (the 6-speed automatic is optional), the Accent offers solid bare-bones motoring. Base models offer many standard features found only on upscale cars such as a height-adjustable driver's seat, four-wheel disc brakes, active front head restraints, a tilt steering wheel, power locks, an incredibly good reliability record, with few complaints relative to safety or quality control; and it's cheap on gas. The absence of some high-tech features is both an advantage and disadvantage in that some convenience is sacrificed for a simpler, more reliable and less expensive package. **Weak points:** Acrobatic rear-seat entry/exit with the hatchback; cramped rear seating; and some noise intrusion into the cabin. Brake rotors fail prematurely.

Prices and Specs

Prices (Soft): *Hatchback L:* $13,599, *Auto:* $14,899, *Sedan L:* $13,299, *Auto:* $14,499, *GL:* $16,249, *Auto:* $16,399, *GLS:* $18,249 **Freight:** $1,495 **Powertrain (Front-drive):** Engine: 1.6L 4-cyl. (138 hp); Transmissions: 6-speed man., 6-speed auto. **Dimensions/capacity:** *Sedan:* Passengers: 2/3; Wheelbase: 101.2 in.; H: 57.1/L: 172/W: 66.9 in.; Headroom F/R: 4.5/2 in.; Legroom F/R: 41.8/33.3 in.; Cargo volume: 13.7 cu. ft.; Fuel tank: 43L/regular; Tow limit: N/A; Load capacity: 850 lb.; Turning circle: 34.1 ft.; Ground clearance: 5.5 in.; Weight: *L:* 2,396 lb., *Auto:* 2,462 lb.

Other opinions: "The 2015 Hyundai Accent ranks #4 in affordable subcompact cars and #15 out of 42 affordable small cars. [It] delivers a smooth ride and provides plenty of cargo space, critics say, but they point out that the car doesn't have a number of tech features." – *U.S. News & World Report.* "Rear seats split 60/40 to produce 600 litres of cargo space – which is about mid-pack for the segment. However, it falls far short of the Honda Fit, which, with its grand total of 1,492 litres, is the undisputed champion of interior flexibility. The Accent has no flashy touchscreen and, as mentioned, no navigation. With the display screen, there's no backup camera, which could be of concern to some buyers. The Accent's tapered roofline and small rear window result in poor rearward visibility." – *driving.ca/ hyundai/accent/reviews/.* **Major redesign:** 2000, 2006, and 2012. **Highway/city fuel economy:** *Man.:* 4.9/6.7 L/100 km. *Auto.:* 4.8/7.8 L/100 km. **Best alternatives:** Honda Fit, Mazda2, or 3, Nissan Versa or Sentra, and the VW Golf.

SAFETY: Child safety seat setup: "Poor." **Crashworthiness:** NHTSA: 2012-16 Accent gets four stars for frontal, side, and rollover crash protection. 1996-2010 models did almost as well with three to five stars in overall crashworthiness. IIHS: Small overlap frontal scores for the 2015 Accent was "Poor" and side crashworthiness was only "Acceptable." 2012 and 2013 Accents are "Good" and 2006-11 models are rated "Acceptable." Side impact results for the 2012 and 2013s are considered "Good," but the 2006-11s are rated as "Poor" performers. 2012-13 model roof strength is seen as "Good" while the 2006-11 models rate only "Acceptable." 2012-13 rear crashworthiness is "Good; 2010-11 versions are "Acceptable;" and 2006-09

Accents were judged "Poor." **Owner-reported safety-related failures:** Sudden unintended acceleration, with brake loss and no airbag deployment:

Owner of a 2013 Hyundai Accent stated that shortly after stopping and parking the vehicle, it suddenly accelerated and crashed into the rear of a parked vehicle. Although the brakes were engaged the accelerator pedal went to the floor and the airbags failed to deploy. Injuries to both knees and to the neck.

Driver's airbag deployed when vehicle was started; driver injured. Sometimes, airbags don't deploy when they should, or there's a sudden loss of power, or the steering locks up. Headlight bulbs burn out because of a voltage spike apparently caused by a faulty voltage regulator. Many complaints of Kuhmo tires' sidewall "bubbling." The air can tire kit inflator is tough for some to figure out and doesn't work as well as a regular spare tire. Keep the car in the garage if you live in a woodsy area – rodents see your yummy wiring insulation as Tim Hortons take out. One owner reports that groundhogs love to snack on the car's undercarriage cables, thereby disabling the tranny and important dash gauges:

I put down moth balls and fox scent to ward them off, but they love Accent wires; losing the transmission and speedometer can make driving a little dangerous.

ALERT! Before signing the contract, insist upon a spare tire instead of a tire repair kit and stay away from Kuhmo low-profile tires.

Accent Profile

	2006	2007	2008	2009	2010	2011	2012	2013	2014
Used Values ($)									
HB /Sedan L	2,500	3,000	3,500	4,000	5,000	6,000	7,500	9,000	11,500
GL	3,000	3,500	4,500	5,000	5,500	7,000	8,500	10,500	12,500
GLS	4,000	4,500	5,500	6,000	7,000	9,000	10,500	12,500	14,000
Reliability	④	④	③	②	②	③	☆	☆	☆
Repairs ($$$)	①	①	①	②	②	②	①	①	①
Electrical	☆	☆	☆	☆	☆	☆	☆	☆	☆
Engine (base)	☆	☆	③	③	③	★	★	★	☆
Fit/Finish	☆	☆	☆	③	③	②	②	②	③
Infotainment	—	—	—	—	—	③	③	③	☆
Transmission (auto.)	☆	☆	☆	③	③	②	②	②	☆

SECRET WARRANTIES, INTERNAL BULLETINS: 2008-11—Some 2008-11 Accents may have a rattle noise coming from underneath the vehicle near the front muffler pipe assembly. This bulletin provides a procedure to replace either the front muffler pipe hanger assembly or the front muffler assembly. 2011-13—Harsh delayed shift diagnosis on the 6-speed automatic transmission. Reducing wind noise from the front door mirror area. 2012-13—A persistent spark knock on heavy acceleration may be due to incorrect canister purge valve flow. 2012-15—An improperly adjusted or improperly operating inhibitor switch (range switch) may result in one or more of the following conditions: Malfunction indicator light (MIL) illuminated, or intermittent no engine crank/no engine start in Park or Neutral. Troubleshooting tips for shift lever concerns. Some Hyundai vehicles may experience brake noise due to improperly adjusted parking brakes. A maladjusted parking brake may cause floating brake shoes that, in turn, may create squealing and judder. Brake noise can be reduced by adjusting the parking brake cable to 0.5mm free play at the adjusting nut, then adjusting the rear shoes.

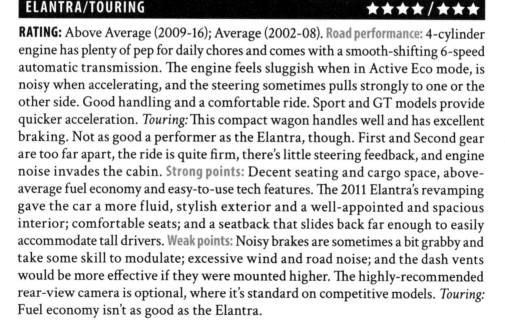

ELANTRA/TOURING ★★★★/★★★

RATING: Above Average (2009-16); Average (2002-08). Road performance: 4-cylinder engine has plenty of pep for daily chores and comes with a smooth-shifting 6-speed automatic transmission. The engine feels sluggish when in Active Eco mode, is noisy when accelerating, and the steering sometimes pulls strongly to one or the other side. Good handling and a comfortable ride. Sport and GT models provide quicker acceleration. *Touring:* This compact wagon handles well and has excellent braking. Not as good a performer as the Elantra, though. First and Second gear are too far apart, the ride is quite firm, there's little steering feedback, and engine noise invades the cabin. Strong points: Decent seating and cargo space, above-average fuel economy and easy-to-use tech features. The 2011 Elantra's revamping gave the car a more fluid, stylish exterior and a well-appointed and spacious interior; comfortable seats; and a seatback that slides back far enough to easily accommodate tall drivers. Weak points: Noisy brakes are sometimes a bit grabby and take some skill to modulate; excessive wind and road noise; and the dash vents would be more effective if they were mounted higher. The highly-recommended rear-view camera is optional, where it's standard on competitive models. *Touring:* Fuel economy isn't as good as the Elantra.

Other opinions: "The 2015 Hyundai Elantra ranks #10 in affordable compact cars and #19 out of 42 affordable small cars." – *U.S. News & World Report.* "Although the Elantra remains a solid choice for a small sedan, some newer rivals have eclipsed it in regards to refinement and comfort." – *Edmunds.* **Major redesign:** 2001, 2007, and 2011. **Highway/city fuel economy:** *1.8L man.:* 4.9/6.8 L/100 km. *Auto.:* 4.9/69 L/ 100 km. *Touring 2.0L man.:* 6.4/8.9 L/100 km. *Touring auto.:* 6.5/8.7 L/100 km. **Best alternatives:** The Honda Fit, Accord or Civic, Mazda2 or 3, Toyota Corolla, and Volkswagen Golf.

SAFETY: Child safety seat setup: "Marginal." **Crashworthiness:** NHTSA: 2001-16 models are rated four and five stars for overall crashworthiness. Earlier models performed poorly in some of the crash tests. *Touring:* 2009-10 models garnered a four- and five-star ranking. IIHS: 2011 through 2015 models generally rate "Good," except for "Acceptable" small overlap frontal scores. 2004-10 Elantras are "Good"; 2001-03 are "Poor"; and 1996-2000 versions are "Acceptable." Side impact results for the 2010 models are "Good;" 2007-10s are rated "Marginal,," and 2001-06 Elantras are classed as "Poor" performers. The worst rating is reserved for 2001-06 Elantras that were judged to give "Poor" protection. **Owner-reported safety-related failures:** Sudden engine shutdown on the highway; hood suddenly flew up while vehicle was underway; dangerous airbag deployment, or failure to deploy:

> Drivers side airbag deployed and metal bracket deployed with airbag from headliner area, also. It sliced my ear in half … Could have been my neck …

At other times, both airbags deployed for no reason; the airbag warning light and tire-pressure monitoring system alert come on for no reason; there was sudden, unintended acceleration accompanied by loss of braking capability; the cruise control suddenly reset itself to a higher speed; throttle sensor sticks when cruising; automatic transmission jumps out of gear; complete electrical shutdown; car may roll away even with the emergency brake applied; faulty electronic stability control; car idles roughly, then refuses to shift into Drive; sudden steering lock-up; the car continually pulls to the right or left: Brakes freeze up when the vehicle is driven through snow; brake rotors rust prematurely producing a grinding noise; a history of front windshield cracks; windshield glare from defroster dish; sunroof implosions; can't trust the fuel gauge; Continental, Kumho Solus, and Hankook original equipment tires are noted for sidewall failures ("bubbling"); and large blind spots caused by the left and right front pillars:

> The positioning of the rear-view mirror only makes the right blind spot larger as there is only the space from the bottom of the mirror to the right pillar to view outside of the car. As a result, I almost hit someone crossing the street from my right to my left.

ALERT! Tire pressure sensors give false alerts. No need for optional equipment; Elantra comes with all the right standard features; one feature missing on some models – a spare tire and jack. Check it out.

Elantra/Touring Profile

Used Values ($)	2006	2007	2008	2009	2010	2011	2012	2013	2014
Sedan GL/L	4,000	4,500	5,000	5,500	6,000	7,000	8,500	10,000	12,500
GLS	4,500	5,000	6,000	7,000	8,000	10,000	11,500	13,500	16,000
LTD	—	6,000	7,000	8,000	9,500	11,000	13,000	15,500	18,000
Touring L	—	—	—	—	6,000	7,500	10,000	—	—
GLS	—	—	—	—	8,500	10,000	12,500	—	—
GLS Sport	—	6,000	7,000	8,000	9,500	11,000	13,500	—	—
Reliability	★	★	★	★	★	☆	☆	☆	☆
Repairs ($$$)	①	①	①	①	①	②	②	②	①
Electrical	☆	☆	☆	☆	☆	☆	☆	☆	☆
Engine (base)	☆	☆	★	★	★	②	②	②	☆
Fit/Finish	☆	☆	☆	★	★	②	②	②	★
Infotainment	—	—	—	—	—	★	★	★	☆
Transmission (auto.)	☆	☆	☆	★	★	②	②	②	☆

SECRET WARRANTIES, INTERNAL BULLETINS: 2007-12—Troubleshooting hard shifts. 2010—Some Elantra and Elantra Touring vehicles may exhibit a noise originating from the front struts when passing over bumps or dips at speeds of 10-16 mph. 2011-12—Free rear door harness and centre muffler rattle noise repair. Excessive driveshaft noise (creaking or popping). Troubleshooting an automatic transmission that stays in Third gear, goes into "failsafe mode," or has an illuminated MIL alert. Touch screen new recalibration. 2011-13—Hard starts may signal the need to clean the electronic throttle control (ETC) throttle body.

SONATA/HYBRID ★★/★★★

RATING: Below Average (2011-16; 2007-09); Not Recommended (2010); Below Average (2002-06). There have been few owner complaints 6 months into Hyundai's 2015 redesign, which is encouraging in that Hyundais don't usually tolerate redesigns very well (see "Weak points" and "Safety," below). *Hybrid:* Average (2013-16); Below Average (2012). Sonata's 2012 Hybrid debut was blasted by car columnists for its poorly-designed powertrain, inadequate braking, and fanciful fuel economy. The 2013-15 models successfully redressed earlier powertrain problems with a quieter and smoother-shifting transmission (no more buzzy drone), and a more refined clutch. Braking is also more confidence-inspiring; the battery has a higher capacity and is smaller, freeing up some cargo space, and the car can reach 75 mph on battery power alone (engine power has been cut from 166 to 159 hp). Road performance: Sizzling, smooth V6 performance; acceptable handling; and a comfortable ride. The suspension is somewhat bouncy and noisy; there's too much body lean under hard cornering; and the steering lacks sufficient feedback. Many complaints of steering wander and pull. Strong points: V6 engine burns only a bit more gas than the 4-banger does. Well-equipped and stylish; user-friendly controls and gauges; spacious trunk, a conveniently low lift-in height; and a fairly quiet cabin that comfortably seats three in the back. Weak points: Noisy shocks/struts; engine alert light comes on for no reason. Sudden, unintended acceleration when passing other cars; same thing happens when shifting to Reverse; cruise control resets itself to a higher speed; and sudden hybrid engine failure due to water intrusion in rainy weather:

> Engine can easily become hydro-locked in heavy rain and road splash-back from other vehicles due to the design of the direct air intake of the Sonata Hybrid. With its design, it does not have any water baffles to prevent water from entering the air filter and once it enters the air filter box, there are no drain holes for it to drain out. This forces the water through the engine. This could lead to damage of the HEV system and battery pack.

Prices and Specs

Price (Negotiable): *GL:* $22,699, *GL auto.:* $24,299, *GLS auto.:* $26,499, *Limited:* $29,899, *2.0T Limited:* $31,799 *Hybrid:* $28,999 **Freight:** $1,565 **Powertrain (Front-drive):** Engines: 1.6L 4-cyl. turbo (177 hp), 2.4L 4-cyl. (185 hp), 2.0L 4-cyl. turbo (245 hp); Transmissions: 6-speed auto., and 7-speed manumatic **Dimensions/capacity:** Passengers: 2/3; Wheelbase: 110 in.; H: 57.9/L: 189.8/W: 72.2 in.; Headroom F/R: 3/3 in.; Legroom F/R: 45.5/34.6 in.; Cargo volume: 16.4 cu. ft.; Fuel tank: 70L/regular; Tow limit: N/A; Load capacity: 860 lb.; Turning circle: 35.8 ft.; Weight: 3,161-3,316 lb.

Other opinions: "The 2015 Hyundai Sonata is rated #3 out of 18 affordable midsize cars." – *U.S. News & World Report.* "My new 2014 Sonata SE is a safety hazard while driving down the freeway at speeds of 60 to 75 mph. The problem is more relevant at high speeds than low speeds but the car still wanders. It will not stay in a straight line. It is a constant fade from left at one point to the right at another point. Hyundai dealership told me it is made to go to the right in case you fall asleep at the wheel." – *safercar.gov*. **Major redesign:** 1999, 2006, 2011, and 2015. **Highway/city fuel economy:** *Auto. 2.0L:* 6.0/9.3 L/100 km. *Man. 2.4L:* 5.7/8.7 L/10 km. *Auto. 2.4L:* 5.7/9.4 L/100 km. *Hybrid:* 4.6/5.5 L/100 km. **Best alternatives:** A Honda Accord, Hyundai Elantra, Nissan Sentra, Mazda5 or 6, and the Toyota Camry.

SAFETY: **Child safety seat setup:** "Marginal." **Crashworthiness:** NHTSA: 2006-16 models get the agency's top five-star rating for overall crashworthiness. 2002-05s did almost as well, with four stars. IIHS: Gave out a "Good" rating for front offset protection, head-restraint effectiveness, roof crush-resistance, and side-impact protection. **Owner-reported safety-related failures:** Not all model years are reliable or safe, judging from the following owner experiences with their 2011-15 Sonatas: Sudden unintended acceleration, electrical shutdown; passenger side airbag disabled when a normal-sized adult occupies the seat; airbags fail to deploy in a high-speed collision; side curtain airbag deploys inadvertently; parked vehicle rolled downhill, even though the transmission was left in Drive; manual transmission lunges forward when shifting from First to Second gear; poorly located cruise control Resume button inadvertently activates the feature; premature wearout of the rear brakes; low-beam headlights give inadequate illumination, left tail light fell out of its mounting inside the trunk due to the plastic mount crumbling; rear windshield exploded after door was closed; trunk opens spontaneously; Hankook original equipment tires continue to fail due to sidewall bubbling; sun visors are not long enough (vertically) to keep sun from blinding the driver; the horn is weak, makes a short sound, and sometimes won't sound at all; and hard starts, no-starts:

> The only reliable solution for starting the car is to depress the brake pedal and depress the Engine Start button for a minimum of 10 seconds. I've placed the key fob in several locations in the car (dashboard, cup holder, smart key holder) with no repeatable success. After a visit to the dealership, they cannot find a problem. However, a search on the Internet shows other owners experiencing the same problem.

Prior to the 2011 model's redesign, only an average number of owner complaints appeared on NHTSA's safety database each year. For example, the 2010 model shows only 151 incidents reported where the 4-year norm would be 250 complaints. Contrast that with the redesigned 2011 model's profile up through June 2015. That model year alone elicited 807 safety-related failures and 46 service bulletins posted on NHTSA's website. Subsequent years show a dramatic reduction of owners' complaints: The 2012, 2013, 2014, and 2015 versions have generated 184, 158, 27, and 18 reports of safety failures, respectively. Although better built, these cars still have far too many life-endangering defects that re-appear year after year. Expect sudden unintended acceleration; loss of power due to a faulty engine cam advance sensor; inadvertent front airbag deployment, sunroof implosions, erratic downshifting with the automatic 6-speed tranny; loss of brakes, original equipment tires blow out or have inadequate traction; the fuel tank won't fill up; and excessive steering wander and severe pulling to the right or left:

> I have had my 2013 Sonata Limited for two weeks. This is my third Hyundai vehicle after owning a 2011 Sonata Limited and 2007 Santa Fe. The steering in the vehicle weaves from left to right (does not track straight) and control of the car is jeopardized by the smallest road contours or gusts of wind requiring constant correction. As a result of the constant driving adjustments, I am experiencing fatigue and shoulder/neck soreness. Equally alarming, the lack of control is extremely noticeable on highways at increased speeds.

ALERT! Check out the car's directional stability and headlight projection:

> Low beams did not project adequately when driving up and down hills and driving around curves. The low beam headlight projection decreased up to 50% and sometimes more than 50% depending on the size of the hill or curve.

Sonata Profile

	2006	2007	2008	2009	2010	2011	2012	2013	2014
Used Values ($)									
GL	4,500	5,000	6,000	7,000	8,000	10,000	12,000	14,500	18,000
VE/GLS	5,500	6,500	7,500	—	—	13,000	15,000	17,500	21,500
GLX/LTD	—	—	8,500	9,500	12,500	14,500	16,000	18,500	23,000
Hybrid	—	—	—	—	—	—	13,000	15,500	19,000
Reliability	★3	★3	★3	★3	★3	★4	★4	★4	★4
Repairs ($$$)	2	2	2	2	2	1	1	1	1
Electrical	★3	★3	★3	★3	★3	★4	★4	★4	★3
Engine (base)	★2	★2	★3	★3	★3	★4	★4	★4	★3
Fit/Finish	★2	★2	★2	★3	★3	★4	★4	★4	★3
Infotainment	—	—	—	—	—	★3	★3	★3	★4
Transmission (auto.)	★2	★2	★2	★3	★3	★4	★4	★4	★3

SECRET WARRANTIES, INTERNAL BULLETINS: 2006-08—Engine hesitation and misfire repair tips. Remedy for seat creaking, squeaking. 2006-09—Correction for a rough idle or display of the MIL warning light on vehicles equipped with the 3.3L engine. The oil temperature sensor may leak. 2006-10—Steering squeaks when turning. 2007-10—Troubleshooting hard starts or a rough idle. 2008—Correction for a steering wheel shimmy/vibration. 2009-10—A cold weather no-start condition may require a new starter solenoid. Water leaking onto the passenger side front floor is likely due to a kinked AC drain hose. 2009-13—If the engine spins, but doesn't crank, replace the starter motor says Hyundai TSB #13-EE-001, issued Feb. 2013. 2011-12—Hyundai is reluctantly recalling nearly a half-million Sonatas equipped with 2.0L or 2.4L engines to replace the engines that may fail prematurely. Hyundai says that metal debris may not have been fully removed from the crankshaft area at the factory. That could cause the car to stall or crash. The prematurely worn connecting rod bearing will make a cyclical knocking noise, and it also could cause the oil pressure warning light to illuminate. Dealers will inspect the cars and replace defective engines at no cost to owners. The company also will increase the engine warranty for 10 years or 120,000 miles. (This is an American announcement, so owners will have to do their own metric conversion.) Automatic transmission malfunctions caused by faulty solenoids and other electronic failures. The transmission may shift harshly, drop into a "safe" default mode, or hesitate between shifts. 2015—Reduced engine performance on cars with a 1.6L turbo-charged engine can be caused by a defective intercooler (TSB #14-01-045). Consider replacing the driveshaft, if the transmission produces a grinding noise, won't move into Drive or Reverse, or the vehicle rolls away with the parking brake applied.

GENESIS COUPE, SEDAN ★★★★★

RATING: Recommended (2013-16); Above Average (2009-12). Coupe or sedan? Both are excellent buys. The Genesis coupe and sedan are impressive upscale rear drive vehicles with different performance characteristics and widely varying retail prices. Cheaper 2012 leftovers are not worth the 2013 upgrades you will miss. Road performance: The 3.8L engine gives breathtaking power to the coupe and quick acceleration when used with the sedan, although the sedan's 5.0L V8 is a real tire burner. The coupe's 4-cylinder turbo is both noisy and hooked to an imprecise 6-speed manual transmission; the optional 4.6L V8 is like having a sixth finger: It's there, but not all that useful. Expect the coupe to have a choppy, stiff ride, while the sedan has some body roll in hard cornering due to its more supple, "floaty" suspension (Infiniti and BMW models have stiffer suspensions that produce a more-secure feeling). Strong points: These luxury cars are loaded with high-tech safety gear and are generally well-appointed with first-class interior fit and finish; a quiet, vibration-free, and spacious cabin; and clear and easy-to-read gauges. The sedan has plenty of room fore and aft and has posted impressive crashworthiness rankings. The 2013s were restyled to look more aggressive, and their new powertrains pack more punch and a few more gears as well. For example, the coupe's 3.8L V6 now generates 348 hp and the 2.0T is rated at 274 hp, a 30% increase over the previous engine. Cabin amenities have also been improved with easier-to-read gauges and extra seat bolstering. Weak points: Cramped rear seating with the coupe; navigation and audio system controls are cumbersome. Hyundai recommends premium fuel for extra horsepower from the 4.6L V8, but it's not worth the higher fuel cost for just a few more horses. V6 reliability is above average; V8s are average. Some early transmission failures; manual transmission knocking while the clutch is disengaged and the transmission is in Neutral; inaccurate fuel gauge (confirmed by Hyundai service bulletin) rattling caused by broken frame spot welds; original equipment, low-profile tires are rough-riding and failure-prone; engine compartment is vulnerable to rodent infestation; chewed plastics and soya-coated wiring can cost $5,000 to diagnose and replace; faulty power seat switch; inadequate power seat cooling; a small pebble damaged the AC condenser ($800); and the windows and windshield produce a moldy-looking condensate.

Prices and Specs

Base – Prices (Firm): *Coupe 2.0T: $26,499, auto.: $28,299, 2.0T GT man.: $31,149, 2.0T R-SPEC man.: $28,799, 3.8 man.: $32,999, 3.8 GT man.: $36,999, auto.: $38,799, Sedan: $39,999* **Freight:** *Coupe: $1,565, Sedan: $1,760* **Powertrain (Rear-drive):** *Engines: 2.0L 4-cyl (164 hp); 1.6L Turbo 4-cyl. (175 hp); Transmissions: 7-speed manumatic* **Dimensions/capacity:** *Coupe: Passengers: 2/3; Wheelbase: 105.2 in.; H: 58.3/L: 176/W: 73.5 in.; Cargo volume: 15.9 cu. ft.; Fuel tank: 65L-73L/regular/premium; Tow limit: 5,000 lb.; Ground clearance: 5.2 in.; Turning circle: 36 ft.; Weight: 3,748 lb.*

Premium – Prices (Firm): *Coupe 3.8 R-SPEC: $29,499, Premium: $32,199, Premium auto.: $33,999, GT man.: $37,199, auto.: $38,999 Sedan Premium: $43,000, Luxury: $48,000, Technology: $53,000, Ultimate: $62,000* **Freight:** *Coupe: $1,795; Sedan: $1,995* **Powertrain (Rear-drive):** *Engines: Coupe: 2.0L Turbo 4-cyl. (274 hp), 3.8L V6 (348 hp); Sedan: 3.8L V6 (311 hp), 5.0L V8 (420 hp); Transmissions: Coupe: 6-speed manual, 8-speed manumatic; Sedan: 8-speed manumatic* **Dimensions/capacity:** *Coupe: Passengers: 2/3; Wheelbase: 111 in.; H: 54.5/L: 182.3/W: 73.4 in.; Cargo volume: 10 cu. ft.; Fuel tank: 65L regular/premium; Tow limit: N/A.; Ground clearance: 5.1 in.; Turning circle: 37.4 ft.; Weight: 3,538 lb Sedan: Passengers: 2/3; Wheelbase: 118.5 in.; H: 58.3/L: 196.5/W: 74.4 in.; Cargo volume: 15.3 cu. ft.; Fuel tank: 65L regular/premium; Tow limit: 5,000 lb.; Ground clearance: 5.2 in.; Turning circle: 36.2 ft.; Weight: 4,295 lb (AWD).*

Other opinions: "The 2015 Hyundai Genesis is rated #4 out of 18 upscale midsize cars… Its well-constructed interior and strong engines deliver high-end features for less money than most competitors, critics say." – *U.S. News & World Report.* "I am very unhappy with my 2013 Genesis Coupe. In fact I hate it. It has a rattle that the dealer can't find … This rattle is so bad I hate to drive the car." – *Cars.com.* **Major redesign:** 2015. **Highway/city fuel economy:** *Coupe 3.8L man.:* 9.9/14.4L/100 km. *3.8L auto.:* 9.6/14.6L/100 km. *5.0L 8-spd. auto.:* 10.5/17.3L/100 km. **Best alternatives:** *Coupe:* The Chevrolet Camaro and Ford Mustang – for sheer sportster thrills without the bills – the Mazda Miata. *Sedan:* The BMW 3 Series, Lexus GS, Mercedes-Benz E-Class, and Toyota Avalon.

SAFETY: Child safety seat setup: Untested. **Crashworthiness:** NHTSA: 2015-16 four-door models get five stars for overall crashworthiness. 2011-14 two- and four-door versions earned five stars for rollover resistance, while the 2009-10 sedan and 2010

coupe garnered a five-star rating for front, side, and rollover occupant protection. IIHS: 2009-15 models were top-scorers with a "Good" designation in all crash categories, including moderate frontal overlap crash protection. **Owner-reported safety-related failures:** Less than 100 safety-related complaints posted during the past six model years – 300 would have been average. Powertrain failures are notable for cruise control malfunctions; sudden unintended acceleration; and a prolonged hesitation when accelerating after slowing down:

> Multiple times I have accelerated the car to get onto the highway, change lanes quickly, and make right turns on reds, only to have it literally do nothing. At times it takes 2 to 3 seconds before it accelerates and then seems to have a tough time shifting through the gears. At low speeds the car seems to hesitate and shift poorly.
>
> *– Safercar.gov*

Electronic stability control can lock the brakes; frequent brake failures; fire caused by overheated brake rotors; various ESC and Bluetooth malfunctions; steering tracks to the right or left; turn signal continues blinking after it is no longer needed; driver's door opens by itself and will not latch; GPS and rear camera malfunction intermittently; and the rear seat belt anchors may be reversed.

ALERT! Fuel consumption figures are not to be believed; expect to get 20% less than what Hyundai promises.

Genesis Profile

	2009	2010	2011	2012	2013	2014
Used Values ($)						
Coupe	—	10,500	12,000	15,500	18,500	21,500
3.8 GT	—	12,500	15,000	17,500	25,000	29,500
Sedan	12,500	15,000	17,500	19,500	24,000	30,000
Tech	15,000	17,500	20,500	24,500	30,000	37,000
V8/V8 R-Spec	17,500	19,500	22,500	28,000	34,000	42,000
Reliability	☆	☆	☆	☆	☆	☆
Repairs ($$$)	💰	💰	💰	💰	💰	💰
Electrical	☆	☆	☆	☆	☆	☆
Engine (base)	☆	☆	☆	☆	☆	☆
Fit/Finish	☆	☆	☆	☆	☆	☆
Infotainment	—	—	—	—	—	☆
Transmission (auto.)	☆	☆	☆	☆	☆	☆

SECRET WARRANTIES, INTERNAL BULLETINS: 2001-12—Remedy for engine ticking at idle. A faulty transmission solenoid may activate the Check Engine alert and send the transaxle into "Fail-Safe" limp mode. Troubleshooting tips for a harsh, delayed automatic transmission shift. Introduction of a new touch screen recalibration. *Coupe:* Free sunroof switch replacement campaign. *Sedan:* Troubleshooting speed sensor malfunctions (replace the valve body assembly). 2009-12—An inoperable or noisy A/C may require an A/C pulley disc limiter (Equus included). 2010—No start in Park or Neutral. 2012—Shift lever can't be moved out of Park. 2012-14—Erratic or unresponsive fuel gauge. 2013—Service Campaign #938 provides for the free replacement of the fuel feed tube assembly if the Check Engine light comes on; there's a hesitation upon acceleration; or the transmission shifts erratically. 2013-14—Hyundai TSB #12-EM-007, issued Nov. 2012, says an engine rattle or buzzing sound "results from the required tolerances in the waste gate pivot point and the waste gate valve. This normal operating characteristic will not affect the performance or durability of the vehicle." Despite what Hyundai says, other turbo-equipped cars don't produce this noise. 2015—Hyundai will replace free of charge the lower cowl to prevent water intrusion into the cabin (Service Campaign TX1, TSB #15-01-016). Power window malfunctions are addressed in TSB #15-BE-007.

TUCSON

RATING: Above Average (2011-16), Average (2004-10). The revamped 2016 version is 1.1 inch wider than its predecessor, 3.0 inches longer, and there's a 1.2-inch greater stretch between the axles – all making for more interior space and cargo volume. The new platform is stiffer, thanks to redesigned front suspension struts and rear control arms. **Road performance:** V6 engine provides smooth, sustained acceleration; sure-footed (thanks to the standard stability control); and effective, easy-to-modulate braking. Owners say the base 4-cylinder engine struggles with a full load, so shoppers with a large family may want the new 1.6L 175 hp turbo 4-cylinder, paired with a 7-speed dual-clutch automatic transmission. This year's refinements make the Tucson a bit more agile, though the electric steering still feels vague and lacks sufficient feedback at highway speeds. **Strong points:** The Tucson is Hyundai's compact crossover that was first introduced for the 2005 model year. It is smaller than the Santa Fe and built on the same Elantra-based platform as the Kia Sportage. It's reasonably priced and well equipped; has a roomy and easily accessed cabin; and above average reliability. **Weak points:** Stiff riding; poor styling limits cargo space; rear seat needs more bolstering for thigh support; some road noise; and advertised fuel economy shouldn't be expected. Automatic transmission jerks and slams into gear:

> Sudden downshifting with loud clunk and lurching of vehicle at 35 mph [55 km/h]. Felt as if I had been hit from behind by another vehicle. Instinctively hit the brakes and pulled over to check for exterior damage, and found none. Continued down the road and experienced unusual increases in rpms. When I arrived at my destination, the vehicle would not go in Reverse. Owned vehicle only 11 days. Incident occurred at 500 miles [800 km].

> ## Prices and Specs
>
> **Prices (Firm):** *2.0L GL man.: $21,999, auto.: $23,999, GL AWD: $25,999, 2.4L GLS: $27,449, GLS AWD: $29,449, Limited AWD Navi.: $33,999* **Freight:** $1,760 **Powertrain (Front-drive/AWD):** Engines: 2.0L 4-cyl. (165 hp), 2.4L 4-cyl. (176 hp); Transmissions: 5-speed man., 6-speed manumatic **Dimensions/capacity:** Passengers: 2/3; Wheelbase: 103.9 in.; H: 65.2/L: 176.2/W: 71.7 in.; Headroom F/R: 5/4 in.; Legroom F/R: 41.2/38.7 in.; Cargo volume: 25.7 cu. ft.; Fuel tank: 58L/regular; Tow limit: 1,000-2,000 lb.; Load capacity: 860 lb.; Turning circle: 34.7 ft.; Ground clearance: 6.7 in.; Weight: 3,139-3,488 lb.

Other opinions: "The 2015 Hyundai Tucson ranks #15 out of 27 affordable compact SUVs … [It] doesn't have as much cargo space as rivals and its base engine could use more power, but it has an attractive cabin and agile handling" – *U.S. News & World Report.* "Hyundai's Tucson is a compact crossover that is certainly likable for its maneuverability, dimensions, and stylish exterior, but up against plenty of excellent competition, it seems to need more to stand out." – *Edmunds.* **Major redesign:** 2005, 2010, 2014, and 2016. **Highway/city fuel economy:** *2.0L man.:* 7.4/ 10.1 L/100 km. *Auto.:* 6.5/9.1 L/100 km. *2.4L man.:* 6.9/10 L/100 km. *Auto:* 6.3/ 9.5 L/100 km. *4WD auto.:* 7.1/10 L/100 km. **Best alternatives:** The Honda CR-V and Toyota RAV4.

SAFETY: Child safety seat setup: Untested. **Crashworthiness:** NHTSA: 2005-15 Tucsons scored a five-star crashworthiness rating for side-impact occupant protection and a four-star rating for frontal and rollover crashworthiness. IIHS: The 2015 Tucson generally "Good," except for the moderate overlap front test result, which was considered to be "Poor." 2010-14 Tucsons continued to perform poorly in the moderate frontal overlap crash test, although they posted a "Good" ranking in other crash categories. 2005-09 models were judged "Acceptable." In the small frontal overlap test, the 2009-13 models got a "Poor" rating; side ratings for 2010-13: "Good;" 2005-09: "Acceptable;" roof strength for 2010-13: "Good;" 2005-09: "Poor;" rear for 2009-13: "Good;" 2006-08: "Poor." **Owner-reported safety-related failures:** Firewall insulation caught fire; rear window shattered spontaneously; key can be taken out of the ignition and transmission placed in Park and the Tucson rolled downhill; loss of brakes for a couple of seconds after passing over speed bumps or small potholes; when accelerating to merge with traffic, the vehicle hesitates and then decelerates while the gas pedal is fully depressed; power steering seized; vehicle sways left and right while cruising; rear of the vehicle slides as if it were on ice; rear-tire lock-up; and speed sensor wires are vulnerable to road debris:

> Wires are located behind the tires and are fully exposed to road debris. They can be easily severed, thereby affecting ABS and traction control. The wire sticks out 3 inches in open air of the undercarriage and are located close enough to the tires that if they kick up any debris, it is in the direct path of the wire.

ALERT! Does the car's rear styling cut your rearward visibility too much? Test the 4-cylinder engine for merging and steep grade performance. Also, check the steering performance and look for excessive road wander.

Tucson Profile

	2006	2007	2008	2009	2010	2011	2012	2013	2014
Used Values ($)									
L	—	—	6,000	7,500	—	10,000	12,500	—	—
GL	5,500	6,500	7,500	8,500	9,000	11,500	14,000	15,500	18,000
GL AWD	—	7,000	8,500	9,500	11,000	13,000	15,000	17,000	19,500
GLS AWD	—	8,500	—	—	12,500	15,000	17,500	20,000	23,000
LTD AWD	—	—	9,000	11,000	13,500	16,500	19,000	22,000	27,500
Reliability	★	★	★	★	★	★	★	★	★
Repairs ($$$)	2	2	2	2	1	1	1	1	1
Electrical	☆	☆	☆	☆	☆	☆	☆	☆	☆
Engine (base)	★	★	★	★	★	★	★	★	★
Fit/Finish	★	★	★	★	★	★	★	★	★
Infotainment	—	—	—	—	—	★	★	★	★
Transmission (auto.)	★	★	★	★	★	★	★	★	★

SECRET WARRANTIES, INTERNAL BULLETINS: 2005-09—No movement in Drive or Reverse. Fluid may leak from the area around the automatic transmission torque converter or between the transaxle and the transfer case. Correcting harsh gear engagement. Tips on silencing a rattling sunroof. 2008-12—Remedy for engine ticking at idle. 2010—Troubleshooting harsh, delayed shifts by the automatic transmission. Incorrect operation of the transmission solenoids will cause the transmission to perform erratically and the Check Engine warning to light up. 2010-15—An improperly adjusted or improperly operating inhibitor switch (range switch) may result in one or more of the following conditions: Malfunction indicator light (MIL) illuminated, or intermittent no engine crank/no engine start in Park or Neutral. Troubleshooting tips for shift lever concerns. Some Hyundai vehicles may experience brake noise/vibration due to improperly adjusted parking brakes.

SANTA FE/HYBRID ★★★★★ / ★

RATING: Recommended (2014-16); Above Average (2006-13); Average (2004-05); Below Average (2001-03). *Hybrid:* Scheduled for late 2015, the new Hybrid is expected to be met by underwhelming enthusiasm, now that fuel prices have cratered (Not Recommended during its first years on the market). This SUV does almost everything right. Road performance: Acceptable acceleration with the base 2.4L 4-cylinder, but the 3.3L V6 gives you more usable power and acceptable fuel economy as well. You will also enjoy the smooth-shifting automatic transmission; fairly agile comportment; and a comfortable, controlled ride. Less enjoyable: The 2.4L 4-cylinder could use more low-end power; vague steering; and the ride quality may be too stiff for some. Strong points: The Santa Fe is a competitively priced family SUV that is at the small end of the mid-size sport-utility lineup. It offers impressive room, good build quality, and many standard safety and performance features that cost a lot more when bought with competing models. Revamped recently, the Santa Fe now has better-performing, fuel-thrifty powertrains, additional cabin space, and more useful tech features. The 6-speed automatic transmission is smooth, responsive, and quiet. A long list of standard equipment; standard stability/traction control and full-body side curtain airbags; a roomy interior that easily accommodates both passengers and cargo; enhanced by comfortable seats; exceptional forward visibility from the front seats; simple, user-friendly controls; improved fuel economy; and better than average quality control. Weak points: Competent handling, but steering is numb. The three-row version rides stiffly when fully-loaded. You will have to get used to some annoying suspension and road noise. Third-row houses Lilliputian seats (a common complaint for vehicles in this class) and provides limited cargo space, as well. The lack of a standard-issue rear-view camera is a major oversight.

Prices and Specs

Prices (Firm): 2.4 Sport: $27,149 2.4 Sport Premium front-drive.: $29,249, 2.0T Premium: $35,449, 2.4 Premium AWD: $31,249, 2.0T AWD: $33,449, 2.4 Luxury AWD: $35,449 **Freight:** $1,595 **Powertrain (Front-drive/AWD):** Engines: 2.4L 4-cyl. (190 hp), 2.0L 4-cyl turbo. (264 hp), 3.3L V6 (290 hp); Transmission: 6-speed auto. **Dimensions/capacity:** Passengers: 2/3; Wheelbase: 106.3 in.; H: 67.9/L: 184.1/W: 74.4 in.; Headroom F/R: 6/4.5 in.; Legroom F/R: 41/28 in.; Cargo volume: 35.5 cu. ft.; Fuel tank: 75L/regular; Tow limit: 2,000 lb.; Load capacity: 930 lb.; Turning circle: 35.4 ft.; Ground clearance: 8.1 in.; Weight: 3,725-3,875 lb.

Other opinions: "The 2015 Hyundai Santa Fe ranks #4 out of 12 affordable midsize SUVs and #5 in affordable SUVs with 3 rows. The 2015 Hyundai Santa Fe impresses critics with its premium materials, clear-cut cabin controls and powerful engines in both the two- and three-row trims." – *U.S. News & World Report.* "Want to know my trick for staying awake during long drives? No, it's not coffee – although let's be real, there will be coffee involved. Just put me behind the wheel of a 2010–12 Hyundai Santa Fe. How's that? This SUV has an engine with a nasty reputation of stalling at any speed, any time, without any warning. That means no acceleration. No power steering. No power brakes. And one change of pants." – *www.hyundai problems.com/trends/engine-stalling/*. **Major redesign:** 2001, 2007 and 2013. **Highway/ city fuel economy:** *2.4L man.:* 7.7/11 L/100 km. *Auto:* 7.2/10.4 L/100 km. *2.4L 4WD:* 8.0/10.6 L/100 km. *3.5L:* 7.6/10.2 L/100 km. *3.5L 4WD:* 7.7/10.6 L/100 km. **Best alternatives:** GM Terrain, Traverse, Acadia, or Enclave; Nissan Xterra; and Toyota RAV4 or Highlander. Although the Santa Fe is 2.1 inches shorter than the Lexus RX330, its seats have more head, leg, and shoulder room than the RX, with additional room for an optional third-row seat, missing in the Lexus. The 2014 Hyundai offers six- or seven-passenger third row seating with its additional length and width.

SAFETY: **Child safety seat setup:** "Acceptable." **Crashworthiness:** NHTSA: 2012 Santa Fe has an overall three-star ranking, while 2002-10 models earned ratings that varied between three and five stars. IIHS: The 2013-15 Santa Fe's frontal, side, rear, and roof crashworthiness as "Good," but small overlap front crashworthiness was seen as "Marginal." 2007-12s were considered "Good" performers, however, the small overlap test was not carried out. **Owner-reported safety-related failures:** Sudden acceleration accompanied by loss of braking:

> Driver was pulling into a parking space when Santa Fe suddenly surged or lunged forward and to the right causing car to jump over a concrete bumper and into another car parked at a 90-degree angle. After the accident investigation was cleared, driver proceeded to the local dealership. Enroute the Santa Fe would not shift out of low gear.

When accelerating, vehicle pulls sharply to the side; and often stalls out:

> Plaintiffs in a California class-action claim 2010-2012 Santa Fe SUVs have a stalling defect and Hyundai waited years to admit the problem. The lawsuit quotes a dealer service bulletin that admits the SUVs can stall because the alternator can't take the extra load and drops the engine rpms. Plaintiffs claim the vehicles shut off completely without warning, particularly when driven at low speeds, turning or coming to a stop. Some owners have also reported experiencing unexplained loss of power resulting in deceleration or stalling while driving at highway speeds. The case was filed August 8, 2014, in the U.S. District Court for the Northern District of California (see *Reniger v. Hyundai Motor America.*or *HyundaiSantaFeProblem.com*).

Raw gas smell both inside and outside the vehicle; Santa Fe frequently shuts down when underway; a loud knock and transmission jerk occurs whenever the vehicle is first started; when shifting, the jerkiness of the transmission feels like someone is hitting the rear end; and loss of brakes, as the pedal descended to the floor.

ALERT! Take a night test drive; low-beam headlight illumination may be insufficient.

Santa Fe Profile

	2006	2007	2008	2009	2010	2011	2012	2013	2014
Used Values ($)									
GL	4,500	6,000	7,000	8,500	10,000	12,500	14,500	—	—
GLS/Premium	5,000	—	—	—	—	13,500	17,500	—	—
3.3/3.5 FWD	6,000	7,000	8,000	10,000	11,500	15,000	18,500	—	—
2.4 AWD	—	—	—	—	—	14,500	17,500	—	—
3.3/3.5 AWD	—	8,000	9,500	11,000	12,500	15,500	18,500	—	—
LTD/GLS/Sport AWD	—	8,500	10,000	12,000	13,500	17,000	20,500	—	—
Sport 2.4	—	—	—	—	—	—	—	19,500	22,000
Sport AWD	—	—	—	—	—	—	—	22,000	25,000
Reliability	☆	☆	☆	☆	★	★	★	★	☆
Repairs ($$$)	🛍1	🛍1	🛍1	🛍1	🛍2	🛍2	🛍2	🛍2	🛍1
Electrical	☆	☆	☆	☆	☆	☆	☆	☆	☆
Engine (base)	☆	☆	☆	☆	☆	☆	☆	★	☆
Fit/Finish	☆	☆	☆	★	★	★	★	★	☆
Infotainment	—	—	—	—	—	★	★	☆	☆
Transmission (auto.)	☆	☆	☆	☆	☆	☆	☆	★	☆

SECRET WARRANTIES, INTERNAL BULLETINS: 2008-12—Tips on reducing excessive driveshaft noise (creaking or popping). **2010**—This bulletin provides an extended warranty to cover the replacement of the intermediate shaft on some 2010 Santa Fe 2.4L 2WD vehicles with automatic transmissions (CAMPAIGN 102). **2010-15**—An improperly adjusted or improperly operating inhibitor switch (range switch) may result in one or more of the following conditions: Malfunction indicator light (MIL) illuminated, or intermittent no engine crank/no engine start in Park or Neutral. Troubleshooting tips for shift lever concerns. Some Hyundai vehicles may experience brake noise/vibration due to improperly adjusted parking brakes. **2013**—Free front and rear door latch replacement under CAMPAIGN TS0. **2013-14**—Cold start misfires with a 2.0L turbo engine can be corrected through an ECM upgrade. **2013-15**—Some (NC) AWD vehicles may experience a buzzing or scraping noise from the transmission area when accelerating at slow speeds. The crank position sensor wheel plate may need to be replaced under warranty. **2015**—Hyundai will replace free of charge original equipment 19-inch Hankook tires that may produce road noise and vibration (TSB #March 2015). These tires continually show up on owner complaint reports.

INFINITI

Unlike Toyota's Lexus division, which started out as softly sprung Camry clones akin to your dad's rear-drive Oldsmobile, Nissan's luxury Infiniti brand took another road that stressed performance over comfort and opulence, and offered buyers lots of high-performance, cutting-edge features at what were initially very reasonable prices. But the company went more mainstream during the mid-'90s, and its vehicles became less original as they lost their price and performance advantage.

Infiniti limped along for another decade with dressed-up Nissans carryng meaningless and confusing alpha numeric names copied from German automakers to hide their cars' more humble origin. For example, the G37 is a rebadged Skyline. The M35/45 is the Nissan Fuga. Even going back to their original lineup, the Q45 was (and still is) a rebadged Nissan Cima, the G20 was a Nissan Primera, the I30 was just a Maxima, and the M30 and later J30 were a Nissan Leopard. Shoppers weren't fooled.

After the 2009 global recession, Infiniti's lineup went into retail freefall and Nissan was ready to shut it down after 24 years on the market. Nissan/Renault CEO Carlos Ghosn was clear, "We don't need Infiniti, we just don't need that brand."

But Infiniti got a reprieve and is now fighting to put performance back into its luxury cars' original styling, and every conceivable high-tech safety and convenience feature imaginable. And it's working, almost.

Sales are on the upswing. The company is considering a plug-in hybrid, mid-engine sports car, and adding more high-performance models to its product mix. However, its newest offerings are meeting with a decidedly mixed reception. Take for example the recently-launched QX60, a re-branded JX35 three-row SUV crossover aimed at Acura and Audi customers.

Says the *Wall Street Journal*'s auto critic, Dan Neil:

> If I'm painting a picture of a big, fat, electronically sedated cow, then I've succeeded. Nimble she ain't. The steering is as numb as a well digger's bottom, the suspension extra plush, and body motions are sometimes hilariously undamped. The ride is pretty comfortable, but the whole affair feels a bit unstuck. Cornering- and handling-wise, the BMW X5 and Acura MDX murder the QX60.

Neil sums up Infiniti's chronic infirmities: Promised high-performance driver participation that's snuffed out by multiple layers of electronics and extra weight.

Infinitis are sold and serviced by a small dealer network across Canada that limits servicing and parts. High-tech components drive up servicing costs by making dealer servicing mandatory and electronic/mechanical complexity practically guarantees a higher failure rate. Since these cars are so dealer-dependent, your luxury dream car can easily morph into a luxury lemon if you choose the wrong dealer.

But what can go wrong with your brand new 2016 $45,495 Infiniti QX60? Or a used 2013 G37? Plenty.

As for performance, a sampling of QX60 reviews collected by *U.S. News & World Report* ranks the car #23 out of 33 luxury crossover SUVs. Quality control? Poor, says *Consumer Reports*; scary, say owners in their NHTSA web postings:

I press the accelerator to turn into traffic, and after the car initially moves forward, it slips out of gear even though it shows that it's in drive. The engine rpms rev with the accelerator pressed, but the car will not accelerate or move. Lifting up and re-pressing the accelerator only makes the tachometer rpms rev up, but after about 10 seconds, the car pops back into gear. When I pull out into traffic, I could cause a serious accident if my car will not accelerate and lies dead in the road! The dealer cannot replicate the problem because it only occurs a few times a month, but it has been going on for 12 months now. I also see dozens of online posts and complaints identical to this from other QX60 owners. This is a serious injury and death risk.

Owners complain of Infiniti and its dealers routinely dismissing their complaints (principally powertrain and airbags) as "not duplicated," or "operating normally." When a correction is carried out, owners say it doesn't last.

One bright spot, a year after an onslaught of negative ratings, the company focused on improving quality control and overall highway performance on its 2015-16 models. In fact, Infiniti was so successful, that the brand was catapulted from 23rd place in 2014 into 5th place in the 2015 J.D. Power Initial Quality Study ranking. The company raised its quality score principally by correcting software snags on the pre-2015 Q50 sedan's InTouch telematics system; enhancing shifting with the QX60 SUV; and giving the Q70 sedan a quieter interior and smoother steering.

G25/G35/G37 ★★★ / ★★★★★ / ★★★★★

RATING: *G25:* Average (2011-12); *G35:* Above Average; *G37:* Above Average (2010-13). **Road performance:** *G25:* This entry level sedan is fitted with a 218 hp 2.5L V6 that skimps on acceleration but burns about 15% less fuel. Generally, the car is fairly agile, quiet, and comfortable, but the engine is noisy when pushed. There is no manual transmission or sports package option. *G35:* Marking Infiniti's return to high-performance cars, the G35 borrowed Nissan's sporty 350Z platform, added a roomy cabin, and lots of rear-drive performance features for an affordable price. The sedan was refreshed inside and out in 2004 and the coupe in 2004 and 2005. In a class action settlement, the G35's standard Brembo brakes were dropped from the 2005 and 2006 models, and better brakes with larger discs were added. Owners had sued for compensation due to the premature wearout of brakes on 2003-04 models. The second-generation model is simply a G37 sedan with a smaller V6. A 2007 or later redesigned G35 is your best bet. You get a solid platform, more responsive handling, a powerful 306 hp 3.5L V6, less dated styling, and the use of better quality interior materials. *G37:* A powerful, smooth, and responsive powertrain; predictable, sporty handling; and a firm but comfortable ride. The convertible (325 hp) has five horses less than the coupe (330 hp) but lots more than you'll find with the competition. An IPL (Infiniti Performance Line) G Convertible joined the 2012 IPL G lineup with an array of special performance and luxury upgrades. **Strong points:** *G25:* Only a handful of owner complaints posted on the NHTSA (*safercar.gov*) website. **Weak points:** *All models:* Powetrain glitches that cause hesitation and surging when slowing down, accelerating or turning, erratic shifting; warped brake rotors and prematurely-worn pads; electrical and electronic system failures, defective tire pressure sensors, and, most surprising, mediocre fit and finish. *G25:* You get less power and less equipment than with the G37, and the resale value for the 2012 has nose-dived to almost half its original $37,000 list price. This entry-level G-car was dropped in December 2012 after barely 2 years on the market. *G35:* Be wary of the poorly-designed unreliable manual tranny on the 2007 model. *G37:* There's a small rear seat and cargo area; towing is not advised; and the convertible model has even less room and has yet to be crash tested. The convertible has some body shake; engine tapping, a clicking sound at start-up, which requires the use of a costlier "factory" oil; transmission may suddenly downshift to 15 km/h from 100 km/h. The manual transmission gears grind when shifting, causing a delayed shift, especially in Sixth gear; transmission was replaced under warranty. The anti-traction feature activated on its own and caused the wheels to lock on a rainy day; defective Bridgestone Pole Position tires; tire pressure light did not come on when tire went flat; premature brake replacement; the area between the gas pedal and centre console gets quite hot; audio system malfunctions; and poor fit and finish. Luxurious and sexy to drivers; tasty and succulent to rodents:

Infiniti G37 has electrical wiring insulation made of soy-based polymer. Soy-based polymer is apparently biodegradable. The problem is that it is also attractive to rodents, who eat the wiring, creating electrical safety hazards. It also creates an economic stress on consumers and insurers who have to pay for repairs done to these automobiles, which Infiniti claims are not covered under any existing warranty.

Specs

G37 – Powertrain (Rear-drive/AWD): Engines: 3.7L V6 sedan (328 hp); coupe (330 hp); convertible (325 hp); Transmissions: 6-speed man., 7-speed auto. **Dimensions/capacity:** Passengers: 2/2, 2/3; Wheelbase: 112.2 in.; H: 54.7-55.3/L: 183.1/W: 71.8 in.; Headroom F/R: 2.5/1.5 in.; Legroom F/R: 41/27.5 in.; Cargo volume: 14 cu. ft.; Fuel tank: 76L/premium; Tow limit: N/A; Load capacity: 900 lb.; Turning circle: 35.4 ft.; Ground clearance: 5.1 in.; Weight: 3,642-3,847 lb.

Other opinions: "The 2013 Infiniti G37 ranked #12 in used upscale midsize cars. Reviewers noted that the manual has a jerky clutch and an imprecise shift quality, so several preferred the quick-shifting automatic." – *U.S. News & World Report.* On the other hand, the same magazine cut its rating dramatically when comparing the G37 to a complete lineup of competitors: The car rated "#25 in used upscale mid-size cars $25K and up." **Major redesign:** 2007 and 2014. **Highway/city fuel economy:** *G37 3.7L 6-speed man.:* 7.9/12.3 L/100 km., *G37 3.7L 6-speed man. convertible:* 8.4/ 12.9 L/100 km., *G37 3.7L 7-speed auto. convertible:* 7.8/11.9 L/100 km., *G37 3.7L 6-speed man. coupe:* 7.9/12.3 L/100 km., *G37 3.7L 7-speed auto. coupe:* 7.4/11.0 L/100 km., *G37x 3.7L 7-speed auto.:* 7.8/11.7 L/100 km. **Best alternatives:** The G37 (later sold as the Q50) is a premium mid-sized car with SUV pretensions. A used G37 attracts shoppers who would normally buy a 2013 Acura RDX or TL, or a BMW 328i or X3. Convertible models are priced right within striking range of BMW's 328i/335i Cabriolet and the Lexus IS 250 or IS 350 convertible. The Mercedes-Benz CLK350 AMG Edition Cabriolet has priced itself out of that market and a used Cadillac ATS or CTS will likely have many quality issues.

 SAFETY: **Child safety seat setup:** Untested. **Crashworthiness:** NHTSA: 2012 G25 awarded five stars for rollover protection, while the 2008 G35 scored five stars in all categories. 2009-10 G37 models also earned five stars for occupant crash protection in all NHTSA categories; 2011-13 models were tested only for rollover protection, which was given five stars. IIHS: Front overlap and side protection "Good," on the 2007-13 models and roof protection "Acceptable" for the same models years. 2011-13 G25s had no serious safety-related incidents reported to NHTSA. Head restraints were judged to be only "Marginal" with the 2007-13 G35s and "Poor" on the 2005-06 models. **Owner-reported safety-related failures:** NHTSA files show the G35 elicites few owner safety-related complaints. Driver's airbag failed to deploy; passenger-side airbag is disabled for no reason; chronic stalling; clutch sticks until it warms up; warped brake rotors and prematurely-worn brake pads; sudden wheel lockup when the anti-traction switch activates in rainy weather; doors won't lock or unlock due to faulty door actuators; and defective tire pressure sensors. 2011 G37 models also generated only a handful of complaints. When the convertible top automatically folds into the trunk it doesn't retract if there is an object in the way, causing damage to the top and posing a safety hazard to children; sudden unintended acceleration; seat belt failed to lock in an emergency stop; long hesitation before accelerating:

> As I was waiting to cross a major highway junction, I almost had a collision after crossing the highway due to what I suspect was a faulty transmission with hesitation in shifting. There was an SUV waiting to turn and while I had the right of way, they pulled off and as I had my chance to cross the 2-lane highway, they did too. I punched the gas and in the middle of the road, the engine took a few seconds to get into gear so I literally was in the road of oncoming traffic that was driving at speeds in excess of 55mph. It happened within 5 seconds but after I crossed avoiding a front and side collision, I pulled off the road because I was shaking.

Side mirrors become distorted in cold weather; and gas station automatic fuelling nozzles shut off after a few seconds. 2012 G37 owner complaints: Head restraints cause driver to sit in a chin-to-chest position which is painful and dangerous; hip pain caused by poor bolstering of the driver's seat; clutch pedal sticks; station automatic fuelling nozzles still shut off after a few seconds; vehicle suddenly accelerated while in Park with the engine running; engine also surges when braking (confirmed by TSB #ITBO7-048), or is slow to brake.

ALERT! Why can't Nissan … er … Infiniti … make decent powertrains that don't jerk you around, stall, or lag and lurch when turning into an intersection? This has been a chronic affliction over the years that's often dismissed by service managers as, "Oh, they all do that."

G25/G35/G37 Profile

	2005	2006	2007	2008	2009	2010	2011	2012	2013
Used Values ($)									
G25	—	—	—	—	—	—	14,000	18,500	—
AWD	—	—	—	—	—	—	16,500	19,500	—
G35	6,000	7,000	8,000	9,500	—	—	—	—	—
G37 Sedan	—	—	—	—	16,500	20,500	23,500	27,500	—
G37 Convertible	—	—	—	—	25,000	30,000	35,500	41,500	—
Reliability	☆	☆	☆	☆	☆	☆	☆	☆	☆
Repairs ($$$)	💰	💰	💰	💰	💰	💰	💰	💰	💰
Electrical	☆	☆	☆	☆	☆	★	★	★	☆
Engine (base)	☆	☆	☆	☆	☆	☆	☆	②	☆
Fit/Finish	☆	☆	☆	③	②	②	③	②	☆
Infotainment	—	—	—	—	—	☆	☆	☆	☆
Transmission (auto.)	④	④	④	④	☆	☆	☆	②	☆

Note: Additional Infiniti ratings are in the Appendix.

SECRET WARRANTIES, INTERNAL BULLETINS: All models—Troubleshooting multiple transmission problems. Tips on reducing excessive driveshaft noise (creaking or popping). Steering pull/drift. Steering wheel is off-centre. Automatic transmission shifter boot may come loose. Drivebelt noise. Navigation screen goes blank (2010-12 models). Paint chipping off the edge of the trunk lid (2007-12 models). Steering noise on left turns (2012s). The warranty is extended under Campaign PO308 in relation to the radio seek function. *G25:* Shift issues (2011 models) Campaign PO385 relative to reprogramming the G25's engine control module (ECM). *G37:* Shift responsiveness issues (2009-12 models). Low battery, or no start (2008-10). Bluetooth voice recognition. Convertible top water leak at windshield header. AC blows warm air at idle. Door accent garnish replacements.

EX35 ★★★

RATING: *EX35:* Average (2008-13). Smaller than the Infiniti FX, the EX35 is essentially a G wagon priced in the same range as the Infiniti G series. Offering the room of a compact station wagon, the EX37 is a small, upscale SUV wannabe that targets shoppers who would normally buy the Acura RDX or the BMW X3. The EX and G series are entry-level Infinitis with the most to offer from a price and quality perspective – as long as you have short legs, don't mind limited headroom, or never ride in the EX's rear seat. **Road performance:** Not as sporty as Infiniti's sport sedans or some of BMW's crossovers; the latest EX performs like a car with power to spare, however; and the smooth, responsive manumatic transmission works flawlessly with the new V6 and 7-speed transmission. Overall, the car is much more agile, quiet, and comfortable than the G series. Wait until late-winter or spring for lower prices when extra rebates and other sales incentives kick in. **Strong points:** Larger V6 engine means there will be more horsepower on tap. Although it's not a car for serious off-road use, it definitely is a comfortable, well-equipped, and versatile vehicle for most driving needs. The new 7-speed manumatic may give a slight boost to fuel economy, but keep in mind that any new powertrain is a risky buy during its first year on the market. **Weak points:** A smallish interior makes the EX a four-seater; limited cargo space; back seat occupants must keep a knee-to-chin posture when the front seats are pushed all the way back; taller drivers will want more headroom (especially with the sunroof-equipped Journey model); voice recognition feature performs erratically; and fuel economy is unimpressive on pre-2013 models. Also, the larger, 18-inch wheels may make for a bumpier ride and also cut your gas mileage.

> ### Specs
>
> **EX35 – Powertrain (Rear-drive/AWD):** Engine: 3.7L V6 (325 hp); Transmission: 7-speed manumatic **Dimensions/capacity:** Passengers: 2/3; Wheelbase: 110.2 in.; H: 61.9/L: 182.3/W: 71 in.; Headroom F/R: 3/3 in.; Legroom F/R: 42/26 in.; Cargo volume: 24 cu. ft.; Fuel tank: 76L/premium; Tow limit: N/A; Load capacity: 860 lb.; Turning circle: 36 ft.; Ground clearance: 5.5 in.; Weight: 3,757-3,979 lb.

Other opinions: "Ranked #2 among luxury compact SUVs. With its powerful V6 engine and sport sedan-like handling, reviewers said the 2013 Infiniti EX37 is one of the most fun SUVs to drive in the class." – *U.S. News & World Report.* "There are only 3 things I would like to see in this car. 1. 2-3 more inches of legroom for the rear seat; 2. a power lift for the rear hatch; and 3. a navigation screen that is easier to see in the daytime." – *www.kbb.com/infiniti/ex/2013.* **Major redesign:** 2008 and 2013. **Highway/city fuel economy:** *(2012) 3.5L 6-speed man.:* 8.5/12.3 L/100 km. **Best alternatives:** Acura RDX, BMW 3 Series or X3, Lincoln MKX, and Lexus 350.

SAFETY: Child safety seat setup: Untested. **Crashworthiness:** NHTSA: 2008-09 EX35 earned four stars for rollover and frontal-impact protection; five stars for side crashworthiness. 2011-12 versions scored four stars for rollover crash safety. The 2013 EX37 scored four stars for rollover protection. IIHS: 2008-13 models have "Good" frontal overlap, side, rear, and roof crash protection. **Owner-reported safety-related failures:** Right-rear visibility is compromised by right-rear head restraint and side pillar and some drivers find the accelerator and brake pedals are mounted too close together. Also, be wary of the Distance Control Assist or DCA. It creates a distracting "safety zone" around the vehicle and may apply the brakes or buzz an alert that could make matters worse. Plus, the system can malfunction if its sensors are snow covered. Almost no safety-related complaints posted at NHTSA relative to the 2008-13 E models. One owner did mention the following brake/transmission failure to NHTSA:

> 2012 Infiniti EX35 journey … the consumer stated she parked the vehicle in the driveway on a moderate slope covered with light snow. The consumer went back outside and stood by the vehicle, when all of a sudden it popped out of park and started rolling down the hill. The consumer managed to catch up with the vehicle, opened the door and put her foot on the parking brake, and the vehicle stopped.

ALERT! Beginning with the 2013 models, the Infiniti EX crossovers are powered by a much better performing 325 hp 3.7L V6, replacing the fuel-slurping 3.5L V6.

EX35 Profile

	2005	2006	2007	2008	2009	2010	2011	2012	2013
Used Values ($)									
EX35	—	—	—	12,000	15,500	17,500	21,000	26,500	30,000
Reliability	—	—	—	★3	★	★	★	★	★
Repairs ($$$)	—	—	—	💰2	💰1	💰1	💰1	💰1	💰1
Electrical	—	—	—	★	★	★	★	★	★
Engine (base)	—	—	—	★	★	★	★	★2	★
Infotainment	—	—	—	—	—	★3	★3	★	★
Transmission (auto.)	—	—	—	★	★	★	★	★2	★

SECRET WARRANTIES, INTERNAL BULLETINS: 2009-10—Some vehicles may have water entry into a wire harness which could cause an engine no-start condition or a warning light illumination when no warning issue exists. Infiniti will repair any damage and install a cover to protect the harness from water entry. This service will be performed at no charge for parts or labour. **2010-13**—Various navigation malfunctions. **2011-12**—Steering pull/drift, or steering wheel is off centre. Bluetooth voice recognition issues. Door accent garnish replacements.

KIA

Crime Pays

What an amazing five-year turnaround by Kia from a quality, performance, and value perspective.

OK, those were the flowers, now, here comes the flower pot. (Or as we say in Quebec: *"Aujourd'hui, des fleurs, demain, les pots."*)

We can't talk about Kia's tremendous gains, without first exposing the company's false horsepower ratings and gas mileage lies. It's shameful that Kia, along with its parent company Hyundai, use bogus claims to sell cars. Who do they think they are? GM and Ford who also roll out dishonest gas mileage and truck payload figures? A class-action lawsuit has been launched in Ontario against Hyundai Canada and Kia Canada after the automakers were found to have overstated their vehicles' fuel mileage. London, Ontario-based law firm, Siskinds LLP, says it filed the legal motion against the two carmakers in Ontario, and expects similar lawsuits to be filed in Quebec and British Columbia.

The lawsuit comes just days after the companies announced they would reimburse the owners of more than 170,000 vehicles in Canada for the difference in the combined fuel consumption rating plus 15%. The fuel mileage revelations came to light after a U.S. Environmental Protection Agency (EPA) audit found fuel economy was inflated by up to six miles per gallon on some vehicles. The affected vehicles for Hyundai are the 2010-13 Elantra, Sonata Hybrid, Accent, Genesis, Tucson, Veloster, Elantra Coupe, Elantra GT, and Santa Fe. For Kia, the affected vehicles are the 2010-13 Rio, Sportage, Soul, Soul ECO, and Optima HEV.

Kia has gone from buffoon to bestseller. Especially now that it doesn't make every model a failure-prone jack-in-the-box, full of costly repair surprises, as it did a decade ago. But, to carry the box metaphor farther, Kias are like Forrest Gump's box of chocolates: "You never know what you're gonna get."

Buyers now have more confidence in Kia cars, SUVs, and minivans that have become more functional, fuel-efficient, and stylish over the last few years. Hyundai and its Kia subsidiary are breaking sales records with a much improved lineup crafted during this economic recession and covering practically all the market niches, with the exception of trucks. While Hyundai goes upscale with high-tech and fuel-frugal models placed throughout its model lineup, Kia is putting its money into a more refined lineup of less-expensive, fuel-efficient vehicles that carry more standard features, are freshly styled, and likely to have fewer reliability problems.

Granted, Kia's quality has dramatically improved over the past few years, but serious safety- and performance-related defects keep appearing year after year. Sudden, unintended acceleration, powertrain failures, steering/suspension wander (a generic problem with many Hyundai/Kia models), and atrocious fit and finish haunt the entire Hyundai Kia lineup, along with automatic transmission and brake failures.

Ignoring the above deficiencies and prevarications, *Consumer Reports* has been recently won over by Kia's improved quality control after decades of listing most of the Kia lineup as "Not Recommended." *CR* has consistently criticized the automaker for making unreliable, unsafe vehicles. Now, in a surprising turnaround, it has many Kia models on its "Recommended" list published in April 2015.

And, that's the truth.

RIO/RIO5 ★★★★/★★★★★

RATING: Recommended (2015-16); Above Average (2011-14); Average (2009-10); Below Average (2007-08); Not Recommended (2000-06). The Rio sedan and Rio5 hatchback return for 2016 practically unchanged, except for a refreshed front and rear end, new colours, and more cabin soundproofing. Actually, the car doesn't need much. It provides good fuel economy and interior room with useful standard features and carries a reasonable base price. **Road performance:** The 1.6L engine with the manual transmission is usually adequate for most chores; handling is exceptionally good, with plenty of steering feedback; good brakes; and a comfortable, though sometimes busy, ride. Slow acceleration with the automatic transmission; insufficient highway passing power; excessive engine noise at higher speeds; and a harsh ride when passing over small bumps. **Strong points:** Lots of standard features that cost extra on other cars; a well-equipped, roomy cabin housing good quality materials, user-friendly controls, and high-end electronics; strong brakes; and responsive steering. Sharing the Accent platform and using more Hyundai components has undoubtedly improved Kia's quality, judging by J.D. Power survey results and the small number of owner complaints registered with NHTSA. In fact, the Rio and Rio5 have registered fewer owner complaints than the newer Kia Soul. **Weak points:** Automatic transmission malfunctions; poor fit and finish; premature brake repairs; electrical shorts; and trunk lid hinges intrude into the trunk area. Also, 5-doors lose their stick-shift tranny for 2016.

Prices and Specs

Prices (Soft): *Rio LX:* $14,295, *Rio, EX:* $19,695, *Rio5 SX:* $20,395 **Freight:** $1,535 **Powertrain (Front-drive):** Engine: 1.6L 4-cyl. (138 hp); Transmissions: 6-speed man., 6-speed auto. **Dimensions/capacity:** *Rio:* Passengers: 2/3; Wheelbase: 101.2 in.; H: 57.3/L: 171.9/W: 67.7 in.; Headroom F/R: 5/3 in.; Legroom F/R: 42/26.1 in.; Cargo volume: 13.7 cu. ft.; Fuel tank: 45L/regular; Tow limit: Not recommended; Load capacity: 925 lb.; Ground clearance: 5.5 in.; Turning circle: 34.5 ft.; Weight: 2,410-2,480 lb.

Other opinions: "The 2015 Kia Rio ranks #2 out of 25 affordable subcompact cars (Honda Fit ranked #1).Critics like the Rio's spry engine, generous warranty, and well-made interior in its higher trims, but some complain the car's ride is too stiff." – *U.S. News & World Report.* **Major redesign:** 2001, 2006, and 2012. **Highway/city fuel economy:** *Man.:* 5.8/7.1 L/100 km. *Auto.:* 5.6/7.7 L/100 km. **Best alternatives:** The

Chevrolet Sonic has a small performance edge and upfront occupant knee airbags. Honda's Fit is roomier, with versatile seating that accommodates five people. Other contenders: The Hyundai Accent, Mazda3, and VW Golf are more-refined small cars that offer better performance while also conserving fuel.

SAFETY: Child safety seat setup: Untested. **Crashworthiness:** Crash protection is a mixed bag. NHTSA: The 2012-16 Rio merits four stars for overall crash protection; earlier models from 2005 through 2010 were generally positive with three- to five-star scores, except for the two-star rating for side protection on 2003-05 models. IIHS: 2012-16 Rio "Good" for moderate overlap front, roof strength, and head restraints and seats. Small overlap front and side protection scored "Marginal" and "Acceptable." The 2011's frontal offset, rear, and roof crash protection was also "Acceptable" but given a "Poor" crashworthiness score for side collisions. **Owner-reported safety-related failures:** Limited rear-corner visibility with the Rio5; airbags failed to deploy in a frontal collision; passenger-side airbag was disabled, even though an average-sized passenger was seated. Fuel hose vent line may leak fuel into the back seat area; sudden acceleration in Reverse, with loss of brakes; brakes locked up when applied; tie rod and ball joints broke away from the chassis while vehicle was turning; and the rear window shattered when the driver's door was closed.

ALERT! Get a better and safer car by making a smart year and trim choice. For example, for $1,000 more, the 2012 Rio EX adds features like mandatory electronic stability control (ESC), air conditioning, power steering, and anti-lock brakes.

Rio/Rio5 Profile

	2006	2007	2008	2009	2010	2011	2012	2013	2014
Used Values ($)									
Rio/Rio5 LX	—	—	—	—	—	—	7,500	9,000	10,500
EX	3000	3,500	4,000	4,500	5,000	6,500	9,000	10,500	12,000
EX/SX Luxury/Navi	—	—	—	—	—	—	10,500	12,500	15,000
EX Convenience	—	4,000	4,500	5,000	6,000	7,000	—	—	—
Rio5 Sport	—	5,000	5,500	6,500	7,000	8,000	—	—	—
Reliability	★1	★2	★2	★2	★2	★3	★3	☆	☆
Repairs ($$$)	◆3	◆2	◆2	◆2	◆2	◆1	◆1	◆2	◆2
Electrical	☆	☆	☆	☆	☆	☆4	☆4	☆	☆
Engine (base)	★2	★2	★2	★2	★2	☆	☆	☆	☆
Fit/Finish	★1	★1	★1	★1	★2	★	★	★	★
Infotainment	—	—	—	—	—	★3	★3	☆	☆
Transmission (auto.)	★1	★1	★1	★1	★2	★3	☆	☆	☆

PART FOUR | ASIANS AND AUTO SAFETY

SECRET WARRANTIES, INTERNAL BULLETINS: 2009-10—How to silence a rear strut creaking noise. *Spectra:* 2006-07—Troubleshooting tips for automatic transmission Second to Third gearshift shock, slip, or flare. 2010-13—Poor windshield wiper performance can be fixed by replacing the washer pump inlet filter. 2011-12—Troubleshooting instrument panel noise. Fixing an outside mirror cover gap. Steering-wheel noise and vibration repair tips. 2011-15—A defective inhibitor switch may cause intermittent no crank and no start; erratic or harsh shifting; and a slight engine stumble when placed into Park position after a long drive. This condition occurs more often following a heat soak, after long periods of driving in regions with high ambient temperatures or during the summer months. 2012—A remedy for a noisy, vibrating steering wheel is detailed in TSB #084, Issued: Nov 2011. 2012-13—An easy fix for AC water leaks onto the front passenger side floor. 2012-14—DTC P0711, P0712, and P0713 can be set due to a faulty PCM, an open circuit, or a bad transaxle oil temperature sensor.

SOUL	

RATING: Above Average (2015-16); Average (2010-14). Fairly well equipped, the Soul is a cheap little four-door hatchback/wagon that combines good fuel economy with acceptable urban performance. The best combination is the 2.0L engine hooked to a 6-speed manual transmission. The redesigned 2014 and later models are much more practical than earlier versions due to their roomier cabin, refined interior, additional infotainment and online connectivity, better powertrain performance, and reliability. Interestingly, following the 2014 upgrades, there wasn't the usual upsurge in safety-related complaints posted by NHTSA (2015 model received two complaints). **Road performance:** Competent engines and fuel-sipping powertrains (again, the 2.0L is a better choice for reserve power), although the base engine could use more grunt at low engine rpm; a compliant suspension, without undue body roll or front-end plow; and fairly agile cornering, with good steering feedback. A busy highway ride. **Strong points:** Inexpensive and well equipped with safety devices like ABS, stability control, six airbags, and active head restraints – features that are rare on entry-level small cars. User-friendly, simple controls; plenty of interior room, especially when it comes to headroom; excellent front and side visibility; and comfortable seats. **Weak points:** Omnipresent rattles; excessive wind and road noise; and many body, fit, and finish glitches. Poor-quality, easily broken, or prematurely worn interior items. Long delays in getting recalled cars fixed. The AC defroster may not clear the windshield; excessive condensation in the headlights, chips in the glass and paint, and door panels that scratch with the slightest touch. Steering-wheel noise and vibration repair. Fuel economy is seriously overstated.

Other opinions: "The Soul ranks #6 out of 42 affordable small cars. The 2015 Kia Soul's high-end interior materials, as well as numerous standard and optional features, impress automotive writers." – *U.S. News & World Report*. "My 2014 had two flat tires and no way to fix them. The "whatever" it is that is in the vehicle to fix a flat tire is of no use. As much as I paid for this car I would expect it to have the proper spare tire and jack. I have been left stranded two times because of Kia's poor service. Whatever the reason for not putting this in the car is ridiculous. It is not safe for women to be out on the road and have a flat (June 9, 2015)." – *www. consumeraffairs.com/automotive/kia.htm.* **Major redesign:** 2014. Except for a few additional colour schemes, the 2016 is a carryover from last year. Kia says the manual transmission option will be dropped. **Highway/city fuel economy:** *1.6L man.:* 4.9/6.6 L/100 km. *1.6L auto.:* 4.9/6.8 L/100 km. **Best alternatives:** Other contenders are the Hyundai Elantra, Mazda3, Nissan Cube, Toyota Corolla, or Volkswagen Golf.

SAFETY: Child safety seat setup: Acceptable. **Crashworthiness:** Soul does well in most crashworthiness tests. NHTSA: 2014-16 models rated five stars for overall crashworthiness; 2011-13 models earned four stars. IIHS considers the 2014-15 Soul as "Good" in moderate frontal overlap, side, and roof crash protection. 2010-13 models got similar Good marks, though, small frontal overlap tests were ranked "Poor." **Owner-reported safety-related failures:** Engine compartment fire; door locks cycled from unlock to lock while passengers were being pulled out of the cabin:

> I should note that while we left the car unlocked when we got out, the doors locked themselves during the fire, and the key fob was inoperable (lock electronics in the car were fried). Had a person or pet been in the car, they would have been trapped.

Airbags failed to deploy; front seat belts allow only a slight body movement before they lock up and don't retract; brake pedal is too small; rear brake failure caused a rear-ender; car hesitates when accelerating from a stop; automatic transmission slips and often sticks in gear or grinds when going into Second gear; sometimes the transmission suddenly downshifts for no reason; when the vehicle is shifted into Park, the doors are automatically unlocked; when parked on an incline, with the emergency brake engaged, vehicle rolled down driveway into a house; fuel spews out when refueling; glass shatters when the rear hatch is closed;

driver's door fails to latch; steering locks up when turning; the steering column came off while the car was cruising on the highway; the electronic stability control may engage for no reason and lock up the steering:

> The steering wheel was locked up and could only be turned if considerable force was applied to it. The Kia dealer service shop ultimately had to replace the entire steering column to "fix" the problem. About two months later I was driving down the interstate and attempted to do a lane change. Again the electronic stability control falsely activated and caused me to collide with the vehicle directly in front of me. When the ESC activated, the steering wheel locked up and caused a sudden loss of control, resulting in the accident.

Although front and side views are fine, rearward visibility is poor due to the small rear windshield and thick rear pillars

ALERT! What? No spare tire? Tell the dealer this is a deal-breaker:

> Most Kia Souls don't come with a spare tire, instead they come with a can of Fix-A-Flat and an air pump. There is no jack either. The flat may be fixed if the damage is on the tread and the hole is under 1/4 inch in diameter. If the damage is on the sidewall or greater than 1/4 inch, the vehicle has to be towed. For those people that have no cell phone or are in an area that gets no reception they will be stranded until another motorist comes along and these days most motorists don't stop for other drivers. Kia offers roadside assistance with the vehicle, but if you are traveling in a remote area, in the southwest (like Death Valley for example) what do you do without a spare? If your cell phone quits, you're done. Even if you have AAA, their driver will have to tow the vehicle as he won't have a spare either.

Soul Profile

	2010	2011	2012	2013	2014
Used Values ($)					
1.6	6,000	7,000	9,000	10,000	11,500
2.0 4d	7,500	9,500	11,500	14,000	17,000
Burner	9,000	12,000	15,500	16,000	—
Luxury	—	—	16,500	17,000	20,000
Reliability	★3	★3	★3	★3	★
Repairs ($$$)	2	2	2	2	1
Electrical	★3	★3	★3	★3	★
Engine (base)	★4	★4	★	★	★
Fit/Finish	★3	★3	★3	★3	★
Infotainment	★3	★3	★3	★	★
Transmission (auto.)	★4	★4	★4	★3	★3

SECRET WARRANTIES, INTERNAL BULLETINS: 2010-13—A steering column clicking noise may require the replacement of the flexible coupling in the MDPS. Steering assemblies should last at least 5 years, so the cost of this repair should be charged back to Kia. Poor windshield wiper performance can be fixed by replacing the washer pump inlet filter. 2011-15—A defective inhibitor switch may cause intermittent no crank and no start; erratic or harsh shifting; and a slight engine stumble when placed into Park position after a long drive. This condition occurs more often following a heat soak, after long periods of driving in regions with high ambient temperatures or during the summer months. 2012—A remedy for a noisy, vibrating steering wheel is detailed in TSB #084, Issued: Nov. 2011. 2012-14—DTC P0711, P0712, and P0713 can be set due to a faulty PCM, an open circuit, or a bad transaxle oil temperature sensor. When either of these codes is set, the default value for the transaxle oil temperature sensor is 176°F (80°C). Prior to replacing the temperature sensor, perform a component and wire harness inspection after confirming proper connections, circuits, and PCM simulation checks.

FORTE 5/FORTE KOUPE ★★★★☆ / ★★★★★

RATING: Above Average (2014-16); Average (2010-13). The car's 2014 redesign blows away most of its earlier deficiencies. Kia slew the poor-quality dragon a few years back; now, Kia's roomy compact sedan, coupe, and hatchback have the engine, suspension, and equipment refinements the lineup lacked in the past. Among the various models, the hatchback is the most versatile for access and storage. Road performance: There are now three different engines available and they all offer more than enough power for most driving needs. Handling is a breeze, thanks to the Forte's front-drive unibody frame and four-wheel independent suspension, which provide a firm and sporty ride with a minimum of noise, vibration, and harshness. Although the standard engine doesn't pack much of a punch, a smooth-shifting automatic transmission and confidence-inspiring handling produce a comfortable, though jittery, ride. Strong points: The restyled and redesigned 2014 Forte is longer, lower, and wider than its predecessor and loaded with standard features that are optional on other cars, like four-wheel disc brakes and easily accessed and intuitive controls, plus Bluetooth and steering wheel controls with voice activation. Nicely bolstered, comfortable front seats; lots of interior room; heated side-view windows; fewer rattles and body glitches; a large dealer network, with both Kia and Hyundai providing servicing; and a comprehensive base warranty. Overall quality is much improved, with few complaints posted on the NHTSA website. Weak points: Five passengers is a squeeze; steering wheel tilts but doesn't telescope (EX trim excepted). Headlights crack; sunroof leaks water; massive amounts of water enter the engine compartment when it rains; windows don't close or open properly when frost or ice are present; front bumper falling down because the mounting clips are easily broken ($1,000 repair); minor audio and fit and finish complaints; major paint defects; and the windshield may not be installed securely at the factory:

> Our technician was able to push most of the windshield out without having to cut the urethane bead. The urethane bead pulled right off the windshield, and was only adhered to about 1/3 of the windshield perimeter. This vehicle was not involved in an accident, but had it been, the windshield would not have remained intact. The safety of the vehicle occupants due to this factory-installed improper installation was compromised.

Prices and Specs

Prices (Firm): *Forte:* $15,995, *Forte5:* $19,495, *Forte Koup:* $19,495 **Freight:** $1,715 **Powertrain (Front-drive):** Engines: 1.8L 4-cyl (148 hp), 2.0L 4-cyl. (173 hp), 1.6L Turbo 4-cyl. (201 hp); Transmissions: 6-speed man., 6-speed auto. **Dimensions/capacity:** Passengers: 2/3; Wheelbase: 104.3 in.; H: 57.5/L: 178.3/W: 69.9 in.; Headroom F/R: 4/2.5 in.; Legroom F/R: 41/27.5 in.; Cargo volume: 15 cu. ft.; Fuel tank: 51.9L/regular; Load capacity: 850 lb.; Turning circle: 33.9 ft.; Ground clearance: 5.9 in.; Weight: 2,729-2,849 lb.

Other opinions: "The 2015 Kia Forte ranks #9 out of 42 affordable small cars. A spacious interior and trunk, supportive seating and a range of tech features make the Forte a good value, critics say." – *U.S. News & World Report.*"**Major redesign:** 2014. **Highway/city fuel economy:** *2.0L man.:* 5.7/8.1 L/100 km. *Auto.:* 5.5/8.0 L/100 km. *2.4L:* 6.2/9.2 L/100 km. **Best alternatives:** Honda Fit might be the best choice. It's the roomiest hatchback in this class and is also the most versatile, thanks to seats that accommodate long and tall items. The Fit is also less expensive than the Forte hatchback, and is a better performer. Other good choices include Honda's Civic, Hyundai Accent and Elantra, Kia Soul, the Mazda2 and 3, Toyota's Matrix (base model), and VW Golf.

SAFETY: **Child safety seat setup:** "Acceptable" **Crashworthiness:** NHTSA: The 2010-16 Forte earned four and five stars for overall crash protection. IIHS: The 2010-13 models were rated "Poor" in the small frontal overlap crash test, however, they scored "Good" for side, rear, and roof crashworthiness. **Owner-reported safety-related failures:** Lousy recall treatment; engine compartment fire; airbags fail to deploy:

> Driver was in middle lane driving around 55 mph. For some unknown reason, driver lost control of vehicle. Car began flipping whiel still in the roadway, eventually hit a guard rail and continued flipping. Driver was ejected and killed. Airbags never deployed.

Force of airbag deployment broke driver's wrist; steering seized and brakes failed after driving through water; engine loses power when accelerating (fuel pump has been ruled out); Nexen tires (original equipment) sidewalls "bubble" and explode:

Three of the four OEM tires that came on my vehicle have needed replacement due to damaged sidewalls. The OEM tires are 16 inch Nexen CP671 205/55R16 tires, and my vehicle currently has less than 23,000 miles on it.

Stalling on turns; broken drive axle; car lost all power and wouldn't start due to a blown fuel pump fuse; rear window shattered for no reason; defogger doesn't clear the windows sufficiently and frequent taillight failures.

ALERT! Kia penny-pinchers can short-change your safety with poor-quality original equipment tires they provide. Stay away from Nexen, Firestone, and Bridgestone tires; they may not perform very well and can fail prematurely. Can you say "Tire Mobility Kit?' Demand a regular-sized spare tire from another tire maker or a more effective repair kit:

2014 vehicle lacks a spare tire, and it was not disclosed at time of purchase, nor does it state this fact in any of its published sales literature or website publications. Kia customer service was contacted and claimed there was not any need for a spare. Customer service indicated that a 'donut spare,' as provided on their other vehicles, is not available, yet, and has no delivery date scheduled. Their mobility kit (tire inflation) will not work on tire cuts and blow outs. The kit usefulness date is one year. The kit is dangerous to operate, especially if one is a senior and disabled. In addition, use of the kit will ruin the tire pressure monitor installed in the tire and void the entire warranty. Kia provides and delivers a full spare tire, rim and tool kit in other markets, namely Australia and New Zealand, at not extra cost.

Forte 5/Forte Koup Profile

	2010	2011	2012	2013	2014
Used Values ($)					
LX	5,500	7,000	9,000	10,000	11,500
EX	7,000	9,000	11,000	13,000	16,500
SX	8,000	10,500	13,500	17,000	19,500
Koup EX	7,500	9,000	11,000	13,000	—
Luxury	—	10,000	14,000	16,500	—
Reliability	★	★	★	★	☆
Repairs ($$$)	2	2	2	2	1
Electrical	★	★	★	★	☆
Engine (base)	★	★	★	☆	☆
Fit/Finish	★	★	★	☆	☆
Infotainment	★	★	★	★	★
Transmission (auto.)	★	★	★	★	☆

SECRET WARRANTIES, INTERNAL BULLETINS: 2009-13—Poor windshield wiper performance can be improved by replacing the washer pump inlet filter. 2011-12—An ECM software upgrade to address the MIL warning light coming on for no reason. 2011-14—DTC P0711, P0712, and P0713 can be set due to a faulty PCM, an open circuit, or a bad transaxle oil temperature sensor. When either of these codes is set, the default value for the transaxle oil temperature sensor is 176°F (80°C). Prior to replacing the temperature sensor, perform a component and wire harness inspection. 2012-14—A steering column clicking noise may require the replacement of the flexible coupling in the MDPS. Steering assemblies should last at least 5 years, so the cost of this repair should be charged back to Kia. 2012-15—An improperly adjusted or improperly operating inhibitor switch (range switch) may result in one or more of the following conditions: Malfunction indicator light (MIL) illuminated, or intermittent no engine crank/no engine start in Park or Neurtal. 2014—Some 2014 Forte vehicles equipped with a Kia accessory spoiler may exhibit a gap forming between the adhesive tape on the spoiler and the trunk lid. Kia will inspect and correct this condition, free of charge.

OPTIMA/HYBRID

RATING: *Optima, Hybrid*: Below Average (2011-16). Optima's rating has been downgraded due to persistent steering failures, stalling and surging when accelerating, imploding sunroofs, and self-destructing engines, problems also seen with the Hyundai Sonata. **Road performance:** The base engine performs well, the ride is comfortable, and handling is secure. The optional 4-cylinder turbocharged engine is powerful and fuel efficient, but V6-equipped rivals give a smoother and quieter performance. Considerable body lean when turning. *Hybrid:* Minimal body roll when cornering, and an excellent ride. On the other hand, the electrically assisted steering is a bit numb, the powertrain's jerky when going from gas to electric power (see "Secret Warranties," below), and the regenerative brakes could be more responsive. **Strong points:** Nicely appointed; has good overall visibility; provides plenty of front headroom; uses firm, supportive front bucket seats with plenty of fore and aft travel; a spacious trunk; and posts better than average fuel economy figures with regular fuel. Another plus: Servicing can be done by both Hyundai and Kia dealers. *Hybrid:* Nicely styled and well appointed; intuitive, easily accessed controls; and plenty of room in front and back. **Weak points:** Mediocre braking; average rear headroom; excessive wind and tire noise; low rear seats; difficult rear access; trunk has a small opening; and fit and finish isn't up to Asian or European automakers' standards. *Hybrid:* Repair parts have been hard to find and can be costly.

Other opinions: "The 2016 Kia Optima is wider and longer than the 2015 model, and these larger dimensions allow for a bit more legroom in the back seat. Additionally, Kia says it has improved the Optima's sound deadening to cut down on road and wind noise entering the cabin. Up front, the center console and control layout are redesigned to reduce the number of buttons." – *U.S. News & World Report.* **Major redesign:** 2001, 2006, 2011, and 2016. This year's redesign gives birth to a 178 hp turbocharged 1.6L 4-cylinder engine, harnessed to a new 7-speed dual-clutch automatic transmission. The returning base 2.4L 4-cylinder 185 hp engine has seven less horses this year, while the carried-over turbocharged 2.0L 4-cylinder 247 hp engine's output drops from 274 to 247 hp, hooked to last year's 6-speed automatic tranny. A new lighter and stiffer chassis should result in improved steering and handling. Now, wider and longer than the 2015 model, passengers will enjoy a bit more legroom in the back seat. Additional sound deadening will mute some road and wind noise entering the cabin. Up front, the center console and control layout are redesigned to reduce the number of buttons. **Highway/city fuel economy:** *2.0L auto.:* 5.8/9.2 L/100 km. *2.4L man.:* 5.7/8.7 L/100 km. 2.4L *auto.:* 6.5/8.6 L/100 km. *Hybrid:* 4.9/5.6 L/100 km. **Best alternatives:** Consider the Chevrolet Cruze, Honda Accord, Kia Rondo, Mazda3, and Toyota Camry.

SAFETY: Child safety seat setup: "Acceptable." **Crashworthiness:** NHTSA: 2011-15 Optima and Optima Hybrid earned five stars for overall crash protection. IIHS: 2011-13 models tested in frontal overlap crashes were rated "Good" and the small frontal overlap score for the same models was "Average." Side impact and roof protection were both rated "Good" as was the 2011-13 Optima head-restraint test. **Owner-reported safety-related failures:** Panoramic sun roof exploded outward; the front passenger seat is too low for some; and limited rear visibility:

> I purchased this new car in January and have had a difficult time adapting to the blind spots out of the rear window. The rear headrests of this car were designed too large. Even in the down position, these headrests block nearly two-thirds of the rear window visibility.

As with its Sonata cousin, the Optima pulls sharply to one side when accelerating:

> Vehicle hard to control and steer straight, especially at highway speeds. Severe pull to the left, though occasionally it drifts to the right. If you let go of the steering wheel, then the car swiftly moves across to the left lanes (see: *www.arfc.org*).

Other scary failures: Airbags failed to deploy; vehicle suddenly loses power when accelerating from a stop or when slowing down to make a turn; unintended acceleration:

> If I press the gas pedal to increase my speed, whether from a stopped position, or to pull into a busy roadway, or to increase my speed to pass another vehicle, the car will start to go then choke, so that no matter how hard I press the gas pedal, the rpm stay the same and my 2014 Optima loses power and will not speed up. If Kia doesn't figure out what is causing this – because I have seen other people with different Optima vehicle years complain about this – someone is going to get killed. I have had numerous near misses because of this problem. I also see many people saying Kia is telling them this is the way the vehicle is supposed to behave – really???

> . . .

> For 3 to 5 seconds, no response from engine at idle when accelerator depressed and the car is stopped (e.g., for traffic signal). Then, without warning, the engine went from idle (about 800 rpm) to rapid (surging) acceleration, often with screeching tires. This occurred each time I started from a stopped position.

Catastrophic transmission failure; a parked car will roll down an incline, despite being put in First gear or having the emergency brake engaged; driver-side floor mat bunches up around the brake pedal; Brake warning light comes on for no reason; side-view mirror fell off while driving along the freeway; no spare tire.

ALERT! Many complaints that the headlights don't provide enough light; check this out during a test drive at night. While you are at it, also check for excessive steering wander.

Optima Hybrid

Kia's Optima Hybrid can be driven on battery power alone, or in blended gas-electric mode. When the car is stopped, the engine shuts off to save fuel. It uses a lithium polymer battery that will hold its charge up to 25% longer than hybrids with nickel metal hydride batteries.

The Hybrid also is one of the first full hybrid systems to use a typical automatic transmission – a compact 6-speed automatic that debuted on the 2011 Kia Sorento SUV. An external electrically driven oil pump provides the pressure needed to keep the clutches engaged when the vehicle is in idle stop mode.

Optima/Hybrid Profile

	2011	2012	2013	2014
Used Values ($)				
LX	12,500	15,000	14,000	19,000
LX+	13,500	16,000	17,000	—
EX	12,500	15,500	16,500	19,500
EX+	14,500	16,500	18,000	—
Hybrid	12,000	16,000	18,500	—
Premium	14,000	17,500	20,000	—
SX Turbo	16,000	19,500	22,000	—
Reliability	☆	☆	☆	☆
Repairs ($$$)	💰2	💰2	💰2	💰2
Electrical	☆	☆	☆	☆
Engine (base)	☆	☆	☆	☆
Fit/Finish	☆	☆	☆	☆
Infotainment	☆	☆	☆	☆
Transmission (auto.)	☆	☆	☆	☆

SECRET WARRANTIES, INTERNAL BULLETINS: 2006-10—Poor windshield wiper performance can be improved by replacing the washer pump inlet filter. **2011-12**—An ECM software upgrade to address the MIL warning light coming on for no reason. Kia says the tire monitor system can be affected by radio signals. Remote Start system module software upgrade. Remedy for vehicles that stick in Park. TSB #040 outlines Kia Campaign #SA150, which covers the free replacement of both corroded rear lower control arms on vehicles driven where heavy amounts of road salt are used. Corrosion will cause a knocking or clunking noise from the affected lower control arm. **2011-13**—(MIL) illuminated with the ECM (Electronic Control Module) system-related DTC P0087. To correct this concern, follow the procedure outlined in Kia's TSB #026, issued Sept. 2013, and, if necessary, replace the high pressure fuel pump, fuel delivery pipe, and mounting bolts. **2011-14**—DTC P0711, P0712, and P0713 can be set due to a faulty PCM, an open circuit, or a bad transaxle oil temperature sensor. Prior to replacing the temperature sensor, perform a component and wire harness inspection after confirming proper connections, circuits, and PCM simulation checks. **2011-15**—An improperly adjusted or improperly operating inhibitor switch (range switch) may result in one or more of the following conditions: Malfunction indicator light (MIL) illuminated, or intermittent no engine crank/no engine start in Park or Neutral. **2012-14**—Remedies for rear-view camera issues. 2014—A steering column clicking noise may require the replacement of the flexible coupling in the MDPS. Steering assemblies should last at least 5 years, so the cost of this repair shouldbe charged back to Kia.

SPORTAGE ★★★★

2014 Kia Sportage.

RATING: Above Average (2014-16); Average (2011-13); Not Recommended (1993-2010). A third-generation redesign improved the overall reliability and road performance. The low rating for early models reflects the Sportage's serious steering problems, "jack-in-the-box" factory-related defects, and low crash-test scores. **Road performance:** Kia's post-2010 Sportage comes with a lively 260 hp 2.0L turbocharged 4-cylinder engine, and lots of performance enhancements that set it apart from its twin, the Recommended Tucson. The boost in power is accompanied by a sport-tuned suspension with tauter shock and strut valving that makes for a ride that may be too stiff for some. The base engine is a competent 4-banger that accelerates at a leisurely pace, though it's adequate for most driving chores. 2010 and earlier versions aren't worth considering; acceleration and handling are mediocre and the driving "experience" includes moments of terror as the car wanders into oncoming traffic. Roadway feedback is barely noticeable, and the car exhibits excess body roll and, like the Optima, wanders all over the road in addition to pulling sharply to one side or the other. The part-time 4x4 system can't be used on dry roads. **Strong points:** A competent powertrain, provides decent fuel economy, and has demonstrated above-average reliability on recent models. **Weak points:** Poor suspension/steering design degrades handling. Interior hard plastic garnishments cheapen the look; the firm leather seats look good but are hard on the butt; noisy, ineffective brakes; brake pedal grip padding falls off; windshield cracking; minor problems with the audio system; cargo space and rear visibility compromised by the car's styling; and the subpar fit and finish produces lots of clunks and rattles. Excessive road noise.

Other opinions: "The 2015 Kia Sportage ranks #12 out of 27 affordable compact SUVs. Reviewers think the Sportage is fun to drive, thanks to its peppy available turbo-charged engine and nimble handling, but they say it has a firm ride and limited cargo space for the class." – *U.S. News & World Report*. **Major redesign:** 1995, 2005, and 2011. **Highway/city fuel economy:** *2.4L man.:* 6.9/10 L/100 km. *2.4L auto.:* 6.2/9.4 L/ 100 km. *2.4L 4WD:* 7.0/9.9 L/100 km. *2.0L 4WD:* 7.7/10 L/100 km. **Best alternatives:** The Honda CR-V, Hyundai Tucson, Kia Rondo, Mazda Tribute, and Toyota RAV4.

SAFETY: **Child safety seat setup:** Untested. **Crashworthiness:** NHTSA: 2012 through the 2016s got four- and five-star scores for overall occupant protection; 1997-2010 models scored three to five stars for overall crash safety. IIHS: Crashworthiness scores were as follows: Moderate frontal overlap protection for 2011-15 models: "Good;" 2005-10 versions: "Average;" and 1998-2002s "Marginal." Small frontal overlap crash results on 2011-15 models: "Poor." Side impact test results on the 2011-13 models was rated "Good;" 2005-10s: "Average." Roof strength on the 2011-13 models: "Good;" 2005-10s were rated "Poor." Rear crash protection on the 2008-13s: "Good;" 2005 through some 2008s were rated "Poor." **Owner-reported safety-related failures:** Seriously unstable on the highway; wanders all over the road; stall and surge acceleration; ineffective brakes; brake pedal grip padding falls off; early rustout of the lower control arms:

> I slowly pulled my car onto the Taconic to get out of the massive traffic. I looked under the rear of the car and saw that the control arm of the strut on the driver's side had rusted through completely and broken. The control arm on the passenger side was also rusted through and would have broken as well.

Snow and ice collects on the "running board" and makes it impossible to open the doors; persistent raw gasoline smell in the cabin; sunroof implosions continue; and windshield cracking without any object hitting it:

> My 2014 Sportage's sunroof exploded. I had just entered the highway (there was no overpass near me) merging into traffic. I heard a loud pop like a gun shot and glass rained down on

me. I immediately called my dealership and drove it in. There was no determination as to the cause. Dealership had to completely replace the sunroof. Had to claim on my insurance and pay the deductible – roughly total repair cost was $1200.00.

ALERT! During your test drive, check the car for excessive wander or pulling when accelerating, turning, or stopping:

While travelling at highway speeds, or any speed above 50 km/h on a straight road, vehicle requires constant correction to track in a straight line. Without constant correction, the vehicle would leave the road surface. This problem, on trips over 45 minutes excessively fatigues the driver. (I thought I was going crazy on a 4.5 hour trip at mostly expressway speeds). Over 110 km/h this problem seems to be eliminated … but not worth the endangerment to others using the roadway.

Sportage Profile

	2006	2007	2008	2009	2010	2011	2012	2013	2014
Used Values ($)									
LX	4,000	5,000	6,000	7,000	8,000	10,000	12,500	15,000	17,500
AWD	—	6,500	7,500	8,500	10,000	12,500	14,500	17,000	19,000
EX	—	—	—	—	12,000	13,500	16,000	18,000	20,500
AWD	—	—	—	—	—	15,000	17,500	19,500	22,500
Reliability	2	2	2	3	4	4	4	4	4
Repairs ($$$)	2	2	2	2	1	1	1	1	1
Electrical	2	2	2	3	3	4	4	4	5
Engine (base)	2	2	2	2	3	3	3	2	2
Fit/Finish	1	1	2	3	3	2	2	3	2
Infotainment	—	—	—	—	—	3	3	3	4
Transmission (auto.)	2	2	2	3	3	3	4	2	4

SECRET WARRANTIES, INTERNAL BULLETINS: 2006-13—Poor windshield wiper performance can be improved by replacing the washer pump inlet filter. **2011-12**—*What?* Outside radio signals may cause the tire-pressure monitoring system to malfunction. Steering-wheel noise and vibration repair tips. **2011-13**—Vehicle may experience a malfunction indicator lamp (MIL) illuminated with the ECM (Electronic Control Module) system-related DTC P0087. To correct this concern, follow the procedure outlined in Kia's TSB #026, issued Sept. 2013, and, if necessary, replace the high pressure fuel pump, fuel delivery pipe and mounting bolts. **2011-15**—DTC P0711, P0712, and P0713 can be set due to a faulty PCM, an open circuit, or a bad transaxle oil temperature sensor. When either of these codes is set, the default value for the transaxle oil temperature sensor is 176°F (80°C). Prior to replacing the temperature sensor, perform a component and wire harness inspection after confirming proper connections, circuits, and PCM simulation checks. 2012—A remedy for a noisy, vibrating steering wheel is detailed in TSB #084, issued Nov. 2011.

SORENTO ★★★★

A 2011 loser: Kia's Sorento … proof-positive that not all that is Asian is top-quality.

RATING: An Above Average buy (2015-16); Average (2014); Below Average (2012-13); Not Recommended (2003-11). The 2016 Sorento comes with a new body structure that's about 3 inches longer, a wheelbase more than 3 inches longer, and it's slightly taller than the 2015 model. Cabin amenities are more refined, infotainment and navigation features have been enhanced, and the car feels much more solid. Other notable changes include a firmer suspension, more responsive braking, and a new 240 hp turbocharged 2.0L 4-cylinder engine coupled to a 6-speed automatic. The Sorento represents good value in theory, with its strong towing capacity and excellent safety ratings. However, early models fall far short on reliability, safety, quality control, fuel economy, and ride quality. The 2011 redesign adopted a new unibody platform and an additional third-row seat, making the Sorento larger and much more reliable. Road performance: While the V-6 might have 50 more horsepower, the 2.0T model is the one that actually felt perkier in most types of driving – all but off-the-line acceleration. Off-roader's will appreciate the low-range gearing and good ground clearance, but there's always that pesky reliability thing hitching a ride in the back of your mind. The base engine will do what is required. Strong points: Sorento is well-appointed and you get more SUV for fewer bucks. There's also a fairly roomy interior and good fit and finish. Weak points: Your off-roading fun may end as soon as the tranny, steering, or brakes give out. Life-threatening defects reported on the 2012 models: Sudden, unintended acceleration, as brakes wouldn't work and airbags failed to deploy; car stalls out when cruising; transmission hesitates or fails to upshift:

> On three occasions during the first month I owned the vehicle, I have experienced uncommanded downshift from Sixth gear to Fourth gear at speed. Transmission then locks in Fourth gear until shut down and restarted. Very violent event when it occurs, with an instantaneous bang and corresponding immediate loss of speed.

Vehicle jerks, stutters, and stalls when accelerating:

> Almost immediately started experiencing the occasional hesitation problem when pulling into traffic from a stop. On a couple occasions it put us in a very dangerous situation as we were crossing 2 lanes of traffic. Took the vehicle to dealer 4 times, they could not duplicate the problem. Finally they got us a 2012 near identical Sorento V6, and on the 3rd day had the same experience w/50 miles [80 km] on the vehicle. We now have 500+ [800 km] on it and have had a total of 7 similar situations.

Early brake wearout; chrome bezel instrument panel creates a painful and annoying reflection; rear sunroof exploded for no reason; headlight illumination is too short; sudden tire blowouts; and poor outward visibility:

> New SUVs are adding huge pillars to the rear of vehicles, shrinking rear third windows, shrinking rear trunk door windows, pushing driver seats tightly up against the driver door — to shrink the car and boost gas mileage. On top of that, they are pursuing "quietness" and part of that is shrinking the exterior mirrors. Add this all up & you can hide a semi in the blind spot of this car. It was like driving a windowless cargo van w/o the big cargo van mirrors. The mirrors are small like what belongs on an economy car. Yes, my driver side mirror was well adjusted to only show a sliver of the vehicle. I just couldn't see. As I continued SUV shopping, I found this new design in many new SUVs. Gigantic blind spots are now the new design. I couldn't see to change into the left lane. When I looked over my shoulder my face was so close to the window, all I could see behind me were the separating pillars. Changing lanes was a guess.

Prices and Specs

Prices (Firm): *LX:* $27,495, *EX:* $36,695, *SX:* $43,195 **Freight:** $1,715 **Powertrain (Rear-drive/4WD):** Engines: 2.4L 4-cyl. (185 hp), 3.3L V6 (290 hp), 2.0L turbo 4-cylinder (240 hp); Transmission: 6-speed auto. **Dimensions/capacity:** Passengers: 2/3; 2/3/2; Wheelbase: 106.3 in.; H: 68.7/L: 183.9/W: 74.2 in.; Headroom F/R/R2: 5.5/5.5/0 in.; Legroom F/R: 41/27/26 in.; Cargo volume: 37.5 cu. ft.; Fuel tank: 80L/regular; Tow limit: 1,650 lb.; Load capacity: 930 lb.; Turning circle: 38 ft.; Ground clearance: 7.5 in.; Weight: 3,571-3,682 lb.

Other opinions: "Most notably, the 2016's suspension has been dramatically reworked to offer a smoother ride and more responsive handling than last year's model, and it works well in practice. That's especially true of the sporty SX version, which offers some of the best steering feel in the midsize-SUV realm." – *www.autotrader.com.* Major redesign: 2003, 2011, and 2016. Highway/city fuel economy: *2.4L man.:7.4/10. 6L/100 km. 2.4L auto.: 6.2/9.5 L/100 km. 2.4L 4WD: 7.1/10.1 L/100 km. V6 4WD: 8.2/11.5 L/100 km.* Fuel consumption is much higher than represented. Best alternatives: The Honda CR-V and Hyundai Tucson.

SAFETY: Child safety seat setup: "Acceptable." Crashworthiness: NHTSA: 2011-16 Sorentos rated four and five stars for overall crash protection. IIHS: 2011-16 Sorento "Good" in all categories, except for a "Poor rating in small front overlap crashes. Owner-reported safety-related failures: Sorento boasts a commanding view of the road, unlike some mid-size-SUV rivals, which continually pinch visibility with increasingly lower roofs and higher window lines.

ALERT! Sorento is a perfect example of how a redesign can screw up a vehicle's reliability and overall quality for several years running.

Sorento Profile

	2006	2007	2008	2009	2010	2011	2012	2013	2014
Used Values ($)									
L/LX/2.4	5,000	6,500	7,500	9,000	—	12,000	14,500	17,500	20,000
AWD	—	—	9,000	10,500	—	13,500	16,000	19,000	22,000
3.3/3.5	—	—	—	—	—	16,000	19,000	22,000	24,000
3.5 AWD	—	—	—	13,000	—	18,500	21,500	24,000	26,000
Reliability	☆2	☆2	☆2	☆2	☆2	☆	☆	★1	☆
Repairs ($$$)	②	②	②	②	②	②	②	❸	◌
Electrical	☆	☆	☆	☆	☆	☆	☆	☆	☆
Engine (base)	☆	☆	☆	☆	☆	☆	☆	☆2	☆
Fit/Finish	☆	☆	☆3	☆2	☆2	☆2	☆3	☆2	☆
Infotainment	—	—	—	—	—	☆2	☆2	☆	☆
Transmission (auto.)	☆	☆	☆	☆	☆	☆	☆	☆2	☆

SECRET WARRANTIES, INTERNAL BULLETINS: 2011-12—Transmission shift improvement. Steering wander or pull troubleshooting. 2011-13—Vehicles equipped with the 3.5L engine may produce a loud engine chatter during initial start-up after sitting for several hours. Kia TSB #140, issued Feb. 2014 says the best way to silence the noise is to replace both intake CVVTs and camshafts with upgraded parts. Oil leakage and/or noise coming from the front struts may require new struts and strut dust covers. New front strut bearings may be needed on some Sorentos that make a creaking noise from the front of the vehicle when turning the wheel, quickly, at slow speeds. This noise is likely caused by front strut bearing corrosion due to water or debris entry into the component. Troubleshooting tips for a difficult to release or inoperative second row seat. 2011-15—DTC P0711, P0712, and P0713 can be set due to a faulty PCM, an open circuit, or a bad transaxle oil temperature sensor. When either of these codes is set, the default value for the transaxle oil temperature sensor is 176°F (80°C). Prior to replacing the temperature sensor, perform a component and wire harness inspection after confirming proper connections, circuits, and PCM simulation checks. An improperly adjusted or improperly operating inhibitor switch (range switch) may result in one or more of the following conditions: Malfunction indicator light (MIL) illuminated, or intermittent no engine crank/no engine start in Park or Neutral. 2012—A cheap fix for a noisy, vibrating steering wheel is detailed in TSB #084, Issued: Nov. 2011. 2012-14—There are various remedies for rear-view camera issues outlined in service bulletins. Vehicle may experience a malfunction indicator lamp (MIL) illuminated with the ECM (Electronic Control Module) system-related DTC P0087. To correct this concern, follow the procedure outlined in Kia's TSB #026, issued Sept. 2013, and, if necessary, replace the high pressure fuel pump, fuel delivery pipe, and mounting bolts. 2013-14—A parasitic drain on your battery may be caused by a faulty power window switch found on vehicles equipped with Integrated Memory System (IMS) seats.

STEERING/SUSPENSION – PULL OR DRIFT CONCERN

BULLETIN NO.: CHA 033   DATE: JULY 2011

SUB-FRAME AND SUSPENSION ADJUSTMENT FOR DRIFT CONCERN

This bulletin provides information related to a drift condition and adjusting/settling the suspension components under load as assembly variation can remain on the suspension. Camber and Caster may need slight adjustment depending on actual road conditions. To improve this condition the dealer is requested to first follow the TSB CHA 032 (Drift/Pull Diagnosis and Best Practices Tips) for specifications and if they are outside the parameters then perform the instructions as directed in this TSB.

LEXUS

"The disregard Toyota/Lexus had for the safety of the public is outrageous," Venizelos said. "Not only did Toyota fail to recall cars with problem parts, they continued to manufacture new cars with the same parts they already knew were deadly. When media reports arose of Toyota hiding defects, they emphatically denied what they knew was true, assuring consumers that their cars were safe and reliable. ... More than speeding cars or a major fine, the ultimate tragedy has been the unwitting consumers who died behind the wheel of Toyota vehicles."

– (March 14, 2014 – George Venizuelos, FBI Assistant Director announces $1.2 billion U.S. fine against Toyota for lying about its runaway vehicles.

Lies and Lost Lives

No one had heard of Lexus vehicles suffering from sudden, unintended acceleration with attendant brake loss – until a few years ago. At that time, Toyota, the owner of the Lexus luxury brand, insisted the accidents and deaths were due to driver error. However, after some delay the automaker did a turnabout and in late 2009 recalled almost its entire lineup (4.4 million vehicles) to better secure floor mats and fix a sticky throttle, while insisting that most of its higher-end Lexus models weren't involved. Even though they were.

Lexus is a luxury automaker on its own merits, even though many models are mostly dressed-up Camrys. Unlike Acura, Infiniti, Cadillac, and Lincoln, Lexus is seen by some as the epitome of luxury, reliability, and comfort, with a small dab of performance thrown in. Lexus executives know that no matter how often car enthusiast magazines say that drivers want "road feel," "responsive handling," and "high-performance" thrills, the truth of the matter is that most drivers simply want cars that look good and that give them bragging rights for safety, performance, convenience, and comfort; they want to travel from point A to point B, without interruption, in cars that are more than fully equipped Civics, warmed-over Maximas, repackaged Chevrolet SUVs, or thinly disguised Ford Fusion or Flex-derived Lincolns. Lexus executives figure that hardcore, high-performance aficionados can move up to its sportier models and the rest will stick with the Camry-based ES series.

Although these high-end cars and SUVs do, in most cases, set advanced benchmarks for quality control, they don't demonstrate engineering perfection, as proven by automatic transmissions that hesitate and then surge when shifting or cars that run away. And, yes, cheaper luxury cars from Acura, Hyundai, Kia, Nissan, and Toyota give you lots of comfort and are almost as reliable, but they don't shout out the luxury cachet and laidback refinement of the Lexus.

Speaking of resale values, let's be real. Buying a Lexus isn't a sure-fire money-maker. Some models are money-losers. Take, for example, a 2010 entry-level ES 350. New, it sold for $41,950; today you can get one for about $17,500. What? A 5-year-old Lexus selling for less than half its original value? Yes, it happens every day.

Technical service bulletins show that recent Lexus models have been affected mostly by powertrain and electrical malfunctions, faulty emissions-control components, computer module miscalibrations, and minor body fit and trim glitches. To Lexus' credit, many owners haven't heard of these problems because Lexus dealers have been particularly adept at fixing defects early.

Nevertheless, these are benchmark cars known for their comfort, convenience features, and good looks. Sports cars, they're not. But if you're looking for your father's Oldsmobile from a Japanese automaker, these luxury cars fit the bill.

When buying used, be especially wary of the redesigned 2010 "active" head restraints. Owners say the restraints push the driver's head down and forward, causing considerable neck and back pain. Worst of all, there is no fix for this problem that doesn't contravene U.S. and Canadian federal safety legislation.

Hybrids

Toyota and Lexus have been leaders in hybrid sales since the Prius was first launched in 2001. Lexus hybrids have gotten good marks for reliability and fuel consumption, however their worth as fuel-savers has taken a beating with lower resale values that match 50% lower fuel prices. Used, a $121,750 2012 LS 600h L is now worth about $65,000. Congratulations, you've just poured over $55,000 down the drain. Other vehicles worth considering are an all-dressed Toyota Highlander LTD hybrid, Avalon, Acura TL, or BMW 328i.

RATING: Above Average (2010-16; 2006 and earlier); Average (2007-09). An over-priced luxury sedan that's really a gussied-up Camry. The 2016 version doesn't have much that's new except for a slightly restyled exterior, additional structural reinforcements to improve body stiffness and handling, and more dashboard insulation to muffle engine noise. There are two ES models: The naturally aspirated ES 350 and the ES 300h hybrid. They are practically identical at first glance – the hybrid model is distinguished by unique 17-inch alloy wheels, a rear decklid spoiler, and a fuel-frugal 2.5L Atkinson-cycle inline-four. **Road performance:** Good acceleration; a pleasantly quiet ride; steering feel is muted; and overall handling (excessive body roll) isn't as nimble as with its BMW or Mercedes rivals. There's a drive-select knob on the centre console that can be dialed to Normal, Eco, and Sport modes, and the steering and throttle response is altered to match your choice. The only problem is that the differences between the Normal and Eco settings are more mental than mechanical. Dangerous erratically performing automatic transmission that hesitates and surges when shifting. **Strong points:** Aggressive styling and a well-appointed interior; lower curb weight and some engine tinkering nudges up fuel economy a bit; and better-than-average quality control. **Weak points:** Brakes are disappointing, in that the small discs are the same size as those found on the much lighter Camry and brake fade after successive stops is evident. The car is primarily a four-seater, as three adults can't sit comfortably in the rear; headroom is inadequate for tall occupants; trunk space is limited (low liftover, though); and some of the dash instruments and controls look a bit outdated. Fit and finish imperfections; Bluetooth cell phone voice distortion; and an inoperative moonroof.

Prices and Specs

Prices (Firm): *Base:* $42,000, *300h:* $44,450 **Freight:** $2,045 **Powertrain (Front-drive):** Engines: 3.5L V6 (268 hp), *Hybrid:* 2.5L 4-cyl. (200 hp); Transmissions: 6-speed auto., *Hybrid:* CVT **Dimensions/capacity:** Passengers: 2/3; Wheelbase: 111 in.; H: 57.1/L: 193/W: 71.7 in.; Headroom F/R: 3/2.5 in.; Legroom F/R: 42.5/30.5 in.; Cargo volume: 15 cu. ft.; Fuel tank: 65L/regular; Load capacity: 905 lb.; Turning circle: 37.4 ft.; Ground clearance: 6.1 in.; Weight: 3,549 lb., *Hybrid:* 3,660 lb.

Other opinions: "The 2015 Lexus ES ranks #10 out of 18 upscale midsize cars. [Its] V6 engine is potent and refined, according to critics. ... Reviewers agree that the ES 350 has a very comfortable ride, but many complain that its handling is clumsy, and that its steering is uncommunicative and slow." – *U.S. News & World Report.*" "For me, then the decider is price (because, again, frugal/meager/penny-pinching/water-man), and the bottom line is this: My test model Camry XSE, with the only option being a $225 paint job, came to $28,245 U.S. for a car that includes almost everything I could ask for (and even if you move up to the 6-cylinder version, it is still only $33,650); and the admittedly more prestigious Lexus ES 350, with no options, priced out at $41,500." – *theautonet.com/.* **Major redesign:** 2001, 2006, and 2013. **Highway/city fuel economy:** 7.5/11.3 L/100 km; *300h:* 6.1/5.8.1 L/100 km. **Best alternatives:** The early ES models are acceptable buys. Other choices include the Acura TL, BMW 3 Series, Infiniti G35, and, of course, the Toyota Camry.

SAFETY: Child safety seat setup: Untested. **Crashworthiness:** NHTSA: 2013-16 models given five stars for overall crash safety, while the 2012 version's side crash protection merited only two stars – unusually low for a higher-end car and four stars for front and side crashworthiness. 2007-10 models had high scores of four and five stars. IIHS: 2007-15 models earned "Good" ratings for front, moderate overlap, side, and roof protection, but the 2012 got a "Poor" rating for small overlap crash safety. Head restraints were rated "Marginal" on the 2007-12s and "Poor" on the 2004-06 ES. **Owner-reported safety-related failures:** Rear-corner visibility is hampered by the high rear end. Dashboard melts from the heat of the sun causing a high shine and glare on the windshield. This bizarre defect is covered by a secret warranty and affects most of the Lexus lineup from 2003-09. (See "Secret Warranties," below). Plastic tabs that hold the front window in place break and the window falls down. Reports of sudden, unintended acceleration, accompanied by brake loss, and failure of the airbags to deploy during the collision:

> When her husband moved the gear from park, to drive, the vehicle shot out like a rocket. The vehicle went through and broke an iron gate, smashed some electrical equipment, took down a tree and another one fell on top of the vehicle crushing and breaking the driver's side window. The vehicle finally stopped under the stairway to an upstairs condo wall. The consumer believed the vehicle went airborne at some point. The vehicle was totaled. Also, the airbags did not deploy.

Stuck accelerator; automatic transmission shifts erratically, suddenly accelerates, or slips and hesitates before going into gear; car lurches forward when the cruise control is reengaged; brake failures and premature tire monitor system malfunctions.

ALERT! Owners say the automatic power window can be a bone crusher:

> Extremely dangerous when right front passenger grasps top of door frame to close door. Driver closes window but is unable to stop window from closing. Once it starts it can't be stopped nor is there a safety stop such as that found in garage or elevator doors. Window crushes finger of passenger and flesh is torn. Flesh retrieved and sewn in emergency room but hospital surgery required 3 weeks later on right ring finger. Potential death trap! Imagine if it closes on a child, a dog, or object.

ES 330/350/300h Profile

	2006	2007	2008	2009	2010	2011	2012	2013	2014
Used Values ($)									
330/350	8,000	10,000	12,000	15,000	17,500	21,500	26,500	31,500	35,500
ES 300h	—	—	—	—	—	—	—	33,000	36,500
Reliability	★	★	★	★	★	★	★	★	★
Repairs	1	2	2	2	1	1	1	1	1
Electrical	★	★	★	★	★	★	★	★	★
Engine (base)	★	★	★	★	★	★	★	★	★
Fit/Finish	★	★	★	★	★	★	★	★	★
Infotainment	—	—	—	★	★	★	★	★	★
Transmission (auto.)	★	★	★	★	★	★	★	★	★

SECRET WARRANTIES, INTERNAL BULLETINS: 1990-2013—Lexus service bulletin says the seat belt pre-tensioner devices "may, or may not, perform as expected." 2003-09—In a Dec. 10, 2014, letter to dealers, Lexus says it will reimburse owners, or replace free of charge melted, sticky dashboards on most of its model lineup. 2003-13—Troubleshooting tips to silence a creaking, or ticking windshield noise. 2007—Engine oil may leak from the front timing cover. The front passenger airbag Disable light may come on for no reason. Idle may fluctuate when the AC is turned on. Steering intermediated shaft noise. 2007-08—The oil supply hose degrades prematurely and leaks oil. Lexus will replace the hose free of charge until Dec. 31, 2021. Some models may experience a torque converter shudder. 2007-09—A rear seat "popping" may be caused by insufficiently-torqued nuts. Silencing an engine ticking noise. 2007-14—Some vehicles may find the HVAC Evaporator Drain Hose obstructed with an insect nest. An insect repellent drain hose tip (ARINIX(R) Tip) is now available to help minimize future occurrences. For some models a new drain hose is required to properly fit the ARINIX Tip. Note: Lexus says "The ARINIX(R) Tip is *not* registered or labeled for sale or use outside the United States or Puerto Rico." So, will Canadian Lexus owners have to keep their insect nests? 2008-10—When the heat is turned on there may be a large variation in temperatures between the vents. 2008-11—Vehicles that have sat in sub-freezing weather may not shift from Park to Drive, or multiple warning lights may come on. A new relay and wire harness may be needed. 2011—A faulty charcoal canister may activate the MIL warning light. Check it first, before spending a bundle on other repairs. 2011-12—Steering wheel noise and vibration repair. Transmission shift improvement. Steering wander or pull troubleshooting. 2013—Bluetooth connection may suddenly cut off.

RATING: Above Average (2010-16); Average (2006-09). A sedan "sport" wannabe, the 2016 version returns with minor trim changes. The car was restyled 2 years ago and given an 8-speed automatic transmission, the GS's platform, a stiffer suspension, and electrically-assisted power steering. **Road performance:** The IS 350 has a competent standard 3.5L engine, but the IS 250's 2.5L feels rather sluggish when pushed. The larger engine has plenty of tire-smoking power and provides thrilling high-performance handling, but your thrills will come with a bone-jarring, teeth-chattering ride. Suspension is too firm for some and there's no manual transmission option. Handling on both the 250 and 350 models doesn't feel as sharp or responsive as with the BMW competition, owing in large part to an intrusive Vehicle Dynamics Integrated Management system that automatically eases up on the throttle during hard cornering. Emergency braking also isn't a confidence builder. **Strong points:** Targeting BMW's 3 Series, Lexus's entry-level IS 250 and IS 350 rear-drive sport-compact sedans come with either a 204 hp 2.5L V6 or a 306 hp 3.5L V6. Both cars handle well and braking is exceptional. The F version ups the ante considerably with its 416 hp 5.0L V8 powerplant. Although Lexus has lost some of its lustre after going through years of non-stop safety-related recalls and increased competition from European and Japanese luxury carmakers, the nameplate continues to outshine Acura, Infiniti, Cadillac, and Ford. Owner comments are mostly positive, except for engine complaints (2006-09), electrical system short-circuits, and fit and finish glitches. Interior amenities were also upgraded for 2014, including an optional navigation screen that is more easily read. A low beltline provides a great view and the high-quality interior is relatively quiet. Get used to paying top dollar for premium fuel and a sky-high freight charge when buying new. **Weak points:** The navigation touch screen will suddenly shut off:

> There is a faulty connector on the 2008 IS 250 touch panel screen. The touch panel is a 4-wire resistive panel, taped to the LCD display. There's a four wire ribbon cable that is improperly bonded to the touch panel. Lexus quoted me $2,800 to fix this problem that is a common problem and a defect in their manufacturing.

The Vehicle Dynamics Integrated Management feature performs erratically. Cramped rear seating and limited trunk space; convertibles lose almost all their trunk space when the top is lowered. Although the 2014 is wider, longer, and more solid-looking than previous models, owners still feel the interior is too small. Two other gripes: Paying top dollar for premium fuel and the dealer's sky-high freight charge when buying new. Excessive window rattling when driving with the top down; transmission fluid leaks; mediocre fit and finish; and the driver-side door won't open automatically from the outside:

> My 2014 Lexus IS 250 driver's side door will not unlock or let me in at random. When approaching the vehicle and pressing the "unlock" button on my key fob, all doors will

unlock except the driver's side door. When this occurs, you must walk to the other side of the vehicle, manually unlock the door, and then it will work again until the next time you need access to the vehicle.

Prices and Specs

Prices (Firm): *IS 250:* $37,900, *AWD:* $40,500, *IS 350:* $50,350, *AWD:* $47,400, *IS C:* $54,850 **Freight:** $2,045 **Powertrain (Rear-drive/AWD):** Engines: 2.5L V6 (204 hp), 3.5L V6 (306 hp), 5.0L V8 (416 hp); Transmissions: 6-speed man., 6-speed auto. **Dimensions/capacity:** Passengers: 2/3; Wheelbase: 108 in.; H: 56/L: 180/W: 71 in.; Headroom F/R: 2/2 in.; Legroom F/R: 41.5/25.5 in.; Cargo volume: 13.0 cu. ft.; Fuel tank: 65L/premium; Tow limit: N/A; Load capacity: 825 lb.; Turning circle: 33.5 ft.; Ground clearance: 4.7-5.3 in.; Weight: 3,814 lb.

Other opinions: "The 2015 Lexus IS ranks #4 out of 14 upscale small cars and #9 in luxury convertibles." – *U.S. News & World Report.* "The exact timing isn't clear, but now that we have the good news we're OK with a little wait: In Europe Lexus just replaced the 2.5-L V6 in the IS 250 with its 241 hp 2.0L, turbocharged 4-cylinder, and we'll get it in early 2016." – *www.autoblog.com/.* **Major redesign:** 2001, 2006, and 2014. **Highway/city fuel economy:** *IS 250 man.:* 7.5/11.4 L/100 km. *IS 250 auto.:* 6.8/9.8 L/100 km. *IS 250 AWD:* 7.6/10.5 L/100 km. *IS 350:* 7.8/10.9 L/100 km. *IS 350C:* 7.9/11.5 L/100 km. *IS F:* 8.5/13.0 L/100 km. **Best alternatives:** Try the Acura TL, a post-2011 Audi A4, the BMW 3 Series, or Infiniti's G37.

SAFETY: Child safety seat setup: Untested. **Crashworthiness:** NHTSA: 2014-15 IS models earned NHTSA's top five-star award for overall crashworthiness; 2013s got four stars overall. The 2010 versions posted similar results. IIHS: 2014-15 models were given an overall "Good" ratings, while 2006-13 models earned "Good" ratings in moderate overlap frontal crashes and "Poor" in small overlap frontal tests. Side crash protection was "Good," but roof strength and head-restraints merited only an "Acceptable" score. **Owner-reported safety-related failures:** Electric seat warmer shorted out and burned through the seat cushion. Engine surges when the vehicle is stopped. Also, many complaints of shattered sunroofs, premature brake wear, and the car jerking to one side when the brakes are applied. Automatic rear-view mirror dimmer takes up to 7 seconds to dim trailing headlights and won't dim at all on roads with brightly lit overhead lighting. Poor instrument visibility:

The visual displays on the center dashboard console indicating HVAC and audio information for the Lexus IS 250 C are so light as to be virtually invisible to the driver, particularly in bright sun and when the driver is wearing sunglasses.

ALERT! Although sunroofs aren't usually a wise buy due to leaks and noise intrusion into the cabin, they are particularly risky with Lexus due to the high number of owners reporting shattered sunroofs and their astronomically high replacement cost.

IS Profile

Used Values ($)	2006	2007	2008	2009	2010	2011	2012	2013	2014
IS 250	8,000	9,500	11,000	13,500	15,500	18,500	23,000	26,500	33,500
AWD	10,000	12,000	13,500	15,500	17,500	20,500	24,500	28,000	35,000
250C	—	—	—	—	23,500	31,000	35,000	42,000	50,000
350	—	13,500	16,500	19,000	21,500	27,000	31,500	36,500	41,000
AWD	—	—	—	—	—	29,500	33,500	38,000	42,500
350C	—	—	—	—	31,000	36,000	41,000	46,000	52,000
F	—	—	25,000	29,500	35,000	40,500	49,000	58,000	66,000
Reliability	3	3	3	3	☆	☆	☆	☆	☆
Repairs ($$$)	2	2	2	2	1	1	1	1	1
Electrical	☆	☆	☆	☆	☆	☆	☆	☆	2
Engine (base)	2	2	2	3	☆	☆	☆	☆	☆
Fit/Finish	3	3	3	3	3	3	3	3	3
Infotainment	—	—	—	3	3	3	3	3	2
Transmission (auto.)	3	3	3	3	☆	☆	☆	☆	☆

SECRET WARRANTIES, INTERNAL BULLETINS: 1990-2013—Lexus service bulletin says the seat belt pre-tensioner devices "may, or may not, perform as expected." 2008-12—Lexus has extended the warranty on 2008-12 IS F models to replace free of charge faulty engine cooling fan motors or screws, and the cooling fan assembly, to prevent the engine from overheating. The extension (#LSC ELE) is in effect through Nov. 30, 2017. 2011-12—Fuel gauge indicates Empty when there is gas in the tank. Bubbled HID headlight housing. 2014-15—IS 250 models with squeaking rear brakes will be given a free brake kit to silence the noise under TSB #L-SB-0105-14, issued Nov. 21, 2014.

RX 300, 330, 350/400H, 450H

RATING: *All Models:* Above Average (2014-16); Average (2000-13). Lexus invented the luxury crossover segment with the RX series in 1998, and since then it has been a perennial bestseller. Unfortunately, over a decade ago, Lexus followed Toyota's example of cutting content to keep prices low, with the result that the car's safety was frequently compromised. At that time, *Lemon-Aid* alerted readers to Lexus safety hazards and our ratings were lowered. Readers' comments, internal service bulletins, and owner complaints showed us that many early models had airbags that failed to deploy, dangerous engine surging and automatic transmission delayed shifts ("lag and lurch"), sudden acceleration, unreliable brakes, inadequate and theft-prone headlights, and weak rear hatches that kept falling on people's heads. Nevertheless, buyers continue to give the RX series high marks for reliability and comfort. *RX 400h and 450h:* Above Average buy (2011-16); Below Average (2006; 2010). There have been far fewer safety-related complaints with hybrids and fuel savings are a given, but you will pay a heavy purchase price in Canada (in the States, the car costs much less). Resale value for the hybrid has dropped along with fuel costs and are expected to fall even faster as you get closer to the battery pack's warranty expiration of 8-10 years. Essentially a more fuel-frugal RX model with plenty of horsepower and full-time AWD, Lexus hybrids are, nonetheless, ridiculously expensive and sometimes hazardous to drive. They can lose their brakes whenever passing over bumpy terrain, and their frequently delayed shifts and engine surges can be deadly either from a rear-ender when you stall, or from a T-bone collision that cuts your car in half as it suddenly accelerates into traffic. If you must go "green," get a cheaper, all-dressed, used Prius RX. **Road performance:** Suspension is independent all around, and the progressive electronic power-steering system is speed-sensing for enhanced control. The front-drive and AWD RX models come identically equipped. Count on a smooth, quiet, car-like ride and a satisfying braking response and feel. Handling is not as positive; the car doesn't feel as agile as its competition and steering gives little road "feel." **Strong points:** The 2016 series doesn't disappoint with its impressive safety and reliability ratings, lots of luxury in a spacious cabin, and plenty of back-seat legroom. Also, the RX has excellent gas mileage for a luxury crossover. Among the cheaper used versions, the best place to start is with the 2013 models; they have increased cargo space over previous versions and are substantially discounted. **Weak points:** No third-seat option; expensive options packages; and modest cargo capacity. This year's restyled exterior is an automotive paella with a soupcon of Nissan Murano, Jeep Cherokee, and Toyota Highlander mixed in with the clams and fish. The mouse pad infotainment screen is outdated, not user-friendly, and distracting. There's also less steering feedback when compared to the RX 450h. Owners report excessive dust/powder blows from the AC vents; tire monitor system malfunctions; inoperative moonroofs; leaky shocks; parts are on national backorder (see "Secret Warranties," below); the vehicle pulls to the right; audio system glitches; and poor fit and finish. *Hybrid 2015 and earlier:* Slow acceleration; the car takes more effort to turn; and the Remote Touch multifunction joystick and screen are distracting features.

Other opinions: "The 2015 Lexus RX 350 ranks #2 out of 18 luxury midsize SUVs. … [It] delivers exceptional comfort, a peaceful ride, roomy rear seats and ample cargo room, but a less-than-entertaining driving experience." – *U.S. News & World Report.* "It looks hideous. If you can get by the ghastly appearance, the underlying car looks like a nice drive and the interior isn't too bad, though less elegant than the current model. The weird D-pillar treatment leaves a huge blind spot from the resultant thick pillar. Dash is busy and the nicely integrated screen of the 2015 model gives way to what looks like a tablet computer mounted on top as an after-thought, and it bucks the (welcome) trend of not relegating too many functions to the screen (not a touchscreen, since it's still controlled by a mouse)." – *carand driver.com/news/2016-lexus-rx-photos-and-info-news.* **Major redesign:** 1999, 2004, 2010, and 2016. In addition to a light restyling that includes an extra 5 inches in length and a 2-inch longer wheelbase, the 3.5L V6 gets about 30 more horses, and the 6-speed transmission will be replaced by an 8-speed, used by the F Sport. The RX 450 hybrid returns, with almost 300 hp, a corralling of 50 more horses. Some new safety features this year: Lane-departure warning, lane-keep assist, rear cross-traffic alert, and adaptive high beams. **Highway/city fuel economy:** *RX 300:* 9.7/13.0 L/100 km. *RX 330:* 9.0/12.8 L/100 km. *RX 350:* 8.2/11.6 L/100 km. *RX 400h:* 8.1/7.5 L/100 km. *RX 450h:* 7.2/6.6 L/100 km. **Best alternatives:** Other vehicles to consider: The BMW 5 Series, GM Acadian or Traverse, Honda Pilot, Hyundai Santa Fe Limited or Veracruz SE, Nissan Xterra, and the Toyota Highlander Limited. Don't overlook the Acura MDX. It seats seven, has comfortable second-row seats, uses high-grade cabin materials, and provides strong acceleration with reasonable fuel economy.

SAFETY: Child safety seat setup: "Marginal." **Crashworthiness:** NHTSA: The 2013-15 RX 350 AWD models earned five-star scores for overall crashworthiness; front-drives of the same years did almost as well, with four stars. 2011-12 RX 350's rankings varied between four and five stars. 2007-10 models earned five-star scores everywhere except for four stars given for rollover protection. IIHS: 1999-2015 models received the agency's top "Good" ranking across the board for crash protection. 2004-09 models were rated as Poor" for head restraint and seat crash-worthiness. **Owner-reported safety-related failures:** Despite reassurances from Toyota and Lexus, and millions of dollars in fines and out of court settlements, sudden, unintended acceleration and airbag failures continue to plague the automaker year after year:

> The contact owns a 2014 Lexus RX 350. While attempting to park the vehicle after a complete stop, during the (gear) shifting from drive to park, the vehicle suddenly accelerated and hit/crashed into a building and spun off, and the impact caused the vehicle to travel for about 15 feet and stopped. Airbags did not deploy and a police report was filed. No injuries to anyone. The vehicle was towed to the lexus dealership and later to dealership's collision shop. Approximate estimate for the repair is $21,000. Manufacturer was notified through the email option in Lexus customer assistance center. Approximate failure mileage was 5,500. It appears to be an issue with the engine or some internal electronic system. Because, when this incident happened, the vehicle was at a complete stop and my (driver) foot was on the brake pedal.

Hundreds of complaints of airbags not deploying in a collision. Some airbags deploy for no reason at all, or disable themselves when a normal-sized passenger is seated up front. When parked on an incline with the parking brake set, the car rolls downhill. Loss of brakes. Windshield distortion cause driver/passenger dizziness. Liftgate crashed down on passenger's head. Passenger side door unlocked and opened slightly while vehicle was underway. Premature failure of Michelin Latitude Tour original equipment tires. Accident reconstructionist believes sudden, unintended acceleration could be caused by electrical interference near electrical plants:

> First part of complaint just in case it did not go thru the first time. Dear sirs, I'm writing to you on behalf of the owner of this vehicle. They have contracted me as a vehicle accident reconstructionist in Puerto Rico. I need to know if you have made any inquiries in the fuel delivery and propulsion system. My concern is that the Toyota, Lexus and Honda vehicles that I know of so far are having some kind of sudden acceleration issues and the computer does not catch the problem. This acceleration surges that I have found out about, all have occurred around high electricity areas. So far that I know of, three of these surges have occurred next to the electrical plant center in Palo Seco Puerto Rico and one caused two deaths. The other one is the one I'm representing which occurred in their home twice … my theory is that electric surges from this high intensity cables interfere with the throttle control and accelerate this vehicles. It is the only logical explanation.

ALERT! Stay away from sunroof-equipped models. Not only is it a non-essential feature and often failure-prone, but it also comes in packages that include other frivolous features. Also, put the Adaptive Cruise Control through its paces; it is known to operate erratically and can be costly to troubleshoot and repair. Rearward visibility is limited by the sloped styling and the rear camera view may be obscured by messages on the screen during startup. All the more reason to verify if the system conforms to your needs. During the test drive, pay careful attention to how the RX 450h 4x4 "On Demand" feature performs (see below and Weak points and Safety (above)). Hybrid suddenly accelerated as it was being parked, brakes were ineffective, and the front tire exploded. Car surges forward when the brakes are applied. RX 450h brake failures are similar to those reported on the Prius:

> I wanted to alert you that other hybrid models that were manufactured with the same braking system as the Prius suffer the same issue. I have a 2010 Lexus 450h RX and its brakes disengage when I am driving on bumpy roads and over pot holes. I live in a northeastern city with many bumps and my brakes stop working often and as a result I have to slam them on much more quickly.

The 4x4 system doesn't perform as advertised:

> The RX 450h powertrain can be downright dangerous. The 4 wheel drive does not switch "on demand" as the advertising says. I live in snowy Massachusetts and do not need permanent 4 wheel drive, but it is essential when the roads are full of snow or ice. I was puzzled at first that the 4 wheel drive only actuated under 25 mph [40 km/h]. I tested it on sharp corners in the snow: The back slid out; and on faster, gradual corners: The car side slipped. Never did the 4 wheel drive switch on and correct the slide. I looked in the manual for the method to manually activate 4 wheel drive but couldn't find it. I contacted Lexus. They said that I should use the snow switch. This is a menu item which annoyingly [must] be switched on every time you drive. It didn't work, as it only changes the gear and acceleration characteristics like any other winter/summer switch. They also said that it should work at high speeds when more power is needed. I tried that and found that at 60 mph [95 km/h] if I absolutely floored the accelerator on a steep hill the 4 wheel drive would switch on briefly.

RX 300, 330, 350, 400h, 450h Profile

	2006	2007	2008	2009	2010	2011	2012	2013	2014
Used Values ($)									
300	11,000	—	—	—	—	—	—	—	—
330	13,000	—	—	—	—	—	—	—	—
350	—	13,000	16,000	19,000	22,000	27,000	32,000	35,000	42,000
400h	15,000	16,000	18,000	21,000	—	—	—	—	—
450h	—	—	—	—	26000	36,000	40,000	46,000	58,000
Reliability	★3	★3	★3	★3	☆4	☆4	☆4	☆3	☆3
Repairs ($$$)	💰2	💰2	💰2	💰2	💰1	💰1	💰1	💰1	💰1
Electrical	★3	★3	★3	★3	★3	☆3	☆3	☆3	☆3
Engine (base)	★2	★2	★2	★2	★2	★2	★2	★3	☆3
Fit/Finish	★3	★3	★3	★3	☆3	☆3	☆3	☆3	☆3
Infotainment	—	—	—	★3	★3	★3	★3	★3	★3
Transmission (auto.)	★2	★2	★2	★2	★2	★2	★2	☆2	☆2

SECRET WARRANTIES, INTERNAL BULLETINS: All models/years: There are dozens of bulletins that address the correction of various squeaks and rattles found throughout the vehicle. 2003-09—Cracked, sticky, or melted dashboards (instrument panels) will be replaced at no charge under Lexus Warranty Enhancement Program – ZLD, issued Dec. 10, 2014. 2003-10—Windshield ticking fix. 2004-06—Rear door-stay improvement. Unacceptable power back door operation. Fuel tank shield rattle. 2004-07—Troubleshooting dash rattles. 2004-08—Front power seat grinding, groaning. 2004-09—Transmission fluid or gear oil leaks from the transfer case vent. Plugging water leaks at the liftgate area. 2004-10—Remedy for brake rattle, buzz heard near the driver's side dash. Power back door noise. 2006-09—Multiple warning lights; can't shift out of Park. Moonroof auto-close function inoperative. 2007—Engine timing cover oil leaks. Engine squealing. Moonroof rattle. 2007-09—Oil leak from the engine camshaft housing. Replace the engine VVTI oil hose for free until 2021 under a Lexus secret warranty extension #LSC9LH; see ES 350 "Secret Warranties." Driver's door rattle fix. 2007-10—Engine ticking noises. 2007-11—An oil control valve will be replaced under warranty to stop a seeping oil leak from the engine oil cooler pipes. 2008-09—Transfer case fluid leak. 2010—Steering groan when turning the steering wheel. Front seat track noise. 2010-11—Steering column rattle. 2010-12—RX 350 and RX 450h vehicles may have a rear end squeak when going over an uneven road surface. In addition, the rear shock absorber(s) may leak oil. TSB #L-SB-0013-13, issued Feb. 28, 2013, addresses these issues. 2010-14—The HVAC Evaporator Drain Hose may be obstructed with insect nests. An insect repellent drain hose tip (ARINIX(R) Tip) will help minimize future occurrences. A new drain hose may be required to properly fit the ARINIX Tip.

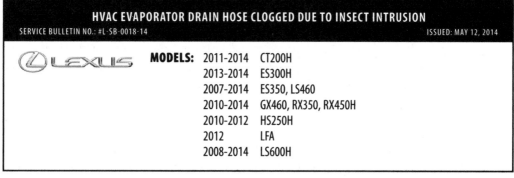

HVAC EVAPORATOR DRAIN HOSE CLOGGED DUE TO INSECT INTRUSION		
SERVICE BULLETIN NO.: #L-SB-0018-14		ISSUED: MAY 12, 2014

MODELS:

2011-2014	CT200H
2013-2014	ES300H
2007-2014	ES350, LS460
2010-2014	GX460, RX350, RX450H
2010-2012	HS250H
2012	LFA
2008-2014	LS600H

Lexus says "The ARINIX(R) Tip is not registered or labeled for sale or use outside the United States or Puerto Rico." Apparently, Canadian Lexus owners will have to live with Lexus-bred spiders, wasps, etc., and their nests.

450h: 2010—The oxygen sensor wire harness will be replaced for free up to May 31, 2018. Fix for a steering groan when turning the steering wheel. 2011-12—Fuel gauge indicates Empty when there is gas in the tank. Bubbled HID headlight housing. Inoperative smart key. Insufficient charging.

Fast and Frugal

The long-lived Mazda B-Series has remained a true compact pickup for its entire run.

Mazda has lots to smile about. But this hasn't always been so. Four decades ago, it was a marginal automaker selling cheap, hard-to-service, here-today-gone-tomorrow rustbuckets. But during the past decade, Mazda trimmed its Ford ties and improved the quality of its lineup, and it now specializes in peppy, fuel-saving, and stylish small cars, family sedans, the bestselling MX-5 Miata sporty roadster, and a number of popular SUV crossovers, the latest being the CX-3 compact.

Mazda's past is a story of missed opportunities. It snared the rights to the innovative Wankel rotary engine from GM (destined for the Vega and Astre) that had a reputation for being relatively small and powerful – but at the expense of poor fuel efficiency. Mazda put the Wankel in its RX-7 series of roadsters (1978–2002) and its RX-8 sports cars (2004–10) and was fairly successful in marketing the cars to the high performance crowd. But once North American fuel prices soared and gas station lineups stretched for blocks, Mazda switched gears, dropped the Wankel, and went back to building conventionally powered, non-descript econocars.

Ford saved Mazda from bankruptcy in 1994 by purchasing part of the company and sharing the production of their cars and trucks. Mazda soon turned profitable through better management and a popular new array of small cars and trucks made in partnership with Ford. The company's sole minivan, the MPV, was both a quality and performance boondoggle and never got any traction. It was put out of its misery in 2006. Mazda went back to its small-car roots with the successful debut of the $13,995 2011 Mazda2, a four-door hatchback powered by a 100 hp

1.5L 4-cylinder engine with a standard 5-speed manual transmission or optional 4-speed automatic. It gets 7.2 L/100 km (39 mpg) in the city and 5.6 L/100 km (50 mpg) on the highway. Best of all, the 2011 has generated only four safety-related complaints spread over 6 years of service. Three-hundred safety failures would be the norm. (See Appendix I for a rating summary.)

Mazda's 2016 product lineup will be augmented by one new model while another bites the dust. This change reflects buyers' taste for less fuel economy and more performance and versatility. According to *Automotive News,* the company will phase out the Mazda5 mini-minivan by year's end, while in early-2016, a new CX-3 subcompact crossover will appear. The Mazda5 didn't have a chance. Minivan sales have generally been hammered by buyers shifting to crossovers, and with Mazda5 sales on the decline since 2011, Mazda had no choice. Chrysler's minivans will likely face the same fate next year. On the other hand, subcompact crossovers are where the action is in a cheap-fuel market that favours trucks, SUVs, and crossovers. The CX-3 will join other crossovers like the Buick Encore and Nissan Juke, and Honda's recently-minted HR-V.

We will also see the return of the redesigned CX-5, followed by the all-new Mazda6, which arrives with a sportier appearance and more fuel-efficient engines. Additionally, Mazda is expected to launch redesigned versions of the Mazda3, MX-5, and CX-9. All the models will have Skyactiv technologies and ride on lightweight platforms.

The slightly upscale Mazda3 does everything the Mazda2 doesn't. There's plenty of interior room, and the powertrain performs flawlessly. In fact, this little pocket rocket, marketed as an urban runabout, remains on back order, due to the performance crowd support since its debut as a 2004 model. This peppy and fuel-efficient compact takes Mazda back to its compact-car roots and adds some performance thrills to its fuel-saving powertrain. Recently the "3" was restyled, the suspension stiffened to enhance handling, and a third engine, a 155 hp 2.0L 4-cylinder, was added along with Mazda's new Skyactiv fuel-saving feature that was introduced several years ago.

MAZDA3	★★★★

RATING: Above Average (2011-16; 2005-09). The 2016 version will be little changed. Below Average (2010). This little Mazda impresses with its dependable reliability, quality workmanship, powerful engines, responsive handling, and well-appointed interior. The car ranks #3 in the *U.S. News & World Report*'s top four list of affordable small cars chosen among 41 small cars. The ranking: #1: Honda Fit; #2: Volkswagen Golf; #3: Mazda3; and #4: The Honda Civic. These cars are similar and have remained relatively unchanged for the past 3 years, so you might consider a cheaper 2014 version. But, keep in mind that resale value is higher than average. Still, buyers can save thousands on freight charges, tax, and insurance. Redesigned for 2014, the car was improved with a more powerful, smoother engine, an upscale cabin and more refined handling to compete with cars costing much more. New-car discounts are paltry. By waiting until early 2016, prices should fall about 5% as new models flush out back inventory. **Road performance:** For day-to-day driving, the Mazda3's base 4-cylinder engine is more than up to the task. For quicker, sustained acceleration, the optional 2.4L 4-cylinder provides plenty of top end power without compromising fuel economy. Whether paired with the standard 6-speed manual or optional automatic, shifting is effortless and driving is a pleasure. Good powertrain set-up, with plenty of reserve power for passing and merging; easy, predictable handling; good steering feedback; small turning radius; and the rear multi-link suspension gives the car solid stability at higher speeds. **Strong points:** The interior's roominess is decent, and seats are comfortably supportive; easy-to-load small trunk; user-friendly instruments and controls; and better-than-average workmanship. **Weak points:** The Mazda3 has a history of automatic transmission malfunctions (similar to what we've seen with Honda and Toyota models) and frequent brake repairs. Owners dislike the small trunk; limited rear footroom; excessive road noise; premature wearout of brake pads and rotors, accompanied by an annoying grinding sound and pulling to one side when the brakes are applied; manual transmission clutch failure; and the rear sway bar link nut may loosen, causing a clunking sound from the rear undercarriage when the car passes over bumps or rough roads. Dash and door gaps are common and radio reception tends to fade in and out. 2004-07 models are rust-prone, and often have AC compressor and engine mount failures. 2004-08s are known for squeaks, rattles, and the early wearout of struts and shocks. 2007-10 models have a limited history of premature suspension and AC failures.

Mazda's 2016 CX-3 is a mini-compact, high-performance, fuel-sipping driver's car with SUV attributes. What more could you want? (Probably more backseat room.)

> ### Prices and Specs
>
> **Price (Firm):** *GX sedan:* $15,995, *Auto.:* $17,690, *GX Sport:* $18,690, *GS sedan:* $19,795 **Freight:** $1,695
> **Powertrain (Front-drive):** Engines: 2.0L 4-cyl. (155 hp), 2.5L 4-cyl. (184 hp); Transmissions: 5-speed man., 6-speed man., 5-speed auto., 6-speed auto. **Dimensions/capacity:** *Sedan:* Passengers: 2/3; Wheelbase: 106.3 in.; H: 57.3/L: 181/W: 70.7 in.; Headroom F/R: 4.5/3 in.; Legroom F/R: 41/25 in.; Cargo volume: 12 cu. ft.; Fuel tank: 55L/regular; Load capacity: 850 lb.; Turning circle (hatchback): 34.2 ft.; Ground clearance: 6.1 in.; Weight: 2,799 lb.

Other opinions: "If you value a cushy ride, there are better choices out there. If you want the most cargo room you can get, you can spring for the Golf or even Mazda's own CX-5. But if you want great driving dynamics and a complement of hitherto-unobtanium advanced technology reserved for the most sybaritic of luxury cars, the Mazda3 is well worth the look. It certainly looks like it's worth it." – *AutoWeek*. **Major redesign:** 1999, 2004, 2010, and 2014. The restyled 2014 is wider and shorter, offers more safety features, comes with two fuel-efficient Skyactiv engines (seven more horses with the 2.0L engine; 17 more with the 2.5L), a new interior, and an upgraded infotainment system. 2016s return with minimal changes. The Mazda3 i Sport is the new standard model with more standard features, most notably a backup camera, radar cruise control, and HID headlights. **Highway/city fuel economy:** *2.0 man.:* 5.9/8.1 L/100 km. *2.5 man.:* 6.9/10.2 L/100 km. **Best alternatives:** A 2013 Honda Civic is the most reliable alternative and combines the latest upgrades with a reasonable purchase price. When compared with the Mazda5, the Mazda3 costs less. The Speed3 has been a bit more problematic (drivetrain and fuel distribution) throughout all model years. The Honda Fit impresses reviewers with its comfy ride, roomy rear seat and better than average gas consumption. The Fit also has a large cargo area, and a back seat that folds flat and in multiple directions for packing versatility. Volkswagen's Golf has good cargo space, first-class interior garnishing, and gives reasonable fuel economy with, or without, the diesel option. The Golf also has nimble handling and a spacious back seat. The Hyundai Elantra is another good new or used alternative.

SAFETY: **Child safety seat setup:** "Acceptable." **Crashworthiness:** NHTSA: A five-star overall crash protection score for 2014-16 models. Front-impact crashworthiness rating for the 2013 model is five stars, rollover resistance earned four stars, and side protection scored only three stars. IIHS: A "Good" score for frontal offset, head-restraint, and rear crash protection. Roof strength was also rated "Good." **Owner-reported safety-related failures:** Normally, a new car would get at least 50 safety-related defect reports posted each year by the NHTSA. Amazingly, the 2015 Mazda3 has only recorded seven incidents; the 2014 generated 22 safety failures (75 would have been normal). Nevertheless, some of the safety failures are quite dangerous: Vehicles that lose power when merging into traffic, or suddenly accelerate without any driver input. Gasoline may leak out through fuel tank seams and the shut-off switch and key fob may keep the engine running:

There was no built-in safety mechanism to prevent the car engine from running while the "key fob" was no where near the car. Imagine the safety concerns associated with this? If the car were parked in a residential garage, why doesn't the engine automatically cut off when the key fob is a certain distance from the vehicle?

. . .

My car is equipped with a push to start/stop (keyless) "feature." I pulled my car into the garage last night (with the radio off), pressed the start/stop button to stop the engine, and went inside. When I woke up this morning, the car was still running, all night inside my attached enclosed garage.

. . .

I am a fire investigator with Lexington fire department. I responded to a structure fire on the listed date. It was determined that the fire originated in the engine compartment of the vehicle and spread to the building. The vehicle belongs to Hertz rental car. The individual renting the vehicle reported that he had experienced problems shutting the engine off and that the vehicle had turned on after he turned it off.

Front passenger-side airbag disabled even though an average-sized adult is seated; sudden, unintended acceleration; parking brake won't hold the car parked on an incline; flickering headlights when braking; a high deck cuts rear visibility; design of the window door posts creates a large blind spot; headlight assembly overheats and melts; and the rear glass window may explode in chilly weather:

Morning: 16 degrees F [−9°C]. Approached my car in the morning and heard a crackling noise. I thought the sound was ice. I started the car and the rear defogger. As I sat in my driveway … approximately 30 seconds after turning on the defogger … the rear glass exploded with a loud noise. … The car is 4 months old and under warranty. … I called Mazda and was told that this could happen in the cold weather. I cannot believe that I should expect that my rear window can explode in cold weather.

In the above-cited incident, the car owner could have easily sought restitution from small claims court on the grounds that the "balance of probabilities" points to a defective rear window.

ALERT! The Mazda3 is a theft magnet. Invest in an engine disabler and GPS tracker. Many drivers have experienced the car losing power when turning, or slowing down. Watch for this in your test drive:

Intermittent lack of acceleration after coming out of a parking lot, making a slow turn and slowing down then needing to speed up on the freeway. I have almost been rear ended multiple times because of the car's inability to speed up immediately. The technician told me it was the transmission valve body that needed to be replaced. I contacted Mazda and they basically told me to pound sand.

Mazda3 Profile

	2006	2007	2008	2009	2010	2011	2012	2013	2014
Used Values ($)									
Sedan GX	3,500	4,000	4,500	5,500	6,500	8,000	10,000	11,500	13,500
2.3/2.5L	4,000	5,500	7,000	8,500	9,500	12,000	15,500	19,500	21,500
GS	4,500	5,000	5,500	7,000	8,000	10,000	12,500	15,000	16,500
GT	5,000	6,000	7,500	9,000	10,000	12.500	16,000	20,000	22,000
Sport GS/GX H/B	4,500	5,500	6,000	7,000	8,000	9,000	10,500	12,000	13,500
Speed3	—	6,500	8,000	9,500	11,000	15,500	19,500	22,500	—
Reliability	☆	☆	☆	☆	★	☆	☆	☆	☆
Repairs ($$$)	💰	💰	💰	💰	💰	💰	💰	💰	💰
Electrical	★	☆	☆	★	★	★	★	★	★
Engine (base)	☆	★	★	★	★	★	☆	☆	☆
Fit/Finish	★	★	★	★	★	★	★	★	★
Infotainment	—	—	—	★	★	★	★	★	☆
Transmission (auto.)	☆	☆	☆	☆	☆	★	★	★	★

SECRET WARRANTIES, INTERNAL BULLETINS: 2004-11—Remedy for intermittent no starts in Park. 2004-12—Correction of brake judder, or dragging. 2007-10—In a January 2012 memo to dealers, Mazda unveiled a Special Service Program (SSP) #87 to extend the warranty to address variable valve timing (VVT) noise and/ or timing chain noise on certain 2007-2010 CX-7 vehicles equipped with a L3T engine; 2007-2010 Mazdaspeed3 vehicles equipped with L3T engines; and 2006- 2007 Mazdaspeed6 vehicles equipped with the same engine. The warranty coverage is extended to 7 years (84 months) from the original warranty start date or 70,000 miles, whichever comes first. 2006-13—Troubleshooting a clunk, bang, or jolt from the front of vehicle upon takeoff. Fuel gauge indicates Empty when there is gas in the tank. Bubbled HID headlight housing. Inoperative smart key; insufficient charging. 2010-12—Corrective measures relative to cleaning rust on the bottom of the rear door guide. 2010-14—A rear windshield or window creak- ing noise is addressed in TSB #09-025-14. 2012-13—Mazda will repair or replace under warranty sticky or warping dash panels. 2012-13—Mazda service bulletin confirms engine may rev above 3,000 rpm with just a slight tap on the accelerator pedal. 2012-14—Engine drain plug oil leak requires a new oil pan covered by war- ranty. Troubleshooting engines that have a rough idle or low oil pressure. High pressure fuel pump may not be generating required fuel pressure. Troubleshooting automatic transmission whining. 2012-15—Manual transmission hard shifts, or jumping out of Third gear may need a new clutch hub. 2013—Excessive condensation in the headlamp assembly requires the replacement of the assembly under warranty. 2014—Repair procedure for an AC that won't blow cold (Mazda says it may be due to a factory-related glitch). Fix for a buzzing dashboard. 2014-15—Repairing squeaky front brakes and addressing groove marks on the front brake discplate. Remedy for master warning light, charging alert, and instrument display coming on for no reason. How to silence a tapping noise from a full fuel tank. Whast to do when the fuel gauge reads Empty, but there is fuel in the tank. Active Driving Display vibrates and/or cannot be adjusted to a viewable position. Seat warmer malfunctions.

MAZDA5

RATING: Above Average (2012-15); Average (2006-10). All the advantages of a small minivan, without the fuel penalty; too bad 2015 is its last model year. Based broadly on the Mazda3, the Mazda5 carries six passengers in three rows of seats. Used mostly for urban errands and light commuting, this people-hauler employs a peppy, though fuel-frugal, 157 hp 2.5L 4-cylinder engine hooked to a standard 6-speed manual transmission or a 5-speed automatic. Since these minivans haven't changed much during the last few years, buy a depreciated 2013 for almost half the price of an "end-of-the-line" 2015. **Road performance:** Agile, no-surprise handling. Drivers will find this Mazda a breeze to park and easy to manoeuvre with its tight turning radius and direct steering. The small 4-cylinder engine doesn't have much torque ("grunt," or pulling power) for heavy loads or hill climbing, and towing isn't recommended. Some body roll when cornering, and steering is somewhat vague. **Strong points:** This small minivan is a relatively tall and narrow car – it looks like a long hatchback – with a thick, obtrusive front A-pillar. Reasonably priced; decent fuel economy; a comfortable ride; dual sliding rear doors; an easy-access liftgate; and relatively quiet interior (except for omnipresent road noise – a common trait with small wagons). The cabin is roomy, and two wide-opening sliding doors make for easy access and are a great help when installing a child safety seat. Anothert advantage is that this mini-minivan is the perfect vehicle for servicing by cheaper independent garages. It hasn't changed much over the years, and its generic parts are available practically anywhere. **Weak points:** So-so fit and finish. There isn't much room for passengers in the third-row seat, and the interior seats may be too firm for some. There's also a history of automatic transmission malfunctions, premature wearout of suspension components and brake rotors and pads. Very few owner complaints recorded by NHTSA, except for the suspension, brakes, and fuel system (fuel pumps, mostly):

The vehicle again suddenly shut down while driving on the highway. During this incident, not only was I about 80 miles [130 km] away from home, but I was traveling with 5 children in the vehicle! At this point, I became very concerned for the safety of my children in the car!

Owners also report a few automatic transmission failures; transmission gear hunting and fluid leaks; power-steering malfunctions; electrical system shorts; frequent failure of the evaporative emission system leak detection pump; rapid tire wear and the airbag warning light and Traction Stability Control (TSC) light may come on for no reason.

Prices and Specs

Prices (Firm): *GS:* $21,995, *Auto.:* $22,995, *GT:* $24,805, *Auto.:* $25,595 **Freight:** $1,695 **Powertrain (Front-drive):** Engine: 2.5L 4-cyl. (157 hp); Transmissions: 6-speed man., 5-speed auto. **Dimensions/capacity:** Passengers: 2/2/2; Wheelbase: 108.2 in.; H: 64.1/L: 181.5/W: 68.7 in.; Headroom F/R1/R2: 4.5/4.5/2 in.; Legroom F/R1/R2: 41/29.5/22 in.; Cargo volume: 39 cu. ft.; Fuel tank: 60L/regular; Tow limit: No towing; Load capacity: 1,020 lb.; Turning circle: 37 ft.; Ground clearance: 5.9 in.; Weight: 3,408-3,465 lb.

Other opinions: "The 2015 Mazda5 ranks #5 out of 7 Minivans. [Its] outstanding fuel economy and responsive handling earn critics' accolades, but its cargo space doesn't measure up to competitors." – *U.S. News & World Report.* "Downsides include modest performance and so-so fuel economy from the 4-cylinder engine, a noisy ride and a lack of feature content compared to larger minivans." – *Edmunds.* **Major redesign:** 2006 and 2010. North American production ended June 2015. **Highway/city fuel economy:** *Man.:* 6.8/9.7 L/100 km. *Auto.:* 6.7/9.5 L/100 km. **Best alternatives:** Honda Civic or Accord, Hyundai Tucson, and Toyota Corolla, Camry, or Matrix.

SAFETY: Child safety seat setup: Untested. **Crashworthiness:** NHTSA: Front- and side-impact crashworthiness rating for the 2008-10 models is five stars, and four stars for rollover protection. IIHS: 2012-15 models rated "Good" for moderate front overlap and roof strength; "Marginal" for side protection; head restraints and seats "Acceptable"; and small front overlap protection considered "Poor." **Owner-reported safety-related failures:** Airbags failed to deploy; sunroof explosions; passenger-side sliding door doesn't remain closed; locks and doors freeze shut; emergency brake won't hold vehicle stopped or parked on an incline; and original equipment Toyo tires sidewall bubbling.

ALERT! Mazda head restraints (especially, on 2013 models) can be pure torture:

> Mazda headrests tilt too far forward. We were ready to buy a Mazda5 but when my wife got behind the wheel in the test drive the headrest pushed her head forward; cannot adjust tilt. She got a headache after the test drive. This is not safe. Should support from bottom of head and around back of head – instead it pushed forward from top of head! Worst headrest I have ever seen – no real support for head. Customers will (and do) turn these around, providing no support and little protection.

Mazda5 Profile

	2006	2007	2008	2009	2010	2011	2012	2013	2014
Used Values ($)									
GS	4,000	5,000	6,000	7,000	8,500	—	12,500	15,500	17,500
GT	5,000	6,000	7,500	8,500	10,000	—	14,000	17,500	20,500
Reliability	★	★	★	★	★	—	★	★	★
Repairs ($$$)	2	2	2	2	1	1	1	1	1
Electrical	★	★	★	★	★	★	★	★	★
Engine (base)	★	★	★	★	★	★	★	★	★
Fit/Finish	★	★	★	★	★	★	★	★	★
Infotainment	—	—	—	—	—	★	★	★	★
Transmission (auto.)	★	★	★	★	★	★	★	★	★

SECRET WARRANTIES, INTERNAL BULLETINS: 2006-10—Water entering the crash sensor connector may cause the airbag warning light to come on. 2008-12—Bluetooth hands-free troubleshooting. Headlights don't come on with parking lights. 2010—Repair tips for condensation/fogging inside the front and rear combination lights. Fix for a steering wheel that has a slight in or out movement when pushed or pulled. 2013—Troubleshooting passenger side airbag deactivation warning light that comes on for no reason. Remedy for excessive headlamp condensation or water accumulation.

MAZDA 626/MAZDA6

RATING: Above Average (2014-16); Average (2000-13). A car enthusiast's family sedan. Although earlier models weren't as refined or as sporty as the competition, notably, the Honda's Accord, the 2014 through 2016 models are all-around winners. Their last redesign makes the car roomier, acceleration smoother and more responsive, increases fuel economy, and adds more interior refinements. Road performance: Good powertrain setup; very agile, with nice overall handling; responsive, precise steering; a tight turning circle; all independent suspension; and impressive braking. Ride quality is relatively firm. Strong points: Comfortable seating, and acceptable workmanship. High prices can be easily bargained down, inasmuch as the few 2016 upgrades aren't worth a premium price. Weak points: Excessive road noise intrudes into the cabin; an unusually low roofline restricts access into the interior; small rear windows; the 2016 navigation system can still be difficult to use and the touch screen interface isn't user-friendly, nor as advanced as systems used by competitors. Mazda has a history of automatic transmission, suspension system, and fit and finish deficiencies. This is reinforced by owner complaints of minor problems with the transmission, electrical, and fuel systems. Also many reports of paint delamination, blistering, and surface rusting.

Prices and Specs

Prices (Soft): *GX I4:* $24,495, *Auto.:* $25,795, *GS:* $27,495, *GT I4:* $32,295 **Freight:** $1,695 **Powertrain (Front-drive):** Engines: 2.5L 4-cyl. (184 hp), 3.7L V6 (272 hp); Transmissions: 6-speed man., 5-speed auto., 6-speed auto. **Dimensions/capacity:** Passengers: 2/3; Wheelbase: 111.4 in.; H: 57.1/L: 191.5/W: 72.4 in.; Headroom F/R: 5/3 in.; Legroom F/R: 40.5/29.5 in.; Cargo volume: 14.8 cu. ft.; Fuel tank: 64L/regular; Tow limit: No towing; Load capacity: 850 lb.; Turning circle: 36.7 ft.; Ground clearance: 6.7 in.; Weight 3,232 lb.

Other opinions: "The 2016 Mazda6 ranks #8 out of 18 affordable midsize cars. It remains one of the best-handling, most fuel-efficient cars in its class, critics say, though it has a firmer, noisier ride than many rivals." – *U.S. News & World Report.* "While powertrains carry over, changes for 2016 are concentrated on the interior. The big news there is a new center stack that makes for an airier cabin. It features a larger, seven-inch touch screen that is a floating-style design. Switching from a mechanical to an electronic parking brake frees up space in the center console. Outside, there are minor tweaks to the grille, the front bumper, and the taillights." – *caranddriver.com.* **Major redesign:** 1998, 2003, 2009, and 2014. Take note that the arrival of the 2016 Mazda6 diesel in Canada has been delayed indefinitely while the company works out engine performance glitches. **Highway/city fuel economy:** *2.5 man.:* 6.6/9.8 L/100 km. *2.5 auto.:* 6.5/9.4 L/100 km. *3.7:* 7.9/11.9 L/100 km. **Best alternatives:** Honda Accord, Hyundai Tucson, Nissan Altima, and Toyota Camry or Matrix.

SAFETY: Child safety seat setup: "Poor." **Crashworthiness:** Almost any year Mazda6 provides occupants with above average crash protection. NHTSA: A five-star score for overall crashworthiness was earned by the 2014-16 models. 2012-13 versions do well with one star less, while 2006 to 2012's post equally good crash ratings that vary between four and five stars. IIHS: The 2016 rates "Good" for overall crashworthiness. 2014-15 models also garner "Good" scores, except for small front overlap protection, which is rated "Acceptable." A decade earlier, 2003 through 2013 model ratings varied from "Poor" to "Good." **Owner-reported safety-related failures:** Premature front brake pad wear and rear door locks inoperative in freezing temperatures.

ALERT! For most people, the 4-cylinder engine has power to spare for most driving needs. Don't opt for a more expensive, less fuel-efficient V6 before test driving a model with the smaller engine.

Mazda 626/Mazda6 Profile

	2006	2007	2008	2009	2010	2011	2012	2013	2014
Used Values ($)									
Mazda6 GS	4,500	6,000	7,000	8,000	9,000	11,500	13,500	16,500	22,500
GT	5,500	7,000	8,000	9,000	10,500	13,500	16,500	20,500	25,000
Reliability	★	★	★	★	★	★	☆	☆	☆
Repairs ($$$)	2	2	2	2	1	1	1	1	1
Electrical	☆	☆	☆	☆	☆	☆	☆	☆	☆
Engine (base)	☆	☆	☆	☆	☆	★	☆	☆	☆
Fit/Finish	☆	★	★	★	★	★	★	★	☆
Infotainment	—	—	—	★	★	☆	☆	☆	☆
Transmission (auto.)	☆	☆	☆	☆	☆	★	☆	☆	☆

SECRET WARRANTIES, INTERNAL BULLETINS: 2003-12—Corrective repairs for brake judder or dragging. 2003-13—Tips on eliminating excessive sulfur odours. 2007-11—Excessive water/condensation in headlamps. 2009—Poor AC performance; engine runs hot. Excessive manual transmission noise when shifting. Transmission servo-cover fluid leaks. Inaccurate fuel gauge. 2009-10—Engine runs hot, poor AC performance. Manual transmission hard to shift into Third or Fourth gear. Diagnosing why the automatic transmission defaults to a "limp home" mode. Silencing drivetrain squeak noises. Front door speaker rattling. An electrical short circuit may cause the horn to intermittently self-activate. Rear taillight heat deformation. 2009-11—Fix for front brakes that click or pop when applied. Repair tips for an inoperative sunroof. 2009-12—Bluetooth hands-free troubleshooting. Improving poor AC performance. 2010—Free fix for A-pillar water leaks. 2011-12—Headlights may not come on with the parking lights. 2012—Plugging water leaks from the left A-pillar/cowl area. 2014—Troubleshooting automatic transmission whining. Tips on freeing up a hard-to-move automatic transmission shift lever. 2014-15—Manual transmission hard shifting, or jumping out of Third gear may need a new clutch hub. Repair procedure for an AC that won't blow cold (Mazda says it may be due to a factory-related glitch). Repair procedure to stop wind noise from door window edges. Fuel gauge reads Empty when there is fuel in the tank. Audio screen and touch screen lock up (black screen). Seat warmer malfunctions. Driver seat gradually moves down by itself.

MIATA MX-5 ★★★★★

Stylistically, all model years look similar. Buy a cheaper three-year-old model; everyone will think it's new.

RATING: Recommended (2012-16); Above Average (1990-2011). The fourth-generation 2016 Miata has a shorter wheelbase and is nearly a half-inch lower, yet, the reworked cabin feels roomier with a bit more headroom helped by a lower seat that reclines farther than before, and a tilting steering wheel for easier access. This year's 2.0L 155 hp 4-cylinder engine works well with the 6-speed transmission and steering is quick and precise. Since the Miata has remained relatively unchanged over the years, consider a cheaper 2012 or later model that will give you sports car thrills without adding thousands of dollars on freight charges, sales tax, and insurance. 2012 and later versions include government-mandated electronic stability control – a good safety feature for any small sports car. For almost three decades, the Miata has proven to be an exceptionally fine-performing, time-tested, and reasonably-priced modern roadster. It's still a stubby, lightweight, rear-drive, two-seater convertible that combines new technology with old British roadster styling reminiscent of the Triumph, the Austin-Healy, and the Lotus Elan. It comes in a variety of trim levels: The three convertibles are the Sport, Touring, and Grand Touring. The fourth model is the Touring (Power-Retractable) Hard Top. The lineup begins with the soft-top-only Sport; a removable hardtop is available as an option. All models come with a heated glass rear window. Road performance: Well-matched powertrain provides better-than-expected acceleration and top-end power at the 7000 rpm range; classic sports car handling; perfectly weighted steering with plenty of road feedback; and a firm but comfortable suspension. Strong points: It's amazing how well the MX-5 is put together, considering that it isn't particularly innovative and most parts are borrowed from Mazda's other models. For example, the engine is taken from the Mazda3 and CX-5, and the suspension belongs to the RX-8. The MX-5 is shorter than most other sports cars; nevertheless, this is a fun car to drive, costing much less than other vehicles in its class. Impressive braking; mirrors are bigger and more effective than those found in most luxury sports cars; engine is fairly quiet, and little road noise intrudes into the cabin; instruments and controls are easy to read and access; good fuel economy; user-friendly trunk; manual top is easy to operate; very few safety- or performance-related defects; and a high resale value. **Weak points:** All the things that make roadsters so much "fun:" a compact cabin, difficult entry and exit, and a can of tire sealant instead of a spare tire. Some minor driveline, fuel system, and fit and finish complaints. Headlight beams that lack adjustment capability may blind oncoming drivers:

> I have to apply tape over the driver side headlight to "fix" the problem and now I get zero bright beam flashes from oncoming cars. Affixing an ugly piece of tape to my car is not what I expected when I paid $34,000 for this automobile.

Prices and Specs

Prices (Firm): *GX:* $29,450, *Auto.:* $31,645, *GS:* $36,045, *Auto.:* $37,245, *GT:* $40,250, *Auto.:* $41,450 **Freight:** $1,695 **Powertrain (Rear-drive):** Engine: 2.0L 4-cyl. (167 hp); Transmissions: 5-speed man., 6-speed man., 6-speed auto. **Dimensions/capacity:** Passengers: 2; Wheelbase: 91.1 in.; H: 48.6/L: 154.1/W: 68.1 in.; Headroom: 1.5 in.; Legroom: 40 in.; Cargo volume: 5 cu. ft.; Fuel tank: 48L/regular; Tow limit: N/A; Load capacity: 340 lb.; Turning circle: 30.8 ft.; Ground clearance: 4.6 in.; Weight: 2,458-2,632 lb.

Other opinions: "[T]he big news was the arrival of the MAZDASPEED Miata for the 2004-05 model years. Blessed with a turbocharged 1.8-L 4-cylinder engine capable of 178 hp and sub-7-second sprints to 60 mph, the MAZDASPEED finally provided the serious sports-car kick that many Miata fans had always wanted. A 6-speed manual was the sole transmission offered, and a slew of performance modifications came standard, including 17-inch wheels, a limited-slip differential and a sport suspension with a lower ride height." – *autotrader.com*. Top repair and maintenance tips from *Repair Pal.com:* "Ticking noise from valve lash adjusters due to infrequent oil changes; check engine light due to improperly manufactured threads on fuel filler pipe; valve cover gasket may fail and leak oil onto spark plug wires; clutch slave cylinder may develop leaks; and a warped flywheel may cause shudder when vehicle is in reverse." – *repairpal.com/mazda/miata+mx-5*. **Major redesign:** 1999, 2006, and 2016. The 2006 redesign gave the car a firmer, more refined chassis, increased engine power, a larger interior, and better interior amenities. **Highway/city fuel economy:** *5-speed man.:* 7.1/9.2 L/100 km. *6-speed man.:* 7.1/9.7 L/ 100 km. *6-speed auto.:* 7.2/10.1 L/100 km. **Best alternatives:** The BMW Z cars, Chevrolet Camaro, Infiniti G37 Coupe, Mercedes-Benz SLK, and Porsche Boxster.

SAFETY: Child safety seat setup: Untested. Crashworthiness: NHTSA: 1990 to 2001 models earned three to five stars for occupant crash protection. NHTSA hasn't crash tested the MX-5 since then. No Miata crash tests have been conducted by the IIHS, either. Owner-reported safety-related failures: Restricted rear visibility with the top up.

ALERT! Car's a neon sign saying "come and get me" to thieves. An engine disabler and GPS tracker are your best anti-theft devices. Forget about lights, alarms, and steering-wheel locks.

Miata MX-5 Profile

	2006	2007	2008	2009	2010	2011	2012	2013	2014
Used Values ($)									
GX	7,000	8,500	10,500	13,000	14,500	17,000	18,500	21,000	25,000
GS/SV	8,500	10,500	12,500	14,500	16,500	19,000	21,500	25,000	31,000
GT	10,500	12,500	15,000	16,500	18,500	21,500	23,500	28,500	34,000
Reliability	☆	☆	☆	☆	☆	☆	☆	☆	☆
Repairs ($$$)	💰	💰	💰	💰	💰	💰	💰	💰	💰
Electrical	☆	☆	☆	★	★	★	☆	☆	☆
Engine (base)	☆	☆	☆	☆	☆	☆	☆	☆	☆
Fit/Finish	★	★	★	★	★	★	★	☆	☆
Infotainment	—	—	—	★	★	★	★	★	★
Transmission (auto.)	★	☆	☆	☆	☆	☆	☆	☆	☆

SECRET WARRANTIES, INTERNAL BULLETINS: 2006-12—Brake judder or dragging. 2006-13—Differential whine may require a new differential; the Mazda powertrain warranty applies, says TSB #03-004/14, issued 09/09/2014. A clunk, bang, jolt from front of vehicle at takeoff is considered "normal" by Mazda. Dealing with excessive sulfur odours. 2007-12—Silencing hardtop rattles at the windshield header. 2009-12—Bluetooth hands-free troubleshooting tips. 2012-13—Attending to leather seat wrinkles.

The Mazda CX-7.

RATING: *CX-5:* Above Average (2013-16); *CX-7:* Average (2007-10); Above Average (2011-12). *CX-9:* Recommended (2008-14); Above Average (2007). The CX-5 is a late arrival to the CX corral. It's a small SUV with taut handling quick shifts, and responsive steering compromised by a sluggish base 4-cylinder engine. Of course due to the car's size, the ride is a bit choppy and there is some road noise. CX-7 is a small five-passenger front-drive and AWD SUV crossover. It debuted as a 2007 model and was one of Mazda's bestselling models until it was axed in 2012. CX-9 is not an extended CX-7. In fact, it shares its platform with the popular Ford Edge and adds a better interior in the process. Ford's DNA makes the "9" a quieter-running and more agile performer than its smaller brothers. There has been strong demand for both cars, and that may be their saving grace because the more CXs sold, the better servicing and supply should become. The ditching of the CX-7 has had little effect on CX-5 and CX-9 sales. **Road performance:** CX-5: The powertrain is adequate for most duties, but the engine quickly loses steam when merging with traffic or going up-hill with a load. Be wary of the Smart' braking feature:

> Our vehicle is equipped with the "smart city braking" feature that automatically prevents collisions at low speed. This system triggers the brakes and brings the vehicle to a stop when an object is detected in front of the vehicle. This system has been triggered by steam clouds coming out of sewer grates and has brought the car to a complete and very unexpected stop several times.

CX-7: Mazda's first mid-size SUV since the Navajo was discontinued in 1994, the CX-7 is well equipped; turbocharged engine has power to spare; and excellent handling, with a relatively tight turning radius and responsive steering. Base engine is a so-so performer, and the turbocharged version is hampered by considerable "turbo lag," which increases the response time from the throttle to the engine. Both engines are also relatively noisy, with the 2.5L producing a coarse drone and the turbo powerplant emitting an annoying whine. Irregular roadways give occupants a shaky ride. *CX-9:* The Ford-sourced 273 hp 3.7L V6, introduced with the 2008 model, delivers plenty of power with little noise or delay. Handling is better than average, and the ride is fairly smooth and quiet over irregular terrain.

Strong points: All models have better than average reliability. *CX-5:* Impressive fuel economy, a relatively roomy cabin with more cargo space than offered by most SUVs in this class, and simple controls. Standard rear-view camera is a safety plus. 2016 models have an improved infotainment system, a bit more storage room, an electric button-controlled emergency brake, and upgraded interior materials. *CX-7:* Plenty of cargo room, and good all-around visibility. *CX-9:* Even roomier, with more headroom, legroom, and storage space. Instruments and controls are nicely laid out and not hard to master. Third-row seating is surprisingly acceptable.

Weak points: *CX-5:* A sluggish base engine; choose the optional 4-cylinder. A diesel powerplant is a year away. The 2.5 isn't available with a stick shift in the CX-5. Car cannot be driven with the rear window partially opened. It immediately changes the air pressure inside the cabin and produces a headache-inducing loud thumping noise. Mediocre speakers. Front seats could use more cushioning. Tall occupants will appreciate the extra headroom. *CX-7:* Ride comfort is so-so and may be a bit too firm for some; rear seating is a bit low and cramped; and interior garnishing seems a bit on the cheap side. Mediocre fuel economy; the turbo-equipped model requires premium fuel. Drivers have reported minor engine problems in addition to fuel system, brake, and fit and finish deficiencies. Excessive condensation in the front headlights; accelerator and brake pedals are mounted too close together; and persistent brake squeaking, groaning. *CX-9:* Braking distance is a bit long. Gas consumption is relatively high. Among the few registered complaints, we find early brake wear, poor fit and finish, and audio system malfunctions.

Prices and Specs

Price (Firm): *CX-5 GX FWD:* $22,995, *GS FWD:* $28,895, *GS AWD:* $30,895, *GT AWD:* $33,495, *CX-9 GS:* $33,995, *CX-9 GT:* $45,995 **Freight:** $1,695 **Powertrain (Front-drive/AWD):** Engines: *CX-5:* 2.0L 4-cyl. (155 hp), 2.5L 4-cyl. (184 hp); *CX-7:* 2.3L 4-cyl. (244 hp); *CX-9:* 3.7L V6 (273 hp); Transmissions: *CX-5:* 6-speed man., 6-speed auto.; *CX-7:* 5-speed auto., 6-speed auto.; *CX-9:* 6-speed auto. **Dimensions/capacity:** *CX-5, CX-7 and CX-9:* Passengers: 2/3, 2/3, 2/3/2; Wheelbase: 106.3 in., 108.2 in., 113.2 in.; H: 65.7, 68/L: 184.3, 200.8/W: 72.4, 73.7, 76.2 in.; Cargo volume: 29.9 cu. ft., 37.5 cu. ft.; Fuel tank: 69L, 76L/regular or premium; Tow limit: 2,000 lb., 3,500 lb.; Load capacity: 1,190 lb.; Turning circle: 37.4 ft.; Ground clearance: 8.5 in., 8.1 in., 8 in.; Weight: 3,212lb., 3,500-4,007 lb., 4,265-4,585 lb.

Other opinions: "The 2016 Mazda CX-5 ranks #3 out of 27 affordable Compact SUVs. [It] earns great fuel economy, and reviewers say its nimble handling makes it one of the most fun-to-drive SUVs in its class." – *U.S. News & World Report*. The same magazine rates the 2012 CX-7 #15 in used compact SUVs in the $15,000-$20,000 range. "While the Honda CR-V and Toyota RAV4 still dominate as sales-volume leaders, neither has the sporty handling or clean, uncluttered instrument panel of the CX-5, nor can they match its impressive highway fuel economy of 35 miles per gallon." – *autoblog.com*. **Major redesign:** *CX-7:* Launched in 2007 and replaced by the 2013 CX-5. *CX-9:* 2008 engine swap and a scheduled redesign in 2016. **Highway/ city fuel economy:** *CX-5 2.5L; CX-7 2.5L:* 7.2/10.4 L/100 km. *CX-7 2.3L:* 8.7/12.2 L/ 100 km. *CX-9 front-drive:* 9.1/13.4 L/100 km. *AWD:* 9.6 /14.0 L/100 km. **Best alternatives:** The Chevrolet Equinox or Traverse, Ford Flex, GMC Acadia or Terrain, Honda Pilot, Hyundai Tucson or Santa Fe, and Toyota Highlander.

SAFETY: Child safety seat setup: *CX-5 and CX-9:* "Acceptable" and "Marginal." **Crashworthiness:** NHTSA: The 2013-16 CX-5 scored between four and five stars for overall crashworthiness and the 2011-12 earned four stars for rollover protection. The 2007-10 CX-7 got similar scores and its 2011-12 models also received four stars for rollover protection. 2013-15 CX-9 overall crash protection was rated four stars. 2011-12 versions got four stars only for rollover protection. IIHS: 2013-16 CX-5 scored five stars in all categories, except for the 2013's "Marginal" qualification for small overlap safety. 2012 CX-7s were rated "Good" for moderate front overlap and side crash protection while roof strength was "Marginal." Earlier CX-7s from 2007-12 continued to score "Good" in moderate front overlap collisions, but posted "Marginal" scores for roof strength and head restraints/seat protection. The 2015 CX-9 was awarded a "Good" score for moderate overlap front and side protection; roof strength/head restraint protection were given "Marginal" scores. Earlier CX-9 2007-14 crash results were disappointing. Although moderate front overlap and side protection were "Good," roof strength and head rerstraint/seat protection continued to be "Marginal." **Owner-reported safety-related failures:** Rear visibility is limited. Windshields cracking; sunroofs imploding, loss of power on the highway, sudden unintended acceleration, and the automatic "smart city braking" feature malfunctioning and making the car come to a dead stop in traffic (I use "dead" advisedly – see complaints below). The vulnerability of the AC compressor to road debris damage (a $1,500 U.S. repair) is also a troublesome deficiency, especially when it happens repeatedly. Most of these problems have been carried over during the past 3 years:

> I pulled out of the parking lot, drove 1 block in no traffic, and when parked at the stoplight, noticed a bit of smoke/steam coming from under the hood. The next day I pulled out of my driveway and noticed the a/c wasn't cooling. The dealership showed me a small pinhole in my a/c compressor and informed me that a rock must've flown through my grill area and left a hole in the compressor, causing the freon to leak. It would cost around $1500 to fix and isn't covered because considered "road debris." The biggest issue I have is that the

design of the grill is so open, I can fit my arm in there. What's to prevent this from happening again? Every time it happens, the passengers breathe in freon and it's released into the environment. Clearly the grill is designed far too openly to prevent large debris, let alone a pebble, damaging the a/c condenser. Something needs to be done to retrofit the opening and prevent this from happening time and time again. I did research and discovered it's not uncommon for this vehicle and one person reported it happening on the 2nd day of her ownership and then again a year later.

ALERT! Owners say gauges on the instrument panel are hard to read at night and in bright sunlight. Others point out that the CX-5 cannot be driven with the rear window partially opened. It immediately changes the air pressure inside the cabin and produces a headache-inducing loud thumping noise. Excessive vibration of the driver-side mirror. Check out these points in your test drive.

CX-5/CX-7/CX-9 Profile

	2007	2008	2009	2010	2011	2012	2013	2014
Used Values ($)								
CX-5	—	—	—	—	—	—	16,000	18,500
AWD	—	—	—	—	—	—	17,000	20,000
GT	—	—	—	—	—	—	22,500	26,000
CX-7	5,500	6,500	8,000	10,500	12,500	15,000	—	—
AWD	6,500	7,500	9,000	13,000	15,500	17,500	—	—
GT	7,500	8,500	—	—	—	—	—	—
AWD	8,500	10,000	12,500	14,500	17,000	19,500	—	—
CX-9	10,000	11,500	14,000	16,000	18,500	21,500	25,000	—
AWD	12,000	14,000	16,500	18,000	20,000	23,500	27,000	—
GT	13,000	—	—	—	—	—	32,000	—
AWD	14,000	15,500	17,500	19,000	22,000	26,000	32,500	—
Reliability	★	★	★	★	☆	☆	☆	☆
Repairs ($$$)	🛢	🛢	🛢	🛢	🛢	🛢	🛢	🛢
Electrical	☆	☆	☆	☆	☆	★	☆	☆
Engine (base)	★	★	★	★	★	☆	☆	☆
Fit/Finish	★	★	★	★	★	★	★	★
Infotainment	—	—	★	★	★	★	★	★
Transmission (auto.)	★	★	★	★	★	★	★	★

SECRET WARRANTIES, INTERNAL BULLETINS: 2006-12—Bluetooth hands-free trouble-shooting tips. Silencing Bose speaker noise. Removing excessive sulfur odours. First-aid for wrinkled leather seats. A remedy for excessive vibration from the floor or steering wheel during acceleration; front brake squeaking. *CX-5:* 2013-14— Engine drain plug oil leaks require a new oil pan covered by warranty. Trouble-shooting automatic transmission whining. Noisy front suspension struts may plague some CX-5 crossovers. In TSB #0200513 issued on May 24, 2013, Mazda says the knocking or squeaking noise is likely caused by a damaged strut bearing that will be replaced under warranty. Front glass rattling while underway is covered under warranty by TSB #09-17-14. 2013-15—Manual transmission hard shifts, or jumping out of Third gear may need a new clutch hub. Fuel gauge reads Empty when there is fuel in the tank. Audio screen and touch screen lock up (black screen). Seat warmer malfunctions. The seat warmer will be replaced under warranty, says TSB #09-033/14, issued Aug. 18, 2014. Driver seat gradually moves down by itself. Warranty repairs for an AC that won't blow cold air. Repair instructions for a rattling instrument panel, or creaking noise from the A-pillar area. Mazda says it will repaint the liftgate area under warranty after removing paint blisters or rust spots. Cite TSB #09-018-15 as your reference for a free paint job in other parts of the vehicle that show up at a later date. 2014-15—"Chirping" rear shock absorbers will be replaced under warranty, says TSB #02-003/14, issued Oct. 23, 2014. *CX-7:* 2007-12—Fixing a partly detached rear spoiler. 2010-12—Door armrest trim peeling. *CX-7 and CX-9:* 2007-11—These Mazdas may leak oil from the rear differential seal. In TSB #0300411 Mazda says the differential breather was placed too low and could easily become clogged by snow or water. A new differential with a raised breather covered by the breather boot will be installed for free on a case by case basis. *CX-9:* 2007-15—Inoperative or noisy power windows usually need the window motor replaced. This repair should be *gratis* under "reasonable durability" guidelines. 2011-13—Correcting engine surge and/or shift lock by recalibrating the transmission control module (TCM) under the more generous emissions warranty. 2013-15—Audio screen and touch screen lock up (black screen).

MITSUBISHI

Mitsus' new Mirage econobox: Less than meets the eye? (See Appendix I for reviews of Mitsubishi models)

Nissan

What is wrong with Nissan? Why has buying one of its cars or trucks become a crap-shoot. Inconsistent quality control, poor reliability, and "Lego"- fixated designers have hurt the brand considerably during the past decade. Why have they made so many crappy cars after building an enviable reputation for manufacturing some extraordinarily good products,

The Cube (2010-13) melting away after four years.

highlighted by run-forever 6-cylinder engines. It's hard to believe that the same automaker that created the iconic 240Z sports car in the '70s, sold gazillions of cheap and reliable Frontier pickups, developed the dependable and innovative mass-market Leaf electric car, and the reasonably-priced, versatile SUV Rogue has now sunk so low.

Sure, the 370Z, 370Z Roadster, and GT-R supercar have helped the brand's image, but it's too little, too late. Some examples of disappointing products include the "here today, gone tomorrow" Quest minivan, mediocre Sentra and Versa small cars, and quality-challenged Altima sedan and Pathfinder SUV. Additionally, the Cube compact, Juke crossover, Maxima full-size sedan, Xterra SUV, Armada SUV, and the Titan full-size pickup haven't achieved much success, either.

The charts below have been sourced through *Automotive News*, R. L. Polk & Company, and *www.goodcarbadcar.net/*. They demonstrate Nissan's drop in sales in just one year. (An * indicates a good buy.)

#	Model	June 2015 YTD	June 2014 YTD	Change
11	Nissan Sentra	7,885	7,626	3.4%
18	Micra	6,024	2,007	200%
25	Versa	4,755	7,977	-40.4%
29	Altima	4,110	4,484	-8.3%
84	*Leaf	488	462	5.6%
88	*Maxima	466	432	7.9%
98	370Z	309	238	29.8%
129	*GT-R	67	76	-11.8%
143	*Cube	2	14	-85.7%

Note: 144 car models are sold in Canada; Nissan anchors the basement dwellers with no car in the top ten.

#	SUV/Crossover	June 2015 YTD	June 2014 YTD	Change
4	*Nissan Rogue	16,902	13,887	21.7%
21	Pathfinder	4,823	4,825	-0.04%
22	Murano	4,429	1,857	139%
40	*Juke	2,308	1,979	16.6%
66	*Xterra	857	576	48.8%
79	Armada	329	201	63.7%

Note: Same story with Nissan's SUV/crossover sales this year, although the Rogue did make #4 of the top ten models sold.

#	Model	June 2015	June 2014	Change
#9	Titan	331	215	54.0%
#10	Frontier	328	317	3.5%

Note: Nissan is found at the bottom of the 13 trucks sold in Canada.

Model	June 2015	June 2014	Change
Chevy Orlando	5	111	-95.5%
Chrysler Town & Country	1863	706	164%
Dodge Grand Caravan	4323	4714	-8.3%
*Honda Odyssey	1311	1367	-4.1%
*Kia Rondo	279	440	-36.6%
*Kia Sedona	258	39	562%
*Mazda5	176	429	-59.0%
Nissan Quest	—	3	-100%
*Toyota Sienna	1711	1279	33.8%

Note: Among minivans, Nissan's Quest minivan sales in Canada have been a maxi-failure.

For 2016, there is some light at the end of this production tunnel where a few redesigned and restyled models may succeed, notably, the stylish entry-level Versa Note hatchback, the Maxima sedan, and the Murano mid-sized SUV.

Nissan has a revised lineup of models that cover almost every marketing niche, with a few models that defy description (like the small Cube and Juke) and other new vehicles like the NV200 Compact Cargo commercial van, the reworked Rogue compact SUV, and an all-new Pathfinder Hybrid.

Judging by the last few years of complaints sent in by *Lemon-Aid* readers and reports received by government and private agencies, Nissan quality control has picked up considerably, though owners still complain about fuel-delivery systems, brake and original-equipment tire durability, climate controls, and fit and finish. The Murano and Rogue models continue to have the fewest complaints.

Nevertheless, Nissan pinches pennies when it comes to its "goodwill" extended warranties used to correct factory-related defects. For example, the company extended its radiator warranty on 2005-10 Frontiers, Pathfinders, and Xterras to eight years or 129,000 km (80,000 mi) to fix a coolant-leak problem, caused by "a cracked oil cooler tube." Nissan assured owners it would cover "damage, repairs, replacement, and related towing resulting from this issue."

But the devil is most certainly in the details. What Nissan doesn't mention is that the radiator cooler tanks are rupturing, which forces the coolant into the transmission through the transmission cooler lines, causing the trannies to self-destruct in as little as 60,000 km (37,000 mi). Nissan insiders says the company is settling claims for transmission replacements on a "case-by-case basis." Angry Nissan SUV and truck owners faced with $6,000 U.S. repair bills want the 8-year extended warranty – extended – to cover transmission damage.

So, "What is wrong with Nissan?" Answer: Excessive cost-cutting and poor, inconsistent management.

VERSA/NOTE

RATING: Average (2013-16); Below Average (2007-12). There are two body styles available for this subcompact – the base, "blue-light special" Versa sedan and the more expensive Versa Note five-door hatchback. All-2016 models return with minor trim tweaks, however, the 2013 is the price/performance leader of the group. It introduced a stylish exterior design, well-appointed interior, more standard features that would cost extra on competing models, and exceptional room for five adults. **Road performance:** Base engine lacks "grunt" at higher rpms and produces an annoying drone when pushed; the manual 6-speed is a bit clunky; the suspension is tuned more to the soft side; the rear drum brakes are less effective; and a 6-speed manual transmission is available, whereas most small cars offer only a 4- or 5-speed gearbox. The car's larger wheelbase makes for a smooth ride. The 1.8L 4-cylinder engine provides plenty of power, and handling is responsive and predictable, thanks to the tight, power-assisted steering and independent front suspension. **Strong points:** Versa offers a lot more interior room than what is found with other compact cars in its class, thanks to a tall roofline that also makes for easy access. Visibility is first rate, and there's minimal road noise. The fuel tank dwarfs the mini-car field, where most tanks are 45L; standard 15-inch wheels are used, versus the competition's 14-inchers; and the Versa carries a 122 hp engine, while the other micro cars get by with 103-109 hp powerplants. **Weak points:** Premature transmission, AC, and coil spring failures. Car has to be turned off to unlock the doors; key sticks in the ignition; mediocre defrosting; condensation collects throughout the car, including the trunk area; doors aren't properly aligned;

speedometer can't be read in daylight; brake howling; rear driver-side tire failures; and complaints of hard starting. Owners also report some problems with the fuel and climate systems, paint, and body integrity. 2015 base models don't have an outside passenger-side door lock:

> The car does not have any way on the passenger side to access the car if the doors are locked. There is no keyhole on the passenger side. The locked car cannot be accessed on the passenger side in an emergency (or if the driver's side is blocked such as by a car parking too close or an object).

Prices and Specs

Prices (Negotiable): *1.6 Note S:* $14,298, *Auto:* $15,598, *SV:* $17,865, *SL:* $19.915, *SR:* $20,365 **Freight:** $1,567 **Powertrain (Front-drive):** Engines: 1.6L 4-cyl. (109 hp), 1.8L 4-cyl. (122 hp); Transmissions: 5-speed man., 6-speed man., CVT, 4-speed auto. **Dimensions/capacity:** Passengers: 2/3; Wheelbase: 102.4 in.; H: 60.4/L: 169.1/W: 66.7 in.; Headroom F/R: 5/3.5 in.; Legroom F/R: 40/30 in.; Cargo volume: 17.8 cu. ft., 13.8 cu. ft.; Fuel tank: 50L/regular; Tow limit: N/A; Load capacity: 860 lb.; Turning circle: 37 ft.; Ground clearance: 5 in.; Weight: 2,538-2,758 lb.

Other opinions: "The Nissan Versa ranks #41 out of 42 affordable small cars. [It] has a bare-bones interior and delivers a dull performance, but critics say it provides a spacious cabin and decent fuel economy for a bargain-basement price." – *U.S. News & World Report.*" The Nissan Versa Note isn't a great inexpensive car. Actually, it is a shambles, a car so out of step with the best in its segment, it almost has an early 1970s, East German vibe to it. The ball pit at IKEA doesn't have this much hard plastic inside. The continuously variable transmission (CVT) moans like it is in the third day of a four-day exorcism." – *Dan Neil, Wall Street Journal.* **Major redesign:** 2007 and 2012. **Highway/city fuel economy:** *1.6L man.:* 5.4/7.5 L/100 km. *1.8L man.:* 6.3/7.9 L/100 km. *1.8L auto.:* 6.2/8.5 L/100 km. *2014 Note:* Combined gas mileage is 4.8L/100 km. Owners say real-world fuel consumption is about 20% higher than what is represented. **Best alternatives:** The Honda Fit, Hyundai Accent, and Mazda2.

SAFETY: **Child safety seat setup:** "Acceptable." **Crashworthiness:** Disappointing crash protection scores. NHTSA: An overall score of four stars, but the 2011 version only scored two stars for overall crash safety. The 2012 merited three stars for front and side crash protection, while rollover resistance garnered four stars. Earlier Versas got better overall scores from NHTSA: Four and five stars for the 2007-10s. IIHS: 2012-15 models scored "Good," except for "Poor" small front over- lap protection. Moderate overlap frontal test results on the 2007-11 models were "Good;" side impacts on the 2011s were "Acceptable," while 2007-10 versions were rated "Good." Rear impact protection for the 2007-11 models was judged "Good," while the same models' roof strength scored only an "Acceptable" rating. **Owner-**

reported safety-related failures: Car suddenly accelerated when stopped; sudden unintended acceleration when driver's shoe gets stuck on the black box located above the accelerator pedal; car hesitates, then surges forward when turning:

> This car hesitates. I push the accelerator all the way down and nothing happens. I just roll. When I make a left turn — I have cars behind me honking at me to get moving, but nothing works. Then, suddenly the car shoots forward. This doesn't happen all the time and not only on left turns, but they are the worst. Before making a left turn, everyone makes sure there is no car approaching. But, every left turn is a real issue for me, because I never know if the car is going to move.

Brake pedal goes to the floor without engaging; antilock brake system failures; and when the AC engages, the car will lurch forward when stopped. "A proposed class-action lawsuit alleges 2007-2011 Nissan Versa cars have dangerous front suspensions with coil springs that can snap. The front coil springs can completely break and cause a loss of vehicle control." (*www.carcomplaints.com/Nissan/Versa/*)

ALERT! Haggle. The Versa's higher cost when compared with other vehicles isn't justified. During your test drive check if the vehicle wanders on the road, there isn't a coolant smell in the interior, or the AC, and heating and defrosting are working properly. Some model years don't come with a cabin air filter (the 2014, for example) and a dealer-installed filter costs $60 U.S. to put in.

Versa, Note Profile

	2007	2008	2009	2010	2011	2012	2013	2014
Used Values ($)								
S Sedan	3,500	4,000	5,000	5,500	6,500	7,000	7,500	8,500
SL	—	—	—	—	—	—	11,000	13,000
Note S	—	—	—	—	—	6,000	7,000	8,000
SV	—	—	—	—	—	—	8,500	10,500
SL	—	—	—	—	—	10,000	11,000	12,500
Reliability	★	★	★	★	★	★	☆	☆
Repairs ($$$)	②ᵇ	②	②	②	②	②	①	①
Electrical	★	★	★	★	★	★	☆	☆
Engine (base)	★	★	★	★	★	★	★	★
Fit/Finish	★	★	★	★	★	★	★	☆
Infotainment	—	—	—	—	★	★	★	★
Transmission (auto.)	★	★	★	★	★	★	★	★

SECRET WARRANTIES, INTERNAL BULLETINS: You won't believe this, but Nissan service bulletin #EL09-010A, Reference NTB09-019A, issued Aug. 27, 2012, says, "[C]ar's rain sensors (windshield wipers) may operate, intermittently or unexpectedly, when exhaust gas, moisture, fingerprints, dirt, or insects are near or around the rain sensors." Lock on door handle doesn't respond or lock/unlock feature won't respond to "intelligent" key. Seats may not move, or adjust, either backwards or forward, or will have some slight movement from side to side. Repairs needed to fix a rear hatch that won't shut in cold weather. 2007-12—Guidelines for fixing water leaks that wet the floor carpets. 2009-11—Odometer racks up more miles than actually driven due to a faulty computer chip. If warranty repairs were refused due to an inaccurate mileage readout or a leased/rented car incurred extra charges, Nissan says it will offer restitution under its Customer Service Campaign #2508. Fix for a horn that doesn't work when pressed. 2011-12—Troubleshooting a rear hatch that is difficult to close in cold weather. Diagnosing CVT oil leaks. Rear brake squealing. Front axle clicking. Front-seat creaking. Key sticking in the ignition, even though vehicle is in Park and shut off. Drivebelt noise troubleshooting tips. Repair tips for a malfunctioning fuel gauge. There's also a voluntary service program (Campaign #PM053) involving the free replacement of the instrument panel cluster and a free correction for seatbacks that won't recline. 2012-14—In hot weather, vehicle will hesitate when accelerating from a stop. Loose fuel cap warning light comes on for no reason. 2015—A low-speed vibration felt when decelerating can be corrected by recalibrating the transmission control module (TCM).

SENTRA   ★★★★

RATING: Above Average (2013-16); Average (2008-12); Below Average (2000-07). The 2016 Sentra will be slightly restyled and offer some interior revisions and tweaks to get better fuel economy. **Road performance:** The 2.0L engine is underpowered, but the 1.8L and 2.5L engines provide lots of power; manual transmission shifter's location may be too high and forward for some drivers; some body lean when cornering under power; occupants are treated to a quiet, comfortable, "floaty" ride; easy handling if not pushed hard; the rear end tends to fishtail a bit; some road wander; and long braking distances, probably due to the use of rear drum brakes instead of the more-effective disc brakes. **Strong points:** Unlike many bare-bones economy cars, entry-level Sentras offer dependable motoring with lots of safety, performance, and comfort. Besides making for a roomier interior, the large body produces a quieter, smoother ride. Plenty of cabin space, and the rear seat cushion can be folded forward, permitting the split rear seatback to fold flat with the floor; a commodious trunk; the locking glove box could house a laptop; and good quality control, with few safety- or performance-related defects. **Weak points:** An underpowered engine; ride may be too firm for some; and limited storage space for small items. Severe rear brake grinding and a noisy rear suspension head the list of complaints. Other reported failures: Faulty oil-pressure sensor gasket; engine piston slap; blown engine head gasket; ABS clanks, grinds, and causes excessive vibration when it is active; unstable front seats; driver's sun visor obstructs the rear-view mirror; bottom of the windshield may be distorted; tire-pressure indicator malfunctions. Problem areas also include fuel, climate, electrical, and audio systems, in addition to horrendous fit and finish deficiencies (a misaligned trunk lid and malfunctioning trunk locks, for example) that produce excessive rattling and water leaks into the interior.

Prices and Specs

Prices (Soft): *Base:* $15,598, *Auto.:* $18,898, *2.0 SR:* $18,698, *SR Premium:* $23,398. *SL:* $24,398 **Freight:** $1,567 **Powertrain (Front-drive):** Engine: 1.8L 4-cyl. (130 hp); Transmissions: 6-speed man., CVT **Dimensions/capacity:** Passengers: 2/3; Wheelbase: 106 in.; H: 59/L: 182/W: 69 in.; Headroom F/R: 6/2 in.; Legroom F/R: 41/26.5 in.; Cargo volume: 15 cu. ft.; Fuel tank: 50L/regular/premium; Tow limit: N/A; Load capacity: 850 lb.; Turning circle: 35.4 ft.; Ground clearance: 5.5 in.; Weight: 2,819-3,079 lb.

Other opinions: " The Sentra ranks #27 out of 42 affordable small cars. Critics don't think the 2015 Nissan Sentra is particularly powerful or entertaining to drive, but they note that its high fuel economy and large interior make it a decent option for daily commutes." – *U.S. News & World Report.* Major redesign: 2000, 2007, and 2013. Highway/city fuel economy: *2.0L:* 6.4/8.4 L/100 km. *2.0L CVT:* 5.8/7.5 L/100 km. *SE-R:* 6.5/8.7 L/100 km. *Spec V:* 7.0/9.8 L/100 km. *1.8L CVT:* 5.8 L/100 km combined. Many owners say advertised fuel consumption figures can't be trusted. Best alternatives: A Honda Civic, Hyundai Elantra, and Mazda3.

SAFETY: Child safety seat setup: "Marginal." Crashworthiness: NHTSA: Four stars for overall crash protection were given to the 1991 through 2016 models. IIHS: 2015s were rated "Good" overall; 2014 and 2013 models were "Good," except for their "Poor" score for small front overlap protection. Moderate overlap frontal tests of the 2007-12 Sentras found them "Good," while side impact scores on the 2011-12s were rated "Acceptable;" and "Good" on the 2007-10 versions. Roof strength results on the 2007-12 models was scored "Acceptable." Head restraint protection varies considerably: 2013 – "Good" and "Marginal;" 2010-12 – "Acceptable;" 2007-09 – "Good;" 2002-06 – "Poor." Owner-reported safety-related failures: Airbags failed to deploy; rear end of the car caught on fire; gas pedal is mounted too close to the brake pedal; sudden, unintended acceleration; defective computer module causes the vehicle to shut down; car can be started without driver's foot on the brake; the front side pillar obstructs the view of what lies ahead, and tall drivers will need to lean back to see the road more clearly. Car was shifted into Drive but went into Reverse instead; early replacement of Bridgestone Turanza EL400 tires; premature wearout of rear tires due to factory misalignment of the rear suspension; sudden brake loss; and brakes are hard to modulate, resulting in abrupt stops; and power-steering failures.

ALERT! Sentras are mobile soup kitchens for rodents:

The contact owns a 2012 Nissan Sentra. The vehicle was parked when owner noticed that mice were building nests inside of the heater vents. As a result, the blower motor failed. The vehicle was taken to an authorized dealer and the nests were cleaned out from the vents, however, mice continue to enter the vehicle and build nests inside of the heater vents.

Sentra Profile

	2006	2007	2008	2009	2010	2011	2012	2013	2014
Used Values ($)									
1.8/2.0	4,000	4,500	5,000	6,000	7,000	7,500	8,500	9,500	11,500
S	4,500	5,000	6,000	6,500	7,500	9,000	10,500	—	—
SE-R	5,000	6,000	7,000	8,000	9,000	10,500	12,500	—	—
SL	—	7,000	7,500	8,500	9,500	11,000	13,500	—	18,500
SE-R Spec V	6,000	7,000	7,500	8,500	9,000	11,000	13,000	—	—
Reliability	★	★	★	★	★	★	☆	☆	☆
Repairs ($$$)	②	②	②	②	②	②	①	①	①
Electrical	☆	☆	☆	☆	☆	☆	☆	☆	☆
Engine (base)	☆	☆	☆	☆	★	★	★	★	★
Fit/Finish	★	★	★	★	★	★	★	★	★
Infotainment	—	—	—	★	★	★	★	★	★
Transmission (auto.)	★	★	★	★	★	★	★	★	★

SECRET WARRANTIES, INTERNAL BULLETINS: 2007-12—Reduced speed due to the CVT transmission over-ride. Troubleshooting an oil leak from the upper end of the oil cooler. Front seats may have a slight movement, or won't adjust. 2011-12—Correcting instrument cluster that may be too dim. 2013-14—If the engine RPM intermittently drops very low while stopped (idling) or the engine stops running while coming to a stop, diagnosis and repair costs may be covered by Nissan under Campaign ID P3212/NTB13-022. Another bulletin gives repair tips when the engine overheats, the AC doesn't cool, and the radiator fan is inoperative. A clunking, popping, or bumping when the steering wheel is turned may require a spacer in the front strut assembly. 2014—A low-speed vibration felt when decelerating can be corrected by recalibrating the transmission control module (TCM).

ALTIMA ★★★

RATING: Average (2015-16); Not Recommended (2011-14); Below Average (2001-10). The Altima is a nicely-styled, roomy sedan that has all the performance features that drivers and techno-philes could ever want. What the car lacks, however, is quality, reliability, a responsive powertrain, and acceptable fit and finish. This conclusion contradicts J. D. Power and *Consumer Reports'* high ratings for the model, but accurately reflects owners' complaints and Nissan internal service bulletins obtained by *Lemon-Aid*. Normally, even the best-made vehicles generate up to 50 NHTSA-registered owner complaints per model year. Yet, the reported life-threatening incidents for the 2013 model, as of October 2015, is 526+ or over three times the NHTSA average; the 2014 got 155 complaints, but the 2015 model generated only 31 owner complaints. Nissan's front-drive, mid-sized sedan stakes out territory occupied by the Honda Accord, Hyundai Sonata and Elantra, Mazda6, and Toyota Camry. The car's base 4-cylinder engine is almost as powerful as the competition's V6 powerplants, and the optional 270 hp 3.5L V6 has few equals among cars in this price and size class. And, when you consider that the Altima is much lighter than most of its competitors, it's obvious why this car produces sizzling acceleration with little fuel penalty. Four-wheel independent suspension strikes the right balance between a comfortable ride and sporty handling. The 3.5 S, 3.5 SE, and SR models add even more performance and luxury enhancements. Road performance: A powerful 4-cylinder engine delivers good fuel economy, and an even better V6 promises scintillating acceleration with only a small fuel penalty. Too bad the car is hobbled by a droaning CVT transmission that makes the vehicle lag and lurch when accelerating. Handling is only so-so, and the car tends to wander, requiring frequent steering corrections. Ride comfort is best with the soft-sprung 2.5 S, whereas the pricier 3.5 SE models come equipped with a firmer suspension and wider tires. Strong points: Good braking; well laid-out instruments and controls; and better-than-average interior room on 2013 and later models. Weak points: Absolutely abysmal quality control; a small trunk; a snug interior with limited headroom and insufficient space for three (2012 and earlier models). Frequent AC, electrical, and fuel system failures; sulfur odour invades the cabin intermittently; and steering vibration, whine, growl, and shimmy:

Power steering was very noisy at all times. Like a high-pitched dentist's drill that only gets worse when wheel is turned. Not sure how long electric power steering system will last. After three weeks, dealer agreed to accept car back and swap it for another one.

Dash and center console reflection in the front windshield and mirrors; and rust perforation in the driver and passenger-side floor boards (2015 model):

I lifted the carpet and noticed a hole on the passenger side floorboard. The hole is as big as my foot. Just yesterday my wife was seated there and felt the floor soft. I went over to the driver's side and noticed that the floor is so rusty that I could put my foot right through.

Prices and Specs

Prices (Soft): *2.5:* $23,798, *2.5 S:* $24,998, *2.5 SV:* $26,998, *2.5 SL:* $29,698, *3.5 SL:* $34,148 **Freight:** $1,595 **Powertrain (Front-drive):** Engines: 2.5L 4-cyl. (182 hp), 3.5L V6 (270 hp); Transmissions: 6-speed man. CVT **Dimensions/capacity:** *2.5S:* Passengers: 2/3; Wheelbase: 109.3 in.; H: 57.9/L: 190.7/W: 70.7. in.; Headroom F/R: 4.5/2 in.; Legroom F/R: 41.5/29 in.; Cargo volume: 7.4-13.1 cu. ft.; Fuel tank: 76L/regular; Tow limit: 1,000 lb.; Load capacity: 900 lb.; Turning circle: 34.6 ft.; Ground clearance: 5.4 in.; Weight: 3,168-3,492 lb.

Other opinions: "The Altima ranks #3 out of 18 affordable midsize cars." – *U.S. News & World Report.* "Drivability is where the Altima stumbles. In our Challenge the car had the lowest numerical rating for handling, and judges cited a tendency to wander and a need for constant correction … The Altima took its lumps regarding acceleration related to its continuously variable automatic transmission … there's often a delay in response when you step on the pedal before the Altima pulls forward – or speeds up proportionally when already in motion … More troubling to our drivers, though, was the noise … engine drone is loud and seems constant." – *www.cars.com/nissan/altima/2015/expert-reviews.* **Major redesign:** 1998, 2002, 2007, and 2013. **Highway/city fuel economy:** *2.5:* 6.2/8.8 L/100 km. *CVT:* 6.0/8.7 L/100 km. *Coupe:* 6.3/9.0 L/100 km. *Auto.:* 6.2/8.9 L/100 km. *3.5 sedan:* 7.2/10.2 L/100 km. *Coupe:* 7.3/11.4 L/100 km. *Auto.:* 7.3/10.2 L/100 km. *Hybrid:* 5.9/5.6 L/100 km. **Best alternatives:** The Honda Accord, Hyundai Elantra, Mazda6, and Toyota Camry.

SAFETY: **Child safety seat setup:** "Poor." **Crashworthiness:** NHTSA: 2011-15 models earned four- and five-star scores following their crash safety tests. Earlier models through 2004 got similar high scores beginning in 1993, though the 1998 side-impact test only gave two stars for passenger protection. IIHS: 2013-14 Altimas provided "Good" overall crash protection, except for small overlap crashworthiness that was rated "Acceptable." 2002-12 Altimas were also rated "Good" in moderate front overlap crashes; small overlap performance was judged "Acceptable" on the 2007-12s and "Poor" for the 2004-06 models. Roof strength was "Acceptable" for the 2007-12 models. Rear crashworthiness was judged "Acceptable" for the

2009-12; "Marginal" for the 2007-08s; and, again, "Acceptable" for the 2005-06 models. **Owner-reported safety-related failures:** Airbags fail to deploy; passenger-side airbag shuts off when the seat is occupied by a normal-sized occupant; sunroof shatters with no impact; and sudden, unintended acceleration:

> I walked in front of the car to get around to the driver's side. I opened the driver's side door and the car accelerated and took off moving forward with nobody in it. I was holding onto the door chasing after my car trying to jump in and put my foot on the brake to stop the car. I was unsuccessful as the car ran into another car in the parking lot and came to an abrupt stop. My car was damaged and still running. The parked car that it hit was damaged. Upon impact, I was thrown against the open door and then onto the pavement … It is fortunate that nobody was hit/run over by this "run-away" car.

Keyless ignition allows car to be left with the engine running; there is no automatic shut-off:

> I went back and opened the garage door. A rush of hot air hit me in the face. To my horror, I realized that I did not shut the car off. Garage temperature had to be about 120 degrees. Who knows what could have happened, had the car run all night … I'm just thankful that my garage was detached. Carbon monoxide deaths via keyless ignition are easily avoidable.

Defective fuel-pump fuse makes it impossible to shut off the engine; vehicle may jerk violently when accelerating; shifts into Neutral, without warning; abrupt downshifts; premature clutch failure; car "drifts" constantly; while cruising, or suddenly veers to the right as the steering freezes; loss of power steering; loss of brakes; headlights don't cast a wide enough beam; windshield cracks for no reason:

> Windshields on 2013 Nissan Altima's have a propensity to easily crack possibly due to weakness or defective manufacturing? Our 2013 Altima which has less than 3000 miles suffered a crack windshield passenger side. Other drivers have also seen this. (*www.carcomplaints.com/Nissan/Altima/2013/windows_windshield/windshield_cracked.shtml*).

And the ignition key may inadvertently start the car:

> If you leave the key outside the vehicle and it is touching the vehicle, the push-button ignition will acknowledge the key and start the vehicle. According to the manual the key must be with you (inside) in order for the vehicle to start. There is no warning stating otherwise.

BRAKE MASTER CYLINDER

BULLETIN NO.: NTB12-001A

DATE: APRIL 3, 2012

VOLUNTARY SERVICE CAMPAIGN

2007–12 Altima Sedan & Coupe Brake Master Cylinder

INTRODUCTION: Nissan is conducting a Voluntary Service Campaign on Model Year 2007–12 Nissan Altima Sedan and Coupe vehicles to inspect the brake systems in vehicles with an illuminated brake warning lamp. If no leak is present, the reservoir will be topped off. If a leak in the brake master cylinder is identified, the brake master cylinder will be replaced for free.

ALERT! In your test drive, check out these four safety-related design deficiencies reported by other owners to NHTSA:

1. **Painful front head restraints:**

   The contact owns a 2013 Nissan Altima. The contact stated that the headrest caused the contact back pain, headaches and numbness in the arm. The contact took the vehicle back to the dealer where the dealer turned the headrest around. The contact stated that after the headrest was turned, there was no more pain.

2. **A crooked driver's seat:**

   The driver's seat is crooked – both across the back and across the seat. This means one's shoulders and torso are twisted and facing the center console, not the steering wheel. Hips are uneven with the right side significantly lower than the left. This is a very uncomfortable and painful position to be in. I have been informed by the dealership that all 2012 Altimas are like this and therefore it is not a warranty item! I have been able to determine the back of the seat is in fact crooked in the more than two dozen examples.

3. **Brake and gas pedals are mounted too close together:**

   My husband complained of this a few weeks ago when he drove my car because his shoe got caught on the brake pedal as he was lifting his foot off the gas pedal. Then, yesterday, the same thing happened to me. I nearly drove my car through the front of the daycare where I was dropping off my son.

4. **Blind spot warning feature gives false alerts:**

   When it was raining or the roads were wet, the BSW would give false alarms that a car was next to me. I was handed a bulletin that shows the issue. I was told by the dealer to contact Nissan customer support for resolution. I just heard back from them on 12/30/14 and their response was that it was working as designed. How can a safety feature that is part of a $1000 package be designed to give false alarms when the roads are wet?

Altima Profile

	2006	2007	2008	2009	2010	2011	2012	2013	2014
Used Values ($)									
S Coupe	—	—	6,500	9,000	11,000	13,000	15,500	19,500	—
SE/SR	—	—	9,500	11,500	13,000	15,500	18,500	—	—
S Sedan	6,000	7,000	8,500	10,000	10,000	11,000	13,500	16,500	19,500
3.5 S	7,500	8,500	10,000	11,500	12,500	13,500	16,500	19,500	24,000
SE/SR/SL	8,500	9,500	11,000	12,500	13,500	14,500	18,000	22,000	25,000
Hybrid	—	7,000	7,500	8,500	10,000	12,500	—	—	—
Reliability	②	②	②	②	②	③	③	③	③
Repairs ($$$)	③	③	③	③	③	③	③	③	③
Electrical	①	①	①	①	①	②	②	②	②
Engine (base)	③	③	③	③	③	③	③	③	③
Fit/Finish	①	①	①	①	①	②	②	②	②
Infotainment	—	—	—	④	④	④	④	④	④
Transmission (auto.)	③	③	③	③	③	③	③	③	③

SECRET WARRANTIES, INTERNAL BULLETINS: 2007-12—Front seats bind, won't move fore or aft. Inoperative driver power seat lumbar support. 2008-12—Buzzing wind noise from the A-pillar/mirror area. 2008-13—Oil cooler leakage. 2009—Nissan set up a special Campaign (#PCO 44) to prevent the front windshield wipers from scraping the windshield. Parts and labour are Nissan's responsibility. Another Campaign (#PC005) provides free replacement of the rear suspension knuckle. 2011-12—Oil may leak from the upper end of the engine oil cooler (see the Sentra profile). Steering/suspension drift. Sunroof water leak. Rear end clunking. Knocking on turns. Brake master cylinder may slowly leak fluid. If the ignition push button doesn't respond, the body control module (BCM) may need recalibrating. 2013—Shuddering at moderate speeds could indicate problems with the transmission torque converter in certain Altimas and Pathfinders. TSB #13-064A issued on June 13, 2013, says the shaking in 2013 V6-equipped models could be a sign that the torque converter is defective and needs to be replaced. The bulletin only covers a shudder occurring at 18-35 mph. 2013-14—Light acceleration shuddering with V6-equipped Altimas and Pathfinders may be corrected by recalibrating the transmission control module. 2013-15—Excessive right rear brake pad wear is covered by TSB #BR15-001 and NTB15-047. 2015—Under a voluntary service campaign (PC346), Nissan will pay for the replacement of the transmission torque converter on all Altimas equipped with a 4-cylinder engine.

VOLUNTARY SERVICE CAMPAIGN REAR SUSPENSION REPLACEMENT/BUSHING REPLACEMENT AND SEALING

On some model year 2002–05 Nissan Altima and 2004–05 Nissan Maxima vehicles, there is a possibility that corrosion of the rear sub-frame may occur. Corrosion is most likely in cold climates where heavy salting of roads is common practice in freezing conditions.... In severe cases, cracking of the rear sub-frame may occur, which may result in a knocking noise coming from the rear of the vehicle.... On most vehicles, Nissan will replace the rear sub-frame assembly. On some 2005 Model Year vehicles, where sub-frame replacement is not necessary, Nissan will replace and seal the front bushings and seal the rear bushings.

WARRANTY EXTENSION: To ensure the highest levels of customer satisfaction, Nissan is also extending the warranty for cracking of the rear sub-frame due to corrosion to a total of 13 years with unlimited mileage on all model year 2002–05 Nissan Altima and 2004–05 Nissan Maxima vehicles. Vehicles included in the Service Campaign (as described above) are also covered by the Warranty Extension.

MAXIMA

RATING: Above Average (2011-16); Below Average (2006; 2010); Average (2007-09). Except for a couple of early model years, Nissan's earlier redesigns didn't produce more than a handful of complaints. Could it be that Nissan has finally shaken the poor-quality Quest and Altima monkeys off its back? Not really. In fact, one month after the Maxima's debut last June, Nissan issued a rarely used "stop-sale" order on the redesigned 2016 to fix some quality problems. Like with the Altima, the same quality glitches continue to re-appear with the Maxima each year: Exploding, malfunctioning sunroofs; engine knocking from the first crankshaft bearing; the passenger-side airbag that's disabled when an average-sized occupant is seated; power steering failures; and broken driver seats that wobble, or won't move fore or aft. In spite of the quality issues noted above, this front-drive, mid-sized model soldiers on as Nissan's luxury flagship. And as such, it's a competent and roomy sedan, that's a far better buy than the bestselling Altima. For 2016, the redesigned front-drive carries an upgraded 300 hp 3.5L V6 (a 10-hp gain) that is still coupled to the same old, problematic CVT automatic transmission. The car is also a little longer (by 2.2 inches) and 1.3 inches lower. Granted, you get plenty of horsepower, comfort, and gadgets, but unfortunately the car isn't backed up with all the standard technical refinements and quality components provided by the competition. Road performance: As always, the powerful V6 engine provides impressive acceleration and this year's CVT tranny's performance is slightly improved. Handling is also much better than with last year's model. Steering takes some getting used to: It's overboosted at low speeds and then suddenly firms up. The 18-inch original equipment tires produce high-speed tire whine. Strong points: Good acceleration without much of a fuel penalty; a restyled interior and exterior; a quiet cabin; and user-friendly controls and instrumentation. **Weak points:** Excessive engine noise; tall occupants may find rear seating a bit cramped; many incidents of the SkyView roof suddenly shattering; and heated seats that leave occupants cold.

Prices and Specs

Price (Negotiable): *SV:* $35,900, *SL:* $38,950, *SR:* $41,100, *Platinum:* $43,300 **Freight:** $1,620
Powertrain (Front-drive): Engine: 3.5L V6 (300 hp); Transmission: CVT **Dimensions/capacity:** Passengers: 2/3; Wheelbase: 109.3 in.; H: 56.5/L: 192.8/W: 73.2 in.; Headroom F/R: 4/2 in.; Legroom F/R: 42/30 in.; Cargo volume: 14.2 cu. ft.; Fuel tank: 70L/premium; Tow limit: 1,000 lb.; Load capacity: 900 lb.; Turning circle: 37.4 ft.; Ground clearance: 5.6 in.; Weight: 3,471 lb.

Other opinions: "The 2016 Maxima is ranked #1 in affordable large cars." – *U.S. News & World Report.* "One beef was the old-fashioned pedal-type parking brake, which robs some space you'd otherwise use for your left leg. Other modern $40,000 U. S. cars have an electronic parking brake operated from the center console." – *www.consumerreports.org/cro/news/2015/04/2016.* **Major redesign:** 2000, 2004, 2009, and 2016. **Highway/city fuel economy:** 7.7/10.9 L/100 km. **Best alternatives:** The Acura TSX, BMW 3 Series, Honda Accord V6, the Lexus IS 5-speed, Mazda6 GT V6, and Toyota Camry V6.

SAFETY: **Child safety seat setup:** "Acceptable." **Crashworthiness:** NHTSA: 1995-2015 models earned four- and five-star scores for overall crashworthiness; 1990-94s' overall crash safety merited three stars. IIHS: 2014 model "Good" for moderate overlap front and side crash safety; "Acceptable" for small overlap front protection and roof strength; and "Marginal" for rear crash protection (head restraints and seats). 2004-13 models qualified as "Good" in moderate overlap front tests; 1997-2003 models rated "Acceptable;" and 1995-96s scored "Poor." Small overlap crashes with the 2009-13s produced "Acceptable" ratings. Side-impact protection was judged "Good" on the 2009-13 cars and "Marginal" on the 2004-08s. Roof strength with 2009-13 models was "Acceptable." Head-restraint effectiveness was rated "Marginal" on the 2007-13 and "Poor" on the 2004-06s. **Owner-reported safety-related failures:** Front airbags failed to deploy or the passenger-side airbag is disabled when the seat is occupied:

The passenger side airbag does not activate with my wife in the seat. She is well over the 80 pound limit for activation. Seat was changed but did not change. Dealer service department says there is no fix.

This second problem represents the majority of owner complaints affecting Nissan's entire lineup over the past 5 years. C'mon Nissan, replace those sensors, as other automakers have done when faced with the same problem.

Other negatives: Sometimes, the Maxima won't shift into Drive; engine surges when brakes are applied; drivers must constantly fight the steering wheel to keep from veering to the left or right; car would not shift out of First as the Check Engine warning light came on; electrical problems knock out the interior lights, door locks, and other controls; headlights may provide insufficient illumination; head restraints obstruct rear visibility, particularly when backing up; and the adjustable steering wheel may stick in its highest position.

ALERT! Owners say the car's low roofline and narrow doorway complicates rear access and blocks visibility. Check this out during a test run.

Maxima Profile

	2006	2007	2008	2009	2010	2011	2012	2013	2014
Used Values ($)									
SV	—	—	—	12,000	14,000	15,500	19,500	24,500	—
SE	6,000	7,000	8,500	—	—	—	—	—	—
SL	7,000	8,500	9,500	—	—	—	—	—	—
Reliability	★	★	★	★	★	☆	☆	☆	☆
Repairs ($$$)	2	1	1	1	2	1	1	1	1
Electrical	★	★	★	★	★	★	★	★	★
Engine (base)	★	★	★	★	★	★	★	★	★
Fit/Finish	★	★	★	★	★	★	★	★	★
Infotainment	—	—	—	☆	☆	☆	☆	☆	☆
Transmission (auto.)	★	★	★	★	★	★	★	★	★

SECRET WARRANTIES, INTERNAL BULLETINS: 2000-03—Driver's seat won't go forward or backward. Abnormal shifting (the control valve assembly is the likely culprit, says TSB #NTB04-035). **2000-06**—Oil leaks from oil-cooler oil seal. **2002-06**—How to silence an engine ticking noise. **2003-04**—Harsh First to Second shifts. **2004**—Cold upshift shock; abnormal shifting. Fuel system misfires. Hard start after a cold soak. Engine won't crank in cold weather. Water leaks from roof. Loose headliner. **2004-05**—Exhaust rattle/buzz when accelerating. Voluntary service campaign entails the free replacement of the rear suspension and bushing sealing for 13 years. If the subframe is too corroded, Nissan will buy back the car. **2004-06**—Erratic fuel gauge, AC operation. Front power-seat malfunction. Hard-to-move shifter. **2004-07**—ABS activates when it shouldn't. Noisy driver's power seat. **2004-08**—Tire-pressure-monitor sensor may leak fluid. Inoperative power-door mirrors. Heat shield rattles. **2007-08**—Front suspension rattling. Inoperative lumbar support.

2007-09—If the vehicle has low power accelerating to 80 km/h, the likely cause is a defective wheel speed sensor. Sunroof is inoperative or operates erratically. 2007—A loose fuel filler cap may be the cause of emissions alert. 2007-12—Loss of power between 0-70 km/h. 2009—Sunroof glass chatter, creaking, or popping. Sunroof wind noise. Power window "Up" and steering column adjustment may both be inoperative. Loose headliner. Front passenger seat shakes at highway speeds. Voluntary Service Campaign #PC005 to replace the steering knuckle for free. 2009-10—Transmission "booming" countermeasures. Front power seats won't move. Driver's seat is wobbly. Can't turn ignition to the On position. Fuel gauge issues. 2009-11—Silencing a rear-end squeak or clunk heard when passing over bumps. 2009-13—Steering wheel switch may need replacing. 2010—Slower than normal acceleration. Lock/Unlock button on outside handle doesn't respond. 2009-14—Number one crankshaft bearing noise. Rain sensor may activate intermittently. 2011-12—If the ignition push button doesn't respond, the body control module (BCM) may need recalibrating. Steering pull/drift; door panel looks faded, discoloured. Rear-end squeak, clunk when driving over bumps. Driver's seat bottom shifts or rocks slightly.

CAMPAIGN PC005 – L/H REAR SUSPENSION KNUCKLE

BULLETIN NO.: NTB09-031   DATE: APRIL 23, 2009

2009 Maxima and 2009 Altima Sedan, Coupe, and Hybrid

INTRODUCTION: On some 2009 Altima and Maxima vehicles, the left hand rear suspension knuckle may not be manufactured to specification, which may result in noise or vibration under certain circumstances. Although no safety issue is presented, Nissan is conducting this service campaign to identify and replace those affected units. This service will be performed at no cost for parts or labor.

DEALER RESPONSIBILITY: Dealers are to inspect each vehicle falling within range of this campaign that enters the service department, and if necessary, perform the indicated knuckle replacement. This includes vehicles purchased from private parties or presented by transient (tourist) owners and vehicles in a dealer's inventory.

ROGUE

RATING: Recommended (2010-16); Above Average (2008-09). A hybrid-electric Rogue will appear in late 2015 or early 2016. **Road performance:** This compact SUV is based on the Sentra sedan and gives car-like handling and better fuel economy than the competition that's still wedded to truck platforms. Nevertheless, the Rogue's car DNA becomes all the more evident as the engine protests going through the upper reaches of the CVT when accelerating. A redesigned 2015 model gave the Rogue more horsepower and torque. **Strong points:** Standard features abound, with stability control, curtain airbags, active head restraints, and anti-lock brakes. Well-crafted interior, comfortable front seating, and impressive braking. **Weak points:** Some of the standard features are fairly basic, and those that are in the premium packages should be standard; engine sounds like a diesel when accelerating, and it could use a bit more "grunt;" lacks cargo space and rear-seat versatility. Poor rearward visibility.

Prices and Specs

Prices (Firm): *S FWD:* 24,248, *AWD:* $26,248, *SV FWD:* $28,148, *AWD:* $30,148, *SL AWD:* $32,048 **Freight:** $1,750 **Powertrain (Front-drive/AWD):** Engine: 2.5L 4-cyl. (170 hp); Transmission: CVT **Dimensions/capacity:** Passengers: 2/3; Wheelbase: 105.9 in.; H: 65.3/L: 182.9/W: 70.9 in.; Headroom F/R: 3.5/4 in.; Legroom F/R: 42/30 in.; Cargo volume: 28.9 cu. ft.; Fuel tank: 60L/regular; Tow limit: 1,500 lb.; Load capacity: 953 lb.; AWD: 1,026 lb.; Turning circle: 37.4 ft.; Ground clearance: 8.3 in.; Weight: 3,315-3,469 lb.

Other opinions: "The Rogue ranks #5 out of 27 affordable compact SUVs. Though reviewers would like a less-noisy, more-refined powertrain, the 2015 Nissan Rogue is recognized for its top-level fuel economy estimates, generous cargo room and stylish cabin." – *U.S. News & World Report.*" "The new Rogue steers with more heft, damps its ride better, and has a more substantial and composed feel than the Rogue Select in every way we can think of." – *www.thecarconnection.com/overview/nissan rogue_2015.* **Major redesign:** 2008 and 2015. The 2016 remains relatively unchanged, except for a foot-activated power liftgate, additional Nissan Connect telematics, and Siri Eyes Free now standard on the SL models. **Highway/city fuel economy:** *Front-drive:* 7.0/ 9.0 L/100 km. *AWD:* 7.7/9.6 L/100 km. **Best alternatives:** The Buick Enclave, and GMC Acadia.

SAFETY: Child safety seat setup: "Marginal." **Crashworthiness:** NHTSA: 2010-16 Rogues earned four stars for overall crashworthiness, while 2008-09 models did better with five stars given for overall crash safety. IIHS: 2014-16 models were designated five-star Top Safety Picks. 2008-13s didn't do as well, scoring "Good" for moderate frontal coverlap crash protection and "Marginal" small overlap protection. Side crashworthiness was rated "Good" for 2006-13 models and roof strength was judged "Acceptable" for the 2008-13s. Head-restraint protection was judged to be "Good" for the 2008-13 models, as well. **Owner-reported safety-related failures:** Few safety-related complaints have been recorded since 2008, but some are deadly serious, like the following:

I was on my way to work and had entered our parking lot and was ready to pull into a parking space. As I pulled in and was at a stop, my car suddenly accelerated and I was unable to stop it. I started to turn the wheel to the right because there was a 2010 Ford Explorer that was parked in front but unfortunately I hit the back end of the car and pushed it at least 30 ft dead straight. My car continued going to the right and over an island and by the time I got it to stop, the airbag had gone off. I'm not sure how this happened since I was stopped.

Transmission, steering wheel, and brake failures (brakes may also suddenly lock up):

Nissan Rogue transmission failure at 16,000 miles [25,750 km]. Transmission began to make strange noises under load from the front end. Dealer replaced transmission and claimed there is no current recall. A check on the internet indicates the problem is pervasive.

Tire-pressure monitoring systems are so sensitive that they often give false alerts, so drivers end up ignoring them. Steering-wheel vibrations may numb your hands:

I think it's absurd my vehicle has 2,100 miles [3,380 km] on it and I've never owned a car that does this. You have to move your hands off the wheel because they go numb. I was told drive faster or take a different route to work.

Driver-side door handle broke, and it took over a month to get the part:

In the meantime, the only way to access my vehicle is by using the passenger side door and climb over the seats. If I were physically unable to climb over the seats, I would not be able to operate my vehicle. Fortunately, I am able, but if a person was not, they would either have to rent a vehicle or use some other means of transportation. I find this problem inexcusable. A simple door handle part must be sent from Japan to fix this problem.

ALERT! Owners say the sunroof doesn't open fully, and dealers say all Rogues are designed that way – check it out.

Rogue Profile

	2008	2009	2010	2011	2012	2013	2014
Used Values ($)							
S	7,500	8,500	10,000	11,500	14,000	16,500	18,500
AWD S/SV	8,500	10,000	10,500	12,500	15,000	17,500	20,500
AWD SL	10,000	11,500	12,500	16,000	18,500	21,500	25,500
Reliability	★	★	★	★	★	★	★
Repairs ($$$)	💰	💰	💰	💰	💰	💰	💰
Electrical	★	★	★	★	★	★	★
Engine (base)	★	★	★	★	★	★	★
Fit/Finish	★	★	★	★	★	★	★
Infotainment	—	—	—	★	★	★	★
Transmission (auto.)	★	★	★	★	★	★	★

SECRET WARRANTIES, INTERNAL BULLETINS: 2007-12—A leak from the oil cooler may be a problem on some Nissans. In TSB #NTB11015A, Nissan says the leak is from the upper end of the oil cooler. Door locks inoperative with Keyless Entry. **2008-12**—Troubleshooting a grinding, knocking noise from the rear on turns. **2008-13**—Oil cooler leakage. **2008-14**—A quick fix for a rattling heat shield (TSB #NTB 14-018, issued March 20, 2014). **2011-12**—Inaccurate ambient display temperature. Troubleshooting water vapour in the exterior lights. Steering/suspension pull or drift diagnosis. Oil may leak from the upper end of the engine oil cooler (see Sentra profile). Noise when turning the steering wheel. **2014**—Free replacement of the engine On/Off button:

CAMPAIGN #PC311 TO REPLACE ENGINE ON/OFF PUSH BUTTON

SERVICE BULLETIN NO.: NTB14-082   DATE: AUGUST 28, 2014

2014

INTRODUCTION: Nissan has a Voluntary Service Campaign covering the free replacement of the engine ON/OFF push-button. Dealers are to correct each vehicle falling within the range of this campaign.

Water leaking onto the driver or front passenger floor may be coming in through the kick panel and/or the cowl end area. **2014-15**—Vehicle may lose power due to snow entering into the air cleaner case. In TSB #BT14015a and #NTB14-069a, issued Dec. 15, 2014, Nissan admits responsibility for sunshades that may bind or come apart. **2015**—Under a voluntary service campaign (PC346), Nissan will pay for the replacement of the transmission torque converter.

GRINDING/KNOCKING NOISE FROM REAR ON TURNS

CLASSIFICATION: RA09-004A   DATE: OCTOBER 5, 2011

2003-12 Murano (Z50, Z51) AWD ONLY and 2008-12 Rogue (S35) AWD ONLY

IF YOU CONFIRM: There is a grinding or knocking noise or vibration from the rear of the vehicle.
ACTION: Remove the Rear Propeller Shaft and test drive the vehicle. If the noise/vibration DOES NOT stop: This bulletin DOES NOT APPLY. Refer to ASIST for further diagnostic assistance. If the noise/vibration DOES stop: Replace the Electrical Coupling Assy. (CPLG ASSY-ELEC) with the one from the Parts Information section of this bulletin.

MURANO

RATING: Above Average (2009-16); Average (2007); Below Average (2004-06); Not Recommended (2003). The mid-sized Murano continues to be the car-based "ying" to the Pathfinder's truck-based "yang." Both vehicles embody strong, in-your-face styling and are loaded with many standard safety, performance, and convenience features. **Road performance:** Nicely equipped with a refined, responsive powertrain that includes a smooth V6, a comfortable, quiet, though, sometimes bouncy ride, and, no-surprise, car-like handling. On the other hand, this engine is mated to Nissan's "save fuel, screw performance" CVT tranny – a noisy, shiftless "automatic" transmission that stays in high revs, and then gradually slows down as accelerator pressure is reduced. Passing/merging power is lethargic; the ride stiffens with 20-inch wheels and the 2015 redesign dumbed down steering feel and response. **Strong points:** A plush, easily accessed, comfortable, and roomy interior; good fuel economy; easy-to-use tech features, and good fuel economy for its class. **Weak points:** Do you really want to pay Lexus-like prices for a mediocre SUV crossover? There is less cargo space behind the second row than what is available in competing models; no height adjustment for passenger seat; limited rear visibility; the sloping windshield and hood make it hard to judge distance; and you better save your loonies for gassing up with premium fuel. Recommended optional active-safety features are tied to the purchase of a problematic sunroof. Frequent brake replacements (calipers and rotors) and poor body fit and finish, including paint defects and water/air leaks. Excessive vibration (sometimes fixed by reducing tire pressure from 41 psi to 36 psi); inoperative sunroof; faulty sun visors suddenly flop down, completely blocking visibility; and power windows open and close on their own. Centre rear seat passengers' legs straddle the centre console.

Prices and Specs

Prices (Firm): *S:* $29,998, *SV AWD:* $35,998 **Freight:** $1,750 **Powertrain (Front-drive/AWD):** Engine: 3.5L V6 (265 hp); Transmission: CVT **Dimensions/capacity:** Passengers: 2/3; Wheelbase: 111.2 in.; H: 66.6/L: 192.4/W: 75.4 in.; Headroom F/R: 3/3 in.; Legroom F/R: 40.5/28 in.; Cargo volume: 31.6 cu. ft.; Fuel tank: 82L/premium; Tow limit: 3,500 lb.; Load capacity: 900 lb.; Turning circle: 38.7 ft.; Ground clearance: 6.9 in.; Weight: 4,034-4,153 lb.

Other opinions: "The 2015 Nissan Murano is ranked #1 out of 12 in affordable SUVs with 2 rows of seating; #2 in affordable midsize SUVs; and #2 in affordable crossover SUVs. [It] has an upscale interior and a smooth ride. It also gets very good fuel economy compared with its rivals" – *U.S. News & World Report.* "There are better options for families – including Nissan's own Rogue and Pathfinder models – but the Murano is an excellent alternative to other premium crossovers if you rank style and value above brand recognition." – *Left Lane News.* By the way, *Lemon-Aid* doesn't consider the Pathfinder to be a better option (see its rating in Appendix 1). **Major redesign:** 2003, 2009, and 2015. The 2016 has a dramatically restyled interior and exterior; not much else. **Highway/city fuel economy:** *AWD:* 8.3/11.2 L/ 100 km. **Best alternatives:** The Buick Enclave, GMC Acadia, Hyundai Santa Fe, Toyota Highlander. On paper, the Jeep Cherokee is a competitor; in real time, it's a quality-challenged disaster. Run, don't walk away.

SAFETY: Child safety seat setup: "Acceptable." **Crashworthiness:** NHTSA: 2012-16 four-star overall crash protection. IIHS: 2012 Murano rated "Good" for frontal offset, side, and head restraint protection. Roof strength considered "Marginal." **Owner-reported safety-related failures:** Sudden unintended acceleration; airbags failed to deploy when needed; passenger-side airbag may be disabled when an average-sized occupant is seated; airbag warning light comes on continually, even after multiple resets by the dealer; vehicle rolls down incline when stopped in traffic; faulty transmission body causes the powertrain to vibrate when cruising; Check Engine light comes on after each fill-up (cap must be carefully resealed); headlights may suddenly shut off; when the headlights are in the Manual position, such as when it is raining; the blind spot warning indicator is just a flicker; the Start/Stop ignition button can be accidently pressed, and this can suddenly shut down the vehicle in traffic; the tilt steering wheel may be unsafe in a crash; steering wheel turns with no effect:

> Adaptive steering failed at below freezing temperature. Lost ability to steer in a curve and hit another car. After, car could not be driven, as steering was totally inoperative. Steering wheel actually turns 360 degrees over and over with no effect on the front wheels. Front wheels actually ended up in a "pigeon toe" alignment and the car could not be towed.

Remote-controlled door locks operate erratically; the rear-view camera image may be fuzzy and distorted:

> I agree with the complaint about the backup camera visibility problem with excessive glare and distortion. My 2006 Murano was somewhat blurry so I was looking forward to my 2013 Murano having a much improved camera similar to my friend's 2013 Honda Accord, but to my dismay my camera visibility is even worse than before, especially in the rain when it is needed the most for safety.

The sunroof may suddenly explode:

> Driving 30 mph [48 km/h] on open asphalt road, no cars ahead of me, no cars behind me, when I heard a loud explosion, similar to a shotgun blast. The moon roof had exploded. Appeared to be an upward explosion. Damage was not caused from any flying objects.

ALERT! The driver's view of the road is seriously limited by the sloped front windshield, sitting position being too far back, and poor hood design (2015 model):

> The inclination of the hood near the wipers reflects the sunlight directly onto the driver eyes and obstructs vision and could lead to fatal front collision and the driver may not asses the distance of braking before the impact in emergency situations.

Pay attention to how the vehicle accelerates; Muranos are known for their "lag and lurch" performance when speeding up:

At low speeds on a slight incline will not accelerate with input to gas pedal rpms will [increase but] vehicle will not respond then suddenly drivetrain will [respond] and engage (a slipping action) vehicle will suddenly launch forward with a slight bang and bucking.

Murano Profile

Used Values ($)	2006	2007	2008	2009	2010	2011	2012	2013	2014
SL/S	7,000	8,500	—	12,500	14,500	16,500	20,000	24,000	26,500
AWD SV	—	—	—	—	—	18,500	22,500	26,000	29,500
SL	9,000	11,000	—	13,500	15,000	20,500	23,500	28,500	31,500
SE/LE	10,500	12,500	—	15,500	16,500	22,000	26,000	31,000	—
Platinum	—	—	—	—	—	—	—	—	35,500
Reliability	★	★	★	☆	☆	☆	☆	☆	☆
Repairs ($$$)	②	②	②	①	①	①	①	①	①
Electrical	★	★	★	☆	☆	☆	☆	☆	☆
Engine (base)	★	★	★	☆	☆	☆	☆	☆	☆
Fit/Finish	★	★	★	★	★	☆	★	★	★
Infotainment	—	—	—	★	★	★	★	★	★
Transmission (auto.)	★	★	★	★	★	★	★	★	★

SECRET WARRANTIES, INTERNAL BULLETINS: 2003-12—Troubleshooting a grinding, knocking noise from the rear on turns. 2009-12—Cold weather hard starting countermeasures. 2009-14—Powertrain transfer assembly oil leaks may require the replacement of the transfer assembly (TSB: #NTB11-017b, March 24, 2014). 2011-12—Intermittent power-steering noises; steering/suspension pull or drift diagnostics; Bluetooth voice recognition issues; and possible reasons for a faulty navigation screen. If the ignition push button doesn't respond, the body control module (BCM) may need recalibrating.

NAVIGATION SYSTEM – SCREEN GOES BLANK

BULLETIN NO.: EL12-010   DATE: MARCH 16, 2012

2010-12 370Z Coupe and Roadster; 2011-12 Murano and Cross Cabriolet; and the 2011-12 Quest.

IF YOU CONFIRM: The customer states the navigation display turns off, goes completely blank, or "blacks out" in DRIVE or REVERSE intermittently, and all functions of the audio system and heater/defroster/air conditioning work normally.

ACTION: Replace the AV display unit (also referred to as monitor or screen).

2014 Nissan Frontier PRO-4X.

RATING: Recommended (2009-16); Above Average (2008); Below Average (2002-07). The few 2016 changes are a standard 6-inch touch screen display on the SV and Runner models, and a standard sunroof and navigation system on the long-wheelbase PRO-4X trucks. **Road performance:** A gutsy, reliable pickup that's compact in name only, the Frontier carries a powerful V6, with towing horsepower to spare; a 4-cylinder engine that's acceptable for light chores; and responsive handling, though steering is a bit slow. **Strong points:** An accommodating interior, especially with the Crew version; plenty of storage in the centre console; and good overall reliability. **Weak points:** Ride is a bit stiff; cabin looks and feels cheap; rear seatroom is tight; and you'll need to eat your Wheaties before attempting to lift the tailgate on earlier models.

Prices and Specs

Prices (Firm): *King S 4x2:* $22,748, *King SV 4x4:* $27,563, *Crew SV 4x4:* $34,148, *PRO-4X:* $30,4588, *Crew PRO-4X:* $35,608 **Freight:** $1,695 **Powertrain (Rear-drive/AWD):** Engines: 2.5L 4-cyl. (152 hp), 4.0L V6 (261 hp); Transmissions: 5-speed man. 6-speed man., 5-speed auto. **Dimensions/capacity:** Passengers: 2/3; Wheelbase: 126 in.; H: 70/L: 206/W: 73 in.; Headroom F/R: 3/3.5 in.; Legroom F/R: 40/27 in.; Cargo volume: 60 cu. ft.; Fuel tank: 80L/regular; Tow limit: 6,100 lb.; Load capacity: 1,160 lb.; Turning circle: 43.3 ft.; Ground clearance: 8.7 in.; Weight: 4,655 lb.

Other opinions: "The Nissan Frontier ranks #4 out of 4 compact pickup trucks. [It] falls short of rivals that have a more spacious back seat, nicer cabin materials and a smoother ride." – *U.S. News & World Report.*" "There's no sugar coating the reality that the Frontier's appeal has slipped in the midsize pickup class. The similarly dated Toyota Tacoma shares many of its faults, but has a more accommodating backseat and a more fuel-efficient 4-cylinder engine, while the GM trucks are far better to drive on paved roads and have much nicer interiors." – *Edmunds.* **Major redesign:** 1998 2005, and 2016. Next year, the Frontier will be redesigned with a new body, altered roofline, higher ground clearance, more cargo space, increased fuel efficiency, and revised styling. A Cummins diesel engine is rumoured to be on the way. **Highway/city fuel economy:** *2.5L man.:* 8.7/10.7 L/100 km. *2.5L auto.:* 9.2/12.6 L/100 km. *4.0L 4x2 auto.:* 9.2/14.2 L/100 km. *4.0L 4x4:* 10.4/13.7 L/100 km. *4.0L 4x4 auto.:* 10.4/14.7 L/100 km. **Best alternatives:** A cheaper 2013 Frontier will give almost everything that's offered with this year's version. Other choices are the Honda Ridgeline and Toyota Tacoma.

SAFETY: Child safety seat setup: "Marginal." **Crashworthiness:** NHTSA: 2011-16 models earned between three and four stars for rollover resistance. IIHS: 2010-15 Frontiers are rated "Good" for overall crash protection, except for head restraints and seats, which qualified for an "Acceptable" rating. 2005-13 models got a "Good" for moderate front overlap crash protection, while 1998-2004s scored "Marginal." The 2010-13 models rated "Good" in side-impact crashes while the 2005-09 models were judged "Marginal." Roof crash protection was "Good" with the 2005-13 models, while head restraints were rated "Acceptable" with the 2010-13s and "Poor" in tests of the 2005-09 Frontier. **Owner-reported safety-related failures:** Passenger-side front airbag is disabled when an average-sized adult occupies the seat; airbags deploy for no reason:

> Myself and one passenger were off-roading in my 2012 Frontier PRO-4X going over a bumpy surface and without warning the side airbags went off! Luckily no one was injured, but we both got quite a scare due to the noise and lack of visibility. There is no damage to the front end nor were we at any degree of an angle. Yes it was bumpy but when you pay for a vehicle that states clearly off road on the side you expect it has the suspension to support the ride.

Delayed acceleration; faulty fuel-level sending unit sensor:

> I went online to nissanhelp.com after performing a search. I came across many others who have experienced the same problem. Apparently it has something to do with the fuel sending unit. A similar problem was found on the 2000–2004 Xterra models and a recall was performed when the vehicle would stop after not getting any fuel.

ALERT! Be wary of the front head restraints on some models:

> The contact owns a 2012 Nissan Frontier. The front driver's seat headrest could not be adjusted. The headrest was positioned downward, causing the driver's head to be forced to look down. The dealer was made aware of the failure and advised the owner that the headrest was designed in that manner and they could not compromise the design of the vehicle.

Frontier Profile

	2006	2007	2008	2009	2010	2011	2012	2013	2014
Used Values ($)									
4x2 XE/S	4,500	5,500	6,000	6,500	7,500	9,500	11,500	14,000	16,000
V6	5,500	6,500	7,000	8,000	9,500	11,000	13,500	16,500	19,000
Crew V6	7,000	8,500	10,000	11,000	12,500	14,500	16,500	18,500	22,000
4x4 SE/SV	8,500	9,500	11,000	12,000	13,000	15,500	18,500	21,500	24,500
Crew PRO-4X	—	—	—	13,500	15,000	17,000	20,000	23,500	26,500
Reliability	☆	☆	☆	☆	☆	☆	☆	☆	☆
Repairs ($$$)	🛈	🛈	🛈	🛈	🛈	🛈	🛈	🛈	🛈
Electrical	☆	☆	☆	☆	☆	☆	☆	☆	☆
Engine (base)	☆	☆	☆	☆	☆	☆	☆	☆	☆
Fit/Finish	☆	☆	☆	☆	☆	☆	☆	☆	☆
Infotainment	—	—	—	☆	☆	☆	☆	☆	☆
Transmission (auto.)	☆	☆	☆	☆	☆	☆	☆	☆	☆

SECRET WARRANTIES, INTERNAL BULLETINS: 2005-11—Correction for a water leak onto passenger-side floor when the AC is on. 2007-12—Front seats bind, won't move fore or aft. Inoperative seat lumbar support. 2008-12—Buzzing wind noise from the A-pillar/mirror area. 2011-12—Oil may leak from the upper end of the engine oil cooler (see the Sentra profile). Steering/suspension drift; sunroof water leak. Rear end clunking, knocking on turns. Brake master cylinder may slowly leak fluid. 2013—Nissan will replace the front air control assembly with a new one, free of charge, under "Campaign 239" outlined in TSB #NTB13-092, issued Oct. 28, 2013. 2013-14—A fuel tank that is hard to fill will likely need a new vent tube that connects the charcoal canister to the fuel tank. This correction should be free under the emissions warranty. 2015—Fix for a sunroof that won't close from the tilt-up position.

SUBARU

An Extraordinary Ordinary Car

Even in these hard economic times, buyers are clamouring for Subaru's AWD Forester, Impreza, and Legacy. And the company doesn't intend to risk its success with any dramatic changes.

WRX and WRX STI

Mechanically both models remain unchanged this year. Nevertheless, WRX Premium and STI Premium models are now available with Subaru's full suite of active safety features; including blind-spot monitoring, lane-change assist, and rear cross-traffic alert. Other changes include larger 6.2-inch touchscreens and voice recognition via the Pandora smartphone app integration. Following its redesign of the Legacy sedan, Subaru isn't making any significant changes on either model for 2016. This said, the automaker will provide upgraded power steering, improved suspension dampers, a new Starlink infotainment system, and additional features to its EyeSight safety package.

Keep in mind, there is nothing remarkable about Subaru's lineup except for the inclusion of AWD in all models. If you don't need the AWD capability, you're wasting your money. Be wary of Subaru's high-performance WRX and STI models. They require special parts and specialized mechanical know-how that may be hard to find in these troubled economic times. Remember, WRX versions are expensive, problematic Imprezas, but when they run right, they'll equal the sporty performance of most of the entry-level Audis and BMWs – cars that cost thousands of dollars more. STIs are just a notch up on the WRX and not worth the extra cash.

Although all Subarus provide full-time AWD capability, studies show that most owners don't need the off-road prowess; only 5% will ever use their Subaru for off-roading. The other 95% just like knowing they have the option of going wherever they please, whenever they please – and they don't seem to care that an AWD burns about 2% more fuel. As one retired Quebec mechanic told me, "AWD simply means that you will get stuck deeper, further from home. It's no replacement for common sense."

FORESTER/IMPREZA/WRX, STI ★★★★★/★★★★★★/★★★

RATING: *Forester and Impreza:* Recommended (2001-16). *WRX and STI:* Average for all years. Subaru redesigned its 2015 Forester crossover SUV, adding cleaner styling, a roomier and better-appointed interior, and increased fuel economy; the 2016 returns with no significant changes and a modest price increase. Choose the base Forester if you want the most cargo space; models with the panoramic sunroof have less room due to the lower roof height. The most affordable version is the Forester 2.5i, fitted with the standard 6-speed manual transmission. Essentially, Forester is a wagon/sport-utility crossover that uses the Legacy Outback's 2.5L engine or an optional turbocharged version of the same powerplant. Road manners are more subdued, and its engine provides plenty of power and torque for off-roading. Both "Boxer" 4-cylinder engines are competitive in terms of power and fuel economy, despite being coupled to an outmoded 4-speed automatic transmission. The Impreza is essentially a shorter Legacy with additional convenience features. It comes as a four-door sedan, a wagon, and an Outback Sport wagon, all powered by a 173 hp 2.5L flat-four engine or a 224 hp turbocharged 2.5L. The rally-inspired WRX STI models have a more powerful turbocharged engine (a 305 hp 2.5L variant), lots of standard performance features, sport suspension, an aluminum hood with functional scoop, and higher quality instruments, controls, trim, and seats. **Road performance:** Good acceleration with the base 2.5L engine; however, the WRX STI and STI Limited models have even more powerful 305 hp engines. But with that power comes complexity – a complexity that requires good access to parts and servicing. *Forester:* Acceptable acceleration without any torque steer; the turbocharged engine is more robust, but fuel consumption increases and premium fuel is required; the 4-speed transmission is Flintstone-dated; 6-speed is required; competent, agile, and secure handling; and gives one of the smoothest rides in its class over good roads; a rough ride over broken pavement. *Impreza:* Not impressive performance. The base Impreza has to split its horsepower between all four wheels. (Yawn.) Some body roll when cornering, but the suspension smoothes things out nicely; the outdated 4-speed automatic transmission shifts roughly and wastes fuel, making the new CVT a must-have, though it augments engine noise; lots of road noise, too. *WRX and STI:* Quick acceleration with some turbo lag; solid handling; precise and responsive transmission, especially with the optional short-throw shifter; easy riding over bumps; good steering feedback; and some turbo whine at full throttle. **Strong points:** Full-time AWD; a roomy cabin; spacious rear seating; lots of storage space with the wagons; a nice control layout; good all-around visibility; large windows; and well placed mirrors. **Weak points:** Excessive oil consumption (*www.edmunds.com/subaru/forester/2015/suv/review/*):

> At around 4000 miles with my 2015 Forester, I started to notice excessive oil consumption. Checked with Subaru National, was given a case number, and was instructed to have the local dealer in Bedford, Ohio, do an oil consumption test. The service managers statement, "One-third of a quart in 1200 miles is acceptable." If that answer sounds scripted, it was. Plus he talked down to me like I was a third grader. So that means that by the time your first scheduled synthetic oil change is due, you have blown through two quarts. That is not acceptable, that is frightening. There are lots of negative comments online about excessive oil consumption with these engines.

CVT transmission a poor performer:

> My 2015 with the change to CVT was bad, really bad. Bucking/surging/hesitating since day one and got worse. Dealer/mechanic saying that it needs to warm up is just wrong. It would never quit bucking, cold, hot or any other time.

Problematic entry and exit; the Bluetooth screen constantly "freezes"; tiny backup camera display washed out in sunlight; short seats require additional lumbar bolstering for better lateral support and more height; hatchbacks have more wind and road noise; high-mounted cabin audio controls are hard to reach; the cargo area needs a light; Impreza interior materials look and feel cheap; slow moving power liftgate; heated seats are slow to warm; and the heater works poorly when the outside temperature is below 40 degrees farenheit:

> I purchased a new 2015 Subaru Forester. The interior windows ice over. Have to continually switch from 100% defrost to 100% side windows to be able to see out one or the other. If anyone is riding in the back seat, the rear side windows are never clear. This poor visibility is a safety hazard. In addition, the car is extremely cold inside, especially in the foot well. My feet are numb from the cold as the heater is blowing cold air on your feet and legs. Even when no air is directed to the foot well, there is a continual cold draft.

WRX and STI bucket seats also need more lumbar support; fuel pump failures; fuel economy much less than advertised; and both cars require premium fuel.

Prices and Specs

Prices (Forester: Firm; Impreza: Firm): *Forester 2.5i:* $25,995, *Convenience Package:* $28,795, *Convenience with PZEV:* $29,495, *Touring Package:* $29,995, *Limited Package:* $34,595, *XT Limited:* $36,795; *Impreza 2.0i:* $19,995, *5d:* $20,895, *Touring Package 5d:* $22,595, *Sport Package:* $23,895, *5d:* $24,795, *Limited Package:* $26,895, *Limited Package 5d:* $27,795; *WRX Sedan:* $29,995, *Sport Package:* $32,795, *STI:* $40,795 **Freight:** $1,675 **Powertrain (AWD):** Engines: *Forester:* 2.5iL 4-cyl. (170 hp), 2.0L 4-cyl. Turbo (250 hp), 2.5L 4-cyl. Turbo (224 hp) and (250 hp with the 2014 model); *Impreza:* 2.0L 4-cyl. (148 hp); *WRX:* 2.5L 4-cyl. Turbo (270 hp); *WRX STI:* 2.5L 4-cyl. Turbo (305 hp); Transmissions: 6-speed man., CVT **Dimensions/capacity:** *Forester:* Passengers: 2/3; Wheelbase: 103 in.; H: 66/L: 180/W: 70 in.; Headroom F/R: 6.5/6.5 in.; Legroom F/R: 41/29.5 in.; Cargo volume: 35.5 cu. ft.; Fuel tank: 64L/regular/premium; Tow limit: 2,400 lb.; Load capacity: 900 lb.; Turning circle: 38 ft.; Ground clearance: 8.9 in.; Weight: 3,064-3,373 lb. *Impreza:* Passengers: 2/3; Wheelbase: 104.1 in.; H: 57.7/L: 180.3/W: 68.5 in.; Headroom F/R: 6/3.5 in.; Legroom F/R: 43.5/35.4 in.; Cargo volume: 12 cu. ft.; Fuel tank: 64L/regular/premium; Tow limit: Not recommended; Load capacity: 900 lb., *WRX, STI:* 850 lb.; Turning circle: 37 ft.; Ground clearance: 6.1 in.; Weight: 2,910-3,384 lb.

Other opinions: "The Forester ranks #9 out of 27 affordable compact SUVs, while the Impreza is #11 out of 20 affordable compacts. Reviewers praise the 2015 Subaru Forester for its ample cargo space, comfortable rear-seat legroom, solid fuel economy and standard AWD ... Critics say the Impreza needs more punch at highway speeds, but they appreciate the standard AWD and ample seating." – *U.S. News & World Report*. "Elevated stadium-type rear seating enhances thigh support and affords a better view, while the Forester's rear legroom is only about an inch shy of what you'll find in a Mercedes-Benz S-Class sedan ... a huge cargo hold offers nearly 4 more cubic feet than the Honda CR-V." – *Edmunds*. **Major redesign:** *Forester:* 1998, 2003, 2009, and 2014; *Impreza:* 1993, 2000, 2007, and 2011. **Highway/city fuel economy:** *Forester:* 7.4/9.9 L/100 km. Auto.: 7.5/9.9 L/100 km. *Impreza:* 5.9/8.3 L/100 km. Auto.: 5.5/7.5 L/100 km. *WRX:* 8.0/11.1 L/100 km. *STI:* 8.8/12.6 L/100 km. **Best alternatives:** If you don't really need a 4x4, there are some front-drives worth considering, like the Hyundai Elantra, Mazda6, and Toyota Corolla or Matrix.

SAFETY: Child safety seat setup: *Forester, Impreza*: "Marginal." Crashworthiness: Excellent crash scores. NHTSA: *Forester:* 2011-15 versions earned four stars in all NHTSA crash scenarios; IIHS: "Moderate" overlap frontal, small overlap, side impact, and roof strength crash tests of 1999-2015 models, confirmed the "Good" rating. 2006-14 Foresters gave a "Good" performance in head restraint protection, as well. *Impreza:* The 2013-16s earned a five-star overall rating; IIHS scores were identical to the Forester's rating. *WRX and STI:* Tested for rollover resistance only, but they each got five stars. Owner-reported safety-related failures: *Forester:* Sudden, unintended acceleration while the vehicle was cruising on the highway; driver-side mirror and bracket detached and swung around wildly; rear-view mirror also falls off; and many reports of windshield cracks without any impact on recent Foresters and Imprezas:

> My 2015 Impreza windshield cracked when the defroster was turned on with temperature outside about 20F. We noticed a crack starting from the right bottom of the windshield (near the passenger side).

Cruise control malfunctions; smell of raw fuel permeates the cabin; front door corners can easily cut one's head when opened, due to their design. *Impreza:* WRX models have had fewer owner complaints (mostly paint, trim, and body hardware) than the STI, which has been afflicted with similar fit and finish deficiencies, plus engine, exhaust, and fuel system complaints. Also, reports of sudden, unintended acceleration:

> While driving approximately 15 mph [24 km/h] on normal road conditions, there was sudden, aggressive, and forceful acceleration. The driver immediately depressed the brake pedal, but there was no response. The driver placed the gear shifter into Park, but the vehicle failed to slow down. The vehicle crashed into a brick wall. The failure occurred without warning. The police and ambulance were called to the scene and a police report was filed. The driver sustained severe back injuries. The vehicle was completely destroyed.

When accelerating, some model years have a serious shift lag, then the vehicle surges ahead; defective engine had to be replaced; head restraints push head forward at an uncomfortable angle, causing neck strain and backache; and the moonroof system cavity allows debris and small animals to enter between the headliner and interior walls – the perfect place for fungi and mould to incubate.

ALERT! Before investing big bucks in Subaru's latest electronic safety gadgets, check out how they work. Some people aren't impressed by the nonstop beeping from features like the lane departure warning and abrupt slowdowns from Eyesight when traffic approaches. Even worse, the backup camera may be useless if you wear polarized sunglasses:

The electronic screen on the 2015 Subaru Forester that includes the back-up display reflects a solid black bar down the middle if you are wearing polarized sunglasses. I've almost backed over walkers in parking lots who were in the obscured area of the screen because of this. I checked at the dealer, and other 2015 Foresters have the same problem, but the Outback does not. Since I first noticed the problem I have driven a number of cars, including Toyotas and BMWs that do not have the problem. Subaru's suggested solution is that I don't wear polarized sunglasses. I wear corrective lenses, and it is virtually impossible to buy corrective sunglasses that aren't polarized.

The passenger side airbag is frequently disabled for some of the most obscure reasons:

This Subaru occupant detection system in my 2014 Forester is defective. It does not detect my wife and the passenger airbag does not turn on. We have been told by Subaru that they have recently changed to an "electrostatic capacitance sensor" to replace the previous "weight sensor." My wife needs to sit on a seat cushion as the seats are too hard for her medical condition. Subaru told us the seat cushion will not allow the ODS to verify a person is sitting in the seat and will not turn on the passenger airbag. I also discovered that wet clothing (wet raincoat) will also defeat the sensor and the airbag will not be turned on. This is totally unacceptable and dangerous to all passengers. The only suggestion from Subaru was for my wife to sit in the back seat.

2014 Subaru Forester 2.5i.

Forester/Impreza/WRX, STI Profile

	2006	2007	2008	2009	2010	2011	2012	2013	2014
Used Values ($)									
Forester 2.5X/i	6,000	7,500	9,000	10,000	12,000	13,500	16,500	19,500	21,500
2.5XT Touring	—	—	—	11,500	13,500	15,500	18,500	21,500	25,000
2.5XT/X LTD	9,000	—	—	13,000	15,500	17,500	20,500	24,000	27,500
Impreza	5,000	6,000	7,000	8,000	10,000	9,500	11,000	13,000	16,000
Touring	—	—	—	—	—	—	12,500	14,500	17,000
LTD	—	—	—	—	11,500	13,000	15,500	17,500	20,500
Wagon	5,500	—	—	—	—	11,000	13,000	14,500	17,500
WRX Sedan	7,500	8,500	9,500	11,500	14,000	17,500	20,000	23,000	26,500
WRX Wagon	8,000	—	—	—	—	19,500	21,500	25,000	28,000
STI Sedan/Wagon	13,000	9,500	12,000	—	—	22,000	24,500	29,000	32,000

Forester

	2006	2007	2008	2009	2010	2011	2012	2013	2014
Reliability	★	★	★	★	★	★	★	★	★
Repairs ($$$)	💰	💰	💰	💰	💰	💰	💰	💰	💰
Electrical	★	★	★	★	★	★	★	★	★
Engine (base)	★	★	★	★	★	★	★	★	★
Fit/Finish	★	★	★	★	★	★	★	★	★
Infotainment	—	—	—	★	★	★	★	★	★
Transmission (auto.)	★	★	★	★	★	★	★	★	★

Impreza

	2006	2007	2008	2009	2010	2011	2012	2013	2014
Reliability	★	★	★	★	★	★	★	★	★
Repairs ($$$)	💰	💰	💰	💰	💰	💰	💰	💰	💰
Electrical	★	★	★	★	★	★	★	★	★
Engine (base)	★	★	★	★	★	★	★	★	★
Fit/Finish	★	★	★	★	★	★	★	★	★
Infotainment	—	—	—	★	★	★	★	★	★
Transmission (auto.)	★	★	★	★	★	★	★	★	★

SECRET WARRANTIES, INTERNAL BULLETINS: 2011-12—*Forester:* TCM computer reboot to cure harsh shifting. TSB #02-113-11R, published Jan. 26, 2011, addresses cold-start engine noise and suggests that the timing chain tensioner be changed.

Excessive oil consumption, white exhaust smoke. **2011-12**—Loose instrument panel vents. **2011-14**—TSB #02-141-13R outlines the design change to the rubber sealing cap oil pressure switch to prevent false low oil alerts. **2014**—TSB #02-152-14R, issued April 22, 2014, and revised June 12, 2014, announces the availability of free revised valve train components developed to reduce a tapping sound (sometimes described as "a sewing machine type" sound) which may be heard coming from the left-hand side of the engine when the engine is warm. The changes consist of:

- Design change to the valve rockers
- Camshaft profile change
- 1. .65mm longer intake and 2.45mm longer exhaust valve stem lengths

If a customer's concern over a tapping sound from the B2 cylinder head is confirmed, the dealer must replace the intake and exhaust camshafts, the four intake valves, four exhaust valves, and all eight rockers. Repair tips for an inoperative liftgate. Details on how to silence a rattling sound from the sunroof air deflector while driving with the roof panel closed. Some changes made to the oil level switch assembly designed to improve its accuracy. **2014-15**—Hard starts and extended cranking time can be correted by re-calibrating the electronic control module (ECM). The rear door power window regulator/motor assembly gearing has been changed to prevent the mechanism from binding. *Impreza:* **2008-14**—Replacement of faulty air intake duct that leaks turbo boost pressure, cuts power, and increases engine noise. **2012-13**—Troubleshooting premature wear of rings and higher oil consumption, Camshaft position sensor clearance could be out of specification, causing the Check Engine light to come on. Loose instrument panel vents. Highway speed, vibration, harshness, and noise diagnostic and correction tips.

LEGACY/OUTBACK ★★★★/★★★

RATING: *Legacy:* Above Average (2005-16); Average (2001-04). Given more info-tainment and safety features for 2016, this is one of the most fuel-efficient mid-size AWD sedans available in North America for drivers who want to move up in size, comfort, and features. Available as a four-door sedan or five-door wagon, the Legacy is cleanly and conventionally styled. Furthermore, although it seems to have similar factory-related defects as its Subaru cousins, they are less frequent in NHTSA postings. *Outback:* Average (2001-16). The car's greater number of safety complaints (related almost entirely to hesitation and stalling) shows sloppy assembly and the use of subpar components. Both cars are distinguished by their standard full-time AWD drivetrain. This AWD feature handles difficult terrain without the fuel penalty or clumsiness of many truck-based SUVs. Without it, the Outback would be just a raised wagon variant that's well equipped but outclassed by most of the import competition. Road performance: A refined and relatively reliable AWD system; a well-balanced 6-cylinder engine; precise, responsive handling, and a comfortable ride; the GT handles best and has power to spare. On the downside, it's the same old "lurch and lag" acceleration; abrupt throttle response when parking; crosswinds require constant steering correction; excessive engine and road noise; the base 2.5L engine remains a sluggish, noisy performer and the more powerful GT version is a fuel hog and available only with a manual gearbox. If you don't mind paying the fuel penalty, the 6-cylinder engine is quicker and quieter. *Outback:* This rugged SUV has all of the above and adds higher ground clearance. Handling degrades with extreme off-road use. **Strong points:** Interior materials and fit and finish have been substantially upgraded (except for crack-prone windshields), and there's a spacious interior, with lots of cargo room (innovative under-floor, rear-car cargo storage area). *Outback:* An even roomier interior. **Weak points:** Oil-burning engines continue to be a problem with almost all 2011-15 Subaru models. Spontaneous windshield/sunroof cracks appear for no reason. Replacement windshields are dealer-dependent and expensive ($700) due to the EyeSight feature:

> When getting into the car in the afternoon, noticed a huge crack on the windshield starting between the wiper blades and going to the top of the windshield. There was no impact to have caused this. The car was parked in the open on a day where temperatures were mild. Looks like there are quite a few complaints in the Subaru forums complaining about the Subaru Legacy and Outback which share the same platform. The issues discussed matches my specific case.

Fuel filler lid often sticks; limited rear access; front seats need more padding; interior garnishes look and feel cheap; the V6 engine requires premium fuel; and the radio display "freezes" until vehicle is re-started.

> Subarus are very dealer-dependent for parts and servicing, resulting in long delays for back-ordered parts.

Prices and Specs

Prices (Firm): *Legacy 2.5i:* $27,995, *Touring:* $31,195, *Limited Package:* $35,995, *3.6R Touring:* $37,195, *Limited with Eyesight Option:* $40,195; *Outback 2.5i:* $27,995, *PZEV:* $29,995, *Touring Package:* $31,195, *Limited Package:* $35,995, *3.6R Touring Package:* $37,195, *3.6R Limited:* $34,495 **Freight:** $1,675 **Powertrain (AWD):** Engines: 2.5L 4-cyl. (173 hp), 2.5L 4-cyl.; Turbo (265 hp) 3.6L V6 (256 hp); Transmissions: 5-speed man., 6-speed man., 5-speed auto. CVT **Dimensions/capacity:** *Legacy:* Passengers: 2/3; Wheelbase: 108.2 in.; H: 59.2/L: 186/W: 72 in.; Headroom F/R: 6/3 in.; Legroom F/R: 43/30 in.; Cargo volume: 15 cu. ft.; Fuel tank: 70L/regular/premium; Tow limit: 1,000 lb.; Load capacity: 850 lb.; Turning circle: 36.8 ft.; Ground clearance: 5.9 in.; Weight: 3,273-3,522 lb. *Outback:* Passengers: 2/3; Wheelbase: 1,078 in.; H: 65.7/L: 188.1/W: 71.6 in.; Headroom F/R: 4/6 in.; Legroom F/R: 39.5/29 in.; Cargo volume: 36.5 cu. ft.; Fuel tank: 70L/regular; Tow limit: 2,700 lb.; Load capacity: 900 lb.; Turning circle: 39 ft.; Ground clearance: 8.7 in.; Weight: 3,540 lb.

Other opinions: "The 2016 Subaru Outback ranks #2 out of 10 wagons. Outback impresses critics with its outstanding AWD traction and substantial passenger and cargo space." – *U.S. News & World Report.* "Snow & water entering the top of my 2015 Legacy's engine bay, drenching/flooding over electrical & mechanical components and causing the toxic burning smell from the burn off of de-icing chemicals/salts used on road surfaces entering the engine bay due to a lack of weather stripping." – *safercar.gov.* **Major redesign:** 2000, 2005, 2010, and 2015. **Highway/city fuel economy:** *Legacy 2.5:* 7.4/10.6 L/100 km. *Auto.:* 6.5/9.2 L/100 km. *GT:* 8.0/11.5 L/100 km. *3.6R:* 8.2/11.8 L/100 km. *Outback 2.5:* 7.4/10.6 L/100 km. *Auto.:* 6.9/9.5 L/100 km. *3.6:* 8.2/11.8 L/100 km. Fuel economy trails rivals like the Chevrolet Malibu, Ford Fusion, and Toyota Camry. **Best alternatives:** The Honda CR-V, Hyundai Tucson or Santa Fe, and Toyota RAV4.

SAFETY: **Child safety seat setup:** *Legacy, Outback*: Untested, "Marginal." **Crashworthiness:** NHTSA: Four- and five-star crashworthiness scores for 2003-16 Legacys. IIHS: 2015 Legacy gets the top, "Good," rating for overall crashworthiness. Small overlap tests results were "Acceptable" on the 2013-14 models. Side impact tests gave mixed results: "Good" for 2006-14 models. **Owner-reported safety-related failures:** *Legacy:* Sudden, unintended acceleration when in Park:

> The vehicle was in Park when it accelerated in Reverse through a yard, crashing into a retaining wall.

Long delay to get up to speed when accelerating; engine may default to very low idle, almost to the point of stalling out; cruise control and brake failures; steering shimmy and wobbles, and car sways from right to left (partially corrected by replacing the steering-column dampening spring and force-balancing the tires); excessive steering wheel, clutch, and brake vibration; airbag warning light comes on for no reason; and driver-side floor mats may "creep" toward the accelerator pedal. The location of the electronic brake button makes it easy to engage the brake inadvertently. EyeSight safety feature often malfunctions. *Outback:* Sudden, unintended downshifting or accelerating when using paddles:

> Situation: Travelling at 60 mph [97 km/h] up a steep hill in left passing lane. Cars following close, and cars in the right lane. For the first time (new car) I used the downshift paddle on the left side of the steering wheel to downshift to accelerate. I tapped it to downshift one gear. It instantly dropped to First gear. The engine rpms went to red line or above. The car decelerated dramatically, and I was tossed forward. I attempted to upshift using the right paddle but there was no response, and the car remained in First gear. The car behind nearly hit me. The only useful control that I had was the steering wheel (brakes or accelerator useless). Further, I assumed the brake lights were not lit. Due to the alertness of the driver behind and the drivers to my right as I slowed dramatically and got off the highway to the right shoulder, a serious accident was avoided.

• • •

Ever since purchasing the 2012 Outback we have had a serious issue when using the paddle shifters to slow down for a stop. When the tach slows to about 1100 rpm in First or Second gear the engine then accelerates to up to 2500 rpm, slowing down and then speeding up again then repeating the cycle over even if you apply the brakes. Sometimes it would just run at 2500 rpm until you braked to a stop.

Faulty cruise control/traction control:

Vehicle stopped cruise control & flashed Brakes & No Traction Control unexpectedly. Came close to a wreck shutting the vehicle down on the side of the road hitting various tire recaps & debris on the side of the road. Not told that this is a regular occurrence with this vehicle.

Passenger-side airbag may suddenly disable itself while vehicle is underway:

Drove the car for approximately 45 minutes, made a quick stop with car turned off, when restarting car, airbag warning light came on and also the passenger side airbag light said it was off even though there was an adult passenger on that side of the car. Light stayed on even after restarting car, readjusting seat belts, etc. Drove with warning light on for about an hour.

Transmission slipped from Neutral to Drive:

I was setting the homelink mirror on my car to recognize a particular garage door opener. The mirror is powered so I needed to leave the car idling. I put the car in Neutral and began the programming process. The last step in the process is to engage the garage door opener from the motor head. To prepare to do this, I [exited] the car and moved on foot into the garage to look for a step ladder. As I was searching for a step ladder and after a period of at least one full minute, the automatic transmission slipped into "Drive" at which point the unoccupied car drove into the garage and hit the rear wall.

Chronic hesitation, stalling; steering shimmy, and wobble. Excessive wander over the roadway:

When driving on the highway the vehicle exhibits very poor straight line stability. Vehicle wanders within the lane and requires excessive steering wheel correction to maintain straight direction. Vehicle 500 miles [800 km] on it (350 driven by owner) but is now sitting in driveway for fear of personal safety if emergency maneuver is necessary on the highway.

ALERT! During the test drive, remember that owners say the head restraints force the driver's head into a painful and unsafe chin-to-chest position (worse for short drivers), a problem plaguing all Subarus for several years. Running lights may not illuminate high or far enough, and headlights have a similar handicap. Owners have to pay up to $50 twice per year to have the federally mandated tire-pressure monitoring system reset when they change tires in the spring and fall.

Legacy/Outback Profile

	2006	2007	2008	2009	2010	2011	2012	2013	2014
Used Values ($)									
Legacy Sedan	5,500	6,500	7,000	8,000	9,500	11,500	13,500	16,000	18,500
LTD	6,500	8,000	9,000	10,500	12,000	15,500	18,500	22,000	24,000
Outback	6,000	7,000	8,500	10,500	11,500	15,000	18,000	20,500	23,000
LTD	8,000	9,500	11,500	13,000	15,000	18,500	24,000	28,500	33,000
Reliability	☆	☆	☆	☆	☆	☆	☆	☆	☆
Repairs ($$$)	💰	💰	💰	💰	💰	💰	💰	💰	💰
Electrical	☆	☆	☆	☆	☆	☆	☆	☆	☆
Engine (base)	☆	☆	☆	☆	☆	☆	☆	☆	☆
Fit/Finish	☆	☆	☆	☆	☆	☆	☆	☆	☆
Infotainment	—	—	—	☆	☆	☆	☆	☆	☆
Transmission (auto.)	☆	☆	☆	☆	☆	☆	☆	☆	☆

SECRET WARRANTIES, INTERNAL BULLETINS: 2005-12—Replacement of the air intake duct that leaks turbo boost pressure, cuts power, and increases engine noise. 2005-14—Remedy for customer concerns of a "Click," "Pop," or "Creak" sound heard coming from either the left or right side around the rear corners of the cowl/engine compartment/base of "A" pillar area. 2010-13—Water leaks from map light area. 2013-14—Revised valve train parts to reduce a warm engine tapping sound from the left cylinder head. Engine chirp, squeak, or squeal (replace the existing V-belt (serpentine drive/accessory belt) with the upgraded version (Part No: #809221160). Sunroof doesn't open properly. 2015—Wind noise from the front door glass and rear door area. Whistling from the rear seat console air vents and side vents. Poor fuel door fit.

SUZUKI

The Suzuki SX4 (above) rides well, handles well, and crashes — not so well. See Appendix I.

Help! Toyota has been hijacked by pirates!
(That's why their trucks are rust-cankered, their brakes
fail, and their cars accelerate on their own, right?)

When Good Cars Go Bad

A quick glance at NHTSA's 2010 safety defects complaint log shows that the Camry, Corolla, and Prius are runaway bestsellers – "runaway" in the sense that you may find yourself an unwilling hostage in a car careening out of control with a stuck accelerator, no brakes, and limited steering.

When running properly, though, Toyotas do hold up very well over the years, are especially forgiving of owner neglect, and cost very little to service at independent garages.

But as far as safety is concerned, Toyota's, "Oh what a feeling" jingle comes to mind – indeed, a "feeling" of fear and betrayal. I have recommended Toyota models since the early '70s, when the company first came to Canada. Their vehicles were reliable and cheap (though rust-prone), and most disputed warranty claims were paid without forcing customers to file small claims court lawsuits.

All this came to an end over a decade ago when bean-counters took over the company and adopted the mantra that profit and market share trump quality and fair prices.

In Canada, Toyota and its dealers subsequently used the Toyota Access program to keep retail prices artificially high. *Lemon-Aid* made a formal complaint to Ottawa, alleging Toyota price-fixing, and the next thing we knew, Toyota settled and agreed to give $2 million to a Canadian charity – without admitting guilt. Slick, eh? Price-fixing charges were never filed and Toyota prices have remained firm.

Fast-forward to Toyota's sudden-acceleration woes over the past two years. Although NHTSA-logged complaints confirm that Toyota reps stonewalled thousands of Toyota car and truck owners, these same Toyota executives, claims managers, and lawyers said they were unaware that the vehicles would suddenly accelerate out of control. Toyota's president cried as he testified before the U.S. Congress in 2010 when confronted with complaint records. Shortly thereafter, Toyota recalled almost its entire lineup to change floor carpets and throttles and paid almost $50 million U.S. in fines. In December 2012 another $1.6 billion was offered to Toyota owners in the States in a class action settlement.

Again, there was no admission of guilt, nor any confirmation by Toyota that its own internal service bulletins (published in *Lemon-Aid*) showed that 2002 and 2003 Camrys can suddenly accelerate due to defective computer modules.

After the congressional hearings, the U.S. government fined Toyota $49 million for dragging its feet in implementing the above recalls. In the meantime, owners swear that electronic component failures are the real culprit and Toyota still stonewalls their pleas. Toyota maintains that the problem isn't electronic-based, but just in case it's mistaken, a brake override feature has been added on all models. European vehicles have had this safety device as a standard feature for years. The problem is that some motorists driving Toyotas with the override feature added, say their cars still suddenly accelerate without warning.

Toyota's Quality Decline

Ten years ago *Lemon-Aid* warned readers that Toyota quality was declining. Reports of "runaway" cars were coming in through NHTSA owner complaint Internet postings and brakes failures were rampant. We immediately lowered our ratings on many Toyota models.

In the late '90s, Toyota's reputation took a battering when angry owners refused to pay $6,000-$9,000 to repair the sludged-up engines used on many Toyota and Lexus models. After first blaming the problem on poor owner maintenance, the automaker relented and quietly settled most claims.

One would think Toyota had learned to "fess up" when it "messed up," but shortly thereafter, its handling of hundreds of sudden, unitended acceleration complaints and lawsuits proved the company preferred to stonewall rather than recall. When caught in the television lights at a Congressional hearing, it made its defense with a mixture of lying, denying, and crying.

But Toyota's crocodile tears cannot erase the memory of Mark Saylor, a California Highway Patrol officer who was loaned a Lexus ES350 by a San Diego dealer. The Lexus accelerated, flipped, and burst into flames. As the car careened out of control, the occupants dialed 911, and on the tape you can hear them screaming in terror. The dispatcher asks their location, and Lastrella, Saylor's brother-in-law, is heard asking someone in the car where they are. He exclaims, "We're going

120 [mph]! Mission Gorge! We're in trouble – we can't – there's no brakes, Mission Gorge … end freeway half mile."

The dispatcher asks if they can turn the car off. Lastrella doesn't answer and says repeatedly, "We are now approaching the intersection, we're approaching the intersection, we're approaching the intersection."

The last sounds heard on the tape are someone saying, "Hold on and"pray." Lastrella says, "Oh shoot … oh … oh." Then a woman screams.

Saylor, 45, his wife, their 13-year-old daughter, and Lastrella died in the crash on August 28, 2009.

Toyota blamed the driver, denied knowledge of similar incidents reported by other Toyota and Lexus owners, and refused to support its own dealer, who claimed Toyota electronics were to blame for the crash. (The dealer was sued separately and in turn sued Toyota.)

Bowing to public pressure, the company finally paid $10 million to the officer's estate on February 25, 2011, in an out-of-court settlement. As with so many other Toyota settlements, the automaker asked that a gag order be issued to prevent disclosure of the settlement sum. This was refused (*John Saylor v. Toyota Motor Corp.*, 37-2010-00086718, California Superior Court, San Diego County).

But the story doesn't end there.

Toyota rejected a petition from Phillip Pretty, the owner of a Ford Explorer that was hit by the above-mentioned, out-of-control Lexus speeding behind him at more than 160 km/h. Pretty was hospitalized with a concussion and injuries to a shoulder and knee. Toyota denied all responsibility – in the same accident it had paid $10 million a few months earlier to settle.

Lemon-Aid is skeptical of Toyota's claim that sudden acceleration is no longer a problem with its vehicles. There are too many complaints coming from owners of recalled models and service bulletins that point to an electronic failure in the throttle system still apparently affecting its latest models.

"Lag and Lurch"

Toyota has systematically rejected owner complaints over dangerously defective drivetrains that possibly affect all of its 1999-2014 lineup. A look at NHTSA's safety complaint database shows a ton of complaints alleging these vehicles have an electronic module glitch that causes a lag and lurch when accelerating, decelerating, or turning.

Toyota knows that if it confirms the defect is electronic in nature, the company re-opens the sudden acceleration polemic and could be forced to replace electronic control modules on millions of vehicles – modules that cost far more than a floormat anchor.

A perusal of *Lemon-Aid* readers' letters and e-mails, as well as NHTSA reports, shows that other recent-model Toyotas have been plagued by engineering mistakes that put occupants' lives in jeopardy. These include cars that pull to one side or the other, requiring constant steering corrections; Corollas that wander all over the road; Prius hybrids that temporarily lose braking ability; and trucks with rear ends that bounce uncontrollably over even the smoothest roadways. Other safety failures include engine and transmission malfunctions; fuel spewing out of cracked gas tanks; gauge lights that can't be seen in daylight; and electrical system glitches that can transform a sliding power door into a guillotine.

$2000 Dashboard Repairs

After a pummeling from owner complaints mounting class-action lawsuits, Toyota finally agreed this year to extend the warranty on 4.5 million vehicles with sticky, cracked, and melted dashboards. The company acted in the face of investigative journalists, a barrage of consumer complaints, and numerous class-action lawsuits alleging that the company's dashboards were "biodegradable."

In light of the warranty extensions, listed below, owners can replace their dashboards free of charge at Toyota and Lexus dealerships. For owners who already paid out-of-pocket to replace their dashboards, Toyota will pay up to $1,500 per dashboard. The extended warranty only applies to dashboards that were damaged by heat and humidity. If the dealers find that the dashboards were damaged by other means, the extended warranty won't apply, unless an independent expert refutes Toyota's appraisal.

All owners of the affected vehicles should have received letters from Toyota in the mail in May of 2015. If no letter was received, contact your local dealer, since only Toyota and Lexus dealers are authorized to do the work.

Affected Vehicles with Defective Dashboards

Toyota	Lexus
Toyota 4Runner (model years 2003-05)	Lexus Es 350 (model years 2007-08)
Toyota Avalon (model years 2005-10)	Lexus GX 470 (model years 2003-08)
Toyota Camry (model years 2007-11)	Lexus IS 250.350 (model years 2006-08)
Toyota Sienna (model years 2004-10)	Lexus LS 460 (model year 2007)
Toyota Solara (model years 2004-08)	Lexus RX 330 (model years 2004-06)
	Lexus RX 350 (model years 200-09)
	Lexus RH 400h (model years 2005-08)

YARIS ★★

RATING: Below Average (2016). The untested Scion iA replaces the Yaris for 2016. Yaris is a form-over-function econobox commuter, where a low price trumps style and driving pleasure. Not a sporty performer by any stretch. Positioned just below the Corolla, the Yaris manages to offer about the same amount of passenger space, thanks to a tall roof, low floor height, and upright seating position. 2015 versions have a more modern look with large windows, and additional legroom. It also has a revised front end, a retuned suspension, and a quieter, roomier interior. A complete redesign for the 2018 or 2019 model year is scheduled. Road performance: Yaris feels underpowered, especially when equipped with the automatic transmission, which often doesn't downshift quickly or smoothly. A tall profile and light weight make the car vulnerable to side-wind buffeting and the base tires provide poor traction in wet conditions. Owners say the car's interior layout makes it hard to find a comfortable driving position. Still, the Yaris passes over uneven terrain with less jarring movements than do other mini-compacts, and is quite nimble when cornering. Better road feel with SE models, thanks to electric power steering. Strong points: Lots of interior space up front; a nice array of storage areas, including a huge trunk and standard 60/40 split-folding rear seats; well-designed instruments and controls don't look as cheap as with earlier models; easy rear access; surprisingly quiet for a small car; and excellent visibility fore and aft. Weak points: Not overly generous with standard features. Interior ergonomics are subpar (an awkward seating position and poorly-placed centre gauges); interior materials look and feel cheap; and rear seating is cramped. There's also excessive torque steer (sudden pulling to one side when accelerating); some wind noise from the base of the windshield; the steering wheel is mounted too far away for some drivers; and gas mileage doesn't match the competition.

Prices and Specs

Price (Soft): *Hatchback CE 3DR.:* $14,595, *Auto:* $15,595, *LE 5DR.:* $16,015, *Auto:* $17,015, *SE 5DR.:* $17,715, *Auto.:* $18,715. The 2016 Scion iA estimated base price is $16,000 **Freight:** $1,660 **Powertrain (Front-drive):** Engine: 1.5L 4-cyl. (106 hp); Transmissions: 5-speed man., 4-speed auto. **Dimensions/capacity:** Passengers: 2/3; Wheelbase: 100.4 in.; H: 57.5/L: 169.3/W: 66.7 in.; Headroom F/R: 3.5/1.5 in.; Legroom F/R: 40.5/27 in.; Cargo volume: 13.7 cu. ft.; Fuel tank: 42L/regular; Tow limit: 700 lb.; Load capacity: 845 lb.; Turning circle: 30.8 ft.; Ground clearance: 5.5 in.; Weight: 2,315-2,355 lb.

Other opinions: "The Toyota Yaris is ranked #37 out of 42 affordable small cars." – *U.S. News & World Report.* "You really have to struggle to portray the Yaris in a positive light, when even the traditional Toyota trait of durability is questionable. And who still offers a 4-speed autobox these days? That's an insult to the prospective buyer's intelligence. It's like saying, 'Here, have this cheap car; everything about it is cheap.' … The latest Yaris is kind-of good looking and cutesy, but from the back it looks too much like a Peugeot and the front is nowhere near as fresh looking as that of a Mazda2, for instance, or even the almost futuristic Honda Fit/ Jazz." – *www.carscoops.com/2015/04/.* Major redesign: 2000, 2006, and 2010. The 2016 Scion iA/Yaris features a 106-hp, 1.5L 4-cylinder engine with both 6-speed manual and automatic transmission options. Standard-equipped features include, power-adjustable heated exterior mirrors, keyless entry, cruise control, power windows, and power door locks. **Highway/city fuel economy:** *Man.:* 5.5/6.9 L/100 km. *Auto.:* 5.7/7.0 L/100 km. **Best alternatives:** The Honda Fit is the best of the competition – it's got more room and is a lot more fun to drive. Nevertheless, the Hyundai Accent, Kia Soul, Rio, or Forte hatchback, Mazda2 or Mazda3 are all worthwhile candidates.

SAFETY: Child safety seat setup: Untested. **Crashworthiness:** NHTSA: 2009-15 models have four- and five-star ratings for crashworthiness; the 2007-08s were similarly rated, except that side protection was cut to three stars. IIHS: Front overlap crashworthiness and side protection rated "Good" on the 2007-12s, but head restraints got only a "Marginal" rating and roof strength passed with an "Acceptable" grade. **Owner-reported saftey-related failures:** Yaris owner safety complaints include airbags that fail to deploy; vehicle wandering all over the road, requiring constant steering corrections; and windows that spontaneously shatter.

ALERT! Steer clear of the poor-performing original tires. MSRP includes an "administration fee;" don't pay it.

Yaris Profile

	2006	2007	2008	2009	2010	2011	2012	2013	2014
Used Values ($)									
CE	3,500	4,000	4,500	5,000	6,000	7,000	8,000	9,500	11,000
LE	4,000	4,500	5,000	6,000	7,000	8,000	9,000	10,500	12,000
RS	5,500	6,000	7,000	7,500	8,500	10,000	12,000	14,000	—
Sedan	—	4,500	5,000	5,500	6,500	7,500	8,500	—	—
Reliability	★	★	★	★	★	★	★	★	★
Repairs ($$$)	2	2	2	2	1	1	1	1	1
Electrical	★	★	☆	☆	☆	☆	☆	★	☆
Engine (base)	☆	☆	☆	☆	☆	☆	☆	☆	☆
Fit/Finish	★	★	★	★	★	★	☆	☆	☆
Infotainment	—	—	—	★	★	★	★	★	★
Transmission (auto.)	☆	☆	☆	☆	☆	☆	☆	☆	☆

SECRET WARRANTIES, INTERNAL BULLETINS: 2002-14—Remedies for vehicle pulling from one side to the other, requiring constant steering corrections. **2003-11**—Eliminating a windshield ticking noise. **2004-10**—Front seat squeak. **2006-09**—Inability to shift out of Park. **2006-11**—Corroded front suspension lower control

No. 2 bolts will be replaced for free up to 7 years/100,000 miles. An abnormal front end noise when accelerating, turning, or braking is one symptom of this problem. 2006-12—Engine intermittently runs rough with engine misfires present after a cold soak startup. The valve lifters and valve springs have been updated. Remedy for a front suspension clunk. 2007—Trunk lid full-open improvement. Engine compartment rattle heard when car is put in Reverse. Intermittent odour in the cabin. Paint staining along horizontal surfaces. 2007-08—Water on front and rear carpets. Noise, vibration with the blower motor on. Rattle from the upper instrument panel area. ABS light stays on (corrosion alert). Noise, vibration on acceleration, or when shifting gears. 2007-09—Engine noise, vibration when vehicle accelerates. Automatic transmission shift cable rattles when car in Reverse. 2007-10—AC blower motor noise and vibration. 2007-11—Front end clunk. 2007-14—AC evaporator drain hose clogged by insect nests. 2011-12—What to do if the passenger-side airbag Off light comes on when the seat is occupied by an average-sized adult. 2012-13—Loose windshield dam fix.

COROLLA/MATRIX/VIBE ★★★★

2015 Toyota Carolla.

RATING: Above Average (2015-16); Average (2011-14); Below Average (2003-10). Last year's 2015 Corolla was reworked to give the car better road performance and a larger interior. This year's model isn't significantly changed. We are several years year into Corolla's last major redesign and guess what incidents reappear in NHTSA's owner-reported, life-threatening defects compendium for the 2013 model? Yep, faulty steering that causes the car to veer into traffic. Just like the falling headliners on its redesigned Avalon (see below) – Toyota doesn't always learn from its mistakes. Some minuses inherent in the car's redesign: The carryover rear drum brakes and torsion-beam rear suspension are pure Jurassic. The handling on the base and LE trim levels stumbles and wanders all over the roadway; and the near-vertical instrument panel is Austin Powers retro.

> The contact owns a 2012 Toyota Corolla. The contact stated that while driving 55 mph, she attempted to turn left but the steering wheel pulled to the right. The contact stated that she applied the brakes but that caused both of the passenger side tires to become lifted off the ground. As result, the vehicle flipped onto the driver's side and rolled over several times.

> . . .

> The contact stated that while driving approximately 70 mph, the 2013 Corolla suddenly veered into another lane. The vehicle was taken to the dealer for diagnosis where the technician stated that there was an electronic steering failure but they were unable remedy the failure.

A step up from the Yaris, the Corolla has long been Toyota's conservative standard-bearer in the compact sedan class. Over the years, however, the car has grown in size and price, to the point where it can now be considered a small family sedan. *Matrix/Vibe:* Corolla spin-offs that are Above Average buys (2004-15). These practically identical small front-drive or AWD sporty wagons are crosses between mini-SUVs and station wagons, but they're packaged like small minivans. Unlike the Matrix, which has soldiered on, GM dropped Vibe from its lineup when it shut down the Pontiac division. The front-drive Matrix/Vibe is equipped with a 1.8L 132 hp engine, a 5-speed manual overdrive transmission, and lots of standard features; however, the weak, buzzy base engine can be felt throughout the car. The AWD models are about 10% heavier and are woefully power-challenged. If you really need a bit more horsepower, get a model equipped with the 2.4L 158-hp 4-cylinder, but keep in mind that there are safer, better-quality high-performance choices out there, such as the Honda Civic Si, Mazda5, or a base Acura RSX. Other front-drives worth considering are the Honda Civic, Hyundai Elantra or Tiburon, Mazda3, Nissan Sentra, and Suzuki SX4. The Subaru Impreza and Forester are two other good choices for the AWD variant. **Road performance:** Average acceleration requires constant shifting to keep in the pack; automatic-transmission equipped versions are slower still; clumsy emergency handling; and poor steering performance:

> The problem is the steering is dangerous over 65+ mph! The front end of the car feels like it floats at highway speeds. I have zero feeling of the road from my hands to the wheels. The car tracks and never stays true on the road. This is constant and not intermittent which means I am focusing more on the steering issue then on the traffic. I am either overcompensating for any slight movement of the steering wheel to barely touching the wheel to keep this car remotely driving straight in the center of the lane, and that doesn't help! It worsens at speeds of 75+ mph. Someone is going to get hurt! Please recall this EPS system now!!!

Strong points: The reworked 2013 Corolla has more interior space, provides a supple ride, and handles much better (except for its "Hail Mary" erratic steering) than previous models. User-friendly interior ergonomics are enhanced by the flat rear floor, which provides more room. **Weak points:** Lots of high-speed wander along with excessive wind and road noise; limited front legroom; and plastic interior panels and trim look cheap; harsh downshift when stopping; seat belt warning alarm isn't loud enough; instrument-panel rattling; front-seat squeaking, and the front power seat grinds and groans. Overall reliability is average to below average.

Prices and Specs

Prices (Negotiable): *CE:* $15,995, *Auto.:* $18,635, *S:* $19,600, *CVT:* $20,585, *LE CVT:* $19,960, *LE ECO CVT:* $20,710, *ECO Tech Package:* $25,435 **Freight:** $1,660 **Powertrain (Front-drive):** Engine: 1.8L 4-cyl. (132 hp and 140 hp-LE Eco); Transmissions: 6-speed man., 4-speed auto., CVT **Dimensions/capacity:** Passengers: 2/3; Wheelbase: 106.3 in.; H: 57.3/L: 182.6/W: 69.9 in.; Headroom F/R: 4/2 in.; Legroom F/R: 41/28 in.; Cargo volume: 13 cu. ft.; Fuel tank: 50L/regular; Tow limit: 1,500 lb.; Load capacity: 825 lb.; Turning circle: 37.1 ft.; Ground clearance: 5.5 in., *XRS:* 5.3 in.; Weight: 2,800 lb.

Other opinions: "The Toyota Corolla ranks #20 out of 42 affordable small cars." – *U.S. News & World Report.* "Toyota denies any defect with the electronic power steering system in the 2009 and 2010 model year Corollas at issue. Under the terms of this settlement, class members who have complained about the on-center steering feel of their vehicle will have their retuned electronic control units installed at no cost. For those who haven't previously complained, the retuned electronic control unit will be available at a 50% discount. Class members who paid out-of-pocket to have the returned electronic control unit installed may be reimbursed up to $695, according to the settlement memorandum." – *Irene Corson v. Toyota Motor Sales USA Inc.* **Major redesign:** 1993, 1998, 2003, 2009, and 2014. With its latest redesign, the 2014 Corolla gains 4 inches in wheelbase and overall length, with a longer wheelbase than a 1996-2001 Camry. Toyota also offers an optional "Eco" version of the same engine with an additional intake-timing actuator that adds 8 hp and boosts highway fuel economy. **Highway/city fuel economy:** *1.8 man.:* 5.6/7.4 L/100 km. *Auto.:* 5.7/7.8 L/100 km. *2.4 man.:* 6.7/9.4 L/100 km. *2.4 auto.:* 6.5/9.4 L/100 km. **Best**

alternatives: Some small cars that are good investments with dependable steering, windshields, and headliners include the Hyundai Elantra and Mazda3 and Mazda6.

 SAFETY: Child safety seat setup: "Marginal." **Crashworthiness:** NHTSA: 2014-16 Corollas have a five-star rating for overall crashworthiness. 2012-13s have an overall four-star score. 2002-09 ratings varied between three and five stars. Over 723 safety-related failures for the 2010 model year alone. IIHS: The redesigned 2014 and 2015 models did a bit worse, scoring a "Marginal" in the tough small overlap frontal crash test. 2009 through 2013 versions qualified as "Good" in all crash categories, while the 2003 to 2008 models posted scores that varied from "Good" to "Poor." **Owner-reported safety-related failures:** Many of the 2010's close calls involved faulty steering that caused the vehicle to veer back and forth, all over the road and sudden, unintended acceleration accompanied by total brake failure:

> While driving 50 mph [80 km/h] the vehicle suddenly accelerated. As the vehicle is accelerating, the contact is trying to slow the vehicle down by applying the brakes. At this time the brakes are malfunctioning and speed is increasing. The contact was unable to slow the vehicle down and crashed into another vehicle.

2009-10 Pontiac Vibes (equipped with an electronic throttle control system) may suddenly accelerate without driver input and against the intentions of the driver. Car speeds up or slows down on its own:

> I see variations of about 500 rpm on the tachometer. Sometimes when letting off the throttle pedal, the car keeps going and doesn't get the message it's supposed to slow down. This is scary, it's almost like the car thinks it's on cruise control when it's not at all (here is a link to a forum where owners of 2011 Toyota Corollas describe exactly the same safety issue with the car: *www.corollaforum.com/showthread.php?p=285#post285*).

Airbags fail to deploy:

> The driver fell asleep at the wheel, awoke and tried to correct his lane position. Upon his attempt, the car could not be stabilized or controlled. This was a front end crash at a speed of approximately 50–55 mph going through a chain link fence, hitting hundreds of stacked lobster crates (like hitting a brick wall). The car was completely totaled, the driver had seat belt on. Not one airbag deployed. The driver side mirror smashed through the driver side window and a piece of wooden lobster crate with nails came through the front windshield and into the vehicle. This caused serious injury to the driver, severe facial and elbow lacerations, and major amounts of glass fragments in his body.

Driver cannot open the rear window with the other windows closed, as it produces a dramatic vibration and shaking inside the vehicle; mysterious windshield cracks; car parked on a small hill and with the parking brake applied will still roll away. Other safety-related reported with the 2013s: Airbag warning light comes on for no reason; sudden brake loss and unintended acceleration; rear defogger doesn't adequately clean the windshield; and the steering veers from one side to the other.

Corolla/Matrix/Vibe Profile

	2006	2007	2008	2009	2010	2011	2012	2013	2014
Used Values ($)									
CE	4,000	4,500	5,000	6,000	6,500	7,500	8,500	9,500	12,500
LE	6,000	6,500	7,000	8,000	9,000	10,000	12,000	16,000	—
XRS	6,500	—	8,000	9,000	10,000	11,500	13,500	—	—
Matrix Wagon	4,000	4,500	5,000	5,500	6,500	8,000	9,000	12,500	15,000
AWD	6,500	7,500	9,000	9,500	10,500	12,000	13,500	18,000	—
XRS/XR	7,500	8,500	9,500	11,000	11,500	12,500	14,000	17,500	—
Vibe Wagon	4,500	5,000	5,500	6,000	6,500	—	—	—	—
AWD	—	—	6,000	6,500	7,500	—	—	—	—
GT	6,000	—	—	7,000	8,000	—	—	—	—
Reliability	★	★	★	★	★	★	★	★	★
Repairs ($$$)	②	②	②	②	②	①	①	①	①
Electrical	★	★	★	★	★	★	★	★	★
Engine (base)	★	★	★	★	★	★	★	④	④
Fit/Finish	★	★	★	★	★	★	★	★	★
Infotainment	—	—	—	★	★	★	★	★	★
Transmission (auto.)	★	★	★	★	★	★	★	★	★

SECRET WARRANTIES, INTERNAL BULLETINS: All models/years: Steering-column noise may require the replacement of the steering-column assembly. Toyota has developed special procedures for eliminating AC odours and excessive wind noise. These problems are covered in TSBs #AC00297 and #BO00397, respectively. *All models*: 2002-14—Remedies for vehicle pulling from one side to the other, requiring constant steering corrections. 2009—According to TSBs #SB002411 and #SB009411, excess oil consumption in the 2.4L 4-cylinder engine was traced to the piston assembly. Toyota will replace the pistons and rings on a "goodwill" case-by-case basis. *Corolla:* 2002-07—Repair tips for correcting a severe pull to one side when underway (TSB #ST005-01). 2003-08—Tips on silencing windshield, automatic transmission whistle or hoot, wind noise, and front brake rattling. 2004-10—Fixing front-seat squeaking. 2005-06—Grille mesh available to protect the AC condenser from road debris. 2005-07—Troubleshooting tips to fix a harsh-shifting automatic transmission and hard starts. 2009-10—Poor steering feel. Steering clunk, pop noise. A-pillar rattles. Premature front brake pad wear. 2009-14—AC evaporator drain hose clogged by insect nests. *Matrix, Vibe:* 2003—Loose or deformed front or rear glass door run. AC doesn't sufficiently cool the vehicle.

Headlights come on when turned off. 2003-06—Correction for rear-end whining, humming, or growling. 2005-06—Troubleshooting no-starts. 2009—Harsh downshift when stopping. 2009-10—No starts. Condensation dripping from the dome lamp. *Vibe:* 2003—Transmission shifts too early when accelerating at full throttle and the engine is cold. Harsh shifting. Water leak from the A-pillar or headliner area. 2003-04—Harsh 1-2 upshifts. Slipping transmission. 2003-08—Silencing a hoot or whistle heard on light acceleration (replace the automatic transaxle cooler hoses).

CAMRY ★★★★

RATING: Above Average (2012-16); Average (2006-11). Carried over to 2016 relatively unchanged, a redesigned Camry will arrive in the fall of 2017 as a 2018 model. That version will likely feature a continuously variable transmission (CVT) and a 2.0L, turbocharged 4-cylinder powerplant. The hybrid varient will also return in 2018. **Road performance:** The 2012's redesign corrected most of the Camry's performance gaps, however vague steering causing excessive road wander remains a problem:

> Steering is vague and not predictable. Never had a car with electric steering. Car follows its own course. It takes a lot of attention to keep it on the road.

The SE trim level delivers sporty handling; the base 4-cylinder is a competent, responsive performer; surprisingly, the 3.5L V6 powertrain set-up delivers fuel economy figures that are almost as good as the base 4-banger; although the ride has smoothed out, the SE suspension is a bit stiff. The 6-speed automatic transmission has a taller final drive ratio, which saves fuel, but slows acceleration. **Strong points:** There's a nice array of standard safety and convenience features that include a telescoping steering column, 10 airbags, stability control, antilock brakes, and four wheel disc brakes. The cabin is relatively quiet; instruments and controls are well laid-out in an interior that has a rich look and feel; and passenger and storage space is better than average. **Weak points:** Paint on the lower plastic bumper is easily chipped. Hybrid fuel economy is overstated by almost 30%, says *Consumer Reports* and many others. Frequent failures of the engine cam head, which is often back ordered; inaccurate speedometer readings; gasoline in the fuel tank hits the tank baffle with a loud bang; driver-seat lumbar support may be painful for some drivers; a strong moldy odour invades the cabin due to a defective air conditioning system that emits "noxious and foul odors from mold growth in the HVAC system" (*topclassactions.com/lawsuit-settlements/lawsuit-news/*) ; windows often stick in the up position; and some complaints of Hybrid AC failures.

Other opinions: "The Toyota Camry ranks #2 out of 18 affordable midsize cars." – *U.S. News & World Report.* "Power steering leaking is one of the more common problems, and sometime the repairs can be tricky. The difficulty lies in the fact that the leak can be coming from different places. Unfortunately, some mechanics will just replace part after part without really looking for the leak. Power steering leak repair can sometimes end up costing you thousands of dollars. This problem appears more often in the V6 model Camry." – *Joe Campanella of CARCHEX.* **Major redesign:** 1997, 2002, 2007, and 2012. **Highway/city fuel economy:** *Hybrid:* 4.9/4.5 L/ 100 km. *XLE:* 5.1/4.7 L/100 km. *2.5:* 5.6/8.2 L/100 km. *3.5 V6:* 6.4/9.7 L/100 km. Owners say fuel-economy figures are much lower than advertised. **Best alternatives:** The Honda Accord, Hyundai Elantra, Mazda5 or Mazda6, and Nissan Sentra or Altima. Stay away from the optional moonroof; it robs you of much-needed headroom and exposes you to deafening wind roar, rattling, and leaks. Original equipment Firestone and Bridgestone tires should be shunned in favour of better-performing tires recommended by *thetirerack.com.*

SAFETY: Child safety seat setup: "Acceptable." **Crashworthiness:** NHTSA: 2012 through 2015 models are rated five stars for overall crashworthiness. 2011s get four-star scores. IIHS: Camry scores the top rating for frontal offset, side, and roof crash protection. Head-restraint effectiveness as only "Marginal." **Owner-reported safety-related failures:** The same safety-related failures are reported year after year. These defects can be especially lethal to older drivers with slower reflexes. Indeed, probably few Camry drivers have the necessary driving skills to confront excessive steering wander, engine stall and surge, when accelerating, merging, passing, or turning. As seen with other Toyota models (like the 2010 Prius, which has received 1,917 complaints as of July 2015), sudden, unintended acceleration without any brakes has been the top reported problem with Camrys for many years, with an added twist – they still speed out of control after having recall work done to correct the problem:

Entering a driveway at 2 mph the car accelerated to approximately 30 mph and struck a brick wall. The airbags deployed causing injury and the car was totaled.

Other safety problems reported: Airbags fail to deploy; when accelerating from a stop, the vehicle hesitates, sometimes to a count of three, before suddenly accelerating; and when decelerating, the vehicle speeds up, as if the cruise control were engaged. The close placement of the brake and accelerator pedals also causes unwanted acceleration due to driver error; however, this cannot explain the large number of incidences of sudden acceleration reported. Transmission shift lever can be inadvertently knocked into Reverse or Neutral when the vehicle is underway; harsh shifting; vehicle may roll backwards when parked on an incline; and electronic power steering operates erratically and is sometimes unresponsive. There have also been reports that the steering constantly pulls the car to the left, into oncoming traffic, no matter how many alignments you get; the centre console below the gear shift becomes extremely hot; Hybrid's low beam lights are inadequate for lighting the highway; excessively bright LED tail/brake lights will impair the vision of drivers in trailing vehicles; and wheels may lock up. Reports of the front windshield cracking from the driver-side upper left corner and gradually extended toward the middle of the windshield. Glass sunroof implodes and in one incident the rear window exploded while the vehicle was stopped in traffic; front windshield distortion looks like little bubbles are embedded in the glass; rear windshield distortion when viewed through the rear-view mirror during night driving; the passenger-side windows may fall out; rear window-defrosting wires don't clear the upper top of the windshield; and head restraints obstruct driver's rearward vision. Trunk lid "beans" people when the weak struts fail:

> A short time after I took delivery of the car, I parked it on my driveway which has a small climb to the garage. The car was parked with the rear end lower than the front. When I opened the trunk to unload it and released the trunk lid it came down and hit me in the head. It happens every time when the trunk is opened under the same conditions and sometimes when the car is level. Obviously the trunk lid needs a tighter spring.

ALERT! Many owners say the Camry is a "rat hostel." Granted, this is a recurrent theme in this year's *Lemon-Aid*, but the problem is pandemic among many automakers who are too cheap to install a grille that blocks rodent access. Besides the safety hazard of half-devoured plastic components, wiring, and fuel/brake lines, there's also the thousands of dollars in repair costs. Hmmm…maybe that's why dealers don't care:

> While driving 40 mph [64 km/h], the driver noticed a rat crawled from under the passenger seat into the glove compartment and into the air conditioner. The [sight] of the rat almost caused the driver to crash. The contact was able to get the rat out of the vehicle. Two days later the contact took the vehicle to the dealer to repair the back seat and the seat belt that the rat had chewed through and also clean the air conditioner.

Can you endure the severe wind buffeting if driving with one window open?

> The wind buffeting that occurs in this car is unbearable. This causes an unsupportable pressure that you feel in your ears and head.

Make sure there's no rear window defroster line reflection at night:

The contact owns a 2012 Toyota Camry. The contact stated that when looking out of the rear window, the defrost lines going across the window and the tint caused the contact to see multiple headlights. The contact stated that one headlight would appear as twenty various headlights, disorientating the driver. The contact took the vehicle to multiple dealers and was told that the design was normal.

Also, inspect the factory-ordered window tinting. Check out the tint in the day and at night before purchase:

The contact stated that she was unable to see out of the factory rear window tint. The vehicle was taken to the dealer. The dealer confirmed the failure was with the factory window tint.

Camry Profile

	2006	2007	2008	2009	2010	2011	2012	2013	2014
Used Values ($)									
LE	6,000	7,000	7,500	9,000	10,000	11,500	13,500	17,000	19,500
SE V6	—	8,000,	8,500	11,000	12,000	14,000	18,000	22,000	24,500
XLE	—	—	—	—	13,500	15,000	16,500	22,500	26,000
XLE V6	8,500	10,000	11,500	12,500	14,500	16,500	20,500	24,500	28,500
Hybrid	—	8,500	10,000	11,500	12,500	15,000	17,000	20,000	23,000
Reliability	⭐	⭐	⭐	⭐	⭐	☆	☆	☆	☆
Repairs ($$$)	①	②	②	②	①	①	①	①	①
Electrical	☆	☆	☆	☆	☆	☆	☆	☆	☆
Engine (base)	⭐	⭐	⭐	⭐	⭐	☆	☆	☆	☆
Fit/Finish	⭐	⭐	⭐	⭐	⭐	⭐	⭐	⭐	⭐
Infotainment	—	—	—	⭐	⭐	⭐	⭐	⭐	⭐
Transmission (auto.)	⭐	⭐	⭐	⭐	☆	☆	☆	☆	☆

SECRET WARRANTIES, INTERNAL BULLETINS: 2002-14—Remedies for vehicle pulling from one side to the other, requiring constant steering corrections. 2006-09—*2006-08 RAV4, 2007-08 Solara, 2007-09 Camry, 2007-11 Camry Hybrid, 2009 Corolla, and 2009 Matrix.* The 2.4L 4-cylinder engine may be an "oil-burner." In TSBs #SB002411 and #SB009411, Toyota says the problem was traced to the piston assembly. The automaker will replace the pistons and rings on a "goodwill" case-by-case basis. No shift from Park; multiple warning lights come on. 2007—Engine oil leaks from the timing cover. Rough idle, stalling; shift flare. 2007-08—No crank; engine starts and dies. Premature brake pad wear; squeaking rear brakes. Excessive steering-wheel vibration, flutter, and noise. Instrument panel rattle. Frame creaking noise. Rear suspension squeaking, rubbing. Engine oil leak from camshaft housing. Engine ticking noises. Torque converter shudder. Moonroof knocking when underway. Troubleshooting brake pulsation/vibration. Rattle from trunk area. 2007-09—The 2.4L 4-cylinder engine burns oil rapidly. 2007-11—Sunroof leaks at headliner and floor areas. 2007-14—AC evaporator drain hose clogged by insect nests. 2009—Silencing engine ticking and floor pan creaking. Inoperative moonroof. 2007-10—Braking vibration, pulsation. A rattle or buzz coming from the driver's side dash may require an updated vacuum check valve. Tips on correcting a roof knocking sound. Intermittent noxious AC odours. Loose sun visor mounts. 2007-11—Uneven rear brake pad wear. Water leaks from sunroof onto headliner and into footwell area. 2008-09—TCM update for shift improvements. 2008-10—Ignition coils may need replacing if the MIL alert is illuminated. *Hybrid:* 2007-09—No shift from Park; multiple warning lights come on. Water leaks onto headliner and footwell area. Inoperative moonroof. 2007-10—Ways to fix a knocking sound from the roof area. 2007-11—The 2.4L 4-cylinder engine burns oil rapidly. Front strut insulator noise. 2011-12—Passenger-side airbag OFF light will come on even though the seat is unoccupied. Uneven rear brake wear. Insufficient alternator charging may be corrected with an updated pulley assembly. Remedy for a front/rear suspension noise that occurs when passing over bumps in the road. A front door trim panel rattle. Underbody rattling. Troubleshooting a windshield back glass ticking noise. 2012-14—Toyota has extended its warranty up to 8 years/150,000 miles (it's an American decision) to cover repairs to correct transmission torque converter shudder. This "goodwill" warranty applies no matter if the Camry was bought new or used. Trunk lid won't stay up on an incline. Condensation drips from the headliner. Transaxle high-pitch whine when cruising.

PRIUS ★★★

The Toyota Prius C.

RATING: Average (2014-16); Below Average (2006-13). Toyota sells four Prius models in Canada – the base Prius, Prius v wagon, Prius c subcompact (set on the Yaris platform), and the Prius Plug-in Hybrid. Toyota's latest third-generation Prius uses a 1.8L DOHC 16-valve 4-cylinder engine. It may sound hard to believe, but the bigger engine doesn't have to work as hard. So at highway speeds, the lower rpms save about 1.3 km/L (3 mpg). With the debut of the Prius v five-door wagon, Prius is now approaching the Camry in size, and its powerplant is more sophisticated, powerful, and efficient than what you get with similar vehicles in the marketplace. Interestingly, because the car relies primarily on electrical energy, fuel economy is better in the city than on the highway – the opposite of what one finds with gasoline-powered vehicles. An electric motor is the main power source, and it uses an innovative and fairly reliable CVT for smooth and efficient shifting. The motor is used mainly for acceleration, with the gasoline engine kicking in when needed to provide power. Braking automatically shuts off the engine, as the electric motor acts as a generator to replenish the environmentally unfriendly NiMH battery pack. The Solar Panel option uses solar energy to keep the vehicle cool when it's parked. Do the math. You will spend a lot of money upfront to save a little money later on. After two decades you may break even. One surprising statistic comes from R.L. Polk, an automotive marketing research company based in the United States. Polk's August 2012 study found only 35% of hybrid owners purchased another gas-electric vehicle when trading in during 2011. Repurchase rates varied across hybrid models, with the highest percentage of hybrid loyalty going to the Toyota Prius. Removing Prius from the mix shows a repurchase rate under 25%. Hybrid resale prices held firm due to the 2012 improvements, until 2014-15 when fuel prices crashed by 50%. Buyers have now shifted to crossovers, luxury cars, trucks, and SUVs, softening heretofore, unreasonably high hybrid prices. **Road performance:** Lethargic acceleration; ponderous, bland handling; slow steering response; has lots of body roll when cornering, and is prone to stalling. Braking isn't very precise, and the car is buffeted by crosswinds. Highway rescuers are wary of the car's 500-volt electrical system, and take special courses to prevent electrocution and avoid toxic battery components. **Strong points:** Standard rear-view camera (2015-16), good fuel economy, a roomy back seat, lots of cargo space, and little engine noise. **Weak points:** A money-saver for taxi fleets, but a big disappointment for everyday drivers. We know the problems: Sudden unintended acceleration, no brakes or weak brakes, the passenger-side airbags are disabled when a normal-sized adult is seated, and a cruise control that doesn't turn off are scary enough. But what about a steering column that becomes unhinged? Or, the transmission that suddenly drops into Neutral? Or, wallet-busting depreciation? Did you know that a 2010 Prius that sold for $27,800 is now worth barely $11,500? That alone wipes out the overblown fuel savings. Owners are still reporting that the brakes give out when they pass over a bump in the road. Of particular interest to Canadians is the car's poor performance in cold weather; battery pack will eventually cost about $3,000 U.S. to replace; on some model years, fuel consumption may be 20% higher than advertised; over 50% depreciation after 5 years; higher-than-average insurance premiums; dealer-dependent servicing means higher servicing costs; sales and servicing may not be available outside large urban areas; and the CVT cannot be easily repaired by independent agencies. Inaccurate fuel readings; and a failure-prone navigation aid:

> My 2014's Entune navigation system randomly freezes and resets. When this happens at high speeds on a highway where a person is depending on the system to get somewhere, it causes a massive distraction and a risk to life and limb. Toyota is offering no resolution to this issue and its dealerships are refusing to even register user complaints.

The hands-free phone system is inordinately complicated to use; a strong, moldy odour permeates the cabin;

> My 2014 Prius smells like a swamp even before it is turned on. There is also humidity inside the car when opening the door, I've asked multiple times to have the evaporator replaced because I fear that it is not draining and causing mold and mildew to form. Breathing in the mold is a sweious health concern and Toyota will not agree to any kind of fix. (Camry owners have launched a class action over this).

Noisy rear brakes; cheap cabin trim, and the driver-side seat can't be adjusted away from the steering wheel on some models. Finally, excessive road noise intrudes into what is ordinarily a quiet cabin.

Prices and Specs

Prices (Soft): *Prius c:* $21,055, *Prius c Technology:* $26,055, *Base Prius:* $23,305, *Moonroof Upgrade Package:* $29,550, *Touring Package:* $31,290, *Technology Package:* $34,390, *Prius Plug-in:* $35,905, *Technology Package:* $41,140, *Prius v:* $28,090, *Luxury:* $30,095, *Technology Package:* $34,095 **Freight:** $1,660 **Powertrain (front-drive):** Engine: 1.8L 4-cyl. (134 hp); Transmission: CVT **Dimensions/capacity:** Passengers: 2/3; Wheelbase: 106.3 in.; H: 58.3/L: 175.6/W: 68.7 in.; Headroom F/R: 4/2 in.; Legroom F/R: 40.5/30 in.; Cargo volume: 15.7 cu. ft.; Fuel tank: 45L/regular; Tow limit: No towing; Load capacity: 810 lb.; Turning circle: 34.2 ft.; Ground clearance: 5.5 in.; Weight: 3,042 lb.

Other opinions: "The Prius ranks #13 out of 42 affordable small cars. [It] gets outstanding fuel economy and has a roomy interior, automotive writers say, but its lackluster acceleration and drab handling contribute to dull performance." – *U.S. News & World Report.* Incidentally, the car is also rated #5 among 18 hybrid cars and #10 among 37 hatchbacks. **Major redesign:** 2001, 2004, and 2010. The fourth-generation Prius comes out this fall with a new modular platform. Toyota says it will be more performance oriented than its predecessors, though it won't be much different than the 2015 verion. **Highway/city fuel economy:** 4.0/3.7 L/100 km. **Best alternatives:** Honda Fit or Insight, Hyundai Accent, and Nissan Versa. In a Prius-versus-Insight matchup, the Prius got better fuel economy but was more expensive; the Insight, despite its fewer horses, was more fun to drive, though it's not as fast as the Prius. On the other hand, the Nissan Insight or Leaf won't abduct you at high speed, or send you head-on into a guardrail with no brakes.

 SAFETY: Child safety seat setup: "Marginal." Crashworthiness: NHTSA: 2015-16 models have a four-star overall crashworthiness score, while 2011-13s did better with five stars. 2004-2010s dropped back to four stars. IIHS: Gave the 2010-15 models a "Good" rating for all tests, except the 2014-15 small front overlap test which was judged "Acceptable." *Prius c:* 2012-15 "Good" scores, except for a "Poor" rating in the small overlap front crash test. *Prius v:* 2015 model was rated "Good" in all categories, however, the 2012-14 versions failed the small front overlap test with a "Poor" score. Owner-reported safety-related failures: Rear windshield spontaneously shatters when the trunk lid closes; sun reflects into the driver's eyes; and the driver's head restraint could be used to interrogate prisoners:

> I finally realized that the driver's side head restraint on my 2014 Prius is causing me chronic head and neck pain.

Furthermore, the low driver's seat and window distortions impede visibility:

> The driver's seat does not raise far enough to allow shorter drivers to see over the dash board, base of windshield and rear of hood. This prevents shorter drivers from being able to see the ground anywhere near the car. This could be fixed with increased travel height for the driver's seat. As I have had to offer several friends chair cushions to prop them up so they could see.

> ...

> Windshields on Prius models 2010 and higher are affected. While most obvious at night, external light sources viewed through the front windshield can be mirrored in triplicate via a "prism" or "refraction" effect.

Only 113 safety-related complaints have been posted against the 2012 Prius and just 40 against the 2014. Contrast this with the 1,962 safety-related failures reported on the 2010 model; 50 reports per model year would be average. Almost all of the earlier complaints concern sudden acceleration, loss of brakes, electrical short-circuits, and cruise control failures. A major complaint with the 2012s is the sudden loss of Drive or Reverse:

> Car becomes immobile – will not shift into Reverse or Drive. Computer keeps sending the message to put it in Park and depress brake, but once that is done, any attempt to shift into Reverse or Drive triggers the message, endlessly. The problem is apparently intermittent.

The car is also extremely vulnerable to side winds, and light steering doesn't help much, causing the vehicle to wander all over the road and need constant steering corrections. Owners of 2012 models continue to report brake failures when their car accelerates out of control. This occurs despite Toyota's much-vaunted brake/throttle override:

> As I was approaching a turn I began to brake and the brakes failed. I tried pressing the brake pedal harder and making sure that I had proper foot placement and it felt like the car accelerated at that point. Since the car was not slowing down I was unable to make the turn and ended up crossing the road diagonally and going up onto the curb. Once the car was over the curb and in the grass the brakes finally engaged and the vehicle came to a stop.

Car lurches forward when brakes are applied; many reports of loss of braking even after having the recalled ECU replaced:

> Since Toyota updated the software for the recall, I still experience the same problem multiple times, and it is not only [happening] during slow and steady application of brakes, also [happening] when I use the brake in more sudden fashion even at moderate speed (30-40 mph [48-64 km/h]).

Cruise control doesn't disengage quickly enough:

> I have to press the brake harder than any prior vehicles I have owned to kill the cruise control and if I release the brake before the cruise control is released then the car lurches forward. Many other people have experienced this issue and have documented their experiences on the forum priuschat.com. They have even fixed the problem themselves by moving the cruise control disengagement closer to the top of the brake pedal.

The steering column may fall out of its mount:

> My wife and 2 daughters were driving on Interstate 90/94 when the entire steering column slowly dropped. I double checked the lever underneath to adjust it, but that was tight. I could see wires and bolts where the column had been dropped several inches. I lifted the column up and thought it would lock in or click back in place. When I did this, the entire column collapsed in my lap. An alarm sounded and I had no control of the steering while going 110 [km/h].

Transmission sometimes goes into Reverse when shifted into Drive, or goes into Drive when Reverse is selected; traction control engages when it shouldn't; airbags failed to deploy; and the headlights go on and off intermittently.

ALERT! Okay, the fuel savings are exaggerated, but how about running out of gas?

> When driving, dashboard [reads] "Hybrid system not working. Pull over..." This was 7/3/2012. It had run out of gas even though there were 2 bars out of 10 still present on gas gauge. On 7/30/12 later this happened again with 4 bars showing. Got the fuel sensor and gauge replaced on 7/30/12. 8/14/12 with 3 bars showing, cruising range of 60 miles and having gone 480 miles the same warning "Hybrid system not working...." I was able to get to a gas station before running out of gas. The Prius manual states the tank holds 9.5 gallons. Filling up the tank took 9.91 gallons. There is clearly something wrong.

During the test drive, verify if you can drive safely with the car's blind-spots:

There are very dangerous blind spots on both rear driver and passenger sides of the Prius v. Vehicles located near the mid to rear of the car cannot be seen in mirrors or by glancing over the shoulder when changing lanes. I have had numerous near collisions due to this design defect.

Finally, check that your child's safety seat can be safely installed in the Prius v – some can't:

The latch system design on the seats on the new Prius V is flawed. Instead of having four latch points, one set of two for the left seat and one set of two for the right seat, they have only three latch points, one in the middle of the left seat, one in the middle of the right seat and one in the middle of the car. Our child safety seat has three buckles designed to work with the latch system, one on the left, one on the right and a top tether. The left and right buckles cannot attach to the same latch point because then the child safety seat will pivot.

Prius Profile

	2006	2007	2008	2009	2010	2011	2012	2013	2014
Used Values ($)									
Base	6,000	7,500	8,500	10,500	12,000	14,000	16,500	19,500	21,500
c	—	—	—	—	—	—	—	14,500	16,500
Plug-In	—	—	—	—	—	—	—	23,000	26,500
v	—	—	—	—	—	—	17,000	20,000	22,500
Reliability	★	★	★	☆	★	☆	☆	☆	☆
Repairs ($$$)	3	3	3	2	3	2	2	2	2
Electrical	★	★	★	☆	★	☆	☆	☆	☆
Engine (base)	★	★	★	☆	★	☆	☆	☆	☆
Fit/Finish	☆	☆	☆	☆	☆	☆	☆	☆	☆
Infotainment	—	—	—	☆	☆	☆	☆	☆	☆
Transmission (auto.)	★	★	★	☆	★	☆	☆	☆	☆

SECRET WARRANTIES, INTERNAL BULLETINS: All years: It is surprising that with so many serious consumer complaints and recall campaigns, most Prius service bulletins are bereft of any reference to major deficiencies. 2000-08—Multiple warning lights on; vehicle won't shift out of Park. Steering pulls to the right. 2002-14—Remedies for vehicle pulling from one side to the other, requiring constant steering corrections. 2003-08—Back windshield glass ticking. 2004-08—Troubleshooting an engine knock and inaccurate fuel gauge readings. Intermittent instrument display in cold weather. 2010—Warped engine cover. 2010-14—AC evaporator drain hose clogged by insect nests. 2011-12—Abnormal noise when brake pedal is released. Excessive roof sun shade noise. Cleaning tips to keep the HV battery cooling fan at peak efficiency. Troubleshooting rear windshield ticking. 2012-13—Warm air comes out of the AC vents.

AVALON ★★★★

RATING: Above Average (2009-16; 1995-2004); Average (2005-08). The redesigned 2013 and subsequent models would be a Recommended choice if not for their on-going fit and finish deficiencies. How many luxury cars have headliners that fall down, a seriously distorted windshield view, or reflective interior trim that blinds drivers? Nevertheless, the revised Avalons are relatively reliable luxury sedans with more compact dimensions, a lighter curb weight and a Camry Hybrid powerplant. Restyled with cleaner lines like those of the Audi A7, the interior has been reworked to increase headroom and trunk capacity, make controls easily accessible, add more supportive seats, and give the cabin a high-end look. For 2016, the car has been slightly restyled; a redesign is scheduled for the fall of 2018 as a 2019 model. **Road performance:** A smooth and responsive powertrain that provides quick acceleration combined with good fuel economy; acceptable handling and the ride is both comfy and quiet. Some negatives: A mushy brake pedal and ultra-light steering that can degrade handling. **Strong points:** This five-passenger, near-luxury, front-engine, front-drive, mid-sized sedan offers more value than do other, more expensive cars in its class. Buying an Avalon means you are getting the equivalent of an entry-level Lexus. It performs well, is loaded with safety, comfort, and convenience features, and costs thousands of dollars less than a Lexus. Owners get a roomy, limousine-like interior with reclining backrests and plenty of rear seat room and storage space; large doors make for easy front- and rear-seat access; comfortable seats; user-friendly controls; and good resale value. **Weak points:** Excessive interior noise; a suspension that may be too firm for some; and serious fit and finish deficiencies. Practically all owner complaints are unrelated to safety concerns, including poor fit and finish, and water leaking into the cabin. For example, water leaks from the roof staining the headliner; or the headliner falls down and takes months to get corrected:

> Purchased showroom 2013 Toyota Avalon with headliner in the rear dropped down. This is brand new ... I was told that probably some kids have pulled the headliner down while in showroom. Next up, seat back covers also was blammed on kids in showroom pulling them down.

Other concerns include engine and rear windshield/window ticking; a front power-seat grinding, groaning noise; transmission control module (TCM) updates needed to improve shifting; problems with the trunk opener; and sunshade switches that are located too close together.

568

Prices and Specs

Prices (Soft): *XLE:* $38,185, *LTD:* $40,280 **Freight:** $1,660 **Powertrain (Front-drive):** Engine: 3.5L V6 (268 hp), Transmissions: 6-speed auto., CVT auto. **Dimensions/capacity:** Passengers: 2/3; Wheelbase: 111 in.; H: 57/L: 195/W: 72 in.; Cargo volume: 16 cu. ft.; Fuel tank: 70L/regular; Headroom F/R: 3/2.5 in.; Legroom F/R: 41/31 in.; Tow limit: 1,003 lbs; Load capacity: 875 lb.; Turning circle: 36.9 ft.; Ground clearance: 5.3 in.; Weight: 3,497 lb.

Other opinions: "The Toyota Avalon ranks #3 out of 11 affordable large cars." – *U.S. News & World Report.* "The Avalon comes up short in one key area: Status. It doesn't boast the luxury badge that Toyota's Lexus division offers, and for many buyers, that alone is the difference between choosing the full-size Toyota and the luxurious Lexus ES, which is largely similar to the Avalon underneath." – *www.autotrader. com/car-reviews/.* **Major redesign:** 1995, 2000, 2005, and 2013. **Highway/city fuel economy:** 7.0/10.7 L/100 km. Expect actual fuel consumption to be about 20% higher than advertised. **Best alternatives:** Honda's Accord V6, the Hyundai Genesis, Mazda6, and Nissan Altima.

SAFETY: **Child safety seat setup:** "Marginal." **Crashworthiness:** NHTSA: 2013s through 2015s merited five stars for overall crash safety, while the 2001-10 Avalons did almost as well, scoring five stars for front and side crash protection and four stars for rollover resistance. IIHS: 2000-15 models are considered overall "Good" performers, except for 2001-08 Avalons, which turned in "Poor" scores for rear crashworthiness. **Owner-reported safety-related failures:** Sudden unintended acceleration; rear-corner blind spots and excessive rear windshield glare and distortion:

> My 2013 Toyota Avalon, has a distorted rear window and one cannot get a clear view of what is behind. All lines are zig-zag and everything behind is fuzzy.

Other reported driving hazards: Loss of brakes; "lag and lurch" when accelerating; when cruise control is engaged, applying the brake slows the car, but as soon as the foot is taken off the brake, the car surges back to its former speed; vehicle rolls backward when parked on an incline; "chin-to-chest" head restraints; a defective telescopic steering-wheel lever may cause the steering wheel to collapse towards the dash when the vehicle is underway; steering column is unusually loose; newly designed high-intensity discharged headlights only partially illuminate the highway; and electrical shorts that may suddenly shut down dash lights.

ALERT! Don't let the dealer sell you poorer-performing Firestone/Bridgestone original equipment tires. Instead, ask for a replacement set of Michelin or Pirellis. Serious glare and reflections throughout the car due to the trim and other instruments: A "must-check" during the test drive:

Avalon dashboard trim causes a dangerous reflection of sunlight directly into driver's eyes. During mid-day sun, blinding beams of sunlight bounce off several areas of the mirrored-chrome-coloured plastic trim that surrounds the dashboard and wraps around the instrument cluster. Sunlight is reflected off chrome trim beneath the tachometer and speedometer. Blinding sunlight also reflects off trim on both sides of the steering wheel, and other points across the trim depending on time of day and direction of car, sunlight bounces off different places on the trim because the trim is beveled, instead of a vertical surface, it focuses the sunlight directly back into the driver's eyes. Drivers need to regularly glance down at the instrument cluster and reflected sunlight from that area and other sections on the dash is dangerously distracting.

Avalon Profile

	2006	2007	2008	2009	2010	2011	2012	2013	2014
Used Values ($)									
XL/Touring/Base	7,500	9,000	11,000	13,000	15,000	17,500	21,500	26,000	30,000
XLS/Premium	9,000	10,500	12,500	14,500	16,000	—	—	—	—
LTD	—	—	—	—	—	—	—	27,000	31,000
Reliability	★	★	☆	☆	☆	☆	☆	☆	☆
Repairs ($$$)	💰	💰	💰	💰	💰	💰	💰	💰	💰
Electrical	★	★	☆	☆	☆	☆	☆	☆	☆
Engine (base)	☆	☆	☆	☆	☆	☆	☆	☆	☆
Fit/Finish	★	★	★	★	☆	☆	☆	★	★
Infotainment	—	—	—	★	★	☆	☆	☆	☆
Transmission (auto.)	☆	☆	☆	☆	☆	☆	☆	☆	☆

SECRET WARRANTIES, INTERNAL BULLETINS: 2005-09—Front power seat grinding, groaning. 2005-11—Sunroof leaks at headliner and floor areas. 2005-12—Telescopic steering column adjustment lever detent clip replacement is at no charge for 10 years under a "goodwill warranty" (Warranty Enhancement Program #ZTY). 2005-14—Front strut insulator noise. 2006-07—Harsh shifting. 2007—Rough idle, stalling. 2007-08—Steering-wheel flutter; body vibration. 2007-14—AC evaporator drain hose clogged by insect nests. 2008-10—High-beam headlight failures. 2008-11—Underbody rattling noises. 2009-11—Front, rear knocking noises when passing over bumps. 2011—Rear window glass fogging. 2011-12—Torque converter shudder at low acceleration. Insufficient alternator charging may require an updated pulley assembly. 2013-14—Free replacement of the driver and passenger front seatback board until July 31, 2017 (Limited Service Campaign #E0J). The driver's seat bottom outer bolster may have a ridge/bulge in it, or the seat is uncomfortable.

Both conditions are caused by the seat heater element twisting or bunching up. Fuel door may be difficult to open.

SIENNA

RATING: Above Average (2014-16); Average (2006-13); Not Recommended (1998-2005) in view of more than 1,827 reports of life-threatening failures for the 2004 model alone. There has been a welcomed decrease in serious safety-related complaints since the dark days of 2004 and later models. Interestingly, the Sienna's 2011 redesign did not produce an inordinate number of owner complaints. **Road performance:** Smooth (most of the time) 3.5L V6 powertrain performance; and optional full-time AWD; standard stability control. Handling isn't as sharp and secure as some of the competing vans. Sienna is in the top of its class when all systems are working correctly, but when they don't:

> Joining highway in a situation where vehicles giving way ... braking then acceleration repeatedly, transmission refused to downshift on kick down, vehicle would not accelerate, actually slowed significantly forcing following vehicles to brake. Vehicle eventually began to pick up speed. Generally poor response from transmission in all modes. Transmission drops out of drive at low speeds causing engine to race before taking up Drive, very hard to operate vehicle smoothly. Excessive engine vibration and noise.

Strong points: Toyota's redesigned, third-generation Sienna has become more car-like than ever in its highway handling and comfort, while offering a larger, restyled interior. It is sold in a broad range of models, and stands out as the only van with an AWD option (though this is not recommended). It's now available only with a 6-cylinder engine and as a seven- or eight-passenger carrier. Toyota built the Sienna for comfort and convenience. Sienna's V6 turns in respectable acceleration times, and the handling is also more car-like, but not as agile as with the Odyssey. **Weak points:** Recommended options are bundled with costly gadgets; an unusually large number of body rattles and assorted other noises. Toyota says slimmer seats and controls add to the feeling of "roominess." How's that for "spin control?" No matter how they spin it, the interior looks less luxurious than before, cabin noise levels are higher, and fit and finish is far from acceptable. Avoid models equipped with the under-powered, noisy, 4-cylinder engine.

Prices and Specs

Prices (Firm): *V6, 7-pass.:* $31,040, *LE 8-pass.:* $34,300, *LE 7-pass., AWD:* $37,125, *SE V6 8-pass.:* $37,845, *XLE AWD:* $41,730, *Limited AWD:* $46,225 **Freight:** $1,660 **Powertrain (front-drive/AWD):** Engine: 3.5L V6 (266 hp); Transmission: 6-speed auto. **Dimensions/capacity:** Passengers: 2/3/2; 2/3/3; Wheelbase: 119.3 in.; H: 69.5/L: 200.2/W: 78.2 in.; Headroom F/R1/R2: 3.5/4/2.5 in.; Legroom F/R1/R2: 40.5/31.5/2.5 in.; Cargo volume: 39.1 cu. ft.; Fuel tank: 79L/regular; Tow limit: 3,500 lb.; Load capacity: 1,120 lb.; Turning circle: 36.7 ft.; Ground clearance: 6.2 in.; Weight: 4,189-4,735 lb.

Other opinions: "The Sienna ranks #2 out of 7 minivans ... cargo space exceeds that of most minivans, and reviewers like its refreshed cabin that features user-friendly controls and high-end materials." – *U.S. News & World Report*. "2004-06 Sienna minivans have an engineering flaw with the design of the plate welded to the door that causes the door strap welds to break loose ... typically just outside of warranty for many owners. Toyota has issued a TSB (download TSBNV003-07.pdf), but refuses to issue a recall to fix the minivans. Repairs typically cost around $2,000 for the replacement of the driver's side door. Re-welding the failure points is not recommended as they are prone to fail again sooner than replacing the door." – *sites.google.com/site/toyotasiennadefects/*. **Major redesign:** 1998, 2001, and 2011. This year's Sienna is a carryover from its 2015 freshening; a redesigned version will debut as a 2018 model. **Highway/city fuel economy:** *(2012) 2.7L:* 7.5/10.4 L/100 km. *3.5L:* 8.1/11.5 L/100 km. *AWD:* 9.0/12.8 L/100 km. The 2.7L 4-cylinder engine burns almost as much fuel as the V6. **Best alternatives:** 2016 prices are higher than last year due to lower fuel costs boosting minivan and truck/SUV sales. As far as quality is concerned, it would be wise to delay your purchase a few months to take advantage of fewer factory-related glitches with later versions. Faster than average depreciation is another important factor to consider. For example, a 2010 LE seven-passenger AWD Sienna that sold for $34,000 now sells for $15,000. If an independent mechanic OK's the deal, this could be a bargain for used car buyers. Other choices: Honda's Odyssey and the Mazda5 (a mini-minivan). Chrysler's minivans bring up the rear of the pack due primarily to their Pentastar V6 and automatic transmission failures. Why not Nissan's Quest? The Quest's persistent powertrain and fit and finish deficiencies over the years preclude the van's consideration.

SAFETY: Child safety seat setup: "Poor." **Crashworthiness:** NHTSA: 2014 through 2016s received five stars for crashworthiness in all categories; 2001-13 models did almost as well with four-star crash protection. IIHS: 2011-14 Siennas have a "Good," overall crash score. However, the 2015 scored a "Poor" in the small front overlap crash test. 1998-2000 models were also generally "Good," except for a "Poor" rating for head restraint and seat protection among the 2005-10 models. **Owner-reported safety-related failures:** Be wary of the power-sliding door and power-assisted rear liftgate. The doors can crush children and pose unnecessary risks to other occupants, while the liftgate can seriously injure anyone standing under it. Also, as unbelievable as it sounds, a decade after all the complaints of "runaway" Toyotas, the 2014 Siennas suddenly accelerate and lose braking capability, in spite of Toyota's much-vaunted brake/throttle override feature:

> I was driving out of the parking lot from the grocery store, making a right turn on to the road, my 2014 Sienna suddenly accelerated, it was all I could do with all of my weight on the brakes to stop the Sienna from hitting another car. It was frightening.

• • •

I parked my 2014 Sienna on an upward inclining driveway and left it in idle. I went inside the house to go and get my dog. I went back inside and was speaking to my in-laws when all of a sudden we heard a loud crash. We went outside and my car had accelerated and crashed into their garage.

When the brakes *do* work, and are applied, the driver's seat moves forward; cruise control won't turn off; and the brakes don't engage:

At around 5 pm on a clear Monday evening I went to turn left into a parking spot. I stepped on the gas and nothing happened, I let up a bit and stepped again and my Sienna shot forward. I slammed on the brake halfway into the parking spot and ran into the tree in front of the van.

Airbags don't deploy when needed; power-sliding rear doors and power rear hatch are two options known more for their dangerous malfunctions than their utility:

My 17-month-old's head got jammed between the right rear wheel and the right rear door panel while the electric door slid open. Even though my wife pulled on the door handle the door kept sliding open. My baby's head was crushed between the tire and door panel. This is a very unsafe design as my wife tried to stop the door from sliding back and the door kept moving.

· · ·

My 2-year-old daughter got her leg caught in the back part of the sliding door of a 2011 Toyota Sienna. She was inside the car. The door was opened. Her leg fell into the space while the door was opening. The door opened as far as it could and constricted her leg. Her leg was so constricted we could not reposition her body to open the door. . . . She was trapped (screaming) for 20–25 minutes. Her leg was cold and turning blue before it was freed. . . . I'm very concerned about the design of the door. I've looked at other minivans (even the same make and model but different year) and they don't have the gap in the back part of the door like the 2011 Toyota Sienna.

· · ·

Couple of months after I got the car, there were several incidents [in which] me and family members were hit on our heads and shoulders by self closing liftgate [and we] didn't know what the cause was. After researching about this problem, Toyota had recalled Sienna in the past about this same problem for older models for weak liftgate struts.

In another reported incident, a driver accelerated to pass another car, and his 2014 Sienna suddenly accelerated out of control, while the brakes were useless. Brakes can take a couple of seconds before they engage; the slightest touch of the gear shifter causes a shift into Neutral or Reverse; multiple warning lights come on, and the vehicle cannot shift; front windshield distorts the view; sunroof may spontaneously explode:

The rear window on my 2013 Sienna hatchback door blew out. The vehicle had been parked in my garage overnite — the next morning it was shattered. I contacted the dealer to find out of this was a common problem — I was told no. However, upon performing a Google search, I found hundreds of instances of of people complaining of the same issue. It was also interesting to learn that rear windows were/are on national backorder from Toyota.

Excessive rearview mirror vibration; factory-installed TV screen obstructs the field of vision through the rearview mirror and lacks an audio warning; rear tires quickly wear out; front passenger seatback tilts forward when braking and second-row seats may be wobbly. Three more things to remember, particularly on the 2013 models: If the battery "dies" you will have to climb over the console to extract kids from the backseat; the AC is known for emiting a foul, moldy smell that may cause respiratory distress; and washing the van in cold weather can freeze the brakes.

ALERT! Dealer-supplied run-flat tires are reportedly fast-wearing and expensive to replace. Buy Michelin or Pirelli original-equipment tires, instead of Bridgestone or Dunlop run-flats. There have also been many owner reports that the brake and accelerator pedals are mounted too close together; see if this affects your driving during the dealership test drive. Finally, ensure the dash digital readouts can be read in daylight:

We cannot see the speed on cloudy days or with sunglasses on sunny days. My previous Toyota 2006 Sienna and 2013 Avalon have illumination anytime the ignition is on for driving. When you can't see the speed easily, this is a safety risk.

Sienna Profile

Used Values ($)	2006	2007	2008	2009	2010	2011	2012	2013	2014
CE	7,500	8,500	9,500	11,000	12,500	16,000	18,500	—	—
LE AWD	9,000	10,000	11,500	13,000	16,000	21,000	23,000	26,000	28,500
XLE	10,500	11,500	13,500	15,500	—	23,000	26,500	30,000	32,500
XLE AWD	—	—	—	—	—	—	28,000	32,500	35,000

	2006	2007	2008	2009	2010	2011	2012	2013	2014
Reliability	★2	★3	★	★	★	★	★	★	★
Repairs ($$$)	🛍2	🛍1	🛍1	🛍1	🛍1	🛍1	🛍1	🛍1	🛍1
Electrical	★2	★2	★3	★	★	★	★	★	★
Engine (base)	★4	★	★	★	★	★	★	★	★
Fit/Finish	★2	★2	★2	★2	★2	★2	★2	★2	★3
Infotainment	—	—	—	★3	★3	★	★	★	★
Transmission (auto.)	★3	★3	★3	★	★	★	★	★	★

SECRET WARRANTIES, INTERNAL BULLETINS: All years: Sliding-door hazards, malfunctions, and noise are a veritable plague affecting all model years and generating a ton of service bulletins. Owner feedback confirms that front brake pads and discs are often replaced under Toyota's "goodwill" policy if they wear out before 2 years/40,000 km (in spite of Toyota's pretensions that brakes aren't a warrantable item) and the customer is adamant that the brakes aren't "reasonably" durable. Rusting at the base of the two front doors will usually be repaired at no cost, often with a courtesy car included. 2002-14—Remedies for vehicle pulling from one side to the other, requiring constant steering corrections. 2003-09—Upper, lower windshield ticking noise. 2004—Rear disc brake groan (TSB #BR002-04). Intermediate steering shaft noise on turns. Front-door area wind noise (TSB #NV009-03). Power-sliding door inoperative, omnipresent rattles (the saga continues). Back door shudder and water leaks. Seat heaters operate only on high.

NOXIOUS AC ODOURS			
SERVICE BULLETIN NO.: #T-SB-0142-13			ISSUED: SEPTEMBER 12, 2013

YEAR(S)	MODEL(S)	ADDITIONAL INFORMATION
2004–2014	4Runner, Avalon, Avalon HV, Camry, Camry HV, Corolla, FJ Cruiser, Highlander, Highlander HV, Land Cruiser, Matrix, Prius, Prius C, Prius PHV, Prius V, RAV4, Sequoia, Sienna, Tundra, Venza, Yaris	

INTRODUCTION: Some 2004–2014 model year Toyota vehicles may exhibit odors naturally occurring from the HVAC system and/or related environmental factors. Although there is no way to eliminate these odors follow the General Procedure in this bulletin to minimize the odors experienced.

OP CODE	DESCRIPTION	TIME	OFP	T1	T2
N/A	Not Applicable to Warranty	–	–	–	–

WARRANTY INFORMATION:

MODEL	MODEL YEAR	PART NUMBER	PART NAME
4Runner	2010–2014	87139-50100	High Performance Charcoal Filter
Avalon	2007–2014		
Avalon HV	2013–2014		
Camry	2007–2014		
Camry HV	2007–2014		
Corolla	2009–2013		

2004-05—Remedy for hard starts in cold weather. Transmission lag, gear hunting. Premature brake pad wear. Fuel-injector ticking. Inoperative AC light flashing. AC blower or compressor noise; seized compressor. 2004-06—Silencing engine ping, knock. Power-hatch door shudder and leakage. Power-sliding door rattles. Excessive steering effort in high road-salt areas. 2004-07—Back power-sliding doors are hard to close. Back power-door shudder. 2004-08—Front power-seat grinding, groaning. Remedy for front brake pads that wear out prematurely. 2004-10—Front seat squeaking. Sliding doors don't operate smoothly (change the lock assembly). Sliding-door rattle. Brake rattle, buzz from driver's side of the dash. The TSB below contains Toyota's admission that its AC system can emit foul, musty, moldy odours. Odours this foul *do not* "naturally" occur in most cars. The bulletin is confusing: It states the warranty doesn't apply to labour and then lists which cars and parts are eligible for warranty coverage. The bottom line is that this "hidden defect" is Toyota's decade-old problem, affecting almost its entire model lineup. If the charcoal canister doesn't work, Toyota should compensate owners and take the vehicle back under provincial consumer protection and business practices laws. 2007— Inoperative front, sliding-door windows. Front-seat squeak. 2006-09—No shift from Park. 2007-08—Engine compartment squeaking. 2011-12—Engine ticking; more ticking from the windshield/back glass. Vehicle may exhibit insufficient charging performance from the alternator. An updated pulley assembly is available to address this condition. Transfer-case fluid leaks. Water puddles in the van's rear storage area near the back door. 2011-13—If the A/C doesn't work properly, an A/C line retainer (piping clamp) may have become unlatched and caused a refrigerant leak. This is a simple and cheap repair; try it first. 2011-14—Some Siennas may have a front brake vibration/pulsation that can be felt while lightly applying the brake pedal. New front brake pads and a new field fix repair procedure have been developed to improve this condition, says TSB # T-SB-0045-14, issued July 8, 2014. Cleaning out an AC evaporator drain hose that is clogged by insect nests.

RAV4 ★★★★

RATING: Above Average (2009-16); Below Average (2006-08); Average (1996-2005). This SUV crossover combines a car-type unibody platform with elevated seating and optional AWD. Although classed as a compact SUV, the RAV4 is large enough to carry a kid-sized third-row bench seat, giving it seven passenger capacity. A powerful V6 makes this downsized SUV one of the fastest crossovers on the market. Road performance: 4-cylinder acceleration from a stop is acceptable with a full load; excellent V6 powertrain performance; transmission is hesitant to shift to a lower gear when under load, and sometimes produces jerky low-speed shifts; some nose plow and body lean when cornering under power; and some road and wind noise. Good handling and a comfortable, and relatively quiet ride are big improvements over earlier, more firmly sprung models. Strong points: Lots of sales incentives available. Base models offer a nice array of standard safety, performance, and convenience features, including electronic stability control and standard brake override; RAV4 seats five, but an optional third-row bench on Base and Limited models increases capacity to seven; comfortable seats; a quiet interior; cabin gauges and controls are easy to access and read; exceptional reliability; and good fuel economy with the 4-cylinder engine (the V6 is almost as fuel frugal). **Weak points:** Resale value is only average. (A "Strong Point" for used SUV shoppers!) Practically all of the owner complaints unrelated to safety involve poor fit and finish and audio system malfunctions. Some drivers say they are sickened by a sulphur smell that invades the interior. Owners also deride the flimsy glove box lid, loose sun visor, constantly flickering traction control light, sticking ignition key, uncomfortable head restraints, squeaks and rattles from the dashboard and rear-seat area.

Prices and Specs

Prices (Firm): *LE:* $24,365, *LE 4WD:* $26,630, *XLE:* $28,700, *AWD:* $30,900, *Limited 4WD:* $33,710 **Freight:** $1,660 **Powertrain (Front-drive/AWD):** Engines: 2.5L 4-cyl. (179 hp), 3.5L V6 (269 hp); Transmissions: 4-speed auto., 5-speed auto. **Dimensions/capacity:** Passengers: 2/3; 2/3/2; Wheelbase: 105 in.; H: 66/L: 181/W: 72 in.; Cargo volume: 39 cu. ft.; Fuel tank: 70L/regular; Headroom F/R: 6.55/4 in.; Legroom F/R: 41.5/29 in.; Tow limit: 1,500 lb.; Load capacity: 825 lb.; Turning circle: 37.4 ft.; Ground clearance: 7.5 in.; Weight: 3,590 lb.

Other opinions: "The Toyota RAV4 ranks #22 out of 27 Affordable Compact SUVs … RAV4's engine is underpowered, but this compact SUV has a spacious cabin, plenty of cargo room and numerous standard features." – *U.S. News & World Report.* **Major redesign:** 2001 and 2006. The 2016 RAV4 gets a minor upgrade; later this year, a new hybrid model arrives. Next redesign is due in the summer of 2018, when the car gets a new platform and a CVT tranny. **Highway/city fuel economy:** *2.5L:* 6.9/9.4 L/100 km, 41/30 mpg. *2.5L AWD:* 7.2/9.7 L/100 km. *3.5L:* 7.4/10.7 L/100 km. *3.5L AWD:* 7.7/11.7 L/100 km. Owners say fuel economy figures are too high by 15%. **Best alternatives:** Other vehicles worth considering are the Honda CR-V, Hyundai Tucson, and Nissan X-Trail.

SAFETY: Child safety seat setup: "Marginal." **Crashworthiness:** NHTSA: The 2012-13 RAV4 received five stars for side crashworthiness and four stars for frontal and rollover protection. 2014s earned five stars for side crash safety; four stars for rollover protection. IIHS: Rates 2004-13s "Good" in moderate overlap front crash tests; 2001-04 models were judged "Acceptable," and 1996-2000 models were considered "Poor." **Owner-reported safety-related failures:** Sudden, unintended acceleration (even after recall repairs were done) and loss of braking:

After attempting to drive in Reverse out of a parking space with the brake pedal engaged, the vehicle suddenly accelerated and crashed into a parked vehicle. The vehicle changed gears on its own, and the gas pedal went to the floor on its own as well.

Other reports: Fire erupted in the engine compartment; steering angle sensor malfunction causes the vehicle to stall out; a "thumping" rear suspension noise; cracking front windshields:

Vehicle is only a few weeks old and the windshield began developing a crack from the passenger side spreading towards the center of and down towards the bottom of the passenger side.

Original-equipment Yokohama tires may blow out their side walls; and the defroster/air circulation system is weak; and wide rear roof pillars that obstruct visibility. And, the mice are back! Rodents routinely enter the vehicle at will through the clean-air filter. One dealer suggested owners buy mouse traps or adopt a cat:

Check Engine light indicated. The car was taken to the dealer, where the dealer mentioned, "Evidence of rodent/small animal has chewed wiring harness at connector completely through." The car will need a new wiring harness.

ALERT! The Sport model has an option that uses run-flat tires and dispenses with the tailgate-mounted spare tire. Stick with the regular tire; it's cheaper and less problematic. If you come across a substantially discounted 2014, buy it. The 2015s don't offer much more.

RAV4 Profile

	2006	2007	2008	2009	2010	2011	2012	2013	2014
Used Values ($)									
Base 4x2	—	—	—	—	11,000	13,500	16,500	19,000	21,000
Base 4x4	7,500	8,500	9,500	11,000	13,000	15,000	17,500	20,500	22,500
Sport V6	7,500	10,000	11,000	12,000	13,500	18,000	20,500	—	—
LTD V6	8,500	10,000	11,500	13,000	15,000	19,500	22,500	26,500	28,500
Reliability	⑫	⑫	⑫	③	③	③	③	③	③
Repairs ($$$)	②	②	②	①	①	①	①	①	①
Electrical	③	③	③	③	③	③	③	③	③
Engine (base)	②	③	③	③	③	③	③	③	③
Fit/Finish	②	②	②	③	③	③	③	③	③
Infotainment	—	—	—	③	③	③	③	③	③
Transmission (auto.)	②	②	③	③	③	③	③	③	③

SECRET WARRANTIES, INTERNAL BULLETINS: 2002-06—Correction for vehicles that pull to the right when accelerating. 2003-11—Windshield ticking noise considered a factory-related problem (TSB-0142-08, published July 29, 2008). 2004-10—Front-seat squeaking. 2006—Engine timing cover oil leaks. 2006-07—Automatic transmission shift lever doesn't move smoothly. Water leaks onto the passenger floorboard. Front-door locks may be inoperative in cold weather. 2006-08—The 2.4L 4-cylinder engine may be an "oil-burner" covered by a Toyota "goodwill warranty" (see Camry section). Engine compartment squeaks. Steering clunk, pop, knock. 2006-09—Engine ticking noise. Multiple warning lamps lit; no shift from Park. Brake rattle, buzz heard from the driver's-side dash area. Inoperative moon-roof. 2006-10—No-crank, no-start requires the installation of a revised neutral switch assembly. Rough idle. Loose sun visor mount. Automatic transmission whining noise. 2006-12—A rear-end clunking sound may signal that one or both rear stabilizer links are damaged. 2006-14—AC evaporator drain hose clogged by insect nests. 2007—Paint stains on horizontal surfaces. 2008—Water drips from the headliner near the front pillar. 2011-12—Vehicle may exhibit insufficient charging performance from the alternator. An updated pulley assembly is available. 2013—One or both power back door actuator units may separate from the ball mounts on the hatch or the body. Additionally, wiring on the actuator may be damaged causing the power back door to become inoperative.

VENZA	

RATING: Above Average (2010-15); Average (2009). Toyota's Venza is a five-passenger wagon sold in two trim levels that match the two available engines. Going into its eighth and last year, the car offers the styling and comfort of a wagon with the flexibility of a small SUV. This combination has proven itself to be relatively problem-free and a good highway performer. **Road performance:** Powerful and efficient engines; pleasant riding though the ride is stiff at times; and handling is acceptable, though there isn't much steering feedback. **Strong points:** Roomy interior; innovative cabin storage areas; an automatic headlight dimmer; easy entry and exit; and a low rear loading height. **Weak points:** No third-row seat; radio station indicator washes out in sunlight; and high-intensity discharge headlights are annoying to other drivers, are often stolen, and are expensive to replace. Resale value is lower than one would expect for a Toyota SUV. For example, a 2010 Venza AWD V6 wagon that sold new for $32,100 is now worth only $14,000. The V6 is a must-have.

Other opinions: "Toyota's Venza ranks #9 out of 12 affordable midsize SUVs ... An underwhelming engine and low-quality interior materials detract from the Venza's abundant cargo and rear-seat space, reviewers say." – *U.S. News & World Report.* **Major redesign:** 1998 and 2005. **Highway/city fuel economy:** *2.7L:* 6.8/10.0 L/100 km. *AWD:* 7.1/10.2 L/100 km. *3.5L:* 7.6/11.0L/100 km. *AWD:* 7.9/11.5 L/100 km. **Best alternatives:** A Subaru Forester or Toyota Highlander.

SAFETY: **Child safety seat setup:** Untested. **Crashworthiness:** NHTSA: 2013-15s given a five-star overall rating for crashworthiness; 2011-13 scored four stars. Ratings varied between four and five stars on 2009 and 2010 models. IIHS: "Good" for overall crash protection. **Owner-reported safety-related failures:** Only one safety-related incident reported with the 2015 Venza and it concerned the poorly-designed driver's head restraint. On earlier models, some reports of the sunroof shattering, brake and airbag failures, and sudden, unintended acceleration:

> We accelerated our Venza to match ongoing traffic speeds, when the throttle stuck wide open and was increasing in speed, I stepped on the brakes, which failed to respond. I then checked the cruise control, to see if I had inadvertently engaged it, but I had not. I then started to pump the accelerator pedal with extreme force, and after numerous pumps, the throttle disengaged.

Transmission would not go into Reverse; the Hill-Start Assist feature doesn't prevent the car from rolling back when stopped on a hill in traffic; sometimes, after the brakes are applied, the car won't accelerate; automatic rear hatch can crush a hand if it is caught when the hatch is closing; seat belt began strangling a three-year-old, who had to be cut free; the radio overheated up to 63 degrees C (145 degrees F).

ALERT! Yikes! Not poorly designed head restraints, again!

> The headrest for the front seats on the Venza makes these seats the most uncomfortable I have ever sat in, let alone drive. I am only 5'4" tall and the way the headrest lands, it pushes my head forward when I drive. I end up with both a headache and a neck ache whenever I drive. It appears this vehicle was designed for someone taller, perhaps a man. The headrest needs to be redesigned for someone of my stature. I would gladly pay for another headrest

if one was available. But the bottom line here is that once again the needs of women (shorter than men) are not what is driving the design. I expect more from all car manufacturers. It is time to recognize that women make up 51% of the population.

Venza Profile

	2009	2010	2011	2012	2013	2014
Used Values ($)						
Base	10,500	12,500	16,000	19,000	21,000	23,500
V6 AWD	12,500	14,500	18,000	21,500	23,500	27,500
Reliability	☆	☆	☆	☆	☆	☆
Repairs ($$$)	💰	💰	💰	💰	💰	💰
Electrical	☆	☆	☆	☆	☆	☆
Engine (base)	☆	☆	☆	☆	☆	☆
Fit/Finish	☆	☆	☆	☆	☆	☆
Infotainment	—	—	—	☆	☆	☆
Transmission (auto.)	☆	☆	☆	☆	☆	☆

SECRET WARRANTIES, INTERNAL BULLETINS: 2007-11—Some vehicles equipped with 2GR-FE/FXE towing package engines may exhibit an oil seep from the engine oil cooler pipes. 2009-10—Wind noise from the front door area can be silenced by adding weather stripping. Rear end squawk noise on bumps. 2009-11—Correction for a steering column rattle. The noise may be caused by rear coil spring contact with the lower strut seat. An updated rear coil spring lower insulator is available. 2009-13—Drivers may hear a "pop" noise from the steering column when turning the steering wheel sharply during low speed maneuvers. Some Venzas equipped with 2GR-FE engines may exhibit difficulty restarting in sub-freezing temperatures (approximately -4°F [-20°C] and lower). A new Engine Room Junction Block Assembly is available to address this condition. Some vehicles equipped with the 1AR-FE engine may exhibit one or more of the following conditions: An inoperative A/C, or rising engine temperature when stopped. Some vehicles may exhibit a condition where the seat heater is inoperative. Cold start engine knock/rattle. 2009-14—Remedies for vehicle pulling from one side to the other, requiring constant steering corrections. AC evaporator drain hose clogged by insect nests. 2011-12—Vehicle may exhibit insufficient charging performance from the alternator. An updated pulley assembly is available to address this condition. 2013—Entune infotainment and navigation issues and concerns.

HIGHLANDER ★★★★★

RATING: Recommended (2009-16); Above Average (2001-08). A crossover alternative to a minivan, this competent, refined, family-friendly SUV puts function ahead of style and provides cargo and passenger versatility along with a high level of quality. **Road performance:** Powerful engines and a smooth, refined powertrain; the Hybrid can propel itself on electric power alone; a quiet interior enhances the comfortable ride; and responsive handling. **Strong points:** Roomy second-row seating is fairly versatile. Third-row seating is much improved with the bigger 2014 and later versions. **Weak points:** The third-row seat is a bit tight and doesn't fold in a 50/50 split.

Prices and Specs

Prices (Firm): *LE V6:* $32,775, *Convenient Package:* $35,575, *AWD:* $35,275, *XLE AWD:* $40,995, *Limited V6 4WD:* $46,195, *LE Hybrid:* $44,915, *XLE:* $47,340, *Hybrid Limited:* $53,890 **Freight:** $1,660 **Powertrain (Front-drive/AWD):** Engines: 2.7L 4-cyl. (185 hp), 3.5L V6 (270 hp), 3.5L Hybrid (280 hp); Transmissions: 6-speed auto., CVT **Dimensions/capacity:** Passengers: 2/3/2, Hybrid: 2/3; Wheelbase: 110 in.; H: 68/L: 191/W: 76 in.; Cargo volume: 40.5 cu. ft.; Fuel tank: 72.5L/regular; Headroom F/R1/R2: 4.0/5.5/1 in. (Ouch! Third-row seat is for only the very young or very short.); Legroom F/R1/R2: 41.5/32/23.5 in.; Tow limit: 3,500-5,000 lb.; Load capacity: 1,385 lb.; Turning circle: 38.7 ft.; Ground clearance: 8.1 in.; Weight: 4,490 lb.

Other opinions: "The Highlander ranks #3 out of 12 affordable midsize SUVs ... [It] delivers roomy seating, generous cabin storage and a hushed, comfortable ride, making it a perfect SUV for families." – *U.S. News & World Report.* **Major redesign:** 2001, 2008, and 2014. The next redesign is scheduled for the 2020 model year. **Highway/city fuel economy:** 7.3/10.4 L/100 km. *V6:* 8.8/12.3 L/100 km. *Hybrid:* 8.0/7.4 L/100 km. **Best alternatives:** From the Detroit SUV side, try the Buick Enclave, Chevrolet Traverse, Ford Flex, and GMC Acadia. A good Asian SUV is the Honda Pilot. The Honda Odyssey is the only suitable Asian minivan choice. V6-equipped models best represent the Highlander's attributes, as the Hybrid models' higher prices aren't justified with fuel costs so low.

SAFETY: **Child safety seat setup:** "Marginal." **Crashworthiness:** NHTSA: 2014-16 Highlander and its Hybrid variant earned five stars for overall crash protection; 2011-13 models scored four stars; and the 2005-10 Highlander crashworthiness rating varies between four and five stars. IIHS: 2014-15s rated "Good" in providing overall occupant protection, except for an "Acceptable" score in small overlap frontal crashes. 2008-13 Highlander judged "Good" for overall crash safety; "Poor" for the 2004-07 models. **Owner-reported safety-related failures:** NHTSA's safety-defect log sheet shows very few complaints registered against the Highlander. Nevertheless, lag and lurch acceleration, unintended acceleration, and brake failures are front and centre:

The driver owns a 2012 Toyota Highlander. While attempting to park with the brake pedal depressed, the vehicle suddenly accelerated and went over the curb. The driver applied the brake with both feet and shifted into Park in order to bring the vehicle to a complete stop.

Other incidents: Airbag failed to deploy; transmission will not hold car parked on an incline; speedometer overstates the car's true speed by about 3 mph; sudden brake failure; brake and steering both went out as driver was making a turn; engine replaced after overheating, due to road debris damaging the radiator; engine loses power in turns; and windshield distortion.

ALERT! Don't open the window while underway:

While driving on the highway, my son opened the rear passenger window. When he opened the window the noise and pressure on our ears was unbearable, it was like an extremely loud helicopter noise. We even tried opening other windows in the car to reduce the pressure and noise, while the noise and pressure were reduced it was still very loud and distracting. Dealer said all cars do that and to just open another window to relieve pressure. When I told him we tried that and it did not work he did not have any other answers. The dealer gave me a phone number to Toyota service, I called them and the rep said she had checked and they have never heard of anything like that. After checking on the Internet I have found multiple instances where other people have had this issue, the noise is so loud it actually hurts your eardrums.

Highlander Profile

	2006	2007	2008	2009	2010	2011	2012	2013	2014
Used Values ($)									
Base	—	—	—	—	—	18,500	22,500	24,500	—
AWD	8,500	9,500	11,500	13,000	15,000	21,000	25,500	29,000	—
Base Hybrid	9,500	10,500	12,000	13,500	15,500	24,500	29,000	35,500	—
Reliability	★	★	★	★	★	★	★	★	★
Repairs ($$$)	💰	💰	💰	💰	💰	💰	💰	💰	💰
Electrical	★	★	★	★	★	★	★	★	★
Engine (base)	★	★	★	★	★	★	★	★	★
Fit/Finish	★	★	★	★	★	★	★	★	★
Infotainment	—	—	—	★	★	★	★	★	★
Transmission (auto.)	★	★	★	★	★	★	★	★	★

SECRET WARRANTIES, INTERNAL BULLETINS: 2002-14—Remedies for vehicle pulling from one side to the other, requiring constant steering corrections. 2008-13—Vehicles equipped with the 5-speed automatic transaxle may exhibit a whine noise from the final drive gear assembly. This noise is noticeable above 50 kph. A new automatic transaxle assembly may be needed. A clunk, pop, or knock-type noise when turning the steering wheel can be silenced by replacing the intermediate shaft. 2008-14—AC evaporator drain hose clogged by insect nests. 2011-12—Insufficient alternator charging may require an updated pulley assembly. Procedures needed to fix a loose roof drip moulding. 2011-13—If the A/C doesn't work properly, an A/C line retainer (piping clamp) may have become unlatched and caused a refrigerant leak. This is a simple and cheap repair; try it first. 2012-13—Difficulty in folding down or stowing the third row seat assembly may be due to binding between the seat frame and the banana bracket guide in the seat assembly.

TACOMA	★★★

RATING: Average (2011-15; 2000-04); Below Average (2005-10). The improved 2016 Tacoma will likely be an Above Average buy, after it gets in more road time. Generally, buying a Tacoma is a roll of the dice. Owners don't report a lot of failures, but those that are reported generally turn out to be major, life-threatening, expensive to repair, and often "unfixable." This cheap light-duty, basic truck would have been rated higher if it weren't for the Tacoma's infamous hazardous drivetrain, decade-old lag and lurch transmission, and sudden unintended acceleration problems spilling over into the 2011-15 lineup. Plus, Toyota's entry-level pickup isn't as utilitarian as its predecessors or some of the competition (watch the payload). Overall, it has sufficient power and is relatively inexpensive if not too gussied up. So, ask yourself that famous Clint Eastwood/*Dirty Harry* question: "Do you feel lucky?" **Road performance:** Well-chosen powertrain and steering set-up; ideal for off-road work with electronic stability control and the optional suspension; good acceleration, although delayed transmission engagement and excessive drivetrain vibration are still omnipresent. Very responsive handling over smooth roads; over rough terrain, the ride can be jolting and steering control reduced. If you decide to go for the optional off-road suspension, you will quickly notice the firmer ride and increased road feedback. The driving position seems low when compared with the competition. **Strong points:** A well-garnished, roomy interior; plenty of storage space; and much improved for 2016. **Weak points:** Excessive driveline vibration:

> We were driving home after the purchase of our 2014 Tacoma. There was severe vibration inside the cab and it felt like the driveshaft was going to fall out. We have had it back to the dealer numerous times for this issue and have been told it is a characteristic of the vehicle by the dealer and 2 other representatives from Toyota. The dealer has changed different components on the suspension and motor mounts; tires have been balanced, re-balanced

and replaced; the driveshaft was trued and balanced; and the driveshaft was replaced, no change. We are told that the vibration is normal and a characteristic of the Tacoma.

Faulty, noisy gear boxes (transmission pops out of gear); premature wearout of the brake rotors and drums; squeaking, howling rear brakes; AC malfunctions; noisy fuel pump; suspension bottoms out at 300-500 lbs; instrument panel is poorly lit; loose front passenger seat; windshield seal lifts in high winds and allows air into the cab:

I heard wind noise coming into the vehicle. I stopped at the next rest area and checked the vehicle out and found that the windshield seal had lifted and was causing wind noise and flexing of the windshield. This could have been catastrophic had the windshield blown completely out.

Rodent marauders continue to snack on wiring, hoses, and plastic components making Tacomas unsafe and running up huge repair bills:

Electronic stability control turns off when check engine light turns on. Vehicle stability is compromised. Almost rolled the truck over. Dealer technician reports that rodents ate the hose connecting fuel injector air pump to valve which triggers the ECU to fault and cascades failure to stability control. Technician reports that Toyota is using edible soy-based plastics for engine hoses and wiring harness and rodents are causing extensive damage in Toyota vehicles. Toyota does not cover related repairs under manufacturers warranty. Was quoted $1000 to replace one hose.

Prices and Specs

Prices (Firm): *Access Cab 4x2:* $24,285, *4x4 V6:* $29,180, *4x4 SR5:* $31,505, *V6 TRD offroad:* $34,220, *Double Cab V6:* $30,670 **Freight:** $1,660 **Powertrain (Rear-drive/AWD):** Engines: 2.7L 4-cyl. (159 hp), 4.0L V6 (236 hp); Transmissions: 5-speed man., 6-speed man., 4-speed auto., 5-speed auto. **Dimensions/capacity:** Passengers: 2/2; Wheelbase: 127.8 in.; H: 70/L: 208.1/W: 75 in.; Fuel tank: 80L/regular; Headroom F/R: 4/3 in.; Legroom F/R: 42.5/28 in.; Tow limit: 3,500-6,500 lb.; Load capacity: 1,100 lb.; Turning circle: 44.6 ft.; Ground clearance: 8.1 in.; Weight: 4,115 lb.

Other opinions: "The Tacoma ranks #3 out of 4 compact pickup trucks ... [It] has durable cabin materials and great off-road capability, but it has an aging design and faces some stiff new competition." – *U.S. News & World Report.* "While the Tacoma has taken great strides forward, it was far, far behind in terms of technology and features, and, at least on paper, the 2016 model doesn't seem to advance the mid-size truck species so much as it simply catches up." – *www.caranddriver.com/.* **Major redesign:** 1995, 2005, and 2016. The 2016 improvements address most of the powertrain, suspension, and infotainment issues of past models. There's the long-standing 2.7L 4-cylinder engine hooked to a 6-speed automatic transmission or the existing 5-speed manual and an all-new aluminum 3.5L V6 that switches from port to direct injection depending on driving conditions. Toyota also added more high strength steel to reduce vibration and weight, plus a re-engineered suspension, rear differential, and rear axle to improve the truck's ride and handling without compromising its off-road prowess. The interior has also been revamped to improve the infotaint system, strengthen the windshield seal, and reduce cabin noise. **Highway/city fuel economy:** *2.7:* 7.8/10.5 L/100 km. *Auto.:* 7.9/11.0 L/100 km. *AWD:* 9.1/12.0 L/100 km. *4.0 4x4:* 10.8/14.7 L/100 km. *Auto.:* 9.9/13.4 L/100 km. **Best alternatives:** The Chevrolet Terrain and Traverse, or Nissan's Frontier and X-Trail.

SAFETY: Child safety seat setup: Untested. **Crashworthiness:** NHTSA: 2004-15 models get a four- and five-star rating across the board. IIHS: "Good" designation for 2009-14 models' head restraints and seat protection. 2005-08 versions rated the seats and head restraints "Marginal." **Owner-reported safety-related failures:** Less than average number of life-threatening incidents were registered for the 2014-15 models, where 50 reports per year would be expected. But the same safety hazards reappear year after year. Airbags fail to deploy; sudden, unintended acceleration accompanied by loss of braking ability; truck surges forward when braking; brakes come on by themselves when turning or slowly release, allowing truck to "drift" into car ahead; there is no brake light warning to others when brakes are applied; and ABS braking is unpredictable:

> The abs system on my 2014 Tacoma is very unpredictable and unsafe. I have had 3 incidents where the abs system disabled all braking power to the wheels and just coasted to a stop narrowly missing other vehicles. This happens maybe 10 percent of the time when driving on snowy roads. When this happens there is no pulsing from the ABS system; it is just a dead brake pedal ... it is well documented online at www.tacomaworld.com. Many people are resorting to removing the ABS fuse from their truck in order to have a safer and more predictable vehicle.

Other common failures: Cracks in the tread of original equipment Goodrich Rugged Trail tires and sidewall "ballooning" with Dunlops; when braking, the driver's foot presses the accelerator pedal, as well; the plastic piece found within the rear seat head restraints can exacerbate head injuries in a collision; clutch pedal sticks in cold weather; steering locks up when entering a tight turn with 4x4 engaged; spare tire fell off the vehicle in traffic; and false low-pressure tire alerts:

> The dealer suggested that I try driving on different roads and to take another route home. The dealer also stated that radio signals are causing the TPS tire light to flash. My 2013's mileage: 158 miles.

ALERT! Payload capacity may be overly optimistic:

> My 2012 Toyota Tacoma TRD Off Road does not meet its payload capacity. It has a limit of 1240 lbs and routinely bottoms out with 300–500 lbs in the bed of the truck. Toyota knows

about the issue on its 2005-11s [and] has issued TSBs on the leaf springs but refuses to solve the issue on the new 2012 trucks.

Front windshield may distort night visibility:

At night, the top 1/3rd of the windshield causes double vision of lights. This occurs for all headlights, taillights, signal lights, and streetlights. This doesn't occur lower in the windshield, but it's unavoidable for taller drivers (I'm over 6' tall). This does occur the entire width of the windshield. It doesn't occur with any of the side windows.

Tacoma Profile

	2006	2007	2008	2009	2010	2011	2012	2013	2014
Used Values ($)									
Acces Cab 4x2	5,500	6,000	6,500	8,000	10,500	12,000	14,000	15,500	17,500
4x4 SR5	—	8,000	9,000	10,000	12,000	14,000	16,000	17,500	19,500
V6	8,000	9,000	10,000	12,000	13,500	15,500	17,500	19,500	21,500
Double Cab/SR5	9,500	11,000	13,000	14,500	16,000	18,000	20,000	22,500	24,500
PR/TRD	11,500	13,500	15,500	17,500	19,000	21,500	24,000	27,000	30,000
Reliability	★	★	★	★	★	★	★	★	★
Repairs ($$$)	3	2	1	2	2	1	1	1	1
Electrical	☆	☆	☆	☆	☆	☆	☆	☆	☆
Engine (base)	★	★	★	★	★	★	★	★	★
Fit/Finish	★	★	★	★	★	★	★	★	★
Infotainment	—	—	—	—	—	★	★	★	★
Transmission (auto.)	★	★	★	★	★	★	★	★	★

SECRET WARRANTIES, INTERNAL BULLETINS: 2002-14—Troubleshooting tips for a vehicle that continually pulls to one side. 2005-12—Passing over rough surfaces may produce a steering shaft rattle. 2005-13—A rear differential whine at 50-60 mph may be heard by some owners of Tacoma pickups. In TSB #005713 issued on April 26, 2013, Toyota said the noise could occur in 2005-13 models with the 5-speed automatic transmission that were not equipped with limited-slip or locking rear differentials. Replacement of the differential is the cure. TSB #0016-13 says some 4x4 Tacomas equipped with an automatic transmission may exhibit a clunk/thunk noise from the rear of the vehicle or a "bump-from-behind" sensation just before a stop or when accelerating from a stop. Improvements have been made to the rear propeller shaft (driveshaft) to reduce this condition. 2006-14—Driveline vibration at 24-40 km/h Canada Bulletin:

DRIVELINE VIBRATION

SERVICE BULLETIN NO.: T-TCI-4089

DATE: FEBRUARY 7, 2014

YEAR(S)	MODEL(S)	ADDITIONAL INFORMATION
2005–2014	Tacoma	Transmission(s): 5AT, 6MT VDS(s): JU4GN, JU62N, KU4HN, KU72N, LU42N, LU4EN, MU4FN, MU52N, TU4GN, TU62N, UU42N, UU4EN

INTRODUCTION: Some 2005–2014 model year Tacoma vehicles may exhibit an excessive vibration felt in the seat, floorboard, and steering wheel between 24–40 km/h (15–25 mph) caused by a second order drivetrain vibration under acceleration. Replace the rear engine insulator (rear transmission mount); install a steering wheel damper; and overhaul the rear leaf springs.

Over a decade and Toyota returns each year with another "MixMaster" vibrating Tacoma drivetrain. At least, the Tundra's "shake" was eventually corrected.

2011-12—A bouncy rear suspension ride with a heavy load can be corrected by installing upgraded rear spring assemblies. 2012-13—A wind whistle from the front of the vehicle may be coming from the radiator grille where it meets the hood. An upgraded radiator grille seal will silence the noise.

EUROPEAN VEHICLES

Mice ate my Audi TT ($18,250 repairs).

hitchhikinganimals.blogspot.com/2009/10/mice-ate-my-car-support-group-needed.html

TECHNICAL BACKGROUND: Animal damage primarily occurs on easily accessible, exposed cables and on thin cables. To avoid future animal bites, advise the customer to clean the engine compartment. Electrical deterrents and cable protection have proven effective, but 100% protection cannot be guaranteed.

WARRANTY: This damage is due to outside influence and is not covered by any Audi warranty.

Audi of America
2012 memo to dealers

Auto Sales "Lag and Lurch"

2015 was a turning point for European makes in Europe and in North America. European car sales bounced back in the first half of the year and rose almost 15% in June alone – even in Greece – marking the first positive sales report since the world financial crisis began in 2007. European car sales in Canada mirrored the European stats with a 15-20% increase through July.

But the sales euphoria hasn't lasted for long. In August, China devalued the yuan and contributed to further market volatility that has stalled the auto industry comeback on both sides of the Atlantic. As China works through its own economic turmoil, it is cutting back substantially on auto production and sales. With this uncertainty, no one knows if hard times or record sales lie ahead.

Imported car bargains will be rare in Canadian dealerships during 2016. With the loonie now devalued by almost 30% the 2016 lineup of European vehicles is more expensive than ever.

Smart shoppers should wait until early 2016 when prices will be discounted and leasing terms sweetened, lower fuel prices will have put a few more dollars in our pockets, and carmakers will liquidate their over-production with dramatic price cuts. Volkswagen and Audi are dramatically chopping prices, following the public disgust over their rigging of emissions tests on diesel-equipped 2009-2015 models (see Volkswagen).

VW has admitted it cheated on diesel engine emissions tests for 8 years and now must recall 11 million VWs and 2.1 million Audis. Shoppers are wary and owners are angry because these recalls screw up performance, fuel economy, and resale values. Co-conspirator Audi says the A1, A3, A4, A5, A6, TT, Q3 and the Q5 were equipped with fraudulent emissions software.

EUROPEAN "ORPHANS"

Orphans are those vehicles that have been sold by their parent builder, or, as in Volvo's case, sold twice to different automobile manufacturers. Usually when this occurs, the purchased companies dwindle into bankruptcy or irrelevancy after a few years. It happened with American Motors, Bricklin, Chrysler, DeLorean, and Saab.

There are many problems with buying orphaned European used cars. First, there's the high cost of servicing, due to increased costs for parts that become rarer and rarer. Second, it's incredibly difficult to find mechanics who can spot the likely causes of some common failures; there isn't a large pool of them who work on those vehicles all the time, and those who can work on them don't have current service bulletins to guide their work. There's also fewer secret ("goodwill") warranties to pay for repairs outside of the warranty period, because the automaker will have dropped the warranty extensions along with the models.

Luxury Lemons

European vehicles are generally a driver's delight and a frugal consumer's nightmare. They're noted for having a high level of performance combined with a full array of standard comfort and convenience features. They're fun to drive, well appointed, and attractively styled. On the other hand, you can forget the myth about European luxury vehicles holding their value – most don't. They're also unreliable, overpriced, and a pain in the butt to service.

This last point is important to remember because in hard economic times dealers skimp on parts inventories or mechanic training to adequately service what they sell. So, if you get a bad dealer, you will likely end up with a bad car.

Servicing problems and costs can be attenuated by purchasing a model that's been sold in relatively large quantities for years and has parts that are available from independent suppliers. If you insist on buying a European make, be sure you know where it can be serviced by independent mechanics in case the dealership's service becomes "lemony." Interestingly, independent BMW, Mercedes, Volkswagen, and Volvo garages seem to be fairly well distributed, while Fiat, Jaguar, and Smart repairers are found mostly in the larger cities.

So what's wrong with European cars? First, they can't compare to cheaper Asian competitors in terms of performance and durability. Who wants a Mercedes when offered a Lexus? Why get a dealer-dependent and quality-challenged VW Passat when you can have more fun with a Mazda3 Sport (even with its stupid grin on the front grille)? Second, when times get tough, European automakers get out of town or go belly up. Remember ARO, Dacia, Fiat, Peugeot, Renault, Saab, Skoda, Yugo, Cadillac's Catera, and Ford's Merkur XR4TI? Finally, European vehicles require constant, expensive maintenance. Shoppers understandably balk at these outrageously high prices, and European automakers respond by adding complicated, failure-prone electronics that drive up servicing costs even more.

British independent automotive journalist Robert Farago, former editor of *The Truth About Cars* website (*www.thetruthaboutcars.com*), writes:

> Once upon a time, a company called Mercedes-Benz built luxury cars. Not elk aversive city runabouts. [An allusion to a Smart Car precursor rolling over at one test track.] Not German taxis. Not teeny tiny hairdressers' playthings. And definitely not off-roaders. … In the process, the Mercedes brand lost its reputation for quality and exclusivity. In fact, the brand has become so devalued that Mercedes themselves abandoned it, reviving the Nazi-friendly Maybach marque for its top-of-the-range limo. Now that Mercedes has morphed with Chrysler, the company is busy proving that the average of something good and something bad is something mediocre.

Now that Chrysler has been thrown out of the Mercedes family and run off with Fiat, Farago's insight seems particularly applicable today. Of course, you won't read this kind of straight reporting from the cowering North American motoring press, as they fawn over any new techno-gadget-laden vehicle hailing from England, Germany, or Sweden. It's easy for them; they get their cars and press junkets for free.

The following European car ratings include some of the most popular offerings from the four major German automakers: Audi, BMW, Mercedes, and Volkswagen. Small-volume vehicles from these and other automakers are covered in Appendix 1.

AUDI

"Only a masochist owns an Audi outside of its warranty period. VW too for that matter."
— Wall Street Journal reader comment (March 13, 2015)

From a quality and safety perspective, both Audi and other European luxury makes have reputations they don't deserve – Audis and Volvos aren't that bad; and Bimmers and Mercedes aren't that good, while Volkswagen is stuck somewhere in the middle. Saddled in the early '80s with a reputation for making poor-quality cars that would suddenly accelerate out of control, Audi fought back for two decades and staged a spectacular comeback with well-built, moderately priced, front-drive and AWD Quattro sedans and wagons that spelled "Performance" with a capital "P." Through an expanded lineup of sedans, coupes, and Cabriolets during the last decade, Audi gained a reputation for making sure-footed, AWD, luxury cars loaded with lots of high-tech bells and whistles – and they look drop-dead gorgeous. Audi's quality control, servicing, and warranty support has not been first-class, however, as the company rebounds from the recession.

Nevertheless, used Audis can be found at bargain prices, even among the models that have a relatively clean record. Take, for example, the TT. A 2010 TT Quattro Coupe that originally sold for $49,350 is now worth barely $21,000 after 5 years – a boon for used-car buyers with independent garage connections, but a bust for owners who bought new. The fact that Audi powertrains are covered under warranty only up to 4 years/80,000 km is far from reassuring, since engines and transmissions have traditionally been Audi's weakest components and many other automakers cover their vehicles up to 5 years/100,000 km. This worry is backed up by *Consumer Reports* surveys showing some engine and transmission problems with the entire Audi lineup. In many cases, both Audi and VW settle these complaints collectively or offer "goodwill" refunds on a case-by-case basis through a warranty extension (like the one below), not widely known to Canadian Audi owners:

SUBJECT: Warranty Extension
Intake Camshaft, Camshaft Follower & High Pressure Fuel Pump
Certain 2005-2007 Model Year Audi 2.0L TFSI Engine Vehicles

Dear Audi Owner of VIN <VIN>

As part of our ongoing commitment to customer satisfaction, we are pleased to inform you of our decision to extend the warranty that covers the intake camshaft, camshaft follower and high-pressure fuel pump (as described in this letter) to 10 years or 120,000 miles, whichever occurs first, from the vehicle's original in-service date. This warranty is fully transferable to subsequent owners.

The vehicle's original in-service date is defined as the date the vehicle was delivered to either the original purchaser or the original lessee; or if the vehicle was first placed in service as a "demonstrator" or "company" car, on the date such vehicle was first placed in service.

What is the Problem?

Audi has determined that under specific conditions, certain production issues affecting the intake camshaft and camshaft follower in your vehicle's engine could make them susceptible to premature wear. If this happens, the premature wearing of these components could, in rare cases, lead to wear in the base of the high pressure fuel pump camshaft follower. This issue does not cause vehicle stalling.

Additionally, the Malfunction Indicator Lamp (MIL) on the instrument cluster may illuminate due to the presence of specific fault codes caused by this condition.

Fit and Finish Glitches

Audi and Volkswagen's fit and finish has been problematic for the past two decades highlighted by a precedent-setting class action settlement in 2012 covering major sunroof water leaks that could ruin expensive electronic components. The case is *John Dewey, Jacqueline Delguercio v. Volkswagen of America, Inc.*, Case Nos. 07-CV-2249-FSH-PS and 07-CV-2361-FSH-PS (see *www.WaterIngressSettlement2.com*). Used Audi shoppers should be wary of the designated model years below. Owners who have paid or are about to pay for these repairs should contact Audi and file a claim in small claims court if Audi doesn't offer a goodwill refund for the repairs, similar to its settlement 3 years ago.

Audi Leaky Sunroof Settlement (Audi and VW)	
1997	AUDI A6 C4
1997-2009	AUDI A8 (including S versions)
2005-2009	AUDI A6 C6 (including S and RS versions)
2005-2008	AUDI A4 (including S and RS versions)

A3

RATING: Average (2003-13). Based on the Volkswagen Golf, the A3 is Audi's entry-level, compact, four-door hatchback. It's a well-appointed, generously powered vehicle that is smaller and less costly than Audi's A4 compacts, more reliable, and just as much fun to drive. Nevertheless, Audi's use of illegal emissions-control software has compromised safety, emissions/performance, and quality, making pre-2009 diesel-equipped Audis a better choice than newer versions. *E-tron Sportback Hybrid:* Not Recommended during its first year on the market (2016). The A3 e-tron is Audi's first plug-in hybrid with a 157 mpg laboratory-tested fuel rating; as always, real world gas mileage will be much less. The e-tron is basically an A3 five-door with a 1.4L turbo four, and an all-electric range of only 50 kms. The sales-leading

Toyota Prius has about half that range (16-24 kms.). Frugal drivers who want a bit more performance should choose a 2008 or earlier Audi diesel, or invest in a used gasoline-powered model, thereby saving money and cleaning the environement by taking one more vehicle out of the national fleet. Smart buyers will want to take a pass on buying the 2016 e-tron until it proves itself to be both reliable and easily serviced. Audi Canada says the delayed e-tron hatchback won't arrive before early 2016. **Road performance:** The car's a superb highway performer, thanks to its powerful and smooth-running engines and transmissions. Handling is crisp, steering is accurate, and cornering is accomplished with minimal body roll. **Strong points:** Loaded with safety, performance, and convenience features, the A3 holds its value and is well-appointed. Audi rates the A3 as capable of carrying five passengers; however, the three back-seat passengers had better be friends. **Weak points:** Fairly expensive for an entry-level Audi; on top of that, depreciation will likely be much faster than average, which increases your losses. Also, a freight fee that nudges $2,000 should be made a felony. Premium gas is required, and insurance premiums are higher than average. Navigation feature is confusing. Numerous factory-related problems affecting primarily the electrical system, powertrain, brakes, and accessories. Fit and finish are not up to luxury-car standards, either.

Prices and Specs

Prices (Firm: Komfort Sedan: $31,600, Progressive S tronic: $35,500, Quattro Technik: $43,300, Komfort Cabriolet: $42,600, Progressive Cabriolet: $45,100, Technik Cabriolet: $48,900, Sportback Komfort TDI: $36,600, Sportback Progressive TDI: $38,700, Sportback Technik TDI S tronic: $42,500, S3 Quattro Progressive Sedan: $45,400, S3 Quattro Technik S tronic: $48,900, e-tron: (Negotiable): estimated $45,000 **Freight:** $2,095 **Powertrain (Front-drive/AWD):** Engines: 2.0L 4-cyl. Diesel (150 hp), e-tron 1.4L 4-cyl. Turbo (150 hp, combined 204 hp), 1.8L 4-cyl. Turbo (170 hp), 2.0L 4-cyl. Turbo (220 hp), 2.0L 4-cyl. Turbo (292 hp); Transmissions: 6-speed man., 6-speed auto. **Dimensions/capacity:** Passengers: 2/3; Wheelbase: 101.5 in.; H: 56/L: 169/W: 69 in.; Headroom F/R: 4.5/2 in.; Legroom F/R: 42/25.5 in.; Cargo volume: 19.5 cu. ft.; Fuel tank: 55L and 60L/premium/diesel; Tow limit: Not recommended; Load capacity: 990 lb.; Turning circle: 35 ft.; Ground clearance: 4.3 in.; Weight: 3,219 lb.

Other opinions: "The Audi A3 ranks #10 out of 14 upscale small cars. The redesigned 2015 Audi A3 earns praise for its peppy turbocharged engines, sporty handling and long list of standard and optional features – *U.S. News & World Report*; "Mercedes-Benz broke new ground with the CLA. Audi walked the same path, with more commitment, and made a better car. The A3 feels like it has more interior space, an airier cabin, more comfort, and fewer blind spots for the driver. It's also a sharper handler." – *Road and Track*; "Since purchasing my Audi A3 on 2/8/2015 I have had four flat tires. My tires are OEM and are Contiprocontact 225/40 18 92H. All four tire failures have happened at low speed (5-20 mph) going over potholes. Online it seems that there are many complaints for Continental tires having sidewall issues (bubbling) with no or minimal road hazard and at low speeds. A dealership service employee said they have been overwhelmed with tire issues, mostly in newly sold Audis." – *safercar.gov.* **Major redesign:** 2006 and 2014. The restyled sedan will arrive at year's end and resemble the larger A4 and A6. Three engines are used: a 2.0L TDI diesel, plus a 1.8L and a 2.0L turbocharged 4-cylinder gasoline engine. A more powerful S version became available in the first quarter of 2014. **Highway/ city fuel economy:** *2.0 front-drive man.:* 6.7/10.4 L/100 km. *2.0 front-drive auto.:* 6.9/ 9.4 L/100 km. *2.0 AWD:* 7.5/9.6 L/100 km. *TDI:* 4.7/6.7 L/100 km. **Best alternatives:** Acura TSX, or a BMW 3 Series.

 SAFETY: Crashworthiness: NHTSA: Five-star crashworthiness award earned by the 2015-16 models. IIHS: "Good" designation for the 2008-13s, however, 2006-07 models were rated only "Acceptable" when the head restraints and seats were tested. **Owner-reported safety-related failures:** Many reports that the A3 stalls out in traffic or hesitates when accelerating. Owners also report a sudden loss of diesel power when accelerating.

> Purchased a used 2013 Audi A3 TDI. I only use diesel fuel. Driving onto I80 west when I heard/felt car hiccup, lost power. Coasted to the stop sign, tried multiple times but car would not start. Dealer said that the fuel pump (HPFP) had come apart spewing metal shards into the system and that the entire system had to be replaced. Internet research shows documented failures in VW TDI (same engine) HPFP in 2010, 2011 and 2012. Is this system safe?

Many incidents where the transmission engages and then disengages when accelerating from a stop or when parking:

> While pulling out into an intersection the DSG transmission briefly went into neutral and I saw the tachometer needle shoot up and heard the engine whine. I was in manual mode at the time. I down shifted and let off the gas and it re-engaged. The following day ... the same thing happened again. This time I was also in manual mode and was again pulling out into traffic from an almost complete stop. I have since learned that this is an ongoing and known issue with VW/Audi DSG transmissions.

ALERT! Since Audi maintenance is highly dealer-dependent make sure good servicing is available from several nearby dealerships and try to keep the car 6 years or more to offset the high buy-in and depreciation loss. Also, be wary of bloated costs from bundled options, poor-quality dealer-supplied tires, unjustified "administrative" fees, and thousands of dollars in delivery charges. One un-named British Columbia Audi dealer lists the following special fees: A Dealer Prep Fee $499, Administration Fee $558, AC and Disposal Fee $125, and a $2,095 Freight/Pre-delivery Inspection Fee. No, his last name isn't Capone.

	2006	2007	2008	2009	2010	2011	2012	2013
Used Values ($)								
A3 Sedan	6,000	7,500	9,500	12,000	14,500	18,000	21,000	25,000
AWD	—	8,500	11,000	13,500	16,000	19,500	22,500	26,500
TDI	—	—	—	—	17,500	20,500	23,500	27,500
S-Line	8,500	—	—	17,000	20,000	22,500	24,500	—
TDI	—	—	—	—	21,500	23,500	25,500	30,500
Reliability	☆	☆	☆	☆	☆	☆	☆	☆
Repairs ($$$)	💰	💰	💰	💰	💰	💰	💰	💰
Electrical	★1	★1	★1	★1	★1	★1	★2	★3
Engine (base)	★2	★2	★2	★3	★3	★3	☆	☆
Fit/Finish	★1	★1	★1	★2	★3	★3	★3	★3
Infotainment	—	—	—	★3	★3	★3	★3	★3
Transmission (auto.)	★1	★1	★1	★1	★1	★2	★3	★3

SECRET WARRANTIES, INTERNAL BULLETINS: 2005-10—Headlights go on and off. 2005-11—Sunroof noises. Inoperative windshield wipers. 2005-13—Audi says in TSB #40 12 28 that "it's normal to hear creaking and squeaking noises coming from the front axle when driving at low temperatures on rough roads. The sound comes from the rubber and metal mounting of the front track control arms. The rubber lip of the rubber metal mounting rubs on the collar of the control arm (Figure 1, B). The resulting stick-slip effect creates this sound, which does not affect the service life and function of the components. However, track control arm bushings that are completely cracked through should be replaced." 2006-09—No acceleration when shifted into gear. Inoperative low beams. Xenon headlights flicker and fail. 2006-10—Cluster lights dim, flicker. Electrical malfunctions in door. 2006-11—Front suspension cracking, rubbing noise. Front, rear brake squealing. 2006-15—A loud cracking or rubbing noise coming from the steering or suspension is likely caused by the shock absorber stop contacting the suspension strut's plastic cap. Check out this possibility before spending lots of dough replacing parts needlessly. 2008-11—Warranty extended on fuel injectors and the intake manifolds up to 10 years/120,000 miles on 2.0L engines. 2008-13—Rattling and/or jarring noises heard from the engine compartment/exhaust system between 1800 and 2900 rpm are likely caused by the wastegate flap and rods vibrating at the start of the boost air control. A spring clip (06J145220A) fitted on the wastegate adjustment should eliminate the noise. Turn signal light may not work due to a cracked lens allowing condensation behind the lens. 2008-15—If the radio turns On and Off and the doors lock and unlock while driving, the S-contact lubricant needs to be changed. 2009—Stiff steering. 2009-10—Airbag light stays on. Hard start; timing chain noise. Automatic transmission control module update. Inoperative headlight washer system. 2010—TDI catastrophic fuel-pump failure; sudden engine shutdown; metal shavings found in the fuel system (an $8,000 repair awaits). Automatic transmission suddenly downshifts to M1, inviting a rear-ender. 2010-11—A faulty thermostat may cause the engine to overheat. 2010-12—Engine exhaust flap will be replaced free of charge up to 10 years/120,000 miles (when it fails the MIL light will come on). 2010-13—Diesel engine won't start, rough running, or excess moisture found in intake piping.

NO START/RUNS ROUGH, OR EXCESS MOISTURE IN THE INTAKE PIPING

SERVICE BULLETIN NO.: 01 01 13 04   DATE: JUNE 6, 2013

Audi

CONDITION: Engine will not start after standing in cold weather below 0°C (32°F). MIL may be illuminated with various induction and/or boost system faults stored in the ECM.

TECHNICAL BACKGROUND: Moisture from the intake air condenses and collects in the charge air cooler. At cold temperatures, this moisture can freeze, causing blockage of the intake air system.

SERVICE: Install a revised charge air cooler kit (1K0198803B) to prevent the formation of moisture in the boost system.

2011-12—Tiptronic DSG transmission malfunctions can be corrected via a software upgrade. Parking Assist System false warnings. Bose Radio erratic sound volume. Cannot pair Bluetooth phone to vehicle. Poor cell phone voice recognition. No-start due to discharged battery. Electrical malfunctions after window tint. Excessive engine noise. Front window binds or is noisy during operation. Inaccurate "distance to empty" display. Noises from the sunroof area. Disc brake squeal. Can't eject navigation DVD. Rattling, humming noise from speakers. Radio turns on/off, locks self-activate. Inoperative remote key. Dash cluster lighting appears to flicker. Fuel system malfunction warning. Moisture accumulation in exterior lights. Expensive harness damage caused by rodent bites. Cold weather intercooler kit. 2015—If the AC doesn't cool sufficiently or the compressor is noisy, a faulty N280 valve may be the culprit. 2015-16—Troubleshooting headliner/sunroof squeaks and rattles.

A4/S4

RATING: Average (2012-16); Below Average (2006-11). Quality has improved measurably since 2011. Nevertheless, servicing is still spotty and warranty claim performance for premature engine and transmission failures continue to be problematic. On the positive side, so many of these vehicles have been sold for so long that sustained digging will usually find you the part and an independent mechanic who can service the vehicle competently. Plus, there has been a large reduction in safety-related problems reported by owners. This series of cars should be kept at least 6 years to compensate for their high initial cost and depreciation losses. **Road performance:** The base 2.0L engine provides gobs of low-end torque and accelerates as well with the automatic transmission as it does with the manual. The turbocharger works well, with no turbo delay or torque steer. The manual gearbox, Tiptronic automatic transmission, and the CVT usually work well, with some exceptions on earlier models. Comfortable ride; exceptional handling, though not as sporty as Acura's TSX; acceptable braking performance. Not as fast as rivals; the ride is stiff at low speeds, and a bit firm at other times; some body roll and brake dive under extreme conditions; braking can be a bit twitchy. **Strong points:** Loaded with safety, performance, and convenience features, and you get lots of cargo room in the wagon. The all-road Quattro offers more ground clearance than the A4 wagon (Avant) it replaces. The Avant wagon performs like a well-equipped sport-utility. **Weak points:** Limited rear seatroom (the front seatbacks press against rear occupants' knees); some tire drumming and engine noise. Infotainment features aren't user-friendly and voice controls and climate adjustments are particularly overly-complicated. Owners report abysmal fit and finish and a trunk that's smaller than the competition. The electrical system is the car's weakest link, and it has plagued Audi's entire lineup for the past decade. Normally, this wouldn't be catastrophic; however, as the cars become more electronically complex and competent mechanics are fired as dealerships open and close, you're looking at a greater chance of poor-quality servicing, long waits for service, and unacceptably high maintenance and repair costs. Overpriced, with an outrageously high $2,000 freight charge and depreciation that is a wallet-buster. For example, a 2011 front-drive A4 sedan that sold for $37,800 is now worth barely $20,000. Not even high-performance variants can escape value-robbing depreciation. For example, the 2011 V8-equipped S5 coupe that originally sold for $60,000 is now worth $32,000. Worse yet, convertibles are no longer a safe haven, either. A 2010 S5 convertible that once sold for about $72,000 is now worth $33,000. Another expense to consider is the car's high maintenance cost, especially because of its costly dealer-only servicing.

Prices and Specs

Prices (Negotiable): *Komfort plus:* $38,500, *Progressiv plus:* $46,600, *Technik plus:* $48,500, *Komfort plus Quattro:* $42,800, *Progressiv plus Quattro:* $46,600, *Technik plus Quattro:* $48,500, *Komfort Allroad Quattro:* $47,300, *Progressiv Allroad Quattro:* $51,300, *Technik Allroad Quattro:* $53,700, *Progressiv plus S4 Quattro:* $55,200, *Technik plus S4 Quattro:* $57,600 **Freight:** $2,095 **Powertrain (Front-drive/AWD):** Engines: 2.0L 4-cyl. (211 hp), 3.0L SC V6 (333 hp); Transmissions: 6-speed man., 8-speed auto., 7-speed auto., CVT **Dimensions/Capacity:** *A4 Sedan:* Passengers: 2/3; Wheelbase: 110.5 in.; H: 56.2/L: 169.5/W: 71.8 in.; Headroom F/R: 3.5/2.5 in.; Legroom F/R: 41.5/24.5 in.; Cargo volume: 16.9 cu. ft.; Fuel tank: 62L/premium; Tow limit: Not recommended; Load capacity: 1,060 lb.; Turning circle: 37.4 ft.; Ground clearance: 4.2 in.; Weight: 3,665 lb.

Other opinions: "The 2016 Audi A4 ranks #4 out of 14 … [It] delivers an attractive, spacious cabin, athletic handling and a comfortable ride." – *U.S. News & World Report*. "The way Audi's service departments and warranties work leaves much to be desired and does not inspire confidence in me with regards to simple fairness and support for their own products." – *www.cars.com/audi/a4/2014/consumer-reviews*. **Major redesign:** 1996, 2002, 2009, and 2016. **Highway/city fuel economy:** *2.0 front-drive man.:* 6.5/8.9 L/100 km. *2.0 front-drive auto.:* 7.0/10.0 L/100 km. *2.0 Quattro man.:* 6.5/9.5 L/100 km. *2.0 Quattro auto.:* 7.0/10.0 L/100 km. *A5 convertible:* 7.0/10.0 L/100 km. *A5 coupe man.:* 6.5/9.5 L/100 km. *S4 man.:* 8.1/12.2 L/100 km. *Auto.:* 7.9/12.1 L/100 km. *S5 convertible:* 8.1/12.9 L/100 km. *Coupe man.:* 9.4/15.1 L/100 km. *Auto.:* 9.8/12.8 L/100 km. *Avant Quattro:* 8.6/13.0 L/100 km. New 3.0L engines have not been sufficiently tested yet. Remember, AWD models exert a heavy fuel economy penalty for better traction. **Best alternatives:** Buy a 2013-14 model, with some of the base warranty left, and use Audi's accelerated depreciation to your advantage. Buying used saves at least $10,000, plus an additional $2,000 in freight fees, and 30% less when servicing the car at an independent garage. S5 convertibles cost about $10,000 more than A5 convertibles mainly due to the V8 engine used by the S5. This is too much to pay for what is only a slightly better performer. Think twice about getting the power moonroof if you're a tall driver or want to avoid a spontaneously shattering panel. If you like the S4 or S5 tire burners, also consider the BMW M3 convertible or 5 Series and the Porsche 911 Carrera. A4 alternatives are the Acura TL or TSX, BMW 3 Series, Hyundai Genesis, Infiniti G37, and Lexus ES 350 or IS series. BMW's 2-Series is another fun-to-drive car in this class. Buyers have a wide choice of powerful engines, in addition to the car's responsive handling, and extra cargo space (more than the A4). Finally, there's the Mercedes-Benz C-Class. Although early models were second-class, these entry-level models now offer reasonable reliability, more cargo space, a luxurious cabin, and a comfortable ride, plus, good fuel economy. The only caveat: Limited dealer servicing and poor reliability with early models.

SAFETY: **Crashworthiness:** NHTSA: 1996-16 models get a four- and five-star rating across the board. IIHS: "Good" designation for 2007-15 models, except for small front overlap crashes which scored "Poor." **Owner-reported safety-related failures:** NHTSA logs show few safety-related complaints. The smattering of reports highlight sudden, unintended acceleration; continued acceleration while braking; acceleration lag and engine surge; vehicle lunging every time the Tiptronic transmission is down shifted; stalling caused by faulty fuel injectors; CVT allows the vehicle to roll down an incline when stopped; and severe road wander.

After 3500 miles the vehicle developed a "notchy" sensation in the steering feel that varied in intensity and would occur at random times. This notchy sensation would occur any speed above 20 mph, as if switched on. When symptoms would occur there would be a heavy, notchy feeling on either side of straight steer that would take a lot of force to overcome and then once feeling like the wheel is over the notch, it would over-correct making it difficult to maintain a lane. The steering wheel could not be placed in those notch positions, as if trying to drive using a click wheel. The notchiness is also felt throughout all wheel travel, not just on center, straight wheel. This makes staying on a given path difficult and unsafe. At random times steering felt so heavy that it felt like there was no power steering in maneuvers. Turning the car off and on or turning the wheel lock to lock alleviates the symptoms. This is the first year Audi has introduced electromechanical steering into their cars in the United States. Many other 2013 Audi (varying models) owners have had the same issue.

Secondary radiator is easily damaged from road debris; sudden water pump failure; and the windshield wipers stop working when the vehicle comes to a stop. The following problems have all taken these cars out of service for extended periods in the past: Airbag fails to deploy; excessive steering shake due to a faulty lower control arm; engine, fuel-system (fuel-injectors, principally), and powertrain component failures; defective brakes; and chronic electrical shorts.

ALERT! The car's notchy steering can be caught during your road test: *www.youtube.com/watch?v=mw9m2ncym4* shows what to look for.

A4/S4 Profile

	2006	2007	2008	2009	2010	2011	2012	2013	2014
Used Values ($)									
Sedan	8,000	10,000	12,000	14,500	17,000	20,000	23,500	28,000	33,000
Allroad Quattro	—	—	—	—	—	—	—	29,000	34,000
Avant	10,000	12,500	14,000	16,000	18,500	23,500	26,000	—	—
S-Line	11,500	13,500	15,500	17,500	19,500	25,500	29,000	34,500	41,500
Reliability	2	2	3	3	3	☆	☆	☆	☆
Repairs ($$$)	3	3	3	3	3	◇	◇	◇	◇
Electrical	1	1	1	1	1	3	3	☆	☆
Engine (base)	2	2	2	2	2	2	3	☆	☆
Fit/Finish	2	2	3	3	3	3	☆	☆	☆
Infotainment	—	—	—	3	3	3	3	3	3
Transmission (auto.)	1	1	1	1	1	2	3	☆	☆

SECRET WARRANTIES, INTERNAL BULLETINS: 2002-04—Oil leak at camshaft adjuster. Hard jerking in Reverse at idle. 2002-06—Audi agreed to refund repair and other expenses to drivers who bought or leased 2002-06 Audi A4s and A6s with factory-installed CVTs. Faulty glove compartment door. Noisy power steering. 2003-04—Service campaign to replace the engine wire harness. 2005-06—Remote won't lock/

unlock doors. 2005-07—Xenon headlights flicker and fail. 2005-08—Remedy for a vehicle that pulls to one side. Dash clicking noises. Headlights vibrate. 2006-07—Inoperative low beams. 2006-08—Front, rear brake squealing. Brakes moan when accelerating or turning. 2007—Multiple electrical failures. 2009-11—Sunroof noises, concerns. 2012-15—Rattling noises can be heard coming from underneath the vehicle. These noises are likely caused by contact between the exhaust heat shield and the body of the vehicle. Apply a section of PVC sealer to the area. *A4, A5, Q5, and A6:* 2009-13—A coolant leak may signal the need for a new water pump, says TSB #191336 issued on April 15, 2013. Replacing the pump, hose, and seal ring ought to stop the dripping. *A4, A5, and Q5:* 2009-14—Stiff steering on turns can be fixed by installing an upgraded intermediate steering shaft under warranty, says TSB: #48-14-61. Improper operation of the AC fresh air blower could be caused by a faulty printed circuit board in the blower control module, or the carbon brushes are losing contact with the fresh air blower's motor commutator. Install an improved fresh air blower or blower module. 2013—Troubleshooting tips to smooth out harsh First to Second upshifts or braking downshifts. Intermittent cruise control malfunctions. Water accumulation in xenon headlights may cause serious electrical short-circuits elsewhere. A constantly lit ABS alert could mean the wiring harness is damaged. *A4, A5, A6, Q5, and TT:* 2009-14—If the engine judders when accelerating or runs erratically, a faulty air mass meter is the likely culprit. 2013-14—The circlip connecting the turbo wastegate actuator rod and the wastegate flap lever can fail due to low tension of the clip. Consequently, the wastegate linkage becomes disconnected, and the car loses power. 2014—Clunking or rattling noises coming from the rear suspension area when driving over bumps is likely caused by an improperly seated rear bump stop. *A4, A5, A6, A8, Q5 Q7, and TT:* 2010-14—Correction for coolant loss from the coolant valve. Symptoms: Engine warning light on, "Limp Home" mode active, and insufficient cabin heating. Water ingress into the connector housing of the brake pad wear indicator can lead to the oxidation of the pins. This oxidation can increase contact resistance in the connector, which can generate a false brake pad wear warning. 2011-14—Ice can form on the locking surface of the touch sensor (inside the door handle), preventing proper locking operation. *A4, A6:* 1998-2004—Noisy power steering. 2005—Fuel gauge reads empty with a full tank. 2005-06—Rough-running cold engine. Inoperative sunroof. 2005-09—Long warm-engine crank time. 2005-11—Sunroof noises. Brakes moan when accelerating or turning. 2006-11—Front, rear brake squealing. 2007—AC doesn't cool. Loose, broken control knobs. 2008-09—Erratic operating radio and door locks. *A4, A5, A6:* Automatic transmission will not engage, or shifts only after key cycle. 2009-15—Illegal emissions software on diesel-equipped models may need to be replaced before vehicle can be registered. Replacement is free. 2013—Coolant leak at water pump and hose area. *A4, A6, S6:* 2002-05—Vehicles equipped with the Multitronic automatic transmission buck when accelerating. 2002-08—Noisy power steering. Inoperative daytime running lights. 2005—Cold engine stumble; warm engine stall. 2005-08—Eliminating brake moan on low-speed turns. Front window reverses direction when closing. Inoperative sunroof switch. Inoperative One Touch window feature. 2005-09—Long warm-engine crank time. 2005-10—Headlights go on and off. 2007-08—Paint spots or stains on upper surfaces. 2009—Hard start; timing chain noise. 2009-10—Airbag light stays on. 2009-13—A coolant leak in some models may mean a new water pump is in order. In TSB #191336, issued on April 15, 2013, Audi said owners of 2009-13 A4, A5, Q5 and A6 models might notice leaks from the hose connecting the water pump to the heater core. Replacing the pump, hose and seal ring under this "goodwill warranty" ought to correct the problem. Water pooling in xenon headlamp assemblies is covered in TSB #941314 issued on April 5, 2013. Audi said the headlight adjustment screw or the bonding channel between the housing and the lens might let water enter. The problem affects some 2013 A4, S4, A5, S5 and RS5 models. Replacing the headlamp assembly will prevent further leakage.

ELECTRICAL—HARNESS DAMAGE FROM ANIMAL BITES

BULLETIN NO.: 2021169/2

DATE: JULY 1, 2010

Audi

MODEL(S)	YEAR	VIN RANGE	VEHICLE-SPECIFIC EQUIPMENT
All Audi	2007–2010 2012–2015	All	Not Applicable
R8	2011	All	
A3	2011	All	
A4, S4	2011	All	
A4 Cabriolet	2011	All	
A5, S5	2011	All	
A5 Cabriolet	2011	All	
A6	2011	All	
Q5	2011	All	
Audi Q7	2011	All	

CONDITION: The customer may report:
- Engine warning light illuminated in IP cluster
- Reduced driving performance
- Engine does not start
- Coolant warning light illuminated
- ABS warning light illuminated
- Parking system warning illuminated in IP cluster
- Cable or rubber hose damages in the engine compartment.

TECHNICAL BACKGROUND: Animal damage primarily occurs on easily accessible, exposed cables and on thin cables. To avoid future animal bites, advise the customer to clean the engine compartment. Electrical deterrents and cable protection have proven effective, but 100% protection cannot be guaranteed.

WARRANTY: This damage is due to outside influence and is not covered by any Audi warranty.

Audis and Hondas represent a "Moveable Feast" to mice, rats, squirrels, etc. Rodent bites can cause up to $18,000 in wire/hose damage, make the car unsafe, and scare the dickens out of some drivers if "Mickey" decides to ride shotgun. Lawyers say Audi is 100% responsible for not building barriers to animal entry as other automakers have done. This means buying back the car, paying for rentals, tags, insurance, and inconvenience along with "mental distress" (See Sharman judgment in Part Three). "Honey, what just scurried under your seat?"

A6/S6/R8

RATING: Above Average (2013-16). The A6 would have been rated higher if its build quality was better and its residual value didn't drop so much. Illegal emissions software on 2009-15 diesel-equipped models may need to be replaced before vehicle can be registered. Replacement is free. Stick with Audi's simpler models. The A6 is a comfortable, spacious front-drive luxury vehicle that comes as a sedan or wagon. The sedan carries a standard 211 hp 2.0L four-cylinder engine or an optional 310 hp 3.0L V6. Both engines are mated to a CVT or an 8-speed automatic transmission with manual-shift capability; Audi's Quattro AWD is also available. The Audi R8 is an AWD, two-seat coupe with a mid-mounted engine. The entry-level 4.0L has a 420 hp V8 engine, but the 5.2L has a 550 hp V10. As with other Audis, depreciation is a value-killer. A 2010 top-of-the-line R8 coupe that sold new for $141,000 is now worth about $75,000 – a huge loss in just over 5 years. **Road performance:** The 2016 has a bit more horsepower, giving the car a more solid feel. Its potent base engine produces incredible acceleration times and gives excellent gas mileage, predictable handling, and good braking. The Servotronic steering is improved, but it is still the car's weakest feature. It is both over-boosted and uncommunicative in "Comfort" mode and ponderous and numb in its "Dynamic" setting. The V8 is a bit "growly" when pushed, and the firm suspension can make for a jittery ride. **Strong points:** Comfortable seating; interior includes a competent navigation system and an analog/digital instrument panel that is a joy to behold and use; plenty of passenger and cargo room (it beats out both BMW and Mercedes in this area); easy front and rear access; and very good build quality. Dropping the failure-prone DSG automatic transmission in favour of the 8-speed automatic on the A6 was smart. Audi has never been a major player in the global mid-size luxury sedan market. For every A6 sold in 2010, Mercedes sold seven E-Series models and BMW moved five 5 Series sedans. This means you can haggle to your heart's delight because Audi dealers have a substantial profit margin, and they'll do almost anything to poach buyers from their competitors. **Weak points:** The restyling looks limp and dated. Overdone lights, ho-hum grille, and a painfully boring interior. Some tire thumping and highway wind noise; uncomfortable centre-rear seating; the wagon's two-place rear seat is rather small; and servicing can be problematic. And, if high servicing costs aren't enough, at the end of 4 years you may find your Audi is worth only a third of its original value. Non-safety related problems concern mostly the electrical and fuel delivery systems, in addition to scads of fit and finish deficiencies.

Prices and Specs

Prices (Negotiable): *A6 Progressiv 2.0 Quattro:* $56,900, *Technik:* $63,300, *4.0:* $88,500, *S6:* $85,600, *R8 Coupe:* $136,100, *Spyder:* $150,300 **Freight:** $2,095 **Powertrain (Front-drive/AWD):** Engines: 2.0L 4-cyl. (211 hp), 3.0L V6 (310 hp) 4.0.L V8 (420 hp) 5.2L V10 (550 hp) Transmissions: 7-speed S tronic, 8-speed auto., 6-speed man., S tronic, CVT **Dimensions/capacity:** Passengers: 2/3; Wheelbase: 114.7 in.; H: 57.8/L: 193.9/W: 73.8 in.; Headroom F/R: 3/3 in.; Legroom F/R: 41.3/37.4 in.; Cargo volume: 14.1 cu. ft.; Fuel tank: 75L/premium; Tow limit: Not recommended; Load capacity: 1,100 lb.; *R8:* 551 lb.; Turning circle: 39 ft.; *R8:* 38.7 ft.; Ground clearance: *A6:* 4.6 in.; *S6:* 4.6 in.; *R8:* 4.5 in.; Weight: 3,891 lb.

Other opinions: "The 2016 Audi A6 ranks #5 out of 17 upscale mid-size cars ... An attractive interior, poised handling and powerful, fuel-efficient engines make the refreshed 2016 Audi A6 one of the most appealing mid-size luxury cars on the market." – *U.S. News & World Report.* "On occasion it is known for the turbo to blow on these vehicles. If you have noticed that there is blue smoke coming from the exhaust, or/and you are hearing a whistling noise coming from the top of the engine, this is an indication of the turbo failing. You will need to a replacement turbo." – *www.breakeryard.com/.* Major redesign: 1998 and 2005. Highway/city fuel economy: *3.0:* 8.0/12.0 L/100 km. *4.2 Quattro:* 8.6/13.0 L/100 km. 3.0 *R8 4.2 Coupe man.:* 10.2/16.3 L/100 km. *Auto:* 11.4/17.0 L/100 km. *S6 5.2:* 10.0/15.2 L/100 km. Best alternatives: Although the base A6 2.0L models are cheaper and more fuel-efficient than many competitors, they are also the least powerful cars in the segment. The A6 4-cylinder base model rivals the more-powerful BMW 528i. On the down-side, the 528i's gas consumption can't match the A6. For the A6 3.0L, Infiniti's M37x is worth test driving. Other vehicles worth taking a look at are the Hyundai Genesis and Lexus GS.

SAFETY: Crashworthiness: NHTSA: 2014-16 models given a five-star crashworthiness rating. IIHS: 2012-16 models' scored "Good" in all tests. Owner-reported safety-related failures: Very few safety-related complaints have been recorded over the past two model years. Among the reports: Sudden, unintended acceleration, brakes barely stop the car at low speeds, power brake failure, and the brake and accelerator pedals are mounted too close together.

ALERT! The multi-tasking joystick control for all the entertainment, naviga-tion, and climate-control functions can be confusing. It's similar in function to BMW's 2002 7 Series feature, based on Microsoft Windows CE. This failure-prone, non-intuitive feature gave new meaning to the phrase "computer crash" and was quickly changed after it was panned as being dangerously distracting and confusing to operate.

A6/S6/R8 Profile

	2006	2007	2008	2009	2010	2011	2012	2013	2014
Used Values ($)									
A6 Quattro	10,000	12,000	14,500	17,000	20,500	29,500	34,000	38,500	44,000
AWD	—	—	—	19,000	22,000	—	—	—	—
S-Line	—	15,500	18,500	22,500	25,000	—	41,000	44,500	51,000
S6	—	25,000	30,000	35,000	39,000	50,000	—	60,000	70,000
R8	—	—	50,000	60,000	77,000	93,000	105,000	—	115,000
Reliability	2	2	3	3	3	3	3	4	4
Repairs ($$$)	2	2	2	2	2	1	1	1	1
Electrical	3	3	3	3	3	3	3	4	4
Engine (base)	2	2	2	3	3	2	3	4	4
Fit/Finish	4	4	4	4	4	4	4	4	4
Infotainment	—	—	—	3	3	3	3	3	3
Transmission (auto.)	1	1	1	1	1	2	3	4	4

SECRET WARRANTIES, INTERNAL BULLETINS: (See also Secret Warranties section of A4/S4 models): *A6, S4, S5 Cabriolet, Q5:* 2011—TSB #131106 says that some models with 3.0L or 3.2L V6 engines may experience problems with the accessory drive belt or its guide due to a guide that is out of line, causing damage to the belt. Audi will do a free inspection of vehicles it suspects of having the problem and replace the guide and the belt for free as needed. 2011-12—Countermeasure to prevent electrical harness damage caused by animal snacking. 2013-14—The circlip connecting the turbo wastegate actuator rod and the wastegate flap lever can fall off and the car loses power.

TT/TTS/TT RS ★★★★

The Audi TT.

RATING: Above Average (2008-16); Average (1999-2007). *Illegal diesels:* Sue for a refund. TT models provide a nice balance of agility, comfort, and sleek styling. The TT Coupe Quattro debuted in the spring of 1999 as a $49,000 sporty front-drive hatchback with 2+2 seating, set on the same platform used by the A4, VW Golf, Jetta, and New Beetle. TT RS, the series' most robust model, is powered by a 360 hp 2.5L 5-cylinder turbocharged engine hooked to a revised 6-speed manual transmission (there is no automatic). This little rocket goes from 0-60 mph in just 4.3 seconds, with a top speed of 174 mph (280 km/h). An impressive performance appreciated mostly by gearheads. **Road performance:** The TT and TTS both come exclusively with the less reliable dual-clutch manumatic 6-speed transmission. The TT RS is available with a 6-speed manual transmission only. Be prepared for a surprisingly low resale value and handling that's not the equal to Hyundai Genesis, Mazda RX8, or Porsche Boxster. **Strong points:** Beautifully styled and with better handling than most sporty cars, TTs are well-appointed and provide a tastefully designed interior; comfortable, supportive seats; and plenty of passenger and cargo space (especially with the rear seatbacks folded). Used bargains abound if you are an experienced Audi mechanic or have access to a competent independent repairer. **Weak points:** A useless back seat; tough rear-seat access; awkward navigation system interface; and lots of engine and road noise. The hatch is heavy to raise, and a rear windshield wiper would be nice. These cars, like most Audis, don't hold their value well.

Other opinions: Surprisingly, not all car critics are enthusiatic over the TT's performance: "The Audi TT ranks #14 out of 16 luxury sports cars..." – *U.S. News & World Report*. "There is slight turbo lag, albeit effectively masked by the swift action of the dual-clutch gearbox. Push the touchy gas pedal and this Audi hisses and whooshes forward in a rush. The TT turns into corners eagerly with very little understeer, and the Sport setting of the stability-control system allows for considerable drift angles before intervening. The electrically boosted power steering is wonderfully precise and nicely weighted; it's one of the best we've driven." – *www.caranddriver.com/reviews/*. **Major redesign:** 2000, 2008, and 2016. **Highway/city fuel economy:** *TT Coupe Quattro 2.0:* 6.4/9.1 L/100 km. *Roadster:* 6.4/9.1 L/100 km. *TTS Coupe:* 7.4/10.7 L/100 km. *Roadster:* 6.4/9.1 L/100 km. **Best alternatives:** A used TTS, priced thousands of dollars less and powered by a torquier small engine. Other vehicles worth considering: The BMW Z Series, Hyundai Genesis Coupe, Infiniti G37 Coupe, and Mazda Miata. Think twice about getting a moonroof-equipped model if you're a tall driver.

SAFETY: **Crashworthiness:** Vehicles haven't been crash-tested. **Owner-reported safety-related failures:** Brake and accelerator pedals are too close together. Outside door handles won't open the car door. Poor rear and side visibility.

ALERT! Buy used. The TT's classic design doesn't betray the car's true vintage and three- to five-year depreciation tables take the sting out of the car's original premium price. Illegal emissions software on 2009-15 diesel-equipped models may need to be replaced before vehicle can be registered. Although this recall "fix" is free, future performance will likely suffer.

TT Coupe/TT Roadster Profile

	2006	2007	2008	2009	2010	2011	2012	2013	2014
Used Values ($)									
Coupe	12,000	—	15,000	18,500	22,000	26,000	31,500	36,500	42,500
TTS	—	—	—	24,500	27,500	33,000	40,500	50,000	53,500
Roadster	—	—	18,000	21,000	24,500	27,500	33,000	38,000	44,000
TTS	—	—	—	26,500	29,000	35,000	42,000	48,000	55,500
TT RS	—	—	—	—	—	—	45,500	52,000	—
Reliability	★	★	★	☆	☆	☆	☆	☆	☆
Repairs ($$$)	②	②	②	①	①	①	①	①	①
Electrical	★	★	★	★	★	★	☆	☆	☆
Engine (base)	★	★	★	★	★	★	★	☆	☆
Fit/Finish	★	★	★	★	☆	☆	☆	☆	☆
Infotainment	—	—	—	★	★	☆	☆	☆	☆
Transmission (auto.)	★	★	★	★	★	★	☆	☆	☆

SECRET WARRANTIES, INTERNAL BULLETINS: 1996-2011—Silencing squealing brakes. 2000-08—Hesitation on acceleration. 2000-10—Low power, won't move after stopping. Inoperative keyless entry. Excessive oil consumption. 2002-11—Front, rear brake squealing troubleshooting tips. 2004—Front stabilizer bar upgrade to reduce noise. 2004-06—Momentary delay when accelerating. Vehicle won't go into gear. 2005-10—Noxious AC odours. 2005-11—Sunroof noises, concerns. 2005-13—Another remedy for squealing brakes. 2006-09—No acceleration when shifted into gear. 2006–10—Cluster lights dim, flicker. 2007—Inoperative windows, locks, and sunroof. Loose, noisy air-intake duct. Rear suspension rumble, rattle. 2007–08—Inoperative One Touch window feature. 2007-10—Multiple electrical malfunctions. Headlights go on and off. Inoperative headlight washer system. 2007-11—Interior buzzing vibrating noises. 2008-11—Front suspension cracking, rubbing noise. 2009—Hard start; timing chain noise. Stiff steering. 2009-11—Steering squeak when turning. 2009-13—Under an extended warranty, Audi will remove excess 3.0L/3.2L engine carbon buildup in the cylinder head secondary air ports, free of charge, up to 10 years/120,000 miles. 2011-12—Countermeasure to prevent electrical harness damage caused by animal snacking. Rattling, jarring engine noise. Door can be opened from the inside only. No-starts due to dead battery. Window tint causes electrical malfunctions. Inaccurate Distance to Empty display. False warnings from the parking-assist system. Radio turns on/off, locks self-activate. DSG transmission software update. Fuel-system malfunction alert. Dash cluster lighting flickers. Moisture accumulation in exterior lights, and possible harness damage from rodents snacking on the car's innards. 2012-13—When the car is underway, squeaks or rattles can be heard coming from the A-pillar area (near the corner of the windshield). This occurs because the openings in the reinforcement panel of the A-pillar structure are slightly off-center from the carrier plate. As a result, the mounting clips for the A-pillar trim are either not fully engaged in the openings, or they are engaged and are unnecessarily tight against the edges of openings. 2013-14—The turbo wastegate actuator rod and the wastegate flap lever can fall off and the car loses power. 2013-15—When the battery is fully charged, the energy generated by the alternator is sometimes too great for the power system to absorb. This may cause the lights to flicker. This is a normal, says Audi. 2014-15—The rear spoiler may extend slowly or operate erratically and an error light for the rear spoiler may be illuminated. It is likely the spoiler operation is restricted due to corrosion in the spoiler drive unit. As a result, the rear spoiler becomes stiff and doesn't reach its end points.

BMW

Cash and Cachet

BMW wants to hold the line on the cost of its 2016 models in order to maintain a high market share in Canada. To this end, the automaker will be offering an array of discounts, rebates, and other sales incentives this year to fend off Audi, Mercedes-Benz, and Volkswagen to keep its number-one spot in Canada's pantheon of European cars.

Nevertheless, temporary discounts may not work. The slide in the Canadian dollar's worth by almost 30% over the past 2 years, the European recession, and the souring of the Chinese economy will force the company to raise prices on many of its high-end models and this will trickle down to higher costs for entry-level models later in 2016.

Canadian buyers haven't balked at BMW's high prices yet, inasmuch as lower fuel prices have put thousands of dollars in their pockets. Shoppers are also beguiled by BMW's reputation (underserved) for offering well-built and reliable vehicles. Entry-level shoppers have the 1 and 3 Series; families with more disposable income may opt for the 5 and 6 Series; and for those who have the cash to buy more comfort, convenience, and snob appeal, there's always the flagship 7 Series. Sport-utility fans have four vehicles to choose from: The X1 "baby SUV," the compact X3, and the larger X5 and X6.

BMW Shortcomings

BMWs have excellent road manners and shout, "Yes, I am smart and successful!" Unfortunately, there's barely a whisper to warn you of a plethora of bizarre and deadly factory-related defects hiding in these beautifully-styled, gadget-infused machines.

These glitches are typical of what we find in many cheaper, entry-level cars and SUVs. Owner surveys show, and internal service bulletins confirm, the cars are afflicted with chronic fuel and electrical system and powertrain deficiencies that can be quite expensive to troubleshoot and repair. Surprisingly, coming from a country that extols its German craftsmanship, BMW fit and finish is embarrassingly bad. Read on about "out-gassing" fumes that permeate the BMW cabins and form a sticky, image-distorting film on windshields; or windshield/sunroofs that suddenly explode like a gunshot; or deadly door locks that suddenly open while underway, throw the dog out through the rear hatch, or hold children hostage unless the window is broken to get them out. Worst of all, these door lock failures span a period of 21 years and involve locks on all doors and the rear hatch.

2014 X5 passenger-side door lock failed while car was underway.

Doors opened (on multiple occasions) by themselves, while my 2014 X5 was in motion. The vehicle has soft close automatic doors; yet driver's door as well as rear passenger doors opened while driving. The dealer claimed to have repaired it (based on BMW service bulletin), yet it occurred again within a few days. Eventually BMW North America bought the vehicle back.

2014 X5 door lock failure trapped toddler in summer heat.

On 3 separate occasions the electric door locks have locked the car with the key fob inside. On the 1st occasion, a 2 y/o child had just been strapped into his car seat, a purse, with the key inside the purse, was placed on the floor behind the driver's seat, the rear door was closed and all locks were activated. This occurred in the heat of summer and required another driver with a spare fob to quickly drive to the site of the parked car and avoid having to break a window. This was a very scary moment! Same thing happened (no child in car); all doors locked when a briefcase containing both key fobs was placed on back seat and rear door was closed. A call to BMW's hot line resulted in the doors being unlocked via the airways. The same incident occured this week with only one key fob in the car.

Family held hostage in a 2007 X5 BMW.

My wife and kids were in the vehicle while I went inside the store. After I got back to the vehicle, my wife told me she saw service lights. I tried to start the vehicle and the vehicle wouldn't start. I drove screen faded in and out, windshield wipers moved slow, and I saw various service messages. In the process of trying to start the vehicle, all doors locked. I tried to unlock the doors and wasn't able to. My family and I were trapped inside the vehicle with our kids. The emergency flashers worked as well as the horn. I noticed the vehicle next to me (driver's side) was backing out. I honked the horn and banged on the window to get the passenger's attention. She was nice enough to notice and her husband got out of the vehicle and called 911. The Good Samaritan tried to unlock the vehicle from the outside without any luck. The vehicle started to fog up and it felt as if there was no air circulating inside the vehicle. I was parked in an area which was not well lighted and it was dark and raining outside. With a dark interior and no lights working inside the vehicle, I wasn't able to find the manual unlock in the back trunk area. About 8-10 minutes into this terrible ordeal, the doors unlocked automatically. BMW Service replaced the battery and wasn't able to reproduce the problem.

2005 BMW door lock failure traps kids, again.

When the rear locks get locked/jammed, do not have any manual override to open the back doors. My kids got trapped in and had to get out from the front door. There are lots of complaints like this on the Internet and the dealer says that there is a fault with the electrical connections to open the door.

2004 BMW door lock failure makes passenger climb over seats.

The external driver door latch is not working, have to climb over from passenger side of vehicle. This is ridiculous.

Germany is also famous for its top electronics firms, but BMW electronic and fuel delivery components head the list of parts most likely to cause owners grief. Three authoritative websites that list BMW problems and fixes are *ALLDATA.com*, *safercar.gov*, and *www.roadfly.com*. Here are just a few incidents from BMW's "Dark Side" found at *safercar.gov*.

2011 X5: Quit stalling, pay up!

Started the car and the engine light came on with "Engine Malfunction – Reduced Power" and drove a few hundred yards and then the car completely died. The 2011 BMW X5 35I Premium just died – no power whatsoever. Because there was no power, the car could not be put into neutral to be put on a flatbed. The X5 had to be put on a crane and lifted onto a flatbed tow truck. (Engine replaced.)

2007 X5: "Raindrops keep falling on my head."

This is my second complaint of problems caused by water intrusion of my 2007 BMW X5. First complaint was the passenger-side floorboard carpet getting wet. Now, I have a problem with electrical components getting wet. My satellite radio receiver was destroyed by moisture.

2005 X5 Not a hot foot!

The contact owns a 2004 BMW X5. He started to smell something burning from under the driver's seat and found that there was a hole under the seat from the heated seat element. The contact then took the vehicle to the dealer where they replaced the heated seat element, but not the actual seat.

Owners also mention slow parts delivery; poor transmission performance with gear hunting and abrupt engaging, believed to be caused by a faulty mechatronic unit; premature fuel and water pump failures leading to stalling, no starts, and engine overheating; exhaust fumes that invade the cabin; faulty TPM tire sensors; no brake power assist; and high maintenance costs with dire consequence if not performed (simultaneous engine shutdown, and loss of brakes and steering):

While driving my 2012 X5, the engine suddenly shut off along with power steering and power brakes. It started again and I took it to a BMW dealer that said I needed a $325 software update. I asked if that meant my engine would shut off while driving should my software ever go out of date. They said yes, it happens but not on all software updates. They also said software updates come out about every 3 to 4 months meaning my engine could be shut off again at any time.

Finally, keep in mind that the base versions of these little status symbols are generally well-equipped, and just a few options can blow your budget. Adding to that, the upscale, gizmo-laden, better-performing high-end models aren't worth their premium price when compared with cheaper Japanese and South Korean competitors.

SECRET WARRANTIES, INTERNAL BULLETINS: *All models:* Many of the service bulletins listed here apply to other cars in the BMW lineup, as well. If you want to check if there is an overlap that includes your car, ask a BMW dealer. If that doesn't work, go to *www.safercar.gov* and look up the service bulletins applicable to your car. As a last resort, pay $26.95 (U.S.) to ALLDATA (*www.alldatadiy.com/buy/index.html*) to get a digital copy of every bulletin applicable to your vehicle. *3 Series:* 2002—Incorrect fuel gauge readings. Rattling, tapping engine noise. Troubleshooting navigation system malfunctions. No First-Second upshifts. 2003—Harsh Third-Second and Second-Third downshifts. 2004—Delayed Park-Drive shift. Numerous malfunctions of telematics components. 2005-06—Reduced engine power. 2007-10—High-pressure fuel pump failue. BMW has extended the emissions warranty to 10 years/120,000 mi. (193,000 km), according to TSB #SI B13 03 09, announced in BMW's November 2010 dealer letter. 2008—Instrument cluster displays go blank. Intermittent engine valve lash adjuster noise. 2008-09—Water leaks into footwell area. 2009—Airbag warning light stays on. No start, or reduced engine power. Poor AC performance. Rattling noise from the radio area. No Reverse or Forward gear. An oil leak at the right-hand side of the V6 engine crankcase may require that the crankcase be replaced. Excessive engine vibration. Silencing brake squeak and squeal. No start, or false fuel reading. Steering column noises. Front suspension creaking and groaning.

3 SERIES/M SERIES ★★★★

2014 BMW 320i.

RATING: Above Average (2013-16); Average (2000-12). With BMW's recent mechanical upgrades, styling changes, and increased exterior and interior dimensions, the 3 Series has come to resemble its more-expensive big brothers, with super-smooth powertrain performance and enhanced handling (when working properly). Still, competitors deliver more interior room and standard features for less money. *M3:* Not Recommended; the transmission hesitation on acceleration or deceleration is too risky for high-performance driving demands. **Road performance:** Good acceleration; the 6-cylinder engines and the transmissions are the essence of harmonious cooperation, even when coupled to an automatic transmission – there's not actually that much difference between the manual and the automatic from a performance perspective. Light and precise gear shifting with easy clutch and shift action; competent and predictable handling on dry surfaces; no-surprise suspension and steering make for crisp high-speed and emergency handling; a somewhat harsh ride (but the M3 is harsher than most); lots of road feedback, which enhances rear-end stability; and smooth, efficient braking that produces short stopping distances. The optional Sport suspension does enhance handling and steering, but it also produces an overly harsh, jiggly ride on rough pavement. Wider tires compromise traction in snow. **Strong points:** Twenty more horses with this year's new 3.0L V6; a better-appointed interior; an improved navigation and infotainment system, and better handling. BMW promises the 2016's retuned power steering, new front struts, and upgraded rear dampers will result in "reduced roll, improved directional stability, and a higher level of steering precision." The jury is still out. **Weak points:** Seriously overpriced and depreciation is only slightly slower than with Audi's lineup. For example, the entry-level models keep their value reasonably well, but as you get into pricier BMWs, the depreciation is mind-spinning. For example, a 2010 323i sedan that once sold for $34,800 is still worth about $15,500, but a 2010 750i that sold for $105,100 is now worth only $30,000. Ouch! Other complaints: High-pressure fuel pumps, electrical and infotainment systems, and some body trim and accessories are the most failure-prone components. Rattles and excessive vibration are also common with older models. Engine overheating is a serious problem experienced by many owners; insufficient front headroom and seat lumbar support for tall occupants; limited rear seatroom and cargo area; tricky entry and exit, even on sedans; confusing navigation system controls; excessive tire noise, especially with the M3; radio buzz; and premium fuel is required.

Prices and Specs

Prices (Firm): *320i Sedan:* $35,990, *320i xDrive Sedan:* $39,990, *328i Sedan:* $42,300, *328i xDrive Sedan:* $46,500, *335i Coupe:* $51,400, *335i xDrive Sedan:* $54,000, *328d xDrive Sedan:* $48,000, *ActiveHybrid 3:* $58,300, *4 Series Coupe:* $44,900, *4 Series Convertible:* $58,200, *5 Series Sedan:* $56,900, *M3 Sedan:* $74,000, *M3 Convertible:* $82,300, *M4 Coupe:* $75,000, *M4 Convertible:* $84,500, *6 Series Coupe:* $99,500, *6 Series Convertible:* $110,500, *7 Series Sedan:* $100,100, *M5 Sedan:* $101,500, *M6 Coupe:* $124,900, *M6 Convertible:* $129,500, *i3:* $45,300, *i8:* $150,000 **Freight:** $2,095 **Powertrain (Rear-drive/AWD):** Engines: 2.0L 4-cyl. (240 hp), 3.0L 6-cyl. (230 hp), 3.0L 6-cyl. Turbo (320 hp), 3.0L 6-cyl. Diesel (265 hp), 4.0L V8 (414 hp); Transmissions: 6-speed man., 8-speed auto. **Dimensions/Capacity:** Passengers: 2/3; Wheelbase: 109 in.; H: 56/L: 178/W: 72 in.; Headroom F/R: 3.5/2.5 in.; Legroom F/R: 40.5/27.5 in.; Cargo volume: 11 cu. ft.; Fuel tank: 63L/premium; Tow limit: No towing; Load capacity: 1,060 lb.; Turning circle: 19.4 ft.; Weight: 3,485 lb.

Other opinions: "The BMW 3 Series ranks #5 out of 14 upscale small cars. [It] has a great mix of outstanding handling, powerful acceleration and top-flight comfort." – *U.S. News & World Report.* "Turbocharged 3 Series tend to be problematic, with high-pressure fuel pumps being the most documented problem component. This issue can be identified by a variety of engine issues including stalling, rough idle, rough running and long crank times. Additionally, BMW's variable valve timing system, VANOS, is also a concern with turbocharged models. The sensors involved with VANOS can get dirty and clogged, causing the car to go into a limp-mode." – *www.autoguide.com/auto-news/2014/08/buy-used-bmw-3-series.html.* **Major redesign:** 1999, 2006, and 2012-13. The 2016 series offers only a few discreet interior and exterior changes, and some upgraded engines like a new 320 hp 3.0L 6-cylinder (340i). One engine we will likely not see any time soon in North America is the entry-level turbocharged 3-cylinder used by BMW in other countries. Low fuel prices are to blame. BMW says by mid-2016, it will add a plug-in hybrid called the 330e. It will come with a 4-cylinder gasoline engine and an electric motor, which combined will produce 250 hp. The company will jettison its ActiveHybrid 3, due to underwhelming sales. **Highway/city fuel economy:** *323i:* 6.9/11.1 L/100 km. *Auto.:* 6.7/11.2 L/100 km. *328i:* 7.0/10.9 L/100 km. *Auto.:* 6.9/11.3 L/100 km. *328i xDrive:* 7.6/12.2 L/100 km. *Auto.:* 7.8/11.9 L/100 km. *335i:* 7.9/11.9 L/100 km. *Auto.:* 7.6/11.9 L/ 100 km. *335i xDrive:* 7.9/12.2 L/100 km. *Auto.:* 7.9/12.2 L/100 km. *335d:* 5.4/9.0 L/ 100 km. *M3:* 9.7/15.3 L/100 km. *M3 Cabrio:* 10.1/15.7 L/100 km. **Best alternatives:** Smart BMW buyers will stick with the simple, large volume, entry-level models until the recession blows over. Used Bimmers with naturally-aspirated engines like the 2006 325i and 330i are your best bet for sustained reliability and cheaper, independent servicing. Other cars worth considering are the Hyundai Genesis Coupe or Sedan and the Lexus IS series. Stay away from run-flats and Bridgestone tires:

> Bridgestone tire exhibits unsafe characteristics in wet weather, with noticeable drift and hydroplaning in any amount of standing water. The tire also flat spots every morning, especially in cool weather, but even in warmer weather as well, leading to vibrations in the initial miles of any drive. It is also especially harsh over roadway expansion joints, and is so loud on concrete pavement that it poses a safety hazard due to driver fatigue induced by the continuous noise.

SAFETY: Crashworthiness: NHTSA: 2012-15 models have an impressive five-star overall crash safety rating; 1996-2011 models do fairly well, too, with a four- and five-star designation. IIHS: 2012-15 models have a "Good" overall crash rating, except in small front overlap collisions that produced a "Marginal" score. Roof strength was judged to be "Good" with the 2012-13 models and "Acceptable" with the 2006-11 versions, 2006-08 models were judged "Acceptable" but earlier models (2002-07) produced "Poor" rear crash scores. Keep this in mind when tempted to buy a cheaper earlier model. **Owner-reported safety-related failures:** A fire originated in the fog light socket; premature tire wear – and owners are forced to pay for tire failures. *325i:* Excessive hesitation on acceleration:

> When the driver demands a sudden increase in acceleration, the car hesitates anywhere from 1.5 to 3 seconds. This is a dangerous condition when someone is making a left turn in traffic, or getting onto a highway, or passing on a 2 lane country road, etc. Other cars traveling at 60 mph [96.5 km/h] are moving at 88 ft./sec. [27 m/s]. The amount of leeway this car needs is much too excessive.

Bridgestone tire-tread separation and side wall buckling:

> Bridgestone Potenza RE050A run-flat tires. The tires buckled on the side wall after less than 8,000 miles [12,870 km]. Out of curiosity I checked the Bimmerfest (www.bimmerfest.com/forums/showthread.php?t=146728) forum and discovered this is a widespread problem among BMW owners.

328: Some of the failures reported during the past few years: Airbags fail to deploy; underhood fire ignited while car was parked; premature tire failure (bubbles in the tread); sudden acceleration; engine slow surge while idling at a stoplight; when accelerating, engine cuts out and then surges forward (suspected failure of the throttle assembly); severe engine vibrations after a cold start as Check Engine light comes on; poor rain-handling; First gear and Reverse are positioned too close together, as are the brake and gas pedals; sunroof spontaneously shattered; a rear-quarter blind spot with the convertibles; seat rails that project a bit into the foot area could catch the driver's feet; and the front passenger head restraint won't go down far enough to protect short passengers. 330i: Side airbag deployed when vehicle hit a pothole; vehicle overheats in low gears; and vehicle slips out of Second gear when accelerating. *335i:* Delay in throttle engagement when slowing to a roll and then accelerating; frequent false brake safety alerts; sunroof suddenly exploded; tires lose air due to defective tire rims; faulty fuel injectors; and engine stalling and loss of power, which was fixed by replacing the fuel pump – now exhaust is booming, fuel economy has dropped, and there's considerable "turbo lag" when accelerating. Many other cases of loss of power on the highway, or the high-pressure fuel pump failing, with some owners having to replace the pump four times. *335d:* After a short downpour, engine started sputtering. Dealer and BMW said there was water in the fuel and held the car owner responsible for the full cost of the repairs. *M3:* Tail light socket overheats, blowing the bulb and shorting other lights – costs $600 to rewire; vehicle loses power due to faulty fuel pumps; transmission hesitates when accelerating in Second gear (see *www.roadfly.com*).

ALERT! Short drivers report the head restraints are uncomfortable; check this out during the test-drive. Don't take diesel power claims as Gospel; the system is much more complicated to service and repair than earlier versions, plus independent researchers say BMW diesels aren't as "clean" nor as fuel-efficient, as advertised.

3 Series/M Series Profile

Used Values ($)	2006	2007	2008	2009	2010	2011	2012	2013	2014
320i/323i/325i Sedan	8,500	10,000	11,000	13,000	15,500	18,500	22,000	25,500	31,000
320i xDrive	—	—	—	—	—	—	—	—	32,500
328i	—	11,500	13,000	15,000	17,500	21,500	26,500	31,500	37,000
328i xDrive	—	—	—	—	18,500	23,000	—	32,500	38,500
328id xDrive	—	—	—	—	—	—	—	—	41,500
330/335i	12,500	15,000	17,500	20,000	22,000	27,000	33,500	38,500	45,000
335d	—	—	—	—	23,000	28,500	—	—	—
Coupe 325i/328i	11,000	12,500	14,000	16,000	18,000	22,000	28,000	32,000	—
Cabriolet	14,500	17,500	20,500	23,500	26,500	32,000	38,500	44,500	—
M/M3	20,000	22,500	26,000	30,000	33,500	42,000	49,000	57,000	—
M5	—	—	—	—	46,000	—	66,000	75,000	87,000
M6	—	—	—	—	44,000	—	70,000	83,000	103,000
Cabriolet	—	—	—	—	—	—	72,000	89,000	106,000
ActiveHybrid 3	—	—	—	—	—	—	—	43,500	51,500
Reliability	★2	★2	★3	★3	★3	★3	★3	★	★
Repairs ($$$)	3	3	2	2	2	2	2		
Electrical	★1	★1	★1	★1	★1	★2	★3	★3	★
Engine (base)	★2	★2	★2	★3	★3	★3	★	★	★
Fit/Finish	★1	★1	★1	★2	★3	★3	★3	★	★
Infotainment	—	—	—	★3	★3	★	★	★	★
Transmission (auto.)	★1	★1	★1	★1	★1	★2	★3	★3	★3

SECRET WARRANTIES, INTERNAL BULLETINS: *All models:* 2011-12—Many of the service bulletins listed here apply to other cars in the BMW lineup, as well. If you want to check if there is an overlap that includes your car, ask a BMW dealer. If that doesn't work, go to *www.safercar.gov* and look up the service bulletins applicable to your car. As a last resort, pay $26.95 (U.S.) to ALLDATA (*www.alldatadiy.com/buy/index.html*) to get an overnite digital copy of every bulletin applicable to your vehicle. *3 Series:* 2002—Incorrect fuel gauge readings. Rattling, tapping engine noise. Troubleshooting navigation system malfunctions. No 1-2 upshifts. 2003—Harsh 3-2 and 2-1 downshifts. 2004—Delayed Park-Drive shift. Numerous malfunctions of telematics components. 2005-06—Reduced engine power. 2007-10—High-pressure fuel pump failue. BMW has extended the emissions warranty to 10 years/120,000 mi. (193,000 km), according to bulletin #SI B13 03 09, announced in BMW's November 2010 dealer letter (see: *www.scribd.com/doc/153404704/BMW-N54-HPFP-Warranty-Extension-TSB#scribd*). An 8 year/82,000 miles warranty extension covers the free correction of turbocharger wastegate rattles (see: *www.scribd.com/doc/151944416/BMW-N54-Turbo-Wastegate-Rattle-TSB-Extended-Warranty*). 2008—Instrument cluster displays go blank. Intermittent engine valve lash adjuster noise. 2008-09—Water leaks into footwell area. 2009—Airbag warning light stays on. No start, or reduced engine power. No start, or false fuel reading. Poor AC performance. Rattling noise from the radio area. No Reverse or Forward gear. An oil leak at the right-hand side of the V6 engine crankcase may require that the crankcase be replaced. Excessive engine vibration. Front suspension creaking and groaning. Silencing brake squeak and squeal. Steering column noises. 2013—During operation with high temperature fluctuations, the different materials used in the ignition coil construction can deteriorate over time, leading to a failure. For vehicles with the N51, N52, and N52K engines, which have been in service for over 24 months or 10,000 miles, during the first service visit due to an ignition coil failure, replace all Bosch ignition coils with the replacement Bosch coils. 2015—The power-assisted steering fails with a warning lamp in the instrument cluster or a check control message (CCM) in the Central Information Display. In some cases, the Dynamic Stability Control warning lamp in the instrument cluster may also be illuminated. Failure may be caused by various software-related issues. A CCM for "luggage compartment open" may come on in the instrument cluster, even though the lid is closed. Additionally, the convertible top cannot be opened as a result of the CCM. Both problems may be caused by a luggage compartment micro-switch that isn't activated.

5 SERIES X1/X3/X5/X6 ★★★★★ / ★★★★★ / ★★★

RATING: *X1:* Recommended (2016); Above Average (2013-15); *X3:* Above Average (2011-16); *X5:* Above Average (2010-16): Average (2011 and earlier X5s); *X6:* Average (2010-16). Despite BMW's sophisticated (and complicated) engineering, mechanical upgrades, styling changes, and increased exterior and interior dimensions, only the redesigned, entry-level 2016 X1 is recommended due to its almost reasonable base price, overall increased interior space, and interior upgrades. The X3 and X5 are competent performers but they are hobbled by a history of electrical and fuel system deficiences, combined with fit and finish glitches. *X3:* A small crossover that has swelled to the size of the previous generation, X5. There is plenty of room for front passengers, while rear legroom is generous and well-paired with comfortable seating, making this one of the most family-friendly SUVs in its class. *X5:* BMW's first crossover SUV has been on the market since 1999. It's a mid-sized seven-seater that has a worse reliability record with its early models than the other "X" SUVs. An unimpressive X5 spin-off in a larger box; ranked #25 out of 32 luxury crossover SUVs by *U.S. News & World Report*. *X6:* Proof that more can mean less. This upscale, X5 sporty spin-off drives, rides, and handles well, but its unusually low, racy styling obstructs rear visibility, cuts storage room, and turns egress and exiting into a Cirque de Soleil performance. All the while you're thinking, "Why did I spend $70,000 for this 'clown' car?" Like most European offerings, these BMWs are overpriced and quickly lose their value. **Road performance:** *X1:* The 2016 version carries the same powerful and responsive 228 hp 2.0L 4-cylinder engine as last year's model. An 8-speed automatic transmission and AWD are standard and deliver power seamlessly. *X3:* A potent 6-cylinder and an efficient, fuel-thrifty 4-cylinder engine; crisp handling; precise, predictable steering. Recent changes provide a more-forgiving suspension; a softer, less choppy ride; and more power-steering assistance. Unfortunately, the car's old nemesis – accelerator lag – is still present. Kickdown response suffers from a similar delay. Some help, though, is offered by leaving the transmission setting in Sport mode, which keeps the transmission in lower gear longer. Jerky stops, caused by the transmission's inherent imprecise shifting, compounded by the standard Brake Energy Regeneration system. *X5:* Engines deliver plenty of power, and there's a turbocharged diesel option; smooth, responsive power delivery; secure handling; and good steering feedback. *X6:* Billed as BMW's "sports activity" coupe because it's loaded with high-performance features. It carries a turbocharged 3.0L 6-cylinder engine or a powerful optional 4.4L V8 and is a bit taller than most coupes. Capable handling, the AWD system can vary the torque from side to side to minimize under-steer. Delayed throttle response continues to be a problem, and the 8-speed automatic transmission makes gearshifts less than luxurious. **Strong points:** *X1:* Essentially a five-seater, this year's restyled model has more headroom, legroom, and cargo space than the outgoing version and is 66 pounds lighter. Its new AWD system and chassis should improve the X1's handling and ride comfort. X1 comes standard with a seven-speaker audio system, BMW's iDrive infotainment system, a 6.5-inch display screen, Bluetooth, a USB port, leatherette upholstery and power-adjustable front seats. *X3:* Carried over this year relatively unchanged, except for an enhanced Bluetooth system, the X3 has abundant cargo space; good cabin access; and a quiet, nicely appointed interior, with a better integrated centre screen. The second-row seats have good leg and elbow room, and rear seating is relatively comfortable. *X5:* The 2015 X5 xDrive35d production was extended through November 2015 production. All other 2015 X5 models ended last July. A new plug-in hybrid Sports Activity Vehicle, the 2016 X5 xDrive40e, started production in August 2015. It will feature advance technology that promises a combined output of 308 hp, a 0-60 run in 6.5 secs, and better fuel economy (55 mpge) through all-electric mobility with zero tailpipe emissions and a 13-mile electric driving range. Comfortable first- and second-row seating and a high-quality cabin. Suspension improvements have smoothed out the ride. *X6:* No significant changes for 2016. Comfortable front seats and solid construction. Few reliability reports from owners. **Weak points:** Parts are scarce outside of major metropolitan areas, and independent mechanics who can service these vehicles are rare. Servicing deficiencies are accentuated by a weak dealer network and unreliable suppliers. Unbelievably fast depreciation. A 2010 X3 28i that once sold for $39,800 is now worth only $16,500. Hold on, it gets worse. A 2010 X5 xDrive 35d sold for $62,700 new, yet its used value is now barely $26,000 – a tremendous 6-year loss. Incidentally, the 2010 X6 M AWD that sold new for $99,800 may eventually take the crown for possessing a reverse "Midas Touch." Its value 5 years later is a disappointing $36,000. General complaints target the fit and finish, power equipment, audio system, fuel system, and transmission as most in need of special attention. *X3:* This little SUV with its somewhat narrow interior is way overpriced; options are a minefield of inflated charges; and mind-spinning depreciation makes Wall Street look tame. Reliability is compromised by powertrain deficiencies, serious fit and finish problems, audio system malfunctions, power equipment failures, and electrical system glitches. Although backseat legroom is adequate, the seat cushions are too low, forcing your knees to your chin. *X5:* A smallish cargo area; bundled options can be pricey; and there have been long-standing quality control issues with the fuel system (chronic stalling), brakes, powertrain, electrical components, climate control, body integrity, and fit and finish. The complicated shifter and iDrive controls can also be hard to master without a lot of patience and frustration; and the third-row seats are a bit cramped. *X6:* A hefty price and heftier weight; numb steering, stiff ride, soft brakes, insufficient back seat headroom with no adjustments on early models; a small cargo area; fit and finish glitches; and the iDrive infotainment system is too complicated for some.

Prices and Specs

X1 – **Prices (Firm):** *28i:* $34,800 **Freight:** $2,095 **Powertrain (Rear-drive/AWD):** Engines: 2.0L 4-cyl. (240 hp) Transmission: 8-speed auto. **Dimensions/capacity:** Passengers: 2/3; Wheelbase: 105.1 in.; H: 63.5/L: 174.8/W: 71.7 in.; Headroom F/R: 4/3 in.; Legroom F/R: 41.5/27.5 in.; Cargo volume: 47.7 cu. ft.; Fuel tank: 67L/premium; Tow limit: 3,500 lb.; Load capacity: 905 lb.; Turning circle: 38.7 ft.; Ground clearance: 8.5 in.; Weight: 3,649 lb.

X3 – **Prices (Firm):** *28i:* $43,600, *28id:* $45,300, *35i:* $49,200 **Freight:** $2,095 **Powertrain (Rear-drive/AWD):** Engines: 2.0L 4-cyl. (240 hp), 3.0L 6-cyl. (240 hp) 3.0L Turbo. 6-cyl. (300 hp) Transmission: 8-speed auto. **Dimensions/capacity:** Passengers: 2/3; Wheelbase: 110.6 in.; H: 67/L: 182.8/W: 74 in.; Headroom F/R: 4/3 in.; Legroom F/R: 41.5/27.5 in.; Cargo volume: 63.3 cu. ft.; Fuel tank: 67L/premium; Tow limit: 3,500 lb.; Load capacity: 905 lb.; Turning circle: 38.4 ft.; Ground clearance: 8.5 in.; Weight: 4,067 lb.

X5 – **Prices (Firm):** *35d xDrive:* $65,500 **Freight:** $2,095 **Powertrain (Rear-drive/AWD:** Engines (Turbo): 2.0L 4-cyl. (240 hp), 3.0L 6-cyl. (300 hp), 4.4L V8 (400 hp); Transmission: 8-speed auto. **Dimensions/capacity:** Passengers: 2/3/2; Wheelbase: 116 in.; H: 70/L: 191/W: 76.1 in.; Headroom F/R: 3.5/3 in.; Legroom F/R: 40.5/26.5 in.; Cargo volume: 36 cu. ft.; Fuel tank: 93L/premium; Tow limit: 6,500 lb.; Load capacity: 1,290 lb.; Turning circle: 42 ft.; Ground clearance: 8.3 in.; Weight: 5,265 lb.

X6 – **Price (Negotiable) Base model:** $68,890 **Freight:** $2,095 **Powertrain (Rear-drive/AWD):** Engines (Turbo): 3.0L 6-cyl. (240 hp), 4.4L 8-cyl. (400 hp), 4.4L 8-cyl. (555 hp), 4.4L 8-cyl. Hybrid (480 hp); Transmissions: 6-speed auto., 7-speed auto., 8-speed auto. **Dimensions/capacity:** Passengers: 2/2; Wheelbase: 116 in.; H: 67/L: 192/W: 78 in.; Headroom F/R: 3.5/2.5 in.; Legroom F/R: 40/27.5 in.; Fuel tank: 85L/premium; Tow limit: No towing; Load capacity: 935 lb.; Turning circle: 42 ft.; Ground clearance: 8.5 in.; Weight: 4,895-5,687 lb.

Other opinions: "The X3 ranks #3 out of 14 luxury compact SUVs." – *U.S. News & World Report.* "Marketed as a cross between an SUV and a high-end coupe, the X6 is engaging to drive but offers little in the way of utility." – *Edmunds.* **Major redesign:** *X1:* 2016; *X3:* 2004 and 2011 (next redesign in 2017); *X5:* 2000, 2007, and 2014; *X6:* 2009 and 2015. The 2015 X6 offers a new base rear-wheel drive sDrive35i and has been restyled without losing its sloping roofline. Occupants got a roomier interior, though, thanks to increases in length, width, and height. **Highway/city fuel economy:** *X3 28i:* 8.3/12.2 L/100 km. *X3 30i:* 8.2/12.5 L/100 km. *X5 30i:* 9.3/13.6 L/100 km. *Diesel:* 7.5/10.7 L/100 km. *X5 48i:* 10.2/15.6 L/100 km. *X5 M:* 11.9/17.2 L/100 km. *X6 35i:* 10.0/14.4 L/100 km. *X6 50i:* 11.0/17.1 L/100 km. *X6 M:* 11.9/

17.2 L/100 km. *X6 Hybrid:* 10.3/12.6 L/100 km. **Best alternatives:** The smaller X3's high buy-in puts it at a disadvantage against larger, mid-size luxury crossover SUVs like the Acura MDX and Lexus RX 350. But the X3 has a generous amount of passenger and cargo room, which outshines "compact" competitors like the Audi Q5 and Mercedes-Benz GLK350. *X1:* The redesigned Mercedes-Benz GLC that replaces the GLK and Audi A3. *X3:* Buy the more fuel-efficient 2013-16 if gas mileage is your main concern, but give preference to the second-series model built in March 2013 or later to make sure the electronics are less glitch-prone. Or, pick up a less-expensive 2012 V6-equipped X3, *sans* the latest changes. The money saved could buy a lot of fuel. *X5:* If the reports of poor quality don't faze you, get an almost identical, cheaper 2012 version, as well. *X6:* A big, brash, and beautiful barge – for potentates and poseurs. If you don't need the extra room, take the savings and run. Also consider the Acura RDX and Honda's CR-V. Other worthy contenders: The GM Acadia, Enclave, Escalade, Terrain, or Traverse, and the Lexus RX Series.

 SAFETY: Crashworthiness: NHTSA: X1 and X6 are unrated. The 2015 X3 has an overall five-star rating; as does the 2003-10 X5 models. IIHS: X1 and X6 not yet crash-tested. Mostly "Good" crash protection scores for 2004-15 X3 models. X5: "Good" designation for 2001-15 X5s. Rear crash protection was "Good" for 2008-13s, but surprisingly "Poor" for 2001-07 models. **Owner-reported safety-related failures:** Poor rearward visibility. *X1:* Sudden uninteneded acceleration; spontaneous shattering of the sunroof and windshield; interior "off-gassing" creates a film on the windshield:

> Creeping sticky-fog across lower portion of my 2013 X1's windshield "diagnosed" as fumes resulting from glue and substances on/in dash, seats, etc. Began in August 2013 as "fog" on passenger side windshield. Eventually spread to driver's side, obstructing driving visibility. All vehicles purchased in US, past year, have same substances and resulting vapors. Besides visibility issues, I need to know if these "fumes" are a health risk!

• • •

> 2013 BMW X1. Consumer writes in regards to spontaneous shattering of sun roof in my 2013 BMW X1. The consumer stated as he was making a right turn, the sun roof suddenly fell apart in tiny fragments of glass all over his seat, floor, clothing and skin. Nothing hit the car.

X3: Fewer than usual safety-related failures reported to the government, nevertheless, the safety implications are evident. Some examples include sudden unintended acceleration, brake failures, airbags fail to deploy, electronic steering shuts off, and defective xenon headlamp wiring:

> During replacement of the xenon headlamp bulbs on my 2014 x3, i noticed that all the vinyl wire covering material had become brittle and cracked off most of the copper wire inside both headlamp assemblies. The now exposed bare wiring posses potential fire hazards and also loss of lighting at night. I believe that the oem headlamp supplier supplied out of spec wire and should remedy this potentially dangerous situation.

Acceleration lag is also a problem for the X3:

The car didn't move for about a second or two when I tried to make a left turn in an intersection and then again when I was on the highway changing lanes. There were cars heading towards me but the initial distance was quite comfortable and safe. With the hesitation of the X3, I was actually in a panic and stepped really hard on the gas pedal to avoid a potential collision. And since then I have been stepping on the gas pedal much harder, guzzling gas, not to mention rough starts off of a full stop. I have seen countless Internet threads of people complaining about the same thing with the X3 model, both versions, however equipped. I would strongly suggest someone look at how this car's software is failing to function and fix this thing.

Car accelerates when the brakes applied; sudden stallouts on the highway; vehicle will roll backwards even if in Park; total shutdown of the electrical system:

The windshield wipers don't work, the headlights operate sporadically, the power door locks and power windows do not operate, the A/C doesn't work, the horn honks periodically, the tailgate won't open to facilitate replacement of fuses. The fuel gauge is inoperative and the cruise control doesn't work.

Run-flat tires are noted for their short tread life; steering failures; car veers to the right with sudden stops; protruding exhaust pipe can burn your leg when unloading cargo through the rear hatch.

X5: Engine surges and stalls:

The vehicle sporadically suffers from engine failure when executing a sharp turn. This has happened so far on three separate and distinct instances during its first 1,000 miles [1,609 km] of service, under the operation of two different drivers, with several passenger witnesses on one occasion. When these failures happen, the vehicle engine stalls or otherwise shuts itself off, which leads to loss of power steering in mid-turn and loss of braking. The only way to recover control of the vehicle is to let it coast to a stop, then put the vehicle in Park, then push the ignition button to re-start the car.

• • •

I leased my 2012 BMW X5 35I in May 2011. I was driving on the interstate with 2 toddlers at around 65 mph [105 km/h], when the car suddenly lost power and the message displayed "Engine Malfunction, Reduced Power." I pulled over on the shoulder, and tried to re-start the car, but it wouldn't start. The next day my wife took the car to the dealer, and the report sheet they provided said that the high pressure pump was faulty.

ALERT! *Lemon-Aid* readers report that dealers are demanding up to $500 "administrative" fees as a contract add-on. Simply tell the salesman that "No" means "No" and threaten to go elsewhere. The charge is unjustified and is nothing more than a shameful ploy to steal your money.

X1/X3/X5/X6 Profile

	2006	2007	2008	2009	2010	2011	2012	2013	2014
Used Values ($)									
X1 28i	—	—	—	—	—	—	23,500	27,500	31,000
X3 2.5i/28i/30i	9,000	10,500	12,500	14,500	17,000	22,500	26,500	31,500	35,500
X5 3.0i/35i	13,000	15,000	17,500	21,000	24,500	31,500	37,000	45,000	52,000
X6 35i	—	—	21,000	24,000	27,500	33,000	39,000	48,000	54,000
Reliability	☆	☆	☆	☆	☆	☆	☆	☆	☆
Repairs ($$$)	3	2	2	2	2	1	1	1	1
Electrical	☆	☆	☆	☆	☆	☆	☆	☆	☆
Engine (base)	☆	☆	☆	☆	☆	☆	☆	☆	☆
Fit/Finish	☆	☆	☆	☆	☆	☆	☆	☆	☆
Infotainment	—	—	—	☆	☆	☆	☆	☆	☆
Transmission (auto.)	☆	☆	☆	☆	☆	☆	☆	☆	☆

SECRET WARRANTIES, INTERNAL BULLETINS: 2008-14—BMW says headlight failures can often be traced to a defective LED main light module. This admission makes BMW liable for part of the replacement cost on a pro-rata basis as to what would be reasonable durability. 2011-12—Oil leak from the transfer case. *X1:* 2012-14—The Service Engine Soon lamp (MIL) may light up; the engine may run poorly or no longer start; and various faults may be stored in the DME memory. This could be caused by water damage and corrosion to the DME pins and harness connectors because the harness connectors aren't properly sealed. 2013—The vehicle judders or surges repeatedly while accelerating in hot ambient temperatures between 3,000 RPM and 5,000 RPM. The Service Engine Soon lamp is not illuminated, and no fault codes are stored in the vehicle memory related to this complaint. The EPDW (electropneumatic pressure convertor) for the turbocharger wastegate valve is probably binding internally. *X3:* 2013—Intermittently noisy cooling fan. Water leaks into the cargo area. In most cases, the customer is not aware of any water in the lower compartments of the cargo area, but complaints of an electrical malfunction or failure, as a result of water intrusion. Water leaks from A/C centre console into the left and right footwell. Condensation is leaking from the HVAC housing water drain connection (not fitted correctly). Various electrical system failures leading to no-starts. Repeated juddering or surging on acceleration. Intermittent loss of power. The EPDW for the turbocharger wastegate valve is binding internally. Vehicle drifts to the right when traveling straight ahead. Possible Causes: Tires or improper tolerance in the coil springs of the front axle. *X5:* 2013—Intermittent loss of power. Computer/controls. Idle may fluctuate or cut off. Lag and lurch acceleration continues; various faults concerning the automatic tailgate that flies open on the highway and BMW's admission that its door locks malfunction on most models.

OIL LEAK FROM TRANSFER CASE

BULLETIN NO.: S1 B27 01 12   DATE: APRIL 2012

Model: X3, X5, and X6.

SITUATION: Oil is leaking from the transmission area, or oil seepage is noticed from the transmission/transfer case area during a service.

CAUSE: The leak can be misdiagnosed as a transmission fluid leak from either the mechatronics sleeve or transmission oil pan. The leak is actually coming from the transfer case (input or output shaft seal).

PROCEDURE: Before attempting to perform any repairs, check the fluid level in both the transmission and transfer case. If the level is low in the transfer case, repair as necessary. Delay in engine response may require recalibration of the software; engine whistling, hooting, or squealing; intermittent engine rattle upon cold start; noise from the transmission bell housing area; faulty various electrical/computer malfunctions; inoperative front window; free replacement of the right front window regulator under Service Action #214, published in March 2012; whistle noise from rear-view mirror; humming noise from front of car; AC blows warm air; wipers/washers self-activate, can't be shut off; revised sun visor repair instructions; Check Gas Cap alert; excessive door mirror vibration; inoperative cell phone; and leather peeling from the steering wheel.

Here are some helpful service bulletins for the 5-Series profiled in the Appendix.

5 Series: All years: Water inside of headlight. Erratic performance of the navigation system. *All 5 Series Models:* 2008-13—A rattling or clattering noise may be heard from the driver's or passenger footwell area while driving. This likely caused by excessive tolerance between the footwell air duct and the securing hooks. 2013—Transmission intermittently goes into Park or Neutral. Loss of performance and turbocharger noise may mean the oil supply is restricted, causing oil starvation and resulting in the seizing of the turbocharger assembly. 2013-15—Clicking noises are heard from the front axle area while maneuvering at low speeds (e.g., parking lot maneuvers). Confirm the noise is coming from the front wheel bearing area and remove the front wheel bearing. Use repair kit P/N 83 19 2 298 825 to clean up the mating surfaces of the wheel bearing and the swivel bearing (steering knuckle). Troubleshooting side-view camera malfunctions. 2014-15—Fixing adaptive headlights that malfunction in cold weather. Tips on correcting speaker cover rattles. *525i:* 2006-07—Troubleshooting AC compressor noise. 2007-09—Automatic transmission jolt or delay when accelerating from a stop. 2009—Reduced engine power. Automatic transmission jumps out of Drive or Reverse into Neutral (requires a software adjustment). Troubleshooting front seat noise. Front brake squeak or squeal upon light brake application. An oil leak at the right-hand side of the V6 engine crankcase may require that the crankcase be replaced. Intermittent engine valve lash adjuster noise. Exhaust system vibration or drone at idle. Poor AC performance. Steering column noises. *530i: 2005-07*—Front brake squeak or squeal upon light brake application. Sunroof wind noise and water leaks.

MERCEDES-BENZ

Quality Decline

"Another noteworthy finding: Numerous luxury brands, including Lexus, Cadillac and BMW, did poorly in this year's survey. Even top-rated Mercedes-Benz (86) dropped 2 percent. Honda's Acura line had the most dramatic decline – 7 percent for a score of 77 – landing it at the very bottom of the list."

– American Customer 2014 Satisfaction Index Report
www.theacsi.org/

Rich Profits, Poor Quality

Daimler AG, Mercedes' governing company, is registering record-breaking profits – mostly generated by strategic cost cutting, generous leasing packages, and new products. These profits are all the more remarkable in that North America, Europe, and Asia are barely emerging from a recession where only the strongest brands (mostly German automakers) survived.

Shoppers want luxury, but they also want powerful, fuel-efficient, comfortable vehicles with a high-performance edge. Automobile alchemists capable of creating fast, fancy, and frugal cars will be the winners in 2016-17. Mercedes is doing just this *and* it is paying off handsomely. In June, global unit sales of Mercedes-Benz increased by 19.3% and, in the first half of the year, by 14.7%. In Canada, half-year overall sales were up 18.7% over the same period last year. Daimler AG made a healthy profit, mostly from strong sales of the lucrative E-Class and S-Class models, a drop in costly sales incentives, and a surprisingly sharp rebound in demand from Chinese and U.S. car buyers.

The company has pulled off this turnaround by increasing sales of smaller and less expensive cars in the United States, while selling fewer – but larger and more expensive – models in Europe and Asia. This means we'll see more subcompacts, electric vehicles, crossovers, and a proliferation of turbocharged engines that have mostly been offered off-shore.

However, as oil prices hover around $45 U.S. a barrel, luxury car sales in North America are shifting to larger, fully-loaded, and expensive European imports that are snapped up by Millennial buyers (age 18-34) using favourable leasing deals. According to data supplied by Polk, leasing accounts for 28.9% of all new car purchases by Millennials in 2015 – a couple of points higher than leasing by the general population. Why the attraction? Simple. Leasees get more car for less money up front; younger buyers are used to carrying a heavy debt load (school or mortgage debt) and in the age of 3-year cellphone contracts, they want a different vehicle every few years. A CL-Class, today, an S-Class, tomorrow?

Edmunds' 2015 poll findings show Millennials want to put no more than $2,999 down and pay about $299 per month. This limits financed purchases to cars costing $20,000 or less. Leasing with the same upfront and monthly payment obligation permits the use of a $35,000 vehicle for 3-5 years. Of course, you pay more during the lease and wind up car-less when the lease expires.

More Models, Less Quality

Mercedes hasn't been very good at making reliable or top-quality cars and SUVs over the past few decades. Industry insiders say quality control went downhill after M-B extended its product lineup in 1997. Since then, the company has settled multimillion dollar lawsuits for engine sludge and other major engine defects.

One recent American settlement outlines the benchmark that Canadian owners can use to get extra-judicial compensation from Mercedes for a common engine failure costing thousands of dollars to fix. On March 23, 2015, Mercedes settled a landmark American class action lawsuit relating to failure-prone engines found throughout its 2005-07 model lineup. This was after stonewalling owner claims during 6 years of litigation. (see *Majeed Seifi v. Mercedes-Benz USA LLC*, Case No. 3:12-cv-05493, in the U.S. District Court for the Northern District of California; *eclaim.kccllc.net/caclaimforms/mse/faqs.aspx*; *www.gaulitics.com/2015/06/mercedes-benz-settlement-rips-off.html*)

Vehicles covered by this settlement are 6- and 8-cylinder engines found in the following 2005-07 cars: ML350, SLK280/300, SLK 350, C230, C280, C350, C350 4Matic, C280 Wagon 4Matic, CLK350, CLK350 Cabriolet, E350, E350 4Matic, E350 Wagon, R350, R350 4Matic, ML550 4Matic, GL450 4Matic, GL550 4Matic, CLK550, CLK550 (Cabriolet), E550, E550 4Matic, CL550, CLS550, S550, S550 4Matic, SL550.

The class action lawsuit alleged:

> M272 engines are equipped with defective gears in their balance shafts or with defective idle gears in the case of the M273 engines. These defective gears wear out prematurely, excessively, and without warning, causing the vehicle to malfunction, the 'check engine light' to remain lit, and the vehicle to misfire and/or stall out.

The amount owners will receive can vary. Repairs not done at an authorized dealer will result in a reimbursement of up to $4,000. Mercedes will also cover the cost to repair future engine problems, up to 10 years or 125,000 miles. Reimbursement will be 100%, 70% or 37.5% of the cost of the repair, depending on the age of the car when the problems first appear.

For example, in a recent U.S. class action, owners say about 1.6 million cars built from 2006 to 2015 were sold with defective wheels. Court documents show approximately 30% of the 50 wheels the plaintiffs' expert tested, including ones that didn't appear to be abused in any way, had visible cracks. The expert determined the cracks were "clearly induced by cyclic deformation" during normal use of the cars. (*Vincent Luppino v. Mercedes-Benz USA LLC, et al.*, Case No. 2:09-cv-05582, in the U.S. District Court for the District of New Jersey.)

In addition to failure-prone components, a number of M-B's new models have been failures as well. The company's 1982-93 190e "mini-Benz" economy car was a poorly-engineered sales dud in North America; first efforts with the C- and M-Class were flops; and the Smart car is still seen as merely a "cute" marginal player out-classed by more refined, reliable Japanese and South Korean mini-compacts. Showcasing Mercedes' deficiencies in the most embarrassing way possible, its much-hyped A-Class drew gasps from auto journalists when the small car did cartwheels in a 1997 press-sponsored "moose-proof," challenge – a performance exercise used for decades in Sweden that calls for the driver to suddenly change lanes while going 70-80 km/h (45-50 mph), as though trying to avoid hitting a moose. What shocked the West Germany-based Daimler dignitaries most was that the Trabant – a much older, widely mocked car from Eastern Germany – passed the test with flying colours.

Although Mercedes quality is improving, especially with the E-Class, some models continue to do much worse than others. For example, the C-Class, M-Class, and GLK-Class still have many quality shortcomings outstanding, like fit and finish and powertrain delays – defects that are also evident in Audi, BMW, and VW models:

I almost had two accidents due to the lag problems, and have attached a more detailed analysis for your review. Turbo Lag: This is the time it takes for the car to go from its naturally aspirated power to the full power of the car as full boost/peak boost is reached relatively low in the reverse range, but it is not instantaneous power like a naturally aspirated engine. Throttle Lag: The drive by wire system has a bit of lag. Under certain conditions, I measured it at .2 of a second or so. Whatever the value, there is always lag there, and we are very sensitive to it. However, driving in S Mode vs. E Mode does make somewhat of a difference. Nonetheless, the car always starts out in E Mode when I get in and start the car. We didn't purchase the car to always drive in S Mode. Transmission Lag: This I notice significantly and it is, in my opinion, probably the most annoying to me. You'll notice this when stomping the pedal to the floor and then doing the wait … wait … wait … downshift. Even if this engine was running only on its naturally aspirated four cylinders, the transmission should respond immediately to a sure footed stomp to the floor with the quickness, as does my four cylinder RAV-4. However, the MB C-250 does not! In my opinion, you can reset the TCU all you want, the delay will remain.

High-end models like the CLK, GL-Class, and M-Class SUV have a history of quality failures that can lighten your wallet and make your life miserable. Most ironic of all, the most expensive models like the $91,850 to $210,900 (U.S.) S-Class can also be troublesome, particularly, the 2007 and 2008 models.

Mercedes' first minivans were a disaster and are still a work in progress. From the very beginning, everyone (except for some clueless buyers) knew that the 1998 M-Class was abysmally bad. You couldn't have made a worse vehicle, judging by the unending stream of desperate-sounding service bulletins sent from head office to dealers after the vehicle's official launch. Two bulletins stand out in my mind. One was an authorization for dry-cleaning payouts to dealers whose customers' clothing had been stained by the dye from the burgundy-coloured leather seats. The other was a lengthy scientific explanation (which the Germans compose so well) as to why it was "normal" for occupants to be "tasered" by static electricity when entering or exiting their vehicles.

Fast forwarding to the present, the CLA model was singled out by *Consumer Reports'* 2014 Annual Auto Reliability Survey as a particularly bad buy. Deputy auto editor Jon Linkov was emphatic, "Not only is the CLA the worst performing Mercedes in the survey, [it] is also 140% worse than the average car." Mercedes fell from the 13th to 24th spot in that year's ratings.

The S-Class, formerly known as "Sonderklasse" (German for "special class") is a series of flagship vehicles built by Mercedes-Benz since 1972. Sadly, owners say these super-luxury cars aren't as "special" as Mercedes says. Costing hundreds of thousands of dollars each, they apparently aren't as reliable as the $30,000 B-Class small compact, as the following two NHTSA sample complaints show:

Collision Avoidance System crashes

Salesman reached across driver and set cruise at 40mph and encouraged driver to test the collision prevention system – traffic ahead was stopped at light – salesman continued to tell driver to not apply brakes – driver did not apply brakes – collision avoidance system failed – seat belt tensioners failed – air bags did not deploy when S550 collided with rear of stopped vehicle (an E-class) at approx 40mph. Back seat passenger (driver's wife) was hospitalized with a cracked sternum.

Sunroof an "Improvised Explosive Device" (IED)

The 2015 S-class 550 was underway on the freeway when the sunroof exploded and broke off in chunks hitting driver repeatedly until approximately 80% of the glass collapsed. Glass shards cut driver. MBworld shows similar incidents reported on other Mercedes-Benz vehicles. Mercedes-Benz would not cover under warranty or admit defect. See sample of postings: http://mbworld.org/forums/e-class-w212/405329-2011-e350-exploding-sunroof.html; http://mbworld.org/forums/c-class-w204/544374-exploding-shattered-sunroof-tristar-mercedes-st-louis-mo.html; http://mbworld.org/forums/c-class-w203/346317-c230-sunroof-exploded.html; http://mbworld.org/forums/c-class-w203/525268-sunroof-blew-out-exploded.html; http://mbworld.org/forums/gl-class-x166/550965-panoramic-roof-blew-up.html.

Although Mercedes sales are on the upswing, its vehicles' residual values have fallen dramatically from the most expensive cars down to the base entry-levels. At the top end, a 2010 65 AMG S-Class Sedan that cost $234,000 new is now worth barely $55,000. Even the entry-level B-Class models feel the depreciation bite. A 2010 B-Class 200 that originally sold for $29,900 is now worth only $11,500, and contrary to popular belief Mercedes' diesel models don't hold their value very well, either. A mid-range 2012 E-Class E350 BlueTEC sedan, once priced at $65,600, now sells for almost half as much – $35,500. Adding to Mercedes' uncertain future, German investigators suspect its emissions software may, like VW diesels, give phony emissions and fuel-economy readings.

So, what should a smart buyer do?

Don't waste money on a new Audi, BMW, or a Mercedes-Benz. Sure, the cars are stylish head-turners, but you make a Faustian bargain with your purchase. Along with the upper-class cachet, buyers going in for servicing end up wearing the equivalent of a sign on their back, reading, "Kick me – and take my wallet, too."

Choose an Asian or South Korean alternative. If a European luxury model is a must, look for a 3-year-old version with some warranty left, or buy it with a supplementary powertrain warranty. This will protect you from some of the more common drivetrain deficiencies and strengthen your case for a buy-back, if corrective repairs don't work.

B-CLASS

RATING: Average (2013-16); Below Average (2006-12). This is the third year of the car's last redesign, which means, most of the first year's production errors have been corrected. Keep in mind, though, that most reworked Mercedes models offer poorly-integrated electronics and hardware during their first few years after a redesign, but so far this mini-Mercedes has performed admirably. Further complicating the reliability and servicing is BMW's world-wide parts redistribution changes put in place several years ago. Owners grumble that the new system is inefficient and parts are unduly delayed for even the most minor repairs. The parts are particularly hard to find in the States due to the B250's absence from the American market. This means possibly longer servicing waits in the States (a problem also facing Mercedes Smart owners), forcing prudent drivers to plan Canada-only driving vacations. Audi, BMW, and VW have better organized nationwide servicing networks throughout the States. **Road performance:** On 2013 and later models, the standard electronic stability control tames wheel spin and maintains directional stability. Brisk acceleration, with good fuel efficiency, thanks to turbocharging and the advent of an ECO stop/start feature that saves on gas in stop-and-go traffic. The 7-speed dual-clutch transmission, that replaces the previous generation's inadequate CVT gearworks, delivers power smoothly and quietly. Considering its small size, the "B" has an unusually large turning circle, which cuts its urban usefulness. **Strong points:** Occupant ingress and egress takes a minimal amount of acrobatics, and rear-seat passengers can sit in relative comfort. B250s are wider and longer, and have a stretched wheelbase, but they sit lower. The back is roomy, with lots of storage space, a wide-opening hatch, and low load height. All cars are feature-laden, with four-wheel disc brakes, nine standard airbags, upgraded suspension and steering, and a classier, more user-friendly interior, and Internet capable. **Weak points:** The retail price could be trimmed by at least $2,000, making this wagon/hatchback more competitive. Furthermore, shoppers would be wise to consider the equivalent Mazda or other Japanese or European compacts that can cost less and be serviced everywhere. Owners decry mostly fit and finish problems, door bottoms (rocker panels) rusting on earlier models, electrical system shorts, and premature brake wear gripes.

Prices and Specs

Prices (Soft): *B 250 Sport tourer:* $31,300, *4MATIC Sport Tourer (AWD):* $33,500 **Freight:** $2,074 **Powertrain (Front-drive):** Engine: 2.0L Turbo 4-cyl. (208 hp); Transmission: 7-speed auto. **Dimensions/capacity:** Passengers: 2/3; Wheelbase: 106.3 in.; H: 61.5/L: 173/W: 79.1 in.; Legroom F/R: 43/38.4 in.; Cargo volume: 23.5 cu. ft.; Fuel tank: 50L/premium; Tow limit: N/A; Turning circle: 39.2 ft.; Weight: 3,252 lb.

Other opinions: "[A]n entry-level runabout that is so downmarket – by Mercedes' standards – that Daimler's sales arm in the United States won't even stock it for fear of degrading the Mercedes brand." – *www.theglobeandmail.com/globe-drive/reviews/new-cars/the-entry-level-mercedes-that-americans-cant-buy/article6842712/*. **Major redesign:** 2013 models are more refined and represent a big step up with additional performance, safety, and convenience features. In 2015, a $41,450 B-Class Electric Drive was launched in the States and has been well-received by independent car critics. It has a driving range of 87 miles (U.S. Mercedes-Benz rating) and the Tesla-supplied battery can be charged at any standard public power outlet or rapid charging terminal. Another 2015 plus: An AWD 4Matic option. **Highway/city fuel economy:** Front-drive: 6.6/9.2 L/100 km. **Best alternatives:** Take a look at the Audi A3, BMW 1 Series, Kia Rondo, Mazda5, Toyota Matrix, or VW Golf/Jetta. AWD alternatives: The Nissan Juke, Buick Encore, Mitsubishi RVR, and Subaru XV Crosstrek.

SAFETY: Crashworthiness: Wasn't tested. **Owner-reported safety-related failures:** The 7-speed transmission can't make up its mind as to which gear it should choose; it randomly shifts up and down and lingers in one gear when it should be in another. Cold starts acerbate the problem. M-B's Eco Start/stop is a fuel-saver that shuts off and re-starts the engine when stopped and accelerating. As with the 7-speed tranny, its performance is anything but smooth and mirrors what drivers find with the same feature on BMW and other brands. Consider de-activating it with the dash-mounted switch.

ALERT! The paddle shifters take getting used to and may discourage spirited driving. Check out the left side-view mirror's blind spot.

B-Class Profile

	2006	2007	2008	2009	2010	2011	2012	2013	2014
Used Values ($)									
200/250	6,000	7,500	8,500	10,000	11,500	13,000	—	21,500	24,000
200T	7,000	8,500	10,000	11,500	13,000	14,500	—	—	—
Reliability	★2	★3	★3	★3	★3	★4	★4	★5	★5
Repairs ($$$)	3	2	2	2	2	1	1	1	1
Electrical	★3	★3	★3	★3	★3	★3	★3	★4	★4
Engine (base)	★	★	★	★	★	★	★	★	★
Fit/Finish	★	★	★	★	★	★	★	★	★
Infotainment	—	—	—	★2	★2	★2	★3	★3	★3
Transmission (auto.)	★	★	★	★	★	★	★	★	★

SECRET WARRANTIES, INTERNAL BULLETINS: All Years—Owners report premature rusting of the rear hatch and door seams. Apparently, M-B is repairing the damage for free, on a case-by-case "goodwill" basis.

C-CLASS ★★★

2014 Mercedes-Benz C 350.

RATING: Average (2008-16); Below Average (2001-07). Do you really want to payC $43,000 for a small car that's only "Average?" These little entry-level cars lack the reliability, simplicity and popular pricing found with the Japanese luxury competition; save up for an E-Class or a Hyundai Genesis. **Road performance:** A big improvement in power and handling with the adoption of V6 power. The ride is generally comfortable, though sometimes choppy, and braking is first-class. The light steering requires constant correction, and there's some tire thumping and engine and wind noise in the cabin. **Strong points:** Plenty of high-tech performance and safety features; a good V6 powertrain matchup; available AWD; and an innovative anti-theft system. **Weak points:** Higher prices than are reasonable when compared with competitors and faster than average depreciation that hits entry-level and moderately-priced models harder than some of the more extravagant offerings. For example, the popular-priced $41,200 2010 C300 AWD Sedan is now barely worth $17,500. Owners report problems with the climate control systems, body hardware, and fit and finish, as well as complicated controls; limited rear-seat and cargo room; and tight entry and exit. Also, these cars are noted for being dealer-dependent for parts and servicing – a problem likely to worsen with newer powertrains and during economic slowdowns that make dealers reluctant to invest in a large inventory.

Prices and Specs

Prices (Soft): *C 300:* $43,000, *C 400 4Matic:* $51,400, *AMG C 63:* $74,000, *AMG C 63 S:* $82,900 **Freight:** $1,995 **Powertrain (Rear-drive/AWD):** Engines: 1.8L 4-cyl. (201 hp), 3.5L V6 (248 hp), 3.5L V6 (302 hp), 6.3L V8 (451 hp); Transmission: 7-speed auto. **Dimensions/capacity:** Passengers: 2/3; Wheelbase: 108.7 in.; H: 56.9/L: 182/W: 70 in.; Headroom F/R: 2.5/1.5 in.; Legroom F/R: 42/26 in.; Cargo volume: 12.4 cu. ft.; Fuel tank: 62L/premium; Tow limit: Not recommended; Load capacity: 835 lb.; Turning circle: 35.3 ft.; Ground clearance: 4.2 in.; Weight: 3,565 lb.

Other opinions: "The 2015 Mercedes-Benz C-Class ranks #2 out of 14 upscale small cars. [It] compares favorably with its competitors, according to reviewers who single out its luxurious interior and composed ride." – *U.S. News & World Report.* **Major redesign:** 2001 and 2008. **Highway/city fuel economy:** *C250, 1.8L:* 6.3/9.6 L/ 100 km. *2.5L:* 8.3/12.4 L/100 km. *Coupe:* 6.4/9.7 L/100 km. *C300:* 7.9/11.8 L/ 100 km. *4Matic:* 10.8/16.3 L/100 km. *C350:* 7.0/10.8 L/100 km. *4Matic:* 7.0/10.7 L/ 100 km. *4Matic Coupe:* 7.1/10.8 L/100 km. *63 AMG:* 10.4/16 L/100 km. *Coupe:* 10.4/16.1 L/100 km. *CL550:* 8.8/13.8 L/100 km. *CL600:* 11.2/18.1 L/100 km. *CL 63 AMG:* 9.3/13.8 L/100 km. *CL 65 AMG:* 10.9/17.4 L/100 km. *CLS 550 4Matic:* 8.2/ 12.7 L/100 km. *CLS 63 AMG:* 8.6/13.6 L/100 km. **Best alternatives:** Take a look at the Audi A4, BMW 3 Series, or a Hyundai Genesis Coupe. The Bose sound system is a good investment.

SAFETY: Crashworthiness: NHTSA: 2002-15 C-Class models were awarded four and five stars for overall crash protection. IIHS: Crash tests gave top marks ("Good") for front moderate overlap protection from 2001 through 2015 model years and a "Poor" score for side crashworthiness. 2005-07 models rated "Acceptable" for side crash safety and "Good" for 2009-13 versions. Roof strength was judged "Good" from 2008 up to the 2013s and head restraints scored "Marginal" for the 2004-05s; "Acceptable" from 2006-07; and "Good" for the 2008-13s. **Owner-reported safety-related failures:** Airbags fail to deploy. *C250:* Turn-signal control light is barely visible in daylight, and steering-column-mounted levers (cruise control, for instance) are hard to see behind the steering wheel. *C300:* Severe injuries following sudden unintended acceleration; original equipment Continental tire sidewall bubbling; and driver's door popped open as interior lights suddenly came on, says this owner of a 2015 C300:

> It was very frightening, and caught me by surprise. Luckily at the time there were no other cars near me. I was told by dealer they couldn't duplicate the door opening. However, looking at forums on the internet, this exact issue has been reported by others in the US and Australia at least. Some were the driver's door, others were the passenger's door. One reported it happening a second time after the dealer inspected the vehicle. I am very concerned about this happening again, and possibly triggering an air bag or auto-park. I do not feel safe in this car.

Vehicle fails to accelerate on the highway:

> The accelerator pedal was depressed but my 2015 C300 would not accelerate. The stability control, collision preventive assistance, and cruise control shut down. Warning indicators illuminated. The failure recurred three times. The radar sensor was replaced, but the failure recurred.

Power steering failures:

> My 2015 C300's steering malfunction light came on and the steering wheel lost power and locked up.

ALERT! Severe noise invades the cabin when the window is rolled down while driving:

> The contact owns a 2012 Mercedes Benz C300. The contact stated that while driving 35 mph [56 km/h], the rear passenger side window exhibited a loud, abnormal noise when opened. As a result, the contact experienced a temporary loss of hearing from the high pitch of the noise. The vehicle was taken to the dealer who stated that the loud noise was common for the vehicle.

C-Class Profile

Used Values ($)	2006	2007	2008	2009	2010	2011	2012	2013	2014
Coupe 230/250	8,500	—	—	—	—	—	23,500	28,000	33,500
350	—	—	—	—	—	—	28,500	34,000	40,000
AMG	—	—	—	—	—	—	36,500	43,000	54,000
Sedan 240/250	8,000	10,000	12,000	15,500	18,000	20,000	22,500	27,500	32,000
AWD	—	11,500	13,500	14,500	16,500	20,000	24,000	30,000	34,000
250	—	—	—	—	15,000	18,500	22,500	27,500	31,500
AWD	—	—	—	—	16,000	20,000	24,000	—	—
280	7,000	8,500	—	—	—	—	—	—	—
AWD	8,000	10,000	—	—	—	—	—	—	—
300	—	—	12,000	14,000	17,500	19,500	—	—	—
AWD	—	—	14,000	16,000	19,000	21,000	25,000	—	—
350	11,000	13,000	16,000	18,500	21,000	23,000	27,000	33,000	38,000
AWD	13,000	15,500	18,000	20,500	22,000	24,500	28,500	35,500	41,000
AMG	—	—	—	24,000	26,500	31,500	37,500	45,000	54,000

	2006	2007	2008	2009	2010	2011	2012	2013	2014
Reliability	★	★	★	★	★	★	☆	☆	☆
Repairs ($$$)	3	3	2	2	2	2	1	1	1
Electrical	★	★	★	★	★	★	★	☆	☆
Engine (base)	★	★	★	☆	☆	☆	☆	☆	☆
Fit/Finish	☆	☆	☆	☆	☆	☆	☆	☆	☆
Infotainment	—	—	—	★	★	★	★	★	★
Transmission (auto.)	★	★	★	★	☆	☆	☆	☆	☆

SECRET WARRANTIES, INTERNAL BULLETINS: *All C-Class (2009-13), CLK-Class (2009-10), E-Class (2009-13), and S-Class (2009) models:* Correction for steering knock. *All C-Class and E-Class models:* 2011-13—Bulletin advises dealers to replace noisy automatic transmissions under warranty. 2013—Oil loss near the rear crankcase-transmission bell housing. Corrosion spreads under wheel hub sealing ring. Dirt and water are washed in front of the sealing ring of the wheel hub via the rpm sensor bore in the steering knuckle or through corresponding gaps between the anchor plate and steering knuckle. Corrosion forms on the contact surface of the sealing ring and spreads under the sealing lips. As a result, moisture can penetrate the wheel bearing and cause corrosion. Moisture in area of A-pillar trim/headliner at front left or right. Replace water drain grommet. Casting porosity in crankcase or leaks in oil filter housing (seal might be damaged at the oil filter housing plate). The steering boot heat shield with aluminum ring may be loose and could scrape on the steering shaft. 2005—Engine oil leaks from the oil-level sensor. Harsh shifts with the automatic transmission. Transmission fluid leaks at the electrical connector. Inoperative central locking system and AC heater blower motor. Steering assembly leaks fluid. Sliding roof water leaks, rattling. Moisture in the turn signal lights and mirrors. Tail lights won't turn off; trunk light won't turn on. A Service Campaign calls for the modification of the lower door seal. 2007—Rough shifting. Automatic transmission shift chatter. Steering rack leaks. Inoperative AC blower motor. Remedy for brake squealing. Front-end/dash noise. Front axle knocking when parking. Torsion bar front-end creaking. Inoperative turn signals. Rear seatback rattle. Loose head restraint. Horn may not work due to premature corrosion of the assembly. *350:* 2009—Oil leaks at the rear of the engine may be fixed by changing the camshaft cover plugs. Hard 1-2 shifts. Harsh engagement when shifting from Park to Drive. Delayed Reverse engagement. What to do if the automatic transmission goes into "limp home" mode. Front axle noise when maneuvering. Front axle dull, thumping noise when going over bumps. Front-end suspension or steering grinding noise. Front seat backrest noise. Interior lights flickering. Four-way lumbar support fails. Internal steering gear leakage. AC is inoperative or supplies insufficient cooling. *C250:* 2011-12—Oil leakage at the seam between the automatic transmission and the transfer case housing. Suspension noise from front axle suspension struts on vehicles equipped with a 1.8L engine. Automatic transmission hard Second-Third upshift or slipping, no Third gear. *C300, C350, C63 AMG, and CL550:* 2013—Vehicle doesn't perform automatic engine stop. Repair tips for engine cylinder head cover leaks. Consumer electrical shut-off intermittently active. Automatic transmission switches default to "limp home" mode for no reason. Automatic transmission hard Second-Third upshifts, slipping, or no Third gear. Oil leaks at the seam between the automatic transmission and the transfer case housing. Front suspension noise. Correcting various Parking Assist malfunctions. *C180, C200, C220, C250, C300:* 2013-15—Sluggish steering; instrument cluster display power steering warning message is activated.

Although the Mercedes has a classy appearance, it's not quite as good looking as the Audi A6 and doesn't handle as well as the BMW 5 Series.

RATING: Above Average (2012-16); Average (2008-11); Below Average (2006-07). Redesigned only a few times during the past decade, these family sedans, wagons, and convertibles manage to hold five people in relative comfort while performing acceptably well. Recently Mercedes added the E400 Hybrid, updated the engine in the E250 BlueTEC diesel, and now sells that model with optional AWD. The E63 high performance AMG sedan and station wagon were revamped for 2015. Road performance: Solid acceleration in the higher gear ranges; 4Matic AWD operates flawlessly; good handling, though not quite as crisp as with the BMW 5 Series; impressive braking with little brake fade after successive stops; and an acceptable ride, although the Sport model may feel too stiff for some. The car feels much slower than it actually is. Strong points: Well-appointed with many safety, performance, and convenience features; good engine and transmission combo; a relatively roomy interior (except for front headroom); lots of cargo room (with the 4Matic wagon); plush, comfortable seats; an innovative anti-theft system; and average quality control, though the AWD version generates more owner complaints. Weak points: E-Class cars have improved incrementally over the years, particularly since 2008, but they have also suffered from unreasonably high base prices, powertrain glitches, overly complex electronics and fuel-delivery systems, and subpar fit and finish. For example, the overly-complicated electronic control centre, and navigation system controls through 2014 are hard to master. Other minuses include transmission, brake system, and fuel pump malfunctions, diesel engine cabin noise; a surprisingly small trunk; and knee bolsters and limited headroom that will annoy tall drivers. Plus, the cleaner-burning diesel-equipped models require costly periodic urea fill-ups at the dealership. Instead, try to get urea off the shelf at auto supply outlets, and pour it yourself. You can save a few hundred bucks. A few years ago, *Consumer Reports* took its own diesel-powered Mercedes-Benz GL320 BlueTEC to a dealer because a warning light indicated that the SUV was low on AdBlue urea. The fill-up cost? $316.99! The GL needed 7.5 gallons, which accounted for $241.50 of the total bill ($32.20/gallon). Labour (twisting a cap and pouring) and tax accounted for the remaining $75.49. It took *CR* about 26,660 kilometres (16,565 miles) to run low on AdBlue, which means spending $1,457.80 on the stuff over 160,935 kilometres (100,000 miles). Faster than average depreciation can also be costly: A $53,900 2011 528i sedan entry-level model is now worth $30,000 – great news if you are buying used, but a lousy price if the car was purchased new.

Prices and Specs

Prices (Negotiable): *E 250 Blue TEC 4MATIC Sedan:* $64,500, *E 300 4MATIC Sedan:* $65,500, *E 400 4MATIC Sedan:* $72,900, *E 550 4MATIC Sedan:* $79,800, *E 400 Coupe:* $64,500, *E 550 Coupe:* $74,500, *E 400 4Matic Wagon:* $70,400, *E 63 AMG S Wagon:* $116,300 *E 400 Cabriolet:* $71,300, *E 550 Cabriolet:* $81,500 **Freight:** $1,995 **Powertrain (Rear-drive/AWD):** Engines: 3.0L V6 turbodiesel (210 hp), 3.5L V6 (302 hp), 4.7L V8 (402 hp), 5.5L V8 (518 and 550 hp); Transmission: 7-speed auto. **Dimensions/capacity:** Passengers: 2/3; Wheelbase: 113.1 in.; H: 57.7/L: 191.7/W: 71.9 in.; Headroom F/R: 3/3 in.; Legroom F/R: 44/28.5 in.; Cargo volume: 16 cu. ft.; Fuel tank: 80L/premium; Tow limit: N/A; Load capacity: 960 lb.; Turning circle: 36.2 ft.; Ground clearance: 4.1 in.; Weight: 4,020 lb.

Other opinions: "The 2016 Mercedes-Benz E-Class is ranked #3 in upscale mid-size cars. [It] is an exceptionally comfortable luxury car with an opulent interior and a lineup of engines that are all capable of vigorous acceleration." – *U.S. News & World Report.* "My 2014's outer transfer case bearing was making a noise related to speed. Dealer ordered and replaced entire transmission at 58,000 miles. There is a service program for all 4-Matic Mercedes relating to this issue due to tolerance stacking." – *www.truedelta.com/2014-Mercedes-Benz-E-Class/repair-histories-186.* **Major redesign:** 1996, 2003, 2007, 2010, and 2014. The 2014s were completely revised, with a new front end, the 3.5L V6 powering the E350 and the 4.7L twin-turbo V8 going into the E500 and E550. For 2016, the E400 Hybrid and standard E63 AMG models are discontinued; only the E63 AMG S remains. **Highway/city fuel economy:** *E350:* 8.3/12.7 L/100 km. *E550:* 8.6/13.8 L/100 km. *E63:* 10.2/16.5 L/100 km. **Best alternatives:** A discounted 2014 is your best bet. Again, old-time diesel lovers beware: Sure, they are quieter and less smelly but there is a price to pay. It is hard to find competent, inexpensive servicing by independent agencies. And we still don't know for sure if M-B cheated the emissions/fuel economy watchdogs. Choose instead, the Hyundai Genesis sedan or high performance coupe. They both have lower price tags, fantastic interiors, rear-drive acceleration, and powerful V8s. Other choices include the Acura RL, BMW 5 Series, Hyundai Equus, Infiniti M35x, and Lexus GS AWD.

SAFETY: Crashworthiness: NHTSA: 2014-16 models were given four-star overall crash protection; 2003-10 sedans were awarded four and five stars in all crash tests. IIHS: Test scores were just as impressive with 2010-15 versions receiving "Good" scores overall. Owner-reported safety-related failures: Owner safety complaints are few, but serious, like airbags failing to deploy in a collision; car constantly stalls in traffic; original equipment Continental tire sidewalls self-destruct after they are punctured by the rim; and run-flat Bridgestone Turanza tires can't be fixed. Replacements are expensive and can be hard to find.

ALERT! During your test drive, look for distracting side mirror reflections coming from the cabin and check out the front seat and seat belts for comfort:

The 2012 EC50 interior dash vents (shiny items) are reflected onto the side mirrors making it dangerous when changing lanes because one cannot be sure what one is seeing in those lanes because the reflection is very pronounced. These vents and other dash items are also reflected on the windshield, almost like an obstruction when one is driving. In addition, the adjustable front seats are so uncomfortable that one is constantly adjusting the seat setting while driving.

E-Class Profile

	2006	2007	2008	2009	2010	2011	2012	2013	2014
Used Values ($)									
Coupe 300/350	—	—	—	—	24,500	28,500	37,500	46,000	—
Coupe 550	—	—	—	—	28,500	33,000	42,000	53,000	—
Sedan 280/350	12,500	15,500	18,000	21,000	24,500	—	—	47,500	54,000
Sedan Diesel	15,000	16,500	19,500	23,500	—	—	36,000	48,000	—
320/350 AWD	13,000	15,500	18,500	21,500	24,500	29,000	36,000	41,000	55,000
500/550 AWD	14,500	18,000	21,000	24,500	28,500	33,000	42,000	54,000	63,000
Cabrio 350	—	—	—	—	—	36,500	43,000	53,500	—
500/550	15,000	—	—	—	—	38,500	45,000	61,000	—
320/350 Wagon	15,500	17,000	20,000	22,000	—	30,500	37,500	49,000	56,500
AMG	—	21,000	25,000	28,000	32,500	37,900	52,000	72,000	82,000
Reliability	2	3	3	☆	☆	☆	☆	3	☆
Repairs ($$$)	2	2	2	1	1	1	1	1	1
Electrical	2	2	3	3	3	☆	☆	4	☆
Engine (base)	2	3	☆	☆	☆	☆	☆	☆	3
Fit/Finish	3	3	☆	☆	☆	☆	☆	4	☆
Infotainment	—	—	—	3	3	3	3	3	3
Transmission (auto.)	3	3	☆	☆	☆	☆	☆	☆	☆

SECRET WARRANTIES, INTERNAL BULLETINS: 2004—Harsh transmission shifts. Steering leaks. Sliding roof-rack cover cracks. Rear axle rumbling. 2005—Oil leaks from the oil-level sensor. Rough automatic transmission engagement, droning, buzzing noises. Transmission leaks fluid at the electrical connector. Campaign to check and repair possible automatic transmission pilot bushing leakage; another campaign recommends the cleaning of the front axle carrier sleeve and bolt replacement. Steering fluid leaks and steering squeal when turning. Sliding roof water leaks, rattling. Moisture in the turn signal lights and mirrors. Fanfare horns may not work due to wiring corrosion. *350:* 2006-07—Rough transmission shifts. Upshift/downshift chatter or shudder. Front axle creaking, grinding, knocking noise when parking, and other front-end noises. Brake squeal. Steering-rack leaks. Rivet replacement to prevent water leakage. Inoperative AC, faulty blower motor, or compressor failure. False oil readings. Loose front centre armrest falls off. *E350 Sedan and BlueTEC Diesel:* 2011-12—Automatic transmission switches to "limp home" mode. Hard Second-Thrid upshifts, slipping, or no Third gear. Oil leakage at the seam between the automatic transmission and the transfer case housing. Also, the vehicle doesn't perform automatic engine stop. The front suspension may be noisy. Repair tips for Parking Assist malfunctions. 2011-13—No crank/no start. 2012-14—Rear brake squeaking, scraping, or rattling may require replacing the brake shoes, stator, and expansion lock. 2013—Navigation feature freezes/slow/delayed response. Battery discharged, vehicle does not start. The cause is the rotary light switch sending a wrong signal after the ignition is turned off. 2014—An engine crank assembly knocking might be attributed to a defective connecting rod in the piston. The repair requires replacing all connecting rods and pistons with wrist pins and the connecting rod's bearing as well. Remedy for harsh shifts when going from Park to Drive. The automatic transmission may default to limp-home mode while driving (gearshifts no longer possible) and/or one or more fault codes will be stored. A knocking/creaking noise from the front axle may occur when maneuvering with steering almost at full lock. This noise is caused by the inner stop plug in the hydro-mount colliding with the outer sleeve. Noise from the front seat backrests can occur when there's contact between the upper rivets inside the backrest cover and the backrest frame. Slight pressure on the center console can cause the rear blower fan wheel to scrape on the housing. Check the rear blower to see whether the cable set is badly installed or trapped. Replacing the blower is not necessary. 2014-15—Even after a software update of the Keyless-Go control unit, the vehicle cannot be opened either via Keyless-Go or via the radio remote control. The failure is caused by a software error in the Keyless-Go control unit. Mercedes says it is developing new software (TSB #L180.61-P-061174). Water can enter into the control unit tray under the driver/front passenger seat and damage the control units installed there. Problems with the on-board power supply voltage may also occur. It's possible the condensation hose (right/left) on the A/C housing may either be dislocated, pinched/crushed (water collects in A/C housing) or leaking, resulting in water entering the interior. 2015—A clunking noise from the front axle on rough roads can be traced to a damaged piston threaded section within the suspension damper. The piston may be bolted incorrectly. Enhancement of transmission shift quality following owner complaints.

Volkswagen

"Liar, Liar, Pants on Fire"

KANATA, Ontario; September 28, 2015 — Volkswagen Canada has vowed to be **completely transparent** in cleaning up the diesel emissions scandal that threatens the global reputation of the largest carmaker in the world.

Company public relations manager, Thomas Tetzlaff admitted the brand has been scrambling to find answers and solutions. The issue involves the U.S. Environmental Agency (EPA) instituting a ban on sales of 2.0-litre turbo diesel engines sold in cars made from 2009 to the present saying VW had **allegedly** installed software that could turn off emission controls except during government pollution tests. Tetzlaff noted there are currently 136 dealers in Canada with some 100,000 vehicles affected in this country and almost 500,000 in the U.S sold between 2009-2015. According to the U.S. Environmental Protection Agency the cars were allegedly polluting up to 40 times the legal limit. Since the news broke, VW Canada has set up a Canadian website (http://www.vwemissionsinfo.ca/customers/) "We want them to **know this is not a safety issue** but a NOx (**nitrous oxide**) issue.

Author's Note: Come clean Volkswagen. This **IS** a safety issue. But first get your facts straight: VW did not **allegedly** install cheat devices. VW U.S. President Horn and German CEO Winterkorn confessed to committing fraud and resigned in disgrace. VW **did** install illegal software. **Nitrous oxide (NOx)**, which you reference is more commonly known as "laughing gas," was once used by dentists. VW's diesels spew out 40 times the maximum amount of **nitric oxide and nitrogen dioxide** – lung-killing, deadly toxins – which are no laughing matter. You should all go to jail.

And you say VW isn't endangering the public health?

Exposure to high industrial levels of nitric oxide and nitrogen dioxide can cause death. It can cause collapse, rapid burning and swelling of tissues in the throat and upper respiratory tract, difficult breathing, throat spasms, and fluid build-up in the lungs. It can interfere with the blood's ability to carry oxygen through the body, causing headache, fatigue, dizziness, and a blue colour to the skin and lips.

But, that's not all. Industrial exposure to nitrogen dioxide may cause genetic mutations, damage a developing fetus, and decrease fertility in women. Repeated exposure to high levels of nitrogen dioxide may lead to permanent lung damage. Industrial exposure to nitric oxide can cause unconsciousness, vomiting, mental confusion, and damage to the teeth. Industrial skin or eye contact with high concentrations of nitrogen oxide gases or nitrogen dioxide liquid can cause serious burns.

And here's the kicker: Long-term exposure to nitrogen oxides in smog can trigger serious respiratory problems, including damage to lung tissue and reduction in lung function. Exposure to low levels of nitrogen oxides in smog can irritate the eyes, nose, throat, and lungs. It can cause coughing, shortness of breath, fatigue, and nausea.

What to do

- Don't buy a new or used VW diesel.
- If selling one, make sure you tell the buyer the car has to be "fixed" – and watch their hasty retreat.
- Sit tight and have the car fixed only after you know what will be done.
- Ask how engine performance and fuel mileage will be affected.
- Ask what will be the long-term effects on the powertain.
- If you decide to leave the car unrepaired, will it be registered? If so:
- Consider a lawsuit against dealer and VW for loss of use, misrepresentation, inconvenience, and loss of value.

VW Year-end Review

It is one of the few automakers that made money and increased market share throughout the worldwide recession that reached its peak in 2008 with the twin bankruptcies of Chrysler and General Motors. This was done through a combination of multi-billion dollar investments in new products, plants, and equipment, all oriented toward building small, high-performance, and fuel-frugal vehicles. Meanwhile, the company's competitors, more exposed to the slumping North American market, and wedded to larger, more expensive, luxury cars and SUVs, lost market share, closed factories, and fired workers. Volkswagen continued to accelerate its dominance of world markets with the right mix of fuel-efficient vehicles that responded well to up-and-down fuel prices, through a solid international footing. In fact, from 2005 to 2012 VW's market share in Europe rose from 18% to 24% as fuel prices stayed relatively high.

Now, crude prices have tumbled during the past year from their peak of $145 U.S. a barrel down to $40. Small and cheap is out, big and expensive is in as VW is caught flat-footed in a market that has changed its tune.

Volkswagen is once again shifting its marketing strategy to meet a new demand for powerful, larger vehicles, fully-loaded with electronic gadgets and innovative drivetrains. It is using superior production techniques, expanding manufacturing operations to span the globe, and offering unmatchable prices through subsidized leases.

Luxury/European Canada Car Sales (2015)

BRAND	June 2015	%	2015 YTD	%
Acura	1860	27.6	9945	8.5
Audi	2696	23.7	13,463	19.6
BMW	3235	-0.2	17,204	12.4
Cadillac	992	13.1	5663	11.4
Fiat	395	53.7	3335	34.3
Infiniti	912	20.2	5230	2.8
Jaguar	139	14.7	701	10.4
Land Rover	664	28.2	3399	6.7
Lexus	1914	25.8	10,300	22.2
Lincoln	546	22.7	3295	22.1
Maserati	56	14.3	205	22.1
Mercedes-Benz	4171	17.3	21,895	18.7
Mini	642	20.5	3191	46.2
Porsche	725	25.9	3057	32.1
Smart	63	68.2	370	-59.1
Volkswagen	6454	3.7	36,974	20.8
Volvo	521	-9.7	2316	-5.6

June 2015 VW sales in Canada gained only about 4%. Nearly seven out of every ten purchases come from the Jetta and Golf. Most other luxury/European automakers increased sales in the two digits, except for Acura, BMW, Smart, and Volvo.

Source: Desrosiers and provincial registrations

Presently, Volkswagen's aging lineup lags other European makes that have been recently redesigned to meet market exigences (e.g., VW's absence of a mid-sized SUV). Consequently, the company is using cheap leasing contracts to buy Volkswagen time to improve its product mix over the next 3 years as leasing contracts expire and owners return to the dealership (leases account for as many as 45% of the company's buyer transactions – double the rate of most other makes).

Still, in spite of discounts, cheap leases, and high-tech drivetrains Volkswagen's products are no dazzlers. They embody stodgy styling and offer only basic safety and infotainment technology – a niche already taken by the conservatively designed bestselling Honda Accord and Toyota Camry.

Going into 2016, VW's lineup beyond Jetta includes the mid-size Passat, small Golf hatchback, and the sportier GTI and Beetle. Its sport utility vehicles, the compact Tiguan and upscale Touareg, have yet to catch on even in a market hungry for SUVs and pickups. A new mid-size SUV is slated to begin production in Tennessee in late 2016.

Meanwhile, Volkswagen is also lowering prices on a few of its models.

For 2016, the CC will get an entry-level 2.0L Trend model and an all new 1.4L turbo engine will power the base Jetta. VW is also installing an upgraded infotainment system with Car-Net App-Connect on almost every model. Prices will be slashed by over $2,000 U.S. on the high-end Tiguan and Touareg and most models will, henceforth, use regular fuel.

VW's E-car

Volkswagen launched its first all-electrc car (EV), the $33,450 E-Golf, last year in the States and is scheduled to bring it to Canada in 2016. With Canadian tax credits and adding a $2,000 freight charge the car should retail for about $28,000 U.S.

The car looks promising with an 83-mile range per charge and an estimated equivalent of 126 mpg in the city and 105 mpg on the highway. This contrasts with the and Nissan Leaf's equivalent of 60 mpg and the Volt's combined 40 mpg claims.

Be Wary of Volkswagen DSG Transmissions

VW's small, fuel-efficient cars and diesel-equipped lineup has touched a nerve with Canadian shoppers in much the same way as the company's first Beetle captured the imagination and support of consumers in the mid-60s. Building on that support, over the past few years Volkswagen has cut prices and features to keep its small cars affordable.

But quality has always been the company's Achilles' heel, from the first Beetle's no-heat heaters that chaperoned your mom and dad on their first date, to gear-hopping, car-wrecking DSG transmissions afflicting Volkswagen's 2007-13 models:

I own a 2009 Jetta TDI with a DSG transmission. I feel like I am going to get hit when I start from a stop. The transmission jumps and hesitates. It has been to the dealer without being *fixed. It is terrifying to drive a car that may or may not accelerate, which also jumps in and out of gear!*

We can all agree that Volkswagens are practical drivers' cars that offer excellent handling and great fuel economy without sacrificing interior comfort. But overall reliability goes downhill after the fifth year of ownership and servicing is often more competent and cheaper at independent garages, which have grown increasingly popular as owners flee more expensive VW dealerships.

Unfortunately, parts are fairly expensive, and both dealers and independent garages have trouble finding them due to VW's frequent addition of more-complex electronic and mechanical components as well as a chaotic parts distribution system, which has resulted from dealer and supplier closures during the ongoing recession.

With rare candor Volkswagen now admits that car buyers see its products as failure-prone, and the automaker vows to change that perception by building a more reliable, durable product and providing timely, no-return servicing. Taking a page out of Toyota's sudden, unintended acceleration/brake failure Congressional testimony in February 2010, Volkswagen says it is now paying more attention, sooner, to problems reported by fleet customers and dealers in order to find and fix problems before they become widespread among individual customers.

VW's quality control efforts seem to be working – more on some models than others. A check of the NHTSA owner complaints log at *safercar.gov* does show safety-related incidents have dropped during the last 4 years, probably as a result of the recall of the DSG transmission and subsequent "goodwill" warranty extension to address DSG claims. In spite of all these efforts, automatic powertrain-related problems are still the number-one failure reported to NHTSA's safety complaint website.

Six years ago, *Lemon-Aid* exposed the DSG problem and rated Audi and VW new and used models equipped with DSG transmissions as Not Recommended and we called for a warranty extension and recall. Since then, VW and Audi have recalled the tranny several times and extended the warranty to 10 years/100,000 miles on 2007-10 models.

Incidentally, Australian VW/Audi car owners, irate that VW stonewalled their DSG complaints, sought the help of local media. *The Sydney Morning Herald* and *The Age* championed their case, leading to Volkswagen pulling its advertising from both publications. Shortly thereafter, VW recalled the affected VW, Audi, and Skoda models.

For a copy of VW's extended warranty, go to *www.dsgproblems.co.uk/Volkswagen %20 of%20America%20Inc.pdf.*

Now there is fresh evidence that tranny failures have spread to the 2012-13 models.

Therefore, be wary in your choice of vehicle and persistent in pursuing your claim.

RATING: Although they use similar components, the Golf is far more reliable than the Jetta, because of the Jetta's greater use of the failure-prone DSG drivetrain. Golf's nemesis has been primarily turbocharger failures and defective high pressure fuel pumps that shoot metal particles throughout the fuel delivery system. *Jetta:* Recommended (2013-16); Above Average (2004-05; 2007-12); Below Average (2000-03; 2006). *Golf:* Above Average (2000-16). *Golf and Jetta:* Not Recommended (2009-15 diesels, and all models using the DSG tranny). All gasoline- and diesel-powered models equipped with the DSG automatic transmission are risky buys with serrious, life-threatening powertrain and fuel-delivery defects. **Road performance:** Drivetrain problems aside, these cars are good all-around front-drive performers when not coupled to a DSG shifter and equipped with an adequate base engine. The sporty GLI, with its turbocharged 200 hp 2.0L 4-cylinder engine, delivers high-performance thrills without much of a fuel penalty, and the 170 hp 2.5L 5-cylinder engine is well suited for city driving and most leisurely highway cruising, thanks mainly to the car's light weight and handling prowess. Be wary of models equipped with the wimpy 115 hp 2.0L 4-cylinder engine. The DSG's shifts are soft in full-auto mode, unreliable, stick in gear, and subject to a three- to 10-second lag when most needed, like on turns, merging from an on-ramp into traffic, passing on two-lane highways, or pulling away from a stop sign or traffic light:

2013 DSG Transmission Issues: When making a left hand turn across traffic, I coasted up to the light when it was my turn, then I pressed the accelerator and the car had no power. It crossed through the intersection at approximately 1 to 2 mph. It took 5 to 10 seconds for the power to return. This has happened at quite a few intersections. Also it happened when I was accelerating then had to release the accelerator due to a vehicle slowing in front of me, I re-engaged the accelerator and there was no power for 5 to 10 seconds.

• • •

> A two week old 2013 VW Jetta became stuck in reverse after being in park and then I tried to put it in drive in the middle lane of an extremely busy street. The car had to be towed away. I hear from others this is a known defect.

> • • •

> We just bought a new 2013 Volkswagen Jetta Sports Wagon with a Diesel TDI engine and DSG transmission. Driving the car home from the dealer the transmission failed at 110 miles on the odometer. It has been towed to the dealer and they tell me that the mechatronic unit has failed. The sympton of the failure was that the transmission seemed to shift into neutral with no notice and the car had severally reduced power available (less than 10 mph). Research on the Internet shows that Volkswagen has had problems with this before.

Strong points: "Practical and fun to drive" pretty well sums up why these VWs continue to be so popular – at least for the first 5 years. They offer an accommodating interior, plenty of power with the higher-end models, and responsive handling. Like most European makes, these VWs are drivers' cars with lots of road "feedback;" a comfortable ride; plenty of headroom, legroom, and cargo space; a standard tilt/telescope steering column; a low load floor; and good fuel economy.
Weak points: Powertrains on the DSG-powered 2011 through 2013s are showing failures similar to the recalled 2007-10 models. Base Jettas come with a 115 hp 4-cylinder engine that is the runt of the litter. It fails to meet the driving expectations of most Jetta buyers, who want both good fuel economy and an engine with plenty of low-end torque and cruising power. Diesels with cruise control can't handle small hills very well, and often slow down by 10-15 km/h. At times, the engine will seize:

> At 13k miles my 2014 Jetta's engine hydrolocked due to icing in the intercooler. Car is a 2014 Jetta TDI value edition. They "fixed it" by a VW TSB. Turns out it is a very well known issue. Condensation freezes in the intercooler at low temps (below 25 deg), then melts and is sucked in when you start your car (or try) the next morning.

> • • •

> My 2014 Jetta was towed to the closest VW dealer. Was told the car was in hydrolock and ice was found in the hose and intercooler. After removing the glow plugs, ice was also found in the cylinders. In addition, ice was also found in the oil and oil pan. I was told by the service manager that this was a known issue for vehicles in the northeast. The "fix" was to install an updated intercooler, pressure sensor and valve in the front of throttle body. My concern is that if this is a "known issue" why is there no recall?

Excessive engine and road noise; cabin fills with diesel exhaust fumes; difficult entry and exit; and restricted rear visibility. Folding rear seats don't lie flat. Maintenance costs increase after the fifth year of ownership; it takes 6 years for fuel savings to equal the car's higher purchase cost; and depreciation accelerates as you approach the end of the 4-year warranty, even with the always-popular, diesel-equipped Jetta. For example, a 2010 Jetta TDI Trendline turbocharged sedan that first sold for $24,475 is now worth only $9,500. Less than average annual maintenance cost while under warranty. After that, repair costs start to climb dramatically… just replacing a fuse can be a head-scratcher. The GLI and TDI offer a DSG 6-speed dual-clutch automated manual that is fuel-frugal and a pleasure to drive… when it's not hesitating, stuck in Reverse, falling into Neutral, or simply falling apart.

Prices and Specs

Prices (Negotiable): *Golf 3d:* $18,995, *5d:* $19,995, *Golf GTI:* $27,995, *Golf Sportwagon:* $22,495, *Jetta:* $14,990, *Jetta GLI:* $28,990, *Jetta Turbo Hybrid:* $36,490, *CC:* $36,375, *EOS:* $42,990, *2.0 TDI Highline:* $28,775, *2.0 TDI Highline DSG:* $30,175, *GTI:* $29,375, *R:* $39,675, *Jetta TDI Trendline:* $24,475, *Jetta TDI Comfortline:* $27,175, *Jetta TDI Highline:* $30,875 **Freight:** $1,605 **Powertrain (Front-drive/AWD):** Engines: 2.0L 4-cyl. (115 hp, 2.0L TDI 4-cyl. (140 hp), 2.0L Turbo 4-cyl. (200 hp), 2.0L Turbo 4-cyl. (256 hp), 2.5L 5-cyl. (170 hp), 3.6L V6 (280 hp); Transmissions: 5-speed man., 6-speed man., 6-speed auto., 7-speed auto., 4 Motion AWD **Dimensions/capacity:** *Jetta:* Passengers: 2/3; Wheelbase: 104.4 in.; H: 57.2/L: 182.2/W: 70 in.; Headroom F/R: 4.5/2.5 in.; Legroom F/R: 43/30 in.; Cargo volume: 15 cu. ft.; Fuel tank: 55L/regular; Tow limit: 1,500 lb.; Load capacity: 1,070 lb.; Turning circle: 35.7 ft.; Ground clearance: 5.5 in.; Weight: 3,090 lb.

Other opinions: "The 2015 Volkswagen Golf ranks #1 out of 27 affordable compact cars … The redesigned Golf delights test drivers with its high-end interior, agile handling and abundant cargo space." – *U.S. News & World Report.* "For comfort, quiet, and highway handling, our drivers found the TDI had significant advantages over every other car in the test. It would have been our choice, in other words, for an easy daytrip on the interstates, regardless of fuel economy. And we topped the hybrids by driving with just a little attention to fuel economy, not making it an obsession." – *Autoweek.* **Major redesign:** *Golf:* 1999, 2006, 2010, and 2015. *Jetta:* 1999, 2005, and 2011. *Eos:* 2007. **Highway/city fuel economy:** *Golf City 2.0L:* 7.0/9.8 L/ 100 km. *Golf 2.5L:* 7.0/10.4 L/100 km. *Auto.:* 6.9/9.2 L/100 km. *TDI:* 4.7/6.7 L/ 100 km. *Auto.:* 4.6/6.7 L/100 km. Jetta fuel economy should be similar. **Best alternatives:** Other cars worth considering are the Honda Civic and Civic Si or Accord, Hyundai Elantra, Kia Forte, Mazda3, Mazda6, and Toyota Corolla or Matrix. Be careful with the Ford Focus as an alternative suggested by reviewers who rave over its "engaging driving dynamics," as "striking cabin design," and "high-quality materials." The Focus isn't as good as they say (see earlier review).

SAFETY: Crashworthiness: This is the deal breaker. Although many VW's will give you excellent crash protection, their inherent powertrain and fuel system failures will increase your chances of crashing. NHTSA: Gave the 2000-16 models its top four- and five-star scores in all crash tests; 1997-99 models earned three stars in most categories. IIHS: 2015-16s are "Good;" 2013-14s have the same rating, except that small front overlap collision protection is given a "Marginal" score.

2009-12 versions got a "Good" overall grade. **Owner-reported safety-related failures:** Many of the NHTSA-posted complaints on 2013 and earlier models involve DSG transmission and high-pressure fuel pump failures:

> The car completely lost power while in motion and I had to pull off the roadway in heavy traffic. The dealer told me that the TDI (diesel) fuel system had a complete failure and imploded into many very small metal parts. VW is replacing the entire fuel system, but not the engine. The car is less than 4 months old and 5500 miles total.

Exhaust leaks on Jetta TDIs may send dangerous levels of exhaust gases into the cabin; some owners report hundreds of foggy-looking spots appear in the rear windshield:

> When these spots appear it is almost impossible to see out of this windshield or into it. This usually happens around dawn and around dusk though it has happened at other times of the day also. I have pursued having this problem resolved by contacting the dealer several times only to be told it is because of the window being polarized. . . . You cannot see out of or in through the windsheild when these foggy spots are there. . . .

Many of the same failures have been reported for almost a decade. Premature brake wear, electrical and electronic failures, and fit and finish defects are the top problems reported by the owners of the 2012 model. Fender sound system rattles (covered by a special service campaign). Water leaks are commonplace. *CC:* When coming to a stop, the car still inches forward; factory-installed GPS tells the driver to turn just moments before the turn must be made; the horn doesn't sound immediately; and the Low Tire Pressure warning indicator gives false alerts. Here are problems that are model-specific: *Golf:* Failure of the high-pressure fuel pump on diesel models is one cause of chronic stalling and unbelievably high repair bills reported for the past several model years:

> I was notified by the dealer that the fuel pump (commonly referred to as HPFP) basically imploded and sent metal throughout the entire fuel system, which now needs to be replaced. . . . This is a design failure and/or oversight on the part of both Volkswagen and Bosch, the HPFP manufacturer. I am a veteran member of the TDI Club VW Diesel online community, and there is extensive information and documentation there of these repeated failures.

DSG automatic transmission failures have returned to haunt owners:

> Leaving a parking lot in my 2012 Golf, put the gear into Reverse and was going forward. Put the gear in Parking 3X and back to Reverse 3X, but still going forward. Couldn't turn off the engine. Opened the door, and after maybe 10 minutes was able to turn off the engine, gave it a minute and then use the Reverse gear and it worked.

GTI: DSG transmission won't shift into gear, and sometimes the engine suddenly surges or stalls, accompanied by total brake failure:

During rush hour traffic, I had to slow down a little in order to allow the car next to me to pass so I could change lanes without hitting the car in front of me. The car seemed to shift into Neutral and did not respond when I hit the accelerator. The accelerator pedal actually sunk down to the floor with no response. After a few seconds, the transmission did shift into gear and took off too fast. In the meantime, I was almost rear-ended. This happens almost every day that I drive in heavy traffic. I can't control it so I have to make sure there is not a car within a mile behind me when I change lanes because the car frequently almost stalls. This also happens sometimes when I make a turn. It generally happens when I decelerate and then accelerate and the transmission is in Drive... The problem still occurs on an almost daily basis. I understand that this problem has been reported in GTIs with DSG transmissions since 2009, but VW still has not corrected it.

Other things for Jetta owners to worry about: Sudden, unintended acceleration; complete loss of braking capability; Reverse lights don't work; fuel filler leaks because some gas pump handles don't fit into the fuel nozzle; left outside mirror blind spot cannot be adjusted; cracked fuel lines from the common rail on diesels; and chronic stalling:

Without warning, the engine shut down while driving down a busy road. Check Engine and Glow Plug warning light came on. Was just able to coast to the shoulder of the road. Car would turn over, but engine would not start. Car towed to dealer. Was told there was a catastrophic failure of the high pressure fuel pump, and metal shards were found throughout the fuel system. VW replaced the entire fuel supply system (including fuel tank) and fuel injection system.

Vehicle was idling on an incline with the brakes depressed, and it started rolling backwards, even though brakes were continuously applied; when stopped on an incline, the automatic transmission holds the car for only a few seconds before the vehicle starts rolling backwards; while attempting to start the vehicle, the steering wheel locked; premature replacement of the rear brakes; windshield distortion; roof design sends excess rainwater to the front windshield, and the wipers push large amounts of water into the driver's viewing range; wipers slow down as engine speed decreases; inoperative wiper motor; delayed horn response; premature original-equipment tire failures; bubbling in the side wall of Continental original equipment tires; the muffler extends too far out from the underbody – one woman was burned on the leg while unloading groceries; and heated seats on 2012-14 models can give occupants much more than a "hot foot," as one owner told government investigators:

My heated seats caught fire and burnt my ass!

ALERT! Before opting for the cheapest Jetta with its glacial 115 hp 4-cylinder engine, take it for a test drive and see if the reduced power is acceptable; guard against tire over-inflation by garages; and don't pay last-minute $475 dealer "administration" or "processing" fees; they're scams. Also, stay away from the electric sunroof; it costs a bundle to repair and offers not much more than the manual sunroof. On top of that, you lose too much headroom and unexpected shattering and water/air leaks are common:

> I was traveling on an interstate highway in my 2015 VW Golf and my sunroof exploded without warning. Temperatures outside were in the mid 90's, time of day was 6:00 pm, I had air conditioning running and sunroof and interior shade totally closed. After the explosion, the sunroof was bowed from the inside out (convex curve) and the safety glass was shattered in weblike pieces. I was missing glass from the middle of the roof about the size of an oblong watermelon.

Jetta/Golf Profile

	2006	2007	2008	2009	2010	2011	2012	2013	2014
Used Values ($)									
Golf CL/City	3,500	4,000	4,500	5,500	6,500	—	—	—	—
GL/GLI	5,000	—	7,000	9,000	—	—	—	—	—
H/B Trendline	—	—	—	—	8,000	9,500	12,000	14,000	—
Highline	—	—	—	—	10,000	12,500	15,500	17,500	—
GL/Highline TDI	5,500	—	—	—	11,500	13,500	16,500	20,000	25,500
Wagon Trendline	—	—	—	—	11,000	13,500	15,500	—	—
Wagon Highline TDI	—	—	—	—	12,000	14,500	17,000	20,500	26,000
GTI	7,500	8,500	10,000	11,500	13,500	16,000	18,500	21,500	—
Jetta GLI	—	9,500	—	—	—	—	15,500	18,500	22,000
City	—	4,000	5,000	6,000	—	—	—	—	—
GLS TDI/Wagon/Trendline	—	—	—	8,000	—	—	—	—	—
Sedan Trendline	—	—	4,500	5,500	6,500	7,500	8,000		10,000
11,500									
2.5/Comfortline	5,000	5,500	6,000	7,000	8,500	9,500	11,000	13,500	15,500
TDI Comfortline	6,500	—	—	8,500	10,000	11,500	13,500	16,500	19,000
Jetta Hybrid	—	—	—	—	—	—	—	—	21,000
Reliability	★2	★3	★3	★3	★3	★3	★3	★	★
Repairs ($$$)	◆3	◆2	◆2	◆2	◆2	◆2	◆2	◆1	◆1
Electrical	★2	★2	★2	★3	★3	★3	★3	★	★
Engine (base)	★2	★3	★	★	★	★	★	★	★
Fit/Finish	★2	★3	★2	★2	★2	★2	★2	★3	★
Infotainment	—	—	—	★2	★2	★2	★2	★3	★3
Transmission (auto.)	★2	★3	★	★3	★3	★3	★3	★3	★

SECRET WARRANTIES, INTERNAL BULLETINS: 1995-2013—Squeak and rattle kit available. 1999-2013—(except Routan) Abnormal vibration when braking caused by excess corrosion or an out-of-round rotor; tackling unpleasant odours coming from the AC vents; reducing exterior light moisture accumulation, removing headlight lens blemishes; and servicing the cooling fan if it runs with the ignition turned off. 2003-10—Headlights dim when vehicle is put into Idle. 2004-11—DSG transmission lag and lurch troubleshooting. 2005-07—Engine knocking noise. Rattle from front passenger-side floor area. 2005-08—Troubleshooting sound system malfunctions. Fix for an inoperative seat heater. Seized AC compressor. 2005-10—Cooling fan runs on after ignition shut off. Poor heater output. 2006-08—Ice deforms leading edge of doors. 2007-10—AC blower motor operates on high speed only. 2008—Loose door mirrors; incorrect fold functions. Engine cooling fan stays on. 2008-11—VW has extended the Emissions Control Systems Warranty for the intake manifold under specific conditions to 10 years or 120,000 miles, whichever occurs first, from the vehicle's original in-service date, for certain 2008-2011 model year Volkswagen 2.0 TFSI engine vehicles. 2008-12—Engine rattling noise correction. 2008-13—Remedy for a hard-starting, noisy, and rough-running engine. 2008-14—A faulty high pressure fuel pump may be the cause for no starts or a rough-running engine. 2011-12—Free engine repairs and injector replacements:

WARRANTY EXTENSION FOR INTAKE MANIFOLD & FUEL INJECTORS

SUBJECT: Warranty Extension for Intake Manifold & Fuel Injectors. Certain 2011-12 Model Year Volkswagen Vehicles with 2.0 TFSI Engine.

"We are informing you of our decision to extend your Emissions Control Systems Warranty for the intake manifold and fuel injectors under specific conditions to 10 years and 120,000 miles, whichever occurs first, from the vehicle's original in-service date." – Volkswagen of America.

VEHICLE MODEL AND YEAR(S):

2011-2012 BEETLE	2211 R3
2011-2012 CC	2011-2012 RABBIT
2011-2012 EOS	2011-2012 ROUTAN
2011-2012 GOLF	2011-2012 TIGUAN
2011-2012 GTI	2011-2012 TOUAREG
2011-2012 JETTA	2011-2012 TOUAREG HYBRID
2011-2012 PASSAT	

2011-12—How to silence a squeaking front seat. 2011-14—A seam sealer skip or hole in the area around hood hinge or behind front fender will allow water to leak into the front passenger compartment. 2011-15—Front outside door handles may stick due to outside temperatures. 2012-13—Correcting an MIL warning light that comes on for no reason. 2013—Engine intermittently shuts off immediately after starting. When restarted, the engine may exhibit rough idle for a few seconds. However, the engine does not shut off again on a restart. UV radiation can cause fading of the burred walnut veneer wood finish trim parts. Various door function control failures. Steering honking/squeaking noises. 2013-14—Rough idling and poor engine timing may be corrected cheaply by first reprogramming the engine control module (ECM). 2014-2015—Sticking camshaft adjuster control valve as the Malfunction Indicator Lamp (MIL) comes on. *Rabbit, GTI, R32:* 2010—Noise from the B-pillar area. Front door gap causes some wind noise. Can't open liftgate after locking. 2010-11—Poor front seat heater performance. 2011-12—How to prevent electrical harness damage caused by animal snacking. If the heater doesn't blow hot enough, reboot the system with upgraded software. Turbo diesels – What to do about engine hesitation; harsh shifting in low gear and cold weather no-starts. *2.0L TDI engine* 2009-11—VW says it may have a remedy for diesels that won't start in cold weather. In TSB #2111-06 Volkswagen confirms that some vehicles might not start if left in temperatures below freezing. Moisture from the air intake may condense in the intercooler. VW suggests adding a cold weather intercooler kit, that will be provided free of charge on a case-by-case basis.

PASSAT ★★

RATING: Below Average (2014-16); Not Recommended for earlier years. The Passat is an attractive mid-sized car that rides on the same platform as the Audi A4. It has a more stylish design than the Golf or Jetta, but it still provides a comfortable, roomy interior and gives good all-around performance for highway and city driving. The car's large wheelbase and squat appearance give it a massive, solid feeling, while its aerodynamic styling makes it look sleek and clean. Not recommend for driving or parking over hilly terrain (see the ALERT! section) or for drivers or passengers who are tortured by the poorly-designed head restraints:

The fault isn't with government regulation, however, it's with VW's design engineers who picked the cheapest, most uncomfortable restraints possible – ones that would give Freddy Krueger nightmares. Ford had a similar inhumane design until buyer protests forced the company to phase in versatile and comfortable head restraints later that year. **Road performance:** Impressive acceleration with the turbocharged engine hooked to the smooth-performing manual gearbox. The sophisticated, user-friendly 4Motion full-time AWD shifts effortlessly into gear; refined road manners; better-than-average emergency handling; quick and predictable steering; handling outclasses most of the competition's; and the suspension is both firm and comfortable. Some negatives: Engine/automatic transmission hesitates when accelerating and the vehicle tends to pull to the right. **Strong points:** Well-appointed and holds its value fairly well. Quiet-running; plenty of passenger and cargo room; impressive interior fit and finish; and exceptional driving comfort. **Weak points:** How'd you like to lose almost two-thirds of your Passat's value after barely 3 years? That's what would happen if you had bought a new 2010 Passat Comfortline sedan for $31,075, that's now worth about $11,000. Despite their rapid depreciation, Passats remain a favourite among thieves – whether for stealing radios, wheels, VW badges, or entire cars. (No, the delayed tranny shifts, fire-prone fuel system, and sticking outside door handles are not anti-theft measures – hmm, that's a thought.) In the 2011 J.D. Power Initial Quality Survey, VW scored 29th among 32 brands. Two years later, the same survey still put VW's models near the bottom third of the rankings at 23 out of 33 carmakers. More recently, 2014-15 models scored Below Average in Power's Dependability Ratings. Traditional deficiencies dating back to the 2006 model year include failure of the powertrain, fuel, and electrical systems, and various fit and finish flaws. Power windows freeze shut in cold weather and driver-side door locks freeze shut on more recent models:

On more recent models, there have been a flood of complaints of turbocharger and fuel pump failures that cause highway stallouts or reduced power (see Secret Warranties section, below).

Other opinions: "The Passat ranks #11 out of 18 affordable mid-size cars. Though reviewers say the navigation system is slow to respond, they praise the 2015 Volkswagen Passat's spacious back seat and gas-sipping diesel trim." – *U.S. News & World Report.* "The Jetta and the Passat have all new powertrains, gas and diesel and are better cars than they were when introduced. Their TDI models are their best offers today. They should also increase the factory warranty to 5/60,000 miles full coverage and 10/120,000 miles powertrain, they say they are building better vehicles now they should stand behind them." – *www.autoblog.com/2014/03/04/vw-passat-2016-refresh-coming/.* **Major redesign:** 1998, 2006, and 2012. The 2016 model arrives with few changes, except for a facelift that includes new sheetmetal, wheels, headlights, and taillights, plus, a reworked infotainment system, instrument panel, and upgraded interior. **Highway/city fuel economy:** *2.5L:* 6.5/10.1 L/100 km. *Auto.:* 6.7/9.6 L/100 km. *3.6L:* 7.4/10.9 L/100 km. *TDI diesel:* 4.4/6.8 L/100 km. *Auto:* 4.9/ 6.9 L/100 km. **Best alternatives:** If you must have a Passat, get it used, without the DSG transmission, and with some warranty left. Other choices, the BMW 3 Series, Honda Accord, Hyundai Genesis, and Toyota Camry.

SAFETY: **Crashworthiness:** NHTSA: 1995-16 Passats scored four and five stars for different crash scenarios and two to four stars for 1990-93 versions. IIHS: 2013-16 models are rated "good," though frontal small overlap collision was given only an Acceptable" rating. Frontal moderate overlap tests of 1999-2013 Passats produced a "Good" rating; 1994-98s were rated "Marginal." Frontal small overlap tests qualified the 2013 performance as "Marginal." Side and roof strength were given a "Good" rating for the 2005-13 models, while the head restraints on the 2009-13s were rated "Good," "Marginal" (2007-08s), and "Acceptable" (2005-06 versions). **Owner-reported safety-related failures:** Owner safety-related complaints are down significantly; however, the failures reported relative to the steering, brakes, and powertrain are just as hair-raising as ever. Sudden unintended acceleration;

vehicle pulls or drifts to the right or shuts off when slowing down; the electronic stability control engages erratically; exploding sunroofs; steering wheel controls and horn don't work; and a problematic navigation system:

> My wife is afraid to drive it because of concerns with the aforementioned radio navigation system. When putting the vehicle in reverse and waiting from 3-7 seconds the rear-view camera shows a picture. When placed in drive it stays on the screen for around 8-9 seconds. Multiple touches to get a channel change, again a distraction to the driver. Now the navigation system in this unit also is a pain. When my wife would use the navigation system the map would freeze up on the original streets

Some of the transmission failures are eerily similar to complaints heard from owners 7 years ago:

> My 2014 Passat suddenly slowed from 75 to 40 mph and the rpm went into the red line zone. The sensation within the car was as if the brakes were being applied in full panic stop. Since there were no brake lights activated or other indication to fast moving motorists, I only avoided an accident (being plowed into from behind) by pulling off on to the shoulder. The dealer service department informed me that the car would need a new transmission.

> . . .

> My 2014 Passat will not stop smoothly and gives whip lashes after pumping the brakes pedal twice to ensure the car stops. The DSG system fails to engage smoothly while in automatic but runs smoothly while in "sport" mode. We have almost rear ended several cars while driving in automatic due to the jerky DSG gear shifting and poor response time in the braking systems while in stop and go traffic conditions.

> . . .

> The vehicle has a significant delay/hesitation upon initial acceleration (2.5L). This is dangerous when pulling into or across traffic. This issue is known to others and is reported elsewhere on the Web.

ALERT! Function is sacrificed to style with rear corner blind spots and head restraints that impede rear visibility. In your test drive, check out the car's head restraints for comfort and the car's ability to parallel park on a hill, after first making sure there are no cars parked nearby that you might hit:

> We have a problem controlling the car while using Reverse on a hill. It appears that VW has tied the accelerator and braking function together in a way that the driver may lose control of the vehicle while in Reverse. If the brake is pressed, the accelerator is disengaged thus allowing the engine [to] fall to an idle and not develop any thrust. If the driver is using both feet to control the vehicle, left foot on the brake, right foot on the accelerator while depressing the brake, the engine develops no power even if the accelerator is depressed fully. By releasing the brake while the accelerator is depressed fully, the vehicle will lurch at full throttle in Reverse in an out of control condition until the driver realizes what is happening and removes the foot from the accelerator.

Passat Profile

	2006	2007	2008	2009	2010	2011	2012	2013	2014
Used Values ($)									
Passat GLS	5,000	—	—	—	—	—	—	—	—
CC	—	—	—	—	12,500	15,500	18,500	22,500	28,000
Base/Trendline	6,000	—	8,000	9,500	11,500	—	13,000	15,500	18,500
Comfortline	—	—	9,000	10,500	12,000	—	16,000	18,000	22,500
TDI Trendline+	—	—	—	—	—	—	9,000	11,500	17,500
CC Sportline	—	—	—	12,000	15,500	16,000	18,000	22,500	27,000
CC Highline AWD	—	—	—	11,000	10,500	11,500	19,500	25,000	38,500
Highline AWD	—	—	—	13,000	—	—	—	30,000	—
Wagon Trendline	—	—	10,000	13,500	14,500	—	—	—	—
Comfort V6 AWD	—	—	12,000	15,000	—	—	—	—	—
Reliability	2	2	2	2	2	2	2	2	3
Repairs ($$$)	3	3	3	3	3	3	3	3	2
Electrical	1	1	1	1	1	1	2	2	3
Engine (base)	2	2	2	2	2	2	2	2	2
Fit/Finish	1	1	1	2	2	2	2	2	3
Infotainment	—	—	—	2	2	2	2	2	2
Transmission (auto.)	1	1	1	1	1	1	1	1	2

SECRET WARRANTIES, INTERNAL BULLETINS: 1997-2009—Class action settlement to pay for and mitigate water damage to components and interiors of numerous models, and reimburse expenses caused by leaking sunroofs (see Class Actions in Part 3). 1999-2008—Correcting excessive brake pulsation, vibration. 2000-11—Removing smelly odours from vents. 2004-11—DSG delay on acceleration. 2005-10—Cooling fan continues to run after ignition has been turned off. Poor heater output. 2006-07—Airbag light constantly lit. 2006-08—Front-seat creaking, cracking. Inoperative AC and seat heater. Inoperative lumbar support. 2006-09—Wind noise from the top of the doors. 2006-10—Inoperative front-seat back recliner. 2008—Inoperative keyless remote. 2008-11—Silencing a front suspension knocking. 2008-13—Remedy for a hard-starting, noisy, and rough-running engine. 2008-14—A faulty high pressure fuel pump may be responsible for hard starts or a rough-running engine. 2011-12—Free engine repair and injector replacements up to 10 years/120,000 miles (see Golf/Jetta section). A transmission whistle or whine at highway speeds requires the installation of an updated shifter cable bracket. A harsh engagement from Park to Drive or Reverse may signal the need for a software update. How to silence a squeaking front seat. **2011-13**—Possible oil leak from the oil filter housing. Troubleshooting tips to correct brake vibration/pulsation when brakes are applied. **2011-15**—Front outside door handles may stick due to outside temperatures. **2012-13**—Troubleshooting tips for a malfunctioning navigation system. **2012-14**—Engine may not operate properly due to a broken turbocharger fan or seized shaft. Models equipped with a 2.0L TDI diesel engine may experience exhaust failure after initial startup. Cold temperatures could compromise the exhaust turbocharger's performance. **2013-14**—Rough idling and poor engine timing may be corrected cheaply by first reprogramming the engine control module (ECM). Sunroof/sun shade won't open. Noise from the right-side door panel when driving. **2015**—Sticking camshaft adjuster control valve; Malfunction Indicator Lamp (MIL) comes on. Steering upgrade will assist in keeping the vehicle straight on the road.

Appendix 1

1990-2017 REVIEWS AND PREVIEWS

In this Appendix we include thumbnail sketches of some of the vehicles that were passed over in Part Four, including models that have been axed, are relatively new to the market, were sold in small numbers, or are scheduled to be introduced during the next few years. Inasmuch as owners in Canada keep their cars more than 11 years according to Polk Auto Data, we also couldn't resist rating some cheap older cars and trucks that are commonly called "beaters" or "minounes" in Quebec.

Back to the Future

Get ready for cars that have more power, are better performers, and carry higher prices. 2015-16 will be a milestone period as auto sales return to their pre-recession levels due to pent-up buyer demand. There will be a slew of 500+ horsepower racers, fuel-efficient, redesigned, and over-priced products that will soon arrive in dealer showrooms (Acura's 2016 NSX 560 hp, $150,000 U.S., for example). Financing has been boosted to 96 months, and GM and Chrysler pickups have rocketed to the top of *Consumer Reports'* good buys. Compact cars are larger, while Cadillacs are downsized, discontinued, or go electric. Lincoln has virtually disappeared, and Tesla is betting on an affordable third electric car for the masses.

But there are some bizarre happenings this year, as well. Fiat, flush with cash from its popular Jeep and Ram sales, is threatening to make a hostile takeover bid for General Motors; Suzuki has skedaddled out of the country; and recalled-airbag manufacturer, Takata, has to supply over 50 million replacement airbags to swap out deadly inflators. The company can make a million airbags a month – do the math.

And, then there's Ford, enjoying good sales, but bedeviled by four years of failure-prone infotainment systems that give wrong info, or simply ignore owner commands. Ford says it now has a fix for its high-tech electronic woes – buttons and knobs. *Lemon-Aid* always knew Ford would come up with a Better Idea.

Redesigned or new vehicles may be good buys, but risk-aversive shoppers should wait for a second-series model (made after March). This will minimize factory gliches and take advantage of lower prices, discounts, and more generous leasing terms, as the 2017s arrive. For a listing of 2015-16 new, upgraded and dropped models, see Part 1, under Something Old, Something New.

Best Vehicles for Students, Families, and Seniors

Students

Young drivers feel they are invulnerable to accidents and would never admit that they are poor drivers, or that they are more responsive to peer pressure than parental admonition. That's why you want to buy a car that gets top marks in crashworthiness and reliability, sips gas, and doesn't look like a Flintstone retread. Advanced safety features, such as electronic stability control (government-mandated on some 2012 and later models) and full-torso side-curtain airbags, are a plus. Large pickups or SUVs can be rollover-prone, hard to control on the highway, and carry too many distracting passengers. Sports cars beg to be driven too fast and inspire a false sense of confidence. Here are some models worth considering.

Acura TSX	Honda Civic	Kia Soul	Subaru Impreza/
Chevrolet Camaro	Hyundai Accent	Mazda3	Outback
Ford Mustang (auto.)	Hyundai Elantra	Mazda Miata	Toyota Matrix
Honda Fit	Hyundai Tucson	Nissan Rogue	

Families and Seniors

Vehicles that are recommended for families and seniors have much in common: A reasonable price, good crashworthiness ratings, and dependable reliability are paramount. Electronic stability control (standard on some 2012 and later model years), full-torso side-curtain airbags, adjustable seats that have a memory for different drivers, easy child safety seat installation, no dash glare onto the windshield, windows, or mirrors, and keyless locks that won't lock you in or out, or be easily hacked. The possibility isn't that far-feched. See these two stories two days apart in Manitoba:

- **Brandon tow truck driver smashes window to save baby from hot car:** Aug 12, 2015 – Brandon to truck driver Jeff Hogg saved a baby from a hot car on Wednesday by smashing the vehicle's windows. (See *www.cbc.ca/news/canada/manitoba/ brandon-tow-truck-driver-smashes-window-to-save-baby-from-hot-car-1.3189105*)

- **Winnipeg mom shocked after car doors lock:** Aug 13, 2015 – A Winnipeg mother had some scary moments this afternoon after her car automatically locked its doors, trapping her 13-month-old daughter inside. (See *www.cbc.ca/news/canada/ manitoba/winnipeg-mom-shocked-after-car-doors-lock-trapping-toddler-inside-1.3190378*).

You want a minivan with sliding side doors that don't have a history of injuring occupants, suddenly opening when under way, or just plain don't work (see 2009 Toyota Sienna owner comment below):

Driver side sliding door broke when rusty frayed cable snapped. Called dealer and they said there were extended warranties/recalls on models from 2003-2007 but not 2008 and above. Told me that it could cost between $1300-$1900. Told me it would take a day to take the door apart. Crazy they would design a part that is so labour intensive to take apart when using cheap, and weak components. What kind of reliabity testing do they do?

Appearance is not as important as access, reliability, and no-hassle servicing. Good visibility, maximum seat and head restraint comfort, a comfortable driving position, a spacious interior, and intuitive, easily-operated controls are key factors worth considering. For more details as to what makes the ideal vehicle for seniors, see Part One, Cars for Seniors).

For the best models for families and seniors, check out these vehicles.

Acura RDX	Honda Accord	Honda Ridgeline	Mazda5
Chevrolet/GMC Silverado/ Sierra (post-2013)	Honda CR-V	Hyundai Azera	Nissan Altima
Chevrolet Malibu (post-2013)	Honda Element	Hyundai Elantra	Subaru Forester
Ram pickup (post-2013)	Honda Odyssey	Hyundai Genesis	Toyota Camry
	Honda Pilot	Hyundai Santa Fe	Toyota Corolla

CHOOSING THE RIGHT CAR OR TRUCK

The price of fuel is a wild card that affects new vehicle prices, depending upon how much and the kind of fuel each model uses. As gasoline prices continue to fall to less than half what they were a year ago, gas-powered econocars, electrics, hybrids, and diesels are taking it on the chin. Shoppers are now turning to high-end cars and trucks loaded with the latest electronic gadgets to convert their muscle car into a mobile Wi-Fi "hot spot."

Yes, these are volatile times as car and truck prices fluctuate dramatically and fuel costs change every day. Still, the longer you wait to buy a new or used car, the less you will pay, thanks to rapid depreciation, increased sales incentives such as dealer or factory rebates, low-cost financing, and free maintenance. You don't want the economic burden of buying a car that's on the market for the first time or one that has been radically changed this model year – the value of these vehicles is yet unproven. Nor should you invest in a vehicle that merely looks nice or is cheap if it doesn't have a positive reliability history. And you certainly don't want to overpay simply to be the first in your town with something "different" or "environment-friendly." Remember the over-priced, no-heat, short-range Chevrolet Volt electric car that debuted as a 2012? Production was halted earlier this year due to poor sales. The car will be re-introduced in 2016 with greater range and thousands of dollars of discounts. All it lacks is a market.

Incidentally, if you were the first owner of a 2012 Volt, your $41,545 "green" car investment is now worth $16,500. Other "unique" vehicles that turned out to be sales duds are the $78,250 Cadillac ELR electric car, Chrysler's PT Cruiser, Pontiac's Aztek SUV, and the Mercedes Smart car. The uniqueness will pass; the costly repairs and rapid depreciation on par with the Venezuelan bolivar will remain forever.

WHY DREAD A HYBRID?

$8,000 (U.S.) BATTERY PACK

BATTERY DISPOSAL?

ELECTROCUTION DURING ACCIDENTS

FUEL SAVINGS OFF BY 40%

DEALER-ONLY SERVICE

EXPENSIVE

50% DEPRECIATION AFTER 3 YEARS

HIGH INSURANCE RATES

$30,000 FOR A PRIUS

A BETTER IDEA: A 2002 HONDA CIVIC ($9,000)...LEAVES $21,000 FOR FUEL!

EUROPEAN IMPORTS

Lemon-Aid readers who own pricey European imports invariably tell me of powertrains that stall, China-made DSG transmissions that jump out of gear, nightmarish electrical glitches that run the gamut from annoying to life-threatening, and computer malfunctions that are difficult to diagnose and hard to fix. Other problems noted by owners include premature brake wear, excessive brake noise, AC failures, poor driveability, hard starts, loss of power, and faulty computer modules leading to erratic shifting. Plus, servicing diesels has gotten costlier and more complicated.

NOT RECOMMENDED/UNRATED EUROPEAN MODELS

Jaguar: "Bad Cars Gone?"

"The times of bad cars are over," said Joe Eberhardt, president and CEO of Jaguar Land Rover North America in a *Los Angeles Times* article in September 2015. "We have been perceived as a low-volume, high-priced brand," the executive said. "Jaguar has the reputation that we build unreliable cars that are expensive to maintain."

Lemon-Aid doesn't give a "Recommended" rating to vehicles built by Jaguar, Land Rover, Saab (now bankrupt), Smart, or Volvo because there are better alternatives available.

For over four decades, I've heard the horror stories. Mostly from embarrassed doctors, lawyers, accountants, and politicians who feel trapped and helpless. They tell me, in a confessional tone, "I'm a Mercedes (Audi, BMW, Land Rover) owner, and I'm mad as hell."

I have heard the stories of $20,000 repair jobs after rodents gobbled up Audi electronic innards (Audi response: "Don't park the car outdoors"). Or tales of self-destructing BMW engines and VW Group DSG dual clutch transmissions (VW Group response: "You don't know how to drive."). Or my two favourites, "My Rabbit's catalytic converter almost caught fire" (VW's written notice to owners: "Don't park the car near anything combustible.") and "What do you mean $300 for my Mercedes tune-up?" (Mercedes response: "It's a luxury car – you pay a luxury price.").

Most European brands quickly lose their value, causing secondary "sticker shock" at trade-in time. Another annoyance is there's not a lot of choice for servicing and little competition that would bring down the cost of servicing. If you get the service manager from hell, well, learn to enjoy the heat.

Jaguar and Land Rover

Not Recommended

Three quick points about Jaguars and Land Rovers: First, as mentioned before, they are overpriced. Secondly, depreciation is so severe that a used Jaguar may look like a bargain, until you are faced with thousands of dollars in repairs from only one available dealer. Finally, most independent reliability surveys show both brands near the bottom of the list.

Ideally, when buying a new or used vehicle you will want a vehicle that will hold its value in case you have to sell it quickly (say within three years, minimal money lost through depreciation). As can be seen by the following table don't expect either Jaguar or Land Rover to give you a fair return on your investment.

2010 Jaguar and Land Rover (September 2015)

JAGUAR			LAND ROVER		
Model	Cost	Used Value	Model	Cost	Used Value
XF	$61,800	$21,000	LR2	$44,950	$17,500
XFR	$85,300	$27,500	LR4	$59,990	$23,500
XJ	$88,000	$31,000	Range Rover	$93,830	$33,000
XJL	$95,500	$33,000	Rover Sport	$73,200	$28,000
XK	$95,500	$37,000			
XKR	$107,000	$42,000			

And, finally, there are good and bad Jaguars. The worst of the used lot are the failure-prone XJ and XF, followed by the X-Type and XJ. Only the XK stands out above the rest, while the jury is still out on the all-new F-Type.

Volvo

Unrated

With the increasing economic turmoil in China and volatility of car sales here and in North America, Volvo's underpinnings are on shaky ground. Owned by Geely, a Chinese truck manufacturer that has limited experience in automobile manufacturing and marketing, Volvo may find itself cut off at the knees, just as it is showing much better sales than ever before. The automaker isn't a huge-volume seller in Canada and its North American sales have been one long roller coaster ride, steered by dueling boards. But if the Chinese cutback in manufacturing continues, the automaker will again face poor sales, demands for new management, and increased insistence from the latest board to market its vehicles as high-end, chauffeur-driven luxury cars. Just the opposite of what Volvo was doing in North America and Europe. This is too bad considering that the thrice-married Swedish automaker is finally recovering from a "reality show" track record in North America, with Sweden, Ford, and China each presenting conflicting visions as to who is Volvo's target clientele.

In the recent past, *Lemon-Aid* has rated the Volvo lineup "Not Recommended" for the same reasons that the uncertainties surrounding pre-bankrupt Saab earned that company a similar low rating.

Jeremy Cato, one of Canada's better auto writers, once had his own misgivings about the company's future. He concludes that despite Volvo's emphasis on research and new products, Canada may not be much of a player in Volvo's future global growth plans (*www.theglobeandmail.com/globe-drive/driving-it-home/volvo-claims-it-has-a-plan-for-the-future/article8896220/*):

> I had all but given up on Volvo in Canada – and truthfully, Volvo in the rest of the world, too – when a prominent Volvo dealer approached me at the Toronto Auto Show. Do I want to meet the new Volvo Canada president? he asked.
>
> That would be Marc Engelen, who took over the top job in Canada on July 1, 2012. He replaced Jeff Pugliese, who seems to have been something of a disaster. But don't believe me; believe the numbers. Volvo Canada's sales were down 18.2 per cent last year, in a market that was up 5.7 per cent. The premium car market in Canada is booming, yet Volvo's sales last year were a bust.

In an exclusive television news story titled "The Worst-Selling Cars in Canada in 2015," presented last May on *CTV News*, researchers concluded:

> After four months of nonexistent sales activity, and after twelve years in which Volvo marketed the first-generation XC90, the new version is finally here. It's an impressive luxury family-hauling device, and if it doesn't sell well, Volvo is in trouble in North America.

In other words, if Mr. Engelen doesn't improve sales of Volvo's most impressive new product to date, after his three-year tenure, Volvo's reputedly schizophrenic Board of Directors will send him packing.

Volvo Canada Monthly Sales	2010	2011	2012	2013	2014	2015
January	396	397	340	280	323	273
February	411	422	349	302	258	217
March	604	563	664	415	419	328
April	633	705	709	477	343	438
May	642	770	751	617	533	539
June	716	800	618	455	577	521
July	712	736	462	381	287	442
August	521	512	371	437	309	483
September	537	486	398	363	428	
October	434	490	332	358	405	
November	497	424	326	328	300	
December	448	510	258	260	284	

Source: Automotive News, Polk, and Good Car, Bad Car

Lemon-Aid leaves Volvo's lineup "Unrated" mainly because the company continues to lose traction in the marketplace and there are so many storms on the horizon that could compromise quality, servicing, and resale value even more so. A small low-volume company like Volvo would once again be unable to meet the requirements of its small, loyal customer base. Shoppers don't want to buy a car with a residual value that flows faster downhill than the Yangtze river. They long for that safe, solid, and understated New Democrat car that was always more functional than fashionable.

On the plus side, Volvo quality and crashworthiness have improved considerably over the past few years. Among the company's products sold in Canada, the S60, S80, XC60, and XC70 have had the fewest "Trouble Spots" reported since 2007, according to *Consumer Reports'* annual surveys. The C30, C70, and XC90 were seen as more troublesome, however. As for passenger crash safety, the 2013 through 2015 Volvo S60 has been recognized as a Top Safety Pick by the Insurance Institute of Highway Safety (IIHS). Not surprising, since Volvo built its reputation upon the active and passive safety features its vehicles provide.

Other Choices

Audi

A4 ALLROAD: *Average.* This is a comfortable and versatile wagon that offers mediocre highway performance with its turbocharged four-banger and extra height. It also has a seemingly small interior, and an unjustifiably high retail price. Launched as a 2013, the Allroad is outclassed by more versatile competitors like the Acura TSX Sports Wagon and BMW's 3-Series Sports Wagon. **Price:** $46,600, but Audi's Q5 is cheaper, more reliable, and features more towing capacity, rear room, and storage areas. A 2013 now sells for $22,000. **Crashworthiness:** No crash data.

Acura

ILX: *Average.* Acura's smallest sedan competitors have better performance, gas mileage, and cargo space. The sluggish base engine perks up only through the addition of the manual transmission. If you want more fuel economy, you'll have even less power to work with. Not a people-hauler. The 2016 is more powerful, better looking, and more luxurious, still its infotainment features and driving dynamics aren't first-class. Consider, instead, the Audi A3 or BMW 3-Series. **Price:** $29,490. **Crashworthiness:** NHTSA: Five stars.

RL: *Average.* The $69,690 flagship of the Acura fleet, the RL is loaded with intuitive high-tech gadgetry and premium luxury features that don't confound or distract the average driver. Nevertheless, equipped with standard all-wheel-drive, the RL still doesn't handle as well as its sporty rivals, offers limited trunk space, and depreciates in an instant. **Price:** A 2010 base model that sold for $63,900 is now barely worth $20,000. A Hyundai Genesis is a good alternative. **Crashworthiness:** NHTSA: 2012 RL scored a five-star rating for rollover protection.

RLX: *Below Average.* As auto journalist, Dan Neil once wrote in referring to another car, "Right plane, wrong airport." With hybrid sales nose-diving and Acura's brand still to be defined, this hybrid can't compete with others in its class. As for non-hybrid versions, They aren't very luxurious, nor are the controls easy to figure out. **Price:** The $50,000 2016s return with additional driver-assistance features. **Crashworthiness:** NHTSA: Five stars.

NSX: *Not Recommended.* Due to an insufficient time on the market, *Lemon-Aid* cannot recommend this model. Predicted to arrive in early-2016, the resurrected NSX (it was dropped in 2005) is a hybrid on steroids. It will employ a mid-mounted 3.7L V6 hooked to a twin turbo, twin-clutch 9-speed transmission, and an electric motor driving the rear wheels. Two more electric motors will spin the front wheels independently, delivering 550+ horsepower. **Price:** Estimated to cost $155,000 U.S. **Crashworthiness:** Not yet crash-tested.

Q3: Above Average. Based on the VW Tiguan platform, the Q3 is a "baby Q" much like the small variants we have seen with BMW, Buick, and Mercedes-Benz. The car has plenty of power, thanks to its 2.0L, 200 hp, turbocharged 4-cylinder engine, mated to a front-drive or AWD drivetrain. Handling is effortless, the ride is firm but comfortable, and the Q3 is well-appointed and nicely-styled. **Price:** *2.0T Progressive:* $35,800 (firm) and the *3.0T Technik AWD:* $40,900 (firm). **Crashworthiness:** Not tested.

Q5: Average. The Q7's smaller brother debuted as a stylish five-passenger luxury crossover compact full of high-tech gadgetry, including an adaptive suspension that allows for firm, sporty handling, if so desired. The 270 hp 3.2L V6 is the better engine. Audi has had a history of factory-related engine and tranny glitches, but owners are apparently satisfied with Audi's servicing of these problems. The 2012-15s generate the fewest complaints and the 6-cylinder models, fewer still. A perusal of Audi service bulletins show repeated drivetrain failures like defective 2.0L engine head gaskets, fuel injectors; intake solenoids on 2011-12 models (covered by a secret extended warranty); harsh shifting with 2011-12s; a campaign to improve the intermediate steering shaft on 2008-14 A5, and Q5 models; a turbocharger warranty extension to 7 years/70,000 miles; another warranty extension for 10 years/120,000 miles covering the intake manifold, fuel injectors, and other emissions components; servicing for clogged parking aid control units; free carbon buildup removal from the engine cylinder head secondary air ports on 2009-2012 models; and Bosch ignition coil premature failures. **Price:** *2.0 Komfort:* $41,900 (firm); *3.0 Progressive:* $46,700 (firm); *TDI Progressive:* $49,200 (firm); *Hybrid:* $57,000 (soft). **Crashworthiness:** NHTSA:Four stars overall on 2014-16 models. IIHS: Gave its top, "Good," rating for frontal offset and side protection. Head restraint effectiveness is also rated "Good."

Q7: Average. These aging, cumbersome to handle, complicated five- or seven-passenger machines offer limited seating and storage space. A smaller, lighter-weight version debuts early next year; it's not recommended during its first year on the market. The Q7 offers both gasoline and diesel powertrains hooked to an 8-speed automatic transmission. **Price:** *3.0T Progressive:* $58,200 (firm); *3.0 TDI Progressive:* $63,200 (soft); and the *3.0T Sport:* $74,200 (soft). **Crashworthiness:** NHTSA: Gives the 2011-15 models four stars for rollover resistance. IIHS: Gives its top, "Good," score for frontal offset, side, and head-restraint protection.

BMW

1 SERIES: Above Average. BMW's entry-level 128i and 135i include either a two-door coupe or convertible with a power-folding soft top. Like the Audi Q3, these mini-Bimmers are a joy to drive – when the powertrain, fuel, and electrical systems aren't acting up. 2013 was the series' last model year, though, servicing hasn't been affected and prices are about 30% less than new. Owners report chronic fuel pump failures covered by a 10-year secret warranty. Fit and finish isn't first-class and servicing requires sustained dealer support, as is the case with all BMWs. **Price**

(2013 Used): 128i Coupe: $27,500; *128i Convertible:* $32,500; *135i Coupe:* $33,500; *135i Convertible:* $34,500. Crashworthiness: Not crash-tested.

I3: Not Recommended. The BMW i3 is an urban electric plug-in car backed up by a scooter engine. Launched as a 2014 model. the car seats four, not comfortably, and rear seat access and exiting is torturous, at best. It has the limited range of a Chevy Volt, and is as ugly as the Pontiac Aztek. There's also an optional 34-horse-power motorcycle engine that is mounted next to the electric motor. Its 2.4-gallon tank doubles the car's range, which is expected to attenuate driver "range anxiety" Really? Price: $43,350 U.S. Crashworthiness: Not crash-tested.

X1: Average. This is a rear-drive, small, luxury SUV, powered by a base 240 hp 2.0L turbocharged 4-cylinder or an optional 3.0L 300 hp V6, coupled to either a 6- or 8-speed automatic transmission. Test drivers recommend the 4-cylinder model for sportier performance. X1 has limited cargo space, tight rear seating, and costly, bundled options. The fuel-saving start-stop system is abrupt at times. Price: $36,990 that drops to only $27,000 used (2013). It's priced lower than some competitors, but has fewer standard features. Buick's Encore is an alternative worth considering. Crashworthiness: Not crash-tested.

X3: Above Average. Unlike the X4, the X3 has been around long enough to get over most of its first-year glitches, except for the fuel-saving stop/start feature that's sometimes slow to restart the car, a delayed turbo response, and limited storage space. First-class handling, firm, comfortable ride, powerful engines, and a roomy cabin. Price: $44,300. Crashworthiness: NHTSA: Top five-star rating for the 2015-16s.

X4: Not Recommended. New for 2015, the X4 is essentially to the X3 what the X6 is to the X5 – the same vehicle with a different roofline. It shares powertrains and almost everything else with the X3, including 4- and 6-cylinder gasoline and diesel engines. Six-and 7-speed dual-clutch transmissions are standard; an 8-speed Steptronic transmission is optional. Price: $46,300. Smart shoppers will head straight for the practically identical X3 and save thousands. Crashworthiness: Unrated.

5 SERIES: Average (2011-16); Below Average (all earlier years). 5-Series models are beautifully-styled, roomy, competent, and problematic vehicles. Owners report frequent engine, transmission, and fuel system failures in addition to fit and fin-ish glitches through the 2010 model year. Since then, powertrain durability has improved, but the fuel-saving stop/start feature has generated many complaints of delayed re-starts and jerky performance. Price: The price range is $56,900 (528i) to $76,750 (550i xDrive) for the sedans; a $71,150 hybrid version; $72,000 to $82,000 for the GT; and $68,150 for the new 535d xDrive. *Note:* Get ready for "sticker shock;" the above prices were set before the Canadian dollar dropped 25%. You can atten-uate this extra cost though by choosing a 2013 528i for $40,000 – a savings of $16,000, and no egregious $2,000 "freight fee." Crashworthiness: NHTSA: Five-stars for 2012-16 models; 2008-10 versions have a similar score, except for passenger protection in frontal collisions that was given only three stars.

MINI COOPER: Average. "Cute" styling with an attractive interior and nimble handling. Mediocre acceleration (Cooper S, excepted); stiff-riding; two-door cramped back seating; and a history of costly, premature mechanical and fit and finish deficiencies. This eye-catching classic British-cum-German car is a competent highway performer, but high maintenance bills makes "cute" costly. Although the base Mini has an average reliability rating, the Cooper S has been much less reliable. The 2016 Mini Cooper hatchback returns relatively unchanged; the convertible is on hiatus. A revised 2016 Clubman will be bigger and more conventionally-styled station-wagon version of the four-door Cooper hatchback, with an extended cargo area. **Price:** *Clubman:* $24,950; *Convertible (2015):* $29,500; *Coupe:* $25,950; *Hatchback:* $23,600; and *Roadster:* $28,900. Normally, we would suggest buying a cheaper 3-year-old model with some original warranty left (a $15,000 2013 Clubman), but used Minis are too often synonymous with "money pit." **Crashworthiness:** NHTSA: Says this little tyke merits a four-star rating for its frontal collision crashworthiness and five stars for side occupant protection and resistance to rollovers. IIHS: Rates the Mini as "Good" for offset crash protection and head-restraint effectiveness; side crashworthiness was given an "Average" score.

Buick

ENCORE: Above Average. The Buick Encore is a small luxury SUV that is only slightly larger than the Chevrolet Sonic with which it shares its platform. Touted as a five-passenger SUV, the Encore can only sit four comfortably. Powered by the Sonic's optional 1.6L 140 hp turbocharged four, the Encore stresses fuel economy over speed. Last year when gas prices were high, Encores were flying off dealers' lots at the full MSRP price, now with cheaper fuel, dealers are offering substantial discounts of 5-10%. **Price:** $26,895 for the base model. Forget haggling. **Crashworthiness:** NHTSA: Four and five stars (2013-16 models).

VERANO: Average. The Verano doesn't have the luxury look or feel of some of its rivals. The $23,000 entry-level returns with no important changes, following its adoption of a new turbocharged 250 hp powerplant. This is not a quick car: The base 180-horsepower, 2.4L 4-cylinder engine will do 0-60 mph in about 9 seconds, but the responsive 6-speed automatic tranny makes those extra seconds uneventful. Very few owner complaints have been posted by NHTSA for the Verano. **Price:** $22,595 for the base model. **Crashworthiness:** NHTSA: Five stars (2013-16 models).

Cadillac

ATS: Average. Essentially a compact Caddy. The ATS is a four-door, five-passenger compact luxury sedan that is Cadillac's smallest vehicle, slotted just below the CTS. Available in either rear- or all-wheel drive, the car comes with a 202 hp 2.5L 4-cylinder engine, but also offers a 272 hp 2.0L turbocharged Four, and a 321 hp 3.6L V6 – all paired to a 6-speed automatic transmission. Owners report serious transmission shifting delay, steering malfunctions, and excessive shaking at idle or when passing over small bumps in the road. **Price:** $35,000, which jumps to $40,000 for the AWD model. A used 2013 ATS shaves almost $10,000 off the base price. **Crashworthiness:** NHTSA: Gives the ATS five stars for overall crash protection (2014-16 models).

DTS: Average. Essentially your father's comfortable, roomy, bouncy, and ponderous Oldsmobile with a Cadillac badge. There have been reports of airbags failing to deploy, loss of braking, and head restraints literally being a pain in the neck (try before you buy). **Price:** Dropped in 2011, that model year sold for $56,540 and is now worth $27,000. The $75,680 Platinum model sells for $38,000. **Crashworthiness:** NHTSA: Good; four- and five-star protection ratings across the board.

SRX: Below Average. Base models are front-drive, while luxury versions include all-wheel drive; both are powered by a 308 hp 3.6L V6 hooked to a 6-speed automatic transmission, with a maximum towing capacity of 3,500 pounds. Alternative vehicles are the Lexus RX or Acura RDX. Other observations: The car is overpriced; the AWD model is slower to accelerate than the rear-drive, and the transmission often hesitates before downshifting; there's insufficient rear passenger room; poor fit and finish; costly, dealer-dependent servicing; and suspension may be too firm for some. **Price:** *FWD:* $41,780; and the *AWD (entry-level):* $48,000. Prices are very negotiable. Depreciation is unbelievably rapid: A $42,000 base 2012 SRX is now worth barely $20,000. **Crashworthiness:** NHTSA: Five star overall rating (2010-16 models) and four stars for the 2004-09 models.

ELR: Not Recommended (2015). A gussied-up Volt sold to well-to-do "green" wannabes, Cadillac's ELR is an upmarket, plug-in hybrid that targets aging baby-boomers who want a sexy, luxury car that projects lots of cachet for lots of cash. The car debuted as a 2014 model. **Price:** Sold originally for $80,050, a 2014 ELR is now worth $60,000. Subsequent models were dropped. **Crashworthiness:** Unrated.

STS: Not Recommended (All years). Dropped in 2011. No matter how hard you try, there is nothing good to say about this touring sedan. **Price:** A 2011 that sold for $61,135 is now worth only $22,000. **Crashworthiness:** NHTSA: Gave the STS four stars for frontal and side protection and five stars for rollover resistance. Ah, something positive to say...

Chevrolet

COLORADO/CANYON: Average (2015-16); **Below Average** (2004-14) **Recommended.** With earlier models, performance and reliability of these mid-size pickups aren't competitive with other vehicles in their class. Redesigned 2015s are better-built, often discounted, handle well, and compare favourably with the Nissan Frontier and Toyota Tacoma. Nevertheless, they also have frequent Stabilitrak, steering, engine, and transmission failures. **Price:** The 2016 Colorado sells for $21,945 while the GMC Canyon equivalent lists for a bit more at $22,645. 2014 models and earlier versions are no bargain, despite their low cost. A 2012 Colorado (there were no 2013 or 2014 models) is now worth about $14,500. Main drawbacks are wimpy engines, poor handling, so-so reliability, and sloppy fit and finish. Buy, instead, a 2010 Honda Ridgeline or Pilot for about $16,000. Crashworthiness: NHTSA: 2015 and 2016 models given a four-star overall crash safety rating, while 2004 through 2009 models get four- and five-star crash ratings.

EXPRESS/SAVANA: Recommended. These full-sized, rear-drive vans have been around forever with relatively few changes. These are easily accessed, capacious, and dependable vans that can be fixed anywhere with cheap parts easily found at dealers, independent suppliers, and junkyards. And the good news doesn't stop there. With fuel prices bottoming out, there's no fuel penalty in choosing one of these large vans. Both vans are also perfect recession buys because most of their reliability issues aren't expensive to correct. Some weak areas: They are fuel-thirsty, are ponderous performers, and frequently are susceptible to water leaks. Price: The base Chevrolet Express sells for $30,595, but with a diesel powerplant, the price jumps to $42,540. An optional compressed natural gas system costs $8,245. The Savana variant costs only a few hundred dollars more. Crashworthiness: NHTSA: *Express 1500 cargo van:* Five stars for frontal protection; *1500 passenger van:* Five stars for frontal protection and three stars for rollover resistance; *2500 and 3500 12-passenger van and the 3500 15-passenger van:* Three stars for rollover resistance. Many auto safety groups ascribe horrific injuries and deaths due to the 15-passenger vans' high propensity to roll over and offer little occupant protection.

HHR: Below Average. This five-passenger compact wagon uses GM's Cobalt/Pursuit platform and an under-powered standard 4-cylinder engine. Dropped in 2011. Servicing is easy and can be done at any independent garage. Price: A $20,395 base 2011 model is now worth $6,500; the SS will cost an extra $1,500. Crashworthiness: NHTSA: 2006-10 models earned five stars for frontal- and side-impact occupant protection; rollover crashworthiness scored four stars.

ORLANDO: Average. This Opel-inspired seven-seater was sold in Canada for three model years (2012-14). It combines reasonable fuel economy with a minivan passenger load in much the same way as the Mazda5, Kia Rondo, and my old favourite, the long-gone, greatly lamented Nissan Axxess – a small minivan sold in Canada as a 1990 model and axed in 1995. Thanks to its European DNA, the $20,000 Orlando rides and handles well and is reasonably fuel-efficient. Price: Valued at $10,000 to $14,500, this minivan's attractive price doesn't compensate for the car's so-so highway performance and uncertain servicing as parts dry up. Crashworthiness: Unrated.

SPARK: Average (2016); Below Average (2013-15). *EV:* Not Recommended (2014-16). Chevrolet's 2016 Spark has been significantly redesigned, returning with a 17% more powerful 98 hp engine, a restyled exterior (gone are the quirky headlights), upgraded interior, lowered roof and seats, and a standard backup camera. OnStar now has a 4G LTE data connection and onboard Wi-Fi is also available, as are rear parking sensors. Even with its 2016 power increase, the Spark has a puny 98 hp engine, and doesn't get any better gas mileage than the 150 hp Honda Civic or 140 hp Chevy Cruze. The steering is a bit light for highway driving; CVT gear shifts are a bit clunky; steering column doesn't telescope; a harsh ride when going over uneven terrain; and refinement that's slow and untested. Chevrolet launched the Spark electric vehicle (EV) several years ago. Buyers should delay their purchase until it has had a few more years on the market. **Price:** The car's $13,995 base price is quite reasonable and the 2013's value barely nudges $8,000. The costlier EV version is sold only in Maryland, Oregon, and California. In Canada it has been available only to fleet customers during the past 2 years, but in 2016, it's scheduled to be sold in British Columbia, Ontario, and Quebec for an estimated $29,995, plus, a $1,700 freight fee. Haggling is encouraged due to soft-prices for electrics and hybrids, generally. **Crashworthiness:** NHTSA: Four stars for 2014-16 models. *EV:* Unrated.

VOLT: Not Recommended. Not an Electric Edsel, but close. Volt is GM's 5-year-old electric compact four-seater. It has just come back from a summer hiatus where GM added power, improved highway performance, restyled the exterior and interior, and cut prices. The 2016 sells for $1,175 U.S. less than the 2015, trimming that car's price to $33,995. It will have a shortened model run from this fall to next spring – when the 2017 debuts and sales will be limited to British Columbia, Ontario, Quebec, and 11 American States. Some negatives: Rear passenger's head likely to strike the glass or the black hard plastic trim; brakes may fail when passing over rough terrain; liftgate strut rod detaching; taillights collect water; steering wheel locks in the centre position; carbon monoxide poisoning due to the car not shutting off in the owner's garage; horn operates spontaneously while engine is idling; home charger may catch on fire; battery can be drained by OnStar, even if OnStar is shut off; and complete electrical shutdown on the highway. Owners say that the Volt has these safety flaws: Front suspension may collapse; rear Reverse lights are too dim; rear windshield distorts the view; rear end "slips" when accelerating; and the charging system may overheat and short out. Also, if one leaves the car without powering down, it may keep running silently. **Price:** Launched in Canada a year late, the 2012 model carried an astoundingly high starting price of $41,545. Disappointing sales forced GM to discount the car by $10,000 2 years ago, in addition to giving a provincial tax credit of up to $7,500. Still, the car is way overpriced if you consider a 2014 Volt can be bought in the States for $25,000, if you live in California. Currency exchange rates included. By the way a $42,000 2013 Volt is now worth $21,000. The car costs more than the Nissan Leaf EV, and $15,000 above a well-equipped compact with a gas engine. **Crashworthiness:** NHTSA: Five stars (2011-16 models).

Chrysler/Dodge

100: Not Recommended. The 100 will be a spin-off of the Dodge Dart platform and built in Illinois. The hatchback version takes the place of the PT Cruiser and will be smaller and lighter than the Dart. Price: $16,000 to $18,000. Crashworthiness: Unrated.

DART: Average. The Dodge Dart is a much better performer than the Caliber it replaces. Buyers have the choice of one of three 4-cylinder engines: A 160 hp turbo 1.4L; a 160 hp 2.0L; or an 184 hp 2.4L. There are three choices of 6-speed gearboxes: One manual, one automatic, and one dual-clutch variant. The interior has some nice features like a central seat cushion that flips up to open a huge storage area for handbags, etc., and the user-friendly Uconnect media screen. Changes for the 2016 Dodge Dart compact sedan are mostly cosmetic. The 2016 Dodge Dart SRT, however, will have a 2.4-L with turbocharger and about 260 hp. Driving the Dart is a breeze, although the base 1.4L engine's turbo takes a bit of time to get the car up to speed. Going head to head with the Chevy Cruze, Ford Focus, Honda Civic, and Toyota Corolla, the Dart leads the pack for highway performance, especially with a manual transmission. Price: *SE:* $15,995; *SXT:* $18,995; *Rallye:* $19,495; and the *Limited:* $22,995. A used 2013 Dart is worth about $11,000. The basic Dodge Dart SRT 2016 price will be around $25,000 U.S. Crashworthiness: NHTSA: Five stars (2013-16 models).

DURANGO: Below Average (2012-14); Not Recommended (1998-2011). The Dodge Durango is an SUV nightmare on wheels that has always been afflicted by serious powertrain, steering, electrical, brake, and climate system failures. A 1998 spin-off of the failure-prone Dakota pickup, the Durango has provided over the years three-row seating and several gas-guzzling V8s, that are underwhelming performers. Despite a 2004 and 2011 redesign, overall performance has improved only slightly and poor reliability continues to be troublesome. The ride continues to be truck-stiff, handling is ponderous, engines are noisy, and braking is far from a sure thing. Price: *SXT:* $38,445 and *Crew Plus V6:* $46,845. A 2011 base Durango sells for $19,500. Crashworthiness: NHTSA: Four stars (2011-15 models). Surprisingly, 2001-09 models got higher safety ratings, except for a two-star rating for frontal crash protection (driver) given to the 2000 model year Durango.

Fiat

500: Average. After walking out on its U.S. and Canadian owners in 1984 and leaving them high and dry with worthless warranties and rust-cankered vehicles, Fiat announced a triumphant return to North America as Chrysler's saviour. When Fiat pulled out of North America, I was in the trenches as president of the Automobile Protection Association and remember only too well the many Fiat owners who were stunned that their rusty, unreliable, and unwanted pieces of crap would never be fixed. Fiat's new products have returned to our shores following its acquisition of Chrysler (FCA). Independent auto critics throughout Europe and North America (U.K.'s *Auto Which*, *Consumer Reports*, J. D. Power, etc., all concur that Fiat's models would not be their first choice. The only Fiat *Lemon-Aid* can recommend is the one driven by Pope Francis, due to the possibility of divine intervention when it lets him down. **Price:** *500:* $14,595; *500HB:* $15,995; *500Turbo:* $18,895; *500L:* $20,495; *500C Convertible:* $19,996; *Abarth:* $22,495; and the *500x:* $21,195. Depreciation will shave almost half of the original value after 3 years (a 2012 base Fiat that sold for $15,995 is worth about $8,500). **Crashworthiness:** NHTSA: Four stars (2013-16 models); three stars (2012 model). The 2012 version earned only two stars for side crash protection.

Ford

C-MAX HYBRID ENERGI: Not Recommended. Part hatchback, wagon, and micro-van, the C-Max Hybrid is a tall five-seater powered by an electric motor and a 2.0L 4-cylinder gas engine. It is barely larger than a Ford Focus, but boasts more passenger volume than the Prius. The only reason to buy the Energi or Hybrid is to save fuel. However, Ford's misrepresentation of the cars' fuel savings and the low cost of fuel means that other choices can be cheaper and just as economical,. Buy a Mazda5, instead. C-Max will operate electrically up to 100 kph, allowing the electric traction motor to power the vehicle, providing maximum fuel-efficiency. Owners report sudden unintended acceleration; failure to go into Reverse and frequent stalling on the highway. Some performance glitches: Poor gas mileage (Ford is refunding owners $500 for the extra fuel cost as part of a class-action settlement); no-starts; dead battery; fuel pump and radio turn themselves on overnite, while car is parked; navigation feature malfunctions; no spare tire; and the backup camera won't shut off. **Price:** *Hybrid SE:* $27,499; *SEL:* $30,199; and *Energi SEL:* $36,999. **Crashworthiness:** NHTSA: Four stars (2013-16 models).

ECONOLINE, E-SERIES: Average. These gas-guzzling, full-sized vans haven't changed much over the years and quickly lose their value, making them a better deal used. Price (2014): *Commercial van:* $31,999; *Passenger van:* $36,999 (very soft). Crashworthiness: NHTSA: Three stars for rollover protection (2012-14; 2005-09 models); four stars for front driver/passenger protection (2005-06 models).

EXPEDITION: Below Average. This gas-guzzling, over-priced, full-sized SUV quickly loses its value and, like Ford vans, is a better deal bought used. **Price:** *XLT:* $48,099 (soft); *Limited:* $59,999 (soft); *4x4 Max Limited:* $62,499 (are you kidding?). Crashworthiness: NHTSA: Four and five stars for overall occupant protection (2013-16 models).

TAURUS: *2013-16 models:* Average. *2012 models:* Below Average. **Price:** *SE 3.5:* $28,999; *SEL 3.5:* $34,199; and *SHO AWD:* $47,299 (firm). A 2013 base model sells for $17,000, which is quite a drop from its original price of $28,800. **Crashworthiness:** NHTSA: Four stars for overall crash protection.

TRANSIT CONNECT: Below Average. This van is available in two wheelbases with seats for up to seven in three rows and a 1200-lb payload. Maximum towing capability is 2000 lbs. The base engine is a 169-hp 2.5L 4-cylinder; the optional turbocharged 178-hp 1.6-L 4-cylinder isn't worth the extra cost. *Price: Cargo XL:* $28,699; *Window Van XLT:* $31,899. Crashworthiness: NHTSA: Five stars for overall passenger protection. (2014-16 models); only two stars for the 2012-13 models. 2010s scored five stars for frontal collision and side protection

Honda

CR-Z HYBRID: Below Average. A city car for "green" enthusiasts, the CR-Z is a sporty ("sporty" by hybrid standards, I suppose), two-passenger, hybrid coupe equipped with a manual/automatic shifter. It doesn't come with the rev-happy powertrain we enjoyed with earlier sporty, fuel-frugal Honda runabouts, like the little CRX, dropped in 1992. A spin-off from Honda's Insight (also dropped – in 2011), the CR-Z has a shorter wheelbase, shorter length, and wider front and rear tracks than its cousin. Parts and servicing may be a problem since Honda dealers won't stock parts for low-volume hybrid repairs. Choose a $1,000 cheaper 2012 Hyundai Veloster, instead. Strong points: Fuel-efficient, agile, strong brakes and responsive brakes; CVT gets 37 mpg on the highway. Weak points: Fuel economy numbers don't compensate for the car's mediocre highway performance. The slanted roof/split rear window restrict rear visibility and compromise interior space. Price: 2011-2015s cost between $11,000 and $22,700 (new). Crashworthiness: NHTSA: Disappointing. Only three stars for overall crash protection and five stars for rollover resistance.

INSIGHT: Not Recommended. One of the least expensive hybrids available in North America, the Insight had such a checkered reliability and performance history that Honda took it off the market for a few years. Its return was short-lived after Honda marketing gurus learned to their dismay that car buyers have long memories. Price: A last-year, 2010 Insight is worth only $9,000, despite its original $24,000 listing. Parts and servicing can be hard to find. Crashworthiness: NHTSA: Four- and five-star crash protection rating (2000-10 models).

Hyundai

EQUUS: Recommended (2011-16). The Hyundai Equus, the Latin word for "horse," is an upscale full-size luxury sedan that is Hyundai's largest and most expensive model. In 2009, the company released a new version on a rear-wheel drive platform aimed to compete with the BMW 7 Series, Mercedes S-Class, Audi A8, and Lexus LS. Owner safety complaints are sparse, but, some are serious, like the following NHTSA-logged incident where the car's suspension suddenly collapsed:

The air suspension system failed and the whole car, mostly the front, dropped a number of inches. We could barely drive home and had to have the vehicle towed. Seems to be a very unsafe item. The first time it was the passenger side; second time it was the driver side.

Price: $64,799. The car has been on the Canadian market since 2011 and that first-year model, which retailed for $62,999, now sells for only $25,000 – a little-known bargain, judging by its high performance and reliability ratings. Crashworthiness: NHTSA: Unrated; IIHS: Gives the car its top "Good" ranking.

VELOSTER: Recommended (2015-16); Above Average (2012-14. Surprisingly fuel-efficient; fuel economy rivals the Honda CR-Z Hybrid. A four-seater hatchback, this two-door sports coupe actually has a hidden rear passenger-side third door that gives access to the two rear seats. Parts and servicing aren't a problem since the Veloster shares most of the Accent's hardware and electronics. Price: $26,999 for the base vehicle. A $19,000 2012 Veloster (its first year) is now worth only $10,000. Crashworthiness: NHTSA: Five stars for overall crashworthiness (2014-16 models).

Jaguar

F-TYPE ROADSTER: Average (2014-16). With this relatively new model, Jaguar makes a play to find its soul after being held captive during its acquisition by Ford. The 2014 F-Type roadster is a bold statement by Jaguar that it has not forgotten its roots. It's a pure two-seater, powered by a supercharged V6 that should make around 380 hp. With its small size, 8-speed ZF transmission and open cockpit, it's more Porsche 911 steak and potatoes than a high-end exotic. Not a single complaint registered for the first year 2014 model, but 13 service alerts were sent out. They involve the transmission, high pressure fuel pump, rear suspension, brakes, electrical system, folding top, and lockable stowage box lid. Price: *F-Type Convertible:* $76,900; *S:* $88,900; *S V8:* $100,900. The 2014 base model that sold new for $76,900, is now worth $65,000, which is good value for a car this expensive. Crashworthiness: Unrated.

Jeep

JOURNEY: Not Recommended. Due to the Dodge Journey's poor reliability, wimpy engine, mediocre handling, and confusing base infotainment system, it has repeatedly anchored the bottom of most car critics' lists. If you must get a Journey, opt for the V6 engine and a 6-speed automatic transmission. Price: *Base:* $21,495; *SXT:* $25,495; *Rallye AWD:* $33,395. Crashworthiness: NHTSA: Four star overall crashworthiness (2012-14 models); five star crash protection (2009-10 models).

LIBERTY: Not Recommended. Introduced in 2002, the Liberty came on the scene equipped with several worthwhile features like an independent front suspension and rack-and-pinion steering. However, its interior is hard to access and relatively small and narrow, plus the ride is unsettled when passing over uneven terrain. As with most Jeeps, poor reliability is the Liberty's most serious problem. Owners complain about costly engine, transmission, electrical system, and AC failures. Premature brake disc and rotor replacements also figure prominently among owner gripes. **Price:** 2012 was the Liberty's last model year, thank goodness. Resale value of a 2012 Sport that sold new for $30,295 is $15,500; the same year Limited that sold for $34,295 is worth only $18,500 today. **Crashworthiness:** NHTSA: The 2012 Liberty's crash safety scores (mostly two- and three-stars) were worse than what earlier models had earned. 2004-10 models got mostly four- and five-star crash protection scores, with the exception of rollover protection which scored two stars (2002-03) and three stars (2004-10).

PATRIOT: Not Recommended. A spin-off of the Dodge Caliber and Jeep Compass, the Patriot arrived in 2007 and quickly sank out of sight. It's a small, upright SUV that comes equipped with the same anemic 2.0L and 2.4L engines that once powered the late, unlamented Caliber. Other shortcomings? A mediocre ride and so-so handling, fit and finish that's early Lada, and frequent brake, electrical, and powertrain failures. **Price:** *Sport:* $17,995; *4x4:* $20,595; *Limited:* $24,795; *4x4:* $27,395. A 2010 Patriot Limited 4x4 sells for $3,500. **Crashworthiness:** NHTSA: Four stars for overall crashworthiness (2007-14 models).

Kia

BORREGO: Below Average. Sold in Canada for only three model years (2009-11), the Borrego lacks the refined ride comfort and easy handling found in other luxury three-row SUVs, due to its truck-like body-on-frame construction. **Price:** Prices range from $9,000 to $13,000 (2011). But, parts, repair agencies, and future buyers will be rare. Look to the 2011 Hyundai Santa Fe or Tucson as better alternatives. Vehicles with more car-like qualities are the Chevy Traverse, Honda Pilot, and Mazda CX-9. A 2011 $39,000 Borrego now sells for $20,000. **Crashworthiness:** NHTSA: Five stars for frontal and side occupant crash protection. Rollover protection was given four stars.

K900: Average. This Kia Luxury "newbie" hasn't fully established itself in North America, so we can only give it an Average rating. Nevertheless, during its first year on the market, the K900 has racked up only three owner safety-related complaints reported to NHTSA. The K900, which sold as the K9 and Quoris in other markets, carries the latest safety and luxury features and offers high performance with a 420 hp powerplant. It's similar in size to the BMW 7 Series and targets both BMW and Audi's high-end sedans. **Price:** Kia Canada is barking up a tall tree with its $49,995 car that targets mostly the Chinese Audi/BMW market. Shoppers buying a used K900 should deduct 20% or $10,000 from the car's advertised price. **Crashworthiness:** Unrated.

CADENZA: Above Average. Only on the market for 2 years, the Kia Cadenza is a well-appointed large car that rides comfortably and supplies sufficient power for most needs. The 6-speed automatic transmission downshifts flawlessly, though it is sometimes slow with upshifts. Handling is acceptable, steering responsive and light, and the cabin is quiet. There's roomy seating both fore and aft and plenty of trunk space, as well. A rear-view camera is standard and the infotainment system is easy to use and read. **Price:** $37,995. A 2014 version sells for about $9,000 less. **Crashworthiness:** No crash data, yet.

RONDO: Above Average (2010-16); Average (2007-09). The 2010 and later models, equipped with a six-cylinder engine, are powerful enough for a full passenger load and can tow 2,000 pounds. The 2014 model with some of the original five year warranty intact is a particularly good buy from a price/quality perspective. Also, the standard electronic stability control has been improved on those models. Repair parts are reasonably-priced and aren't hard to find, plus competent independent mechanics can easily repair most problems. Overall reliability is Average and gets better with more recent models. Some owner concerns have been expressed relative to the instability of 2007-09 models on wet roads and airbags that fail to deploy when needed. Owners do complain of inadequate interior heating; paint delamination/peeling; poor performance of the 4-speed tranny (a 5-speed is more fuel-efficient); an underpowered 4-cylinder engine; limited cargo room; some interior road and wind noise; and limited rear-view visibility. A final word about the electronic stability control – it's touchy. If the system senses some slip, it cuts engine power ... not good, when stuck in a snowbank. Fortunately, drivers can shut this feature off if necessary to get out of a snowy driveway, though adding winter tires might be a better option. Many reviewers recommend the Mazda5 as a viable alternative. **Price:** $21,495. A 2014 Wagon LX five-passenger costs $16,500; a seven-passenger version: $2,000 more. **Crashworthiness:** NHTSA: Four-star rollover protection (2011 model); four- and five-star crashworthiness scores (2007-10 models).

Lexus

CT 200H: Not Recommended. A small hybrid that uses the Prius powerplant, the CT 200h gives modestly better fuel economy along with a cramped cabin, a stiff and choppy ride, excessive road noise, tight rear seats, limited cargo space, and poor rear visibility. **Price:** The last model year in Canada was 2013 when it sold for $31,450. That same car is now worth $22,000. **Crashworthiness:** Never crash-tested. *Safercar.gov* complaints include spontaneous sunroof explosion, hard starting, brake failures, and front windshield image distortion.

NX 200T/300H: Not Recommended. A *faux* Lexus. The NX twins are spinoffs of Toyota's RAV4 launched on the Canadian market last year as 2015 models. They don't provide as much Lexus luxury for their excessively high price as one would expect. Turbo lag when accelerating; considerable understeer at higher speeds; erratic upshifting; a firm ride, handling outclassed by European and Asian competitors, the interior lacks a luxury "feel" and is too snug, and the infotainment system's touchpad isn't very user-friendly. Lexus enthusiasts should buy a "real" 3-year-old Lexus ES with some warranty left. **Price:** *NX200t:* $41,450; *NX300h:* $59,450. **Crashworthiness:** NHTSA: Five stars for overall crash safety (2015-16 models).

Lincoln

MKC: Below Average. A luxury compact SUV, that's well-appointed, has plenty of power, and handles well. The best choice is the turbocharged 4-cylinder engine paired to the 6-speed automatic transmission. However, the tranny shifts erratically, the EcoBoost system has a rotten record from previous years, the MyLincoln Touch is problematic, there's insufficient legroom in the rear, and cargo space doesn't equal the competition. Price: $39,940; *2.3 EcoBoost:* $49,650. Crashworthiness: NHTSA: Four-star occupant protection (2015-16 models).

Mazda

MAZDA2: Below Average. This subcompact five-seater (really, it's a four-seater) comes only as a four-door hatchback equipped with a power-challenged 100 hp 1.5L 4-cylinder engine. The engine can be paired to either a 4-speed automatic transmission or a 5-speed manual gearbox. This mini-minicar is roomier in the rear than the Ford Fiesta, costs less, and highway/city fuel economy is quite good. Highway cruising isn't recommended, but city driving is a breeze due to the car's superb handling and small size. However, it's slow when carrying a full load and the transmission needs more gears. Also, the interior is rather Spartan when compared with the competition. Price: *GX:* $13,450; *GS:* $18,300. A 2013 can be bought for $9,500. Crashworthiness: IIHS: Frontal offset and roof crash protection is rated "Good," while side and rear crashworthiness is judged "Acceptable." Small overlap front protection is "Marginal" (2011-14 models).

Mercedes-Benz

ML 350: Not Recommended. Since they first came on the market as 1998 models, these luxury SUVs haven't been recommended due to their low quality and high cost. Following a 2012 redesign, some of the more serious engineering faults and poor quality control were corrected. But the ML Series has continued to be highly overpriced and loses its value quickly. The 2016 version is renamed the GLE, a restyled update of the M-Class, with an improved infotainment system. There's also a new 436 hp GLE550e 4Matic hybrid SUV based on the S-Class plug-in and paired with AWD. ML350 owners report steering suddenly locks up, fuel pump failures, stalling, vehicle rolls away when parked on an incline, transmission sometimes slips out of gear, liftgate can suddenly fall, premature brake rotor replacements, dim headlights, and chrome bumper peeling. Price: *2016 GLE 350d 4MATIC SUV:* $63,200; *2015 Base ML350:* $59,900; *ML350 BlueTEC:* $61,400; *ML63:* $103,200. Imagine spending that amount of money for an SUV that inhabits the middle of the pack. Crashworthiness: NHTSA: *ML350:* Five-star overall crash protection (2006-15). *GLE:* Hasn't yet been crash-tested.

SMART: Below Average (2016); Not Recommended (2015 and earlier). This subcompact is miscast for Canada. We are not Europe. Our cities are not so congested that we need to sacrifice so much with a car so minimal. This said, the 2016 Smart Fortwo's third-generation improvements add some important upgrades to an econocar that has always stressed size and fuel economy over performance. For example, an optional dual-clutch 6-speed automatic transmission coupled to the turbocharged 3-cylinder engine results in smoother shifts and acceleration times that are measured with a watch, instead of an hourglass. The car now rides more comfortably and a low centre of gravity adds to its stability when cornering. The automated manual shifter is annoyingly slow and rough with 2015 and earlier models; and you must use premium fuel. Indeed, the Smart is fuel-frugal; highly practical for city driving and parking; and is relatively reliable. But, it's highly dealer-dependent and seriously outclassed by the Honda Fit, Hyundai Accent, Kia Rio, and Nissan Versa. The electric variant needs 16 hours for a 120-volt recharge, or 8 hours with a 240-volt system. **Price:** *Fortwo Pure:* $14,400; *Passion:* $17,500; *BRABUS:* $20,900; *Fortwo ED (Electric Drive):* $27,000; *Passion Cabriolet:* $20,500; *BRABUS Cabriolet:* $23,900; *ED Cabriolet:* $27,000. **Crashworthiness:** NHTSA: Three stars for rollover protection (2011-12 models). Five stars for side protection, four stars for frontal collision occupant protection, and three stars for rollover resistance (2008-10 models).

Mitsubishi

MIRAGE: Below Average (2014-15). Mitsubishi says its 3-year-old Mirage compact will take a break for 2016 and will introduce next spring an early 2017 model with some powertrain and chassis updates. Dealers have a large inventory of unsold 2015s and the automaker needs to liquidate the old stock before bringing in a 2017 version. Mitsubishi officials know the car is disappointing. Especially, when compared with other models in its niche that are more refined and have a proven track record. Mirage is an import from Thailand that comes with a 1.2L 3-cylinder engine that delivers a paltry 74 hp to the front wheels through a standard 5-speed manual or optional CVT transmission. Reliability is better than average; during the few years the Mirage has been on the Canadian market only 17 safety-related complaints have been registed at *safercar.gov.* However, one of the more frequent defects reported that appears to have no solution is chassis misalignment affecting 2014-15 vehicles. Mirage owners say the car tilts to one side at rest and wanders over the highway when underway. It lags and lurches when accelerating from a stop; and brakes lock up when applied. **Price:** *ES:* $12,498; *SE:* $15,398. **Crashworthiness:** NHTSA: Four-star overall crashworthiness (2015-16 models).

Nissan

CUBE: Above Average. This five-passenger front-drive compact has so far has proven to be a reliable and competent, though odd-looking, small car. Essentially a box on wheels, the Cube has plenty of room, but no personality. It is ugly stylistically and induces a feeling of instant claustrophobia. In comparison with the Kia Soul, the Cube is a better buy. Although the Kia is cheaper, neither the ride nor the handling can touch the Nissan. Then add the fact that the Cube is fairly reliable, and offers a high level of quality. As for the initial cash savings with the Soul, they will be wiped out by the Kia's higher rate of depreciation. Still the Cube does have its failings, like a power-challenged engine, and subpar fuel economy. Some negatives: Airbags failed to deploy; axles may be misaligned; loss of power on the highway as the vehicle apparently goes into "limp mode;" and the too-vertical windshield is often shattered because rocks won't bounce off. **Price:** 2013 was the Cube's last model year; that vintage sells for $11,500. **Crashworthiness:** NHTSA: Four-star rollover protection (2011-14 models); five stars for side crash protection; and four stars for frontal crashworthiness and rollover resistance (2009-10 models). IIHS: Awarded the Cube "Good" marks in frontal offset, side, and rear occupant protection (2009-14 models).

JUKE: Above Average. This funky-looking small wagon crossover makes no attempt to blend into the crowd; it also makes no attempt to provide an outstanding driving experience or offer good fuel economy, unlike the Mini Cooper. No, the Juke takes a cheap shot and targets young consumers who want a well-performing car with a unique look. Esthetics aside, this front-drive, five-door compact crossover uses a direct-injection, turbocharged 188 hp 1.6L 4-cylinder engine coupled to a 6-speed manual or hooked to an optional CVT automatic transmission. Some of the Juke's positive features: A reasonable new and used price; good acceleration; agile, with steering that is quick and sensitive; a comfortable ride; decent seating in front and back, complemented by reasonable storage space; a well-appointed interior; and reliability that has been outstanding. **Price:** *SV FWD:* $20,498 (without freight fee); *Auto.:* $21,298; *SV AWD auto.:* $23,978; *Nismo RS FWD:* $28,798; *SL FWD auto.:* $24,848; *SL AWD auto.:* $30,178. **Crashworthiness:** NHTSA: Four stars for overall crash protection (2012-16 models).

LEAF: Recommended (2015-16); Above Average (2012-14). Nissan's first all-electric car beats the competition, until we see what the 2016 Chevy Volt's upgrades provide. Good acceleration in city traffic; comfortable seats, with an interior about the size of a Toyota Prius; quiet running; and user-friendly and easily read infotainment features. Minuses: Lethargic steering, excessive leaning when cornering, and a few, ahem, electrical problems. The Leaf is advertised as being able to travel up to 160 kilometres without stopping to recharge – a process the automaker tells us would normally take "only" eight hours on a 220-volt circuit (wink, wink; nudge, nudge). But, just after reassuring us with the above claims, Nissan then adds this caveat (i.e., don't believe what we just said): "Battery capacity decreases with time and use. Actual range will vary depending upon driving/charging habits, speed, conditions, weather, temperature, and battery age." Age, weather, temperature, speed? Yikes! Overall reliability has been better than average. Some sample complaints: Front side view blocked by huge window pillars; non-responsive brakes; front wheels lock up when braking; driving range is about half that advertised (car's Range Meter is commonly called the "Guess-O-Meter"); head restraints are angled too far forward; rear seat buckle design makes it hard to latch the seatbelts. **Price:** $31,998. Interestingly, a 2012 Leaf that originally sold for $38,395, is now worth $14,500. **Crashworthiness:** NHTSA: Four- and five-star overall crash safety (2011-16 models).

NV (NISSAN VAN): Above Average. Launched as a 2012 model, the NV (Nissan Van) represents Nissan's first attempt at breaking into the lucrative full-sized commercial van market monopolized by Ford and General Motors. There are two engines available: A 261 hp 4.0L V6 and a 317 hp 5.6L V8, both coupled to a 5-speed automatic transmission. These vans combine convenience and utility, as well as roominess and comfort. You don't have to take apart the interior to access the engine and you don't have to worry about tucking your work boots into a cramped footwell. During the past 3 years, there have been only 7 complaints posted at *safercar.gov.* They include premature roof corrosion (fixed under warranty); cruise control failure; parked vehicle rolled down an incline; and door locks that freeze up in cold weather. No complaints of back-ordered parts or poor servicing. **Price:** A 2013 NV 1500 that sold new for $32,300 is now worth $20,000; an NV 3500: $2,500. **Crashworthiness:** NHTSA: Only two stars, indicating below average rollover crash safety for the NV 3500 – a common van shortcoming.

370Z, GT-R: Recommended. Nissan does have a couple of sports cars that are worth considering. The 350hp V6-equipped 370Z is available as a coupe or a roadster. Is either model worth the price? Yes. Both are speedy and attractive alternatives to the Chevrolet Corvette, which costs much more. The Nissan GT-R is the first AWD sports car to be fitted with an independent rear axle and is powered by a 530 hp twin-turbo V6. **Price:** *370Z coupe:* $38,428; *370Z roadster:* $47,470; *GT-R:* $106,930; *Black edition:* $116,565. **Crashworthiness:** Not yet tested.

PATHFINDER: Not Recommended (2006-2013); Below Average (2014-16). Launched in 1985, this SUV is a derivative of Nissan's compact pickup, which makes early models good off-road performers, but fuel thirsty and ponderous on the highway, with an overall reputation for powertrain and electrical system malfunctions. Following its 2013 switch to the Altima platform, the Pathfinder's fuel-economy, handling, and interior amenities improved, however, service bulletins and owner complaints confirm that reliability and overall performance weren't much better than with previous models. Pathfinder's biggest drawbacks to ownership are principally poor reliability, powertrain malfunctions, an erratic fuel supply, mediocre brakes, electrical system short-circuits, poor-quality audio components, and subpar fit and finish. Some good alternative models are the GMC Acadia, if maximum interior room is a priority, or the Buick Enclave, Chevrolet Traverse, Honda Pilot, Toyota Highlander, and Mazda CX-9. If you want to stick with Nissan, the smaller redesigned 2014 Nissan Rogue or large Xterra are worth considering. **Price:** *S V6:* $31,198 (plus a $1,760 freight fee). A 2013 model is worth about $15,000 less. **Crashworthiness:** NHTSA: Four and five stars (2005-16); three stars rollover protection (2005-10).

TITAN: Above Average (2011-16); Average (2010 and earlier). Also consider a 2014 or later Chevrolet Silverado or Dodge Ram. The Titan is a full-sized truck that performs well and is more reliable and durable than most of its rivals. It has a large cabin and handles well, though the ride is a bit busy over irregular roadways. Powerful V8 engine that shifts smoothly. Fit and finish is mediocre. Owners report these problems, however: Airbags failed to deploy; rodents chewed through fuel lines (only) requiring replacement of lines and fuel tanks; excessive vibration when underway linked to propeller shaft U-joint, which may be replaced for free under a Nissan voluntary service campaign; and fractured exhaust manifolds; also sometimes replaced *gratis*, as "goodwill." Inadequate heaters are covered by a Nissan "voluntary service campaign;" leaking wheel seals can affect braking; premature brake rotor repairs; early rustout of the exhaust flange; strut tower bracket may separate from the frame; tonneau cover flew off the back of the truck; and when the armrests are down it is practically impossible to latch or unlatch the seatbelts. **Price:** *King Cab S 4x2:* $33,898; *4x4:* $39,898. A 2013 Titan that sold for $33,898 is now worth $26,500. **Crashworthiness:** NHTSA: 2012-14 Titans get three and four stars for rollover protection; 2005-09 models earned five stars for frontal crash safety and four stars for rollover safety. IIHS: Gives the 2012-15 models a "Good" rating for front overlap and rear-end collisions; roof strength was scored "Acceptable."

XTERRA: Above Average (2008-15). An exceptionally reliable, no-frills, rugged SUV that's almost as good off road as the Jeep Wrangler and far more reliable than any Jeep rival. A good, inexpensive choice, if bought used. Acceptable off- and on-road performance, a spacious cabin and adaptable cargo area, distinctively aggressive looks, adequate power and acceleration from a stop, but limited passing ability. Other minuses: A rough ride, dated interior, and poor fuel economy. From a reliability perspective the 2008-2015 models aren't very troublesome although the powertrain and fuel delivery systems have had some minor problems. Overall, the Xterra has way fewer problems reported than the Nissan Pathfinder and comes in second to the Toyota 4-Runner that is relatively glitch-free, except for some trim item fit and finish. The spacious and versatile cargo area hasn't changed. **Price:** $34,013, plus a $1,760 freight fee. A 2013 version is worth $21,000 (like the Pathfinder, about a $15,000 difference). **Crashworthiness:** NHTSA: Three stars for rollover protection (2011-2015); four and five stars for front and side protection, though rollover crashworthiness remained problematic, earning two and three stars (2001-10).

Porsche

BOXSTER AND 911: Average; *Cayenne:* Average; *Cayman and Panamera:* Average. Porsches have become more reliable during the past few years, although parts availability and dealer servicing continue to generate owner complaints. The small dealer network means customers don't have much choice when buying a Porsche and have no independent repair facilities to cut servicing costs. Forget about haggling over the price of a new or used Porsche sold by dealers – the cars are so popular that many buyers are willing to pay full MSRP. This leads to price – gouging, which in the past was attenuated by bad publicity generated by *Lemon-Aid* and others. This year, however, Porsche and its dealers can use the falling value of the loonie to justify price increases that aren't justifiable. Buckle your seatbelt and hold onto your wallet. Legendary racers, these cars can't outrun repair overcharges, theft, depreciation, high insurance costs, and premature wear and tear from cold and snow. Recent consumer complaints show that even the entry-level Boxster hasn't escaped the typical Porsche factory-induced defects affecting the engine, transmission, electrical system, brakes, and fit and finish. On the 911 and Cayenne, the powertrain, climate system, suspension, and fit and finish should be your main concerns. Don't count on "goodwill" extended warranties to assuage the high cost of powertrain repairs. Porsches *do* depreciate quickly. For example, a 2010 Boxster that originally retailed for $59,600 is now worth less than half as much – about $26,500. All Porsche models lose much of their value after 5 years on the road. That's why frugal shoppers look for used Porsches whose first owners have absorbed depreciation shock. **Price:** *Boxster:* $57,500-$70,900; *911:* $94,100-$213,200; *Cayman:* $62,800-$75,000; *Panamera:* $88,000-$155,000. **Crashworthiness:** Not tested.

Subaru

TRIBECA: Not Recommended. A Subaru version of the ugly and unpopular Pontiac Aztek, the Tribeca's odd rounded styling and triangular grille has turned off buyers since the car was first launched in 2005. Now the Tribeca has a new look, but it, too, is failing to catch on with an unimpressed public. Ranked #48 among mid-size SUVs $25K and up, the Tribeca is noted for tiny third-row seating, limited cargo space, and poor fuel economy. Consider a Chevrolet Traverse or Toyota Highlander, instead. **Price:** *3.6:* $38,995; *LTD:* $43,195; *Premier:* $45,495. A 2010 3.6 Tribeca is now worth only $15,500 – an unusually high rate of depreciation for a Subaru. **Crashworthiness:** NHTSA: Four stars for rollover protection (2011-14 models); five stars for overall crash safety; rollover protection was awarded four stars (2006-10 models). IIHS: Crash test results are unbelievably good; not a single score less that "Good" (2006-14).

Suzuki

KIZASHI: Below Average. Sold in Canada for only three years (2011-13), this homeless, front-drive, five-door, compact crossover offers nothing exceptional for its original $30,000 price. The Kizashi is a relatively well-equipped family sedan with standard electronic stability control. Handling is better than average, especially with the Sport model's precise steering. The trunk has a useful pass-through to the folded rear seats. A perusal of NHTSA owner-safety complaints and Suzuki's internal service bulletins shows no evidence of any quality problems. A few minuses: The car has been "orphaned" since Suzuki abandoned the North American market a few years ago; insufficient power, a firm ride, and a narrow interior that's invaded by engine noise. **Price:** The 2011 and 2013 are worth $10,000 and $16,000, respectively. **Crashworthiness:** NHTSA: Four stars awarded for rollover resistance (2011-14 models). IIHS: Rated head restraints as "Good" and roof crashworthiness as "Acceptable."

Tesla

MODEL S AND MODEL X: Recommended (2013-17). The Tesla brand has distinguished itself for top-quality vehicles during the past years. These electric cars are also exceptional performers that leave similarly-priced sports vehicles like the Chevrolet Corvette and Dodge Viper in the dust. European and Asian rivals haven't fared much better. In fact, Teslas are so exceptional, *Consumer Reports* was forced to toughen its test benchmarks because the Tesla blew past the consumer magazines's test parameters. **Price:** The 2016 Tesla Model S electric car ($79,000 (U.S.)) is going after mainstream luxury car buyers by adding all-wheel-drive and more range and power to the base S version. Last April, Tesla stopped selling the 2015 Model S, called the 60 – its $70,000 (U.S.) rear-drive powered by a 380 hp motor with a 330 kilometre range and a 0-60 mph (almost 100 kilometres per hour) acceleration time of 5.9 seconds. The 514 hp 2016 version can go 384 km per charge, with a 0-60 mph time of 5.2 seconds. Tesla's next vehicle, the 2017 Model X SUV, is due out in early 2016 and undoubtedly will cost more than last year's base $79,900 four-door Model S sedan. It will be followed in 2018 by a more affordable $35,000 U.S. compact sedan, named Model 3 that targets the lucrative family sedan market presently dominated by Honda, Toyota, and a handful of American cars.

What's the downside to Tesla ownership? One drawback is the distribution of dealerships and charging stations. Not a problem for most urban dwellers, however, with two more dealerships set to open in downtown Calgary later this year. Saskatchewan and the eastern provinces, though, aren't as well served. Another negative is the declining value of the Canadian dollar giving rise to a price difference with the States that can be one third higher than U.S.-posted prices. Finally, it's hard to find a price guide for used models, since traditional resale percentages don't apply due to the models' over-the-top popularity. Tesla insiders confide, however, that used models are not only rare, they hardly depreciate at all. Rule of thumb: 5% a year during the first 3 years.

The Tesla's performance stats are astounding. It is the safest car in North America based on independent crash test scores and *Consumer Reports*' driving tests. *U.S. News & World Report* ranks the Model S #1 in luxury large cars; #1 among hybrid luxury vehicles; and #2 of 10 super luxury cars. This rating is based on an analysis of published reviews and test drives, as well as reliability and safety data. The top car: The gasoline-driven Mercedes-Benz S-Class, a car that retails for $90,000-$200,000 U.S.). Go figure.

Toyota

FJ CRUISER: Average for general use; Above Average for off-roading. FJs are powered by a competent 258 hp 4.0L V6 that can be used for either two- or four-wheel drive. A 5-speed automatic transmission comes with both versions, and a 6-speed manual gearbox is available with the all-wheel drive. The Cruiser beats the pants off of its off-road rivals. On the other hand, the FJ's turning circle is larger than those of similar-sized SUVs, making for limited maneuvrability in close quarters. The rear side doors are taken from the Honda Element, which means rear and side visibility are severely restricted. There is also some side-wind vulnerability; a jiggly, busy ride; and annoying wind noises generated by the large side mirrors. Although touted as a five-passenger conveyance, a normal-sized fifth passenger in the back seat may consider litigation for cruel treatment. Front-seat headrests may be uncomfortably positioned for short occupants. Another minus is that premium fuel must be used to obtain mediocre gas mileage. *Price: Base:* $33,540; *Offroad:* $37,950. A 2007 and 2012 are worth $7,500 and $20,000, respectively. Crashworthiness: NHTSA: A big surprise. Rollover protection merits only three stars (2011-14 models). This is disappointing and is almost never seen with vehicles that are equipped with electronic stability control. Better scores were earned by the 2007-10 models which posted four- and five-star ratings in all categories, except rollover protection, which continued to merit only three stars. Apparently, the addition of ESC had no effect upon rollover protection.

SOLARA: Recommended. Shhhh, this is a "hidden" gem. Introduced in the summer of 1998 as a '99 model, the Solara is essentially a two-door coupe or convertible Camry that's longer, lower, and more bare-bones, with a more stylish exterior, sportier powertrain and suspension, and fewer quality problems. The stiff body structure and suspension, as well as tight steering, make for easy, sports-car-like handling with lots of road feel and few surprises. Convertibles have seating for four and resemble the two-seat Lexus SC 430 hardtop convertible. For 2008, the Solara's last model year, the standard powertrain was a 3.3L V6, coupled to a 5-speed automatic transmission. Price: A 2008 Solara convertible that sold originally for $40,000, now costs $10,000. SHHHH, keep it quiet. Crashworthiness: NHTSA: 2004-08 Solaras earned a five-star rating in all crash categories; 2003 models earned only three stars for side impact protection.

TUNDRA: Recommended (2014-16); Above Average (2004-13). Tundras offer a roomy interior and better than average off-road ability and reliability, but the truck lags behind more modern rivals in terms of ride quality ("bed bounce" and excessive vibrations throughout the vehicle since 2007), brake glitches, engine compartment rodents snacking on the wires and plastics, poor fuel economy, and mediocre interior appointments. Although all Tundras are relatively good buys, a 2014 or later will incorporate the latest redesign improvements. Tundra's larger V8 is responsive and powerful, with plenty of low-end torque for trailering. But be careful. Some owners say the cargo ratings are over-rated. Fuel economy is an oxymoron. You get a firm ride and controlled handling, except for recurring vibrations. Standard features include a rearview camera (which I highly recommend) and Toyota's user-friendly and dependable Entune infotainment system. The Chevrolet Silverado 1500 is a worthy alternative for its fuel economy, towing capability, comfortable ride, and quiet interior. **Price:** *2x4 Regular Cab:* $29,035 plus a $1,600 freight fee; *4x4:* $33,295. These same Tundras, as 2013 models, would cost about $18,000 and $20,000, respectively. And no $1,600 freight fee. **Crashworthiness:** NHTSA: 2015 models post a four-star ranking across the board; the 2014 has only a three-star crashworthiness rating on the 2WD regular, extended, and 4WD regular cab models. IIHS: Top "Good" scores (2008 to 2015).

Volkswagen

THE "NEW" NEW BEETLE: Not Recommended. More sizzle than steak, the New Beetle isn't really so "new;" Volkswagen took the familiar Beetle design and literally flattened it to increase cabin and cargo space and add 3.5 inches to the car's length. Early base models are powered by an underwhelming, noisy 2.5L engine (a turbocharged variant is available). A Premium TDI, won't be sold until their fraudulent emissions system has been replaced – cutting performance and fuel economy. Some of the Beetle's shortcomings: Steering is over-assisted; the DSG dual-clutch automatic transmission's past high failure rate doesn't bode well for long-term reliability; and, although diesel fuel economy is good, it's still not as good as VW claims; the car is easily buffeted by crosswinds; large head restraints and large front roof pillars obstruct front visibility; rear visibility is limited; there's insufficient rear legroom and headroom; and you won't find much storage and trunk space. 2016 models don't change much, except for a new infotainment system that allows for Android Auto and Apple CarPlay connectivity, as well as a new value-packed 1.8T S model. The Beetle's competitors are better handling and provide higher fuel economy (legally!) and more cargo space for a lower price, **Price:** *Comfortline:* $22,675; *TDI Comfortline:* $24,675; used, these models sell from $14,000 for a 2013 to $16,500 for the diesel variant (wear a disguise). Consider the Golf as an alternative: It has a lower base price than the Beetle and provides much more cargo space. **ALERT!** Beetle diesel owners can petition VW to buy back their car and include compensation for inconvenience and embarrassment. **Crashworthiness:** NHTSA: Five-star overall occupant crash protection (2013-16 models); four-star overall crashworthiness (2012 models). The 2005-10 models provide mostly four- and five-star crash protection, while IIHS gives the 2012-15s a "Good" score, except for the small front overlap test which earned a "Marginal" rating.

EOS: Below Average. Watch out for the unpredictable, failure-prone transmission. Eos is agile, handles well, and provides a comfortable, taut ride. Braking is smooth, effective, and easy to modulate. The triumph of style over practicality: Limited interior access, rear legroom, and rear headroom; and excessive cabin engine noise. Owners give the Eos a below-average reliability score. **Price:** *Comfortline:* $42,990;

2012s sell for $20,000. **Crashworthiness:** NHTSA: Hasn't crash tested the Eos. IIHS: Gives the 2009-15 models its top, "Good" rating for frontal offset and side crashworthiness and head-restraint effectiveness. 2007-08 models got a similar score, except that head restraints were rated "Marginal."

TOUAREG: Not Recommended. Volkswagen's third-generation, mid-sized Touareg comes with lots of style, a plush and comfortable cabin, and some of the most impressive off-road capabilities in its class. For those benefits, you pay an outrageously high price to get an SUV that doesn't offer third-row seating, has a pitifully poor reliability record, and needs pampering. Its problem areas include the powertrain, fuel, and electrical systems; brakes; and fit and finish. There will be no 2016 hybrid model. **Price** (2014): *Comfortline:* $38,500; *TDI:* $42,000 (not sold until 2017). **ALERT!** If VW's diesel deception extends to the 2009-2015 Touaregs, shoppers should steer clear of the car. The impending recall fix will likely compromise the car's performance, cut fuel economy, make the car difficult to resell, and accelerate its depreciation. Touareg owners should petition VW to buy back the car and include compensation for their inconvenience. **Crashworthiness:** NHTSA: Five-star overall crash safety, except for four-star rollover award (2009 models); five-star overall crashworthiness award, except for four-star score for front driver and passenger; rollover protection not tested (2004-06 models).

Phil's "Beater" Beat 1970+

Automobiles are getting so complicated (infotainment, Wi-Fi "hot" spots, navigation aids, 50-75 computer modules per vehicle, and high-tech emissions controls) that the average car owner has little choice for servicing and must go to the dealership where that vehicle was sold. This is a scary thought because it gives dealers a servicing monopoly and cuts out independent repairers who build their customer base through honest and competent service, and often serve as indispensable small claims court witnesses.

"Beaters," "tacots," and "minounes" got us through our college years, that first job, and the love of our life. As unforgettable as our first date, our first car will forever be a symbol of our optimism and a reminder of our past stuggles.

Cheap, cast-off cars have their own charm. They break the chains of automaker/dealer service monopolies and allow us to go where our wallets dictate.

Plus, the cars have been pre-rusted and a few more dents and scratches don't matter. There are plenty of cheap, reliable used cars, vans, and trucks out there that will suit your driving needs and budget. In the 1970s, the average car was junked after around seven years or 160,000 km (100,000 mi); two decades later, the average car was driven for almost eight years or 240,000 km (150,000 mi). Industry experts now say that most new models should last eleven years or more before they need major repairs. This means you can get good high-mileage vehicles for a few thousand dollars, or less, and expect to drive them for five years or more.

But having said that, it can be tough to find a ten-year-old vehicle that's safe and reliable. Personally, I'd be reluctant to buy any decade-old vehicle from someone I didn't know, or one that has been brought in from another province. All of that accumulated salt is a real body killer, and it's just too easy to fall prey to scam artists who cover up major mechanical or body problems resulting from accidents or environmental damage.

Nevertheless, if you know the seller and an independent mechanic gives you the green light, you might seriously consider a ten-year-old, beat-up-looking car, pickup, or van (but heed my advice about old SUVs, following). Look for one of those listed in this Appendix, or, if you have a bit more money to spend and want to take less of a risk, look up the Recommended or Above Average models found in Part Four.

Old Sport Utilities

Anyone buying a sport utility that's a decade old or more is asking for trouble, because many SUVs are worked hard off-road. The danger of rollovers for vehicles not equipped with electronic stability control is also quite high, particularly with Ford, Isuzu, and Suzuki versions; safety features are rudimentary, dangerous, and unreliable (especially airbags and ABS); overall quality control is very poor; and performance and handling cannot match today's models.

It's no wonder that many buyers are opting for new or almost-new SUVs manufactured during the past three years. During that time, prices came down considerably because more products were in the supply line, electronic stability control and full-torso side airbags were more widely available as standard safety features, and crashworthiness scores climbed higher.

Just two words of caution relative to buying a diesel-equipped vehicle. Be careful. Following Volkswagen's "diesel-gate" scandal, where the company installed engine software to cheat on emissions tests from 2009-2015, regulators will inspect more diesel engines and probably "detune" diesel engines from many other carmakers. This means all makers of diesel-equipped vehicles will trade performance and low fuel consumption for cleaner emissions. Used models won't generally be affected, however, those that have been brought in to be fixed for registration purposes will be "neutered" and lose their performance edge.

Beaters You Will Love

Acura

The 5-cylinder **VIGOR** is a 1992-94 Honda Accord sedan spin-off that sells for $1,000-$2,000 and is rated an Above Average buy. This compact has power to spare, handles well, and has an impressive reliability/durability record. Problem areas: Premature brake wear, electronic malfunctions and fit and finish deficiencies. The 1992 Vigor turned in below-average crash test scores.

The 1989-95 **LEGEND** is another Above Average $2,000-$2,500 buy, except for the 1986-88 model years which are Not Recommended. Resale values are high on all Legend models, especially the coupe. Shop for a cheaper 1989 or later base Legend with the coupe's upgraded features and fewer reports of sudden, unintended acceleration. Pre-1990 Legends were upscale, enlarged Accords that were unimpressive performers with either of the two 6-cylinder powerplants. The 3.2L V6 that appeared in 1991 is by far a better performer.

Chrysler

DART, VALIANT, DUSTER, SCAMP, DIPLOMAT, CARAVELLE, NEWPORT, REAR-DRIVE NEW YORKER FIFTH AVENUE, AND GRAN FURY—Problem areas are electrical systems, suspensions, brakes, body and frame rust, and constant stalling when humidity is high. The Caravelle, Diplomat, and New Yorker Fifth Avenue are reasonably reliable and simple-to-repair throwbacks to a time when rear-drive land yachts ruled the highways. Powered with 6- and 8-cylinder engines, they will run practically forever with minimal care. The fuel-efficient "slant 6" powerplant was too small for this type of car and was changed to a gas-guzzling but smooth and reliable V8 after 1983. Handling is vague and sloppy, though, and emergency braking is often accompanied by rear-wheel lock-up. Still, what do you want for a $300-$500 1984-89 "retro rocket"? Other problem areas include the carburetor (don't ask what that is; your dad knows), ignition, and suspension (premature idler-arm wear). It's a good idea to adjust the torsion bars frequently for better suspension performance.

The **STEALTH** is a serious, reasonably priced sports car that's as much go as show. Although 1995 was its last model year in Canada, it was still sold in the United States as the Mitsubishi 3000GT. Prices range from $2,500-$3,000 for the 1991-93 base or ES model. A '95 high-performance R/T will go for about $4,000 – not a bad price for an old "orphaned" sports car, eh? Problem areas are engine, transmission, front brake, and electrical failures. Parts availability has also been problematic. The 1993 model excelled in crash tests.

Ford

MAVERICK, COMET, FAIRMONT, ZEPHYR, TRACER, (1964-2004) MUSTANG, CAPRI, COUGAR, THUNDERBIRD V6, TORINO, MARQUIS, GRAND MARQUIS, LTD, AND LTD CROWN VICTORIA—"Rustoleum" models from the king of rust-prone, biodegradable bodies by Fisher. Problems areas are trunk, wheelwell, and rocker panel rusting as well as brake, steering, and electrical system failures. Yet, these cars are tanks, mechanically. Price varies from $300 to $2,000 for the late-model, full-sized versions. The Marquis and Crown Victoria are the best of this lot.

The 1990-97 **PROBE** is essentially a Mazda MX-6 sporty two-door coupe in Ford garb. It's fairly reliable and gives better-than-average highway performance. Problem areas are AC, CV joints, suspension, steering, electrical, and body glitches.

Good crashworthiness ratings, but limited servicing support. Prices range from $1,000-$1,500.

General Motors

The **1982-96 CAPRICE, IMPALA SS, AND ROADMASTER** are Above Average-rated, comfortable, and easy-to-maintain large cars that have been off the market since the 1996 model year. Overall handling is acceptable, but expect a queasy ride from the too-soft suspension. The trunk is spacious, but gas mileage is particularly poor. Despite the many generic deficiencies inherent in these rear-drives, they still score higher than GM's front-drives for overall reliability and durability. The Impala SS is basically a Caprice with a 260 hp Corvette engine and high-performance suspension. Good, cheap cars for first-time buyers, the 1991-93 models can be bought for $700-$1,000, while later models will cost $1,500-$2,000. Maintenance is inexpensive and easy to perform, and any corner garage can do repairs.

The 1991-96 models have shown the following deficiencies: AC glitches; prematurely worn brake (lots of corrosion damage), steering, and suspension components, especially shock absorbers and rear springs; serious electrical shorts; and poor-quality body and trim items.

GM's 1984-96 rear-drive Cadillac **BROUGHAM** and **FLEETWOOD** are Above Average-rated luxury "land yacht" buys that sell for $2,000-$3,000. Originally front-drives (terrible buys), these big sedans adopted the rear-drive, stretched platform used by the Buick Roadmaster and Chevrolet Caprice in 1993. Equipped with a 185 hp V8 mated to a 4-speed automatic transmission, all models came with standard traction control and anti-lock brakes. The rear-drive configuration is easy to repair and not hard to diagnose, unlike the cars' front-drive brethren. A Cadillac worth considering is the DeVille. The most serious problem areas are the fuel-injection system; engine head gasket failures; automatic transmissions that shift erratically; a weak suspension; computer module glitches; and brake rotors and pads. From a reliability/durability standpoint, the rear-drives are much better made than their front-drive counterparts.

Pontiac's 1991-95 **SUNBIRD** was GM's smallest American-built car, along with its twin, the Chevrolet **CAVALIER**. Available as two-door coupes, four-door sedans, and two-door convertibles, both models are Average buys. Nearly all Sunbirds were powered by a wimpy 96 hp 2.0L 4-cylinder engine as standard equipment, mated to a clunky, performance-sapping, fuel-wasting 3-speed automatic tranny. GT models featured a 165 hp turbocharged version of the same engine. A better-quality, optional 140 hp 3.1L V6 came on the scene in 1991. In 1992, ABS became a standard feature. Not worth more than $500.

Honda

The 1984-91 **CRX** is a highly Recommended and seriously quick two-seater sports car – a Honda Civic spin-off that was replaced in 1991 by the less sporty and much less popular Honda del Sol. Prized by high-performance "tuners," a well-maintained CRX is worth between $3,500 and $4,500.

The 1985-2001 **PRELUDE** is an Above Average buy. It's unimpressive as a high-performance sports car, but instead it delivers a stylish exterior, legendary reliability, and excellent resale value. Preludes are, nevertheless, a bit overpriced and over-hyped; cheaper, well-performing makes such as the Ford Mustang or Probe, GM Camaro or Firebird, Mazda Miata, and Toyota Celica should be checked out first. Prelude repair costs are average, though some dealer-dependent repairs to the steering assembly and transmission can be quite expensive. Price: $3,500 to $5,000.

The year for big Prelude changes was 1997, while 1998-2001 models just coasted along with minor improvements (their prices vary from $4,000 to $6,000). The '97 was restyled and repowered, and given handling upgrades that make it a better-performing, more comfortably riding sports coupe. There's no crashworthiness data, though head-restraint protection has been given a "Marginal" designation. On these more-recent models, owners report that the engine tends to leak oil and crank bolts often loosen (causing major engine damage

Mazda

Sports-car thrills, minus the bills. The 1992-96 **MX-3**'s base 1.6L engine supplies plenty of power for most driving situations, and it's reasonably priced at $1,500. When equipped with the optional 1.8L V6 powerplant (the smallest V6 on the market at the time) and high-performance options, the car transforms itself into a 130 hp pocket rocket. Reverse gear is sometimes hard to engage, and brake and wheel bearing problems are commonplace. Most of the MX-3's parts are used on other Mazda cars.

Toyota

All '80s and early '90s models are Above Average buys, except the **LE VAN**, which is a terrible choice with a history of chronic brake, chassis, and body rusting problems. Chassis rusting and V6 engine head gasket failures are common problems with the 1988-2000 sport-utilities and pickups.

From its humble beginnings in 1979, the **SUPRA** became Toyota's flagship sports car by 1986, and it took on its own unique personality – with the help of a powerful 3.0L DOHC V6 powerplant. Supra prices range from a low of $3,500 for a '90 model up to $5,500 for a '97. It's an attractively styled high-performance sports car that had been quite reliable up until it caught the Corvette/Nissan 300ZX "bigger is better" malady in 1993. Early models (pre-'93) are more reasonably priced and are practically trouble-free, except for some premature front brake wear and vibrations. On later models, owners report major turbocharger problems; frequent rear differential replacements; electrical short circuits; AC malfunctions; and premature brake, suspension, and exhaust system wear. The 3.0L engine is an oil-burner at times. Seat belt guides and the power antenna are failure-prone. Body deficiencies are common.

Rated Above Average, the **1999-2005 TOYOTA CELICAS**, all handle competently; the extra performance in the higher-line versions does come at a price, but this isn't a problem, given their high resale value ($9,000 for a 2005). Nevertheless, 1997 and later models sacrifice quality for performance. This is offset a bit by the proliferation of independent Toyota garages that perform most repairs for about a third less than what many dealers charge. Other vehicles to consider are the Ford Mustang, GM Camaro or Firebird, Honda Civic Si, Hyundai Tiburon, and Mazda3 or Miata. Incidentally, crashworthiness scores have generally been Above Average in most categories.

Another subset of problems shows up on the redesigned 2000-05 models. This includes engine failures while driving ("weak" valves blamed), not much power when the accelerator is floored, stalling after a cold start, engine knocking, excessive oil consumption, early replacement of the belt tensioner and airflow meter, a failure-prone 6-speed transmission, insufficient AC cooling, lights dimming and heater lagging when shifting into idle, seat belt tabs that damage door panels, interior panels that separate, a driver's window that catches and doesn't go all the way up, a leaky convertible top and sunroof, drivebelt squeaks when turning, a squeaking gearshift lever, a grinding noise emanating from the front wheels and brakes, paint peeling, and limited rear visibility. The audible reverse alarm isn't Toyota's brightest idea: Audible only inside the vehicle, it adds a forklift cachet to your Celica.

A final Celica caveat: Keep your head up (or down, whichever the case may be). The rear hatch can suddenly collapse and "bean" you.

Toyota's 1991-99 **TERCEL** and **PASEO** models are Above Average buys, while the 1987-90 Tercel remains a good Average pick. Prices vary little: A 1992-1995 Tercel will cost about $1,000, while the 1996-99 versions sell for about $2,000. These economy cars are dirt cheap to maintain and repair, inexpensive parts are everywhere, and repairs can be done by almost anybody. Tercels are extraordinarily reliable, and the first-generation improvements provided livelier and smoother acceleration and made the interior space feel much larger than it was. Updated 1995-99 Tercels are noted for sporadic brake, electrical system, suspension, and body/accessory problems. Frontal crashworthiness was rated two stars on the 1992 Tercel, four stars on the 1993-94, and three stars on the 1995-97. Head restraints were always rated Poor.

The Recommended 1996-99 Paseo is a baby Tercel. Its main advantages are a peppy 1.5L 4-cylinder engine, a smooth 5-speed manual transmission, good handling, a supple ride, great fuel economy, and above-average reliability. This light little sportster is quite vulnerable to side winds; there's lots of body lean in turns; plenty of engine, exhaust, and road noise; front headroom and legroom are limited; and there's very little rear-seat space.

NEW AND USED CAR CHECKLIST

Now, let's assume you're dealing with an honest seller and have chosen a vehicle that's priced right and seems to meet your needs. Take some time to assess its interior, its exterior, and its highway performance with the checklists below. If you're buying from a dealer, ask to take the vehicle home overnight in order to drive it over the same roads you use in your daily activities. Of course, if you're buying privately, it's doubtful that you'll get the vehicle for an overnight test – you may have to rent a similar one from a dealer or rental agency.

Here's how to check out a new or used vehicle without a lot of hassle. But if you are deceived by a seller despite your best efforts, don't despair. As discussed in Part Three, Canadian federal and provincial laws dish out harsh penalties to new- and used-car dealers who hide or embellish important facts. Ontario's *Consumer Protection Act (www.e-laws.gov.on.ca/html/statutes/)*, for example, lets consumers cancel a contract within one year of entering into an agreement if a seller makes a false, misleading, deceptive, or unconscionable representation. This includes using exaggeration, innuendo, or ambiguity about a material fact, or failing to state a material fact, if such use or failure deceives or tends to deceive.

Just keep in mind these three points:

1. Dealers are presumed to know the history, quality, and true performance of what they sell.

2. Dealers and private sellers cannot mislead you as to the condition of what you are buying, although judges are more lenient with private parties.

3. Even details like a vehicle's fuel economy can lead to a contract's cancellation if the dealer gave a higher-than-accurate figure. In *Sidney v. 1011067 Ontario Inc. (c.o.b. Southside Motors)*, the plaintiff was awarded $11,424.51 plus prejudgment interest. The plaintiff claimed the defendant advised him that the vehicle had a fuel efficiency of 800-900 km per tank of fuel when, in fact, the maximum efficiency was only 500 km per tank.

Catalytic Converter

Make sure the catalytic converter is present. In the past, many drivers removed this pollution-control device in the mistaken belief that it would improve fuel economy. The police can fine you for not having the converter, and you'll be forced to buy one (for $400+) in order to certify your vehicle.

Tires

Be wary of tire brands that have poor durability records. NHTSA's *www.safercar.org* will show you tire complaints and recalls, while *www.tirerack.com* will give you grass-roots owner experiences. Stay away from the Firestone/Bridgestone tires sold with many new vehicles; their poor reliability histories nearly guarantee future problems. Look at tire wear for clues that the vehicle is out of alignment, needs suspension repairs, or has serious chassis problems. Getting an alignment and new shocks and springs is part of routine maintenance, and it's relatively inexpensive to do with aftermarket parts. However, if your vehicle is an AWD or the MacPherson struts have to be replaced, you're looking at a $1,000 repair bill.

Interior Check

New vehicles often have a few hundred kilometres on the clock; used vehicles should have 20,000 km (12,500 mi) per model year. Thus, a three-year-old vehicle would ordinarily have been driven about 60,000 kilometres. The number of kilometres on the odometer isn't as important as how well the vehicle was driven and maintained. Still, high-mileage vehicles depreciate rapidly because most people consider them to be risky buys. On new cars, a few thousand kilometres showing may indicate the car was used as a demonstrator or sold and then taken back. Be suspicious. With used cars, subtract from your offer about $200 for each additional 10,000 kilometres above the average the car shows. Confirm the odometer figure by checking the vehicle's maintenance records.

The condition of the interior will often give you an idea of how the vehicle was used and maintained. For example, sagging rear seats plus a front passenger seat in pristine condition indicate that your minivan may have been used as a minibus. Delivery vans will have the paint on the driver's doorsill rubbed down to the metal, while the passenger doorsill will look like new.

Most inspections will undoubtedly turn up some defects, which may be major or minor (new vehicles have an average of a half-dozen major and minor defects). Ask an independent mechanic for an estimate, and try to convince the seller to pay part of the repair bill if you buy the vehicle. Keep in mind that many three- to five-year-old vehicles with 60,000-100,000 km on their odometers run the risk of having an engine timing belt or timing chain failure that can cause several thousand dollars' worth of repairs. If the timing belt or chain hasn't been replaced, plan to do it and deduct about $300 from the purchase price for the repair.

It's important to eliminate as many duds as possible through your own cursory check, since you'll later invest two hours and about $100 for a thorough mechanical inspection. Garages approved by the Automobile Protection Association (APA) or members of the Canadian Automobile Association (CAA) usually do a good job. CAA inspections run from $100 to $150 for non-members. Remember, if you get a bum steer from an independent testing agency, you can get the inspection fee refunded and hold the garage responsible for your subsequent repairs and consequential damages, like towing, missed work, or a ruined vacation. Part Three has the Alberta jurisprudence.

Appendix 11

HOMEMADE LEMON-AID

Why not draw up your personal *Lemon-Aid* guide to find the cheapest, safest, and most reliable vehicle on the market? All it takes is a trip to the library, a computer (available for free at the library), and a couple days of research. Check out at least three top choices in: *Consumer Reports, Lemon-Aid, U.S. News & World Report,* and *safercar.gov.*

1. Read *Consumer Reports'* December or April editions that rate the best new and used vehicles and their relative crashworthiness. Alternative models are listed and the latest sales scams are exposed. Prices, however, have no relevance to Canada.

2. Use *Lemon-Aid* to get a Canadian take on much of *Consumer Reports'* findings (although some ratings will be quite different). *L-A* also rates new and used vehicles and includes Canadian prices, service bulletins to confirm defect trends, and adds legal tips and Canadian jurisprudence to get you out of a bad deal.

3. Get more info about where your three choices stand from a performance perspective. *U.S. News & World Report* will do just that. It is a compilation of new and used car critiques from a dozen different sources. Readers will find performance stats, pros and cons from other journalists' test drives, and

a numerical rating for the best and worst cars in each model category. Again, no Canadian prices are listed. Access the magazine's ratings through Google by typing in the car and year you are interested in, followed by: U.S. News and. When the webpage appears, then do the same search on the alternative cars listed in the rating.

4. *safercar.gov* will give you information on crashworthiness, consumer complaints, service bulletins, ongoing safety investigations, and recalls. The consumer complaints registry presents eye-popping, jaw-dropping, safety-related failures that are early warning alerts as to what may happen. Consumers write their own story with details related to safety defects, corrective parts, and secret warranties. Speaking of secret warranties, the service bulletins found on this website expose many little-known warranty extensions and show which common problems are the manufacturer's responsibility. The kicker? All this info is neatly packaged by car model and model year, from 1972 to 2015.

5. Complete your *Lemon-Aid* guide by adding new and used price information from three online resources: *The Black Book, The Red Book,* and *VMR.ca.* These publications' prices will vary, somewhat, but they give you a fairly accurate idea of what to pay, or how much your car is worth in an insurance settlement. Readers can also find out when a model debuted, when it ceased production, and which upgrades appeared in each model year. This will help determine if a higher price is justified. Simply type the name of the car model into Google and add: *Wiki.*

There, you have it. Your own "homemade" *Lemon-Aid.*

Negotiating Prices

Dealer profit margins on new and used cars vary considerably – giving lots of room to negotiate a fair price if you take the time to find out what the vehicle is really worth. A new vehicle's selling price as suggested by the manufacturer (MSRP) is just that – a suggestion. Most savvy buyers beat the MSRP by at least 10 percent by shopping when inventories pile up and automakers/dealers double-down on sales incentives (usually during the first quarter of the year).

Getting the Lowest Price

If you want a low price and abhor dealership visits and haggling, search out a reliable new- or used-car broker. For years, *Lemon-Aid* has recommended Dealfinder, an Ottawa-based auto broker that helps clients across Canada. Go to *www.deal finder.ca* for all of the particulars. Ottawa-based Bob Prest, a small broker who believes in big discounts, has helped many people find great deals.

For those readers who feel comfortable negotiating all of the transaction details with the dealer themselves, here's what to do.

1. Compare a new vehicle's "discounted" MSRP prices published on the auto-maker's website with invoices downloaded from the Automobile Protection Association (*www.apa.ca*), the Canadian Automobile Association (*www.caa.ca*), and a host of other agencies.

2. Check the prices you find against the ones listed in this book.

3. Pay particular attention to the prices charged in the States by accessing the automaker's U.S. website – just type the company name into Google and add "USA." For example, "GM USA" will take you directly to the automaker's American website, whereas "GM Canada" gives you the Canadian headquarters, models, and prices. If you find the U.S. price is substantially lower than what Canadian dealers charge, take your U.S. printout to a Canadian dealer and ask that the price not vary more than the 30 percent difference in value between our loonie and the American dollar. There is no reason why you should pay more than the Canadian exchange rate. And this includes freight and pre-delivery inspection fees.

Real Trade-in Values

If you have a trade-in, it's important to find out its true value to decide whether selling it privately would put more money in your pocket than selling it to the dealer. Right now, there is a shortage of good three- to five-year-old used cars on the market and private buyers are paying a premium for them.

Problem is, how do you find how much your trade-in is worth? In the past dealers had a monopoly on this information because only they could afford the hundreds of dollars in annual subscription fees charged by the publishers of *Black Book* and *Red Book*. That has now changed with the advent of the Internet.

There is now an excellent alternative to the traditional *Red* and *Black Book* price guides. Go to *www.vmrcanada.com/* for free listings of trade-in values for 1984 to 2014 cars and trucks, reliability predictions, and three- to five-year residual value projections. Better yet, subscribe to the publication in eBook format. A year's subscription for $9.95 U.S. is more comprehensive and much cheaper than either the *Black Book* or *Red Book* (although the other two publications give current new and used prices for 2013-14 models and are more popular with car dealers, insurance companies, and government agencies). The *Black Book* gives used values online for free at: *www.canadianblackbook.com/*; *Red Book*: *www.canadianredbook.com/* gives values online to subscribers for an annual fee of $195.95.

Now available in eBook format, *VMR Canadian Used Car Prices* delivers our unbiased, market-based values in an easy-to-use format. The smart PDF has a simple, built-in menu system incorporated with the Table of Contents, allowing fast and easy navigation to anywhere in the publication. Download it once to your computer or device and access it anytime, anywhere – just like a book. Only $9.95 U.S. for full year (published quarterly).

Recent surveys show that close to 80 percent of car buyers get reliability and pricing information from the Internet before visiting a dealer or private seller. This trend has resulted in easier access to confidential price margins, secret warranties, and lower prices – if you know where to look.

Automobile companies have helpful – though self-serving – websites, most of which feature detailed sections on their vehicles' histories and research and development, as well as all sorts of information of interest to auto enthusiasts and bargain hunters. For example, you can generally find out the freight fee before you even get to the dealership; sales agents prefer to hit you with this charge at the end of the transaction when your guard is down. As said earlier, cut the freight fee by 50 percent. Manufacturers can easily be accessed through a search engine like Google or by typing the automaker's name into your Internet browser's address bar followed by ".com" or ".ca". Or for extra fun and a more balanced presentation, type the vehicle model or manufacturer's name into a search engine, followed by "lemon," "problems," or "lawsuits."

Consumer Allies

Automobile Protection Association *(www.apa.ca)*

A motherlode of honest, independent, and current car-buying information, the non-profit APA has been protecting Canadian motorists for over 40 years from its offices in Toronto and Montreal. This dynamic consumer group fights for safer vehicles for consumers and has exposed many scams associated with new-vehicle sales, leasing, and repairs. For a small fee, it will send you the invoice price for most new vehicles and help you out if you get a bad car or dealer. The APA also has a useful free online guide for digging out court judgments.

Canadian Legal Information Institute *(www.canlii.org)*

Be your own legal "eagle" and save big bucks. Use this site to find court judgments from every province and territory all the way up to the Supreme Court of Canada.

Car Help Canada *(www.carhelpcanada.com)*

Founded by former director of the Toronto Automobile Protection Association, Mohamed Bouchama, the ACC's Car Help Canada website provides many of the same services as does the APA; however, the ACC is especially effective in Ontario and Alberta and uses a network of honest garages and dealers to help members get honest and fair prices for vehicles and repairs. The ACC has been particularly successful in getting new legislation enacted in Ontario and obtaining refunds for its members.

CBC TV's Marketplace *(www.cbc.ca/marketplace)*

Marketplace has been the CBC's premier national consumer show for almost forever. Staffers are dedicated to searching out scammers, airbag dangers, misleading advertising, and unsafe, poor-quality products. Search the archives for auto info, or contact the show's producers to suggest program ideas.

Class Actions in Canada *(www.classproceedings.ca)*

After successfully kicking Ford's rear end over its front-end thick film ignition (TFI) troubles and getting a million-dollar out-of-court settlement, this powerhouse Ontario-based law firm got a similar settlement from GM as compensation for a decade of defective V6 intake manifold gasket failures. Estimated damages were well over a billion dollars. The firm has also worked with others to force Liberty Mutual and other insurers to refund money paid by policy holders who were forced to accept accident repairs with used, reconditioned parts instead of new, original-equipment parts.

Class Actions in the U.S. *(www.lawyersandsettlements.com)*

This is a useful site if you want to use a company's class action woes in U.S. jurisdictions as leverage in settling your own Canadian claim out of court. If you decide to go the Canadian class action route, most of the legal legwork will have been done for you. The site is easy and free to search. Just type in the make of the vehicle you're investigating and read the results.

Competition Bureau Canada *(www.competitionbureau.gc.ca)*

Imagine, consumers can file with the federal government an online complaint regarding misleading advertising or price fixing. The Competition Bureau's role is to promote and maintain fair competition so that Canadians can benefit from lower prices, increased product choices, and quality services.

This website includes a handy online complaint form that gives Ottawa investigators the mandate to carry out an official probe and lay charges. Most auto-related complaints submitted to the Bureau concern price-fixing and misleading advertising. After *Lemon-Aid*, the APA, and Mohamed Bouchama from the ACC submitted formal complaints to Ottawa against Toyota's Access pricing program a few years ago, the automaker settled the case for $2.3 million. The Bureau agreed to drop its inquiry into charges that the automaker rigged new car prices.

Almost 28 years earlier, an APA complaint forced GM to pay a $20,000 fine for lying in newspaper ads, touting the Vauxhall Firenza's triumphant cross-Canada "reliability run." The cars constantly broke down, and one auto journalist brought along for the ride spilled the beans to Ottawa probers. GM took the car off the market shortly thereafter.

Consumer Affairs *(www.consumeraffairs.com/automotive/manufacturers.htm)*

Expecting some namby-pamby consumer affairs site? You won't find that here. It's a "seller beware" kind of website, where you'll find the scandals before they hit the mainstream press.

Consumer Reports and Consumers Union *(www.consumerreports.org/cro/cars.htm)*

It costs $6.95 (U.S.) a month ($30 a year) to subscribe online, but *CR*'s database is chock full of comparison tests and in-depth stories on products and services. The group's $29.95 New Car Price service is similar to what the APA offers.

Protégez-Vous (Protect Yourself) *(www.protegez-vous.qc.ca)*

Quebec's French-language monthly consumer protection magazine and website is a hard-hitting critic of the auto industry. *Protégez-Vous* has supported the APA in testing dealer honesty and ratings of new and used cars in Quebec and throughout Canada. The magazine publishes dozens of test-drive results as well as articles relating to a broad range of products and services sold in Canada.

Supreme Court of Canada *(scc.lexum.umontreal.ca/en/index.html)*

It's not enough to have a solid claim against a company or the government. Supporting your position with a Supreme Court decision also helps. Three pro-consumer judgments rendered in February 2002 are particularly useful.

- *Bannon v. Thunder Bay (City):* An injured resident missed the deadline to file a claim against Thunder Bay; however, the Supreme Court maintained that extenuating factors, such as being under the effects of medication, extended her time to file. A good case to remember next time your vehicle is damaged by a pothole or you are injured by a municipality's negligence.

- *R. v. Guignard:* This judgment says you can protest as long as you speak or write the truth and you don't disturb the peace or harass customers or workers.

- *Whiten v. Pilot Insurance Co.:* The insured's home burned down, and the insurance company refused to pay the claim. The jury was outraged and ordered the company to pay the $345,000 claim, plus $320,000 for legal costs and $1 million in punitive damages, making it the largest punitive damage award in Canadian history. The Supreme Court maintained the jury's decision, calling Pilot "the insurer from hell." This judgment scares the dickens out of insurers, who fear that they might face huge punitive damage awards if they don't pay promptly.

Auto Safety

Center for Auto Safety *(www.autosafety.org)*

A Ralph Nader-founded agency that provides free online info on model-specific safety- and performance-related defects.

Crashtest.com *(www.crashtest.com)*

This website has crash-test information from around the world. You can find additional crashworthiness data for cars just recently coming onto the North American market that have been sold for many years in Asia, Europe, or Australia. The Honda Fit (Jazz), Mercedes Smart, Magna's Opel lineup, and Ford's upcoming European Fiesta and Focus imports are just a few examples.

Insurance Institute for Highway Safety *(www.iihs.org)*

A dazzling site that's long on crash photos and graphs that show which vehicles are the most crashworthy in side and offset collisions and which head restraints work best.

SafetyForum *(www.safetyforum.com)*

The Forum contains comprehensive news archives and links to useful sites, plus names of court-recognized experts on everything from unsafe Chrysler minivan latches to dangerous van conversions.

Transport Canada *(www.tc.gc.ca/eng/roadsafety/safevehicles-defectinvestigations-index-76.htm)*

A ho-hum site that's in no way as informative as the NHTSA or IIHS sites. You can access recalls for 1970-2010 models, but owner complaints aren't listed, defect investigations aren't disclosed, and service bulletin summaries aren't provided. A list of used vehicles admissible for import is available at *www.tc.gc.ca/roadsafety/ safevehicles/importation/usa/vafus/list2/menu.htm* or by calling the Registrar of Imported Vehicles (RIV) at 1-888-848-8240.

U.S. National Highway Traffic Safety Administration *(www.safercar.gov)*

This site has a comprehensive free database covering owner complaints, recall campaigns, crashworthiness and rollover ratings, defect investigations, service bulletin summaries, and safety research papers.

Information/Services

Alberta Government's Vehicle Cost Calculator *(www.agric.gov.ab.ca/app24/costcalculators/ vehicle/getvechimpls.jsp)*

Your tax dollars at work! This handy calculator allows you to estimate and compare the ownership and operating costs for any business or non-business vehicles. Eleven types of vehicles can be compared and the ownership cost can be calculated by modifying the input values. Alternatively, you may select the same model if you wish to compare one vehicle but with variations in purchase price, options, fuel type (diesel or gas), interest rates, or length of ownership.

ALLDATA Service Bulletins *(www.alldata.com/recalls/index.html)*

Free summaries of automotive recalls and technical service bulletins are listed by year, make, model, and engine option. You can access your vehicle's full bulletins online by paying a $26.95 (U.S.) subscription fee.

GM Inside News *(www.gminsidenews.com/forums)*

Kelley Blue Book and Edmunds *(www.kbb.com; www.edmunds.com)*

Prices and technical info are American-oriented, but you'll find good reviews of almost every vehicle sold in North America – plus there's an informative readers' forum.

Online Metric Conversions *(www.sciencemadesimple.net/conversions.html)*

A great place to instantly convert gallons to litres, miles to kilometres, etc.

Roadfly's Car Forums and Automotive Chat Rooms *(www.roadfly.org/forums)*

Another site that's no butt-kisser. Here you'll learn about BMW fan fires, upgrades, and performance comparisons. It also contains message boards for Bentley, Cadillac, Chevy, Jaguar, Lotus, Porsche, Mercedes-Benz, and others.

Women's Garage *(www.womensgarage.com)*

Three Canadian mechanics with a combined 100 years' experience set up this site to take the mystery out of maintaining and repairing vehicles. Don't be deterred by the site's title – men will learn more than they'll care to admit.

INFREQUENTLY ASKED QUESTIONS

Since the early '70s I have been interviewed hundreds of times on subjects ranging from auto consumer advocacy, my years as an Army Medic in Panama, and my time in Ottawa as the New Democratic Party's first elected Quebec Member of Parliament. Here are some questions I wish I had been asked over the years.

What's the difference between Canadian and American consumers?

Americans *publicly complain and then act* with an arsenal of laws and agencies that stoke confrontation and end in a compromise for restitution and a large fine. In rare cases, jail time may be served.

Canadians *quietly grumble and then seek a compromise* after the issue has been studied ad infinitum. This isn't surprising when you recognize that Canada doesn't have a bulwark of consumer protection laws or aggressive regulatory agencies. We deliberately opt for compromise rather than confrontation. Our country was created by compromise rather than revolution – commissions instead of cannons. And that works out fine for both countries.

Isn't auto industry fraud just a few bad apples spoiling the rest?

No, the industry is founded upon fraud where profit trumps principle. It's not a capitalist-socialist debate, either, as I once told Renault's Board in Paris how shameful it was that the state-owned automaker made cars for Canadians in St. Bruno, Quebec, with safety features not available in France. How about Volkswagen's 6-year "diesel-gate" scandal that came to light this year. It shows clearly that VW cheated 11 million owners and its competition by faking pollution tests. And don't forget that both Toyota and Honda were fined over $70 million this year for hiding owner complaints of accidents and failures caused by safety-related defects. As the Pogo cartoon character said, "We have met the enemy, and he is us."

VW's "in your face" dishonesty has had several positive effects: Consumer protection agencies around the world are energized in passing new regulations with teeth and enforcing laws already on the books. This radicalization of consumer protection swaps the traditional do-nothing "Buyer Beware" mantra for a "Seller Beware" activism. Hopefully, this will lead to auto executives going to jail.

How do we combat unsafe cars, corruption, and misrepresentation?

By applying strong laws forcefully and equally and instilling the fear of certain, quick punishment that includes incarceration. It's done all the time in Scandinavian countries that always lead in independent surveys of honest governments. Diplomacy while holding a big stick works wonders in getting a fair settlement. And courts don't have to be your first recourse.

Back in the '70s Ford built "rust magnet" cars and trucks that were practically biodegradable. I, along with a few dozen Ford owners, formed the Rusty Ford Owners Association. We sold bumper stickers (one Prime Minister's wife put it on her car), picketed dealers, got thrown out of auto shows, and filed class actions. This drove Ford's sales into the basement. We called in federal Liberal Consumer Affairs Minister Bryce Mackasy to intervene and got a settlement. Ford gave $2.8 million in free rust repairs and agreed on a voluntary Anti-corrosion Code we set up that strengthened warranties. Almost all auto companies in Canada adopted the Code that year and the Code was expanded to the States following the APA's U.S. Senate testimony as to how well the Code worked.

Aren't all car companies the same?

No. It all depends upon the leadership at the top. Ford of Canada has been both the best and the worst auto company in Canada. During the Rusty Ford campaign, Ford Canada President **Bob Bennett** was about as responsive as a stone. As Ford sales nose-dived, Ford goons threw me out of the Toronto Auto Show. Bennett was aghast and called to apologize and negotiations got back on track. Shortly thereafter, Bennett signed the Mackasy-inspired settlement and made sure it was respected.

Bobbie Gaunt, another Ford of Canada President, settled hundreds of Ford Taurus, Mercury Sable, and Ford Windstar tranny and engine claims. Plus she set up an extended warranty for thousands of other owners of these vehicles. No picketing, no class-actions, no bumper stickers, just a few meetings and lots of phone calls. Gaunt's team went to Detroit to convince Ford CEO **Jac Nasser** to make the warranty extension and refunds a North American program. Nasser and his staff were adamant. No way did they want this Canadian contagion infecting them in Detroit. Shortly thereafter, Nasser quit Ford and Gaunt retired. But her honesty and courage to face up to Nasser is unforgettable.

Honda and Nissan Canada were two of the worst-behaving car companies in Canada when they came to Canada in the early '70s. Nissan's 240Z models had failure-prone brakes that made the vehicles "Kamikaze" cars, and Honda's lineup included rust-cankered bodies and defective CVCC engines. Instead of recalling their cars, the presidents of both companies decided to sue me for $5 million. They both dropped the suits and finally improved their cars.

Another bad car company executive was GM Canada President **John Baker** who refused to meet with an association of angry Firenza owners in March 1973. Then he signed off on a dishonest newspaper ad extolling the Firenza's virtues and was hit by a $20,000 fine for false advertising. The car was taken off the market shortly thereafter.

Finally, we come to the worst of the worst of auto execs. Fiat Chrysler Automobile's CEO **Sergio Marchionne**. A Canadian ex-pat, Marchionne has an arrogant, anti-consumer attitude toward safety recalls and Canadians, generally, who he called "guppies" when his bullying tactics failed to get Ottawa subsidies 2 years ago for renovating Winndsor's minivan plant. Ironically, his egocentric leadership style has managed to tick off both government regulators and fellow car company executives.

Over the past four decades, who were the most effective pro-consumer politicians?

- **Andre Ouellett, Liberal federal Consumer Affairs Minister.** He believed passionately in consumer protection and grass-roots protests. In fact, his statements against what he called the "sugar cartel" kept him in the courts for a year.

- **Bill Tetley, Liberal provincial Consumer Affairs Minister.** The "father" of Quebec's Consumer Protection Bureau, Tetly passed Bill 45 in the '70s. That law laid the foundation for Quebec's leadership, along with British Columbia and Saskatchewan, in guaranteeing effective consumer protection legislation.

- **Lise Payette, Parti Quebecois provincial Consumer Affairs Minister.** Minister Payette took the embryonic consumer legislation passed by Tetley and extended its provisions to almost every aspect of the economy. A brilliant tactician, she managed to tap the resources of Quebec's different consumer groups and use them to propose and support a panoply of innovative laws.

- **Barry Mather NDP MP** from Surrey, British Columbia. A former *Sun* columnist, Barry always asked questions in the House relative to consumer complaints and supported activist consumer groups like the Automobile Protection Association. In fact, I decided to run federally for the NDP mainly as a result of my friendsip with, and respect for, Barry Mather.

- Finally, there's **Heward Graffety**, who worked tirelessly for the passage of the *Canadian Motor Vehicle Safety Act* (1971). I met with him at his home in the Eastern Townships after he retired and was impressed by his commitment to auto safety.

What car do you drive?

I have a 2007 Hyundai Tucson. During the past four decades I have owned a 1959 Chevy Impala, a 1967 Ford Mustang, several Ford Mavericks, a Toyota Camry, a Ford Probe, and two Chevrolet Vanduras. All bought used.

MODEL INDEX

MODEL INDEX